T0140122

ONTOLOGIES

A Handbook of Principles, Concepts and Applications in Information Systems

INTEGRATED SERIES IN INFORMATION SYSTEMS

Series Editors

Professor Ramesh Sharda
Oklahoma State University

Prof. Dr. Stefan Voß
Universität Hamburg

Other published titles in the series:

E-BUSINESS MANAGEMENT: *Integration of Web Technologies with Business Models*/ edited by Michael J. Shaw
VIRTUAL CORPORATE UNIVERSITIES: *A Matrix of Knowledge and Learning for the New Digital Dawn*/ Walter R.J. Baets & Gert Van der Linden
SCALABLE ENTERPRISE SYSTEMS: *An Introduction to Recent Advances*/ edited by Vittal Prabhu, Soundar Kumara, Manjunath Kamath
LEGAL PROGRAMMING: *Legal Compliance for RFID and Software Agent Ecosystems in Retail Processes and Beyond*/ Brian Subirana and Malcolm Bain
LOGICAL DATA MODELING: *What It Is and How To Do It*/ Alan Chmura and J. Mark Heumann
DESIGNING AND EVALUATING E-MANAGEMENT DECISION TOOLS: *The Integration of Decision and Negotiation Models into Internet-Multimedia Technologies*/ Giampiero E.G. Beroggi
INFORMATION AND MANAGEMENT SYSTEMS FOR PRODUCT CUSTOMIZATION/ Thorsten Blecker et al
MEDICAL INFORMATICS: *Knowledge Management and Data Mining in Biomedicine*/ edited by Hsinchun Chen et al
KNOWLEDGE MANAGEMENT AND MANAGEMENT LEARNING: *Extending the Horizons of Knowledge-Based Management*/ edited by Walter Baets
INTELLIGENCE AND SECURITY INFORMATICS FOR INTERNATIONAL SECURITY: *Information Sharing and Data Mining*/ Hsinchun Chen
ENTERPRISE COLLABORATION: *On-Demand Information Exchange for Extended Enterprises*/ David Levermore & Cheng Hsu
SEMANTIC WEB AND EDUCATION/ Vladan Devedžić
INFORMATION SYSTEMS ACTION RESEARCH: *An Applied View of Emerging Concepts and Methods*/ Ned Kock

ONTOLOGIES
A Handbook of Principles, Concepts and Applications in Information Systems

edited by

Raj Sharman
Rajiv Kishore
Ram Ramesh

Raj Sharman
SUNY Buffalo
New York, USA

Rajiv Kishore
SUNY Buffalo
New York, USA

Ram Ramesh
SUNY Buffalo
New York, USA

ISBN-10: 0-387-37019-6
ISBN-13: 978-1-4899-7730-4
ISBN-10: 0-387-37022-6 (eBook)
ISBN-13: 978-0387-37022-4 (eBook)
DOI 10.1007/978-0-387-37022-4
Printed on acid-free paper.

Softcover re-print of the Hardcover 1st edition 2007

9 8 7 6 5 4 3 2 1

springer.com

Dedicated to

To my wife Janie, my children Kristi, Kristin and Krissie and my parents T.S. and Sushila Visvanathan

– Raj Sharman

To Sujata, Anant, and Aseem for your love, support, inspiration, and patience

– Rajiv Kishore

To the countless individuals who have helped, guided and shaped my life and continue to do so

– Ram Ramesh

CONTENTS

ODIS Architectures

Foreword

Ontology, or the nature of being, has been a focal area of study in the philosophical disciplines for a long time. Interpreted simply, the term ontology refers to the question "what kinds of things exist?" to a philosopher, while a computer scientist grapples with the question "what kinds of things should we capture and represent?" Together, research on the two questions yield a broad framework for the analysis of a discourse universe, its representation in some abstract form and the development of organizations and systems within the universe.

The philosophical perspective on ontology provides a description of the essential properties and relations of all beings in the universe, while this notion has been expanded as well as specialized in the fields of computer science and artificial intelligence. The AI/CS communities now use this notion to refer to not one but multiple ontologies. In the AI/CS perspective, an ontology refers to the specification of knowledge about entities, and their relationships and interactions in a bounded universe of discourse only. As a result, a number of bounded-universe ontologies have been created over the last decade. These include the Chemicals ontology in the chemistry area, the TOVE and Enterprise ontologies for enterprise modeling, the REA ontology in the accounting area, organizational knowledge ontology in the knowledge management area, an ontology of air campaign planning in the defense area, and the GALEN ontology in the medical informatics area.

Of late, however, there is a growing recognition that ontological principles and concepts need not be restricted to the traditional domains of knowledge inquiry, and can be fruitfully applied to and developed further in various fields within the broader information systems area. This has led to the notion of *ontology-driven information systems (ODIS)*, a concept that, although in preliminary stages of development, opens up new ways of thinking about ontologies and IS in conjunction with each other, and covers both the structural and the temporal dimensions of IS.

In the structural dimension, ontologies can provide mechanisms for structuring, storing and accessing generic IS content including database schemas, user interface objects, and application programs that can be customized and integrated into a functioning IS. Unlike the well-established data modeling paradigms, the structural foundations of ontological systems are still in infancy; there is a growing need for a unified theory of structural representations of ontologies. Some of the key research questions in this dimension include: What representational formalisms for ontologies are needed? How are these distinguished from the traditional relational, predicate-based and object formalisms? Can algebras and calculi be developed for specific ontology representation formalisms? How can ontologies yield efficient frameworks for systems design? There are many more important questions in this dimension.

In the temporal dimension, ontologies can guide the development of new information systems by helping analysts and designers choose appropriate processes, algorithms, rules, and software components depending upon their needs. It has also been suggested recently that ontologies, frameworks, and systems are essentially knowledge artifacts at different levels of knowledge abstraction and, therefore, systems can be generated from bounded-universe ontologies through specialization and combination. It also appears that the emerging paradigms such as web services and the semantic web will enable the large-scale development, deployment, and sharing of ontologies and ontology-driven information systems. Some of the key research questions in this dimension include: How can both the static and dynamic elements of a universe be captured in an ontology? Can ontologies be sound and complete? Can ontologies be verified and validated? What are the relationships between ontologies and the systems development life cycle? What theories of ontologies are needed for ontological system integration, interoperability of ontologies and knowledge discovery through ontology mining? Can ontologies be used in organization design, besides their well known applications in systems engineering? And there are numerous other questions.

The primary objective of this book is to mobilize a collective awareness in the research community to the leading and emerging developments in ODIS, and consequently, highlight the enormous potential of ODIS research to both fundamentally transform and create innovative solutions to several problems in various domains. This book is a compendium of some of the leading research of the community working in various fundamental and applied disciplines related to ODIS. These contributions deal with the design, technical, managerial, behavioral, and organizational aspects of

ODIS. They clearly demonstrate the synergies derived from cross-disciplinary efforts in ODIS research and also open up the numerous challenges and opportunities in the road ahead.

This book contains a total of 32 leading-edge research contributions presented as chapters. These chapters are organized into the following broad themes: *Foundations of ODIS, Ontological Engineering, ODIS Architectures,* and *ODIS Applications.* These four themes together describe the state-of-the-art in ODIS and give a complete perspective on the problems, solutions and open research questions in this field. We briefly outline these contributions in the following discussion.

Foundations of ODIS

The foundations of ODIS are addressed in Chapters 1–6. Chapter 1 provides an introduction to ontologies and a justification of their need in various domains. They expound on how the concept of ontology has expanded from Philosophy into Computer Science and is an excellent introduction to those who are new to the area. Chapter 2 discusses how taxonomies and ontologies can help in making sense of huge amount of content that gets generated across the locations in different languages and format. Chapter 3 illustrates how an ontological evaluation of business models can be used to compare them for equivalency of representation of business requirements, especially when re-engineering legacy systems into component-based information systems.

The semantic web is a mechanism of representing information on the web in a form that makes it processable by machines on a global scale. Semantic Web based applications are being developed in all disciplines, although the area is still in its infancy. Chapter 4 provides a detailed introduction to the use of ontologies, ontology languages and editors in the context of the semantic web and highlights their advantages through real-world applications. Chapter 5 examines the differences between positivism and non-positivism ontologies and concludes that those differences are indeed irreconcilable. Interestingly, this chapter studies the relationships of epistemology and methodology with ontology and concludes that there are clear epistemological and methodological consequences of the ontological divide, but these are less clear-cut than the ontological opposition. This opens up the pragmatic implications of this ontological divide on IS research and raises the question of whether a tolerant coexistence of the two approaches is feasible within IS research. Finally, Chapter 6 argues that a large number of moral and ethical issues, such as privacy, intellectual property, access to data, and digital divide, are related to and even created by the use of information technology. This chapter proposes that these ethical and moral issues can be viewed through the lens of responsibility in information systems and examines this notion of responsibility through positivist ontology as well as ontology of life-world which represents a reality that is created by intentional perception and hermeneutic interaction.

Ontological Engineering

The principles and techniques of Ontological engineering in the contexto f ODIS are addressed in Chapters 7–14. Chapter 7 presents an ontological engineering approach to knowledge-intensive Case Based Reasoning (CBR) systems development. This chapter addresses knowledge acquisition through cases, knowledge representation, ontology development and systems engineering. Chapter 8 presents an overview of the state-of-the-art research on the subject of applications of Model Development Architecture (MDA) standards for ontology development, including a discussion on similarities and differences between MDA languages and semantic web languages. A new ontology language M-OWL that supports an ontology designed for multimedia applications is presented in Chapter 9. M-OWL is an extension of the standard ontology language OWL. Chapter 10 addresses a basic problem in implementing ontology-based information systems, that of ontology growth and evolution through revisions. New knowledge, essentially justified true beliefs, that needs to be incorporated in an ontology for its growth may contradict the current knowledge stored in the ontology in terms of definitions and agreements. When this happens, the ontology may need to be revised to reflect the changes. This chapter shows that belief revision theory provides a way to revise an ontology ensuring that new knowledge does not cause inconsistencies with existing knowledge when it is incorporated in the system, and develops a three-phase ontological reengineering methodology based on this theory.

Knowledge changes over time and domains evolve. The ontology supporting domain knowledge has to keep up with this growth. Chapter 11 presents a framework for representing ontological evolution over time and provides an ontology developer with an intuitive change model for expressing local ontological changes in a declarative way. Chapter 12 develops an interesting incremental ontology population methodology that exploits machine learning techniques to tackle the problem of ontology maintenance. This chapter also includes experimental results to establish the applicability and effectiveness of the proposed methodology. This chapter is an excellent complement to Chapter 11, and together they present effective tools for ontological engineering. Chapter 13 develops a tool called MnM that helps during the ontology maintenance process. Using natural language processing, information extraction, and machine learning technologies, MnM uses information extracts from texts and populates an ontology. MnM has the potential to become an important part of standard ODIS repertoire, given its integrated web-based ontology editor, open APIs to link to ontology servers and integration with the information extraction tools.

The last chapter in this cluster (Chapter 14) deals with the selection of an appropriate requirements elicitation (RE) technique in ontological engineering from a huge set of such methods and their variations. This issue has become very important due to the development of numerous new and innovative RE techniques used by various researchers and practitioners. Chapter 14 creates an ontology describing the context for requirements elicitation, elicitation techniques and their selection criteria, key characteristics of elicitation techniques and their similarities and differences. This chapter presents an approach that can be used by systems developers for selecting an appropriate elicitation technique in a given context.

ODIS Architectures

A collection of ODIS architectures in a variety of contexts is presented in Chapters 15–24. Chapter 15 examines the evolution of knowledge intensive business processes and develops an architecture for systems supporting such processes using ontology principles. The central idea here is design automation of high-end systems that are typically needed in knowledge management. Chapter 16 develops an approach to creating an object model from a problem domain description by using ontologies as a basis for object identification and abstract data modeling. This chapter yields a nice framework for conducting the analysis and conceptual modeling phases of systems design leading to the development of object-oriented architectures in a variety of domains. Chapter 17 develops interesting insights into the ontology metaphors. The notion of ontology is used to discover and define the source domain knowledge in terms of metaphors. Integrating the Conceptual Mapping Model between a source domain and its target domain with an ontology-based knowledge representation, this chapter demonstrates how a conceptual metaphor analysis could lead to automated architectural designs. Chapter 18 introduces the notion of Knowledge Collective, which is a realization of Expert agents who may need to have their own ontologies and to work together as a team to tutor students. A multi-layered, multi-agent framework for developing and maintaining intelligent knowledge bases that can be used in areas such as Intelligent Tutoring Systems is developed in this chapter.

Chapter 19 argues that hypermedia documents are essentially knowledge assets of an organization and uses a knowledge management ontology to integrate technical hypermedia concepts with organizational information systems. The core elements of the hypermedia ontology are derived from the existing Labyrinth model while the knowledge management concepts come from Holsapple and Joshi's knowledge management ontology. The resulting ontological framework provides ground for the development of ontology-based Information Systems in which hypermedia assets are managed. Chapter 20 introduces an architecture and ontology model for an ontology-enabled database management system. This chapter also introduces many extensions to the RDF/S-based ontology models that are emerging as standards, and provide a graph-based abstraction for the model.

Designing for interoperability among system architectures using underlying ontological principles is the focus of Chapter 21. This chapter addresses the scope and limitations of a web service choreography standard in providing standardized descriptions of business processes both in terms of process flow and control flow. Focusing on the set of limitations arising out of a lack of a general ontology for enterprise systems interoperability domain, this chapter develops a comprehensive ontological representation model for such descriptions.

Dynamic discovery and invoke ability are very important components of Service Oriented Architecture (SOA). Chapter 22 presents a context-aware ontology selection framework, which allows an increase in precision of the retrieved results by taking the contextual information into account. The main component of the context-aware ontology selection framework is the matching algorithm that attempts to find a semantic match between a declarative description of the service being offered and the service in demand. Chapter 23 argues that a focus on users is crucial in the design of a knowledge management system (KMS) to account for the heterogeneity of users, differences in their responsibilities, their different domains of interests, their different competencies, and their different work tasks that are to be handled by the KMS. Emphasizing the role of user models, this chapter proposes an ontology-based user modeling approach that manages extended user profiles containing not only user competencies and their preferences but their behaviors as well including types of activity, levels of activity, and levels of knowledge sharing. User modeling addresses two important user needs: a need for enhanced support for filtering and retrieving the knowledge available in the system, and a need to better manage the tacit knowledge that is generally believed to be the more important types of knowledge.

Finally in this cluster of chapters, Chapter 24 presents the architecture of a personalized search system. This system employs user profiles, the browsing-history and profiles built from system interactions to improve the performance of search engines. This chapter provides an insightful discussion on a variety of mechanisms for automated profile creation leading to several open issues in this process.

ODIS Applications

A set of important and emerging ODIS applications is presented in Chapters 25–32. Chapter 25 presents an ontological approach to design information systems that support supply chain operations. By separating domain knowledge from IS solutions, an ontology-based application architecture that effectively complements its three other components – interface, management, and knowledge gathering is developed for the supply chain integration context. Chapter 26 discusses the problem of interoperability in the manufacturing parts arena. This chapter argues that while imposing a standard terminology and classification system for manufactured components by an organization on its suppliers would increase interchange and interoperability, this may not be always feasible due to resistance by the suppliers. To overcome this problem, this chapter proposes a three-phase methodology for developing a harmonized ontology of an enterprise's product models in use. This methodology has been applied and tested in the Intelligent Manufacturing Systems (IMS) SMART-fm program (www.ims.org) and European ATHENA project (www.athena-ip.org) under real industrial environments. Chapter 27 classifies the concepts of ADACOR (ADAptive holonic COntrol aRchitecture) ontology for distributed manufacturing systems using the DOLCE (Descriptive Ontology for Linguistic and manufacturing scheduling and control environments. This ontology is conceptually transparent and semantically explicit due to the use of a sound foundational ontology and formal semantics and is appropriate for information communication, sharing, and retrieval in manufacturing environments.

Chapter 28 presents the Babylon Knowledge Explorer (BKE) system which is an integrated suite of tools and information sources to support the prototyping and implementation of ODIS and several other ontology-enhanced knowledge applications. Chapter 29 investigates the development of a software-based ontology within the context of a rural wireless emergency medical (EMS) services. Using an inductive, field-based approach, this study devises and tests a new ontology-based framework for wireless emergency response in rural Minnesota. This ontology is expected to yield effective solutions to several technical and non-technical problems in EMS deployment, especially in rural settings.

Smart card (SC) technology is emerging as a technology that offers a solution for the current problems of secure communication and data handling with reasonable privacy by fulfilling simultaneously the main demands of identification, security, and authentication besides the functions of the main application (e.g., payments). Chapter 30 uses the notions of ontology in this area and develops a General Reference Architecture for Smart Card systems

(GRASC) that can help address some of the problems in configuration, reconfiguration, interoperability, and standardization of smart card systems. Chapter 31 develops the ontological foundations of Mobile Surveyor, a model-based monitoring system that provides a novel approach to software monitoring by incorporating data models throughout the monitoring process. Focusing on the construction and deployment of the underlying concept ontologies, this chapter also develops a design environment for ontology development and knowledge-base querying and management. The last chapter in this set, Chapter 32 integrates current journalistic standards with existing top level ontologies and other metadata-related standards to develop an ontology for journalistic applications.

Putting It All Together

This book is a significant contribution to research on ontologies, ontological engineering and ODIS development. With its foundations in the fields of philosophy, computer science, artificial intelligence and information systems, the domain of ODIS is rapidly expanding due to numerous multi-disciplinary efforts in various research communities over the years. Our attempt has been to spotlight the themes emerging in ODIS research and weave them into a tapestry of thought giving ODIS a unique identity in the arts and sciences. Research on ODIS holds tremendous promise for future advances. We hope this book will give the research communities a refreshing perspective on ODIS and a new view of the future. We also expect this book to trigger innovative thought processes that will open up significant new domains in ODIS research. Numerous open research questions, challenges and opportunities can be found throughout this book and we hope this will stimulate significant research over the years.

Acknowledgements

This book was produced with the help of many people. At the outset we wish to thank Ramesh Sharda, Oklahoma State University; Stephan Voss, Universität Hamburg and Gary Folven, Springer Verlag for the Springer's Integrated Series in Information Systems, of which this book is a part of. Thanks are also due to Gary Folven, Carolyn Ford, Denise Gibson of Springer Verlag and Ina Talandiene of VTeX Limited for their support and the enormous patience they have shown us through this publication process. Special thanks also go to Dinesh Satheshan, Tejaswini Herath and Valerie Bartkowiak for their assistance with ensuring that the chapters conform to Springer guidelines and for help with the management of the process in general. This book would obviously not have been possible without the contributions from our authors and we are deeply grateful to them for contributing their papers to this edited volume. We would also like to offer our very special thanks and gratitude to the many reviewers who spent their time and efforts to give valuable feedback to our authors. Their feedback has made a significant improvement in the quality of this book.

Finally, we would like to convey our deepest thanks to our families who endured many hours of our being locked away in our offices to work on this project.

Raj Sharman
Rajiv Kishore
Ram Ramesh

June 2006

Foundations of ODIS

Chapter 1

THE ROAD TOWARD ONTOLOGIES

Diana Marcela Sánchez, José María Cavero and Esperanza Marcos Martínez
Universidad Rey Juan Carlos Departamento de Informática, Estadística y Telemática

Abstract: One of thc most important characteristics of today's society is that a huge amount of information is shared by many participants (people, applications). This information must be characterized by a uniformity of terms. This means that, in similar contexts, everyone should understand the same meaning when reading or hearing the same word and everyone should use the same word to refer to the same concept. In different Computer Science disciplines one of the methods that satisfies this need for "common understanding" of concepts is thc creation of *ontologies*. Curiously, there are different interpretations of what ontology is. In this chapter, we show the way that the concept of ontology has expanded from Philosophy into Computer Science.

Key words: Ontology; Philosophy; Computer Science

1. INTRODUCTION

As in many other disciplines, in Computer Science new terms emerge and become fashionable. In recent years one of these terms is the concept of *ontology*. It has been adopted by Computer Science with a different meaning than it had in its origin. Ontology in Computer Science, broadly speaking, is a way of representing a common understanding of a domain.

Perhaps one of the consequences of the World Wide Web is the idea that all of the world's knowledge is available to everyone. Although this is obviously not correct, it has created new demands on Computer Science. The idea of sharing knowledge requires that all participants (not only people, but also applications) must share a common vocabulary, that is, a consensus about the meaning of things. Ontologies, therefore, are one of the solutions for representing this common understanding. However, the concept of ontology had a long history in Philosophy before being used in Computer Science.

The rest of this chapter is organized as follows. In section two, we summarize the traditional (philosophical) definition of ontology. Section three presents how the *ontology* concept came to be used in Computer Science and later reviews the meaning of this concept in that discipline, including different classifications of ontologies within Computer Science. Section four shows how ontologies are used in the development of Information Systems, including techniques and methodologies for developing ontologies, and applications based on ontologies. Finally, Section five offers conclusions and suggests possible future work.

2. PHILOSOPHICAL ONTOLOGY

The concept of ontology was taken from Philosophy and applied to Computer Science with a meaning different from the one traditionally accepted since Classical Greece. In the following paragraphs, we take a look at the classical definition of ontology and related concepts, starting with Aristotle. We conclude by discussing the adoption of the concept by some of the Computer Science disciplines.

Since early human history, people have asked themselves about the "essence" of things. Aristotle, in his *Metaphysics*, was one of the first philosophers to ask and to write about "*What is being?*" In an attempt to answer that question, he concluded that all beings in the world must have some "thing", some characteristic, which gives the property of "being" to objects.

Aristotle starts his Metaphysics with a compilation of the different approaches to the meaning of the primary constitutive element (the essence of things) and how that essence or primary element generates all things in the world. For example, Anaximenes thought that air was the first principle of all things, and Tales thought that the water was the beginning, reason and substance of all things. Aristotle, nevertheless, thought that those approaches dealt with the primary principle rather than the essence of things.

He distinguished between principle and essence. Principle is the "source point of something" while essence is the "intrinsic reason of existence of being" (Aristotle, 1994).

Nevertheless, neither Ontology nor Metaphysics were concepts used by Aristotle in his essays. Andronicus of Rhodes, who divulged Aristotle's writings for the first time, was the one who observed that the main subject of Aristotle's writings went *beyond* Physics. It was he who coined the term Metaphysics. In the middle ages, metaphysics studies were influenced by the idea of God. God is presented as *the Creator* of all things, a divine, transcendent and mystic being capable of giving life, that is, of giving "essence". But God is a particular being; therefore, the study of God (Theology) could not replace Metaphysics in its search for the intrinsic reason common to *all* beings. Philosophers of the Modern Ages applied the "divide and conquer" strategy, so they divided the study of beings according to the nature of objects studied. Nevertheless, their discussions and conclusions were still grouped around Metaphysics.

By the end of XVII century, Christian Wolff divided Metaphysics into "*metaphysica generalis*" and "*metaphysica specialis*". *Metaphysica generalis* (general metaphysics) was also called "*ontologia*" (Ontology), with the meaning to investigate the most general concepts of being. Meanwhile "*metaphysica specialis*" (special metaphysics) was divided into three branches: Rational Theology (the study of God), Rational Psychology (the study of the soul) and Rational Cosmology (the study of the universe as a whole) (García Sierra, 1999).

Traditionally, philosophers have adopted two attitudes about General Metaphysics (that is, Ontology). Both look for the "essence" of things, but with different approaches:

1. The first approach looks for the intrinsic reason that might allow us to give the name "being" to objects that possess it. The method to obtain that *essence* must be through observation of and reflection on all things and behaviors in the world, and then put such reasoning into words.
2. The second approach also looks for essence, but through a hierarchical classification of beings. In this classification, high levels are generated by general properties and could be composed by lower levels, which represent more specific characteristics. An organization of beings permits us to find common characteristics (physical or not). The top level of this classification must be the essence, that is, the property that all beings (animated or not) possess and permit them to exist.

3. FROM PHILOSOPHY TO COMPUTER SCIENCE

It could be thought that ontologies entered Computer Science through Philosophy of Science, which is a branch of Philosophy that looks for the reason and justification of sciences (Mosterin, 2000). Nevertheless, the path followed by the Ontology concept from Philosophy to Computer Science was the result of different requirements in various fields (Smith and Welty, 2002). Artificial Intelligence, Software Engineering and Database communities independently concluded that knowledge representation was important for the evolution of their areas.

In the field of Artificial Intelligence (AI), this need for knowledge representation is most evident because its goal is to make an agent do tasks autonomously and systematically (Guarino and Giaretta, 1995). To do a job well, agents must make decisions; these decisions must be made based on knowledge. So, AI's researchers' goal is to incorporate knowledge into agents, that is, to find a method of representing knowledge in a computational environment. Epistemology, which is "the field of Philosophy which deals with the nature and sources of knowledge" (Nutter, 1987) can help to find answers and tools to create a way of representing knowledge. Regarding Epistemology, if we speak about the nature of knowledge, then we ask ourselves about its components. If we speak about the sources of knowledge, we try to understand the inference process we use to generate it. One of the most widely accepted ideas in the epistemological field is that knowledge is made up of concepts.

The object-oriented paradigm gave Software Engineering a new style of representing elements involved in a problem. This paradigm classifies the world into objects that may be the representation of anything of the world. Those elements have two basic characteristics: attributes (or properties) and methods (or possible actions that objects could do) (Booch, 1993). Object-orientation is a hierarchical way of thinking about the world where an object inherits properties and methods from its parents. Objects may have different behaviors depending on the situation, due to the *overloading* mechanism, which allows giving multiple meanings to the same concept. Polymorphism is a property of the objects that allows them to answer a specific requirement in different ways, according to their particular properties. At a higher level, software engineers found that representing concepts, that is, representing the meaning of things, may also help to simplify some problems, like systems interoperability.

Finally, the Database community also needed conceptual, high level models. The purpose of such models was to give an abstract representation of a problem domain without considering implementation issues.

Therefore, three different areas had the same problem: the representation of concepts. This representation can be used, for example, as a starting point to generate knowledge.

According to the Oxford Dictionary (Oxford, 1993) a concept is an abstract idea and has a Latin origin which means "something conceived". So, a concept is the representation of the meaning of a thing or, in other words, the mental representation of an object when a human being thinks about that object. Concepts take on the main characteristics of things, that is, their essence.

However, each Computer Science discipline addressees the problem of knowledge representation in a different manner, because each one is interested in a specific problem, called problem domain (Guarino, 1998). Therefore, researchers elaborate a valid representation for a specific part of reality.

In 1980, John McCarthy proposed, in the field of Artificial Intelligence, the concept of an environment's ontology (McCarthy, 1980). An environment's ontology comprises not only a list of concepts involved in a problem (environment) but also their meanings in that context, that is, what we mean by each one of them. He applied ontologies for establishing an order in the concepts within a domain. Since then, ontologies have been associated with the representation of concepts.

Before continuing, it is important to take into account two issues:

1. We are talking about concepts. Therefore, we have to think about a *conceptualization* process, that is, the process by which concepts are generated.
2. We are talking about representation. Therefore, we want to "present" something; in other words, we want to express the characteristics and structure of things easily (McCarthy, 1980). In Computer Science, the mechanism used to show the structure (to present) has always been the creation of models.

Doing a rough comparison with philosophical Ontology, one might come to some preliminary conclusions: Computer Science does not give an answer about what is the essence (it is not its goal). It assumes that everything that can be represented is "real". In this context, concepts are primary principles, so all the things that exist in the world are susceptible to being represented by a concept which tries to capture its meaning (essence). Computer Science models are constructed for small, reduced domains; if those models were hierarchical, then when modeling, we were looking for the primary elements of our reduced domain. That is the same goal that philosophical ontology has for the entire world.

Currently, the most common definition of ontology in Computer Science is Gruber's (Gruber, 1993): ontology is an "explicit specification of a conceptualization". This definition is based on the idea of conceptualization: a simplified view of the world that we want to represent. Conceptualization is the process by which the human mind forms its idea about part of the reality. This idea is a mental representation free of accidental properties and based on essential characteristics of the elements. Therefore, the (Computer Science) ontology concept is joined to a domain or mini-world and the specification represented in ontology is concerned with that domain. In other words, if the domain (or part of it) changes, the conceptualization must also change and consequently the ontology that represents this mini-world changes too.

Regards the Gruber definition, a lot of comments and new definitions has been proposed by several authors– within Computer Sciences disciplines-. All these definitions are based on the idea that Computer Science ontology is a way of representing concepts.

Some authors have compared philosophical and Computer Science ontology concepts. Guarino proposes that both concepts be distinguished using different terms. He proposes "ontology" as the Computer Science term and "conceptualization" for the philosophical idea of "*search for the essence of beings*" concept (Guarino and Giaretta, 1995). He argues that currently the Ontology concept has taken on a concrete meaning and that it is associated with the development of a model which often represents a particular situation. He observes that the term "conceptualization" should be used for the abstract and non palpable process of reasoning, and "ontology" for the concrete process of reasoning. Nevertheless, as we have previously said, that "process for the creation of concepts" belongs to Epistemology (the way how knowledge is generated) more than to philosophical Ontology.

The next step in the construction of ontologies is to explicitly represent conceptualization, that is, select which tool may be used to represent knowledge. One attempt to formally represent conceptualizations is the concept of Formal Ontology. It looks, using Logics, like "an axiomatic and systematic study about all forms of being" (Cocchiarella, 1991).

Formal Ontology is, for several authors, the Theory of Distinctions at all levels (Guarino, 1998). Theory of Distinctions may be applied to entities or to categories of entities, or even to categories of categories (meta-categories) that used the world for modeling. For other authors, it is the study of formal structures to represent knowledge and its relations. However, for both approaches, there are two important study fields associated with Formal Ontology: Mereology, or the study of part-whole relations, and Topology, or study of connection relationships (Guarino, 1998; Smith, 1998).

The purpose of Mereology is to identify when an object (that may be composed of other objects) stops being itself and turns into something else (by aggregating a new component or subtracting one of its components) (Mosterin, 2000). This is very important in Computer Science's ontologies, because in a hierarchical model, where a concept is divided into its components, it is important to distinguish where the limit between essential and non essential elements is. Essential elements are those components of the element that if they disappear, the (composed) element changes or no longer exists. At this point, Topology can help. Topology analyzes the strength of the relationships between elements. Using Topology, we can compare two elements and decide if they are the same element; or if an element is essential for another element, which means that they can not "live" separately.

Those previous concepts may be applied to interoperability between systems. If we were able to know what the essential characteristics that distinguish an object are, then it might be possible to analyze another information system and find the element that possesses the same characteristics.

We have previously said that the purpose of ontologies is to represent concepts. But, how do those concepts end up being "real" in some (human or artificial) system? We could say that any representation needs a language to be expressed; ontologies are no exception.

Formal ontology distills, filters, codifies and organizes the results of an ontological study (in either it's local or global settings). (Poli, 2004). So, in Computer Science, Formal Ontology represents ontologies through logical structures. A formalization of ontology is given in a logical language, which describes a structure of the world that considers all objects involved within the domain of study, their possible states and all relevant relationships between them.

3.1 Classification of Ontologies

There are several classifications of Computer Science's ontologies, based on different parameters. Guarino (1998) classifies them by their level of generality in:

- top-level ontologies, which describe domain-independent concepts such as space, time, etc., and which are independent of specific problems;
- domain and task ontologies which describe, respectively, the vocabulary related to a generic domain and a generic task;
- and, finally, application ontologies, which describe concepts depending on a particular domain and task.

Van Heijst, Schereiber and Wieringa (1996) classify them according to their use in:

- terminological ontologies, which specify which terms are used to represent the knowledge;
- information ontologies, which specify storage structure data; and
- knowledge modeling ontologies, which specify the conceptualization of the knowledge.

Fensel, (2004) classifies ontologies in:

- domain ontologies, which capture the knowledge valid for a particular domain;
- metadata ontologies, which provide a vocabulary for describing the content of on-line information sources;

- generic or common sense ontologies, which capture general knowledge about the world providing basic notions and concepts for things like time, space, state, event, etc;
- representational ontologies, that define the basic concepts for the representation of knowledge; and
- finally, method and particular tasks ontologies, which provide terms specific for particular tasks and methods. They provide a reasoning point of view on domain knowledge.

Gómez-Perez, Fernández-López and Corcho (2003) classify ontology based on the level of specification of relationships among the terms gathered on the ontology, in:

- Lightweight ontologies, which include concepts, concept taxonomies, relationships between concepts and properties that describe concepts.
- Heavyweight ontologies which add axioms and constraints to lightweight ontologies. Those axioms and constraints clarify the intended meaning of the terms involved into the ontology.

4. WORKING AROUND ONTOLOGIES

Since their appearance, ontologies have been one of the most important branches of development in Computer Science. As in any new area of knowledge, when researchers started to work with ontologies almost everything had still to be done. However, the needs of researchers in this area focused on three specific activities: Techniques, Methodologies and Applications. All of these activities could be compiled under Ontological Engineering. According to Gómez-Perez, Fernández-López and Corcho (2003), Ontological Engineering refers to the set of activities that concerns the ontology development process, the ontology life cycle, and the methodologies, tools and languages for building ontologies.

In the following sections, we briefly summarize some techniques, methodologies and applications related to ontologies, with the aim of giving a general outlook about work in this field of study.

4.1 Techniques

Any formalism used to materialize ontology must contain elements for representing concepts and their relations. Those elements are always based on a set of basic axioms that set the parameters and the representation rules.

Some initiatives for the modeling of ontologies are:

- (Gruber, 1993) proposes using frames and first order logic. This schema uses classes, relations, functions, formal axioms and instances. Classes are the representation of relevant concepts (no matter if they are abstract or specific concepts) in the domain; classes are organized in taxonomies. Relations represent different types of associations between concepts in a domain. Functions are a special case of relations. Other elements are the formal axioms, which are sentences that are always true; these axioms are used to generate new knowledge and to verify consistency of the ontology. Finally, instances are used to represent elements or individuals in the ontology.

- Another proposal for modeling ontologies is using Description Logics (DL) (Baader, Horrocks and Sattler, 2004). DL is a logical formalism that is divided in two branches: TBox and ABox. The TBox contains the definitions of concepts and roles, also called intentional knowledge; the ABox contains the definitions of individuals, also called extensional knowledge. Therefore, systems based on DL use three elements to represent ontologies' components: concepts, roles and individuals. Concepts represent classes of objects, roles describe relations between concepts, and individuals represent instances of classes. Concepts and roles are specified based on a set of pre-existing terms and constructors whose elements can be mixed to obtain any kind of DL language. Primitive concepts are those whose specification does not need to be based on other concepts, but only on conditions that individuals must satisfy. Derived concepts are those concepts whose specification is based on another concept, from which it inherits some properties. Individuals represent an instance of the concepts and their values.
- Software Engineering Techniques like Unified Modeling Language (UML) are also used for modeling ontologies. Several authors argue that basic UML is enough to represent lightweight ontologies (Cranefield and Purvis, 1999 ; Kogut et al., 2002), however, for heavyweight ontologies it is necessary to enrich UML with, for example, the Object Constraint Language (OCL). OCL is the language for describing constraints in UML and helps us to formalize its semantics. UML class diagrams are the diagrams used to represent concepts where each class represents a concept. The instances of classes are represented by objects, which are instances of a concept. Concept taxonomies are represented through generalization relationships. Binary relations are represented through association relationships.
- Database Technologies are another possibility to represent ontologies (Gómez-Perez, Fernández-López and Corcho, 2003) using, for example, Entity-Relationship (ER) diagrams. In these diagrams, concepts can be represented using entities, which have attributes that are the properties of the concept. These attributes have a name and a type. Relations between concepts are represented by relationships, which have cardinality and

permit expression not only of associations but also generalization relations to create taxonomies of the concepts. Formal axioms can be represented using integrity constraints.

4.2 Methodologies

Like any piece of software, the construction of ontologies may be improved if some kind of methodology is applied. The goal of using a methodology is to obtain a good result following a set of steps which usually are based on best practices.

Most of the methodologies for building ontologies are based on the experience of people involved in their construction. In several cases, methodologies are extracted from the way in which a particular ontology was built.

Nowadays, methodologies are more focused on modeling knowledge than on developing applications. So, such methodologies are good alternatives for modeling knowledge instead of good alternatives for managing an information technology project centered on ontologies.

Next, we briefly summarize some significant methodologies that can be found in the literature. First we are going to list methodologies designed to build ontologies. The steps that confirm the methodologies are the result of analyzing the good choices and the mistakes in projects formulated to create ontology for a particular case:

- *Cyc* is based on the experience during the development of the Cyc knowledge base (Lenat and Guha, 1990), which contains a great quantity of common sense knowledge. In this process three basic tasks were carried out:
  - First, manual extraction of common sense knowledge;
  - Second, the knowledge coding was aided by tools using the knowledge already stored in the Cyc knowledge base;
  - Third, computer managed extraction from common sense knowledge.

  CycL was the language used to implement Cyc and two activities were carried out to specify the ontology:
  - First activity: development of a knowledge representation and a top level ontology with the most abstract concepts, and
  - Second activity: representation of the knowledge for different domains
- (Uschold and King, 1995) is one of the first specific proposals for building ontologies. It was used for developing *Enterprise Ontology* and for describing a set of guidelines to create an ontology:
  - To identify the purpose of the ontology.
  - To build the ontology through three activities. The first activity consists of capturing the ontology, in which we capture the concepts and the

relationships between concepts. The second activity consists of codifying the ontology using a formal language. The third activity consists of integrating the resulting ontology with previously existing ones.
- To evaluate the ontology, that is, "to make a technical judgment of the ontology, their associated software environment, and documentation with respect to a frame of reference".

- (Grüninger and Fox, 1995) methodology was developed to implement Toronto Virtual Enterprise (TOVE) ontology and is divided into six steps:
- To identify motivating scenarios: to capture the why? And what for? for which the ontology is built
- To elaborate informal competency questions: this consists of asking some questions written in natural language that must be answered by the ontology. These questions will be used to delimit the restrictions of the ontology and to evaluate the final ontology.
- To specify the terminology using first order logic.
- To write competency questions in a formal way using formal terminology: the questions used in step 2, are re-written in first order logic.
- To specify axioms using first order logics: this methodology proposes using axioms to specify the definitions of terms in the ontology and constraints in their interpretation.
- To specify completeness theorems: To define several conditions to assure that the ontology is finished.

- *Amaya* methodology is the result of ESPRIT KACTUS project (KACTUS, 1996), which investigates the possibility of reusing knowledge in complex technical processes. The method has three stages:
- To specify the application, where we identify context and the elements that we want to model.
- Preliminary design based on relevant top-level ontological categories. The elements identified in the previous step are used as inputs to obtain a global vision of the model. During this process it is possible to establish the reuse of ontology that already exist.
- Ontology refinement and structuring. To specialize terms of ontology for obtaining a definitive design with the maximum modularization.

The following methodologies address the development of ontologies in the framework of software projects. Therefore, their purpose is more focused on developing software applications which main elements are ontologies.

- *CommonKADS*: (Schreiber et al., 1999). Although it is not a methodology, it covers several aspects from corporate knowledge management to implementation of knowledge information systems.

CommonKADS has a focus on the initial phases for developing knowledge management applications.

- *Methontology* (Gómez-Perez, Fernández-López and Corcho, 2003) is inspired by software development methodologies. This methodology divides the process into three phases:

1. Project management activities. Those activities involve the planning, tracking of task and control of quality to obtain a good result.
2. Development-oriented activities: Specification of the ontology, formalization of resources used to build the ontology, design, implementation and maintenance.
3. Support activities: Knowledge gathering, ontology evaluation, ontology reuse and documentation.

This methodology divides the process for modeling knowledge process into eight tasks:

- Task 1: To build the glossary of terms. Those terms must have their natural language definition, their synonyms and their acronyms.
- Task 2: To build concept taxonomies to classify the concepts.
- Task 3: To build ad hoc binary relation diagrams to identify ad hoc relationships between concepts of the ontology or concepts of other ontologies.
- Task 4: To build a concept dictionary. A concept dictionary contains all the domain concepts, their relations, their instances and their classes and instance attributes.
- Task 5: To describe in detail each *ad hoc* binary relation that appears in the binary relation diagram. Results of this task are shown in an *ad hoc binary relation table.*
- Task 6: To describe in detail each instance attribute that appears on the concept dictionary.
- Task 7: To describe in detail each class attribute that appears on the concept dictionary.
- Task 8: To describe each constant, which specifies information related to the knowledge domain.

4.3 Applications

Several branches of Computer Science have used ontologies to model their knowledge. Database Systems, Software Engineering and Artificial Intelligence are the three most important fields where ontologies have been used to construct solutions to satisfy their needs.

The main purpose for using ontologies in previous branches of Computer Science is as a means of integrating several platforms or applications. The problem of integration between platforms consists of looking for the most natural way to inter-communicate two applications. To obtain such communication, it is important to have a set of concepts that compile vocabulary used by the applications and a set of rules for solving semantic heterogeneity that could exist between the concepts in each application. The association of these two elements allows transforming data from one application to another. So, the solution developed must allow information sharing and have efficient communication (Rubin, 2003), (Zhibin, Xiaoyong, Ishii, 1998), (Dehoney, Harte, Lu, Chin, 2003), (Tosic and Agha, 2004).

Another common use of ontologies is for domain modeling. Ontologies constitute a good alternative for representing the shared knowledge about a domain. Leaving aside accidental characteristics, ontologies hope to represent an objective point of view of a part of the reality, so its representation is more universal and includes the main characteristics that would be used by any application that is expected to give a particular solution in a modeled domain (Wagner and Taveter, 2004; Dehoney, Harte, Lu, Chin, 2003; Sallantin, Divol, Duroux, 2003).

It is also possible to apply ontologies to support specific tasks in different fields of study. In Database Systems, the ontologies help to model a specific domain and facilitate the integration with other databases. In addition, they improve information search (Kohler, Lange, Hofestadt, Schulze-Kremer, 2000). In Software Engineering, a specific ontology could be taken as reference point to validate a model that acts over a particular domain (Ambrosio, de Santos, de Lucena, da Silva, 2004; Conesa, de Palol, Olivé, 2004), likewise several paradigms of Software Engineering, like, for example, Extreme Programming could be used to build ontologies (Ceravolo, Damiani, Marchesi, Pinna, Zavaterelli, 2003). In Artificial Intelligence, ontologies help to ease the inference process (Rubin, 2003).

Figure 1-1 shows, by means of a use case diagram, the different ways ontologies could be used in Software Engineering, Artificial Intelligence and Database Systems.

So, ontology is found in a wide range of applications and may take different forms. In the following, some application examples of different topics are briefly summarized:

- FLAME 2008 is a platform to model a provider system of services for mobile devices based on ontologies (Weißenberg, Voisard and Gartmann, 2004).
- ONTOLOGER is an application for optimizing the searching on the Web according to user profiles (Stojanovic, González and Stojanovic, 2003).
- Carr et al. (2001) create a conceptual hypermedia service which provides hyperlinks for searching on the web. Hyperlinks are obtained by an improved ontological processing.

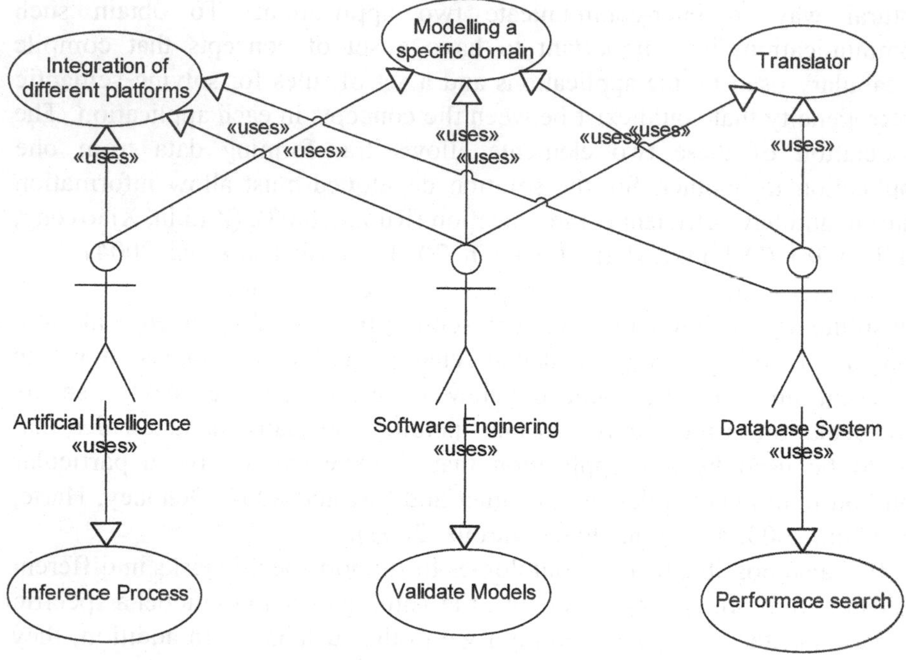

Figure 1-1. [Uses of Ontologies]

- *OntoWeb Project* is a thematic network created to exchange information in fields like knowledge management or e-commerce using ontologies. (Oberle and Spyns, 2004).
- *Onto-Share* is an application for virtual communities where ontologies specify a hierarchy of concepts (Davies, Duke and Sure, 2003).
- *SweetDeal* is a rule-based approach based on an ontology for the representation of business contracts (Grosof and Poon, 2003).
- Corcho et al. (2003) present a three-layer ontology-based mediation framework for electronic commerce applications.
- *CoursewareWatchdog* use ontologies to model an easy e-learning system (Tane, Schmitz and Stumme, 2004).
- *Edutella* is a P2P network based on the use of an ontology (KAON) for the exchange of educational resources between German universities (Nejdl et al., 2001).
- *OntoVote* is a mechanism for the development of ontologies in P2P environments, so ontology is produced by the consensus of all members of P2P application (Ge et al., 2003).
- SAMOVAR (Systems Analysis of Modeling and Validation of Renault Automobiles) is a system developed based on ontologies to optimize the

design of automobiles through management of past design experiences (Golebiowska et al., 2001).

- Stevens et al. (2004) show us a general panorama of using ontologies in bioinformatics which is a discipline that uses computational and mathematical techniques to manage biological data.
- Thesaurus and tools that organizes knowledge in concepts and relations, such as The Art and Architecture Thesaurus (AAT, 2005), WordNet (WordNet, 2004), ACM Computing classification system (ACM, 1998).

A survey about the relationship between ontologies and information systems can be found on (Chandrasekaran, Josephson, Benjamins, 2003)

5. CONCLUSIONS AND FUTURE WORK

The concept of *ontology* has been taken up by Computer Science with a different meaning than the one that it traditionally has had in Philosophy for centuries. In this work we have summarized the evolution of the concept of ontology as it passed from Philosophy to Computer Science, and we have examined the new meaning that this term has acquired. In future works, a profound comparison of this concept with related Computer Science terms (for example, the concept of *model*) will be addressed.

ACKNOWLEDGEMENTS

This research was carried out in the framework of the MIFISIS project (*Research Methods and Philosophical Foundations in Software Engineering and Information Systems*) supported by the Spanish Ministry of Science and Technology (TIC2002-12378-E), and of the PPR-2004-15 project, financed by Rey Juan Carlos University.

REFERENCES

AAT, 2005, Art & Architecture Thesaurus Online; (March 7, 2005) http://www.getty.edu/research/conducting_research/vocabularies/aat/.

ACM, 1998, The ACM Computing Classification System, 1998 Version. http://www.acm.org/class.

Ambrosio, A.P., de Santos D.C., de Lucena F.N., da Silva J.C., 2004, Software engineering documentation: an ontology-based approach, *WebMedia and LA-Web, 2004. Proceedings*. pp. 38 – 40.

Aristotle, 1994, *Metaphysics*. Chapters I and V. Oxford: Oxford University Press. Oxford.

Baader, F., Horrocks, I., Sattler, U., 2004, Description Logics. In: Staab S and Studer R, ed. *Handbook on Ontologies*. Berlin: Springer-Verlag, pp. 03-28.

Booch, G., 1993. *Object-oriented Analysis and Design with Applications* (2nd edition). Canada: Addison-Wesley Press.

Carr, L., Hall, W., Bechofer, S., Goble, C., 2001, Conceptual Linking: Ontology-Based Open Hypermedia. *International World Wide Web Conference 2004,* pp. 334-342. New York: ACM Press.

Chandrasekaran, B., Josephson, J.R., Benjamins, V.R., 2003, What are ontologies, and why do we need them? *Intelligent Systems and Their Applications, IEEE. IEEE Intelligent Systems* Volume 14, Issue 1. pp. 20 – 26.

Cocchiarella, N.B., 1991, Formal Ontology. In: Burkhard, H. and Smith, B. (eds), *Handbook of Metaphysics and Ontology*. Munich: Philosophia Verlag.

Conesa, J., Palol, X. de, Olivé, A., 2003, Building Conceptual Schemas by Refining General Ontologies. In *Marik, V, et al (ed). DEXA 2003*. pp: 693-702.

Corcho, O., Gómez-Pérez, A., Leger, A., Rey, C., Toumani, F., 2003, An Ontology-based Mediation Architecture for E-commerce Applications. *IIS 2003*; pp. 477-486.

Cranefield, S., Purvis, M., 1999, UML as an Ontology Modelling Language. In: Fensel D, Knoblock C, Kushmeric N and Rousset MC, ed. *IJCAI'99 Workshop on Intelligent information integration. Stockholm, Sweden.* Amsterdam, 5.1-5.8.

Davies, J., Duke, A., Sure, Y., 2003, OntoShare - A Knowledge Management Environmental for Virtual Communities of Practice. *International Conference On Knowledge Capture Sanibel Island 2003*. New York. ACM Press

Dehoney, D., Harte, R., Lu, Y., Chin, D., 2003, Using natural language processing and the gene ontology to populate a structured pathway database. *Bioinformatics Conference, 2003. CSB 2003. Proceedings of the 2003 IEEE*. pp. 646 – 647.

Fensel, D., 2004, *Ontologies: A Silver Bullet for Knowledge Management and Electronic Commerce.* 2nd ed. Berlin: Springer-Verlag

García Sierra, P., 1999, *Diccionario filosófico. Manual de materialismo filosófico. Una introducción analítica.* Oviedo: Biblioteca Filosofía en español.

Ge, Y., Yu, Y., Zhu, X., Huang, S., Xu, M., 2003, OntoVote: A Scalable Distributed Vote-Collecting Mechanism For Ontology Drift On A P2P Platform, *The Knowledge Engineering Review,* 18(30): 257-263. New York: Cambridge University Press.

Golebiowska, J., Dieng-Kuntz, R., Corby, O., Mousseau, D., 2001, Building And Exploiting Ontologies For An Automobile Project Memory, *International Conference On Knowledge Capture,* pp. 52-59. New York: ACM Press

Gómez-Pérez, A., Fernández-López, M., Corcho, O., 2003, *Ontological Enginering*. London, Springer-Verlag.

Grosof, B., Poon, T., 2003, Sweetdeal: Representing Agent Contracts With Exceptions Using XML Rules, Ontologies And Process Descriptions, *International World Wide Web Conference.* pp: 340-349. New York: ACM Press.

Gruber, T.R., 1993, A translation approach to portable ontology specifications. *Knowledge Acquisition* 5(2): 199-220

Grüninger, M., Fox, M.S., 1995, Methodology for the design and evaluation of ontologies, In: Skuce, D., ed. *IJCAI 95 Workshop on basic ontological issues in knowledge sharing.*, 6.1-6.10.

Guarino, N., Giaretta, P., 1995, Ontologies and Knowledge Bases: Towards a Terminological Clarification. In: NJI Mars, ed. *Towards very large knowledge bases.* Amsterdam: IOS Press, pp: 25-32

Guarino, N., 1998, Formal Ontology and Information Systems. In: *FOIS'98*, Trento, Italy. Amsterdam: IOS Press. pp. 3-15

KACTUS, 1996, The KACTUS Booklet version 1.0 Esprit Project 8145 KACTUS, (April 5, 2005); http://www.swi.psy.uva.nl/projects/NewKACTUS/Reports.html.

Kogut, P., Cranefield, S., Hart, L., Dutra, M., Baclawski, K., Kokar, M., Smith, J., 2002, UML for Ontology Development. *The Knowledge Engineering Review,* 17(1); 61-64

Kohler, J., Lange, M., Hofestadt, R., Schulze-Kremer, S. Logical and semantic database integration, 2000, *Bio-Informatics and Biomedical Engineering, 2000. Proceedings. IEEE International Symposium on,* pp. 77 – 80.

Lenat, D.B., Guha, R.V., 1990, Building large knowledge-based systems: Representations and Inference in the Cyc Project. Addison-Wesley, Boston Massachusetts.

McCarthy, J., 1980, Circumscription – A form of non-monotonic reasoning. *Artificial Intelligence,* 13; 27-39

Mosterín, J., 2000 *Conceptos y teorías en la ciencia*. Editorial Alianza. Madrid

Nejdl, W., Wolf, B., Staab, S., Tane, J., 2001, EDUTELLA: Searching and Annotating Resources within an RDF-based P2P Network. (April 27, 2005); http://edutella.jxta.org

Nutter, J.T., 1997, Epistemology. In: S. Shapiro, ed. *Encyclopedia of Artificial Intelligence.* Wyley Press.

Oberle, D., Spyns, P., 2004, The Knowledge Portal "OntoWeb", In: Staab, S. and Studer, R., ed. *Handbook on Ontologies*. Berlin: Springer-Verlag, pp: 499-516.

Oxford, 1993, *Compact Oxford Dictionary*. Oxford University Press

Poli, R., 2004, *Descriptive, Formal and Formalized Ontologies*. University of Trento. Mitteleuropa Foundation

Rubin, S.H., 2003, On the fusion and transference of knowledge. II. *Information Reuse and Integration, 2003. IRI 2003. IEEE International Conference on*. pp. 150 – 159

Sallantin, J., Divol, J., Duroux, P., 2003, Conceptual framework for interactive ontology building, *Cognitive Informatics, 2003. Proceedings. The Second IEEE International Conference on*. pp. 179 – 186.

Schreiber, G., Akkermans, H., Anjewierden, A., Hoog, R. de, Shadbolt, N., Velde, W. van de, Wielinga, B., 1999, Knowledge Engineering And Management – The CommonKDAS Methodology. The MIT Press, Cambridge, Massachusetts.

Smith, B., Welty, C., 2002, Ontology: Towards a New Synthesis. *FOIS Introducction 2002*. Amsterdam: IOS Press

Smith, B., 1998, The Basic Tools of Formal Ontology, In: Nicola Guarino (ed.). *Formal Ontology in Information Systems.* Amsterdam, Oxford, Tokyo, Washington, DC: IOS Press (Frontiers in Artificial Intelligence and Applications), pp. 19-28.

Stevens, R., Wroe, C., Lord, P., Goble, C., 2004, Ontologies In Bioinformatics. In: Staab, S. and Studer, R., ed. *Handbook on Ontologies*. Berlin: Springer-Verlag, pp. 635-657

Stojanovic, N., Gonzalez, J., Stojanovic, L., 2003, ONTOLONGER – A System For Usage-Driven Management Of Ontology-Based Information Portals, *International Conference On Knowledge Capture* Sanibel Island, New York: ACM Press, pp. 172-179

Tane, J., Schmitz, C., Stumme, G., 2004, Semantic Resources Management for the Web: An E-Learning Application, *International World Wide Web Conference,* pp. 01-10. New York: ACM Press.

Tosic, P. T., Agha, G. A., 2004, Towards a hierarchical taxonomy of autonomous agents. *Systems, Man and Cybernetics, 2004 IEEE International Conference on*. 4:3421–3426

Uschold, M., King, M., 1995, Towards a Methodology for building ontologies . In: Skuce D, ed. *IJCAI'95m Workshop on Basic Ontological Issue in Knowledge Sharing*. Montreal, 6.1-6.10.

Van Heijst, G., Schereiber, A. T., Wielinga, B. J., 1996, Using Explicit Ontologies in KBS Development. *International Journal of Human and Computer Studies*.

Wagner, G., Taveter, K., 2004, Towards radical agent-oriented software engineering processes based on AOR modeling. Intelligent *Agent Technology, 2004. (IAT 2004). Proceedings. IEEE/WIC/ACM International Conference on*. pp. 509 – 512.

Weißenberg, N., Voisard, A., Gartmann, R., 2004, Using Ontologies In Personalized Mobile Applications. *The 12th Annual ACM International Workshop on Geographic Information Systems*. New York: ACM Press.

WordNet, 2005, WordNet A lexical database for the English language. 2005, (February 3, 2005); http://wordnet.princeton.edu.

Zhibin, L., Xiaoyong, D., Ishii, N., 1998, Integrating databases in Internet. *Knowledge-Based Intelligent Electronic Systems, Proceedings KES '98. 1998 Second International Conference on*. 3: 21-23.

Chapter 2

USE OF ONTOLOGIES FOR ORGANIZATIONAL KNOWLEDGE MANAGEMENT AND KNOWLEDGE MANAGEMENT SYSTEMS

Vasudeva Varma
International Institute of Information Technology, Hyderabad, India

Abstract: This chapter describes the role of ontologies and corporate taxonomies in managing the content and knowledge within organizations. Managing content in a reusable and effective manner is becoming increasingly important in knowledge centric organizations as the amount of content generated, both text based and rich media, is growing exponentially. Search, categorization and document characterization, content staging and content delivery are the key technology challenges in knowledge management systems. This chapter describes how corporate taxonomies and ontologies can help in making sense of huge amount of content that gets generated across the locations in different languages and formats Different information silos can be connected and workflow and collaboration can be achieved using ontologies. As the KM solutions are moving from a centralized approach to a distributed approach, a framework where multiple taxonomies and ontologies can co-exist with uniform interfaces is needed.

Key words: Knowledge Management; Knowledge Management Systems (KMS); corporate taxonomy; categorization; document classification

1. INTRODUCTION

In this era of knowledge economy, every organization is producing a lot more content than before, resulting in a situation where we need to deal with the problem of information overload. As documents of structured and unstructured nature are growing exponentially; we have to find most relevant document(s) in the least possible time. Hence, obtaining very high precision and recall in information retrieval systems is very important. In addition, mergers and acquisitions are major hurdles faced by the architects of information technology. As a number of organizations are being merged or acquired, making sure that the content of organizations can also be merged seamlessly is very important.

Recent studies in enterprise content management [Venkata, 2002] [Winkle, 2004] have estimated that 85% of the corporate content is in the form of unstructured data that doesn't fit neatly into relational database tables. Considering the effort and money that goes into creating such volumes of data, there is a compelling need for the organizations competing in today's economy to leverage unstructured data. Product development, sales and marketing, as well as executive planning and decision-making all depend upon information that resides within corporate documents. It is, hence, a challenge to manage the critical information that is scattered amongst various kinds of documents originating from various sources such as emails and web pages, various document-authoring applications, file systems, document management systems. In many corporations, it is a well known fact that decision makers are unable to leverage unstructured data to gain valuable business insights as these systems cannot easily exchange information and as a result users cannot easily explore and navigate documents from multiple sources.

The latest University of California at Berkeley study [Berkeley] into information growth estimates that 5 exabytes of recorded information were created worldwide in 2002 (equivalent to 800 Mb for each person on the planet). If access to these volumes of information is to be a benefit rather than a burden, then order and control become prerequisites. Information management techniques must be improved if we are to gain more control over these information flows, and taxonomies should be a key part of it.

To address this major challenge, companies need a platform to establish a shared vocabulary across disparate sources of unstructured information. If a company cannot provide a transparent view of its unstructured data, employees will neither be able to consistently locate nor share documents, thereby significantly hindering their ability to act effectively. The shared vocabulary is the backbone of the entire content and knowledge management infrastructure. This well-crafted vocabulary resides in the corporate taxonomy[1] or ontology. Corporate taxonomy is the key to success for building effective content and knowledge management systems. Content management system is an important sub-system of any corporate knowledge management initiatives.

1 A simple definition of taxonomy is that it is a hierarchy of categories used to classify documents and other information. A corporate taxonomy is a way of representing the information available within an enterprise.

A classical taxonomy assumes that each element can only belong to one branch of the hierarchical tree. However, in a corporate environment, such formal ordering is neither feasible nor desirable. For example, a document on a competitor's product may be of interest to different departments in the organization for different reasons--forcing it into a single predefined category may be neater, but it also reduces its usefulness. Corporate taxonomies need to be flexible and pragmatic as well as consistent.

In the context of corporate intranet and knowledge organization, I would like to make note of two important characteristics of ontologies and taxonomies.

- **Ontology is more than an agreed vocabulary:** Ontology provides a set of well-founded constructs that can be leveraged to build meaningful higher level knowledge. The terms in taxonomies and ontologies are selected with great care, ensuring that the most basic (abstract) foundational concepts and distinctions are defined and specified. The terms chosen form a complete set, whose relationships to each other are defined using formal techniques. It is these formally defined relationships that provide a semantic basis for the terminology chosen.
- **Ontology is more than a classification of terms:** Although taxonomy contributes to the semantics of a term in a vocabulary, ontologies include richer relationships between terms. It is these rich relationships that enable the expression of domain-specific knowledge, without the need to include domain-specific terms.

Taxonomy-based knowledge management solutions are well known and widely practiced in the industry today. However, the limitations of corporate taxonomies are the entry points for ontology-based approaches. This issue will be discussed in detail later in the chapter. However, it is important to note that the organizational content management systems and knowledge-management systems make use of ontologies and taxonomies at several functional points that include: document categorization, indexing, document retrieval (whole or partial), user query expansion, query matching, and result verification. Since rich media documents are also becoming pervasive and important (perhaps more important than the textual documents) there is an emphasis on extending the ontologies work for multimedia documents as well.

In this chapter we first take a general look at the knowledge management (KM, henceforth) problems and issues, and the role of technology in KM in section two. The importance of categorization in KM arena is discussed in section three, where the limits of categorization and how taxonomy improves on categorization is our main emphasis. In section four, I will discuss the role of ontology in knowledge management systems and discuss how ontologies can help where taxonomies expose their limitations. A framework called as UTON, Uniform Taxonomy and Ontology Network, where several ontologies and taxonomies can co-exist and accessible through uniform interface is also described here. Section five discusses future trends in using ontologies in knowledge management applications and presents our conclusions.

2. KNOWLEDGE MANAGEMENT TECHNOLOGIES

In the last decade, knowledge management (KM) has developed into an important success factor for organizations. KM has matured to provide a substantial insight into some of the fundamental challenges facing modern organizations, including the management of intellectual and social capital, the promotion of innovation and support for new forms of collaborative working [Woods, 2004]. As organizations could no longer draw sustainable competitive advantage by further improvements in operational effectiveness, knowledge has turned into a crucial competitive factor in business. Increasing complexity of products and services, globalization, virtual organizations and customer orientation are the major developments that demand more thorough management of knowledge – within and between organizations.

2.1 Knowledge Management Challenges

While it is easy to win the intellectual argument for KM, arguing for any kind of technology poses certain challenges. A chief knowledge officer or anyone else who is responsible for organizational KM initiatives will have a tough time while answering questions like “How KM can help company manage the knowledge that it needs in order to increase profits?” At times when business pressure is growing on KM groups to make costs and benefits transparent, it is of utmost importance to come up with a cogent elevator-ride answer to such a simple question.

Even though we will focus mostly on the technology aspects of KM in this chapter, I would like to emphasize that KM is more of a culture than a technology, a fact that is well documented. KM requires a strong commitment from all the stake holders, specially the top management, to information sharing, collaboration in order to deliver on its potential. KM can be defined simply as “The process of turning information into useful knowledge that is accessible when needed.”

The goal of KM is to enable all the individual knowledge workers and their communities to gain instantaneous access wherever, whenever and however needed to most relevant information so that they can make better decisions. It should also help in improving efficiency and in saving money. Organizations are putting an increasing amount of investment into their overall information architecture to provide a framework for managing data, information and knowledge. The growing value being placed on corporate taxonomies, metadata management and XML-based standards for information description are all part of that trend. But these solutions need also to be implemented in the light of a deep and rigorous understanding of the information needs of an organization. It means that knowledge management methodologies and practices have a vital role to play in guiding the evolution of a new generation of information architectures.

Various enterprise applications and content databases are designed keeping the specific user needs and business functions as major drivers. Although this helped to make these systems valuable and indispensable, this narrow focus has also created information silos that are difficult to integrate and harness. Some of the major issues with fragmented enterprise application are: proprietary data formats, non-standard interfaces, non-extensible and application-specific search and information access tools. This phenomenon across the organizations worldwide has given birth to disciplines such as Enterprise Application Integration (EAI) and many middleware software tools. Organizations spend a lot of money and effort in integrating enterprise wide applications.

2.2 Technology in Knowledge Management

In the past we have seen that much of technology has been abused in Knowledge Management. Especially during the early days of the KM adoption in organizations, technology was projected as a panacea for all knowledge needs. One major reason for this is the vendors of information management and CRM products have projected their products as solution to KM problems by hastily trying to re-label their offerings as KM solutions. After realizing the inadequacy of these solutions, the second generation KM implementers made the mistake of substituting enterprise application integration (EAI) and business intelligence projects for KM solutions. The current generation KM solutions are riding the wave of intranets and portals by externalizing internal information and by providing access to so called "corporate knowledge" to knowledge workers any where, any how and any time. We can also notice that the process and people aspects of KM, such as workflow applications, collaborative work spaces, project management tools etc. are also appearing in the KM implementation agenda.

The current KM implementations illustrate a strong disillusionment that followed the misuse of many of these technologies in the past. It is important to use technologies as tools that help in implementing KM solutions. Most KM architects typically put together the technology infrastructure after studying the organizational need for knowledge management and identifying right KM solutions. The typical technology infrastructure is built using KM technology enablers that are listed in the following subsection.

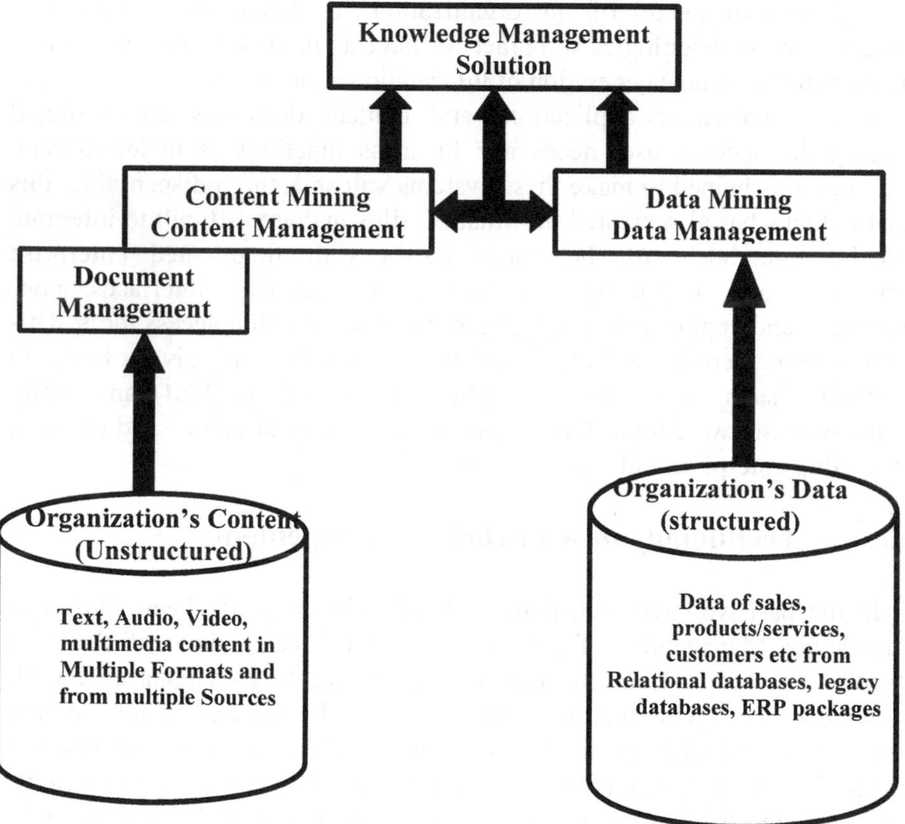

Figure 2-1. Knowledge Management Solution

A typical knowledge management solution will consist of document management, content management (including content analysis, content categorization, and search technologies), together with data mining and data warehousing sub systems that collaborate with each other to manage both tacit and explicit organizational knowledge. The above diagram shows how a knowledge management solution can be seen as a confluence of data and content management solutions.

2.3 Technology Infrastructure for KM

The two most important and widely used components of the technology infrastructure of KM systems are search and categorization. These two provide an alternative to expensive content-integration projects. These information access and discovery tools must harness the information residing in disparate enterprise applications and information repositories.

Full-featured advanced search technologies are required to access, manage, and organize information stored in many and varied sources throughout the enterprise. Intuitive yet powerful search capabilities that enable users to look for mission-critical information and have it presented in a variety of formats to suit their particular need or preference is essential. Superior search and retrieval tools are capable of indexing and accessing information stored in a wide range of business systems, e-mail packages, document management systems, file systems and other repositories, regardless of whether the information is structured or unstructured.

It is important to find the right digital content in the shortest interaction time and in a very intuitive manner. We need to employ techniques such as "pearl growing" (improving and building upon the initial query). Ability to combine keyword or text-based approach with sample image or image parameter based approach. An example query would look some thing like: "show me all the Toyotas which are shaped like this [insert or select an image] and are in black color and registered in New Delhi".

The system should be able to navigate through vast digital content with ease and efficiency. Users should be able to interact with the digital content servers in a very meaningful manner using the latest technologies such as conversational systems to arrive at the right content in the fastest possible manner.

Categorization tools are the lifeblood of knowledge management initiatives. They are a key building block in that they add context to content. These tools leverage and enrich an existing corporate taxonomy. Solid categorization engines develop an intuitive, precise "table of contents" that enables users to find the information they require faster by providing them with a contextual map of search results—organizing related information by similar theme or concept.

There is another aspect to categorization that is called as media specific categorization. Once the document is parsed and various media objects are extracted from the document, we need to index the sub-documents (or media objects) based on the media type. For example, video objects need to be parsed and indexed by the video indexers, similarly, textual objects need to be indexed by text indexers, image objects need to be indexed by the image indexers. There may be specializations and more than one indexer may be applicable for any specific media type. The content management system architecture needs to be extensible to add new indexing engines.

Besides the search and categorization, some knowledge management systems are equipped with the following tools and technologies:

- **Organizational knowledge network:** One of the main objectives of KM is to connect people and create communities that interact with each other for mutual benefit. To achieve this objective, KM architects build a soft infrastructure with the help of information technology, which includes: Email, creating user groups, building extranet bridge, creating corporate portals, online events (such as Virtual meeting interfaces, the corporate showcase) and virtual discussion forums (such as chat or instant messaging, peer-to-peer networking, video, file sharing, conversation, seminars and conferences). Some advanced KM systems also feature external knowledge hang-outs including activities such as touring customer hangouts and creating customer hangouts.
- **Crawlers and Agents:** Another key feature of a knowledge management solution is the provision of "intelligent agents" capable of pushing the required information to users. Agents allow users to define criteria, alerts or changes to documents, Web site content, or new information from other sources. Crawlers are enabling technologies that provide for Internet content and other external information sources to be included in user- and agent-based searches. This can also involve "brokered" searches whereby a search and retrieval solution brokers out searches to Internet-based search engines and then organizes those results as part of its own search. It is important to capture the digital assets from various sources and systems including that of file storage, web, databases and storage networks. The multi-media content can originate from any sources. The content crawlers and document filters can automatically 'grab' content from content databases, video sources, voice sources, XML Sources, emails etc. The content from various sources is being captured by crawlers. Depending on the document type and document format, various filters can be used to separate the media specific content.
- **Document Summarization:** Providing contextual summaries of documents, offering a "preview" format of the related result. This enables readers to see the document in a minimized form. Summarization is important for textual documents as well as rich media documents. For

example, video summarization is possible using the techniques that include video skimming or fast flipping of select frames and video information collages. For audio and text media we will use the summarization techniques developed in natural language processing and linguistics research. For images we can create thumb nails.

- **Personalization:** Customization of the content for an individual requires mixing and matching content elements. Personalization has become very important in web content management systems and this area has proven to be highly specialized and complex. A new trend of personalization of results obtained by search engines is gaining popularity within search community. Personalization takes into account various parameters such as past and present user behavior, the context in which the search is being made, and the predicted information need of the user.
- **Multiple Language Support:** In today's global economy, the ability to search and return result sets across a variety of not only major European languages but also Asian languages is essential.
- **Application "Hooks":** The ability of knowledge management tools to access and categorize enterprise business systems is critical. Hooks, or activators, that enable knowledge management technologies to index, categorize, retrieve, and display comprehensive, flexible result sets from packages such as Siebel, SAP, and J.D. Edwards are extremely valuable to organizations looking to ensure that the entire range of business content is available to knowledge workers conducting information-based activities.
- **Application Programming Interface (API):** The ability of organizations to tailor knowledge management tools, including information search and retrieval and categorization tools is essential. From an information search and retrieval perspective, this equates to enabling organizations to develop custom interfaces, leverage a variety of advanced features, and include natural language capabilities. From a categorization standpoint, API enables organizations to develop, manage, and modify business taxonomy, provide a variety of knowledge agents for users, and initiate supervised or unsupervised categorization; or a combination of the two to monitor and fine-tune the contextualization of enterprise content.

In sum, knowledge management tools are rapidly emerging as the primary means of leveraging business information. Typical KM implementations combine these tools and techniques with the benefits and capabilities of an enterprise portal and organizations can begin truly realizing and capitalizing on the wealth of information available to them.

I would like to end this section with a word of caution. KM is a controversial subject with no clearly defined boundaries. We can be more comfortable discussing the technical aspects that can aid the KM architecture rather than discuss about feasibility, strategy or planning of knowledge management. The technical approaches to managing knowledge have some known limitations. Information professionals are or should be involved in the creation and maintenance of the intellectual infrastructure of their organization. While technology and organizational infrastructures have received more attention and resources, some of the imbalance could be corrected through the intelligent utilization and integration of new software, new methods of working with both content providers and content consumers, and new ways of presenting information.

3. CATEGORIZATION AND TAXONOMY IN KM SYSTEMS

An important problem in content and knowledge management systems is that of organizing a large set of documents either in response to a query or during the staging phase or characterization phase of the document. Text categorization and text clustering are two techniques that are applied to achieve this task. Text categorization refers to an algorithm or procedure that assigns a category(s) to a given document and clustering refers to an algorithm that sorts documents into a finite set of groups based on associations among the intra-document features.

Categorization is a supervised process where as clustering is unsupervised. Various studies as mentioned in [Hearst, 1999] explored the advantages and disadvantages of both these approaches. In this section, it is not our main focus to distinguish between the two but to treat them as text classification methods that play a major role in knowledge management systems in organizing documents.

There are also a very large number of companies offering their version of this new software and, of course, most claim that their approach is the best, the fastest, and the smartest (an informal survey in 2004, puts the number of categorization companies at nearly fifty). Further, more and more search and content management companies are scrambling to incorporate categorization into their products. The reason why search engine companies now are taking categorization very seriously is that when users can't find anything, the categorized content enables a browse or search/browse functionality. Often users prefer browsing, which is more successful than simple keyword search and facilitates knowledge discovery.

3.1 Document Categorization

As we saw before, one of the most central pieces of KM infrastructure is categorization. Moreover, like all infrastructure activities, integration with other components is essential. Categorization needs to be incorporated into content creation through content management tools and at the same time incorporated into content consumption through search and collaboration software. Categorization software classifies documents using taxonomy and a classification model. There are several algorithms that can be used in a classification model. Among them are:

- Statistical classifiers, which provide accurate classification for broad and abstract concepts based on robust training sets;
- Keyword classifiers, which excel at defining granular topics within broad statistically generated topics;
- Source classifiers, which leverage pre-existing definitions from sources; for example, documents from a Web site or news service that are already categorized;
- Boolean classifiers, which can accommodate complex classification rules, as well as many legacy information systems.

Each of these classifiers provides optimum results for different use cases, which occur in a normal document corpus and taxonomy. Often it makes sense to create rules between classifiers as to when and how they should operate. In many situations the optimal use of keyword and Boolean classifiers is to provide more granular topic distinctions under broad-based, statistically derived topics. In this case, it can be necessary not only to create a hierarchical relationship between topics, but also to create an explicit rule regarding how and when a classifier should operate based upon an earlier classification or condition being satisfied. Some of the most recent research in text classification indicates that a parallel classification architecture utilizing multiple classifiers provides the best results.

As regard to all these above-mentioned classification techniques, it should be noted that none of them categorizes the way humans do, which is both strength and a weakness. Typically, each category is represented as a multi-nominal distribution of sets of terms. These parameters are estimated from the frequency of certain sets of words and phrases in the training sets of documents. The probability that a document with such a distribution of terms would belong to a given category is given be *P(document | Category)*. The category chosen for the document is the one with maximum *P(Document | Category)* [Gutherie et al, 1999].

Text categorization has been mostly influenced by the statistical information retrieval models. But, some text categorization systems have been built that exhibit strong performance using hand-coded knowledge bases [Hayes and Weinstein, 1991] and [Goodman, 1991]. There is also a middle path as suggested by [Riloff and Lorenzen, 1999] that benefits from a strong domain knowledge but acquires this domain knowledge in an automated fashion.

Categorization software can very quickly scan every word in a document and analyze the frequencies of patterns of words and based on a comparison with an existing taxonomy and assign the document to a particular category in the taxonomy. Some other things that are being done with this software are clustering or taxonomy building in which the software is simply pointed at a collection of say 10,000 to 100,000 documents, and search through all the combinations of words to find clumps or clusters of documents that appear to belong together. It's not as successful as the first use, but it can be an interesting way of aiding a human in creating or refining a taxonomy.

Another feature of categorization software is metadata generation. The idea is that the software categorizes the document and then searches for keywords that are related to the category. This can be useful even if the suggested metadata isn't simply taken, since authors or editors work better selecting from an existing set of keywords than when starting fresh with a blank field.

One reason for preferring auto-categorization on intranet is the sheer amount of unstructured but very valuable content that resides on corporate intranets. However, because of the factors noted above, it requires a different mix of automatic and manual categorization and also calls for a better auto-categorization than has been adequate for news feeds. The "browse and post" feature, which is guided by the corporate taxonomy, aids human editors to manually categorize the content.

3.2 Applications of Categorization

There are various areas where categorization software worked wonders. For example, news and content provider arena depends on auto categorization. The reason is clear, it is an environment in which you have tens of thousands of documents a day to categorize and so obviously it has to be done in an automated fashion. Various characteristics such as that the material is written by professionals who know how to write good titles and opening paragraphs helps the auto categorization software perform better. A related market is in sites that categorize web sites on the Internet into browse taxonomy. Though the pioneer in this area, Yahoo, started with all human editors, it uses auto categorization to make editors more productive by supporting, not replacing them.

A new and intriguing market is in the intelligence industry. They, like the publishing industry, have huge volumes of content to categorize. However there are two features of the intelligence industry that are different; they need a finer granularity of categorization and not coincidentally, the material is not designated for a community of readers but is routed to one or a few experts. Not only does the intelligence industry need more specific categories, they also need to categorize content, not just at the document level, but at the paragraph level. This requires a level of sophistication beyond the early simple Bayesian statistics.

Finally, the corporate intranet and organizational knowledge management is a very important area where categorization has a major role to play. It is difficult because all the things that make news feeds work very well when pushed through the auto-categorizer are missing on almost all corporate intranets.

3.3 Role of Taxonomy in Categorization

There are several challenges we face while dealing with content available on the internet or even on an organization's intranet. The content is written by a really wild mix of writers. Some of the content may be pure literature, which unfortunately may sits next to an accounting document which may be next to a scientific research paper. Some of the content may have good titles, some may have very bad titles and some may have every page on the site with the same title. Some of the documents may be a single page of HTML, some may be book-length PDF documents and some may have about a paragraph of content but links to all sorts of other pages or sites.

Given this situation, there is every reason to believe that the corporate information organization systems such as content and knowledge management systems will see the most lucrative employment of auto-categorization software. Certainly the need is great and there are a very large number of corporate intranets which makes the challenge worthwhile.

Taxonomy enables "disambiguation" based on word meanings–for example, to distinguish the meanings of "java" as coffee, a country or a programming language. One advantage of using Taxonomy for categorization is that the system does not need to be "trained" with representative documents, as systems based on statistical techniques do. Furthermore, having an existing knowledge base enables accurate categorization for very short documents as well as longer ones.

The most important challenge is to create a corporate taxonomy rather than to categorize thousands of documents. Another challenge is to create either a very broad taxonomy or else integrate a number of taxonomies.

Finally, there is a need for both general categorization to support browsing and a very deep, specific taxonomy that supports quickly finding a particular document or even a paragraph.

3.4 Role of Taxonomy in KM systems

Software support for the corporate taxonomy is not limited to the provision of automatic classification tools. More effort is now being invested in software that can increase the usability of taxonomies for both corporate users and consumers and in tools to support taxonomy design and management.

The experience gained in building intranet and e-commerce sites is driving the development of more flexible technologies for the definition, management and use of taxonomies. The goal is to combine:

- The need for control and order in information management,
- An understanding of how users navigate through large volumes of information, and
- The realities of corporate and e-commerce information models.

Anyone trying to implement a corporate taxonomy would know that the world does not fit easily into neatly labeled boxes.

The enterprise search industry realized that it cannot provide very relevant results without making use of taxonomy. In the early stages of KM solutions, knowledge workers spent more time looking for information than using it. A solution to this problem that has become very popular is to combine search with browse functionality. When the user knows exactly what she wants, she will use search functionality and when she is not sure, a combination of search and browse is more effective. The backbone of browse functionality is the corporate taxonomy. Browse and search works better than search. When the entire document collection is held together by taxonomy, the information access becomes easy for the user. Any organization that needs to make significant volumes of information available in an efficient and consistent way to its customers, partners or employees needs to understand the value of a serious approach to taxonomy design and management.

Without an up-to-date Enterprise Content Taxonomy database to understand the inter-relationships, controls, and potential liabilities of structured and unstructured content, we suspect regulations such as Sarbanes-Oxley, and concerns over possible shareholder and other litigation, would result in a gridlock over any future document destruction.

Most organizations skip formal taxonomy development and rush into deployment by building their classification system around index keywords for retrieval. This is not a complete taxonomy and causes many problems later with their document management system, as well as missing many reengineering and process improvement opportunities. Taxonomy incorporates the practice of characterizing the context and relationships among documents and their retrieval aspects.

In the following, we list some scenarios resulting from the lack of a consistent taxonomy across all areas of the enterprise:

- Isolated silos of information systems and processes expand, causing significant cost, duplication of effort, and liabilities to the organization. How many times do you have to give your personal and insurance information to different departments of the same hospital?
- One group calls a form or report one name, another group another name. Both groups file them. Retention rules are applied to the form under one name, but not the other. When litigation occurs and a discovery action results, the information which was properly destroyed in one system is discovered in another and becomes a liability
- One department creates a business form with many data fields. Another form already exists with the same fields in a different layout. A third version exists as an electronic web form.
- Different courts, social services agencies, and prison systems file the same paper documents. Most of this paper is created by other government agencies. When courts or other agencies request the information, it is copied and exchanged on paper. 90% of this paper was originally generated electronically, yet a half-dozen agencies each undertake the labor to scan and index or file this paper in their own systems—and then exchange the data on paper.
- A bank forecloses on someone's unpaid mortgage, while that same bank issues them a new credit card.

3.5 Creation and Maintenance of a Corporate Taxonomy

The task of creating taxonomy can be daunting. Whereas Web sites are often organized using at most a few hundred topics, enterprise taxonomies can often contain upward of 5,000 to 15,000 nodes. Developing such taxonomies manually is an extremely labor-intensive effort. We have encountered situations where companies developing taxonomies have averaged three person-days per topic for several thousand topics. Finally, in the absence of a neutral analysis of a document corpus, manual taxonomy development can easily run afoul of internal political agendas.

There are some significant efforts in building ontologies and ontology systems like CYC [Guha et al, 1990], [Lenat and Guha, 1990] [Lenat, 1995] and IEEE SUMO [Niles and Pease, 2001a], [Niles and Pease, 2001b]. The Upper CYC project captures 3000 most significant concepts of common knowledge and creates ontology. The SUMO (Suggested Upper Merged Ontology) project at IEEE Standard Upper Ontology Working Group addresses the problem of capturing high level, meta, philosophic and general kind of concepts and presenting them in more details. Some domain specific ontologies are also built using these formalisms. From these previous efforts, we know that building large scale ontologies pose a new set of problems, especially in an environment where ontologies are viewed as "live repositories" rather than frozen resources [Farquhar et al., 1996]. For example, any large scale ontology design teams will have to consider the following major issues: adding a new domain in the existing ontology network, changing the knowledge format, performance issues and guaranteed quality of service, scalability and ease of making any modifications. There are some engineering approaches [Varma, 2002] to build ontologies and to provide access to them by making use of existing resources such as WordNet [Fellbaum, 1999] and Open Directory Project called Directory Mozilla [DMOZ].

Maintaining a corporate taxonomy consists of two primary activities: incorporating new documents into the existing structure and changing the structure to accommodate new information that cannot fit into the existing one. Those processes are usually carried out through a combination of automation and human intervention. Classification techniques include keywords, statistical analyses that look for patterns of words, and use of a semantic network or ontology that analyzes words for their meaning in context. Analytical capabilities can help determine when a new category is needed, and how the documents would be redistributed. According to Laura Ramos, director at the Giga Information Group, maintenance is the most expensive part of a taxonomy project, yet is often overlooked in the planning process.

Leading industry analysts and solution providers focus on taxonomies that can bring a consistent and predictable sense of structure. For example, a geographic taxonomy is a hierarchical, general-to-specific representation, such as: world > continent > region > nation > state > city. Employing such taxonomy against all of an organization's information repositories allows the search system to automatically identify documents with references to the taxonomy nodes, thus allowing the information to be organized and analyzed (in this case) from a geographic perspective. The application of additional taxonomies, such as MeSH2, GO3 or DTIC®4 and others, can organize information that is relevant to an organization's primary areas of interest and operation.

Much standard or industry-accepted taxonomy are readily available. Applying these enables a new realm of information categorization that can be either industry- or domain-specific, or general and horizontal. Taxonomies provide well-defined, stable organizational frameworks that cut across disparate data sets and functional areas, adding structure and the ability to find information that would otherwise be difficult to recognize. Once categorized, information can be populated into browsable folders or classifications allowing users to intuitively navigate to relevant concentrations of information. These classifications can mirror the taxonomy hierarchy used to categorize the information, or be constructed and populated to meet the specific organizational structures and perspectives of an enterprise.

Although difficult, creating a corporate taxonomy is just the first, albeit crucial, step to leveraging informational resources in support of organizational agility. The ongoing challenge that an enterprise must overcome is how to keep the taxonomy accurate and up-to-date. Because taxonomies exist within dynamic organizational and market environments, they must constantly change to accurately reflect the state of informational resources as well as organizational imperatives.

4. USE OF ONTOLOGY IN KNOWLEDGE MANAGEMENT

Typical Knowledge organization software can be divided into two types: content staging that includes content characterization, indexing, metadata creation, concept extraction, categorization, and summarization; and content delivery that includes data visualization, retrieval, broadcasting, and packaging. An example of content staging is categorization that automatically funnels documents into pre-defined hierarchical structures. We discussed this issue in detail in section three and saw how taxonomies can help in categorization. An example of content deployment is visualization tools such as animated or hyperbolic trees. These tools graphically represent large amounts of data and translate enterprise knowledge into an animated tree or web structure. In a visually stunning interface, wire frame graphics link a category with all its sub-categories.

Simple taxonomies that have a fixed relationship (e.g. "is-a") or no clearly defined relationship (e.g. "is related to") have many limitations effectively staging and delivering knowledge. However, ontologies are richer than taxonomies as they allow different kinds of relations between concepts. In addition, these relations are governed by definable set of axioms such as Disjoint-ness, covering, equivalence, subsumption etc.

Ontology help in organizational knowledge management in several ways both in content and information staging as well as in content deployment. Though the way in which ontologies are used may be completely different. For example, ontological parameters for automatic document classification and for visualization tools such as animated or hyperbolic trees can be very different, though both share the goal of easing information access; they employ different techniques of information organization. Another difference between classification and visualization tools is that animated trees do not materially reorder content. Classification directories physically catalog documents in an enterprise portal. In contrast, visualization tools graphically link similar content together regardless of where material is located. A simple taxonomy will not be bale to provide this flexibility.

4.1 How Ontologies help KM

Similar to the role played by taxonomies in knowledge management applications, ontologies also act as repositories to organize knowledge and information based on a common vocabulary. They provide access to and optimize knowledge retrieval and support the mechanisms for communications and, therefore, the exchange of knowledge. They also help in reusing existing knowledge and facilitating reasoning and inferences on existing knowledge.

Ontology in knowledge management contributes directly to the application functionality. Ontologies help in all three fundamental knowledge management processes, namely, communication, integration, and reasoning. Once ontology has been created, it serves as a base for communication, facilitating knowledge transfer. To do this, it provides precise notation for queries on the domain of interest. Likewise, it facilitates the interpretation of messages, establishing a proper interpretation context. Then it serves to integrate varied knowledge sources. Finally, the most complex applications can use the ontologies to find new rules or patterns that had not appeared before.

The main purpose of any ontology is to enable communication between computer systems in a way that is independent of the individual system technologies, information architectures and application domain. The key ingredients that make up ontology are a vocabulary of basic terms and a precise specification of what those terms mean. The rich set of relations between these terms guide knowledge workers and knowledge systems navigate through the corporate semantic space. Categories or directories provide a meaningful context for retrieved information because they delineate conceptual relationships. Within a category, searchers can hop from one associated concept to another, learn about related terms, or begin their search at a broader term in the hierarchy and move down to more specific instances of a concept.

Searching is an iterative venture, and people often cannot fully articulate what they are looking for. This type of information structure takes the pressure off users. Directories contextualize the search and knowledge management process. Because classification schemes explicitly delineate a structure of conceptual relationships, the meaning of a discrete term is not presented as "a thing in itself" but is understood in the context of surrounding terms.

Ontology also helps in improving communication. Directories and ontologies function to hook people and context together. They provide a common language, and workers better relate concepts across departments, divisions and companies. For example, what one company calls "CRM" another may term "infrastructure management," "one-to-one marketing" or "front-office applications". Ontologies promote collaboration by matching up users with similar interests. Research is more cumulative when, for example, an analyst studying European Union banking policies is linked to an employee researching French fiscal policies.

Ontology classifies information into logical categories that allow users to readily browse through content. They are often used in tandem with search and retrieval tools (keyword- or concept-based) to help locate target information. However, unlike search technology alone, ontologies reveal the overall structure of a knowledgebase, in a hierarchy that is visible to the user. The user navigates through sub-categories to narrow the search, a process that helps avoid false hits that are outside the area of interest. When used with search and retrieval tools, ontologies aid in efficiency by limiting the volume of material that must be searched.

4.2 Central versus Distributed Ontologies

There are two technologically different approaches in designing KM solutions. The first one looks at the organizational knowledge converging from various sources into a central repository. This Centralized KM approach focuses on providing central control, standardization. The second approach takes a distributed approach to managing organizational knowledge and attempts to coordinate the exchange of knowledge across different autonomous entities.

It was shown [Ehring et al, 2003] that the KM solutions need to move away from traditional approach of centralized knowledge repository to the realization of one or a few repositories of documents, organized around a single ontology or other meta-structures. In the past, it has been the experience of many KM implementers that the centralized KM systems are often deserted by end-users. The reasons for this may have been the social, distributed and subjective nature of working groups in any large organization, each with its own languages, process or tools. There is a major directional change for all the KM solutions from a stand alonc KM application to Global-Ontology-Local-Application to Local-ontology-local-application to completely distributed applications.

The Semantic Web and Peer-to-Peer (SWAP) project (swap. semanticweb.org) demonstrates that multiple and distributed ontologies will allow support for decentralized KM applications. Participating knowledge work groups can maintain individual knowledge structures, while sharing knowledge in such ways that minimize the administration efforts and knowledge sharing and finding is easy. Considering this major paradigm shift in building knowledge management systems, we need to find a way in which we can work with multiple, distributed ontologies and corporate taxonomies. There should be a provision to shift from one ontology to another by the core knowledge staging and deployment engines with ease. The next subsection presents one such framework.

4.3 UTON - Universal Taxonomy and Ontology Network

Content and knowledge management systems should be able to operate with multiple taxonomies and ontologies at the same time. It should be possible to switch between taxonomies or ontologies depending on the context and the input document. Hence it is important to come up with a framework where multiple taxonomies or ontologies can co-exist and accessed using unified protocols.

In this section we briefly describe a framework that can be used to co-locate different taxonomies and ontologies, called Universal Taxonomy and Ontology Network (UTON). UTON stores concepts, relations among these concepts, cross linkages, language dependencies in its repository and provides interfaces to storage and retrieval functionality and the administrative functionality (including user and version management). The knowledge and semantic information is stored within the network in the form of a DAG (Directed Acyclic Graph). The storage and retrieval interfaces provided by ontology network are used by various media indexing and categorization components. Ontology developers, editors and administrators have different interfaces depending on their needs.

All these interfaces interact with higher level UTON objects such as Ontology, Concept, term and relation. If ontology consists of concepts belonging to more than one domain or sub domains, then another higher level object called context will come into play to help disambiguate concepts belonging to more than one domain. In the following, we describe each of the higher-level objects.

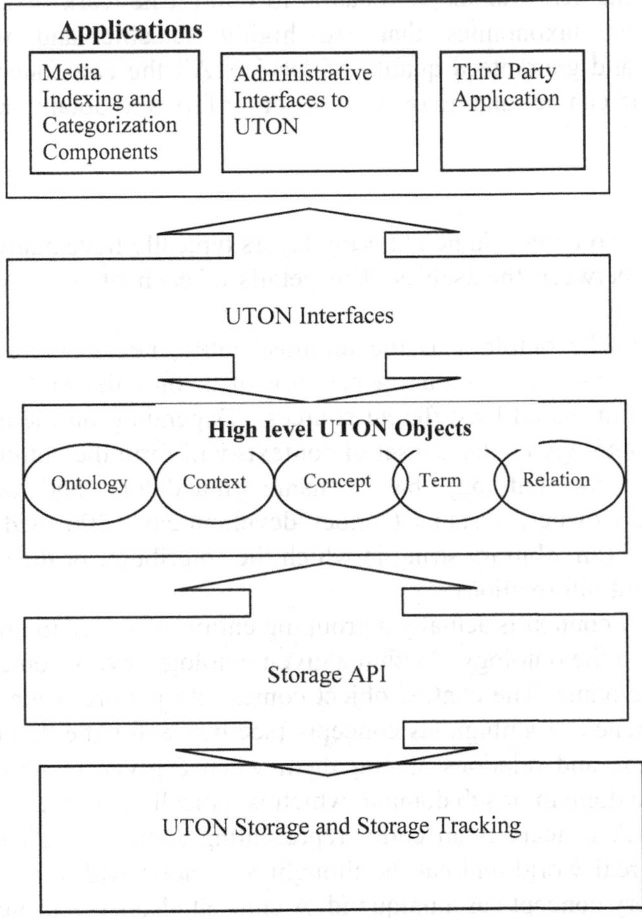

Figure 2-2. Architecture of UTON

As shown in the above figure, the general architecture components are:

- UTON Storage: The storage system is the place where the UTON data is stored – typically a Relational Database Management System (RDBMS).
- Storage API: Provides a unified access to the basic structures of UTON. The API should be accessible from any high level programming language.

- Higher level UTON objects: UTON objects are expressed in a data description language format, or as objects in any high level programming language. They are retrieved and stored using the storage API.
- Applications: Applications can use the UTON by integrating the ontology objects returned from the storage API in their program code.

This architecture and design of UTON [Varma, 2002] enables multiple ontologies and taxonomies to co-exist and makes it possible to access them in a unified manner. Our major focus is to build a network of large scale ontologies and taxonomies that are highly scalable and with high performance and guaranteed quality of service. All the components can be distributed and can be running on a set of server forms to obtain the required scalability and performance.

The UTON objects Ontology, Context, Concept, Term and Relation are independent entities and are related to each other in a loosely hierarchical fashion. Any two objects in neighboring layers typically have many-to-many relationships between themselves. The details of each of these objects are given below.

Ontology: The ontology is the topmost entity, necessary because the intention of UTON is to contain a network of taxonomies and ontologies, likely to be contributed by different sources. Depending on the number of domains the ontology contains a set of contexts will form the ontology itself. As attributes, the ontology has a name (mandatory and unique), a contributor, an owner, a status ("under development", "finished" ...) and documentation (an arbitrary string in which the contributor or the owner can specify relevant information).

Context: A context is actually a grouping entity; it is used to group terms and relations in the ontology. Within a given ontology, every context should have a unique name. The context object comes into picture when there is a possible existence of ambiguous concepts (see below for the description of concept), terms and relations among them when a given ontology covers more than one domain or sub domain, which is typically the case.

Concept: A concept is an entity representing some "thing": the actual entity in the real world and can be thought as a node within the ontology structure. Every concept has a unique id. A concept also has a triple "source-key-value", which is the description for that concept. The “source” identifies the source from which the description originates, the “key” is a string which gives a hint to the user on how he should interpret the value, and finally the “value” is the description of the concept. One concept can have more than one source-key-value triple, and thus have its meaning described in different ways. As an example, let's consider WordNet [Fellbaum, 1999]. In WordNet synsets denote a set of terms (with their "senses") which are equivalent. Every term also has a glossary, which is an informal description of the meaning for that (particular sense of the) term. In this respect, from WordNet, we can extract two different descriptions for a concept, two different source-key-value triples, namely the glossary (Source: WordNet – Key: Glossary – Value: "<informal description denoted as a glossary in WordNet>") and the synset (Source: WordNet – Key: Glossary – Value: <enumeration of synonyms forming the synset>). As a different example, when a concept exists in various media (text, video, audio and image), a concept represented using source-key-value triple will give the appropriate media value, when retrieved using appropriate key.

Term: A term is an entity representing a lexical (textual) representation of a concept. Within one context, a term is unambiguous and, consequently, it can only be associated with one concept and of course, several different terms within one context can refer to the same concept, implicitly defining these terms as synonyms for this context. Terms in different context can also refer to the same concept, and in this way implicitly establish a connection between these two contexts.

Relation: A relation is a grouping element; it can be interpreted as a set of triples consisting of a starting term (also called the "headword" of the relation), a role (relation name) and a second term (also called the "tail" of the relation).

UTON was developed in the context of building information extraction, indexing and categorization engines for a content management system that is heavily rich media oriented. There was a compelling need to switch between ontologies depending on the domain and the context in which the application was running.

5. FUTURE TRENDS

As organizations realize the need to break down existing silos of information and question the established limits on information flow in the organization, there is an emerging trend to take a more holistic view of information architecture. This trend is due to the failure of many companies to respond quickly enough to changing conditions and being able to adopting themselves to information overflow.

The rising interest in ontologies and information classification, hopefully, will result in a better management of information assets across an organization. With the emergence of usable standards for information representation, information exchange and application integration (such as XML, RDF, WSDL, SOAP), we can finally start to overcome the recurrent barriers to developing a unified approach to managing information and knowledge across an organization. The increasing use of XML as a standard for information description holds out the hope of developing semantically rich infrastructures in which new forms of information publishing, information discovery and information sharing will be possible.

All these developments in terms of standards and awareness in organizations regarding the role of ontologies bring up various possibilities in building and utilization of ontologies within the corporate world. Some such important possibilities are:

Multifaceted ontologies: Multi-faceted ontologies enable the user to navigate through a number of facets of ontology. An example of this is a search feature in a music library by artist, genre, instrument or composer. They also allow the different facets to be cross-referenced to narrow or widen a search as the user browses the categories. For example, in a cooking recipe portal, one can browse and select recipes by a combination of ingredients, cuisine and occasions. Developments in multifaceted taxonomies are also closely linked to new analytical and visualization capabilities that offer to transform our experience of search and navigation through large volumes of information.

Workflow and collaboration: Developing and managing ontologies is a collaborative project involving multiple stakeholders. It also needs clear procedures for change management. Integrated workflow tools and collaborative editing tools make it easier to manage ontologies in large organizations and places where ontologies have to monitored and adapted on a regular basis, such as shopping sites.

Search analytics and ontology management: Search analytics refers to the collection, analysis and exploitation of information about the way search technologies are used. The initial impetus for this development came from the need for e-commerce sites to know how users are searching their sites. The next step is for those techniques to be used within the enterprise. Better information on what users are searching for, and the ability to tailor results and navigation paths, offers a relatively easy way to improve information retrieval within an organization. There is a great opportunity for using search analytics in the design and maintenance of better ontology structures.

Visualization tools: Improved visualization capabilities can enhance the value of ontologies at two levels:

- **Usability**–providing visualization capabilities to the user enhances their ability to take advantage of the investment in an underlying ontology. Ontologies provide a basis for implementing existing visualization tools in a useful way and open the way for new tools that can help users visualize the multidimensional space in which they are searching.
- **Design and management**–improved means of visualizing ontology structure make it easier to ensure an efficient balance among categories and better fit with user expectations. Such developments are closely

linked to improved support for the rapid design, test and refinement of ontologies.

In order to develop the promise of the "knowledge-based economy," organizations have to develop a much better understanding of the nature of information and knowledge capital. Ontologies are linked into that development at a number of levels: The development of ontologies and corporate taxonomies is part of a general move toward developing methods and techniques for the management of intellectual capital. Those developments are also linked with the evolution of a mature information management architecture based on technologies such as content management, portals, search and data warehousing. Thirdly, a new generation of enterprise IT architectures based on Web services and other open standards is making possible new levels of information integration and interoperability.

As organizations evolve their information management processes, methodologies and technologies in coming years, ontology development will be given a much more prominent role within organizations. Ontology methods and technologies will themselves have to evolve if they are to meet the requirements of this general transformation in information management.

6. CONCLUSIONS

Observing current day KM implementations makes it clear that there is a sluggish adoption of ontology-based tools and technologies within the mainstream KM community. Poor understanding of the relationship between KM and ontology research is the major culprit behind this.

Modern organizations cannot survive without the help of technology in managing its information and knowledge. Architecting information and Knowledge management systems is increasingly becoming complex with a constant growth in the amount of content that gets generated. Corporate taxonomies and ontologies play a key role in building effective content management and knowledge management systems for organizations. In this chapter, I have discussed technology enablers in building content and knowledge management systems. These include search, categorization, creating knowledge network and infrastructure, crawlers and agents, summarization, personalization, multiple language support. Each of these features can benefit from the corporate taxonomies and ontologies.

There is a movement away from centralized Knowledge Management solutions towards distributed and peer-to-peer knowledge management systems. There is an urgent need to technically support this paradigm shift. UTON kind of frameworks can help in providing uniform interface to co-located ontologies and help in implementing distributed knowledge management solutions.

The emerging trends in ontologies such as multi-faceted ontologies, workflow and collaboration, search analytics, ontology management tools and visualization tools will hopefully make the creation, usage and maintenance of ontologies in organizations easier and help in creating the much needed awareness on benefits of ontology use.

ACKNOWLEDGEMENTS

I would like to thank Bipin Indurkhya for reviewing this chapter at various stages and providing very useful comments. I thank the co-editors and other reviewers whose comments helped in making this chapter more readable.

REFERENCES

[Berkely] Berkey study on information growth http://www.sims.berkeley.edu/research/projects/how-much-info-2003.

[Davies et al., 2002] Davies, J., Fensel, D., and van Harmelen, F. (eds.), 2002. Towards the semantic web: ontology-driven knowledge management. John Wiley & Sons.

[DMOZ] The Open Directory Project, http://dmoz.org.

[Ehring et al., 2003] Ehrig, M., Tempich, C., Broekstra, J., van Harmelen, F., Sabou, M., Siebes, R.,Staab, S., Stuckenschmidt, H.: "SWAP – ontology-based knowledge management with peer-to-peer technology". In Sure, Y., Schnurr, H.P., eds.: Proceedings of the1st National "Workshop Ontologie-basiertes Wissensmanagement (WOW2003)".

[Farquhar et al., 1996] Farquhar, A., R. Fikes, J. Rice. "The Ontolingua Server: a Tool for Collaborative Ontology Construction". KAW96. November 1996. Also available as KSL-TR-96-26.

[Fellbaum, 1999] Fellbaum, Christiane (Ed). "WordNet: An electronic lexical database", MIT Press, 1999.

[Feldman, 2001] Feldman, Susan "Content Management" in eInform Volume 3, Issue 7, IDC News letter.

[Guha et al., 1990] Guha, R. V., D. B. Lenat, K. Pittman, D. Pratt, and M. Shepherd. "Cyc: A Midterm Report." *Communications of the ACM* 33, no. 8 (August 1990).

[Lamont, 2003] "Dynamic taxonomies: keeping up with changing content" Judith Lamont, KMWorld May 2003, Volume 12, Issue 5.

[Lenat and Guha, 1990] Lenat, D. B. and R. V. Guha. "Building Large Knowledge Based Systems". Reading, Massachusetts: Addison Wesley, 1990.

[Lenat, 1995] Lenat, D. B. "Steps to Sharing Knowledge." In *Toward Very Large Knowledge Bases*, edited by N.J.I. Mars. IOS Press, 1995.

[Niles and Pease, 2001a] Niles, I., and Pease, A., "Origins of the Standard Upper Merged Ontology: A Proposal for the IEEE Standard Upper Ontology" *in Working Notes of the IJCAI-2001 Workshop on the IEEE Standard Upper Ontology*, 2001.

[Niles and Pease, 2001b] Niles, I., & Pease, A., "Toward a Standard Upper Ontology", *in Proceedings of the 2nd International Conference on Formal Ontology in Information Systems (FOIS-2001).* 2001.

[PWC, 2003] Price Waterhouse Coopers, "Technology forecast 2003-2005".

[Sanda, 1999] Harabagiu Sanda M, Moldovan Dan I, "Knowledge processing on an extended WordNet" appeared in [Fellbaum, 1999].

[SemWeb] Semantic web: http://www.semanticweb.org.

[SWAP] Semantic web and Peer-to-Peer: http://swap.semanticweb.org.

[Staab et al., 2001] "Knowledge Processes and Ontologies" IEEE Intelligent Systems, 2001.

[Varma, 2002] Vasudeva Varma "Building Large-scale ontology networks", Language Engineering Conference, University of Hyderabad, December 13-15, 2002. IEEE Computer Society Publications, Pages: 121-127, ISBN 0-7695-1885-0.

[Venkata, 2002] "Taxonomies, Categorization and Organizational Agility", Ramana Venkata, Best Practices in Enterprise Knowledge Management, Volume II, October 2002, A Supplement to KMWorld, Vol 11, Issue 9.

[Woods, 2004], "KM past and future—Changing the rules of the game" Eric Woods, KMWorld-Volume 13, Issue 1, January 2004 Content, Document and Knowledge Management.

[Winkle, 2002] "Maximizing the Value of Enterprise Information by Leveraging Best of Breed Search and Categorization Software", Jon Van Winkle, Best Practices in Enterprise Content Management, Vol. IV, A Supplement to KMWorld, March 2004, Vol. 13, Issue 3.

Chapter 3

ONTOLOGICAL EVALUATION OF BUSINESS MODELS: COMPARING TRADITIONAL AND COMPONENT-BASED PARADIGMS IN INFORMATION SYSTEMS RE-ENGINEERING

Raul Valverde[1] and Mark Toleman[2]

[1] *Concordia University 1455 de Maisonneuve Blvd. W. H3G 1M8 Montreal, QC Canada;*
[2] *University of Southern Queensland West Street Towoomba Qld 4350 Australia*

Abstract: The majority of current information systems were implemented using traditional paradigms which include business modeling techniques applied during the analysis phase such as System Flow Charts, Data Flow Diagrams and Entity-Relationship Diagrams. These legacy systems are now struggling to cope with recent developments, particularly trends towards e-Commerce applications, platform independence, reusability of pre-built components, capacity for reconfiguration and higher reliability. Many organizations now realize they need to re-engineer their systems using new component-based systems approaches and object-oriented computer languages. Although the traditional and component-based approaches have different grammars for representing business models, these business models can be compared, based on their ontological grammars. This paper illustrates how an ontological evaluation of business models can be used to compare them for equivalency of representation of business requirements, when re-engineering legacy systems into component-based information systems.

Key words: Re-engineering; component-based systems; structured systems; business models, ontological evaluation; legacy systems

1. INTRODUCTION

The vast majority of Information Systems were implemented in the early days of computing using traditional software development paradigms with procedural computer languages such as Cobol (Longworth, 2003). The traditional paradigm consists of modeling techniques such as System Flow

Charts, Data Flow Diagrams (DFD) and Entity Relationship (ER) Diagrams used by system analysts during the design phase to capture the activities within a system. These particular models have been used since the early times of computers and were considered, for the most part, the documentation of legacy systems (Longworth, 2003).

However, with recent developments, particularly the trends towards e-Commerce applications and platform independence, many companies are realizing that they have to migrate their systems to new improved systems in order to meet these trends since legacy systems are not capable of coping with these new challenges. The migration of a *legacy* system to a new target system is a process of *re-engineering* that requires the system's examination and alteration to reconstitute it in a new form (Chikofsky and Cross, 1990). This new form may result in the need for a shift in the information systems paradigm serving the architecture and the business domain. Modern computer languages such as Java, offer many advantages in such a re-engineering process; in particular, good web-application development capabilities, platform independence for applications and security. However, Java is an object-oriented language and changing from the procedural language often used in traditional systems to an object-based language would represent a fundamental paradigm shift.

Although object technology has become the vogue for re-engineering information systems, many projects regarded as being object-oriented have failed in recent years due to organizational and technical troubles. Wolfgang (1997) mentions some the problems associated with the object-oriented paradigm as: classes/objects implemented in one programming language cannot interoperate with those implemented in other languages, some object-oriented languages require the same compiler version, composition of objects is typically done at the language level, and composition support is missing, that is, visual/interactive tools that allow the plugging together of objects.

On the other hand, the *Component-Based (CB) paradigm* is now heralded as the next wave to fulfill the technical troubles that object technology could not deliver (Wolfgang 1997). In addition, the component-based paradigm allows a fast delivery of information systems due to its capacity of reconfiguring and reassembling pre-built business components, easy maintainability and higher quality due to the reusability of pre-tested components (Szyperski, 1999). However, regardless of the systems paradigm used in the development of information systems, business models need to be created in order to describe the requirements (Jacobson Christerson and Jonsson, 1993) collected by the system analyst.

These business models can be used as the blueprint for information systems development, however, they can become quite different depending on whether the project team uses the traditional or the component-based paradigm. The former maintains a process-oriented view of systems, providing a decomposition based on processes (namely, data flow diagrams), whereas the component-based paradigm constructs a system around a set of interacting components (Satzinger, Jackson and Burd 2002).

Within the context of an information systems paradigm shift, the continuity, robustness and integrity of the business processes and functions of the system are of prime concern when re-engineering legacy systems. This means that the business model of the re-engineered information system should represent the same business requirements as the ones from the original legacy system in order to preserve this integrity.

Although the traditional and component-based approaches have different grammars for representing business models, these business models can be compared for equivalency of representation of business requirements (Wand and Weber 1993). An evaluation of business models would reveal the limitations of representing the legacy system business requirements in the component-based re-engineered model.

The chapter is structured as follows: The problem definition and scope is described in the next section. In section three, the Bunge-Wand-Weber (BWW) model (Wand and Weber 1988, 1993, 1995) is discussed and justified for this research. In the next section the research approach is described and then the case study software system is explained. The following section describes the ontological evaluation, finally preliminary results are shown and conclusions are drawn.

2. PROBLEM DEFINITION AND SCOPE

During the life cycle of the information system, changes can occur that require a change of its scope. One of these changes is the availability of better technology (Whitten, Bentley and Dittman, 2000). A decision analysis would need to be performed in order to assess if the new technology would be feasible in the system (Whitten, Bentley and Dittman 2000). If the analysis reveals that the implementation is not feasible, the information systems will require re-engineering in order to adapt to the new technology requirement.

This re-engineering of a legacy information system would require a paradigm shift. However, there is a high degree of interest and concern in establishing whether or not a full migration to a more portable and scaleable component-based architecture will be able to represent the legacy business requirements in the underlying business model of the re-engineered information systems.

The aim of research therefore becomes an evaluation of the business models of the traditional and component based information systems in the re-engineering process in order to verify that both models are equivalent and represent the same business requirements.

The main purpose of research would be to investigate the following research question:

Is the resulting component based business model equivalent to the legacy business model when shifting paradigms in the re-engineering process?

A substantial information systems evolution can be a major concern of any company considering a paradigm shift since this represents the ability of the new information system to accommodate the company's essential business processes.

The study concentrates on re-engineering projects that do not include new requirements. The main reason for this is to simplify the comparison of business models that should be equivalent in this particular case.

Over the years, much different ontology has emerged as a way to model reality. A general ontology that has been frequently applied for the evaluation of modeling methods in Systems Analysis and Design is the Bunge-Wand-Weber model (Wand and Weber, 1988, 1993, 1995).

In the next section, the BWW model will be discussed as tool for business model evaluation in order to detect the limitations of representing the legacy system business requirements in the component-based re-engineered model.

3. BUNGE-WAND-WEBER MODEL

The BWW (Bunge-Wand-Weber) model's (Wand & Weber, 1988, 1993, 1995) fundamental premise is that any Systems Analysis and Design modeling grammar (set of modeling symbols and their construction rules) must be able to represent all things in the real world that might be of interest to users of information systems; otherwise, the resultant model is incomplete. If the model is incomplete, the analyst/designer will somehow have to augment the model(s) to ensure that the final computerized information system adequately reflects that portion of the real world it is intended to simulate. The BWW models consist of the representation model, the state-tracking model, and the decomposition model. The work reported in this chapter uses this representation model and its constructs. The representation model defines a set of constructs that, at this time, are thought to be necessary and sufficient to describe the structure and behavior of the real world.

The BWW model is not the only ontology available to evaluate information systems since alternatives exist both in the form of general philosophical ontology, e.g., Chisholm (1996), or special enterprise and IS ontology, e.g., the enterprise ontology (Uschold et al., 1998) and the framework of information systems concepts (FRISCO) (Verrijn-Stuart et al., 2001). However, the use the BWW-model is justified for two reasons: first, the model is based on concepts that are fundamental to the computer science and information systems domains (Wanda & Weber 1993). Second, it has already been used successfully to analyze and evaluate the modeling constructs of many established IS and enterprise modeling languages such as dataflow diagrams, ER models, OML and UML (Evermann and Wand 2001; Green and Rosemann 2000; Opdahl and Henderson-Sellers 2002; Weber and Zhang 1996) and for the evaluation of enterprise systems (Green et al. 2005) and business component frameworks (Fettke and Loos 2003b).

For brevity, we do not introduce the BWW-model in detail. Instead, table 3-1 summarizes its main constructs.

Table 3-1. Constructs of the BWW-model (source: (Wand and Weber 1993; Weber and Zhang 1996))

Ontological Construct	Ontological Construct
THING	The elementary unit in our ontological model. The real World is made up of things. A composite thing may be made up of other things (composite or primitive).
PROPERTY	Things possess properties. A property is modeled via a function that maps the thing into some value. A property of a composite thing that belongs to a component thing is called a hereditary property. Otherwise it is called an emergent property. A property that is inherently a property of an individual thing is called an intrinsic property. A property that is meaningful only in the context of two or more things is called a mutual or relational property.
STATE	The vector of values for all property functions of a thing.
CONCEIVABLE STATE SPACE	The set of all states that the thing might ever assume.
STATE LAW	Restricts the values of the property functions of a thing to a subset that is deemed lawful because of natural laws or human laws.
EVENT	A change of state of a thing. It is affected via a transformation (see below).

Ontological Construct	Ontological Construct
EVENT SPACE	The set of all possible events that con occur in the thing.
TRANSFORMATION	A mapping from a domain comprising states to a codomain comprising states.
PROCESS	An intrinsically ordered sequence of events on, or state of, a thing.
LAWFUL TRANSFORMATION	Defines which events in a thing are lawful.
HISTORY	The chronologically ordered states that a thing traverses.
ACTS ON	A thing acts on another thing if its existence affects the history of the other thing.
COUPLING	A thing acts on another thing if its existence affects the history of the other thing. The two things are said to be coupled or interact.
SYSTEM	A set of things is a system if, for any bi-partitioning of the set, couplings exist among things in the two subsets.
SYSTEM COMPOSITION	The things in the system.
SYSTEM ENVIRONMENT	Things that are not in the system but interact with things in the system.
SYSTEM STRUCTURE	The set of couplings that exist among things in the system and things in the environment of the system.
SUBSYSTEM	A system whose composition and structure are subsets of the composition and structure of another system.
SYSTEM DECOMPOSITION	A set of subsystems such that every component in the System is either one of the subsystems in the decomposition or is included in the composition of one of the subsystems in the decomposition.
LEVEL STRUCTURE	Defines a partial order over the subsystems in a decomposition to show which subsystems are components of other subsystems or the system itself.

Ontological Construct	Ontological Construct
STABLE STATE	A state in which a thing, subsystem or system will remain unless forced to change by virtue of the action of a thing in the environment (an external event).
UNSTABLE STATE	A state that will be changed into another state by virtue of the action of transformation in the system.
EXTERNAL EVENT	An event that arises in a thing, subsystem or system by virtue of the action of some thing in the environment on the thing, subsystem or system. The before-state of an external event is always stable. The after-state may be stable or unstable.
INTERNAL EVENT	An event that arises in a thing, subsystem, or system by virtue of lawful transformations in the thing, subsystem, or system. The before-state of an internal event is always unstable. The after state may be stable or unstable.
WELL DEFINED EVENT	An event in which the subsequent state can always be predicted given the prior state is known.
POORLY DEFINED EVENT	An event in which the subsequent state cannot be predicted given the prior state is known.
CLASS	A set of things that possess a common property.
KIND	A set of things that possess two or more common properties.

4. RESEARCH METHODOLOGY

In order to address the research question, the case study methodology is chosen to emphasize and explore factors, which may lead to directions for the question (Benbasat, Goldstein and Mead, 1987).

There are many reengineering methodologies that help to cope with the problem of transforming legacy systems originally developed with structural methodologies into component-based systems. However, the Jacobson & Lindstrom (1991) approach for reengineering of legacy systems was chosen for the following reasons:

It contemplates cases of a complete change of implementation technique and no change in the functionality, which is the case of this research.

- It does not require the use of source code. In the case study used for this research there is no access to the source code used to develop the system.

- It also covers reverse engineering. This is useful for this research given the need to capture the original business model for the legacy system.
- It is relatively simple to use.

Although the original methodology was proposed for object-oriented systems, it can be easily adapted for component-based systems since components can be viewed as a higher level of abstraction that is based on object oriented methodology.

In order to capture the business model of the legacy system, the researcher will apply reverse engineering as specified in the Jacobson and Lindstrom (1991) methodology. To do this, the following steps need to be used:

1. A concrete graph that describes the components of the system and their interrelationship.
2. An abstract graph showing the behavior and the structure of the system.
3. A mapping between the two, i.e. how something in the abstract graph relates to the concrete graph and vice versa.

The abstract graph should be free of implementation details. For example, mechanisms for persistent storage or partitioning into processes should not appear on this graph. The concrete graph must, on the other hand, show these details. The mapping between the two should tell how the ideal world of analysis is implemented by way of the concrete graph (Jacobson & Lindstrom 1991).

This abstract graph is in fact the business model. The business model will be represented in terms of Data Flow diagrams, Context Model, Functional Decomposition Diagram and Entity Relationship Diagrams. Once the business model is reverse engineered from the legacy system, the legacy system will be re-engineered by using the following steps (Jacobson & Lindstrom 1991):

1. Prepare an analysis model.
2. Map each analysis object to the implementation of the old system.

In order to prepare the analysis model step, it is important to assimilate the existing information about the system. The existing information has many different forms, e.g. requirements specifications, user operating instructions, maintenance manuals, training manuals, design documentation, source code files, and database schema descriptions. These are called description elements (Jacobson & Lindstrom 1991).

From the set of description elements, an analysis model can be prepared. This is done by using the criteria for finding objects that are described in the object-oriented methodology of Jacobson et al. (1993). After the analysis model is completed, a map of each analysis object to the implementation of the old system is required. The map must show that all analysis objects and dependencies must be motivated by at least one primitive description element. We can express that with *is-motivated-by*, a mapping from the analysis model to the set of primitive description elements. All the dependencies in the analysis model must be motivated by at least one primitive description element.

A methodology by Fettke & Loos (2003a) is used to evaluate the business models generated by the reverse engineering (legacy business model) and the one generated by the reengineering process (component model), for the following reasons:

- It provides a mechanism for evaluation of business models
- Business models can be compared based of their normalized referenced models
- Its simplicity
- It is based on the BWW model

The ontological normalization of a reference model consists of four steps (Fettke and Loos 2003a):

1. Developing a transformation mapping,
2. Identifying ontological modeling deficiencies,
3. Transforming the reference model, and
4. Assessing the results.

In the first step of this method, it is necessary to develop a transformation mapping for the grammar used for representing the business model. This transformation mapping allows converting the constructs of the used grammar to the constructs of the BWW-model. The first step is based on the method for the ontological evaluation of grammars proposed by Wand and Weber (1993).

The transformation mapping consists of two mathematical mappings: First, a representation mapping describes whether and how the constructs of the BWW-model are mapped onto the grammatical constructs. Second, the interpretation mapping describes whether and how the grammatical constructs are mapped onto the constructs of the BWW-model (Fettke and Loos 2003a).

In the third step, the reference model will be transformed to an ontological model. The outcome of this step is an ontologically normalized reference model. The objective of both techniques is to represent the domain of interest in a normalized way by applying specific transformation patterns (Fettke and Loos, 2003a). The two models will be compared based on their ontologically normalized models. The result of a comparison will be that the compared models are equivalent, complementary or in conflict.

In order to generate these normalized reference models in BBW terms, the Rosemann and Green (2002) BBW meta models will be used. This meta model is based on the original E-R specification from Chen (1976) with extensions made by Scheer (1998). This version is called the extended ER-model (eERM).

The methodology used for the study is summarized in figure 3-1.

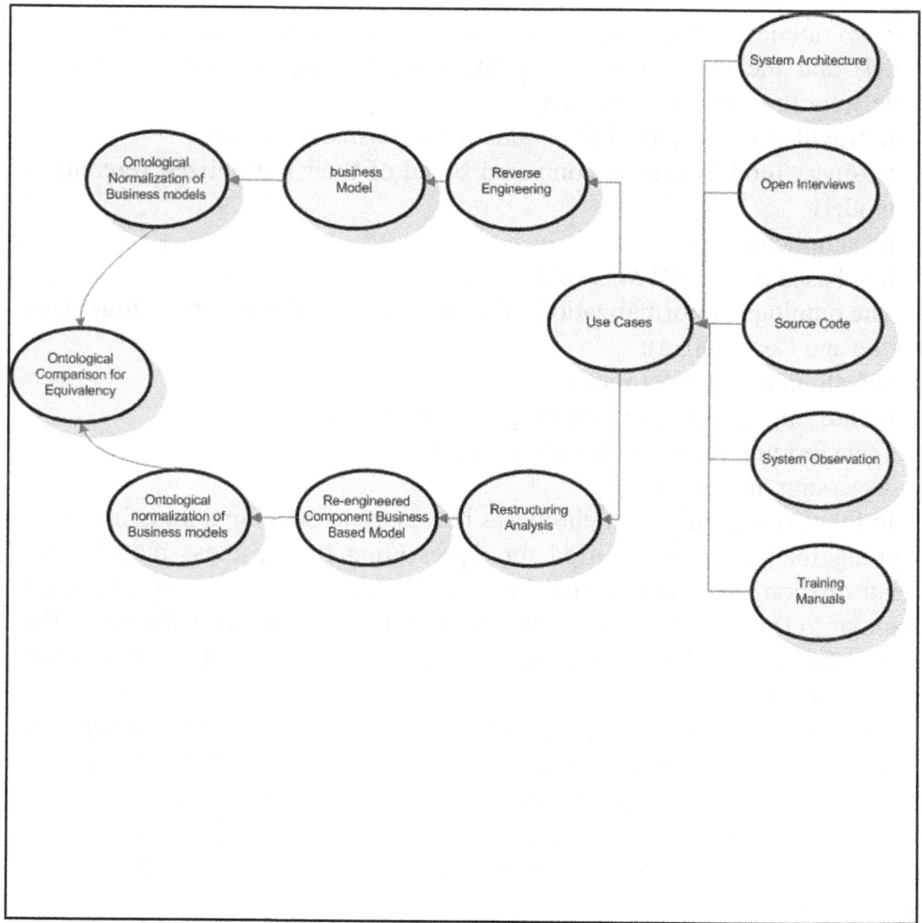

Figure 3-1. Methodology used for study

5. CASE STUDY

The case-study system selected is a *Home Loan* information system developed by a consultant company in the Netherlands. The system was customized for a mid-sized home loan bank that specializes in the marketing, sales and administration of its own home loan products. The information system was designed for use on Unisys A-Series mainframes.

Due to the large scale and complexity of the system, the study is focused on one sub-system that is representative of the main types of business processes. This includes an on-line user interactive component, a procedural business flow component and a batch-processing component. The sub-system for this research is the Offer and Application system.

The technique used to recover the original business model from the legacy system is the one proposed by Jacobson and Lindstrom (1991). For this case study, the following elements were collected to describe the information system:

1. Architecture diagram
2. Database files
3. Manuals
4. Interviews with users and developers

The description of the business process, business events and responses are essential in recovering the business model (Whitten et. al 2000). One of the most popular and successful approaches for documenting business processes, events and responses is a technique called *use cases*, developed by Dr. Ivar Jacobson (Jacobson et al. 1993). Use cases describe the business process, which documents how the business works and what the business goals are of each interaction with the system. Use cases are not just useful to document business processes, they are also used to generate the target component based business model.

The following use-cases were identified to describe the Offer and Application Sub System:

- Process Application
- Process Offer Regional office
- Process Offer Head office
- Maintain Offer
- Loan Generation

In order to generate the DFD diagrams required to construct the legacy business model, business events to which the system must respond and appropriate responses were identified with the help of the use cases. For example, in the case of the process application use case, the applicant (actor) responds to the event "Completes loan application" that was triggered by a "new application" with "storing the application in a file cabinet" response.

Once these events were identified, Data Flow Diagrams were drawn with the help of the list of transformations suggested by Whitten el al. (2001). The list of recommendations is:

- The actor that initiated the event will become the external agent.
- The event will be handled by a process.
- The input or trigger will become the data or control flow
- All outputs and responses will become data flows

Figure 3-2 depicts the context diagram for the events of table 3-1. The data model was generated by examining the database files and by identifying the data stores in the DFD diagram. An ERD diagram for the process application is shown in figure 3-3.

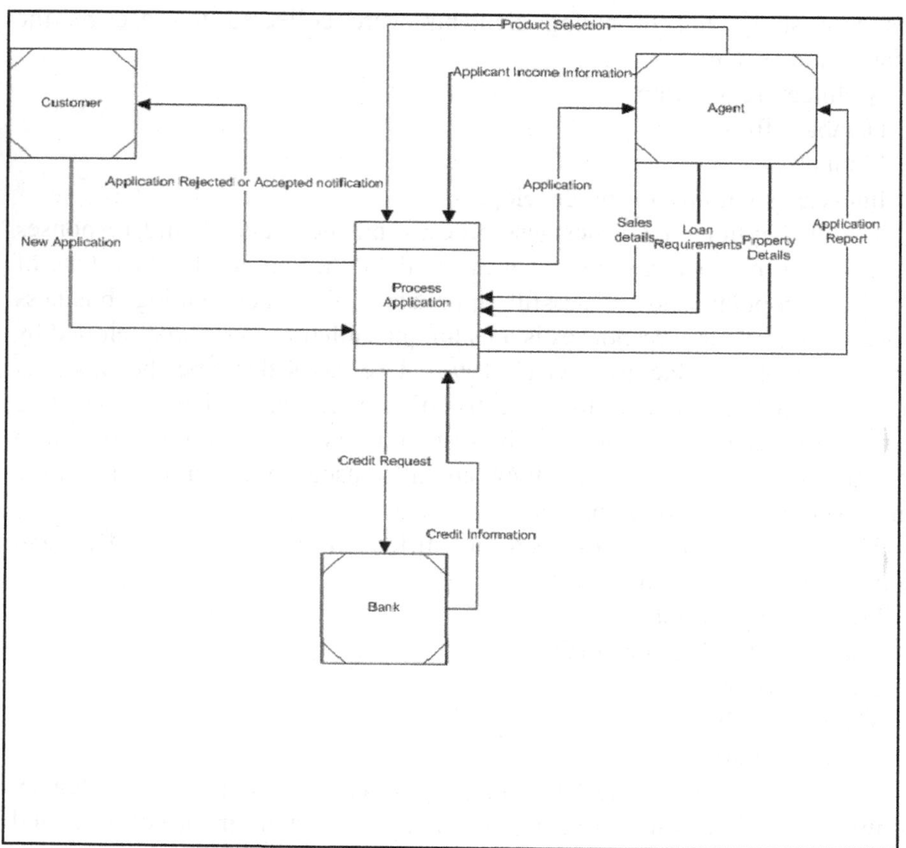

Figure 3-2. Context diagram for the Process Application use case

After the business model is recovered, the system is re-engineered and component based models are generated with the help of the use cases. UML was chosen to model the target system as it is the most accepted standard modeling language based on current best practice (Reed 2002). The type of UML diagrams used for this purpose were:

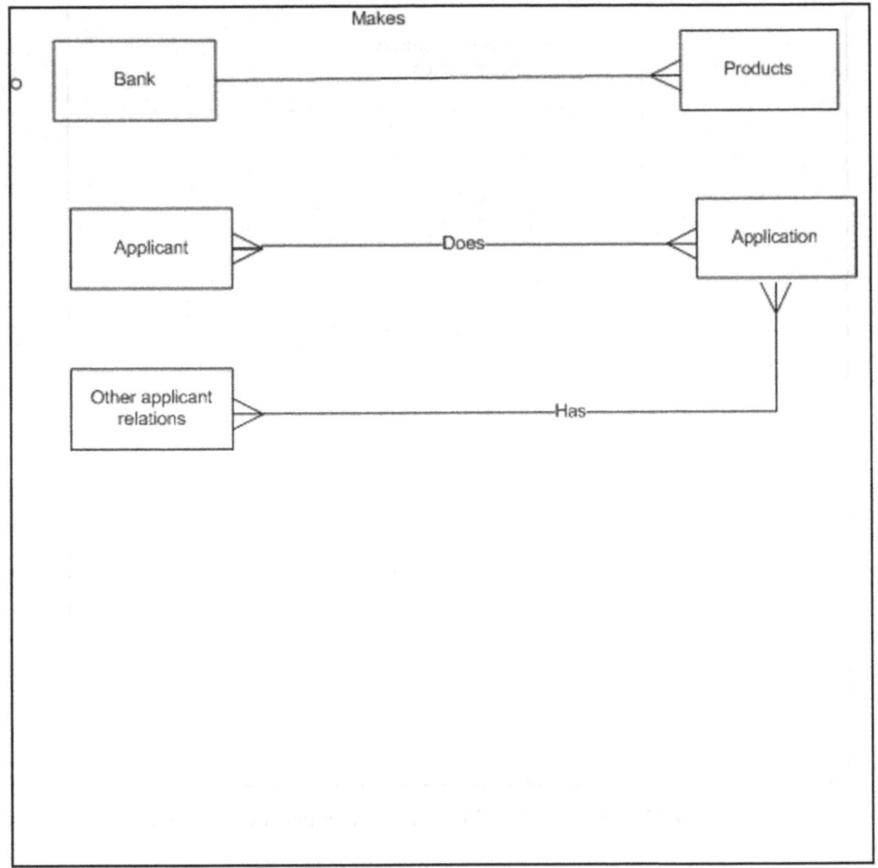

Figure 3-3. ERD for the Process Application Use Case

1. Use case diagrams
2. Sequence diagrams
3. State diagrams
4. Activity Diagrams
5. Class diagrams

Figure 3-4 shows the use case diagram and figure 3-5 the class diagram for process application of the re-engineered system. One of the main differences of class diagrams for component-based systems is the inclusion of interface classes. These classes are used by components in order to interact with each other.

Once the legacy business model is recovered and the re-engineered business model generated, an ontological evaluation of business models by using the BWW model will be applied in order to verify that the requirements captured in the legacy business model are also reflected in the re-engineered business model.

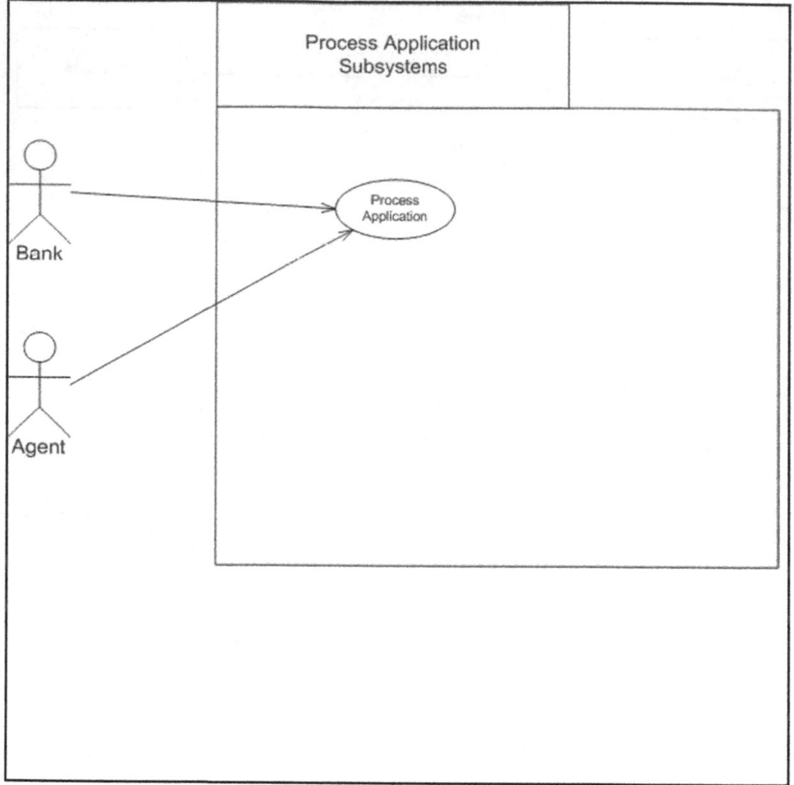

Figure 3-4. Use case diagram for the process application use case

6. ONTOLOGICAL EVALUATION

In this section of the study, diagrams are mapped into BBW constructs and then normalized reference models generated as part of the ontological evaluation of business models. There are four types of diagrams that depict legacy systems by using the Yourdon (1989) structured analysis:

1. Context diagram
2. Functional decomposition diagram
3. Data flow diagram
4. Entity relationship diagram

The DFD and Context diagrams mapping to BWW constructs is based on the work of Rosemann et al. (2005). A context diagram is constructed to establish the initial scope of the system. It shows the main interfaces with its environment. It shows the relation (data flows in and out) of the "system" to external entities. External agents can be interpreted as BWW system environment since they define a person, organization unit, other system, or

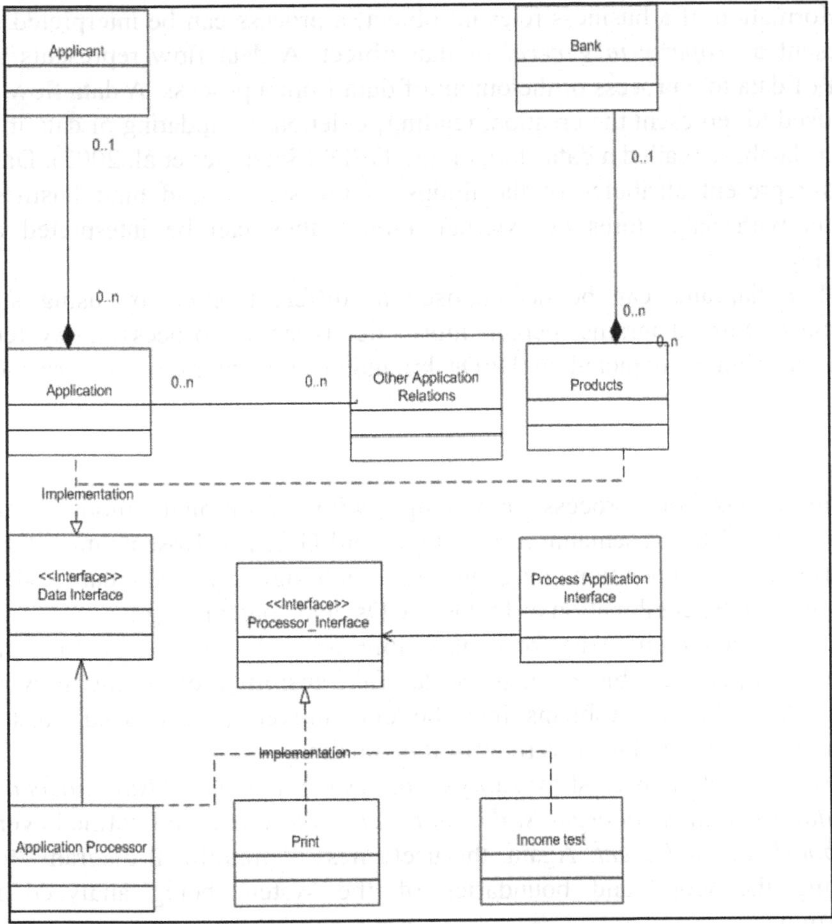

Figure 3-5. Diagram for the process application use case

other organizations that lie outside the scope of the project but interact with the system being studied. The same can be said for external data stores that represent external data repositories that are not part of the system modeled.

A DFD is a graphical system model that shows all the main requirements for an information system in one diagram: inputs and outputs, processes, and data storage. In the DFD, the external agent is a person or organization, outside the boundary that supplies data input or accepts data output (Satzinger et al. 2002 pp 196). In the mapping for legacy system models, external entities and data stores are represented by BBW things. Transformations are represented by processes because they represent a procedure by which data inputs are transformed into data outputs (Satzinger et al. 2002 pp 196).

Data stores and externals agents in a DFD and context diagram can be interpreted as the system composition. Because a process can be seen as the transformation of a business relevant object, a process can be interpreted to represent a *property in general* of that object. A data flow represents an input of data to a process or the output of data from a process. A data flow is also used to represent the creation, reading, deletion, or updating of data in a file or database (called a data store on the DFD) (Satzinger et al. 2002). Data flows represent attributes of the things in the system and bind business objects with data stores or external agents; they can be interpreted as coupling.

DFD diagrams can be decomposed at different levels by using sub diagrams. Sub diagrams depict more detail about processes. System decomposition is depicted in DFDs by using sub diagrams. A series of processes and data flows at different levels define a partial order over the subsystems in a decomposition to show which subsystems are components of other subsystems or the system itself.

Limitations of process modeling with traditional models are acknowledged by Rosemann et al. (2005) and Green & Rosemann (2005). Functional decomposition diagrams are ontologically redundant when compared to the combination of DFDs, ERDs, and context diagrams.

No representations exist for conceivable state, state space, lawful state space, event, conceivable event space, lawful transformation or lawful event space. Accordingly, problems may be encountered in capturing all the potentially important business rules of the situation.

No representations exist for subsystem, *system structure, history, acts on, external event, internal event, stable state, unstable state*, well defined event and *poorly-defined event.* Again, the usefulness of traditional diagrams for defining the scope and boundaries of the system being analyzed is undermined.

Component based models were generated by using UML diagrams and mapped into BBW constructs in table 3-3.

UML actors in use case diagrams can be interpreted as BWW things since they act on the proposed system. UML-extend and UML-include can be mapped as a BWW-binding mutual property and UML-use cases as a BWW processes. The UML-system and UML-sub-system boundaries can be mapped as a UML system composition. UML actors can be also considered BBW environment since they are external entities that interact with the system (Opdahl and Henderson-Sellers 2004).

Irwin and Turk (2005) propose that the use case construct represents a BBW thing and a process at the same time and therefore ontologically overloaded. The system construct in a use case diagram represents a BWW composite thing (Irwin and Turk 2005). The UML actor is also overloaded as it also corresponds to a kind in the BWW ontology (Irwin and Turk 2005).

Table 3-2. Mapping between traditional and BWW constructs

BWW construct	Context Diagram	DFD	Functional	ERD
THING	External agents	External Agents Data Store		
PROPERTY: IN PARTICULAR IN GENERAL INTRINSIC MUTUAL EMERGENT HEREDITARY ATTRIBUTES	Data Flows	Data Flows Data Stores	Function	Attribute type
CLASS				Entity type
KIND			Specialization/ generalization (IS-A)	Specialization/ generalization (IS-A)
CONCEIVABLE STATE SPACE				
STATE LAW			Specialization/ generalization descriptors	Specialization/ generalization descriptors; [Min, max] cardinalities
LAWFUL STATE SPACE				
EVENT				
PROCESS		DFD diagram Process	Function type Process oriented function decomposition	
CONCEIVABLE EVENT SPACE				
TRANSFORMATION		Process	Function Type	
LAWFUL TRANSFORMATION				
LAWFUL EVENT SPACE				
HISTORY				
ACTS ON				

BWW construct	Context Diagram	DFD	Functional	ERD
COUPLING: BINDING MUTUAL PROPERTY		Data Flow		Relationship type (no symbol for relationship in grammar)
SYSTEM	System			
SYSTEM COMPOSITION	External agents and external data stores in a context diagram	External agents and data stores in a DFD diagram		
SYSTEM ENVIRONMENT	External Agent External data stores	External Agent		
SYSTEM STRUCTURE				
SUBSYSTEM				
SYSTEM DECOMPOSITION		DFD Diagrams and subdiagrams		
LEVEL STRUCTURE		Series of processes decomposed at different levels	Series of function type decomposition indicators	
EXTERNAL EVENT				
STABLE STATE				
UNSTABLE STATE				
INTERNAL EVENT				
WELL-DEFINED EVENT				
POORLY DEFINED EVENT				

The UML-system is consistent with the BWW definition, and thus there is technically no ontological discrepancy with BWW system construct (Irwin and Turk 2005). In a use case diagram, an association represents a specific type of relationship; namely that an actor initiates a use case, or that an actor interacts with the system to accomplish the goal of the use case. Association in use case diagrams corresponds to a BWW binding mutual property (Irwin and Turk 2005).

The interpretation for the mapping of BWW constructs for the activity, state, class and sequence diagrams comes from the work of Dussart et al. (2004). The BWW ontological construct "Thing" can be associated with the object in the sequence, activity and state diagrams. The activity chart can show the transformations made on objects during activities and therefore interpreted as BWW transformation and property constructs (Dussart et al. 2004).

Class diagrams can contain symbols for classes, associations, attributes, operations, generalizations. Class and Kind are respectively represented in the UML in the class diagram with the class and the generalization constructs (Deursan et. al 2004). UML operations can be depicted by BWW transformations and UML-attribute a BWW-characteristic intrinsic property (Opdahl, A.L. and Henderson-Sellers 2004).

Class diagrams can also show the subsystem architecture, where the primary elements are UML system and subsystems. Subsystems represent components during development (Opdahl and Henderson-Sellers 2004). Subsystems and systems can be represented using a stereotyped package (Dussart et. al. 2004).

Relations between classes are depicted by UML associations; these can be represented by using the BWW mutual binding property construct and UML-multiplicity represented by state law. (Opdahl & Henderson-Sellers 2004).

Table 3-3. Mapping between UML diagrams and BBW constructs

BWW construct	Use Case	Sequence	Class	State	Activity
THING	Actor Use Case	Object		Object	Object Swimlane Actor
PROPERTY: IN PARTICULAR IN GENERAL INTRINSIC MUTUAL EMERGENT HEREDITARY ATTRIBUTES			UML attribute		Activity Swimlane

BWW construct	Use Case	Sequence	Class	State	Activity
CLASS			Class		
KIND	Use Case		Generalization UML aggregate class UML composite class		
STATE				State	
CONCEIVABLE STATE SPACE				State machine	
STATE LAW			UML-multiplicity	State> Transition> State	
LAWFUL STATE SPACE				Sub states	
EVENT				Trigger	Activity
PROCESS	Use Case				Activity diagram Activity
CONCEIVABLE EVENT SPACE				All triggers	
TRANSFORMA TION			UML operation		Activity
LAWFUL TRANSFORMA TION					Guard conditions On transitions
LAWFUL EVENT SPACE					
HISTORY				Shallow history state construct	
ACTS ON					
COUPLING: BINDING MUTUAL PROPERTY	UML association UML extend UML include	Messages	UML association UML interface		

BWW construct	Use Case	Sequence	Class	State	Activity
SYSTEM	System Boundary	Sequence Diagram	Package with <<system>>		
SYSTEM COMPOSITION	System Boundary Sub-system Boundary	Object			
SYSTEM ENVIRONMENT	Actor	<<Stereotype>> Messages			Actor
SYSTEM STRUCTURE					
SUBSYSTEM			Package with <<subsystem>>		
SYSTEM DECOMPOSITION			Composition		
LEVEL STRUCTURE			Generalization		
EXTERNAL EVENT				<<Stereotype>	
STABLE STATE				Final State	
UNSTABLE STATE				Initial State	
INTERNAL EVENT				<<Stereotype>> Trigger	
WELL-DEFINED EVENT					
POORLY DEFINED EVENT					

States of the thing are represented by the state of the object in the activity diagram or by the state construct in the state diagram. A state machine in the state diagram represents the conceivable State Space, defined as all the states that a thing may ever assume. A Lawful State Space can be represented in a state diagram using substates. Stable States and Unstable States can respectively be represented by the final state or the initial state in a state diagram (Dussart et al. 2004).

Events are represented as the trigger for a transition in the state diagram. But events can also be represented as an activity in the activity diagram. There is no grammatical differentiation for External and Internal events but the use of the Uses Cases for human-machine interaction diagram or the use of stereotypes could help make the differentiation possible. The Conceivable Event Space can be observed on the state machine of a thing by looking at all transitions triggers. There exists no construct for a poorly defined event, and well-defined events use the same grammatical construct as a normal event (Dussart et al. 2004).

Lawful transformations are represented by guard conditions on transitions. There is no grammatical construct for Lawful event space. History can be modeled using the shallow history state construct in the state diagram. Acts on cannot be represented in the same way as it is defined in the definitions of the ontological constructs but could eventually be associated to the composition relationship in the class diagram, for example, in a composition relation between a thing "Activity" and a thing "Project" (Dussart et al. 2004)

A system can be represented using the sequence diagrams, the System composition is represented using the object construct and the System environment, that is to say external and internal things to the system cannot be differentiated without a stereotype. The System structure BWW construct is represented using the UML-message in the sequence diagram and the decomposition by UML-composition (Dussart et. al. 2004).

For an analysis of ontological completeness, several constructs cannot find representation in any diagrams: lawful event space, acts on, poorly defined event. A construct overload is found for the activity construct in the activity diagram that can represent a transformation, a process, a property in general or an event. Construct overload was also observed for the swimlane of the activity diagram that can represent either a thing (such as an organization) or a hereditary property of the thing (a user of the organization). Finally, overload was also identified for the trigger construct (that can represent either an event or a well-defined event). There is construct redundancy in the case of the process ontological construct that can be either represented by a complete activity diagram or by the activity construct in an activity diagram. In the case of the activity diagram, construct excess can also be identified since the branching construct could not find any matching ontological construct. Overlaps occur in the activity diagram and the state diagram (Dussart et. al. 2004).

As for the transformation of legacy business models using traditional diagrams into UML models, the ontological analysis reveals that all the BWW constructs represented in the traditional models can be represented in the UML models. Context diagrams can be depicted by use case diagrams as these contain all the BWW constructs required for equivalent representation. ERD diagrams are represented by property, class, kind, state law and coupling constructs. The class diagram is able to represent the same constructs therefore able to represent the same requirements. DFD diagrams are able to represent thing, property, transformation, process, coupling, system composition, system environment, system decomposition and level structure constructs. These could be represented with the help of activity, class and use case diagrams. Finally, functional decomposition diagrams can be depicted with the use of the same diagrams.

The use of state and sequence diagrams is redundant in the representation of structured diagrams. The main reason is that structured traditional diagrams are not able to represent states and the overlap of sequence with use case diagrams.

Although the ontological mappings provide evidence that component-based models derived from the traditional models of a legacy system are able to represent the same BWW constructs, a normalized reference model comparison can be used as a tool to verify that the same requirements captured in the legacy system traditional business models are represented in the component-based models. Figures 3-6, 3-7, 3-8 and 3-9 show the BWW normalized reference models for the ERD, class, context and use case diagrams of the legacy and reengineered systems. The reference models were created by using the Rosemann and Green (2002) meta models for the representation of BBW constructs.

By comparing the normalized reference models from the ERD and class diagram (figures 3-6 and 3-7), it is possible to verify that the same classes represented in the ERD diagram are represented in the class diagram. The same relationships are present in both reference models. On the other hand, the class diagram reference model is able to complement the ERD by including classes for things that are also part of the original system but were not able to be represented in the traditional diagrams and by including classes that will help to implement the interfaces needed for component interaction.

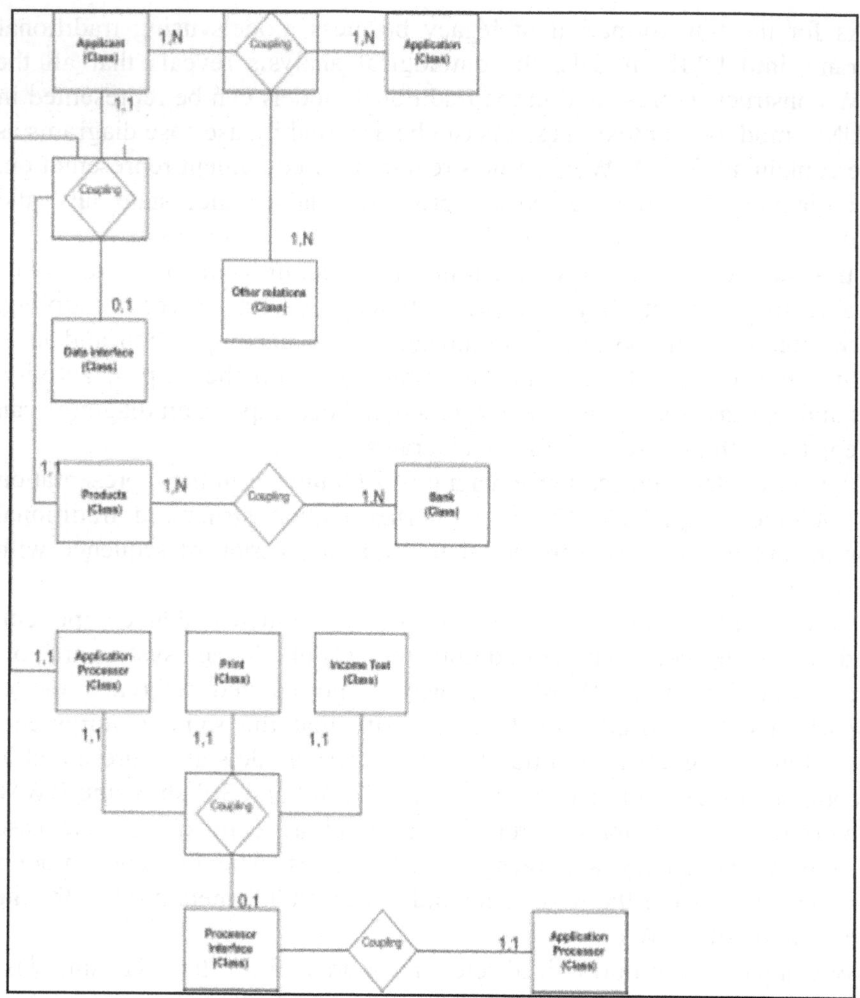

Figure 3-6. Normalized referenced model for the class diagram of the case study

The comparison of normalized reference models for the context and use case diagrams (figures 3-8 and 3-9) reveals that the applicant (BWW thing) originally represented in the legacy system is not included in the use case diagram of the re-engineered system. Although this actor is included in the original use case, process modeling includes manual functions while use cases diagram boundaries only include automated systems. Since the applicant fills an application manually, this component is left out of the use case diagram but it is part of the context diagram. The representation of the applicant is therefore no longer part of the re-engineered system.

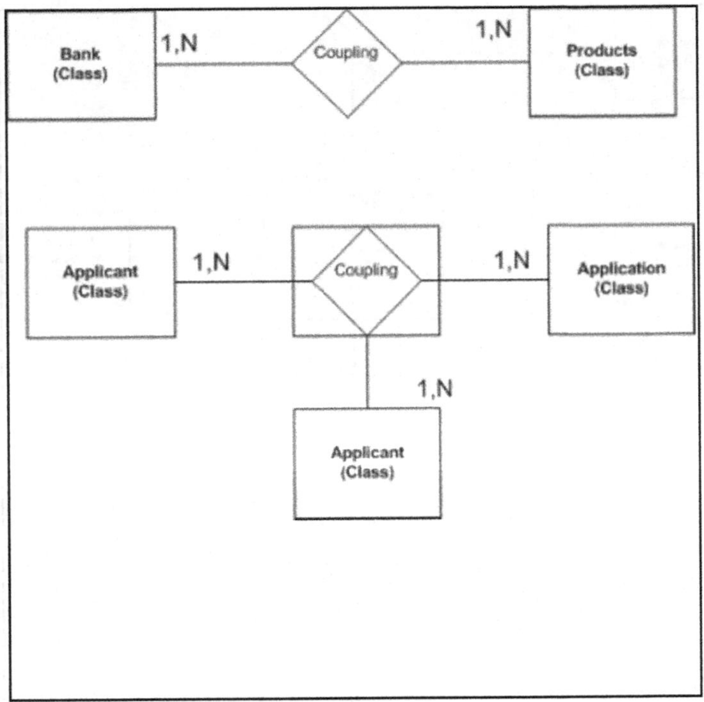

Figure 3-7. Normalized referenced model for the ERD diagram of the case study

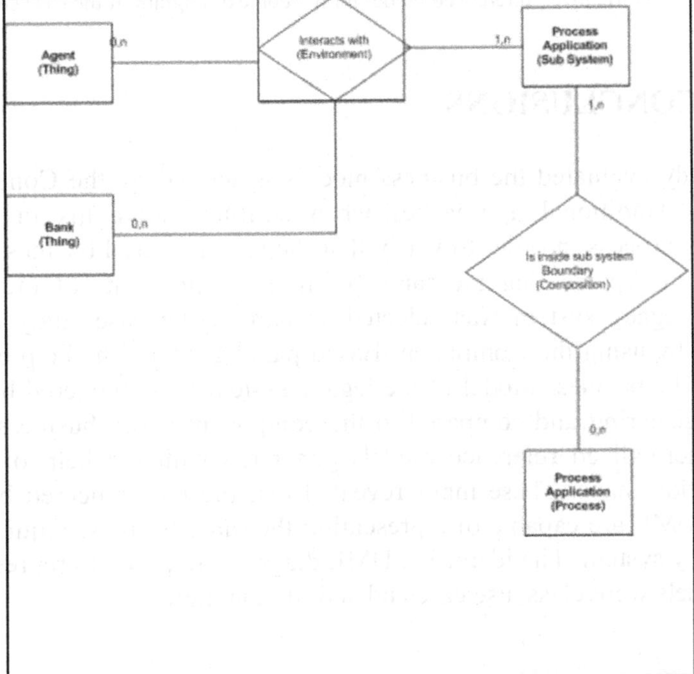

Figure 3-8. Normalized referenced model for the use case diagram of the case study

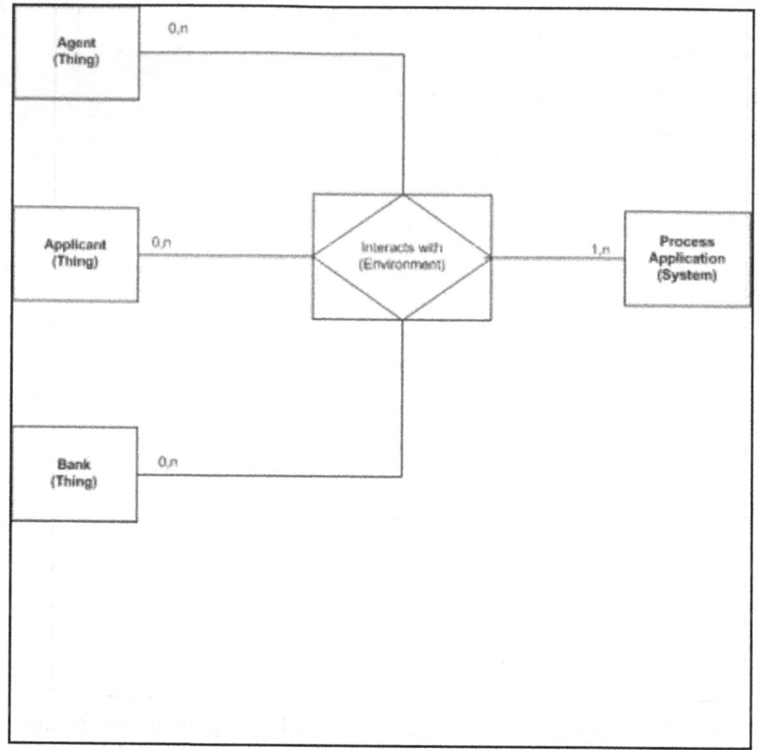

Figure 3-9. Normalized referenced model for the context diagram of the case study

7. CONCLUSIONS

The study evaluated the business models generated by the Component-Based and Traditional approaches when shifting paradigms in the re-engineering process in order to verify that the re-engineered business model is capable of representing the same business requirements of the legacy system. A legacy system was selected as part of the case study and re-engineered by using the Component-Based paradigm with the help of UML diagrams. The business model of the legacy system was recovered by using reverse engineering and compared to the component-based business model by using normalized reference models generated with the help of BWW transformation maps. These maps revealed that the re-engineered business models in UML are capable of representing the same business requirements of the legacy system. The identified UML diagrams required to represent the legacy models were class, use case and activity diagrams.

Normalized reference models in BWW terms were generated for the ERD, context, use case and class diagrams as a way to illustrate their use for business model comparison. A conflict was detected in this comparison as actors in the context diagram might not appear in the use case diagram as the latter only depict automated systems while context diagrams depict manual processes. On the other hand, component models complement legacy models by including objects that were not represented before re-engineering.

Although the study showed that these normalized reference models are useful tools to verify that component-based models represent the same requirements as the original traditional models of the legacy systems, further research will need to be conducted in order to find how to generate normalized reference models for the complete suite of traditional and UML component based models. As a result, business rules could be elaborated in order to re-engineer legacy systems into modern component-based systems for business requirements equivalency.

REFERENCES

Benbasat, I., Goldstein, D. and Mead, M. 1987, The Case Research Strategy in Studies of Information Systems *MIS Quarterly*, 4, pp. 368-386.

Chikofsky E.J and Cross J.H. 1990, Reverse Engineering and Design Recovery - a Taxonomy. *IEEE Software*. No. 7 Vol. 1. pp. 13-17.

Chisholm, R.M. 1996, A Realistic Theory of Categories: An Essay on Ontology. *Cambridge University Press*.

Chen, P. P.-S. 1976, The Entity-Relationship Model: Toward a Unified View of Data, *ACM Transactions on Database Systems*, 1, Vol. 1, pp. 9-36.

Dussart, A., Aubert, B. A. and Patry, M. 2004, An Evaluation of Inter-Organizational Workflow Modelling formalisms, *IDEA group publishing*.

Evermann, J.; Wand, Y. 2001, An Ontological Examination of Object Interaction in Conceptual Modeling. *Proceedings of the 11th Workshop on Information Technologies and Systems (WITS 2001)*. New Orleans, Louisiana.

Fettke P., Loos P. 2003a, Ontological Evaluation of Reference Models using the Bunge-Wand-Weber Model, *North America Conference in Information Systems*.

Fettke, P.; Loos, P. 2003b, Onthological Evaluation of the Specification Framework proposed by the "Standardized Specification of Business Components" Memorandum – Some Preliminary Results. *In S. Overhage, K. Turowski (Eds.): Proceedings of the 1st Int. Workshop on Component Engineering Methodology*. Erfurt, pp. 1-12.

Green, P and Rosemann, M. 2000, Ontological Analysis of Integrated Process Modeling: Some Initial Insights, in *Proceedings of the Australian Conference on Information Systems (ACIS 2000)*, Brisbane, Australia, 6-8 December.

Green, P, Rosemann, M & Indulska M 2005, Ontological Evaluation of Enterprise Systems Interoperability Using ebXML *IEE transactions in knowledge and data engineering* Vol. 17. No. 5.

Jacobson, I.,Christerson, M., Jonsson, P. and Overgaard, G. 1993, Object-oriented Software Engineering: A Use Case Driven Approach, *Addison-Wesley*, Wokingham, Englad

Jacobson and F. Lindstrom 1991, Re-engineering of Old Systems to an Object-Oriented Approach, *Proceedings OOPSLA 1991*, pp. 340-350.

Irwin, G. Turk D, 2005, An Ontological Analysis of Use Case Modeling Grammar, *Journal of the Association for Information Systems* Vol. 6 No.1, pp.1-36

Longworth, R. 2003, Modeling Events for Today's System Requirements available from Internet (http://www.cips.ca/it/resources/eventviews.pdf (255Kb)) Accessed 20 Oct 2003.

Opdahl, A.L., and B. Henderson-Sellers 2002 Ontological Evaluation of the UML Using the Bunge-Wand-Weber Model, *Software Systems Model*, 1, pp. 43-67.

Opdahl A and Henderson-Sellers B 2004, A template for defining enterprise modeling constructs *Journal of Database Management*, 15(2), 39-73, April-June 2004.

Reed, Jr, P.R. 2002, *Developing Applications with JAVA and UML*, Addison-Wesley, Boston.

Rosemann, M., Recker J., Indulska M. and Green P. 2005, Process Modeling – A Maturing Discipline? *BPMI.org: Business Process Modeling Notation (BPMN)*, available at: http://www.bpmi.org/ accessed June 5 2005.

Rosemann, M. and Green, P. 2002 Developing a meta model for the Bunge-Wand-Weber Ontological Constructs, *Journal of Information Systems*, 27, 75-91.

Satzinger, J.W., Jackson R.B., and Burd S.D. 2002, *Systems Analysis ad Design in a Changing World,* 5th ed. Course Technology, Boston, Mass.

Serrano, M., Carver, D., de Oca, C. 2001, Reengineering legacy systems for distributed environments, *Journal of Systems and Software*, 64(1), 37-55.

Scheer, A.-W. 1998, : *ARIS–Business Process Frameworks.* 2nd edn. Springer-Verlag, Berlin

Szyperski. C., 1999. *Component Software: Beyond Object-Oriented Programming*, 1th edn Addison-Wesley, New Jersey.

Uschold, M., King, M., Moralee, S. & Zorgios, Y. 1998, The enterprise ontology. *The Knowledge Engineering Review*, vol. 13.

Yourdon, E. 1989 *Modern Structured Analysis*. 1th edn Yourdon Press, Englewood Cliffs.

Wand, Y. and Weber, R. 1988,. An ontological analysis of some fundamental information systems concepts. In DeGross, J.I. & Olson, M.H. (eds.), *Proceedings of the Ninth International Conference on Information Systems, Minneapolis/ USA, November 30-* December 3, 1988, 213–225.

Wand, Y.; Weber, R. 1989, An Ontological Evaluation of Systems Analysis and Design Methods, *In: E. D. Falkenberg; P. Lindgreen (ed.): Information Systems Concepts: An In-Depth Analysis*. North-Holland, pp. 79-107.

Wand, Y. & Weber, R. 1990. An ontological model of an information system. *IEEE Transactions on Software Engineering (TSE)*, 16(11), 1282–1292.

Wand, Y.; Weber, R. 1993, *On the ontological expressiveness of information systems analysis and design grammars*, Journal of Information Systems (3:4), 1993, pp. 217-237.

Wand, Y. & Weber, R. 1995. On the deep structure of information systems. *Information Systems Journal*, 5, 203–223.

Wand, Y.; Weber, R. 2002, Research Commentary: Information Systems and Conceptual

Weber, R.; Zhang, Y. 1996, An analytical evaluation of NIAM's grammar for conceptual schema diagrams, *Information Systems Journal* (6), 1996, pp. 147-170.

Weber, R. 1997 *Ontological Foundations of Information Systems*, Coopers and Lybrand Accounting Research Methodology. Monograph No. 4. Melbourne.

Whitten, J. L., Bentley D. L. and Dittman K.V. 2000, *Systems Analysis and Design Methods,* 5th edn, McGraw-Hill, New York.

Wolfgang P. 1997, Component-Based Software Development - A New Paradigm in Software Engineering? *Software-Concepts and Tools Software - Concepts and Tools* vol 18 no. 4 pp. 169-174.

Verrijn-Stuart, A.A. 2001. A Framework of Information System Concepts — *The Revised FRISCO Report*. Web document, draft version.

Chapter 4

USING ONTOLOGIES IN THE SEMANTIC WEB: A SURVEY

Li Ding, Pranam Kolari, Zhongli Ding and Sasikanth Avancha
University of Maryland Baltimore County

Abstract: The Semantic Web is well recognized as an effective infrastructure to enhance visibility of knowledge on the Web. The core of the Semantic Web is "ontology", which is used to explicitly represent our conceptualizations. Ontology engineering in the Semantic Web is primarily supported by languages such as RDF, RDFS and OWL. This chapter discusses the requirements of ontology in the context of the Web, compares the above three languages with existing knowledge representation formalisms, and surveys tools for managing and applying ontology. Advantages of using ontology in both knowledge-base-style and database-style applications are demonstrated using three real world applications.

Key words: Ontology; Semantic Web; survey; tools

1. INTRODUCTION

In philosophy, ontology studies the nature of being and existence. The term 'ontology' is derived from the Greek words "onto", which means *being*, and "logia", which means *written or spoken discourse*. Smith [1] reviewed the studies on the metaphysical aspect of ontology since Aristotle's time, and summarized the essence of ontology as follows: "provide a definitive and exhaustive classification of entities in all spheres of being". In contrast to these studies, Quine's *ontological commitment* [1] [2] drove ontology research towards formal theories in the conceptual world. Computer scientists further extended Quine's work into a new interpretation of ontology as "a specification of a conceptualization" [3].

[1] That is, one is committed as an existing thing when it is referenced or implied in some statements, and the statements are commitments to the thing.

In computer science and information science, knowledge reuse is facilitated by the use of explicit ontology, as opposed to implicit ontology, i.e., knowledge encoded into software systems [4]. Hence, appropriate ontology languages are needed to realize explicit ontology with respect to three important aspects:

- **Conceptualization.** The language should choose an appropriate reference model, such as *entity-relationship model* and *object-oriented model*, and provide corresponding ontology constructs to represent factual knowledge, such as defining the entities and relations in a domain, and asserting relations among entities.
- **Vocabulary.** Besides the semantics, the language should also cover the syntax such as symbol assignment (i.e., assigning symbols to concepts) and grammars (i.e., serializing the conceptualism into explicit representation).
- **Axiomatization.** In order to capture the semantics for inference, rules and constraints are needed in addition to factual knowledge. For example, we can use rules to generate new facts from existing knowledge, and to validate the consistency of knowledge.

On the other hand, web based knowledge sharing activities demand that human and/or machine agents agree on common and explicit ontology so as to exchange knowledge and fulfill collaboration goals. In order to share knowledge across different communities or domains, three requirements should be considered when developing explicit ontology:

- **Extensibility.** In the context of the Web, ontology engineers should be able to develop ontology in an incremental manner: reusing as many existing popular concepts as possible before creating a new concept from scratch. For example, the concept "woman" can be defined as a *sub-class* of an existing concept "person" in WordNet [2] vocabulary. This requirement demands an expressive common reference model as well as distributed symbol resolution mechanisms.
- **Visibility.** Merely publishing knowledge on the Web does not guarantee that it can be readily understood by machines or human users. In order to make knowledge visible on the Web, additional common ontological ground on syntax and semantics is required between information publishers and consumers. This requirement is especially critical to machines since they are not capable of understanding knowledge written in an unfamiliar language.
- **Inferenceability.** Ontology not only serves the purpose of representation, i.e. enumerating factual domain knowledge, but also serves the purpose of computation, i.e., enabling logical inference on facts through axiomatization. Hence, ontology on the Web should provide constructs

[2] See http://wordnet.princeton.edu/.

for effective binding with logical inference primitives and options to support a variety of expressiveness and computational complexity requirements.

The Semantic Web inherits the power of representation from existing conceptualisms, such as *Semantic Networks* [5], and enhances interoperability at both syntactic and semantic levels. It can function as a distributed database or a collaborative knowledge base according to application requirements. In particular, *extensibility* is offered not only by the underlying URI based vocabulary but also by the simple graph data model of *Resource Description Framework* (RDF) [6]. *Visibility* is offered by web based publishing mechanisms (i.e. "Anyone Can Make Statements About Any Resource") which uses URI based vocabulary, XML syntax, RDF graph data model and some common ontology languages. *Inferenceability* is offered by the ontology constructs from *RDF Schema* (RDFS) [7] ontology language and *Web Ontology Language* (OWL) [8] which connect knowledge statement to logical inference at different levels of expressiveness and computational complexity. Formally defined semantics of RDFS and OWL plays an essential role in inferenceability.

This chapter surveys the current deployment status of Semantic Web ontology and corresponding tools, and draws a practical road map on using ontology in the Semantic Web. Section two reviews the evolution of Semantic Web ontology languages by comparing them with existing approaches in database and knowledge representation literature. Section three surveys tools for creating, publishing, extending and reasoning with Semantic Web ontology. Section four surveys storage and integration tools used for applying Semantic Web ontology. Section five discusses three applications to demonstrate the use of ontology in building knowledge-base-oriented and database-oriented applications in the Semantic Web with respect to the three requirements.

2. ONTOLOGY IN THE SEMANTIC WEB

Ontology play an important role in fulfilling semantic interoperability as described in the seminal article on the Semantic Web [9]. W3C has standardized a layered stack of ontology languages that possess the advantages of both knowledge representation (KR) formalisms and conceptual modeling methods for databases. Such standardization activities encouraged creating new ontology and translating pre-existing ontology into the Semantic Web.

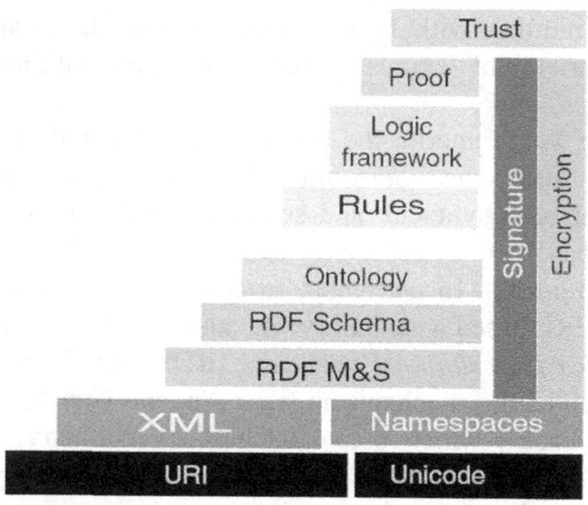

Figure 4-1. The layer cake: enabling standards and technologies for the Semantic Web. Adapted from Tim Berners-Lee (http://www.w3.org/2002/Talks/04-sweb/slide12-0.html)

2.1 Evolution of Semantic Web Ontology Languages

In the Semantic Web layer cake (see Figure 4-1), the semantic part is enabled by a stack of evolving languages: Resource Description Framework (RDF) [6] offers a simple graph reference model; RDF Schema (RDFS) [7] offers a simple vocabulary and axioms for object-oriented modeling; and Web Ontology Language (OWL) [8] offers additional knowledge base oriented ontology constructs and axioms.

Figure 4-2 shows similar evolutionary trends among three paradigms: KR formalisms, conceptual modeling methods for databases, and the Semantic Web. The built-in semantics increases in each paradigm along the vertical axis driven by the demand of porting implicit semantics into explicit representation. For example, *Semantic Networks*, developed between the mid-60s and early 70s, are highlighted by their simple but powerful relational reference model in supporting conceptualization; *Frame Systems* [10], which emerged in the mid-70s, incorporate additional constructs that model classes and instances in a user-friendly manner; *Description Logics* [11], which came out in the 80s as descendents of Semantic Networks and Frame Systems, are highlighted by their formal semantics and decidable inference. Similar evolutions can be observed in the development of the databases and the Semantic Web. RDF was proposed in 1998 as a simple graph model, followed a year later by RDFS. Independent contemporary efforts in DARPA Agent Markup Language (DAML) [3] and Ontology

[3] See http://www.daml.org/.

Inference Layer (OIL) [12] merged into DAML+OIL [13] in 2001 and finally evolved into OWL, which was drafted in 2002 and became a W3C recommendation in 2004.

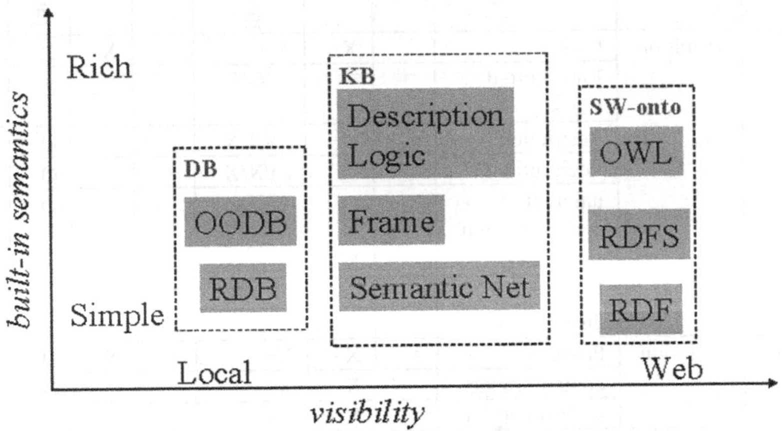

Figure 4-2. A comparison of knowledge representation formalisms (KB), conceptual modeling methods in databases (DB), and Semantic Web ontology languages (SW-onto)

The rapid evolution of Semantic Web ontology languages was enabled by learning from the experiences in developing existing knowledge representation formalisms and database conceptual models, and by inheriting and extending some of their useful features. In particular, the Semantic Web significantly improves visibility and extensibility aspects of knowledge sharing in comparison with the previous approaches. Its URI-based vocabulary and XML-based grammar are key enablers to web scale knowledge management and sharing.

2.2 A Comparison of Ontology Constructs

In order to gain insight into built-in semantics, Table 4-1 summarizes ontology constructs in RDF/RDFS and OWL and compares them with other formalisms in knowledge base (KB) as well as formal models in databases (DB).[4]

[4] Some auxiliary functional constructs are not included in this table: datatype constructs (e.g. rdf:Literal, rdf:XMLLiteral); RDF reification (i.e. rdf:Statement, rdf:subject, rdf:predicate, rdf:object); collections and container (e.g. rdf:List, rdf:Alt, rdf:Bag, and rdf:Set).

Table 4-1. A comparison of ontology constructs*

Cat-1	Cat-2	Ontology Constructs	RDF	RDFS	OWL Lite/DL/Full	RDB	OODB	KB (Frame)	KB (DL)
class	definition	Class		X	X+		X	X	X
		Enumerated Class			–/X/X				O
		Restriction			()/X/X			O	X
		intersectionOf			()/X/X			O	X
		unionOf, complementOf			–/X/X			O	X
	axiom	subclassOf		X	X=		X	X	X
		Equality			()/X/X			O	O
		disjointWith			–/X/X			O	X
relation	definition	Property	X	X=	X+	X	X	O	X
		domain, range		X	X=			O	O
		subPropertyOf		X	X=				
	axiom	(Inverse) Functional			()/()/X	X			
		Equality, inverseOf			X				
		transitive, symmetric			()/()/X				
instance	definition	Type	X	X=	X=		X	X	X
	axiom	(In)Equality			()		O	O	O

* Cat-1 divides constructs into those describing either a class, a property (i.e., relation), or an individual (i.e., class instance); and Cat-2 divides constructs into those describing concepts/relations or specifying axioms. Table cells are marked to show how an ontology construct is supported by an ontology language or formalism: 'X' means fully supported; 'X=' means fully support via inheritance, 'X+' means extended fully support, '( )' means supported with restriction; '-' means not supported; and 'O' means optionally supported.

2.2.1 RDF

RDF offers a simple graph model which consists of nodes (i.e. resources or literals) and binary relations (i.e. statements). It is a type of Semantic Network and is very similar to the *Relational Model* [14]. Such a simple model embodies a small amount of built-in semantics and offers great freedom in creating customized extensions; however, an extended or specialized semantic network is usually required in practice. John Sowa identifies six categories of semantic networks based on relation semantics [15]: (i) *Definitional networks*, which build taxonomies for conceptualisms with inheritance (subclass) and membership (instance) relations; (ii) *Assertional networks*, which represent cognitive assertions about the world with modal operators; (iii) *Implicational networks*, which focus on implication relations, e.g. belief network; (iv) *Executable networks*, which focus on temporal dependence relations, e.g. flowchart, PetriNet; (v) *Learning networks*, which focus on causal relations encoded in numerical value, e.g. neural network; (vi) *Hybrid networks*, which combine features of previous types. In the Semantic Web, most ontology are defined using RDF(S)/OWL and thus fall in the first category; the second category (assertional networks) emerges in the context of sharing instance data and evaluating trustworthiness of such data, e.g., [16, 17, 18, 19, 20, 21]; and the third category (implicational networks) gains interests in ontology mapping study [22, 23]. A variation of definitional networks is natural language encyclopedia such as dictionaries and thesaurus which uses a different set of relations rather than class-property relation. WordNet and Simple Knowledge Organization System (SKOS, http://www.w3.org/2004/02/skos/) are their representative Semantic Web versions respectively.

2.2.2 RDFS

Under the influence of *Frame Systems* and the *Object Oriented Model*, RDFS has been used to augment RDF to provide better support for definition and classification [24]. These models organize knowledge in a concept-centric way with descriptive ontology constructs (such as frame, slot, and facet) and built-in inheritance axioms. Frame Systems enable users to represent the world at different levels of abstraction with the emphasis on entities, and this aspect makes it quite different from the planar graph model offered by most semantic networks. In addition to inheriting basic features from Frame Systems, RDFS provides ontology constructs that make relations less dependent on concepts: users can define relations as an instance of *rdf:Property*, describe inheritance relations between relations using *rdfs:subPropertyOf*, and then associate defined relations with classes using *rdfs:domain* or *rdfs:range*.

2.2.3 DAML+OIL and OWL

DAML+OIL and OWL extend RDFS and emphasize support for richer logical inference. Besides inheriting advantages from Frame Systems, these ontology languages provide a rich set of constructs based on formal Model Theoretic Semantics[5]. Three variants of OWL trade off computational complexity and the expressiveness of ontology constructs.

[5] See http://www.w3.org/TR/rdf-mt/ (RDFS), http://www.w3.org/TR/owl-semantics/ (OWL).

- *OWL-Lite* is the simplest variant for building a basic frame system (or an object oriented database) in terms of class, property, subclass relation, and restrictions. OWL-Lite does not use the entire OWL vocabulary and some OWL terms are used under certain restrictions.
- *OWL-DL* is grounded on Description Logics, and focuses on common formal semantics and inference decidability. Description logics offer additional ontology constructs (such as conjunction, disjunction, and negation) besides class and relation, and have two important inference mechanisms: subsumption and consistency. Horrocks and Sattler [25] argued that basic inference in most variations of Description Logics is decidable with complexity between polynomial and exponential time. The strong Set Theory background makes Description Logics suitable for capturing knowledge about a domain in which instances can be grouped into classes and relationships among classes are binary. OWL-DL uses all OWL ontology constructs with some restrictions.
- *OWL-Full* is the most expressive version of OWL but it does not guarantee decidability. The biggest difference between OWL-DL and OWL-Full is that class space and instance space are disjointed in OWL-DL but not in OWL-Full. That is, a class can be interpreted simultaneously as a set of individuals and as an individual belonging to another class in OWL-Full. The entire OWL vocabulary can be used in without any restrictions in OWL-Full.

2.3 Swoogle's Survey of Semantic Web Ontology

This subsection surveys ontology with emphasis on the Semantic Web context, in contrast to prior surveys on ontology development [26, 27]. According to a recent report by Swoogle[6], a search engine that indexes the Semantic Web on the Web, over ten thousand Semantic Web ontology have been discovered on the Web. Table 4-2 (a, b) lists some well populated Semantic Web ontology discovered by Swoogle. Existing Semantic Web ontology can be classified into the following four major categories (without clear-cut boundaries): meta-ontology, comprehensive upper ontology, systematic domain specific ontology, and simple specialized ontology.

Table 4-2a. Usage of Semantic Web meta-ontology (Swoogle, July 2005)

Ontology prefix	Namespace URI	# of Docs. Populated
rdf	http://www.w3.org/1999/02/22-rdf-syntax-ns#	382*K*
rdfs	http://www.w3.org/2000/01/rdf-schema#	82*K*
owl	http://www.w3.org/2002/07/owl#	64*K*
daml	http://www.w3.org/2001/03/daml+oil#	5*K*

6 See http://swoogle.umbc.edu.

Table 4-2b. Popular Semantic Web ontology (Swoogle, July 2005)

Ontology prefix	Namespace URI	# of Docs. Populated
dc	http://purl.org/dc/elements/1.1/	250*K*
rss	http://purl.org/rss/1.0/	165*K*
admin	http://webns.net/mvcb/	130*K*
sy	http://purl.org/rss/1.0/modules/syndication/	90*K*
foaf	http://xmlns.com/foaf/0.1/	77*K*
cc	http://web.resource.org/cc/	74*K*
content	http://purl.org/rss/1.0/modules/content/	60*K*
trackback	http://madskills.com/public/xml/rss/module/trackback	56*K*
iw	http://inferenceweb.stanford.edu/2004/05/iw.owl#	47*K*
bio	http://purl.org/vocab/bio/0.1/	35*K*
geo	http://www.w3.org/2003/01/geo/wgs84_pos#	25*K*
vCard	http://www.w3.org/2001/vcard-rdf/3.0#	20*K*

2.3.1 Meta-Ontology

The ontology languages, namely RDF, RDFS, DAML+OIL and OWL, are in fact meta-ontology themselves; and their instances are Semantic Web ontology. Such meta-ontology offers a small vocabulary and corresponding axioms as the building blocks for any conceptualisms, and they are backed by inference engines with built-in support for their ontology constructs and axioms. For example, a RDFS inference engine can understand the semantics of *rdf:subClassOf* and infer RDF triples by propagating *rdf:type* statement through sub-class relations. Such ontology only provides necessary parts for the reference model without considering any domain concepts.

There are also some additional candidate ontology languages. In order to represent the semantics of rules, rule/policy languages have been proposed, such as Semantic Web Rule Language (SWRL) [7], which is a combination of OWL and RuleML, and Rei declarative policy language [28]. In additional to the object-oriented constructs provided in RDF(S) and OWL, ontology constructs for thesaurus like concept organization (e.g. concept, narrower-concept, and related-concept) have been modeled in SKOS.

2.3.2 Comprehensive Upper Ontology

Upper ontology provides a high level model about the world using the meta-ontology. Currently, Semantic Web researchers are working to translate existing upper ontology, such as Cyc [29], WordNet [30, 31], OntoSem [32], and IEEE's Standard Upper Ontology (SUO) [33], into

[7] See http://www.daml.org/2003/11/swrl/.

RDF(S) or OWL versions. OpenCyc (http://www.opencyc.org/) has published a 700MB OWL files encoding part of the CYC ontology. There is also a RDFS version of WordNet ontology using the namespace http://xmlns.com/wordnet/1.6/, and a W3C's task force [8] has been formed recently aiming at better RDF(S)/OWL based representation of WordNet. OntoSem is being translated into OWL [34, 35].

2.3.3 Systematic Domain Specific Ontology

Unlike upper ontology which require agreements across multiple domains, *domain specific ontology* have been developed to build systematic vocabulary for certain domains long before the inception of the Semantic Web, e.g. legal ontology [36], gene ontology [37], chemical ontology [38], bio ontology [39], and spatial ontology [40]. Again, the Semantic Web makes it possible to improve the visibility of such domain ontology; hence, translation efforts such as building an RDF version of CIA world fact book are ongoing. Domain ontology can also contain some well-known class instances besides class/property definition, e.g. airport ontology not only defines the class "airport", but also enumerates all three-letter airport codes.

2.3.4 Simple Specialized Ontology

One difficulty with comprehensive or systematic ontology is that they are usually too big to use. For example, no existing ontology inference engine can store and use the complete OpenCyc ontology which has over 60,000 terms and is stored in a 700MB file. Hence, much simple specialized Semantic Web ontology have been developed to overcome this difficulty by concentrating on a set of basic and commonly-used concepts. Such ontology is often used as interchange languages in knowledge sharing.

Dublin Core (http://dublincore.org/) brought about a series of ontology for document metadata, e.g., the well-known RDFS based ontology – Dublin Core Metadata Element Set ontology. RSS news digest ontology (including rss, sy, trackback, and content as listed in Table 4-2 is driven by the blogging community and has now become one of the most popular domain ontology. W3C is also driving the Friend-Of-A-Friend (FOAF) [9] ontology for person information. The Inference Web ontolog [10] focuses on explicit representation of justification steps produced by inference engines. The Creative Commons ontology aims at recording copyright related information. Similarly,

[8] See http://www.w3.org/2001/sw/BestPractices/WNET/tf.html.
[9] See http://www.foaf-project.org.
[10] See http://inferenceweb.stanford.edu.

ontology such as 'geo', 'vCard', and 'admin' have been developed with small vocabulary sets specialized to capture relevant domain information.

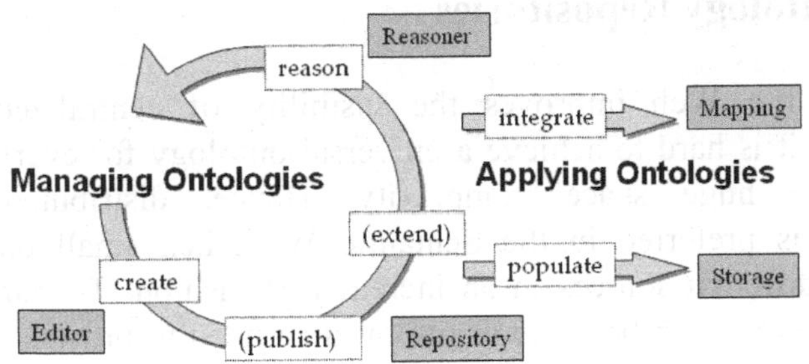

Figure 4-3. Ontology tools for managing ontology and applying ontology. The 'publish' and 'extend' steps are parenthesized to indicate they are optional

3. SEMANTIC WEB ONTOLOGY TOOLS

Our discussion thus far has shown how ontology play a critical role in Semantic Web applications. Effective enabling tools are needed in order to implement Semantic Web ontology. Figure 4-3 depicts typical steps in managing ontology, i.e., create, publish, extend, and reason; and two common scenarios in applying ontology: populating instances of ontology and integrating information encoded by different ontology. Accordingly, five tool classes are placed close to relevant steps or scenarios: tools for managing ontology are covered in this section; and tools for applying ontology are covered in Section four.

3.1 Ontology Editors

A good editor can save a significant amount of time when developing ontology by helping ontology engineers focus on the semantics without worrying much about syntactic organization. This section offers a brief introduction to some popular and Semantic Web related ontology editors for collaborative or independent ontology development. A more comprehensive survey can be found in [41].

Protege [42] provides a standalone ontology development environment. It is highlighted by its syntax grammar independent user interface and pluggable infrastructure. It is suitable for independent ontology development and has a large user community.

SWOOP [43] takes advantage of both Protege and Ontolingua [44] (a web-based environment for editing, publishing, and sharing ontology developed before the Semantic Web) and provides a convenient web-based ontology browsing, editing, debugging [45] and publishing interface.

3.2 Ontology Repositories

Although the Web improves the visibility of centralized ontology development, it is hard to achieve a universal ontology for everything (e.g. Cyc) due to huge space complexity. Hence, distributed ontology development is preferred in the Semantic Web, i.e., small ontology are authored by different sources in an incremental fashion. To reuse existing ontology, effective web based tools are in great need to browse, search and navigate distributed ontology. Table 4-3 compares some popular repositories for publishing and searching ontology on the Web, and their technical highlights are detailed below.

Table 4-3. A comparison of Semantic Web ontology access services

	DAML ontology Library	SchemaWeb	Ontaria	Semantic Web Search	Swoogle
Indexed documents/ ontology	282/282	203/203	N/A	N/A	>1M / >10K
search ontology	listAll	listAll; Full-text;	keyword	use resource search	keyword
search document	no	no	yes	use resource search	yes
search class/ property	keyword	triple pattern	keyword	keyword	keyword; alphabetical index
search RDF resource	no	triple pattern	N/A	keyword	no
navigation	no	no	yes	no	yes
annotation	by user	by user	no	no	auto digest
auto discovery	no	no	no	yes	yes

- **DAML Ontology Library** (http://www.daml.org/ontology/) indexes user submitted ontology and provides browse/search services. It organizes ontology by their URI, users' annotations supplied during ontology submission (e.g. submission date, keyword, open directory category, funding source, and submitter's organization), the defined class/property, or the used namespace. Users can run sub-string queries over a defined class/property.
- **SchemaWeb** (http://www.schemaweb.info/) provides services similar to DAML ontology library with better human/machine user interface (i.e. both HTML and web service interface). It adds more services: (i) for human user, it provides full-text search service for indexed ontology, and

a customizable resource search interface by letting users specify triple pattern; (ii) for machine agents, it searches the "official" ontology of a given namespace or the resource with user specified triple pattern; it also navigates RDF graph through RDFS properties (i.e. subClassOf, subPropertyOf, domain, range), and publishes RSS feeds about new ontology submissions.

- **W3C's Ontaria** (http://www.w3.org/2004/ontaria/) stores RDF documents (including ontology) and provides search/navigation services in the repository. It allows a user to (i) browse a RDF file as a list of triples, a list of used properties, or a list of populated classes, and (ii) browse relations between RDF files.
- **Semantic Web Search** (http://www.semwebcentral.org/) provides an object oriented view of the Semantic Web, i.e. it indexes instances of well-known classes including *rdfs:Class*, *rdf:Property*, *foaf:Person*, and *rss:Item*. It partially supports ontology search by finding instances of *rdfs:Class* and *rdf:Property*; however, its search results are biased to terms from the namespace of *WordNet 1.6*.
- **Swoogle** (http://swoogle.umbc.edu) indexes millions of Semantic Web documents (including tens of thousand of ontology). It enables users to search ontology by specifying constraints on document metadata such as document URLs, defined classes/properties, used namespaces, and RDF encoding. Moreover, it provides detailed metadata about ontology and classes/properties in an object oriented fashion. It has an ontology dictionary that enables users to browse the vocabulary (i.e. over 150KB URIrefs of defined/used classes and properties) used by Semantic Web documents, and to navigate the Semantic Web by following links among classes/properties, namespace and RDF documents. In addition, it is powered by automatic and incremental Semantic Web document discovery mechanisms and updates statistics about the use of ontology in the Semantic Web on a daily basis.

3.3 Ontology Language Reasoners

An ontology construct conveys descriptive semantics, and its actionable semantics is enforced by reasoners (i.e. inference engines). Table 4-4 introduces several popular reasoners by comparing how they support the inferenceable semantics of Semantic Web ontology languages. A detailed developers' guide is available online[11], and experimental evaluation can be found in W3C's OWL Test Cases report[12].

[11] See http://www.wiwiss.fu-berlin.de/suhl/bizer/toolkits/.

[12] See http://www.w3.org/2003/08/owl-systems/test-results-out.

Table 4-4. Capabilities of reasoners for the Semantic Web ontology*

	OWLJessKB	JTP	Jena	F-OWL	FaCT++	Racer	Pellet	TRIPLE	Sweet Rules
RDFS	()	()	+	()	()	()	()	()	-
OWL-Lite	()	()	()	()	+	()	()	()	-
OWL-DL	-	()	()	()	()	()	()	()	-
OWL-Full	-	()	()	()	-	-	-	()	-
RuleML	-	-	-	-	-	-	-	-	+
Language	Java	Java	Java	Java	C++	Lisp	Java	Java	Java

* Here, '+' means full-support, '-' means no support, and '()' means partial support.

- **OWLJessKB** (http://edge.cs.drexel.edu/assemblies/software/owljesskb/) is the descendent of DAMLJessKB [46] and is based on the Jess Rete inference engine.
- **Java Theorem Prover (JTP)** (http://www.ksl.stanford.edu/software/JTP/), developed at Stanford University [47], supports both forward and backward chaining inference using RDF/RDFS and OWL semantics[13].
- **Jena** (http://jena.sourceforge.net/), developed at HP Labs at Bristol [48], is a popular open-source project. It provides sound and almost complete (except for blank node types) inference support for RDFS. Current version of Jena also partially supports OWL inference and allows users to create customized rule engines.
- **F-OWL** (http://fowl.sourceforge.net/), developed at UMBC [49], is an inference engine which is based on Flora-2[14].
- **FaCT++** (http://owl.man.ac.uk/factplusplus/), developed at the University of Manchester [50], is the descendent of FaCT [51] reasoning system. It provides full support for OWL-Lite. Its future releases aim at providing complete support for OWL-DL reasoning.
- **Racer** (http://www.sts.tu-harburg.de/r.f.moeller/racer/) is a description logic based reasoner [52]. It supports inference over RDFS/DAML/OWL ontology through rules explicitly specified by the user.
- **Pellet** (http://www.mindswap.org/2003/pellet/), developed at the University of Maryland, is a 'hybrid' DL reasoner that can deal both TBox reasoning as well as non-empty ABox reasoning [53]. It is used as the underlying OWL reasoner for SWOOP ontology editor [43] and provides in-depth ontology consistency analysis.

[13] See http://www.ksl.stanford.edu/software/JTP/doc/owl-reasoning.html.

[14] Flora-2 is an object oriented language with Frame System background.

- **TRIPLE** (http://triple.semanticweb.org/), developed by Sintek and Decker [54], is a Horn Logic based reasoning engine (and a language) and uses many features from F-logic. Unlike F-logic, it does not have fixed semantics for classes and objects. This reasoner can be used by translating the Description Logics based OWL into a language (named TRIPLE) handled by the reasoner. Extensions of Description Logics that cannot be handled by Horn logic can be supported by incorporating other reasoners, such as FaCT, to create a hybrid reasoning system.
- **SweetRules** (http://sweetrules.projects.semwebcentral.org/) is a rule toolkit for RuleML. RuleML is a highly expressive language based on courteous logic programs, and provides additional built-in semantics to OWL, including prioritized conflict handling and procedural attachments. The SweetRules engine also provides semantics preserving translation between various other rule languages and ontology (implicit axioms).

4. APPLYING SEMANTIC WEB ONTOLOGY

In many practical scenarios, ontology tools introduced in the previous section are not sufficient for application development on the Semantic Web. The rest of this section surveys two important issues: (i) providing inference support in populating and storing instances of Semantic Web ontology in large scale applications; (ii) mapping concepts from different ontology in ontology based information integration.

4.1 Storing Ontology Instances

Though technology in large scale relational models is relatively mature, the inferenceability feature of ontology introduces additional requirements on storing instances of ontology. Users should now be able to access the asserted knowledge as well as the inferred knowledge which can be derived by ontology based inference. In the Semantic Web, instances of ontology (i.e, knowledge represented in RDF triples) are stored in so-called *triple stores* or *RDF databases*.

There are three alternative strategies to manage inferred knowledge in triple store as influenced by logic inference [55].

- **Forward Chaining** applies entailment rules as soon as RDF triples have been added into a triple store. This approach eliminates run-time inference by enumerating and storing all possible knowledge; hence it will result in fast query response at the cost of increased load time and storage space. Unfortunately, this approach is not so promising since (i) there is no guarantee that the inferred triples will be queried in the future and (ii) the additional storage space for inferred triples can be prohibitively large and impose overhead in access.

- **Backward Chaining** applies entailments rules when the triple store is queried. This approach performs run-time inference without the need of storing inferred knowledge; hence it will result in short load time at the cost of increased query response time. Since query response time is an important benchmark of ease-of-use, too slow response time will decrease users' adoption.
- **Hybrid Inference** combines both forward and backward chaining so as to avoid the disadvantages of both.

There are two well-known storage options, namely in-memory storage and persistent storage. Their performance has been evaluated by comparing the efficiency of load/save operations [56], soundness and completeness of inference [57], and scalability [58]. Table 4-5 compares basic features of some popular triple stores with the emphasis on the persistent storage option since knowledge in the Semantic Web is expected to be in large amount. In the following text, the term 'model' is used to signify the RDF graph including both asserted and inferred triples.

Table 4-5. Capabilities of persistence triple stores *

	Query Language	Level of Inference	Inference Strategy
Jena	RDQL	RDFS, OWL(partial)	F, B, H
RSSDB	RQL	RDFS	-
Kowari	iTQL, RDQL	Explicit Rules	F
Sesame	SeRQL	RDFS	-
3Store	OKBC, RDQL	RDFS	H
Instance Store	Racer, FaCT++ based	OWL-Lite, OWL-DL	-
DLDB	conjunctive KIF	OWL-DL	F

* The three kinds of inference strategies are abbreviated as follows: 'F' for Forward Chaining, 'B' for Backward Chaining and 'H' for Hybrid. '-' is used when corresponding information is not available.

- **Jena** [59] offers both in-memory and persistent storage options. It provides physical data independence through its Java based data access library which hides the physical storage details; hence there is not much difference between accessing persistence store or in-memory store.
- **RSSDB** [60] implements persistent storage option. In addition to being a general triple store, it improves data storage efficiency by storing instances of a class in a specialized (Object-Relational) table at the expense that it assumes that domain ontology are fixed and have defined classes with significant amount of instances.

- **Kowari** (http://www.kowari.org/) implements persistent storage using flat files instead of conventional database products. It allows users to explicitly associate various inference rules (e.g. axioms) with the asserted triples, and separates the storage of asserted triples from that of the inferred triples.
- **Sesame** (http://www.openrdf.org/) [61] implements persistent storage option using Forward Chaining and RDFS level inference, i.e., it enumerates and stores all inferred triples according to RDFS semantics and domain ontology.
- **3Store** [55] supports hybrid inference mechanisms. It classifies inference axioms into those which generate comparatively fewer entailments and apply forward chaining inference on them, and uses backward chaining to handle the rest.
- **Instance store** (http://instancestore.man.ac.uk/) [62] provides Description Logics level persistent storage, and it relies on the FaCT++/Racer inference engine.
- **DLDB** [63] supports persistent triple store by explicitly using the FaCT reasoner which support Description Logics inference. Similar to Sesame, entailment is pre-computed based on the assumption that ontology change less frequently. Similar to RSSDB, it uses a class-centric view for efficient query processing.

The query languages provided and the ontology languages supported by the above triple stores are listed in Table 4-5. A detailed discussion can be found in [64]. In addition, W3C is standardizing SPARQL [65], a new common query language for triple stores.

Existing triples stores are weak in the scalability aspect, i.e., in-memory approaches are limited by the size of main memory and persistent stores are not sufficiently scalable. Two research directions are tackling this issue. First, distributed storage approach [66], Peer-to-Peer system based approach [67], and efficient index based approach [68] have been proposed in contrast to the current centralized storage. Second, researchers are also exploring efficient hybrid inference strategies which prevent full exploration of search space and keep the inference overhead in processing users' queries in an acceptable range.

4.2 Ontology-Based Information Integration

The Semantic Web puts the onus of ontology creation on the user by providing common ontology languages such as RDF(S) and OWL. However, ontology defined by different applications or agents usually describe their domains in different terminologies, even when covering the same domain. The semantic-level heterogeneity between two information sources refers to the use of conflicted or mismatched terms about concepts in their corresponding ontology, which can be identified into one of the following categories: (i) *ambiguous reference* – the same term (i.e., the symbolic identifier of a concept in an ontology) means differently in different ontology; (ii) *synonymous reference* – two terms from different ontology have the same meaning; (iii) *one-to-many matching* – one term from one of the ontology matches [15] to several terms of the other ontology; (iv) *uncertain matching* – one term from one of the ontology has similar but not exactly the same meaning to any terms of the other ontology; and (v) *structural difference* – two terms with the same or similar meaning are structured differently in different ontology (e.g., different paths from their respective root concepts).

In order to support ontology-based information integration, tools and mechanisms are needed to resolve the semantic heterogeneity problem and align the terms in different ontology. This section reviews the literature about the existing works in this topic, which is grouped into five different research directions in tackling the problem.

- **A Centralized Global Ontology.** Enforcing a centralized global ontology prevents semantic heterogeneity since no more ontology exists and everyone is using the same ontology. However, this approach is obviously impractical since (i) the creation and maintenance of such ontology is usually prohibitively expensive and (ii) it is usually impractical to develop ontology with consent from the user community at large.
- **Merging Ontology.** Merging different ontology into a unified one is another natural approach to semantic integration when those ontology overlap significantly over a common domain. There are many heuristics to merge two terms, such as (i) linguistic heuristics which uses term spelling or additional natural language processing (NLP) techniques with manual validation, e.g., *FCA-MERGE* [69, 70], (ii) syntactic and semantic heuristics, e.g., *PROMPT* [71] [16] and *Chimaera* [72], and (iii) hybrid approaches [73]. However, this approach is usually costly and not scalable. The merging procedure has to restart from scratch when any of the input ontology has been modified. When merging a large number of ontology, the merging result may not always meet application.
- **Mapping Ontology.** Building a set of mappings (or matches) between two ontologies is an alternative way to merging ontology. A mapping between two terms from two different ontologies conveys the fact that the terms have similar or same meaning. Besides manually specifying

15 A subject 'matches' an object if they refer to exactly the same concept.

16 It initializes term-matching suggestions using linguistic similarity among class names, and then updates suggestions by resolving newly detected syntactic and semantic conflicts.

mappings, there are some semi-automated methods such as: (i) lexical similarity analysis on linguistic or lexical ontology [74, 75] such as WordNet, Cyc, and SENSUS; (ii) textual description analysis, which assigns a set of relevant documents to each term so as to capture the meaning of the term, measures similarity between terms using machine learning based text classification techniques, and searches for mappings based on the similarity matrix obtained, e.g., *CAIMAN* [76], *OntoMapper* [77], and *GLUE* [78, 79, 80]; (iii) ontology algebra and articulation, e.g., *ONION* [81], which is semi-automatic, with good scalability, easy to maintenance, but slow; (iv) information flow and channel theory based approach [82]; (v) structural analysis, i.e., 'similarity flooding' – a graph matching algorithm based on fixpoint computation [83]; and (iv) hybrid heuristics, sometimes combined with the structural information of the ontology taxonomy, e.g., *Anchor-PROMPT* [84] and *PROMPTDIFF* [85]. A brief survey of existing approaches is provided by [86], however, most of these approaches only study exact mappings, without taking the degree of uncertainty [17] into consideration [18]. Since semantic similarities between concepts can be easily represented probabilistically (but not logically), Bayesian Networks (BNs) [87] stand out as a natural choice in tackling this problem: (i) Mitra et al. [88] improve existing mapping results by applying a set of meta-rules to capture the structural influence and the semantics of ontology relations; (ii) Ding et al. [89] and Pan et al. [90] proposed a principled methodology by first translating the source and target ontology into BNs, and then mapping the concepts from the two ontology based on evidential reasoning between the two translated BNs.

- **Ontology Translation.** Given two ontology, ontology translation is to translate one of the ontology into a target ontology which uses the representation and semantics of the other ontology, sometimes with the help of an intermediate shared ontology. Based on a set of defined rules and transformation operators, *Ontomorph* [91] offers syntactic rewriting and semantic rewriting to support the translation between two different knowledge representation languages. *OntoMerge* [92], an online ontology translation system [19] based on ontology merging (which requires a set of ontology bridging axioms produced manually by domain experts) and automated reasoning, achieves term translations using a first order

[17] It is often the case that a concept defined in one ontology can only find partial matches to one or more concepts in another ontology.

[18] Note that the methods in (ii) fail to completely address uncertainty in mapping since the degree of similarity found between concepts will not be considered in further reasoning.

[19] See http://cs-www.cs.yale.edu/homes/dvm/daml/ontology-translation.html.

theorem prover built on top of PDDAML (PDDL-DAML Translator) [20] (based on Jena) and OntoEngine [21] (an inference engine based on JTP), in either forward or backward chaining way. Ontology translation takes a further step after mapping or merging, and is one of the most difficult tasks towards information integration.

- **Runtime Ontology Resolution.** Semantic differences can arise in run-time interaction in a multi-agent environment since it is impractical to restrict all agents to use the same ontology. Merging, mapping, or translating ontology are impractical too since they are usually offline approaches which need to be done before the deployment of the multi-agent system. One family of approaches [93, 94, 95, 96] is inspired by language games, where agents identify and resolve ontology conflicts through incremental interpretation, clarification, and explanation by negotiating with one another when semantic differences have been detected. An alternative approach utilizes approximate classification methods for semantic-preserving context transformations, such as rough set theory, fuzzy set, or probabilistic Bayes' Theorem [97, 98].

Since the interoperability between different knowledge systems or agents relies on their full understanding of the terminologies used by the peers, the resolution of semantic heterogeneity between different information sources is necessary and important. Hence, this aspect currently attracts significant attention from the Semantic Web research community.

5. USING SEMANTIC WEB ONTOLOGY

The semantics conveyed by ontology can be as simple as a database schema or as complex as the background knowledge in a knowledge base. By using ontology in the Semantic Web, users can leverage the advantages of the following two features: (i) data is published using common vocabulary and grammar; and (ii) the semantic description of data is preserved in ontology and ready for inference. This section presents three real-world Semantic Web based applications to show the different roles of Semantic Web ontology played in different context.

The first application is called *semantic service discovery*, which builds an extensible ontology to describe the various data services in ad-hoc networks, and uses ontology to reason the capability of sensors. It is highlighted by the *extensibility* aspect of the Service ontology. The second application is called *ontology based personal profile integration*, which builds a web scale database for personal profiles. It is highlighted by the *visibility* aspect of

[20] See http://www.cs.yale.edu/homes/dvm/daml/pddl_daml_translator1.html.

[21] See http://projects.semwebcentral.org/projects/ontoengine/.

FOAF ontology. The third application is called *description logic reasoning for adaptive sensors*, which infers sensor states using the axioms in OWL-DL. It is highlighted by the *inferenceability* aspect of Sensor State ontology.

5.1 Semantic Service Discovery

Avancha et al. [99] have used ontology to represent the profile and infer the capability of services in ad-hoc networking environment like Bluetooth.

5.1.1 Service Ontology

Ontology-based service description is superior to UUID-based descriptions [100] because of the following merits of the former: (i) it enables extensible and richer description about the services, entities and the relationships between entities in application domain; (ii) it supports inferring implied knowledge from the asserted descriptions; and (iii) it captures domain knowledge in the explicitly represented ontology (instead of in source code) and thus make domain ontology independent to source code.

The Service Ontology is created through the following two steps.

1. *Choosing an appropriate Semantic Web ontology language.* In order to achieve successful semantic service discovery, a simple but powerful model is needed for describing domain knowledge. It should be lightweight - easy to parse, easy to manipulate and easy for a reasoning engine to use. It should be extensible, so that any organization or person can create classes or properties that can be added to ontology. It should be scalable enough to handle huge number of resources in a given ontology. Hence, RDFS was chosen as the ontology language because it meets all the above requirements and no advanced feature from OWL is needed in this application.
2. *Building the service ontology which captures background knowledge.* The root of the service ontology is a class called *Service*. It has one subclass called *AdHocNetworkService*. Specific services are described as subclasses of the latter. The Service class has two properties – *ServiceCost* and *ProvidedBy*. The latter "points" to a class called *ServiceProvider* that contains *ProviderName* and *ContactURI* as its properties. Every property of the *AdHocNetworkService* class, except *MemoryCapacity*, is associated with a *value* and a *priority*. The priority field is used to decide the ordering of properties, so that the highest priority property (specified by the client in the query or assigned by the server) is used to determine the correct service instance to match against. The client is allowed to leave the *priority* field(s) unspecified. The client may also leave the *value* field(s) unspecified. In such cases, the server uses a set of predefined priority values for the properties.

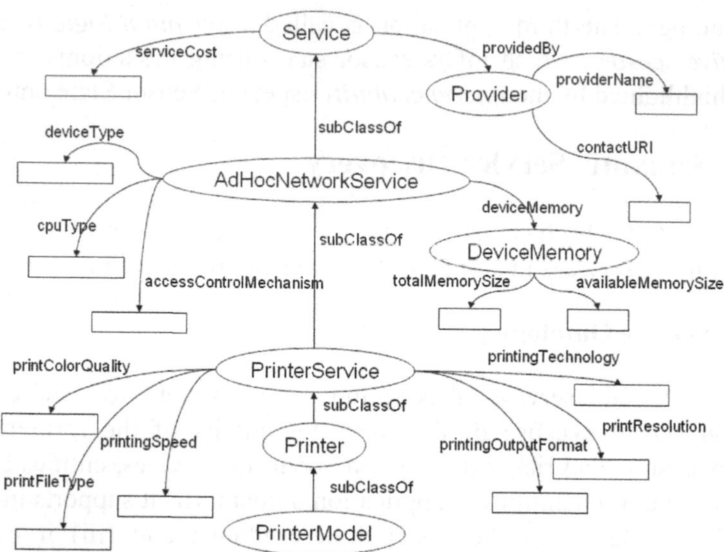

Figure 4-4. The service ontology. Oval nodes represent classes (concepts) and rectangular nodes represent literal values. Labels on the arcs represent properties between concepts

Figure 4-4 shows a graphical representation of the Service Ontology using an example *PrinterService*. The *priority* and *value* property-types for all of the property-types of the *AdHocNetworkService*, *PrinterService* and *Printer* subclasses are not shown for conciseness. The *PrinterService* subclass has six property-types and the *Printer* subclass has only one. However, it is emphasized that the *Printer* subclass inherits all property-types from its ancestors. Therefore, all the property-types can be associated with values at the level of the *Printer* subclass.

5.1.2 Applying Service Ontology and Evaluation

By reusing the service ontology written in RDFS, *extensibility* feature can be best demonstrated when incorporating new devices or services, resources, capabilities and constraints into the ac-hoc network. Description of new service can be greatly reduced by inheriting property-types using sub-class relation. In addition, extending domain knowledge does not require any code level changes.

By using inference engine which supports RDFS, *inferenceability* feature can be demonstrated when matching service request with service description. The inference engine combines the asserted and implied domain knowledge into the complete service descriptions, and thus gets better matching results.

Readers interested in the details of the approach and experimental results are referred to [101].

5.2 Ontology-based Personal Profile Integration

Recently, the "Friend of A Friend" (FOAF) project has gained attention from both academic and industrial communities. Aiming at publishing information about people using machine understandable language, the FOAF project is highlighted by the following features: (i) publishing personal profile with better visibility; (ii) enforcing unique reference to a person on the Web and supporting integration of partial data from difference sources; and (iii) representing and facilitating large scale social networks on the Web.

5.2.1 FOAF Ontology

The core of FOAF project is the FOAF ontology which is identified by namespace URI *http://xmlns.com/foaf/0.1/*. The core concepts of FOAF ontology are shown in Figure 4-5 an agent could be a person, a group, or an organization, among which person is the most used; a *foaf:Person* usually has her name, mbox, depiction(personal photo), homepage, and etc.; and social network could be captured by the *foaf:knowns* property between two instances of *foaf:Person*.

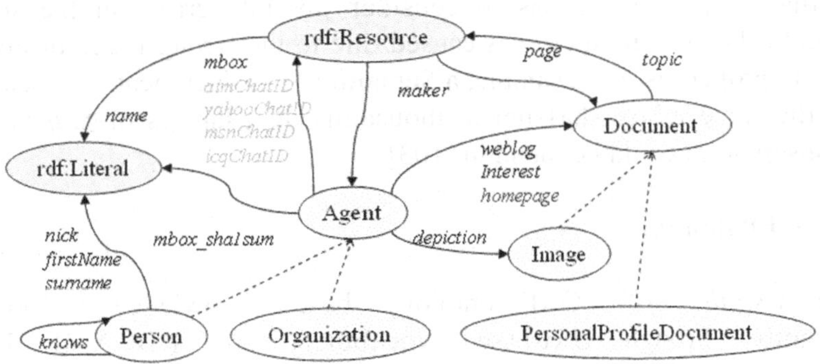

Figure 4-5. Important classes and properties in FOAF Ontology. Solid arcs refer to properties linking domain-class to range-class, and dashed arcs refer to subClassOf relation

5.2.2 Integrating FOAF Personal Profile

The simple and commonly adopted FOAF ontology make it possible to build a distributed database for personal information. Among millions of Semantic Web documents discovered by Swoogle [102], a large portion of them contribute a significant amount of instances of *foaf:Person*. An interesting observation shows that the person "Tim Finin" has been mentioned by some Semantic Web documents from UMBC and CMU, and several of his email addresses have been mentioned in different documents. According to the entity-equality semantics of FOAF ontology, the RDF graphs in those RDF documents can be merged into a more complete personal profile. The integration procedure is described as the following steps:

1. Swoogle discovers and indexes Semantic Web documents on the Web.
2. Search Swoogle for all Semantic Web documents that populate instances of *foaf:Person*.
3. Parse those documents and store all instances of *foaf:Person* in a triple store.
4. Merge instances using the following heuristics: (i) two instances with the same URIref; (ii) compare the identities of instance obtained from (inverse) functional properties; and (iii) use *owl:sameAs* assertions over instances. In practice, most instances are anonymous (i.e., without URI identifier) and the second heuristic is heavily used. The merge could be implemented by computing connected component on a graph where each node is a class instance and each arc conveys one instance-equivalence relation.
5. Output each connected component as a merged personal profile.

Figure 4-6 shows the merged profile for "Tim Finin". It should also be noted that such merging has to consider possible errors in the source documents. The common error is caused due to the wrong usage of inverse functional properties. For example, a Semantic Web document [22] mistakenly assign the same mbox_sha1sum to thousands of instances of *foaf:Person*. More observation could be found in [103].

5.2.3 Evaluation

The *visibility* of FOAF ontology based knowledge is boosted significantly through URI-based vocabulary and RDF/XML based serialization. On the publisher side, many social network websites, such LinkedIn.com, Okurt.com, and LiveJournal.com, have adopted FOAF ontology in publicizing their users' profile and millions of Semantic Web documents are published on such websites [103]. On the information consumer side, many XSL based tools, such as *Foaf Explorer* and *Foafnaut* (http://www.foafnaut.org), have been developed to visualize FOAF data in a user friendly format.

[22] See http://blog.livedoor.jp/rusa95/foaf00756.rdf.

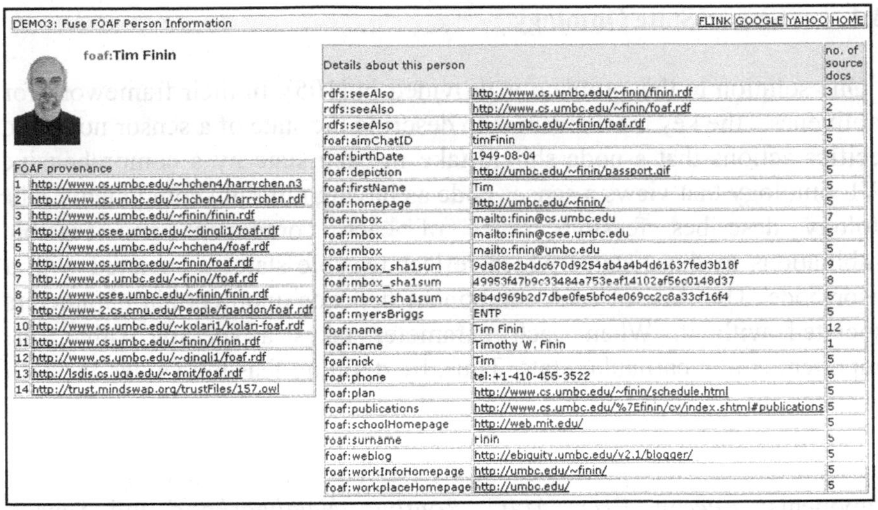

DEMO3: Fuse FOAF Person Information FLINK GOOGLE YAHOO HOME

foaf:Tim Finin

FOAF provenance	
1	http://www.cs.umbc.edu/~hchen4/harrychen.n3
2	http://www.cs.umbc.edu/~hchen4/harrychen.rdf
3	http://www.cs.umbc.edu/~finin/finin.rdf
4	http://www.csee.umbc.edu/~dingli1/foaf.rdf
5	http://www.cs.umbc.edu/~hchen4/foaf.rdf
6	http://www.cs.umbc.edu/~finin/foaf.rdf
7	http://www.cs.umbc.edu/~finin//foaf.rdf
8	http://www.csee.umbc.edu/~finin/finin.rdf
9	http://www-2.cs.cmu.edu/People/fgandon/foaf.rdf
10	http://www.cs.umbc.edu/~kolari1/kolari-foaf.rdf
11	http://www.cs.umbc.edu/~finin//finin.rdf
12	http://www.cs.umbc.edu/~dingli1/foaf.rdf
13	http://lsdis.cs.uga.edu/~amit/foaf.rdf
14	http://trust.mindswap.org/trustFiles/157.owl

Details about this person		no. of source docs
rdfs:seeAlso	http://www.cs.umbc.edu/~finin/finin.rdf	3
rdfs:seeAlso	http://www.cs.umbc.edu/~finin/foaf.rdf	2
rdfs:seeAlso	http://umbc.edu/~finin/foaf.rdf	1
foaf:aimChatID	timFinin	5
foaf:birthDate	1949-08-04	5
foaf:depiction	http://umbc.edu/~finin/passport.gif	5
foaf:firstName	Tim	5
foaf:homepage	http://umbc.edu/~finin/	5
foaf:mbox	mailto:finin@cs.umbc.edu	7
foaf:mbox	mailto:finin@csee.umbc.edu	5
foaf:mbox	mailto:finin@umbc.edu	5
foaf:mbox_sha1sum	9da08e2b4dc670d9254ab4a4b4d61637fed3b18f	9
foaf:mbox_sha1sum	49953f47b9c33484a753eaf14102af56c0148d37	8
foaf:mbox_sha1sum	8b4d969b2d7dbe0fe5bfc4e069cc2c8a33cf16f4	5
foaf:myersBriggs	ENTP	5
foaf:name	Tim Finin	12
foaf:name	Timothy W. Finin	1
foaf:nick	Tim	5
foaf:phone	tel:+1-410-455-3522	5
foaf:plan	http://www.cs.umbc.edu/~finin/schedule.html	5
foaf:publications	http://www.cs.umbc.edu/%7Efinin/cv/index.shtml#publications	5
foaf:schoolHomepage	http://web.mit.edu/	5
foaf:surname	Finin	5
foaf:weblog	http://ebiquity.umbc.edu/v2.1/blogger/	5
foaf:workInfoHomepage	http://umbc.edu/~finin/	5
foaf:workplaceHomepage	http://umbc.edu/	5

Figure 4-6. Fusing Tim Finin's person profile. For each statement (i.e. triple), the number of supporting sources listed to the right. All supporting sources are listed on left column

The *extensibility* feature of FOAF ontology is exhibited in an *open source* manner – the latest FOAF specification only lists one stable term – 'homepage' and leaves many others in 'testing' or 'unstable' stages. FOAF ontology uses WordNet ontology to define its concepts such as foaf:Agent, and foaf:Person has been used by many other ontology to restrict the *rdfs:domain*. This feature differs from distributed databases in that it preserves a common schema and allows additional customized schema provided by different publishers.

The *inferenceability* feature of FOAF ontology is supported by part of OWL ontology language. Some FOAF properties, such as *foaf:mbox* and *foaf:homepage*, are defined as instance of *owl:InverseFunctionalProperty* and linked the unique identifier of a person.

5.3 Description Logic Reasoning for Adaptive Sensors

A wireless sensor network consists of energy-constrained nodes that are capable of sensing their surrounding environment and communicating that information to a central entity in the network for further processing. Such networks face many challenges including energy management, network management, data management and security [104]. An important and open research problem that combines the above challenges is to design a wireless sensor network that can determine its current state (in terms of energy, communications, security and sensor accuracy) and modify its behavior, if required, to ensure continuous operation as desired by its users.

5.3.1 Sensor State Ontology

One solution to this problem is provided in [105]. In their framework for adaptiveness, the key mechanism is to describe the state of a sensor node and specifies actions that a node should take in each state by a comprehensive OWL ontology that views a sensor node as having multiple components. The ontology describes feasible states of each component and feasible combinations of those states which reflect feasible states associated with a sensor node. The state of each component depends upon certain parameters associated with it. When each parameter takes a specific value, the component is in a particular state. Thus, by defining feasible values for each parameter, we arrive at feasible states of the component.

The hierarchical design of the ontology places the *SensorNode* class at its root. *SensorNode* has properties that describe it in terms of its various components: *Energy*, *PHY*, *MAC*, *Routing*, *Neighborhood* and *Sensor*. Figure 4-7 shows a snippet of the OWL-DL ontology describing its top-level hierarchy. The first two properties only are shown, due to lack of space. The other properties are defined in a similar manner.

```
<owl:Class rdf:ID="SensorNode"/>
<owl:ObjectProperty rdf:ID="hasEnergyComponent">
    <rdfs:domain rdf:resource="#SensorNode"/>
    <rdfs:range rdf:resource="#Energy"/>
</owl:ObjectProperty>
<owl:ObjectProperty rdf:ID="hasPHYComponent">
    <rdfs:domain rdf:resource="#SensorNode"/>
    <rdfs:range rdf:resource="#PHY"/>
</owl:ObjectProperty>
```

Figure 4-7. Top-level Hierarchy of SensorNode Ontology

5.3.2 Reasoning about Sensor State Using Subsumption

In order to show how the ontology enables a sensor node to determine its state, the energy component of the sensor node requires further investigation. The energy component is defined as shown in Figure 4-8. The state of the energy component depends upon two parameters: *remainingEnergyCapacity* and *energyConsumptionRate*. The former takes its value from a class called *Amount*, which consists of two symbols *Amount_Normal* and *Amount_ Abnormal*. Similarly, the second parameter takes its values from the *Rate* class. The task of mapping numerical values of these two parameters to logical symbols is performed in a separate module of framework [105] and is beyond the scope of this chapter.

```
<owl:Class rdf:ID="Energy" />
<owl:ObjectProperty rdf:ID="remainingEnergyCapacity">
    <rdfs:domain rdf:resource="#Energy"/>
    <rdfs:range rdf:resource="#Amount"/>
</owl:ObjectProperty>
<owl:ObjectProperty rdf:ID="energyConsumptionRate">
    <rdfs:domain rdf:resource="#Energy"/>
    <rdfs:range rdf:resource="#Rate"/>
</owl:ObjcctPropcrty>
```

Figure 4-8. Energy Component Definition

Figure 4-9 shows the definition of a *LowEnergyState* associated with a sensor node. A sensor node is in a low-energy state if the remaining energy capacity has an abnormal value *and* the rate of energy consumption is normal. *LowEnergyState* is an intersection of three classes: *Energy* and two anonymous classes that assign particular values to the two parameters. Thus, *LowEnergyState* is an implicit sub-class of *Energy*.

```
<owl:Class rdf:ID="LowEnergyState">
  <owl:intersectionOf rdf:parseType="Collection">
      <owl:Class rdf:about="#Energy"/>
      <owl:Restriction>
        <owl:onProperty rdf:resource="#remainingEnergyCapacity"/>
        <owl:hasValue rdf:resource="#Amount_Abnormal"/>
      </owl:Restriction>
      <owl:Restriction>
        <owl:onProperty rdf:resource="#energyConsumptionRate"/>
        <owl:hasValue rdf:resource="#Rate_Normal"/>
      </owl:Restriction>
  </owl:I ntersectionOf>
</owl:Class>
```

Figure 4-9. Low Energy State Definition

Figure 4-10 shows how a sensor node in a low energy state is defined in the ontology. *SensorNodeInLowEnergyState* is defined as a sub-class of

SensorNode and has the property that its *Energy* Component is in a low energy state.

```
<owl:Class rdf:ID="SensorNodeInLowEnergyState">
    <rdfs:subClassOf rdf:resource="#SensorNode"/>
    <owl:intersectionOf rdf:parseType="Collection">
        <owl:Restriction>
            <owl:onProperty rdf:resource="#hasEnergyComponent"/>
            <owl:someValuesFrom rdf:resource="#LowEnergyState"/>
        </owl:Restriction>
    </owl:intersectionOf>
</owl:Class>
```

Figure 4-10. Sensor Node in Low Energy State

The rest of the *SensorNode* ontology is designed along similar lines and thus, comprehensively describes feasible states associated with a sensor node. By asserting the ontology into a forward-chaining or backward-chaining reasoning engine that supports OWL-DL, e.g., Java Theorem Prover (JTP), a system that can reason over a given *instance* of a sensor node and respond with a value that indicates the state of the node is created. Thus, in the current example, when the complete instance of a sensor node is presented to a JTP instance containing the ontology, it responds with the correct state of the node. Figure 4-11 shows a snippet of a sensor node instance; only the Energy component is shown due to lack of space.

```
<wsn:SensorNode rdf:ID="SN175">
    <wsn:hasEnergyComponent rdf:resource="#E_SN175"/>
    <wsn:hasPHYComponent rdf:resource="#PHY_SN175"/>
    <wsn:hasMACComponent rdf:resource="#MAC_SN175"/>
    <wsn:hasRoutingComponent rdf:resource="#Rt_SN175"/>
    <wsn:hasNeighborhoodComponent rdf:resource="#Nb_SN175"/>
</wsn:SensorNode>
<wsn:Energy rdf:ID="E_SN175">
    <wsn:remainingEnergyCapacity rdf:resource="#Amount_Abnormal"/>
    <wsn:energyConsumptionRate rdf:resource="#Rate_Normal"/>
</wsn:Energy>
```

Figure 4-11. Complete Instance of a Sensor Node

The response from JTP is shown in Figure 4-12; again only the relevant responses are shown. The reasoning process is automated by designing it as a client-server system. The JTP engine containing the *SensorNode* ontology runs as the server (either on each node or centrally), waits for and receives a sensor node instance, reasons over the instance, responds to the "client" and deletes the current instance from the system. This process continues as long as the node functions.

```
> ask
Enter query: (rdf:type dawsn_v4_embed.owl:SN175 ?x)

Query succeeded.

Bindings 4:
  ?x = |#|::|SensorNodeInLowEnergyState|
Bindings 5:
  ?x = |#|::|SensorNode|
```

Figure 4-12. Query and Response in JTP

5.3.3 Evaluation

The *inferenceability* feature of ontology has been highlighted in this application through the above subsumption inference over sensor network state. The use of OWL-DL inference also makes inference procedure decidable, which is very important to those intelligent but constrained devices which have limited computing capabilities.

6. CONCLUSION

This chapter provides a pragmatic view on Semantic Web ontology via comparison, survey and case-study. The comparison on chronological evolution and built-in semantics reveals how the Semantic Web inherits the merits from pre-existing knowledge representation formalisms and reference models of databases. It also highlights the advantages of using Semantic Web ontology in terms of better visibility, extensibility and inferencability. The practical aspects of Semantic Web ontology is demonstrated through both (i) the significant amount of Semantic Web ontology and instances, and (ii) the rich set of enabling tools for managing and applying Semantic Web ontology. Finally, the three case-studies demonstrate how to use Semantic Web ontology in different application contexts with benefit evaluation in each of them.

ACKNOWLEDGMENTS

Partial support for this research was provided by DARPA contract F30602-00-0591 and by NSF awards NSF-ITR-IIS-0326460 and NSF-ITR-IDM-0219649.

REFERENCES

[1] Smith Barry. Ontology: Philosophical and Computational. http://ontology.buffalo.edu/smith/articles/ontologies.htm; 2000.
[2] Quine WVO. On What There Is. Review of Metaphysics 1948; p. 21–38.
[3] Gruber ThomasR. A Translation Approach to Portable Ontology Specifications. Knowledge Acquisition 1993; 5(2):199–220.
[4] Uschold Mike, Grüninger Michael. Ontologies: principles, methods, and applications. Knowledge Engineering Review 1996; 11(2):93–155.
[5] Sowa John, editor. Principles of Semantic Networks: Explorations in the Representation of Knowledge. San Mateo: Kaufmann; 1991.
[6] Klyne Graham, Carroll JeremyJ. Resource Description Framework (RDF): Concepts and Abstract Syntax. http://www.w3.org/TR/2004/REC-rdf-concepts-20040210/; 2004.
[7] Brickley Dan, Guha RV. RDF Vocabulary Description Language 1.0: RDF Schema. http://www.w3.org/TR/2004/REC-rdf-schema-20040210/; 2004.
[8] Dean Mike, Schreiber Guus. OWL Web Ontology Language Reference. http://www.w3.org/TR/2004/REC-owl-ref-20040210/; 2004.
[9] Berners-Lee T, Hendler J, Lassila O. The Semantic Web. Scientific American 2001; 284(5):35–43.
[10] Minsky Marvin. A Framework for Representing Knowledge. MIT. 1974.
[11] Baader Franz, Calvanese Diego, McGuineness Deborah, Nardi Daniele, Patel-Schneider Peter. The Description Logic Handbook. Cambridge University Press; 2003.
[12] Horrocks Ian, Fensel Dieter, Broekstra Jeen, Decker Stefan, Erdmann Michael, Goble Carole, et al. OIL: The Ontology Inference Layer. Vrije Universiteit Amsterdam; 2000.
[13] Horrocks Ian, Patel-Schneider PeterF, van Harmelen Frank. Reviewing the Design of DAML+OIL: An Ontology Language for the Semantic Web. In: Proceedings of the Eighteenth National Conference on Artificial intelligence. 2002. p. 792–797.
[14] Codd EF. A relational model of data for large shared data banks. Commun ACM 1970; 13(6):377–387.
[15] Sowa John. Semantic Networks. http://www.jfsowa.com/pubs/semnet.htm, 2002.
[16] Gil Yolanda, Ratnakar Varun. Trusting Information Sources One Citizen at a Time. In: Proceedings of International Semantic Web Conference 2002; 2002. p. 162–176.
[17] Golbeck Jennifer, Parsia Bijan, Hendler James. Trust Networks on the Semantic Web. In: Proceedings of Cooperative Intelligent Agents; 2003.
[18] Richardson Matthew, Agrawal Rakesh, Domingos Pedro. Trust Management for the Semantic Web. In: Proceedings of the 2nd International Semantic Web Conference; 2003.
[19] da Silva PauloPinheiro, McGuinness DeborahL, McCool Rob. Knowledge Provenance Infrastructure. Data Engineering Bulletin 2003; 26(4):26–32.
[20] Carroll JeremyJ, Bizer Christian, Hayes Patrick, Stickler Patrick. Named Graphs, Provenance and Trust. HP Lab; 2004.

[21] Ding Li, Kolari Pranam, Finin Tim, Joshi Anupam, Peng Yun, Yesha Yelena. On Homeland Security and the Semantic Web: A Provenance and Trust Aware Inference Framework. In: Proceedings of the AAAI Spring Symposium on AI Technologies for Homeland Security; 2005.

[22] Ding Zhongli, Peng Yun. A Probabilistic Extension to Ontology Language OWL. In: Proceedings of the 37th Hawaii International Conference On System Sciences, 2004.

[23] Ding Zhongli, Peng Yun, Pan Rong. A Bayesian Approach to Uncertainty Modelling in OWL Ontology. In: Proceedings of 2004 International Conference on Advances in Intelligent Systems - Theory and Applications (AISTA2004). 2004.

[24] Lassila Ora, McGuinness DeborahL. The Role of Frame-Based Representation on the Semantic Web. Stanford University; 2001.

[25] Horrocks Ian, Sattler Ulrike. Description Logics Basics, Applications, and More. Tutorial at ECAI-2002, http://www.cs.man.ac.uk/~horrocks/Slides/ecai-handout.pdf; 2002.

[26] Noy NatalyaFridman, Hafner CaroleD. The State of the Art in Ontology Design: A Survey and Comparative Review. AI Magazine 1997; 18(3):53–74.

[27] Chandrasekaran B, Josephson JohnR, Benjamins VRichard. What Are Ontologies, and Why Do We Need Them? IEEE Intelligent Systems 1999; 14(1):20–26.

[28] Kagal Lalana, Finin Tim, Joshi Anupam. A Policy Based Approach to Security for the Semantic Web. In: Proceedings of the 2nd International Semantic Web Conference; 2003.

[29] Lenat DouglasB, Guha RV. Building Large Knowledge-Based Systems; Representation and Inference in the Cyc Project. Addison-Wesley; 1989.

[30] Miller George. Wordnet: A Dictionary Browser. In: Proceedings of the First International Conference on Information in Data; 1985.

[31] Fellbaum Christiane, WordNet:An Electronic Lexical Database. MIT Press; 1998.

[32] Nirenburg Sergei, Raskin Victor. Ontological Semantics. MIT Press; 2001.

[33] Niles Ian, Pease Adam. Towards a standard upper ontology. In Proceedings of the international conference on Formal Ontology in Information Systems. 2001. p. 2–9.

[34] Beltran-Ferruz PJ, Gonzalez-Calero PA, Gervas P. Converting Frames into OWL: Preparing Mikrokosmos for Linguistic Creativity. In: Workshop on Language Resources for Linguistic Creativity; 2004.

[35] Java Akshay, Finin Tim, Nirenburg Sergei. Integrating Language Understanding Agents Into the Semantic Web. In: Proceedings of AAAI Fall Symposium Series; 2005.

[36] Bench-Capon TrevorJM, Visser PepijnRS. Ontologies in legal information systems; the need for explicit specifications of domain conceptualisations. In: ICAIL-97: Proceedings of the sixth international conference on Artificial intelligence and law. 1997. p. 132–141.

[37] Smith Barry, Williams Jennifer, Schulze-Kremer SchulzeKremer. The Ontology of the Gene Ontology. In: Symposium of the American Medical Informatics Association; 2003.

[38] Lopez MarianoFernandez, Gomez-Perez Asuncion, Sierra JuanPazos, Sierra AlejandroPazos. Building a Chemical Ontology Using Methontology and the Ontology Design Environment. IEEE Intelligent Systems 1999; 14(1):37–46.

[39] Sklyar Nataliya. Survey of existing Bio-ontologies. Univ. of Leipzig; 2001.

[40] Fonseca FredericoT, Egenhofer MaxJ. Ontology-Driven Geographic Information Systems. In: ACM-GIS; 1999. p. 14–19.

[41] Denny Michael. Ontology Tools Survey, Revisited. http://www.xml.com/pub/a/2004/07/14/onto.html; 2004.

[42] Gennari JohnH, Musen MarkA, Fergerson RayW, Grosso WilliamE, Crubezy Monica, Eriksson Henrik, et al. The evolution of Protege: an environment for knowledge-based systems development. Int J Hum-Comput Stud 2003; 58(1):89–123.

[43] Kalyanpur A., Parsia B., Hendler J.. A Tool for Working with Web Ontologies. In: International Journal on Semantic Web and Information Systems. vol. 1; 2005.

[44] Fikes R, Farquhar A. Large-Scale Repositories of Highly Expressive Reusable Knowledge. IEEE Intelligent Systems 1999; 14(2).

[45] Parsia Bijan, Sirin Evren, Kalyanpu Aditya. Debugging OWL Ontologies. In: In the 14th International World Wide Web Conference (WWW-05); 2005.

[46] Kopena Joseph, Regli William. DAMLJessKB: A Tool for Reasoning with the Semantic Web. IEEE Intelligent Systems 2003; 18(3):74–77.

[47] Fikes Richard, Jenkins Jessica, Frank Gleb. JTP: A System Architecture and Component Library for Hybrid Reasoning. Stanford University; 2003.

[48] Carroll JeremyJ, Dickinson Ian, Dollin Chris, Reynolds Dave, Seaborne Andy, Wilkinson Kevin. Jena: implementing the semantic web recommendations. In: WWW (Alternate Track Papers & Posters); 2004. p. 74–83.

[49] Zou Youyong, Finin Tim, Chen Harry. F-OWL: an Inference Engine for the Semantic Web . In: Formal Approaches to Agent-Based Systems. vol. 3228 of Lecture Notes in Computer Science. Springer-verlag; 2004.

[50] Tsarkov Dmitry, Horrocks Ian. Implementing new reasoner with datatypes support. WonderWeb:Ontology Infrastructure for the Semantic Web Deliverable; 2003.

[51] Horrocks Ian. The FaCT System. In: Automated Reasoning with Analytic Tableaux and Related Methods: International Conference Tableaux-98. 1998. p. 307–312.

[52] Haarslev Volker, Moller Ralf. Description of the RACER System and its Applications. In: Proceedings of the International Workshop in Description Logics (DL2001); 2001.

[53] Sirin Evren, Parsia Bijan. Pellet: An OWL DL Reasoner. In: Description Logics; 2004.

[54] Sintek Michael, Decker Stefan. TRIPLE - A Query, Inference, and Transformation Language for the Semantic Web. In: Proceedings of the 1st International Semantic Web Conference (ISWC-02). Springer-Verlag; 2002. p. 364–378.

[55] Harris Stephen, Gibbins Nicholas. 3store: Efficient Bulk RDF Storage. In: Proceedings of the First International Workshop on Practical and Scalable Semantic Systems; 2003.

[56] Lee Ryan. Scalability Report on Triple Store Applications. http://simile.mit.edu/reports/stores/; 2004.

[57] Guo Yuanbo, Pan Zhengxiang, Heflin Jeff. An Evaluation of Knowledge Base Systems for Large OWL Datasets. In: International Semantic Web Conference; 2004. p. 274–288.

[58] Beckett D., Grant J. Semantic Web Scalability and Storage: Mapping Semantic Web Data with RDBMSes. http://www.w3.org/2001/sw/Europe/reports/scalable_rdbms_mapping_report/; 2003.

[59] Wilkinson K, Sayers C, Kuno H, Reynolds D. Efficient RDF Storage and Retrieval in Jena2. In: Proc. of the 1st International Workshop on Semantic Web and Databases; 2003.

[60] Alexaki Sofia, Christophides Vassilis, Karvounarakis Gregory, Plexousakis Dimitris, Tolle Karsten. The ICS-FORTH RDFSuite: Managing Voluminous RDF Description Bases. In: Proc. of the 2nd International Workshop on the Semantic Web; 2001.

[61] Broekstra Jeen, Kampman Arjohn, van Harmelen Frank. Sesame: A Generic Architecture for Storing and Querying RDF and RDF Schema. In: Proceedings of the 1st International Semantic Web Conference (ISWC-02); 2002. p. 54–68.

[62] Horrocks Ian, Li Lei, Turi Daniele, Bechhofer Sean. The Instance Store: DL Reasoning with Large Numbers of Individuals. In: Description Logics; 2004.

[63] Pan Zhengxiang, Heflin Jeff. DLDB: Extending Relational Databases to Support Semantic Web Queries. In: Proceedings of the First International Workshop on Practical and Scalable Semantic Systems (PSSS); 2003.

[64] Haase Peter, Broekstra Jeen, Eberhart Andreas, Volz Raphael. A Comparison of RDF Query Languages. In: International Semantic Web Conference; 2004. p. 502–517.

[65] Prud'hommeaux Eric, Seaborne Andy. SPARQL Query Language for RDF. http://www.w3.org/TR/rdf-sparql-query/; 2004. W3C Working Draft 12 October 2004.

[66] Stuckenschmidt Heiner, Vdovjak Richard, Broekstra Jeen, Houben GeertJan. Towards Distributed Processing of RDF Path Queries. In International Journal on Web Engineering and Technology; 2005

[67] Cai Min, Frank Martin. RDFPeers: a scalable distributed RDF repository based on a structured peer-to-peer network. In: WWW-04: Proceedings of the 13th international conference on World Wide Web. ACM Press; 2004. p. 650–657.

[68] Harth A., Decker S. Yet Another RDF Store: Perfect Index Structures for Storing Semantic Web Data With Contexts. http://sw.deri.org/2004/06/yars/doc/summary, 2004.

[69] Stumme G., Maedche A. Ontology Merging for Federated Ontologies on the Semantic Web. In: Proceedings of the International Workshop for Foundations of Models for Information Integration (FMII-2001); 2001.

[70] Stumme G., Maedche A. FCA-Merge: Bottom-up Merging of Ontologies. In: Proceedings of 7th Intl. Conf. on Artificial Intelligence (IJCAI-01); 2001. p. 225–230.

[71] Noy N.F., Musen M.A. PROMPT: Algorithm and Tool for Automated Ontology Merging and Alignment. In: Proceedings of the Seventeenth National Conference on Artificial Intelligence (AAAI-2000); 2000.

[72] McGuinness D.L., Fikes R., Rice J., Wilder S. An Environment for Merging and Testing Large Ontologies. In: Proceedings of the Seventh International Conference on Principles of Knowledge Representation and Reasoning (KR-00); 2000. .

[73] Hovy E. Combining and Standardizing Large-Scale, Practical Ontologies for Machine Translation and Other Uses. In: Proc. of 1st Intl. Conf. on Language Resources and Evaluation; 1998.

[74] Guarino Nicola. Semantic Matching: Formal Ontological Distinctions for Information Organization, Extraction, and Integration. In: SCIE-97: International Summer School on Information Extraction. London, UK: Springer-Verlag; 1997. p. 139–170.

[75] Kiryakov A., Simov K.I. Ontologically Supported Semantic Matching. In: Proceedings of NoDaLiDa-99 Conference; 1999.

[76] Lacher Martin S., Groh Georg. Facilitating the Exchange of Explicit Knowledge through Ontology Mappings. In: Proceedings of the Fourteenth International Florida Artificial Intelligence Research Society Conference. AAAI Press; 2001. p. 305–309.

[77] Prasad S., Peng Y., Finin T. A Tool For Mapping Between Two Ontologies Using Explicit Information. In: AAMAS-02 Workshop on Ontologies and Agent Systems, 2002.

[78] Doan A.H., Madhavan J., Domingos P., Halevy A. Learning to Map between Ontologies on the Semantic Web. In: WWW 2002; 2002.

[79] Doan AnHai, Madhavan Jayant, Dhamankar Robin, Domingos Pedro, Halevy Alon. Learning to match ontologies on the Semantic Web. The VLDB Journal 2003; 12(4):303–319.

[80] Doan A.H., Madhavan J., Domingos P., Halevy A. Ontology Matching: A Machine Learning Approach; 2004. p. 397–416.

[81] Mitra Prasenjit, Wiederhold Gio, Kersten MartinL. A Graph-Oriented Model for Articulation of Ontology Interdependencies. In: EDBT-00: Proceedings of the 7th International Conference on Extending Database Technology; 2000. p. 86–100.

[82] Kalfoglou Y., Schorlemmer M. Information Flow Based Ontology Mapping. In: Proceedings of 1st International Conference on Ontologies, Databases and Applications of Semantics (ODBASE-02); 2002.

[83] Melnik S., Molina-Garcia H., Rahm E. Similarity Flooding: A Versatile Graph Matching Algorithm. In: Proceedings of the Intl. Conf. on Data Engineering (ICDE); 2002.

[84] Noy N.F., Musen M.A. Anchor-PROMPT: Using Non-local Context for Semantic Matching. In: Workshop on Ontologies and Information Sharing at IJCAI-2001; 2001.

[85] Noy N.F., Musen M.A. PROMPTDIFF: A Fixed-Point Algorithm for Comparing Ontology Versions. In: AAAI-2002, Edmonton, Canada; 2002.

[86] Noy N.F. Semantic Integration: A Survey Of Ontology-Based Approaches. SIGMOD Record, Special Issue on Semantic Integration 2004; 33(4).

[87] Pearl J. Probabilistic Reasoning in Intelligent Systems: Networks of Plausible Inference. San Mateo, CA: Morgan Kaufman; 1988.

[88] Mitra P., Noy N.F., Jaiswal A.R. OMEN: A Probabilistic Ontology Mapping Tool. In: Workshop on Meaning Coordination and Negotiation at ISWC-04; 2004.

[89] Ding Z., Peng Y., Pan R., Yu Y. A Bayesian Methodology towards Automatic Ontology Mapping. In: First international workshop on Contexts and Ontologies: Theory, Practice and Applications, held in AAAI-05; 2005.

[90] Pan R., Ding Z., Yu Y., Peng Y. A Bayesian Network Approach to Ontology Mapping. In: Proceedings of the 4th International Semantic Web Conference (ISWC-05); 2005.

[91] Chalupsky H. Ontomorph: A Translation System for Symbolic Knowledge. In: Proceedings of the Seventh International Conference on Principles of Knowledge Representation and Reasoning (KR-00). Morgan Kaufman; 2000. p. 471–482.

[92] Dou D., McDermott D., Qi P. Ontology Translation by Ontology Merging and Automated Reasoning. In: Proc. of EKAW Workshop on Ontologies for Multi-Agent Systems; 2002.

[93] Wiesman F., Roos N., Vogt P. Automatic Ontology Mapping for Agent Communication. MERIT; 2001.

[94] Bailin S., Truszkowski W. Ontology Negotiation between Agents Supporting Intelligent Information Management. In: Workshop on Ontologies in Agent-based Systems; 2001.

[95] Bailin S., Truszkowski W. Ontology Negotiation as a Basis for Opportunistic Cooperation between Intelligent Information Agents. In: Proceedings of the Fifth International Workshop on Cooperative Information Agents (CIA 2001); 2001.

[96] Peng Y., Zou Y., Luan X., Ivezic N., Gruninger M., Jones A. Semantic Resolution for E-Commerce. In: Proceedings of the 1st International Joint Conference on Autonomous Agents and Multiagent Systems (AAMAS-02); 2002.

[97] Ciociou M., Nau D. Ontology-Based Semantics. In: Proceedings of the Seventh Intl. Conf. on Knowledge Representation and Reasoning; 2000. p. 539–560.

[98] Stuckenschmidt H., Visser U. Semantic Translation Based on Approximate Re-classification. In: Workshop on Semantic Approximation, Granularity and Vagueness; 2000.

[99] Avancha Sasikanth, Joshi Anupam, Finin Timothy. Enhanced Service Discovery in Bluetooth. Computer 2002; 35(6):96–99.

[100] Farnsworth Dale. Service Discovery Protocol (in Bluetooth Specification). http://www.bluetooth.com/link/spec/bluetooth_e.pdf; 2001.

[101] Avancha Sasikanth. Enhanced Service Discovery in Bluetooth. Master's thesis. UMBC; 2002.
[102] Ding Li, Finin Tim, Joshi Anupam, Pan Rong, Cost RScott, Peng Yun, et al. Swoogle: A Search and Metadata Engine for the Semantic Web. In: Proceedings of the Thirteenth ACM Conference on Information and Knowledge Management; 2004.
[103] Ding Li, Zhou Lina, Finin Tim, Joshi Anupam. How the Semantic Web is Being Used:An Analysis of FOAF. In: Proceedings of the 38th International Conference on System Sciences; 2005.
[104] Raghavendra Cauligi S., Sivalingam Krishna M., Znati Taieb, editors. Wireless Sensor Networks. Kluwer Academic Publishers; 2004.
[105] Avancha S., Joshi A., Pinkston J. SWANS: A Framework for Secure, Adaptive Wireless Sensor Networks. UMBC; 2005.

Chapter 5

POSITIVISM OR NON-POSITIVISM – TERTIUM NON DATUR

A Critique of Ontological Syncretism in IS Research

Bernd Carsten Stahl

Centre for Computing and Social Responsibilty, De Montfort University, Leicester LE1 9BH, UK, bstahl@dmu.ac.uk

Abstract: This paper revisits the debate between positivism and its alternatives in the field of information systems from a philosophical point of view. It will argue that the heart of the debate is the ontological difference between the views of reality as observer-independent versus observer-dependent. The logical axiom of the excluded third (*tertium non datur*) informs us that two contradictory options cannot simultaneously be true. The paper will discuss what the incompatibility of the ontological positions of positivism and its alternatives means for IS research. It will discuss why scholars attempt to mix the two and will spell out the consequences of an acceptance of their incompatibility. The paper will end by arguing that this debate needs to be contextualized with the problem of positivism versus non-positivism in society and it will ask whether a tolerant coexistence of the two approaches is feasible. Without this contextualized understanding of ontology in general, regional ontologies in IS are not likely to be successful as they will be based on unclear bases.

Key words: positivism; non-positivism; interpretivism; ontology; epistemology; methodology

1. INTRODUCTION

"In my view, it is time to assign the rhetoric of positivism versus interpretivism to the scrap heap. It no longer serves a useful purpose. On the contrary, it promotes unhelpful schisms among scholars." (Ron Weber, Editor-in-Chief, MISQ (2004, p. xi))

Many information systems (IS) scholars probably sympathize with Weber's sentiment and agree that they have heard enough of the discussion of positivism versus interpretivism. There seems to be little progress in the debate and it has the potential to hurt the discipline. This paper will nevertheless address the issue of positivism and its alternatives as philosophical foundations of IS research. The reason for this is that there seems to be a growing tendency to mix positivist and non-positivist research. The paper will argue that such philosophical syncretism is suspicious for logical reasons.

The argument presented here is a philosophical one. First, the main argument is based on the ontological assumptions of research. Ontology is one of the classical sub-disciplines of philosophy. Second, it will argue that, in order to understand the current state of philosophical syncretism of IS research, one need to look at the relationship between ontology, epistemology, and methodology, which opens the doors to other philosophical areas. Third, the central problem discussed here is a conceptual one. "Philosophy has always been concerned with conceptual clarifications" (Tugendhat, 1992 p. 113; cf. Ricoeur, 1995; Wittgenstein, 1963). Finally, the heart of the argument, the *tertium non datur*, the proposition of the excluded third, is an integral part of Aristotelian propositional logic.

It is generally accepted that research is based on several interconnected philosophical assumptions. This paper will follow Davies (1991) in concentrating on the relationship of ontology (theory of being / reality / essence), epistemology (theory of knowledge), and methodology (theory of method / action). The question of which research philosophy or approach is appropriate in IS has a long history (cf. Pettigrew, 1985) but is not likely to be resolved (Petter & Gallivan, 2004). The ontological divide between different research philosophies has been a continuing topic of debate in the philosophy of science and can be traced back to the great philosophers (cf. Monod, 2002) and even to the earliest writings on western philosophy. The aim of the paper is therefore not to "solve" the problem, which may be impossible (Fitzgerald & Howcroft, 1998), but to clarify its roots and meaning and to spell out the theoretical and practical consequences of the dichotomy between positivism and non-positivism.

The paper thus aims to clarify some questions of general philosophical ontology in the area of information systems. One should note that such a general ontology is of central importance if one wants to discuss regional ontologies, as suggested by Kishore, Sharman & Ramesh (2004). Regional ontologies and the universes of discourse they are based upon rely on general ontology. The very idea that there are regional universes of discourse and that these allow the classification of specific ontological structures is already a strong ontological claim, which, as the present paper will argue, is likely to be contentious. The dichotomy between positivism and non-positivism is therefore of decisive importance for most questions of ontology in IS.

1.1 Contribution

This paper is written from a non-positivist point of view. The author was motivated by the intrinsic contradictions created by attempts to mix positivism and alternative ontological positions. The paper is positioned outside the traditional ways of doing research in IS. Leading scholars of information systems suggest that researchers following a non-traditional (meaning non-positivist) approach should explain their research to the reader and provide criteria for evaluating it (Klein & Myers, 2001; Lee, 2001). Accordingly, Klein & Myers (1999) suggest a set of criteria for evaluating interpretive research. Similar criteria for philosophical/conceptual research in IS do not exist. Some criteria can nevertheless be distilled from the aims of philosophical research and the overlap it has with other IS research in creating accessible knowledge.

Jenkins (1985, p.112) defines philosophical research as a mental pursuit where the "researcher thinks and logically reasons causal relationships". Logical stringency will thus be one criterion for the evaluation of this paper. The paper should furthermore address a topic that "should be directly related to the future interest that key stakeholders [...] are likely to hold in a topic" (Benbasat & Zmud, 1999 p. 8). The argument should be convincing to the reader, it should ring true, be persuasive, and "convince the reader that a believable story is being told" (Trauth & Jessup, 2000 p. 68). Since the topic of the paper concerns the theoretical underpinnings of IS research, one might ask what a good theory is (van de Ven, 1989). Weick (1989 p. 517) suggests that a good theory should be "interesting rather than obvious, irrelevant or absurd, obvious in novel way:, a source of unexpected connections, high in narrative rationality, aesthetically pleasing, or correspondent with presumed realities". Maybe the ultimate quality criterion of the paper will be whether the author can "convince and cajole [his] colleagues about the directions we should now pursue" (Benbasat & Weber, 1996 p. 398).

2. ONTOLOGY

Ontology, which etymologically means "speaking of being", is the philosophical discipline that asks "what is?" and "what does it mean to be" (cf. Heidegger, 1993). It researches the fundamental questions of being, and thus, in everyday parlance, one could say that it studies the nature of reality. Ontological assumptions form one of the most important building blocks of our worldview and they are so fundamental that we rarely question them. They are therefore of central importance to any research in any discipline (cf. Klein, Hirschheim & Nissen, 1991). One needs to know what is or what exists in order to research it. There are profoundly different ontological theories, which in this paper will be called ontologies used by different individuals. This paper will argue that the concept of positivism can be defined primarily in terms of its ontological assumptions and that ontological questions are at the basis of many of our epistemological and methodological differences. There are numerous questions of importance to be found in the history of ontology. The paper will concentrate only on the question whether reality is independent of the observer or not.

2.1 Positivism

I will argue in this paper that positivism can be defined as a research approach that is based on the ontological doctrine that reality is independent of the observer. Most scholars interested in the philosophy of IS research agree with this definition. The independent and objective existence of reality can be found as a definition of positivism in a number of texts (cf. Orlikowski & Baroudi 1991; Visala, 1991; Jönsson, 1991; Landry & Banville, 1992; Darke, Shanks & Broadbent, 1998; Iivari, Hirschheim & Klein, 1998; Myers & Avison, 2002; Varey, Wood-Harper & Wood, 2002). Some authors use different terms to denote this ontological position, such as "objectivism" or "realism" (Burrell & Morgan, 1979; Hirschheim, 1985; Chua, 1986; Hirschheim & Klein, 1989; Weber, 2003). These authors typically see positivism as comprising epistemological (Olaison, 1991; Lee, 1991; Walsham, 1995), methodological (Benbasat & Weber, 1996), and sometimes other philosophical aspects, such as ethics (Wynn, 2001). Such a collection of different philosophical aspects under the term "positivism" is understandable for several reasons and some of these aspects will be discussed later.

The division between positivism and non-positivism is so deep that the very term "positivism" has taken on a pejorative meaning for non-positivist (Burrell & Morgan 1979; Lee 2001). It seems to be used predominantly by opponents of the idea, whereas proponents prefer the adjective "positive" instead of "positivist" (cf. Friedman 1994).

The realist ontology on which positivism is based, namely the conviction that reality exists independent of the observer, is a remnant of the successful ontology of the mechanistic natural sciences of the Enlightenment period. It is still wide-spread in parts of natural and technical sciences. Our current use of the term is shaped by the attempt to import this scientific ontology into humanities and social sciences with the declared aim of copying the success of the natural sciences (cf. Habermas, 1974).

It is not the purpose of this paper to discuss the shortcomings of positivism. Intellectual honesty requires nevertheless that some of the main arguments against positivism are reviewed. This will also help the reader comprehend the thrust of the argument. Positivism, especially the elaborate set of theories developed by the Vienna Circle called "logical positivism", has largely been discredited in the philosophy of sciences. It nevertheless continues to be a strong "logic in use" (Landry & Banville, 1992) or "ontology in use" (Lee, 2004) in the social sciences, and arguably in information systems. The probably most important critique of positivism in information systems is that the idea of an independent reality and the consequent impartial observation of this reality does not lead to an adequate understanding of the phenomena in question (Adam, 2001). This often implies a distinction between natural and social reality. Positivism seems to be a deficient basis for research at least in the latter realm (Nissen, 1985; Orlikowski & Baroudi 1991). Other points of critique address the epistemological problems resulting from positivist ontology. There are problems of induction and generalisation (Pettigrew, 1985; Lee & Baskerville, 2003). Philosophy has not found a convincing explanation how the mind can adequately represent a mind-independent reality (Khlentzos, 2004). Then there is the charge that positivism is self-contradictory because it is not itself a natural occurrence independent of the observer and related problems of the final foundation of positivism (Quine, 1980). Resulting from this it can be argued that positivism is structurally circular and that despite its alleged objectivity it can only investigate phenomena that are created by the investigator (Stahl 2003).

2.2 Non-Positivism

If positivism is not the only ontological position, then the question arises as to which alternatives to positivism there are. In the light of our definition of positivism, the alternatives are those ontological positions that do not depend on a reality independent of the observer. The history of philosophy offers a number of different non-positivist ontological viewpoints. Since the observer plays a part in the constitution of reality, and is usually believed to do this using his or her mind, some authors hold that the opposite of positivism is rationalism (Hollis, 1994). But the field of rationalism is wide and contains many different theories. One is the doctrine that the observer constructs reality and that, at the extreme, all of reality is just a figment of the individual's imagination. This solipsist theory is mirrored in the doctrine of radical constructivism (Glasersfeld, von, 2000; Watzlawik, 2001).

Another non-positivist stream of thought that was hugely influential in the philosophy of the 19th and 20th century is idealism, or more specifically German idealism. It is linked with the names of Hegel, Schelling, Fichte, and others who argued for the supremacy of the mind or spirit over any external reality.

In contemporary IS research these ontological positions do not play a major role. They can be seen, however, as the basis of some of the ontological alternatives to positivism prevalent today. The two most important concepts opposed to positivism are constructionism and interpretivism. Constructionism (or social constructivism) holds that reality is constructed by the observer, but, in opposition to (radical) constructivism, it states that reality is a collective construction. It emphasises the role of interaction and communication in the process of constructing reality (Gergen, 1999). Its intellectual history can be traced back to idealism (Burrell & Morgan 1979). IS researchers who subscribe to the constructionist ontology typically call themselves interpretivists rather than constructionists. The difference between constructionism and interpretivism appears to be that constructionists are more radical and extend their ontological views to all aspects of reality whereas interpretivists limit it to social reality. Since IS researchers are usually interested in aspects of technology having to do with social phenomena, they can mostly refrain from defending the more contentious claims of constructionism and concentrate on those aspects of reality that are easily recognisable as socially constituted.

In current IS research interpretivism is probably the most important alternative to positivism. This paper argues that this is possible because the heart of the interpretivist position is an ontological position which views reality as a social construct. The constructionist ontology of interpretivism can be found in many of the texts on interpretivism (Orlikowski & Baroudi 1991; Walsham, 1995; Darke, Shanks & Broadbent, 1998; Varey, Wood-Harper & Wood, 2002). The concept of interpretivism has to contend with some of the same problems as positivism in that it often refers to epistemological (Myers & Avison 2002; Klein & Myers 2001; Trauth & Jessup, 2000; Walsham, 1995b) and methodological (Lee 1991; Yin, 2003) aspects of research simultaneously. The term "interpretivism" is often not sharply defined. Also, "interpretivism" is a term that is relatively new but at the same time ubiquitous among non-positivist IS researchers. A brief comparison of the uses of "positivism" and "interpretivism" may shed some light on this. If one compares the proceedings of the IFIP WG 8.2 conferences 1984 (Mumford et al. 1985) and 2002 (Wynn et al. 2003) then one finds a marked difference between use and acceptance of these terms. In 1984 the main thrust of the conference was to break the perceived stranglehold of positivism on IS research. Consequently, terms starting with "positivi..." were used 158 times in 9 of the 18 essays. "Interpretiv" was used only 15 times, mostly with references to Burrell & Morgan (1979). "Interpretivism" or "interpretivist" was not used at all. In 2002, when non-positivist IS research was firmly established, "interpretive" was used 30 times in 10 out of 30 essays whereas "positivi..." was used only twice, one of which was a reference. This indicates that the struggle against positivism seems to have been successful and interpretivism is recognised as a term in IS research.

2.3 Tertium Non Datur

The paper has so far been set up to sharpen the contradiction between positivism and non-positivism. It has defined positivism as the ontological claim that reality is independent of the observer and non-positivism as the logically contradictory view that reality depends on the observer. The advantage of this definition is that it allows the application of a fundamental logical axiom, namely the proposition of the excluded third. This proposition was developed by Aristotle in his Metaphysics. It means that a sentence must be true or false. In the notation of propositional logic it can be represented as follows:

$$\neg(p \wedge \neg p)$$

The history of logic has given rise to several attempts to show that this axiom is not sufficient and that logical states do not have to be bivalent. Examples of such non-bivalent logics are modal logic, deontic logic (Garson, 2003) or fuzzy logic (Hajek, 2002). The proposition is nevertheless widely accepted and forms one of the basic tenets of our scientific system. An example can easily show the strength of the axiom. If A is the proposition "X is a dog", then $\neg$A is the proposition that "X is not a dog". *Tertium non datur* informs us that it is impossible that A and $\neg$A are true, thus that X can not be a dog and not a dog (or a non-dog: $\neg$dog) at the same time.

If the proposition A means: "reality is independent of the observer" then $\neg$A can be translated as "reality is not independent of (thus dependent on) the observer". According to *tertium non datur*, both cannot be true simultaneously. This statement is the heart of this paper. The irreconcilable opposition between positivism and non-positivism is simply based on a logical axiom and the ontological root of the terms.

This does not solve all ontological problems in IS research but it allows for a much more concise discussion of several issues. We can now say, for example that, if interpretivism is a form of non-positivism (as was argued earlier), then a researcher cannot follow a positivist and an interpretivist research approach at the same time. That does not mean that all researchers must be either positivists or interpretivists. Similarly, if a cat is a non-dog then X cannot be a dog and a cat. X does not have to be a cat or a dog, however, since X might be, say, a fish. An analogue conclusion is that an IS researcher can choose a non-positivist ontology that is not interpretivist.

This position should not be equated with some of the theories concerning the relationship between positivism and its alternatives viewed as paradigms, such as purism (Petter & Gallivan, 2004), supremacism (Klein, Hirschheim & Nissen, 1991), or paradigm incommensurability (Brooke, 2002; Mingers, 2001). It only states that the ontological assumptions of positivism and non-positivism are not commensurable. What this means for research epistemology and methodology will be explored in the following sections.

3. EPISTEMOLOGY

Epistemology is the "theory or science of the method or grounds of knowledge" (OED 2004). If research wants to produce knowledge then it has to rely on an implicit or explicit epistemology. This paper will follow Chua (1986) in distinguishing between epistemology and methodology where the former refers to the principles of knowledge, the latter to ways of acquiring it. Epistemology is closely linked to ontology. One can only gain knowledge about entities that exist. In return, one needs to have a way of gaining knowledge in order to make statements whether something exists. While the exact relationship between given ontologies and epistemologies is not always clear-cut, it is important to note that every epistemology requires a corresponding ontology (Iivari, Hirschheim & Klein, 1998). There is no ontology-free epistemology (cf. Feyerabend, 1980).

If epistemology is the philosophical discipline concerned with knowledge then it needs to define what knowledge is. One definition sometimes used by philosophers is that knowledge is "true, justified beliefs" (Steup, 2001). This is helpful because it allows us to distinguish the question when a statement is true from the question when we are justified in believing a statement to be true. While the latter question is much-discussed in IS research, the former, arguably more important one, is usually ignored.

3.1 Truth Theories

The question when a statement is true is addressed by theories of truth. There are at least four major types of such theories using different criteria for determining the truth of a proposition: correspondence, consensus, coherence, and pragmatist. The correspondence theory of truth holds that a statement is true if it corresponds with the reality it describes. This is probably closest to our everyday understanding of truth (McCarthy, 1992) and assumes an objectively given describable reality. Proponents of onsensus theories believe that truth is defined by the agreement of those who are knowledgeable in the area in question (Wellmer, 1986; Habermas 1991). Coherence theories hold that statements are true if they are can be supported in a formal system of statements. Typical examples of this are mathematical theorems (Weizenbaum, 1976; Wittgenstein, 2001). Pragmatist theories hold that those statements are true that fulfil their purpose, that lead to desirable outcomes (Rorty, 1991).

These different theories of truth are of highest importance for any research, including IS research, because they determine what can count as a successful attempt to produce truth and thus knowledge. They also indicate ways in which knowledge can or must be acquired. Differences in the underlying truth theory lead to problems in appreciating why a piece of research may be considered valuable. This leads us to the second problem of knowledge, the question when a belief is justified.

3.2 Empiricism

Among the different ways of acquiring knowledge and defending the claim for truth, the most prominent one is probably empiricism. Empiricism can be defined as the "doctrine that experience rather than reason is the source of our knowledge of the world" (Morick, 1980 p. 1; cf. Gergen, 1999). Empiricism is the traditional epistemology of the natural sciences (Ciborra, 2002) where its adherents usually search for causal relationships. An empiricist tries to discover the laws governing reality and use a hypothetico-deductive approach (Vitalari, 1985). Empiricists set up hypotheses which they then try to prove of falsify (Popper, 1980). The ultimate aim of empiricist research is to be able to make well-founded predictions (Orlikowski & Baroudi, 1991; Westland, 2004)

Empiricism is closely associated with several assumptions about the nature of scientific inquiry. First, it holds that observation is objective (Klein & Myers, 1999) and value-free (Walsham, 1995). It is also seen as a universally valid approach to knowledge which means that it is often associated with calls for a unity of science which would include the natural sciences as well as arts, humanities, and social sciences. Objectivity can be assured through an observer who is detached from the object of observation and who does not interfere (Introna, 1997; Yin, 2003). An important ingredient to this of approach to academic inquiry is a certain kind of detached and aloof rationality which is interested in relationships without being intimately involved in them (Wilson, 2003).

As a reaction to the perceived weaknesses of empiricism, which includes the problem of the possibility of objectivity in social science, the question of appropriateness of empirical observation of humans, the alleged circularity of empiricism, the complexities of the notion of causality, a resistance to the underlying rationality, and other problems, other epistemological approaches have been developed. The most frequently quoted alternative to empiricism in philosophy is rationalism, which is the doctrine the reason, instead of sensation, is the foundation of knowledge.

3.3 Phenomenology

Phenomenology is an ambiguous term because it can refer to a general first-person description of human experience or, more specifically, to a philosophical method for analyzing consciousness developed by Edmund Husserl (Beavers, 2002). The term has been used by Kant and Hegel, but Husserl redefined it in reaction to the detached academic discussion in philosophy in the 19th century. Heidegger, the possibly most important phenomenologist, defines the term "phenomenon" using its Greek etymology as "that which shows itself in itself, the manifest" (Heidegger, 1993 p. 28; cf. Moran, 2000)

Heidegger sees phenomenology as ontology but it can also be understood as an epistemology. The central idea of phenomenology is that the world is opened up by consciousness. Every perception is a conscious act. Phenomena are given to consciousness and phenomenology tries to go back to the things themselves. These things are not objectively given things, but rather the content of consciousness (Lyotard, 1993). The phenomenologist tries to bracket out the non-essential aspects of perception to end up with the essence of the phenomenon.

In phenomenology the essences of the objects of research cannot be divided from the subject who researches them. The classical subject-object dichotomy of empiricism is not valid here (Moran 2000). An important aspect emphasised by Heidegger is that the subject of perception is never an independent entity but that it is a human with all the lived experiences and background, what he calls being-in-the-world, and for which he uses the term "*Dasein*". Dasein has to contend with the realities of human existence. It is embodied, it faces death, it is lonely and at the same time subjected to fashions, to the One (*das Man*) as Heidegger calls it (Dreyfus, 1993; Introna, 1997; Capurro & Pingel, 2002; Stuart, 2002; Introna & Whittaker, 2003). Since humans cannot live a detached and objective existence, they live in their own, partly idiosyncratic world, which Husserl calls life-world. The life-world is the strange thing that disintegrates before our eyes. It is the horizon within which we always move (Habermas, 1985; Stahl, 2003b).

Phenomenology is thus a way of achieving knowledge and can be seen as an epistemology. It differs essentially from empiricism and is based on completely different assumption what knowledge is and how it can be acquired. But it is not the only possible alternative to empiricism.

3.4 Hermeneutics

Hermeneutics is another alternative to empiricism as a way of acquiring knowledge. Etymologically it is derived from the Greek word for "to interpret" (Hirschheim & Klein, 1989). The original purpose of hermeneutics was the understanding of religious texts, more specifically of the bible. It has developed into a general approach to the understanding of texts. The underlying problem is that every reader of a text has a different understanding of that text depending on his or her own experiences and life-world. This understanding differs from the understanding of the author. Originally, hermeneutics tried to find ways of determining the true sense of the text as intended by the author (or God). Hermeneutics has moved away from the idea of such a "correct" understanding and has expanded into the art of understanding all communication, not just written text.

One important aspect of contemporary hermeneutics is the hermeneutic circle. The idea behind this is that there is a circular relationship between the prior knowledge of a recipient of a text and her understanding of the same text. A text can only be read if the reader has a general understanding of its content but this understanding will be modified through the reading of the text (cf. Gadamer, 1990).

The current version of hermeneutics was explicitly developed to counter the natural science approach to humanities and social sciences. The opposition to natural sciences can best be demonstrated by looking at a pair of concepts associated with the German words *erklären* und *verstehen* (Hausman, 1994). *Erklären*, literally "to explain" refers to the natural sciences where causal relations can be established which can be used to explain phenomena. Such causal explanations are not useful in the humanities and social sciences because they negate the ability of agents to act. An explanation of human actions is thus not an application of natural laws but rather a description of humans that allows the reader to understand what the agent did and why she did it. This is what *verstehen*, literally "to understand" will achieve. Hermeneutics aims at facilitating this understanding. In hermeneutics there can be no unity of sciences. Social and natural sciences have different research objects and thus need different epistemologies (cf. Ricoeur, 1982; Mill, 1994).

According to this description of hermeneutics, the role of the researcher must be different from that in empiricism. The researcher cannot be detached and needs to admit that his or her understanding of the situation affects the outcome of the research (Myers & Avison, 2002).

A final remark on the relationship between hermeneutics and phenomenology: In its current form hermeneutics has been shaped by phenomenology. The most important hermeneutic philosophers, among them Gadamer and Ricoeur, were strongly influenced by phenomenology. If the phenomenon in question is a social one, as is typically the case in IS research, then a phenomenological researcher needs to acquire an understanding of the social exchange that constitutes it. For this, the researcher must apply hermeneutic means. He or she must follow the hermeneutic circle by starting with a given understanding, engaging with the phenomenon and thereby changing the initial understanding (cf. Boland, 1985).

3.5 Positivist and Non-Positivist Epistemology

Empiricism, phenomenology, and hermeneutics are the most important epistemologies in current IS research. In the context of this paper it is interesting to ask what their relationship to positivism and its alternatives is. There are tendencies that link ontologies and epistemologies. Positivism typically goes with empiricism whereas non-positivist approaches such as interpretivism tend to use hermeneutics or phenomenology as means to acquire knowledge. The question is whether these are necessary or contingent relationships. This paper will argue that these relationships are not necessary but that a change in the typical configurations requires rethinking the meaning of concepts.

There is, for example, no reason why a positivist should not use hermeneutics. The history of hermeneutics is actually based on a positivist understanding where one real and existing God put His thoughts to paper (using human instruments) and these words had one right meaning. Hermeneutics can be used as a tool to find out what this correct meaning of a divine text is. This meaning of "hermeneutics" is different from the post-Heideggerian hermeneutics described above. Conversely, an interpretivist can use an empiricist approach to research and try to observe reality and find objective truth. In this case, however, "objective truth" will mean something different from the positivist use of the term. It cannot be a correct description of an independent reality but must be something different, for example a validity claim that is not disputed (cf. Habermas, 1981).

While these questions are discussed frequently in IS research, particularly with regards to methodology (cf. next section), an equally important but generally not discussed problem is that of the relationship of ontology with truth theory. This is important because the assumed truth theory will determine what can count as valid research results. The dichotomy of positivism and non-positivism is mirrored more clearly with respect to truth theories. A correspondence theory of truth is only valid if there is a detached reality which one can describe correctly. Similarly, a consensus theory of truth is highly adequate to constructionist ontology but holds no merits in an objective world. The coherence theory will play a role in the mathematical modelling, which is again best suited to positivism. Pragmatic truth theories, finally, can be appropriate for different ontologies but their meaning, the question what works; can reflect the ontology in different ways. For the positivist, a proposition is successful because it describes the world adequately, for the constructionist because it fulfils the criterion of being successfully constructed.

4. METHODOLOGY

While epistemology deals with the question what knowledge is, methodology asks how valid knowledge can be acquired. Methodology is thus the study of methods (Mingers, 2001), and it analyses the different methods used in research. There are numerous attempts to collect and classify research methods. Jenkins (1985), for example, identifies thirteen. The most important divide between methods is that between quantitative and qualitative methods. There has been an intensive discussion between proponents of the two sides in IS research for at least the last 20 years. I will not recount this discussion here.

The interesting question in this paper is whether research methodologies have a clearly defined relationship to the ontology upon which the research is based. Again, there are typical combinations between methods, epistemologies and ontologies, which are not always necessary. Positivists using a correspondence theory of truth and an empiricist epistemology will often use quantitative methods. However, there is no fundamental reason why they could not use qualitative methods (Urquhart, 2001). In order to find out the reality of a social phenomenon and to describe it as it objectively is, it may be helpful to observe agents or interview them, to write "realist tales" (van der Blonk, 2003). On the other hand, there is the typical combination of constructionist ontology, consensus theory of truth, hermeneutic/phenomenological epistemology and qualitative methods. Again, there is on *a priori* reason, however, why quantitative methods should not be used here. Numbers and statistics can be seen as ways of clarifying meanings and shared realities (Miranda & Saunders, 2003).

A related question of interest is whether different research methods can be combined, which is usually discussed under the heading of "multi-method" research or "pluralist research" (Landry & Banville, 1992; Sawyer, 2001; Brooke, 2002). This is a question on which the discussion of positivism versus non-positivism has a profound influence and to which we will return later.

Due to space constraints I will have to leave the questions of methodology at this rather superficial level. The reader should remember that there are typical methodological predispositions depending on the underlying ontology but no strictly necessary relationships.

5. ONTOLOGICAL SYNCRETISM IN IS RESEARCH

Syncretism is the "combination of different beliefs, the attempted combination of different systems of philosophical or religious belief or practice" (Encarta, 1999, p. 1893). It is usually regarded with skepticism by adherents of a given philosophy or religion. The fundamental question concerning syncretism is always whether the combined belief systems are compatible. This paper has argued that positivism and non-positivism are mutually exclusive and a syncretistic approach therefore cannot be acceptable. The consequent questions for this paper are: 1. is there indeed a philosophical syncretism to be observed in IS research? and 2. if so, how can it be explained?

5.1 The Existence of Philosophical Syncretism in IS Research

Analyzing examples of philosophical syncretism in IS research is made difficult by the fact that most scholars follow their own definition of philosophical terms. An added difficulty is that some concepts seem to imply a mixture of positivism and non-positivism, such as multi-method research (Hirschheim, 1985; Cavaye, 1996), critical realism (Mingers, 2001; Mingers 2001b), but that the fundamental ontological issues are rarely spelt out.

The typical form of ontological syncretism in IS research is the assurance that positivism and non-positivism (usually interpretivism) can peacefully coexist and pose no threat to one another. If this paper is correct in arguing that positivism and non-positivism are logically mutually exclusive, then this constitutes syncretism. One typical example of this is the interpretivist researcher who wants to promote understanding for her research approach but who is careful not to offend positivist researchers by insisting that both approaches are valuable. "We must clearly state that it is not our intention to replace the positivist perspective with critical or interpretive ones"

(Orlikowski & Baroudi, 1991 p. 24). Others see a more complex relationship where positivist and non-positivist research enters into some kind of dialectical process whereby higher level knowledge is produced (Klein, Hirschheim & Nissen, 1991). There are few examples of actually mixing positivist and non-positivist research approaches and contrasting the results of doing research on the basis of different ontologies and their resulting choices of epistemology and methodology (cf. Trauth & Jessup 2000). Nevertheless, most non-positivists seem to imply that positivism and non-positivism can coexist (Lee, 1991; 1994). The frequency of these syncretistic approaches allows Walsham (1995b) to identify four rhetorical figures used in the literature to justify the syncretistic approach.

5.2 Reasons for Syncretism

If syncretism between positivism and non-positivism is wide-spread in IS research despite the fact that the two approaches are based on contradictory ontologies, and then the question must be why researchers try to combine the two. There are several reasons for this. The most important ones are lack of clarity of the concepts, confusion of the levels, research interests, metaphysical convictions, and the history and politics of the IS discipline.

The possibly most wide-spread reason for mixing positivism and non-positivism is the lack of clarity of the terms. This paper has made the point that we are looking at ontological positions which are associated with epistemological, methodological and arguably other research-relevant aspects. One should concede, however, that there is no unanimity on the exact limits and definition of the concept of positivism, and less so on its alternatives. The situation is worsened by the used of the term "paradigm". For Kuhn (1996) a paradigm is a set of assumptions that scientists agree on and that set the frame for scientific research. This theory is interesting and fruitful because it can explain fundamental changes in the development of science. It is widely used in social sciences and information systems research (Burrell & Morgan, 1979; Chua, 1986, Hirschhein & Klein, 1989; Orlikowski & Baroudi, 1991; Goles & Hirschheim, 2000; Petter & Gallivan, 2004) where it has taken on a slightly different meaning. When IS researchers speak of paradigms they mean some sort of worldview, a general understanding of the world. Paradigms encompass all the aspects discussed in this paper and often others, such as ethical stances, social order, or the relationship between theory and practice. The problem with this use of the word paradigm is that it makes it very difficult to delimit and define meanings and contrast different paradigms. Typically, we speak of the positivist, the interpretivist, and the critical paradigm. Since methodologies used in the positivist paradigm can be used in conjunction with methodologies associated in the interpretive paradigm, some authors conclude that the two can coexist, thereby (wrongly) implying that the underlying ontologies can also coexist.

The unclear use of the term paradigm is partly responsible for the next reason for syncretism, namely the confusion of levels. It was argued here that the ontological assumptions of positivism and non-positivism are mutually exclusive. However, the same is not necessarily true for the associated epistemologies and methodologies. Typical examples of this are given by Lee (1991; 1994) when he tries to integrate the positivist and interpretivist approaches to organisational research. This mistake is closely related to the equating of ontology and methodology, where positivism stands for a certain methodology (usually quantitative methods) and interpretivism for non-quantitative methods (Benbasat & Weber, 1996; Cavaye, 1996; Landy & Banville, 1992; Eisenhardt 1989; Weber 2004). In these cases, the dichotomy between positivism and non-positivism becomes indistinguishable from the dichotomy between quantitative and qualitative research. Since the latter pair does not actually constitute a contradiction, the (wrong) conclusion is that positivism and non-positivism are also compatible.

Another reason of syncretism is research interest. This, too, is based on the confusion of the different philosophical levels. The argument here states that one gets a richer picture of a research object by looking at it from several sides. Similarly, the application of positivist and non-positivist research approaches is supposed to help IS researchers understand their object of interest better. The two positions are seen as complementary rather than contradictory. One can help explain (*erklären*) whereas the other helps understand (*verstehen*) (Lee, 1994). They allow triangulation through different methods and thus improve understanding. On the basis of these convictions one can call for a pluralism of methods. This understandable argument leads to the untenable conclusion that one should also mix the different ontologies.

Such attitudes may partly be explained by the history and politics of the IS discipline, which determines the constraints and requirements that IS researchers are subject to. A look at the history of IS (or MIS) shows that the discipline has been established for 30 to 50 years (Hirschheim & Klein, 2003; Ward & Peppard, 1996). The established "reference disciplines" (Keen, 1991), such as computer sciences, management sciences, organisation sciences, or economics (Benbasat & Weber, 1996), tend to use positivist assumptions. Given the traditional strength of positivism in IS, researchers are under strong pressure to recognise it as valid in order to get their PhD recognised or their research published (Baskerville, 2001). Then there are the politics of the IS discipline which has to survive among competing academic disciplines and which, according to some, lacks a recognisable core and definition (Benbasat & Zmud, 2003). It has been called a "fragmented adhocracy" (Landry & Banville, 1992) which does not bode well if it wants to survive among the other positivist subjects. Independent of the truth and usefulness of such statements, they serve to exert pressure on academics not to be seen as divisive. As a result, history and politics of the discipline combine to strongly pressure non-positivist researchers to accept positivist approaches even if they agree with the argument of this paper.

All of the above arguments allowed for syncretism by shirking the issue of the ontological contradiction between positivism and its alternatives. There are, however, some arguments that directly oppose my thesis of the contradictory nature of positivism and its alternatives. The most problematic of these is the denial that there is a difference between positivism and non-positivism. This seems to be grounded in the positivists' fundamental inability to understand that there are alternatives to their realist ontology. Weber (2004, v) exemplifies this position when he incredulously exclaims that "[...] surely some kind of reality exists beyond our perceptions of it!" and posits that it is inconceivable that anybody might contradict this statement. As proof he offers the certain reality of death faced by everybody who jumps out of his office window. He neglects to see that, for the phenomenologist, death is always-mine (*jemeinig*, as Heidegger (1992) would have said) and thus the epitome of an idiosyncratic and thus non-objective experience. On a possibly more accessible level, the problem has also been discussed by Grint & Woolgar (1997) under the heading of "what is social about being shot?"

There are also more sophisticated attempts to reconcile the ontological differences. These can be based on post-positivism, postmodernism, critical realism, Heglian dialectics, pragmatism or others (cf. Petter & Gallivan, 2004; Hirschheim, 1985; Varey, Wood-Harper & Wood, 2002; Achterberg, van Es & Heng, 1991; Goles & Hirschheim, 2000). There is no space here to discuss these but, briefly, there seems to be no way they can avoid the dichotomy between an observer-independent and an observer-dependent reality. At best they open up a new meta-theoretical approach to reality, which typically depends on the observer and is thus non-positivist.

6. CONSEQUENCES OF THE DICHOTOMY OF POSITIVISM AND NON-POSITIVSM

If the ontological foundations of positivism and non-positivism are not compatible; if, at the same time, IS researchers tend to mix them, then one should ask what consequences it would have to change this practice and own up to the unbridgeable dichotomy of ontologies. Is Weber (2004, p. vi) possibly right when he says that it "makes no difference to the fundamental goals [...]" of researchers? This section will briefly look at implications in the area of research, politics, and ethics.

6.1 Research Implications

There is no algorithmic way of doing research according to one's ontological position. This paper does not support the thesis of the incommensurability of different methods (quantitative vs. qualitative). The main conclusion to be drawn is that the combination of different methods, epistemologies, and ontologies has to be justified in every single instance. It may be completely acceptable and logically stringent to use quantitative methods from an interpretivist viewpoint or to use semi-structured interviews from a positivist viewpoint. At the same time, the same research method will mean different things depending on one's ontology. A positivist doing interviews will expect to find social reality as it is, whereas the constructionist will be part of the collective construction of the relevant reality. Two researchers using the exact same approach and getting the same results may thus come to opposing conclusions, based on their ontological underpinnings.

A related but more difficult question is that of the compatibility of epistemologies. Empiricist and hermeneutic / phenomenological approaches seem to be more difficult to combine than quantitative and qualitative methods. This is probably based on their greater closeness to the underlying ontology. One problem results from the fact that most interpretive IS research is based on the collection of empirical evidence. That means that empirical research is not necessarily empiricist. It also means that non-empiricist researchers doing empirical research should spell out why they believe that this will help them. In the light of non-positivist ontology and a non-empiricist epistemology it is not immediately obvious that empirical research is superior to other kinds, such as philosophical or conceptual research (Stahl, 2003)

The main research implications of the positivism - non-positivism divide is that there are individual and collective responsibilities with regards to the combinations of methodologies, epistemologies and ontologies (Robey, 1996). A simple pick-and-choose approach guided by considerations of expediency cannot be acceptable. That means that the individual researcher should be clear about these questions and should address them in his or her research design. On the collective side, the discipline as represented by conferences or journals, chairs, reviewers, or editors needs to make sure that these questions are properly and satisfactorily reflected.

A related aspect, leading us to the politics of IS research, are standards of research quality, validity, rigour, or relevance. These much-debated problems will not be compatible for positivists and non-positivists. While they are in some instances related to specific methods, the underlying ontology determines whether a certain piece of research is acceptable. A central point here will be the truth theory used to assess these issues. These are very closely linked to the underlying ontology and they are currently rarely reflected in detail.

For readers more familiar with the discussion of ontology in IS rather than general philosophical ontology, a question of interest may be what the above debate has to do with computational or IS ontology. I believe that any discussion of specific ontologies requires a foundation in philosophical ontology. There are numerous issues of philosophical ontology that this paper has not addressed. But the question whether reality is independent of the observer is pertinent to all ontologies. If Kishore, Sharman & Ramesh (2004) are right and there are different "universes of discourse" which establish different ontologies, then the question is what ontological status these ontologies have. The existence of multiple ontologies seems to imply that there is not one reality as assumed by positivism but a number of them. These are then presumably dependent on the observer and the situation she finds herself in. Computational ontologies, which have as a main purpose to provide a taxonomy that will allow dealing with computational entities, are thus non-positivist (even if they are typically not explicitly or intentionally linked to a philosophical ontology). If this is true, we need to ask where the influence of the observer can be seen in the resulting taxonometic systems. These should play a role in the verification, validation, and assessment of ontologies. A cursory glance at the literature suggests that this is not the case. Computational ontologies seem to claim objective validity and thus aim for a positivist description of reality (Kishore, Sharman & Ramesh, 2004b). Again, if this is true, then there may be a potential contradiction in the ontological foundations of regional ontologies which would need to be addressed.

6.2 Political Implications

Research does not take place in a vacuum (cf. Lee, 2001) but is embedded in social systems where politics play a great role. This should be quite obvious particularly for non-positivist researchers who recognize the social construction of reality. Yet, non-positivist research politics are much less visible or successful than their positivist counterpart. Representatives of the positivist view are openly trying to set the agenda of IS research according to their ideas. They try to define legitimate research subjects like the IT artifact and to impose an "identity" on the field (Benbasat & Zmud, 2003). They promote certain research methodologies and theories, favoring formal and mathematical methods, which are typically more useful to their ontology than to others (Weber, 2003).

While these attempts to promote the positivist agenda have created a lively debate (see the "Core of IS" debate in the Communications of the AIS), no concerted non-positivist action is visible. The reasons for this are manifold, but among the most important ones one can find the historical prevalence of positivism (Walsham, 1995b; Trauth, 2001) and the lack of coherence among non-positivist. This paper may help alleviate the problem by offering the idea that the overarching characteristic of non-positivist research is its ontological belief of the dependence of reality on the observer.

6.3 Ethical Implications

A final important implication of recognizing the incommensurability of positivism and non-positivism has to do with the ethics of research, and more specifically with how humans are perceived in research. Positivism requires ethical behavior by the researcher (Hausman & McPherson, 1994) and it can even be described as an ethically motivated endeavor that promised to develop society (Wynn, 2001) and "limitless progress" (Chomsky, 1998 p. 128). It would thus be wrong to see positivism as fundamentally "un-ethical" but in effect it develops worrying ethical consequences. These are the result of the perceived possibility of distinguishing clearly between research object and subject and between objective description and subjective evaluation. This allows positivists to argue that they are detached observers which negates the necessity to become involved and therefore roots for the status quo (Orlikowski & Baroudi, 1991).

Positivist ontology suggests that all things exist in some sort of objective universe and this includes human beings. This, combined with methodological individualism, can create a disposition to treat humans as objects. Treating humans as objects means that one can treat them as means rather than ends, thus violating Kant's (1995, p. BA 67) famous version of the Categorical Imperative according to which humans should never be treated as means. Or to put it in more contemporary words: "Such research may end up by recommending most people to be handled like billiard balls" (Nissen, 1985 p. 40).

7. CONCLUSION: A TIME FOR TOLERANCE?

The paper has argued that positivism and non-positivism as ontological positions are irreconcilable. There are epistemological and methodological consequences of the ontological divide, but these are less clear-cut than the ontological opposition. The paper has outlined some of the implications a recognition of the divide as they would arise for research, politics, and ethics.

Given the philosophical and conceptual nature of the argument, it is impossible to "prove" it wrong by using contradicting empirical data. Ontology is not subject to empirical investigation because any empirical research must be based on an ontology which it cannot prove wrong because it determines which phenomena can be observed. The main area of contention will lie in the use of the concepts themselves. One potential weakness of the paper is that the general use of the concepts such as positivism, interpretivism, empiricism, etc. does not always follow the definitions offered here. The paper has tried to show that these definitions are tenable and well-grounded in the literature but it is also true that some authors use them differently. The answer to such a claim would be that a different use of terms does not affect the content of the argument. A researcher must base his or her research on an understanding of the nature of reality. He or she will be faced with the dichotomous choice of an observer-independent or observer-dependent reality. The two sides cannot be bridged for logical reasons. Resulting from or at least affected by the choice, the researcher will use certain epistemologies or methodologies. The argument thus stands as it is, even if one does not agree with the definitions of "positivism" or "non-positivism".

But even if this problem exists as suggested in the paper, do IS researchers or practitioners need to worry about it? Are there conclusions that need to be drawn or consequences that arise from it? In the light of the current debate about the core and definition of the field of information systems, the answer has to be affirmative. For many everyday purposes, researchers may be able to rely on their ontology in use and not worry about the underlying problems. This is at least true for those who use the predominant ontology of positivism. Researchers who prefer a different approach are put more often in a position where they have to justify their ontology. But in the overall climate of scarcity of resources (university chairs, research positions, studentships, funding, etc.) we need to consider which criteria constitute valuable work in IS and these criteria are inherently dependent on the underlying ontology. If the paper is right and positivism and non-positivism are not commensurable, then the discipline of IS should ask itself how it should view and possibly compare research from these two traditions. A radical solution would be to say that they are so fundamentally different that they do not in fact belong to the same discipline and that we therefore should establish two different disciplines. For the political reasons mentioned above, this may not be a desirable position. A less radical solution would be to continue to coexist under the roof of "information systems" but to generally ignore each other. One can probably argue that this is the current state of the discipline. But if we want to coexist, will we be able to tolerate one another well enough to remain under the same roof despite competition for the same resources?

Finally, there is the crucial question of the overall context of this discussion. This paper has concentrated on philosophical arguments in the context of IS research. The question of ontology is by no means confined to research or to a specific discipline. On the contrary, it is a central assumption in our individual and collective world-views. It strongly influences questions of politics, social distribution, of war and peace. The problem of tolerance between positivist and non-positivist IS researchers would thus have to be viewed in the context of tolerance between positivists and non-positivists in general. To stay within the religious terminology of the title of this paper, tolerance might be translated into an ecumenical approach. A brief look at the history of religious wars and the ensuing ecumenical movements suggests that peaceful coexistence of contradictory beliefs may be possible but tends to be very fragile. It is also only possible if the different sides desire it deeply and are willing to accept the other position as possibly misguided but legitimate. It is open to debate whether these conditions are met in contemporary IS research.

REFERENCES

Achterberg, J. S., van Es, G. A. & Heng, M. S. H., 1991, Information systems research in the postmodern period. In: *Information Systems Research: Contemporary Approaches & Emergent Traditions*, Nissen, H. -E.; Klein, H. K. & Hirschheim, R., eds., North Holland, Amsterdam, pp. 281 – 294.

Adam, A., 2001, Gender and Computer Ethics. In: *Readings in Cyberethics*, Spinello, R. A. & Tavani, H. T., eds., Jones and Bartlett, Sudbury, Massachusetts, pp. 63 – 76.

Baskerville, R., 2001, Conducting Action Research: High Risk and High Reward in Theory and Practice. In: *Qualitative Research in IS: Issues and Trends*, Trauth, E., ed., Idea Group Publishing, Hershey, pp. 192 – 217.

Beavers, A. F., 2002, Phenomenology and Artificial Intelligence, *Metaphilosophy* (33:1/2), Special Issue: *Cyberphilosophy: The Intersection of Philosophy and Computing*. Edited by J.H. Moor and T.W. Bynum, 70 – 82.

Benbasat, I. & Weber, R., 1996, Research Commentary: Rethinking “Diversity” in Information Systems Research. *Information Systems Research* (7:4), 389 – 399.

Benbasat, I. & Zmud, R. W., 2003, The Identity Crisis Within the IS Discipline: Defending and Communicating the Discipline's Core Properties, *MIS Quarterly, (*27:2), 183 – 194.

Benbasat, I. & Zmud, R. W., 1999, Empirical Research in Information Systems: The Practice of Relevance. *MIS Quarterly, (*23:1), 3 – 16.

Boland, R. J. jr., 1985, Phenomenology: A Preferred Approach to Research on Information Systems. In: *Research Methods in Information Systems* (IFIP 8.2 Proceedings), Mumford, E.; Hirschheim, R.; Fitzgerald, G. & Wood-Harper, T. (eds), 1985,, North-Holland, Amsterdam, pp. 193 – 201.

Brooke, C., 2002, Critical Perspectives on Information Systems: An Impression of the Research Landscape. *Journal of Information Technology* 17, 271 – 283.

Burrell, G. & Morgan, G., 1979, *Sociological Paradigms and Organizational Analysis*, Heinemann, London.

Capurro, R. & Pingel, C., 2002, Ethical Issues of Online Communication Research, *Ethics and Information Technology* (4:3,, Special Issue on *Internet Research Ethics*, edited by C. Ess, 189 – 194.

Cavaye, A. L. M., 1996, Case Study Research: A Multi-Faceted Research Approach for IS, *Information Systems Journal* 6, 227 – 242.

Chomsky, N., 1998, Reflections on Language (orig. 1975,. Reprinted in: *On Language)*, Chomsky, N., The New Press, New York.

Chua, W. F., 1986, Radical Developments in Accounting Thought. *The Accounting Review* (61:4), 601 – 632.

Ciborra, C., 2002, *The Labyrinths of Information - Challenging the Wisdom of Systems*, Oxford University Press, Oxford.

Darke, P.; Shanks, G. & Broadbent, M., 1998, Successfully Completing Case Study Research: Combining Rigour, Relevance and Pragmatism. *Information Systems Journal* (8), 273 – 289.

Davies, L. J., 1991, Researching the Organizational Culture Context of Information Systems Strategy: A Case Study of the British Army. In: *Information Systems Research: Contemporary Approaches & Emergent Traditions*, Nissen, H. -E.; Klein, H. K. & Hirschheim, R., eds., North Holland, Amsterdam, pp. 145 – 167.

Dreyfus, H. L., 1993, *What Computers Still Can't Do*, MIT Press, Cambridge, Massachusetts / London.

Encarta, 1999, Encarta World English Dictionary, Bloomsbury, London.

Eisenhardt, K. M., 1989, Building Theories from Case Study Research, *Academy of Management Review*, (14:4), 632 – 550.

Feyerabend, P. K., 1980, How to Be a Good Empiricist - A Plea for Tolerance in Matters Epistemological. In: *Challenges to Empiricism*, Morick, Harold, ed., Methuen, London, pp. 164 – 193.

Fitzgerald, B. & Howcroft, D., 1998, Towards Dissolution of the IS Research Debate: from Polarization to Polarity, *Journal of Information Technology* 13 (Special Issue on Interpretive Research in Information Systems, edited by M. Myers and G. Walsham), 313 – 326.

Friedman, M., 1994, The Methodology of Positive Economics. In: *The Philosophy of Economics: An Anthology*, Hausman, D. M., ed., pp. 180 – 213, 2nd edition Cambridge University Press , Cambridge.

Gadamer, H. -G., 1990, *Wahrheit und Methode - Grundzüge einer philosophischen Hermeneutik*. 6th edition, J.C.B. Mohr (Paul Siebeck), Tübingen.

Garson, J., 2003, Modal Logic. In: *The Stanford Encyclopedia of Philosophy (Winter 2003 Edition)*, Zalta, Edward N., ed., URL = <http://plato.stanford.edu/archives/win2003/entries/logic-modal/>, [accessed 09.07.2004].

Gergen, K. J., 1999, *An Invitation to Social Construction*, Sage, London.

Glasersfeld, von, E., 2000, Konstruktion der Wirklichkeit und des Begriffs der Objektivität. In: *Einführung in den Konstruktivismus*, Carl Friedrich von Siemens Stiftung, ed., 5th edition, Piper, München, pp. 9 – 40.

Goles, T. & Hirschheim, R., 2000, The Paradigm is Dead, the Paradigm is Dead... Long Live the Paradigm: the Legacy of Burrell and Morgan, *Omega, (2*8:3), 249 – 268.

Grint, K. & Woolgar, S., 1997, *The Machine at Work: Technology, Work, and Organization*, Blackwell, Cambridge.

Habermas, J., 1991, *Erläuterungen zur Diskursethik*, Suhrkamp, Frankfurt a. M.

Habermas, J., 1985, *Die neue Unübersichtlichkeit*, Suhrkamp, Frankfurt a. M.

Habermas, J., 1981, *Theorie des kommunikativen Handelns,* Suhrkamp Verlag, Frankfurt a. M.

Habermas, J., 1974, *Erkenntnis und Interesse*, Suhrkamp, Frankfurt a. M.

Hajek, P., 2002, Fuzzy Logic. In: *The Stanford Encyclopedia of Philosophy (Fall 2002 Edition)*, Zalta, E.N., ed., URL = <http://plato.stanford.edu/archives/fall2002/entries/logic-fuzzy/> [accessed 09.07.2004].

Hausman, D. M., ed., 1994, *The Philosophy of Economics: An Anthology*, 2nd edition, Cambridge University Press, Cambridge.

Hausman, D. M & McPherson, M. S., 1994, Economics, rationality, and ethics. In: *The Philosophy of Economics: An Anthology*, 2nd edition, Hausman, D. M., ed., Cambridge University Press, Cambridge, pp. 252 – 277.

Heidegger, M., 1993, *Sein und Zeit*, 17th edition, Max Niemeyer Verlag, Tübingen.

Hirschheim, R. A., 1985, Information Systems Epistemology: An Historical Perspective. In: *Research Methods in Information Systems* (IFIP 8.2 Proceedings), Mumford, E.; Hirschheim, R.; Fitzgerald, G. & Wood-Harper, T. (eds), North-Holland, Amsterdam, pp. 13 – 36.

Hirschheim, R. & Klein, H. K., 2003, Crisis in the IS Field? A Critical Reflection on the State of the Discipline, *Journal of the Association for Information Systems* (4:5), 237 – 293.

Hirschheim, R. & Klein, H. K., 1989, Four Paradigms of Information Systems Development. *Communications of the ACM* (32:10), 1199 – 1216.

Hollis, M., 1994, *The Philosophy of Social Science: an Introduction*. Cambridge University Press, Cambridge.

Iivari, J.; Hirschheim, R. & Klein, H. K., 1998, A Paradigmatic Analysis Contrasting Information Systems Development Approaches and Methodologies, *Information Systems Research* (9:2), 164 – 193.

Introna, L., 1997, *Management, Information and Power: A narrative of the involved manager*, MacMillan, London.

Introna, L. D. & Whittaker, L., 2003, The Phenomenology of Information Systems Evaluation: Overcoming the Subject/Object Dualism. In: *Global and Organizational Discourse About Information Technology*, Wynn, E.; Whitley, E.; Myers, M. D. & DeGross, J., eds., Kluwer Academic Publishers, Dordrecht, pp. 156 – 175.

Jenkins, Milton A., 1985, Research Methodologies and MIS Research. In: *Research Methods in Information Systems* (IFIP 8.2 Proceedings), Mumford, E.; Hirschheim, R.; Fitzgerald, G. & Wood-Harper, T. (eds), North-Holland, Amsterdam, pp. 103 – 117.

Jönsson, S., 1991, Action Research. In: *Information Systems Research: Contemporary Approaches & Emergent Traditions*, Nissen, H. -E.; Klein, H. K. & Hirschheim, R., eds., North Holland, Amsterdam, pp. 371 – 396.

Kant, I., 1995, *Kritik der praktischen Vernunft, Grundlegung zur Metaphysik der Sitten,*: Suhrkamp, Frankfurt a. M.

Keen, P. G. W., 1991, Relevance and Rigor in Information Systems Research: Improving Quality, Confidence, Cohesion and Impact. In: *Systems Research: Contemporary*

Approaches & Emergent Traditions, Nissen, Hans-Erik; Klein, Heinz K. & Hirschheim, Rudy, eds., North Holland, Amsterdam, pp. 27 – 49.

Khlentzos, Drew, 2004: *Naturalistic Realism and the Antirealist Challenge.* Cambridge, Massachusetts: The MIT Press.

Kishore, Rajiv; Sharman, Raj & Ramesh, Ram, 2004, Computational Ontologies and Information Systems: I. Foundations. In: *Communications of the Association for Information Systems* 14, 158 – 183.

Kishore, Rajiv; Sharman, Raj & Ramesh, Ram, 2004b, Computational Ontologies and Information Systems: II. Formal Specifications. In: *Communications of the Association for Information Systems* 14, 184 – 205.

Klein, H. K.; Hirschheim, R. & Nissen, H. -E., 1991, A Pluralist Perspective of the Information Systems Research Arena. In: *Information Systems Research: Contemporary Approaches & Emergent Traditions*, Nissen, H. -E.; Klein, H. K. & Hirschheim, R., eds., pp. 1 - 17 North Holland, Amsterdam.

Klein, H. K. & Myers, M. D., 2001, A Classification Scheme for Interpretive Research in Information Systems. In: *Qualitative Research in IS: Issues and Trends*, Trauth, Eileen, ed., pp. 218 – 239, Idea Group Publishing, Hershey.

Klein, H. K. & Myers, M. D., 1999, A Set of Principles for Conducting and Evaluating Interpretive Field Studies in Information Systems. MIS Quarterly, (23:1), 67 – 94.

Kuhn, T. S., 1996, *The Structure of Scientific Revolutions*, 3rd edition, The University of Chicago Press, Chicago and London.

Landry, M. & Banville, C., 1992, A Disciplined Methodological Pluralism for MIS Research. *Accounting, Management & Information Technology, 2*:2, 77 – 92.

Lee, A., 2004,: Thinking about Social Theory and Philosophy for Information Systems. In: *Social Theory and Philosophy for Information Systems*, Mingers, John & Willcocks, Leslie, eds., Chichester: Wiley, pp. 1 – 26.

Lee, A., 2001, Challenges to Qualitative Researchers in IS. In: *Qualitative Research in IS: Issues and Trends*, Trauth, E., ed. Idea Group Publishing, Hershey, pp. 240 – 270.

Lee, A., 1994, Electronic Mail as a Medium for Rich Communication: An Empirical Investigation Using Hermeneutic Interpretation. *MIS Quarterly*, (18:2), 143 – 157.

Lee, A., 1991, Integrating Positivist and Interpretive Approaches to Organizational Research. *Organization Science, (2*:4), 342 – 365.

Lee, A. S & Baskerville, R. L., 2003, Generalizing Generalizability in Information Systems Research. *Information Systems Research, (14*:3), 221 – 243.

Lyotard, J. -F., 1993, *Die Phänomenologie*, Junius Verlag, Hamburg.

Miranda, S. M. & Saunders, C. S., 2003, The Social Construction of Meaning: An Alternative Perspective on Information Sharing. *Information Systems Research*, (14:1), 87 – 106.

McCarthy, T., 1992, Philosophy and Social Practice: Avoiding the Ethnocentric Predicament. In: *Philosophical Interventions in the Unfinished Project of Enlightenment*, Honneth, A.; McCarthy, T.; Offe, C. & Wellmer, A., MIT Press, Cambridge, Massachusetts & London, pp. 241 – 260.

Mingers, J., 2001, Combining IS Research Methods: Towards a Pluralist Methodology, *Information Systems Research*, (12:3), 240 – 259.

Mingers, J., 2001b) Embodying Information Systems: the Contribution of Phenomenology, *Information and Organization*, (11:2), 103 – 128.

Mill, J. S., 1994, On the definition and method of political economy. In: *The Philosophy of Economics: An Anthology*, Hausman, D. M., ed., 2nd edition, Cambridge University Press, Cambridge, pp 52 – 68.

Monod, E., 2002, For a Kantian Foundation of IS Research: Proposals for an Epistemological Pluralism. In: Proceedings of the Eighth Americas Conference on Information Systems 2002, 1751 – 1759.

Moran, D., 2000, *Introduction to Phenomenology*, Routledge, London / New York.

Morick, H., 1980, Introduction: The Critique of Contemporary Empiricism. In: *Challenges to Empiricism*, Morick, Harold, ed., Methuen, London, pp. 1 – 25.

Myers, M., D & Avison, D., 2002, An Introduction to Qualitative Research in Information Systems. In: *Qualitative Research in Information Systems: a Reader*, Myers, M., D & Avison, D., eds., Sage, London, pp. 3 12.

Mumford, E.; Hirschheim, R.; Fitzgerald, G. & Wood-Harper, T. (eds), 1985, *Research Methods in Information Systems* (IFIP 8.2 Proceedings), North-Holland, Amsterdam.

Nissen, H. -E., 1985, Acquiring Knowledge of Information Systems – Research in a Methodological Quagmire. In: *Research Methods in Information Systems* (IFIP 8.2 Proceedings), Mumford, E.; Hirschheim, R.; Fitzgerald, G. & Wood-Harper, T. (eds), North-Holland, Amsterdam, pp. 39 – 51.

OED (Oxford English Dictionary), 2004, http://athens.oed.com/ [accessed 01.06.2004].

Olaison, J., 1991, Pluralism or Positivistic Trivialism: Important Trends in Contemporary Philosophy of Science. In: *Information Systems Research: Contemporary Approaches & Emergent Traditions*, Nissen, H. -E.; Klein, H. K. & Hirschheim, R., eds., Amsterdam: North Holland, pp. 235 – 264.

Orlikowski, W. J. & Baroudi J. J., 1991, Studying Information Technology in Organizations: Research Approaches and Assumptions. *Information Systems Research, (2*:1), 1 – 28.

Petter, S. C. & Gallivan, M. J., 2004, Toward a Framework for Classifying and Guiding Mixed Method Research in Information Systems. In: Proceedings of the 37th Annual Hawaii International Conference on Systems Sciences, Hawaii, January 5-8, 2004.

Pettigrew, A., 1985, Contextualist Research and the Study of Organisational Change Processes. In: *Research Methods in Information Systems* (IFIP 8.2 Proceedings), Mumford, E.; Hirschheim, R.; Fitzgerald, G. & Wood-Harper, T. (eds), North-Holland, Amsterdam, pp. 53 – 78.

Popper, K. R., 1980, Science: Conjectures and Refutations. In: *Challenges to Empiricism*, Morick, Harold, ed., Methuen, London, pp. 128 – 160.

Quine, W. V. O., 1980, Two Dogmas of Empiricism. In: *Challenges to Empiricism*, Morick, H., ed., Methuen, London, pp. 46 – 70.

Ricoeur, P., 1995, *Le Juste*, Editions Esprit, Paris.

Ricoeur, P., 1983, *Temps et récit - 1. L'intrigue et le récit historique*, Editions de Seuil, Paris.

Robey, D., 1996, Research Commentary: Diversity in Information Systems Research: Threat, Promise, and Responsibility, *Information Systems Research* (7:4), 400 – 408.

Rorty, R., 1991, *Objectivity, Relativism and Truth*, Cambridge University Press, Cambridge.

Sawyer, S., 2001, Analysis by Long Walk: Some Approaches to the Synthesis of Multiple Sources of Evidence. In: *Qualitative Research in IS: Issues and Trends*, Trauth, E., ed., Idea Group Publishing, Hershey, pp. 163 – 190.

Stahl, B. C., 2003, How We Invent What We Measure: A Constructionist Critique of the Empiricist Bias in IS Research In: Proceedings of the Ninth Americas Conference on Information Systems, Tampa, 04 to 06 August 2003, 2878 – 2884.

Stahl, B. C., 2003b, When does a Computer Speak the Truth? The Problem of IT and Validity Claims. In: *Global and Organizational Discourse About Information Technology*, Wynn, E.; Whitley, E.; Myers, M. D. & DeGross, J., eds., Kluwer Academic Publishers, Dordrecht, pp. 91 – 107.

Steup, M., 2001, The Analysis of Knowledge, *The Stanford Encyclopedia of Philosophy (Spring 2001 Edition)*, Edward N. Zalta, ed., URL = http://plato.stanford.edu/archives/spr2001/entries/knowledge-analysis/, [accessed 01.06.2004].

Stuart, S., 2002, A Radical Notion of Embeddedness: A Logically Necessary Precondition for Agency and Self-Awareness. *Metaphilosophy* (33:1/2), Special Issue: *Cyberphilosophy: The Intersection of Philosophy and Computing.* Edited by J.H. Moor and T.W. Bynum, 98 – 109.

Trauth, E., 2001, The Choice of Qualitative Method in IS Research. In: *Qualitative Research in IS: Issues and Trends*, Trauth, Eileen, ed., Idea Group Publishing, Hershey, pp. 1 – 19.

Trauth, E. M & Jessup, L. M., 2000, Understanding Computer-Mediated Discussions: Positivist and Interpretive Analyses of Group Support System Use. *MIS Quarterly, (*24:1), 43 – 79.

Tugendhat, E., 1992, Reflections on Philosophical Method from an Analytic Point of View. In: *Philosophical Interventions in the Unfinished Project of Enlightenment*, Honneth, A.; McCarthy, T., Offe, C. & Wellmer, A, eds., MIT Press, Cambridge, Massachusetts & London, pp. 113 – 124.

Urquhart, C., 2001, An Encounter with Grounded Theory: Tackling the Practical and Philosophical Problems. In: *Qualitative Research in IS: Issues and Trends*, Trauth, E., ed., Idea Group Publishing, Hershey, pp. 104 – 140.

van de Ven, A. H., 1989, Nothing Is Quite So Practical as a Good Theory. *Academy of Management Review*, (14:4), 486 – 489.

van der Blonk, H., 2003, Writing Case Studies in Information Systems Research. *Journal of Information Technology* 18, 45 – 52.

Varey, R. J.; Wood-Harper, T. & Wood, B., 2002, A Theoretical Review of Management and Information Systems Using a Critical Communications Theory. *Journal of Information Technology* 17, 229 – 239.

Visala, S., 1991, Broadening the Empirical Framework of Information Systems Research. In: *Information Systems Research: Contemporary Approaches & Emergent Traditions*, Nissen, H. -E.; Klein, H. K. & Hirschheim, R., eds., North Holland, Amsterdam, pp. 347 – 364.

Vitalari, N. P., 1985, The Need for Longitudinal Designs in the Study of Computing Environments. In: *Research Methods in Information Systems* (IFIP 8.2 Proceedings), Mumford, E.; Hirschheim, R.; Fitzgerald, G. & Wood-Harper, T. (eds), North-Holland, Amsterdam, pp. 243 – 265.

Walsham, G., 1995, Interpretive Case Studies in IS Research: Nature and Method. *European Journal of Information Systems* 4, 74 – 81.

Walsham, G., 1995b) The Emergence of Interpretivism in IS Research, *Information Systems Research* (6:4), 376 – 394.

Ward, J. & Peppard, J., 1996, Reconciling the IT/business relationship: a troubled marriage in need of guidance, *Journal of Strategic Information Systems* 5, 37 – 65.

Watzlawik, P., ed., 2001, *Die erfundene Wirklichkeit*, 13th edition, Piper, München, Zürich

Weber, R., 2004, The Rhetoric of Positivism Versus Interpretivism: A Personal View (Editor's Comment), *MIS Quarterly, (*28:1), iii – xii.

Weber, R., 2003, Theoretically Speaking (Editor's Comment), *MIS Quarterly, (*27:3), iii - xii

Weick, K. E., 1989, Theory Construction as Disciplined Imagination. *Academy of Management Review*, (14:4), 516 – 531.

Weizenbaum, J., 1976, *Computer Power and Human Reason*, W. H. Freeman and Company, San Francisco.

Wellmer, A., 1986, *Ethik und Dialog: Elemente des moralischen Urteils bei Kant und in der Diskursethik*, Suhrkamp, Frankfurt a. M.

Westland, J. C., 2004, The IS Core XII: Authority, Dogma and Positive Science in Information Systems Research. *Communications of the Association for Information Systems* 13, 136 – 157.

Wilson, M, 2003, Rhetoric of Enrollment and Acts of Resistance: Information Technology as Text. In: *Global and Organizational Discourse About Information Technology*, Wynn, Eleanor; Whitley, Edgar; Myers, Michael D. & DeGross, Janice, eds., Kluwer Academic Publishers, Dordrecht, pp. 225 – 248.

Wittgenstein, L., 2001, *Philosophical Investigations / Philosopische Untersuchungen* (translated by G.E.M. Anscombe), 3rd edition, Blackwell, Oxford.

Wittgenstein, L., 1963, *Tractatus logico-philosophicus – Logisch-philosophische Abhandlungen*, Suhrkamp, Frankfurt a. M.

Wynn, E., 2001, Möbius Transitions in the Dilemma of Legitimacy. In: Qualitative Research in IS: Issues and Trends, Trauth, E., ed., Idea Group Publishing, Hershey, pp. 20 – 44.

Wynn, E.; Whitley, E.; Myers, M. D. & DeGross, J., eds., 2003, *Global and Organizational Discourse About Information Technology*: Ifip Tc8/Wg8.2 Working Conference on Global and Organizational Discourse About Information Technology, December 12-14, 2002, Barcelona, Spain, Kluwer Academic Publishers, Dordrecht.

Yin, R. K., 2003, *Case Study Research: Design and Methods*, 3rd edition, Sage, Thousand Oaks / London / New Delhi.

Chapter 6

ONTOLOGY, LIFE-WORLD, AND RESPONSIBILITY IN IS

Bernd Carsten Stahl

Centre for Computing and Social Responsibilty, De Montfort University, Leicester LE1 9BH, UK, bstahl@dmu.ac.uk

Abstract: This paper discusses the influence which philosophical ontology has on the ascription of responsibility in IS. It starts out with a description of two ontological positions which are treated under the heading of "positivism" and "life-world". Positivism is defined as being based on the assumption of an observer-independent objective reality whereas the life-world represents a reality that is created by intentional perception and hermeneutic interaction. In the subsequent section the paper introduces the concept of responsibility as a possible approach to the ethical and moral questions raised by the use of information systems. The final part then proceeds to discuss the influence that the ontological underpinning has on the ascription of responsibility. In conclusion it will be argued that these questions are of fundamental importance to information systems and that philosophical ontology therefore deserves a more explicit place in IS than it currently has.

Key words: ontology; life-world; ethics; morality; IS research; hermeneutics; phenomenology

1. INTRODUCTION

When information systems (IS) scholars or practitioners hear the word "ontology" they tend to think about database design. Such ontology refers to the entities that can be found within a database. Indeed, the guiding idea of ontology in IS seems to be that there are specific ontologies that can be used for codifying knowledge in "universes of discourse". These ontologies then take the form of categorizations of relevant entities (Kishore, Sharman &

Ramesh, 2004). What is often overlooked is the fact that the concept of ontology has a long and distinguished history as one of the main areas of philosophy. All regional ontologies must be based on general ontological assumptions. Therefore questions of general ontology are important in specific areas such as IS. In a philosophical context, the term "ontology" is used to denote questions pertaining to being. What is, what does it mean to be, what is the meaning of being – are possible questions to be asked in ontology. While these may sound like very abstract questions with little relevance to IS, a second look quickly reveals that they are in fact of high importance. Ontology plays a role in questions such as: what is the status of data? Is hardware more real (and thus possibly more important) than software? Do people and machines share the same type of reality (thus: can machines replace humans)? Are IS nothing but tools but do they develop their own higher level of reality (problem of AI)? These are just a few examples that show the importance of ontology in IS. An additional problem here is that these questions are rarely discussed explicitly despite the fact that the stakeholders' implicit answers to them determine in large parts how IS are developed and used.

Another philosophical discipline with high relevance for IS is that of ethics. Ethical problems are of central importance for information systems theory and practice. Ethics plays a role in systems design and implementation. It determines the adoption of systems and in many cases can decide about success or failure of a system. There is a range of ethical problems in information systems or related to the use of ICT in more general terms. To name some of the more frequently discussed ones, there are problems of access and the digital divide, privacy / surveillance / data protection, intellectual property rights, data accuracy and software reliability, computer crime, business implications, power shifts, or effects of technology on our perception of the other.

This paper will combine the questions regarding ontology and ethics in IS. The main starting point is that ontology has a decisive influence upon ethics. In IS there are two main ontological positions: positivism and non-positivism (cf. Myers & Avison, 2002). Positivism holds that reality is given independent of the observer whereas non-positivism stands for the belief that the observer constitutes reality, or at least the perception thereof. The most prominent non-positivist position is interpretivism, which, in terms of ontology, is based on a social constructivist viewpoint. It is closely linked to phenomenology and hermeneutics. This is where the idea of the life-world enters the picture. The life-world is a concept developed in the phenomenological tradition. It represents the horizon within which we all live. Everybody has an idiosyncratic life-world which overlaps with the life-worlds of others to some degree (cf. Gadamer, 1990). Ontologically the life-world can be interpreted as the prevalent reality. This would mean that there are multiple realities which partially overlap.

The influence of ontology on ethics will be developed using the notion of responsibility. Depending on whether one believes that reality is objectively given or subjectively / collectively constituted, the understanding of responsibility will differ. This, in turn, has a serious impact on how individuals and collectives can or should use IS. In order to develop this argument, the paper will start out by defining and discussing the concept of ontology and the different ontological positions open to IS researchers. It will then proceed to a discussion of ethics and morality and introduce the notion of responsibility. The main contribution of the paper will be the subsequent discussion of the relationship between different ontological positions and responsibility ascriptions. The conclusion will then highlight which consequences the entire argument has for IS researchers and practitioners.

A final introductory word on the place of this paper in the scholarly IS discourse: It will quickly become clear that this is not a positivist paper. But it cannot be considered an interpretivist paper either. In fact, it is best understood as a piece of critical research. Critical research is often portrayed as the third alternative next to positivist and interpretive research (Chua, 1986; Orlikowski & Baroudi, 1991). Leaving aside the usefulness of this grouping of research approaches in "paradigms", the main reason why the paper can be called critical is that it follows the critical intention to change the status quo. Inspired by the Marxist critique of capitalism, critical research has traditionally set out to make a difference (Mingers, 1992; Alvesson & Deetz, 2000; Ngwenyama & Lee, 1997). This has often been translated as meaning that critical research tries to empower or emancipate the subject of its research (Lyytinen & Hirschheim, 1988; Alvesson & Willmott, 1992; Cecez-Kecmanovic, 2001). In our case empowerment and emancipation must be understood to be aimed at scholars and practitioners who have been socialized in the dominant ontology of positivism. This suggests that ethical issues in IS can be dealt with similar to technical issues by subsuming them under the right rule and applying this correctly. The choice of a non-positivist ontology, which is arguably more appropriate for ethical problems, reveals that ethics and responsibility are integral parts of IS and that they cannot be dealt with algorithmically. Indeed, IS, as part of social reality, are one aspect of the greater question of the good life, which cannot and must not be ignored when talking about technology. Emancipation in this case will thus be an emancipation of a limited and limiting understanding of what IS is about.

2. ONTOLOGY IN IS

This section will discuss some of the main ontological positions to be found in IS research. It will discuss these under the headings of "positivism" and "life-world". This should not be misread as meaning that either of the terms is predominantly viewed as ontological terms in the current literature. It also should not be understood to mean that they cover all possible ontologies in the field. Rather, they have been chosen because they are based on ontological assumptions and will form a suitable basis for the subsequent discussion of the relationship between ontology and responsibility.

2.1 Positivism in IS

The predominant research "paradigm" in IS, as in most other social sciences and the sciences in general, is that of positivism. Positivism can be seen as a research approach that, like all research approaches implies certain assumptions about ontology, epistemology, and other aspects of the (social) world (Klein, Hirschheim & Nissen, 1991). Positivism is built on the ontological assumption that reality is given independent of the observer (Myers & Avison, 2002). This ontological position has also been called "realism" as it indicates that there is a reality, which exists whether or not it is observed (Burrell & Morgan, 1979; Hirschheim, 1985; Hirschheim & Klein, 1989). It is interesting to note that the very word "realism" contains ontological assumptions. It stems from the Latin "*res*", meaning "thing". This can be read to imply that things, typically physical things such as stones, hammers, or computers are *real*, whereas non-physical entities, such as thoughts, theories, emotions, are less real.

The ontology underlying research is important because it determines in large parts what can be observed and thus how research can or should be done. In positivism, given an external and stable world, the task of science and research is to investigate and describe reality. If reality is objectively given, then it can be objectively mapped and represented. Research finds true statements by describing the world as it (really) is. This is closely linked to empiricism, which holds that useful knowledge must result from experience (Mingers, 2004). Positivism and empiricism combined entail a vision of science and research that sees the researcher as seeking true descriptions of the world with the purpose of developing appropriate theories, which can then be used to make predictions (Darke, Shanks & Broadbent, 1998; Varey, Wood-Harper & Wood, 2002; Weber, 2003). This complexity of thought is closely linked to the idea of unity of science, that there must be generally agreed ways of describing the world independent of the specific research object (Olaison, 1991; Landry & Banville, 1992).

The realist ontology of positivism seems to be what comes most naturally to us. We are socialized by learning what the reality surrounding us is and it is hard to believe it could be different. Our everyday life is "shot through" with positivist assumptions (McCarthy, 1992). Another argument for positivism is that it originally aimed to do the right thing. It can be seen as part of the project of enlightenment. Going hand in hand with utilitarian philosophy, it attempted to eradicate obscurantism and prejudice and replace these with scientific knowledge of the world. This was supposed to improve society, eradicate illiteracy, and emancipate humans. Originally, positivism and empiricism can thus be seen as critical approaches in the sense of the word introduced earlier (Wynn, 2001).

Nevertheless, the term positivism has lost some of its positive sound. This has to do with the decline and demise of logical positivism, the philosophical school that formulated its ideas most clearly. Today it sometimes even carries a pejorative connotation (Burrell & Morgan, 1979; Lee, A., 2001). Indeed, positivist scholars according to the definition offered above rarely call themselves positivist but prefer to talk about "positive" or "objective" research (Friedman, 1994; Westland, 2004).

One problem that leads to confusion is that positivism is often defined in terms of epistemology. Lee (1991 p. 343), for example, defines positivism as involving "the manipulation of theoretical propositions using the rules of formal logic and the rules of hypothetico-deductive logic, so that the theoretical propositions satisfy the four requirements of falsifiability, logical consistency, relative explanatory power, and survival". While this definition spells out the epistemology of positivism correctly, it hides the fact that this epistemology is only feasible on the basis of the ontological assumption of an objective reality. The concentration on epistemology has led to an equation of positivism with certain methods, usually quantitative ones, which cloud the issue even further (Benbasat & Weber, 1996).

As indicated earlier, positivism is still the predominant research "paradigm" in most sciences and social sciences, including information systems. However, it is no longer uncontested. A majority of criticism of positivism hinges on the pragmatic problem that it is not very successful in social sciences. While it has led to spectacular successes in the sciences which have allowed the development of the scientific-technical civilisation we live in, it has been far less successful in describing human beings and addressing social issues. One example is the persistently high failure rate of information systems, which endures despite decades of intensive, IS research (cf. Keil et al., 1998; Schmidt et al., 2001). However, the main argument against positivism in this paper is of an ontological nature. It is philosophically difficult to sustain the idea that the world is independent of the observer. The main argument against the ontological realism of positivism is that it is completely unclear how an observer-independent reality can be represented correctly in the mind of the observer. Even outspoken proponents of ontological realism have to concede that no satisfactory answer to this millennia-old problem has been found (Khlentzos, 2004). That means that we have no model that could explain how we could know what the alleged objective reality is upon which positivism is built. But if we don't know how we represent reality, then the question arises why we think we know it. And, consequently, we need to ask what the point is of saying that there is an objective reality if we don't know how we can know about it.

2.2 Life-World in IS

Dissatisfaction with the orthodox positivist approach to social science, including its realist ontology, empiricist epistemology and lack of useful results, has led to the development of alternatives. The most frequently discussed alternative research approach in the field of information systems is that of interpretivism (Klein & Myers, 1999). Unlike "positivism" the term "interpretivism" has no relevant etymological history and is generally used to denote some sort of opposition to positivism. It thus variously refers to ontological, epistemological, methodological and other issues. Most writers agree that interpretivism is less about finding out the absolute truth of a phenomenon but rather giving a convincing account of a situation (Trauth & Jessup, 2000; Lee & Baskerville, 2003). It thus has to concentrate on how social actors make sense instead of identifying quantifiable variables that describe social settings (Schultze & Leidner, 2002). In terms of ontology, interpretive researchers are skeptical about the claim that there is an observer-independent external reality that can be correctly represented (Walsham, 1995). This rises the question what the ontological alternative is. Before we can answer this question, we need to briefly look at two philosophical traditions which are closely linked to interpretivism, namely hermeneutics and phenomenology.

2.2.1 Phenomenology

The link between interpretivism and phenomenology is so close that the two have been equated (Galliers, 1991). Phenomenology is a somewhat ambiguous term that. In a wider sense, it can refer to all first-person accounts of human experience (Beavers, 2002). In a narrower sense, the one used here, it stands for philosophical approaches following Edmund Husserl. Phenomenology was created as a reaction to scholarly philosophy that seemed arid and self-referential. Husserl wanted to overcome idealist speculation about the object of cognition and look at the things themselves. He chose the term phenomenology which had previously been used by Kant and Hegel to describe how things appear to us (Moran, 2000). The phenomenologist most frequently cited in IS, presumably because he specifically discussed technology, is Martin Heidegger (Introna & Ilharco, 2004). He explained the term "phenomenology" by looking at its etymology as being made up of the Greek terms "phainomenon" and "logos". This allowed him to translate phenomenology as "that which shows itself in itself, the manifest" (Moran, 2000 p. 229; cf. Heidegger, 1993 p. 28), which means that phenomenology has to do with self-manifestation.

For Heidegger phenomenology was primarily a type of ontology, because it investigates the beingness of being. The novel aspect of phenomenology is that it does not try to look at the objectively given being, but recognizes that the most important being is the human being, which is never objectively given but always already in a situation or, as he would say, being-in-the-world. This primordial being is what Heidegger called *Dasein*. Dasein perceives the world not by being a passive recipient of sensory data but by actively and intentionally constructing the object of cognition. Such perception can also not be objective because it is based on the prior experience of the individual. This is where the idea of life-world (*Lebenswelt*) enters the picture. The life-world is the horizon within which each individual is always already caught up. Only from this horizon of the life-world can we experience the external world. One can thus state that the ontological basis of phenomenology is captured in the concept of life-world. The life-word is the "container" of reality because all perception of reality must start from it and lead back to it. Dasein cannot leave the life-world and everything outside of it therefore cannot properly said to be "real".

This raises a number of fundamental philosophical questions that we cannot discuss here. One of the problems we must address, however, is the question how life-worlds can be made to overlap. A critical reading of the above introduction to phenomenology could charge it with being solipsist because it cannot explain why and how individuals interact or why individual life-worlds contain similarities. However, they must be similar to some degree, otherwise it would be impossible to communicate and collaborate. Since communication and collaboration are central to the study of information systems, this problem must be addressed. This is the point where hermeneutics enters the picture.

2.2.2 Hermeneutics

Etymologically hermeneutics is derived from "Hermes", the Greek messenger god. He is credited with giving humans speech and with helping them understand the will of the gods. The term was used to describe ways of finding the right meaning of a text, originally biblical scriptures (Rathswohl, 1991). From its theological starting point, hermeneutics has developed into the discipline that deals with understanding and interpreting texts (Boland, 1985; Boland, 1991).

Hermeneutics originally aimed to understand the "real" meaning of a text as intended by the author. However, this objectivist understanding of hermeneutics has given way to a more individualistic one. It became clear that two people reading the same text rarely have the same understanding of it. Furthermore, there is no external and objective position that can be used to judge which interpretation is the "right" one. Hermeneutics thus became the discipline that is interested in how sense and meaning can be derived from texts. This is closely linked to the idea of the "hermeneutic circle" (Gadamer, 1990). The concept of the hermeneutic circle represents the fact that one can never understand a text without preconceptions. Rather, the reader of a text creates his or her understanding of the text on the basis of prior knowledge. This knowledge will then be affected and modified by the reading of the text. The reader's understanding and the message of the text are thus in a circular relationship. Hermeneutics in this sense does not try to cover up the tension between the text and its present understanding but to bring it out into the open (Klein & Myers, 1999).

Hermeneutics is concerned with understanding, which means that it has to consider how meaning is created and how sense can be made of texts. The word text here should be understood in a wide sense that includes everything that can be understood, including the use of information systems (Myers & Avison, 2002). Hermeneutics is often seen as pertaining in particular to the social sciences whose purpose is to understand what agents do and why rather than make predictions (Hausman, 1994). The difference between natural and social sciences is then said to be the difference between understanding and explaining (*verstehen* and *erklären*). Where social sciences aim to understand what agents mean, using hermeneutic means, natural sciences want to explain phenomena by offering causal explanations (Lee, 1994). This distinction leads to a number of consequences for research, which is partly reflected in the quantitative v. qualitative debate in IS. For this paper, the main interest of hermeneutics is its influence on the life-world as an ontological concept.

2.2.3 Life-World as Ontology

The life-world is a concept that was developed in the context of phenomenology. If perception is an intentional activity of the individual then it is no longer useful to suppose the classical Cartesian distinction between subject and object of perception. Instead, the observer who creates the phenomenon by perceiving it cannot be divided from it. Consequentially, it makes little sense to speak of an objective reality that is fundamentally the same for everybody. That means that reality is (at least partly) idiosyncratic, that everyone has their own reality. This personal reality is what Husserl has termed the life-world (*Lebenswelt*). Habermas has called it the strange thing that disintegrates before our eyes when we want to inspect it in detail (Habermas, 1985 p. 186). It is the horizon within which we always already live but whose limits we can never explore completely.

This idiosyncratic concept of life-world requires hermeneutic interaction in order to be a possible basis of social action. The individual agents need to ensure that their life-worlds correspond to some degree if they want to interact and collaborate. This can only be done through communication. In a phenomenological world without external fix points, understanding must follow the hermeneutic circle. The individual understands the utterances (or texts) of others on the basis of her prior knowledge and uses the new-found understanding of the text to improve her knowledge and communicate on a different level.

The idea of a life-world is clearly not exclusively an ontological one. It can be used for epistemological and methodological purposes. However, it should also be recognized that at its heart it contains an ontological assumption, namely that it is an alternative to positivist realism. Information systems scholars who use the concept of the life-world thereby implicitly state that they believe the positivist assumption of an objective and observer-independent reality is not tenable (cf. Walsham, 1993). It is therefore justified in the context of this paper to see the life-world as an ontological opposition to positivism. The rest of the paper will explore what this means for the ascription of (moral) responsibility in IS.

3. RESPONSIBILITY IN INFORMATION SYSTEMS

The first part of the paper has developed two alternative ontological positions under the headings of "positivism" and "life-world". This second part will prepare the ground for the analysis of the chosen ontology on what ethical and moral issues are. For this purpose it will start out with a discussion of the importance and a subsequent definition of responsibility and a discussion of the strengths and weaknesses of the concept.

3.1 Importance of Responsibility

There are several reasons why scholars as well as practitioners in the field of information systems should be interested in questions of responsibility. A large number of moral and ethical issues are related to, and in some cases even created by the use of, information technology. These include issues such as privacy, the use of intellectual property, access to data, the "digital divide", power issues in IS, justifications of truth (regimes of knowledge), the way we interact and spend our time. A comprehensive discussion of these issues is far beyond the confines of this paper. It is nevertheless useful to introduce a distinction here, namely that between ethics and morality. Morality can be understood to refer to the set of norms that rule individual and collective behavior in a society. Ethics can then be used to denote the theory and justifications of morality (Brenkert, 1998; De George, 1999). While this distinction is not etymologically necessary and is more prominent in European continental philosophy (Ricoeur, 1990; Wunenburger, 1993; Homann, Blome-Drees, 1992) than in English language publications on the topic, it is nevertheless useful because it allows avoiding several problems.

Morality as the set of rules governing behavior is directly linked to the prevailing perception of good and bad, of right and wrong. Most of the issues enumerated above are thus of a moral nature. When we talk about issues such as downloading mp3 files from the Internet then the arguments are usually informed by an assumption that such action is "right" or "wrong". In order to justify such moral assumptions one would have to change the level of discussion and engage in ethical debate. What are the reasons that make us evaluate something as good or bad? How can we balance different goods?

The reason why this distinction between ethics and morality is important in this paper is that the solution to the moral problems produced or exacerbated by the use of ICT depends on both levels. There are moral problems and in order to address the moral problems, one needs an ethical understanding of these problems. Solutions to, say, the moral problem of employee surveillance, are only conceivable if there is some degree of agreement why we think it is a moral problem or why it has moral advantages. However, there is no generally agreed-upon ethical theory that would allow us to identify, describe, and solve moral problems. The history of moral philosophy has produced a large number of ethical theories that are not always in agreement. Worse, even if one agrees on an ethical theory (and in contemporary IS research and practice the most likely contender is the theory of utilitarianism), there is no guarantee that this theory will produce an unambiguous solution.

In this complex and muddled context, one apparent solution is to choose the concept of responsibility because it seems to promise a manageable approach to moral issues without requiring ethical expertise. Sentences such as "users are responsible for not misusing the computer" seem to have the value of addressing moral issues and producing manifest results without being overly contentious.

Furthermore, the use of the term responsibility is quite familiar in organizational contexts where information systems are mostly used. Managers are responsible for their "area of responsibility"; the CIO is responsible for the information infrastructure of the organization, the CEO is responsible for the entire organization etc. Responsibility here has a positive connotation which includes moral issues but is not limited to them. Being responsible is something most people in organizations strive for. Responsibility can thus be seen as an answer to the moral (and ethical) issues of IS. Unfortunately it is usually not clear what the term responsibility actually means.

3.2 A Preliminary Definition of Responsibility

For the reasons just explained, the term "responsibility" can be seen as a potential answer to the problem of morality and ethics in the field of information systems. However, it is not always clear what "responsibility" means. It can denote different facts or circumstances in different contexts. When we say that the flood was responsible for the destruction of the crop then this stands for a causal relationship. This is different from the prime minister's responsibility for his extramarital affair. This is again different from parents' responsibility for their children. (For a more in-depth discussion of the concept of responsibility cf. Stahl, 2004.)

A good starting point for the types of responsibility to be found in IS is the etymology of the word. Responsibility has a direct link to the response, the answer. Responsibility can thus be seen as a "liability to answer" (Lewis, 1972 p. 124f). This is true in English as well as in a number of other languages such as German (*Verantwortung*) (Lenk & Maring, 1995) or French (*responsabilité*) (Etchegoyen, 1993). This liability to answer is a first indication of the moral and ethical content of responsibility. The fact that an agent perceives a duty to answer to someone else implies that this other is taken seriously and deemed worthy of respect. It also indicates that responsibility is a deeply social issue that can only come to fruition in social contexts. The question remains: who answers to whom and why?

This leads us to the dimensions of responsibility. These include the subject and the object. The subject is the entity which is thought to be responsible. The object is that which the subject is responsible for. If A is responsible for B, then A is the subject and B the object. The point of responsibility is to establish a link between the subject and the object. This is why responsibility can be seen as a concept of ascription. The object is ascribed to the subject (Bayertz, 1995; Hart, 1948). This holds true for most, if not all types of responsibility. In legal responsibility the crime is ascribed to the accused, in moral responsibility the misdeed is ascribed to the person, in theological responsibility the sin is ascribed to the sinner etc. A complete ascription of responsibility will usually require more than just subject and object. There is typically an independent dimension, the authority, which decides whether ascriptions are feasible and which sanctions are linked to them. In legal responsibility this is the judge or the jury. Then there also needs to be an agreed-upon normative basis. Responsibility ascriptions are only valid if there are norms, be they moral rules, laws, customs or others, that the parties believe to be valid. Beyond this, there is a large number of conditions and other aspects of responsibility that need to be taken into account for an ascription to be successful. Before we return to these in the light of differing ontological assumptions, a final important question is why responsibility is ascribed.

French (1992 p. 18), drawing on Pincoffs, identifies three reasons for the practice of ascribing responsibility: "One is determining who merits punishment or reward. The second is setting the targets of (usually financial) burden shifting, and the third is identifying appropriate subjects of blame and praise." These aims of ascribing responsibility are not always free of conflict. What they seem to have in common, however, is that they establish a link between the object and the subject in order to impute sanctions based on the object to the subject. These sanctions can be positive (reward, praise, money) or negative (blame, punishment, exclusion). Why do we want to sanction subjects? In the case of negative sanctions, two motives have been described: retribution and deterrence (Staddon, 1999). Again, we have two possibly contradictory motivations for ascribing responsibility. As a general rule one can nevertheless say that responsibility ascriptions aim to modify behavior in order to achieve a desired social state. The same can also be said for positive sanctions. We reward people in order to motivate them and others to behave in a specific way.

Responsibility thus can be seen as a social mechanism that intends to steer human behavior in such a way as to come to a desired social state. This is important to recognize for several reasons. First, it again shows the moral relevance of responsibility ascriptions. The desired aim of responsibility is what the ancient Greeks would have called the "good life". This stands for the shared view of how one should live one's life as a member of a community. Today it is usually not clear what constitutes a good life. There are too many different life-plans for any one to be universally accepted. And yet, we ascribe responsibility in order to make people live their lives in a specific way. This raises the question: who gets to determine the aims of responsibility ascriptions and on what grounds; a question we will return to below. Second, the (moral) purpose of responsibility is important to be aware of because it indicates that responsibility is not an end in itself but rather a means to an end. This raises the problem of how one can be sure that the intended purpose of responsibility ascription is actually fulfilled, and what one is to do if this is not the case. These are fundamental problems that all responsibility ascriptions have to deal with. They are related to questions of epistemology (how can I know the results of an ascription?) and politics (who gets to set goals of responsibility?). The main contention of this paper is that all of these issues are closely related to the underlying ontology. The answer to who gets to ascribe responsibility in IS on what grounds for what purpose will be different depending on the ontological stance of the people involved. In order to develop this point, it is necessary to take a brief look at the problems that arise during the process of ascribing responsibility.

3.3 Problems of Responsibility Ascriptions in IS

In order to avoid becoming too abstract, it may be a good idea to take a look at a conceivable situation in which responsibility is of importance in IS. Let us assume that a large international corporation intends to introduce a new system, say, an ERP system to streamline and optimize its business processes and to satisfy its information needs. It is relatively easy to think of a large number of responsibility ascriptions that could become relevant here. There would be responsibility for the technical functioning of the system, for the alignment of business strategy and technology, for a fit between software and business processes, or for the correct identification of information needs by different levels of the hierarchy. Apart from such obviously business-related responsibilities, there would also be less obvious but equally important issues. These would include responsibility for user acceptance, for smooth transitions from one system to another, for the political agreement to the system. This will also touch on clearly ethical issues such as responsibility for job losses or redesign, deskilling, physical relocation etc. We thus have something resembling a web of responsibilities, rather than an individual responsibility. Keeping this case in mind will make it easier to understand the discussion of the problems of responsibility. These will now be explored by looking at the dimensions and conditions of responsibility.

3.3.1 Conditions of Responsibility

A possible way of discussing the problems of responsibility in such a context would be to look at the dimensions of the ascription and their potential shortcomings. The first one, related to the subject of responsibility, is the area of conditions. Conditions of responsibility are usually taken to be necessary in order for ascription to be successful. They can refer to the subject or to the relation of subject and object. A first condition frequently named is that of causality. In order for responsibility to be useful, there must be a causal relationship between subject and object. The subject must have caused the object or at least have been able to avoid the object to some degree (Moore, 1999). However, causality is not enough. The subject must be aware of the causal relationship and in a position to change it. This is where the conditions of freedom, power, and knowledge enter the picture (Fischer, 1999). The subject must be free (at least to some degree) to play the role of subject or to avoid being responsible. That implies knowledge of the relationship as well as freedom to leave it or to affect it in a relevant manner. These are philosophically difficult conditions to fulfill. From a philosophical perspective causality is a complex matter whose ontological status is unclear. The idea of freedom may be even worse. What does it mean to be free, can humans be free, is there a difference between freedom of will and freedom of action? On top of these fundamental philosophical questions, there are the more mundane problems of responsibility ascription in modern organizations. Does the CIO know of the consequence of the ERP system? Is the project manager causally related to the failure of the server? Does the data worker have the freedom to enter certain data? We will return to these problems in the context of the discussion of the impact of ontology on responsibility ascription.

3.3.2 Subject of Responsibility

Apart from the general conditions of responsibility, there are also questions relating to the subject itself. There are assumptions about the personal qualities of the subject built into the texture of responsibility. In order for the ascription to be successful the subject must have certain intellectual and emotional qualities (cf. Wallace, 1996). It must be able to act intentionally and to use some sort of reason. This can be translated into personality traits which include a basic level of education and formation, self-control, the ability to react to sanctions, and, arguably, a bodily existence (Velasquez, 1991). This list of assumptions about the subject points clearly to the traditional subject of responsibility and ethics in general, namely the individual human being, the person. Indeed, there is a long history of mutual definitions of persons and responsibility. The person is defined as the entity that can be responsible and responsibility is to be ascribed to persons (Flynn, 1984).

This is a problematic assumption in modern responsibility ascriptions. While individuals or persons act within social groups, it is often not clear whether they still fulfill the conditions of responsibility. They often no longer understand causal relationships and they lack the knowledge and power to change the course of events. The CIO will usually not be aware of all of the consequences of the system and the data entry worker will not be able to change anything about the system. This has led to the search for other subjects, notably collective subjects such as corporations (French, 1979; Werhane, 1985). This extension of the role of the subject, while well established in legal responsibility, can contradict the conditions linked to the subject. It is contentious whether collective entities can rightfully be said to act at all and they certainly lack the personality attributes of the subject. On the other hand, they often have more resources at their disposal and therefore may find it easier to acquire knowledge and act effectively.

3.3.3 Object of Responsibility

Other problems of responsibility are linked to the object of ascription. Most of them refer to the relationship between subject and object including the existence of some sort of causality and the subjects control over the object. This causality and the related control of the subject over the object are particularly endangered because of complexity, cumulative effects, side effects and the problem of doing and omitting. Complexity stands for the fact that the world consists of a potentially infinite number of facts and relationships and it is hard to determine which ones are relevant for responsibility (Beck, 1998). The example of the web of responsibilities in our ERP system should demonstrate the point. The different responsibilities of CEO, CIO, project managers, line managers, individual employees are multiple and interlinked. Changing one of them may have results on others that are amplified in other parts of the system and that are not accounted for.

Another responsibility problem is that of cumulative effects. This refers to such activities that are individually unproblematic but, over a longer time or done in parallel, produce problems of responsibility which cannot be reduced to the individual act. An example is the collection of personal data. If an employee collects data about customers, say, birthdays and gift preferences, and does so on a paper list, then this is not fundamentally problematic. If the same thing is done as a matter of policy and the data is computerized and used for business purposes, then the moral quality may change and we may have a problem of data protection, privacy, respect for the customer and others. However, the individual action of collecting data is not the problem but the accumulation of data is. This changes the moral evaluation of the individual act even though the act itself did not change.

A fundamental problem of all responsibility ascriptions is represented by side effects. We usually consider responsibility only for those acts that were intended. However, all acts can have unintended consequences as well. The question is whether and under which conditions side effects become legitimate objects of responsibility. If the project manager mismanages the risk assessment of the project and the project consequentially fails, then we can say that the manager is responsible because risk avoidance was an intended consequence. But what if, because of the project constraints and increased workload, the marriage of programmer Smith breaks up during the project. There is a clear causal relationship between the project manager who asked Smith to work so much and the end of the marriage. But is the manager responsible? And will there be sanctions? If so what sort? This example should have shown that side effects are a serious problem for responsibility ascriptions. At the same time we know that causal chains are infinite and every action can have an unknown number of results that were not intended. Establishing responsibility between the subject and all of the results of her actions is therefore fundamentally impossible. But the question remains, which side effects do we need to consider? Because surely it will not be good enough to say that responsibility will only be ascribed for those effects that were intended. If nothing else, this would lead to the wide spread of the excuse: "I did not intend to do this."

A final and related problem is that of doing and omitting. We usually assume that responsibility will be ascribed primarily for the results of actions. However, in some cases it is also ascribed for inaction. If I can easily save a drowning child from a river with no danger to myself, but fail to do so, then surely I am responsible for the death of the child even though, or better: because I did nothing. Similarly, a project manager can be responsible for the failure of a project when she fails to take certain precautions. But this exacerbates our problem of complexity and side effects. Instead of "only" being responsible for the infinite number of consequences of my actions, I am all of a sudden also responsible for the infinite number of consequences of my inaction.

3.3.4 The Instance of Responsibility

And, if these complications of responsibility are not enough, there is still the third major dimension, the instance or authority of responsibility. This is the person or institution that ascribes specific sanctions to the subject on the basis of the agreed-upon rules. The instance combines several areas of problems. First, it must make decisions about responsibility based on norms or rules that are not always clear. While legal responsibility has the advantage of being able to refer to statutes and case law (where applicable), the same cannot be said for moral or other forms of responsibility. Furthermore, legal responsibility shows that even in the presence of clearly identifiable rules, the application of these rules is often far from clear. This means that the instance must be concerned with the existence, validity, acceptance, and application of the rules that underlie a responsibility ascription.

This requires the instance to be visible and powerful, which, again, is not always the case. Judge and jury in a court of law fulfill these requirements but for other responsibility ascriptions such clear instances are not always visible. Possible instances of moral responsibility may be God or the personal conscience but they raise new problems of inter-subjective acceptability. That means that even in those cases where the subject and the object are relatively clear and unambiguous, there is no guarantee that the ascription of responsibility will actually work because there may be no instance with the necessary power and acceptance to execute and enforce the ascription, i.e. the sanctions.

In the case of responsibility for and in IS, there are some examples where the problem does not appear. If the CIO, for example, is held to be responsible for the implementation of the ERP system, then she will be measured by looking at the achievements and sanctions will be administered by the CEO or the board of directors. But what about responsibility of the systems analyst who overlooks the moral right to privacy of the customer? How can this be addressed, by whom, and on what grounds? The more uncertain subject and object become, the more uncertain the success of responsibility will be. If the software design requires certain business processes that lead to the redundancy of personnel and if the person in question, partially resulting from this develops depression, it is hard to see how sanctions, even if they were clearly visible and attributable, could be enforced.

It should now be clear that responsibility, albeit a useful term for dealing with a number of normative issues in IS, is also problematic. The next section will discuss which role ontology plays in the process of responsibility ascription by contrasting responsibility based on a positivist position with responsibility in a life-world.

4. RESPONSIBILITY AND ONTOLOGY IN IS

From a philosophical position, it is relatively clear that there is a close relationship between ontology and ethics. Questions of good and bad are linked to questions of reality. An important question is whether good and bad are "real" in any sense, and how this relates to the interpretation of ethical theories. Another problem is whether we need to understand the reality of the world before we can judge ethical matters. In this section, I will discuss the problems of responsibility based on ontological stances.

4.1 Positivist Responsibility

The positivist ontology was characterized as being based on the belief that reality is externally given and independent of the observer. This is of course a very brief summary and does not reflect the possible richness of ontological nuances within positivism. While the independent external existence of physical things is probably generally recognized, it is much less clear whether other entities, ranging from emotions and morality to theory, have a comparable ontological status. For the purpose of this discussion, I will submit that positivist ontology supposes the objective existence of subjects, objects, and instances of responsibility as well as of the underlying norms and rules. The objective positive existence of these entities does not necessarily mean that they are easily identifiable but that they are there and can be found. Indeed, a considerable percentage of the literature in legal responsibility is based on this assumption.

If we assume the objective reality of the relevant entities, then responsibility becomes problematic in many cases. It may still be possible for relatively clear-cut examples such as the criminal responsibility of a villain for his acts. The acts are the object that can be identified, the villain is the object, judge and jury are the instance and the law provides the norms. The ascription of responsibility is meant to protect society by sanctioning the criminal which will deter him and others from repeating the crime. This shows that a positivist approach to responsibility can be successful. However, it does not live up to the challenges that can be found in modern societies and organizations.

The first and maybe most fundamental problem is that of the subject. Individuals, usually acknowledged as being ontologically unproblematic, are the typical subjects of responsibility. Unfortunately they usually do not fulfill the conditions of responsibility ascriptions. They have all the personality characteristics of responsibility such as emotions, intellect, or fear of sanctions but they do not have the necessary knowledge or power to affect the outcomes of IS in such a way as to discharge of responsibility successfully. The individuals at the top of the hierarchical ladder such as a CEO or a CIO may have considerable power but they do not have the knowledge of complex social and organizational impacts of technology. Those individuals who do have such knowledge, usually the ones who are affected, will frequently lack formal power to address issues. Holding them responsible will therefore not lead to the changes in social fabric that the ascription is meant to achieve.

One possible remedy for this is to hold collectives responsible. These could be companies or other organizations such as professions, departments, groups of programmers or users and the like. This, however, raises new problems. It is philosophically doubtful whether collectives have an ontological status independent of their members. This raises the question whether holding collectives responsible is a shorthand expression for holding several individuals responsible. If the answer to this question is yes, then nothing is gained. If it is no and collectives are recognized as subjects *sui generis*, then new problems arise. Collectives may overcome the problems of individuals; they may be more powerful and have more resources. They can accumulate knowledge and have a longer life-span than individuals. However, they do not have the personality attributes, it is unclear whether it is useful to speak of them as agents (do they have a *mens rea*?) and it is not obvious how their ontological status compares to that of individuals. That means that the tenet of positivist responsibility, namely that the subject is clearly identifiable is doubtful.

Similar arguments can be made for the object. Most interesting responsibility objects in IS are located in the future. The successes of the ERP system that the company installs or the return on investment of the CRM system are initially future matters. Planned sanctions are based on future estimates of these objects. Unfortunately, the future is by definition uncertain. We may plan and optimize our knowledge base but we never know what will happen. For the positivist this raises the question whether future occurrences are real. This would be an assumption that would be difficult to defend, which is where the help of statistics can come in handy. Instead of viewing future states of affairs as existing, they are given probabilities, which allow us to make decisions using decision theoretical tools. However, these probabilities are fundamentally as uncertain as the events they describe. We cannot know in advance whether we covered all of the possible outcomes, which renders the statistical solution as uncertain as the deterministic one. Also, there is the problem of unintended consequences of side effects. It was said earlier that these are infinite. We simply do not know what will follow from our actions. Responsibility for an infinite amount of consequences will render the ascription impossible. There must be a limit. But how is the positivist to make the decision among the infinite number of possible outcomes, all of which are not even real yet, knowing that he may have overseen the most important one.

The instance, finally, produces comparable problems. If we assume that the instance is positively given, then we should be able to determine who or what it is. One problem with this is that the instance shifts; that it is not the same for all ascriptions of responsibility. When we look at the examples of a CIO responsible for the success of an ERP implementation, a programmer responsible for a program module and a company responsible for the IT-related redundancies, it becomes clear that the responsibility ascriptions are so different, that they will require different types of instances. A related problem is that of the underlying rules and norms. These may be clear for some ascriptions but they are completely unknown in other cases. If the rules are not known, then how can responsibility be successful?

All of this should have shown that responsibility ascriptions in IS based on a positivist ontology are deeply problematic. None of the major dimensions, subject, object, or instance is unequivocally known despite the positivist assumption that they should exist. An added problem is that different responsibilities may contradict each other. The CIO's responsibility for producing a working system may go counter to the company's social responsibility for maintaining employment. The project manager's responsibility for designing a CRM system which captures an optimum amount of data on customers may collide with the same person's responsibility to keep customer data private.

Despite these difficulties, responsibility can and will be ascribed on the positivist assumption that reality, including ethical matters, are objectively given. In order to overcome the problems just described, however, these responsibility ascriptions must be simplified in order to reflect the underlying ontology. That means that subject, object, and instance must be chosen in such a way as to produce a minimum amount of ontological problems. The result is that the subject is usually a natural person, the object is quantifiable (typically profit), the instance is higher management and the underlying norms are those of economic liberalism. Indeed, a brief look in any newspaper will confirm that this seems to be the prevalent description of responsibility in business. It is the basis of "heroic management" (Gosling & Mintzberg, 2003). The disadvantage of this approach is that it simplifies responsibility ascription to such a degree that they can no longer fulfill their original purpose, namely to contribute to the good life of society.

4.2 Responsibility in the Life-World

The idea of a life-world was introduced earlier as an ontological alternative to the positivist perception that reality is objectively given. The life-world is based upon the personal perception of individuals but its meaning is created through hermeneutic interaction with other individuals. Reality is thus not given and open to objective discovery but outcome of the intentional activity of perception and interpersonal communication. This means that the dimensions of responsibility must be discovered through communication, which has a direct influence on what can count as subject, object, and instance and how these can lead to the attribution of sanctions.

Since the life-world is the product of individual perception and hermeneutic interaction, it is always given as a totality. The individual is not able to extract him or herself from it and to describe it objectively. He or she is always already in the world and experiences it in the light of prior knowledge. Also, most aspects of the life-world are not problematic and therefore not realized by the individual. This means that responsibility is not a matter of general consideration but only becomes relevant and a focus of attention in the case of a breakdown. It will only be of interest when it does not function, when it is missing, or when something goes awry. In this case the individual will have to reconsider his or her assumptions and start communicating with others about the meaning of the breakdown. Different aspects of responsibility will therefore typically be discussed in conjunction with each other, e.g. the subject and the object form part of one discourse.

This means that the dimensions of responsibility are not assumed to be objectively given but they are part of a social construction by discourse which produces an overall phenomenon of responsibility. These discourses will be caused by a breakdown; they are therefore problem-centered. To return to our IS examples, the question will be how a certain problem can be addressed by ascribing responsibility. This might be the problem that an organization is perceived to have an unsatisfactory relationship with its customers. The solution to the problem will not be the installation of a particular information system (e.g. CRM) but rather a discourse about the problem and resulting ascriptions. This discourse must consider the overall aim of the problem solution and contextualize this with the overarching narratives of the social and individual good life. It will then identify subject(s) and object(s) that can address the problem. That means that it is quite conceivable that one result will be the introduction of a CRM system with the CIO as the subject of responsibility and the board of directors as the instance. However, it will include other responsibilities that affect the life-worlds of other individuals which will then cover issues such as privacy, or continued employment.

This approach to responsibility avoids many of the problems encountered by positivists. The ascription is defined holistically which means that subject, object, instance, and norms are part of a simultaneous discussion. That means that the problem whether a collective can be a subject is not discussed in isolation. Instead, the question is whether the ascription of responsibility and thus sanctions to a collective can be realized and can lead to desired results. Similarly, questions of distant objects or side effects lose their problematic aspects. The constructivist approach to responsibility can define the object or ways of limiting it in conjunction with questions of observation and suitable objects. Objects are only of relevance if they are perceived by the participants of the communication that establishes the life-world. There is therefore no claim that all objects of responsibility are considered and taken care of. Instead, only those objects that are of relevance to someone and that are problematic in some way are addressed.

Another advantage of the life-world centered approach to responsibility is that it does not take the entire responsibility process to be objectively given and closed. Instead, responsibility is recognized as an ongoing process which requires continuous interaction to be viable. That means that responsibility ascriptions that are not successful can be revised and redefined. New responsibilities can be found and instituted while others may be discarded. There are no absolute standards but only continuous attempts to achieve a desirable outcome. What this means is not given *a priori* but needs to be negotiated in every instance.

From a positivist point of view this type of responsibility ascription may seem inadequate. Instead of covering all potential problems and providing general advice on how responsibility needs to be ascribed, the non-positivist ontology requires a less comprehensive approach. Responsibility based on the life-world is more an act of improvisation, of muddling through, of bricolage (Ciborra, 2002). It cannot claim to be comprehensive and always needs to be open to new breakdowns which require new responsibility ascriptions. It is a protracted endeavor that never comes to a successful conclusion. It goes counter to the idea of heroic management because it sees everybody always entangled in a web of responsibilities that are interlinked, mingled and not clearly differentiable.

5. CONCLUSION

The paper has suggested that there are two fundamentally different philosophical ontologies that can be found in information systems: positivism and the life-world. Positivism assumes an observer-independent reality whereas the life-world is a result of the intentional perception of phenomena which are contextualized through the hermeneutic act of communication. It has then introduced the concept of responsibility as an answer to the manifold ethical and moral problems caused by the use of information systems. In the final section it has discussed the influence that the choice of ontology has on the process of ascribing responsibility.

The result of this discussion was that responsibility encounters different problems depending on the ontology it is based on. In a positivist view of the world, the problems are that subjects often do not fulfill the requirements necessary for the ascription to be successful. Furthermore, the objective reality of objects is problematic. Since every action has a potentially infinite number of results and most of them are not intended, it is hard to see how responsibility can be limited. Additionally, there is the question of who will attribute sanctions and who will enforce them. An ontological perspective based on the idea of the life-world, on the other hand, will overcome these problems by simultaneously discussing and constituting subject, object, and instance. However, it does not offer the clear-cut and clean solutions assumed by positivists. Responsibility becomes a matter of improvising. Ascriptions result from communicative interaction but they are not always stable and they may have to be revised. Responsibility does not lead to one recognizable outcome but is part of a web of interpersonal relationships.

This raises the question what an IS professional or academic is to do: Should we go down the positivist route or not? The question in this form probably makes no sense. We do not usually consciously decide which ontology we want to follow. Instead, ontological beliefs are deeply ingrained in our everyday life as well as in the basics of our research. Ontologies are given and they are implied as ontologies-in-use (Lee, 2004). Positivism is the predominant approach to information systems. It does not stand to reason that this will change any time soon. However, given the problems of positivism in general and with regards to responsibility ascriptions in particular, it may be worth considering alternatives. In terms of phenomenology, positivism produces may breakdowns, represented by systems failure, unsatisfactory descriptions of phenomena, blindness to context and social fabrics, and last but not least, an inability to address ethical issues other than from a descriptive point of view. Where such breakdowns become obvious, it may be worth considering whether one of the reasons for the failure of positivism may be its ontology. If so, it might be worthwhile to consider alternatives such as the concept of the life-world.

The above discussion has shown that a different choice of ontology will not automatically solve all of our problems. It may take care of some of them but produce new ones. The question of ontology can thus not be answered satisfactorily by reference to questions of responsibility. Indeed, it goes far beyond this. It refers to the underlying philosophical question which ontological position most adequately describes reality. Given several millennia of discussion of this question, we should not expect to find an unambiguous answer to this any time soon. However, it is certainly worthwhile reflecting on these questions because, as this paper has argued, they have a great influence on different aspects of life, including how we deal with ethics, morality, and responsibility. They also determine the adequacies of regional ontologies and are thus an important underpinning for all considerations of ontology in IS.

REFERENCES

Alvesson M, Deetz S., 2000, *Doing Critical Management Research.* London: SAGE.

Alvesson M, Willmott H., 1992, On the Idea of Emancipation in Management and Organization Studies. *Academy of Management Review* (17:3), 1992, pp. 432 – 464.

Bayertz K., 1995, Eine kurze Geschichte der Herkunft der Verantwortung. In: Bayertz K. ed. *Verantwortung: Prinzip oder Problem*? Darmstadt: Wissenschaftliche Buchgesellschaft, pp. 3 – 71.

Beavers AF., 2000, Phenomenology and Artificial Intelligence. *Metaphilosophy* (33:1/2), Special Issue: *Cyberphilosophy: The Intersection of Philosophy and Computing*. Edited by J.H. Moor and T.W. Bynum, 70 – 82.

Beck U., 1998, *Was ist Globalisierung? Irrtümer des Globalismus – Antworten auf Globalisierung*. 5th edition, Frankfurt a. M.: Edition Zweite Moderne, Suhrkamp Verlag.

Benbasat I, Weber R., 1996, Research Commentary: Rethinking "Diversity" in Information Systems Research. *Information Systems Research* (7:4): 389 – 399.

Boland RJ., 1991, Information Systems Use as a Hermeneutic Process. In: Nissen, HE, Klein HK, Hirschheim R. eds. *Information Systems Research: Contemporary Approaches & Emergent Traditions*. Amsterdam: North Holland, pp. 439 – 458.

Boland RJ., 1985, Phenomenology: A Preferred Approach to Research on Information Systems. In: Mumford E, Hirschheim R, Fitzgerald G, Wood-Harper T. eds. *Research Methods in Information Systems* (IFIP 8.2 Proceedings). Amsterdam: North-Holland, pp. 193 – 201.

Brenkert G., 1998, Trust, Morality and International Business. *Business Ethics Quarterly* (8:2): 293 – 317.

Burrell G, Morgan G., 1979, *Sociological Paradigms and Organizational Analysis*. London: Heinemann.

Cecez-Kecmanovic D., 2001, Doing Critical IS Research: The Question of Methodology. In: Trauth E. ed. *Qualitative Research in IS: Issues and Trends*. Hershey: Idea Group Publishing, pp. 141 – 162.

Chua WF, 1986, Radical Developments in Accounting Thought. In: *The Accounting Review* (61:4); 601 – 632.

Ciborra C, 2002, *The Labyriths of Information - Challenging the Wisdom of Systems*. Oxford: Oxford University Press.

Darke P, Shanks, G, Broadbent, M., 1998, Successfully Completing Case Study Research: Combining Rigour, Relevance and Pragmatism. *Information Systems Journal* (8): 273 – 289.

De George RT., 1999, *Business Ethics*. 5th edition Upper Saddle River, New Jersey: Prentice Hall.

Etchegoyen A., 1993, *Le temps des responsables*. Paris: Editions Julliard.

Fischer J.M., 1999, Recent Work on Moral Responsibility.: *Ethics* 110: 93 – 139.

Flynn TR., 1984, *Sartre and Marxist Existentialism: The Test Case of Collective Responsibility*. Chicago, London: The University of Chicago Press.

French PA., 1992, *Responsibility Matters*. Lawrence, Kansas: University Press of Kansas.

French, PA., 1979, The Corporation as a Moral Person.: *American Philosophical Quarterly* (16: 3): 207-215.

Friedman M., 1994, The methodology of positive economics. In: Hausman, DM. ed. *The Philosophy of Economics: An Anthology*. 2nd edition Cambridge: Cambridge University Press, pp. 180 – 213.

Gadamer HG., 1990, *Wahrheit und Methode – Grundzüge einer philosophischen Hermeneutik*. 6th edition Tübingen: J.C.B. Mohr (Paul Siebeck).

Galliers R.J., 1991, Choosing Appropriate Information Systems Research Approaches: A Revised Taxonomy. In: Nissen HE, Klein HK, Hirschheim R. eds.: *Information Systems Research: Contemporary Approaches & Emergent Traditions*. Amsterdam: North Holland, pp. 327 – 345.

Gosling J, Mintzberg H., 2003, The Five Minds of a Manager. *Harvard Business Review* (81:11): 54 – 63.

Habermas J., 1985, *Die neue Unübersichtlichkeit*. Frankfurt a. M.: Shrkamp.

Hart HLA., 1948, The Ascription of Responsibility and Rights. *Proceedings of the Aristotelian Society* 1948: 171 – 194.

Hausman DM., 1994, *The Philosophy of Economics: An Anthology*. 2nd edition Cambridge: Cambridge University Press.

Heidegger M., 1993, *Sein und Zeit*. 17th edition, Tübingen: Max Niemeyer Verlag.

Hirschheim R., 1985, Information Systems Epistemology: An Historical Perspective. In: Mumford E, Hirschheim R, Fitzgerald G, Wood-Harper T. eds. *Research Methods in Information Systems* (IFIP 8.2 Proceedings). Amsterdam: North-Holland, pp. 13 – 36.

Hirschheim R, Klein, HK, 1989, Four Paradigms of Information Systems Development. *Communications of the ACM* (32:10), 1199 – 1216.

Homann K, Blome-Drees F., 1992, *Wirtschafts- und Unternehmensethik*. Göttingen: Vandenhoek & Ruprecht.

Introna LD, Ilharco FM., 2004, Phenomenology, Screens, and the World: A Journey with Husserl and Heidegger into Phenomenology. In: Mingers J, Willcocks L, eds. *Social Theory and Philosophy for Information Systems*. Chichester: Wiley, pp. 56 – 102.

Keil, Mark et al., 1998, A Framework for Identifying Software Project Risks. *Communications of the ACM* (41:11): 76 – 83.

Khlentzos D., 2004, *Naturalistic Realism and the Antirealist Challenge*. Cambridge, Massachusetts: The MIT Press.

Khisore R, Sharman R, Ramesh R., 2004, Computational Ontologies and Information Systems: I. Foundations, *Communications of the AIS* 14: 158 – 183.

Klein HK, Hirschheim R, Nissen, HE. A Pluralist Perspective of the Information Systems Research Arena. In: Nissen HE, Klein HK, Hirschheim R. eds. *Information Systems Research: Contemporary Approaches & Emergent Traditions*. Amsterdam: North Holland, 1991, 1 – 17.

Klein HK, Myers MD., 1999, A Set of Principles for Conducting and Evaluating Interpretive Field Studies in Information Systems. *MIS Quarterly* (23:1): 67 – 94.

Landry M, Banville C., 1992, A Disciplined Methodological Pluralism for MIS Research. *Accounting, Management & Information Technology* (2:2): 77 – 92.

Lee AS., 2004, Thinking about Social Theory and Philosophy for Information Systems. In: Mingers J, Willcocks L. eds. *Social Theory and Philosophy for Information Systems*. Chichester: Wiley, pp. 1 – 26.

Lee AS., 2001, Challenges to Qualitative Researchers in IS. In: Trauth E. ed. *Qualitative Research in IS: Issues and Trends*. Hershey: Idea Group Publishing, pp. 240 – 270.

Lee AS., 1994, Electronic Mail as a Medium for Rich Communication: An Empirical Investigation Using Hermeneutic Interpretation. *MIS Quarterly* (18:2): 143 – 157.

Lee, AS.,1991, Integrating Positivist and Interpretive Approaches to Organizational Research. *Organization Science* (2:4): 342 – 365.

Lee AS, Baskerville RL., 2003, Generalizing Generalizability in Information Systems Research. In: *Information Systems Research* (14:3): 221 – 243.

Lenk H, Maring M., 1995, Wer soll Verantwortung tragen? Probleme der Verantwortungsverteilung in komplexen (soziotechnischen-sozioökonomischen) Systemen. In: Bayertz K ed. *Verantwortung: Prinzip oder Problem*? Darmstadt: Wissenschaftliche Buchgesellschaft, pp. 241 – 286.

Lewis HD., 1972, The Non-Moral Notion of Collective Responsibility. In: French P. ed. *Individual and Collective Responsibility – Massacre at My Lai*. Cambridge, Massachusets: Schenkman Publishing Company, pp. 116 – 144.

Lyytinen K, Hirschheim R., 1988, Information Systems as Rational Discourse: an Application of Habermas Theory of Communicative Action. *Scandinavian Journal of Management* (4:1/2): 19 – 30.

McCarthy T., 1992, Philosophy and Social Practice: Avoiding the Ethnocentric Predicament. In: Honneth, A, McCarthy T, Offe C, Wellmer A. (eds.) *Philosophical Interventions in the Unfinished Project of Enlightenment*. Cambridge, Massachusetts & London: MIT Press, pp. 241 – 260.

Mingers J., 1992, Technical, Practical and Critical OR – Past, Present and Future? In: Alvesson M, Willmott H. eds. *Critical Management Studies*. London: SAGE, pp. 90 – 113.

Moore M., 1999, Causation and Responsibility. In: Paul E, Miller F, Paul J, eds. *Responsibility*. Cambridge et al.: Cambridge University Press, pp. 1 – 51.

Moran D., 2000, *Introduction to Phenomenology*. London / New York: Routledge.

Myers MD, Avison D., 2002, An Introduction to Qualitative Research in Information Systems. In: Myers MD, Avison, D. eds.: *Qualitative Research in Information Systems: a Reader*. London et al.: Sage, pp. 3 – 12.

Ngwenyama OK, Lee AS., 1997, Communication Richness in Electronic Mail: Critical Social Theory and the Contextuality of Meaning. *MIS Quarterly* (21:2): 1997, 145 – 167.

Olaison J., 1991, Pluralism or Positivistic Trivialism: Important Trends in Contemporary Philosophy of Science. In: Nissen HE, Klein HK, Hirschheim R. eds. *Information Systems Research: Contemporary Approaches & Emergent Traditions*. Amsterdam: North Holland, pp. 235 – 264.

Orlikowski WJ, Baroudi JJ., 1991, Studying Information Technology in Organizations: Research Approaches and Assumptions. *Information Systems Research* (2:1): 1 – 28.

Rathswohl, EJ., 1991, Applying Don Ihde's Phenomenology of Instrumentation as a Framework for Designing Research in Information Science. In: Nissen HE, Klein HK, Hirschheim R. eds. *Information Systems Research: Contemporary Approaches & Emergent Traditions*. Amsterdam: North Holland, pp. 421 – 438.

Ricoeur P, 1990, *Soi-même comme un autre*. Paris: Edition du Seuil.

Schmidt, Roy et al. (2001): Identifying Software Project Risks: An International Delphi Study. *Journal of Management Information Systems* (17:4): 5 – 36.

Schultze U, Leidner D., 2002, Studying Knowledge Management in Information Systems Research: Discourses and Theoretical Assumptions. *MIS Quarterly* (26:3): 213 – 242.

Staddon J., 1999, On Responsibility in Science and Law. In: Paul EF, Miller FD, Paul J, eds. *Responsibility*. Cambridge et al.: Cambridge University Press, pp. 146 – 174.

Stahl, BC., 2004, *Responsible Management of Information Systems*, Hershey, Idea Group Publishing.

Trauth EM, Jessup LM., 2000, Understanding Computer-Mediated Discussions: Positivist and Interpretive Analyses of Group Support System Use. *MIS Quarterly* (24:1): 43 – 79.

Varey RJ, Wood-Harper T, Wood B., 2002, A Theoretical Review of Management and Information Systems Using a Critical Communications Theory. *Journal of Information Technology* 17: 229 – 239.

Velasquez M., 1991, Why Corporations Are Not Morally Responsible for Anything They Do In: May L, Hoffman, S, eds. *Collective Responsibility: Five Decades of Debate in Theoretical and Applied Ethics*. Savage, Maryland: Rowman & Littlefield Publishers Inc., pp. 111 – 131.

Wallace R., 1996, *Responsibility and the Moral Sentiment*. Cambridge, Massachusetts / London, England: Harvard University Press.

Walsham G., 1995, Interpretive Case Studies in IS Research: Nature and Method. *European Journal of Information Systems* 4: 74 – 81.

Walsham G., 1993, *Interpreting Information Systems in Organizations*. Chichester: Wiley.

Weber R., 2003, Theoretically Speaking (Editor's Comment). *MIS Quarterly* (27:3): iii – xii.

Werhane P., 1985, *Persons, Rights, and Corporations*. Englewood Cliffs, New Jersey: Prentice-Hall Inc.

Westland, JC., 2004, The IS Core XII: Authority, Dogma and Positive Science in Information Systems Research. *Communications of the Association for Information Systems* 13: 136 – 157.

Wunenburger JJ,, 1993, *Questions d'éthique.* Paris: Presses Universitaires de France, PUF.

Wynn E., 2001, Möbius Transitions in the Dilemma of Legitimacy. In: Trauth E. ed. *Qualitative Research in IS: Issues and Trends*. Hershey: Idea Group Publishing, pp. 20 – 44.

Ontological Engineering

Chapter 7

AN ONTOLOGICAL APPROACH TO DEVELOP KNOWLEDGE INTENSIVE CBR SYSTEMS

Belén Díaz-Agudo and Pedro A. González-Calero
Facultad de Informática, Universidad Complutense de Madrid, Spain

Abstract: Our approach to Case Based Reasoning (CBR) is towards integrated applications that combine case specific knowledge with models of general domain knowledge. In this paper, we describe a domain independent architecture to help in the design of knowledge intensive CBR systems. It is based on knowledge acquisition from a library of application-independent ontologies and the use of CBROnto, ontology with the common CBR terminology that guides case representation; allows the description of flexible, generic and reusable CBR Problem Solving Methods; and allows to reason about the description of CBR systems.

Key words: Knowledge intensive CBR; Ontologies; Problem Solving Methods; Description Logics

1. INTRODUCTION

Any Knowledge-Based System (KBS) achieves its reasoning power through the explicit representation and use of different kinds of knowledge about a certain domain of application. There is a problem typically associated with the development of KBSs: knowledge acquisition often becomes an irremediable problem. This is the so-called *knowledge acquisition bottleneck*.

Trying to solve this problem, main knowledge engineering approaches and methodologies to develop KBSs agree in aspects related with the conceptualization and representation of reusable knowledge *components*. A KBS is viewed as consisting of separate but interconnected collaborating components. Typically, components of a KBS include domain knowledge, task structures and Problem Solving Methods (PSMs), which represent commonly occurring, domain-independent problem-solving strategies.

Case Based Reasoning (CBR) emerges as a more appealing approach to KBS development than the traditional rule based approach mainly due to the more intuitive nature of cases as a knowledge representation and reasoning formalism. CBR is based on remembering past experiences and using them to solve current situations that are *similar* to the ones already solved and stored. CBR has been often motivated also as an alternative to solve the knowledge acquisition bottleneck, because it is easier to tell histories than to model the domain behaviour. There are domains and applications –such as help-desk, medicine, law, engineering... – where experience makes a crucial role and CBR is the natural paradigm to apply. Besides there are many application domains, like help-desks or medicine, where historic databases of solved problems are typically stored, making the case acquisition process even easier. Since cases capture much of the knowledge implicitly, a deep understanding of the domain is not essential for developing CBR applications. Indeed, CBR has become more successful in weak theory domains –such as law– where experts solve problems by using their experience.

In traditional CBR systems, reasoning capabilities rely on the set of previous experiences –cases– plus application-specific methods where similarity and simple, and often inexistent, adaptation knowledge is implicitly codified. Instead, a *knowledge-intensive* CBR approach (KI-CBR) assumes that cases, in some way or another, are enriched with explicit general domain knowledge (Aamodt 1990; Díaz-Agudo & González-Calero 2000 (a)). The role of the general domain knowledge is to enable a CBR system to reason with semantic and pragmatic criteria, rather than purely syntactic ones. By making the general domain knowledge explicit, the CBR system is able to reason in a more flexible and contextual manner than if this knowledge is compiled into predefined similarity metrics or feature relevance weights (Richer 1995) (Aamodt 2004). Besides, it provides a great advantage from the knowledge reusability point of view. Meanwhile explicit domain models are reusable through different applications in the same domain, specific similarity functions, or relevance weights or adaptation formulas is *compiled knowledge* that is application specific and hard to be reused out of the application in which they were codified. With compiled knowledge we mean that it has been distilled in development time. “Compilation” is taken in a very general sense including human knowledge engineering activities.

CBR systems may be more or less knowledge intensive. Next we characterize some aspects of CBR methods along the *knowledge intensiveness dimension* (Aamodt 2004), from the nearest-neighbor based methods at the one end of the scale to the COLIBRI or CREEK like methods closer to the other end. Some typical characterizations of KI-CBR methods (right part) and knowledge poor methods (left part) are listed.

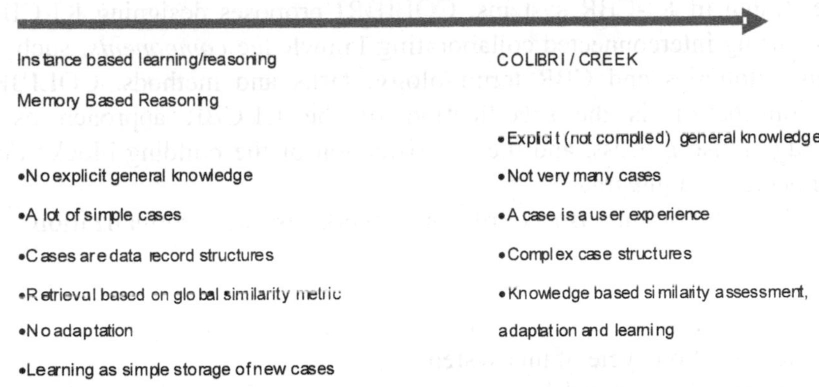
Instance based learning/reasoning
Memory Based Reasoning
•No explicit general knowledge
•A lot of simple cases
•Cases are data record structures
•Retrieval based on global similarity metric
•No adaptation
•Learning as simple storage of new cases
COLIBRI / CREEK
•Explicit (not compiled) general knowledge
•Not very many cases
•A case is a user experience
•Complex case structures
•Knowledge based similarity assessment,
adaptation and learning

Figure 7-1. Knowledge Intensiveness line

The major problem associated with this knowledge intensive CBR approach is the knowledge acquisition bottleneck that CBR tried to solve in its early ages. For a long time the CBR approach to KBS development was seen as a possible solution to the knowledge acquisition and maintenance problems associated with rule based systems. However, as the field of CBR has matured, support has grown for the view that CBR has not alleviated these problems as hoped, but in many ways compounded them. It has become apparent that as opposed to just the need to acquire domain (case) knowledge there is also a need to acquire vocabulary knowledge, retrieval (similarity / indexing) knowledge, adaptation knowledge, and maintenance knowledge before a CBR system can be regarded as operational. The knowledge required for these containers can be obtained from domain experts or through automated learning methods.

In this situation, the KI-CBR approach seems even more promising because – as we have already mentioned – it facilitates the reusability of explicit domain models through applications.

To assist forward domain knowledge acquisition from experts, we propose taking advantage of the ontological engineering community's efforts that could help in the acquisition of the knowledge needed in KI-CBR systems. The main idea behind our work is promoting knowledge reuse to help designing KI-CBR systems. More specifically, we are interested in two active areas of Artificial Intelligence research: Ontologies and PSMs.

The core of our proposal is CBROnto, an ontology incorporating common CBR terminology that provides the vocabulary for describing CBR systems and reasoning about them. CBROnto provides with consistent semantics associated with the domain of CBR and with CBR terminology that guides case representation and allows the description of flexible, generic and homogeneous CBR PSMs.

Based on CBROnto we propose COLIBRI: an architecture that focuses on the design of KI-CBR systems. COLIBRI proposes designing KI-CBR systems using interconnected collaborating knowledge *components*, such as domain ontologies and CBR terminology, tasks and methods. COLIBRI main contribution is the specification of the KI-CBR approach as a knowledge reuse process, and the identification of the building blocks that are connected and integrated.

Another important aspect of our work is the formalization of CBROnto/COLIBRI using Description Logics (DLs). We have formalized CBROnto into DLs to experiment how its associated reasoning mechanisms are well suited to solve the tasks involved in the design of a KI-CBR system and in the execution cycle of this system.

This paper is organized in seven sections apart from this introduction. Section 2 revises the main ideas of CBR systems in general, and KI-CBR systems in particular. Section 3 cites other classical approaches that propose to build KBS within the basis of knowledge sharing and reuse. We briefly explain the main building blocks used in these approaches (and also used in COLIBRI): Ontologies and Problem Solving Methods. In this section, we also review the basic ideas of the knowledge formalization approach that we use in our work: Description Logics. The core of our work begins in Section 4 where COLIBRI/CBROnto architecture is described. It focuses on the knowledge components that participate in a KI-CBR system and how they are integrated. Section 5 describes our CBR ontology, CBROnto, which captures terminology that is semantically important in a CBR system and includes knowledge about the CBR tasks and methods. The design of KI-CBR systems using COLIBRI is exemplified in Section 6 with an application to generate Spanish poetry. Section 7 describes the evolution of our work and the current implementation of the COLIBRI architecture into jCOLIBRI[1] an object-oriented framework codified in Java. Section 8 concludes this paper, reviews its main contributions and describes our current and future lines of work.

2. CASE BASED REASONING (A BRIEF INTRODUCTION)

Development of AI systems so far has concentrated in distilling experiences and examples to extract the knowledge and then representing

[1] http://sourceforge.net/projects/jCOLIBRI-cbr/.

that knowledge directly in the computer – as rules, frames, procedures, etc. Case Based Reasoning provides an alternative model. Experiences are represented as they are and use them directly in problem solving. The processing required to analyse the experience is delayed until the time the case is retrieved for solving a new problem. However, now the task is less haunting, because we only need to understand how the difference between the problem in the recalled experience and the current problem affects the solution proposed in the recalled experience. We do not need to understand the significance of all parameters or try to frame a general model of the problem. This briefly is the essence of the CBR approach.

CBR approaches have been applied to a wide range of problem types. This includes configuration (Clavier for auto-clave layout), diagnosis (Casey for heart diseases), interpretation (Hypo examines a legal case and based on previous cases, prepares arguments for and against the claim in the case), planning (Chef for recipe planning), classification (Protos for hearing disorders), design (Julia for meals), etc. They have been used in automated form as well as in the role of assistants to human decision making.

Case-Based Reasoning is both a paradigm for computer-based problem solvers and a model of human cognition. As a paradigm for computer-based problem solvers, the basic tasks in CBR are (Aamodt & Plaza 1994):

1. **Retrieving** a past case (a problem and solution) that resembles the current problem. Past cases reside in case memory. Case memory is similar to a database but it contains rich descriptions of prior cases stored as units and it allows for approximate retrieval. Retrieving a past case involves determining what features of a problem should be considered when looking for similar cases and how to measure degrees of similarity. This is referred to as the Indexing Problem.
2. **Reusing or adapting** the past solution to the current situation. Although the past case is similar to the current one, it may not be identical. If not, the past solution may have to be adjusted slightly to account for differences between the two problems.
3. **Revising** or applying the adapted solution and evaluating the results.
4. **Retaining, learning or updating** case memory. If the adapted solution works, a new case –composed of the problem just solved and the solution used– can be formed. If the solution at first fails, but can be repaired so the failure is avoided. The new case is composed of the problem just solved and the repaired solution. This new case is stored in case memory so that the new solution will be available for retrieval during future problem solving. In this way, the system becomes more competent as it gains experience.

Not all case-based problem solvers use all of the tasks. In some, there is no adaptation step. The retrieved solution is already known to be good enough without adaptation. In others, there is no memory update step. The case memory is mature and provides adequate coverage for problems in the domain.

Besides our work, there are other knowledge intensive approaches that assume that cases are enriched with explicit general domain knowledge, like CREEK/TrollCreek[2] (Aamodt 1990-2005), ROCADE (Fuchs and Mille 2000) and RESYN-CBR (Napoli et. al. 1996) and DIAL(Leake 1993). The role of the general domain knowledge is to enable a CBR system to reason with semantic and pragmatic criteria, rather than purely syntactic ones. By making the general domain knowledge explicit, the CBR system is able to interpret a situation in a more flexible and contextual manner than if this knowledge is compiled into predefined similarity metrics or vector of feature weights.

Next section introduces components that are suitable to be reused and could alleviate the knowledge acquisition burden.

3. KNOWLEDGE SHARING AND REUSE

Since the mid-1980s, knowledge engineers have developed a number of principles, methods and tools that have considerably improved the process of KBS development. For instance *Generic Tasks* (Chandrasekaran 1986), Role Limiting Methods (McDermott 1988), PROTÉGÉ (Musen 1989), *Components of Expertise* (Steels 1990), KADS (Wielinga *et al.* 1992) and CommonKADS (Schreiber *et al.* 1994).

These knowledge engineering approaches view a KBS as consisting of separate but interconnected collaborating components. Typically, components of a KBS include domain knowledge and Problem Solving Methods, which represent commonly occurring, domain-independent problem-solving strategies.

Our work shares the vision of KBS development as a process of knowledge component reuse (both domain and problem resolution knowledge), the integration, assembling and configuration of these components, and the vision of problem resolution as a task decomposition process into subtasks.

One of the main motivations underlying both ontologies and PSMs is to enable sharing and reuse of knowledge and reasoning behaviour across domains and tasks. PSMs and ontologies can be seen as complementary reusable components to construct KBSs from reusable components. They are complementary in the sense that ontologies are concerned with static domain

[2] http://dionysus.idi.ntnu.no/newcreek/.

knowledge while PSMs with dynamic reasoning knowledge. To build full applications of information and knowledge systems from reusable components, both PSMs and ontologies are required in a tightly integrated way. The integration of ontologies and PSMs is a possible solution to the interaction problem (Chandrasekaran et al. 1998), which states that representing knowledge for solving some problem is strongly affected by the nature of the problem and the inference strategy to be applied to the problem. Through ontologies and PSMs, this interaction can be made explicit and taken into consideration (Gómez-Pérez & Benjamins 1999).

The word *ontology* is used as a technical term by different groups to mean slightly different things. The better-known definition for ontology is: "*An ontology is a specification of a conceptualization*" (Gruber 1993).

Ontologies aim at capturing domain knowledge in a generic way. Ontology, therefore, provides a commonly agreed understanding of a domain, which can be reused and shared across applications and groups (Uschold and Gruninger 1996). Ontologies provide a common vocabulary of an area and define--with different levels of formality--the meaning of the terms and the relations between them. Ontologies are usually organized in taxonomies and they typically contain modelling primitives such as classes, relations, functions, axioms, and instances (Gruber 1993).

3.1 Problem-Solving Methods

PSMs describe the reasoning process of a Knowledge Based System in an implementation- and domain-independent manner. A PSM defines a way to achieve the goal of a task. It has input and output and can decompose a task into subtasks. In addition, a PSM specifies the data flow between its subtasks. Control knowledge determines the execution order and iterations of the subtasks of a PSM. Control knowledge can be specified in advance, if known, or can be determined opportunistically at run time depending on the dynamic problem-solving situation (Benjamins 1995). PSMs can be used to efficiently achieve goals of tasks through the application of domain knowledge. They can play several roles in the knowledge-engineering process, such as guiding the acquisition process of domain knowledge and facilitating knowledge-based system development through their reuse.

Work on PSMs covers different areas such as the identification of task-specific PSMs (for diagnosis, planning, assessment, and so on), the storing and indexing of PSMs in libraries, and the formalizing of PSMs. The difficulty of reusing PSMs is that one has to find the right PSM (that does -part of- the job), check whether it is applicable in the situation at hand, and modify it to fit the domain. To reuse PSMs successfully in a real-life application, one has to understand these processes. For applications, see (Benjamins and Fensel 1998).

3.2 Ontology formalization with Description Logics

Several languages can be used to formalize the content of an ontology at the symbol level. Usually, a language is attached to a given ontology server. The most representative languages are ONTOLINGUA (Gruber 1993), CYCL (Lenat and Guha 1990), LOOM (MacGregor 1991), EXPRESS (Spibey 1991), CML (Schreiber et al. 1994), and KIF (*Knowledge Interchange Format*) (Genesereth and Fikes 1992). Each language is based on different knowledge representation paradigm, like DLs, Frame systems or predicate logic.

DLs based languages (like LOOM or RACER) root in the KL-ONE family (Brachman and Schmolze 1985), are commonly used to implement ontologies, and it is the technology we use in our model to formalize aspects of representation and reasoning.

The idea of developing knowledge representation systems based on a structured representation of knowledge was first pursued with Semantic Networks and Frame Systems. One problem of these solutions is the need of a formal ground to define the semantics of the knowledge representation. In this way, DLs were born trying to provide knowledge representation with this formal ground. In DLs, there are three types of formal objects (Donini et al. 1996):

- Concepts: Descriptions with a potentially complex structure, formed by composing a limited set of description-forming operators.
- Roles: Simple formal terms for properties.
- Individuals: Simple formal constructs intended to directly represent objects in the domain of interest as concept instances.

Concepts can be either primitive or defined. Defined concepts are represented in terms of necessary and sufficient conditions that individuals have to satisfy in order to be recognized as instances of those concepts. Primitive concepts are just represented as necessary conditions, so it is impossible to infer that individuals are instances of primitive concepts. However, if it is explicitly asserted that an individual is an instance of a primitive concept, the system will apply all the concept restrictions to the individual. Roles also can be primitive or defined.

Primitive roles introduce new necessary conditions in the role, and defined role introduce both necessary and sufficient conditions.

Concepts, roles and individuals are placed into taxonomy where more general concepts/roles will be above more specific concepts/roles. Likewise, individuals are placed below the concept(s) that they are instances of. Concepts and individuals inherit properties from descriptions that are more general as well as combine properties as appropriate. Thus, DL-Systems has two main components: A general schema concerning the classes of individuals to be represented built from primitive concepts and role restrictions, usually referred as *TBox*, and a partial or total instantiation of this schema, containing assertions relating either individuals to concepts or individuals to each other, usually referred as ABox.

A key feature of DLs is that the system can reason about concept descriptions, and automatically infer subsumption relations. We say that a concept C subsumes the concept D (C < D) if all the individuals that satisfy the description of D, also satisfy the description of C. There are several variations of deductive inferences, depending on the particular DL. Some of the most typical are Completion and Classification (Brachman and Schmolze 1985). In Completion, logical consequences of assertions about individuals are inferred, and in Classification, each new concept is placed under the most specific concepts that subsume it.

The core of DL-Systems is its concept language, which can be viewed as a set of constructs for denoting concepts and relationships among concepts. An assertion language is also defined which lets express individual features.

4. COLIBRI/ CBRONTO ARQUITECTURE

COLIBRI (*Cases and Ontology Libraries Integration for Building Reasoning Infrastructures*) was born to design KI-CBR systems that combine specific cases with other types of general knowledge and reasoning methods. COLIBRI views KI-CBR systems as consisting of collaborating knowledge components and uses a CBR Ontology (CBROnto) as the unifying framework that structures and organizes different types of knowledge according to the role that each one plays. CBROnto captures knowledge about CBR tasks and methods, includes CBR dependent but domain-independent terms, and aims to unify case specific and general domain knowledge representational needs.

We propose the two-layered architecture shown in Figure 7-2. The lower layer provides with domain specific knowledge while the top layer is used as a bridge between the domain knowledge and the generic PSMs. This way, the specific domain model is interchangeable and the same knowledge could play different roles within different contexts of problem resolution (Díaz and González 2000).

For each designed CBR system, COLIBRI integrates different knowledge sources, namely: general domain knowledge, acquired by reusing ontologies; cases, described using this domain knowledge and CBROnto terms; knowledge extracted from the case base using inductive techniques such as Formal Concept Analysis; DLs inference mechanisms, and CBROnto knowledge about tasks and methods.

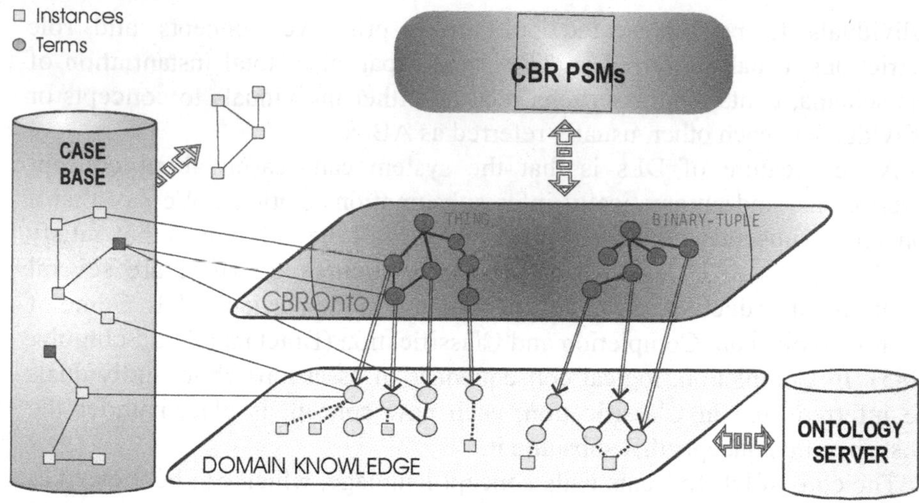

Figure 7-2. COLIBRI Architecture

To take advantage of the domain knowledge acquired by reusing ontologies, the knowledge needed by the CBR methods, or at least part of it, should be expressed in a similar way. CBROnto provides terminology about CBR, captures CBR semantically *important* terms and provides vocabulary for describing issues involved in the CBR methods. CBROnto includes CBR dependent but domain-independent terms that make possible different types of CBR. These terms are used as the junction between the domain knowledge and the Problem Solving Methods that are defined using CBR terminology but with a domain-independent perspective (see Figure 7-2). CBROnto aims to unify case specific and general domain knowledge representational needs.

After domain modelling, during the phase of integration the designer classifies the domain terms (concepts and relations) with respect to the CBROnto terms to "type" knowledge elements according to the role they play in the CBR methods. CBROnto terminology serves as the syntactic and semantic "glue" between the domain terminology and the reusable and generic PSMs.

That mechanism allows the CBR methods to be domain independent because they only refer to the CBROnto terms that are correspondingly linked to the domain terminology by a classification mechanism. Note the designer doesn't classify one by one every domain term because due to the inheritance mechanism only the top-level terms in the hierarchies should be classified.

Table 7-1. Knowledge Components

Knowledge Component	How?
0. CBROnto terminology	• Reuse (see section V)
1. Model of domain knowledge	• Reuse domain ontologies when possible (see next subsection)
2. Initial Case Base 2.1. Formal Concept Analysis	• Define case structure using the domain terminology (1) together with CBROnto terminology (0) (see section V) • Populate the case base • Apply FCA to extract knowledge from the cases and complement the domain knowledge model
3. Reasoner	(see Section V) • Reuse PSMs from COLIBRI library • Classification based Integration = bridge the gap between CBROnto terminology used in PSMs and domain terminology • Method configuration (adjust parameters)

Besides ontological knowledge, the other main source of knowledge in our system is the expert user who, helped and guided by CBROnto, *tells* the CBR methods that perform the tasks how to use the domain knowledge. CBROnto integrates the overlapping roles of the domain knowledge in all the CBR tasks, namely CBROnto represents the way each one of the tasks will take advantage of the available domain knowledge.

Table 7-1 summarizes the knowledge components that participate in the design of a KI-CBR system and how they are integrated. The table also references the section in this paper where a complete description of the corresponding knowledge component and how it is integrated in the KI-CBR system.

4.1 Domain Knowledge acquisition

We make an issue of domain knowledge acquisition and study how the ontological engineering community efforts could help us to acquire the knowledge needed in a KI-CBR application. Most of the KBSs –including the KB CBR systems– have some reusable ontological content but it is often influenced by the specific task, the restrictions of the representation language, and the specific inference procedures employed.

We state that ontologies can be useful for designing KI-CBR applications because they allow the knowledge engineer to use knowledge already acquired, conceptualised and implemented in a formal language, reducing considerably the knowledge acquisition bottleneck. Moreover, the reuse of ontologies from a library also benefits from their reliability and consistency.

We know of little interactions among the CBR community and the ontological community although the knowledge in ontologies is especially well suited to be shared, and many CBR systems codify this kind of domain knowledge. Ontologies may help in the creation of complex, multirelational knowledge structures to support the CBR methods.

We are mainly interested in two types of ontologies:

- Domain ontologies provide the vocabulary for describing a domain and interpreting a description of a problem in that domain;
- Task ontologies provide the vocabulary for describing terms involved in the PSMs, which could be attached to similar tasks that may, or may not, be in the same domain.

The activities performed by the CBR application designer to model a domain are summed up as follows:

1. The designer begins with a preliminary idea of what domain is to be modelled, and selects from a library those ontologies that are potentially useful. For example, if we were modelling the used-car domain, a sensible choice would be the Vehicles ontology –available in the Ontology Server (Farquhar et al. 1997)–, which comprises knowledge about "*vehicles that are typically bought and sold through the classified ads*".
2. The designer must solve the integration problems detected. We must point out that the issue of coherent integration of definitions from different ontologies is still an open problem.
3. Because ontologies are very general and reusable, sometimes all the definitions inside an ontology are not useful for our concrete domain model. The elimination of not relevant terms is not essential but, in our approach, will effect on the final system efficiency and quality because the search space will be smaller and contain only relevant terms. Notice that the selection of a definition can provoke the automatic inclusion of others interrelated definitions that cannot be eliminated and conversely, the elimination of some definitions could cause others to be erased.
4. The designer includes new definitions, just in case some useful specific definitions for our domain are not included in the chosen ontologies.
5. Unfortunately, when there are not appropriate ontologies to be reused, an effort is needed to build a new ontology or knowledge base.

5. CBRONTO

CBROnto is an ontology including general terminology related to CBR systems. CBROnto is conceptually structured in:

- Terminology related with the tasks and methods hierarchies.
- Terminology related with the definition of the case structures; and related with different knowledge roles used in the PSMs; and terms used to organize and classify the domain knowledge.

5.1 Terminology to define the case structure

Cases in the case base should be described by means of the vocabulary provided by the domain terminology. The issue of case representation involves deciding the type and the structure of the domain knowledge within the cases. To help in the case structure authoring tasks, we propose a framework to represent cases based on the CBROnto terminology together with a set of PSMs that works with such representations.

We work with a general structured case representation where individuals are concept instances and concepts are organized in a hierarchy with inheritance. In our approach, cases are linked within a semantic network of domain knowledge and will be described by using both the domain vocabulary provided by the domain model, and the CBR vocabulary provided by the CBROnto. Cases in the case base won't have, in general, the same structure but the designer could define different *types of cases*.

Domain ontologies facilitate the system designer defining possible case structures, because they provide with standardized vocabulary. Besides, CBROnto provides with semantic CBR terminology to define cases structures and express (using classification) domain terminology in CBR terms.

CBROnto captures representation primitives commonly used in the case-based representation languages, as HAS-DESCRIPTION, HAS-SOLUTION, HAS-RESULT, SIMILARITYMEASURE, WEIGHT, GOAL, PRECONDITION, DESCRIPTION, SOLUTION, RESULT or DESCRIPTION-PROPERTY, TEMPORAL-RELATION, DEPENDENCE, STRUCTURAL-RELATION, SPATIAL-RELATION, PART-OF, STEP, AFTER, BEFORE, DURING, DESIGN-CASE, ADAPTATION-CASE, PLANNING-CASE, DIAGNOSIS, EVALUATE, EXPLAIN, DESIGN, SOLVE, SEARCH, KIND_OF_REASONING, ...

Beside the representation primitives, as CBROnto is CBR-wise, it offers predefined types of cases and methods, that can be particularized, to be used within certain prototypical types of CBR (planning, design, diagnostic, prediction), implying the use of certain "type" of CBROnto terms, for example, temporal relations, goals and precondition for planning, or spatial and structural relations for design.

Our representational framework allows complex structures and does not restrict the possible relations among the parts of a case, facilitates the definition of cases having different structures, is able to handle incomplete cases and allows default values (by inheritance).

5.1.1 Case Organization: Formal Concept Analysis

Regarding case organization, the straight alternative in our system is the use of the domain terminology as the case organization structure. Although our framework allows this choice, the alternative we are using is the computation of a different index structure by Formal Concept Analysis (FCA), an inductive technique that elicits knowledge embedded in a given case library (Díaz and Gonzalez 2001a). The lattice induced through FCA provides an efficient indexing scheme for the cases available when the lattice was computed. In (Díaz and González 2001 a-c) we describe classification-based retrieval and the utility of Galois lattices as structures to classify and retrieve cases.

The use of Galois lattices and Formal Concept Analysis can support CBR application designers, in the task of discovering knowledge embedded in the cases. FCA applied on a case library provides an internal sight of the conceptual structure and allows finding patterns, regularities and exceptions among the cases. Moreover, it extracts certain dependence rules between the attributes describing the cases, which will be used to guide the query formulation process.

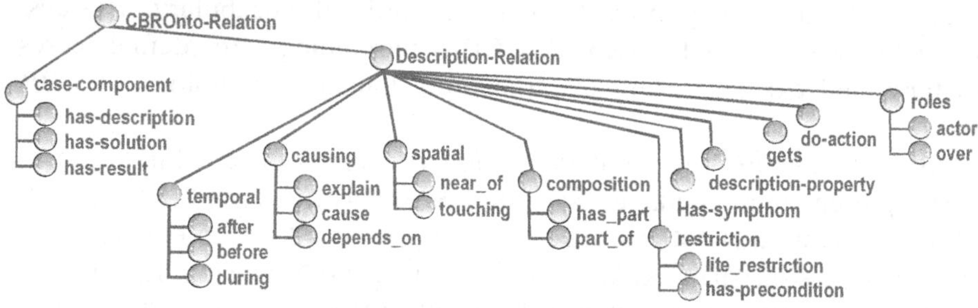

Figure 7-3. Types of relation in CBROnto (excerpt)

What we propose is the application of FCA as an inductive technique, guided by the domain knowledge, to elicit the attribute dependency knowledge inside a case library, and use it to complete the knowledge already acquired by other techniques of domain modelling.

Besides the dependency rules, FCA application to a case library provides an internal sight of the case base conceptual structure, because it extracts the formal concepts and the hierarchical relations among them, where related cases are clustered according to their shared properties. The explicit construction and use of the concept lattice to organize the cases in the library provides us with certain benefits. The concepts in the lattice represent maximal groupings of cases with shared properties. The utility of these groupings is that for a given query we can access all the cases that share properties with the query at the same time, so that they are grouped under the same concept. The order between the lattice elements allows structuring the library according to the attributes describing the cases. The lower in the graph, the more characteristics can be said about the cases, i.e., the more general concepts are higher up than the more specific ones.

5.1.2 Typing the domain relations

CBROnto provides with a hierarchical classification of different types of relations that typically appear when describing cases. The explicit representation of the types of relations is useful to find relational patterns into the case base, and to define generic PSMs. Each relation in Figure 7-3 can be used either directly into the case structure definition or indirectly through the integration process. Remember that this integration is based on classifying the domain relations below the CBROnto relations.

Relations in Figure 7-3 identify the roles that the domain relations play in the CBR system and in its PSMs. For example, identify the case composing parts, which are the symptoms, which are the goals achieved by the case, or the steps of the solution. This allows for a semantic classification of the domain relations from the CBR point of view, i.e., from the role they play into the CBR PSMs. Subsection "similarity types" shows an example. Different types of case similarities are defined depending on the types of relations that appear in the cases.

5.1.3 Example: case structure and integration CBROnto-domain

Within COLIBRI two layered architecture shown in Figure 7-2, we use classification to relate the specific domain terms with the CBROnto terms. Suppose a domain relation that is used to describe a property of the domain cases. For example, `color`. With our framework, it will be classified as a subrelation of `description-property` because is a relation used to describe a domain property. The same mechanism is used to classify other kinds of relations as `temporal`, `composition` or `spatial`.

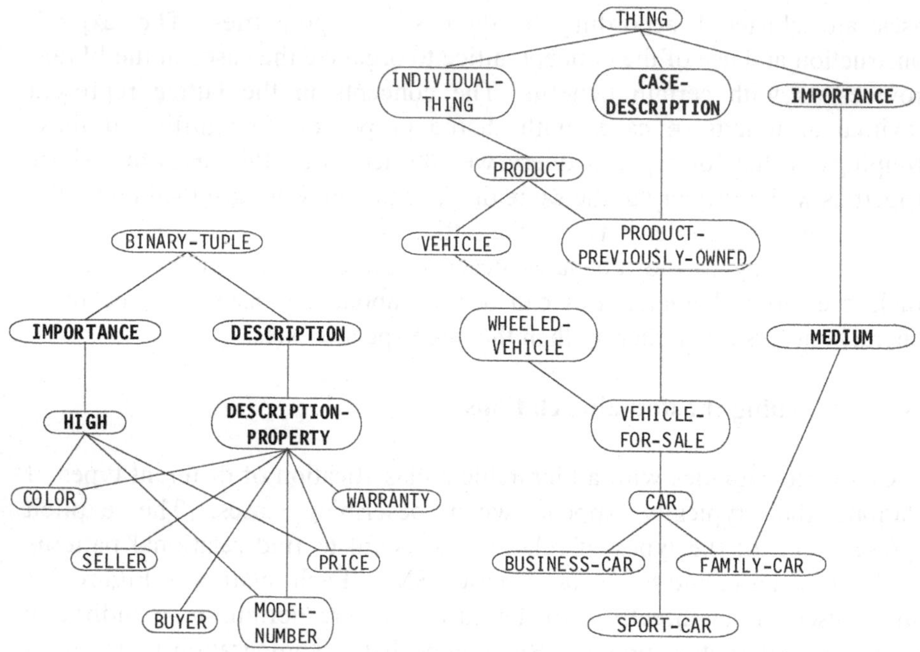

Figure 7-4. Integration based on classification (CBROnto terms in bold)

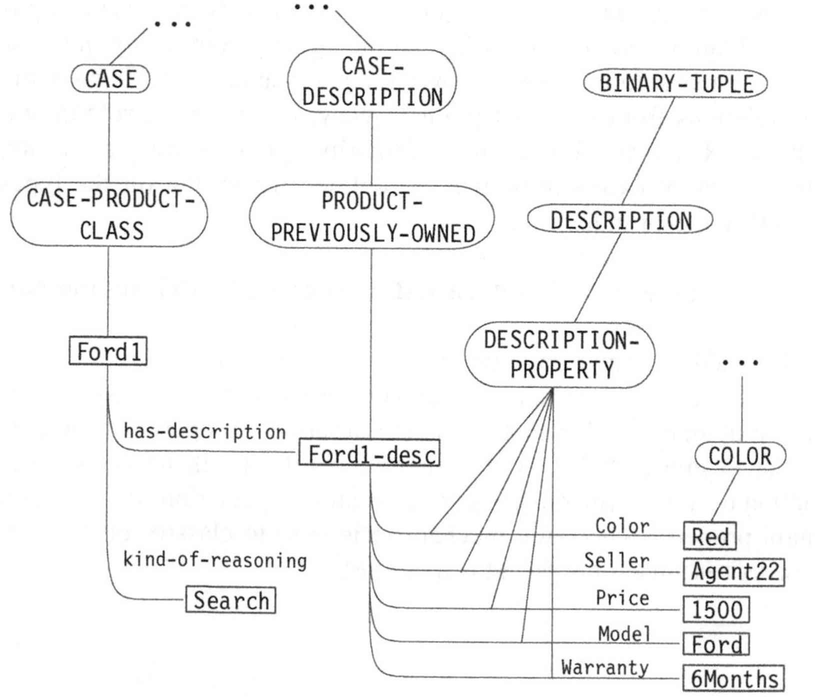

Figure 7-5. Case Structure

We are using relation classification here, but the mechanism is similar in the concept hierarchy. For example, once we have modelled the used-car domain by means of the `Vehicles` and `Product` Ontologies we want to represent the different types of cases. We would like to have cases representing second-hand products and without solution. Each case can include one or more products. We are building the case-type concept `CASE-PRODUCT-CLASS` with the structure of Figure 7-5. The integration mechanism classifies the `PRODUCT-PREVIOUSLY-OWNED` domain concept below the CBROnto `CASE-DESCRIPTION` concept. With this representation, the `PRODUCT-PREVIOUSLY-OWNED` instances –from the `Product` ontology– are used as the description components of the `CASE-PRODUCT-CLASS` cases. Due to the classification mechanism, instances of `FAMILY-CAR`, `SPORT-CAR`, `BUSINESS-CAR`, `CAR`, and `VEHICLE-FOR-SALE`, are appropriate instances to be used to describe a `CASE-PRODUCT-CLASS` case.

Also based on classification, our framework provides with a way to express preferences between the terms. This mechanism can be used for many purposes, and either by the designer, by the final user of the designed CBR application, or by the organization methods.

The importance for the case descriptors used during retrieval can be expressed by classifying them under the `IMPORTANCE` terms: `HIGH`, `MEDIUM`, `LOW`, and `NONE`. The domain independent CBR methods will prefer the domain relations classified under the `HIGH` relation and avoid the `NONE` classified ones. Figure 7-4 illustrates the use of the `HIGH` relation to strengthen the `color`, `model-number` and `price` domain relations; and the use of the `MANDATORY` concept to indicate that only the `FAMILY-CAR` type of `CASE-DESCRIPTION` should be considered for this retrieval.

5.2 Tasks and Methods

In Section 4 we defended the acquisition of domain knowledge for KI-CBR systems by reusing domain ontologies. In this section, we consider problem solving knowledge and we focus on the task/method view of CBROnto.

We describe CBROnto task/method hierarchies and the method description language. Then we are describing how CBROnto solves two problems that are typically found when applying PSMs. The first problem is because PSMs may use different terminology than the one used in the domain. CBROnto bridges the gap between domain knowledge and PSMs using a mapping mechanism that is based on classification. The second problem refers to PSM knowledge requirements. Again, classification is the mechanism we use to check if the method knowledge requirements are satisfied by the application context –made of the domain knowledge and the case base.

5.2.1 CBROnto as a Task and Method Ontology

A useful way to describe problem-solving behaviour is in terms of the tasks to be solved, the goals to be achieved, the methods that will accomplish those tasks, and the domain knowledge that those methods need. A description along these lines is referred to as a *knowledge level* description (Newell 1982). Although various authors have applied knowledge level analysis to CBR systems, the most relevant work is the CBR task structure developed in (Aamodt & Plaza 1994) influenced by the Components of Expertise Methodology (Steels 1990). At the highest level of generality, they describe the general CBR cycle in terms of four tasks (Figure 7-6): *Retrieve* the most similar case/s, *Reuse* its/their knowledge to solve the problem, *Revise* the proposed solution and *Retain* the experience. Each one of the four CBR tasks involves a number of more specific sub-tasks. There are methods to solve tasks either by decomposing a task in subtasks or by solving it directly.

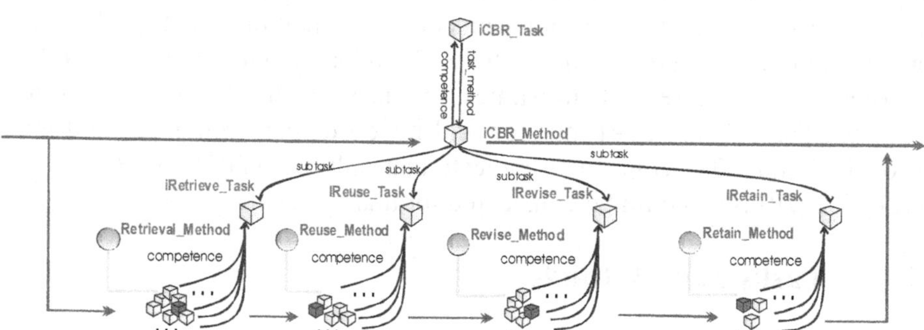

Figure 7-6. CBR Task decomposition into the four "RE" subtasks

CBROnto includes the capabilities for describing a library of PSMs associated to the main CBR tasks. CBROnto describes CBR PSMs by relating them to terms and relations regarding tasks, requirements and domain characteristics. CBROnto includes terms of the method description language that are used to formalize PSMs. CBROnto also includes a simple task ontology influenced by Aamodt and Plaza's task structure that defines the terminology related to the CBR tasks from a domain and method independent point of view. Methods in our library are organized around the tasks they resolve.

Our approach relates to other systems like HICAP (Muñoz et al. 1999) that solves problems with HTNs (*Hierarchical Task Networks*) retrieving methods for decomposing tasks into subtasks. The main difference is that HICAP considers methods to solve problem-specific tasks, and cases in the case base are methods themselves that are retrieved in a case based sense. Our task/method structure only refers to CBR tasks and methods –and not problem-specific tasks and methods.

We represent the task-method structure by using two related concept hierarchies. The task hierarchy is rooted by the `cbr_task` concept representing the generic task of "*solve a problem and learn from the experience*" (Figure 7-7). The method used to solve this task is CBR itself, which is represented by `cbr_method` that is the root concept in the method hierarchy. There are four subconcepts of the `cbr_task` concept regarding the four basic CBR tasks: `retrieve_task`, `reuse_task`, `revise_task` and `retain_task`. Each one of these concepts represents a subtask that results from the application of the decomposition method `CBR_method` to solve `CBR_task`.

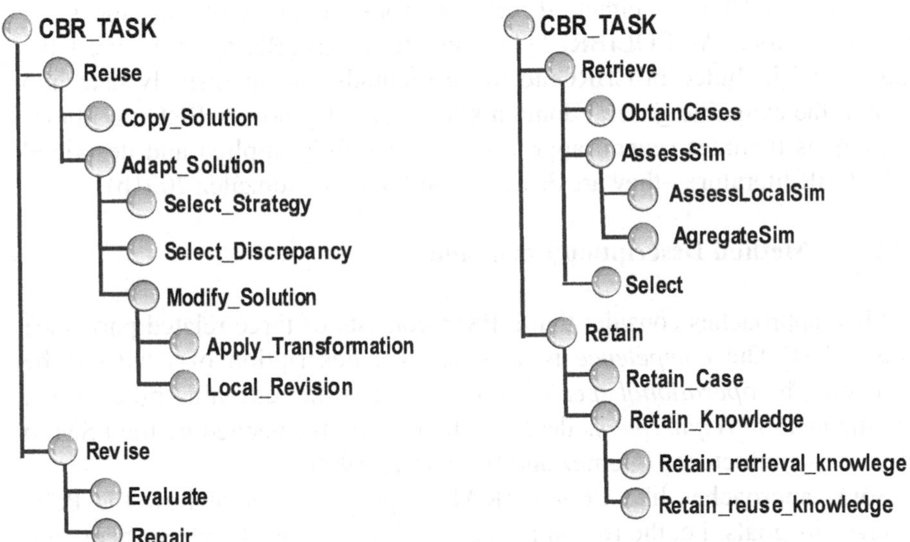

Figure 7-7. CBROnto Task Decomposition Structure

Depending on the method applied to solve a task, it results on a different set of subtasks to be solved themselves. In the task taxonomy, below the concepts corresponding to the four basic CBR tasks, there are concepts for all the subtasks resulting from the different methods. For example, below `retrieve_task` we find concepts for all the subtasks resulting from all the retrieval methods. Each one of the methods represents the information about the subtasks applied for it.

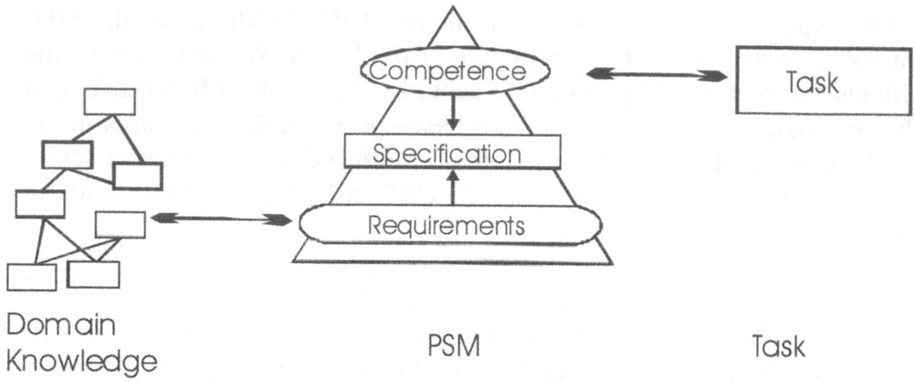

Figure 7-8. PSMs architecture (Benjamins & Fensel 98)

As a corresponding taxonomy, below the `cbr_method` concept there is a subconcept hierarchy classifying different types of methods regarding the task they solve. The two hierarchies allow the representation of certain ontological assumptions in CBROnto. For example, instances of `retrieval_methods` –either direct or not– relate with instances of `retrieve_task`. As COLIBRI helps designing KI-CBR systems, we have studied and included in CBROnto those methods that intensively take into account the available general domain knowledge. By now, CBROnto library of methods includes several approaches successfully applied and described in the CBR literature –they are described in (Díaz & González 2001b).

5.2.2 Method Description Language

Most approaches consider that a PSM consists of three related parts (see Figure 7-8). The *competence* is a declarative description of *what* can be achieved. The *operational specification* describes the reasoning process, i.e. *how* the method *requirements* describe the knowledge needed by the PSM to achieve its competence (Gómez and Benjamins 1999)

Some approaches like CommonKADS specify much of how the PSM achieves its goals, i.e. the reasoning steps, the data flows between them, and the control that guides their execution. As we focus on PSM applicability assessment, we consider what the method does, i.e. the task it solves, and its knowledge requirements, and leave control-flow issues to informal documentation and method implementation code. This allows us to use a black box type of method reuse.

Our approach to the specification of PSMs competence and requirements makes use of ontologies and provides two main advantages. First, it allows formal specifications that add a precise meaning and enables reasoning support. Second, it provides us with important benefits regarding reuse because task and method ontologies can be shared by different systems. Each method in the library is represented as a `cbr_method` instance (direct or not) that relates with:

- The method name.
- The method informal description.
- The `cbr_task` representing the method competence.
- The method knowledge requirements.
- The input requirements that must be satisfied to apply the method.

Method internal reasoning processes are not formalized as part of the descriptions used to reason with. Instead, PSM descriptions relate to functions that implement them. Input to a PSM is a list of instances, representing either values or structured individuals, whose defining concepts reside in the CBROnto method ontology.

5.2.3 PSMs Mappings through Classification

As PSMs are used to accomplish tasks by applying domain knowledge, the external *context* of a PSM is formed by the task to be solved and the domain knowledge to be applied (see Figure 7-8). When we want to use PSMs to build a KBS, we have to connect the PSMs with both the tasks and the domain knowledge. Since PSMs are generic and reusable components, they may not always perfectly fit in a context, or in other words, there may be gaps.

In our model, it is not necessary to consider task-method gaps because tasks and PSMs are defined using CBROnto as unifying terminology. Instead, we take care of gaps between methods and domain knowledge. They exist mainly for two reasons.

The PSMs may use different terminology than that of the domain knowledge in which case a *renaming* process can bridge the gap. When designing a KI-CBR system using COLIBRI, after domain knowledge acquisition, the system designer performs an integration phase based on classifying the domain terms –concepts and relations– with respect to CBROnto terms. Due to the inheritance mechanism, only the top-level terms in the hierarchies should be classified. This mechanism allows CBROnto's methods to capture the problem-solving behaviour in a domain-independent manner, referring only to CBROnto terms that are correspondingly linked to the domain knowledge terms by classification.

McDermott (McDermott 1988) coined the term *knowledge roles* to refer to the way in which problem solving knowledge requires domain knowledge of certain types. PSMs represent different strategies to solve a task, and these strategies determine the roles that domain-dependent knowledge plays. Our approach relies on the use of CBROnto terminology and classification to "type" knowledge elements according to their role in the CBR methods. The roles that domain knowledge terms play in the CBR methods depend on how they are classified below CBROnto terms, i.e., classification integrates the acquired domain knowledge with the task/method knowledge of CBROnto and it defines the role that domain knowledge plays in the PSMs.

The second reason for the domain-method gap is that the knowledge required by a PSM may not be fully given by the available domain knowledge, in which case additional knowledge needs to be acquired. We describe in this paper how CBROnto method applicability in a certain context can be checked thanks to the described integration phase together with a declarative description of contexts of application and the knowledge requirements of PSMs.

Issues involved in reusing PSMs from a library include finding a suitable method and checking whether it is applicable in the current context. In the CBROnto library of methods, selection is simple because methods are organized around the tasks they resolve.

5.2.4 Method Requirements Representation

PSMs are defined in a domain independent way although they include certain knowledge requirements determining their applicability in a particular context. In this section, we propose a formalization of PSMs and method knowledge requirements using DLs[3]. This representation allows using its reasoning mechanisms to check the applicability of a method in a certain context.

Below the CBROnto `requirements` concept there is a taxonomy representing the knowledge requirements for each type of method. These requirements represent situations in which these types of methods are applicable. Each method individual is related with an instance of one of the `Requirements` subconcepts of the hierarchy according to the corresponding ontological assumptions. Figure 7-9 shows the requirements of the `CBR_Method`. It is applicable if there is a case base that is not empty, and there is a query to be solved.

`Requirements` descriptions include information about:

- The domain knowledge model. For example, depth and width properties of the concept and relation taxonomies are relevant to apply the retrieval methods using classification. (Díaz and González 2001b-c)
- The case base size. For example, the number of cases is relevant to assess the efficient use of the retrieval method by similarity computation.

[3] This is only an example of representation at the symbol level although other formalizations could also be applied to the conceptualization.

- The case types. For example, to apply an adaptation method there must be cases with solution.
- The knowledge roles that "type" domain knowledge terms according to their classification below CBROnto terms. For example, a term plays the "goal" role in the retrieval method by goal matching (Díaz and Gonzalez 2001 c) if it is classified below the `goal` CBROnto concept.
- Other CBROnto related knowledge, for example, instances of the `Similarity Measure` concept determine the applicability of the retrieval method by similarity computation, instances of the `RelevanceCriteria` concept determine the applicability of the retrieval method by relevance criteria (see (Díaz and González 2001 a-b-c) for a complete description of the retrieval methods), the adaptation cases –instances of the `AdaptationCase` concept– determine the applicability of the case-based adaptation method, etc.

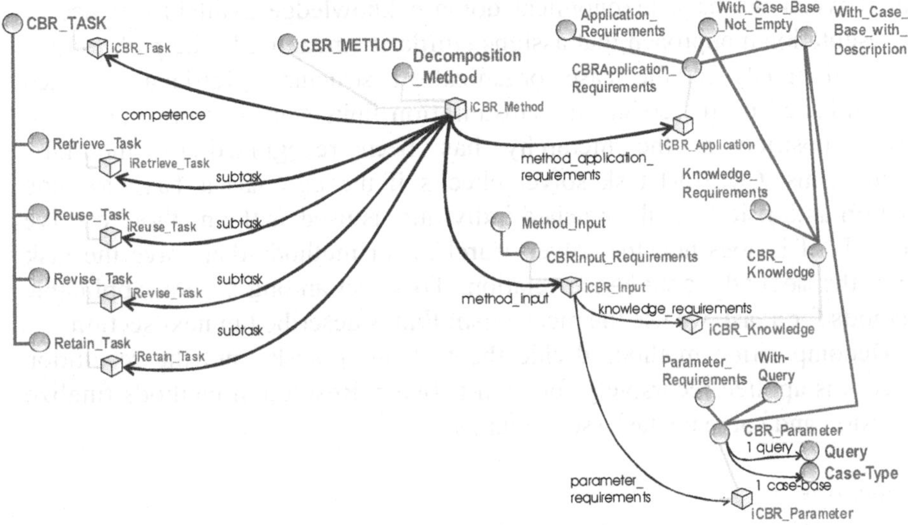

Figure 7-9. Requirements of the CBR method

Method competence is the task the method solves. In a particular KI-CBR system, several alternative methods can be applied to solve each task. In our model, each task can be linked with a preferred method instance. The `Task-method` relation links `cbr_task` instances with `cbr_method` instances maintaining CBROnto ontological assumptions. If a CBR system designer fixes a preferred method to solve the task, then a `task_method` link is asserted between the corresponding individuals.

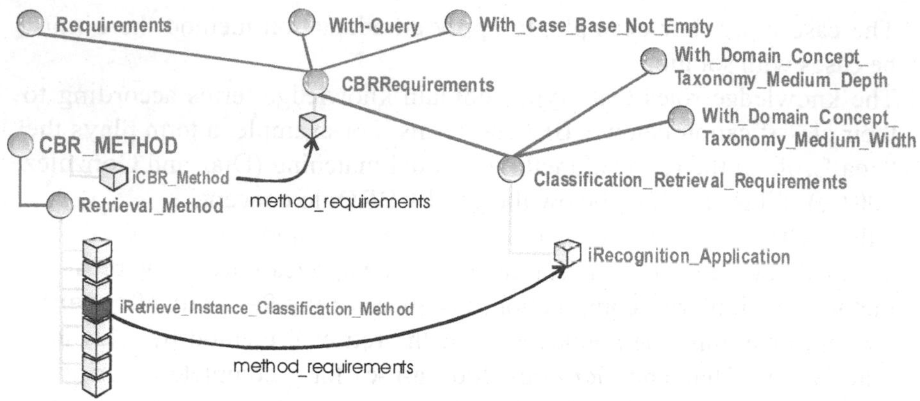

Figure 7-10. Requirements representation for one retrieval method

As an example, we use one retrieval methods that is particularly well suited when we have taxonomical domain knowledge available. It uses a representational approach that assigns similarity meaning to the path joining two individuals in the case organization structure. Retrieval is then accomplished by traversing the subsumption links starting from the query, whose position at the hierarchy has been recognized by the DLs mechanisms. COLIBRI task solver checks if the task has a `task_method` relation and, if it does, the reached individual is used as the method to solve the task. If it does not, the solver searches for methods that solve the task using the `method_competence` relation. To select among several applicable methods for a task we use the mechanism that is described in next section.

Decomposition methods divide the task in subtasks and the resolution process is applied recursively for each subtask. Resolution methods finalize recursion and solve the task (see Figure 7-11).

```
Resolve (iT)
1.Get the method individual to resolve the task: iM
2.Get the method functional specification iEF
4.If iM is a decomposition_method,
      Apply iEF to get the sequence of subtaks
      to be solved: iST1, ...., iSTn
      ResolveSeq(iSTn,ResolveSeq(iSTn-1, ... Resolve(iST1)...))
  Else % iM is a resolution method
   Apply iEF to solve the task iT
```

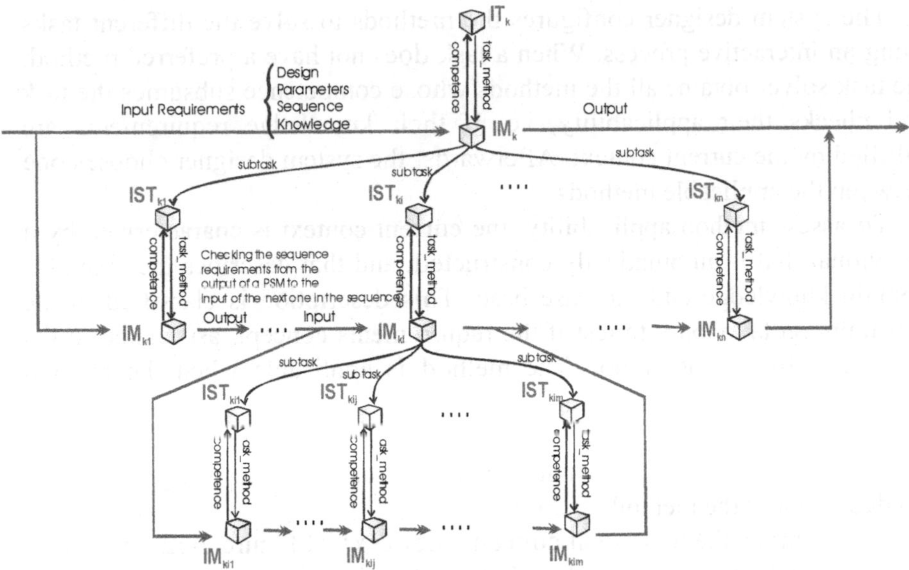

Figure 7-11. Task resolution process in COLIBRI

5.2.5 Selecting Applicable Methods for a Task

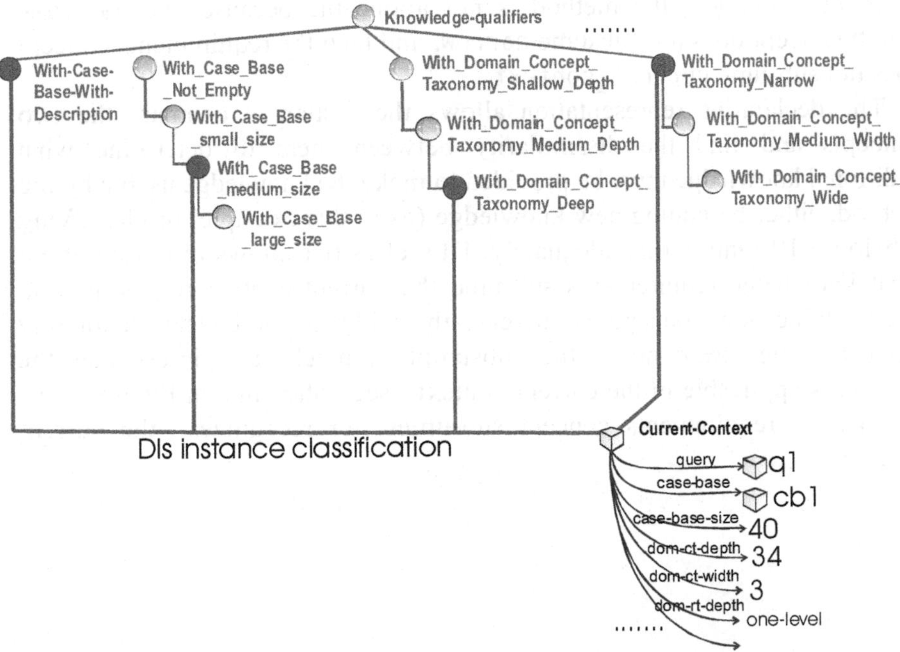

Figure 7-12. Context representation

The system designer configures the methods to solve the different tasks using an interactive process. When a task does not have a preferred method, the task solver obtains all the methods whose competence subsumes the task and checks their applicability, i.e. if their knowledge requirements are fulfilled by the current context. Afterwards, the system designer chooses one between the applicable methods.

To assess method applicability, the current context is characterized by a individual that is automatically constructed, and that describes the available domain knowledge and the case base. This description is classified in the subsumption taxonomy to test if the requirements concept, associated to the method, subsumes it or not. The method is applicable when the method requirements concept subsumes (recognizes) the context. Besides, if a method is not applicable, this mechanism makes possible to explain why the method does not fit the situation and what additional knowledge would be needed to apply the method.

For example, the individual `current_context` of Figure 7-12, represents a situation where there are a deep but narrow domain concept taxonomy, a relation taxonomy with only one level and a case base of medium size. We know that the retrieval method by instance classification behaves adequately when the domain concept taxonomy has enough concepts, i.e. the domain concept taxonomy depth and width are at least of medium level.

In this situation, the method is not applicable because, the `medium-width` concept does not subsume `narrow`, and then the requirements concept does not subsume `current_context`.

The declarative representation allows the system to compare the two concepts and find the dissimilarity between them to determine what additional knowledge must be provided to make the knowledge usable by the method, either by adding new knowledge (as in this example) or classifying it below CBROnto terms adequately. DLs classifier allows to reason about what knowledge requirements subsume the current context representation. After adding new concepts to increase the width of the concept taxonomy –that becomes *wide* now– the subsumption mechanism infers that the method is applicable in the current context –see dotted line in Figure 7-13– because its requirements concept subsumes –or recognizes– the current context.

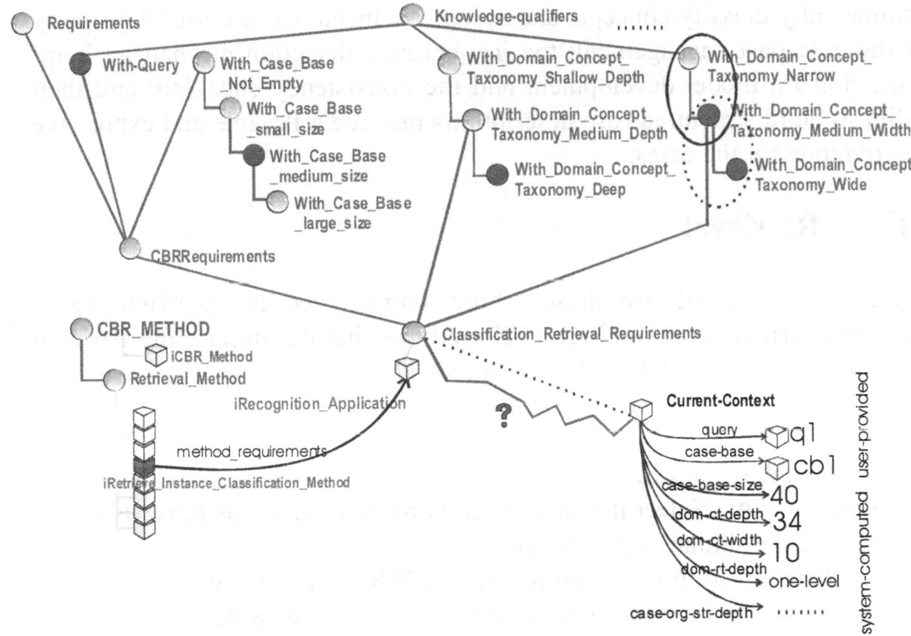

Figure 7-13. Method requirements checking with DLs reasoning

5.3 PSMs for CBR

In previous section, we have described the automatic, general and recursive task resolution mechanism that COLIBRI uses. It starts with the task to solve, and finds the alternative methods whose competence subsumes it. These methods are offered to the CBR system designer who fixes a preferred method to solve the task. Decomposition methods divide the task in subtasks and the resolution process is applied recursively for each subtask. Resolution methods finalize recursion and solve the task.

Although it is not the purpose of this paper to review all the methods in the CBROnto library, in this section we are describing some representative retrieval methods. We focus in the methods doing an intensive use of the knowledge and the DLs reasoning capabilities.

During the last few years, Description Logics (DLs) have become systems of great interest for the Case-Based Reasoning community. There has been a body of work on taking advantage of the DL reasoning mechanisms for the tasks involved in the CBR cycle. Although a number of different approaches are considered, they all focus on the intuition that the formal semantics and the capability of DLs to maintain a terminological taxonomy are interesting properties to manage a case base. Moreover, DL declarative semantics helps in the domain comprehension; their ability to automatically classify concepts and recognise instances is a useful property for the case base management; the incoherence detection mechanism helps in the domain model development and the consistency checking; and their ability to build structured case descriptions provide a flexible and expressive way to represent the cases.

5.4 Retrieval

Retrieval methods are those whose competence is `retrieve_task`. CBROnto formalizes several retrieval methods that decompose the retrieval task into one or more of the following subtasks:

- `Obtain cases`. Select the initial case set (CS)
- `Assess similarity`. Assess the similarity between the query and each one of the cases in CS.
- `Select cases`. Select the case or cases to be returned as retrieval result based on the similarity assessment.

COLIBRI is useful for prototyping CBR systems. When it offers different methods to solve a task, the user (i.e., the system designer) is required to choose one of them. CBROnto's retrieval methods can be described in terms of their knowledge requirements, the subtasks they solve and the methods that are suitable to resolve each one of their subtasks.

As an example, we describe now the PSMs implementing two typical approaches of CBR retrieval: the computational and the representational approach.

- **Computational Method.** The most straightforward CBR approach to retrieval is the one that computes all the similarity values during the retrieval process. The CBROnto similarity framework allows representing, in a declarative way, several alternatives to compute numerical similarity values for complex case representations. Intuitively the domain knowledge base contains similarity knowledge that should participate in the similarity assessment. Apart from the concrete values filling the common attributes, objects that are closer in the hierarchy should be more similar than those that are further apart. Taking this consideration into account there should be two components in the similarity result: one due to the closeness in the class hierarchy (*position similarity*) and other due to the attribute values (*contents similarity*), that are combined using a certain *combination* function.

– Knowledge requirements: Query, Case Base, Similarity Measures
– Subtasks:
  - `Obtain cases` task is solved by a resolution method that returns the whole case base as the initial case set (CS).

- `Assess similarity` task is solved by the numeric similarity computation method, a resolution method that computes the similarity measure between the query and each one of the cases in CS (ordered by their similarity with the query).
- `Select cases` task can be solved by:
  a) `Select all` method: a resolution method that selects all the cases from CS.
  b) `Select best` method: a resolution method that selects the best case according the similarity results obtained in the `assess similarity` task.

- **Representational Method.** This approach assigns similarity meaning to the path joining two cases in the case organization structure and the domain knowledge basc, and retrieval is accomplished by traversing that structure starting from the position of the query. We have applied this choice using an instance classification method that uses the subsumption links to define the distance between two individuals. The usefulness of this kind of approach will depend on the knowledge structure where the cases are located.

– Knowledge Requirements: Query, Case Base, Relation Path (from the query to the individual that is going to be classified)

– Subtasks:

- `Assess similarity` task is solved by instance classification method.
- `Select cases` task can be solved by select all method, select one method or select computation method[4].

5.4.1 Similarity Types

CBROnto supports a declarative similarity framework to represent semantic similarity measures in KI-CBR systems, where the domain knowledge should strongly influence similarity. Our similarity framework allows representing similarity measures for structured case representation where individuals are concept instances and concepts are organized in a hierarchy with inheritance. This approach requires similarity assessment methods that allow comparing two differently structured individuals and that take into account the influence of the domain term hierarchies over similarity (Díaz & González 2001 (b)). CBROnto allows representing different similarity types depending on the contributing terms, namely it allows defining different similarity types depending on a semantic classification of the attributes –relations– below the CBROnto terms. The structural

4 Note that with this choice the case base is filtered by classification and then the retrieved cases are filtered a second time using the (more expensive) numerical computation to a fewer number of cases.

similarity (represented by the STRUCTURAL-TYPE instance) will be computed based on the composition relations (classified below the STRUCTURAL CBROnto relations, as PART-OF or HAS-PART), the semantics similarity (SEMANTIC-TYPE instance) is due to all the concepts and relations describing the meaning of the case, the temporal similarity (TEMPORAL-TYPE instance) is computed due to the temporal relations(classified below the TEMPORAL CBROnto relation, as DURING, BEFORE or AFTER), the causal similarity (CAUSAL-TYPE instance) uses the CBROnto causal relations (DEPENDS-ON, CAUSE, EXPLAINS), and so on.

6. AN EXAMPLE: POETRY GENERATION WITH KI-CBR

The knowledge that a human writer puts into play when carrying out when composing poetry can be formalised in terms of CBR by considering how a prose message has been converted into poetry in the past. A CBR application that generates Spanish poetry versions of texts –also in Spanish– provided by the user is presented as an example of how the theory described so far can be put into practice (Díaz et al. 2002–2003).

For such an application, a case would correspond to a a sentence of prose – the description of the problem or the content for the poem – paired with a corresponding poem fragment – the solution of the problem or the resulting poem. Such a formulation stores the necessary information about how a particular sentence is broken up into lines or fragments of lines, how and where words are added or eliminated, and how the relative order of words is altered.

Adaptation takes place by combining phonetic, metrical and lexical information about the words in the different sources – the prose message, the retrieved case, and additional vocabulary available to the system. This general process is guided by: domain information about the elements involved – words, stanzas, rhyme, verse, line, syllable, feet –, and conceptual information about CBR (CBROnto).

6.1 The CBR System Design using COLIBRI/CBROnto

There were various reasons involved in the choice of poetry generation as an example of the use of COLIBRI. First, it concerns a domain with a hierarchy of concepts rich enough to test the representation capabilities of COLIBRI, both in terms of concept structure and relations between concepts. Second, poetry generation involves reasoning about the meanings of words. The example discussed so far does not consider meaning. This is done with the double intention of paraphrasing previous work in terms of the COLIBRI architecture, and to ensure that the basic procedures can be successfully applied before complicating the problem. Nonetheless, the capabilities of COLIBRI could be tested further as soon as appropriate representation is provided for the meaning of words.

6.1.1 The Domain Knowledge

The COLIBRI approach to building KI-CBR systems takes advantage of the explicit representation of domain knowledge. Given that words are divided into syllables and each word has a unique syllable that carries the prosodic stress, the constraints that have to be taken into account are the following:

1. Specific strophic forms require different number of syllables to a line.
2. Not all possible stress patterns for a line are valid (depending on the length, there will only be certain combinations of feet that 'sound right').
3. The rhyme of a line is made up of the end of its last word, and each strophic form requires a different rhyming pattern between its lines. Domain knowledge should include terminology and the representations of a number of concepts and the relations between them.

The concept of PROSE, a text made up of WORDS appearing in a specific order, possibly broken up into LINES. In order to represent the correct order between words, the relation PRECEDES must be defined between words.

The concept of POEM, a text made up of WORDS appearing in a specific order, possibly broken up into POEM LINES. A poem may built up as a series of STANZAS, which are groups of a definite NUMBER OF LINES of a specific LENGTH IN SYLLABLES, matching specific PATTERNS OF STRESS, and satisfying a certain RHYME PATTERN.

It is important to know whether a line of a poem is also the end of a sentence or whether the sentence follows on onto the next line. A relation FOLLOWS ON is defined between lines of poem that correspond to the same sentence.

The vocabulary must include metric information for each available word – NUMBER OF SYLLABLES, RHYME, and whether it is OPEN-ENDED or not with respect to syllabic recombination with adjacent words.

The result of the domain knowledge representation phase is a knowledge base containing 86 concepts, 22 relations and 606 individuals.

6.1.2 The Cases

Cases describe a solved problem of poem composition. We describe cases using the CBROnto case description language and domain knowledge terminology. A case description is made of a prose description of the poem that constitutes the case solution. The case representation capabilities of CBROnto allow us to represent cases with different granularity levels, namely we define the following case types:

- *MessagePoemType* each stanza of a poem is taken as a case, encoding how the message is distributed over lines, fitted into a pattern of rhyme. Full poems are retrieved to provide structure and then adapted constructively by building each of its lines.
- *PoemType* the poem itself is taken both as description and solution of the case
- *LineType* each line of a poem is taken as a case, encoding how a fragment of language is made to fit the restrictions over a line. Patterns of poem lines are retrieved to provide structure and a new line is built over each one of them using the words of the query.

Each one of these types can be considered as a different case base over which the CBR methods will work. When solving a CBR task, one of the knowledge requirements for all the retrieval methods is to specify which case base we will search in, and what the query is.

Each case that is added to the system adds an average of 50 individuals to knowledge base.

6.1.3 Knowledge Integration

After domain-modelling phase an integration phase must take place to bridge the gap between domain terminology and CBROnto terminology. This integration phase is based on classification. Examples of this integration:

- `precedes` and `follow-on` domain relations are classified under `before` – relation of CBROnto.
- `follow-on` is classified under `depends_on` CBROnto relation. This affects the adaptation process. If a line, which follows onto the next, is modified, the next one may be affected, and its adaptation should be considered.
- relations `has-stanza`, `has-poem-line`, `has-word`, `has-line`, `precedes`, `follow-on`, and some others of the domain are classified under the `has-part` CBROnto relation.

That integration provides the semantic roles that will be used in the predefined *similarity types*. For example, when using *structural similarity* the similarity measures only will consider the domain relations classified under has-part CBROnto relation and the fillers of these relations, and no others. This result indicates the similarity according to the parts that make up the case.

6.1.4 The CBR Methods

The key processes of the CBR cycle must now be defined in terms of the elements presented so far. There are many possibilities to be considered. If creative poetry generation is desired, striking results can be obtained by retrieving cases other than the most similar. This forces the system to employ a higher degree of adaptation, resulting in more innovative poems. If we already know the stanza that we would like the result to follow, this can be included as part of the query, to ensure that the retrieved case will match that stanza. In this sense, structural similarity is very useful. If the query is provided with some specification of its structure, structural similarity will retrieve cases with that structure without taking into account the query contents in a first similarity assessment phase.

In (Díaz et al. 2002) we have detailed the **retrieval** methods we use for this system where the cases whose description does not contain any word in common with the query are filtered. We are assuming that the words provided in the query should set the theme of the desired poem. Then we solve the Select Cases retrieval subtask by computing a measure of similarity between the query and each one of the cases obtained. Predefined similarity measures do exist, but they tend to be too generic, so a special effort of defining domain specific similarity measures must be made. For instance, we must define how we compare two cases depending on their lines, the apparition of words, taking into account the position of the words in the lines, the stress pattern, the rhyme....

When we want to specify how to compute similarity between the instances of a concept –for example, two lines, two words... – using CBROnto similarity framework we define and associate a similarity measure to this concept. For example, in order to compare words we take into account the similarity between two *Word* instances according to the concepts they belong to, and the instances they relate to, i.e., the word characteristics (stress, rhyme, etc.) that satisfy the similarity type specification, binary-tuple by default, although the designer could define a more specific one, to indicate for example, that we want to consider only the stress and length but not the rhyme.

Adaptation takes place by combining phonetic, metrical and lexical information about the words in the different knowledge sources –the prose message, the retrieved case, and additional vocabulary available to the system.

There are many possible ways of adapting a retrieved case. For instance, complete lines of the retrieved poem may be substituted for others. In this case, the similarity criterion for substitutes will search for poem lines with the same length and the same rhyme.

A finer way would be to substitute individual words. In this case, the similarity criterion for substitutes will search for words that preserve the stress pattern for the line, that have the same syntactic category, and the same rhyme if the word is at the end of the line.

Words may also be grouped together (using dependencies) and complete word blocks be substituted. In that case the criteria would also take into account the stress pattern of the line and the syntactic structure, making sure that the appropriate constraints on gender, number and person are satisfied.

7. jCOLIBRI

Our architecture CBROnto/COLIBRI was first implemented in LISP using LOOM as the Description Logics engine. Although this implementation has been useful for testing and prototyping KI-CBR systems, it is not very usable by non-DLs-expert users. For that reason, and in order to open these ideas to a wider community of CBR developers, we have undertaken the development of jCOLIBRI[5], an object-oriented framework in Java, based on CBROnto, built to support COLIBRI architecture (Bello et. al 2004).

jCOLIBRI is a technological evolution of COLIBRI that incorporates in a distributed architecture (see Figure 7-14) a DLs engine, GUI clients for assembling a CBR system from reusable components and an object-oriented framework in Java. The design of the framework comprises a hierarchy of Java classes plus a number of XML files organized around the following elements:

- **Tasks and Methods.** XML files describe the tasks supported by the framework along with the methods for solving these tasks.
- **Case Base.** Different connectors are defined to support several types of case persistency, from the file system to a data base. Additionally, a number of possible in-memory case base organizations are supported.
- **Cases.** A number of interfaces and classes are included in the framework to provide an abstract representation of cases that support any type of actual case structure.
- **Problem Solving Methods.** The actual code that supports the methods included in the framework.

[5] http://sourceforge.net/projects/jCOLIBRI-cbr/.

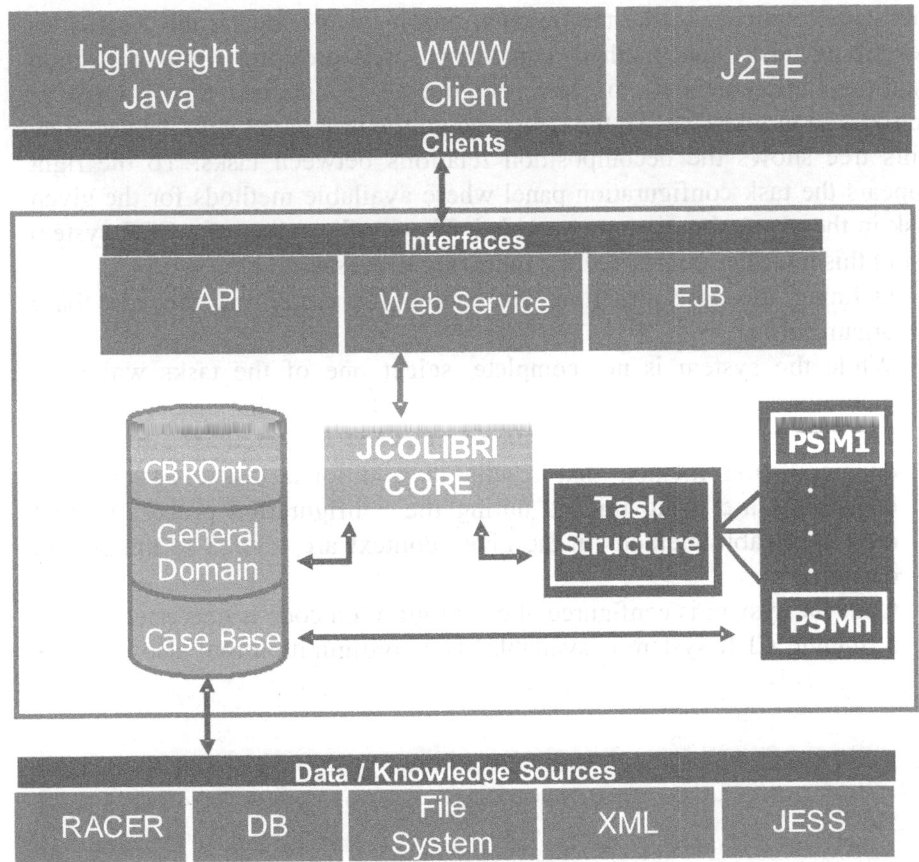

Figure 7-14. JCOLIBRI Architecture

jCOLIBRI is designed to easily support the construction of CBR systems taking advantage of the task/method division paradigm described in previous sections. Building a CBR system is a configuration process where the system developer selects the tasks the system must fulfil and for every task assigns the method that will do the job. Ideally, the system designer would find every task and method needed for the system at hand, so that she would program just the representation for cases. However, in a more realistic situation a number of new methods may be needed and, less probably, some new task. Since jCOLIBRI is designed as an extensible framework, new elements will smoothly integrate with the available infrastructure as long as they follow the framework design.

One of the biggest problems with frameworks is learning how to use them. In order to alleviate framework instantiation effort, jCOLIBRI features a semiautomatic configuration tool that guides the instantiation process through a graphical interface. This interface is dynamically built to reflect the actual contents of the task/method ontology, relying on the XML files describing task and method constraints and profiting from reflection facilities implemented in Java. Figure 7-15 shows the jCOLIBRI configuration interface. To the left is shown the task panel with the task tree. This tree shows the decomposition relations between tasks. To the right appears the task configuration panel where available methods for the given task in the given situation are provided. The configuration of a CBR system using this interface consists of the following processes:

- Defining the case structure, the source for cases and the case base organization.
- While the system is not complete, select one of the tasks without a method assigned, select and configure a method for that task. At start-up the task tree has only one element, *CBRTask*, which is solved by a decomposition method that results in additional tasks. Task/method constraints are being tracked during the configuration process so that only applicable methods in the given context are offered to the system designer.
- Once the system is configured, the configuration code is generated so that a running CBR system is available. The configuration tool also provides

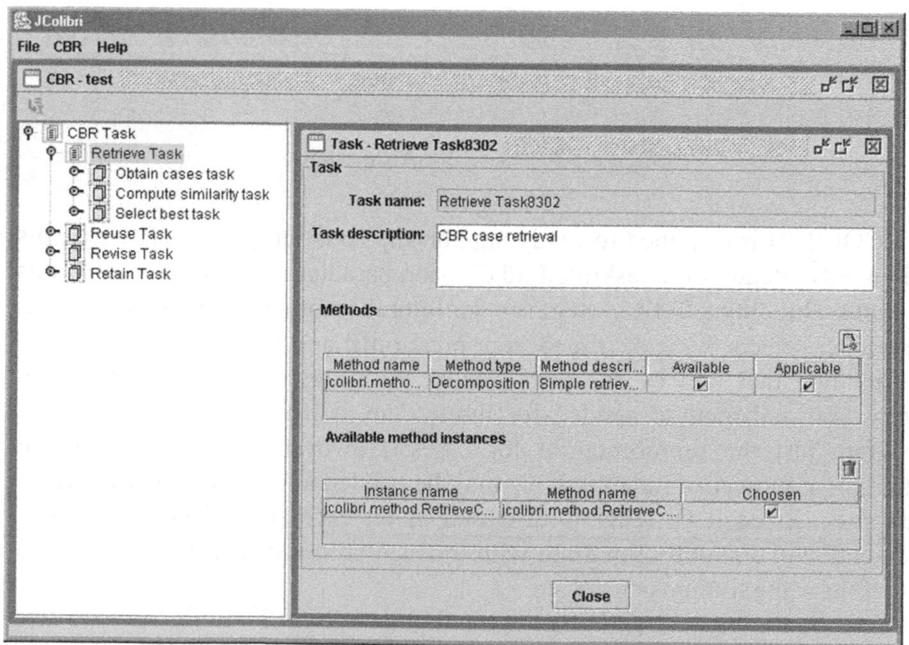

Figure 7-15. jCOLIBRI configuration interface

a default interface for running the configured CBR system although in a real settlement an application specific interface should be developed.

The framework implementation is evolving, as new methods are included, although it is already publicly available at *http://jCOLIBRI-cbr.sourceforge.net*. Our goal is to provide a reference framework for CBR development that would grow with contributions from the community. This reference would serve for pedagogical purposes and as bottom line implementation for prototyping CBR systems and comparing different CBR approaches to a given problem.

8. CONCLUSIONS

In this paper, we have described COLIBRI –architecture to design KI-CBR systems– and CBROnto –ontology that includes knowledge about CBR. The main contribution of our approach is the use of CBROnto as a bridge that allows the connection of expert knowledge with previously defined ontologies. Besides, CBROnto terminology provides a unified declarative framework for describing and reasoning about KI-CBR applications.

CBROnto helps about issues associated with modelling and discovering the knowledge needed in a CBR system. In our approach, the domain expert is used as a knowledge source to relate the domain knowledge to CBROnto. CBROnto helps the domain expert to make explicit his own knowledge about the domain and about the CBR methods, guiding him/her when telling the CBR methods how to use the available domain terminology to solve the CBR tasks. CBROnto makes explicit certain CBR terms that are useful as a junction between the domain knowledge and the CBR methods defined with a domain-independent perspective.

The use of domain ontologies provides a CBR application with the vocabulary for describing a domain, guides the construction of cases and queries, and constitutes a warehouse of vocabulary to solve lexical, semantic and synonym problems. The main drawback of our approach arises when there are not appropriate ontologies to be reused, then an effort is needed to build new ontologies or to integrate definitions from different ontologies. Anyway, we consider this effort is not waste time if this knowledge is reused for other applications.

Our knowledge intensive approach to CBR:

- Guides case representation because it provides with domain and CBR terminology and avoids misunderstandings if cases are given by different sources in the same domain.
- Allows for a seamless integration of cases without requiring all the cases to have the same structure.

- Guides the CBR methods:
  - Allowing semantic vs. syntactic similarity, extensively using the domain knowledge.
  - Helping in the case organization, either using the domain knowledge to directly organize the cases or help constructing a different structure to organize the cases (like the lattice resulting from FCA).
  - Guiding the adaptation process by learning and explicitly representing certain adaptation knowledge.

COLIBRI/CBROnto represents architecture at the knowledge level, but it has been formalized in DLs to show how its associated reasoning mechanisms are well suited to solve the tasks involved in the design of a KI-CBR system and also in the execution cycle of the final designed-system. These ideas are now evolving into jCOLIBRI, a reference framework for CBR development, which has been recently released to the community.

ACKNOWLEDGEMENTS

The work presented here is a summary of the Phd-Thesis of Belén Díaz-Agudo that was supervised by Pedro A. González Calero. We would like to specially express our gratitude to the Group of Artificial Intelligence Applications people (gaia.sip.ucm.es) for their support and assistance.

This work has been supported by the Spanish *Committee of Science & Technology* (TIC2002-01961).

REFERENCES

Aamodt, A. (1990) “Knowledge-intensive case-based reasoning and learning”. ECAI-90, Ninth European Conference on Artificial Intelligence, Stockholm.

Aamodt, A., (1993) “A case-based answer to some problems of knowledge-based systems”. In E. Sandewal and C.G. Jansson (eds): Scandinavian Conference on Artificial Intelligence. IOS Press, 1993. pp. 168-182.

Aamodt A., Plaza E., (1994) “Case-Based Reasoning: Foundational Issues, Methodological Variations, and System Approaches”. Artificial Intelligence Communications, Vol. 7, no. 1, pp. 39-59.

Aamodt A. (1995) “Knowledge Acquisition and Learning from Experience - The Role of Case-Specific Knowledge”, In Gheorge Tecuci and Yves Kodratoff (eds): Machine learning and knowledge acquisition; Integrated approaches, (Chapter 8), Academic Press, 1995, pp. 197-245.

Aamodt, A. (2004) “Knowledge Intensive CBR in CREEK”. Invited Talk. 7 th European Conference on CBR (ECCBR’2004).

Bello-Tomás, J.J., González-Calero, P.A., Díaz-Agudo, B. (2004) "jCOLIBRI: an Object-Oriented Framework for Building CBR Systems". In Funk, P., González-Calero, P.A., (Eds.): Advances in Case-Based Reasoning, Procs. of the 7th European Conference on

Case-Based Reasoning, ECCBR 2004. Lecture Notes in Artificial Intelligence, 3155, Springer, 2004.

Benjamins, R., (1995) "Problem Solving Methods for diagnosis and their role in knowledge acquisition", International Journal of Expert Systems: Research&Applications, 8 (2), pp. 93-120.

Benjamins, R and Fensel, D. (1998) "Special Issue on problem solving methods", International Journal of Human Computer Studies.

Brachman, R., & Schmolze, J. G., (1985). "An overview of the kl-one knowledge representation system". Cognitive Science, 9 (2), pp. 171-216

Chandrasekaran B., (1986). "Generic Tasks for knowledge-based reasoning: High-level building blocks for expert system design", IEEE Expert, 1(3), pp. 23-30.

Chandrasekaran, B., Josephson, J.R, & Benjamins, R., (1998). "Ontology of tasks and Methods", AAAI Spring Symposim. Also in Procs of the 11th Workshop on Knowledge Acquistion, Modeling, and Management, (KAW'98).

Díaz-Agudo, B., & González-Calero, P.A., 2000 (a). "An Architecture for Knowledge Intensive CBR Systems". Advances in Case-Based Reasoning (EWCBR'00), Blanzieri, E., Portinale, L., (Eds.), Springer, LNAI 1898, pp. 37-48.

Díaz-Agudo, B., & González-Calero, P.A., 2001 (a). "Formal Concept Analysis as a Support Technique for CBR". Knowledge-Based Systems, 14 (3-4), June, Elsevier. (ISSN:0950-7051), pp. 163-172.

Díaz-Agudo, B., & González-Calero, P. A., 2001 (b). "A Declarative Similarity Framework for Knowledge Intensive CBR". Case-Based Reasoning Research and Development (ICCBR'01), Aha, D., Watson, I., (Eds.), Springer LNAI 2080, pp. 158-172.

Díaz-Agudo, B., & González-Calero, P. A., 2001 (c). "Classification Based Retrieval Using Formal Concept Analysis". Case-Based Reasoning Research and Development (ICCBR 01), Aha, D., Watson, I., (Eds.) Springer LNAI 2080, pp. 172-187.

Díaz-Agudo, B., & González-Calero, P. A., 2001 (d). "Knowledge Intensive CBR Made Affordable". In Weber, R., Gresse von Wangenheim, C., (Eds.): Procs. of the Workshop Program at ICCBR'01, Technical Note AIC-01-003, Navy Center for Applied Research in Artificial Intelligence, Washington, DC, USA.

Díaz Agudo, B., & González Calero, P.A., (2002). "CBROnto: a task/method ontology for CBR". Procs. of the 15th International FLAIRS'02 Conference (Special Track on Case-Based Reasoning). Haller, S., &, Simmons, G., (Eds.). AAAI Press, pp. 101-106.

Díaz-Agudo, B., Gervás, P. & González-Calero, P., (2002). "Poetry Generation in COLIBRI". Advances in Case-Based Reasoning, Procs 6th European Conference on Case Based Reasoning, Aberdeen, Scotland, 4-7 September 2002 (ECCBR'02). Springer LNAI 2416, pp.73-87.

Díaz-Agudo, B., & González-Calero, P. A., (2003). "Knowledge Intensive CBR through Ontologies". Expert Update, Vol. 6, Num. 1.

Díaz-Agudo, B., Gervás, P. & González-Calero, P., (2003). "Adaptation Guided Retrieval Based on Formal Concept Analysis" In Procs. 5th International Conference on Case-Based Reasoning (ICCBR'2003) K.D. Ashley & D. Bridge (eds). Springer Verlarg, LNAI 2689.

Donini, F., Lenzerini, M., Nardi, D., & Schaerf, A., (1996). "Reasoning in Description Logics". Principles of Knowledge Representation and Reasoning, Brewka; G. (Ed.), CLSI Publications, pp. 193-238.

Farquhar, A., Fikes, R., & Rice, J., 1997. The ontolingua server: a tool for collaborative ontology construction. International Journal of Human-Computer Studies, 46(6), pp. 707-728.

Fuchs, B. and A. Mille (2000). "Representing Knowledge for CBR: The ROCADE system". In Advances in Case-Based Reasoning (EWCBR 2000) (Blanzieri, E., Portinale, L., eds.), Springer-Verlag.

Genesereth, M.R., & Fikes, R.E., (1992). "Knowledge Interchange Formal. Version 3.0. Reference Manual". Technical Report, Logic-92-1, Computer Science Dep., Stanford University.

Gómez-Pérez, A., (1998) "Knowledge Sharing and Reuse". The handbook on Applied Expert Systems. (Liebowitz, ed.), CRC press.

Gomez-Perez, A. and R. Benjamins (1999) Applications of Ontologies and Problem-Solving Methods – workshop at Thirteenth Biennial European Conference on Artificial Intelligence. AI Magazine.

González-Calero, P.A., Gómez-Albarrán, M., and Díaz-Agudo, B., (1999) "A Substitution-based Adaptation Model". Workshop on Formalisation of Adaptation in CBR, (ICCBR'99).

Gruber, T. R. (1993). Toward Principles for the Design of Ontologies Used for Knowledge Sharing, KSL-9304, Knowledge Systems Laboratory, Stanford University.

Leake, D., (1993). "Learning Adaptation Strategies by Introspective Reasoning about Memory Search".*Procs AAAI-93 Case-Based Reasoning Workshop*, volume WS-93-01, Leake, D., (Ed.), pp. 57-63.

Lenat, D.B. & Guha, R.V., (1990). "Building large knowledge-based systems. Representation and inference in the Cyc Project". Addison-Wesley, Massachusetts.

McDermott, J. (1988). Toward a taxonomoy of problem solving methods. In Marcus, S. (Ed.), Automating Knowledge Acquisition for Expert Systems. Kluwer Academic Publishers.

Mac Gregor, R., (1991). "The Evolving Technology of Classification-Based Knowledge Representation Systems". Principles of Semantic Networks. Sowa, J. F. (Ed.), Morgan Kaufmann, pp. 385-400.

Muñoz-Avila, H., Aha D., & Breslow L., (1999) "HICAP: An Interactive Case-Based Planning Architecture and its Application to Noncombatant Evacuation Operations",Orlando, FL: AAAI Press, pp. 870-875.

Musen, M.A., (1989). "Automated Support for building and extending expert models". Machine Learning, 4, pp. 347-376.

Napoli A., Lieber J., and Courien R., (1996) "Classification-Based Problem Solving in CBR", in Advances in CBR (EWCBR'96) (Smith, I., and Faltings, B., eds.), Springer-Verlag.

Newell, A., 1982. "The Knowledge Level". Artificial Intelligence, 18 (1).

Orsvärn, K. (1996). Principles for Libraries of Task Decomposition Methods – Conclusions from a Case-Study. In Nigel Shadbolt, Kieron O'Hara & Guus Schreiber, editors, Advances in Knowledge Acquisition, pages 48--65. Springer-Verlag, Berlin Heidelberg, Germany.

Richer, M.M. (1995). The knowledge contained in similarity measures. Invited Talk on the ICCBR 1995.

Schreiber, A.Th., and Wielinga, B.J. and Breuker, J.A. (1993). KADS: A Principled Approach toKnowledge-Based System Development. Academic Press, London.

Schreiber, Th., Wielinga, B., Akkermans, J., Van de Velde, W. & de Hoog, R., 1994. "CommonKADS: A comprehensive methodology for KBS development". IEEE Expert, 9(6), December.

Schreiber, A. TH and B. Wielinga, J. M. Akkermans, W. Van De Velde, and R. de Hoog, (1994): CommonKADS. A Comprehensive Methodology for KBS Development. IEEE Expert 9 (6), pp. 28-37.

Spibey, P., 1991. Express language reference manual. Technical Report ISO 10300/TC184/ SC4/WG 5, CADDETC.

Steels, L. (1990). Components of Expertise. AI Magazine, 11(2): 29–49.

Uschold, M. & Gruninger, M., (1996). Ontologies: Principles, methods and applications. Knowledge Engineering Review, 11(2).

Wielinga, B.J., Schreiber, A.T., & Breuker, J.A., (1992). "KADS: A modelling approach to knowledge engineering". Knowledge Acquisition, 4 (1), pp. 5-53, Special Issue "The KADS approach to knowledge engineering". Reprinted in: Buchana, B and Wilkins, D (Eds.), 1992, Readings in Knowledge Acquisition and Learning, Morgan Kaufmann, pp. 92-116.

Chapter 8

MDA STANDARDS FOR ONTOLOGY DEVELOPMENT

Dragan Djurić[1], Dragan Gašević[2] and Vladan Devedžić[1]
[1]FON – School of Business Administration, University of Belgrade, POB 52, Jove Ilića 154, 11000 Belgrade, Serbia and Montenegro, [2]School of Interactive Arts and Technology, Simon Fraser University Surrey, 2400 Central City, 10153 King George Hwy, Surrey, BC V3T 2W1, Canada; dragandj@gmail.com, devedzic@fon.bg.ac.yu, dgasevic@acm.org, http://goodoldai.org.yu

Abstract: Ontologies and Model-Driven Architecture (MDA) are two modeling approaches being developed in parallel, but by different communities. They have common points and issues and can be brought closer together. Many authors have so far attempted to bridge gaps and have proposed several solutions. The result of these efforts is the recent OMG's initiative for defining an ontology development platform. In this chapter, we are giving an overview of the state-of-the-art research on the subject of applications of MDA standards for ontology development. The chapter is a result of our experience in developing the MDA-based ontology infrastructure as well as a series of tutorials we gave at many international conferences. The chapter tries to indicate the most important definition for both of the considered modeling approaches. Using those definitions, we depict their mutual similarities and differences. Then, we show the present solution pursuing to apply MDA standard to ontology development with the main stress on OMG's standardization efforts.

Key words: Ontology modeling; Model-Driven Architecture; The Semantic Web; Ontology development; Web Ontology Language (OWL); Resource Description Framework (RDF); RDF Schema (RDFS) Ontology Definition Metamodel (ODM)

1. INTRODUCTION

With the development of the Semantic Web initiative, the importance of ontologies increases rapidly. Semantic Web researchers try to make ontology development and ontologies in general closer to software practitioners

[Knublauch, 2004]. However, ontologies have more rigorous foundation closely related to the well-known AI paradigms (e.g. description logic, semantic networks, frames, etc.). Thus, most of the current Semantic Web ontologies are developed in AI laboratories. Accordingly, we should answer some questions such as: How can we increase the extent of ontologies developers? How can we motivate software engineering practitioners to develop and use ontologies? Can we use software development tools to develop ontologies? Therefore, we need some ways to integrate software development and ontologies.

The integration of the ongoing software engineering efforts with the concept of the Semantic Web is not a new idea [Kogut et al, 2002]. Many researchers have previously suggested using UML in order to solve this problem. However, UML is based upon object-oriented paradigm, and has some limitation regarding ontology development. Hence, we can only use UML in initial phases of ontology development. We believe that these limitations can be overcome using UML extensions (i.e. UML profiles) [Duddy, 2002], as well as other Object Modeling Group (OMG) standards, like Model Driven Architecture – MDA. In addition, if we want to offer a solution consistent with MDA proposals, we should also support automatic generation of completely operational ontology definitions (e.g. in OWL language) that are model driven [Selic, 2003]. Currently, the most important direction toward this goal is the one pursued by a dedicated research group within OMG that tries to converge many different proposals of solutions to this problem [OMG ODM, 2003]. The result of this effort should be a standard language (i.e. a metamodel) based on the MDA standards [Miller & Mukerji, 2003] and the W3C Web Ontology Language (OWL) recommendation [Dean & Schreiber, 2004].

In this chapter, we try to address the current efforts towards the use of MDA standards for ontology development in order to have a comprehensive reference covering recent research on this subject. The chapter is a result of our experience on developing MDA-based infrastructure for ontologies [Djuric et al., 2005b] as well as a series of tutorials on this subject we have given at several international conferences (e.g. UML Conference, Conference on Web Engineering, World Wide Web Conference, etc.). Accordingly, the next section gives the most important definition of both ontologies and the Semantic Web. Section 3 briefly discusses basic MDA concepts, while section 4 attempts to clarify different modeling origins of both MDA and ontologies in terms of modeling spaces. In section 5, we list the previous work on the use of software engineering languages for ontology development, whereas in section 6 we show the starting points for developing an MDA-based infrastructure for ontologies. Finally, sections 7 and 8 present parts of the future OMG standards, Ontology Definition Language (ODM) and Ontology UML Profile (OUP), respectively.

2. ONTOLOGIES AND THE SEMANTIC WEB

Ontologies have been around for quite some time now. Since early 1990s, researchers in the domain of artificial intelligence and knowledge representation have studied ontologies as means for knowledge sharing and reuse among knowledge-based systems. However, even an early survey of the field of ontologies [Fridman-Noy et al, 1997] has identified a number of application classes that benefit to a large extent from utilizing ontologies although some of them are not necessarily knowledge-based systems in the traditional sense. Some of the application classes it mentioned include natural language processing, library science, intelligent information retrieval (especially from the Internet), virtual organizations, and simulation and modeling. Later on, researchers have recognized explicitly that ontologies are not just for knowledge-based systems, but for all software systems – all software needs models of the world, hence can make use of ontologies at design time [Chandrasekaran et al, 1999]. Nowadays, ontologies and ontological engineering span such diverse fields as qualitative modeling, language engineering, database design, information retrieval and extraction, knowledge management and organization, ontology-enhanced search, possibly the largest one, e-commerce (e.g., Amazon.com, Yahoo Shopping, etc.), and configuration [McGuinness, 2002].

2.1 Definitions of Ontologies

There are at least a dozen definitions of ontologies in the literature. A recent one says that ontology provides the basic structure or armature around which a knowledge base can be built [Swartout & Tate, 1999]. Another one specifies that ontology should provide a set of knowledge terms, including the vocabulary, the semantic interconnections, and some simple rules of inference and logic for some particular topic or service [Hendler, 2001]. Although informal, these definitions capture the central idea of ontologies – they are structured depictions or models of known (and accepted) facts about some topics. Ontologies appear most effective when the semantic distinctions that humans take for granted are crucial to the application's purpose [Denny, 2002].

Each ontology provides the vocabulary (or names) for referring to the terms in a subject area, as well as the logical statements that describe what the terms are, how they are related to each other, how they can or cannot be related to each other, as well as rules for combining terms and relations to define extensions to the vocabulary. Hence, ontologies represent a common machine-level understanding of topics that can be communicated between users and applications, i.e. domain semantics independent of reader and context. For a recent more comprehensive discussion of ontologies, see [Kalfoglou, 2001].

2.2 The Semantic Web

One of the central roles of ontologies is to establish further levels of interoperability, i.e. semantic interoperability, between agents and applications on the emerging Semantic Web [Berners-Lee et al, 2001], as well as to add a further representation and inference layer on top of the Web's current layers [Decker et al, 2000] [Hendler, 2001]. When put on the Web, ontologies specify standard terms and machine-readable definitions. The Semantic Web is based on the idea of numerous ontologies providing vocabularies, definitions, and constraints that information resources, agents, and Web-based applications can commit to in order to reuse data and knowledge effectively [Hefflin & Huhns, 2003]. This way, ontology conveys the same meaning of its terms to any two or more sources that commit to it. Any source, agent, or application can commit to any ontology or create a new one. Thus, the Semantic Web is essentially a distributed approach to creating standard vocabularies.

2.3 Ontology Languages

The best picture for understanding ontology languages is the Semantic Web "layer cake", Figure 8-1. While XML with XML Schema enables common, well-defined and easy processable syntax, it tells nothing about semantics of data it describes. That means that some standard must be built on top of XML that will describe semantics of data. The first step in that direction is Resource Description Framework (RDF), a general model in metadata layer and Resource Description Framework Schema (RDFS) [Brickley, 2004], language at schema layer. The RDF data model defines a simple model for describing interrelationships among resources in terms of named properties and values. RDF properties may be thought of as attributes of resources and in this sense correspond to traditional attribute-value pairs. RDF properties also represent relationships between resources. As such, the RDF data model can therefore resemble an entity-relationship diagram [Berners-Lee, 1998]. The RDF Schema declares these properties, and provides mechanisms for defining the relationships between these properties and other resources. RDF and RDFS specifications are available in several documents ([Beckett, 2004], [Manola & Miller, 2004], [Klyne & Carroll, 2004], [Hayes, 2004]).

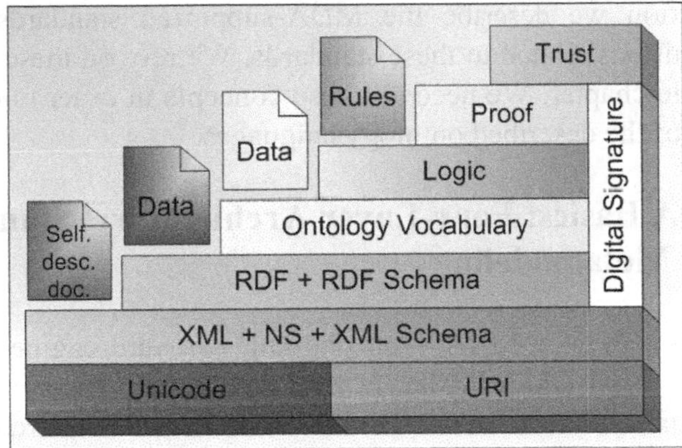

Figure 8-1. Tim Berners-Lee's vision of the Semantic Web "layer cake"

To enable reasoning services for the Semantic Web, another layer is needed on top of RDF(S). That (logical) layer introduces ontology languages, that are based on meta-modeling architecture defined in lower layer. It introduces a richer set of modeling primitives which can be mapped to Descriptive Logic. This enables using of tools with generic reasoning support, independent of specific problem domain. Common examples of such languages are OIL and DAML.

The newest emerging standard is W3C's OWL. The Web Ontology Language (OWL) ([Dean & Schreiber, 2004], [McGuinness & van Harmelen, 2004], [Smith et al, 2004], [Patel-Schneider et. al., 2004]) is a semantic markup language for publishing and sharing ontologies on the World Wide Web. OWL is developed as a vocabulary extension of RDF and is derived from the DAML+OIL Web ontology language. Since World Wide Web is almost unconstrained, OWL must provide open world assumption and allow importing and mixing various ontologies. Some of them may be even contradictory, but new information can never retract existing information, it can be only added to it. In order to provide such capabilities and, in the same time, to support calculations and reasoning in finite time with tools that can be built on existing or soon available technologies, OWL introduces three increasingly expressive sublanguages for various purposes: OWL Full, OWL DL and OWL Lite.

3. MODEL-DRIVEN ARCHITECTURE: AN OVERVIEW

In this section we describe the MDA-supported standards and give important definitions related to these standards. We rely on these definitions in the rest of the chapter. We need all these concepts in order to explain the metamodeling of the described ontology languages.

3.1 MDA Basics: Four-Layer Architecture, Standards, and Metamodeling

Our work is based on MDA – an ongoing software engineering effort under the auspices of OMG [Miller & Mukerji, 2003]. The central part of MDA is the four-layer architecture that has a number of standards defined at each of its layers (see Figure 8-2). Most of MDA standards are developed as metamodels using metamodeling. The topmost layer (M3) is called meta-metamodel and the OMG's standard defined at this layer is Meta-Object Facility (MOF) [OMG MOF, 2002]. This is a self-defined language intended for defining metamodels. In terms of MDA, a metamodel makes statements about what can be expressed in the valid models of a certain modeling language. In fact, a metamodel is a model of a modeling language [Seidewitz, 2003].

Examples of the MDA's metamodels are UML and Common Warehouse Metamodel (CWM). The MDA's metamodel layer is usually denoted as M2. At this layer we can define a new metamodel (e.g., a modeling language) that would cover some specific application domains (e.g., ontology development). The next layer is the model layer (M1) – the layer where we develop real-world models (or domain models). In terms of UML models, that means creating classes, their relations, states, etc. There is an XML-based standard for sharing metadata that can be used for all of the MDA's layers. This standard is called XML Metadata Interchange (XMI) [OMG XMI, 2002]. The bottom layer is the instance layer (M0). There are two different approaches to explaining this layer, and we note both of them:

1. The instance layer contains instances of the concepts defined at the model layer (M1), e.g. objects in programming languages.
2. The instance layer contains things from our reality – concrete (e.g. Mark is an instance of the Person class, Lassie is an instance of the Dog class, etc.) and abstract (e.g. UML classes – Dog, Person, etc.) [Atkinson and Kuhne, 2003].

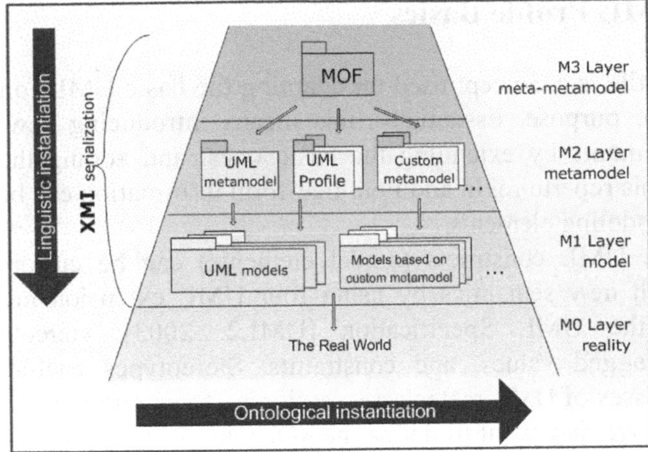

Figure 8-2. The four-layer Model Driven Architecture and its orthogonal instance-of relations: Linguistics and ontological

In this chapter we advocate the second approach, but we should give more details about its impact on UML. In UML, both classes and objects are at the same layer (the model layer) in the MDA four-layer architecture. Actually, MDA layers are called linguistic layers. On the other hand, concepts from the same linguistic layer can be at different ontological layers. Hence, UML classes and objects are at different ontological layers, but at the same linguistic layer.

3.2 Specific MDA metamodels

One possible solution for using MDA capacities in a specific domain is to develop a metamodel that would be able to model relevant domain concepts. That means creating a domain language (i.e. the metamodel) using metamodeling; such a language is created using MOF. Having defined a domain specific metamodel, we should develop suitable tools for using that metamodel. However, it is rather expensive and time-consuming to develop new tools (e.g. for ontology development compliant with an MDA-based language), so we try to use existing, well-known tools. Current software tools do not implement many of the MDA basic concepts. However, most of these tools are currently oriented primarily towards UML and the M1 layer (i.e., the model layer) [Gašević et al, 2003]. Generally, UML itself is a MOF-defined general-purpose language (i.e. a metamodel) that contains a set of core primitives. The problem of tools can be overcome using UML Profiles – a way to adapt UML to specific domains (e.g. ontology development). With Profiles, UML can be seen as a family of languages [Duddy, 2002].

3.3 UML Profile Basics

UML Profile is a concept used for adapting the basic UML constructs to some specific purpose. Essentially, this means introducing new kinds of modeling elements by extending the basic ones, and adding them to the modeler's tools repertoire. In addition, free-form information can be attached to the new modeling elements.

The basic UML constructs (model elements) can be customized and extended with new semantics by using four UML extension mechanisms defined in the UML Specification [UML2, 2003]: stereotypes, tag definitions, tagged values, and constraints. Stereotypes enable defining virtual subclasses of UML metaclasses, assigning them additional semantics. For example, we may want to define the «OntClass» stereotype, Figure 8-3, by extending the UML Class metaclass to denote the modeling element used to represent ontological classes (and not other kinds of concepts).

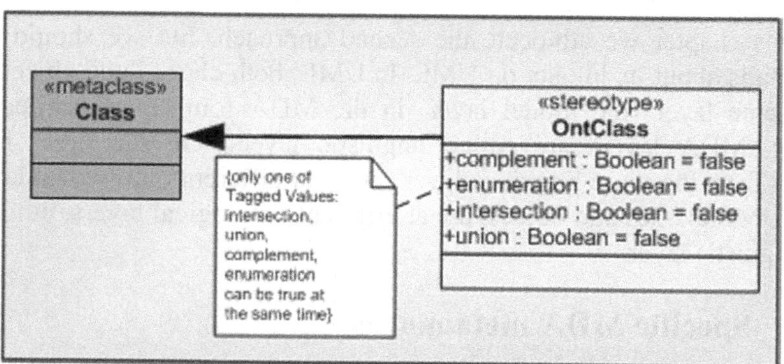

Figure 8-3. New stereotype definition

Tag definitions can be attached to model elements. They allow for introducing new kinds of properties that model elements may have and are analogous to metaatribute definitions. Each tag definition specifies the actual values of properties of individual model elements, called tagged values. Tag definitions can be attached to a stereotype to define its virtual meta-attributes. For example, the «OntClass» stereotype in Figure 8-3 has a tag definition specifying four tagged values (for enumeration, intersection, etc.).

Constraints make possible to additionally refine the semantics of the modeling element they are attached to. They can be attached to each stereotype using OCL (Object Constraint Language) or English language (i.e. spoken language) in order to precisely define the stereotype's semantics (see the example in Figure 8-3).

More details about UML extension mechanisms can be found in [Rumbaugh, 1998] and [UML2, 2003]. A coherent set of extensions of the basic UML model elements, defined for specific purposes or for a specific modeling domain, constitutes a UML profile.

4. THE CLOSE ENCOUNTERS OF THE SEMANTIC WEB AND MDA

In this section, we will see how Semantic Web and MDA technologies can be compared and put in parallel in order to get the big picture of what is going on when we talk of ontology modeling in MDA or MOF-based RDFS and OWL metamodels. To do this, we need to briefly introduce the concept of Modeling Space (MS) [Djuric et al, 2005a]. Then, we will treat RDFS-based languages and MOF-based metamodels as they are at M2 layer of RDFS MS and MOF MS, and show how they are related. As the Semantic Web is a technical space (TS) based on RDFS MS and MDA is a TS based on MOF MS, we relate them by relating MSs they are built on.

4.1 Modeling spaces essentials

The most fundamental definition of model is that it is the simplified abstraction of reality [Hagget and Chorley, 1967]. This definition applies not only to models in technology, but in art or everyday life. Having this definition in mind, we can draw two important conclusions. First, something can be taken as a model if it is an abstraction of things from the real world, but it is simultaneously a thing from the real world. Whether we take it as a model or as a real/world thing depends on the context, i.e. on the point of view. Second, models can be defined using metamodeling concepts formally or implicitly. Since implicit metamodels cannot be precisely defined using formalisms, as in the case of art, in the rest of this discussion we analyze only formal models. Nevertheless, much of the conclusions can also be applied to implicit metamodels.

Figure 8-4 shows a general modeling architecture that was inspired by MDA and is in fact its generalization. In such a modeling architecture, the M0 layer is the real world as in [Bezivin et al, 2005] and [Atkinson and Kuhne, 2003]. It includes all possible things that we try to represent using the models residing at the M1 layer. That representation is more or less abstract and simplified, depending on how rich our models are. Models are defined using concepts de-fined in metamodels, so each metamodel determines how expressive its models can be. M2 is the layer where the metamodels are located. The metamodels are also defined using some concepts. A set of concepts used to define metamodels resides at the separate M3 layer at the top of this architecture and is called meta-metamodel. Meta-metamodel is nothing more than a metamodel that is conventionally elected to be used for other metamodels' definition; it also defines itself. The architecture is generalized to comprise not only models and metamodels based on an object-oriented meta-metamodel like MOF is, but also other systems, for instance: ontologies, Semantic Web technologies or non-technical representations.

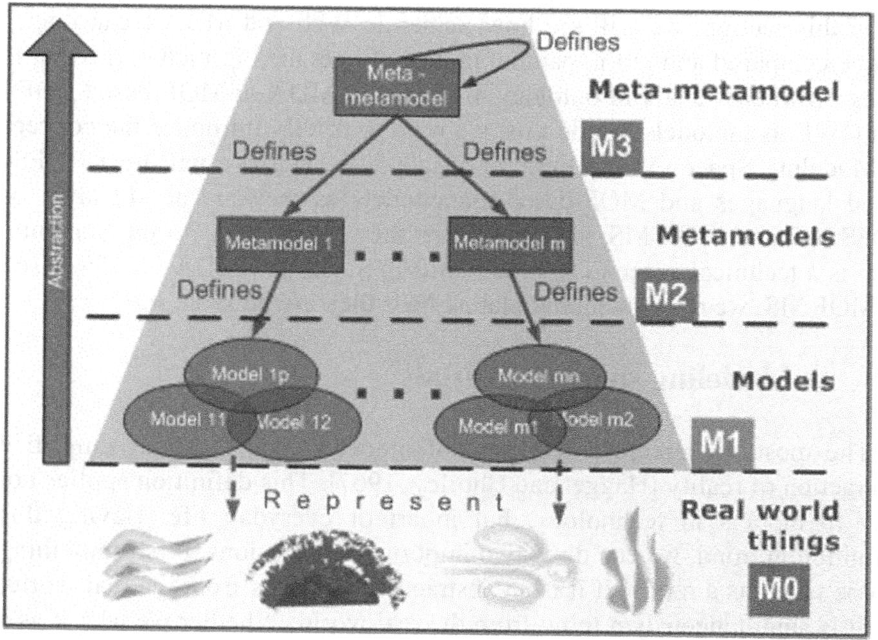

Figure 8-4. General four-layer modeling architecture three modeling layers and the real world)

This is a convenient place to introduce the concept of modeling spaces. A modeling space (MS) is a modeling architecture defined by a particular meta-metamodel. Meta-models defined by the meta-metamodel and models defined by those metamodels represent the real world from one point of view, i.e. from the point of view of that MS. As the meta-metamodel defines the core concepts used in defining all other metamodeling concepts, it is defined by itself. If it was defined by some other concepts, it would not be a meta-metamodel; it would be an ordinary metamodel in some other MS.

4.2 RDFS and MOF modeling spaces

Figure 8-5 shows a few examples of well-known MSs. The most straightforward example from this picture is the MOF MS. It is defined by the MOF meta-metamodel, which in turn is self-defined. It defines various metamodels, for instance Unified Modeling Language [UML2, 2003] or Ontology Definition Metamodel [Djuric et al, 2005b], that are used to describe models that represent things from the real world. The same reality is described in the context of other MSs, like RDF(S) or EBNF spaces.

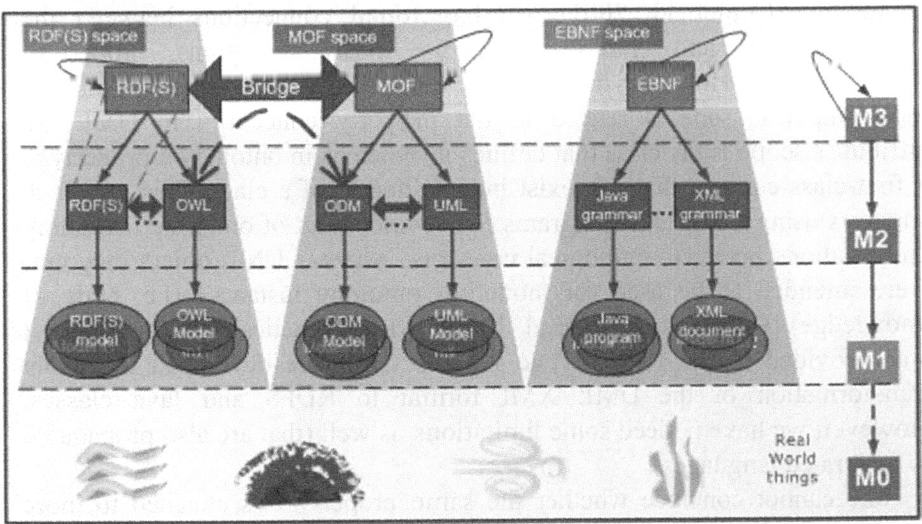

Figure 8-5. RDFS, MOF and EBNF modeling spaces

Although some ontology practitioners may make difference between ontologies and models in the sense of UML or other OO models, RDF(S), OWL or other ontologies are models (but not OO models), because they are abstractions of reality. Therefore, in MS view, RDF(S) and OWL language are metamodels, defined by the RDF(S), which is a meta-metamodel. Don't be confused seeing RDF(S) two times at different layers. It is the same set of concepts, but with different purposes; at M2 it is used to create ontologies and at M3 it is used to define languages (metamodels).

The correlation is obvious; to do the transformation from some RDF(S) based language (RDF(S) or OWL to a corresponding MOF metamodel, RDFS metamodel or OWL metamodel, we should create a bridge which relates their defining concepts at M3. For example, rdfs:Class is related to the most similar MOF concept, MOF Class etc. More on this issue can be found in [Djuric et al, 2005].

5. A BRIEF HISTORY OF ONTOLOGY MODELING

In this section we describe existing efforts to enable using UML, current UML tools, as well as MDA-based standards in ontological engineering. Our goal is to explain the formal background of each approach and their mappings to ontology languages. Table 8-1 summarizes the analyzed frameworks, their formal definitions, the kinds of model interchange description they use, their proposals for implementing the mappings, and the target ontology languages.

The idea to use UML in ontological engineering was firstly suggested by Cranefield [Cranefield, 2001]. He has found connections between the standard UML and ontology concepts: classes, relations, properties, inheritance, etc. However, there is some dissimilarity between them, and the most important one is related to the property concept – in UML, an attribute's scope is the class that defines it, whereas in ontology a property is a first-class concept that can exist independently of a class. This approach suggests using UML class diagrams for development of ontology taxonomy and relations between ontological concepts, whereas UML object diagrams were intended to be used for modeling ontology instances (i.e. body of knowledge) [Chandrasekaran et al, 1999]. Also a practical software support was provided in the form of two XSLTs that were developed to enable transformation of the UML XMI format to RDFS and Java classes. However, we have noticed some limitations as well (that are also propagated to generated languages):

- one cannot conclude whether the same property was attached to more than one class;
- one cannot create a hierarchy of properties;
- target RDFS ontology description does not have advanced restriction concepts (e.g. multiplicity).

Backlawski and his colleagues have introduced two approaches to ontology development. The first one extends the UML metamodel by introducing new metaclasses [Baclawski, 2001]. For instance, these metaclasses define a property as a first class concept, as well as a restriction on a property. This way they solved the "property problem" in UML. This solution is mainly based on the DAML+OIL ontology language [McGuinness et al, 2002]. In order to enable using standard UML tools, they propose a UML profile and its mapping to DAML+OIL. The authors realized that this solution was fairly awkward because it introduced some new concepts in the UML metamodel. Therefore, they have developed an independent ontology metamodel using the MOF, which they named the Unified Ontology Language (UOL) [Baclawski, 2002]. This metamodel was also inspired by DAML+OIL. We have been unable to find any practical software tool that would be able to map these two MDA-based ontology languages into a Semantic Web language.

Falkovych and her associates [Falkovych et al., 2003] do not extend the standard UML metamodel in order to enable transformation of UML models into equivalent DAML+OIL descriptions. They use a UML-separated hierarchy to define the kinds of ontology properties. A practical mapping from UML models to DAML+OIL is implemented using XSLT. The main limitations of this solution are:

1. the lack of mechanisms for formal property specification (e.g. defining property inheritance, or inverseOf relation between properties);
2. it is based on UML class diagrams, which contain only graphical artifacts of real UML elements included in a model (e.g. all associations titled with the same name are assumed to represent the same property, although each association is a distinct model element in UML). Of course, this diagram problem can be partly overcome with XMI for UML 2.0 that supports diagram representation.

Protégé is the leading ontological engineering tool [Noy et al., 2001]. It has complex software architecture, easily extensible through plug-ins. Many components that provide interfaces to other knowledge-based tools (Jess, Argenon, OIL, PAL constraint, etc.) have been implemented in this way, as well as support for different ontology languages and formats like XML, DAML+OIL (backend), and OIL (tab). In fact, Protégé has a formally defined MOF-based metamodel. This metamodel is extensible and adaptable. This means that Protégé can be adapted to support a new ontology language by adding new metaclasses and metaslots into a Protégé ontology. Introduction of these new metamodeling concepts enable users to add necessary ontology primitives (e.g. the Protégé class has different features from OWL class). In that way it can, for instance, support RDFS [Noy et al., 2000] or OWL. It is especially interesting that Protégé has backends for UML and XMI. These two backends use the NetBeans' Metadata Repository (MDR – http://mdr.netbeans.org). The first backend exchanges UML models (i.e. classes, and their relations) using the standard UML XMI format, while the second one uses the XMI format that is compliant with the Protégé MOF-defined metamodel. It is obvious that one can share ontologies through Protégé (e.g. import an ontology in the UML XMI format and store it in the OWL format). However, Protégé has one limitation in its UML XMI support – it does not map class relations (i.e. associations) into a Protégé ontology (i.e. it does not attach instance slots to classes). This limitation was expected since Protégé imports UML models without any extension (i.e. a UML Profile).

The software tool called DUET (http://codip.grci.com/Tools/Tools.html), which enables importing DAML ontologies into Rational Rose and

ArgoUML as well as exporting UML models into the DAML ontology language [McGuinness et al., 2002], has been developed in order to support ontological engineering. This tool uses a quite simple UML Profile that contains stereotypes for modeling ontologies (based on UML package) and properties (based on UML class). Additionally, DUET uses an XSLT that transforms RDFS ontologies into equivalent DAML ontologies. That way, an RDFS ontology can be imported into UML tools through the DAML language. Of course, this tool has constraints similar to approaches we have already discussed (e.g. Falkovych et al.) since it has no ability to define advanced class and property relations (e.g. inverseOf, equivalentProperty, equivalentClass, etc.). On the other hand, this is the first UML tool extension that enables ontology sharing between ontology language (i.e. DAML) and a UML tool in both directions.

Xpetal (http://www.langdale.com.au/styler/xpetal) is another tool implemented in Java that transforms Rational Rose models from the mdl format to RDF and RDFS. This tool has limitations similar to those that we have already mentioned while discussing Cranefield's software (XSLTs), since it uses only standard UML and does not provide a convenient solution for representing properties, their relations, advanced class restrictions, etc. Actually, this tool is even more limited than the Cranefield's one, since it is oriented to Rational Rose, in contrast to the Cranefield's XSLT that is applicable to every UML XMI document and independent of UML tools.

Visual Ontology Modeler (VOM) is a result of the collaborative work between Sandpiper Software Inc and Knowledge System Lab (KSL) at Stanford University. This tool extends Rational Rose and enables ontology development with user-friendly wizards, automatically creating the logical model and related diagrams. The tool is based upon a UML profile for ontology development that is closely related to Protégé's metamodel for ontologies as well as to Gruber's Frame ontology [Gruber, 1993]. Apart from the use of well-known UML-based graphical notation for ontology development VOM supports widely accepted Semantic Web ontology languages such as DAML+OIL and OWL. The transformations between UML models and those ontology languages are built-in into programming logic of the Rational Rose add-in, so Rational Rose can only perform them. Although, this approach uses UML, we cannot say that is a real MDA-based approach, but it is rather an MDA-compatible approach, as it is not based on an ontology metamodel. This compatibility is achieved through the support for the UML Profile and XMI.

Our opinion is that all these approaches we have explored above are useful, but none of them gives a full solution that contains:

- a formal description of the new MDA-based ontology language;

- a related UML profile and necessary transformations between these two languages, as well as transformations to contemporary Semantic Web languages (i.e. OWL) [OMG ODM, 2003].

Table 8-1 gives an overview of present UML and MDA based ontology development frameworks and their transformations to the Semantic Web languages

Table 8-1. Overview of present UML and MDA based ontology development frameworks and their transformations to the Semantic Web languages

Approach	Metamodel	Model description	Transformation mechanism	Generated ontology language
Cranefield [Cranefield, 2001]	Standard UML	UML XMI	XSLT	RDFS, Java classes
Backlawski et al. [Baclawski, 2001] [Baclawski, 2002]	UML Profile, MOF-based ontology language	(not given – UML XMI, and MOF XMI can be used)	–	DAML
Falkovych et al. [Falkovych et al., 2003]	Standard UML	UML XMI	XSLT	DAML+OIL
Protégé	Protégé metamodel Standard UML	Protégé XMI UML XMI	Programmed	OWL, RDF(S), DAML+OIL, XML, UML XMI, Protégé XMI, …
Visual Ontology Modeler (VOM) [Kendall et al., 2002] [Ceccaroni & Kendal, 2003]	UML Profile	Rational Rose	Programmed	OWL, DAML+OIL, RDFS
DUET	UML Profile	Rational Rose, ArgoUML	Programmed	DAML+OIL
Xpetal	Standard UML	Rational Rose mdl files	Programmed	RDFS

We believe that full usage of MDA provides us with considerable benefits when defining metamodeling architecture and enables us to develop new languages (i.e. ontology language). Actually, there is a RFP at OMG that should enclose all these requirements, but it is still in its initial stage (http://ontology.omg.org).

6. MDA-BASED ONTOLOGY MODELING INFRASTRUCTURE

6.1 An overview

To be widely adopted by users and to succeed in real-world applications, knowledge engineering and ontology modeling must catch up with mainstream software trends. It will provide a good support in software tools and ease the integration with existing or upcoming software tools and applications, which will add values to both sides. To be employed in common applications, software knowledge management must be taken out of laboratories and isolated high-tech applications and put closer to ordinary developers. This issue has been addressed in more details in Cranefield's papers [Cranefield, 2001a].

MDA and its four-layer architecture provides a solid basis for defining metamodels of any modeling language, so it is the straight choice to define an ontology-modeling language in MOF. Such language can utilize MDA's support in modeling tools, model management and interoperability with other MOF-defined metamodels. Present software tools do not implement many of the concepts that are the basis of MDA. However, most of these applications, which are mostly oriented to the UML and M1 layer, are expected to be enhanced in the next few years to support MDA.

Currently, there is a RFP (Request for Proposal) within OMG that tries to define a suitable language for modeling Semantic Web ontology languages in the context of MDA [ODMRFP, 2003]. According to this RFP, the authors give their proposal of such architecture. In our approach of ontology modeling in the scope of MDA, which is shown in Figure 8-6, several specifications should be defined:

- Ontology Definition Metamodel (ODM)
- Ontology UML Profile – a UML Profile that supports UML notation for ontology definition
- Two-way mappings between: OWL and ODM, ODM and other metamodels, ODM and Ontology UML Profile and from Ontology UML Profile to other UML profiles.

Ontology Definition Metamodel (ODM) should be designed to comprehend common ontology concepts. A good starting point for ODM construction is OWL since it is the result of the evolution of existing ontology representation languages, and is a W3C recommendation. It is at the Logical layer of the Semantic Web [Berners-Lee, 1998], on top of RDF Schema (Schema layer). In order to make use of graphical modeling capabilities of UML, an ODM should have a corresponding UML Profile

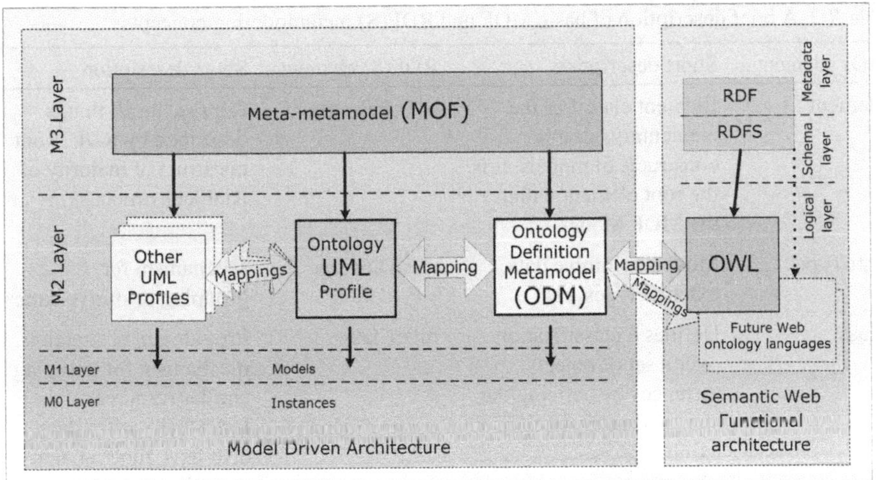

Figure 8-6. Ontology modeling in the context of MDA and Semantic Web

[Sigel, 2001]. This profile enables graphical editing of ontologies using UML diagrams as well as other benefits of using mature UML CASE tools. Both UML models and ODM models are serialized in XMI format so the two-way transformation between them can be done using XSL Transformation. OWL also has representation in the XML format, so another pair of XSL Transformations should be provided for two-way mapping between ODM and OWL. For mapping from the ODM into other metamodels or from Ontology UML Profile into another, technology-specific UML Profiles, additional transformations can be added to support usage of ontologies in design of other domains and vice versa.

6.2 Bridging RDFS and MOF

Before we start with a more detailed description of ODM, we must clarify differences between metamodeling in the Semantic Web world, which is based on RDFS constructs, and in the object-oriented MDA, which is based on MOF. Obviously, if we want to make transformation from RDFS MS to MOF MS, we need to make transformation rules, which have to determine which target concept (defined in MOF) we should get from a source concept (defined in RDFS). The main task is to identify the most important differences and similarities between main constructs from both spaces and decide how to overcome these differences. These concepts are briefly compared in the Table 8-2, grouping the most similar concepts from both spaces.

Table 8-2. A brief description of basic MOF and RDF(S) metamodeling concepts

MOF element	Short description	RDF(S) element	Short description
Element	Element classifies the elementary, atomic constructs of models. It is the root element within the MOF Model.	rdfs:Resource	Represents all things described by RDF. Root construct of majority of RDF constructs.
DataType	Models primitive data, external types, etc.	rdfs:Datatype	Mechanism for grouping primitive data.
Class	Defines a classification over a set of object instances by defining the state and behavior they exhibit.	rdfs:Class	Provides an abstraction mechanism for grouping similar resources. In RDF(S), rdfs:Class also have function that is similar to a MOF concept of Classifier.
Classifier	Abstract concept that defines classification. It is specialized by Class, DataType, etc.		
Association	Expresses relationships in the metamodel between pairs of instances of Classes	rdf:Property	Defines relation between subject resources and object resources.
Attribute	Defines a notional slot or value holder, typically in each instance of its Class.		
TypedElement	The TypedElement is an element that requires a type as part of its definition. A TypedElement does not itself define a type, but is associated with a Classifier. Examples are object instances, data values etc.		In RDF(S), any rdfs:Resource can be typed (via the rdf:type property) by some rdfs:Class.

There are both good and bad news derived from this comparison. The good news is that there is a significant similarity: they both are a sort of entity-relationship based worlds. In RDFS, rdfs:Class is a sort of entity, while rdf:Property is a sort of relation. In MOF, Classifier represents an entity that is related to other entities via associations or attributes. Basically, a concept (at M2 in RDFS MS) that is modeled as a rdfs:Class (at M3 in RDFS space) becomes concept (at M2 in MOF space) that is a MOF Class (at M3 in MOF space), a concept modeled as a rdfs:Property becomes a MOF Association or a MOF Attribute and so on. For Example, owl:Class (M2) is defined as a rdfs:Class (M3) in RDFS. In MOF, it will be OWLClass, a MOF Class. rdf:Property is also an rdfs:Class, so in MOF MS it becomes a MOF Class RDFProperty. An example of an rdf:Property is rdfs:subclassOf; it should be transformed to a MOF Association RDFSsubClassOf.

The bad news is that corresponding concepts (rdfs:Class and Classifier and rdf:Property and Association or Attribute) have different natures. The concept of Class in RDFS (rdfs:Class) is not completely identical as a concept of Class that is defined in UML and MOF. Every rdfs:Class is a set of resources, called class extension. These resources are instances of that class. Two classes can have the same class extension but still be different classes. Classes in RDFS are set-theoretic, while traditional OO classes are more behavioral. Unlike an OO class, an rdfs:Class does not directly define any attributes or relations with other resources, and there is no any concept similar to methods. Attributes and relations are defined as properties.

In RDF, a property is a concept that represents relation between a subject resource and an object resource. Therefore, it might look similar to a concept of Attribute or Association in traditional, object oriented sense. However, the important difference is that rdf:Property is a stand-alone concept; it does not depend of any class or resource as associations or attributes are in MOF. In ontology languages, a property can be defined even with no classes associated to it. That is why a property can not be represented as an ordinary association or attribute, its closest object-oriented relatives.

6.3 Design Rationale for Ontology UML Profile

In order to customize UML for modeling ontologies, we define UML Profile for ontology representation, called Ontology UML Profile.

In developing our Ontology UML Profile we used experiences of other UML Profile designers (e.g., see [Juerjens, 2003]). Applying such experiences to our case, we wanted our Ontology UML Profile to:

- offer stereotypes and tags for all recurring ontology design elements, such as classes, individuals, properties, complements, unions, and the like;
- make specific ontology modeling and design elements easy to represent on UML diagrams produced by standard CASE tools, thus keeping track of ontological information on UML models;
- enable encapsulating ontological knowledge in an easy-to-read format and offer it to software engineers;

- make possible to evaluate ontology UML diagrams and indicate possible inconsistencies;
- support Ontology Definition Metamodel, hence to be able to represent all ODM concepts.
- Currently, several different approaches to ontology representation in UML have been proposed. We note two major trends among them:
- Extending UML with new constructs to support specific ontology concepts (Property for example) [Baclawski, 2001].
- Using standard UML and defining a UML Profile for ontology representation [Baclawski, 2002].

We believe that ontology representation in UML can be achieved without non-standard UML extensions, hence our approach belongs to the latter of the above two trends. In our Ontology UML profile, specific ontology concepts are annotated using the standard UML extension mechanisms described above. Models created with such a UML Profile will be supported by standard UML tools, since they do not add non-standard concepts to UML, thus they are UML models. Since in our approach UML is used to support ODM, not as a stand-alone tool for ontology modeling, Ontology UML Profile will not cover all of the essential ODM (Ontology Definition Metamodel) concepts. Ontology UML Profile should define only constructs for concrete concepts, such as OWLObjectProperty, OWLClass or OWLThing, leaving ODM to deal with abstract constructs like Property, etc, which are not used in development of real ontologies (models), and do not relate to real-world things; they are only introduced to ODM in order to create a coherent hierarchy.

A UML Profile definition in the context of the MDA four-layer metamodeling architecture means extending UML at the metamodel layer (M2). One can understand these extensions as a new language, but also UML as a family of languages [Duddy, 2002]. Each of these languages uses UML notation with the four UML extension mechanisms. Recent UML specifications enable using graphical notation for specifying stereotypes and tagged definitions [Kobryn, 2001]. Thus, all stereotypes and tagged values that are defined in this paper can be shown in this way.

The notation used for stereotype creation of Ontology UML Profile («OntClass» stereotype) accommodates UML's Class («metaclass»). Having this graphical notation for the UML extension mechanism can be useful for explaining certain relations between UML constructs and new stereotypes, but also between stereotypes themselves.

Since stereotypes are the principle UML extension mechanism, one might be tempted to think that defining Ontology UML Profile is a matter of specifying a couple of stereotypes and using them carefully in a coherent manner. In reality, however, it is much more complicated than that. The reason is that there are a number of fine details to take care of, as well as the existence of some conceptual inconsistencies between MDA and UML that may call for alternative design decisions.

7. ONTOLOGY DEFINITION METAMODEL

There were four separate ODM proposals responding to OMG's ODM RFP [ODMRFP, 2003] submitted by the following OMG members: IBM [OMG IBM, 2003], Gentleware [OMG Gentleware, 2003], DSTC [OMG DSTC, 2003], and Sandpiper Software Inc and KSL [OMG Sandpiper&KSL, 2003]. However, none of those submissions gave a comprehensive proposal. For example, none of them proposed XMI bindings for ODM, none of them proposed mappings between ODM and OWL, only IBM [OMG IBM, 2003] and Gentleware proposed Ontology UML profile, etc. Accordingly, the OMG partners decided to join their efforts, and the current result of their efforts is the ODM joint submission [ODMJoint, 2004]. In the rest of this section we introduce the main concepts of that common initiative.

7.1 ODM joint submission

To create a joint ODM, OMG ODM submitters decided to organize it as composition of several metamodels. We show the architecture of the current ODM submission in Figure 8-7.

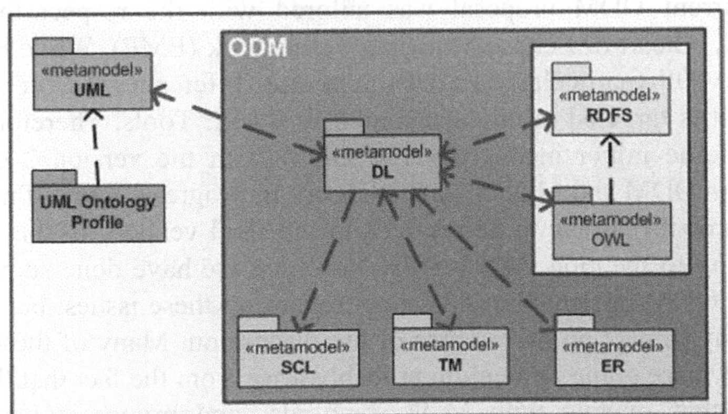

Figure 8-7. ODM Metamodels

The central metamodel is the Description Logics (DL) metamodel since the most of current ontology languages (e.g. OWL) are based upon some of

DL classes. The role of this metamodel is to mediate all metamodels defined in ODM. In order to support well-known Semantic Web ontology languages ODM has two separate metamodels, namely OWL and RDFS. Considering the role of the DL metamodel, mappings between those two languages are done through the DL metamodel. Since ODM needs an expressive logics language that can be used on the Semantic Web to describe string-based expressions, the ODM has the Simple Common Language (SCL) metamodel. Apart from W3C ontology languages, ODM supports other ontology language standards (ISO) by having defined the Topic Maps (TM) metamodel. Finally, to provide connection with many existing systems grounded on databases, the ODM defines the Entity Relationship (ER) metamodel.

Taking into account the importance of UML ODM developers want to create mappings between the standard UML metamodel and the DL metamodel, and hence establish a way for employing present UML models in ontology development. Furthermore, they define Ontology UML Profile (OUP) using standard UML extension mechanisms. The purpose of OUP is to enable the use of the standard UML graphical notation for developing ontologies.

7.2 A few issues regarding the joint submission

Before we start a more detailed explanation of OMG's Ontology Definition Metamodel (ODM), we are going to briefly discuss a few issues that might be interesting in respect to the upcoming version 2 of the MOF standard.

The current ODM proposal was tailored with the respect to ECore metamodel, a heart of Eclipse Modeling Framework (EMF). While ECore is similar to MOF (particularly EMOF) there are differences. ECore is much simpler and is targeted to implementation in CASE Tools. Therefore, there might be some minor incongruities in ODM with the version 2 of MOF standard. As ODM and MOF v2 are still work in progress, some, if not all of them are probably going to be resolved in the final version. In this section, we are going to mention them briefly. Note that we have done some minor changes in ODM presented in this paper regarding these issues, but they do not have any impact on the essence of the discussion. Many of these minor flaws that we are going to mention probably arise from the fact that there are any tools that operate with MOF standards, and proposals have been constructed using CASE tools (EMF for example) that all have their non-standard way of handling some things.

There are lots of associations having the same name in the metamodel proposal that resist in the same package. An example of such situation are two different associations in DL metamodel both having the same name – contains. However, MOF specification clearly states that the name of any element within the same namespace must be unique. A solution could be found in renaming one of these associations, or refactoring by extracting class. The first solution seems less intrusive for this discussion and the second is more elegant from the point of view of software engineering.

Many associations were left unnamed in ODM joint submission. MOF specification states that every Type must be named, and Association inherits Type, so this must be fulfilled. Also note that UML2 Infrastructure specification allows unnamed Types but EMOF adds a constraint that every Type must be named. In this discussion, we have added names to associations, but his can be also solved in CASE tools, which can generate random names. However, random names are not convenient if some human should work with them. Would it be pleasant to have to work with associations named "mnrt90490789" or "FF0AD3458B0BB"?

Associations models relationships between classes. If classes are subjects and objects, associations should represent verbs. Thus, their names should be verbs. The good rule would be that ODM should name associations after the names of properties that are their counterparts in RDF(S), even if they are not verbs. In our opinion, if an association does not have direct RDFS counterpart, verbs should be used for names. In the joint submission, most of the names of properties were used in naming association ends, not associations.

In OWL, owl:Ontology is specified as subclass of rdfs:Resource. ODM introduces a concept of Vocabulary as a means of grouping similar resources in RDFS metamodel, which does not inherit RDFSResource. OWLOntology concept inherits Vocabulary, but then it means it is not RDFSResource, and it should be according to the OWL language.

7.3 Resource Description Framework Schema (RDFS) metamodel

Resource is one of the basic RDFS concepts; it represents all things described by RDF and OWL. It may represent anything on the Web: a Web site, a Web page, a part of a Web page, or some other object named by URI. Compared to ontology concepts, it could be viewed as a root concept, the Thing. In RDFS MS, rdfs:Resource is defined as an instance of rdfs:Class. Since we use MOF as a meta-metamodeling language, this concept will be defined as an instance of MOF Class named RDFSResource. It is the root class of most other concepts from RDFS and OWL metamodels that will be described: RDFSClass, RDFSProperty, RDFStatement etc. The RDFS metamodel concepts hierarchy of is shown on class diagram in Figure 8-8.

Other class diagrams depict these concepts in more detail. Note that, since RDFS is self-defined and rdfs:Class inherits rdfs:Resource, in RDFS MS rdfs:Resource is an instance of itself. However, in MOF MS, RDFSResource is an instance of MOF Class, not RDFS Resource, because MOF is meta-metamodel, not RDFS.

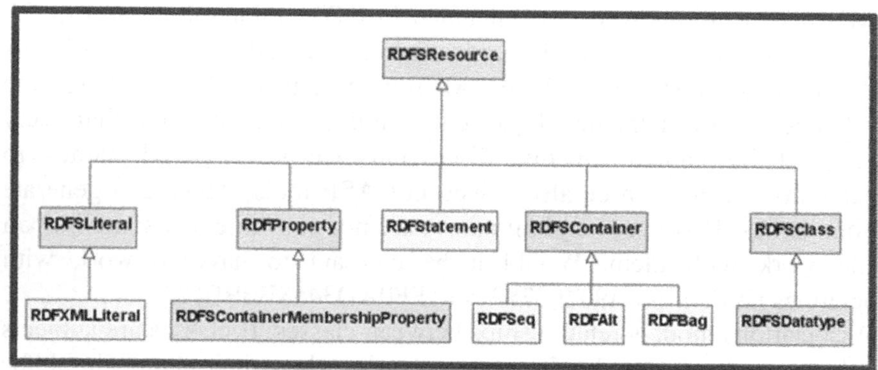

Figure 8-8. RDFS metamodel – hierarchy of concepts

Among shown concepts, the most important ones are

- RDFSResource,
- RDFSClass,
- RDFProperty, and
- RDFStatement.

They are the base for forming Subject-Predicate-Object triples, like “this section – describes – RDFS metamodel”.

Figure 8-9 shows the basic characteristics of RDFSResource and RDFSClass concepts. RDFSResource has three attributes, all of String type, which are primarily intended to identify an instance of RDFSResource (and all concepts that inherit it):

- localName, for the name of the resource, unique within a namespace,
- namespace, for a namespace in which resource resides and grouping similar resources,
- uri, unique resource identifier (may be constructed from namespace and localName and vice versa).

RDFS specification also defines that an rdfs:Resource can have comments and labels attached. As these characteristics in RDFS MS are described using rdf:Property instances, rdf:comment and rdf:label, in MOF MS we model them using MOF Association concept. On the other end of these associations is RDFSLiteral, a concept that is used to represent simple data, like numbers, text etc. Therefore, using these two associations, we can add various textual, numeric or other comments and labels to our data. A special kind of RDFSLiteral is RDFXMLLiteral, which represents XML textual data.

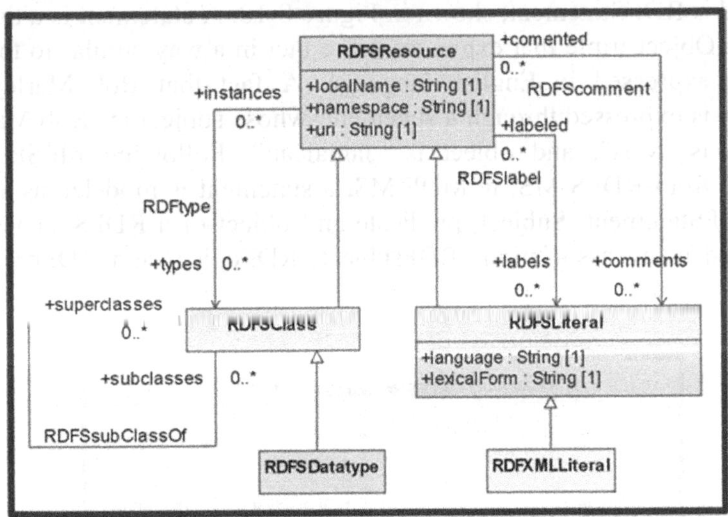

Figure 8-9. RDFSClass and RDFSResource

RDFS specification also defines that an rdfs:Resource can have comments and labels attached. As these characteristics in RDFS MS are described using rdf:Property instances, rdf:comment and rdf:label, in MOF MS we model them using MOF Association concept. On the other end of these associations is RDFSLiteral, a concept that is used to represent simple data, like numbers, text etc. Therefore, using these two associations, we can add various textual, numeric or other comments and labels to our data. A special kind of RDFSLiteral is RDFXMLLiteral, which represents XML textual data.

RDFS also defines a concept that is used for grouping similar resources – rdfs:Class. In MOF-based metamodel, it can be represented using MOF Class named RDFSClass, that, following the specification, inherits RDFSResource. This is determined by RDFtype (rdf:type property from RDFS MS). An RDFSResource can have many types, and multiple RDFSResource instances can have the same type. RDFSsubClassOf models inheritance at M1 layer, ontological inheritance, among various instances of RDFSClass. An RDFSClass instance can inherit many other RDFSClass instances and can be inherited by many other RDFSClass instances, forming complex inheritance hierarchies. Yet again, do not confuse RDFSsubClassOf with generalization between RDFSClass and RDFSResource. It is the same property in RDFS MS because RDFS is both metamodel and meta-

metamodel, but in MOF MS, we use generalization association to model inheritance at M2 layer, not RDFSsubClassOf.

The next important concept from RDFS metamodel that needs to be explained is RDFStatement, shown in Figure 8-10. A statement is a Subject-Predicate-Object triple that expresses some fact in a way similar to the way facts are expressed in English language. A fact that Bob Marley was Jamaican, is expressed through a statement, whose subject is "Bob Marley", predicate is "was", and object is "Jamaican". Following rdf:Statement definition from RDFS MS, in MOF MS, a statement is modeled as a MOF Class RDFStatement. Subject, predicate and object of a RDFStatement are determined using associations RDFsubject, RDFobject and RDFpredicate, MOF MS counterparts of properties rdf:subject, rdf:object and rdf:predicate.

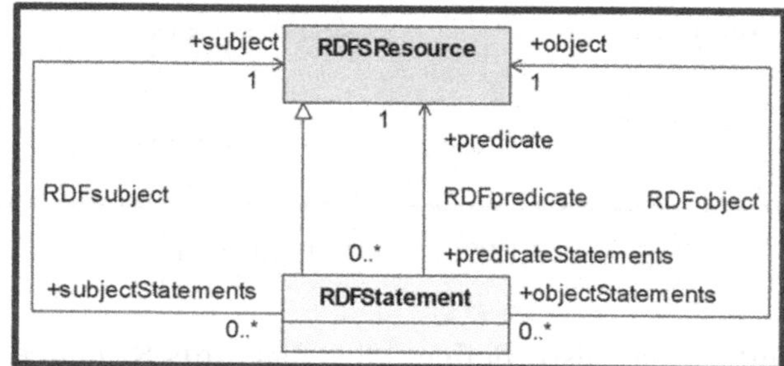

Figure 8-10. RDFS Statement

From the definition of RDFStatement, we can see that all three associations, subject, object and predicate, link RDFStatement to RDFSResource. This design is widely open for any kinds of statements, even those that do not mean anything, for example "Bob Marley"-"Cuba"-"Jamaican". Therefore, predicate should usually be a resource that represents some verb, like "be" or "memorize", or some characteristic of a resource, like "name". In RDFS MS, this is rdf:Property, a concept that represents a type of relationship between resources.

At M2 layer, RDFS defines two properties, rdfs:domain and rdfs:range that connects an rdf:Property with rdfs:Class, making possible to distinguish various types of relations between various types of resources at M1 layer. In MOF MS, RDFS metamodel represents a property using MOF Class named RDFProperty, a descendant of RDFSResource, as shown in Figure 8-11.

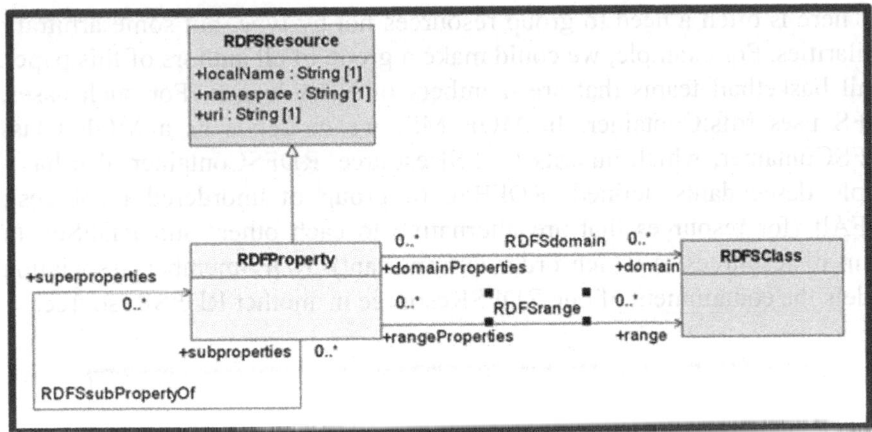

Figure 8-11. RDFSProperty

RDFSdomain and RDFSrange associations represent corresponding rdfs:domain and rdfs:range relations from RDFS MS. RDFSdomain determines which types of resources can be at the "source" end of relation and RDFSrange determines the type of the "destination" end. Another difference between properties and its object-oriented counterparts is that properties can form complex hierarchies, just as classes do. This is modeled by RDFSsubPropertyOf association, a MOF MS counterpart of rdfs:subPropertyOf from RDFS MS.

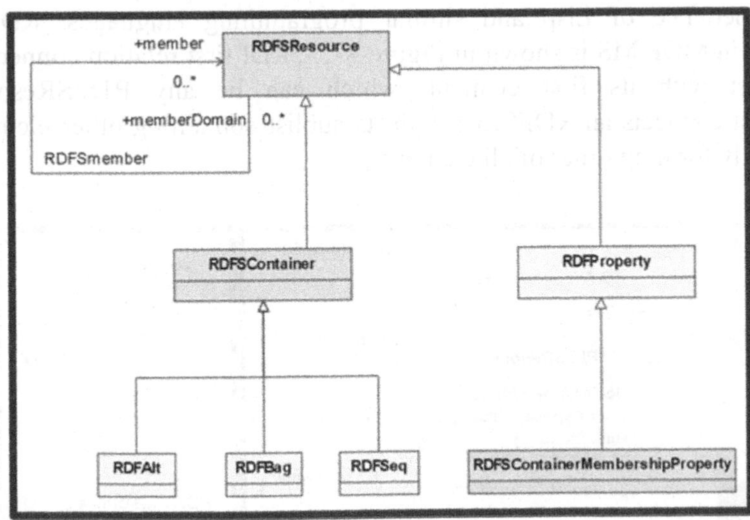

Figure 8-12. RDFS Containers

There is often a need to group resources not by type, but some arbitrary similarities. For example, we could make a group of all authors of this paper, or all basketball teams that are members of NBA league. For such cases, RDFS uses rdfs:Container. In MOF MS, we model is as a MOF Class RDFSContainer, which inherits RDFSResource. RDFSContainer also has a couple descendants defined: RDFBag (a group of unordered resources), RDFAlt (for resources that are alternative to each other) and RDFSeq (a group of resources in which order is important). RDFSmember association models the containment of one RDFSResource in another RDFSResource.

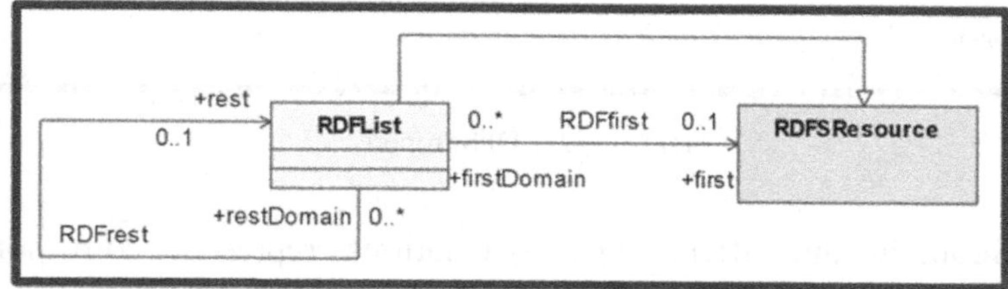

Figure 8-13. [Please provide a caption for this figure]

RDF containers are open in the sense that the core RDF specifications define no mechanism to state that there are no more members. The RDF Collection vocabulary of classes and properties can describe a closed collection, i.e. one that can have no more members. A collection is represented as a list of items, a representation that will be familiar to those with experience of Lisp and similar programming languages. RDFList modeled in MOF MS is shown in Figure 8-13. RDFfirst relation connects an RDFSList with its first element, which can be any RDFSResource. RDFSrest connects an RDFSList with its sublist containing other elements, recursively forming order of all elements.

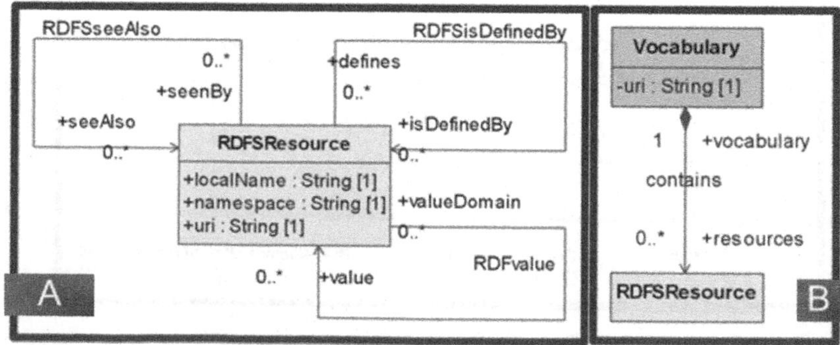

Figure 8-14. (RDFS Utilities, B) Vocabulary

In Figure 8-14A we can see a couple properties from RDFS modeled in MOF MS as associations: RDFSseeAlso, RDFSisDefinedBy and RDFvalue. These properties are also known as "utilities". RDFSseeAlso points to another resource that could be useful to look at. RDFSisDefinedBy points to another RDFSResource that defines the first one. RDFvalue association is used in describing structural values.

Vocabulary, shown in Figure 8-14B, is the concept that is not explicitly defined in RDFS (modeled in RDFS MS). Vocabulary is a concept similar to a concept of Ontology in ontology modeling or Package in UML. It is a concept used for grouping other concepts that belong to similar domains. Containment is denoted by contains association, which links one Vocabulary to one or more RDFSResource.

Giving graphical diagrams in this place as an example of using RDFS metamodel would not be easily possible, because RDF(S) does not have standard graphic representation. Any plain UML diagram given at this place would not represent concepts from RDFS metamodel, but concepts from UML metamodel, which are not the same. Fortunately, in the next section we will define a UML Profile for modeling RDFS concepts using standard UML extension mechanism. In that section, we are providing a couple examples of RDFS and OWL ontologies.

7.4 Web Ontology Language (OWL) metamodel

Web Ontology Language is built on top of RDF(S), using RDF(S) as both meta-metamodel (M3) and a metamodel that is a base for extension (M2). In MOF MS, the first dependency (RDFS as a meta-metamodel) is replaced by using MOF as a meta-metamodel. The second dependency means that OWL metamodel concepts extend RDFS metamodel concepts. Figure 8-15 shows the hierarchy or OWL concepts – we can see that most OWL concepts inherit RDFS concepts RDFSResource, RDFProperty and RDFClass. RDFSClass is a base concept of OWL concepts that represents classes (OWLClass, OWLRestriction and OWLDeprecatedClass), RDFProperty is inherited by a plenty of concepts that represent properties in OWL (OWLObjectProperty, OWLDatatypeProperty and so on). A little difference in regards to OWL in RDFS MS is that OWLOntology inherits Vocabulary, which is not defined in RDF(S).

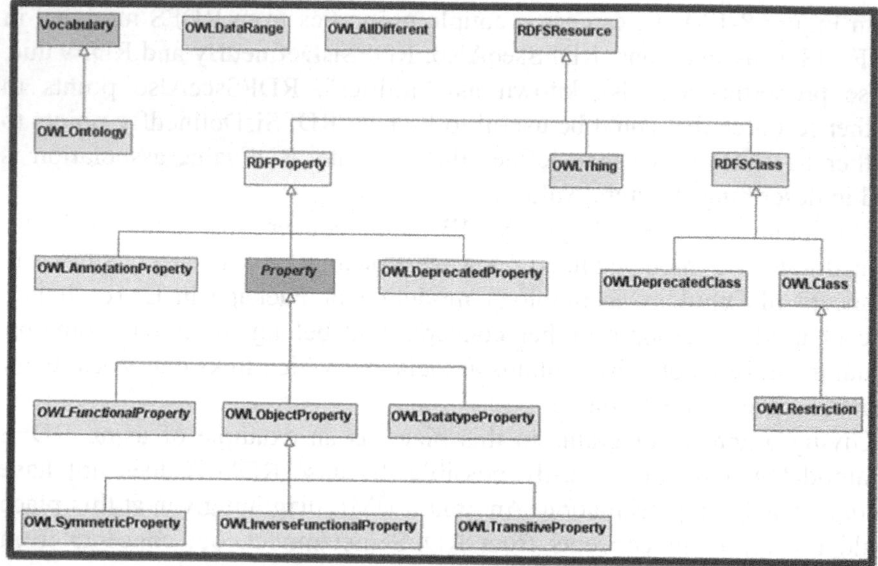

Figure 8-15. OWL Hierarchy

Classes provide an abstraction mechanism for grouping resources with similar characteristics. Like RDF classes, every OWL class is associated with a set of individuals, called the class extension. As OWL in many cases refines the concept of a class, it needs to model it separately, e.g. to inherit RDFSClass with a new concept, OWLClass. Figure 8-16 shows how OWLClass is modeled.

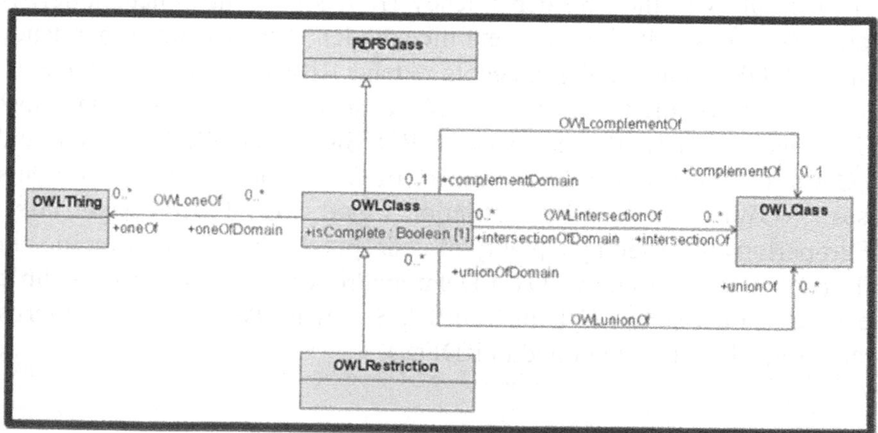

Figure 8-16. OWL Classes

OWLClass inherits RDFSClass. Because OWL Full fully supports RDFS, we can also use RDFSClass concept if we model using OWLFull.

However, it is more convenient to use OWLClass concept, because it is valid in OWL Lite and OWL DL also.

OWL Class is a set of individuals, which in OWL are modeled with OWLThing concept. Thanks to the fact that OWLClass extends RDFSClass, it also extends RDFSClass' associations from RDFS metamodel. One of these is RDFtype which enables various RDFSResources to state that some OWLClass is their type. Other associations in which RDFSClass takes part, among which RDFSsubTypeOf is one of the most important, are also inherited.

Besides defining a class by name and connecting individuals using RDFtype association, in OWL classes can be defined in several other ways. Enumeration is defined exhaustively enumerating its instances so OWLoncOf association is provided for building classes by enumeration. As in OWL a class can be constructed as a complement of another class or a union or intersection of other classes, OWLcomplementOf, OWLunionOf, and OWLintersectionOf associations are provided. These associations and their association ends multiplicities are also shown in Figure 8-16.

OWLRestriction is a special kind of OWLClass, thus it inherit OWLClass concept. It is not a "real" class, but a concept that enables constraints in OWL. Before we describe how restrictions are modeled, we should see the details of concepts that model properties in OWL, because OWLRestiction is a concept tightly connected with properties.

OWL refines concept of rdf:Property distinguishing two basic kinds of properties, owl:ObjectProperty and owl:DatatypeProperty. Recall from our discussion on RDFS metamodel that RDFProperty has its domain and range that both could be RDFSClass and that RDFSDatatype is a subclass of RDFSClass. This means that RDF does not distinguish relations between classes and relations between data types. OWL metamodel, following the OWL language from RDFS MS, introduces two distinct types of properties: OWLObjectProperty (a relationship between two OWLClasses) and OWLDatatypeProperty (a relationship between OWLClass and RDFSDatatype).

OWL metamodel from the joint submission include abstract MOF Class Property (see Figure 8-17) that is not included in standard OWL language as a common superclass of OWLObjectProperty and OWLDatatype Property. This concept is introduced to solve impedance mismatch between RDFS and MOF concepts. Particularly, MOF Association is dependent on classes that are on its ends, and Class have to have "know" which association ends it hosts. However, adding OWLequivalentProperty association directly to RDFProperty, as it is defined in OWL's owl:equivalentProperty would imply difference in RDFS metamodel when it is used alone or as a base of OWL metamodel.

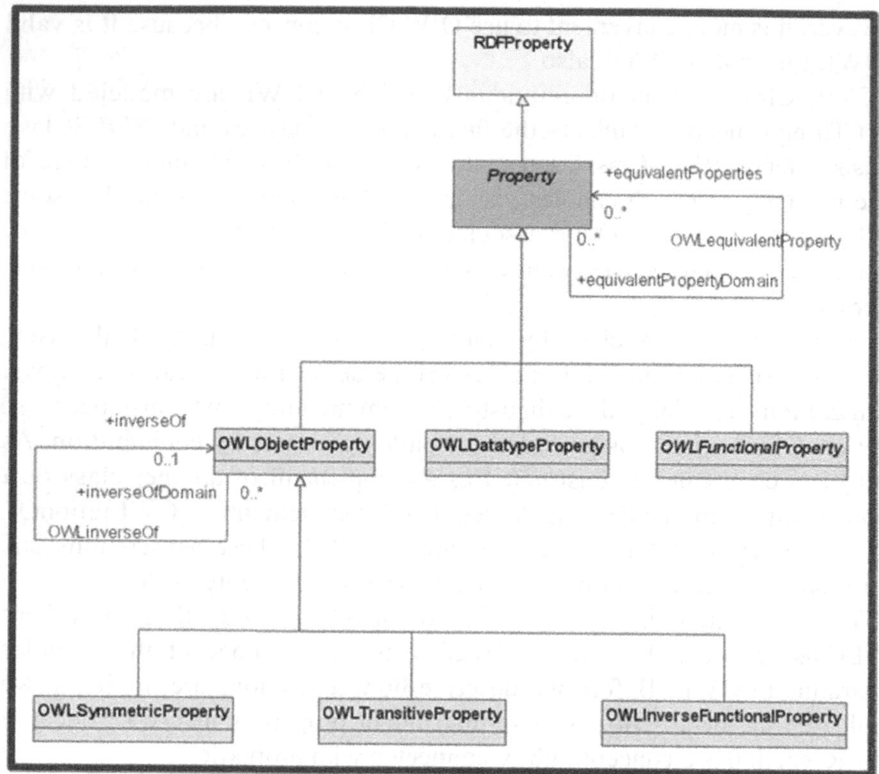

Figure 8-17. – OWL Properties

Properties in OWL cannot have a Datatype as a domain, only as a range. That is why OWLinverseOf association is applicable only to OWLObjectProperty. OWL also defines several other refined kinds of properties. owl:FunctionalProperty for relationships that have functional characteristics, owl:TransitiveProperty for transitive relationships, owl:SymmetricProperty for symmetric relationships and owl:Inverse FunctionalProperty. These types of properties are represented in MOF MS as MOF Classes with adequate inheritance analogous to that in RDFS MS.

OWLRestriction, shown in Figure 8-18, is an anonymous class of all individuals that satisfy certain property restriction. Obviously, it is a MOF counterpart of owl:Restriction concept from RDFS MS. OWLonProperty association connects OWLRestriction and a property on which that restriction is applied. There are two kinds of property restrictions: value constraints and cardinality constraints. A value constraint puts constraints on the range of the property when applied to this particular class description. Value constraints are modeled using OWLhasValue, OWLsomeValuesFrom and OWLallValuesFrom associations. A cardinality constraint puts constraints on the number of values a property can take, in the context of this particular class description. Cardinality constraints are modeled using OWLminCardinality, OWLcardinality and OWLmaxCardinality associations.

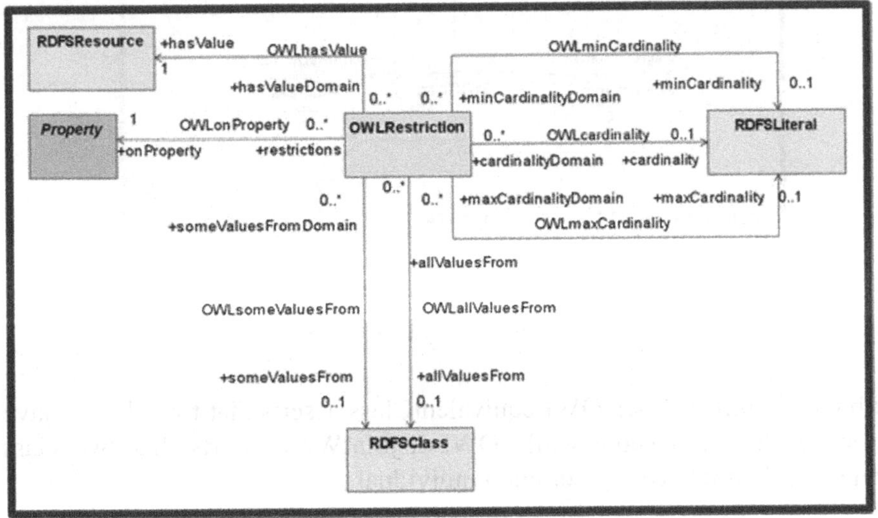

Figure 8-18. OWL Restriction

We mentioned that OWL makes a significant difference between named individuals ("objects"), and plain data values. In OWL metamodel, individuals are modeled using OWLThing concept, which is shown in Figure 8-19. As OWLThing inherits RDFSResource, it also inherits all its associations with other concepts, among which one of the most important is RDFtype, which connects RDFSResource with its type, RDFSClass. In the case of OWLThing, RDFtype association has a constraint that the other end has to be an OWLClass. OWL also introduces properties that are used to state that some individuals are the same (owl:sameAs) or different (owl:differentFrom) as others. In OWL metamodel they are modeled as associations OWLsameAs and OWLdifferentFrom.

Connecting many OWLThing instances with a bunch of single owl:differentFrom (or OWLdifferentFrom in MOF MS) connections would overcrowd the model. That is why OWL introduces owl:AllDifferent class and owl:distinctMembers property to connect that class with all individuals that are different among each other. In OWL metamodel, they are modeled as OWLAllDifferent MOF Class and OWLdistinctMembers MOF Association.

OWL metamodel also defines two associations, counterparts of properties from OWL language; OWLequivalentClass and OWLdisjoint

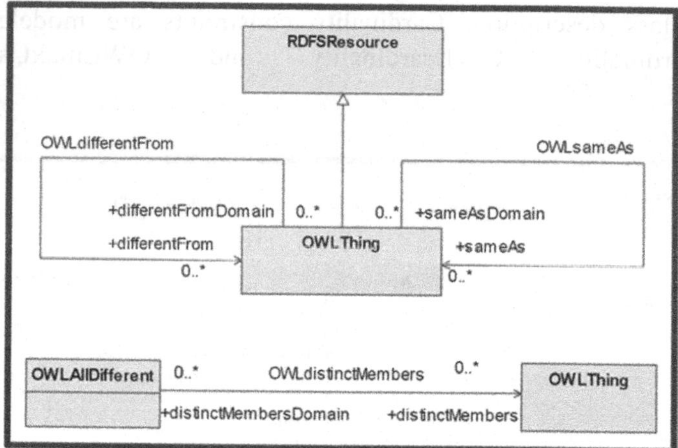

Figure 8-19. OWL Individuals

With (see Figure 8-20A). OWLequivalentClass asserts that two classes have the same class extension, while OWLdisjointWith asserts that two class extensions do not have any common individual.

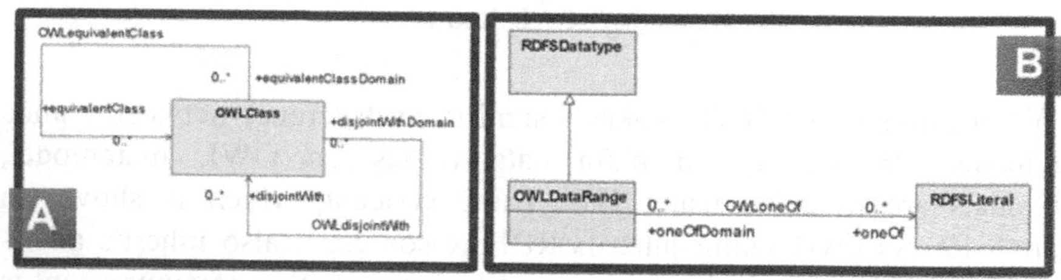

Figure 8-20. A) OWL Class associations, B) OWLDataRange

A data range represents a range of data values. It can be either a datatype or a set of data values. Data ranges are used to specify the range of datatype properties. They are modeled as OWLDataRange MOF Class (see Figure 8-20B), descendant of RDFSDatatype, connected with RDFSLiteral via OWLoneOf association.

OWL groups similar concepts in an ontology using owl:Ontology concept. This concept does not extend any other concept explicitly, but as RDFS defines that everything can be a resource, it is owl:Ontology as well. However, joint submission defines OWLOntology as descendant of Vocabulary, which is not an RDFSResource. You can see the details of OWLOntology and its associations in Figure 8-21. There is OWLimports association, which enables using of data from other ontologies in a particular ontology that import them. Other associations, OWLbackwardCompatible-

With, OWLincompatibleWith, and OWLpriorVersion are intended to support different ontology versions.

An OWLversionInfo statement generally has a string giving information about this version as its object; for example RCS/CVS keywords. An OWLpriorVersion statement contains a reference to some other ontology. This identifies the specified ontology as a prior version of the containing ontology. An OWLbackwardCompatibleWith statement contains a reference to another ontology. This identifies the specified ontology as a prior version of the containing ontology, and further indicates that it is backward compatible with it. In particular, this indicates that all identifiers from the previous version have the same intended interpretations in the new version. An OWLincompatibleWith statement contains a reference to yet another ontology. This indicates that the containing ontology is a later version of the referenced ontology, but is not backward compatible with it.

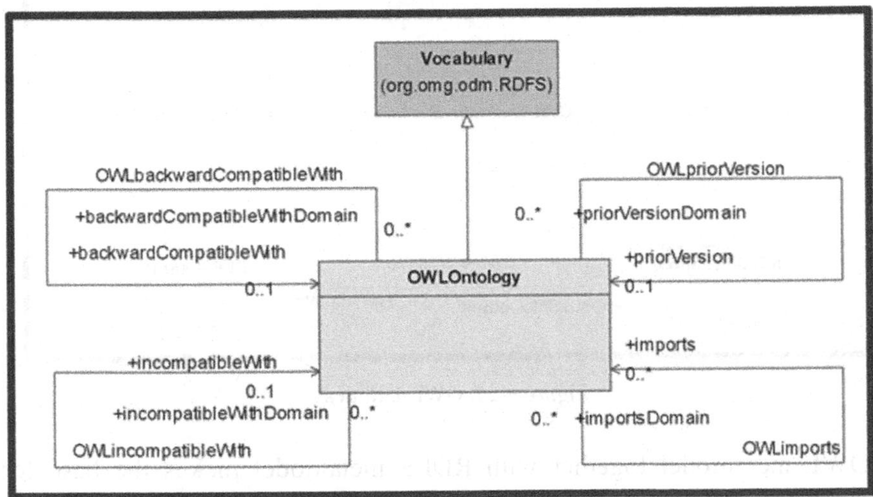

Figure 8-21. OWLOntology

Figure 8-22 shows OWL Utilities – concepts that are not the base of OWL but are intended for version control, deprecated concepts, etc. Deprecation is a feature commonly used in versioning software (for example, see the Java programming language) to indicate that a particular feature is preserved for backward-compatibility purposes, but may be phased out in the future. By deprecating a term, it means that the term should not be used in new documents that commit to the ontology. This allows an ontology to maintain backward-compatibility while phasing out an old vocabulary. In the OWL language both classes and properties can be deprecated. OWL DL allows annotations on classes, properties, individuals and ontology headers.

That is why OWLAnnotationProperty is included in the OWL metamodel. An example of annotation property is the dc:creator property defined in the DC vocabulary (http://dublincore.org/) if one wants to use it to annotate who the creator of an OWL ontology concept is.

The support for all annotations, ontology header, imports, and version information the OWL metamodel is the first comprehensive attempt that covers all those features of the OWL language. In previous similar solutions, only the IBM's submission to the ODM [OMG IBM, 2003] had considered them, and hence it was used as the basis for the present OWL metamodel.

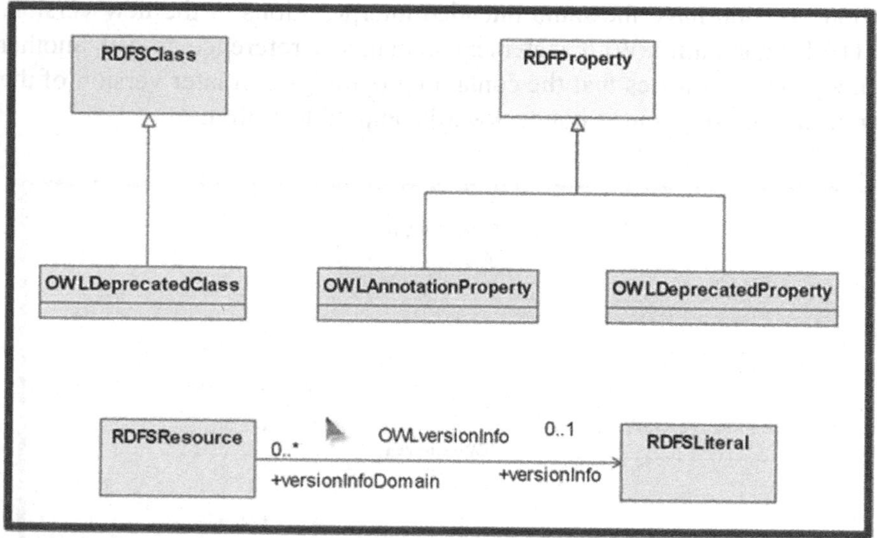

Figure 8-22. OWL Utilities

OWL metamodel together with RDFS metamodel makes the base for ontology development in Model Driven architecture. The main advantage is that it is compatible with Web Ontology Language, which is one of the key technologies of the Semantic Web.

7.5 Description Logic Metamodel (DL)

The next important metamodel that is a part of ODM is Description Logic (DL) metamodel, a weakly constrained abstract formulation of Description Logic (DL). DL is included to avoid an n-squared set of mappings among ODM metamodels, being the target of bidirectional mappings from the other metamodels. For example, to map a legacy application from UML to OWL, we would first map it to DL then from DL to OWL. The DL metamodel is not intended to be used for ontology development in its own right.

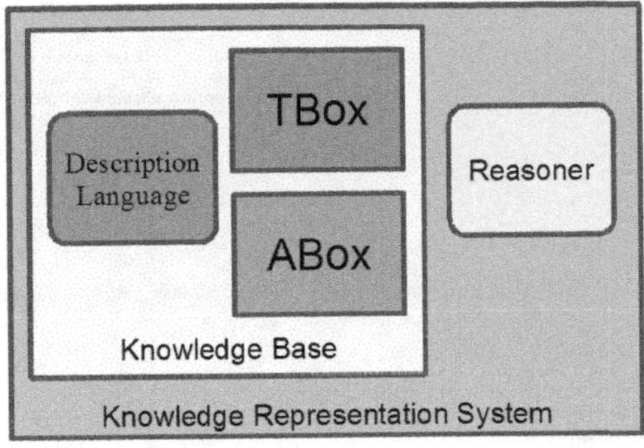

Figure 8-23. Description Logic overview

Traditionally, a DL knowledge base is divided into three parts (Figure 8-23):

- TBox – the vocabulary of the application domain (terminology or schema);
- ABox – named individuals expressed in terms of the vocabulary (assertions);
- Description Language that define terms and operations for build expressions

Basic containment concepts of DL metamodel (Figure 8-24) follow this description. TBox and ABox are connected by defines, where TBox contains concepts that model terminology, while ABox contains concepts used in modeling instances. TBox contains (via tContains relationship) all subclasses of Term that are not subclasses of Instance. Instance and its subclasses belong to ABox (aContains relationship). Term is the concept inherited by most other DL metamodel concepts.

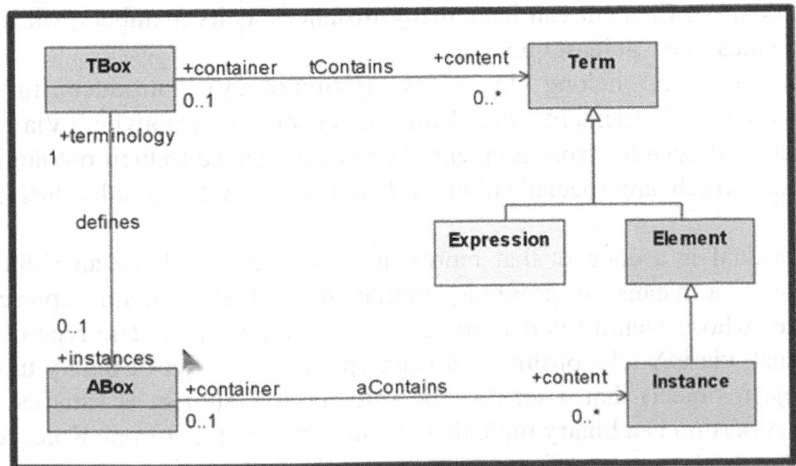

Figure 8-24. DL Basic Concepts

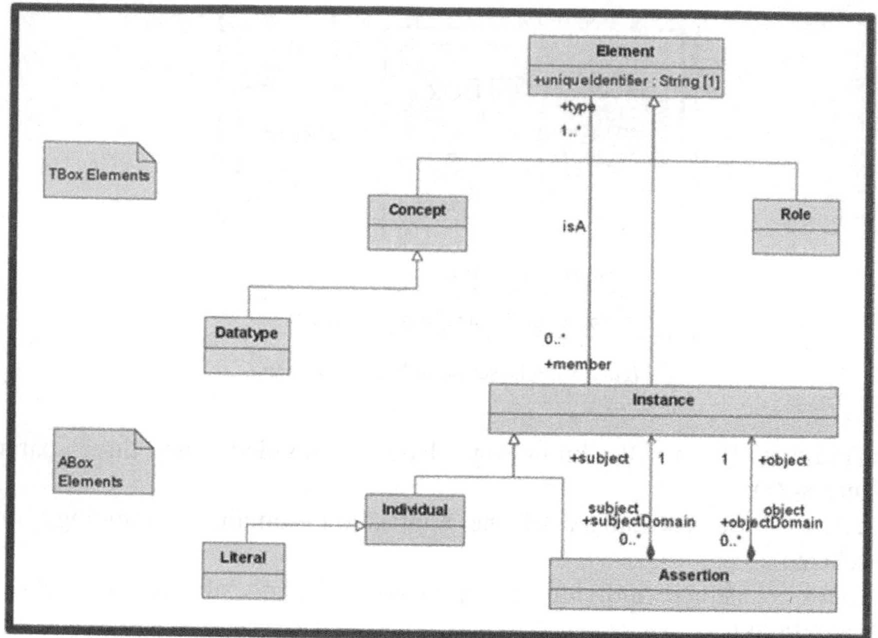

Figure 8-25. DL Elements

Figure 8-25 shows the most interesting concepts contained in TBox and their corresponding ontological instances from ABox. Element defines the notion of unique identity. It has one attribute, uniqueldentifier, which uniquely identifies an Element and all Elements. If the uniqueldentifiers of two Elements are different, then the Elements are different. Instance is the base class of ABox constructs a specialization of Element. In the same time, it is an ontological instance of Element, which is modeled by isA association. An Element can have many Instances as its members, while an Instance must have at least one type.

Concepts that belong to TBox (terminology) introduce further specialization of Element into Role, Concept, or Datatype. Via isA relationship descended from Element, they are connected to their ontological instances, which are specialization of Instance: Assertion, Individual and Literal.

Individual is a concept that represents Instances that have an identity. Concept is a means of grouping similar Individuals. Literal represents Instances whose identity is determined only by their value. The type of an Individual, via isA relationship, is a Datatype. Role is a set of binary tuples of (subject, object) that asset that the role for this subject is satisfied by object. Assertion is a binary tuple that is a member of at least one Role. As a Role represents a type of an Assertion and an Assertion represents an instance of a Role, Role inherits Element, while Assertion inherits Instance.

Role and Assertion are means for relationship (property, association) building in DL models. Therefore, Element, Concept, Datatype and Role represent types of Instance, Individual, Literal and Assertion respectively.

Note that there are corresponding inheritance subtrees among these concepts. Datatype inherits Concept, Concept and Role inherits Element, while on the other hand Literal inherits Individual and Individual and Assertion inherit Instance. The Instance inheritance tree is a sub tree of Element tree because Instance inherits Element. Members of these trees are put into type-member relationship by isA association.

DL metamodel supports another kind of grouping Instances that have something in common, other than typing. It supports collections introducing Collection concept (see Figure 8-26) and its specializations, List and Set.

Collection is a concept that belongs to TBox. It inherits Element, having isA relationship with Extent. Extent represents concrete collection of instances. Using contains association, it establishes a container-content relationship with a number of similar Instances. Collection has a bag semantic, meaning that it is unordered and can contain duplicate elements. List is a Collection that maintains order of elements and Set does not allow duplicate elements.

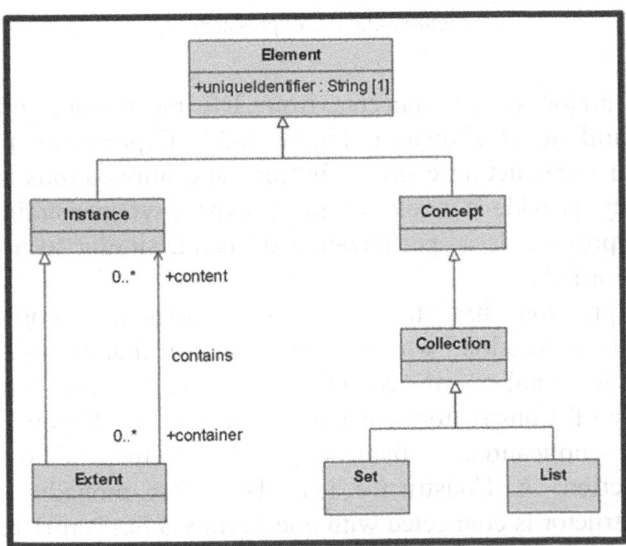

Figure 8-26. DL Collections

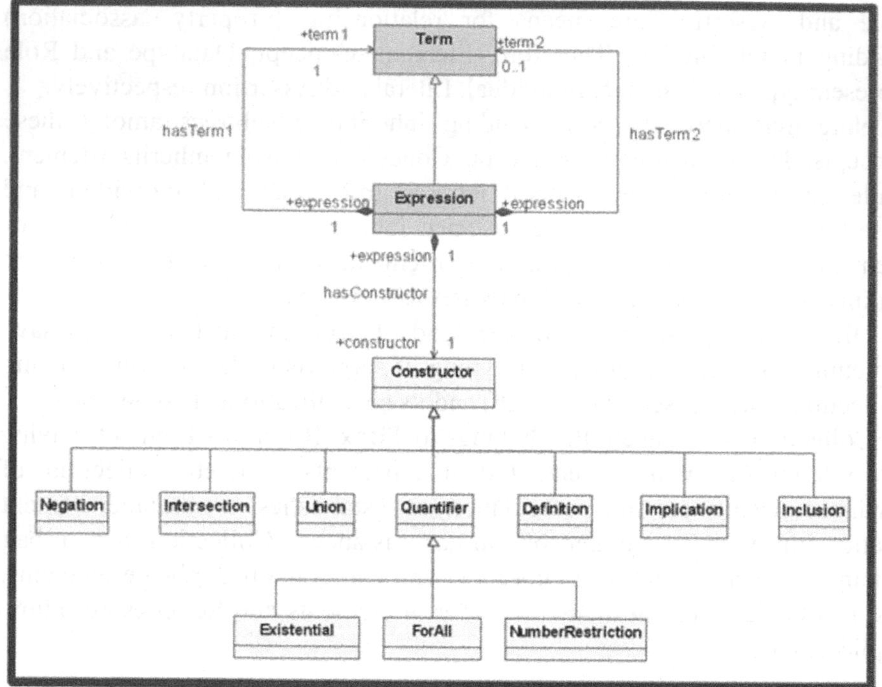

Figure 8-27. DL Expressions

The next major set of concepts from DL metamodel, intended for expression building, is shown in Figure 8-27. Expressions provide the mechanism for constructing class, definitions and implications about TBox elements. They provide a hook for more expressive constraint and rule languages. Expression is a specialization of Term, similar to a concept of Statement or Formula.

Every Expression has to have its Constructor, connected via hasConstructor association, which is an operator that is used to build expressions. A number of common constructors are provided as specializations of Constructor: Negation, Intersection, Union, Quantifier, Definition, Implication, Inclusion, Existential, ForAll and NumberRestriction. A Constructor may be either monadic or dyadic. Monadic constructor is connected with one Term via hasTerm1 relationship, while dyadic constructors are connected with two terms via hasTerm1 and hasTerm2.

8. ONTOLOGY UML PROFILE

UML Profile is a concept used for adapting the basic UML constructs to some specific purpose. Essentially, this means introducing new kinds of modeling elements by extending the basic ones, and adding them to the modeler's tools repertoire. Also, free-form information can be attached to the new modeling elements. Ontology UML Profile extends UML in a standard way to enable ontology modeling in widespread UML modeling tools.

8.1 Ontology classes and individuals

Class is one of the most fundamental concepts in ODM and Ontology UML Profile. As we noted in the discussion about the essential ODM concepts, there are some differences between traditional UML Class or OO programming language Class concept and ontology class as it is defined in OWL (owl:Class). Fortunately, we are not trying to adopt UML as stand-alone ontology language, since that might require changes to UML basic concepts (Class and other). We only need to customize UML as a support to ODM.

In ODM, concepts that represent classes, RDFSClass and OWLClass, AllDifferent, Restriction are modeled using MOF Class concept. These constructs in the Ontology UML Profile are inherited from the UML concept that is most similar to them, UML Class. But, we must explicitly specify that they are not the same as UML Class, which we can do using UML stereotypes. An example of Classes modeled in Ontology UML Profile is shown in Figure 8-28.

RDFSClass and OWLClass, ontology classes identified by a class identifier have the stereotype «RDFSClass» or «OWLClass», OWLAllDifferent – «OWLAllDifferent» and OWLRestriction – «OWL Restriction».

Figure 8-28 shows various types of ontology classes modeled in UML. The «OWLClass» Person is an example of an owl:Class class that is identified by a class identifier, while TheRollingStones is enumeration. There is a class All non-members of The Rolling Stones that represents complement of The Rolling Stones – all individuals which type is not The Rolling Stones belong to this class. AllDifferent is an auxiliary class whose members are different individuals. Also shown is an «OWLClass» Human and the Dependency «equivalentClass», which means that Person and Human are classes that have the same class description (i.e. all Persons are Humans and vice versa). Note that in object-oriented modeling it would be highly unusual to model The Rolling Stones as a class rather than as another

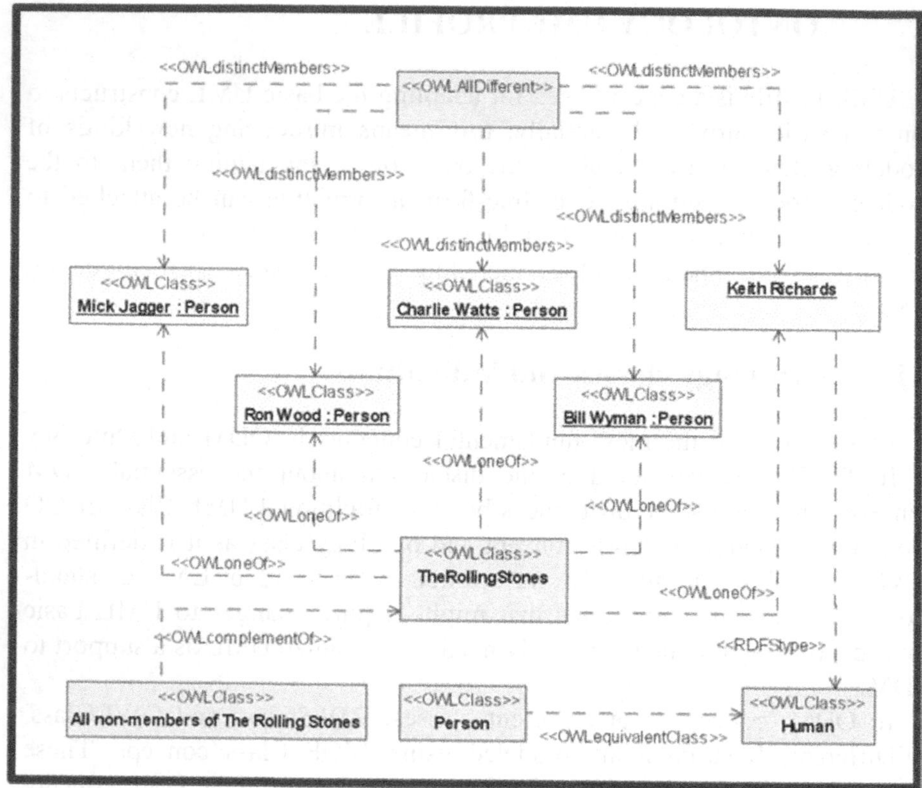

Figure 8-28. Class Diagram showing relations between Ontology Classes and Individuals in the Ontology UML Profile

object of type RockNRollBand. However, ontology classes are not behavioral, but sets, and how would you call a set of all members of The Rolling Stones? Obviously – The Rolling Stones.

In ODM, an instance of OWLClass is OWLThing, an individual. An instance of RDFSClass is RDFSResource, which means that it can be anything. In UML, an instance of a Class is an Object. OWLThing and UML Object have some differences, but they are similar enough, so in Ontology UML Profile, OWLThing is modeled as an UML Object, which is shown in Figure 8-28 and Figure 8-29. The stereotype of an object must match the stereotype of its class («OWLClass» in this case). «OWLThing» stereotype could be added as well. We can state that some individual has some type in three ways:

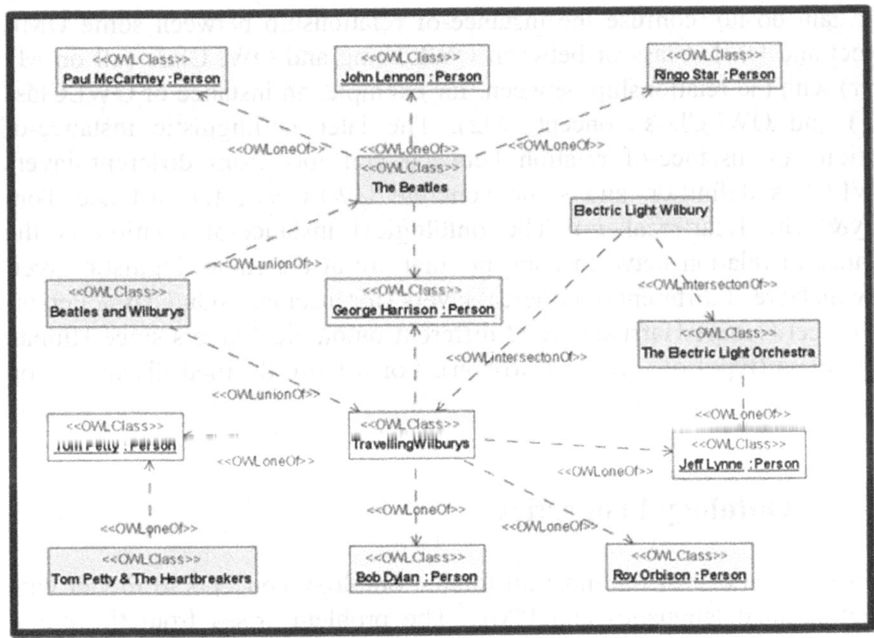

Figure 8-29. Constructing union and intersection in Ontology UML Profile

- by using an underlined name of an individual followed by ":" and its «OWLClass» name. For example, Mick Jagger:Person is an individual (OWLThing) whose type is Person. This is the usual UML method of stating an Object's type.
- by using a stereotype «RDFStype» between an individual and its «OWLClass». This method is also allowed in standard UML using stereotype «instanceOf». For example, Keith Richards has «RDFStype» dependency link to Human, which is equivalent with Person («OWLequivalentClass»). Thus, he is also a Human, just like other members of The Rolling Stones.
- indirectly – through logical operators on «OWLClass». If some «OWLClass» is a union, intersection or complement, it is a class of individuals that are not explicitly defined as its instances. For example, in Figure 8-29 Bob Dylan is not explicitly defined as a member of Beatles and Wilburys union class, but it is its member since he is a member of Travelling Wilburys, which is connected with Beatles and Wilburys through an «OWLunionOf» connection. The similar thing is with Jeff Lynne and Electric Light Wilbury Class. Since he is a member of Travelling Wilburys and The Electric Light Orchestra, he is a member of Electric Light Wilbury, an «OWLintersectionOf».

Again do not confuse the instance-of relationship between some UML Object and UML Class or between OWLThing and OWLClass (all on M1 layer) with the relationship between, for example, an instance of OWLClass (M1) and OWLClass concept (M2). The later is linguistic instance-of relation, an instance-of relation between concepts from different layers (OWLClass definition and some concrete OWLClass, for instance Tom Petty& The Heartbreakers). The ontological instance-of relation is the instance-of relation between concepts that are at the same linguistic layer, but which are at different ontological layers (for instance, «OntClass» Person and object George Harrison are at different ontological layers since Human is the class (type) of George Harrison). For a more detailed discussion on ontological vs. linguistic instance-of relations, see [Atkinson and Kuhne, 2003].

8.2 Ontology Properties

Property is one of the most unsuitable ontology concepts to model with object-oriented languages and UML. The problem arises from the major difference between Property and its similar UML concepts – Association and Attribute. Since Property is an independent, stand-alone concept, it can not be directly modeled with Association or Attribute, which can not exist on their own. Some authors [Baclawski, 2001] suggested extending UML with new constructs to support the stand-alone Property, introducing aspect-oriented concepts into UML. In our view, this solution is rather extreme, since it demands non-standard changes to UML.

Since Property is a stand-alone concept it can be modeled using a stand-alone concept from UML. That concept could be the UML Class' stereotype «RDFProperty», «OWLObjectProperty», «OWLDatatypeProperty». However, Property must be able to represent relationships between Resources (Classes, Datatypes, etc. in the case of UML), which the UML Class alone is not able to do. If we look at the ODM Property definition more closely, we will see that it accomplishes relation representation through its range and domain. According to the ODM Model, we found that in the Ontology UML Profile, the representation of relations should be modeled with UML Association's or UML Attribute's stereotypes «domain» and «range». In order to increase the readability of diagrams, the «range» association is unidirectional (from a Property to a Class).

OWL defines two types (subclasses) of Property – OWLObjectProperty and OWLDatatypeProperty. OWLObjectProperty, which can have only individuals in its range and domain, is represented in Ontology UML Profile as the Class' stereotype «OWLObjectProperty». OWLDatatypeProperty is modeled with the Class' stereotype «OWLDatatypeProperty».

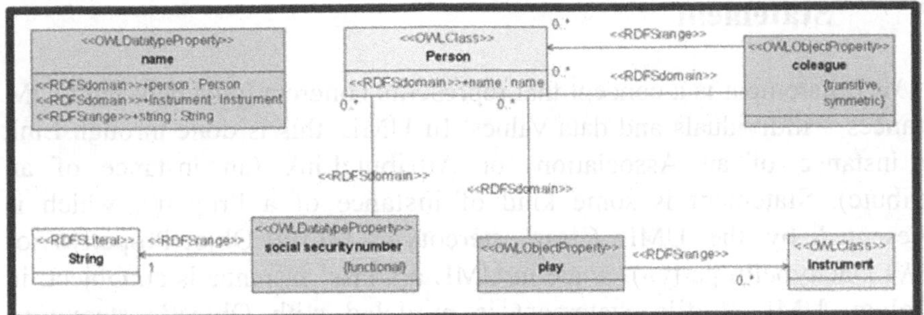

Figure 8-30. Ontology Properties shown in UML Class Diagram

An example of a Class Diagram that shows ontology properties modeled in UML is shown in Figure 8-30. It contains four properties: two «OWLDatatypeProperty»s (name and socialSecurityNumber) and two «OWLObjectProperty»s (play and colleague) UML Classes. In cooperation with «RDFSdomain» and «RDFSrange» UML Associations, or «RDFSdomain» and «RDFSrange» UML Attributes, they are used to model relationships between «OWLClass» UML Classes. Tagged values describe additional characteristics, for example, «OWLObjectProperty» colleague is symmetric (if one Person is a colleague of another Person, the other Person is also a colleague of the first Person) and transitive (if the first Person is a colleague of the second Person, who is a colleague of the third Person, the first and third Person are colleagues).

There is an important issue that must be clarified with this diagram. In UML, relations are represented by Associations (graphically represented as lines) or Attributes, which looks nice and simple. Ontology UML Profile diagrams may look overcrowded, since each relationship requires a box and two lines to be properly represented. The solution shown in this paper uses standard graphical symbols, but UML allows custom graphical symbols for a UML Profile. For example, a custom graphical symbol for Property could be a tiny circle with lines, which reduces the space on diagrams. Additional custom settings, like distinct colors for «OWLClass» (green), «OWLObjectProperty» (orange) or «OWLDatatypeProperty» (orange) in this paper, can be used to increase the diagram readability. For the sake of readability, this UML Profile allows two styles of «OWLDatatypeProperty» domain and range presentation. An example of the first style (a UML Class with two UML Associations) is socialSecurityNumber, and an example of the second one (a Class with Attributes as domain or range) is name. The second style is allowed only for «OWLDatatypeProperty» whose range multiplicity is equal or less than one. So, if an «OWLDatatypeProperty» has range multiplicity of 0..1 or 1, the style with Attributes can be used to reduce the clutter.

8.3 Statement

OWLStatement is a concept that represents concrete links between ODM instances – individuals and data values. In UML, this is done through Link (an instance of an Association) or AttributeLink (an instance of an Attribute). Statement is some kind of instance of a Property, which is represented by the UML Class' stereotype («OWLObjectProperty» or «OWLDatatypeProperty»). Since in UML a Class' instance is an Object, in Ontology UML Profile Statement is modeled with Object's stereotype «OWLObjectProperty» or «OWLDatatypeProperty» (stereotype for Object in UML must match the stereotype for its Class' stereotype). UML Links are used to represent the subject and the object of a Statement. To indicate that a Link is the subject of a Statement, LinkEnd's stereotype «RDFsubject» is used, while the object of the Statement is indicated with LinkEnd's stereotype «RDFobject». LinkEnd's stereotype is used because in UML Link can not have a stereotype. These Links are actually instances of Property's «RDFdomain» and «RDFrange». In brief, in Ontology UML Profile Statement is represented as an Object with two Links – the subject Link and the object Link, which is shown in Figure 8-31. The represented Persons Mick Jagger and Keith Richards are colleagues. Keith Richard also plays an Instrument, guitar.

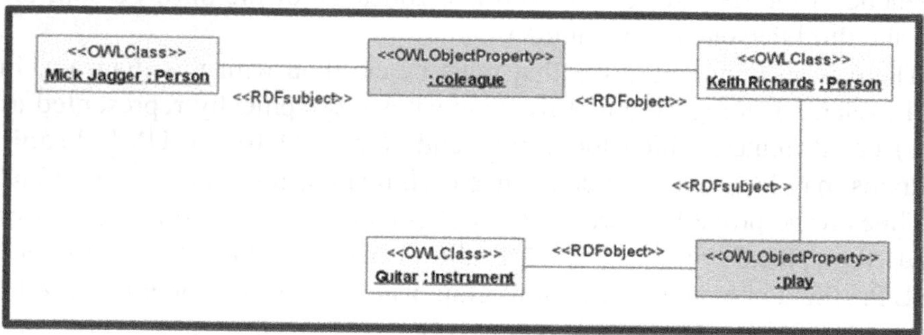

Figure 8-31. Individuals and statements shown in a UML Object Diagram

As with Ontology Properties, the diagram's readability can be further increased by using distinct colors and custom graphical symbols. A tiny circle can be used instead of the standard box for representing a Statement in order to reduce clutter on a diagram.

9. CONCLUSIONS

In this chapter we tried to give a comprehensive overview of the current solution for the use of MDA standards for ontology development. We first described the Semantic Web, ontologies, and ontology languages. Then, we briefly introduced important aspects of MDA and related standards. We also explain similarities and differences between MDA languages (i.e. MOF) and semantic web languages, as well as listed previous research on applying software engineering languages (i.e. UML) for developing ontologies. Finally, we showed the on-going OMG's initiative to create standard ontology metamodel, Ontology Definition Metamodel (ODM), as well as its corresponding Ontology UML Profile.

We hope that the overview given in the chapter can be a solid starting point for software practitioners to understand ontologies, as well as to start using them in real world software applications. On the other hand, we believe that results presented in this chapter can be useful for the researchers from the Semantic Web community who are trying to benefit from ontology development with MDA standards. Both of these communities should be aware of the fact this chapter contains just an initial points for both research and application on the subject of the chapter. We recommend those willing to know more about the presented ideas to continue their research by reading some of the references listed at the end of the chapter.

REFERENCES

[Atkinson and Kuhne, 2003] Atkinson, C., Kühne, T., "Model-Driven Development: A Metamodeling Foundation" (Spec. issue on Model-Driven Development), IEEE Software, Vol. 20, No. 5, Sep/Oct, 2003, pp 36-41.

[Baclawski, 2001] Baclawski, K., Kokar, M.K., Kogut, P., Hart, L., Smith, J.E., Letkowski, J. and Emery, P. Extending the Unified Modeling Language for ontology development. International Journal Software and Systems Modeling (SoSyM), 1(2), 2002.

[Baclawski, 2002] Baclawski, K. Kokar, M., Smith, J.E., Wallace, E., Letkowski, J., Koethe, M.R. and Kogut, P. UOL: Unified Ontology Language. Assorted papers discussed at the DC Ontology SIG meeting, (2002), http://www.omg.org/cgi-bin/doc?ontology/2002-11-02.

[Beckett, 2004], Beckett, D. (ed.) RDF/XML Syntax Specification (Revised), W3C Recommendation 10 February 2004,http://www.w3.org/TR/2004/REC-rdf-syntax-grammar-20040210/.

[Berners-Lee et al, 2001] T. Berners-Lee, J. Hendler, and O. Lassila, The Semantic Web, Scientific American, Vol. 284, No. 5 (2001) 34-43.

[Berners-Lee, 1998] Berners-Lee, T., "Semantic Web Road Map", W3C Design Issues, http://www.w3.org/DesignIssues/Semantic.html, 1998.

[Bezivin et al, 2005] Bezivin, J., et al "A M3-Neutral infrastructure for bridging model engineering and ontology engineering," 1st International Conference on Interoperability of Enterprise Software and Applications, Geneva, Switzerland, 2005 (forthcoming).

[Brickley, 2004] Brickley, D., Guha, R. V., "RDF Vocabulary Description Language 1.0: RDF Schema", W3C Recommendation 10 February 2004, http://www.w3.org/TR/2004/REC-rdf-schema-20040210/, last accessed, 18. Dec. 2004.

[Ceccaroni & Kendal, 2003] Ceccaroni, Luigi & Kendall, Elisa "A Graphical Environment for Ontology Development," In Proceedings of the 2nd International Joint Conference on Autonomous Agents and Multiagent Systems, Melbourne, Australia, pp. 958 - 959, 2003.

[Chandrasekaran et al, 1999] Chandrasekaran, B., Josephson, J.R. and Benjamins, V.R. What Are Ontologies, and Why Do We Need Them?. IEEE Intelligent Systems, 14(1), 1999. 20-26.

[Cranefield, 2001] Cranefield, S. Networked Knowledge Representation and Exchange using UML and RDF. Journal of Digital information, 1(8), 2001. http://jodi.ecs.soton.ac.uk

[Cranefield, 2001a] Cranefield, S., "UML and the Semantic Web", In Proceedings of the International Semantic Web Working Symposium, Palo Alto, 2001, www.semanticweb.org/SWWS/program/full/paper1.pdf.

[Dean & Schreiber, 2004] Dean, M., Schreiber, G. (eds.), "OWL Web Ontology Language Reference, W3C Recommendation 10 February 2004", http://www.w3.org/TR/2004/REC-owl-ref-20040210/, 2004.

[Decker et al, 2000] S. Decker, S. Melnik, F. van Harmelen, D. Fensel, M. Klein, J. Broekstra, M. Ederman, and I. Horrocks, The Semantic Web: The Roles of XML and RDF, IEEE Internet Computing, Vol. 4, No. 5 (2000) 63-74.

[Denny, 2002] M. Denny, Ontology Building: A Survey of Editing Tools (2002) [Online]. Available: http://www.xml.com/pub/a/2002/11/06/ontologies.html.

[Djuric et al, 2005] Djuric, D., Gasevic, D., Devedzic, V., "Adventures in Modeling Spaces: Close Enounters of Semantic Web and MDA Kinds", The 9th International EDOC Conference (EDOC 2005) The Enterprise Computing Conference", 19-23 September 2005, Enschede, The Netherlands, 2005 (submitted).

[Djuric et al, 2005a] Djuric, D., Gasevic, D., Devedzic, V., "Modeling Spaces", submitted to IEEE Computer, 2005.

[Djuric et al, 2005b] Djuric, D., Gasevic, D., Devedzic, V., "Ontology Modeling and MDA", in Journal of Object Technology, vol. 4, no. 1, January-February 2005, pp. 109-128. http://www.jot.fm/issues/issue_2005_01/article3

[Duddy, 2002] Duddy, K., "UML2 Must Enable A Family of Languages", Communications of the ACM, Vol. 45, No. 11, November 2002, pp 73-75.

[Falkovych et al, 2003] Falkovych, K., Sabou, M. and Stuckenschmidt, H. UML for the Semantic Web: Transformation-Based Approaches. in Omelayenko, B. and Klein, M. eds. Knowledge Transformation for the Semantic Web, Frontiers in Artificial Intelligence and Applications, Vol. 95, IOS Press, 2003, 92-106.

[Fridman-Noy et al, 1997] N. Fridman-Noy and C.D. Hafner, The State of the Art in Ontology Design: A Survey and Comparative Review, AI Magazine, Vol. 18, No. 3 (1997) 53-74.

[Gašević et al, 2003] Gašević, D., Damjanović, V. and Devedžić, V., Analysis of the MDA Standards in Ontological Engineering. in Proceedings of the 6th International Conference of Information Technology, (Bhubaneswar, India, 2003), 193-196.

[Gruber, 1993] T. R. Gruber, A translation approach to portable ontology specifications, Knowledge Acquisition, Vol. 5, No. 2 (1993) 199-220.

[Hagget and Chorley, 1967] Hagget, P., Chorley, R. J. Models, Paradigms and New Geography, In Models in Geography, London, Methuen & Co., 1967.

[Hayes, 2004] Hayes, P., RDF Semantics, W3C Recommendation 10 February 2004, http://www.w3.org/TR/2004/REC-rdf-mt-20040210/.

[Hefflin & Huhns, 2003] J. Hefflin and M. N. Huhns, The Zen of the Web, IEEE Internet Computing, Vol. 7, No. 5 (2003) 30-33.

[Hendler, 2001] J. Hendler, Agents and the Semantic Web, IEEE Intelligent Systems, Vol. 16, No. 2 (2001) 30-37.

[Juerjens 2003] Juerjens, J., Secure Systems Development with UML. Springer-Verlag, Berlin, 2003.

[Kalfoglou, 2001] Y. Kalfoglou, Exploring Ontologies, In S. K. Chang (ed.) Handbook of Software Engineering and Knowledge Engineering, Vol. I – Fundamentals (World Scientific Publishing Co., 2001) 863-887.

[Kendall et al, 2002] Elisa F. Kendall, Mark E. Dutra, and Deborah L. McGuinness, "Towards A Commercial Ontology Development Environment," Poster presentation at 1st International Semantic Web Conference, Sardinia, Italy, 2002 [Online]. Available: http://iswc2002.semanticweb.org/posters/mcguiness_a4.pdf.

[Klyne & Carroll, 2004] Klyne, G., Carroll, J., Resource Description Framework (RDF): Concepts and Abstract Syntax, W3C Recommendation 10 February 2004, http://www.w3.org/TR/2004/REC-rdf-concepts-20040210/

[Kobryn, 2001] Kobryn, C., "The Road to UML 2.0: Fast track or Detour", Software Development Magazine, April 2001, 73-75. http://www.sdmagazine.com/documents/s=732/sdm0104b/0104b.htm.

[Manola & Miller, 2004] Manola, F., Miller, E., (eds.), RDF Primer, W3C Recommendation 10 February 2004, http://www.w3.org/TR/2004/REC-rdf-primer-20040210/

[McGuinness et al, 2002] D. McGuinness, R. Fikes, J. Hendlerand , and L. A. Stein, "DAML+OIL: An Ontology Language for the Semantic Web," IEEE Intelligent Systems, Vol. 17, No. 5, September/October 2002, pp 72-80.

[McGuinness & van Harmelen, 2004] McGuinness, D., van Harmelen, F., (eds.), OWL Web Ontology Language Overview, W3C Recommendation 10 February 2004, http://www.w3.org/TR/2004/REC-owl-features-20040210/.

[McGuinness, 2002] L. McGuinness, Ontologies Come of Age, In D. Fensel, J. Hendler, H. Lieberman, and W. Wahlster (eds.) Spinning the Semantic Web: Bringing the World Wide Web to Its Full Potential (MIT Press, Boston, 2002) 171-194.

[Miller & Mukerji, 2003] Miller, J. and Mukerji, J. (eds.), MDA Guide Version 1.0. OMG Document: omg/2003-05-01, (2003) http://www.omg.org/mda/mda_files/MDA_Guide_Version1-0.pdf.

[Noy et al, 2000] Noy, N.F., Fergerson, R.W. and Musen, M.A., The knowledge model of Protégé-2000: combining interoperability and flexibility. in Proceedings of the 12th International Conference, (Juan-les-Pins, France, 2000), 17-32.

[ODMJoint, 2004] Ontology Definition Metamodel – Preliminary Revised Submission to OMG RFP ad/2003-03-40, Volume 1, http://codip.grci.com/odm/draft, 2004.

[ODMRFP, 2003] Ontology Definition Metamodel Request for Proposal, OMG Document: ad/2003-03-40, http://www.omg.org/cgi-bin/doc?ad/2003-03-40, 2003.

[OMG DSTC, 2003] Ontology Definition Metamodel, DSTC Initial Submission, OMG Document ad/2003-08-01, http://www.omg.org/cgi-bin/doc?ad/03-08-01, 2003.

[OMG Gentleware, 2003] Ontology Definition Metamodel, Gentleware Initial Submission, OMG Document ad/03-08-09, http://www.omg.org/cgi-bin/doc?ad/03-08-09, 2003.

[OMG IBM, 2003] Ontology Definition Metamodel, IBM Initial Submission ad/03-07-02, OMG Document http://www.omg.org/cgi-bin/doc?ad/03-07-02.

[OMG MOF, 2002] Meta Object Facility (MOF) Specification v1.4. OMG Document formal/02-04-03, (2002), http://www.omg.org/cgi-bin/apps/doc?formal/02-04-03.pdf.

[OMG Sandpiper&KSL, 2003] Ontology Definition Metamodel, Sandpiper Software Inc and KSL Initial Submission, OMG Document ad/03-08-06, http://www.omg.org/cgi-bin/doc?ad/03-08-06, 2003.

[OMG XMI, 2002] OMG XMI Specification, v1.2. OMG Document formal/02-01-01, (2002), http://www.omg.org/cgi-bin/doc?formal/2002-01-01.

[Patel-Schneider et. al., 2004] Patel-Schneider, P., Heyes, P., Horrocks, I., OWL Web Ontology Language Semantics and Abstract Syntax, W3C Recommendation 10 February 2004, http://www.w3.org/TR/2004/REC-owl-semantics-20040210/

[Rumbaugh, 1998] Rumbaugh, J., Jacobson, I., Booch, G., "The Unified Modeling Language Reference Manual", Addison-Wesley, 1998.

[Seidewitz, 2003] Seidewitz, E. What Models Mean. IEEE Software, 20(5), 2003. 26-32.

[Sigel, 2001] Sigel, J., "Developing in OMG's Model-Driven Architecture", Revision 2.6, Object Management Group White Paper, ftp://ftp.omg.org/pub/docs/-omg/01-12-01.pdf, 2001.

[Smith et al, 2004] Smith, M. K., Welty, C., McGuinness, D., (eds.), OWL Web Ontology Language Guide, W3C Recommendation 10 February 2004, http://www.w3.org/TR/2004/REC-owl-guide-20040210/.

[Swartout & Tate, 1999] W. Swartout and A. Tate, Guest Editors' Introduction: Ontologies, IEEE Intelligent Systems, Vol. 14, No. 1 (1999) 18-19.

[UML2, 2003] OMG spec., "Unified Modeling Language: Superstructure, version 2.0, Final Adopted Specification", http://www.omg.org/cgi-bin/apps/doc?ptc/03-08-02.zip, August 2003.

[Knublauch, 2004] Holger Knublauch, "Ontology-Driven Software Development in the Context of the Semantic Web: An Example Scenario with Protégé/OWL," In Proceedings of the 1st International Workshop on the Model-Driven Semantic Web at the 8th International IEEE Enterprise Distributed Object Computing Conference, Monterey, California, USA, 20-24 September 2004.

[Selic, 2003] Selic, B. The Pragmatics of Model-Driven Development. IEEE Software, 20 (5), 2003. 19-25.

Chapter 9

ONTOLOGY SPECIFICATION AND INTEGRATION FOR MULTIMEDIA APPLICATIONS

Hiranmay Ghosh[1], Santanu Chaudhury[2], Karthik Kashyap[2] and Brindaduti Maiti[2]

[1]Tata Infotech Limited, Research Group, Ground Floor, Library Building, IIT Campus, New Delhi 110016, India; [2]Department of Electrical Engineering, Indian Institute of Technology, New Delhi 110016, India

Abstract: An ontology designed for multimedia applications should enable integration of the conceptual and media spaces. We present M-OWL, a new ontology language, that supports this capability. M-OWL supports explicit definition of media properties for the concepts. The language has been defined as an extension of OWL, the standard ontology language for the web. We have proposed a new Bayesian Network based probabilistic reasoning framework with M-OWL for semantic interpretation of multimedia data. We have also proposed a new model for ontology integration, based on the similarity of the concepts in the media domain. It can be used to integrate several multimedia and traditional ontologies.

Key words: Semantic Web; Ontology; Multimedia; Bayesian Network; Reasoning; OWL; M-OWL; Ontology Integration

1. INTRODUCTION

Late twentieth century has seen an explosive growth of the Internet. Availability of a huge volume of information on the net has resulted in a need for its effective utilization by automated means. The *Semantic Web* [1] envisages an environment, where user agents and other web based applications can make intelligent use of data and services available on the Internet. The technology is maturing fast with rapid inventions in knowledge representation and reasoning schemes, software agent technology, and other related subjects. We have also witnessed a remarkable growth of on-line multimedia data in recent times.

Medical imagery, on-line music, movies, news and sports video are just some of the examples of such collections. This has motivated research in automated semantic access of media data. However, there is a large semantic gap between the information seekers' perspectives and the media features that are machine-detectable in the multimedia documents. Thus, on-line multimedia data poses significant challenge to the development of the semantic web. Knowledge-based multimedia data processing generally employs application and media specific methods for media data interpretation. Little attention has so far been paid to the standardization and re-usability of the knowledge resources for the web based media processing applications. This chapter has been motivated by the need for multimedia data processing in the Semantic Web environment.

Ontology is an essential ingredient for the Semantic Web. It is a formal specification for conceptualization of a domain [2]. This declarative form of knowledge enables reasoning with the concepts in a domain and facilitates semantic interpretation of information. Development and maintenance of a non-trivial ontology for a practical information system is human-intensive and an extremely expensive process. Today's networked world provides an opportunity for sharing ontologies by several information systems, leading to economics in their development and maintenance efforts. W3C forum[1] has taken up the task for standardizing ontology representations with formal semantics to promote such sharing. These efforts have led to a number of standard languages for information markup to knowledge representation. OWL or the Ontology Language for the Web, approved in 2004 being the latest in the series. The problem of ontology integration to promote reuse has also attracted attention of several researchers [3–8].

The present day ontology deals with abstract entities, namely the "concepts" and their "properties". As a result, they help us to reason with a symbolic description of the world. We can use this conceptual reasoning framework for modeling and interpreting textual information embedded in the web-pages and other distributed data sources. In contrast, multimedia information is perceptual in nature. Semantic processing of multimedia data requires a bridge across the perceptual media world and the abstract conceptual world. The present day ontology languages do not support this feature. Moreover, the bridge between the conceptual and the perceptual worlds is characterized with inherent uncertainties [9–12]. The crisp Description Logic [13] based reasoning scheme for present day ontologies is not amenable to uncertain reasoning and cannot be applied for conceptual interpretation of media data.

In this chapter, we present an ontology language that enables semantic processing of multimedia data. It supports explicit specification of media proper-

[1] www.w3c.org.

ties with concepts and reasoning with them. This language, **Multimedia OWL** or **M-OWL** in short, has been defined as an extension of OWL to protect the investments in the existing ontologies. We have complemented M-OWL with a new Bayesian Network based probabilistic reasoning framework to cope up with the inherent uncertainties with semantic interpretation of multimedia data. Moreover, we have proposed a new scheme for ontology integration, based on the media property description of the concepts. Since several ontologies are already existing and will continue to be developed in OWL, we have also addressed the issue of integrating multimedia ontologies expressed in M-OWL with the traditional ones expressed in OWL.

The rest of the chapter is organized as follows. Section 2 provides a brief account of evolution for ontologies and knowledge based applications and establishes the need for a multimedia ontology language. Section 3 describes new constructs introduced in the proposed ontology language, M-OWL. The probabilistic reasoning model for M-OWL is described in section 4. Section 5 deals with a new integration scheme for M-OWL and OWL ontologies, based on media property description of concepts. Section 6 concludes this chapter.

2. TOWARD MULTIMEDIA ONTOLOGY

Knowledge based systems of the earlier generation used custom, and often implicit, knowledge bases. The evolution of techniques like the *first-order logic*, *frame-based systems* and *semantic net* led to declarative knowledge representations and formal reasoning schemes. These developments have further evolved into the modern subject of "ontological engineering". The primary motivation behind explicit knowledge representation has been separation of domain knowledge from the operational (procedural) knowledge, so that each of them can be independently updated in an information system. Moreover, an explicit declarative knowledge has the potential to be reused in several application contexts. A number of knowledge representation schemes have been based on the logical formalism of Description Logic (DL) [13], which provides a set theoretic framework for reasoning. Cyc[14], Ontolingua [15], KL-ONE [16], CLASSIC [17] and LOOM [18] are some of the notable examples of such pioneering works.

The last years of the twentieth century saw a rapid growth of the Internet across the globe and a change in its character. While the web was originally conceived as a host to passive information sources, it increasingly started hosting active services. The availability of huge amount of information and numerous services resulted in the need for automated discovery and utilization of the web resources by intelligent agents on behalf of human beings. These agents required a shared ontology, for common interpretation of the messages exchanged. SHOE [19] has been one of the earliest attempts to define an ontology language for the web through a simple extension of the HTML. Subsequently, the W3C forum has undertaken standardization activities and has come up with a series of specifications. *Extended Markup Language (XML)* specifies the basic syntax for semantic mark-up of information. *RDF* and *RDFS* [20] build on XML to provide the semantic net like structure for knowledge representation in terms of concepts and properties. *Web Ontology Language (OWL)*[2] [21], approved in 2004, builds on RDF(S), adds more vocabulary for describing properties and classes and supports Description Logic based reasoning. It is an improvement over its predecessor, DAML+OIL [22] based on application experiences. OWL provides three increasingly expressive sub-languages *OWL Lite*, *OWL DL* and *OWL Full*, each of which is an extension of its simpler variant. Formal ontologies have been used in several application domains, e.g. semantic retrieval [23, 24], personalized navigation in hyperspace [25], machine processable e-mail [26], GIS [27], bio-medical informatics [28], etc.

Another development during the last decade has been massive proliferation of multimedia collections aided by the falling price of computational power, storage and multimedia I/O devices. This motivated many researchers [29–31] to develop tools for constructing multimedia databases. On-line multimedia data exists in various audiovisual media formats, e.g. still image, graphics, animation, speech, music and video. These media formats require different content based processing techniques. Most of the existing multimedia information systems deals with one or at best, a few media formats and are application-specific. These systems deal with essentially two forms of information:

1. Description of the concepts, or meta-data, associated with the media, e.g. the caption "Tajmahal" with a photograph depicting the monument, and
2. Description of the media contents, e.g. color, texture and shape contours in the images.

Conventional ontologies have been successfully used in multimedia systems to deal with the concept descriptions [32–37]. However, processing media based description of multimedia information poses some additional requirements.

Semantic processing of media data requires a different form of knowledge representation, where media features need to be linked to the subject domain concepts. Traditionally, multimedia applications have used multi-tier domain specific knowledge representation schemes [38–41]. The knowledge representation and reasoning schemes used in these systems have been media and application specific, and without a formal semantics. Thus, it is not possible to share such knowledge representations across multiple applications without making implicit assumptions.

[2] http://www.w3c.org/2004/OWL/.

The description of a multimedia document contents can be at different levels of abstractions. At the lowest level, it can include aggregate statistical media features, e.g. color histogram of still images and motion vectors for video. At a higher level it can include media objects identified in the medium and their spatio-temporal interactions. Sharing of content descriptions by multimedia applications requires standardization. The Motion Picture Engineering Group (MPEG) of ISO has defined the MPEG-7[3] standard [42] for this purpose. The standard provides a flexible mechanism to describe the contents of a multimedia document in terms of commonly defined media features, semantic objects and their spatio-temporal relations. It is also possible to introduce new user defined media features and extend MPEG-7 using the DDL. MPEG-7 MDS enables semantic description of a single multimedia object or a group of objects. However, MPEG-7 standard is defined on XML schema, which does not permit reasoning [43]. Several researchers [44–48] have suggested use of core and domain ontologies to complement MPEG-7 description for semantic access to media data. These ontologies are expressed in RDF(S)/OWL and have formal semantics. The core ontology establishes the semantics of the MPEG-7 descriptors and the domain ontology helps in interpreting the meta-data. However, the semantic interpretation of media features are still left to the individual applications.

A multimedia ontology should provide a bridge between the conceptual world and the media world. It should enable a semantic multimedia application to translate the conceptual model of a media event into a media based model and vice-versa. The media world is a perceptual recording of the real world. In contrast, the conceptual world is an abstraction of the real world in terms of "concepts" and their interactions. The two seemingly disparate worlds are, however, closely coupled with cause-effect relationships. Concepts are mental models of real world objects (or events) formed out of several observations of different instances of the objects (or events). For example, the concept "steam locomotive" is an abstraction of several observations of specific body-shapes, compositional structure, audio properties and motion characteristics that signify the concept [49]. The occurrence of the concept "steam locomotive" in a media event *causes* some of these media properties to appear on a multimedia document, which is a perceptual record of the event. Thus, the symbolic description "steam locomotive" gives rise to expectations of these media properties. On the other hand, perception of sufficient resemblance with these media properties in a multimedia document can be the basis of recognition of the concept.

[3]Formally known as *Multimedia Content Description Interface*.

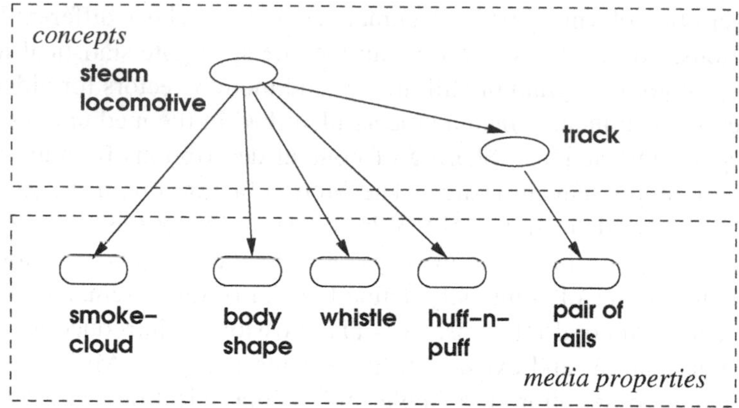

Figure 9-1. A typical Observation Model

We have proposed "Observation Model" (OM) [50] as a representation of a concept in terms of its media properties. In general, it consists of all observable (detectable) audiovisual properties associated with the concept, as well as those associated with some of the related concepts. Figure 9-1 depicts a simple (non-exhaustive) Observation Model for a "steam locomotive". The media features associated with this concept can be specific body shape, color and texture of the smoke-cloud (that a locomotive emits), and parallel lines (the rails on which it runs) in the visual domain and its characteristic whistle notes and huff-and-puff noise in the audio domain. An Observation Model is organized as a Bayesian Tree[4] to represent the uncertainties that are associated with the observation of the media features when the concept materializes[5]. Use of Observation Model in information retrieval is illustrated in [51].

A multimedia ontology should enable formulation of Observation Models for the domain concepts and concept recognition from "observations" on multimedia documents. Thus, a multimedia ontology language should have provision for expressing media properties explicitly for the concepts in a domain. There should be adequate flexibility in the language to express different types of media feature descriptions, for different media formats and at different levels of abstractions. It should have the capability to express spatial and temporal relations between the media properties that generally characterize multimedia objects and events. It should also enable reasoning with the media properties for formulating an Observation Model of a concept.

[4] In general, an Observation Model can be a multiply connected DAG. However, we simplify the graph to a tree by replicating the nodes with multiple parents for computational convenience [50].

[5] We defer further discussions on the probabilities till a later section of this chapter.

The ontology languages, such as OWL, enable formal description of the conceptual domains but do not address the media world. On the other hand, MPEG-7 provides flexible description of multimedia documents in terms of media features at different levels of abstraction, but lacks the rigor of formal semantics of ontology languages. Neither OWL nor MPEG-7 supports specification of uncertainties that are associated with observation of media properties when a concept materializes. These limitations motivate us to develop a formal ontology language, which can meet the demands of the multimedia applications. Description Logic (DL) [13], that has been adopted as the formal reasoning tool with existing ontology languages, provides a crisp reasoning framework and cannot cope up with uncertainties in the multimedia world. We propose a probabilistic reasoning framework based on Bayesian Networks with multimedia ontology. Finally, property inheritance in the frame based languages like OWL is strictly determined by the concept hierarchy. A child concept inherits the properties of its parents. Multimedia ontologies need a more flexible propagation rules for media properties of a concept. For example, if a monument is built with marble, the former "inherits" the color and texture properties of the latter. Thus, the media properties need to flow along a relation *built with*, which does not signify concept hierarchy.

3. EXTENDING ONTOLOGY FOR MULTIMEDIA APPLICATIONS

The discussions in the previous section brings out the requirements of multimedia ontologies that are not catered to by the existing ontology languages such as OWL and the DL based reasoning framework that complements such languages. The requirements can be summarized as follows.

1. A multimedia ontology language should allow flexible specification of media properties, in different media formats and at different levels of abstractions. It should be possible for an author to create new media features and formally define their semantics.
2. A multimedia ontology language should allow formal specification of spatial and temporal relations that exist between the different media properties characterizing a media object or an event, and enable reasoning with them.
3. A multimedia ontology language should allow formal specification of uncertainty between the concepts and their media properties and define a reasoning framework that can cope up with such uncertainty.
4. A multimedia ontology language should allow specification of flexible propagation rules for media properties, independent of the concept hierarchy in the domain.

An ontology is essentially represented as a semantic web, where a node represents a concept and an edge represents the relation between a pair of concepts. A multimedia ontology is an extension of this structure with additional node types, e.g. multimedia properties, and additional types of relations, e.g. probabilistic associations and spatio-temporal relations. The design goal of OWL[21] is consistent with this structure. This makes OWL amenable to extensions to support multimedia ontologies. M-OWL has been proposed as an extension of OWL with new class definitions. The expressive power of MPEG-7 has been exploited for specifying media properties in M-OWL. These extensions are applicable to all flavors of OWL, namely OWL Lite, OWL DL and OWL Full.

3.1 Concepts and Media Properties

Classes and *Individuals* are the basic elements in OWL to describe the real world entities and their hierarchical structure. We use the same elements in M-OWL to represent the concepts. For example, `Tajmahal` can be an individual, which is an instance of the class `monument`. This is expressed in M-OWL in the following way.

```
<owl:Class rdf:ID="monument"/>
<monument rdf:ID="Tajmahal">
```

A multimedia ontology should be able to specify a media property and associate it with a concept. We define a class `mowl:MediaObject` to describe media feature and examples. A `MediaObject` is an observable media property which would be associated with a concept.

```
<mowl:MediaObject rdf:ID="MediaObject">
  <rdfs:label>MediaObject</rdfs:label>
  <rdfs:comment>
    Media Object describes a Media property
  </rdfs:comment>
  <rdf:subClassOf>
    <rdf:resource="http://www.w3.org/2001/01/rdf-schema#Class"/>
  </rdf:subClassOf>
</mowl:MediaObject>
```

Following the general MPEG-7 media property description scheme, we define MediaObject as a 4-tuple: $\langle \mathcal{M}, \mathcal{F}, \mathcal{V}, \mathcal{D} \rangle$, where

$\mathcal{M}$ defines a media format, e.g. still image, video, etc.

$\mathcal{F}$ defines a media feature, e.g. dominant color, motion vector, etc.

$\mathcal{D}$ is a descriptor that describes the content in the value field. It can be one of the standard media descriptors defined in MPEG-7, e.g. Histogram for color, Chain Codes for shape, etc. It is also possible for a user to define new media property descriptors using MPEG-7 DDL.

$\mathcal{V}$ (value) is actual specification of the media property. This field can either contain the property itself (by value), or can be specified by the address of its container, i.e. a URI (by reference), using MPEG-7's `MediaLocator` and `MediaUri` constructs.

We use the same XML schema as defined in MPEG-7 to represent the different components of the media objects. For example, we define media format `video` as

```
<Mpeg7 ... xmlns: ...
  <MediaFormat>
    <Content>Video</Content>
  </MediaFormat>
</Mpeg7>
```

We distinguish between two ways of specifying media properties, either by specifying a constraint on a media feature (e.g. color = white), or by specifying a media example, e.g. an example photograph of a monument. Consequently, we define two media property classes `mowl:MediaFeature` and `mowl:MediaExample` each of which is a subclass of `MediaObject` as shown in the figure 9-2.

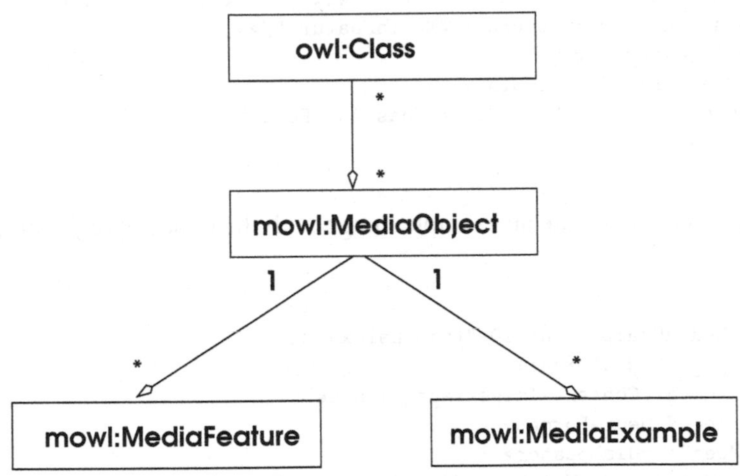

Figure 9-2. MediaObject, MediaFeature and MediaExample

In order to associate a media feature with a concept, we define an `owl:Object Property` which has a domain as any concept and range as a MediaFeature. For example, we can associate the media feature `color=white` with a concept `marble` (see figure 9-3) as follows.

```
<mowl:MediaFeature rdf:ID="whiteColor">
  <Mpeg7: ...
    ...Descriptor specifying color = white..
```

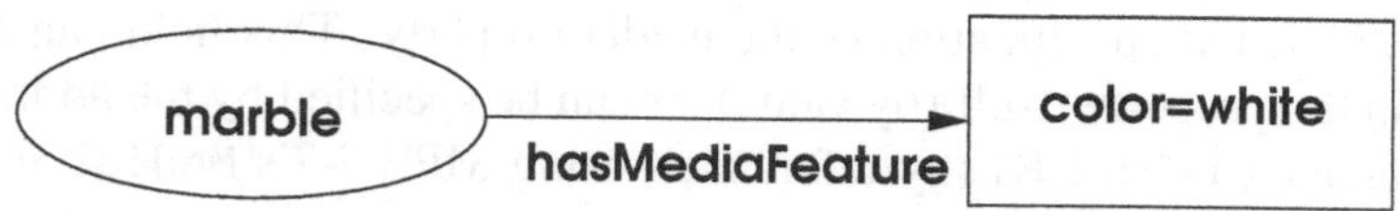

Figure 9-3. Specifying MediaFeature of marble as color=white

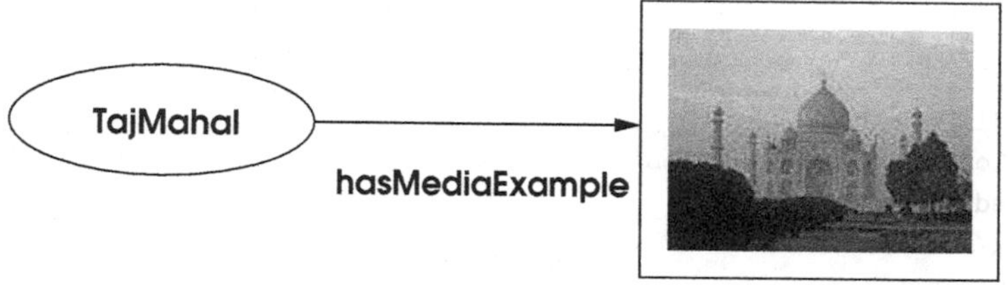

Figure 9-4. Specifying MediaExample for a concept

```
  </Mpeg7>
</mowl:MediaFeature>
<owl:ObjectProperty rdf:ID="hasMediaFeature">
  <rdfs:domain rdf:resource="http://www.w3.org/2002/07/owl#Thing" />
  <rdfs:range rdf:resource="#MediaFeature"/>
</owl:ObjectProperty>
<owl:Class rdf:ID="Marble">
  <hasMediaFeature>WhiteColor</hasMediaFeature>
</owl:Class>
```

Similarly, we can associate an example image with the concept `Tajmahal` (see figure 9-4) as

```
<mowl:MediaExample rdf:ID="tajmahalexample">
    <Mpeg7:MediaFormat>
      <Mpeg7:Content>Image</Mpeg7:Content>
    </Mpeg7:MediaFormat>
    <Mpeg7:MediaLocator>
      <Mpeg7:MediaUri>http://.../img.jpg</Mpeg7:MediaUri>
    </Mpeg7:MediaLocator>
</mowl:MediaExample>
<owl:ObjectProperty rdf:ID="hasMediaExample">
  <rdfs:domain rdf:resource="http://www.w3.org/2002/07/owl#Thing" />
  <rdfs:range rdf:resource="MediaExample"/>
</owl:ObjectProperty>
<owl:Class rdf:ID="Tajmahal">
  <hasMediaExample>tajmahalexample</hasMediaExample>
</owl:Class>
```

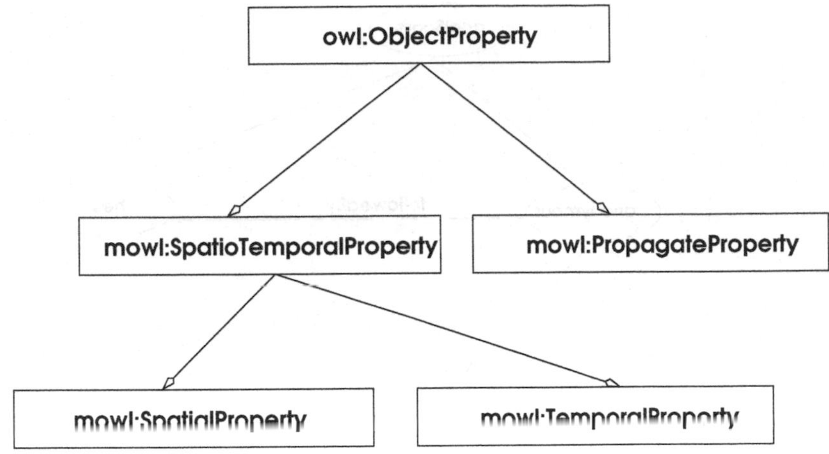

Figure 9-5. Extensions to ObjectProperty

3.2 M-OWL Properties

A `Property` in OWL is a binary relation. OWL defines two types of properties:

- **DatatypeProperty:** a binary relation between an instance of a class and XML schema data-types.
- **ObjectProperty:** a binary relation between instances of two classes.

M-OWL extends `owl:ObjectProperty` into several subclasses as shown in figure 9-5. These extensions define the semantics for spatio-temporal relations and media property propagation in a multimedia ontology. Each of these extensions are described in the following sections.

3.2.1 Spatial and Temporal Relations

Multimedia concepts are often characterized by spatial and temporal relations that exist between the different sub concepts and media objects that constitute such concepts. For example, a *goal scored* event in sports is signified by a specific spatial arrangement of the *ball* and the *goal box* followed by the audio-pattern signifying *cheer* of the crowd in time. In order to specify such spatio-temporal relations, we define a property `SpatioTemporalProperty` as an extension of `owl:ObjectProperty`. `SpatioTemporalProperty` is again extended to `SpatialProperty` and `TemporalProperty`.

The individual spatio-temporal relations can now be defined as the instances of `SpatialProperty` or `TemporalProperty` classes. MPEG-7 provides normative declarations for a fairly comprehensive set of spatio-temporal properties, some of which can be declared and be used in a specific domain. These spatio-temporal relations are classified into three broad classes.

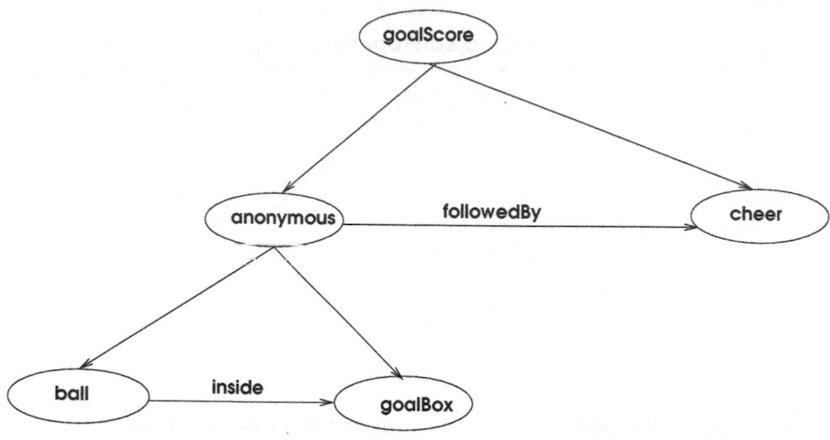

Figure 9-6. A Spatio Temporal Property Example

- **Topological Relations** like *overlap, adjacent* in spatial domain and *co-Begin, co-End* in temporal domain.
- **Metric Relations** like *near* and *far* in both spatial and temporal domains.
- **Directional relations** like *leftOf* in spatial domain and *before,after* in temporal domain.

It is also possible for ontology authors to declare new spatio-temporal relations depending on the specific needs of the domain. These relations can include Allen's temporal relations [52], the RCC-8 spatial relations [53], etc. For example, a `goalScored` event in a soccer match can be described in terms of some spatial arrangements of the `ball` and the `goalBox` followed by the audible pattern of `cheer`, e.g.

`goalScored` = (`ball` *inside* `goalBox`) *followedBy* `cheer`.

The event can be described in M-OWL by declaring the relation `inside` as an instance of `SpatialProperty` and `followedBy` as instances of `Temporal Property` and using them to relate the concepts `ball`, `goalBox` and `cheer` shown as follows. Figure 9-6 provides a graphical representation for the description.

```
<mowl:SpatialProperty rdf:ID="inside"/>
<mowl:TemporalProperty rdf:ID="followedBy"/>
<owl:Class rdf:ID="goalScored">
  <mowl:followedBy rdf:parseType="Collection">
    <owl:Class rdf:ID="cheer"/>
    <mowl:inside rdf:parseType="Collection">
      <owl:Class rdf:ID="goalBox"/>
      <owl:Class rdf:ID="ball"/>
    </mowl:inside>
```

```
    </mowl:followedBy>
  </owl:Class>
```

3.2.2 Media Property Propagation

Another important requirement of multimedia ontologies is flexible media property propagation rules, independent of the concept hierarchy. For example, if a monument is built with a certain type of stone, the former generally "inherits" the visual properties of the latter, though the relation *built with* does not imply a concept hierarchy. The relations like *built with* are domain specific and cannot be a-priori defined in the language. In order for an ontology author to define new properties (relations) between objects which imply media property propagation, we define `PropagateProperty` as an extension to `owl:ObjectProperty` class as follows.

```
<mowl:PropagateProperty rdf:ID="PropagateProperty">
  <rdf:label>PropagateProperty</rdf:label>
  <rdfs:comment>
    Propagate Property is a link between two classes which has
    the propagate property true i.e. the media properties flow
    from the domain to range
  </rdfs:comment>
  <rdfs:subPropertyOf rdf:resource=
    "http://www.w3.org/1999/02/22-rdf-syntax-ns#Property"/>
</mowl:PropagateProperty>
```

The individual relations, e.g. `builtWith` can now be defined as instances of `PropagateProperty` and be used to connect two classes, say `marble` and `Tajmahal` (see figure 9-7) as

```
<mowl:PropagateProperty rdf:ID="builtWith">
  <rdfs:domain rdf:resource="#marble">
  <rdfs:range  rdf:resource="#Tajmahal">
</mowl:PropagateProperty>
```

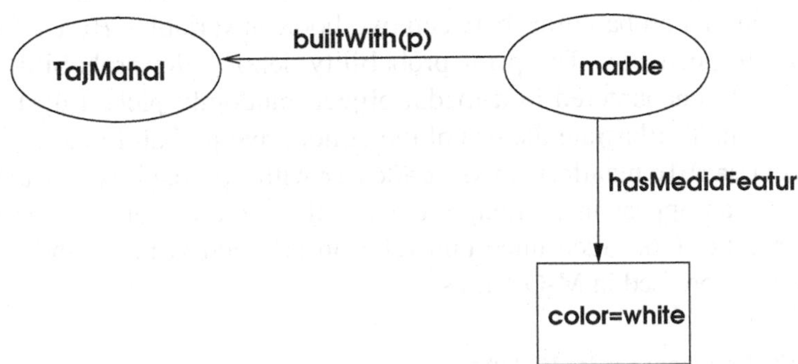

Figure 9-7. PropagateProperty

3.3 Uncertainty Specification

Several real world domains are characterized by uncertain knowledge, which cannot be represented by ontology languages like OWL and cannot be reasoned with crisp Description Logic. Ding and Peng [54] have defined a Bayesian network based extension of OWL for uncertain ontology representation and reasoning. We adopt a similar scheme for representing the uncertainties that exist between two concepts and between a concept and a media property in M-OWL.

A Bayesian Network is a directed acyclic graph, where every node represents a variable that can assume one of finitely many states. The uncertainty in a Bayesian Network is represented by a set of conditional probability tables, $P(X_i \mid \pi_i)$ for every node X in the network. Here, X_i represents a state of the variable X and π_i a state of its parent variables. A Bayesian Network has a causal interpretation: $P(X_i \mid \pi_i)$ implies the state X_i of variable X is caused by the state π_i of the parent set with a probability P.

In multimedia domain, a media property is considered as the manifestation of an abstract concept in a multimedia document and the causal relation implied by a Bayesian Network holds good. For example, a *clear day* manifests itself as a *blue sky* in a landscape, or a *lesion* in the brain manifests in a particular observable shape in an MRI image. Each of these manifestations are however associated with some uncertainty. A photograph taken at dawn on a clear day may not depict a blue sky. Similarly, a certain shape in an MRI image may not be a conclusive evidence for a lesion. These uncertainties can be represented by a probability table between a pair of boolean variables $P(M \mid C)$ and $P(M \mid \neg C)$, where M represents a media pattern and C represents a concept. Similar uncertain causal relation exists between concepts in the multimedia domain, for example, *cheer* will be manifested in a soccer video during a *goal scored* only with a certain probability.

Following [54], we define the constructs `PriorProbObj`, `CondProbObjT` and `CondProbObjF` to denote prior probability of a boolean variable $P(A)$, and the conditional probabilities between two boolean variables $P(A \mid B)$ and $P(A \mid \neg B)$ respectively. The prior probability denotes the probability of a concept A to be encountered in a media object, randomly picked up from a given collection. To illustrate the use of the conditional probabilities, consider that a concept `marble` manifests in `whiteColor` with a probability 0.8 and that `whiteColor` can appear in an image, even without the presence of `marble` with a probability 0.6. Such uncertain relation between `marble` and `white color` can be expressed in M-OWL as

```
<mowl:MediaFeature rdf:ID="whiteColor">
  <Mpeg7: ...
    ...  Descriptor specifying white color
```

```
  </Mpeg7: ...
</mowl:MediaFeature>
<owl:Class ref:ID="Marble">
  <hasMediaFeature>whiteColor</hasMediaFeature>
</owl:Class>
<prob:CondProbObjT rdf:ID="P(whiteColor/Marble)">
  <prob:hasVariable>Marble</prob:hasVariable>
  <prob:hasCondition>whiteColor</prob:hasCondition>
  <prob:hasProbValue>0.8</hasProbValue>
</prob:CondProbObjT>
<prob:CondProbObjF rdf:ID="P(whiteColor/NotMarble)">
  <prob:hasVariable>Marble</prob:hasVariable>
  <prob:hasCondition>whiteColor</prob:hasCondition>
  <prob:hasProbValue>0.6</hasProbValue>
</prob:CondProbObjF>
```

It is not necessary to specify the prior probability or the conditional probability tables with every concept in M-OWL. In absence of the specifications, we assume a crisp relation between the nodes and assign a conditional probability pair $\langle P(A \mid B) = 1, P(A \mid \neg B) = 0$. These default probabilities are also used when an OWL ontology is integrated with an ontology expressed in M-OWL (see section 5). Pradhan [55] observes that inferencing in Bayesian Network is more sensitive to network topology than the conditional probability tables. Thus, the quality of inferencing is unlikely to have significant degradation with such default probabilities. The default prior probabilities of a node are assigned the unbiased value of $\frac{1}{2}$.

4. REASONING FRAMEWORK

An ontology description scheme is not complete unless it is complemented with a reasoning framework for inferencing. The inferencing scheme in M-OWL has been motivated by the need to construct Observation Models for concepts and to recognize concepts by observing expected media patterns in the multimedia documents. The semantics of the additional constructs introduced in the language plays an important role in the reasoning framework.

M-OWL defines the semantics of three classes of relations:

- **Hierarchy relations:** these include `subClassOf` and `instanceOf` properties of OWL.
- **Propagation relation:** these include instances of `PropagateProperty`.
- **Spatio-Temporal relation:** these include instances of `SpatioTemporal Property`.

Thus, an M-OWL ontology can be viewed as an overlay of three distinct semantic networks, each corresponding to a class of properties. We call these graphs as *hierarchy*, *propagate* and *spatio-temporal* graphs respectively. The *hierarchy graph* is useful in reasoning with the media examples, while the *propagate graph* and the *spatio-temporal graph* are useful in reasoning with the media feature specifications. Each of these graphs is a directed acyclic graph (DAG)[6]. Moreover, the adjacent nodes in the graphs are related by Bayesian probability pairs. Thus, the graphs assume the nature of Bayesian Networks. We have used this model to implement a probabilistic reasoning framework to handle the uncertainty in interpreting multimedia data.

The first step in the reasoning scheme is to construct the three Bayesian Networks from an M-OWL ontology. We have extended the rules presented in [54] to account for the new constructs in M-OWL. The rules for constructing the Bayesian Networks are summarized as follows.

1. The *hierarchy* graph is constructed by drawing directed arcs from superconcept nodes to subconcept nodes as in [54]. In addition, all the individuals which are in the range of `hasMediaExample` are linked to their respective domain individuals.
2. The rules for constructing the *propagate* and the *spatio-temporal* graphs are as follows.
   (a) Every concept "C" is mapped to a node in the translated BN.
   (b) Every Property "P" defined with domain "D" and range "R" is mapped to a node, which contains the subset of individuals in "D" who have this property "P".
   (c) Every property node has one more node as its child which has the individuals of the global range of the property.
   (d) All the individuals which are in the range of `hasMediaFeature` are linked to their corresponding domain individuals.
   (e) Prepare prior probability tables for the nodes and conditional probability tables between the nodes using `PriorProbObj`, `CondProbObjT` and `CondProbObjF`, wherever supplied.

In the following text, we introduce the rules for reasoning with the individual classes of relations, followed by an example of construction of the Observation Model for a concept with these rules.

4.1 Reasoning with the Propagate and the Hierarchy Relations

The recognition of a concept in a multimedia document is often facilitated by the recognition of media features of some related concepts. For example, detection of a parallel pair of rails can facilitate recognition of a railway loco-

[6] Acyclic property of the graphs is necessary to prevent indefinite computational loops in the reasoning scheme. It is enforced by inhibiting backward reference; a concept in M-OWL needs to be defined before it is referenced.

motive. Similarly, the detection of the texture of marble reinforces the belief in recognition of a monument, like the Tajmahal. Thus, the Observation Model of a concept should comprise not only the media features of itself but those of the related concepts also. The reasoning with *propagate* and *hierarchy* graphs achieves this objective. The rules of the reasoning are summarized as follows.

1. Media examples propagate upward in a hierarchy graph. If a concept c_2 is a child of the concept c_1 in the hierarchy graph, media examples of c_2 are inherited by c_1. Simply stated, a media example of a sub-class is also an example of its super-class.
2. Media features flow downward in a propagate graph. If a concept c_2 is a child of the concept c_1 in the hierarchy graph, media feature of c_1 are inherited by c_2. Simply stated, the propagation property implies inheritance of media features (constraints).

4.2 Reasoning with the Spatio-Temporal Relations

The reasoning with spatio-temporal relations results in generation of a composite media feature description for a concept, which is described in terms of several sub-concepts interconnected with spatio-temporal relations. Each of the sub-concepts are assumed to have some media features associated with it. The media feature of the composite concept is an aggregate of the media features of its sub-concepts interconnected with appropriate spatio-temporal relations. For example, let us assume that an event `goalScored` is defined using a spatial relation between two sub-concepts `ball` and `goalBox` as

$$\texttt{goalScored} = \texttt{ball}\ \textit{inside}\ \texttt{goalpost}$$

We also assume that

1. The concepts `ball` and `goalBox` are defined and appropriate set of media properties $\mathcal{M}_B$ and $\mathcal{M}_G$ are associated with them.
2. A spatial relation *inside* between concepts ball and goalpost is defined.
3. A probability pair `CondProbT` and `CondProbF` is defined between the composite concept and each of the sub-concepts and between a sub-concept and each of its media properties.
4. A probability pair `CondProbT` and `CondProbF` is defined between the concepts `ball` and `goalBox` (in context of the event `goalScored`).

The composite media feature of the concept `goalScored` is now constructed as follows:

1. Draw a node for the composite concept and a node for each of the sub-concepts. Link them with parent-child relationships.
2. Draw a node for each of the media properties for each the sub-concepts. Link a sub-concept to its media properties with parent-child relationships.

3. Each of the spatial and temporal relations between the sub-concepts is translated into a node and linked as a child to the composite concept.
4. The conditional probabilities `CondProbT` and `CondProbF` are assigned to every pair of adjacent nodes in this graph.

4.3 Reasoning for Concept Description and Recognition

The reasoning schemes with the different types of properties defined in M-OWL as described in the previous section can be used to derive an Observation Model for a concept. An Observation Model is a description of a concept in terms of its observable media properties. It is organized as a Bayesian tree, where the root node represents the concept and the leaf nodes represent a set of expected media properties for the concept. The conditional probability tables in the OM represent the "causal strength" between the concept and the individual media properties. The leaf nodes are also called the "observation nodes" since they provide a basis for observation of media properties toward recognition of the concept.

The rules of constructing the Observation Model for a concept C are as follows.

1. Find the structural components of the concept C. Repeat this step recursively to find the set of elementary concepts $\mathcal{C}$, which do not have structural components. For example, the elementary concepts for the `goalScored` event described in section 3.2.1 are `ball`, `goalBox` and `cheer`.
2. Derive the Observation Model for each of the elementary concepts in $\mathcal{C}$ using example propagation in the *hierarchy* graph and feature propagation in the *propagate* graph using the rules specified in section 4.1.
   (a) The property inheritance is done in a recursive manner, starting with the furthest nodes in the networks and progressively converging to the concept.
   (b) If any of the nodes involved in property propagation has a compositional structure, the rules described in this section are applied recursively on those nodes.
3. Combine the media properties of the constituent elementary components at each level of compositional hierarchy, starting at the bottom-most node and progressively working upward. In the example of `goalScored`, the Observation Models for `ball` and `goalBox` are combined first and then the Observation Model of `cheer` is combined.
4. If the resulting network has multiple connectivity (i.e. not a tree), replicate the nodes with multiple parents to convert the network to a tree. For example, if a node C has two parents X and Y, have two instances of C in the graph – one as a child of X and the other a child of Y.

We propose use of belief propagation [56] in an Observation Model for concept recognition. The "observation"[7] of a media property in a multimedia document, either by the action of a feature detector or by interpretation of a MPEG-7 like content description, provides some evidential support for the respective observation nodes. In general, an "observation" results in a similarity score, which is a number in the range [0, 1]. We interpret this similarity score as a virtual evidence [56] for an observation node. The assignment of the virtual evidences to the observation nodes result in belief propagation in the Bayesian Network. The posterior probability of the root node as a result of such belief propagation represents the degree of belief in the concept. Generally, it is not necessary to observe all media properties specified in an OM for concept recognition, since observation of a selected few can generate enough confidence in the result. Selection of a sufficient and computationally optimal subset of observation nodes through a distributed planning process has been discussed in [51].

4.4 An Example

To illustrate the construction of the Observation Model with the above reasoning framework, consider a small illustrative ontology for the Tajmahal as depicted below. The ontology has been expressed in M-OWL and incorporates media property descriptions of the concepts. In summary, it relates the monument to the material (marble) it is built with, provides its compositional structure in terms of its domes and minaret (simplified for illustration purposes) and associates some example images with it.

```
<mowl:MediaExample rdf:ID="TajmahalExample">
  <Mpeg7:MediaFormat>
    <Content>Image</Content>
  </Mpeg7:MediaFormat>
  <Mpeg7:MediaLocator>
    <MediaUri>http://...jpg</MediaUri>
  </Mpeg7:MediaLocator>
</mowl:MediaExample>

<owl:ObjectProperty rdf:ID="hasMediaFeature">
  <rdfs:domain rdf:resource=
                  "http://www.w3.org/2002/07/owl#Thing" />
  <rdfs:range rdf:resource="#MediaFeature"/>
</owl:ObjectProperty>
<owl:ObjectProperty rdf:ID="hasMediaExample">
  <rdfs:domain rdf:resource=
                  "http://www.w3.org/2002/07/owl#Thing" />
```

[7] We use the term "observation" in a more general sense than visual perception to include any type of feature detection in a multimedia document.

```
  <rdfs:range rdf:resource="MediaExample"/>
</owl:ObjectProperty>

<owl:Class rdf:ID="Tajmahal">
  <hasMediaExample>TajmahalExample</hasMediaExample>
</owl:Class>
<prob:CondProbObjT rdf:ID="P(TajmahalExample/Tajmahal)">
  <prob:hasCondition>TajmahalExample</prob:hasCondition>
  <prob:hasVariable>Tajmahal</prob:hasVariable>
  <prob:hasProbValue>0.8</prob:hasProbValue>
</prob:CondProbObjT>
<prob:CondProbObjF rdf:ID="P(TajmahalExample/NotTajmahal)">
  <prob:hasCondition>TajmahalExample</prob:hasCondition>
  <prob:hasVariable>Tajmahal</prob:hasVariable>
  <prob:hasProbValue>0.6</hasProbValue>
</prob:CondProbObjF>

<mowl:MediaFeature rdf:ID="WhiteColor">
  <Mpeg7:DescriptionSchema>
    The actual schema which specifies the color of marble
  </Mpeg7:DescriptionSchema>
</mowl:MediaFeature>
<owl:Class rdf:ID="marble">
  <hasMediaFeature>WhiteColor</hasMediaFeature>
</owl:Class>
<prob:CondProbObjT rdf:ID="P(WhiteColor/Marble)">
  <prob:hasVariable>Marble</prob:hasVariable>
  <prob:hasCondition>WhiteColor</prob:hasCondition>
  <prob:hasProbValue>0.9</hasProbValue>
</prob:CondProbObjT>
<prob:CondProbObjF rdf:ID="P(WhiteColor/NotMarble)">
    <prob:hasVariable>Marble</prob:hasVariable>
    <prob:hasCondition>WhiteColor</prob:hasCondition>
<prob:hasProbValue>0.2</hasProbValue>
</prob:CondProbObjF>

<mowl:PropagateProperty rdf:ID="builtWith">
  <rdfs:domain rdf:resource="Tajmahal">
  <rdfs:range rdf:resource="marble">
</mowl:PropagateProperty>

<mowl:MediaFeature rdf:ID="minaretshape">
  <Mpeg7:DescriptionSchema>
    The actual schema which specifies the shape of a minaret
  </Mpeg7:DescriptionSchema>
</mowl:MediaFeature>
<owl:Class rdf:ID="minaret">
  <hasMediaFeature>minaretshape</hasMediaFeature>
</owl:Class>
<prob:CondProbObjT rdf:ID="P(Minaretshape/Minaret)">
```

```
  <prob:hasVariable>minaretshape</prob:hasVariable>
  <prob:hasCondition>minaret</prob:hasCondition>
  <prob:hasProbValue>0.85</hasProbValue>
</prob:CondProbObjT>
<prob:CondProbObjF rdf:ID="P(Minaretshape/NotMinaret)">
  <prob:hasVariable>minaretshape</prob:hasVariable>
  <prob:hasCondition>minaret</prob:hasCondition>
  <prob:hasProbValue>0.7</hasProbValue>
</prob:CondProbObjF>

<mowl:MediaFeature rdf:ID="domeshape">
  <Mpeg7:DescriptionSchema>
    The actual schema which specifies the shape of dome
  </Mpeg7:DescriptionSchema>
</mowl:MediaFeature>
<owl:Class rdf:ID="dome">
  <hasMediaFeature>domeshape</hasMediaFeature>
</owl:Class>
<prob:CondProbObjT rdf:ID="P(Domeshape/Dome)">
  <prob:hasVariable>domeshape</prob:hasVariable>
  <prob:hasCondition>dome</prob:hasCondition>
  <prob:hasProbValue>0.77</hasProbValue>
</prob:CondProbObjT>
<prob:CondProbObjF rdf:ID="P(Domeshape/NotDome)">
  <prob:hasVariable>domeshape</prob:hasVariable>
  <prob:hasCondition>dome</prob:hasCondition>
  <prob:hasProbValue>0.66</hasProbValue>
</prob:CondProbObjF>

<mowl:MediaExample rdf:ID="duskExample">
  <Mpeg7:MediaFormat>
    <Content>Image</Content>
  </Mpeg7:MediaFormat>
  <Mpeg7:MediaLocator>
    <MediaUri>http://...jpg</MediaUri>
  </Mpeg7:MediaLocator>
</mowl:MediaExample>
<owl:Class rdf:ID="TajAtDusk">
  <rdfs:subClassOf rdf:resource="Tajmahal"/>
  <hasMediaExample>duskExample</hasMediaExample>
</owl:Class>
<prob:CondProbObjT rdf:ID="P(duskExample/TajAtDusk)">
  <prob:hasCondition>duskExample</prob:hasCondition>
  <prob:hasVariable>TajAtDusk</prob:hasVariable>
  <prob:hasProbValue>0.83</prob:hasProbValue>
</prob:CondProbObjT>
<prob:CondProbObjF rdf:ID="P(duskExample/NotTajAtDusk)">
  <prob:hasVariable>duskExample</prob:hasVariable>
  <prob:hasCondition>TajAtDusk</prob:hasCondition>
  <prob:hasProbValue>0.66</hasProbValue>
```

```
</prob:CondProbObjF>

<owl:Class rdf:ID="Structure"/>
<owl:ObjectProperty red:ID="hasStructure">
  <rdfs:domain rdf:resource="Tajmahal"/>
  <rdfs:range rdf:resource="Structure"/>
</owl:ObjectProperty>

<mowl:SpatioTemporalProperty rdf:ID="between"/>
<owl:Class rdf:ID="Structure">
  <mowl:between rdf:parseType="Collection">
    <owl:Class rdf:ID="dome"/>
    <owl:Class rdf:ID="minaret"/>
  </mowl:between>
</owl:Class>

<prob:CondProbObjT rdf:ID="P(Between/Dome-Minaret)">
  <prob:hasCondition>minaret</prob:hasCondition>
  <prob:hasVariable>dome</prob:hasVariable>
  <prob:hasProbValue>0.9</prob:hasProbValue>
</prob:CondProbObjT>
<prob:CondProbObjF rdf:ID="P(Between/NotDome-Minaret)">
  <prob:hasVariable>minaret</prob:hasVariable>
  <prob:hasVariable>dome</prob:hasVariable>
  <prob:hasProbValue>0.2</prob:hasProbValue>
</prob:CondProbObjF>
```

An overlay of the hierarchy, propagate and spatio-temporal graphs derived from this description is depicted in figure 9-8. We can deduce following media properties of the concept `Tajmahal` from the graph, using the inferencing rules mentioned in the previous section.

1. `Tajmahal` has a media example associated with it.
2. The media feature `color = white` is inherited by `Tajmahal` from `marble`, since `Tajmahal` is a child of `marble` in the propagate graph.
3. The `dome` and the `minarets` are sub concepts of `Tajmahal` connected by spatial relations. Thus, a spatial relation of the media properties of the domes and the minarets gets associated with `Tajmahal`.
4. `Tajmahal` "inherits" the media example of the concept `TajAtDusk`, since the latter is a subclass of the former.

The Observation Model for `Tajmahal` so constructed is depicted in figure 9-9. Conditional probability tables are associated with the pair of adjacent nodes in the graph. These probabilities are derived from the `CondProbObjT` and `CondProbObjF` values wherever specified. Default probabilities (not shown in the figure) are associated where such values are not explicitly specified. The leaf nodes in this tree represent the media patterns that are expected to manifest in a media instance of the Tajmahal. Any of these media patterns, if observed

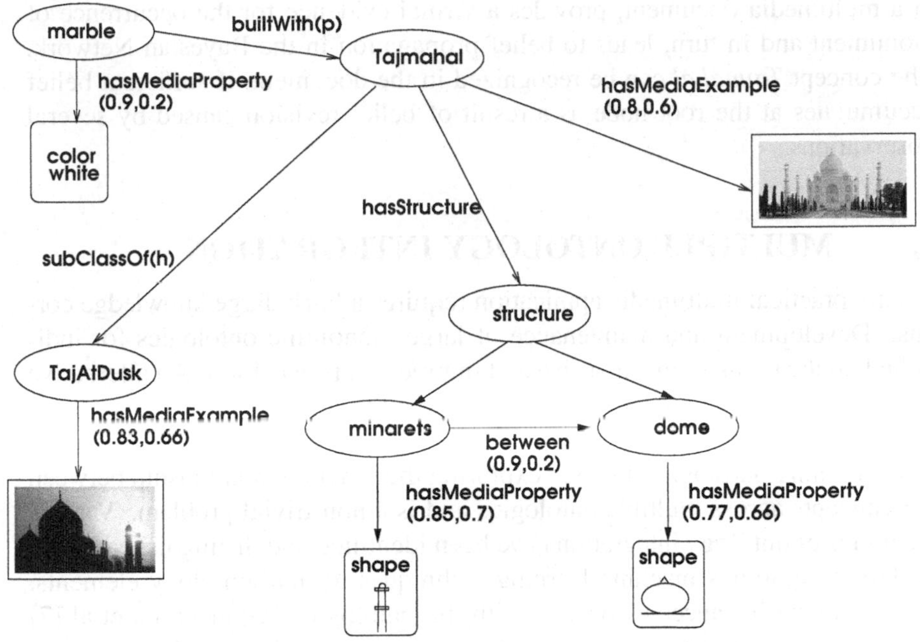

Figure 9-8. Overlay of hierarchy, propagate and spatio-temporal graphs for the "Tajmahal" ontology

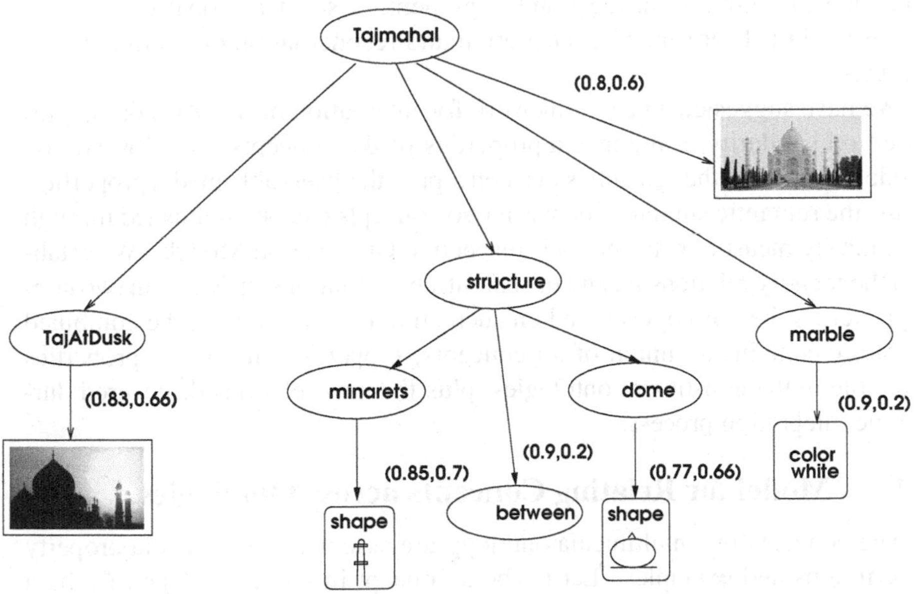

Figure 9-9. Derived Observation Model for "Tajmahal"

in a multimedia document, provides a virtual evidence for the occurrence of monument and in turn, leads to belief propagation in the Bayesian Network. The concept *Tajmahal* can be recognized in the document, if sufficient belief accumulates at the root node as a result of belief revision caused by several observations.

5. MULTIPLE ONTOLOGY INTEGRATION

Any practical multimedia application requires a fairly large knowledge corpus. Development and maintenance of large monolithic ontologies for individual applications is an expensive and impractical proposition. An alternative and more prudent approach is to integrate and reuse a number of existing ontologies, each of which partially fulfill the requirements of the application.

Combining ontologies involves exploring the semantic relationship between the concepts across multiple ontologies and is a non-trivial problem. Various meanings of ontology integration have been identified and distinguished in [3]. GLUE [5] employs machine learning techniques to map ontology elements, based on data instances associated with the ontologies. Giunchiglia et al [7] use a semantic matcher, which analyzes the similarity of the knowledge graphs. The Rainbow classifier [6] uses similarity scores between concepts based on their associated example documents. PROMPT [8] provides a semi-automatic approach to ontology merging and alignment. Use of a global ontology is suggested in [4] for semantic integration and reconciliation of distributed ontologies.

We have suggested a new framework for integration of M-OWL ontologies based on similarity of the media properties of the concepts. An Observation Model establishes the semantics of a concept with observable media properties. Thus, the semantic similarity between two concepts can be established through a similarity measure between their respective Observation Models. We establish the identity relationship and the parent-child relationship between two concepts across the ontologies based on such similarity measures. The combined ontology contains an union of all concepts, properties and media properties available in the constituent ontologies, plus the new relations discovered during the integration process.

5.1 Model for Relating Concepts across Ontologies

The concepts in a multimedia ontology are associated with media property descriptions and examples. Let C_a be a concept in ontology A and C_b be a concept in ontology O_b. Let $D_a = \{d_{a1} \ldots d_{am}\}$ and $D_b = \{d_{b1} \ldots d_{bn}\}$ be the sets of media property descriptors in the OM's for concepts C_a and C_b

respectively. The following algorithm establishes equivalence between C_a and C_b.

1. Compare each of the m property descriptors of C_a with each of the n property descriptors of C_b. Let $D'_a \subseteq D_a$ be the set of descriptors of C_a, each of which has sufficient similarity with at least one descriptor in D_b.
2. Instantiate the property nodes D'_a. Do a belief propagation in OM for C_a and find out the posterior belief value P_{ab} of concept C_a.
3. Similarly, find out the posterior belief value P_{ba} of concept C_b with the subset of property descriptors in D_b, each of which is sufficiently similar with at least one descriptor in D_a.
4. If both of P_{ab} and P_{ba} are greater than a threshold τ_{eq}, then the two concepts C_a and c_b are equivalent.

The above algorithm implies that there should be a sufficient mutual overlap between the media property descriptions between two concepts for them to be declared equivalent. An asymmetric overlap implies parent-child relationship, when the concepts C_a and C_b are not equivalent. We use a more relaxed matching criteria for ascertaining parent-child relationship. We define two other thresholds, τ_p and τ_c ($\tau_c \leq \tau_p \leq \tau_{eq}$) for this purpose. If $P_{ab} > \tau_p$ and $P_{ba} > \tau_c$, the concept C_b is a parent of C_a. Similarly, when $P_{ba} > \tau_p$ and $P_{ab} > \tau_c$, the concept C_a is a parent of C_b. We apply this principle with little variations to integrate two ontologies expressed in M-OWL and in integrating an ontology expressed in OWL with one expressed in M-OWL.

5.2 Integrating M-OWL Ontologies

The Observation Model of a concept consists of media property descriptors and examples. If two descriptors are alike (e.g., both are dominant colors in still images), then a direct comparison is possible using appropriate feature analysis tools. Each of these tools can have their own thresholds to determine sufficiency of match. If the descriptors are of different kinds, a comparison may still be possible by effecting some transformation on one or both of the descriptors and then applying appropriate feature comparison tool. For example, if one of the features is a color histogram and the other is a raw image example, color histogram can be extracted from the latter and be compared with the former. In some other cases (e.g. an audio-clip and a still image), comparison is not possible.

In order to establish the cases where comparison is possible, we need a knowledge base which provides information about various Multimedia descriptors and relations among them. We have introduced a new knowledge structure called *PropertyNet*, which is a multimedia descriptor reference system and whose design is inspired by current MPEG-7 activities. The PropertyNet is essentially an ontology written in OWL expressing the the equivalence and transformation relation between different audio and visual features. For example, two nodes, "color histogram" and "dominant color" in the ontology are linked by a property that is the pointer (URI) to a procedure that can derive dominant color of an image from its color histogram. Once the comparability of the media properties have been established, we apply the algorithm described above to establish the relation between two concepts.

5.3 Integrating OWL and M-OWL Ontologies

A large corpus of ontologies already exist in OWL and continue to be developed in OWL. Though these ontologies may be developed for other types of applications, the knowledge can be gainfully utilized in multimedia systems. This has been the prime motivation for us to explore the possibility of integrating traditional ontologies expressed in OWL with multimedia ontologies expressed in M-OWL. Though an ontology in OWL does not contain any media property definition, it can lead to new relations being found between two concepts in one or more M-OWL ontology(ies).

In general, textual descriptors (keywords or key-phrases) and parametric descriptors (in the form of $\langle attribute, value\rangle$) can be associated with concepts in M-OWL, over and above the media features. These descriptors can be subjected to the same reasoning techniques described in the previous section. Thus, a generalized Observation Model for a concept comprises media, textual as well as parametric descriptors. A textual Observation Model (OM_T) for a concept is a subgraph of the generalized Observation Model, comprising the concepts and their textual and parametric descriptors.

We construct a similar textual Observation Model from OWL ontology for comparing a concept in an M-OWL ontology. The `sameClassAs` construct is used for representing equivalent concepts in OWL. Other relations between the concepts are expressed with the `ObjectProperty` construct. These two constructs form the basis of construction of the textual Observation Model of a concept in an OWL ontology. The names of the concept itself and of the equivalent concepts constitute a set of textual descriptors for a concept. An `ObjectProperty` construct links a concept c_0 to another concept c_1 with a property p_1. Each of such properties can be expressed as a parametric descriptor in the form $\langle p_1, c_1\rangle$ for the concept c_0. The set of textual and parametric descriptors so defined is used to construct the textual Observation Model (OM_T) for a concept.

The concepts in OWL and M-OWL ontologies are compared on the basis of similarity of these textual Observation Models. A term in a textual descriptor is conceptually compared with another using the *similarity* function of WordNet [57]. Application specific thesaurus or other similarity measures can also be used for this comparison. In order to establish the similarity of

Table 9-1. Description of Ontologies used

Ontology	Language	Coverage	No. of Concepts	No. of Descriptors	Overlap
O_1	M-OWL	Categories of Paintings, the themes, origin, and such other details	106	123	All
O_2	M-OWL	Indian Mythology	2	4	O_1, O_5
O_3	M-OWL	Nature, places	5	29	O_1
O_4	OWL	Wild-life in perspective of Hinduism	28	0	O_1
O_5	OWL	Mythology and Indian Paintings	5	0	O_1, O_2

two textual descriptors, D_{ta} and D_{tb} for concepts C_a and C_b having m and n terms respectively, we construct a similarity matrix T_{SM} of dimension $m \times n$. $T_{SM}[c][d](\alpha)$represents the degree of match between c^{th} word of D_{ta} and d^{th} word of D_{tb}. We define a threshold τ_t for textual similarity. If there exists at least one α for each row of T_{SM} where $\alpha \geq \tau_t$, then D_{kiA} is retained.

The parametric descriptors are in the form of $\langle A, V\rangle$ tuples, where A is an attribute and V is a value. To compare two parametric descriptors $\langle a_1, v_1\rangle$ and $\langle a_2, v_2\rangle$, we construct a list of equivalent attributes. If $a_1 \equiv a_2$ in the list and the similarity (ρ) between v_1 and v_2 exceeds a threshold, then the descriptors are considered to be sufficiently similar. The value fields of the parametric descriptors contain the names of concepts, and the similarity of the values can be established using extended WordNet as described earlier.

5.4 An Example of Ontology Integration

We illustrate the effect of ontology integration with a set of five ontologies pertaining to Indian arts and heritage. Three of these ontologies have been specifically developed for multimedia applications using M-OWL. The other two have been originally developed for different applications and encoded in OWL. Table 9-1 summarizes the content of these ontologies.

Let us consider a concept *Krishna*[8]. The concept is defined in the ontology O_1. The Observation Model for the concept derived from the ontology is depicted in figure 9-10(a). Ontology O_2 contains the concept *Madhusudan*. The Observation Model for the concept derived from the ontology is depicted in figure 9-10(b). A comparison of these two Observation Models shows strong similarity in terms of textual keywords and some common image examples.

[8] *Krishna* is a divine character in Hindu mythology, with several aliases like *Madhusudan*, *Gopal*, etc.

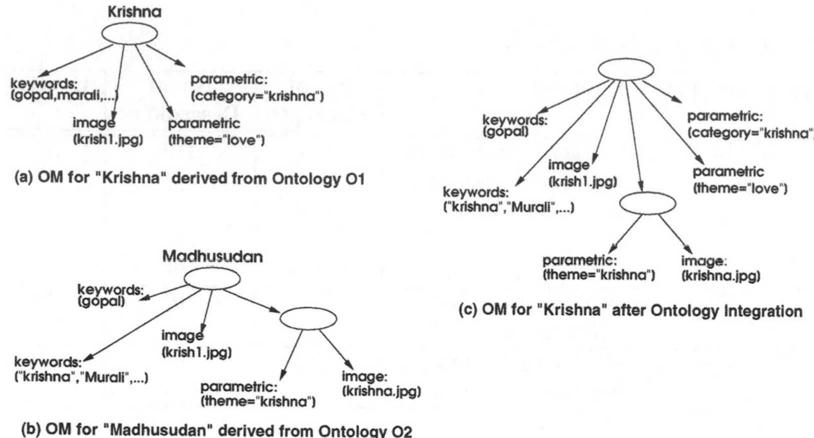

(a) OM for "Krishna" derived from Ontology O1

(b) OM for "Madhusudan" derived from Ontology O2

(c) OM for "Krishna" after Ontology Integration

Figure 9-10. Ontology Integration and its impact on Observation Model

Thus, the concept *Krishna* in O_1 is equated to the concept *Madhusudan* in O_2 and the two ontologies are merged. The Observation Model generated by the combined ontology is a union of all media property descriptions in the two Observation Models and is depicted in figure 9-10(c). The concept *Krishna* (or its equivalent) being a common concept in Hindu mythology was found in some of the other ontologies too and the Observation Model is further augmented. The enrichment of the Observation Model results in more flexibility in recognizing the concept in multimedia documents.

6. CONCLUSIONS

We have proposed M-OWL as an extension of OWL for expressing multimedia ontologies for the web. Additional constructs have been added in M-OWL to express media property descriptions of the concepts and the inherent uncertainties associated. However, the semantics of the M-OWL properties are quite different from that of OWL. We have proposed a Bayesian Network based representation of the domain and a probabilistic reasoning scheme for semantic interpretation of media data. We have proposed a new model for ontology integration using Observation Models of the concepts, which can be used to integrate multimedia and traditional ontologies.

In contrast to the earlier approaches of extending MPEG-7 with core and domain ontologies, we have extended the ontology language itself to include constructs to support media features and the uncertainties that characterize the multimedia world. The extended ontology language provides for the much required bridge between the conceptual and the media worlds with formal semantics. The reasoning with media properties to derive the Observation Models of concepts is a novel feature of our work. The ontology language proposed by us can express the inherent uncertainties in the world of multimedia and the accompanying reasoning scheme exploits them for media data interpretation.

Proposal of the a new standard has generally been greeted in industry with skepticism, because of the lost investments. Our proposal of M-OWL builds on OWL. Moreover, OWL ontologies can be integrated with M-OWL ontologies and reused in the context of multimedia retrieval. In principle, it is also possible to integrate ontologies expressed in earlier ontology languages, e.g. DAML+OIL, with M-OWL. Thus, M-OWL protects the investments in existing ontology development efforts. Moreover, we envisage a scenario where new domain ontologies for non-media applications will continue to get developed in OWL. M-OWL ontology fragments will integrate these OWL ontologies to be utilized in context of multimedia applications.

REFERENCES

[1] T. Berners-Lee, J. Hendler, and O. Lassila. The semantic web. *Scientific American*, May 2001.

[2] T. R. Gruber. Towards principles for the design of ontologies used for knowledge sharing. In *International workshop on formal ontology in conceptual analysis and knowledge representation*, 1993.

[3] H. S. Pinto and A. G. Perz. Software architecture of SETA, an adaptive Web store shell. In *Proceedings of the IJCAI-99 workshop on Ontologies and Problem-Solving Methods(KRR5)*, August 1999.

[4] D. Calvanes, G. D. Giacomo, and M. Lenzerini. A framework for ontology integration. In *Proc of the International Semantic Web Conference*, 2001.

[5] A. Doan, J. Mahadevan, P. Domingos, and A. Halevy. Learning to map between ontologies on the semantic web. In *Online Proceedings of the 11th World Wide Web Conference (WWW2002)*, pages 662–673, 2002.

[6] S. Prasad. A tool for mapping concepts between two ontologies. Technical Report, CSEE, UMBC, 2002.

[7] F. Giunchiglia, P. Shvaiko, and S. Zanobini. Semantic matching. DIT Technical Report DIT-03-013, February 2003.

[8] N. F. Noy and M. M. Musen. PROMPT: algorithm and tool for automated ontology merging and alignment. *International Journal of Human-Computer Studies*, 59(6):983–1024, 2003.

[9] N. Fuhr, N. Govert, and T. Rolleke. DOLORES: a system for logic-based retrieval of multimedia objects. In *Proceedings of the 21st annual international ACM SIGIR conference on Research and development in Information Retrieval*, pages 257–265, 1998.

[10] T. Westerveld and A. P. de Vries. Multimedia information retrieval: Experimental result analysis for a generative probabilistic image retrieval model. In *Proceedings of the 26th annual international ACM SIGIR conference on Research and development in informaion retrieval*, july 2003.

[11] A. Graves and M. Lalmas. Multimedia: Video retrieval using an MPEG-7 based inference network. In *Proceedings of the 25th annual international ACM SIGIR conference on Research and development in information retrieval*, August 2002.

[12] B. Bradshaw. Semantic based image retrieval: a probabilistic approach. In *Proceedings of the eighth ACM international conference on Multimedia*, October 2000.
[13] F. Badder, D. Calvanese, D. L. McGuinnes, D. Nardi, and P. F. Patel-Schneider. *The Description Logic Handbook*. Cambridge University Press, 2003.
[14] D. B. Lenat and R. V. Guha. *Building Large Knowledge-based Systems: Representation and Inference in the Cyc Project*. Addison-Wesley, 1990.
[15] A. F., R. Fikes, and J. Rice. The Ontolingua server: A tool for collaborative ontology construction. *International Journal of Human Computer Studies*, 46(6):707–727, 1997.
[16] R. J. Brachman and J. G. Schmolze. An overview of KL-ONE knowledge representation system. *cognitive Sciences*, 9(2):171–216, 1985.
[17] A. Borgida, R. J. Brachman, D. L. McGuinness, and L. A. Resnick. CLASSIC: A structural data model for objects. In *ACM SIGMOD International Conference on the Management of data*, pages 58–67, 1989.
[18] R. MacGregor. Inside the LOOM classifier. *SIGART Bulletin*, 2(3):70–76, 1991.
[19] S. Luke and J. D. Heflin. SHOE 1.01. proposed specification. Technical Report. Parallel Understanding Systems Group. Department of Computer Science. University of Maryland, 2000.
[20] O. Lassila and R. Swick. Resource description framework (RDF) model and syntax specification. W3C Recommendation (rec-rdf-syntax-19990222), www.w3.org/TR/REC-rdf-syntax/, 1999.
[21] D. L. McGuinness and F. van Harmelen. OWL web ontology language overview. W3C Recommendation. http://www.w3c.org/TR/owl-features/, 2004.
[22] I. Horrocks and F van Hermelen. Reference description for the DAML+OIL (march 2001) ontology markup language. Technical Report. www.daml.org/2001/03/reference.html, 2001.
[23] A. Kiryakov, B. Popov, D. Ognyanoff, D. Manov, A. Kirilov, and M. Goranov. Semantic annotation, indexing and retrieval. *Journal of Web Semantics*, pages 49–79, 2004.
[24] R. Fikes, P. Hayes, and I. Horrocks. OWL-QL: a query language for deductive query answering on the semantic web. *Journal of Web Semantics*, 2004.
[25] L. Carr, W. Hall, S. Bechhofer, and C. Goble. Conceptual linking: ontology-based open hypermedia. In *WWW '01: Proceedings of the tenth international conference on World Wide Web*, pages 334–342, 2001.
[26] L. McDowell, O. Etzioni, and A. Halevy. Semantic email: Theory and Applications. *Journal of Web Semantics*, pages 153–183, 2004.
[27] F. T. Fonseca and M. J. Egenhofer. Ontology-driven geographic information systems. In *GIS '99: Proceedings of the 7th ACM international symposium on Advances in geographic information systems*, pages 14–19. ACM Press, 1999. Talks about Ontology in GIS.
[28] C. Rosse and J.L.V. Mejino Jr. A reference ontology for biomedical informatics: the foundational model of anatomy. *J. of Biomedical Informatics*, 36(6):478–500, 2003.
[29] S. Marcus and V.S. Subrahmanian. Foundations of multimedia database systems. *Journal of the ACM*, 43(3):474–523, May 1996.
[30] A. P. de Vries and H. M. Blanken. Database technology and the management of multimedia data in Mirror. In *Multimedia Storage and Archiving Systems III*, volume 3527 of *Proceedings of SPIE*, pages 443–445, Boston, MA, November 1998.
[31] S. C. Chen and R.L. Kashyap. A spatio-temporal semantic model for multimedia database systems and multimedia information systems. *IEEE Transactions on Knowledge and Data Engineering*, 13(4):607–622, July-August 2001.
[32] L. Khan and D. McLeod. Audio structuring and personalised rertieval using ontologies. In *Proceedings of the IEEE Advances in Digital Libraries*, pages 116–126, 2000.

[33] A. Th. (Guus) Schreiber, B. Dubbeldam, J. Wielemaker, and B. Wielinga. Ontology-based photo annotation. *IEEE Intelligent Systems*, 16(3):66–74, 2001.

[34] S. Jiang, T. Huang, and W. Gao. An ontology based approach to retrieve digitized art images. In *Proceedings of the IEEE International Conference on Web Intelligence*, pages 131–137, 2004.

[35] P.J. Kuo, T. Aoki, and H. Yasuda. Building personal digital photograph libraries:an approach with ontology-based mpeg7 dozen dimensional digital content architecture. In *Proceedings of the Computer graphics International*, 2004.

[36] R. Sarvas, E. Herrarte, A. Wilhelm, and M. Davis. Metadata creation system for mobile images. In *MobiSYS '04: Proceedings of the 2nd international conference on Mobile systems, applications, and services*, pages 36–48. ACM Press, 2004.

[37] N. Arora and H. Ghosh. Concept based retrieval in a painting database. In *Proceedings of Knowledge Based Computer Systems (KBCS 2004)*, 2004.

[38] W. W. Chu, C. C. Hsu, A. F. Cardenas, and Ricky K. Taira. Knowledge based image retrieval with spatial and temporal constructs. *IEEE Transactions on Knowledge and Data Engineering*, 10(6):872–888, November-December 1998.

[39] R. Goularte, E. dos Santos Moreira, M. da Graca, and C. Pimentel. Structuring interactive tv documents. In *DocEng '03: Proceedings of the 2003 ACM symposium on Document engineering*, pages 42–51, 2003.

[40] H. Luo and J. Fan. Concept-oriented video skimming and adaptation via semantic classification. In *MIR '04: Proceedings of the 6th ACM SIGMM international workshop on Multimedia information retrieval*, pages 213–220, 2004.

[41] K. Hornsby. Retrieving event based semantics from images. In *Proceedings of the Sixth IEEE Symposium on Multimedia over Software Engineering*, 2004.

[42] B. S. Manjunath, P. Salembier, and T. Sikora. *Introduction to MPEG-7*. John Wiley and Sons Ltd., 2002.

[43] F. Nack, J. van Ossenbruggen, and L. Hardman. That obscure object of desire: Multimedia metadata on the web, part 2. *IEEE Multimedia*, 12(1):54–63, January-March 2005.

[44] J.Hunter. Enhancing the semantic interoperability of multimedia thrugh a core ontology. *IEEE transcations on Circuits and Systems for Video Technology*, 13(1), January 2003.

[45] S.Hammiche, S.Benbernou, M.S.Hacid, and A.Vakali. Multimedia database query processing and retrieval: Semantic retrieval of multimedia data. In *Proceedings of the Second ACM international workshop on Multimedia Databases*. ACM Press, November 2004.

[46] C. Tsinaraki, P. Polydoros, N. Moumoutzis, and S. Christodoulakis. Coupling OWL with MPEG-7 and TV-Anytime for domain-specific multimedia information integration and retrieval. In *Proceedings of RIAO 2004*, April 2004.

[47] K. Petridis, S. Bloehdorn, C. Saathoff N. Simou, V. Tzouvaras, S. Handschuh, Y. Kompatsiaris Y. Avrithis, S. Staab, and M. G. Strintzis. Knowledge representation and semantic annotation for multimedia analysis and reasoning. *IEE Proceedings on Vision, Image and Signal Processing*, 2005 (accepted for publication).

[48] A. Chebotko. The development of a linguistic multimedia ontology. Presentation Slides, 2005.

[49] H. Kangassalo. Conceptual level user interfaces to data bases and information systems. In Hannu Jaakkola, Hannu Kangassalo, and Setsuo Ohsuga, editors, *Advances in information modelling and knowledge bases*, pages 66–90. IOS Press, 1991.

[50] H. Ghosh. *R-MAGIC: A Cooperative agent based architecture for retrieval of multimedia documents distributed over heterogeneous repositories*. PhD thesis, Indian Institute of Technology, Delhi, 2003.

[51] H. Ghosh and S. Chaudhury. Distributed and reactive query planning in R-MAGIC: An agent based multimedia retrieval system. *IEEE Transactions on Knowledge and Data*

Engineering, 16(9), September 2004.

[52] J.F. Allen. Maintaining knowledge about temporal intervals. *Communications of the Association of Computing Machinery*, 26(11):832–843, November 1983.

[53] A. G. Cohn, B. Bennett, J. Gooday, and N. M. Gotts. Qualitative spatial representation and reasoning with the region connection calculus. *Geoinformatica*, 1(3):275–316, October 1997.

[54] Z. Ding and Y. Peng. A probabilistic extension to ontology language OWL. In *Proceedings of the 37th Hawaii International Conference On System Sciences*, January 2004.

[55] M. Pradhan, M. Henrion, G. Provan, B. Del Favero, and K. Huang. The sensitivity of belief networks to imprecise probabilities: an experimental investigation. *Artificial Intelligence*, 85:363–397, 1996.

[56] R. E. Neapolitan. *Probabilistic reasoning in expert systems: Theory and Algorithms*, chapter 6, pages 226–228. John Wiley & Sons, Inc., 1990.

[57] Y. A. Aslandogan, C. Thier, C. T. Yu, J. Zou, and N. Rishe. Using semantic contents and WordNet in image retrieval. In *Proceedings of the ACM SIGIR Conference*, July 1997.

Chapter 10

ONTOLOGY REVISION

An Application of Belief Revision Approach

Seung Hwan Kang and Sim Kim Lau

School of Economics and Information Systems, University of Wollongong, Wollongong, NSW, 2522, Australia

Abstract: One of the difficulties in the development of ontology is the issue of revising ontology. When the system accepts new information or knowledge, this new information may contradict what was initially agreed or defined in the ontology. When this happens, the ontology may need to be revised to reflect the changes. The belief revision theory provides a way that ensures new information does not cause inconsistencies with the existing system when it is introduced. This paper discusses the feasibility of using the concept of belief revision as a basis for ontology revision.

Key words: Ontology Revision; Ontology; Belief Revision; the Semantic Web

1. INTRODUCTION

Gruber (1993 p.2) notes that, for the aspect of knowledge engineering, "ontology is an explicit specification of conceptualization". In relation to the Semantic Web, ontology is used as a way of representing the semantics of the web documents and enabling it to be used by Web applications and agents (W3C 2003). Ontology also provides a constructive way to structure and define the meaning of metadata of the Web documents. The materialization of the Semantic Web also provides an approach to bring well-formed content of Web pages and create an environment that allows agents to be used and deployed to perform tasks for the users (Berners-Lee et al. 2001). Agents and human users use ontologies to reference a well-defined, agreed and organized definition of terms or concepts when they are performing tasks such as gathering, filtering and distributing information over the World Wide Web (WWW).

One of the problems identified in the development of ontology is the difficulty in maintaining ontology when there is a change in knowledge or perhaps a change in the perception about things within the community of practice. When the system accepts new information or knowledge, or when people change perceptions about certain things, the new information may contradict what was initially agreed or defined in the ontology. When this happens, the ontology may need to be revised to reflect the changes (Kang and Lau 2004). Thus, the concept of belief revision is proposed as a means to ensure that when new information is introduced, it does not cause inconsistency with the existing ontology (Stojanovic et al. 2002, Stojanovic et al. 2003).

This paper aims to show the concept of belief revision theory as a feasible way to frame a mechanism that enriches ontology revision. The feasibility of using the concept of belief revision as a mechanism for ontology revision to deal with consistency issues of ontology will be discussed.

The paper is organized as follows. Section II presents literature about ontology in general and the needs for ontology revision. Section III discusses the concept of belief revision. Section IV discusses the method that employs the belief revision concept to revise ontology. Section V discusses implementation issues in ontology revision operations. Finally, Section VI presents conclusion and future research direction.

2. ONTOLOGY

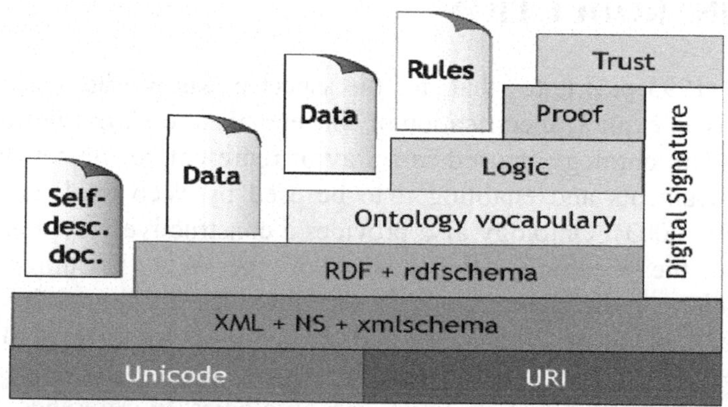

Figure 10-1. The Semantic Web as a "layer cake" (Hendler 2001 p.30)

There are various definitions of ontology in the literature. Commonly used definitions include: "ontology is a formal explicit specification of a shared conceptualization" (Gruber 1993 p.2); "ontology is a particular theory of the nature of being or existence" (Russell and Norvig 2003 p.261). In addition, Zúniga (2001) points out that the term ontology is derived from cognitive semantics which relate to expressions of conceptual structures. Gärdenfors (1997) elaborates the relationship of cognitive semantics as follows: "meanings are not in the head of a single individual, but they emerge from the conceptual schemes in the heads of the language users together with the semantic power structure." Gómez-Pérez (1999) points out that ontology should aim at capturing domain knowledge in a generic way so that it provides a commonly agreed understanding of domains that can be reused and shared.

In particular, ontology has been widely used and engaged in the development of the Semantic Web. Berners-Lee et al. (2001) define the Semantic Web as an extension of the current web "in which information is given well-defined meaning, better enabling computers and people to work in cooperation". Berners-Lee (2001 p.37) presents the Semantic Web as a "layer cake" in terms of knowledge terms, ontology vocabulary, logic, proof, rules, trust and others as shown in Figure 10-1.

A support of ontology is essential in order to achieve the vision of Semantic Web Ontology as proposed by Hendler (2001). The first step of this vision is its use to create web pages with ontological information. Logic experts or individuals will develop decentralized small-sized ontologies. Afterwards, one or more ontologies will be linked to other ontologies to share repositories. The second vision of the Semantic Web Ontology is the definition of services in a machine-readable form. This refers to using the ontologies to agree on terms and constraints for Web Services. The final vision of the Semantic Web Ontology is the use of logic and rules. Logic and rules are being used to improve the description of agents' services. Agents communicate with each other using ontologies, exchanging and merging portions of other agents' ontologies. To achieve this vision a support of ontology change is essential in relation to the Semantic Web.

In an aspect of applications, Jasper and Uschold (1999) classify categories of ontology application scenarios into: neutral authoring, ontology as specification, common access to information and ontology-based search. Each of the ontology application scenarios have the underlying assumption that ontology remains unchanged, that is, the status of ontology remains the same. In particular, the application scenario of common access to information, which is a scheme of using shared or mapped ontologies to enable various developers or multiple target applications to have access to heterogeneous sources of information. Once the ontology has been written and integrated to applications little or no consideration is given regarding changing the ontology. However, a specification or conceptualization of domain knowledge tends to change when we learn something new or when the system accepts new information. When this happens, it may be necessary to change applications that are relying on the unchanged ontology in terms of a set vocabulary or relations. Thus, if we propose ontology into metadata modeling as an application scenario, we have to make sure that changes in ontologies should not contradict the application. Otherwise, a change in our belief may instigate a need for modification of ontologies as well as the application itself.

It is not surprising to see that ontology will evolve over time. Ontologies may change as a result of extensions from previous ontologies or as a result of revision over time. Noy and Klein (2004) identify three causes of ontology changes: changes in domain, changes in conceptualization and changes in the explicit specification. When this happens, issues such as ontology interoperability and handling of multiple ontologies need to be addressed (Ding and Fensel 2001, Klein and Fensel 2001, Stojanovic et al. 2002). Thus the ability of understanding a situation is important whether ontologies remain constant or not. Sowa (1984 p.359) quotes that "An analysis of the concept of mind is an important philosophical issue, but the analysis cannot be reduced to programming or physiological terms." It remarks the importance of questioning "the way people think and the way computers can simulate thinking." (Sowa 1984 p.359). With regard to this question, it motivates thoughts of expressiveness and vagueness from ontological aspects and evolution of ontologies.

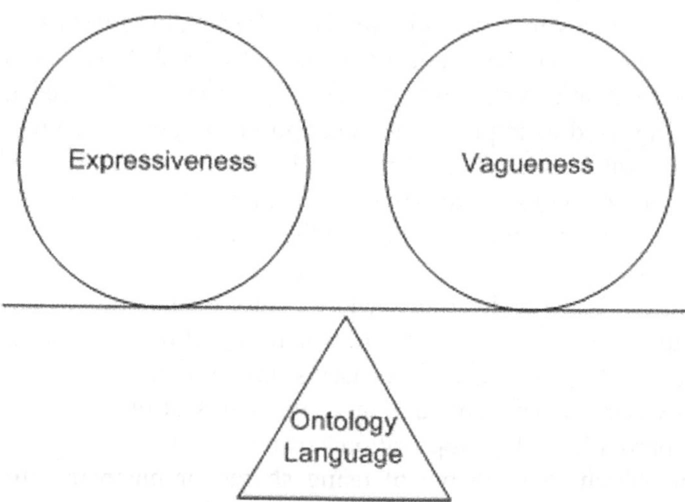

Figure 10-2. A relationship between expressiveness and vagueness

In terms of expressiveness, an ontology language can state anything precisely as any other natural language such as English, if and only if the ontology language has a capability for being precise, otherwise the ontology defined in terms of the ontology language could not be accurate. Paradoxically, the ontology language minimizes vagueness by increasing its range of expression. In fact, ontology is defined for a special purpose with constraints, syntax and limiting the terms or concepts. In this way, constraints limit the syntax to a single concept or small number of concepts. It means that the expressiveness of the ontology language can limit ambiguities on the concepts. Figure 10-2 depicts a balance of ontology language between two different aspects of expressiveness and vagueness.

The vagueness of a concept is also necessary in a natural language because it shows differences relevant to the question of the concept. For example, a concept can be expressed in different ways or asked in different forms. When the ontology language is used in a comprehensive manner for a particular ontology, it may have the vocabulary and means of expression for a purpose about anything within the scope of its use. On the other hand, what if the concept cannot be expressed in a concrete manner due to overlapping definitions? In this case, the world is stated vaguely in the way that the ontology may be loosely expressed or empirical terms somehow specified. As a matter of fact, this vagueness of the concept is necessary and even essential in natural languages.

Although complexity of the expressiveness and vagueness of ontology is not avoidable, few possible approaches to tackle the ontology revision matter have been discussed in the literature in the area of ontology versioning (Klein and Fensel 2001), ontology library system (Ding and Fensel 2001) and ontology evolution management (Stojanovic et al. 2002, Stojanovic et al. 2003). An ontology versioning system refers to the system that allows comparability issues to be taken into consideration when new knowledge is added to the system over time. An ontology library system is described as "a system capable of offering various functions for managing, adapting and standardizing groups of ontologies." (Ding and Fensel 2001 p.1) Ontology Evolution management presents a way to change ontologies with the consistency concerns. For an instance of adding, removing and even revising concepts are discussed in semi-automatic discovery of changes and the evolution strategies. Stuckenschmidt and Harmelen (2005 p.239) also propose an idea of managing ontological changes in the similar way that "is based on a taxonomy of ontological changes and their impact of the class hierarchy in combination with the position of the effected class in that hierarchy." The aforementioned approaches have been widely used to address the ontology maintenance issue as a result of evolving ontologies but have not been considered for an ontology revising perspectives that need a way to revise its ontology via "foreign" ontologies in the Semantic Web environment.

3. BELIEF REVISION

The study of belief revision is a cross-discipline research in the area of artificial intelligence, philosophy and cognitive science. According to Segal (1994 p.2), "belief revision is the process of revising a knowledge base to be consistent with new information." For an instance, when new information is encountered or added to the system, it is important to ensure that new information does not cause inconsistent beliefs and contradict the existing beliefs in the system (Gärdenfors 1992a, Segal 1994). This area of study is well published in agent negotiation and belief changes (Dragoni and Giorgini 2002, Tohmé and Sandholm 1999, Williams and Rott 2001, Zhang et al. 2004). In ontologies, changes may also occur in a way that new information may contradict what was initially agreed or defined. When this happens, the ontology may need to be revised to reflect the changes in a consistent manner. In this sense, the concept of belief revision theory, in particular the coherence theory is a feasible way to frame a mechanism that can enrich ontology revision.

There are two approaches to describing belief revision: the foundation theory and the coherence theory. The foundation theory focuses on keeping track of justifications for one's belief (Gärdenfors 1992b, Gärdenfors 1997). For example, the Truth Maintenance System (TMS) is based on the foundation theory. A TMS allows the system to decide on their actions based on available information and revise their beliefs when new information invalidates previous assumptions (Doyle 1979). The TMS aims to detect inconsistencies during the reasoning process and will revise its knowledge base if any inconsistency is detected. In addition, it is able to provide justifications for conclusions in the problem solving process. McAllester (1978 p. 1) notes that a TMS "is designed to be used by deductive systems to maintain the logical relations amongst the beliefs which those systems to maintain the logical relations amongst the beliefs which those systems manipulate."

On the other hand, the coherence theory highlights the logical structure of the things in a "world" which are semantics in a form of logically consistent structure. The AGM model proposed by Alchourrón, Gärdenfors and Makinson (1985) is based on the coherence theory of justification. This AGM model deals with modeling and analyzing the belief revision process based on epistemic states. The coherence theory highlights the logical structure of the things in a "world". That is, the things are in a form of logically consistent structure. It is an idea where all justification of beliefs relies on coherence within a belief system. For example, p is true if only if p is a member of coherent set. An idea of truth here is that it is a relation or coherence between propositions or beliefs. The coherence theory has the following two notable questions: "What kind of coherence relation is essential to justification?"; "What kind of belief system must a justified belief cohere with?"

Firstly, logical entailment relations are considered as kinds of coherence relations that are essential to justification. It implies that one belief logically entails another if the truth of the first one is assured the truth of the second one. For an instance, if p is a set of sentences, we say that p logically entails a sentence q if and only every model of p is also a model of q. Explanatory relations are also considered as kinds of coherence relations because these relations explain why some other beliefs are true. Let us assume the following set of beliefs:

P: $y - 3x = 0$

Q: $x^2 - y = 0$

R: $x + y = 12$

To believe or not to believe S: $\langle x, y\rangle = \langle 3, 9\rangle$, S must be justified in the following relations.

$(P \& Q \& R) \Rightarrow (S \text{ must be true})$

$(P \& R \& S) \Rightarrow (Q \text{ must be true})$

$(Q \& R \& S) \Rightarrow (P \text{ must be true})$

$(P \& Q \& S) \Rightarrow (R \text{ must be true})$

The above relation shows that adding S to (P & Q & R) increases the number of explanations. It indicates that the more a set can explain, the more coherent it is. Therefore, the more justified are the beliefs in that set. On contrast, deleting S reduces that number of explanations. Thus, based on explanatory relations, S is justified because it belongs to a coherent set.

Secondly, regarding the second question of coherent belief systems, most explanatorily set can be attained. Though Moser et al. (1998 p.84) note that "not just any coherent belief system will confer the kind of justification relevant to epistemic coherentism." In other words, truth is correspondence between a proposition and the world. That is, p is true if and only if p corresponds to the fact. Otherwise, there is no way to examine unconceptualized reality without access to reality except through beliefs. Thus it is not possible to know where there is existence between a belief and reality. As a result, this correspondence view makes truth epistemitically unreachable.

3.1 Belief Revision Operators

The AGM model provides three methods for updating the belief set *K*: expansion, revision and contraction. In this section, a belief set *K* is used as a model of belief state in the AGM model.

Let a belief set *K* be represented by a set of sentences in the logical language *L*. Sentences in the language *L* contains the standard sentential connectives: negation ($\neg$), conjunction ($\wedge$), disjunction ($\vee$), implication ($\Rightarrow$), and two sentential constants of truth (T) and falsity ($\perp$). In a consistent belief set *K*, any sentence *A*, there is only three possible epistemic attitudes exist: accepted, rejected and unknown.

A is accepted ($A \in K$)

A is rejected ($\neg A \in K$)

A is unknown ($A \notin K$ and $\neg A \notin K$)

Accepting *A* in a belief set *K* refers to accepting a proposition *A* in an epistemic state *K* in the sense that in *K* there is no doubt that *A* is true. It is worth pointing out that *A* is unknown means that both accepting *A* and $\neg A$ (negation *A*) are not allowed because it became inconsistent in a belief set *K*. In order to determine which sets of sentences make up belief sets, ideally, the set of accepted sentences should be logically consistent so that it is possible to draw the consequences of what is accepted or not.

3.1.1 Expansion

An expansion of a belief set can be thought of as a set operation that changes the value of a well-formed formula from unknown to true or unknown to false. When a new sentence *A* is added to a belief set *K* together with its logical consequences. The belief set that results from expanding *K* by a sentence *A* will be denoted K^+_A. For an expansion operator, the following postulates from (K^+1) to (K^+6) should be satisfied accordingly. The first postulate requires that the output of expansion operation applied to a belief set is also a belief set.

(K^+1) K^+_A is a belief set

The second postulate requires that a sentence *A* can be treated as a requirement that *A* is accepted as an expansion of the belief set *K*.

(K^+2) $A \in K^+_A$

The third postulate for the expansion is related to "informational economy." According to Gärdenfors (1988), beliefs should be retained as much as possible and unnecessary losses of information are to be avoided. The following postulate expresses an expanded belief set K^{+}_{A} that includes the original belief set *K*.

($K^{+}3$) $K \subseteq K^{+}_{A}$

The fourth postulate is expanding a belief set *K* with a formula that is already in *K*. Thus the expansion of *K* by *A* does not change *K*.

($K^{+}4$) If $A \in K$, then $K^{+}_{A} = K$

The fifth postulate, the expansion of *K* by the same the state of belief *A* on a belief set *K* that is a subset of a belief set *H*, preserves the set-inclusion relation between *K* and *H*. This means that any beliefs that are not included in K^{+}_{A} should not be included in H^{+}_{A}.

($K^{+}5$) If $K \subseteq H$, then $K^{+}_{A} \subseteq H^{+}_{A}$

The sixth postulate for expanded *K* is a smallest possible belief set. It does not include beliefs admitted by an operation that does not satisfy from ($K^{+}1$) to ($K^{+}5$).

(K+6) For all belief sets *K* and all sentences *A*, K^{+}_{A} is the smallest belief set that satisfies ($K^{+}1$) – ($K^{+}5$).

3.1.2 Revision

A revision of a belief set can be thought of as a set operation that changes a value of a well-formed formula from true to false or vice versa. When a new sentence *A* is added to a belief set *K*, it may contradict with the beliefs that are already in *K*. When this happens, it is necessary to revise a belief set in order to maintain consistency. Thus the result of revising *K* by a sentence *A* will be denoted K^{*}_{A}. There are six basic AGM revision postulates from (K*1) to (K*6).

The first postulate requires that the output of revision operation applied to a belief set is also a belief set.

(K*1) K^{*}_{A} is a belief set

The second postulate expresses that revision always succeeds. It guarantees that the epistemic input *A* is accepted in K^{+}_{A}.

(K*2) $A \in K^{+}_{A}$

The next postulate means that a revision never incorporates the epistemic input *A* that are not in the expansion of the belief set *K* by the same epistemic input *A*.

(K*3) $K^{+}_{A} \subseteq K^{*}_{A}$

The fourth postulate indicates that if the negation of a target epistemic input *A* is not in a belief set *K*, then the result of expanding the belief set *K* by that target epistemic input *A* is a subset of the result of revising the theory by the target epistemic input *A*.

(K*4) If $\neg A \notin K$, then $K^{+}_{A} \subseteq K^{*}_{A}$

The fifth postulate express that, given a belief set *K* is consistent, K^{*}_{A} is a consistent belief set unless $\neg A$ is logically necessary. This is the case when revision is applied to a consistent belief set that result in an inconsistent belief set.

(K*5) $K^{*}_{A} = K_{\perp}$ if and only if $\vdash \neg A$

The sixth postulate expresses that logically equivalent sentences should lead to identical changes.

(K*6) If $\vdash A \rightarrow B$, then $K^{*}_{A} = K^{*}_{B}$

The seventh postulate states that if K^{*}_{A} is a revision of *K* and K^{*}_{A} is to be changed by adding further sentences, such a change should be made by using expansion of K^{*}_{A} whenever possible. The minimal change of *K* to include both *A* and *B* ($K^{*}_{A \wedge B}$) should be the same as the expansion of K^{*}_{A} by *B*, as long as *A* does not contradict the beliefs in K^{*}_{B}.

(K*7) $K^{*}_{A \wedge B} \subseteq (K^{*}_{A})^{+}_{B}$

The final postulate states that as long as an epistemic input *A* is consistent in the revised belief set *K* by another epistemic input *B*, then the resulting belief set K^{*}_{A} by *B* is a subset of revising K using the conjunction $A \wedge B$.

(K*8) If $\neg B \notin K^{*}_{A}$, then $(K^{*}_{A})^{+}_{B} \subseteq K^{*}_{A \wedge B}$

3.1.3 Contraction

Finally contraction occurs when some sentences in the belief set are retracted without adding any new beliefs. In order that the resulting belief set be closed under logical consequences, some other sentences from the belief set may need to be given up (Gärdenfors 1990). Thus the result of contracting *K* with respect to *A* will be denoted K^{-}_{A}.

The first postulate requires that the out of contraction operation applied to a belief set is also a belief set.

(K⁻1) K^-_A is a belief set

The second postulate expresses that the resulting belief set K^-_A is a subset of revising *K*. That is, no new sentences are added to the belief set *K*.

(K⁻2) $K^-_A \subseteq K$

The third postulate states that if the target sentence *A* to be contracted is which is not included in the original belief set *K*, then the resulting belief set K^-_A is identical to the original theory.

(K⁻3) if $A \notin K$, then $K^-_A = K$

The fourth postulate states that a retracted belief cannot remain in the belief set *K*, unless it is a tautology.

(K⁻4) if not A, then $A \notin K$

The fifth postulate defines a notion of minimal change where all beliefs removed by the contraction of the epistemic input *A* can be recovered by following contracting and expanding with respect to the same input *A*.

(K⁻5) if $A \in K$, then $K \subseteq (K^-_A)^+_A$.

The sixth postulate expresses that logically equivalent sentences *A* and *B* should lead to identical contractions.

(K⁻6) if $\vdash A \Leftrightarrow B$, then $K^-_A = K^-_B$

The seventh postulate states that beliefs in both the belief sets contracted by the epistemic inputs *A* and *B* are also in the belief set that is contracted by their conjunction $A \wedge B$.

(K⁻7) $K^-_A \cap K^-_B \subseteq K^-_{A \wedge B}$

The last postulate expresses that when contracting *K* by the input *A* with respect to $A \wedge B$, either *A* or *B* or both *A* and *B* have to be rejected.

(K⁻8) if $A \notin K^-_{A \wedge B}$, then $K^-_{A \wedge B} \subseteq K^-_B$

One of the concerns of the underlying idea of revision and contraction methods is removing potentially useful information in the process of removing conflicting beliefs (McAllester 1978, Segal 1994). Segal (1994 p. 9) notes that "removing all beliefs in a candidate is the simplest way to ensure no conflicts occur, but it has the cost of removing potentially useful information." In fact, there is no formal way to decide what to remove or modify in a belief set. Gärdenfors (1990 p. 13) explains that "what is needed here is a (computationally well defined) method of determining the revision."

4. PROPOSED METHOD

A variety of approaches are introduced for building ontologies as a method or a methodology. The goal of these efforts is to present means to design, build, reuse and merge ontologies (Fensel 2004, Gómez-Pérez et al. 2004). Our proposed ontology revisioning method is based on an ontological reengineering method proposed by Gómez-Pérez et al (2004). This method refers to "the process of retrieving a conceptual model of implemented ontology and transforming this conceptual model to a more stable one." (Gómez-Pérez et al. 2004 p. 154) There are three phases in their approach: reverse engineering, restructuring and forward engineering.

The reverse engineering phase refers to deriving "the ontology conceptual model from its implementation code." (Gómez-Pérez et al. 2004 p. 154) This process may include the means of analyzing an existing ontology to identify its components, their relations to create a so called conceptual model that is a representation of the ontology at a higher level of abstraction. Thus this process can be performed for re-designing better maintainable ontologies. The second phase of restructuring, firstly evaluates the ontology to re-design the conceptual model through new concepts, then all changes are recorded accordingly such as description of the change, need for the change, and so on. In this phase, expanding new concepts are discussed in a way that is to create a new concept under the super-class of existing concepts. On the other hand, removal of existing concepts is unobserved. The forward engineering refers to implementing the ontology based on the new conceptual model. Such an example can be found in Protégé ontology editor where it is capable of exporting Flogic, Jess, OIL, XML, Prolog and others.

Figure 10-3 shows our proposed method for revisioning ontologies that is derived and extended from the ontological reengineering process of Gómez-Pérez et al (2004) with belief revision operators applied in the restructuring phase which is now called the revise phase. Thus our method includes three phases of reverse, revise and forward. The three belief revision operators of expansion, contraction and revision are resided in the phase of revise. Figure 10-3 presents our proposed method for revisioning ontologies.

The reverse phase is similar to the reverse phase of Gómez-Pérez et al (2004). It refers to deriving the ontology conceptual model from its implemented ontology. The implemented ontology may have been written with a specific ontology language such as OWL (Web Ontology Language). The conceptual model uses a conceptual hierarchy which shows parent-child relations to illustrate the conceptual relationship of different concepts.

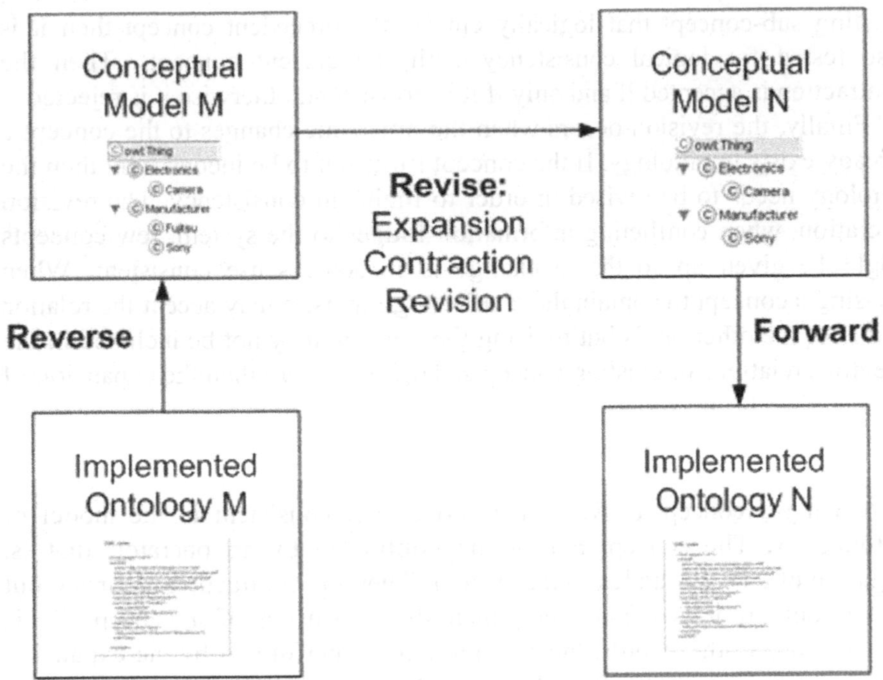

Figure 10-3. Proposed Ontology Revisioning Framework

The revise phase revises the initial conceptual model *M* to a different model *N*. The revise phase is implemented with either one or more revision operators of expansion, revision and contraction. Firstly, the expansion occurs when the system learns something new such as the epistemic attitude towards certain concept *c* is changed from unknown to known (accepted). Let expand (*m*, *n*) denotes the expansion of an ontology *M* by an ontology *N*, where m is the model of ontology *M*, and where *n* is the model of ontology *N*. When the new concept is to be expanded by an operator, the concept is tested for logical consistency with the current concepts. Then the expansion is accepted if and only if it is consistent with existing ones otherwise it is rejected.

Secondly, the contraction occurs when incorrect semantic classification is introduced to the system. It is also possible to obtain contradictory conclusions from the individual concept that is no longer established with a valid definition. Thus the inconsistency needs to be removed. Using the contraction operator, the system can give up the concept and its relation. It is worth nothing if the relation is considerably valuable to other concepts. It may be kept in the concept hierarchy if and only if the relation still remains consistent after the contraction. Let contract (*m*, *c*) denotes the contraction of an ontology *M* by a concept *c*, where *c* no longer exists in the model of ontology *M*. The concept is to be contracted by an operator, if there is any existing sub-concept that logically entails the precedent concept then it is also tested for logical consistency with the current concepts. Then the contraction is accepted if and only if it is consistent, otherwise it is rejected.

Finally, the revision occurs when the epistemic changes to the concept *c* already exists in ontology. If the concept turns out to be inconsistent then the ontology needs to be revised in order to maintain consistency. The revision operation, when conflicting information lodges to the system, few concepts might be given up so that a change is in some sense consistent. When revising a concept to contain the conflicting inputs, it may accept the relation that is of the other one's but revising the concept may not be included in the previous relations of existing concepts. Thus it is more than the expansion of a concept. The revision also needs to follow a minimal change principle. That is, giving up entire concepts to accept particular ones does not meet the minimality requirement. Let revise (n, *c*) denotes the revision of an ontology *N* revising a concept *c*, where *c* is no longer consistent in the model of ontology *N*. The concept *c* is to be contracted by an operator, that is, negation of *c* ($\neg c$) is added to the system. Then the contraction is carried out if and only if it is inconsistent, then the expansion of a concept $\neg c$ is performed. In other words, the revision can be performed by the expansion following by the contraction. It is worth nothing that not all of existing concepts are retained as a result of the revision. Further illustrations of each operation will be discussed with implementation in the next section.

The forward phase transforms the new ontology conceptual model to a new implemented ontology. It is a process of moving from high-level abstractions to the physical implementation of ontology. The implemented ontology can be written into a specific ontology language such as OWL using existing tools such as a Protégé ontology editor.

5. ILLUSTRATION OF IMPLEMENTATION

We will use the following scenario to illustrate the process of ontology revision; in particular, we will explain the revise phase which uses the expansion, contraction and revision operators. Assume a scenario of an online purchase of a digital camera and there is a buyer agent which is triggered by a user to buy a camera in an e-commerce environment. Based on the item specification that is provided, the buyer agent roams on the WWW to find the "right" product to buy. Assume that the buyer agent has access to an ontology which stored concept and information of a camera such as "all cameras are electronics products", "Sony is a manufacturer of electronic products", "Sony manufactures cameras", "Sony is a brand name" and "DSCV1 is a camera produced by Sony". We use concept hierarchy to illustrate the conceptual relationship, in which the relationships of different concepts are shown using parent-child relationship. Figure 10-4 shows part of the ontology of the buyer agent, which describes a brief concept of a camera that includes industry, manufacturer and brand. Notice that we are making the assumption that in this ontology the concept of camera does not include the concept of digital camera.

Now let us consider the request that triggers from the purchase order is to purchase a digital camera with 3 mega pixels. Using the current information stored in the ontology that the buyer agent has accessed, it only contains the conceptual model of the camera as "Sony is a manufacturer and Sony is a manufacturer of electronic products". The ontology does not show the relationship between digital camera and camera and the concept of resolution. Thus, we can envisage that the buyer agent will not be able to process the purchase order unless the buyer agent learns new concepts such as the concept and property of resolution, the relationship between camera and digital camera and so on. Let us assume that the buyer agent is able to learn that "a digital camera is a type of a computer that can be described using the concept resolution which is measured in mega pixels", then the ontology on the concept of camera needs to be updated to reflect this new learning.

In our implementation we develop the ontology using the Protégé ontology editor. The Jena 2 ontology API (Application Program Interface) provides a collection of toolkits to build a hierarchy of concepts as well as to manipulate ontology information in OWL (HPL 2002). To model the implemented ontology, a particular OWL model is created with in-memory storage model using the Jena ontology model. In our research the three revision operations are implemented using the Jena API.

We use the concept hierarchy to depict the conceptual relationship that shows the relationship of different concepts connected using a parent-child relationship. Figure 10-4 shows the concepts related to the camera such as "all cameras are electronics", "Sony is a manufacturer", which are stored in the ontology *M*.

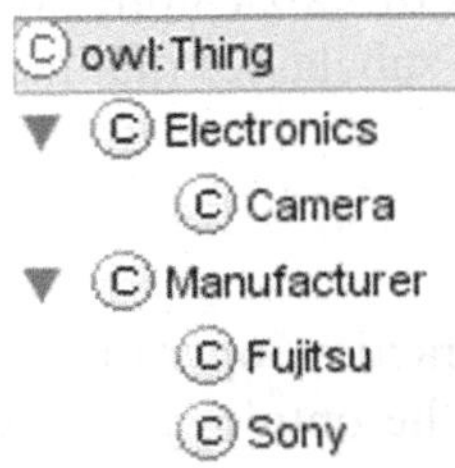

Figure 10-4. Ontology *M*

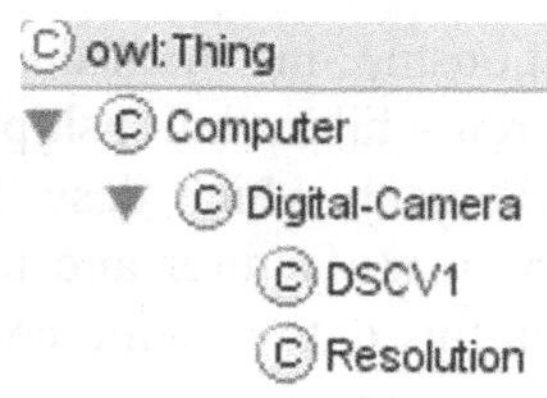

Figure 10-5. Ontology *N*

Figure 10-5 shows a portion of the ontology *N* which includes the concept of digital camera as a form of "Computer" as well as additional concept of "Resolution".

As discussed in the previous section, there are three phases in our proposed method, reverse, revise and forward. The reverse phase derives the conceptual model from an implemented model. The revise phase is used for ontology revision using the three operators of expansion, contraction and revision. Finally the forward phase deals with implementing the new ontology as a result of revised conceptual model. In this section we will focus on the revise phase that deals with expansion, contraction and revision operators.

5.1 Expansion

The expansion operation will be performed to allow the ontology to expand the concept of digital camera into the current ontology *M*. Let us assume that the new information is learnt from ontology *N* that explains the concept of "resolution" is a characteristic of the "digital camera", and it can be measured by number of pixels. In this case, a new concept known as "resolution" that is used to describe the "digital camera" is learnt. This new concept can be included in the ontology if and only if this new concept is consistent with the existing concepts. For example, if there is a same concept such as "Sony", and a relation "Sony is a manufacturer" already exists, it cannot be expanded. Figure 10-6 shows the result of the new conceptual model that represents a series of expansions which illustrate the expanded concept of "Computer" and its subclasses that include resolution.

5.2 Contraction

In this example, the contraction operation removes inconsistencies in order to retain consistency in the ontology. We will contract the concept of "Fujitsu" from the "Manufacturer" but the relation to the concept "Manufacturer" is remained. The reason is the minimum change principle, whenever it is possible all remaining concepts in a contracted concept hierarchy must have exactly the same concept hierarchy as it did before the contraction was carried out. Figure 10-7 shows the result of the new conceptual model that represents the contraction which illustrates the removed concept of "Fujitsu".

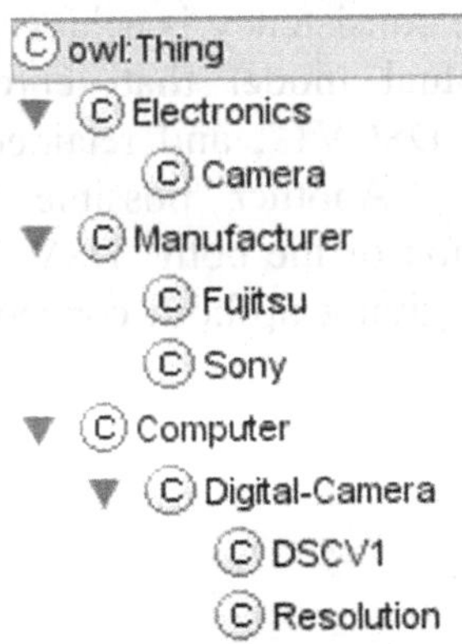

Figure 10-6. Result of expansion for ontology *M*

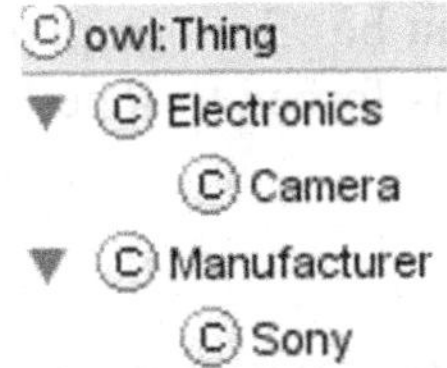

Figure 10-7. Result of contraction for ontology *M*

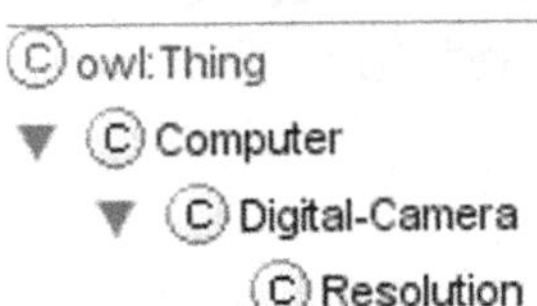

Figure 10-8. Result of revision of ontology *N*

Another example of the contraction may include a logical consequence of the concept. It refers to retracting a concept *A* from ontology *M* with closed logical consequences. If the concept gives an explanation about other concepts, it is necessary to give up other concepts as well. For example, when we contract the concept "Manufacturer", it is included in ontology *M* just because it is a logical consequence of "Sony" and "Fujitsu" which are both in ontology *M* (See Figure 10-4). Then either of "Sony" or "Fujitsu" or both must be removed with the minimum change principle.

5.3 Revision

The next type of ontology change is when new concept is introduced it may contradict with the concepts that are already in ontology *N*. For example, "DSCV1" turns out to be false. When this happens, the revision operator is applied to ensure consistency is achieved. Figure 10-8 shows the result of the new conceptual model that represents the revision that contracted the concept of "DSCV1", and retained the concepts "Digital-Camera" and "Resolution". Another possible implementation of this example is to have disjunction of the both "DSV1" is no longer valid, and "DSV1" is still valid. Then giving up both concepts to keep consistencies, but in this way it does not meet the minimum change principle. That is, it gives up too much information.

5.4 Other Issues

A default value needs to be incorporated to specify a default choice for the value of some concepts. This method is particularly useful if by using some other values it will lead to inconsistency. For example, a default value of the concept "Resolution" can be "3 mega pixels" unless it is specified. In this way, the default semantic is forced to inherit the default value otherwise the asserted value is used.

```
...
<SHIPMENT>30</SHIPMENT>
<SALESDATE>01/01/2005</SALESDATE>
<IF> <SHIPMENT> <LE>30 <THEN>
// accept returned item
</IF>
...
```

Figure 10-9.

A default rule can also be used as a way that specifies a default choice when contraction or revision occurs. A possible consideration can be found on the Semantic Web such as logic and rules that often limits knowledge. For example, we can include a return policy such as: "a return is allowed if it is within 30 days of a receipt of the shipment and the item is in its original condition". Even though vocabularies used in the return policy can be clearly described in the ontology, certain rules offer apparent semantic identification. For example in Figure 10-9, <SHIPMENT> and <SALESDATE> are used as variables, and <IF> is a rule statement than enforce a comparison operator <LE>, less than equal to, to evaluate one of terms in the return policy. If and only if all terms are satisfied, then possible revision operators may be performed to revise ontology.

Another issue is related to epistemic entrenchment, certain concepts are more important and valuable than others (Gärdenfors 1988). For example, the knowledge about resolution might be more important than other features during buying and selling of a digital camera in an online environment. Nevertheless when the owner of shop identifies a supplier, knowledge about the manufacture or a company name is much more important than the resolution. Thus reflecting this difference of entrenchment is useful. Secondly, when ontology *M* is revised or contracted, the concepts in *M* that are given up are those having the lowest degrees of epistemic entrenchment. This concept of epistemic entrenchment may provide a mechanism to select a unique contraction and revision operation. If the knowledge about manufacturer needs to be revised, removing the concept of "Sony" might be considered rather than "Fujitsu". Even though both belong to the concepts of "Manufacturer" (See Figure 10-4), in terms of classification both have the same parent's concept. In an aspect of the epistemic entrenchment, it says that "Sony" has greater epistemic entrenchment due to more comprehensive association with other concepts such as its relationship with "DSCV1" which is a product of Sony.

The above examples illustrate the application of belief revision of AGM model to revise ontologies. From the implementation perspective, in the simplest level, if the concept hierarchy matches, it concludes that both ontologies match. In this case, there is no need to revise ontologies. Otherwise learning is said to occur and the system needs to use the information learnt to extend, remove and revise what is currently stored in its ontology.

6. CONCLUSION

Ontology provides a constructive way to structure and define the meaning of metadata of the Web resources. Even though ontology provides a useful way to construct information semantically, there is still an issue of adjusting concepts and relations in ontologies. Few approaches have been considered in terms of dealing with difficulties in versioning ontologies, maintaining series of ontologies and managing changes in ontologies. But these approaches have not been considered from the ontology revisioning perspectives. However, it is necessary to revise ontologies to reflect changes as a result of changes in conceptualization of domain interests. This revision approach should also maintain consistency in ontologies. In other words, there is a need to ensure that changes in ontologies should not contract with existing concepts and relations in ontologies. To ensure that the revised ontology is consistent, new information is reproduced to its current ontology using operators such as expansion, contraction and revision to achieve this purpose. We attempted that ontology revision is in demand and therefore using the belief revision theory to meet the need of maintaining consistency in ontologies is beneficial. Further investigation concerning handling of comparability issues in ontologies as a result of ontology revision will be conducted.

REFERENCES

Alchourrón, C., Gärdenfors, P. and Makinson, D. (1985) "On the Logic of Theory Change: Partial Meet Contraction and Revision Functions", *The Journal of Symbolic Logic*, 50(2), pp.510-530.

Berners-Lee, T., Hendler, J. and Lassila, O. (2001) "The Semantic Web", *Scientific American*, 284(5), pp.34-43.

Ding, Y. and Fensel, D. (2001) Ontology Library Systems: The key to successful Ontology Re-use, in *Proceedings of International Semantic Web Working Symposium (SWWS) on Ontology and Ontology Maintenance*, 30 Jul. – 1 Aug., Stanford University, California, USA, pp.93-112.

Doyle, J. (1979) A Glimpse of Truth Maintenance, in *Proceedings of the Sixth International Joint Conference on Artificial Intelligence*, 20-23 Aug., Tokyo, pp.232-237.

Dragoni, A. and Giorgini, P. (2002) "Distributed Belief Revision", *Journal of Autonomous Agents and Multi-Agent Systems*, 6(2), pp.115-143.

Fensel, D. (2004) Ontologies: A Silver Bullet for Knowledge Management and Electronic Commerce, 2nd edn, Springer, Berlin, New York.

Gärdenfors, P. (1988) Knowledge in Flux: Modeling the Dynamics of Epistemic States, The MIT Press, London.

Gärdenfors, P. (1990) "The Dynamics of Belief Systems: Foundations vs. Coherence Theories", in *Revue Internationale de Philosophie*, (Eds, Brennan, G. and Walsh, C.), Cambridge University Press, Cambridge, pp.24-46.

Gärdenfors, P. (1992a) "Belief Revision: An Introduction", in *Belief Revision*, Cambridge University Press, pp.1-20.

Gärdenfors, P. (1992b) *Belief Revision*, Cambridge University Press.

Gärdenfors, P. (1997) *Mindscopes: Philosophy, Sciences, and the Mind*, University of Pittsburgh Press, Konstanz.

Gómez-Pérez, A. (1999) Applications of Ontologies and Problem-Solving Methods, in *Proceedings of Workshop at Thirteenth Biennial European Conference on Artificial Intelligence*, 1 - 4 Oct., Berlin, Germany.

Gómez-Pérez, A., Fernandez-López, M. and Corcho, O. (2004) *Ontological Engineering: with examples from the areas of Knowledge Management, e-Commerce and Semantic Web*, Springer, London, Berlin, Heidelberg, New York, Hong Kong, Milan, Paris, Tokyo.

Gruber, T. (1993) *A Translation Approach to Portable Ontology Specifications*, KSL 92-71, Knowledge Systems Laboratory, Computer Science Department, Stanford University, Stanford, California, 23 pages.

Hendler, J. (2001) "Agents and the Semantic Web", *The IEEE Intelligent Systems*, (Mar./Apr.), pp.30-37.

HPL (2002) "*Jena Semantic Web Toolkit*", Hewlett-Packard Company, <http://www.hpl.hp.com/semweb/jena.htm>, (Accessed: 19 Jul. 2002).

Jasper, R. and Uschold, M. (1999) A Framework for Understanding and Classifying Ontology Applications, in *Proceedings of the Sixteenth International Joint Conference on Artificial Intelligence Workshop on Ontology*, 31 Jul. - 6 Aug., City Conference Center, Stockholm, Sweden, pp.11-1-11-12.

Kang, S. and Lau, S. (2004) "Ontology Revision Using the Concept of Belief Revision", *Lecture Notes in Computer Science*, 3215/2004, pp.8-15.

Klein, M. and Fensel, D. (2001) Ontology Versioning on the Semantic Web, in *Proceedings of International Semantic Web Working Symposium*, 30 Jul. - 1 Aug., Stanford University, California, USA, pp.75-91.

McAllester, D. (1978) *A Three Valued Truth Maintenance System*, A.I. Memo 473, Massachusetts Institute of Technology AI Lab, Cambridge, MA., 31 pages.

Moser, P., Mulder, D. and Yrout, J. (1998) *The Theory of Knowledge: A Thematic Introduction*, Oxford University Press, New York.

Noy, N. and Klein, K. (2004) "Ontology Evolution: Not the Same as Schema Evolution", *Knowledge and Information Systems*, 6, pp.428-440.

Russell, S. and Norvig, P. (2003) *Artificial Intelligence: A Modern Approach*, 2nd edn, Prentice Hall.

Segal, R. (1994) "*Belief Revision*", Department of Computer Science and Engineering, FR-35. University of Washington, <http://citeseer.nj.nec.com/segal94belief.html>, (Accessed: 12 Feb. 2003).

Sowa, J. (1984) *Conceptual Structures: Information Processing in Mind and Machine*, Addision-Wesley Publishing Company, Reading, Massachusetts.

Stojanovic, L., Maedche, A., Motik, B. and Stojanovic, N. (2002) User-Driven Ontology Evolution Management, in *Proceedings of the 13th International Conference on Knowledge Engineering and Knowledge Management*, 1 - 4 Oct., Sigüenza, Spain, pp.285-300.

Stojanovic, L., Maedche, A., Stojanovic, N. and Studer, R. (2003) Ontology Evolution as Reconfiguration-Design Problem Solving, in *Proceedings of International Conference On Knowledge Capture*, 23 - 26 Oct., Sanibel Island, FL, USA, pp.162-171.

Stuckenschmidt, H. and Harmelen, F. (2005) *Information Sharing on the Semantic Web*, Springer.

Tohmé, F. and Sandholm, T. (1999) "Coalition Formation Processes with Belief Revision among Bounded-Rational Self-Interested Agents", *Journal of Logic Computation*, 9(6), pp.793-815.

W3C (2003) "*OWL Web Ontology Language Use Cases and Requirements*", World Wide Web Consortium, <http://www.w3.org/TR/webont-req/>, (Accessed: 27 Sep. 2003).

Williams, M.-A. and Rott, H. (2001) *Frontiers in Belief Revision*, Kluwer Academic Publishers, Dordrecht, Boston, London.

Zhang, D., Foo, N., Meyer, T. and Kwok, R. (2004) Negotiation as Mutual Belief Revision, in *Proceedings of the 19th National Conference on Artificial Intelligence*, 25-29 Jul., San Jose, California, pp.317-322.

Zúniga, G. (2001) Ontology: Its Transformation From Philosophy to Information Systems, in *Proceedings of the International Conference on Formal Ontology in Information Systems*, 17 - 19 Oct., Ogunquit, Maine, USA, pp.187-197.

ABOUT THE AUTHOR

Mr. Seung Hwan Kang is a PhD Candidate in the Information Systems Discipline, School of Economics and Information Systems at the University of Wollongong. His PhD research is in Ontology Revision and Belief Revision. He has published several papers in refereed international conferences. His research interest is in the areas of the Semantic Web, ontology, applications of web technology to knowledge management system.

Dr. Sim Kim Lau is a Senior Lecturer in the Information Systems Discipline, School of Economics and Information Systems at the University of Wollongong. She has published widely in refereed Information Systems journals and international conferences. Her research interest is in the area of application of artificial intelligence and optimization techniques to business problems, and more recently in the area of ontology.

Chapter 11

MODELING AND REASONING ABOUT CHANGES IN ONTOLOGY TIME SERIES

Tomi Kauppinen and Eero Hyvönen

University of Helsinki, Department of Computer Science and Helsinki University of Technology Media Technology and HIIT, P.O. Box 5500, Otaniementie 17, FIN-02015 TKK

Abstract: Ontologies evolve when the underlying domain world changes at different points of time. The result then is a series of ontologies whose concepts are related with each other not only within one ontology valid at a moment but through the time, too. This chapter presents a model for representing ontology time series. The focus is on modeling partial overlap between concepts evolving over long periods of time, and the domain of application is historical geospatial reasoning. A framework is presented for representing and reasoning about conceptual overlap of concepts that evolve over an ontology time series. The idea is to provide the ontology developer with an intuitive change ontology for expressing local ontological changes in a declarative way. An algorithm is presented for reasoning about overlapping concepts globally over long periods of time. This algorithm can be applied, e.g., in concept-based information retrieval for ranking search results according to their relevance.

ONTOLOGY CHANGE AND INFORMATION RETRIEVAL

Ontologies are a key technology underlying the Semantic Web (Fensel, 2004). They are used for defining vocabularies by which the metadata describing web contents is represented in a machine-interpretable way. Based on ontologies, intelligent content-based web services can be created and semantic interoperability of web systems enhanced.

An important area of semantic web applications is information retrieval. In ontology-based search, content annotations and queries are based on concepts rather than on keywords. This leads not only to better precision and recall, but ontologies can be used as a navigational aid to help the end-user in formulating the queries and results. For example, in the semantic portal MuseumFinland[1] (Hyvönen et al., 2004) a location partonomy[2] is used for annotating museum artifacts with metadata about the place of manufacture and usage. The same ontological resources are exposed to the end-user as a hierarchical view[3] of categories to be selected when searching semantically related artifacts. A problem in applications like this is that the content in the underlying history-related databases is annotated using historical location concepts that have evolved as time has gone by. For example, an artifact may have been manufactured in East Germany—a country that does not exist any more in the location ontology used today. If the today's ontology is used for formulating a query concerning modern Germany, which may be natural from the end-user's viewpoint, then finding artifacts made or used in East Germany becomes problematic. To solve the mapping problem between query and annotation concepts, a spatiotemporal model of the ontological change from East Germany to current united Germany is needed.

More generally, the problem of areal change is quite common in the area of geospatial ontologies and reasoning, but is not discussed much in the literature (Visser, 2004; Stuckenschmidt and Harmelen, 2004). We investigated, for example, how Finnish counties and cities have been merged together, split into parts, changed name, and annexed to and from the neighboring countries. It turned out (Väätainen, 2004) that after the year 1900 alone there have been nearly 900 changes in the borders and names of the counties and cities in Finland. The number of changes at similar level of granularity in Europe from the times of the Roman Empire until today would be extremely large. Think only how the map of Europe has changed during the last 100 years at the level of countries.

Outline of the Chapter

In this chapter we address the problem of ontological change from the information retrieval point of view. We investigate how to answer to a query based on concepts at a time t_q by using metadata annotated in terms of spatiotemporally related concepts from another point of time t_a. The time of the query concept is often after the metadata concept time, like in the query

"What modern British towns (t_q) are former Viking settlements (t_a)?",

but also the other way around, like in the query

"What Czechoslovakian cities (t_a) are within the current area of EU (t_q)?".

To deal with the problem, the concepts used at different times should somehow be mapped with each other.

In the following, we first formulate the information retrieval task addressed above. Then a model for representing a time series of ontologies is defined, a method for representing ontological changes in a partonomy time series is presented, and an algorithm for computing a partial overlap relation of concepts of different times is developed and illustrated with a realistic example.

The overlap relation can be used for retrieving conceptually related objects and for ordering them according to their relevance. In conclusion, contributions of the work are summarized, related work discussed, and directions for further research outlined.

REASONING OVER ONTOLOGY TIME SERIES

We focus on one aspect in the field of spatial reasoning (Visser, 2004; Stuckenschmidt and Harmelen, 2004): spatial overlap of regions. The other dimensions of spatial relevance, such as topology (of neighboring regions), directions (of related regions), and distances (between regions) are not considered here but could in principle be combined with partonomical relevance, as discussed in (Stuckenschmidt and Harmelen, 2004), chapter 8. Location partonomy will be used as the example domain, but the ideas presented could probably be extended to other domains dealing with other forms of conceptual overlap.

When dealing with historical data, the ontological vocabulary has to cover relevant location categories through different times of interest. There is a time series of location ontologies each of which is valid during a limited period of time. The next ontology in the series is needed whenever a set of simultaneous changes in the modeled domain occurs. This kind of evolution of ontology time series is due to changes in the underlying domain and should not be confused with ontology versioning (Klein and Fensel, 2001), database schema evolution, or ontology evolution (Noy and Klein, 2003) that deal with ontology refinements or other changes in the conceptualization (Klein, 2004; Stojanovic, 2004).

There has been an active philosophical discussion about how and whether things of the word endure or perdure as time goes by (Sider, 2001; Stell and West, 2004; West, 2003; Grenon and Smith, 2004). According to three-dimensionalism, things have only spatial parts, they endure, and are wholly present throughout the time interval of their existence. Four-dimensionalism challenges this view by asserting that things also have temporal parts in addition to their spatial parts. For example, the notion of a person has temporal parts such as childhood and death. According to this view, things can be seen as "space worms" that spread out in spacetime. In the SNAP/SPAN-approach (Grenon and Smith, 2004), both views are supported by a combination of a three-dimensional SNAP-ontology and a four-dimensional SPAN-ontology.

Our approach will use a sequence of three-dimensional models (actually, only two-dimensional areas are considered). Each member ontology in an ontology time series defines a snapshot, where the objects representing two-dimensional regions stay the same. Every ontology may be used quite rightly for both annotations and for querying. We will represent areal changes between regions in successive ontologies, but the identity of a region is changed after each change. We therefore do not have the four-dimensional notion of the same concept, say, "Finland" changing — or merely having different temporal parts — through its history as time goes by, although the change chains between areas in successive ontologies can be seen as a kind of space worms in spacetime.

As in (Holi and Hyvönen, 2004) the reasoning problem of this chapter is formulated as follows: Given is a set of regions whose extensions are geospatial areas that may overlap with each other. If a resource has been annotated using a concept A, and the user makes a query by using another concept Q, then our task is to determine how *relevant* is A with respect to Q.

It is argued that the notion of relevance can be expressed in a natural way as the *proportional overlap*:

$$p = |A \cap Q| / |A| \tag{11.1}$$

Here the notation $|X|$ denotes the extensional size of the set X. For example, if the annotation concept A denotes the area of the Nato countries in 1960, and the query concept Q denotes the area of EU represented as a geospatial area (e.g., a polygon of points or pixels), then p tells how much EU covers Nato (1960) and gives a measure of how likely it is that an object within the range of the Nato (1960) is also within the range of EU.

The practical result of this chapter will be a method and an algorithm for deriving the *global proportional overlap relation*

$$o : Q, A \rightarrow p, p \in [0, 1] \tag{11.2}$$

between any query concept Q and annotation concept A in an ontology time series. By using the relevance relation o, all overlapping concepts for a query concept Q can be found both in the past and in the future. Moreover, the values p can be applied as a measure of relevance to sort the search results and to visualize the mutual relevance of evolved concepts. For example, Figure 11-1 depicts the merger of East and West Germany that constitutes modern Germany. If we query with the area of East Germany, and the metadata is annotated with the newer concept of Germany, we get relevance $o(E.Germany, Germany) = 0.3$, because East and West Germany cover Germany exhaustively and exclusively in proportion 30%/70%. Since East and West Germany are disjoint we get $o(E.Germany, W.Germany) = 0$, and so on. This kind of reasoning based on one *local* change is straightforward, but when the change chains become longer and are intermingled, determining *global* overlaps becomes a challenge.

An obvious approach to determine o would be to map the concepts to physical areas in the real world represented as polygons (Visser, 2004; Stuckenschmidt and Harmelen, 2004). In this way, overlaps between concepts can be determined by geometrical intersection algorithms as customary in Geographical Information Systems (GIS). A problem of this approach is, however, that the physical areas corresponding to the concepts have to be known exactly, which is not always the case when dealing with historical areas. For example, in our case study for modeling counties and cities in Finland, such information is not available. We therefore decided to take another avenue, where the idea is to model the changes, that were known and easier to represent, and then compute the global overlap relation based on local proportional overlaps related to individual changes. In this way one can determine not only the overlap table but also explicate the series of changes and ontology versions that evolves through time in a concise, semantically interpretable ontology. This representation can be used in other reasoning and visualization tasks, too, like for selecting query concepts from an ontology valid at a particular historical time.

A MODEL OF ONTOLOGY TIME SERIES

This section presents a model of ontology time series. The model will be used as the basis for deriving the global proportional overlap relation between concepts.

Ontology Time Series

A *temporal ontology* $O =< R, T >$ is a set of ontology resources R that persist over a time span interval T. An ontology resource $r \in R$ is a tuple $< name, T_r, P >$ where *name* is the name, $T_r \supset T$ is the time span, and P is the set of additional *properties* of the resource. An ontology resource $r \in R$ represents, e.g., a two dimensional geospatial region and its characteristics in the world. We will consider semantic web ontologies represented in terms of RDF triples (Brickley and Guha, 2004), where a resource is characterized by an identity (URI) and related property triples of form $< uri, property, value >$. Intuitively, each ontology resource can be identified by a URI associated with a name, an interval T_r representing the time span during which the resource persists, and other properties. All resources persist over the whole time span of the ontologies in which they belong.

At certain *change points* t_i of time, one or more resources r become obsolete or new resources emerge due to a change in the underlying domain conceptualized by the ontology. For example, East and West Germany were reunited into Germany in 1991. This means that the old notions of East and West Germany became obsolete after 1991, and the new concept of Germany was introduced as depicted in Figure 11-1. New concepts are typically related to old ones in various ways. Here, for example, the geospatial area of Germany is the union of that of the two disjoint merged countries.

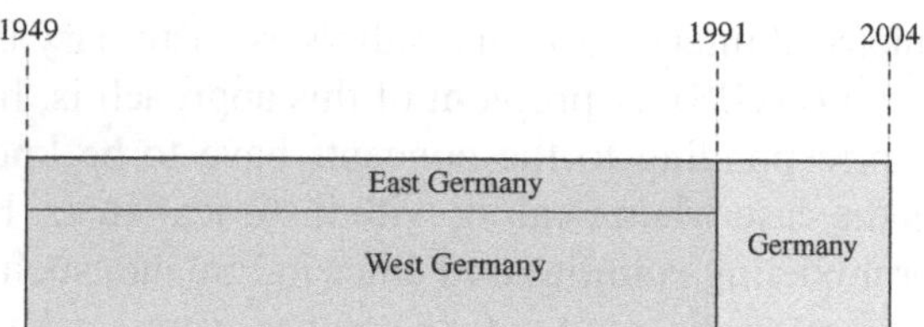

Figure 11-1. Individuals *West Germany*, *East Germany* and *Germany* of an ontology. X-axis depicts time and y-axis the relative areas of the countries

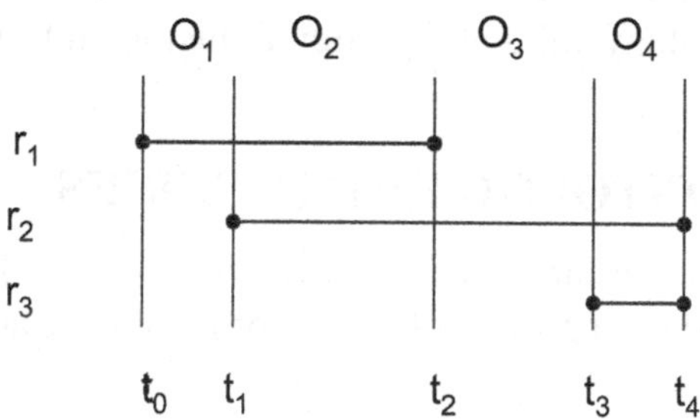

Figure 11-2. An ontology time series of four ontologies O_i and three resources r_j, whose time span is depicted by the horizontal lines over the five successive change points of time t_k

An *ontology time series* is a tuple $< O, S >$, where $O =< R, T >$ is a temporal ontology and $S = [t_0, ..., t_n]$ is a sequence of change points $t_i < t_{i+1}$, $i = 0 \ldots n-1$, such that $T = [t_0, t_n]$. It is assumed that the time span limits of the ontology resources $r \in R$ define exhaustively and exclusively the set of change points, which means that an ontology time series with change points $t_i, i = 0 \ldots n$, define a series of n successive *period ontologies*. Figure 11-2 illustrates the idea: there are three ontology resources r_j whose end-points define five distinct change points t_k and four period ontologies O_i, such as the ontology

$O_1 =< \{r_1\}, [t_0, t_1] >$ and
$O_2 =< \{r_1, r_2\}, [t_1, t_2] >$.

In an ontology time series, each resource belongs to, and its persistence time spans over at least one period ontology. An individual ontology in the series corresponding to a period T can be constructed by collecting all ontology resources that span over T.

Modeling Spatial Relationships by Change Bridges

We introduce the notion of the *change bridge* for representing overlap changes in an ontology time series. A change bridge is associated with a change point and tells, what current concepts become obsolete (if any), what new concepts are created (if any), and how the new concepts overlap with older ones. A bridge is defined by the tuple

$$< t, OLD, NEW, covers, coveredBy >, \tag{11.3}$$

where t is a change point of time, OLD is the set of resources that become obsolete at t, and NEW is the set of new resources introduced at t. The function

$$covers : n, r \rightarrow p \in [0, 1] \tag{11.4}$$

tells how much each new resource $n \in NEW$ covers the other resources $r \in R \cup NEW$ in the ontology time series $O =< R, T >$ at the moment t. It is represented in terms of proportional overlap $p = covers(n, r) = |r \cap n|/|r|$. In the same vein, $coveredBy$ is a function

$$coveredBy : n, r \rightarrow p \in [0, 1] \tag{11.5}$$

that tells how much each new resource is covered by the other older ones. Its value is the proportional overlap $p = coveredBy(n, r) = |r \cap n|/|n|$. For brevity of descriptions, we make the assumption that new resources do not overlap with other resources unless otherwise stated.

For example, the areal merger involved in the reunion of the two Germanies (Figure 11-1) can be represented by the bridge below:

$$t = 1991 \tag{11.6}$$

$$OLD = \{E.Germ., W.Germ.\} \tag{11.7}$$

$$NEW = \{Germ.\} \tag{11.8}$$

$$covers = \{< Germ., E.Germ. >= 1, < Germ., W.Germ. >= 1\} \tag{11.9}$$

$$coveredBy = \{< Germ., E.Germ. >= 0.3, < Germ., W.Germ. >= 0.7\} \tag{11.10}$$

The $covers$-values tell how much the new concept Germany covers the old resources, and the $coveredBy$-values tell how much the old concepts East and West Germany cover the new one. It follows from the absence of other $covers$ and $coveredBy$ values that East and West Germany exhaustively and exclusively cover the area of Germany. Since East and West Germany are in the list OLD their persistence is terminated at t, and since Germany is in the list NEW, a new resource whose persistence starts at t is added into the ontology. Notice that resources are never removed from the ontology, only their time span is updated.

Generating a Time Series by Bridges

A set of bridges at a moment t can be used to introduce a new period ontology in the following way.

1. For each resource in OLD, the upper limit of the time interval is opened and set to t.
2. For each resource in NEW, the time interval $[t, +\infty)$ is set and the resource is added into the ontology of the time series.
3. A new change point t is added into the time series ontology.

An initial time series ontology can be created by a set of simple bridges that introduce new concepts and their partonomy. After this, bridges for renaming, merging, and splitting areas can be used. After each change point t, a new period ontology is implicitly defined as the set of resources that persist after t.

During this evolutionary process, the global overlap relation between concepts could in principle be automatically constructed as a table in the following way. The rows i and columns j represent the resources in the order $X_0, X_1, \ldots, X_n$ in which these have been introduced. When a new n:th resource is introduced, the cells $[i, n]$, $i = 0 \ldots n-1$, of the n:th row can be filled based on the $cover$-function of the corresponding bridge. The cell $[n, n]$ has value 1. In the same vein, the cells $[n, j]$, $j = 0 \ldots n-1$, of n:th column can be filled with the values of the $coveredBy$-function. This means that cells $[i, j]$, $j \leq i$, will always contain the global mapping $coveredBy(X_i, X_j)$ and, in a symmetrical way, cells $[i, j]$, $i \leq j$, will contain the values $covers(X_i, X_j)$ for all resource pairs (X_i, X_j).

By using such a table, the problem of determining proportional overlap of a resource X_i with respect to any other resource X_j can be solved by a simple table lookup at position $[i, j]$ of the table. A major problem, however, remains: a set of bridges has to be defined which is easy to use from the human viewpoint and is yet sufficient for modeling the changes in the domain. Obviously, it is not usually feasible in practice to consider the global $covers$- and $coveredBy$-functions explicitly when creating bridges. Otherwise, for example, modeling a modern county border change in Italy would involve considering overlaps with areal concepts used during the times of the Roman Empire. What is needed is a mechanism that can infer such global overlaps over long periods of time based on local change descriptions that can be modeled easily by the humans. In the following we show how this can be accomplished.

A METHOD FOR DETERMINING GLOBAL COVERINGS

Change Bridges for Expressing Changed Situations

Our method, called ONTOFLUX, uses a set of change bridges to form mappings between concepts from different period ontologies. Each bridge type specifies a typical territorial change type. Our initial analysis of a database (Väätainen, 2004) suggests that at least the following types are needed in practice: *addition* (a new region is formed), *usedtobe* (the name of a region is changed), *removal* (a region ceases to exist), *merged* (several distinct regions are merged into a new region), and *split* (a region is divided exhaustively into several distinct regions). We consider here the *merged* and *split* bridges whose interplay causes problems from the modeling and reasoning points of view.

The *merged* bridge is defined by

$$< t, \{old_1, \ldots, old_n\}, \{new\}, covers, coveredBy > \quad (11.11)$$

where $\cap\{old_i\} = \emptyset$ and $new = \cup\{old_i\}$. The functions $covers(new, r)$ and $coveredBy(new, r)$ have a non-zero value for each older resource r that intersects with new.

The *split* bridge is defined symmetrically by

$$< t, \{old\}, \{new_1, \ldots, new_n\}, covers, coveredBy > \quad (11.12)$$

where $\cap\{new_i\} = \emptyset$ and $old = \cup\{new_i\}$. The functions $covers(new_i, r)$ and $coveredBy(new_i, r)$ have a non-zero value for each older resource r that intersects with new_i.

In our implementation, these bridges are represented as instances of the *change bridge classes* in RDF(S) (Brickley and Guha, 2004) and are created using the Protégé-2000-editor[4]. For example, an instance of the *merged* bridge is depicted in Figure 11-3. The property *before* refers to the concepts before the change time point *hasTime*, and property *after* refers to the merged new concept after the change. The values for *covers*- and *coveredBy*-functions are determined by considering the areas involved.

Bridge Chains

Local bridges relating concepts of successive period ontologies form chains that span over wider time intervals. For example, Figure 11-4 represents some geographical regions at the eastern border of Finland during 1906-1989. These regions have been split and merged over the years, and in 1944 a new country border between Finland and the Soviet Union was established, which makes the ontological modeling of the regions even more challenging.

Figure 11-5 depicts the changes in the same region during the 20th century as a set of chained bridges in more detail. In the first split on the left, a part was

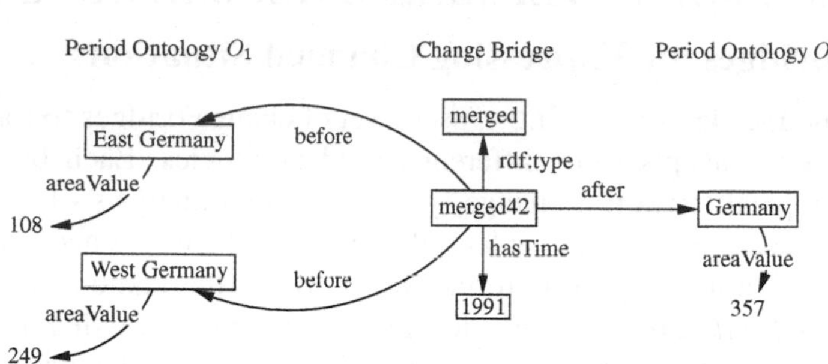

Figure 11-3. An RDF instance of the *merged*-bridge (Equation 11.11) from the change bridge ontology

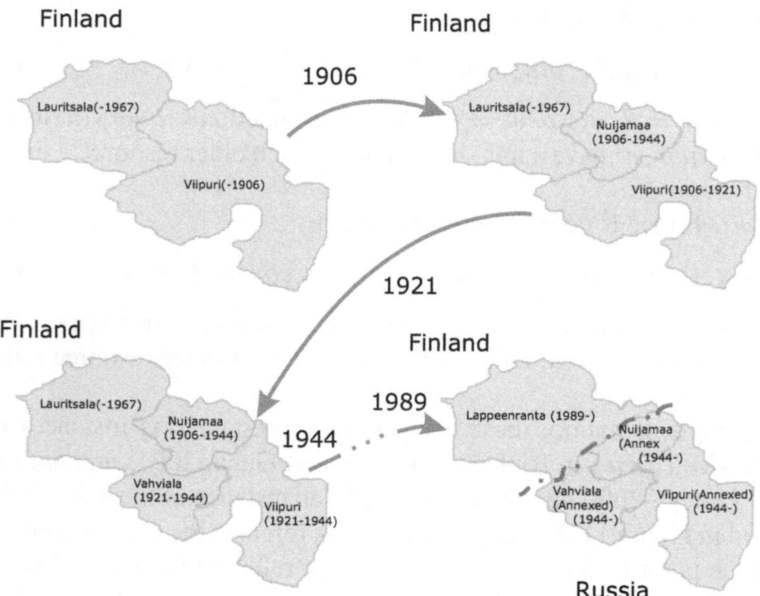

Figure 11-4. An example map that represents geographical regions of Lauritsala, Vahviala, Viipuri, Nuijamaa, and Lappeenranta in different periods of time. The small area inside Lauritsala (-1967) is Lappeenranta (-1967). The gray thicker dotted line represents the border between Finland and Russia (and the former Soviet Union)

separated from Viipuri in 1906 into a new county Nuijamaa that was later in 1944 divided into two halves: one for Finland and one (annexed) for the Soviet Union. The Finnish half was finally merged into Lappeenranta in 1989. The property $areaValue$ tells the geographical size of the attached region in square kilometers. Notice that the concepts Viipuri (-1906) (upper left corner) and Lappeenranta (1989-) (upper right corner) are related with each other through two different chains of bridges.

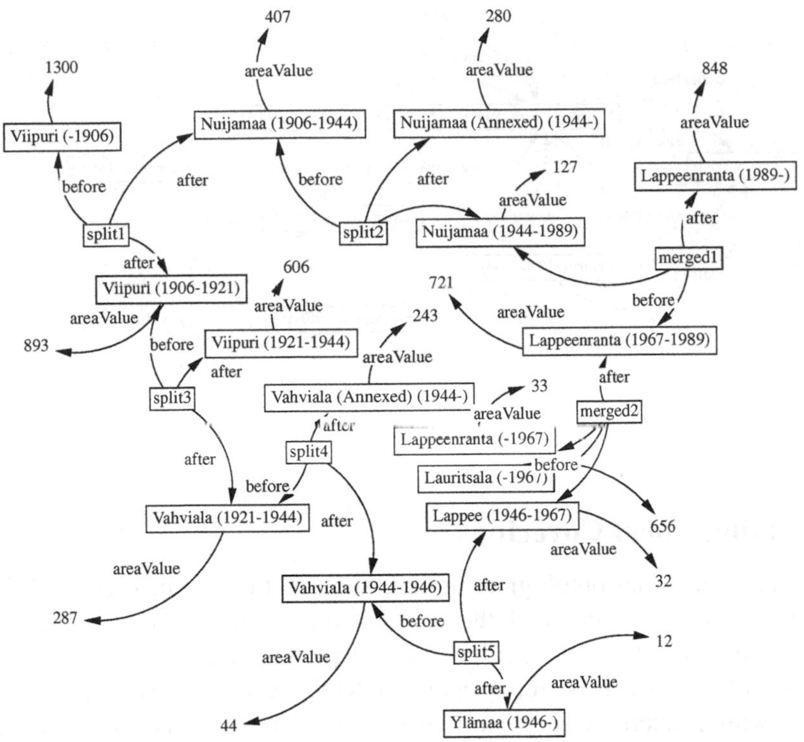

Figure 11-5. An example of chained change bridges. Each region is associated with a literal value for its area in square kilometers

Each local bridge can be defined easily but the global areal relations are not necessarily so obvious. For example, if a museum artifact x has been manufactured in the region of Viipuri (-1906), and the end-user is looking for material that has been manufactured within the area of modern Lappeenranta (1989-), how likely is it that the artifact x indeed is what the end-user is looking for? In the following we show, how the local bridges created at different instants of time can be used for deducing the global covering between arbitrary two concepts over a complete ontology time series.

The method has the following phases:

1. Local Bridges. Changes are modeled as instances of the bridge ontology.
2. Local Coverings. The bridges of the ontology time series, represented in RDF, are transformed into a form where the local covers- and coveredBy-functions are made explicit.
3. Global Coverings. Global overlaps are calculated by chaining local coverings and by considering different change paths between concepts.

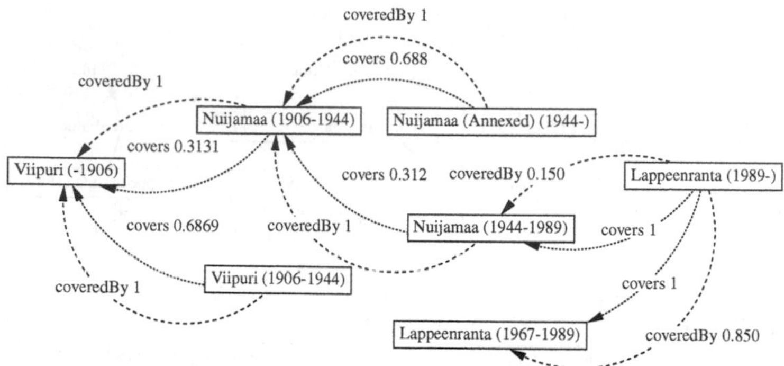

Figure 11-6. Local *covers*-mappings created from the upper part of the bridges of Figure 11-5. Dotted arcs *cover p* and *coveredBy p* tell quantitatively how much related concepts overlap, i.e., cover each other in terms of geographical area

Calculating Local Coverings

The meaning of an ontological bridge, such as the one in Figure 11-3, is essentially defined in terms of the *covers*- and *coveredBy*-mappings. We therefore first transform the bridges into such mappings. A local mapping $covers(a, b) = p$ can be represented in RDF by an instance of the class $Covers$ with property values $hasCoverValue = p$, $coverer = a$, and $coveree = b$; a mapping $coveredBy(a, b) = p$ is an instance of the class $CoveredBy$ with property values $hasCoverValue = p$, $coverer = b$, and $coveree = a$. Functions $covers$ and $coveredBy$ are inverse relations of each other.

For example, Figure 11-6 depicts the covering that can be generated from the upper part of the bridges of Figure 11-5 by using the semantic definitions of the *merged* and *split* bridges. Dotted arcs $covers$ p and $coveredBy$ p are a short-hand notation for corresponding instances of classes $Covers$ and $CoveredBy$ with overlap value p. The value p is calculated based on the areal sizes of the concepts given in Figure 11-5. For example, since the size of Nuijamaa (1906-1944) is 407 and the size of Viipuri (-1906) is 1300, Nuijamaa covers Viipuri by value $407/1300 = 0,3131$ and is coveredBy by Viipuri by value $407/407 = 1$.

The coverage graph, based on split and merged bridges, is always a directed acyclic graph (DAG), because these bridges always introduce new concepts in time by definition.

By traversing the $covers$-arcs, the coverage of a newer concept with respect to an older one (in terms of creation time) can be determined. By traversing $coveredBy$-arcs, the coverage of an older concept with respect to a newer one is determined. These coverage chains will be used as the basis for calculating global coverages.

Calculating Global Coverings

Calculating the coverings of the global overlap relation table can be done in two steps. First, the coverings of newer concepts with respect to older ones are calculated by traversing the local *covers* arcs and by accumulating coverings. Second, the covered-by relations from an older concept to a newer ones are computed in the same way by traversing *coveredBy*-arcs. Due to the similarity in the computation, we describe below only how to deal with the first case of traversing *covers* arcs.

The global cover value $covers(A, B)$ between concepts A and B can be determined by first enumerating all possible paths (chains) $CoveringChain_k$ of local coverings from A to B. The value for each chain is the product of the local *covers*-values of each edge:

$$CoveringChain(A, B)_i = \prod_{k=1}^{n} covers_k, i = 1 \ldots n, \tag{11.13}$$

where i is an index for the covering paths between A and B and n is the number of *covers*-edges on the i:th path between A and B. Multiplication is possible because at each node the outgoing *covers*-arc tells how much the node covers the next one.

It is possible that the covering is accumulated through different paths. Then the global covering between A and B is accumulated by the different covering chains between A and B. Depending on the bridges used on the path, four different cases arise. First, if there are only *split* bridges on the path, then the global accumulated covering is simply the sum of path coverings:

$$GlobalCovering(A, B) = \sum_{i=1}^{n} CoveringChain(A, B)_i, \tag{11.14}$$

The formula is based on the observation that when a split is made, the parts are mutually exclusive, i.e., the parts do not overlap. Therefore, all concepts on alternative *covers*-paths between two nodes are mutually exclusive and their effect on global covering is purely additive.

Second, if there are only *merged* bridges on the path, then the same formula 11.14 is applicable by analogous reasons.

Third, it is easy to see that the formula is also applicable for paths in which a *split* is followed later by a *merged* bridge: alternative coverings remain purely additive.

The fourth remaining case, where a *merged* is followed later by a *split* is a bit more complicated. Figure 11-7 illustrates the situation. Here East Germany (EG) and West Germany (WG) are merged into Germany. Let us assume a hypothetical future, where Germany is split again into two parts, North Germany

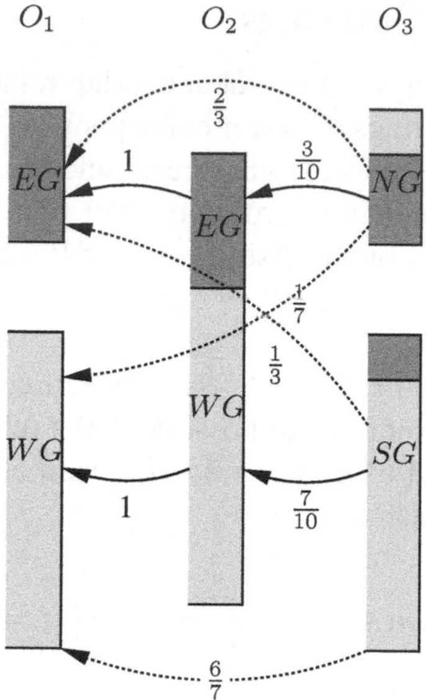

Figure 11-7. Resources EG, WG, G, NG and SG of an ontology time series

(NG) and South Germany (SG), whose sizes are the same as those of East and West Germany, respectively. If we multiply the local arcs using Formula 11.14, then we would get, e.g., the following overlap value:

$$covers(NG, EG) = 3/10 * 1 = 3/10$$

However, it is clear that this result is wrong: we cannot automatically say anything about the global coverings between South/North Germany and East/West Germany because there is no information telling us where the north-south boundary lays.

However, this information should have been provided directly by the user when (s)he created the $merged$ bridge, because its definition demands that the functions $covers$ and $coveredBy$ are given. This information is illustrated in the figure by darker and lighter grey that indicate the areas of East and West Germany, how they are merged into Germany, and how they are redistributed further between North and South Germany. For example, roughly two thirds of East Germany will be within North Germany. This information is given by the following global $covers$ functions:

$$covers(NG, EG) = 2/3, covers(NG, WG) = 1/7$$
$$covers(SG, EG) = 1/3, covers(SG, WG) = 6/7$$

Therefore, the formula 11.14 for accumulating the global covering of paths in situations where a $merged$ is followed later by a $split$ must be modified by the following additional condition: if there is a direct arc $covers(A_1, A_2)$ on a path (from A to B) given by a bridge (i.e., by the user), then any (indirect) path $A_1, \ldots, A_2$ should be omitted from the enumeration.

The same kind of situation arises, when a new areal concept A is introduced by an *addition* bridge, and other concepts intersect with A. This corresponds to a merger. If A or a part of A is later split, then the *covers* relation must be specified between the split parts and the original areas overlapping with A.

To sum up, the global overlap table can be created easily in most cases by enumerating covering paths and adding the effects. The problematic case is the *split* bridge, where local covering definitions are not always sufficient for determining global coverings. The user is obliged to specify some additional global covering values. This situation may occur if 1) the split area *old* intersects with an original region created by the *addition* bridge or 2) *old* is a part of a region created formerly by a *merged* bridge. Luckily, such regions can be found by inspecting the topology of the bridge DAG, and the potentially overlapping concepts can be pointed out to the bridge modeler. The user then has to consider the mappings *covers* and *coveredBy* only with respect to these problematic areal concepts.

AN APPLICATION CASE

We are applying ONTOFLUX to build a Finnish Temporal Region Ontology (Suomen Ajallinen PaikkaOntologia, SAPO) based on a real dataset from (Väätainen, 2004). The dataset defines different areas of Finland and the changes that have occurred from the beginning of the 20th century. The descriptions of the dataset are not fully machine-understandable, and the idea is to change them into an ontology time series. A Perl script was written that created an initial RDF(S) ontology of the dataset and this ontology is being edited further by hand as a Protégé-2000 project. The bridges of Figure 11-5 are one part of the ontology being constructed.

Currently SAPO consists of 667 different regions in time, that is, Finnish counties that have existed during a period from the beginning of the 20th century until today. We have created the change bridge knowledge base of Figure 11-5 to test our method in determining global coverings of regions. An initial analysis of the dataset suggests that there will be in total 887 different change bridges (Table 11-1) between the regions, excluding the *addition* bridges that introduce new concepts.

The method of determining global coverings using the RDF(S) ontology has been implemented in Java with the help of the Jena library[5]. Table 11-2 depicting the global overlap table corresponding to Figure 11-5 was computed using this software. The x- and y-axis list the concepts in the order of their creation. Some concepts are not shown in the table in order to save space. The

Table 11-1. It is expected initially that 887 change bridges are needed to define the changes of 667 different temporal regions of Finland from the beginning of the 20th century until 2004

change bridge	*count*
Merged	302
Split	421
Usedtobe	164
all bridges	887

Table 11-2. Table describing some of the global coverages between ontology concepts illustrated in Figures 11-5 and 11-6

covers(X,Y)	**Viipuri (-1906)**	**Nuijamaa (1906-1944)**	**Viipuri (1906-1921)**	**Vahviala (1921-1944)**	**Viipuri (1921-1944)**	**Lappeenranta (1967-1989)**	**Lappeenranta (1989-)**
Viipuri (-1906)	1	0.31	0.69	0.22	0.47	0.025	0.12
Nuijamaa (1906-1944)	1	1	0	0	0	0	0.31
Viipuri (1906-1921)	1	0	1	0.32	0.68	0.036	0.036
Vahviala (1921-1944)	1	0	1	1	0	0.11	0.11
Viipuri (1921-1944)	1	0	1	0	1	0	0
Lappeenranta (1967-1989)	0.044	0	0.044	0.044	0	1	1
Lappeenranta (1989-)	0.19	0.15	0.038	0.038	0	0.85	1

value in a cell $[X, Y]$ tells the global value $covers(X, Y)$ or, conversely, the global value $coveredBy(Y, X)$. For example, the current city of Lappeenranta (1989-) covers the area of historical Viipuri (-1906) by 0.12, i.e. 12%, and Lappeenranta (1989-) is covered by Viipuri (-1906) by 19%.

When querying a database with Lappeenranta (1989-), an object annotated with Viipuri (-1906) would match with this value with relevance value 12%—a result that many users could find a bit surprising due to the turbulent changes on the Finnish eastern border. A more obvious result in the table is that Lappeenranta (1989-) does not overlap with Viipuri (1921-144) at all (0%). In general, the table $covers(X, Y)$ tells, what annotations Y match the query X and the $covers(X, Y)$ values tell their order of relevance.

The complete global overlap table of the concepts in Figure 11-5 is visualized in Figure 11-8. Here the black color indicates a full 100% coverage between the temporal regions and the white color a 0% coverage, accordingly. Different shades of grey indicate the level of coverage: the darker the box, the higher is the coverage. From this illustration it is easy to see the mutual asym-

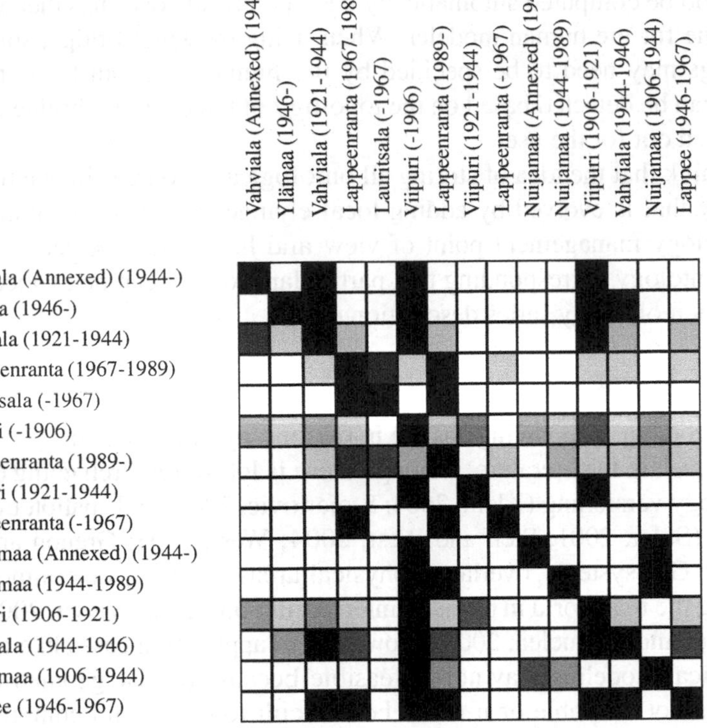

Figure 11-8. All the coverages visualized using colored boxes. The black color indicates a full 100% coverage between the temporal regions and the white colour a 0% coverage, accordingly. Different shades of grey indicate the level of coverage between regions: darker the box, the higher is the coverage between the regions

metric coverages between the regions, and that the overlapping relation in this case is fairly complicated.

DISCUSSION

This chapter formulated the problem of reasoning over a time series of evolving ontologies. The focus was on modeling partial overlap between concepts that change over long periods of time. The domain of application was information retrieval using spatiotemporal reasoning.

A method, ONTOFLUX, was presented for computing a consistent set of global covering relations between overlapping resources in an ontology time series. The method was based on a bridge ontology that was used for expressing local ontological changes in a declarative way. In most cases global coverings could be computed automatically based on local coverings that are easy to determine for the human modeler. When using the *split* bridge, some global coverings may need to be specified by the human user, but the concepts involved can be detected based on the topology of the covering bridge graph and be pointed out for the user.

We think that the idea of storing all ontological resources in one time series ontology that is evolved by adding local change bridges is economical from the ontology management point of view and helps the modeler's work. The period ontology corresponding to a particular moment can be explicated from the implicit ontology series description easily.

Related Work

The problem of modeling change in partonomy time series has not been discussed much in the literature, although there is lots of research going on related to ontology versioning (Klein, 2004; Stojanovic, 2004) and spatiotemporal ontologies (Sider, 2001; Stell and West, 2004; West, 2003; Grenon and Smith, 2004). In GIS systems, overlap of physical areas is usually determined by representing the real world in terms of intersecting polygons (Visser, 2004; Stuckenschmidt and Harmelen, 2004). However, in application cases like ours, such geometrical modeling may not be feasible because precise geometrical information is not available or it could be difficult to create and computationally difficult to use. Local change bridges could be expressed more easily, be used for deriving the global covering information needed in the application, and for presenting the ontologies at different times. An additional benefit of dealing with change mappings is that this notion is more general than that of areal two-dimensional overlap. This suggest that the same approach could perhaps also be used in other more complex application domains dealing with other forms of conceptual overlap, e.g., by using more than two dimensions.

Spatial reasoning is a research field of its own (Cohn et al., 1997). Approaches such as RCC-8 (Randell et al., 1992), however, typically deal with qualitative reasoning and provide relations like $PO(x, y)$, i.e., x partially overlaps y, without quantitative values. Our approach, in contrast, is quantitative. We are interested in the amount of overlap between x and y. These values are provided by the functions $covers(x, y)$ and $coveredBy(x, y)$.

Further Research

The work of modeling the Finnish SAPO ontology has just started and is continued based on the initial promising results presented in this chapter. We plan to further examine the problematic combinations of merge and split bridges, and how the human modeler can be supported in specifying the covering relations of the bridges as easily as possible.

We believe that there are many useful ways to use partonomical coverage data in, e.g., information retrieval and in visualizing partonomical ontologies and their changes. At the moment, an ontology browser for ontology time series is being implemented in order to visualize the changes through time, and for using the ontologies in actual annotation work.

ACKNOWLEDGMENTS

Discussions with Mirva Salminen, Jari Väätäinen, Arttu Valo, Eetu Mäkelä, Markus Holi, Miikka Junnila, and Eero Carlson are acknowledged. Our research was funded mainly by the National Technology Agency Tekes.

NOTES

1. http://museosuomi.cs.helsinki.fi
2. This partonomy is a part-of hierarchy of individuals of the classes Continent, Country, County, City, Village, Farm etc.
3. The idea of view-based search in general is discussed e.g. in (Hearst et al., 2002).
4. http://protege.stanford.edu
5. http://www.hpl.hp.com/news/2004/jan-mar/jena2.1.html

REFERENCES

Brickley, D. and Guha, R. V. (2004). RDF Vocabulary Description Language 1.0: RDF Schema W3C Recommendation 10 February 2004. Recommendation, World Wide Web Consortium.

Cohn, A., Bennett, B., Gooday, J., and Gotts, N. (1997). Representing and reasoning with qualitative spatial relations about regions. In Stock, O., editor, *Temporal and spatial reasoning*. Kluwer.

Fensel, D. (2004). *Ontologies: Silver bullet for knowledge management and electronic commerce (2nd Edition)*. Springer-Verlag.

Grenon, P. and Smith, B. (2004). SNAP and SPAN: Prolegomenon to geodynamic ontology. *Spatial Cognition and Computation*, (1):69–105.

Hearst, M., Elliott, A., English, J., Sinha, R., Swearingen, K., and Lee, K.-P. (2002). Finding the flow in web site search. *CACM*, 45(9):42–49.

Holi, M. and Hyvönen, E. (2004). A method for modeling uncertainty in semantic web taxonomies. In *Proceedings of WWW2004, Alternate Track Papers and Posters*, New York, USA.

Hyvönen, E., Junnila, M., Kettula, S., Mäkelä, E., Saarela, S., Salminen, M., Syreeni, A., Valo, A., and Viljanen, K. (2004). Finnish Museums on the Semantic Web. User's perspective on museumfinland. In *Selected Papers from an International Conference Museums and the Web 2004 (MW2004), Arlington, Virginia, USA*.

Klein, M. (2004). *Change Management for Distributed Ontologies*. PhD thesis, Vrije Universiteit Amsterdam.

Klein, M. and Fensel, D. (2001). Ontology versioning on the Semantic Web. In *Proceedings of the International Semantic Web Working Symposium (SWWS)*, pages 75–91, Stanford University, California, USA.

Noy, N. and Klein, M. (2003). Ontology evolution: Not the same as schema evolution. *Knowledge and Information Systems 5*.

Randell, D. A., Cui, Z., and Cohn, A. (1992). A spatial logic based on regions and connection. In Nebel, B., Rich, C., and Swartout, W., editors, *KR'92. Principles of Knowledge Representation and Reasoning: Proceedings of the Third International Conference*, pages 165–176. Morgan Kaufmann, San Mateo, California.

Sider, T. (2001). *Four-Dimensionalism. An Ontology of Persistence and Time*. Clarendon Press, Oxford.

Stell, J. G. and West, M. (2004). A 4-dimensionalist mereotopology. In Varzi, A. and Vieu, L., editors, *Formal Ontology in Information Systems*, pages 261–272. IOS Press.

Stojanovic, L. (2004). *Methods and Tools for Ontology Evolution*. PhD thesis, University of Karlsruhe, Germany.

Stuckenschmidt, H. and Harmelen, F. V. (2004). *Information Sharing on the Semantic Web*. Springer-Verlag, Berlin Heidelberg, New York.

Visser, U. (2004). *Intelligent information integration for the Semantic Web*. Springer-Verlag, Berlin Heidelberg, New York.

Väätainen, J. (2004). A database containing descriptions of changes of counties in Finland. The Geological Survey of Finland (GSF), Espoo, Finland.

West, M. (2003). Replaceable parts: A four dimensional analysis. In *COSIT-03 - Workshop on fundamental issues in spatial and geographic ontologies*, Ittingen, Switzerland.

Chapter 12

MACHINE LEARNING-BASED MAINTENANCE OF DOMAIN-SPECIFIC APPLICATION ONTOLOGIES

Alexandros G. Valarakos[1,2], George Vouros[2] and Constantine Spyropoulos[1]
[1]Software and Knowledge Engineering Laboratory Institute of Informatics and Telecommunications, National Centre for Scientific Research "Demokritos", 153 10 Ag. Paraskevi, Athens, Greece; [2]Department of Information and Telecommunication Systems Engineering, School of Sciences, University of the Aegean, 83200 Karlovassi, Samos, Greece

Abstract: Ontologies are an essential component in Information Systems since they enable knowledge re-use and sharing in a formal, homogeneous and unambiguous way. A domain ontology captures knowledge in a static way, as it is snapshot of knowledge from a particular point of view in a specific time-period. However, in open and dynamic settings, where knowledge changes and evolves, ontology maintenance methods are required to keep knowledge up-to-date. In this chapter we tackle the problem of ontology maintenance as an ontology population problem of the evolving ontologies proposing an incremental ontology population methodology that exploits machine learning techniques and is enforced with a bootstrapping technique in order to tackle large scale problems. The methodology is enriched with fine-tuning methods towards improving the quality and the number of the discovered instances. Finally, experimental results are shown, which prove the applicability and effectiveness of the proposed methodology.

Key words: ontology maintenance; ontology population; ontology enrichment; evolving ontologies; machine learning; compression-based clustering; bootstrapping ontology population

1. INTRODUCTION

Ontologies are engineering artifacts that formally model a specific view of reality using a specific vocabulary and a set of axioms that constrain the intended meaning of terms. Terms lexicalize ontology concepts, relations and instances. Ontologies provide a well-defined meaning of the concepts they model, advancing the potential for information to become machine, as well as human understandable and exploitable. Once the meanings of terms are organized in such a formal model, information can be searched and retrieved more effectively, shared between interested groups, maintained and re-used in knowledge-intensive tasks, and be exploited for inferring new knowledge. Technologies that have been implemented towards the realization of the semantic web aim to facilitate the development, maintenance and exploitation of ontologies. These constitute the *Semantic Web Technologies (SWTs)*. *SWTs* are catalytic to the development of knowledge-intensive methods and Information Systems *(IS)* that exploit huge amounts of distributed and continually evolving information. This results to a new generation of information systems, the *Semantic Web-enabled Information Systems (SWIS)*. The maturity and evaluation of the promising *SWTs* for the realization of *SWIS* passes through the accomplishment of various research projects. Through successful stories of these research projects, *SWIS* must show what they promise and must convince the *IS's* community that it worths to migrate from the current *IS* to *SWIS*.

For *SWIS* to be deployed successfully, we need to advance methods for the continuous maintenance of loosely controlled and dynamically evolving ontologies. Maintaining ontologies is an issue for many ontology engineering methodologies (Pinto and Martin, 2004; Kotis and Vouros, 2005; Tempich et al., 2005): It involves the evolution of the conceptualization through enrichment, as well as the population of the ontology concepts and relations. The aim of the research described in this chapter is to develop methods for the population of ontologies with the minimum involvement of domain experts, by exploiting web documents.

The problem of populating ontologies has made itself evident in the context of the CROSSMARC[1] research project. In the context of this project it has been developed an agent-based multilingual information extraction system that uses a domain-specific ontology to integrate information from different web-sites (Karkaletsis et al., 2004). This is a *SWIS* whose functionality is driven by ontologies concerning highly evolving domains, such as the "laptop descriptions" domain. For the system to perform properly and prove itself, the maintenance of ontologies' population must be a continuous task with highly qualitative results. Although, ontologies can be maintained manually, information overload and sparseness of relevant information sources make ontology population a tedious, time consuming and error-prone process, hence an expensive one.

[1] CROSSMARC was an IST project partially funded under the EC contract (IST-2000-25366) (Home page: http://www.iit.demokritos.gr/skel/crossmarc).

To cope with the ontology population problem in highly evolving and fine-grained domains, we propose an incremental ontology population methodology that exploits web-pages (such as those shown in Fig. 12-1 and 12-2), with the minimum intervention of a domain expert. The methodology is based on a combination of information extraction and machine learning techniques in order to extract new instances and discover relations between them. The involvement of the domain expert is limited to the correction of the lexicalizations of the extracted instances and to the validation of the discovered instances associations.

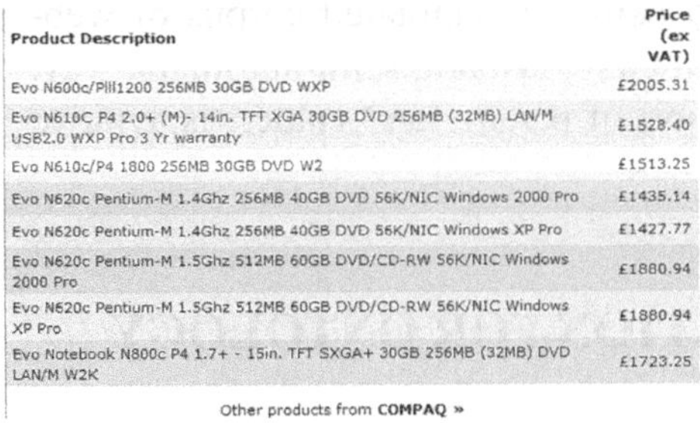

Product Description	Price (ex VAT)
Evo N600c/PIII1200 256MB 30GB DVD WXP	£2005.31
Evo N610C P4 2.0+ (M)- 14in. TFT XGA 30GB DVD 256MB (32MB) LAN/M USB2.0 WXP Pro 3 Yr warranty	£1528.40
Evo N610c/P4 1800 256MB 30GB DVD W2	£1513.25
Evo N620c Pentium-M 1.4Ghz 256MB 40GB DVD 56K/NIC Windows 2000 Pro	£1435.14
Evo N620c Pentium-M 1.4Ghz 256MB 40GB DVD 56K/NIC Windows XP Pro	£1427.77
Evo N620c Pentium-M 1.5Ghz 512MB 60GB DVD/CD-RW 56K/NIC Windows 2000 Pro	£1880.94
Evo N620c Pentium-M 1.5Ghz 512MB 60GB DVD/CD-RW 56K/NIC Windows XP Pro	£1880.94
Evo Notebook N800c P4 1.7+ - 15in. TFT SXGA+ 30GB 256MB (32MB) DVD LAN/M W2K	£1723.25

Other products from **COMPAQ** »

Figure 12-1. 1st web-page sample

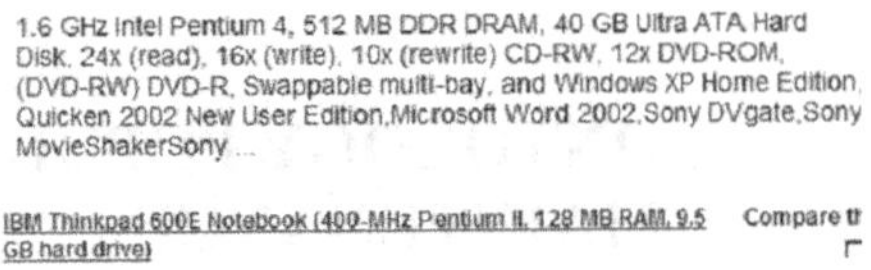

1.6 GHz Intel Pentium 4, 512 MB DDR DRAM, 40 GB Ultra ATA Hard Disk, 24x (read), 16x (write), 10x (rewrite) CD-RW, 12x DVD-ROM, (DVD-RW) DVD-R, Swappable multi-bay, and Windows XP Home Edition, Quicken 2002 New User Edition,Microsoft Word 2002,Sony DVgate,Sony MovieShakerSony ...

IBM Thinkpad 600E Notebook (400-MHz Pentium II, 128 MB RAM, 9.5 GB hard drive) Compare t

Figure 12-2. 2nd web-page sample

In particular, the methodology iterates through the following stages: In the first stage it exploits the instances that exist in the initial domain ontology (seed ontology) to annotate a domain specific corpus using a string matching technique. In this way, it automatically produces a training corpus for the information extraction system. Using this corpus the information extraction system is trained for the extraction of new instances and provides new candidate instances for each concept of the ontology. These candidate instances are grouped into lexicalizations of the same instance by a partition based clustering algorithm (named COCLU (Valarakos et al., 2004a)) that exploits intrinsic characteristics of the instances. Doing so, *"P4" and "Intel Pentium 4"* are grouped into the set of lexicalizations for the instance *"Pentium 4"*. Lexical variants of the same instance are related by a formal relation named *"has typographic variant"*. The proposed methodology pays special attention to this implicit relation between instances, as a domain ontology should not include duplicated information and must include information concerning the different lexicalizations of an instance. At the end of this stage, domain experts tide up the extracted instances, i.e. they erase non-valid extracted instances and remove redundant words from valid instances. Domain specific rules can further enrich the ontology by associating extracted instances by means of ontology relations. Finally, at the last stage, domain experts validate the populated ontology (i.e. the instances and their relations). These stages are repeated iteratively until no further improvement is made in the ontology.

The necessity of domain experts is high for the methodology to populate an ontology with meaningful instances. Ontologies should not contain misleading information e.g. wrong instances and wrong associations between instances. However, as already stated, one of the main objectives of the proposed methodology is the qualitative population of ontologies with the minimum human involvement. Towards this objective, we have investigated the automatic fine-tuning of the parameters involved so as to advance the precision, recall and accuracy of the proposed methodology. This tuning of parameters is performed using an annotated corpus of web-pages. The annotation is performed in an easy, fast and semi-automatic way. Over-fitting, which leads to poor selection of parameters' values, is avoided by the proper selection of web-pages.

2. ONTOLOGY POPULATION FOR ONTOLOGY MAINTENANCE

Ontology maintenance has gained research focus as the exploitation of ontologies and semantic web technologies shift to more complex, real-world, large scale applications. Maintaining an ontology with concept instances and thoroughly associating these instances using domain relations is a challenging and valuable task. Due to its particular interest and necessity, this task is distinctively named ontology population. In general, ontology maintenance (a sub-task of which is ontology population) is a time-consuming, error-prone and labor-intensive task when it is performed manually, especially for loosely controlled and highly evolving ontologies. Machine learning techniques and information extraction systems are the main components towards an automatic ontology population method.

Ontology population can be made in two ways according to the ontology component that drives the task: One can acquire instances of particular concepts or one can acquire pairs of concepts' instances that instantiate a particular relation. Although, the population task is fully accomplished if new instances and their corresponding associations have been asserted, population can focus on a particular concept or on a specific relation. In general, in case the population task is driven by relations between concepts, it is more difficult to be successfully accomplished. This is due to that this approach requires the exploitation of language resources and large sets of training examples. Furthermore, training examples are difficult to be selected, as relations are only implicit in natural language texts.

The ontology population task needs information-rich repositories to acquire the required knowledge. Current population approaches exploit repositories of textual documents. Large scale applications open new challenges to the ontology population task since information extraction systems must be trained to extract valid instances without imposing the necessity to produce the annotated (training) corpus manually. Automatic annotation methodologies (Valarakos et al., 2004b; Dingli et al., 2003; Etzioni et al., 2004; Brin, 1998) tackle this problem. These constitute bootstrapping methods to the machine learning-based information extraction system and are further presented in section 2.2. Recent information extraction systems have addressed the scalability problem by combining weak supervised learning methods (Dingli et al., 2003; Blum and Mitchell, 1998) and by employing unsupervised methods to bootstrap the learning process (Etzioni et al., 2004; Valarakos et al., 2004b; Ciravegnia et al., 2003; Brin, 1998).

Another point of major importance to the population task concerns the recognition of instances that already exist in the domain ontology. This is a challenging issue, since domain or syntactic knowledge should be integrated in the process to discriminate between new and already existing instances. This problem seems relatively easy when instances are lexicalized with only a string that usually stands for their name. However, as already shown above, a single instance may have different surface appearances. Things become more complicated when an instance is described by its distinguishing characteristics, as it is done in expressive logic-based ontology languages (e.g. OWL[2]). In this case distinctions can be made by exploiting concept attributes. This problem is a new challenge for the ontology-related research. The work described in this chapter deals with instances that are lexicalized in different ways. These lexicalizations are treated as typographic variants of an instance's name. For example, the instance *"Pentium II"* has typographic variants *"PII"*, *"P2"*, *"Pentium 2"* as well as *"Intel Pentium 2"*. Lexicalizations of the same entity that are typographic variants are related with the transitive and reflexive relations *"has typographic variant"*. This chapter deals with the automatic grouping of instances' lexicalizations that are typographic variants, relating the different surface appearances of a single entity. This allows the proper and consistent handling of domain instances during ontologies' population.

Although, the minimum human involvement is the aim of this work, domain experts must validate the inferred ontology population. The resulting populated ontology should contain validated data to be of worth and (re-) usable.

[2] Web Ontology Language (OWL): http://www.w3.org/2004/OWL/.

2.1 Ontology Population is more than Semantic Annotation

Towards the realization of the semantic web, the research community has developed ontology-driven indexing methods via the semantic annotation of information items. Focusing on textual information items, the task of semantic annotation (Dill et al., 2003; Buitelaar and Declerck, 2003) differs from that of ontology population as it starts with an ontology and aims to provide a semantic category to each content word. Therefore, semantic annotation classifies entities that are lexicalized by content words to ontology concepts. Advanced semantic annotation approaches (Dingli et al., 2003; Ciravegnia et al., 2003; Handschuh et al., 2002; Vargas-Vera et al., 2002) aim to extract distinct domain entities that form proper concept instances. These techniques can be considered one step before ontology population, as new instances are discovered but are not asserted in the ontology. Ontology population is a complementary task to the above tasks, as it exploits an ontology to semantically annotate documents and, based on these annotations, it discovers new instances that it further classifies and asserts in the ontology.

Instance-based annotation (Dill et al., 2003; Buitelaar, 2003) characterizes the traditional semantic annotation approaches that aim to annotate a content word (which denotes specific entities) with a concept (i.e. the semantic category in which these entities belong). The main problem that these approaches face is the sense disambiguation problem, as a content word can have more than one senses i.e. it may denote entities that may belong to more than one concepts. On the other hand, *concept-based annotation* (Dingli et al., 2003; Ciravegnia et al., 2003; Kiryakov et al., 2003; Handschuh et al., 2002; Vargas-Vera et al., 2002) approaches intend to locate and annotate all the instances (content words that lexicalize them) of a concept. These approaches usually use an information extraction system to extract instances, exploiting the context in which they occur along with the grammatical and syntactical information in that context. All these information extraction systems are machine learning-based; an exception to this is the work of Kiryakov et al. (2003) which is based on hand crafted rules.

Ontology population methods, to be usable in a real setting such as the semantic web, have to be automated, requiring the minimum human involvement, to be efficient, and of course, to advance their performance. The main barriers towards the minimization of human involvement, and thus automation, are: The bootstrapping of the information extraction system towards creating an annotated corpus for its training, the validation of the candidate instances, and the fine-tuning of machine-learning algorithms' parameters. The approach described in this paper proposes the use of a bootstrapping technique to create annotated corpora for the training of the information extraction system and the use of techniques for the fine-tuning of the machine learning-algorithms' parameters.

The first complete ontology population effort was accomplished by Craven et al. (2002). They stated the need for constructing and maintaining knowledge bases with information coming form the Web and they successfully claimed that knowledge bases will provide information in a machine-understandable way, supporting more effective information retrieval, inference, and a variety of tasks performed by intelligent knowledge-based agents. Towards this, in the context of the WEBKB[3] research project, they devised a complete ontology population approach. Given a domain ontology and a set of manually provided training examples, the WEBKB system learns to extract new concept instances and relation instances from the Web. Redundancy of information is exploited by training independent classifiers to recognize concept instances on different segments of a web-page, aiming to capture different contextual information. The combination of these classifiers bootstraps the information extraction system.

The most recent successful story of ontology population is the KnowItAll system (Etzioni et al., 2004). It is an ontology population system that incrementally extracts information from the web in an unsupervised way given only that the ontology concepts follow a particular representation formalism. The system works without human involvement and consists of two main modules the *Extractor* and the *Assessor*. The system starts by instantiating eight domain-independent generic extraction patterns, inspired from Hearst (1992) work, using the labels of the concepts and relations of the initial ontology, producing a set of extraction rules. Then the *Extractor* uses the keywords that are associated with each rule to query a web search engine and collect relative web-pages on which the extraction rules will be applied to produce candidate instances. The web-pages are pre-processed with a shallow syntactic analyzer. After that, the *Assessor* is responsible for the assessment of the candidate instances. It tests the plausibility of candidate instances using statistics computed from the web. The decision concerning the candidate instances is driven by a threshold value whose value range can affect the trade-off between precision and recall of the method. The best n candidate instances are selected, where n is a parameter set manually. The bootstrapping in this work is used to instantiate generic template rules and to train a classifier that is used by the *Assessor* to discriminate concept instances based on features.

[3] Project's home page: http://www-2.cs.cmu.edu/~webkb/.

Between the above research works, several other approaches have been proposed (Brewster et al., 2002; Harith et al., 2002; Valarakos et al., 2004a). Brewster et al. (2002) employees a machine learning-based iterative approach to acquire concepts (their lexicalization) that participate in a particular binary relation, i.e. the "is-a" relation. Although, this effort has been applied in the conceptual level of a domain ontology it can be also used to discover concept instances that participate in any concrete relation. However, further issues should be taken into account during an ontology population task: The works of Valarakos et al. (2004b) and Harith et al. (2003) study such issues towards an appropriate population of a domain ontology. The former work concerns with the recognition of instances' variants, while the later one pays special attention to the various referential and quality problems that arise during the integration of information from various sources in an ontology-based knowledge service.

2.2 Bootstrapping Ontology Population

A major barrier towards the large-scale deployment of ontology population methods is the bootstrapping of the machine learning-based information extraction task. Various *bootstrapping techniques* have been developed for automating the ontology population task. As already pointed, these techniques aim to bootstrap the learning module of the information extraction system by providing well-annotated training corpora. The key idea for this bootstrapping is the exploitation of *information redundancy*: This is based to the fact that an information unit (i.e. a content word) can appear in different contexts that can further train the recognition engine of the information extraction system. The idea of using the redundancy of information to bootstrap an information extraction learning is not new, having already proposed by others (Valarakos et al., 2003; Dingli et al., 2003; Craven et al., 2000; Riloff and Jones, 1999; Brin, 1998;) in various forms. The various bootstrapping techniques used in the context of the ontology population task are presented based on the selection restrictions they impose in order to initially create the training corpus. The presentation goes from the less biased; those that locate lexicalizations of instances without taking into account any contextual restrictions, to the more biased techniques; those that identify and select instances exploiting contextual restrictions and external background knowledge.

According to the less biased bootstrapping variation proposed by Valarakos et al. (2003), a context-independent string matching technique has been employed to annotate occurrences of instances (content words) on the corpus. Then an information extraction system learns to identify instances using the created annotated corpus and the new recognized instances are used to further annotate the corpus. The annotation-training-extraction loop continues until no new instances are extracted. This bootstrapping technique also belongs to the *mutual bootstrapping techniques* coined in Riloff and Jones (1999) in the context of information extraction. Brin (1998) employs a relations-driven population which forces the selection of lines from web-pages where instances of the concepts that participate in a target relation appear. In this way this approach creates the examples from which it will produce patterns to extract more instances. Although, the information extraction system uses a limited class of regular expressions to represent the learned patterns, it performs well.

A more biased bootstrapping technique is used by Dingli et al. (2003). They proposed a methodology that uses information integration techniques to annotate domain-specific information in an unsupervised way by employing hand-crafted strategies. Bootstrapping is accomplished by using patterns to extract information from easy-to-mine structured sources, such as databases and digital libraries, in order to provide seed annotation to more sophisticated information extraction modules. Hand-crafted strategies specify which of these sources should be used and what services should be employed in order to validate the extracted information. Although, this technique incorporates highly domain-dependent configurations, generic resources and services can emerge towards a fully automated ontology population task. Also, Etzioni et al. (2004) proposed an augmented set of extraction patterns based on the work of Hearst (1992). These patterns form extraction rules for matching instances in a corpus of web-pages. This corpus is automatically selected by exploiting rules to query a search engine. Moreover, they validate candidate instances using a component whose training is also bootstrapped by the produced candidate instances. The bootstrapping bias is restricted from the specific grammatical forms that are used in the creation of the extraction rules. Finally, the most biased bootstrapping technique is used by Craven et al. (2000). They combine different information extraction systems using different views of the manually provided annotations.

The various bootstrapping techniques exploit the redundancy of information partially, as they are restricted by the various selection restrictions they use. The adoption of the Valarakos et al. (2003) bootstrapping technique was mainly driven by our intention to take full advantage of the web's potential on information redundancy.

3. MACHINE LEARNING-BASED ONTOLOGY MAINTENANCE

As already pointed, our objectives to the problem of maintenance of evolving ontologies are to populate the ontologies with new instances and enrich them with domain relations as well as with the *"has typographic variant"* relation between instances' lexicalizations. Towards these objectives we employ an information extraction system that is based (a) on Hidden Markov Models (HMMs) to discover new instances, (b) on domain specific rules, and (c) on an unsupervised machine learning algorithm to associate instances of specific concepts with relations. The above constitute a full realization of the ontology population task.

Specifically, Fig. 12-3 shows the specific stages that the proposed method follows, until no further improvement is made to the population of a domain ontology:

1. **Ontology-based Annotation.** The seed domain ontology is exploited to semantically annotate a domain specific corpus. The annotation of the domain-specific corpus is made automatically using an unbiased context-independent technique: string matching. Doing so, the annotated corpus constitutes the training dataset for the training (bootstrapping) of the HMM-based information extraction system.
2. **Knowledge Discovery.** The supervised machine learning-based information extraction system is employed to discover more instances from the corpus. By exploiting information redundancy, it can discover new instances that appear in contexts where the instances of the training cases appear. The new extracted instances constitute the candidate instances.
3. **Knowledge Refinement.** This stage employs methods for associating instances discovered during the previous stage. This stage applies the COCLU compression-based clustering algorithm to the set of candidate instances to group them according to their lexical similarity. The members of the resulting groups are associated with the *"has typographic variant"* relation. Furthermore, domain specific rules are used to associate instances of specific concepts with domain specific relations.
4. **Validation.** This applies in two stages: After the application of COCLU and after the association of instances with domain specific relations. In the first case a domain expert validates the candidate instances and their grouping to sets of typographic variants. In the second case the domain expert validates the discovered associations between instances. During validation, the domain expert inspects the discovered instances in the actual context they appear.

At the end, the ontology has been enhanced with new domain knowledge, and it has been populated with new validated instances, enriched with the *"has typographic variant"* relation and with domain specific associations between instances.

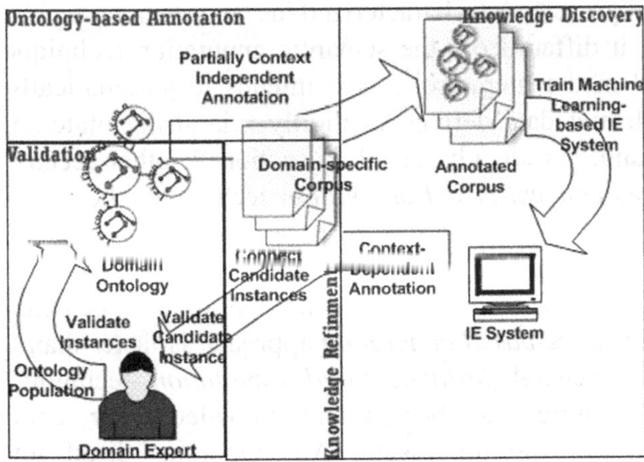

Figure 12-3. Incremental ontology maintenance methodology

3.1 Ontology-based Annotation

The ontology-based annotation stage exploits the instances in the domain ontology, to automatically annotate the corpus. The annotated corpus will be used by the information extraction system in the next stage. The instances are fed to a regular expression machine that finds all their occurrences in the corpus. Context-independent regular expression patterns are constructed using only the space class. For example, the pattern *"p\s+iii"* corresponds to the instance *"P III"*. Problems arise when some instances are substrings of other instances. This is the case for the lexicalization of the instance *"Pentium 3"*, which is a substring of the instance *"Intel Pentium 3"*. To deal with this, we bias the annotation method to select the maximum spanning annotated lexical expression for each instance. Moreover, this is supported by expanding the annotation for the grammatical forms that are specified through the following examples: *"windows 98, me, 2000 and XP"* and *"windows 98, me, 2000, XP"*. In case the annotation is not expanded, then a string matching would always find the first part (*"windows 98"*) of the two instances, missing the following parts and misleading the information extraction system. During the population process the strings between commas and *"and"* are glued together with the tokens of the first part. For example, concerning the phrase *"windows 98, me"*. Its first part *"windows"* is glued with *"me"* excluding the token *"98"*, to construct the instances. The instances identified are *"windows 98"*, *"windows me"*. This string matching expansion method supports the information extraction method to identify instances without being mislead in inappropriate contexts where commas, and *"and"* exist. In general, these forms are hard cases in semantic annotation and have not been studied systematically.

This technique can be characterized as an *instance-based annotation* technique and it differs from the semantic annotation techniques that have been proposed in the literature[13], as it intends to automatically annotate a document with metadata derived explicitly (via string matching) from the ontology at hand. As already stated in section 2, other techniques can be characterized as *concept-based annotation* techniques, because they intend to annotate all the potential instances of a concept that can be found in a corpus. These techniques usually are driven by various contextual information such as part of speech information, token types etc. Obviously, the proposed *instance-based annotation* approach is faster than the *concept-based* and the general *instance-based annotation* techniques, as it is shallower; it requires no background knowledge or computationally expensive linguistic pre-processing. An important disadvantage of the instance-based approach proposed is that it cannot discriminate between different roles that an instance can play, i.e. cases where an instance belongs to more than one concepts. However, when there are no instances that belong to more than one concepts, as it is the case in fine-grained, highly technical domains, our instance-based annotation is sufficient.

The proposed *instance-based annotation technique* is beneficial in the context of our overall approach in two ways. Firstly, it provides a starting point for the information extraction system by automatically annotating the corpus. Secondly, it supports identifying the contexts in which instances appear, providing a very effective way to bootstrap the information extraction system: The instances of the seed ontology are identified in the documents of the corpus and specify the contexts in which they appear. Then, the information extraction system is trained to discover new instances that appear in the same contexts. Therefore, instances provide examples to the information extraction system, which is trained to refine its model in order to recognize new cases. This kind of bootstrapping is performed in each method's iteration, enhancing the number of potential contexts that the information extraction system recognizes.

The absence of a human annotator speeds-up the training of the information extraction system and partially tackles a challenging issue in large scale information extraction tasks: the creation of a training dataset with a big number of examples. However, this technique cannot be generalized so as to be used in cases where there is not a domain specific corpus or in cases that a string may lexicalize more than one concept instances. Despite this fact, the annotation technique can be supported and be further advanced by means of disambiguation techniques. However, this is an issue of further investigation.

3.2 Knowledge Discovery

The knowledge discovery stage aims to locate new instances in the domain specific corpus. For this purpose, we selected to use ergodic first-order discrete Hidden Markov Models (HMMs) to train an information extraction system on the corpus derived from the previous stage. HMMs exploit tokens that intend to capture the contexts in which the instances of particular concepts occur. The information extraction system aims to recognize new instances that are not included in the ontology and appear in the contexts where the training instances appear.

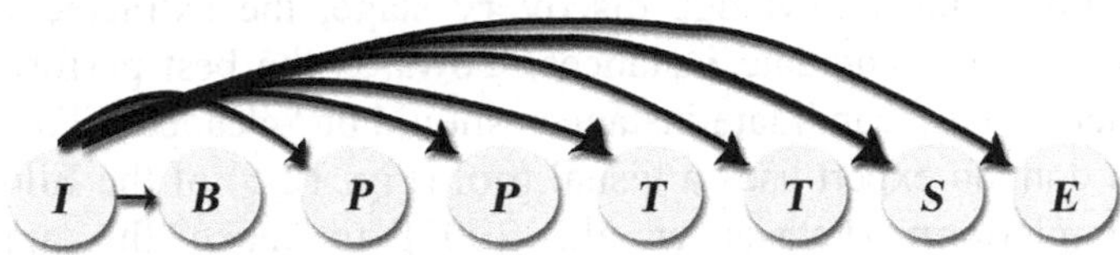

Figure 12-4. Sample of HMM's structure

A single HMM was trained for each concept, as it is proposed in (Freitag and McCallum, 1999) and (Seymore et al., 1999), and we apply it in entire documents. The structure of an HMM consists of six different type nodes which are associated with HMM's states through one-to-one mapping. The *start (I)* node type models the first token of a document, the *end (E)* node type models the last token and is always the end of file symbol, the *target (T)* node type models the tokens that represent the instance, the *prefix (P)* node type models the tokens that exist directly before the tokens that represent the instance, the *suffix (S)* node type models the tokens that exist directly after the tokens of the instance representation, and finally the *background (B)* node type models all the other tokens in the document. Except form the *start, end* and the *background* node types, the number of nodes of the other types is set by hand. For example, a particular HMM structure can comprise the sequence of nodes depicted in Fig. 12-4, and consist of two *prefix type* nodes, two *target type* nodes and *one suffix type* node. The arrows represent the transitions between the nodes. For simplicity and space reasons, Fig. 12-4 depicts only transititions from I node to all other nodes, whereas there are transitions between other nodes as well.

The transitive probabilities are estimated in a single pass over the training dataset by calculating ratios of counts (maximum likelihood estimation). At runtime, each HMM is applied to one document in the corpus, using the Viterbi procedure to identify matches.

As we can easily perceive, the configuration of an HMM can be different for different concepts. This configuration affects the performance of the information extraction system, resulting in extracting entirely or slightly erroneously instances. We define as entirely erroneous instances those that are not relative to the concept to which they are classified (e.g. *"office xp"* is not an instance of "*Processor*"). Similarly, we define as slightly erroneous instances those that include irrelevant words beyond the target instance (e.g. *"have Pentium III"*). Many trial-and-error attempts are needed towards the selection of an optimal or near optimal HMM structure to identify instances with accuracy. The manual selection of the optimal HMM structure is a tedious and time consuming process for small magnitude datasets and impractical for large ones. Section 5.4 describes experiments and provides results towards deciding the configuration of HMMs automatically.

At the end of the knowledge discovery stage, the extracted instances constitute the set of candidate instances. Towards the best performance of the subsequent stages, candidate instances should be "cleaned". Towards this objective, a domain expert uses a visual tool (Fig. 12-5) of the Ellogon text engineering platform (Petasis et al., 2005) to make the appropriate corrections on the extracted instances, i.e. to discard erroneous candidate instances and to delete redundant words from the lexicalizations of the candidate instances. Candidate instances are highlighted in the document and they are annotated with the concept they belong to. This tool helps the validation of the candidate instances, since validation is a hard task even for a domain expert, especially in cases where instances are not introduced in the context they have been found. For example, consider the difficulty of validating the instances of the *"Model"* concept, which are most of the times meaningless alphanumeric-codes (e.g. nx9120).

This extra responsibility of the domain expert to tide up instances is another point that slows down the maintenance approach. To cope with this, as section 5 describes, we managed to control the quantity and the quality of the extracted instances through the selection of HMM's parameter values (i.e. of the HMM configuration) semi-automatically.

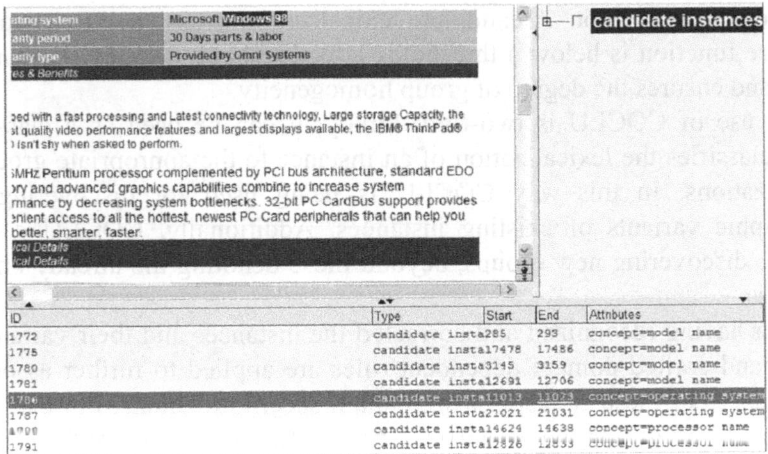

Figure 12-5. Screenshot of the tool for validating candidate instances

3.3 Knowledge Refinement

At the knowledge refinement stage we employ methods for discovering relations that hold between the extracted instances. Firstly, an unsupervised machine learning-based algorithm that groups instances depending on the similarity of their lexicalizations was used. For example, the processor name *"Pentium 2"* can be written as *"Pentium II"*, *"p2"*, *"P II"* or *"Intel Pentium 2"*. As already pointed, doing so, the ontology is enriched by relating instances via the *"has typographic variant"* relation. As already said, the identification of the lexical variants of a single instance is performed by the COCLU compression-based clustering algorithm. The algorithm exploits instance's intrinsic characteristics (i.e. characters) and is based on the assumption that different lexicalizations of an instance use a common set of "core" characters. Therefore, lexicalizations that are "close" to this set are potential alternative appearances of the same instance, while those that are "far" from this set are potentially related to a different instance.

COCLU is a partition-based clustering algorithm that groups the data (i.e. the set of lexicalizations) into several subsets and searches the space of possible subsets so as to classify a new lexicalization, using a greedy heuristic. Each cluster (herein named group) is represented by a model which is realized by a Huffman tree. This tree is constructed incrementally as the algorithm dynamically generates and updates the members of the group, (members are the lexicalizations of a single instance) by processing them one by one. The algorithm employs a score function that measures the compactness and homogeneity of a group. This score function is defined as the difference of the summed length of the coded strings that are members of the group and the length of the same group updated with the candidate instance's lexicalization. A candidate lexicalization is assigned to a group if the score function is below a threshold. This threshold is set by the domain expert and ensures the degree of group homogeneity.

The use of COCLU is two-fold. Firstly, it can be used as a classifier which classifies the lexicalization of an instance to the appropriate group of lexicalizations. In this way COCLU is being used for discovering the typographic variants of existing instances. Additionally, COCLU can be used for discovering new groups, beyond those denoting the already known instances.

After having recognized and corrected the instances and their variants, a set of hand crafted domain dependent rules are applied to further associate the instances of these concepts with domain specific relations. For example, such a case holds for the instances of the *"Manufacturer"* and *"Model"* concepts of the CROSSMARC laptop ontology. This set of rules exploits the instances of those two concepts and the order that they appear in the documents. The objective is to relate instances, by instantiating the relation *"disposes"* that exists between the two concepts in the ontology. Rules specify that sequentially encountered pairs of *"Manufacturer"* and *"Model"* concept instances should be linked together. Pairs are created by associating a recognized instance of a concept with all the subsequent recognized instances of the other concept. A grouping starts with an instance of a concept and ends when another instance of the same concept is encountered. Examples of such cases are shown in Fig. 12-6.

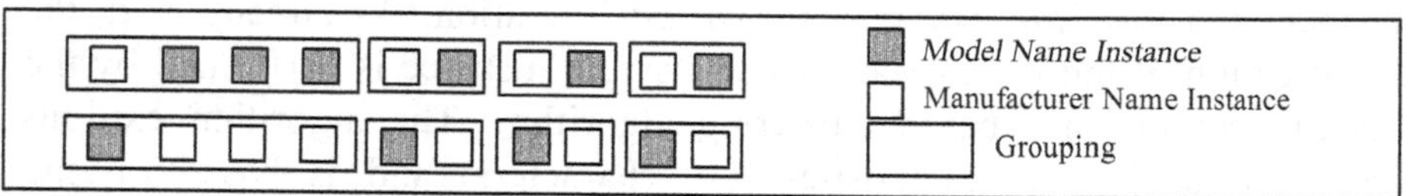

Figure 12-6. Examples of admissible manufacturer and model name pairs

3.4 Validation

Finally, at the stage of validation the domain expert validates the acquired knowledge (extracted instances and discovered relations between instances) via a visual tool (Fig. 12-7). This tool organizes and integrates all the acquired knowledge, making the validation easier and faster.

When this stage ends, an iteration of the ontology population process is considered to have finished. The new version of the ontology, updated with the validated instances and relations, is used as a seed ontology, starting a new iteration. The process stops when no changes are made in the ontology.

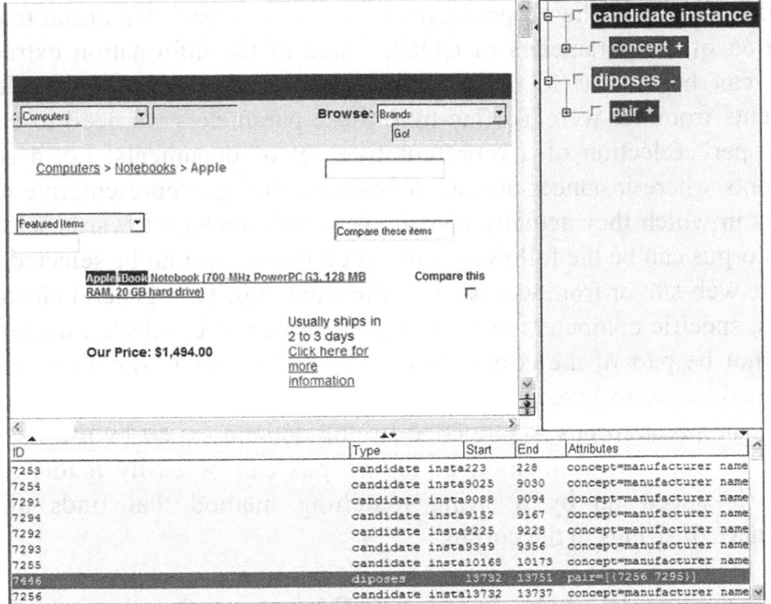

Figure 12-7. Screenshot of the tool for inspecting candidate instances

4. CONTROLLING THE POPULATION PROCESS

One of the main issues of the ontology population approach is to minimize the human involvement, automating the process as much as possible. To automate the population process described in section 3, one needs to automate the parameter settings selection for the machine learning-based methods (HMM and COCLU) that are employed. Of course, the main concern towards automation is the advancement of the quantity and quality of the instances recognized. Random selection of parameters' values leads, in the majority of the cases, to poor results, whereas manual tuning in large scale applications is impractical.

While the parameter values for the information extraction system can be selected manually, this is time consuming and not realistic in large scale applications. Manual selection of parameter values requires many experiments with different parameter settings in order to find the best ones, together with the appropriate magnitude of training and testing dataset. The set of parameters for the information extraction system include the number of prefix (p), target (t) and suffix (s) type nodes of an HMM. Furthermore, automating the selection of the COCLU threshold value is another concern towards automating the population approach. The threshold controls the homogeneity of typographic variants in groups.

In the context of the proposed maintenance approach we argue that the estimation of the parameters of COCLU and of the information extraction system can be automated using a pivot corpus that consists of selected documents from the web. To fine-tune these parameters we need to ensure the "proper" selection of a representative set of documents; i.e. a set of documents where instances appear in contexts that are representative to the contexts in which they actually appear. A simple strategy towards selecting such a corpus can be the following one: Web pages must no be selected from the same web-site or from web-sites of the same type (e.g. general electronic retailers, specific computers retailers etc.). Furthermore, selected documents should not be part of the corpus from which the domain ontology will be maintained so as to avoid the fine-tuning of the parameters to a specific corpus. The pivot corpus is annotated by the domain expert by means of an annotation tool. The annotation of the corpus can be easily made, as the process is speed up by a string matching method that finds all the occurrences of strings in the corpus.

4.1 Controlling the Instances Discovery Process

The selection of parameters' values that would lead a machine-learning task to achieve an optimal generalization performance on new data has occupied the machine learning community since the beginning of its endeavor. One of the proposed methods for arriving at optimal parameter settings is the "wrapper" method (Kohavi and John, 1997). We formalize the parameter value selection problem as a *state search problem*. Each state is the vector (p,t,s) where p stands for the number of prefix type nodes, t for the number of target type nodes and s for the number of suffix type nodes that exist in a HMM. All these parameters range in the set of natural numbers. The initial state is the vector $(1,1,1)$ and the operator increases the value of a vector cell by one. The heuristic function is the formula *A=2*Recal+Precision.* This heuristic is used to evaluate the states of the hypotheses space by measuring the precision and recall of the information extraction system for the particular setting of its parameters. We measure *Recall* and *Precision* against the correct instances in the pivot corpus. Recall is the ratio of the correctly extracted instances to all the correct instances that exist in the pivot corpus, whereas precision is the ratio of the correctly extracted instances to all the extracted instances. Searching the state search space, we employ a best-first strategy that stops when no better (in terms of A) state than the current state can be uncovered. It must be noticed that the heuristic function A is biased to prefer high *Recall* to high *Precision*.

4.2 Typographic Variation Discovery Control

The pivot corpus is further annotated in order to be appropriate for evaluating the discovery of typographic variants. For each instance in the corpus we provide a "normalized lexicalization" which serves as the representative for the grouping of its variants. The groups produced from the human annotated corpus provide the "gold" groups, in contrast to the groups produced by COCLU using the candidate instances.

In order to measure the performance of COCLU we define two measures: *"merge"* and *"split"* (Eqs. (1)–(2)). *Merge* is defined as the ratio of the number of *gold groups*[4] fired to the number of *test groups* created. On the other hand, *split* is defined as the ratio of the number of *test groups* created to the sum of the number of times a *gold group* has been fired in the *test groups* for all the *gold groups*. The measures are in the [0.1] interval. An exception to this occurs for the *merge* measure in cases that the number of *gold groups* is greater than the number of *test groups*. In these cases the right boundary of the interval is equal to the ratio of the number of *gold groups* to the number of *test groups*. The closer or greater these values are to 1, then no merging or splitting actions are required.

$$Merge = \frac{\#gold\_groups\_fired}{\#test\_groups\_created} \quad (1)$$

$$Split = \frac{\#test\_groups\_created}{\sum_{gold\_groups} \#times\_gold\_group\_fired} \quad (2)$$

Scheme 1 and 2 shows two examples of COCLU's results that are evaluated by means of the *"merge"* and *"split"* measures. Scheme 3 shows the gold groups. Squares with the same filling motif belong to the same gold group. Every line in schemes 1 and 2 is a group that has been produced by COCLU (i.e. a test group). The objects in such a group are the squares in that line. For example, for the groups in scheme 1, the *merge* measure is equal to 5/4 since the number of *gold groups* fired is equal to 5 and the number of *test groups* created is 4, hence no merging is needed. The *split* measure is equal to 4/5 since the number of *test groups* created is 4 and the sum of the number of times a *gold group* is fired for all the *gold groups* is equal to 5. In this case the first *test group* (first line) should be splitted. In

[4] When the number of objects in a gold group have been identified and classified in a test group, then the *gold group* is considered to be fired.

the case depicted in scheme 2 the *split* measure is equal to 4/4, whereas the *merge* measure is equal to 3/4, indicating the necessity of merging actions.

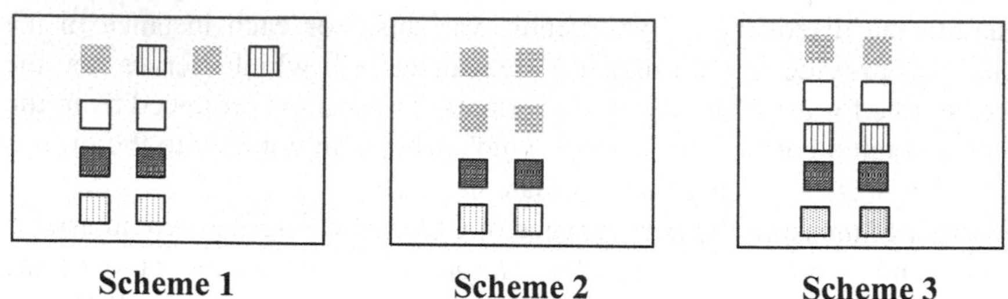

Scheme 1 **Scheme 2** **Scheme 3**

The pivot corpus is used along with the merge and split measures to select the parameter (threshold) value of COCLU. These measures are complementary and there is a trade-off to selecting the parameter value that best fits our needs. In our experiments, we have set that we prefer merging to splitting, preferring high split measure values to high merge values. We reflect this in a search space problem, formalized in a way that is analogous to the HMM parameter estimation problem. Each state is represented by a single natural number *n* equal to the COCLU threshold value. The operator increases n by 1 whereas the initial state is equal to 1. The heuristic function for evaluating each state is defined to be *B=2*Split+Merge,* where *"Split"* and *"Merge"* are measured by applying COCLU with the corresponding threshold value in the pivot corpus.

5. EXPERIMENTAL RESULTS AND DISCUSSION

We evaluated the performance of the incremental ontology population methodology presented in section 3 on the "laptop description" domain ontology created in CROSSMARC project. Figure 12-8 depicts four concepts used in our experiments as well as the relation *"disposes"* that holds between the instances of the concepts *"Manufacturer"* and *"Model"*. Every concept has an attribute *name* whose attribution produces the various concept instances. The relation between the *"Model"* and *"Manufacturer"* concepts has been used for demonstration purposes. Instances of concepts can also be associated using other relations as well.

During evaluation we have used the most highly evolving concepts of this ontology, which are: *"Processor"*, *"Model"*, *"Manufacturer"* and *"Operating System"* (Fig. 12-8). Our intention is to evaluate the performance of the proposed method to acquire the knowledge that exists in a given corpus, populating the ontology with new instances and interlinking the acquired instances via relations, such as the *"disposes"* and the *"has typographic variant"* relation. Furthermore, we experiment with tuning the ontology population method by automatically selecting the machine learning-based algorithms parameters that influence the efficiency of the overall approach.

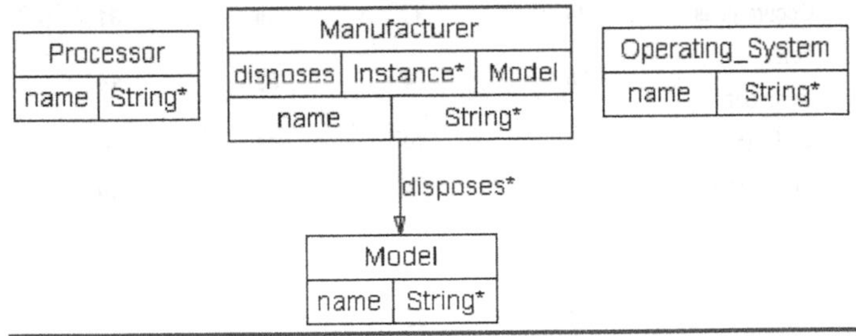

Figure 12-8. Ontology used in our experiments

To evaluate the population approach we compared the populated ontology against a gold ontology that contains the instances that appear in the corpus. The gold ontology has been constructed by a domain expert. The corpus is in English and consists of 69 web-pages containing laptops' descriptions. We conducted experiments using two different starting (seed) ontologies that have a different number of instances. The pre-processing of the corpus has been done using the text engineering platform Ellogon. The proposed method requires the pre-processing of the corpus only from a tokenizer which identifies text tokens (e.g. words, symbols, etc.) in the web-pages. This minimal pre-processing makes our method promising enough as it has a lot of potential for improvements through richer information pre-processing techniques and methods (e.g. shallow part of speech parsing, background information integration methods etc.).

Table 12-1 gives statistical information concerning the gold and the two seed ontologies. For each concept of the ontology, Table 12-1 provides the number of *total instances*. The number of *variants* specifies the number of groups that include typographic variants of the same instances. *Occurrences* refer to the number of appearances of an instance in the corpus.

The quality of the extracted instances is mostly connected with the values of the machine learning-based information extraction system parameters. In order to further investigate the influence of the pivot corpus size in selecting the optimal parameters we compiled 5 different pivot corpora by randomly selecting documents following the corpus selection strategy stated in section 4. Table 12-2 provides statistics about the number of documents each pivot corpus contains, the number of tokens it consists of and the number of instances it includes for each ontology concept.

Table 12-1. Statistics for the gold and seed ontologies

		Operating System	Processor	Model	Manufacturer	Total
1st starting Ontology	Total instances	*8*	*9*	*22*	*9*	*48*
	Variants	*5*	*6*	*12*	*2*	*25*
	Occurrences	*18*	*30*	*35*	*31*	*114*
2nd starting Ontology	Total Instances	*26*	*24*	*52*	*16*	*118*
	Variants	*19*	*19*	*33*	*3*	*74*
	Occurrences	*62*	*107*	*130*	*107*	*406*
Gold Ontology	Total Instances	*50*	*82*	*271*	*28*	*431*
	Variants	*41*	*69*	*239*	*5*	*352*
	Occurrences	*257*	*605*	*602*	*401*	*1865*

Table 12-2. Summary of pivot corpus's characteristics

	Tokens	Documents	Processor	Model	Manufacturer	Operating System
Pivot corpus 1	31.933	13	37	71	19	28
Pivot corpus 2	52.345	26	44	96	21	36
Pivot corpus 3	70.433	36	53	132	22	43
Pivot corpus 4	83.335	46	57	146	25	47
Pivot corpus 5	107.643	56	72	224	27	49

5.1 The Population Task

The population task starts by exploiting the instances included in the seed ontology to semantically annotate the corpus. As already pointed, this approach of producing training examples for the information extraction system bootstraps the information extraction task of the population method. After the end of the information extraction stage, candidate instances are passed to the validation stage. The number of the candidate instances and their "cleanness" (as it has been specified in section 3.2) depends on the performance of the information extraction system. The performance of the information extraction system is controlled by the parameters specifying the configuration of the HMM. Arguing that the parameters' values can be estimated through its evaluation of the system on sample documents form the corpus, we use a pivot corpus to guide the selection of these parameters. In subsection 5.2 we experiment with different sizes of the pivot corpus in order to investigate the size that suffices to drive the learning process to the optimal selection of the parameter values.

5.2 Populating Ontology's Concepts

We measure the improvement of the results as the proposed population method is iteratively applied starting from the two different seed domain ontologies whose statistics are specified in Table 12-1. An instance is considered to populate an ontology correctly, if it does not exist in the ontology, if it has been correctly classified to the appropriate concept and if it has been associated correctly with other existing instances.

Figure 12-9 depicts the results obtained by the application of the population method using the first starting ontology. The percentage of the initial number of instances for each concept appears on the vertical axis. *"Operating Systems"* starts with 16%, *"Manufacturer"* with 32%, *model* with 8% and *"Processor"* with 11% of the total number of instances that exist in the corpus. The horizontal axis represents the number of method's applications. At each iteration, we measure the accumulative coverage of concept's instances discovered, i.e. the percentage of the extracted instances. Thus, the instances of the concept *"Operating System"* have been increased from 16% to 36% at the first application of the method. The method achieves the highest success for the concept *"Operating System",* since it increases the number of instances in the ontology from 16% to 82%. This happens as the instances appear in quite similar contexts and are progressively identified by the information extraction system. Also, the smooth slope of the corresponding line is explained by the fact that the instances are uniformly distributed in different contexts. On the contrary, the instances of the *"Manufacturer"* and *"Model"* concepts appear in less frequent and uniformly distributed contexts. Also, it is worth noting that the method locates all the instances that it can discover until the 4th iteration and manages to increase five times (average on 4 concepts) the initial number of instances. Finally, the method managed to increase the overall number of instances discovered from 17% to 70% (see Table 12-3).

Figure 12-10 shows the results from the overall population approach using the second seed ontology. The coverage of the instances in this case increases faster, as the bigger number of instances in the seed ontology introduces a bigger variety of contexts and provides more examples to the learning algorithm. In general, the bootstrapping technique works well and guides the discovery of more instances in each iteration. The particular use of this technique is depicted in relation to the results for the *"Model"* concept in Fig. 12-9 and for the *"Processor"* concept in Fig. 12-10. In these cases, a slightly small number of new instances are enough to unveil the contextual information needed to discover the new instances and to steadily improve the results. These results recommend the application of the population approach on a regular basis, in order to keep the domain ontology highly up-to-date.

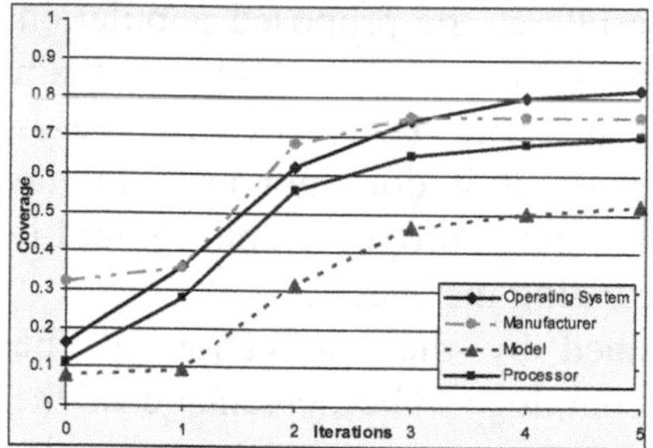

Figure 12-9. Results for the 1st starting ontology

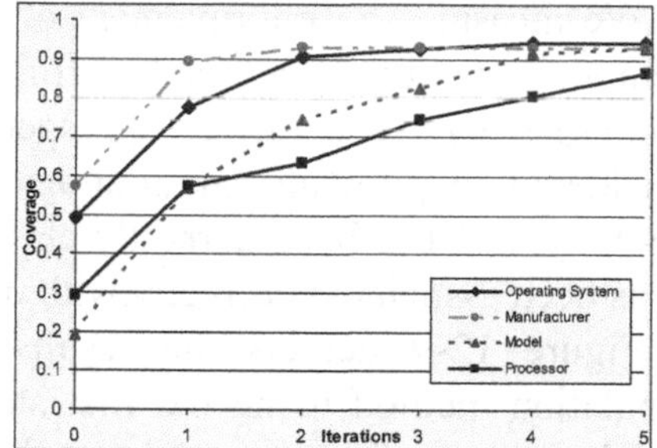

Figure 12-10. Results for the 2nd starting ontology

One of the main problems of the supervised machine learning-based approaches that have been proposed for information extraction is that they rely on the assumption that the documents which contain the information to be extracted have similar structure and the information to be extracted appears in similar context. This is an assumption that seems quite unrealistic considering the heterogeneity of the information in the web. Hence, the collection of the corpus for the training of the information extraction system should be done in a way that will secure a representative enough sample following the corpus selection strategy stated in section 4. Our innovative bootstrapping technique overcomes this barrier by using a context-independent technique i.e. string matching. Newly extracted instances might appear in different contexts not learned before, but are easily identified by the context-independent string matching technique. However, this is admissible in strictly fine-grained domain specific tasks and in cases where instances belong only to one concept. Otherwise, as already pointed, disambiguation techniques should be employed to correctly annotate an instance by exploiting contextual information.

Table 12-3 summarizes the capability of the proposed method to populate the ontology. The column labeled "Initial Coverage" presents the percentage of the known instances initially known, with respect to the number of instances included to the gold ontology. The column labeled "Final Coverage" presents the percentage of the instances that exist in the populated ontology with respect to the number of instances in the gold one. Results are provided for all four concepts used in the experiments, as well as in average (last row of each table).

Table 12-3. Summary of results using 1st and 2nd starting ontology

	1st starting ontology		2nd starting ontology	
	Initial Coverage	Final Coverage	Initial Coverage	Final Coverage
Operating System	0.16	0.82	0.49	0.94
Manufacturer	0.32	0.75	0.57	0.93
Model	0.08	0.52	0.19	0.93
Processor	0.11	0.70	0.29	0.87
Average	0.17	0.70	0.38	0.92

5.3 Populating Ontology's Relations

The information extraction stage results to a list of strings that constitute the sets of candidate concept instances. Amongst them, there exist instances that refer to the same object (e.g. processor Intel Pentium 3) but they have different lexicalizations (e.g. *"P3"*, *"PIII"*, *"Intel Pentium 3"*, *"Pentium 3"* and *"Pent.3"*). As it has been pointed, this valuable information can be acquired and formally encoded into the ontology by a new relation named *"has typographic variant"* between the instances of the same concept. We employ COCLU to obtain this relation and to formally encode it into the ontology.

We evaluate the performance of COCLU to discover typographic variants and new instances in each iteration of the methodology. COCLU takes as input already existing groups of instances (if any), the list of strings that correspond to candidate instances, and assigns each new string to an existing group, or it creates a new group when there is no sufficient evidence for similarity between the candidate string and the strings that represent an existing group. A group contains typographic variants of an instance, as well as the instance itself. Therefore, the members of a group are strings which are similar "enough" for being associated with the *"has typographic variant"* relation (their similarity measure is less than the specified threshold). The similarity of two strings is configured through the setting of COCLU's threshold parameter.

We measure COCLU's capability to discover new instances beyond the existing ones. These new instances have significantly different lexicalizations of the existing concept instances. We measure the performance of COCLU in standard information retrieval terms using the recall and precision measures. Recall is defined as the ratio of the correctly generated groups to all the correct groups, whereas precision is defined as the ratio of the correctly generated groups to all generated groups. Results for each concept are provided in Table 12-4 for each iteration of the method. COCLU has generated almost all correct groups in most of the cases. Its performance increases as the number of pre-existing groups increase. Pre-existing groups provide evidence of surely different instances and helps COCLU to decide whether a string is a variant of them or it constitutes a new group. In most of the cases COCLU was splitting a group to smaller sub-groups. Table 12-5 provides average results for all concepts as well as the average results from all the experiments. In general, the performance of COCLU is quite high, making it appropriate for the instance discovery and for the detection of typographic variants.

Table 12-4. Ontology population results in each iteration

	1st iteration		2nd iteration		3rd iteration		4th iteration	
	Recall	Prec.	Recall	Prec.	Recall	Prec.	Recall	Prec.
Operating System	0.75	0.86	0.88	0.78	1.00	0.90	1.00	0.93
Manufacturer	1.00	1.00	1.00	0.95	1.00	1.00	1.00	1.00
Model	0.76	0.90	0.96	0.96	0.96	0.87	1.00	0.96
Processor	1.00	0.41	0.91	0.83	1.00	0.83	1.00	0.83

Furthermore, we evaluate COCLU's accuracy to assign an instance to the correct class. Hence, we measure the homogeneity of the generated instance groups and COCLU's capability to discover typographic variants. Correctly assigned instances' lexicalizations are counted as correct assignments whereas erroneously assigned instances' lexicalizations are counted as incorrect assignments. Table 12-6 presents the accuracy results for each iteration (rows) and for each concept in the ontology (columns). The accuracy increases as the number of iterations increases. This happens because it is easier for COCLU to correctly assign an instance to a group which has a large number of members rather than if the group has a few member instances.

Table 12-5. Average results on all iterations

	Recall	Precision
Operating System	*0.91*	*0.87*
Manufacturer	*1.00*	*0.99*
Model	*0.89*	*0.92*
Processor	*0.98*	*0.73*
Overall	*0.95*	*0.88*

Table 12-6. COCLU's Accuracy: Instance assignment evaluation

	Operating System	Manufacturer	Model	Processor	*Average*
1st Iteration	0.86	1.00	0.86	0.84	*0.89*
2nd Iteration	0.89	1.00	0.89	0.89	*0.92*
3rd Iteration	0.98	1.00	0.92	0.90	*0.95*
4th Iteration	0.98	1.00	0.97	0.90	*0.96*

5.4 Tuning the Population Task

To tune the population approach in an automatic way we devised methods for deciding the values of the machine learning algorithms' (HMM and COCLU) parameters. Concerning the information extraction system we have used the method described in 5.1 to locate optimal parameters. We experimented with the pivot corpus sizes shown in Table 12-2 to investigate the minimum pivot corpus size that is needed for estimating optimal parameter values. The size of the corpus is measured in terms of the number of documents included.

Table 12-7 provides the results for parameters value selection using different pivot corpus sizes (these label tables' columns). Due to space restrictions, we provide only four sets of parameter values *(hmm0, hmm1, hmm2* and *hmm3)*. Every set of parameter values is a specific attribution to the HMM parameters prefix *(p),* target *(t)* and suffix *(s)*. These sets of parameter values label the rows of tables. Table 12-7 shows the decision formed concerning the values of these parameters for each concept in relation to the pivot corpus used. A table entry is marked with a capitalized "x" (X) when the choice is equal to the optimal one (made also by the domain expert) and with a lower "x" (x) in other cases (when derived automatically but not selected by the domain expert). Blank entries denote that the optimal value decision has been made in another parameter value set. As it can be seen, optimal parameter values for the concept *"Processor"* can be selected with a corpus size of eleven documents. For the concept *"Operating System"* a corpus size of 26 documents is needed, whereas for the concepts *"Manufacturer"* and *"Model"* a corpus size of at least 36 documents is needed. In general, the selection of optimal parameter values can be made with a corpus consisting of at least 36 documents.

Furthermore, a domain expert examined the results of the information extraction system with different parameters values as well as with the automatically derived optimal parameters values. The expert categorized the resulting candidate instances as *"correct"*, when the whole string represent an instance, *"wrong"* when the string does not represent an instance and *"not wrong/correct"* when removing words from the beginning or the end of the string (correcting process) results to an instance. Figures 12-11, 12-12, 12-13 and 12-14 provide the results of the evaluation for the 4 sets of parameters *(hmm0, hmm1, hmm2* and *hmm3)* in terms of the above stated qualitative characterizations. The automatically derived optimal parameters value set (parameter set: *hmm1*) was truly producing the results with the more correct and the less erroneous extracted instances. In Fig. 12-11, 12-12, 12-13 and 12-14 we can see that HMM performed best, discovering more in magnitude correct instances, for the concept *"Model"* and *"Processor"* with the *hmm0* parameters' value set, while for the concepts *"Manufacturer"* and *"Operating System"* it performed best with the *hmm1* parameters' value set. Examining the decision made in Table 12-7, and the portion of the correctly extracted instances in Fig. 12-11, 12-12, 12-13 and 12-14, we come up with the conclusion that the parameter selection method performs optimally and can be used to safely select the parameters of the supervised machine learning-based information extraction system.

Table 12-7. hmm0, hmm1, hmm2 and hmm3 on 1st Iteration

		11	26	36	46	56
hmm0	Processor	**X**	X	X	X	X
	Operating System					
	Model	x	**X**	X	X	X
	Manufacturer					
hmm1	Processor					
	Operating System	x	**X**	X	X	X
	Model	x				
	Manufacturer	x	X	**X**	X	X
hmm2	Processor					
	Operating System	x				
	Model	x				
	Manufacturer	x	x			
hmm3	Processor					
	Operating System					
	Model					
	Manufacturer	x	x			

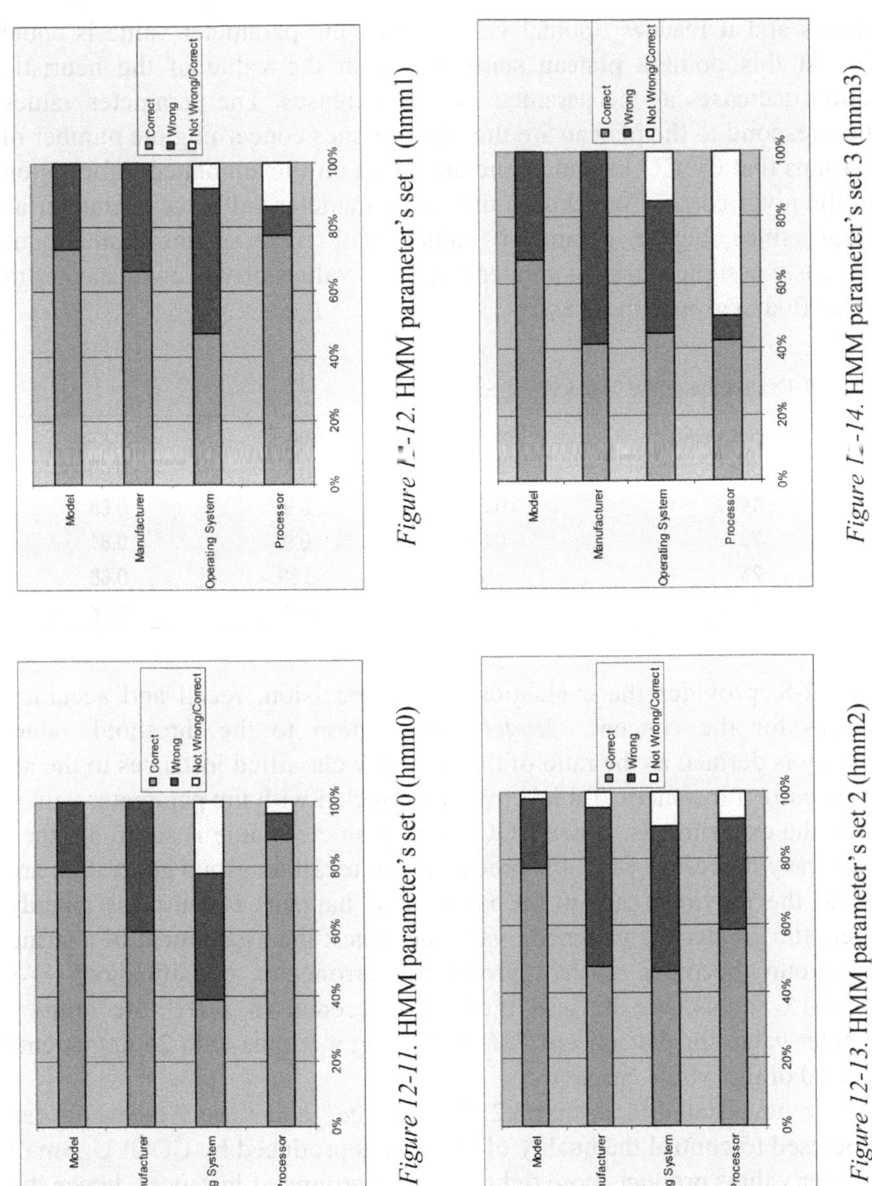

Figure 12-11. HMM parameter's set 0 (hmm0)

Figure 12-12. HMM parameter's set 1 (hmm1)

Figure 12-13. HMM parameter's set 2 (hmm2)

Figure 12-14. HMM parameter's set 3 (hmm3)

Concerning the decision about the COCLU parameter value we exploit the *merge* and *split* measures introduced in section 4.2. To determine the parameter value we have used different pivot corpus sizes. Figure 12-15 presents the values space of the heuristic function used in our experiment for the concept "*Model*". It shows that its value increases as the parameter value increases and it reaches optimal values when the parameter value is equal to 26. At this point a plateau starts and then the value of the heuristic function decreases as the parameter value increases. The parameter values that correspond to the plateau are the optimal ones concerning the number of the groups that COCLU should generate based on the annotated information from the pivot corpus. We choose the first parameter value we encounter as optimal, since bigger parameter values will increase the number of erroneously assigned strings: greater threshold values drive new instances to be classified in groups more easily.

Table 12-8. Evaluation of the "Model" concept

Parameter value	Precision	Recall	Accuracy
8	0.41	0.9	0.90
14	0.53	0.9	0.88
20	0.64	0.9	0.84
26	0.8	0.89	0.88
33	0.8	0.89	0.86

Table 12-8, provides the evaluation of the precision, recall and accuracy measures for the concept *"Model"*, in relation to the threshold value. Accuracy is defined as the ratio of the correctly classified instances to the all the true correct instances. Table's rows are labeled with the parameter values used in the experiments. When COCLU's parameter value is set to 33, then the accuracy decreases while the precision and recall on group generation are equal to the previous case in the table. This happens because, as already pointed, the greater the parameter value becomes, the assignment of a string to a group becomes easier, producing erroneous classifications. As Fig. 12-15 shows, the devised method succeeded to select the optimal parameter value for the concept *"Model"* using a corpus with 26 documents (one third of the whole corpus).

As we have stated in section 5.2, the *"merge"* and *"split"* measures can also be used to control the quality of the results produced by COCLU. Small parameter values produce more tightly similar groups of instances, hence the *"split"* measure is close to one and the *"merge"* measure is decreasing towards zero. On the other hand, bigger parameter values produce loosely similar classes of instances, hence the *"split"* measure decreases to zero and the *"merge"* measure increases to one. It is up to the domain expert to decide the most appropriate configuration.

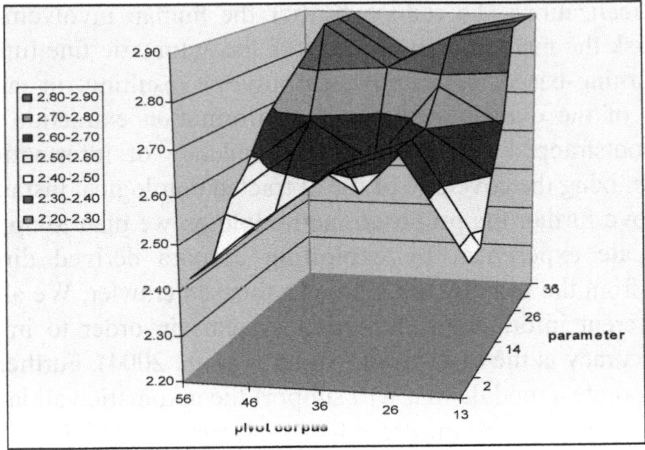

Figure 12-15. Heuristic's values space for "Model" concept

Figures 12-16 and 12-17 show the *"merge"* and *"split"* measure values respectively for various parameter values (i.e. 2, 8, 14, 20, 26 and 32) and different samples sizes (i.e. 13, 26, 36, 46, and 56) and reflect the complementary nature of these two measures. Due to space restrictions we provide figures only for the *"Model"* concept, which is a well representative case. In Fig. 12-16 we see that as the parameter value increases, the less merging actions between derived groups are needed since the value of *merge* measure becomes closer or equal to 1. This is the case as large COCLU's parameter values results in the creation of less tightly similar groups of instances. Analogously, Fig. 12-17 shows that less splitting actions are required when COCLU's parameter value decreases as the *split* measure is close to or equal with 1. This happens due to the creation of more tightly similar groups of instances. These figures depict the complementary nature of these two measures. Nevertheless, as we have shown before, the optimal parameter value is "26" and it is determined with the pivot corpus which contains at least 26 documents. As Fig. 12-16 and 12-17 show, at this point the merge and split measures take their maximum values. Thus the least actions for merging and spitting are required.

6. CONCLUDING REMARKS

In this chapter, we have presented an incremental ontology population method that exploits machine learning and information extraction techniques to automatically maintain a domain-specific application ontology with new instances and typographic variants from a corpus of web-pages. One of our major concerns is to discover instances that refer to the same entity but have different lexicalizations. To reduce further the human involvement in the population task the methodology introduces the automatic fine tuning of the machine learning-based algorithms employed, resulting in an optimal performance of the overall method. The information extraction system is iteratively bootstrapped exploiting the redundancy of information in the corpus, maximizing the coverage of the extracted ontological instances.

To improve further the proposed methodology, we plan to apply it on a real large scale experiment by exploiting corpora derived directly and dynamically from the web, by the help of a focused crawler. We also plan to combine different information extraction systems in order to improve the extraction accuracy at the meta-level (Sigletos et al., 2004). Furthermore, we plan to incorporate a module that will support the automatic validation of the discovered instances and to integrate the implemented modules in a suite of tools that will support the maintenance of ontologies

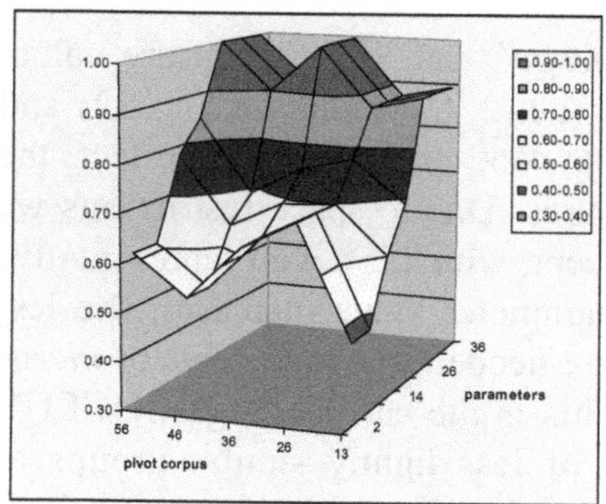

Figure 12-16. Merge Measure for grouping

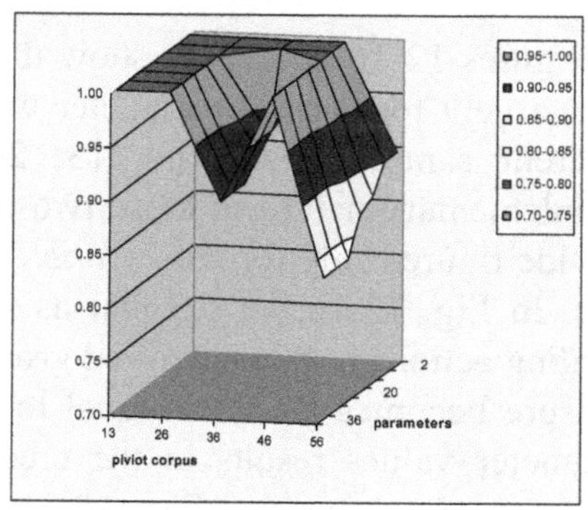

Figure 12-17. Split Measure for grouping

ACKNOWLEDGEMENTS

The authors are grateful to George Sigletos for providing the HMMs implementation. Thanks also go to our colleagues at SKEL laboratory who supported this work and CROSSMARC coordinator for providing the English corpus.

REFERENCES

Blum A., and Mitchell T., 1998, Combining Labeled and Unlabeled Data with Co-training, in: Proceedings of the Workshop on Computational Learning Theory, Morgan Kaufmann Publishers.

Brin S., Extracting Patterns and Relations from the World Wide Web, 1998, in: Proceedings of the WebDB Workshop at 6th International Conference on Extending Database Technology (EDBT'98).

Brewster C., Ciravrgnia F., and Wilks Y., 2002, User-Centered Ontology Learning for Knowledge Management, in: Proceedings of the 7th International Conference on Applications of Natural Language to Information Systems, LNCS, Springer-Verlag, vol. 2553, pp. 203-207.

Buitelaar P., and Declerck T., 2003, Linguistic Annotation for the Semantic Web, in: Annotation for the Semantic Web, edited by Handschuh S. and Staab S., IOS Press.

Ciravegna F., Dingli A., Guthrie D., and Wilks Y., 2003, Integrating Information to Bootstrap Information Extraction from Web Sites, in: Proceedings of the Workshop on Information Integration on the Web, pp. 9–14.

Craven M., DiPasquo D., Freitag D., McCallum A., Mitchell T., Nigam K., and Slattery S., 2000, Learning to Construct Knowledge Bases from the World Wide Web, Journal of Artificial Intelligence, vol. 118, no. 1/2, pp. 69 113.

Dill S., Eiron N., Gibson D., Gruhl D., Guha R., Jhingran A., Kanungo T., Rajagopalan S., Tomkins A., Tomlin J.A., and Zien J.Y., 2003, Semtag and seeker: Bootstrapping the semantic web via automated semantic annotation, in: Proceedings of the 12th International World Wide Web Conference (WWW2003), Budapest, Hungary.

Dingli A., Ciravegnia F., and Wilks Y., 2003, Automatic Semantic Annotation using Unsupervised Information Extraction and Integration, in: Proceedings of the K-CAP Workshop on Knowledge Markup and Semantic Annotation, Sanibel, Florida.

Etzioni O., Kok S., Soderland S., Cagarella M., Popescu A.M., Weld D.S., Downey, Shaker T., and Yates A., 2004, Web-Scale Information Extraction in KnowItAll (Preliminary Results), in: Proceedings of the 13th International World Wide Web conference (WWW2004), New York, pp. 100-110.

Freitag D., and McCallum A., 1999, Information extraction using hmms and shrinkage, in: Proceedings of the Workshop on Machine Learning for Information Extraction (AAAI-99), pp. 31-36.

Handschuh S., Staab S., and Ciravegna F., 2002, S-CREAM–Semi-automatic CREAtion of Metadata, Expert Update, vol. 5, no. 3, pp. 20-31.

Harith A., Sanghee K., Millard D.E., Weal M.J., Hall W., Lewis P.H., and Shadbolt N., 2003, Web based knowledge extraction and consolidation for automatic ontology instantiation, in: Proceedings of the Workshop on Knowledge Markup and Semantic Annotation (KCap'03), Sanibel Island, Florida, USA.

Hearst M.A., 1992, Automatic Acquisition of Hyponyms from large Text Corpora, in: Proceedings of the 14th International Conference on Computational Linguistic (COLING), vol. 2, pp. 539-545.

Karkaletsis V., Spyropoulos C.D., Grover C., Pazienza M.T., Coch J., and Souflis D., 2004, A Platform for Cross-lingual, Domain and User Adaptive Web Information Extraction, in: Proceedings of the 3rd Prestigious Applications Intelligent Systems Conference (PAIS).

Kiryakov A., Popov B., Ognyanoff D., Manov D., Kirilo A., and Goranov M., 2003, Semantic Annotation, Indexing, and Retrieval, in: Proceedings of the 2nd International Semantic Web Conference (ISWC2003), LNAI, Springer-Verlag , vol. 2870, pp. 484-499.

Kohavi R., and John G., 1997, Wrappers for feature subset selection, Artificial Intelligence Journal, vol. 97, issue 1–2, pp. 273-324.

Kotis k., Vouros G.A., 2005, Human-Centered Ontology Engineering: the HCOME Methodology, to appear in: International Journal of Knowledge and Information Systems (KAIS), Springer.

Petasis G., Karkaletsis V., Paliouras G., Androutsopoulos I., and Spyropoulos C.D., 2003, Ellogon: A New Text Engineering Platform, in: Proceedings of the 3rd International Conference on Language Resources and Evaluation (LREC-2002), Las Palmas, Canary Islands, Spain, pp. 72-78.

Pinto H.S., and Martin J.P., 2004, Ontologies: How can they built? Knowledge and Information Systems, Springer-Verlag, pp. 441-464.

Riloff E., and Jones R., 1999, Learning Dictionaries for Information Extraction by Multi-Level Bootstrapping, in: Proceedings of the 6th national Conference on Artificial Intelligence (AAAI-99), pp. 474-479.

Seymore K., McCallum A., and Rosenfeld R., 1999, Learning hidden markov model structure for information extraction, Journal of Intelligent Information Systems, pp. 5–28.

Sigletos G., Paliouras G., Spyropoulos C.D., and Stamatopoulos T., 2004, Stacked Generalization for Information Extraction, in: Proceedings of the 16th European Conference on Artificial Intelligence (ECAI), Valencia, Spain, IOS Press.

Tempich C., Pinto H.S, Sure Y., and Staab S., 2005, An Argumentation Ontology for DIstributed, Loosely-controlled and evolvInG Engineering processes of oNTologies (DILIGENT), in: The Semantic Web, Research and Applications, edited by Gómez-Pérez A. and Euzenat J., LNCS, Springer-Verlag, vol. 3532, pp. 241-256.

Valarakos A., Sigletos G., Karkaletsis V., and Paliouras G., 2003, A methodology for semantically annotating a corpus using a domain ontology and machine learning, in: Proceedings of the Recent Advances in Natural Language Processing International (RANLP) Conference, Bulgaria.

Valarakos A.G., Paliouras G., Karkaletsis V., and Vouros G., 2004a, A Name Matching Algorithm for Supporting Ontology Enrichment, in: Methods and Applications of Artificial Intelligence, edited by Vouros G.A. and Panayiotopoulos T., LNAI, Springer-Verlag, vol. 3025, pp. 381-389.

Valarakos A.G., Paliouras G., Karkaletsis V., and Vouros G., 2004b, Enhancing Ontological Knowledge through Ontology Population and Enrichment, in: Engineering Knowledge in the Age of the Semantic Web, edited by Motta E., Shadbolt N., Stutt A., and Gibbins N., LNAI, Springer Verlag, vol. 3257, pp. 144-156.

Vargas-Vera M., Domingue J., Lanzoni M., Stutt A., and Ciravegna F., 2002, MnM: Ontology driven semi-automatic support for semantic markup, in: Knowledge Engineering and Knowledge Management (Ontologies and the Semantic Web), edited by Gomez-Perez A. and Benjamins V.R., LNAI, Springer-Verlag, vol. 2473.

Chapter 13

MNM: SEMI-AUTOMATIC ONTOLOGY POPULATION FROM TEXT

Maria Vargas-Vera [1], Emanuela Moreale [1], Arthur Stutt [1], Enrico Motta [1] and Fabio Ciravegna [2]

[1] Knowledge Media Institute, The Open University, Walton Hall, Milton Keynes, MK7 6AA, UK, {m.vargas-vera}@open.ac.uk; [2] Department of Computer Science, University of Sheffield, Regent Court, 211Portobello Street, Sheffield S1 4DP, UK

Abstract: Ontologies can play a very important role in information systems. They can support various information system processes, particularly information acquisition and integration. Ontologies themselves need to be designed, built and maintained. An important part of the ontology engineering cycle is the ability to keep a handcrafted ontology up to date. Therefore, we have developed a tool called MnM that helps during the ontology maintenance process. MnM extracts information from texts and populates ontology. It uses NLP (Natural Language Processing), Information Extraction and Machine Learning technologies. In particular, MnM was tested using an electronic newsletter consisting of news articles describing events happening in the Knowledge Media Institute (KMi). MnM could constitute an important part of an ontology-driven information system, with its integrated web-based ontology editor and provision of open APIs to link to ontology servers and to integrate with information extraction tools.

Key words: information extraction; ontology population; ontology-driven information systems

1. INTRODUCTION

Hicks [1] defines an information system (IS) as a "formalized computer information system that can collect, store, process and report data from various sources to provide the information necessary for managerial decision making".

In this chapter, we present MnM, a tool that supports knowledge acquisition/collection, the first function of an IS (as defined by Hicks). This knowledge acquisition is ontology-driven: MnM supports ontology population, an important stage in ontology building. Therefore, MnM could be used as a part of an ontology-driven IS (ODIS).

ISs can clearly benefit from the use ontologies because it will promote interoperability between different ISs. In particular, interoperability will be promoted by domain ontologies and task ontologies. The former consist of static relations and axioms describing the vocabulary related to a generic domain and the latter focus on the dynamic aspects of a domain by describing generic tasks or activities characterising that domain.

Ontology building has been conceptualised in different ways. A somewhat "traditional" view of ontology building (modified from [2]) would see it as consisting of the following four main steps: identifying the purpose of the ontology, ontology capture and population, evaluation and documentation. After deciding on the level of specialisation of the ontology (e.g. core ontology or domain ontology), ontology engineers would proceed with ontology capture by identifying concepts in the domain and proceed to disambiguate the text definition of these concepts. They would then define the classes in the ontology and arrange them in a hierarchy. Properties and constraints (i.e. allowed values) need to be defined through coding in a formal language. Integration with existing ontologies would also take place through these last two steps. Next, ontology population follows: here values for the properties of instances are filled in and individual instances of these classes are defined, filling in specific property value information and additional property constraints.

Grüninger and Fox's approach to ontology building [3] starts not from concepts in the domain, but rather from motivating scenarios that are not covered by current ontologies. They then envisage formulating internal competency questions to be used to see if the ontology meets the requirements (i.e. evaluate the ontological commitments). A formal language step follows, during which terms are taken from the competency questions and translated into a formal terminology. Then the formal competency questions are formulated in terms of the ontology and axioms and definitions are specified. Finally, a completeness check is carried out.

Ontology building has also been approached as ontology engineering, with similarities to software engineering [4]. The *methontology* framework defines three main types of activities: project management activities, development oriented activities and support activities. Project management activities include planning, control and quality assurance. Planning the tasks to be performed and times and resources required is essential in case of ontologies that need to use already existing ontologies (either to build an abstraction/generalisation or specialisation of current ontologies). Development-oriented activities include remindful of software engineering stages: specification, conceptualisation, formalization, implementation and maintenance. Specification states the purpose of the ontology being built and its end users. Conceptualization is building domain structures at the domain level. Formalization is the translation of these knowledge structures into a formal language. The formal description is then translated into a computable model (implementation). Finally, ontology updating and corrections are made (maintenance). The third type of activities – support activities – include knowledge acquisition of the domain, integration of ontologies and documentation and configuration management. By ontology integration, the authors seem to refer to a design-time ontology integration process that occurs when existing ontologies are reused in creating a new ontology. Documentation is a thorough description of all the phases completed and products built. All the versions of the documentation, software and ontology are also kept (configuration management).

It should be noted that, while these different methodologies strive to define stages of ontology building, these stages may not be so clear-cut as the methodologies seem to suggest. Just like in software engineering, it is likely that iteration will be involved in the development of ontologies, with concepts being iteratively refined in the early stages and even in later stages some degree of revision may be required (e.g. addition of a new class or property). MnM, the tool described in this chapter, may be useful in exactly this stage of maintenance (ontology updating and corrections), as well as the more general step of knowledge acquisition.

Ontology population (by means of information extraction) is the method of knowledge acquisition that MnM employs. In general, ontology population can be carried out either manually or automatically. In the manual approach, the knowledge engineer will select the concept to be extract from the document and manually fill the slots. An example is Knote, the Planet knowledge editor used in OntoPlanet [5]. In the automatic approach, the knowledge engineer defines a library of patterns that are then matched against the documents; alternatively, machine learning technologies are used to generate this library of patterns automatically. The manual approach has the disadvantages of being labor-intensive and usually leading to an incomplete library, therefore extraction is very poor. By contrast, the automatic approach based on machine learning automatically generates the patterns but requires a learning phase (training with examples).

Our approach uses machine learning for ontology population. Therefore, one of our first steps in ontology population is the training phase: this comprises the marking up of documents with semantics (slot names in the ontology). For example, in describing the class visiting-a-place-or-people, the ontology contains as slot names "visitor", "organization" being visited etc. So these concepts are highlighted in the text in the document can be marked up with these types.

MnM, as well as being an ontology populator, could be used to annotate resources with semantics, one of the goals of the semantic web [6]. We therefore envision the use of MnM to play an important role in the semantic web as a tool that allows semantic annotation of documents. In order to carry out this task, users need appropriate *knowledge representation languages*, *ontologies*, and *support tools*. The knowledge representation language provides the semantic interlingua for expressing knowledge precisely. RDF [7][8] and RDFS [9] provide the basic framework for expressing metadata on the web, while current developments in web-based knowledge representation, such as DAML+OIL [1] and OWL the language[2], are building on the RDF base framework to provide more sophisticated knowledge representation support. Further details about these knowledge representation languages and semantic web layers can be found in [10].

Ontologies and representation languages provide the basic semantic tools to construct the semantic web. Obviously a lot more is needed; in particular, tool support is required to facilitate the development of semantic resources, given a particular ontology and representation language. This problem is not a new one: knowledge engineers realized early on that one of the main obstacles to the development of intelligent, knowledge-based systems was the so-called *knowledge acquisition bottleneck* [11]. In a nutshell, the problem is how to acquire and represent knowledge, so that this knowledge can be effectively used by a reasoning system. Automated knowledge extraction technologies are likely to play an ever-increasing important role, as a crucial technology to tackle the semantic web version of the knowledge acquisition bottleneck.

In this chapter we present *MnM*, a central part of a knowledge acquisition module within an IS. In particular, it acts as an ontology populator providing both automated and semi-automated support for marking up web pages with semantic content. MnM is an ontology-based information extraction engine based on unsupervised learning. It learns extraction rules from a training set and then applies these rules on unseen news articles to populate an ontology. As a first case study, we used an electronic newsletter of 200 news articles describing academic life at the Knowledge Media Institute[3].

The rest of the chapter is organized as follows: the next section (Section 2) covers ontologies and their use, particularly within ISs. In section 3, we show the Event ontology from our repertoire of ontologies.

[1] http://www.daml.org/2001/03/reference.html.

[2] http://www.w3.org.

[3] http://news.kmi.open.ac.uk/rostra/.

Section 4 presents the process model underlying the design of the MnM tool. Section 5 outlines an example of the tool in use. Section 6 gives an evaluation of MnM using two information extraction engines: Amilcare from Sheffield and Marmot, Badger and Crystal tools from UMass. Section 7 presents related work. Finally section 8 re-states the main tenets and results from our research.

2. WHAT ARE ONTOLOGIES AND HOW ARE THEY USED?

Ontologies are explicit formal specifications of the terms in the domain and the relations among them [12]: they provide the mechanism to support interoperability at a conceptual level. In a nutshell, the idea of interoperating agents able to exchange information and carrying out complex problem-solving on the web is based on the assumption that they will share common, explicitly-defined, generic conceptualizations. These are typically models of a particular area, such as product catalogues or taxonomies of medical conditions.

The main use of ontologies is to make the meaning of concepts explicit in order to improve communication, In particular, interoperability of distributed and heterogeneous computing environments. Ontologies can also be used to support the specification of reasoning services [13][14][15], thus allowing not only 'static' interoperability through shared domain conceptualizations, but also 'dynamic' interoperability through the explicit publication of competence specifications, which can be reasoned about to determine whether a particular semantic web service is appropriate for a particular task.

2.1 Role of Ontology in Information Systems

ISs have been around since the middle of the 1960s. They are concerned with chunks of information like bank balances, tickets reservations, etc. This information can change frequently. Therefore, dynamic information has always been fundamental to ISs. Information items usually need to be interpreted in relation to other items. Then relations need to be defined so the network of connected information can be traversed/navigated for automated procedures. Therefore, the use of ontologies for the application program component can be beneficial. In traditional ISs, some parts of the knowledge are encoded in the static part of the program, such as class declarations or others parts implicitly stored as procedural part of the program. As several services (from different ISs) can be subscribed to the same ontology (in the same IS), we can argue that, using an ontology within an IS allows knowledge sharing between different ISs.

Guarino [16] characterizes an IS as consisting of components of three different types: application programs, resources like databases/knowledge bases and user interfaces. These components are integrated in order to accomplish a concrete purpose.

Using Guarino's terminology, MnM makes use of ontologies in the user interface component. MnM has been equipped with an ontology browser which could be utilised by the user to understand the vocabulary used by the IS. The information extraction is performed using a chosen ontology and this gives flexibility to our MnM system, which could therefore be used as be part of an IS endowed with a whole library of ontologies.

If we follow Guarino's characterization of the temporal dimension of ODIS, our MnM framework can be said to use ontology at run time. We use event ontology for extracting information from news articles and then populate the same ontology using the extracted information. The event ontology is discussed in more detail in the next section.

3. SCENARIO

3.1 Event Ontology

In our laboratory, an electronic newsletter allowing communication between researchers has been in use for approximately five years. This electronic newsletter consists of articles describing events happening in our laboratory. Our lab currently uses a system called OntoPlanet. This system supports the following activities:

- *Article submission.* A journalist (member of the Institute) submits a news article to KMi planet by writing an email or filling in a web page. Then the story is formatted and stored.
- *Article reading.* A Planet reader browses through the latest news articles using a standard Web browser.
- *Article annotation.* Either a journalist or a knowledge engineer manually annotates the story using Knote (the Planet knowledge editor).
- *Provision of customized alerts.* An agent (called Newsboy) builds user profiles from patterns of access to PlanetOnto and then uses these profiles to alert readers about relevant news articles.

The drawback to this system is that it requires manual annotation of the articles, which is time-consuming and may delay news delivering if the annotator(s) are unavailable. To address this problem, MnM was devised for the purpose of performing semi-automatic extraction from news articles.

Because we are dealing with news articles relating to our institute (KMi), MnM uses a local ontology that describes types of events (activities happening in our institution). These activities are defined formally in an ontology consisting of classes and slots. Figure 13-1 gives a snapshot from a fragment of the event ontology. Examples of event are Conferring-an-Award, Visiting-a-Place-or People, etc. The first in turn for example describes someone obtaining an award.

Description: Class of an event describing an event of presenting an award to someone

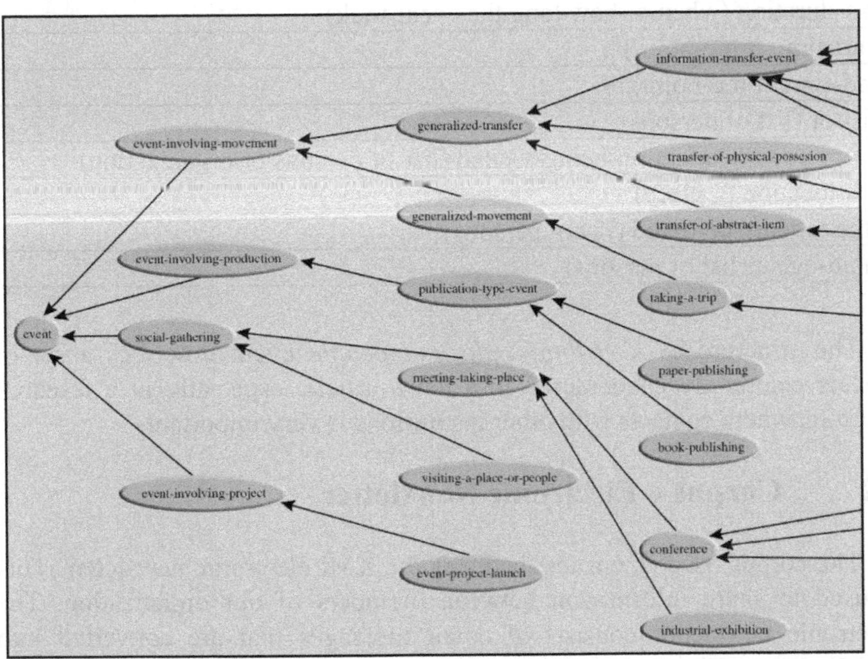

Figure 13-1. Event Ontology

Conferring-an-award class definition

Slots:
has-duration (when or how long the event took)
start-time (time-point)
end-time (time-point)
has-location (a place where it took place)
recipient-agents (the agents who received the award)
has-awarding-body (an organization, donor)
has-award-rationale (for what the award is)
object-acted-on (award, name of the award or amount of money)

The notion of events introduces temporality (time stamp). In our ontology, temporality is also modelled by giving an event a start and end time.

Another example of a class (*visiting-a-place-or-people*) with its slots is given below.

Slots:
has-duration (when or how long the event took)
start-time (time-point)
end-time (time-point)
visitor (list of persons)
people-or-organization-being-visited (list of persons or organization)
has-location (a place)
other agents-involved (list of persons)
main-agent (list of persons)

The structure of a *visiting-a-place-or-people* event describes a set of objects commonly encountered in a news article, especially in a research institute, where contacts with other institutions is very important.

3.2 Corpus – Electronic Newsletter

The corpus used as our test-bed was the KMi electronic newsletter. This is used to share information between members of our organization. The electronic newsletter consists of email messages that are converted into HTML pages. The text used in the news articles is generally unstructured. For example, the writers sometimes use slang, break conventions for capitalization, incorrectly use punctuation, etc. Also, styles of writing in the archive can vary tremendously, as news is submitted by dozens of individuals writing in their personal writing styles. Moreover, some are not native speakers of English and people's backgrounds range from multimedia to formal languages. All this makes it difficult to successfully apply heuristics to identify proper nouns. Natural language processing (NLP) approaches use heuristics such as "if a word is capitalized and is not starting a sentence then it is a proper name". Another example may be that of a string containing "& Co" or "Ltd", which would then be tagged as proper noun of a type of company. However, in our domain, we expect these methods to be so fragile that we are instead required to use patterns.

4. PROCESS MODEL

In previous sections, we described some of the components that will be used within MnM. Now we will focus on the description of the main processes that MnM supports.

MnM follows a sequential model, whereby the first three activities need to be performed for the automatic construction of the library of patterns, whereas the last two are concerned with knowledge acquisition.

These are five main activities supported by MnM:

- *Browsing*. A specific ontology can be selected from our repertoire of ontologies.
- *Markup*. Ontology is selected and its slot names are used to mark-up documents from the corpus.
- *Learning*. A learning algorithm is run over the marked-up corpus (training corpus) to learn the extraction rules.
- *Extraction*. An information extraction mechanism is selected and run over a set of test documents. Then information is extracted to populate the selected ontology. Further details of each component will be provided in the following sections.
- *Population*. A set of extracted concepts/relations is offered to the user for confirmation.

4.1 Browsing

Users browse a library of ontologies located on a web-based ontology server. The user can see an overview of the existing ontologies and can select which one to focus on. Our server has educational, academic, science ontologies, etc. Within a selected ontology, the user can browse the existing items – e.g. the classes and slots of a specific class. For instance, if a user selects the *akt-kmi-planet-ontolog (akt)*, then they can explore people, organizations, publications, technologies and events. Items within the *akt* reference ontology can be selected as the starting point for the information extraction process. More specifically, the selected class forms the basis for the construction of a template that will eventually be instantiated in the extraction activity.

An example of a template is that for the *visiting-a-place-people* class which consists of the slots visitor, *people-or-organization-visited*, *has-location*, *other-agents*, *main-agent*, *has-duration*, *start-time* and *end-time*.

The MnM ontology browser window is composed of five viewers: QSearch, Ontology viewer, Instance, Information and Status viewer. Each of these components is described below.

- QSearch viewer allows users to perform incremental searches in the ontology viewer (if *on* is selected) or in the instance viewer (if *in* is selected). The ontology browser composed by 5 viewers is a new feature that was not implemented in an earlier version of MnM described in [17].
- The Ontology Viewer displays the ontology structure as a tree structure (ontologies, classes and slots). A class might have different icons depending on whether or not it has associated with it a library of information extraction rules.
- The Instance Viewer presents the user with information about instances belonging to the selected class. A right click on an instance will pop up a menu with the following options: import mark-up, rename and remove. A double click on an instance will open a new dialog box. In this box the user can modify the instance manually if needed.
- The Information Viewer shows information about the selected ontology and the selected instances. All information provided is in HTML format. A double click on a piece of text means that the user wants more information. The viewer has some basic features such as go back, go forward, home and history management.
- The Status Viewer monitors the progress of background learning and background knowledge.

4.2 Mark-Up

The activity of semantic tagging refers to the activity of annotating text documents (written in plain ASCII or HTML) with a set of tags defined in the ontology. In particular, we work with the hand-crafted *akt* reference ontology (an ontology describing people, organizations, publications, research areas, technologies and events/news).

MnM provides the means to browse the event hierarchy (defined in the *akt* ontology). In this hierarchy, each event is a class and the annotation component extracts the set of possible tags from the slots defined in each class. Once a class has been selected, a training corpus of manually marked up pages needs to be created. Here, the user views appropriate documents within MnM's built-in web browser and annotates segments of text using the tags based on the slot names of a selected class as given in the ontology (this is ontology driven mark-up). As the text is selected, MnM inserts the relevant XML tags into the document. MnM also offers the possibility of removing tags from a document.

4.3 Learning

Once the corpus has been marked up, a library of patterns has to be built for the extraction. This could be built manually or automatically using a learning algorithm. According to [18], building a library of patterns manually for any specific domain takes approximately 1,500 person-hours. Therefore, there is a good reason for using machine learning technologies to build a library of patterns and this is what we decided to do.

There are several tools around for information extraction. Some of them work very well in structured text, others perform better in unstructured or telegraphic text. These tools are rather difficult to use, as they are aimed at natural language processing experts. So, in MnM we go further by offering this functionality to ordinary users.

In fact, MnM easily allows the selection of alternative information extraction engines and the integration of information extraction tools. In particular, MnM has been integrated with two information extraction engine suites which are described below.

4.3.1 MnM using Marmot, Badger and Crystal

MnM was integrated with Marmot, Badger and Crystal from the University of Massachusetts (UMass) [18] and our own NLP components (i.e. OCML preprocessor).

Background for Crystal, Badger and Marmot

The background for Marmot, Badger and Crystal is presented below.

- **Marmot**

Marmot (from UMass) is a natural language preprocessing tool that accepts ASCII files and produces an intermediate level of text analysis that is useful for information extraction applications. Sentences are separated and segmented into noun phrases, verb phrases, and prepositional phrases. Marmot splits at clausal boundaries (given a generous notion of sentence). In short, Marmot provides an idiosyncratic syntactic analysis which is sufficient for Badger to use in applying its extraction rules. Marmot has several functionalities: it preprocesses abbreviations to guide sentence segmentation, it resolves sentences boundaries, it identifies parenthetical expressions, recognizes entries from a phrasal lexicon and it replaces them, it recognizes dates and duration phrases, it performs phrasal bracketing of noun, preposition and adverbial phrases. Finally, it scopes conjunctions and disjunctions.

- **Crystal**

A second component that we integrated in our information extraction tool is called Crystal [19](Soderland *et al.* 1995). Crystal is a dictionary induction tool: it derives a dictionary of concept nodes (CN) from a training corpus.

Crystal initializes a CN dictionary for each positive instance of each type of event. The initial CN definitions are designed to extract the relevant phrases in the training instance that creates them, but are too specific to apply to unseen sentences. The main task of Crystal is to gradually relax thc constraints on the initial definitions and also to merge similar definitions. Crystal finds generalizations of its initial CN definitions by comparing definitions that are similar. This similarity is deduced by counting the number of relaxations required to unify two CN definitions. A new definition is then created with constraints relaxed. Finally, the new definition is tested against the training corpus to ensure that it does not extract phrases that were not marked with the original two definitions. This means that Crystal takes similar instances and generalizes them into a more general rule by preserving the properties from each of the CN definitions that are generalized. The inductive concept learning in Crystal is similar to the inductive learning algorithm described in [20], a specific-to-general data driven search to find the most specific generalization that covers all positive instances. Crystal finds the most specific generalization that covers all positive instances but uses a greedy unification of similar instances rather than breadth-first search.

- **Badger**

A third component called Badger (from UMass) takes each sentence in the text and sees if it matches any of our CN definitions. If no extraction CN definition applies to a sentence, then no information will be extracted; this means that irrelevant text can be processed very quickly.

An example of the use of MnM using UMass components can be found in [21] and [22].

4.3.2 Extensions to the UMass Tools

One of the main problems we encountered when using the libraries of patterns generated by Crystal is that these libraries contain large amounts of spurious rules. Therefore, some way of discriminating the good (or bad) rules is required. Spurious rules could be removed manually, but this is very time consuming: Riloff [18] reports several experiments on this. One of the most striking results was one experiment in which two thirds of the over 32,000 rules obtained had to be filtered out. Although she does not report how long this took, we can safely conclude that this is a time-consuming and laborious task. A better approach to filtering rules may involve generating a confidence value in each rule. This approach is described next.

Confidence values associated with the Crystal extraction rules

Our most recent work has concentrated on associating confidence values with the extraction rules. This arose from the fact that spurious rules were generated by Crystal (when Crystal is used a learning component of MnM). Previous work has reported that spurious patterns were deleted manually from the library of rules under the assumption that they were not likely to be of much value [18]. Our expectation was that this problem could be solved by associating confidence values to the extraction rules [23][24]. The experiments indeed confirmed our expectation that we would get rid of spurious rules by associating confidence with the rules automatically [25].

The confidence value for each rule was computed by a 10-fold cross-validation methodology on the training set. According to this methodology, the training set is split into ten equally sized subsets and the learning algorithm is run ten times. Each time, nine of the ten pieces are used for training and the tenth is kept as unseen data (test set) for the evaluation of the induced rules. The final result is the average over the ten runs. At run time, each instance extracted by Badger will be assigned the precision value of that rule. The main feature of using confidence values is that, when presented with ambiguous instantiations, we can still choose the one with the highest estimated confidence. We believe that the confidence value could be used as one way of getting rid of extraction rules that are below a given threshold.

The experiments conducted showed that using the rule confidence might increase precision by around 15% depending on different models and parameters [25]. In addition, it was observed that using the 10-Fold-Cross methodology for its computation seems to be a better choice than the simple method of taking Coverage and Error values computed by the learning component Crystal [25].

In the next section, we will look at a different information extraction engine also integrated within MnM.

4.3.3 MnM using Amilcare

MnM can also use, as information extraction engine, Amilcare[4] from Sheffield University [26].

Amilcare is designed to accommodate the needs of different user types. While naïve users can build new applications without delving into the complexity of Human Language Technology, information extraction experts are provided with a number of facilities for tuning the final application. Induced rules can be inspected, monitored and edited to obtain some additional accuracy, if required. The interface also allows precision (P) and

[4] Amilcare, a tool for adaptive information extraction (Ciravegna 2001a).

recall (R) to be balanced. The system can be run on an annotated unseen corpus and users are presented with statistics on accuracy, together with details on correct matches and mistakes. Retuning the precision-recall (P&R) balance does not generally require major retraining and facilities for inspecting the effect of different P&R balances are provided. Although the current interface for balancing P&R is designed for information extraction experts, a future version will provide support for naïve users [27].

At the start of the learning phase, Amilcare preprocesses texts using Annie, the shallow information extraction system included in the Gate package[5] [28]. Annie performs text tokenization (segmenting texts into words), sentence splitting (identifying sentences), part of speech tagging (lexical disambiguation), gazetteer lookup (dictionary lookup) and named entity recognition (recognition of people and organization names, dates, etc.). Amilcare then induces rules for information extraction. The learning system is based on LP^2, a covering algorithm for supervised learning of information extraction rules based on Lazy-NLP [26][29]. This is a wrapper induction methodology [30] that, unlike other wrapper induction approaches, uses linguistic information in the rule generalization process. The learning system starts inducing wrapper-like rules that make no use of linguistic information, where rules are sets of conjunctive conditions on adjacent words. Following this, the linguistic information provided by Annie is used in order to create generalized rules: conditions on words are substituted with conditions on the linguistic information (e.g. condition matching on either the lexical category, or the class provided by the gazetteer, etc). Examples of rules and a detailed description of the (LP^2) algorithm can be found in [29].

All the generalizations are tested in parallel by using a variant of the AQ algorithm [31] and the best generalizations are kept for Information Extraction. The idea is that the linguistic-based generalization is deployed only when the use of NLP information is reliable or effective. The measure of reliability here is not linguistic correctness, but effectiveness in extracting information using linguistic information as opposed to using shallower approaches. Lazy NLP-based systems learn which the best strategy for each information/context is separately. For example, they may decide that using the result of a part of speech tagger is the best strategy for recognizing the speaker in seminar announcements, but not in spotting the seminar location. This strategy is quite effective for analyzing documents with mixed genres, a common situation in web documents [32].

The learning system induces two types of rules: tagging rules and correction rules. A tagging rule is composed of a left hand side, containing a pattern of conditions on a connected sequence of words, and a right hand side that is the action of inserting an XML tag in the texts. Correction rules

[5] GATE is a software architecture for language engineering (http://www.gate.ac.uk/).

shift misplaced annotations (inserted by tagging rules) to the correct position. These are learnt from the errors found whilst attempting to re-annotate the training corpus using the induced tagging rules.

Correction rules are identical to tagging rules, but 1) their patterns also match the tags inserted by the tagging rules and 2) their actions shift misplaced tags rather than adding new ones. The output of the training phase is a collection of rules for information extraction that are associated with the specific scenario (a domain).

Therefore, unlike the UMass tool suite, Amilcare learns tagging rules from the tagging examples. Next time it comes across the same entities in new documents, it will automatically mark them up.

4.4 Extraction

Once a library of induced rules is available, it can be used to extract information from unseen texts.

For example, in the case of Amilcare working in extraction mode, the input will be a (collection of) text(s) with the associated scenario. Amilcare preprocesses the text(s) through Annie and then applies its rules and returns the original text with the added annotations made with the Gate annotation schema [28]. Annotation schemas provide means to define types of annotations in Gate since Amilcare is part of Gate. Gate uses the XML schema language supported by W3C for these definitions. However, Gate version 2 supports annotations in SGML/XML. Finally, the information extracted is presented to the user for approval.

When using the UMass tools, Badger produces templates filled with the values extracted from unseen documents in a file. This file needs to be parsed to present to the user in a more readable format through the user interface.

For both information extraction engines, the extracted information is sent to the ontology server which will populate the selected ontology.

4.5 Population

During the population phase, the information extraction mechanism fills predefined slots associated with an extraction template. Each template consists of slots of a particular class as defined in the selected ontology. For instance, the class *conferring-an-award* has the slots *recipient-agents* and *has-awarding-body*. More detail about the population phase is given in the following section.

The goal of MnM is to automatically fill as many slots as possible. However, some of the slots may still require manual intervention. There are several reasons for this:

- there is information that is not contained in the text,
- none of the rules from the information extraction libraries match with the sentence that might provide the information (incomplete set of rules). This means that the learning phase needs to be tuned.

The extracted information could be validated using the ontology. This is possible because each slot in each class of the ontology has a type associated with it. Therefore, extracted information not matching the type definition of the slot in the ontology can be highlighted as incorrect. However, our current prototype of MnM does yet not provide this feature. After the extraction phase, the user can accept or reject each single extracted piece of information or, alternatively, accept or reject all of the extracted information.

5. WORKING EXAMPLE USING AMILCARE AS INFORMATION EXTRACTION ENGINE

We will now explain the process model we described earlier by walking through a specific example.

The domain of our example is a web-based newsletter, *KMi Planet* [33], that has been running in our laboratory for five years. The *Planet* front page, individual articles and archive views are generated automatically from news articles that are submitted by email or through a web-based form. Over the years, we have extended *Planet* to include semantic retrieval, smart layout and personalization services [34][35]. Over time, we became concerned that the knowledge base is maintained by hand. Therefore, we selected this domain to apply MnM to.

Both information extraction engines embedded in MnM (UMass and Amilcare) were trained using news articles that we had been collected in KMi. These news articles describe events such as visits and project awards. Amilcare is designed to support active annotation of documents. It performs information extraction by enriching texts with XML annotations. To use Amilcare in a new domain, the user simply has to manually annotate a training set of documents. Extensive knowledge of Natural Language Technologies is not required.

Figures 13-2–13-5 show a user setting up an information extraction mechanism for extracting *Planet* news articles about visits to KMi. In Figure 13-2, the user is looking at one of the 200 news articles from our electronic archive which is displayed in the right pane. The left top panel shows all the knowledge models on the server (shown in the left panel). The user selects *akt-kmi-planet-kb* and notes from the documentation that it implements the latest Planet knowledge services. Opening *akt-kmi-planet-kb* displays all of the classes within the knowledge base – note that the majority of the classes are inherited from the ontologies used by *akt-kmi-planet-kb*.

The user now enters a markup phase. In Figure 13-3, the user has selected the story "Lord Rooker discusses community impact of KMi" to mark up. He/She adds an entry to mark Lord Rooker as the visitor with the following simple steps:

- selcct the slot visitor,
- highlight the text "Rt Hon Lord Rooker" and
- double-click on the slot

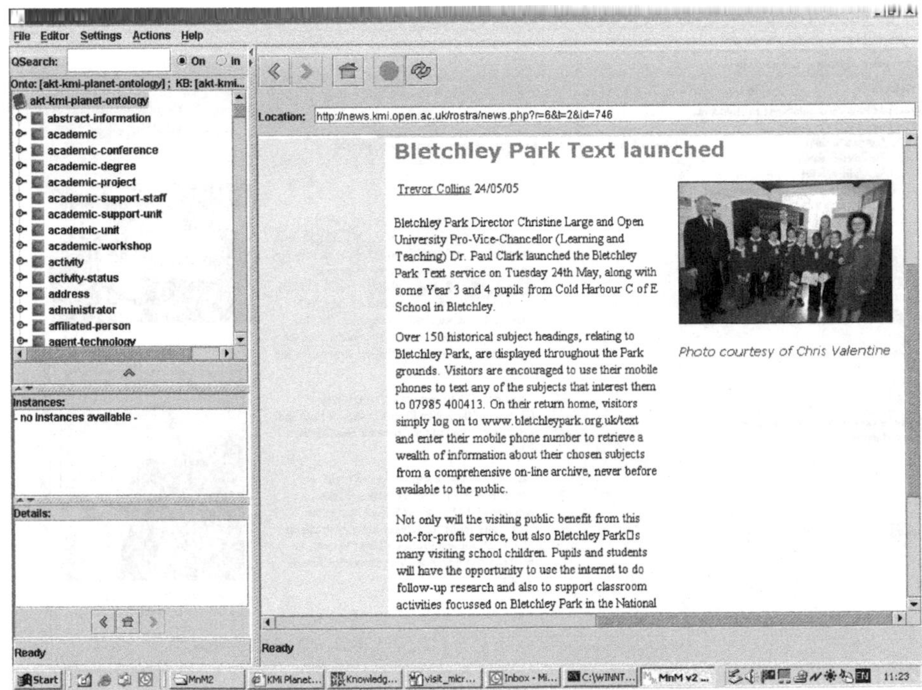

Figure 13-2. A screen snapshot showing a user browsing and selecting the library of knowledge models held on the WebOnto server

Moreover, in the example in Figure 13-3, KMi is the place visited. The XML tags <vapop_visitor> and </vapop_visitor> are inserted into the page around the mention of Lord Rooker. The tag is derived by abbreviating *visiting-a-place-or-people* to vapop plus appending a slot name, in this case -visitor. In the same way, <vapop_peopleororganizationbeingvisited> is added to the text around "KMi". The user continues to mark up a number of visit event news articles in a similar fashion before moving into the learn phase. It is possible to reuse annotated news articles. This might be important if we want to use the training set for a different extraction purpose (i.e. we might want to add or remove tags).

The user initiates the learning phase of the information extraction mechanism to produce rules for visit news articles by specifying the location of the corpus of marked up visit news articles and selecting the 'Learn' button from the "Actions menu''. At this stage, Amilcare learns rules for the event *visiting-a-place-or-people* by analyzing the user's manual markup.

During the extraction phase, the user selects a set of rules and the input set of documents. The input set can either be a directory on the local disk or a URL pointing to a directory of documents. In our example, the user has selected a local directory containing a set of planet news articles.

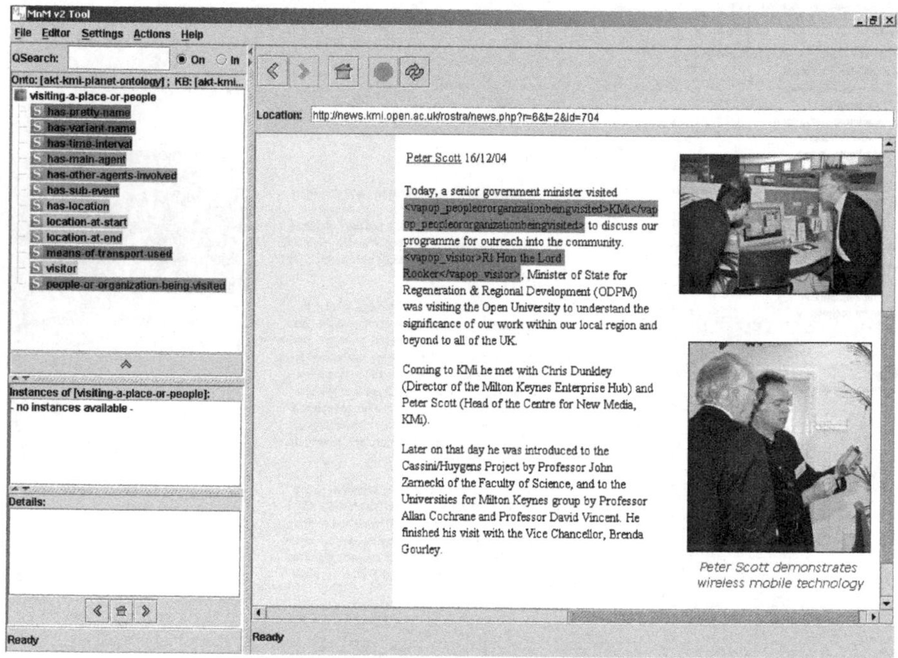

Figure 13-3. A screen snapshot showing a marked-up KMi Planet article

In Figure 13-4 below, Amilcare has finished extracting instances from the input set and the user is checking the created instances. In the top left panel the user has selected one of the articles in the test set. The bottom left panel shows the instance slot values extracted and the web browser on the right shows the source KMi Planet news article with the matched text segments highlighted. This view enables the user to quickly determine if the extracted data is correct. Moreover, Figure 13-4 shows that Amilcare can work on HTML documents.

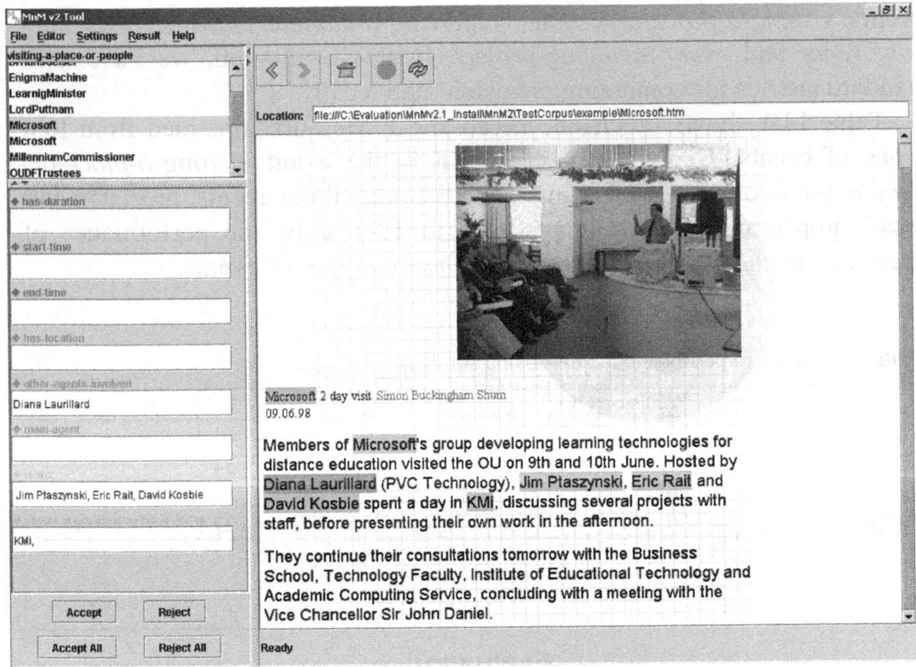

Figure 13-4. A screen snapshot showing the result of the extraction phase

6. EVALUATION

Evaluation has been done using two information extraction engines. Section 6.1 gives an evaluation using Amilcare and section 6.2 presents an evaluation using Crystal, Badger and Marmot.

6.1 Evaluation using Amilcare

MnM using Amilcare (as information extraction engine) was tested using an electronic archive consisting of news articles. The corpus for our experiment were the 200 *KMi Planet* news articles illustrated earlier (section 3.2 and Figures 13-4). A training phase was performed using 4 events: *visiting-a-place-or-people*, *conferring-a-monetary-award*, *academic-conference* and *event-involving-project.* In this evaluation, we have used standard metrics for computing precision[6] and recall[7].

Table 13-1 shows Precision, Recall and F-Measure[8] obtained from four types of events. Experiments show that in the event *visiting-a-place-or-people*, precision was good whilst with the other three events, precision and recall drop dramatically. Figures 13-5 to 13-7 show the performance of Precision, Recall and F-Measure across the four types of events.

Table 13-1. MnM Experimental Results Using Amilcare

Event	Precision (%)	Recall (%)	F-Measure
Visiting	83	40	61.5
Award	75	33	54
Conference	66	7	36.5
Project	50	5	27.5

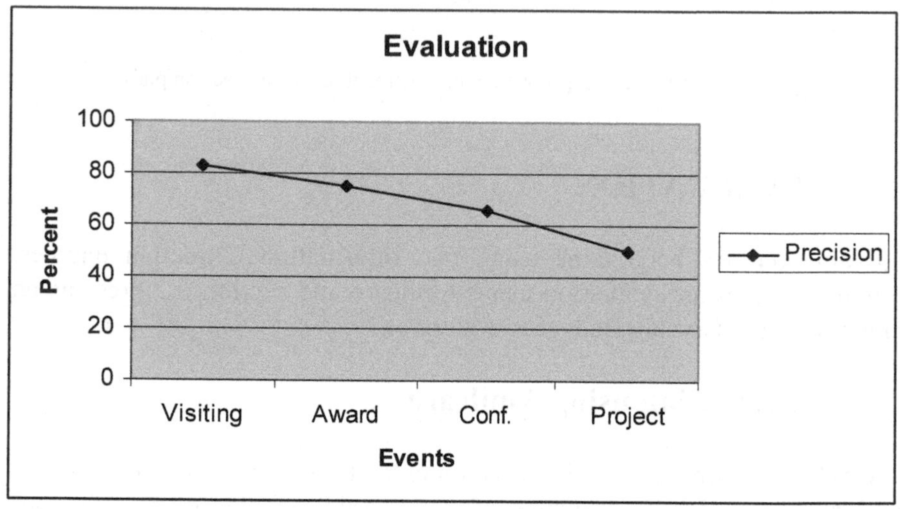

Figure 13-5. Precision for the four types of events

6 Precision was estimated as number of items correctly extracted divided by total number of items extracted by the system.

7 Recall was estimated as number of items correctly extracted divided by total number of items needed to be extracted by the system.

8 F-measure was estimated as $(b^2 + 1)$Precision*Recall divided by (b^2 * Precision + Recall) where b=0.5 means recall is half as important as precision.

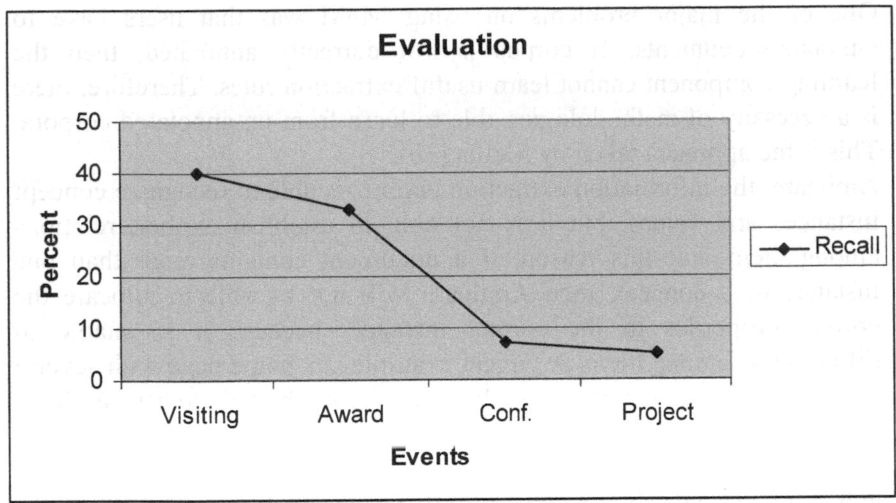

Figure 13-6. Recall for the four different types of events

The F-measure is shown as follows:

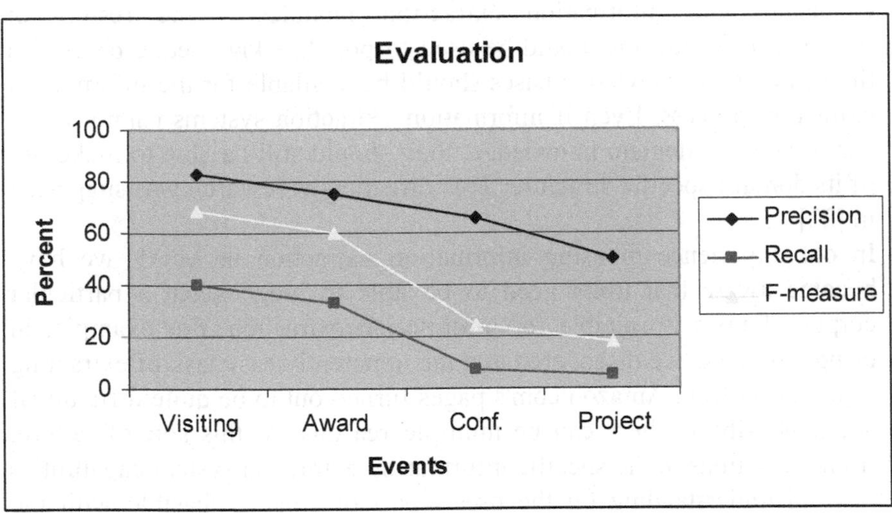

Figure 13-7. Precision, recall and F-measure

6.2 Lessons Learnt From Using Amilcare with MnM

Experience in using MnM with Amilcare suggests that the following issues need to be addressed if information extraction is to be a viable solution to the problem of populating ontologies. From our experiences using MnM, we can conclude the following points:

1. One of the major problems on using MnM was that users have to annotate documents. If corpus is not correctly annotated, then the learning component cannot learn useful extraction rules. Therefore, there is a necessity of methodologies able to learn from un-annotated corpora. This is the approach taken by Melita [36].
2. Amilcare, the information extraction engine, is able to recognize concept instances and values, but it is not able to establish explicit relations among them. For this reason, if a document contains more than one instance of a concept, then Amilcare will not be able to allocate the correct properties to the correct instance, because it is unable to differentiate among them. A typical example is a home page with several names and phone numbers. Amilcare would not be able to assign phone numbers to persons. This can be avoided by ensuring that no document has more than one instance of a concept. Ideally, however, information extraction systems should make use of concept-property structures when suggesting annotations. Since ontology contains the conceptual structure of a domain and the populated ontology contains domain specific knowledge, it would seem sensible to make use of this when performing information extraction. This suggests that there should be a two-way exchange with information extraction modules – the results of information extraction should be used to populate knowledge bases and the contents of knowledge bases should be available for the information extraction process. Even if information extraction systems cannot make use of specific domain knowledge, they should still be able to make use of its domain-specific structure. This direction of research was suggested in [22].
3. In our experience in using information extraction in MnM, we have become aware that users need to be able to judge when a particular corpus of texts is suitable for information extraction. For example, in using Amilcare, we discovered that the apparently easy task of extracting information from Amazon.com's pages turned out to be quite difficult (if not impossible). There can be multiple reasons for this sort of failure, from limitations in the specific information extraction system capabilities to a misunderstanding on the user's part of what is feasible with the existing technology. We need to investigate how to overcome this opacity problem. One solution may be to provide assistance either by training users or providing sets of guidelines which, for instance, map different information extraction modules to different types of corpus. We also need to indicate how many texts need to be marked up manually. For example, for some specific text types (e.g. free texts) a quite large number of cases is needed in order to train the information extraction system properly. Inexperienced users could think that the texts are not

suitable because they do not receive the same early feedback from the information extraction system as they have when using quite structured documents. Again, understanding why the problem arises becomes of fundamental importance for the usability of these technologies.

6.3 Evaluation using Marmot, Badger and Crystal extraction rules with confidence values

Table 13-2 and Graph 4 show Precision, Recall and F-Measure for 3 events. In this evaluation the rules generated by Crystal have associated confidence values. Experiments showed that precision can be incremented by using confidence values to the rules. When populating ontologies, precision is an important factor. Therefore, it seems that by associating confidence values it is possible to increase precision. As a remark to the reader, confidence values are generated over the training set at run time (as described in section 5).

Table 13-2. Precision Recall and F-Measure for 4 events using k-fold-cross validation

Event	Precision (%)	Recall (%)	F-Measure
Visiting	92	14	53
Award	81	3	42
Conference	67	7	37

In conclusion, we can say that it seems that k-fold-cross validation is a better choice than rules generated by Crystal without confidence values. It is important to note that the dataset was not very large. Therefore, learning from such a dataset leads to a very specific or overly generalised rule.

6.3.1 Qualitative Evaluation of UMass tools

Point 1 given in section 6.2 is also present using MnM (with UMass tools). We face the same problem that, if a corpus is not correctly annotated, then the learning component cannot learn useful extraction rules. Therefore, there is a need for methodologies able to learn from un-annotated corpora.

Point 2 defined in section 6.2 can be handled with Crystal with an extra processing to trim extraneous words from the extracted phrase. For example, in the management succession domain, Crystal would report that a PersonIn is to be found somewhere in the subject field "David Brown, Chairman and Vice-president of Motorola," without specifying which phrase is the actual PersonIn.

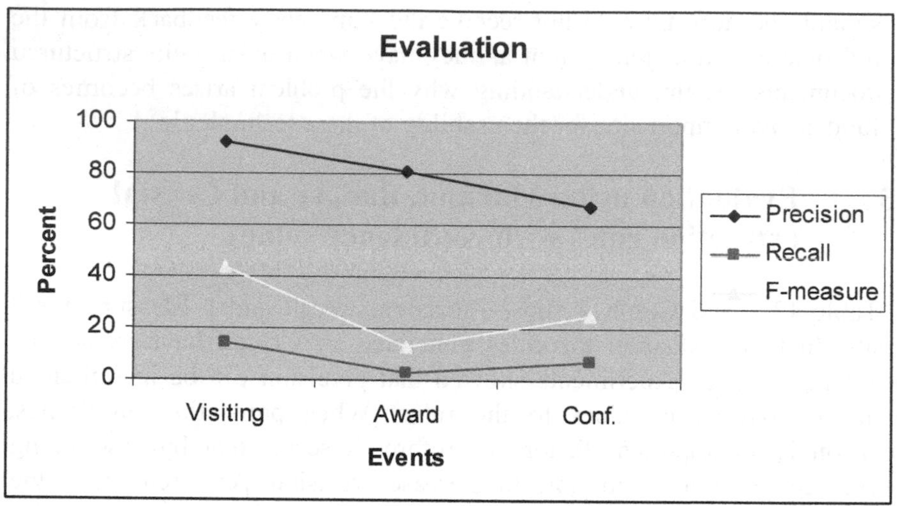

Figure 13-8. Evaluation using extraction rules with confidence values

Succession event
PersonIn: David Brown
PersonOut: John Davison
Post: president

Point 3 given in section 6.2 is also present using UMass tools. Our tool needs an advice module that can guide users during the training phase. For example, criteria specifying how many documents need to be annotated.

6.4 Comparison with other results

Comparison with similar results is problematic. There is currently no standardised methodology for evaluating Machine Learning methods for NLP systems. Moreover, performance usually varies depending on the set of documents used. Even worse, as a recent paper pointed out [37], even in the presence of a standardized evaluation methodology and the availability of standard annotated corpora, it would not be possible to guarantee that the experiments performed with different approaches and algorithms proposed in the literature can be reliably compared.

Some of the Machine Learning-wide problems causing this situation are the difficulty of exactly identifying the effects on performance of the data used (both the sample selection and the sample size), of the information sources used (the features selected and of the algorithm parameter settings [38]. The main of these issues is perhaps that of the exact split between training set and test set, considering in terms of the ratio between the two sets (e.g., a 50/50 vs. a 80/20 split) and the procedure adopted to partition the documents (e.g. *n* repeated random splits vs. *n*-fold cross validation).

In addition to these problems, comparison of our system with other systems suffers from issues specific to the evaluation of Information Extraction systems. These problems include how to deal with issues related to tokenization, how to evaluate an extracted fragment (exact criteria for matching reference instances and extracted instances), allowed number of possible answers per slot (exactly one, one or more, multiple instances) and what software was used to evaluate performance.

Given all these issues, it is apparent that – at least for the moment – any comparison of MnM with other system will not be very reliable and will be a kind of approximation. We will however attempt to outline a limited comparison, based on the results reported in the literature.

MnM integrates two information extraction engines, one of them being Crystal [19]. Soderland annotated 385 hospital discharge reports and reported an evaluation of precision and recall that is dependent on the error tolerance. When the tolerance is 0, precision is high (around 80%) but recall is around 45; however, when tolerance is 0.4, precision dips to around 60 and recalls increases by about 20 percentage points.

To compare this with MnM, we can report that we obtained 92% for the visiting event and 67% precision for the conference event (using k-fold-cross validation)[25]. However, earlier work [17] achieved 95% precision and 90% recall for the visiting event. This differential across events can be explained in terms of how well defined the visiting event is and thus how specific the patterns obtained are. On the other hand, in the case of a conference, paper titles can be nearly anything and therefore the rules generated for this event are overly generalised, leading to lower precision and recall.

7. RELATED WORK

7.1 Events-related work

Identification of events using similarity context is described in [39]. This work is different to our proposal in the sense that it does not learn patterns. Furthermore, it does not uses semantic classes to constraint the slots values of a frame (i.e. there is no constraint associated to slots agent, action, theme or dependent clause, the four slots in their frames).

In our view, the way MnM works is closer in spirit to the frame acquisition described in [40]. However, in our MnM, we are not generating case frames. Our frames are pre-defined in the selected ontology.

7.2 Related work: annotation tools

MnM is mostly used by the semantic web community who see it mainly as an annotation tool. A number of annotation tools for producing semantic markup exist. The most interesting of these are Annotea [41]; SHOE Knowledge Annotator [42]; the COHSE Mozilla Annotator [43]; AeroDAML [44]; Melita [45] and, OntoMat-Annotizer, a tool developed using the CREAM annotation framework [46].

Annotea provides RDF-based markup but does not support information extraction nor is it linked to an ontology server. It does, however, have an annotation server which makes annotations publicly available.

SHOE Knowledge Annotator allows users to mark up pages in SHOE guided by ontologies available locally or via an URL. SHOE-aware tools such as SHOE Search can query these marked up pages.

The COHSE Mozilla Annotator uses an ontology server to mark up pages in DAML. The results can be saved as RDF.

AeroDAML is available as a web page. The user simply enters a URL and the system automatically returns DAML annotations on another web page using a predefined ontology based on WordNet.

Melita adopts an approach similar to MnM in providing information extraction-based semantic annotation. Work on Melita has focused on Human Computer Interaction issues such as limiting intrusivity of the information extraction system and maximizing proactivity and timeliness in suggestions. Melita does not provide sophisticated access to the ontology, as MnM provides. In this sense Melita explores issues that are complementary to those explored in developing MnM and indeed the two approaches could be integrated.

OntoMat is closest to MnM both in spirit and in functionality. Both allow browsing of predefined ontologies as a means of annotating the web pages displayed using their HTML browsers. Both can save the annotations in the document or as a knowledge base.

8. CONCLUSION

In this chapter we have described MnM, an ontology-based annotation and ontology population tool which can be used as a component of an IS during the ontology development process and ontology maintenance phases.

MnM can be used as part of an ontology-driven IS and employs ontologies in the user interface.

MnM has now been completed and tested with both Amilcare and the UMass set of tools. The early results are encouraging in terms of the quality and robustness of our current implementation.

Evaluation proved to be problematic. In the lack of a standard evaluation methodology, we were unable to make a direct comparison of our recall and precision results to other research results. In some cases, no recall and precisions results were reported for us to compare with [39] and in others, when such results were reported and obtained using the same tools [19], they were achieved on a different corpus (different in subject area and format of the text). As recently pointed out [37], more elements need to be specified and explicitly set before the performance of two systems can be directly and reliably compared.

Finally, as far as we know, MnM has been used by several other people (from the Semantic Web community), who have only made use of part of its functionality by using it mostly as an annotation tool, not as an ontology populator.

ACKNOWLEDGEMENTS

This work was funded by the Advanced Knowledge Technologies (AKT) Interdisciplinary Research Collaboration (IRC), which is sponsored by the UK Engineering and Physical Sciences Research Council under grant number GR/N15764/01. The AKT IRC comprises the Universities of Aberdeen, Edinburgh, Sheffield, Southampton and the Open University.

REFERENCES

[1] Hicks JR. Management Information Systems: a User Perspective (3rd Ed). West, 1993.

[2] Uschold M, King M. Towards a Methodology for Building Ontologies. Workshop on Basic Ontological Issues in Knowledge Sharing. 1995.

[3] Grüninger M, Fox MS. The Role of Competency Questions in Enterprise Engineering. IFIP WG 5.7 Workshop on Benchmarking. Theory and Practice. Throndhein, Norway. 1994.

[4] Fernandez M, Gomez-Perez A, Juristo N. METHONTOLOGY: From Ontological Art to Towards Ontological Engineering. In Proceedings of AAAI97 Spring Symposium Series, Workshop on Ontological Engineering, 1997; 33-40.

[5] Domingue J. Tadzebao and WebOnto Discussing, Browsing, and Editing Ontologies on the Web. Proceedings of the 11th Banff Knowledge Acquisition Workshop, Banff, Alberta, Canada. 1998.

[6] Berners-Lee, T., Hendler, J. and Lassila, O. (2001). The Semantic Web, Scientific American, May 2001.

[7] Hayes P. RDF Model Theory, W3C Working Draft, February 2002. URL: http://www.w3.org/TR/rdf-mt/.

[8] Lassila O, Swick R. Resource Description Framework (RDF): Model and Syntax Specification. Recommendation, World Wide Web Consortium, 1999. URL: http://www.w3.org/TR/REC-rdf-syntax/.

[9] Brickley D, and Guha R. Resource Description Framework (RDF). Schema Specification 1.0. Candidate recommendation, World Wide Web Consortium, 2000. URL: http://www.w3.org/TR/2000/CR-rdf-schema-20000327.

[10] Moreale E, Vargas-Vera M. Semantic Services in E-Learning: an Argumentation Case Study. IFETS Journal Special issue Ontologies and the Semantic Web for E-learning, IEEE Educational Technology & Society Journal, Volume 7 Issue 4 October 2004.

[11] Feigenbaum E A. The art of artificial intelligence 1: Themes and case studies of knowledge engineering. Technical report, Pub. no. STAN-SC-77-621, Stanford University, Department of Computer Science. 1977.

[12] Gruber T R. A Translation Approach to Portable Ontology Specifications. Knowledge Acquisition 1993; 5(2), 199-220.

[13] McIlraith S, Son TC, Zeng H. Semantic Web Services, IEEE Intelligent Systems, Special Issue on the Semantic Web, 2001; Volume 16, No. 2, pp. 46-53.

[14] Motta E. Reusable Components for Knowledge Models. IOS Press, Amsterdam, 1999.

[15] Fensel D, Motta E. Structured Development of Problem Solving Methods. Transactions on Knowledge and Data Engineering 13(6):9131-932, 2001.

[16] Guarino N. Formal Ontology and Information Systems. Proceedings of FOIS'98, Trento, Italy, 6-8 June 1998. Amsterdam, IOS Press, 3-15.

[17] Vargas-Vera M, Motta E, Domingue J, Lanzoni M, Stutt A, Ciravegna F. MnM: Ontology Driven Semi-Automatic and Automatic Support for Semantic Markup. The 13th International Conference on Knowledge Engineering and Management (EKAW 2002), Lecture Notes in Computer Science 2473, ed Gomez-Perez, A., Springer Verlag, 2002, 379-391.

[18] Riloff E. An Empirical Study of Automated Dictionary Construction for Information Extraction in Three Domains. The AI Journal, 1996; 85, 101-134.

[19] Soderland S, Fisher D, Aseltine J, Lehnert W. Crystal: Inducing a Conceptual dictionary. Proceedings of the Fourteenth International Join Conference on Artificial Intelligence, 1995; 1314-1321.

[20] Mitchell T. Generalization as search. Artificial Intelligence, 18:203–226, 1982.

[21] Vargas-Vera M, Domingue J, Kalfoglou Y, Motta E, Buckingham-Shum S. Template-driven information extraction for populating ontologies. Proc of the IJCAI'01 Workshop on Ontology Learning, 2001, Seattle, WA, USA.

[22] Vargas-Vera M, Motta E, Domingue J, Buckingham Shum S, Lanzoni M.. Knowledge Extraction by using an Ontology-bases Annotation Tool. First International Conference on Knowledge Capture (K-CAP 2001). Workshop on Knowledge Markup and Semantic Annotation, Victoria B.C., Canada.

[23] Vargas-Vera M, Celjuska D. Ontology-Driven Event Recognition on News Stories. KMI-TR-135, Knowledge Media Institute, The Open University, 2003.

[24] Vargas-Vera M, Celjuska D. Event Recognition on News Stories and Semi-Automatic Population of an Ontology. IEEE/ACM International Joint Conference on Intelligent Agent and Web Intelligence (WI 2004), Beijing, China, September 20-24 2004, IEEE Computer Society Press, 2004.

[25] Celjuska D and Vargas-Vera M. Ontosophie: A Semi-Automatic System for Ontology Population from Text. International Conference on Natural Language Processing ICON 2004, Hyderabad, India.

[26] Ciravegna F. Adaptive Information Extraction from Text by Rule Induction and Generalisation, Proc. of 17th International Joint Conference on Artificial Intelligence (IJCAI - 2001) .

[27] Ciravegna F and Petrelli D. User Involvement in Adaptive Information Extraction: Position Paper in Proceedings of the IJCAI-2001 Workshop on Adaptive Text Extraction and Mining held in conjunction with the 17th International Conference on Artificial Intelligence (IJCAI-01).

[28] Maynard D, Tablan V, Cunningham H, Ursu C, Saggion O, Bontcheva K, Wilks Y. Architectural Elements of Language Engineering Robustness. Journal of Natural Language Engineering – Special Issue on Robust Methods in Analysis of Natural Language Data, 2002; 8:257-274.

[29] Ciravegna F. LP^2 an Adaptive Algorithm for Information Extraction from Web related Texts. Proc. of the IJCAI-2001 Workshop on Adaptive Text Extraction and Mining held in conjunction with the 17th International Conference on Artificial Intelligence (IJCAI-01).

[30] Kushmerick N, Weld D, Doorenbos R. Wrapper induction for information extraction, Proc. of 15th International Conference on Artificial Intelligence, IJCAI-97.

[31] Michalski RS, Mozetic I, Hong J, Lavrack H. The multi purpose incremental learning system AQ15 and its testing application to three medical domains, in Proceedings of the 5th National Conference on Artificial Intelligence, 1986, Philadelphia. Morgan Kaufmann publisher.

[32] Ciravegna F. Challenges in Information Extraction from Text for Knowledge Management in IEEE Intelligent Systems and Their Applications, November 2001, (Trend and Controversies).

[33] Domingue J, Scott P. KMi Planet: A Web Based News Server. Asia Pacific Computer Human Interaction Conference (APCHI'98), Shonan Village Center, Hayama-machi, Kanagawa, Japan.

[34] Domingue J, Motta E. Planet-Onto: From News Publishing to Integrated Knowledge Management Support. IEEE Intelligent Systems Special Issue on Knowledge Management and Knowledge Distribution over the Internet, May/June, 2000, 26-32. (ISSN 1094-7167).

[35] Kalfoglou Y, Domingue J, Motta E, Vargas-Vera M, Buckingham Shum S. MyPlanet: an ontology-driven Web based personalised news service. Proceedings of the IJCAI'01 workshop on Ontologies and Information Sharing, Seattle, WA, USA.

[36] Ciravegna F, Dingli A, Guthrie D, Wilks Y. Integrating Information to Bootstrap Information Extraction from Web Sites. Proceedings of the IJCAI 2003 Workshop on Information Integration on the Web, workshop in conjunction with the 18th International Joint Conference on Artificial Intelligence (IJCAI 2003). Acapulco, Mexico, August, 9-15.

[37] Lavelli A, Califf ME, Ciravegna F, Freitag D, Giuliano C, Kushmerick N, Romano L. A Critical Survey of the Methodology for IE Evaluation. In Proceedings of the AAAI-04 Workshop onAdaptive Text Extraction and Mining (ATEM-2004), San Jose, California, 26 July 2004.

[38] Daelemans W, Hoste V. Evaluation of machine learning methods for natural language processing tasks. In Proceedings of the Third International Conference on Language Resources and Evaluation (LREC 2002). Las Palmas, Spain.

[39] Jones D, Thompson C. Identifying Events using Similarity and Context, in Proceedings of the Conference on Computational Natural Language Learning, Edmonton, Canada, 2003.

[40] Riloff E, Schmelzenbach M. An Empirical Approach to Conceptual Case Frame Acquisition. Proceedings of the Sixth Workshop on Very Large Corpora , 1998.

[41] Kahan J, Koivunen M-J, Prud'Hommeaux E, Swick R. Annotea: An Open RDF Infrastructure for Shared Web Annotations. In Proc. of the 10th International World Wide Web Conference. 2001. Hong Kong.

[42] Heflin J, Hendler J. A Portrait of the Semantic Web in Action. IEEE Intelligent Systems 2001; 16(2), 54-59.

[43] Bechhofer S and Goble C. Towards Annotation Using DAML+OIL. First International Conference on Knowledge Capture (K-CAP 2001). Workshop on Semantic Markup and Annotation. Victoria, B.C., Canada. 2001.

[44] Kogut P, Holmes W. AeroDAML. Applying Information Extraction to Generate DAML Annotations from Web Pages. First International Conference on Knowledge Capture (K-CAP 2001). Workshop on Knowledge Markup and Semantic Annotation, Victoria, B.C., Canada.

[45] Ciravegna F, Dingli A, Petrelli D, Wilks Y. User-System Cooperation in Document Annotation based on Information Extraction. Proceedings of the 13th International Conference on Knowledge Engineering and Knowledge Management, EKAW02, Springer Verlag. 2002.

[46] Handschuh S, Staab S, Maedche A. CREAM – Creating relational metadata with a component-based, ontology-driven annotation framework. First International Conference on Knowledge Capture (K-CAP 2001).

Chapter 14

AN ONTOLOGICAL APPROACH TO REQUIREMENTS ELICITATION TECHNIQUE SELECTION

Ann M. Hickey and Alan M. Davis

University of Colorado at Colorado Spring, 1420 Austin Bluffs Parkway, P.O. Box 7150, Colorado Springs, CO 80933-7150

Abstract: Too many systems constructed by the software industry fail to meet users' needs. Requirements elicitation is the set of activities performed to understand users' needs for a system. Although most texts focus on a few elicitation techniques, there are numerous variations of these basic techniques. So, the question arises, how can an analyst understand all these techniques and their variations? Moreover, most experts today agree that the selection of an appropriate technique must be a function of the situation. But, a seemingly infinite number of situational characteristics exist. So, how can an analyst know which of these many situational characteristics should be taken into account when trying to select elicitation techniques? And, how does an analyst select a technique that makes sense given those situational characteristics?

The overarching goal of this research is to construct an information system to aid novice analysts in selecting the most effective requirements elicitation techniques for their project situation. Fundamental to the success of this endeavor is the creation of an ontology which: (1) sets the context for requirements elicitation and elicitation technique selection; (2) defines key characteristics of elicitation techniques that highlight their essential similarities and differences; and (3) identifies the important characteristics of a situation that should be considered when selecting an elicitation technique. This chapter describes the iterative ontology engineering approach used, summarizes the proposed requirements elicitation ontology, and demonstrates how the ontology will be used as a basis for an information system to assist analysts in selecting an appropriate elicitation technique. As a result, this chapter, rather than focusing on ontology research per se, focuses on the application of ontologies to improve the state of research and practice in one specific information systems discipline – requirements elicitation.

Key words: Requirements engineering; Elicitation; Systems analysis; Ontology

1. INTRODUCTION

More than half the systems constructed by the software industry fail to meet users' expectations (Standish, 1995), often because developers do not understand users' needs (Hofmann and Lehner, 2001). Requirements elicitation (aka systems analysis[1]) is the set of activities performed with the primary goal of understanding users' needs, i.e., the requirements for a system (Thayer and Dorfman, 1994). The ultimate quality of a product is driven by the quality of the requirements gathered by the analysts during elicitation which in turn is directly impacted by effectiveness of the elicitation process and the appropriateness of the techniques used during that process (Hickey and Davis, 2002). Although most recent requirements books (Davis, 2005; Gottesdiener, 2002; Leffingwell and Widrig, 2000; Macaulay, 1996; Wiegers, 2003) describe a dozen or so primary approaches, there are actually hundreds, and perhaps thousands, of variations of alternative elicitation techniques. But many analysts seem to know and use just a few of these techniques (Hickey et al., 2003). So, the question arises, how can an analyst understand all these techniques and their variations? Moreover, while proponents of many elicitation techniques claim that their techniques are universally applicable in all situations; most experts today agree that the selection of an appropriate technique must be a function of the situation (Glass, 2002; Kotonya, 1998; Maiden and Rugg, 1996). But, a seemingly infinite number of situational characteristics exist. So, how can an analyst know which of these many situational characteristics should be taken into account when trying to decide which elicitation technique would make the most sense? And, how does an analyst select a technique that makes sense given those situational characteristics?

The primary goal of this research is to construct an information system to aid novice analysts in selecting the most effective requirements elicitation techniques for their project situation. While often thought to just focus on more traditional, structural (e.g., data modeling) issues, the emerging field of ontology-driven information systems also offers potential in "the temporal (i.e., development and operation processes) dimensions of IS" which can form the basis of more "effective and efficient conceptual analysis and design processes" (Kishore et al., 2004c, p69). Therefore, the goal of the research reported in this chapter is to develop an ontology and explore how well it supports requirements elicitation and elicitation technique selection.

[1] There is much agreement in the industry concerning the need to better understand user needs, but little uniformity concerning what to call the activity. The IS industry calls it systems analysis, problem analysis, business analysis, or just plain analysis. The engineering community calls it requirements analysis, elicitation, knowledge engineering, or requirements engineering. In this chapter, we use the word elicitation.

2. BACKGROUND

The application domain of this research is requirements elicitation. Before exploring the development of ontology to support requirements elicitation, it is important to ensure that all readers have at least a basic understanding of the domain. Therefore, this section provides a brief introduction to requirements management in general and the role of requirements elicitation in that management process.

If requirements are the externally observable characteristics of a desired system, then requirements management (aka requirements engineering) is the set of activities of determining the requirements (i.e., performing elicitation), deciding which are the "right" ones to satisfy (i.e., performing triage), and documenting them (i.e., performing specification) (Davis, 2005). These three components are not sequential, but instead are symbiotic and performed iteratively and concurrently, with the results of each component feeding subsequent iterations of that component and the others as shown in Figure 14-1.

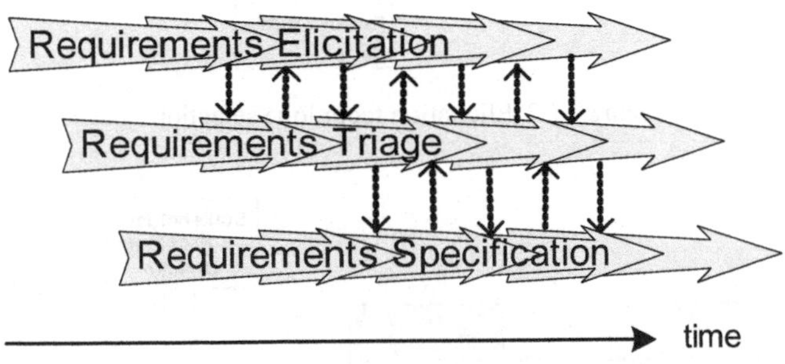

Figure 14-1. Concurrency of requirements activities

Myriad techniques are available to support each of the three activities, for example,

- Elicitation techniques include interviewing, questionnaires, observation, and collaborative workshops, to name but a few.
- Triage techniques include WinWin, prioritization, balancing candidate requirements against schedules and cost, and so on.
- Specification techniques include natural language, standards-adherence, finite state machines, use cases, and data flow diagrams, to name a few.

And yet, few of the above listed techniques can be characterized as solely for just one activity. It is easy to imagine how an analyst could use any of the so called specification techniques for elicitation, e.g., an analyst could ask a potential customer, "does this model describe your needs?" In the current research, we consider most techniques suitable for any requirements activity as a candidate technique for requirements elicitation if it can aid in the discovery of requirements. However, not all techniques may be appropriate in all situations. In particular, every situation demands an elicitation technique that is appropriate for that situation, as shown in Figure 14-2. More specifically, it is the match between the situation and the specific attributes of an elicitation technique which makes that technique appropriate for that situation, as shown in Figure 14-3.

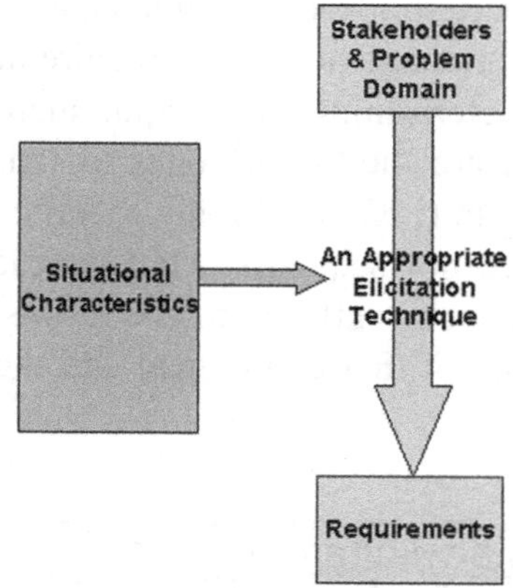

Figure 14-2. Elicitation technique selection

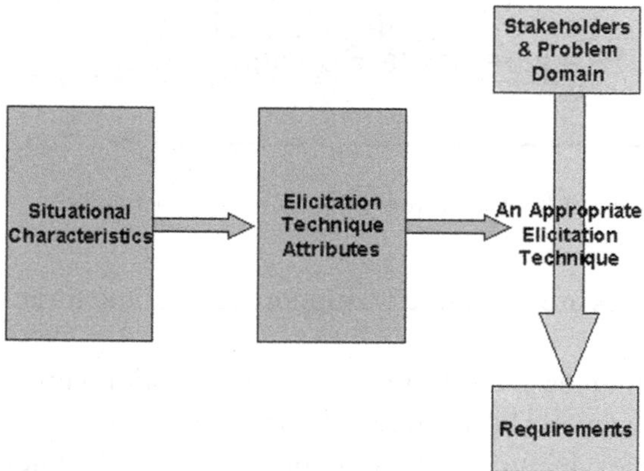

Figure 14-3. Selection based on technique characteristics

Therefore, to select an appropriate elicitation technique, an analyst must first understand what techniques are available, and how they are different or similar. To this end, we created an ontology that defines key characteristics of elicitation techniques, so they can be understood, compared and contrasted. This ontology can then be used to assign clear semantics to the wide range of current elicitation techniques and help all analysts understand, for example, if there are or are not any significant differences between Joint Application Design (JAD) sessions (Wood and Silver, 1995) and the other collaborative or facilitated requirements workshops described by many authors (e.g., (Gottesdiener, 2002; Macaulay, 1996; Robertson and Robertson, 1999)). Given the explosion of possible elicitation techniques, some of which may vary in name only, this ability will be extremely valuable for even the most experienced analysts by increasing awareness and aiding comparison of new techniques. It will also help reduce the "information overload" of less experienced analysts when presented with extensive lists of techniques.

To know which technique to select, one needs to understand what characteristics of a situation are important. While experienced analysts seem to intuitively sense which characteristics are critical in a given situation, less experienced analysts need assistance in identifying key situational characteristics. These situational characteristics were represented in a second ontology, one of characteristics of the domain (Liebowitz, 2001). The situational characteristics used in this ontology are those that are relevant to selection of elicitation techniques.

The two ontologies were later integrated into a single, requirements elicitation ontology to enhance understanding of the requirements elicitation process and facilitate development of an information system to help inexperienced or novice analysts select elicitation techniques for their projects. This chapter reports the iterative development and evaluation of the usefulness of these ontologies for the selection of appropriate elicitation techniques.

3. RESEARCH APPROACH & METHOD

3.1 Research Overview

As stated in the introduction, the overarching goal of this research is to construct an information system to aid analysts, especially novice and other less-experienced analysts, in selecting the most effective requirements elicitation techniques for their project situation. Fundamental to the success of this research is the development of requirements elicitation ontology focused on elicitation technique selection. The purpose of this chapter is to continue the research begun in Hickey and Davis (2003a) and address the following research questions:

- Does the proposed ontology assign clear semantics to currently available requirements elicitation techniques and identify those characteristics of the techniques that are important for effective elicitation technique selection?

- Does the proposed ontology identify those characteristics of a situation that are most important for effective elicitation technique selection?
- Does the proposed ontology support identification of how the characteristics of the situation interact with the characteristics of the techniques to drive effective elicitation technique selection, and ultimately, more effective elicitation?

Numerous authors broadly characterize elicitation techniques. For example, Lauesen (2002) characterizes elicitation techniques with an ontology based on outputs the techniques produce. Gottesdiener (2002) organizes elicitation techniques in terms of top-down/bottom-up, and the underlying models produced as a result of applying the technique. Macauley (1996) provides a long list of elicitation techniques and describes each in terms of its characteristics, but falls short of defining an ontological basis. Byrd et al. (1992) characterize elicitation techniques based on communications obstacles, facilities, and the controller of the process.

Similarly, a few authors have studied characteristics of situations that drive elicitation technique selection. For example, Bento (1994) defines a simple three-dimensional ontology consisting of the need to understand the broadness of the problem, wickedness of the problem, and relative task vs. decision emphasis in the problem domain. Maciaszek (2001) presents a model of the influences that affect the success of requirements elicitation. Maiden and Rugg (1996) provide a framework for elicitation technique selection consisting of six facets.

Our research stands on the shoulders of the above research efforts to create a more complete ontology necessary for elicitation technique selection. We are following the research approach shown in Figure 14-4. (Note: The emphasized (bold) research tasks and links are directly related to the development of the requirements elicitation ontology – the focus of this chapter.)

We have completed tasks 1-4, creating a unified model of requirements elicitation (Hickey and Davis, 2004) and draft versions of separate ontologies for technique and situational characteristics and their interrelationships (Hickey and Davis, 2003a). This chapter summarizes the results of those tasks as well as those of task 5, where we have integrated our model and the two draft ontologies into a single ontology focused on elicitation technique selection. We are currently in the process of interviewing expert elicitors (task 6), and thus far have completed interviews with Grady Booch, Alistair Cockburn, Larry Constantine, Tom DeMarco, Donald Gause, Soren Lausen, Tim Lister, Lucy Lockwood, Shari Lawrence Pfleeger, Neil Maiden, Reifer, James Robertson, Suzanne Robertson, Karl

Wiegers, Edward Yourdon, and Didar Zowghi (see (Hickey and Davis, 2003b) for preliminary interview results). As we complete interviews with these experts, we continue to revise our integrated ontology (task 7) and the mapping between the elicitation technique and situational characteristics included in that ontology (task 8). During task 9, we will validate our findings and implement our results in a tool that can be used by less experienced analysts to assist them in selecting the 'right' elicitation technique for their situation.

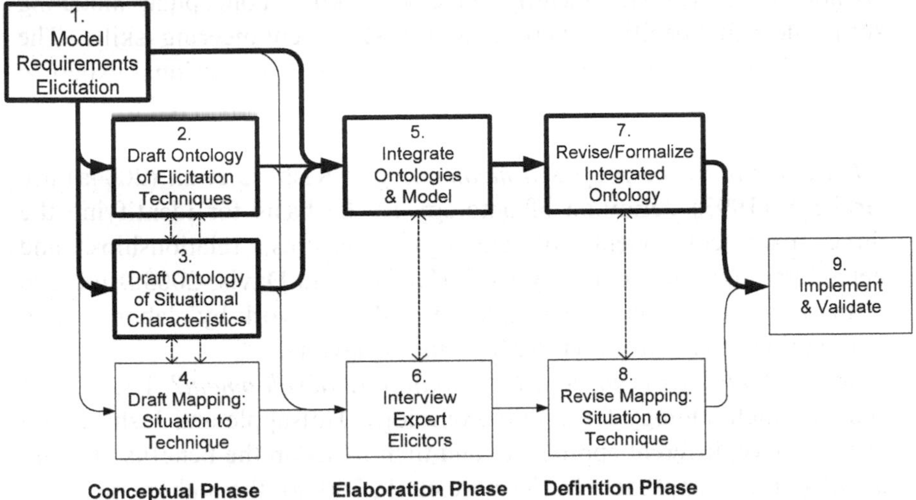

Figure 14-4. Research approach

This overall research approach directly aligns with the conceptual (tasks 1-4), elaboration (tasks 5-6), and definition (tasks 7-9) phases of the Helix-Spindle Model for ontological engineering (Kishore et al., 2004c) as shown in Figure 14-4 and described in more detail in the next section.

3.2 Ontological Engineering

Ontological engineering "refers to the set of activities that concern the ontology development process, the ontology life cycle, and the methodologies, tools and languages for building ontologies" (Gomez-Perez et al., 2004, p5). Kishore et al. (2004a) define some fundamental questions that must be answered as the first step in ontological engineering. These questions and our answers are as follows:

1. *What is the purpose for which ontology is needed?* The primary purpose of the ontology is to improve understanding of requirements elicitation and elicitation technique selection. More specifically, the ontology will

provide a language for capturing and providing guidance on elicitation technique selection to novice analysts. Additionally, it will enable requirements researchers and practitioners to more crisply define and understand the subtle differences between alternative elicitation techniques. As such, the proposed ontology would generally be classified as a domain ontology, or, more specifically, as a task ontology providing "terms specific for particular tasks" and a "reasoning point of view on domain knowledge" (Fensel, 2004, pp. 5-6).

2. *What skills are needed in conceptualizing and building the ontology?* Kishore et al. (2004a) identify three key skills: conceptual modeling skills, domain-specific expertise, and systems engineering skills. The authors have over 25 years each of academic and professional expertise in all three of these skill areas and are therefore well-prepared to take the lead in developing the proposed ontology.
3. *What constitutes the proposed methodology?* Kishore et al. (2004a) use Gruber's (1993) definition of ontology as the basis for identifying the three main components of ontology: concepts, relationships, and behaviors. Our early ontology work (Hickey and Davis, 2003a) focused primarily on concepts. This chapter extends that work by elaborating on our ontology to include relationships and behaviors.
4. *What methodology is to be used in ontology development?* There is no standard methodology for building ontology. Holsapple and Joshi (2002) describe five different approaches and then focus on the benefits of using a collaborative approach. In (Kishore et al., 2004a), the authors discuss a Cue-N-Anchor guided strategy for constructing ontology. However, their Helix-Spindle Model (Kishore et al., 2004c) seems a better fit for this research, as described below.

Just like software development today, successful development of ontology is an iterative and incremental process. In fact, many authors (e.g., (Kishore et al., 2004a)) recognize that ontology is never complete or final. As a result, the ontological engineering methodology chosen should reflect this sort of iterative development process, which interleaves ontology building and testing phases, each of which increases the maturity/completeness (and formality) of the ontology. The Helix-Spindle Model for ontological engineering (Kishore et al., 2004c) provides such an approach and was used to guide development of our Requirements Elicitation Ontology. The Helix-Spindle Model has three phases:

1. Conceptual Phase. In this phase, the initial ontology is built based on existing content and foundation theories, represented informally (e.g., natural language), and then tested for adequacy by actually using the ontology within its application domain. For our research, the initial conceptual ontology of elicitation techniques (task 2) was derived from

the aforementioned works of Lauesen (2002), Gottesdiener (2002), Macauley (1996), and Byrd et al. (1992), selected textbooks (e.g., Conger, 1994; Dennis and Haley Wixom, 2000; Hoffer et al., 2002), as well as our own personal experience. The initial conceptual ontology of situational characteristics (task 3) was derived from the aforementioned works of Bento (1994), Maciaszek (2001), and Maiden and Rugg (1996) as well as criteria influencing life-cycle model selection from Alexander and Davis (1991), multipliers influencing cost estimation from Boehm et al. (2000), factors influencing requirements approaches from Davis (1993), factors influencing software engineering experimental design from Juristo and Moreno (2001), characteristics influencing the definability of a system from Scharer (1981), problems in deriving needs from Yeh and Ng (1990), as well as our own personal experience. The ontologies were represented using a faceted classification described using natural language. They were tested by representing sample elicitation techniques using the technique ontology. We also constructed the initial mappings from the situational characteristic ontology to the elicitation technique ontology (task 4) based on our own experiences and the limited guidance available from the above references. Results of the Conceptual Phase were first reported in (Hickey and Davis, 2003a) and are summarized in Section 4 of this chapter.

2. Elaboration Phase. During this phase, the ontology is refined based on the testing results from the previous phase and/or additional content theories/information; represented using a semi-formal notation (e.g., UML or Ontolingua); and then retested. For our research, the ontology was refined based on testing results from the first phase and initial results of interviews with experts (task 6). We also integrated the elicitation technique and situational characteristic ontologies into a single, integrated ontology representing both the requirements elicitation and elicitation technique selection processes. Results of previous research to create a mathematical model of these processes (Hickey and Davis, 2004) provided the foundational theory for these portions of the ontology. UML was chosen as the representation notation because of its recognition and acceptability as a semi-formal notation by the ontology community (Kishore et al., 2004b; Gomez-Perez, 2004) and as the standard object-oriented modeling notation by the software development community. The refined ontology was tested using the results of additional expert interviews and by a more detailed mapping between elicitation technique and situational characteristics. Results of the Elaboration Phase are reported in Section 5 of this chapter.
3. Definition Phase. It is during this phase that the complete ontology is formally defined using a rigorous, formal notation (e.g., predicate logic).

For our research, formal definition of the complete ontology will be addressed as part of tasks 7-9. The final representation will be chosen to match the implementation environment. Testing and refinement will continue as we validate the implementation. See section 6.2 for an overview of future research related to this phase.

4. CONCEPTUAL PHASE RESULTS

During the conceptual phase, existing foundational knowledge and theories were used to develop two separate ontologies. The first, described in detail in section 4.1, was designed to help analysts understand what elicitation techniques are available, their key characteristics, and how they are different/similar. This ontology is a multi-faceted classification represented as a vector that can then be used to assign clear semantics to the wide range of current elicitation techniques and is designed such that if two techniques are suitable in similar situations, they will be located close to each other within the ontology vector space. To know which vector to select from the technique ontology's vector space, the analyst needs to understand what characteristics of a situation are important. These situational characteristics are represented in a second ontology, one of characteristics of the domain (Liebowitz, 2001). The situational characteristics used in this ontology are those that are relevant to the selection of elicitation techniques. This situational ontology is described in section 4.3. Testing results are reported in sections 4.2 and 4.4.

4.1 Building the Conceptual Elicitation Technique Ontology

The conceptual foundations for the initial elicitation technique ontology are described in the previous section. The ontology developed from these foundations is driven by an attribute vector that locates each technique in a multi-dimensional vector space. The techniques are organized so that any two techniques that are equally applicable in all situations are clustered very closely together in the overall vector space. The vector space includes the following ten dimensions:

- *Physical Co-Location.* This attribute has two possible values: "same place" and "different place." It captures whether or not the technique demands that participating parties be located at the same physical location, e.g., in the same room. We call the value of this attribute PHYS.
- *Temporal Co-Location.* This attribute has two possible values: "same time" and "different time." It captures whether or not the technique

demands that participants collaborate at the same time. We call the value of this attribute TEMP.

- *Record-Keeper*. This attribute has three possible values: "individuals," "analyst," and "no record." It captures whether the results of the elicitation event are recorded for the future by every individual contributor, or by the analyst, or by no one. We call the value of this attribute RECO.
- *Analyst Role*. This attribute has three possible values: "passive," "facilitate," and "lead/direct." Passive indicates that the analyst is observing the elicitation event, but is not participating directly in it. Facilitate indicates that the analyst is aiding the event, helping to ensure that it has positive results. Lead/direct indicates that the analyst drives the activity. We call the value of this attribute ANAL.
- *Convergence/Divergence*. This attribute has two possible values: "convergent" and "divergent." Divergent techniques create new ideas; convergent techniques group, filter, or rank ideas. We call the value of this attribute CONV.
- *Anonymity*. This attribute has two possible values: "anonymous" and "public." Techniques that are anonymous protect each participant from other participants knowing which ideas they generated. Public techniques allow participants to know who generates which ideas. We call the value of this attribute ANON.
- *Stakeholder Count*. This attribute has four possible values: "many," "few," "one," and "none." It captures the number of stakeholder classes involved. A stakeholder class is one or more stakeholders representing identical opinions. We call the value of this attribute STAK.
- *Tool Based*. This attribute has two possible values: "tool" and "no tool." It captures whether the technique requires the use of a software tool. We call the value of this attribute TOOL.
- *Product/Human Focus*. This attribute has two possible values: "product" and "human." It captures the fact that some techniques focus on identifying the requirements for the "product" that solve the users' problems, while other, socio-technical approaches assume that requirements emerge as a result of the interactions between humans (stakeholders and analysts) in a situational context (Coughlan and Macredie, 2002). We call the value of this attribute FOCU.
- *Direct/Indirect*. This attribute has two possible values: "direct" and "indirect." It captures the fact that some elicitation techniques are performed to directly elicit needs (direct), whereas other techniques (e.g., team-building exercises) are performed to alter the situation to make it more conducive to elicit needs. We call the value of the attribute DIRE.

Any attribute may also have a value of "don't care," represented by a "—" in the following examples, indicating that the attribute is not significant or can take on any of the possible attribute values.

We can thus represent any elicitation technique by its attribute vector: (PHYS, TEMP, RECO, ANAL, CONV, ANON, STAK, TOOL, FOCU, DIRE).

4.2 Testing the Conceptual Elicitation Technique Ontology

The elicitation technique ontology was tested by evaluating its ability to accurately represent existing elicitation techniques. Let's look at how these attributes map for some representative techniques.

- *Interview a Single Customer Face-to-Face* (Gause and Weinberg, 1989). The values for the attribute vector are (same place, same time, analyst, lead/direct, —, public, one, no tool, —, direct).
- *Conduct a Distributed Brainstorming Session Where Nobody Knows Who Else Is Involved* (Romano et al., 1999). The values are (different place, same time, individuals, facilitate, divergent, anonymous, many, tool, product, direct).
- *Perform a Demographical Market Analysis* (Higgins, 2003; Schewe and Hiam, 1998). The values are (different place, different time, individuals, passive, divergent, anonymous, many, no tool, product, direct).
- *Observe a Few Stakeholders* (Goguen and Linde, 1993). The values are (same place, same time, analyst, passive, divergent, —, few, no tool, human, direct).
- *Do a Group-Voting Session in One Room Where Voting is Anonymous* (Nunamaker et al., 1991). The values are (same place, same time, individuals, facilitate, convergent, anonymous, —, tool, product, direct).
- *Use Soft Systems Methodology* (Checkland and Scholes, 1991). The values are (same place, same time, individuals, facilitate, —, public, many, no tool, human, direct).
- *Do a Team-Building Exercise.* The values are (same place, same time, —, —, —, public, —, —, human, indirect).
- *Use a Bulletin Board.* The values are (different place, different time, individuals, —, divergent, —, many, tool, product, direct).

Theoretically, the vector space contains 3,456 discrete vectors, and thus could be used to categorize that many techniques. However, there are two observations that make this incorrect: First, many techniques are incredibly similar, often with just different names being applied to the same approach. In these cases, the techniques coexist in the same vector space. Second, we have found some vectors to be meaningless. For example, (same place, different time, —, —, —, —, —, —, —, —) could represent a message board physically located in one location, but does not correspond to any known elicitation techniques. Similarly, (same place, same time, analyst, —, —, anonymous, many, no tool, —, —) makes no sense because if the stakeholders are all co-located and the analyst is recording everybody's ideas without a tool, then obviously the stakeholders are stating their ideas aloud, and there is no way to preserve anonymity.

Finally, as shown in Figure 14-4, this ontology will be revised, integrated with the situational characteristic ontology, and validated as we continue our interviews with experts to ensure that we include all dimensions in the ontology that differentiate techniques based on their appropriateness in various situations. Therefore, we do not claim that the taxonomy created during the Conceptual Phase is complete. However, we can claim that it does identify ten of the key dimensions that differentiate the large number of available elicitation techniques and that are critical in selecting techniques for specific situations, as discussed next.

4.3 Building the Conceptual Ontology of Situational Characteristics

The characteristics of the immediate situation determine which values for which elicitation technique attributes are applicable for that situation. Relevant situational characteristics were derived from the literature as described in the previous sections and fall into five broad categories. Techniques should be selected based on:

- *Characteristics of the Problem Domain.* Inherent characteristics of the problem, including the fuzziness of its definition (FUZZ), its complexity (CPLX), the existence of conflicting needs (CNFL), the maturity of the application (MATU), and the importance of non-functional requirements such as security (SECU), response time (RESP), safety (SAFE) and reliability (RELI), have a major impact on the techniques that should be used. Thus, for example, a totally new, unprecedented application may require more extensive use of divergent techniques, but an upgrade of a well-established legacy application would not. A problem for which a fast response time becomes life-critical may necessitate different, possibly more formal, elicitation techniques than one that has no deleterious effect.
- *Characteristics of the Solution Domain.* Similarly, the type of solution anticipated (e.g., application vs. system vs. embedded software (TYPE), custom development vs. customizing vs. commercial-off-the-shelf software (COTS)) may also impact the selection of elicitation techniques. An embedded system may demand different elicitation approaches than a

software-only system. Planning to purchase (OUTS) vs. build in-house may also make a difference.

- *Characteristics of the Stakeholders.* Inherent characteristics of all the people involved in a software development project, especially the stakeholders (e.g., customer, users, other sources of needs), are major drivers of the selection of appropriate elicitation techniques. The number of different stakeholders and stakeholder roles (#STK) directly impacts whether individual techniques such as interviews can be used virtually exclusively or various collaborative meeting or mass contact (e.g., questionnaires) should be considered. If the stakeholders are novices (STEX) in the application domain or in the use of similar applications they may have a hard time articulating their requirements, so techniques that facilitate that process such as prototyping may be appropriate. If the situation is such that your customers are major competitors of each other (STCM), then only a technique that enforces anonymity is appropriate. Other key questions that may impact the selection of an elicitation technique include: Do the key stakeholders get along with each other (STCP)? Can the stakeholders travel to a common location (STTV)? Are they accessible (STAC)? Do the stakeholders speak with one voice, or do they represent many different roles with quite different needs (STDV)?
- *Characteristics of the Solution Builders.* The knowledge and expertise of the system builders may also impact the selection of elicitation techniques. For example, if the system builders are experts in the problem and solution domains (SOEX), then elicitation techniques that record requirements using problem domain terminology may be appropriate. Their communication skills (SOCO), software development experience (SOSW) and knowledge of specific tools (SOTO) and techniques may also be factors that should be considered.
- *Characteristics of the Bridge-Builders.* Bridge-builders are the individuals who serve as the communication conduit (or bridge) between stakeholders and solution builders. Bridge-builders may be systems analysts, requirements engineers or any individual from the user or developer side of the project assigned to perform this role. Experience has shown that quality bridge-builders are critical to the success of requirements elicitation. Therefore, the match between the characteristics of the bridge-builders and the elicitation techniques used is essential. These characteristics include experience in the problem domain and application type (BBEX), knowledge and experience with specific elicitation techniques (BBTE), and communication/facilitation negotiation skills (BBCO). For example, if bridge-builders have limited experience in a domain, they should initially focus on techniques such as interviews with key stakeholders and/or document reviews that enable

them to develop their domain knowledge. If they have little or no experience facilitating a group meeting, then a group meeting may not be appropriate. One very interesting observation from the expert interviews we have conducted so far is the importance of the bridge-builders experience with a specific technique. We had assumed that inherent characteristics of the technique were the primary driver in its appropriateness for a specific situation. However, our interviews showed us that a moderately good technique for a specific situation in the hands of an experienced "master" can become an ideal technique for that situation, because of the expert's ability to mold the technique to the situation. Thus, masters in specific techniques tend to rely on their favorite technique except under special situational circumstances. However, for less experienced analysts, this approach may lead to disaster because they simply do not have the skills required to adapt the technique to those situations for which it is not a "good fit."

We have isolated over fifty situational characteristics that could influence the decision to select one or more elicitation techniques. As mentioned before, many of these have been adapted from situational characteristics specified for other purposes. We are using our expert interviews (Figure 14-4, task 6) to identify which of those characteristics are the primary drivers for technique selection. We are 75% done with the process of interviewing many of the world's experts in systems analysis to improve our understanding of how situations affect the elicitation techniques they chose to utilize. Without exception to date, we have found that these experts are not *consciously* analyzing situational characteristics to select the technique. However, when we ask questions like "what would you have done if" the situation was slightly different; the experts invariably say they would have selected an alternative approach. Thus, we are receiving consistent evidence that the selection process is in fact situational.

4.4 Testing the Conceptual Ontologies: Mapping from Situational Characteristics to Elicitation Techniques

Testing of the ontologies developed during the conceptual phase primarily focused on the ontologies' ability to support the mapping of characteristics of the situation to appropriate characteristics of the elicitation techniques. The initial mapping was created as part of task 4 of our overall research approach (see Figure 14-4). In general, it is the complete set of situational characteristics that imply the suitability of a set of elicitation techniques. However, some values for some characteristics may be sufficient by themselves to imply such suitability. We captured the initial mapping in a series of cascading tables. Entries in these tables can be any of the following:

- *NO*. The techniques that possess *these* characteristics are incompatible with situations that possess *those* characteristics.
- *OK*. The techniques that possess *these* characteristics are compatible with situations that possess *those* characteristics.
- *HI*. The techniques that possess *these* characteristics are strongly suggested in cases where *those* situational characteristics exist.

There are so many possible combinations of situational characteristics that it is impossible to describe how they map to specific elicitation techniques. Therefore, this section will present a few representative examples, some where multiple characteristics are relevant to the decision, and some where just a few of the characteristics are sufficient.

Example I: The stakeholders are many (#STK=many) and diverse (STDV=high), but are easily accessible (STAC=easy) and available for travel (STTV=yes). They have never worked together before, but we have no reason to believe they would be combative (STCP=high). The application is an unprecedented (MATU=low) decision support system (TYPE=dss). In this situation, the analyst should first seek a technique that supports the many stakeholders. Since the stakeholders have not worked together before and are accessible, techniques that support a same time, same place meeting (PHYS=same, TEMP=same) that can be used to build a sense of team would be preferred in the early stages of the project. The diversity of the stakeholders could also indicate a need to start with team-building exercises (FOCU=human, DIRE=indirect). Because of the unprecedented nature of the application, divergent techniques (CONV=divergent) should also be considered early in the process. With either of the latter two types of techniques, the presence of a large group of stakeholders indicates the need for strong facilitation (ANAL= facilitate). With larger groups of stakeholders it may also be more efficient to have the individual stakeholders record their own ideas (RECO=individual). Optionally, efficiency could also be increased through the use of a tool (TOOL=tool) if an appropriate tool was available.

Example II: We are a company with a customizable base product. We sell a highly modified version of the base to each of our customers (COTS=customize, OUTS=in). These customers are strong competitors of each other (STCM=yes). Critical to our business strategy is to never allow our customers to know who our other customers are. In this situation, techniques that preserve stakeholder anonymity (ANON=anonymous) are critical to the company's business strategy. Therefore, techniques that require same time, same place interaction (TEMP=same time, PHYS=same place) of *all* stakeholders would not be appropriate (although they could work if applied separately to each company's stakeholders). This need for anonymity and separation, when combined with the existence of the current product, would be a strong indicator for product-focused techniques (FOCU=product).

Example III: We are part of an internal IT organization with a very vocal set of stakeholders within the operating divisions of the company located around the world. These stakeholders have worked together well many times in face-to-face meetings (STCP=high). In this situation, because the stakeholders know each other and have worked together, team-building is not required so they can immediately working on the problem (DIRE=direct, FOCU=product). That prior experience when combined with the geographical dispersion of the stakeholders would be strong indicators for the use of distributed techniques (PHYS=different place), which generally require tool support (TOOL=tool) and would benefit from strong facilitation (ANAL=facilitate) to ensure the team stays on task.

Example IV: We are working as a new analyst (BBEX=low) at a small company developing software (OUTS=in) for a 5-person accounting office. Since the analyst's knowledge of the problem domain is low and the number of stakeholders is few, passive techniques such as observation of a few stakeholders (ANAL=passive, STAK=few) would allow the analyst to gain the required problem domain knowledge rapidly.

The above examples clearly show the relationship between the two ontologies we have created for techniques and situations and the interdependent nature of those ontologies. We feel that these ontologies by themselves represent a significant contribution to the elicitation and ontology literature bases. However, the next section of this chapter reports on our efforts to revise, enhance, and integrate the two ontologies during the Elaboration Phase.

5. ELABORATION PHASE RESULTS

The elicitation and situational characteristic ontologies from the Conceptual Phase were refined and integrated with our model of requirements elicitation (Hickey and Davis, 2004) to create our proposed requirements elicitation ontology. The Unified Modeling Language (UML) was used to represent the concepts, relationships, and behaviors of this ontology. An overview of the complete ontology, showing the role of requirements elicitation in the overall requirements process, is shown in Figure 14-5 and described in the following section. Then, in section 5.2, we focus on those elements of the ontology directly related to elicitation technique selection (the primary purpose of the ontology). Figure 14-6 shows detailed attributes, relationships, and critical behaviors for the selected elements.

5.1 Requirements Elicitation Ontology Overview

The requirements elicitation ontology shown in Figure 14-5 expands on the discussion of the requirements process begun in Section 2. The ontology is specifically designed to be general enough to cover the wide variety of requirements processes used in the software development industry. The key elements of the ontology are as follows:

- A *Requirements Process* is initiated by an organization to create or update (i.e., *manage*) an *SRS* (system or software requirements specification) for a project/system.
- An *SRS* is an aggregation of the *Requirements* identified for that project/system. The specific content, format, and even the formality of the *SRS* and information about the *Requirements* are dictated by the

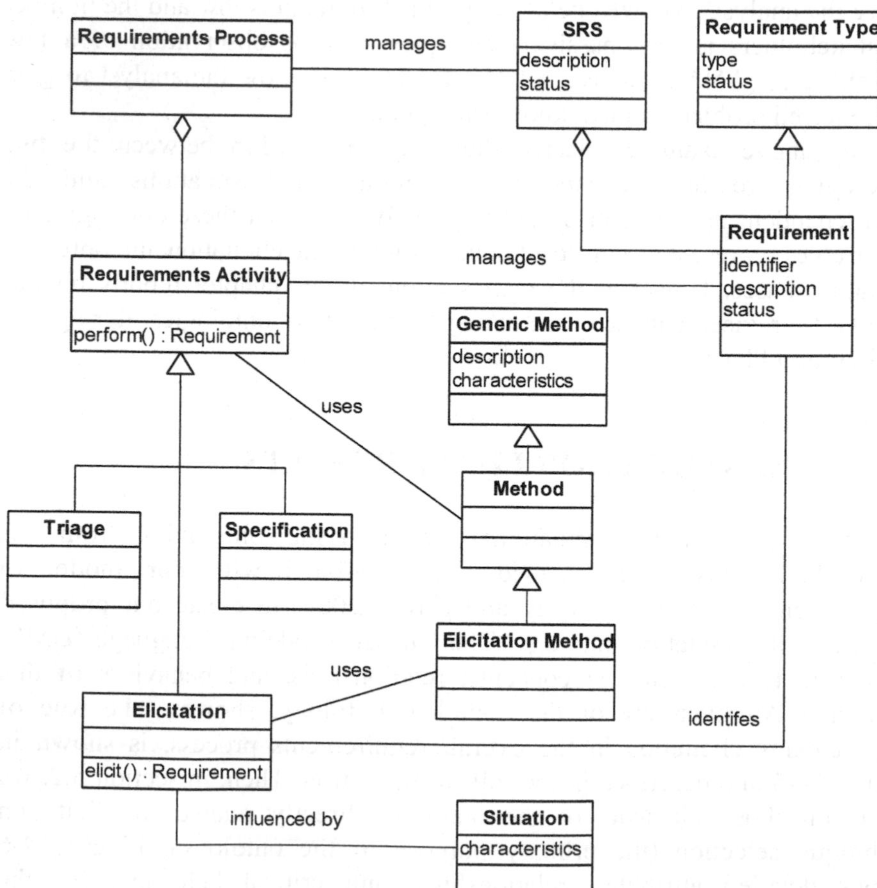

Figure 14-5. Overview of Requirements Elicitation Ontology

organization. Each *Requirement* may also be classified as a specific *Requirement Type* (e.g., functional vs. non-functional requirement, data vs. process requirement). This classification, as well as the *status* (e.g., incomplete, complete, approved) of the *SRS*, the various *Requirement Types*, and the individual *Requirements* are important considerations during elicitation and when selecting elicitation techniques.

- A *Requirements Process* is made up of one or more *Requirements Activities* which analysts *perform* (using one to many *Methods*) to identify, select, document, or otherwise update/maintain (i.e., *manage*) one or more *Requirements*.
- Although there is no standard name or number of requirements activities, at the most basic level, a *Requirements Activity* can be classified as: (1) *Elicitation* if it seeks to identify requirements, (2) *Triage* if it seeks to prioritize/select requirements or (3) *Specification* if it seeks to document requirements. Other classifications of requirements activities easily fit in this same framework.
- Focusing in on requirements elicitation, analysts *elicit* requirements using an *Elicitation Method*, which is any type of *Method* that helps identify, discover, uncover, create, or otherwise determine *Requirements*. Moreover, it became clear during the Conceptual Phase testing and the interviews with experts (Task 6, Figure 14-4), that many *Methods* have very similar characteristics and are often considered together as a single *Generic Method*. For example, an interview could be face-to-face or via phone or video-conference, with one or a few users, formal or informal – but all these variations are generically considered an interview. There are similar variations for collaborative workshops and many other *Methods*, therefore the super-class *Generic Method* was added to the ontology during this phase.
- To effectively elicit requirements, the analyst must take into account the context within which elicitation occurs. Therefore, the ontology recognizes that *Elicitation* is *influenced by* (and also influences) the *Situation*. The next section explores the specific *characteristics* of the *Situation* that most directly influence *Elicitation*.

5.2 Focusing on the Elicitation Technique and Situational Components of the Ontology

Once the overall requirements elicitation context was set for the ontology (see Figure 14-5), the next step in the Elaboration Phase was to add detailed concepts, relationships, and behaviors to those elements of the ontology specifically related to requirements elicitation and elicitation technique selection. Specific elements of concern include: Elicitation, Elicitation

Method, Requirement, Requirement Type, and Situation. Figure 14-6 provides the detailed ontology for these elements as follows:

- When evaluating the ontologies created during the Conceptual Phase and discussing elicitation techniques during the expert interviews (Task 6, Figure 14-4), it become very clear that there was a great deal of confusion on the differences between an elicitation technique and method, the notation used to document information learned while utilizing a technique, and any automated software tools that may be used to support a technique. Many in the software development industry use these terms interchangeably, often leading to confusion or incomplete understanding of how elicitation is actually being performed. Therefore, one of the first enhancements made during the Elaboration Phase was to explicitly define an *Elicitation Method* as a combination of an *Elicitation Technique* which specifics of how to elicit requirements (e.g., interview users, conduct a collaborative workshop); the *Notation(s)* which may be used to record requirements elicited using that technique (e.g., natural language, a modeling language like UML); and *Tool(s)* which may be used with that technique (e.g., a word processor, CASE or diagramming tool, group support system).
- The next step was to elaborate on the detailed characteristics of an *Elicitation Technique*. First, an attribute for the basic *description* of the technique was added. The ten dimensions of the elicitation technique ontology developed during the Conceptual Phase (described in section 4.1) were expanded into twelve attributes to increase accuracy, clarity, and flexibility. This flexibility was essential since some techniques could take on multiple values for a given dimension, making an either/or choice unacceptable. For example, the Convergence/Divergence (CONV) dimension was split into two separate Boolean attributes, *converges* and *diverges*, since the Conceptual Phase evaluation and interview results indicated a technique could support both. Product/Human Focus (FOCU) was similarly split into separate *product-focus* and *human-focus* attributes. The other eight dimensions of the initial elicitation technique ontology are directly represented as individual attributes of an *Elicitation Technique.* The remaining attributes were added during the Elaboration Phase testing, and are described in conjunction with the discussion of testing results in section 5.3.
- An overview of the initial situational ontology created during the Conceptual Phase is provided in section 4.2. During the Elaboration Phase, this ontology was formalized and documented as part of the detailed elicitation ontology shown in Figure 14-6. The *Situation* was divided into three main classes representing situational characteristics

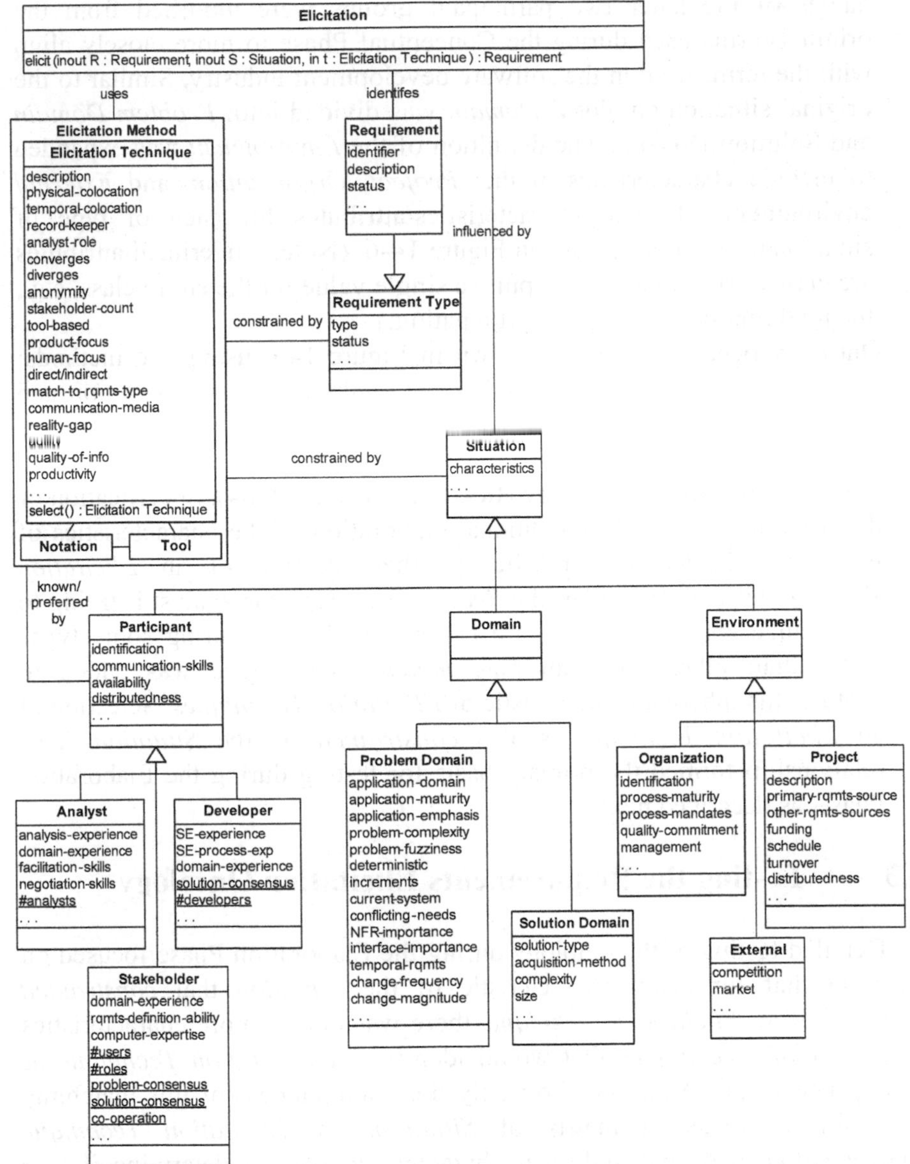

Figure 14-6. Detailed Elicitation Technique Selection Ontology

relating to the *Participants* in the requirements process, the *Domain* for which requirements are being elicited, and the *Environment* in which that elicitation occurs. *Participants* are further classified as: *Stakeholders* (i.e., all customers or users who may be involved in the requirements process or serve as the source of requirements), *Analysts* (originally called Bridge-Builders), *Developers* (originally, Solution Builders). The names of the latter two participant groups were modified from the original terms used during the Conceptual Phase to more closely align with the terms used in the software development industry. Similar to the original situation ontology, *Domain* was divided into: *Problem Domain* and Solution Domain. The definition of the *Environment* was expanded to include characteristics of the: *Project*, *Organization*, and *External* environment. Detailed characteristics/attributes for each of type of situational factor are shown in Figure 14-6. (Note: Underlined attributes are class attributes used to capture a single value for the entire class, e.g., the total number of analysts participating.)

- Ontology behaviors are also shown in Figure 14-6 using two methods: (1) specification of the *elicit* and *select* methods for the *Elicitation* and *Elicitation Technique* classes and (2) relationships between concepts (classes) in the ontology. These behaviors are based on the mathematical model of elicitation defined by Hickey and Davis (2004). Specification of the behaviors also led to additional elaboration of the characteristics of *Elicitation Technique.* Specifically, the selection of an *Elicitation Technique* is *constrained by* the *Requirement Type* the analyst is trying to elicit since some techniques are better suited to capturing some types better than others. The attribute *match-to-rqmts-type* was added to capture this inherent characteristic of *Elicitation Techniques.* Selection of an *Elicitation Technique* is also *constrained by* the *Situation.* This relationship formed the primary basis for testing during the Elaboration Phase, as described next.

5.3 Testing the Requirements Elicitation Ontology

Detailed testing of the ontology during the Elaboration Phase focused on ensuring that for every characteristic of the *Situation* that *constrained* selection of an *Elicitation Technique*, there was one or more characteristics of *Elicitation Techniques* that would identify an *Elicitation Technique* as appropriate in that *Situation.* To verify the completeness of this matching, the authors created a matrix of *Situation* vs. *Elicitation Technique* characteristics and analyzed each characteristic pair to determine if that *Situation* characteristic drove the need for that *Elicitation Technique* characteristic. This analysis identified the need for several additional *Elicitation Technique* characteristics.

- *Participants* in a project may vary significantly in the history and degree of *co-operation*, but the original ontology did not include a specific Elicitation Technique characteristic that directly related to this situation. Media richness theory (Daft and Lengel, 1986) indicates that communication media inherently vary in their ability to communicate information. However, many researchers hypothesize that this communication richness is a function of both the media and a variety of situational factors such as the history of the group communication (Burke and Aytes, 1998; Dennis and Valacich, 1999; Te'eni et al., 2001). In situations with little-to-no history of cooperation or when co-operation problems are anticipated, an *Elicitation Technique* using a richer communication media would generally be preferred. In contrast, when Participants have an excellent history of co-operation, leaner communication media may be sufficient. To capture these relationships, the *communication-medium* characteristic was added to *Elicitation Technique*.

- *Stakeholders* also vary in their ability to define requirements (*rqmts-definition-ability*). Prototyping and other elicitation techniques like scenarios that provide more concrete representations of reality can be very useful when individuals have difficulty defining requirements. Other techniques use more abstract representations of requirements (e.g., many of the modeling techniques commonly used by analysts). These techniques may work well with those with greater experience and expertise in defining requirements. The *reality-gap* characteristic was added capture the gap between reality and a specific *Elicitation Technique*.
- Analysis of the *Environment* and *Domain* characteristics drove the addition of the *agility*, *quality-of-info*, and *productivity* characteristics of *Elicitation Techniques*.

6. DISCUSSION

Building ontologies is a difficult process (Gruninger and Lee, 2002) that is never fully complete (Kishore et al., 2004a). Therefore, it should not be surprising that there are limitations to the current research and many future research opportunities. These limitations and opportunities are discussed in the following sections. However, regardless of the on-going nature of this research, this research currently provides significant contributions for researchers and practitioners. A few of these contributions are highlighted in section 6.3.

6.1 Limitations

The major limitation of this research is that the proposed ontology has not been explicitly agreed to by the requirements elicitation community. Virtually all ontology researchers emphasize the need for such agreement. For example, Gruber (1993) defines ontology as a "shared conceptualization." Fensel (2004) refers to ontology as a "community-mediated and accepted description." This lack of agreement may be less of a problem for this research for the following reasons:

- As described in the earlier sections of this chapter, the ontology was built from commonly-used requirements resources and information from experts in the field. Therefore, as a minimum, it should be understood by members of the requirements elicitation community.
- The ontology will be used to build a single information system for use by analysts in selecting elicitation techniques. At the current time, we do not anticipate information exchange between information systems or broader automated use of the ontology. Therefore, common understanding may be sufficient at this stage of research in the relatively new field of requirements elicitation technique selection.
- Given the diversity of the requirements elicitation community, reaching consensus will be extremely difficult. As mentioned earlier, the two major arms of the community, information systems (IS) and requirements engineering (RE), do not even agree what to call elicitation or those who perform that activity. However, even with their differences, IS and RE have been able to co-exist and communicate, indicating at least a basic understanding of both sets of terms.

Regardless of these mitigating circumstances, the need for consensus will be addressed during the Definition Phase of this research, as discussed next.

6.2 Future Research

As described in Section 3, the primary focus of future research will be the Definition Phase. After we complete interviewing experts (Figure 14-4, task 6), we will revise and finalize the ontology (task 7) and mapping between technique and situation characteristics (task 8). As occurred during the earlier research phases we anticipate that the mapping will identify additional characteristics which should be included in the revised ontology. The final task (task 9) of this research effort will be to implement and validate the ontology-based mapping in a tool to aid novice analysts in selecting an appropriate elicitation technique.

We have implemented a prototype tool called CoStar (Colorado Selector of Techniques for Acquiring Requirements). CoStar presents analysts with a list of questions. The responses to these queries identify the characteristics present in the current situation. These characteristics are then mapped to a vector in the elicitation technique attributes vector space. Finally, the tool presents to the analyst a list of techniques corresponding to that vector. Much more work is necessary before this tool is ready for widespread use. Elicitation technique and situational characteristics will be updated to reflect the final, integrated ontology resulting from the Elaboration and Definition Phases. Then, relationships between situational characteristics and between situational and technique characteristics (missing from the initial tabular/faceted ontologies, but captured in the final ontology) will be analyzed to streamline the questions that the analyst must answer. Research to date indicates that while all characteristics are important for some possible situation, a much smaller set will be critical to any given situation (Hickey and Davis, 2003b). So, the goal will be leverage the power of the comprehensive ontology and sequence the questions that the analyst must answer (1) to rapidly focus on that situation, (2) eliminate unnecessary questions, but (3) continue to ask questions until a workable set of recommended techniques are identified from which the analyst may choose based on personal preference (Hickey and Davis, 2004). Technique recommendations will be updated to reflect the final results of the expert interviews and to fully implement our iterative model of requirements elicitation (Hickey and Davis, 2004) which requires a series of technique recommendations to parallel each of the steps of the elicitation process.

Validation will need to address evaluation of the tool as well as the ontology itself. The tool will be extensively tested to ensure that practical recommendations are generated for the majority of common situations. Validation of the ontology will take place in two stages: (1) initial evaluation as required to complete the proposed analyst information system and (2) a broader evaluation and refinement to attempt to reach consensus on the ontology across the requirements elicitation community. If this effort proves successful, the community may also want to pursue expanding the ontology beyond elicitation to the entire requirements management process.

6.3 Contributions

The research presented in this chapter directly contributes to both elicitation research and practice. It demonstrates how ontologies can be used to compare the many, often similar, available requirements elicitation techniques and help choose between them for a given situation. The ontology defined herein is solidly based in the existing literature and on more than 25 years of the researchers' experience in elicitation. Even though the proposed ontology has not yet been validated, the testing we have completed so far and feedback from our expert interviewees indicates that only limited enhancements may be required. As a result, the ontology and technique selection process presented in this chapter can be used now in research and practice as follows:

- Researchers and practitioners can use the elicitation technique characteristics included in the ontology to sort through the hundreds of existing and proposed techniques to understand techniques' essential similarities and differences.

- Researchers can use the situational characteristics identified in the ontology to explicitly describe the situations their new techniques are designed to support, thereby aiding practitioners in identifying the 'right' techniques for their situation.
- Practicing analysts can use the situational portion of the ontology to alert them to the factors that may impact the effectiveness of their elicitation process. Analysts with some experience should also be able to use the ontology and technique selection examples to improve their current technique selection process, thereby improving the current state of the practice of requirements elicitation.

7. SUMMARY

This chapter has walked the reader through the iterative development of an integrated, requirements elicitation ontology, created to assist inexperienced analysts in selecting elicitation techniques that are applicable to a situation.

During the Conceptual Phase of the ontological engineering process, two ontologies were created. The first ontology identified 10 key characteristics of elicitation techniques that highlight the similarity and differences between the seemingly endless variations of elicitation techniques. The second ontology highlighted situational characteristics relevant to the selection of elicitation techniques. The technique ontology also took into account this situational ontology so that the closeness of two elicitation techniques is proportional to their relative applicability in similar situations. The proposed mapping between these ontologies was explored for selected examples and provides the basis for the evaluation of the effectiveness of elicitation techniques for specific situations.

In the Elaboration Phase, the two ontologies were revised and integrated with the authors' model of requirements elicitation to create a single, integrated, requirements elicitation ontology. This ontology was represented using the Unified Modeling Language and included concepts, relationships, and behaviors critical for requirements elicitation and elicitation technique selection. The ontology was tested for completeness by comparing individual situational characteristics to elicitation technique characteristics with additional technique characteristics added as necessary.

Finally, the chapter discusses the limitations and contributions of this research and explores areas for future research. Future research will focus on the Definition Phase to formalize the ontology and implement it into an effective tool for the selection of elicitation techniques by inexperienced analysts. Current research results can be used by analysts to improve the state of requirements elicitation practice, with even more wide-spread improvements anticipated when that tool is implemented and validated.

REFERENCES

Alexander, L., and Davis, A., 1991, Criteria for the selection of a software process model, *15th IEEE COMPSAC*, IEEE Computer Society, Los Alamitos, CA, pp. 521-528.

Bento, A., 1994, Systems analysis: A decision approach, *Info. & Mgmt* **27**(8):185-193.

Boehm, B., Abts, C., Brown, A., Chulani, S., Clark, B., Horowitz, E., Madachy, R., Reifer, D., and Steece, B., 2000, *Software Cost Estimation with COCOMO II*, Prentice Hall, Upper Saddle River, NJ.

Burke, K., and Aytes, K., 1998, A longitudinal analysis of the effects of media richness on cohesive development and process satisfaction in computer-supported work, *31st Hawaii Int. Conf. on the System Sciences* **1**, IEEE Computer Society, Los Alamitos, CA,, pp. 135-144.

Byrd, T., Cossick, K., and Zmud, R., 1992, A synthesis of research on requirements analysis and knowledge acquisition techniques, *MIS Quarterly* **16**(1):117-138.

Checkland, P., and Scholes, J., 1991, *Soft Systems Methodology in Action*, Wiley, Chichester, UK.

Conger, S., 1994, *New Software Engineering*, Wadsworth, Belmont, CA.

Coughlan, J., and Macredie, R., 2002, Effective communication in requirements elicitation: A comparison of methodologies, *Req. Eng.* **7**(2):47-60.

Daft, R., and Lengel, R., 1986, Organizational information requirements, media richness and structural design, *Mgmt Science* **32**(5):554-571.

Davis, A., 1993, *Software Requirements: Objects, Functions and States*, Prentice Hall, Upper Saddle River, NJ.

Davis, A., 2005, *Just Enough Requirements Management*, Dorset House, New York.

Dennis, A., and Haley Wixom, B., 2000, *Systems Analysis and Design: An Applied Approach*, Wiley, New York.

Dennis, A., and Valacich, J., 1999, Rethinking media richness: Towards a theory of media synchronicity, *32nd Hawaii Int. Conf. on System Sciences*, IEEE Computer Society, Los Alamitos, CA.

Fensel, D., 2004, *Ontologies: A Silver Bullet for Knowledge Management and Electronic Commerce*, Springer, Berlin.

Gause, D., and Weinberg, J., 1989, *Exploring Requirements: Quality Before Design,* Dorset House, New York.

Glass, R., 2002, Searching for the holy grail of software engineering, *Comm. of the ACM* **45**(5):15-16.

Goguen, J., and Linde, C., 1993, Software requirements analysis and specification in Europe: An overview, *1st Int. Symp. on Req. Eng.,* IEEE Computer Society, Los Alamitos, CA, pp. 152-164.

Gomez-Perez, A., Fernandez-Lopez, M., and Corcho, O., 2004, *Ontological Engineering: With Examples from the Areas of Knowledge Management, e-Commerce, and the Semantic Web*, Springer, London.

Gottesdiener, E., 2002, *Requirements by Collaboration*, Addison-Wesley, Reading, PA.

Gruber, T., 1993, A translational approach to portable ontologies, *Knowledge Acq.* **5**(2):199-220.

Gruninger, M., and Lee, J., 2002, Ontology: Applications and design, *Comm, of the ACM* **45**(2):39-41.

Hickey, A., and Davis, A., 2002, The role of requirements elicitation techniques in achieving software quality, *Req. Eng.: Foundations for Software Quality WS*, Essen, Germany.

Hickey, A., and Davis, A., 2003a, A tale of two ontologies: The basis for systems analysis technique selection, *Americas Conf. on Info. Sys.*, Association for Information Systems, Atlanta.

Hickey, A., and Davis, A., 2003b, Elicitation technique selection: How do experts do it? *11th IEEE Int. Req. Eng. Conf.*, IEEE Computer Society, Los Alamitos, CA.

Hickey, A., and Davis, A., 2004, A Unified Model of Requirements Elicitation, *J. of Mgmt Info. Sys.* **20**(4):65-84.

Hickey, A., Davis, A., and Kaiser, D., 2003, Requirements Elicitation Techniques: Analyzing the Gap Between Technology Availability and Technology Use, *Comparative Tech. Transfer & Society* **1**(3):279-302.

Higgins, L., 2003, *Principles of Marketing*, www.principlesofmarketing.com.

Hoffer, J., George, J., and Valacich, J., 2002, *Modern Systems Analysis and Design*, 3rd ed., Prentice Hall, Upper Saddle River, NJ.

Hofmann, H., and Lehner, F., 2001, Requirements engineering as a success factor in software projects, *IEEE Software* **18**(4):58-66.

Holsapple, C., and Joshi, K., 2002, A collaborative approach to ontology design, *Comm. of the ACM* **45**(2):42-47

Juristo, N., and Moreno, A., 2001, *Basics of Software Engineering Experimentation*, Kluwer Academic, Boston.

Kishore, R., Sharman, R., and Ramesh, R., 2004a, Computational ontologies and information systems: I. Foundations, *Comm. of the Assoc. for Info. Sys.* **14**:158-183.

Kishore, R., Sharman, R., and Ramesh, R., 2004b, Computational ontologies and information systems: II. Formal specification, *Comm. of the Assoc. for Info. Sys.* **14**:184-205.

Kishore, R., Zhang, H., and Ramesh, R., 2004c, A helix-spindle model for ontological engineering, *Comm. of the ACM* **47**(2):69-75.

Kotonya, G., and Sommerville, I., 1998, *Requirements Engineering: Processes and Techniques,* Wiley, Chichester, UK.

Lauesen, S., 2002, *Software Requirements: Styles and Techniques,* Addison-Wesley, Harlow, UK.

Leffingwell, D., and Widrig, D., 2000, *Managing Software Requirements*, Addison-Wesley, Reading, PA.

Liebowitz, J., 2001, *Knowledge Management: Learning from Knowledge Engineering,* CRC Press, Boca Raton, FL.

Macaulay, L., 1996, *Requirements Engineering*, Springer, London.

Maciaszek, L., 2001, *Requirements Analysis and System Design,* Addison-Wesley, Harlow, UK.

Maiden, N., and Rugg, G. 1996, ACRE: Selecting methods for requirements acquisition, *Software Eng. J.* **11**(5):183-192.

Nunamaker, J., Dennis, A., Valacich, J., Vogel, D., and George, J., 1991, Electronic meeting systems to support group work, *Comm. of the ACM* **34**(7):40-61.

Robertson, S., and Robertson, J., 1999, *Mastering the Requirements Process*, Addison-Wesley, Harlow, UK.

Romano, N., Nunamaker, J., Briggs, R., and Mittleman, D., 1999, Distributed GSS facilitation and participation: Field action research, *32nd Hawaii Int. Conf. on Sys. Sciences*, IEEE Computer Society, Los Alamitos, CA.

Scharer, S., 1981, Pinpointing Requirements, *Datamation* (April):139-154.

Schewe, C., and Hiam, A., 1998, *Portable MBA in Marketing*, 2nd ed., Wiley, New York.

Standish Group, 1995, *The Chaos Report*, www.standishgroup.com.

Te'eni, D., Sagie, A., Schwartz, D., Zaidman, N., and Amichai, Y., 2001, The process of organizational communication: A model and field study, *IEEE Trans. on Prof. Comm.* **44**(1):6-20.

Thayer, R., and Dorfman, M., 1994, *Standards, Guidelines, and Examples on System and Software Requirements Engineering*, IEEE Computer Society, Los Alamitos, CA.

Wiegers, K., 2003, *Software Requirements*, Microsoft, Redmond, WA.

Wood, J., and Silver, D., 1995, *Joint Application Development*, Wiley, New York.

Yeh, R., and Ng, P., 1990, Software requirements – A management perspective, in: *Systems and Software Requirements Engineering*, R. Thayer and M. Dorfman, eds., IEEE Computer Society, Los Alamitos, CA, pp. 450-461.

ODIS Architectures

Chapter 15

USE OF ONTOLOGY FOR AUTOMATING KNOWLEDGE INTENSIVE BUSINESS PROCESSES

Jyoti M. Bhat, Krishnakumar Pooloth, Manohar Moorthy, Renuka Sindhgatta and Srinivas Thonse

Software Engineering and Technology Labs, Infosys Technologies Limited

Abstract: Knowledge intensive business processes are a category of business processes that rely on experience and expert judgment. Automating such processes is a challenge for most enterprises. This chapter introduces the characteristics of such processes, provides some examples and describes the architecture for implementing a system that caters to knowledge intensive business processes.

Key words: Business Process; Ontology; Automation

1. INTRODUCTION

Businesses have adopted Information Technology (IT) for automation from the early ages of computing. Starting with information storage in the fifties, enterprises have adopted data processing, decision support systems, automation packages like ERP and Internet-delivered services. This has helped in improving the efficiency of the business and contributed to faster cycle times and improved throughput.

The knowledge economy of today is revealing some interesting patterns on evolution of certain business processes. Many business activities in such processes rely on experience and expert judgment. Possible outcomes of the processes are many. The pace of process change is rapid requiring high degree of flexibility.

This chapter describes a category of processes called "Knowledge intensive business processes" with the characteristics as described above. It details out examples of such processes. It then describes the design of a system using ontology to automate one illustrative process in exception management domain. It finally explains the limitations of adopting this design approach.

1.1 Business Process

Business processes enable the organization to successfully deliver its products and services. *A business process can be defined as a sequence of activities performed by roles in the business, accomplishing an end-deliverable for the customers* [1]. Each business process has inputs, methods and outputs. A business process can be part of a larger, encompassing process and can include other business processes that have to be included in its method cutting across organizational units.

Business processes form the core differentiation for organizations, because the sequence of activities is unique to every organization. Repeatable and well-engineered business processes lead to operational excellence in an organization. Optimization of business processes is hence gaining importance in the industry.

1.2 Knowledge Intensive Business Processes

Certain categories of business processes are not very well structured. These are usually executed by people who need to be knowledgeable in the domain. These processes usually get overlooked in process re-design and improvement programs. [1] [2]

Knowledge intensive processes rely on specialized professional expertise, continuous learning and transformation of information. They are performed by knowledge workers with high degree of expertise and experience. Knowledge workers usually enjoy a high degree of empowerment to take decisions on how they perform their activities and to develop new ways of performing their activities as their process knowledge increases. They perform these activities in a fluid, unconscious manner, rather than discrete steps. It is difficult to describe and document them in process terms. Knowledge intensive processes have the following characteristics as described by Tautz [3].

- they involve a creative element, that is, their sequence of activities cannot be fully predefined,
- the overall process description can only be given at an abstract level,
- they involve complex process with numerous steps and agents,
- they contain a few central decision steps which require personal judgment based on experience, comprehensive historical knowledge,

Eppler et al. provide attributes for describing knowledge intensiveness and complexity of business processes [4]. They define the attributes of knowledge intensiveness as

- contingency – outcomes are numerous and depend on chance events and environmental factors
- decision scope – choices and possibilities for the agent (participant) are many
- agent innovation – execution requires creativity and innovation
- knowledge half-life – obsolescence is fast and relevance of process related knowledge is short
- agent impact – process outcome depends on agent skill and performance
- learning time –time to master the process is long

They describe the complexity dimension of business processes by defining additional attributes involving number of process steps and number of agents in the process, interdependencies between steps and between agents, dynamic sequencing of steps based on events.

On classifying business process along the dimensions of knowledge intensiveness and complexity it can be clearly identified that the processes falling under the categories of weak knowledge intensity and low/high process complexity like order fulfillment, inventory control, order configuration and editing can be handled by conventional process redesign and IT automation. Optimization of processes with strong knowledge intensiveness needs a different approach from both process redesign and application of IT systems.

2. OPTIMIZATION OF KNOWLEDGE INTENSIVE PROCESSES

Characteristics of knowledge intensive business processes described in preceding section reveal many areas where optimization can be explored. Can the processes, rules, policies and related operations be documented formally? Can the IT systems be built to execute or enact this knowledge? Can this knowledge be so documented that it can be changed as the context changes? Can experiential knowledge such as past situations, actions and outcomes (cases) be documented in structured manner? Can experiential knowledge of past cases be documented formally? Can this knowledge also be used for training incumbents? Can this knowledge be made searchable by participants in the process for quick reference during execution?

Knowledge intensiveness of business processes arise from business practices which evolve within the organization. While processes depict the 'what' of the activities and are governed by procedures, the practices are about how the activities are done, tasks managed and are under the control of individuals. As an example, tellers in banks have very strict processes for handling money, but the people developing new trading instruments develop their own practices within the framework of the overall process. These knowledge processes also need to adhere to certain business rules, procedures, standards and policies. Hence redesign of the knowledge intensive processes needs to consider both the practices and the process steps [5]. The entirc process needs to be studied by breaking down the process into distinct parts, ones which are structured and repetitive and those which are dynamic and contingent.

We can model and analyze knowledge intensive process based on their structure in two parts, **content-based** – in terms of the knowledge used in executing the activities of the process, and **process-based** – the way the process is currently implemented as activities and tasks among the participants. [4], [6]

The content-based knowledge is about knowledge required to execute the process like knowledge of previous events and outcomes, intermediate process outcomes, critical decision points, lessons learnt, process improvements and critical success factors. Formalisms have been developed for modeling the knowledge distribution between agents and the coordination mechanisms. But not much research is available on modeling the attributes of creativity, learning time, adaptive and knowledge half life.

The process-based knowledge is knowledge about the business implemented in systems and processes of the company. This type of knowledge is found in process documentation, workflow applications, quality assurance of processes, resource allocation decisions, etc. Several formalisms and modeling methods exist for modeling this type of knowledge. As proposed by Leijen & Baets [7], business process re-engineering typically involves process modeling, analysis to find improvements and assessing the impact, implementing the changes through systems and processes.

Certain improvements can be implemented based on process-based knowledge. These fall in the area of classical automation such as replacing paper forms with software forms, reducing hand-offs between workers by communication, saving business data in persistent storage such as database and performing automated computation. These are usually implemented as IT systems. New technologies such as BPM (Business Process Management) are enabling documentation and execution of this process-based knowledge.

Enhancing the structure of the content-based knowledge is the final form of process improvement. The knowledge intensive process can be viewed as resolving a problem having a set of situations and choosing the appropriate response by decomposing and recognizing the stimulus. This implies two parts to the solution: first would be the stimulus-response function (number of possible responses for a stimulus) and the second is the interleaving among the responses (actions are taken even before all information is available). Deepening the stimulus-response function increases the cost and effort of recognizing a response, but will save effort and add value as time progresses. Increasing interleaving will improve speed but at the cost of accuracy, as some atypical situations will be misjudged and lead to rework and backtracking. This approach to process improvements provides flexibility because the two aspects of the solution can be manipulated as required by the knowledge intensive process. The learning which is part of all knowledge intensive processes can be incorporated into the process and can be positioned either before or after the problem. In new product development, learning is often done up front by looking at similar projects in the past and identifying success factors whereas in branches of medicine or insurance the learning is at the end of a problem or series of problems.

3. ILLUSTRATIVE BUSINESS PROCESSES

In this section we describe examples of knowledge intensive business processes and identify a few common characteristics of these processes.

3.1 Insurance Policy Underwriting

Consider ***insurance policy underwriting***. The process involves an expert (underwriter) who uses his/her professional knowledge and experience, interacts with other agents like applicants and doctors/hospitals, based on certain events/ decision points in the process, and provides the decision on the insurance application acceptance or rejection (process outcome). The process outcome is based on decisions made by the expert after weighing all facts and information. The interactions with the other agents will be at various points in the process and may iterate several times during the entire process. The exact sequence of steps in the process will vary between process instances and also across experts. The process documentation would be very high level and would not include best practices developed by the experts. Experts would be required to adhere to certain standard operating procedures.

3.2 Software production support

A process similar in structure to insurance underwriting is found in software application maintenance. ***Production support*** is the heartbeat process of software maintenance services. Any error in the software in the field needs to be corrected immediately so that the business users can continue their activities. The software may fail at any point of usage under various conditions. The problem statement given to the production support personnel would be – the point of failure during usage like screen, field, program and job, with relevant usage history. The support engineer needs to pinpoint the incident or problem to an error such as programming error, data errors, illegitimate usage of the software function, and wrong interpretation of a correct software response.

This type of diagnoses would require the person to know the details of the software application like the input and output files/fields, individual programs, modules, jobs, job flows, program flows and screens. Detailed application knowledge is available only through experience and detailed documentation of the system. Typically system documentation in the form of flow charts and workflows do not help in identifying the root cause of a software failure. The system knowledge (content-based knowledge) needs to be complemented by incident diagnoses knowledge (process-based) which would have details of the exact steps used to pinpoint the problem to an error.

3.3 Exception Management

Another scenario is ***Exception management.*** In certain industries such as Financial Securities, automation levels are high. Trades usually happen in fully automated mode with no manual activities. When exceptions occur, the handling is manual. Exceptions are those transactions cannot be automatically processed by systems. Usually expert human intervention is needed to resolve the exception. Most exception management systems are workflow systems which help in managing the exceptions better by assigning exceptions to experts but do not remove dependency on the humans. The experts spend time and refer to prior knowledge to diagnose and resolve the exception.

3.4 Sales Commission Calculation

Some knowledge intensive processes are complex due to the large amount of laws, rules and data used by the process. These processes typically involve calculation of some monetary benefit by the knowledge worker. There are thousands of situations and many hundreds of rules of calculations that the workers are expected to know.

One such process is the ***sales commission calculation*** process in ***broker dealer domain***. Securities firms pay their traders commissions based on agreements between the traders and the firm. The traders usually have a say in how their commission is calculated for the trades they are involved in. There are hundreds of possible rules and almost equal number of traders associated with a firm. The commission calculation rules change time to time depending on how the trader negotiates his commission with the firm. The rules are based on factors such as type of instruments traded; type of client traded for, volume/amount of the portfolio, percentages or fixed amount, period of trade, vacation time, in absentia and group trading. No standard definition exists for some terms and certain parameters used in the rules, though the concept is well understood. Volume of money getting transacted is large and hence commissions would involve to a substantial monetary outflow for the firm. Calculating the commission involves various combinations and sequences of the individual rules. The commission calculation is predominantly done by people (calculators) with the help of rule-engine based systems and simple spreadsheets. Such systems help in the calculations only to a limited extent.

3.5 Calculation of retirement benefits and old age pensions

A similar process can be found in administrative processes in e-governance. One such process is in the social security area like ***calculation of retirement benefits and old age pensions*** [8], [9]. This process involves lot of data capture, data interpretation, knowledge of rules and changing laws and multiple roles & departments.

The process involves in-depth knowledge of the legislations for two major decision steps, first for deciding whether the applicant is entitled to a pension, and second for calculating the amount of the pension. For a specific case, more than one regulation may be applicable, hence knowledge is required to identify all these regulations and choose the most appropriate one. If the applicant can establish a pension rightly under more than one regulation, the different pension amounts are calculated and the highest one is chosen. The decisions should comply with all binding regulations. Often, issues of incomplete information and documentation to start the pension processing arise, in which case interactions and communications between the pension department and applicant come into play. The people approving and calculating pension payments do not all possess the same education and expertise; hence knowledge of past decisions would help.

3.6 Corporate Actions Processing

Corporate actions processing is a risk-intensive and manual process in the securities industry. Any activity by a public firm which changes its capital structure or financial condition is termed a corporate action e.g. mergers, spin-offs, stock splits and dividends. The process starts with data capture of the corporate actions from various sources. The action data may be messages with standard formats (SWIFT ISO 15022) from data vendors and non-standard messages from newspapers, and custodians. Next is event validation and certification where the corporate action is verified and certified for entitlement calculation and decision making. These steps are people centric and paper based.

4. DESIGN CONSIDERATIONS FOR AUTOMATING KNOWLEDGE INTENSIVE PROCESSES

4.1 Design Approach

Systems to automate the illustrative business processes described in section 3 can be designed using a common design approach as shown in figure 15-1. Systems for automating these processes can be seen as having three parts

- Knowledge definition for capturing knowledge regarding the processes using ontology.
- Knowledge enactment for automating the processes based on the defined knowledge
- Knowledge support for associated functions such as learning, search and query, and simulation

The IT system to address the above requirements would involve

- Knowledge capture tools to capture the domain knowledge using ontology, process steps and practices rules using decision trees and process maps. Ontology editors supporting reading and review would be required to build the ontology. The knowledge can be verified by defining domain constraints on the ontology.
- Knowledge Enactment tools such as workflow systems and rule engines to assign cases requiring human intervention.
- Knowledge support tools such as an information assistant to provide context based help and store annotated knowledge. Various process scenarios can be simulated using the operations simulator to enable a novice learn the process of arriving at a decision. The operations assistant and the learning assistant train the user through the decision steps.

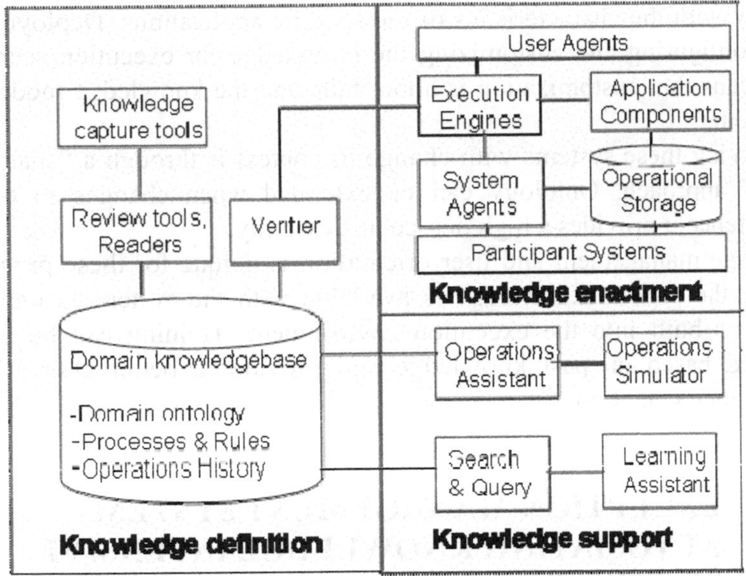

Figure 15-1. Illustrative Environment for Knowledge Intensive Business Processes

In knowledge enactment, well-defined decisions would be assigned to systems for processing. For complex decisions, incomplete data or other types of cases requiring human intervention parallel processing between the system and expert should be designed. The system would recommend decisions based on the knowledge base and capture the decisions and continuously learn in the form of an information assistant which observes the workflow and information retrieval.

4.2 Highlights

This approach reveals a few interesting insights for automation.

Requirements specification for developing systems for these processes is about capturing knowledge. For an exception management process, requirement specification is about capturing exception knowledge. This knowledge also forms the design of the system. The phases of requirements and design are thus replaced by knowledge capture activity

Ontology that models the business understanding such as process knowledge and rule knowledge can be referenced by knowledge execution part of the system. This means that the ontology captured in knowledge definition can also be used for execution. This makes the knowledge capture and implementation phases seamless.

The ontology can be configured to suit specific scenarios. For example, customizing a production support system is about extending the application ontology with the characteristics of the specific applications. Deployment is about configuring and customizing the knowledge for execution scenarios. This means that customization is about tailoring the knowledge modeled in the system.

Evolving these systems with change in context is through a "change-as-you-go" approach. Ontology can be extended when changes in context occur. Hence it provides a high degree of flexibility.

Change management and user orientation is unique for these processes. Because the process knowledge is available with the system as ontology, training is built into the execution environment. Training can be live or simulated based on past knowledge and provides a better alternative to reading documentation.

5. EXCEPTION MANAGEMENT SYSTEM – AUTOMATING KNOWLEDGE INTENSIVE PROCESSES

This section illustrates the architecture of an automated knowledge intensive process using the example of an Exception Management system in a financial securities domain. The architecture, however, is generic and can be used to implement any similar process. The need for exception management system is shown in figure 15-2. A business process requires the execution of a sequence of tasks. An error in the execution of the tasks for certain scenarios of user inputs results in exceptions. These exceptions go through the exception management process to enable the successful execution of the task and hence the process. In the exception management process, an exception is identified, classified, allocated to specific experts and resolved.

The types of exceptions that need to be handled depend on the business of the enterprise and the execution of the various steps in the life-cycle of the exception types involves knowledge that is very specific to the enterprise.

Exception Identification involves identifying those transactions which need to be flagged off as exceptions. The basis for identification of exceptions is very specific to an enterprise. A transaction which needs to be flagged off as an exception by an enterprise may not be an exception for another enterprise.

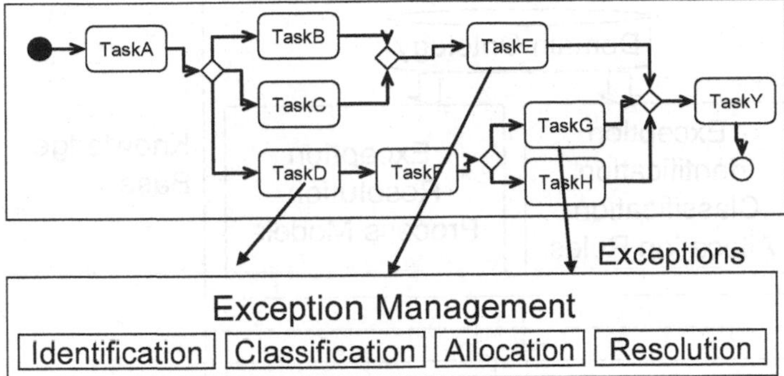

Figure 15-2. Exception Management Process

Exception Classification is the process of tagging an exception with a type. The type determination is done based on values of certain fields in the exception transaction.

Exception Allocation (for investigation and resolution) is based on the organization structure. Exceptions of a particular type or those originating from a particular system or belonging to a specific region of the company's business may need to be assigned to specific operational teams.

Exception Investigation & Resolution is the process of experts identifying the root cause of an exception and taking necessary steps to resolve the exception. Steps involved in exception investigation and resolution may differ based on the exception type. An expert responsible for executing a particular step often looks at data present in various systems within the enterprise and data from its partners/customers. The set of systems which provide this data differ based on the type of exception. Enterprises have a myriad of systems implementing business processes and hence experts, who handle exceptions, use their knowledge of systems relevant to each exception to process the exceptions.

Exception management is enterprise specific and is highly dependent on the expert's knowledge of the domain, processes and systems involved. Hence, it is classified as knowledge intensive. The following section presents the architecture of an exception management system.

6. ARCHITECTURE OF AN EXCEPTION MANAGEMENT SYSTEM

The architecture of any system which implements a Knowledge Intensive Business Process (such as the Exception Management Process) must make provisions for capturing knowledge which is specific to the business process. It must also provide for implementing applications which make use of this knowledge.

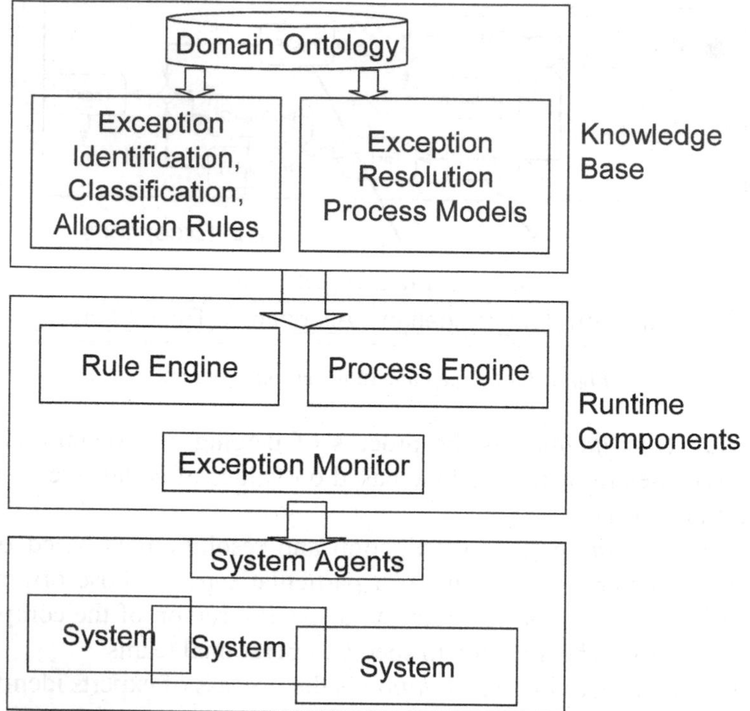

Figure 15-3. Components of Exception Management System

For the purpose of illustration, we will take examples from the financial securities domain. The financial securities domain involves various business processes like trading, accounting settlement etc. and there are various parties involved (Asset Managers, Custodians, Sub-Custodians, Brokers/Dealers etc.) in these business processes. There are various systems (Trading system, Ledger system, Settlement system, Reconciliation system etc.) which participate in the fulfillment of these business processes. One such system is the Reconciliation system which is responsible for reconciliation of trades (related to stocks) and balances (related to cash) coming in from an external party with data obtained from an internal Ledger system. Reconciliation is done by the various parties involved in a trade. The exceptions occur when there is a mismatch between transactions recorded in the Ledger system and that present in the Reconciliation system. These exceptions have to be resolved to ensure that the processing proceeds to the next stage in the fulfillment. Architecture should therefore capture the knowledge of all the systems, concepts in a knowledge base and implement applications components that use the knowledge base to resolve exceptions. Figure 15-3 shows the knowledge base components used for capturing the knowledge of the exceptions and the run time execution components that use the knowledge to manage and resolve exceptions.

6.1 Knowledge Base

The knowledge base comprises of the domain ontology, the rules related to identifying, classifying and allocating exceptions and the process models for resolving exceptions. The knowledge base is built using the knowledge obtained from a set of experts who are involved in handling exceptions at different stages of exception management.

6.1.1 Domain Ontology

The set of concepts and relationships between concepts in the business domain along with their instances constitutes the Domain Ontology. The domain concepts associated with the reconciliation (with respect to data obtained from a Custodian and data present in its internal Ledger system) is shown in figure 15-4. There are various reconciliation exceptions that can occur. The hierarchy of exceptions is captured in the ontology. The systems that participate in the reconciliation process are modeled along with the details of the different operational user groups responsible for managing exceptions.

Once the ontology definition is complete, the instance information for some of the concepts is captured. For example the instances of systems (version, IP address, operating platform etc.) and User groups captured in the ontology would be used by runtime components to identify the system an exception originates from, the process it corresponds to, and other related attributes that are required for processing the exception.

6.1.2 Exception Identification, Classification and Allocation Rules

The identification, classification and allocation of exceptions is based on certain rules. Various systems in an enterprise generate exceptions. The logic used for identifying exceptions is very specific to each process/system in an enterprise. For example, a reconciliation system generates exceptions when it doesn't find a match between transactions data (stock or cash) present in internal ledger systems with the data obtained from an external party. The logic for identifying an exception is often implemented in the system which generates the exception.

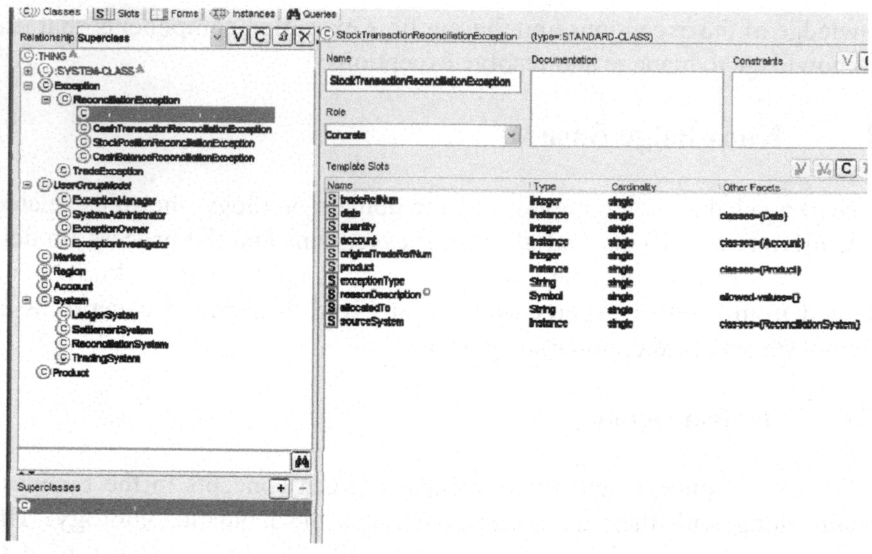

Figure 15-4. Domain Ontology for Reconciliation Exception

When an Exception Management system receives exceptions generated by various systems, they need to be classified. The classification of exceptions involves tagging each exception based on certain rules. Once the domain ontology has been modeled, such exception classification rules can be expressed formally using elements of the domain ontology. A sample classification rule in CLIPS is shown in figure 15-5. CLIPS [10] has been used due to its support for frame based knowledge bases through COOL (CLIPS Object oriented language) extension.

The classification rule checks for an occurrence of "Ledger Transaction Not Found" string in the reason description. If the reason description matches the string, it classifies the exception type as Missing Ledger Stock Transaction.

```
   ; A Classification Rule
   (defrule    ClassifyStockTradeReconciliationExp
   ?ExceptionObj <- (object (is-a
  StockTradeReconciliationException))
   (test( eq (send ? ExceptionObj get-
reasonDescription)     "Ledger Transaction Not
Found"))
   =>
   (send ?ExceptionObj put-exceptionType
  "MISSING_LEDGER_STOCK_TX")
   )
```

Figure 15-5. Classification Rule

The classified exception requires to be allocated to users/user groups responsible for resolving exceptions. The allocation rules are captured in the knowledge base as shown in figure 15-6. The user/user group to whom the exception is allocated owns the exception and is responsible for taking the exception to closure. An enterprise may have a specific organization structure for dealing with exceptions of various types. For example all Stock Trade Reconciliation Exceptions of type "Missing Ledger Stock Transaction" belonging to the APAC region may need to be allocated to the desk responsible for such exceptions. Such policies can be expressed formally using rules as shown in figure 15-6:

```
; An Allocation Rule
(defrule allocateApacStockTradeReconciliationExp
?ExceptionObj <- (object (is-a
StockTradeReconciliationException))
(test( eq (send ? ExceptionObj get-exceptionType)
 "MISSING_LEDGER_STOCK_TX"))
(test( eq (send ? ExceptionObj get-regionName)
APAC))
=>
 (send ?ExceptionObj put-allocatedTo
STOCK_APAC_DESK1)
)
```

Figure 15-6. Exception Allocation Rule

The allocation rule checks for the type and the region name of the exception. If the exception is of type Missing Ledger Stock Transaction and the region where the exception has occurred is Asia Pacific, the exception is allocated to the STOCK_APAC_DESK1 which is an instance of the concept ExceptionOwner in the Domain Ontology. The interrelationship of the Exception, Product, Market and Region captured in the domain ontology, enables easy editing of allocation and classification rules.

6.1.3 Exception Investigation and Resolution Process Models

Once an exception has been assigned an owner, it then needs to go through a sequence of steps to investigate and resolve the exception. The sequence of steps can be captured as a sequence of tasks using a process model. A task may be manual wherein a person performs some actions or automated wherein a software agent looks up some information in a system. Based on the outcome of each task, the next task to be executed is determined. Irrespective of whether a particular task is manual or automated, the business domain ontology can be used as an effective aid for capturing information that is required for execution of tasks. BPMI.org has defined the BPML [11] standard for modeling and defining processes. Process models are captured using BPML. Use of BPML allows us to model both manual and automated tasks in a process. When a process is modeled, each task can be associated with the software function that performs the task. For example, a manual task can be associated with a user interface and an automated task can be associated with a system agent. When a process engine orchestrates such a process, it would invoke the software function that is associated with the current task. When a manual task is encountered, the user interface would be displayed to the concerned user, so that the user can input the necessary information after performing the manual task. Similarly, when an automated task is encountered, the corresponding system agent would be invoked so that it can fetch the relevant data from a system. The use of domain ontology helps in formally defining the information to be displayed to the user for performing a manual task and the information required by a software agent for performing an automated task. When the process actually runs, the instances of the domain ontology concepts are used as actual values for the manual/automated tasks.

Figure 15-7 shows a snippet of the process model for the investigation/resolution of a Stock Trade Reconciliation Exception with Exception Type as "Missing Ledger Stock Transaction". This process model is only illustrative.

The domain ontology can be used to express the information required for executing the conditions/tasks. For example, the condition labeled as "Trade Ref No. Present?" can be represented formally using the expression referring to the ontology elements as "StockTransactionReconciliationException.trade RefNum == NULL?". Similarly, the task labeled "Check Ledger System" may be mapped to a software agent, which accepts as inputs "Stock TransactionReconciliationException.sourceSystem.ledgerSystem", "Stock TransactionReconciliationException.tradeRefNum" etc.

When the process engine orchestrates the process, the instances of the ontology concepts used in the process can either be passed to the process engine or the process engine can retrieve the instances as and when needed. Thus for example, when the process engine executes the task "Check Ledger System", it would need to know the actual ledger system to check and the trade reference number of the transaction to check for. This information can be retrieved from the instance information stored against the domain ontology.

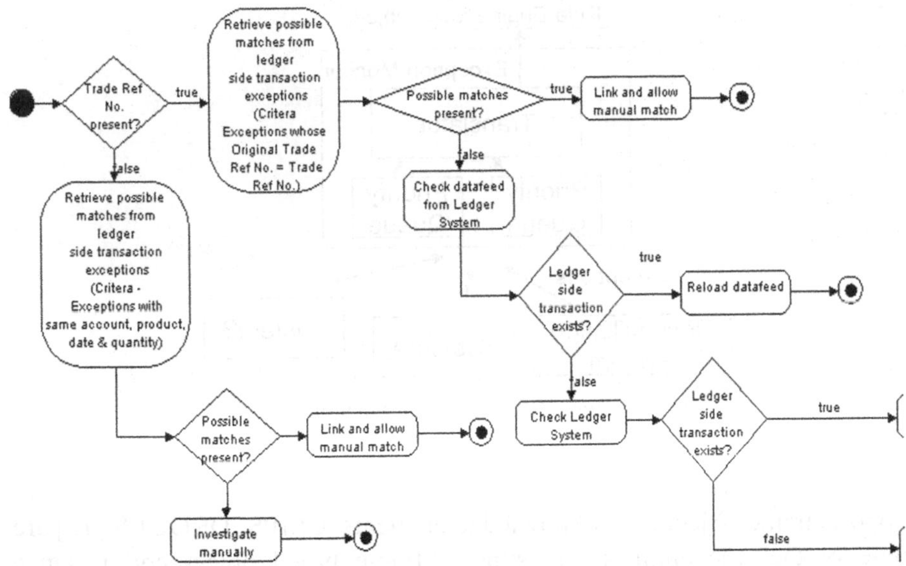

Figure *15-7. Process Model to resolve a Stock Trade Reconciliation Exception*

6.2 Exception Management Run time Components

The run time components use the knowledge base to manage exceptions. The run time components use the knowledge base and interact with users and systems to resolve exceptions.

6.2.1 Exception Monitor

The Exception Monitor is responsible for prioritizing exceptions it receives from multiple systems and triggering the rule engine. As shown in the figure 15-8, the Exception monitor consists of multiple queues. Exceptions from multiple systems are posted on to the appropriate queue based on the priority. The translator picks up the exceptions from the queue. The exceptions in XML format, are translated to instances of appropriate concepts existing in the domain ontology. The instance of the ontology class created by the translator triggers the rule engine for further steps to be taken on the exception.

6.2.2 Rule Engine

The rule engine runs the respective classification and allocation rules. The domain ontology is used by the rule engine to create a set of facts or

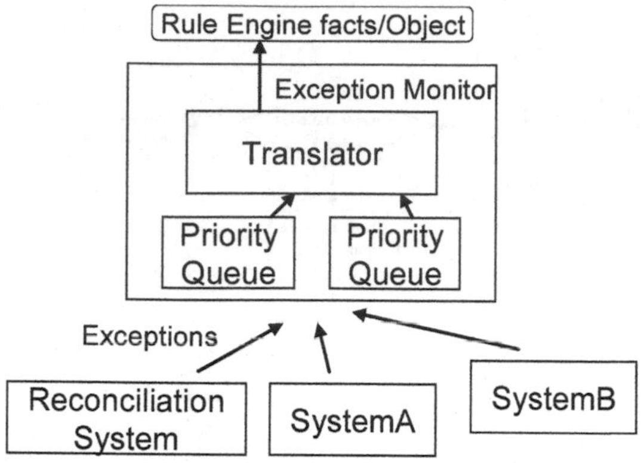

Figure 15-8. Exception Monitor

objects in its working memory. Hence, it is required to use a rule engine that supports frame/object based knowledge elements. CLIPS, DROOLS [12] are some of the rule engines that support frame based object and instance definitions. The exception instances are created and inserted into the working set of the rule engine. The rule engine classifies the exceptions and allocates it to an exception owner. The allocated exceptions are stored in the exception management database.

6.2.3 Process Engine

The process engine picks up the exceptions from the exception management database and executes the relevant process. The process could have tasks that need human intervention. Such tasks would be performed by the exception owner. The automated tasks are executed by the process engine using agents. The activities in the process engine are authored using the domain ontology. Hence, the process engine constantly interfaces with the domain ontology to execute the tasks in the process.

6.2.4 System Agents

The System Agents interface with the various software systems that are involved in the financial business process. The agents are responsible for creating exceptions and posting them to the exception monitor. They also act as an interface to the process and rule engine when additional inputs are required from the system for rule or task execution. The details of the systems and its respective system agents are stored in the domain ontology. The rule engine or the process engine could invoke a system agent and query required system information. The agent provides the relevant data in an XML format. The system agents could be platform and system specific. For extensibility it would be preferable to have the system agents as web services as the rule or the process engine could follow a generic implementation for interfacing with system agents.

7. TECHNOLOGIES INVOLVED

This section looks at some of the key technologies that can aid in the implementation of an Exception Management system.

7.1 Ontology Editor

A frame-based ontology representation language provides a way of modeling business domain ontology. An editor (like Protégé [13], an open source ontology/knowledge-base editor developed by Stanford University) which provides visual modeling of frame based ontology can be used for modeling the ontology. Such editors provide an intuitive and powerful way of modeling concepts and inter-relationships between concepts.

7.2 Ontology Representation Language

Once the business ontology has been modeled using frame-based ontology representation techniques, it needs to be serialized for aiding machine interpretation. XML represents a standards-based serialization technique. The W3C has come up with standards like RDF(S) [14] and OWL [15] for representing ontology in XML format. Ontology once converted to such machine-interpretable standard formats can be used by other components of the Exception Management system.

7.3 Ontology Storage

The ontology and knowledge (instances) need to be stored. For large systems (like an exception management system), persistence of ontology/knowledge in a relational database provides its own advantages. An ontology middleware like Sesame [16] can be used for persisting/querying ontology/knowledge present in a relational database.

7.4 Business domain ontology to system meta-data Map

Data corresponding to the instances of the business domain ontology concepts may be present in systems spread across the enterprise. Such systems have their own meta-data for representing/storing data. If a system uses a relational database for data persistence, the database scheme defines the system meta-data. The business domain ontology forms a common conceptual model of data spread across the organization. Hence, this needs to be mapped to the system meta-data so that data in heterogeneous systems can be easily referred/extracted using a common conceptual model. Ontology representation languages like RDF(s) and OWL provide features for expressing mapping of concepts across different models. RDF(s)/OWL aware inferencing engines can then be used to translate queries expressed using the common conceptual schema to system meta-data format.

7.5 Ontology based Rule Builder

The business domain ontology serves as the basis for the composition of various kinds of rules (exception identification, classification, allocation etc.). This can be achieved if we provide an interface for ontology based rule building. Commercial/open-source rule engines currently don't provide mechanisms for composing rules using elements from an underlying ontology. But an ontology based rule building layer can easily be built on top of existing rule engines. The ontology can be parsed and relevant portions of the ontology can be made available for use in building rules. Rules thus composed can be stored in a format which can be executed using a rule engine.

7.6 Ontology based process Modeler

The business domain ontology serves as a foundation for modeling processes (like the exception investigation/resolution processes). Again, process modelers available currently, don't provide support for ontology based process modeling, but a layer can be built easily on top of existing process modelers to enable modeling of tasks using the domain ontology. The ontology can be parsed and concepts related to the exception for which the exception investigation/resolution process is modeled can be made available to facilitate modeling of tasks in the process. Processes, thus modeled can be stored in the form of a process language like BPML/BPEL, which can be understood by standards-compliant process engines.

7.7 Rule Engine

The rules composed using the ontology, need to be executed in a rule engine. A rule engine that supports frame based knowledge base is required. There are several rule engines that provide support for facts and objects. (like CLIPS and DROOLS). DROOLS provides XML syntax for representing rules. Expressions and statements in the condition/action part of the rules can be represented using a Java like syntax. The ontology modeled earlier can be converted to simple Java classes with methods for retrieving and storing values corresponding to the ontology slots. These classes are invoked when the rule engine receives a fact (for example an exception) and tries to fire a rule (for example to allocate the exception).

7.8 Process Engine

The activities involved in a process need to be orchestrated, based on the exception which needs to be investigated/resolved. A process engine which provides support for execution of manual/system activities can help here. A BPM/Workflow product can serve as a process engine. The tasks that use ontology descriptions should be translated to the BPML Language. An Ontology access API would be required for the process engine to execute the tasks based on ontology specification.

8. ADVANTAGES OF USING ONTOLOGY BASED EXCEPTION MANAGEMENT SYSTEM

8.1 Common and Consistent Vocabulary

Enterprises have a suite of applications automating their business processes. Each of these applications would have been developed at different times by different people. The business analysts involved in process improvement take a long time to understand the systems and their respective vocabulary. Ontology enables the creation of common concept definition which can be mapped to different applications. This ontology then forms the vocabulary which is used by business analyst to model the rules and processes involved in the exception life cycle. It also serves as a mechanism by which the system agents communicate with each other and the exception monitor by mapping their respective system information to the domain ontology. A well defined ontology also helps new staff in learning the well defined concepts of the business process. A new team member would find it easier to understand the details of the exceptions, the systems, the processes, rules and tasks using the ontology.

8.2 Improved Manageability

Enterprise processes vary with changes in business policies and process improvements. The systems automating these processes require constant support and maintenance. As with most systems today, the business knowledge is embedded into the systems. A change in the process requires the system support and development team to change the implementation. Hence, the change cycle is very long. The use of ontology, process models and rules improves flexibility in adding and modifying exceptions, the associated tasks and rules as they can be edited by a knowledge engineer with more ease. Faster turn around time for a change in the business process is a key advantage of using the architecture comprising the ontology, rule and process engine.

9. LIMITATIONS OF USING ONTOLOGY IN KNOWLEDGE INTENSIVE PROCESSES

Knowledge Intensive processes involve several tasks and systems for execution. The processes deal with large amount of work products thus requiring the automating system to be highly scalable. Use of ontology for such systems has the following limitations.

9.1 Scalability

Scalability in use of ontology should provide for easy storing, accessing and managing. Storing and accessing ontology is linked to volume of data and usage. Managing deals with ease of updates or changes to the ontology. Storing of large domain ontology requires existing tools that map ontology to relational database. However, current techniques do not provide the scalability and performance compared to relational databases modeled conventionally with entities and relations.

Traditional database applications frequently use efficient retrieval mechanisms such as indices. The indices of a relational table can uniquely identify each record in the table. Use of indices enables faster access to a given record. However, most of the tools (like Protégé) and standards (RDF) in the ontology world do not support the notion of identifying or indexing an instance in the ontology. Although, they create a unique identifier for each frame/resource, it is not possible to define multiple attributes as a unique identifier for a concept or efficiently retrieve a resource from the ontology.

Another commonly used facility in RDBMS is trigger. A trigger is a fragment of code that RDBMS execute before or after a table is modified. Triggers can be used to fill a column with default information, to insert an audit row, to roll back a transaction after detecting some inconsistency etc. This feature is often required while managing ontology. For e.g., while adding a new instance of a resource, ability to define some action, like inserting a related instance or updating the value of a property is very much required. Most of the ontology capturing tools or standards does not support this feature.

9.2 Query Languages

As ontology is a mechanism to define and store domain knowledge, it is important to have universally accepted standards for querying data stored in the ontology. While W3C's RDF standard provides features required for defining and representing ontology, as of now there are no widely accepted standards for querying into ontology. Most of the ontology editors provide some proprietary mechanism to query the ontology. Some of the proposed standards for this are SquishQL [17] and RDQL [18].

Most of the proposed standards only provide constructs to access the data and its structure stored in the ontology. These languages do not support constructs to define the ontology or RDF Schema. They also do not specify anything for transaction control or access controls that are required in enterprise application. For development and maintenance of a large ontology by a set of users from multiple locations, many of these features are a must. A universally supported standard, which supports different types of operations on ontology, something akin SQL, is required to make this programming paradigm more accessible to the user.

9.3 Standard API

Programmatic access to ontology is equally important to declarative access to ontology as far as developing applications are concerned. Currently, there is no universally accepted standard for programmatically accessing ontology. OKBC[19] (Open Knowledge Base Connectivity) is an application-programming interface for accessing knowledge bases stored in knowledge representation systems (KRSs). Protégé model semantics is compliant to OKBC standard. Similarly there are several other attempts to define an API to programmatically access an RDF data sources. Frameworks such as HP Labs' Jena [20] and KAON [21] are prominent in this area. However, none of these API has been accepted as a universal standard. Definition of a standard Ontology access API, akin to ODBC or JDBC standards will help users develop applications that use ontology.

10. SUMMARY

The paper presents architecture for implementing knowledge intensive business processes. Ontology is used as a basic knowledge element on which the process models and rules are defined. A large scale deployment would require a process engine that supports task specification using ontology. Adoption of new techniques with ontology as the infrastructure component would require more support form the industry with well accepted standards and tools. However, the adoption of an architecture using ontology and process engines would result in improved manageability. Currently, manageability of automated business processes in a challenge faced by most enterprises. Enterprise systems embed the domain knowledge that is difficult to identify and change. Use of process engine would result in faster changes to the existing processes and increased automation of tasks in the process resulting in higher efficiency. Ontology development process would however have to provide mature tools and techniques for maintenance as version management, large knowledge base and multi-user development support are essential for it to be perceived as a mature development platform.

REFERENCES

[1] Davenport, T.H. Process Innovation – Reengineering work through information technology. Boston: Harvard Business School Press, 1993.

[2] Davenport, T.H. Process Innovations: When inmates run the asylum. www.bptrends.com, May 2004.

[3] Tautz, C. Traditional Process representations are Ill-suited for Knowledge Intensive processes. Proceedings of the workshop program at the Fourth International Conference on Case-based reasoning, 2001.

[4] Eppler, M. J., Seifried, P. M., Röpnack, A. Improving Knowledge Intensive Processes through an Enterprise Medium. ACM Conference on Managing Organizational Knowledge for Strategic Advantage, 1999.

[5] Miers, D. The split personality of BPM. www.bptrends.com, 2004.

[6] Massey, Anne P., Montoya-Weiss Mitzi & O'Driscoll Tony. A methodology to structure Ill- Structured Processes: Performance Centered Design. Proceedings of the Hawaii International Conference on System Sciences (HICSS)- 34, 2001.

[7] Leijen, Hans Van, Baets, W.R.J. A Cognitive Framework for Reengineering Knowledge–intensive processes. Proceedings of 36th Hawaii International Conference on System Sciences (HICSS), 2003.

[8] Levine, P., Pomeral, J.-Ch.: Two experiences in knowledge management in Knowledge intensive organizations in the French social sector, Proceedings of the HICSS- 35, IEEE Pub, 2002.

[9] Abecker, A., Mentzas, G.: Active knowledge delivery in semi-structured administrative processes, 2nd Int'l Workshop on Knowledge Management in Electronics Government (KMGov-2001), May 2001, Siena, Italy.

[10] CLIPS WWW Page: http://www.ghg.net/clips/CLIPS.html.

[11] Assaf Arkin, Business Process Modeling Language, Working Draft, June 2002. http://www.bpmi.org.
[12] DROOLS WWW Page http://www.drools.org.
[13] Protégé Ontology Editor WWW Page http://protege.stanford.edu/.
[14] RDF/XML Syntax Specification WWW Page http://www.w3.org/TR/rdf-syntax-grammar/.
[15] OWL Web Ontology Language Overview WWW Page http://www.w3.org/TR/owl-features/.
[16] Sesame WWW Page http://www.openrdf.org/.
[17] Miller, L.(2001) RDF Squish query Language and Java implementation . Public Draft, Institute for Learning and Research Technology See http://irlt.org/discovery/2001/02/squish.
[18] Seaborne, A. (2004) RDQL – A Query Language for RDF http://www.w3.org/Submission/RDQL.
[19] Chaudhri VK,Farqhar A, Fikes R, Karp PD, Rice JP (1998) Open Knowledge Base Connectivity 2.0.3 Technical Report http://www.ai.sri.com/~okbc/okbc-2-0-3.pdf.
[20] B. McBride, Jena: Implementing the RDF Model and Syntax Specification, Proceedings of the Second International Workshop on the Semantic Web - SemWeb'2001, May 2001
[21] Raphael Volz, Daniel Oberle, Steffen Staab, and Boris Motik. KAON SERVER - A Semantic Web Management System. Proceedings of WWW-2003, Budapest, Hungary, May 2003 http://km.aifb.uni-karlsruhe.de/kaon/Members/rvo/rdf_api.

Chapter 16

USING ONTOLOGIES TO CREATE OBJECT MODEL FOR OBJECT-ORIENTED SOFTWARE ENGINEERING

Dencho N. Batanov[1] and Waralak Vongdoiwang[2]

[1]*School of Advanced Technologies, Asian Institute of Technology, Klong Luang, Pathumthani, 12120, Thailand;* [2]*University of the Thai Chambers of Commerces, Din Daeng, Bangkok, 10400, Thailand*

Abstract: In this paper we introduce and discuss our approach to creating an object model from a problem domain text description as a basic deliverable of the analysis phase in Object-Oriented Software Engineering using ontologies. For this purpose we first briefly compare object models with ontologies. The object model of a system consists of objects, identified from the text description and structural linkages corresponding to existing or established relationships. The ontologies provide metadata schemas, offering a controlled vocabulary of concepts. At the center of both object models and ontologies are objects within a given problem domain. The both concepts are based on reusability using intensively libraries. The major difference is that while the object model contains explicitly shown structural dependencies between objects in a system, including their properties, relationships and behavior, the ontologies are based on related terms (concepts) only. Because ontology is accepted as a formal, explicit specification of a shared conceptualization, we can naturally link ontologies with object models, which represent a system-oriented map of related objects. To become usable programming entities these objects should be described as Abstract Data Types (ADTs). This paper addresses ontologies as a basis of a complete methodology for object identification and their modeling as (converting to) ADTs, including procedures and available tools such as CORPORUM OntoExtract and VisualText, which can help the conversion process. This paper describes how the developers can implement this methodology on the base of an illustrative example.

Key words: Object Model; Ontologies; Software Engineering; Object-Oriented; Knowledge base

1. INTRODUCTION

Ontology is a specification of a representational vocabulary for a shared domain of discourse: definitions of classes, relations, functions, and other objects (Gruber, 1993) or, more generally, a specification of conceptualization (Gruber, 1994). The basic components of an ontology are concepts, relationships between concepts and attributes. Concepts, relationship types and attributes are abstracted from the objects and thus describe the schema (the ontology). On the other hand, the objects populate the concepts, values and relationships, instantiate the attributes of those objects and relationships among them respectively. Three types of relationships that may be used between classes or concepts in ontology are generalization, association, and aggregation. Ontology is well known as a structured description of declaration and abstract way to express the domain information of an application (Angele, Staab & Schurr, 2003). The concepts in an ontology are similar with objects in object oriented software engineering. To solve the problem of heterogeneity in developing software applications, there is a need for specific descriptions of all kinds of concepts, for example, classes (general things), the relationships that can exist among them, and their properties (or attributes) (Heflin, Volz, and Dale, 2002). Ontologies described syntactically on the basis of languages such as eXtensible Markup Language (XML), XML Schema, Resource Description Framework (RDF), and RDF Schema (RDFS) can be successfully used for this purpose.

Object models are different from other modeling techniques because they have merged the concept of variables and abstract data types into an abstract variable type: an object. Objects have identity, state, and behavior and object models are structural representation of a system of those objects [based on concepts of type, inheritance, association, and possibly class (ChiMu Corporation, 2003)]. In the artificial intelligence (AI) area, ontology has been focused on knowledge modeling. On the other hand, a lot of industry standards and powerful tools for object-oriented analysis, design, and implementation of complex software systems have been developed. And because of the closed connection between ontologies and object models, these maturing standards and tools can be used for ontology modeling (Cranefield & Purvis, 1999).

Object orientation is a commonly accepted paradigm in software engineering for the last few decades. The motto of object-oriented software development may be formulated in different ways, but its essence can be stated simply: "Identify and concentrate on objects in the problem domain description first. Think about the system function later." At the initial analysis phase, however, identifying the right objects, which are vital for the system's functionality, seems to be the most difficult task in the whole development process from both theoretical and practical point of view. Object-oriented software development is well supported by a huge number of working methods, techniques, and tools, except for this starting point - object identification and building the related system object model. Converting the text description of system problem domain and respective functional requirement specifications into an object model is usually left to the intuition and experience of developers (system analysts). One commonly accepted rule of thumb is, "If an object fits within the context of the system's responsibilities, then include it in the system." However, since the members of a development team are likely to have different views on many points, serious communication problems may occur during the later phases of the software development process. Recently there has been great research interest in applying ontologies for solving this "language ambiguity problem" as either an ontology-driven or ontology-based approach (Deridder & Wouters, 1999). This is especially true for object-oriented software engineering mainly because of the similarity in the principles of the two paradigms. Moreover, the object systems similar to ontologies, which represent conceptualized analysis of a given domain, can be easily reused for different applications (Swartout, 1999).

Representation of objects as Abstract Data Types (ADTs) is of primary importance in developing object-oriented software because it is actually a process of software implementation of ADTs. Any ADT is a named set of attributes, which show the characteristics of and formalize the relationships between objects and methods (operations, functions) for putting into effect the behavior of objects, making the system functional enough to be of practical use. Building an accurate, correct and objectively well-defined object model containing objects, represented as ADTs, is the basis for successful development of an object-oriented software system (Weiss, 1993; Manola, 1999). The basic idea is that the implementation of ADTs as a code allows all working objects (instances of classes) to have one and the same behavior, which can be changed dynamically in a centralized manner for higher efficiency and effectiveness. Objects are transformed during the software development process from "real things" to concepts, and finally to Abstract Data Types, as shown in Fig. 16-1.

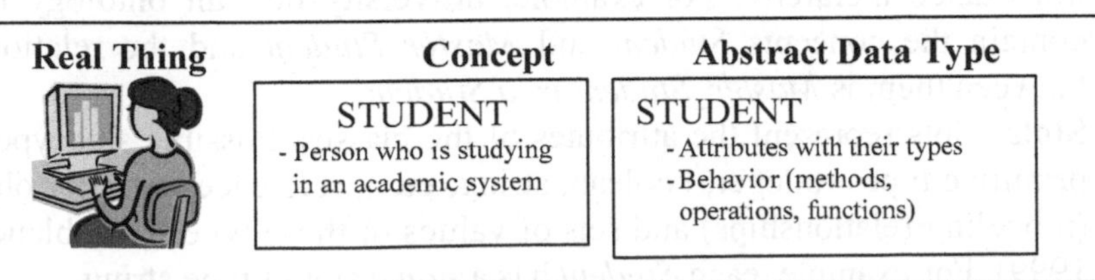

Figure 16-1. Conceptualization and ADTs

Our approach to converting text description into object model, described in this paper, is based on eight different models, only two of which, namely the text description model (T-model) and class (object) model (C-model), are included in the classical object-oriented software development process. The rest of the models used represent specific analysis work, which the developers should do, to get benefit from using ontologies for semi-formal identification of objects, which are to be responsible for the system functionality and their respective ADTs. The basic idea is to ensure suitable transformation of the models from one to another using respective procedures and tools, which can be considered as potential elements for integrating ontologies into CASE tools for object-oriented systems. The paper is structured as follows: Section 2 compares the similarities and differences between object models and ontologies in modeling, languages used, implementation, and reusability. Section 3 presents the overview of the approach to converting text description using ontology to object model. Section 4 introduces the models used and describes the overall procedure for their transformation. This section also shows the techniques and tools, which can be practically used for model transformation. An illustrative example of a part of the information system for the domain of academic management is used throughout the paper to support the explanations. Finally, in section 5 conclusions and some recommendations for future work are outlined.

2. SIMILARITIES AND DIFFERENCES BETWEEN ONTOLOGIES AND OBJECT MODEL

2.1 Modeling

2.1.1 Ontologies Modeling

In this section, we present two commonly employed ontology modeling approaches. The first is formalized using mainly four kinds of components: classes, slots, facets, and instances.

- **Concepts/classes:** the concepts in ontologies are arranged in an inheritance hierarchy. For example, university domain ontology might contain the concepts *Student* and *Master_Student* and the relationship between them is *Master_Student is_a Student.*
- **Slots:** slots represent the attributes of the classes. Possible slot types are primitive types (integer, boolean, string, etc.), references to other objects (modeling relationships) and sets of values of those types (Knublauch H. 1999). For example, each *Student* has a *name* slot of type string.

- **Facets:** they are attached to classes or slots and contain meta information, such as comments, constraints and default values. For example, in order to verify the status of a *Student*, a *Student* has to enroll at least one *Course*.
- **Instances:** instances represent specific entities from the domain knowledge base (KB). For example, the knowledge base of the university ontology might contain the specific student *John* and course *Database*.

Another approach to modeling of ontologies is formalized using five kinds of components: classes, relations, functions, axioms and instances (Corcho, Fermandez, & Perez, 2001).

- **Classes:** classes are usually organized in taxonomies. Sometimes, the taxonomies are considered to be full ontologies (Studer, Benjamins, & Fensel, 1998). Classes or concepts are used in broad sense. Concepts can be anything about which something is said and, therefore, could also be the description of a task, function, action, strategy, reasoning process, etc.
- **Relations:** they represent a type of interaction between concepts of the domain. They are formally defined as any subset of a product of n sets, that is: R: C1 x C2 x ... x Cn. For instance, binary relations may include: subclass-of and connected-to.
- **Functions:** they are a special case of relations in which the n-th element of the relationship is unique for the n-1 preceding elements. Formally, functions are defined as: F: C1 x C2 x ... x Cn-1 x Cn. An example of function is *update*, which gets lists of students and titles of their theses, then returns one list of names with added titles. This function belongs to object *Thesis*.
- **Axioms:** they are used to model sentences that are always true. They can be included in an ontology for several purposes, such as defining the meaning of ontology components, defining complex constrains on the values of attributes, the arguments of relations, etc., verifying the correctness of the information specified in the ontology or deducing new information.
- **Instances:** they are used to represent specific elements of classes.

As we can see the two approaches to modeling ontologies are quite similar. The difference is in the included elements, which lead to lightweight (the first case) or heavyweight (the second case) ontologies and respective differences in the details of available output information.

2.1.2 Object Modeling

Object modeling is formalized using mainly four kinds of components: Objects/classes, attributes/properties, methods/operations/functions, and relationships/relations.

- **Object/class:** everything known in the real world. For example, a university system might contain the objects *Student*, *Course, Registry, Assignment, etc.* Every class serves as a pattern of describing its instances (objects).
- **Attributes/properties:** objects must have at least one attribute. Possible slot types are primitive types (integer, boolean, string etc.), references to other objects (modeling relationships) and sets of values of those types. For example, each *Student* has *identification number* as an attribute and its type is string.
- **Methods/operations/functions:** they are declared and defined on the object's attributes and may contain meta information, such as comments, constraints and default values. For example, in order to verify the status of a *Student* (a *Student* has to enroll at least one *Course*), a method/function *get_course()* can be declared and defined respectively.
- **Relationships/relations:** they represent an abstraction of a set of association, that hold systematically between different objects in the real world. For example, the relationship between object *Student* and object *Course* is *take_course*; on the other hand, object *Course* has relationship *taken_by* with object *Student*. The major types of relationships are classification, generalization/specification, associations, aggregation.

The brief comparisons between ontology and object modeling shows close similarity especially in the elements (components) used. However, the most substantial difference is in the deliverables. While ontologies represent well structured description (explanation) of mutually related terms, the object model is to represent a system as structure of modules (objects) ready for implementation in software. This is actually the basic differences between ontologies and object models, which remains valid for all following comparisons.

2.2 Languages

Object-oriented modeling is used in a growing number of commercial software development projects. There are many languages that have been considered as mature and well accepted by the community of object oriented software developers. Examples of some of the most popular of them are Ada95, C++, Java, C#, Eiffel, Smalltalk, etc.

A large number of languages have been used for ontologies specification during the last decade. Many of these languages have been already used for representing knowledge in knowledge-based applications, others have been adapted from existing knowledge representation languages. There is however also a group of languages that are specifically created for the representation of ontologies such as Ontolingual[1], LOOM[2], OCML[3],

FLogic[4], etc. Recently, many other languages have been developed in the context of the World Wide Web (and have great impact on the development of the Semantic Web) such as RDF[5] and RDF Schema[6], SHOE[7], XOL[8], OML[9], OIL[10], DAML+OIL[11], etc. Their syntax is mainly based on XML[12], which has been widely adopted as a standard language for exchanging information on the Web. More specifically SHOE, whose syntax is based on HTML[13], RDF and RDF Schema cannot be considered as pure ontology specification languages, but as general languages for the description of metadata in the Web. Most of these "markup" languages are still in a development phase, they are continuously evolving. Fig. 16-2 shows the main relationships between the above mentioned languages (Corcho, Fernandez & Perez 2001).

In addition, there are other languages that have been created for the specification of specific ontologies, such as CycL[14] or GRAIL[15] (in the medical domain).

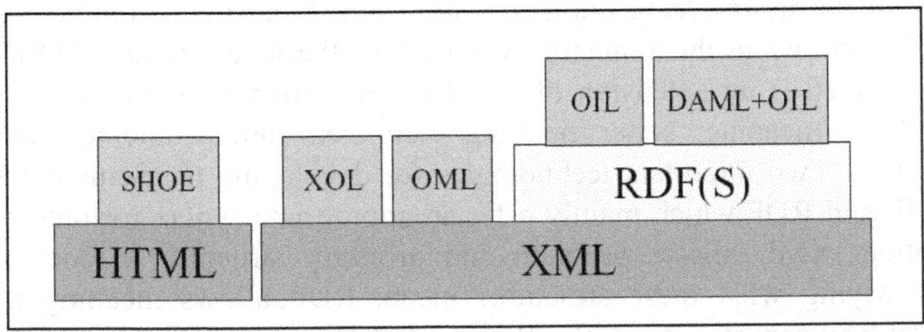

Figure 16-2. Pyramid of Web-based languages (Corcho, Fernandez & Perez, 2001)

In summary, the languages used for object-oriented software development and describing ontologies are definitely different. The former are programming languages while the latter are declarative by nature. This leads to the requirement specific methods and techniques to be used if we need to work with information from ontologies for the purposes of object orientation.

2.3 Implementations

The languages are used to help implementation of object models and ontologies. The basic approach for implementing objects is to have a class, which serves as a pattern for creating instances (objects). A class defines what types the objects will implement, how to perform the behavior required for the interface and how to remember state information. Each object will then only need to remember its individual state. Although using classes is by far the most common object approach, it is not the only one. For example, using prototypes is another approach, but it is considered as and is really peripheral to the core concepts of object-oriented modeling (Mohan & Brooks, 2003).

The Object Data Management Group (ODMG) Object Model is intended to allow portability of applications among object database products. In particular, the ODMG model extends the OMG core to provide for persistent objects, object properties, more specific object types, queries and transactions. The basic concepts are objects, types, operations, properties, identity and subtyping. Objects have state (defined by the values of their properties), behavior (defined by operations) and identity. All objects of the same type have common behavior and properties. Types are objects so may have their own properties. A type has an interface and one or more implementations. All things are instances of some type and subtyping organizes these types in a lattice. A type definition can declare that an extent (set of all instances) be maintained for the type (Cranefield & Purvis, 1999).

One of the more recent implementation developments of ontologies on the Web is known as the Semantic Web (Volz, Oberle, & Studer, 1999). The Semantic Web is an extension of the Web, in which information is given well-defined meaning, better enabling computers and people to work in cooperation. Two important technologies for developing the Semantic Web are XML and RDF which mainly offer an appropriate syntax for ontologies description. XML allows users to add arbitrary structure to documents without saying what these structures mean. RDF allows meaning to be specified between objects on the Web and was intentionally designed as a metadata modeling language. An important aspect of the Semantic Web is a set of ontologies.

2.4 Reusability

Reusability is the most desired goal of the entire software development cycle and is based on the reluctance of reinventing something when it has already been invented. Object-oriented development supports reusability, especially through the principles of abstraction. Inheritance supports continual iterations of analysis until unique objects are found in a class hierarchy. These unique objects inherit characteristics from the higher level classes and this allows reusing information from the previously defined classes, eliminating the need to reinvent it. Class structure leads to the development of class libraries that allow sharing of models and programming throughout a system. The development process can be simplified, from analysis to requirements to implementation, through the use of building blocks of classes and objects (Thomason, & Sauter, 1999).

Examples of some of the most popular commercial libraries are Booch Components[16] (Ada95, C, and C++ versions), KISS – [Keep It Simple Series of Generics, by Osiris], Object Space C++ Libraries, etc.

As the number of different ontologies is arising, the maintaining and re-organizing them in order to facilitate the re-use of knowledge is challenging. If we could share knowledge across systems, costs would be reduced. However, because knowledge bases are typically constructed from scratch, each one with its own idiosyncratic structure, sharing is difficult. Recent research has focused on the use of ontologies to promote sharing. An ontology is a hierarchically structured set of terms for describing a domain that can be used as a skeletal foundation for a knowledge base. If two knowledge bases are built on a common ontology, knowledge can be more readily shared, since they share a common underlying structure (Swartout, Patil, Knight, and Russ, 1996). Ontology plays an important role in knowledge sharing and reuse. Ontology library systems are an important tool in grouping and re-organizing ontologies for further re-use, integration, maintenance, mapping and versioning. An ontology library system is a library system that offers various functions for managing, adapting and standardizing groups of ontologies. It should fulfill the needs for re-use of ontologies. In this sense, an ontology library system should be easily accessible and offer efficient support for re-using existing relevant ontologies and standardizing them based on upper-level ontologies and ontology representation languages. An ontology library system requires functional infrastructure to store and maintain ontologies, an uncomplicated adapting environment for editing, searching and reasoning ontologies, and strong standardization support by providing upper-level ontologies and standard ontology representation languages (Ding & Fensel, 2001). In the computer science area, ontologies aim at capturing domain knowledge in a generic way and provide a commonly agreed understanding of a domain, which may be reused and shared across applications. Assuming an ontology library is available, how can we select ontologies from this library that are potentially useful for a new application? Typically, application development is in fact a combination of ontology construction and reuse. Some ontologies already exist and can be taken from a library. Others might not be provided by the library, and has to be constructed from scratch. Some available important ontology library systems are WebOnto[17], Ontolingual[1], DAML Ontology library system[18], SHOE[7], Ontology Server[19], IEEE Standard Upper Ontology[20], OntoServer[21], ONIONS[22], etc. Ontologies allow the specification of concepts in a domain, which are actually objects. Shared ontologies allow for different systems to come to a common understanding of the semantics of participating object (Mohan & Brooks, 2003). Central is the reuse role of library of ontologies. Such library contains a number of existing definitions organized along different levels of abstraction in order to increase sharing and minimize duplicate efforts, (Ding & Fensel, 2001).

3. OVERVIEW OF THE APPROACH TO CONVERTING TEXT DESCRIPTION TO OBJECT MODEL USING ONTOLOGY

Our approach is based on transformation of models. Models are inseparable and one of the most significant parts of any methodology. They help developers to better understand complex tasks and represent in a simpler way the work they should do to solve those tasks. Object-oriented analysis of a system under development is a good example of such a complex task. The complexity stems from the fact that in object-oriented development everything is based on objects but their identification in a given problem domain is completely left to the intuition of the developer. All that he/she has as a starting point is the text description of the problem domain, which is itself an extended model of the usually very general and ambiguous initial user requirements. Following the existing practice we accept this text description (T-model) as available model, which serves as a starting point of our transformation process. According to the object-oriented software development methodology the analysis work on the T-model leads to two major deliverables: functional specification of the system, expressed as either text or graphically as Use Case diagrams and the object (class) model (we call it C-model).

The ultimate goal of the developer's efforts is actually the creation of the C-model. This is because the objects included in the C-model should contain the complete information necessary for the next phases of design and implementation of the software system. In other words the objects should be represented as ADTs – ready for design and implementation software modules. It is clear now the problem with "language ambiguity" – different interpretations of the T-model, without any formal support of the choice of participating objects, would lead to creating C-models, which are quite probably inconsistent, incomplete or inefficient for the further steps of design and implementation. We believe that using ontology as a tool of conceptualization working on the T-model can make semi-formal, if not fully formal, the process of creating the C-model and in this way help developers in this complex and imprecise task. This is the major motivation of our work described briefly in this paper.

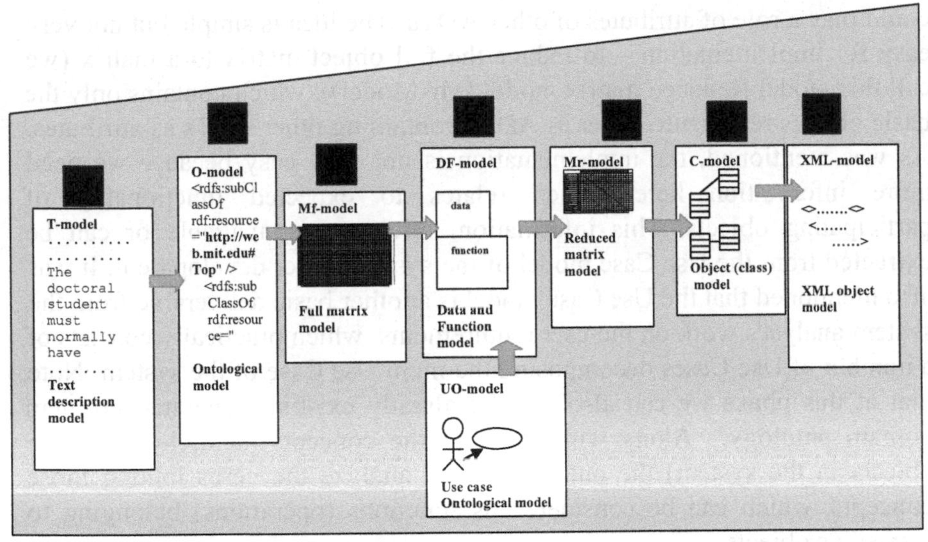

Figure 16-3. Models for converting a text description into an object model

Fig. 16-3 shows the basic idea of the proposed approach, models used, and transformation process on them. The starting point of the transformation is the T-model, which represents a concise description of the problem domain, where the software system under development will work, written in a natural language, in our case English. If not available, the T-model is a deliverable from a system analyst's work on the general user requirements for the system functionality. The presumption is that this problem domain description contains the main objects, which will participate in ensuring that functionality. Of course, at this level the objects are represented by their natural names only and as such are very far from the form we need to reach – represented as ADTs. To help this process we refer to a tool of conceptualization – an ontological engine, which applied on the T-model generates an ontological description (O-model) of the problem domain at hand.

We use the fact here that any ontology is a systematic description of concepts (objects) in a given domain of interest along with expressed relationships between all or part of them. This is actually the crossroads between the object-oriented and ontology-based paradigms. The O-model is a straightforward and practically useful source of information for identifying the participating objects. We use this information to build a so called Full matrix model (Mf-model), which represents in a simple form those objects as well as the linkages (relationships) between them. However, it is worth noting that the processing of the Mf-model is semi-formal in nature. This means that at this phase the developer should take important decisions about which objects could be considered as basic ADTs and which, and where, could play a role of attributes of other ADTs. The idea is simple but not very easy for implementation – to reduce the full object matrix to a matrix (we call this model Reduced matrix model (Mr-Model)), which contains only the basic objects represented later as ADTs containing other ADTs as attributes. As was mentioned, the implementation is not very easy because we need more information here, which relates to expected functionality of participating objects. This information, however, is available or can be extracted from the Use Case model of the system under development. It was also mentioned that the Use Case model is another basic deliverable from the system analyst's work on the user requirements, which practically consists of a number of Use Cases decomposing the main Use Case of the system. Note that at this phase we can also use the already existing generated problem domain ontology. Along with showing the concepts hierarchy (possible objects in the system) the ontologies also analyze the verbs linking those concepts, which can be considered as functions (operations) belonging to respective objects.

We use the text descriptions of different Use Cases to extract different functionality of the system by the ontological engine and as a result we get the so called Use Case Ontological model (UO-model). We show later in section 4 that the functionality, expressed by the UO-model, can be used successfully at this particular phase along with the ontological information about the objects in the Mf-model to create a Data and Function model (DF-model). As a matter of principle DF-model can be used for each of the objects in the DF-model but this would lead to a high degree of redundancy and quite complicated matrix presentation even for relatively simple T-models. To avoid this we propose using so called business object patterns, which can be a result from ontology-based analysis. The idea is to use ontological libraries existing recently for a great number of application domains and to rely on the ontological description of the concepts (objects), which according to the developer's decision have the highest degree of likelihood of being selected as basic objects in the system. This will allow for significant reduction of the number of possible objects in the DF-model, or we can transform it to the Mr-model.

We assume that this model contains all the necessary information for building the C-model, which is actually the goal of this first phase of analysis of object-oriented software systems. The representation of the C-model is significantly different from Mr-model however, as far as the former shows not only the object hierarchy but the objects' structure as well. In other words, the C-model is a model representing ADTs. The last model, the XML-model is optional but can be very important in practice because it allows the C-model to be published on the Web in a unified (XML-based) format supporting in this way the collaborative work, which is a commonly accepted technology nowadays.

Finally, an interesting question may arise here. Do the models proposed in this approach replace or ignore the well known and widely used in practice models applied to the analysis of object-oriented systems? The answer is certainly not. All models, such as the information model, state model, process model, functional model, etc,, along with their accompanying methods, techniques and tools (for example those included in Rational Rose CASE tools) remain absolutely necessary for completing the phase of object-oriented analysis. Moreover, all of them are created to be applied on the object model of the system under development and therefore, they will use the basic deliverable of the transformation process, shown above. What we have proposed is a semi-formal procedure for converting a text description of a given problem domain into an object model, which should be considered as a basis for further analysis work. Identification of objects and representing them as ADTs using ontologies is the major objective and achievement of the proposed approach.

4. THE MODELS USED

In this section we will briefly show the foundation, role and structure of the models used in the transformation process, explained generally in section 3. In addition, we will show some of the tools, mainly the ontological ones, which can be used for implementing the models. One and the same example – a part of a university information system regarding PhD students – is used as an illustration where needed.

4.1 T-model: Text description model

The T-model or text description of a problem domain model that we were working on is an English text description of a part of a specific problem domain, shown on the left side of Fig. 16-4.

This text is represented as an ontology description after processing by an ontological engine tool, in our case CORPORUM OntoExtract (Engles, 2001). It is a Web-based version of CORPORUM, which is able to extract ontologies and represent them in XML/RDF/OIL (default in RDF schema(RDFS)) and also to communicate with and negotiate the final format of the to-be-submitted ontology extracted from a specific text (Engles, 2001). This tool can interpret text, in the sense that it builds ontologies that reflect world concepts as the user of the system sees and expresses them. So

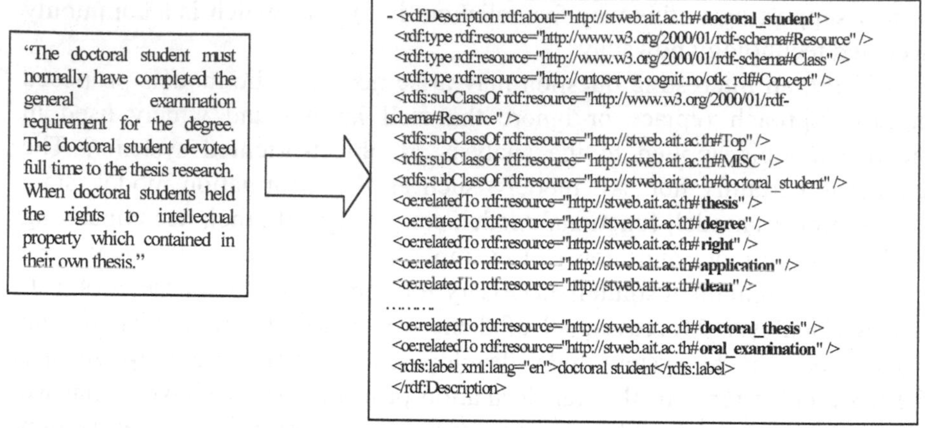
"The doctoral student must normally have completed the general examination requirement for the degree. The doctoral student devoted full time to the thesis research. When doctoral students held the rights to intellectual property which contained in their own thesis."
- <rdf:Description rdf:about="http://stweb.ait.ac.th#doctoral_student">
<rdf:type rdf:resource="http://www.w3.org/2000/01/rdf-schema#Resource" />
<rdf:type rdf:resource="http://www.w3.org/2000/01/rdf-schema#Class" />
<rdf:type rdf:resource="http://ontoserver.cognit.no/otk_rdf#Concept" />
<rdfs:subClassOf rdf:resource="http://www.w3.org/2000/01/rdf-schema#Resource" />
<rdfs:subClassOf rdf:resource="http://stweb.ait.ac.th#Top" />
<rdfs:subClassOf rdf:resource="http://stweb.ait.ac.th#MISC" />
<rdfs:subClassOf rdf:resource="http://stweb.ait.ac.th#doctoral_student" />
<oe:relatedTo rdf:resource="http://stweb.ait.ac.th#thesis" />
<oe:relatedTo rdf:resource="http://stweb.ait.ac.th#degree" />
<oe:relatedTo rdf:resource="http://stweb.ait.ac.th#right" />
<oe:relatedTo rdf:resource="http://stweb.ait.ac.th#application" />
<oe:relatedTo rdf:resource="http://stweb.ait.ac.th#dean" />
....
<oe:relatedTo rdf:resource="http://stweb.ait.ac.th#doctoral_thesis" />
<oe:relatedTo rdf:resource="http://stweb.ait.ac.th#oral_examination" />
<rdfs:label xml:lang="en">doctoral student</rdfs:label>
</rdf:Description>

Figure 16-4. Text description model

at this point in the process, the text is automatically processed and converted into ontologies, which can be done online.

4.2 O-model: Ontological model

The ontology described in RDFS defines the names and relations of the extracted concepts, or object names. RDFS provides a mechanism to define domain-specific properties and classes of resources to which developers may apply those properties (Klein, 2001). More specifically, an ontology description is recognizable as an ontology language. Classes are specified with <rdfs:class>. Subclasses and subproperties are specified using <rdfs:subClassOf> and <rdfs:subPropertyOf> (the top class defined in the schema is "Resource") respectively. When a class is a subclass of several superclasses, this is interpreted as a conjunction of superclasses (Gil and Ratnakar, 2000). CORPORUM OntoExtract basically generates taxonomies that represent classes, subclasses, and instances. A class described in the text may also be defined as a subclass of the universal "rdf:resource" if no more information about the class can be found. A class may also be defined as a subclass of other classes if evidence is found that the class is indeed a subclass. A subclass relationship found by this tool is based on information about the term (Engles, 2001).

An important category that is exported by the CORPORUM OntoExtract engine is the *cross-taxonomic* relations. While a typical ontology often represents taxonomy, <isRelated> refers to cross-taxonomic links that may exist within a domain and, if represented, can make a difference in finding needed information based on context descriptions. In short, it can identify the possible relations between objects. For example, in the box on the right side of Fig. 16-4, the class "doctoral_student" has certain relations with other classes, for instance, "thesis", "degree", "right", etc.

4.3 Mf-model: Full matrix model

The O-model describes only the type (object) name and provides relations between possible objects. However, this model is in a form difficult to understand and work with identified objects. That is why we use the RDFS description as an input to create a simple matrix-based model, which can serve as an intermediate model. It contains all identified objects, approved by the developer and allows easy manipulation on this full set of objects. This is the reason to call this model a full matrix model (Mf-model).

The relationships between objects in the system can be represented as simple mapping as shown in Fig. 16-5 below. Generally speaking, we can always define two sets of k and n objects (k ≠ n in the common case) in a system between elements where relationships exist or can be established. If the objects are numbered differently each X in the table of Fig. 16-5 will represent those relationships.

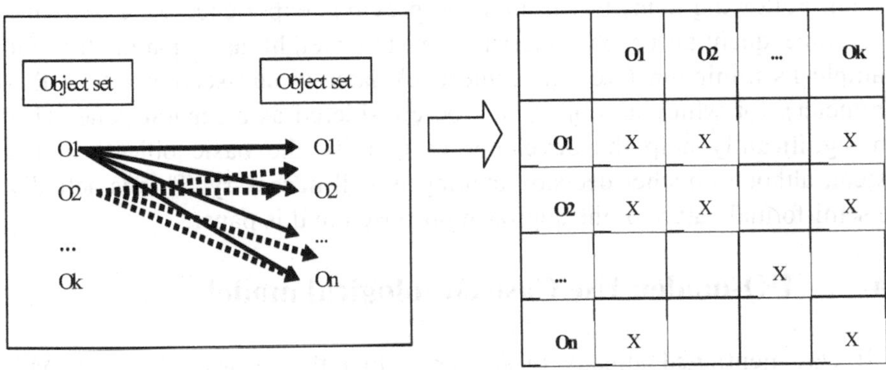

	O1	O2	...	Ok
O1	X	X		X
O2	X	X		X
...			X	
On	X			X

Figure 16-5. Example of relationships between objects

Based on the above general considerations, we can build a full matrix as depicted in Fig. 16-6 to show every relationship that occurs between already identified objects.

The total number of relationships an object has with other objects is called the weight of that particular object. It determines how many relationships one object has to other objects participating in this problem domain. One may infer that higher is the weight the higher the relevance of that object in the domain or, in other words, the higher the likelihood is that this particular object can be considered as a separate ADT in the software

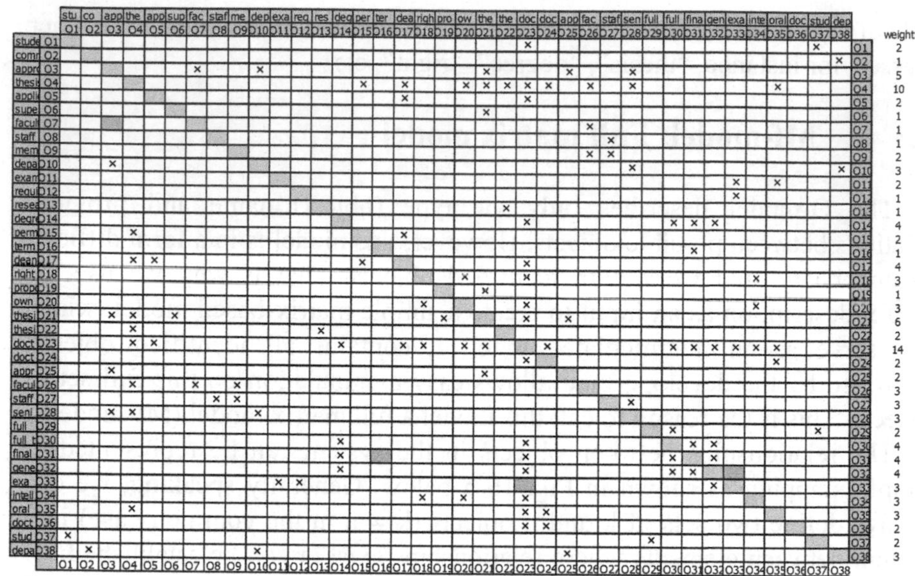

Figure 16-6. Full matrix model (Mf-model)

system. Following heuristics from some previous experience we can define here some quantitative characteristics of the weight as a parameter, for example its minimum (we will come back later in sub-section 4.6 to this parameter), for which an object may be considered as a separate one. This can significantly help the developer to identify the basic objects in the system, although his/her decision making is still necessary. This is actually the semi-formal nature of the approach proposed in this paper.

4.4 UO-model: Use Case Ontological model

It was mentioned already in section 3 that the information from Mf-model, although useful, is perhaps redundant and certainly far from complete. Thanks to the ontological analysis the system analyst may have information about the possible objects in terms of names and partially as their attributes (other objects) but has no any information about the system behavior of objects. This means that at this phase we cannot talk about ADTs. Obviously, additional information is necessary related to system functionality, in which different objects are involved. Such information is of vital importance for identifying the complete contents of objects as data and behavior (objects' functions, operations), which are fundamental elements of the object model (Batanov and Arch-int, 2003). Moreover, considering system functionality at this early stage of analysis may help the system analyst to define more precisely the basic objects in the system, to add new objects or to remove/replace already identified objects, which are not important for any of the system functions. This is the place where we should turn our attention to the Use Case modeling.

Use Case Modeling is the process of identifying and modeling business events, who/what initiates them and how the system responds to them. Use cases capture requirements from the perspective of how the actor will actually use the system, in other words each of them describes a given functionality of the system (Bennett, McRobb, and Farmer, 1999). Any Use Case can be represented either graphically (as a Use Case diagram) or as a text description. We use the text description of functionality in order to apply the same ontology-based approach for creating the O-model (see Fig. 16-7 for clarifying the difference between Use Case diagram, Use Case text description and functionality text description). In this situation however another ontological engine, VisualText is used as a tool.

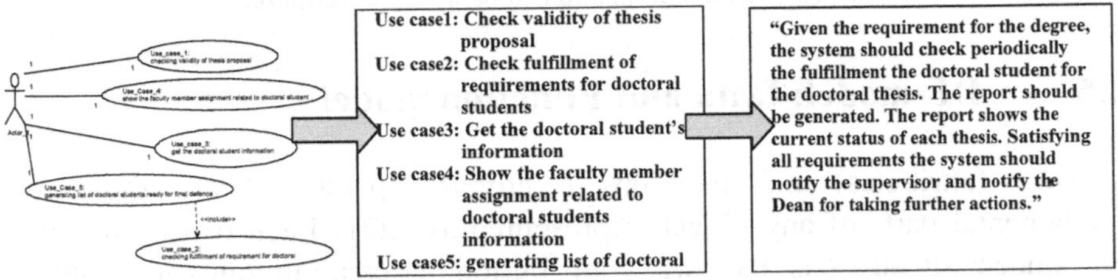

Figure 16-7. Use case diagram, use case description, and functionality text description

VisualText is a tool for information extraction, natural language processing and text analysis systems. It makes possible to find out the function within an event or action assigned to particular actors and/or objects in the system. Thus, the goal of UO-model is to analyze the functionality description and as a result to add functions/operations to respective objects.

As illustrated in Fig. 16-8, several use cases may be used to describe one well-defined functionality of the system to be built within the problem domain. The ontological analysis of such a functionality description helps the system analyst to identify more precisely the real objects, which will play a substantial role in implementing the respective system functions. This can be done comparing (matching) the objects, already identified in the O-model. Obviously, if we have more than one functionality description to analyze, respective objects will be defined for each of them. It becomes easier now for the developer to decide which object should be considered as a separate ADT and which as an element of another ADT. For example, if a new object appears as a result of the ontological analysis of a functionality description but is not identified as a separate object from the O-model, it must be considered as an additional separate object now. Fig. 16-8 illustrates how the two tools OntoExtract and VisualText can help determining which functions are relevant to the working objects in our problem domain description. The figure also shows that it is possible for new relationships to appear between the objects generated by the two tools, which means that they should be formalized in respective new attributes.

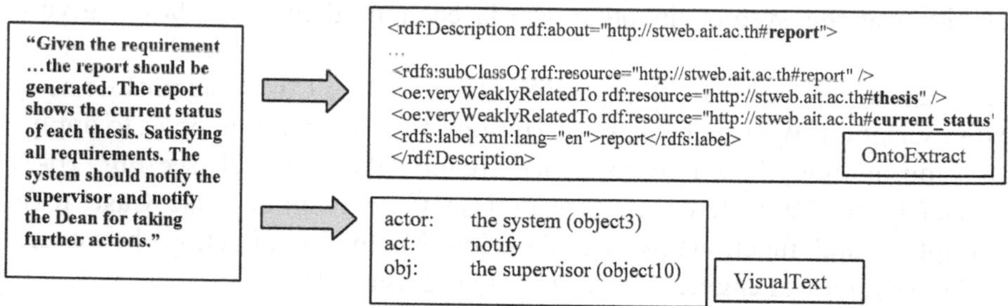

Figure 16-8. Output from a functionality text description

4.5 DF-model: Data and Function model

Data (attributes) and functions (methods, operations) are the two fundamental parts of any object, represented as ADT. Each of the models introduced already has its own contribution to creating one or another element of those two parts. We can continue in this way relying on the decision making abilities of the developer regarding the final acceptable object model of the system containing ADTs. However, because of the requirement for decision making this process can still be characterized as subjective or even intuitive. To avoid this situation we can recall the most powerful feature of both object and ontology orientation – they allow for a high degree of reusability of their artifacts in different application domains. The idea is very simple – if something is defined already and checked successfully, and has been used in practice, perhaps with some adjustments, it can be used for another developer's needs. This idea is implemented and used broadly in object-oriented software engineering through business objects and related patterns, shown in more detail for example in (Batanov and Arch-int, 2003). We propose here an extension of this idea introducing the notion of Ontological Business Object Pattern (OBOP). An OBOP is an ontology-based description of a business object that presumably will be included as a working object in the object-oriented software system. We actually rely on the fact that there are a great number of ontological descriptions of concepts (objects) in different problem domains, existing already and available from ontology library systems such as WebOnto,

Ontolingua, DARPA Agent Markup Language (DAML), SHOE (Simple HTML Ontology Extensions), etc.

We use the DAML ontology library and SHOEntity library in our work, more specifically their catalogs of ontologies, which are available in XML, HTML and DAML formats. Here classes are called categories and these categories constitute a simple "is-a" hierarchy while the slots are binary relations. The relations between instances or between instances and data are allowed to have any number of arguments (Noy, et al., 2001). What the developer should do at this phase is to select the suitable ontology for the respective problem domain. Fig. 16-9 shows an example of how available ontological description for our particular problem domain can be considered as OBOP.

Class Hierarchy

- **Person** (age*, **doctoralDegreeFrom***, emailAddress*, mastersDegreeFrom*, researchInterest*, undergraduateDegreeFrom*)
  - **Student** (advisor*, takesCourse*)
    - GraduateStudent ()
    - UndergraduateStudent ()
  - Worker ()
    - AdministrativeStaff ()
      - Chair ()
      - ClericalStaff ()
      - Dean ()
      - Director ()
      - SystemsStaff ()

```
<Class ID="Student">
  <label>student</label>
  <subClassOf resource="#Person"/>
</Class>
<Property ID="takesCourse">
  <label>is taking</label>
  <domain resource="#Student" />
  <range resource="#Course" />
</Property>
<Property ID="doctoralDegreeFrom">
  <label>has a doctoral degree from</label>
  <domain resource="#Person"/>
  <range resource="#University"/>
</Property>
```

Figure 16-9. Ontological class hierarchy used as a pattern

Representation of ontology specifications is standardized in a form of object description and this provides a great advantage for software developers. For example, the ontological description shown in Fig. 16-9 is found in the ontology library and has a structure, which can be used by the developer directly as not only class hierarchy but as a structured content of respective classes. Therefore, this description can be considered as OBOP. Within this pattern the concept (object) "student" possesses exactly the properties (attributes) necessary for the system under development. We can say the same for the root concept (object, class) "person". Moreover, in the ontology the attributes themselves are treated as concepts (objects) just like in object orientation, which means that we can follow and extract the description of all objects which we are interested in within the class hierarchy. More specifically, the relationships are formalized through the arguments (attributes), which are either types (Atomic ADTs) or categories (objects, classes). If the argument is a category, any subcategory of that category is also valid in the ontology. In addition, the relationship between any two concepts (objects) is a commitment and all commitments are specific to objects and phenomena in one particular domain (Chandrasekaran, Josephson, and Benjamin, 1999). Fig. 16-10 shows that if a relationship exists between two concepts (objects), they are both objects in our problem domain (for example, "takesCourse" has a relationship with argument1 "Student" and argument2 "Course", which should be considered as working objects). The phenomenon "age" is related to argument1 "Person" and argument2 "NUMBER" (type or Atomic ADT), which is different from the first relation ("takesCourse"), so in this case, we should consider the "age" only as an attribute of "Person". It is clear, however, that this attribute "age" will be valid also for objects "Student" and "GraduateStudent" because of the generalization/specialization relationship.

Relation	Argument 1	Argument 2
takesCourse	Student	Course
age	Person	.NUMBER
emailAddress	Person	.STRING
head	Organization	Person
undergraduateDegreeFrom	Person	University
mastersDegreeFrom	Person	University
doctoralDegreeFrom	Person	University
advisor	Student	Professor

Figure 16-10. The relations pattern

4.6 Mr-model: Reduced matrix model

In order to emphasize the necessity of this model we will review what information the developer has up to this point working with the models described above:

1. Set of objects in the problem domain PD = $\{O_1, O_2, O_3,.., O_a\}$ with their names and relationships, extracted from the T-model by an ontological engine (in our case CORPORUM OntoExtract). The result is represented in the Mf-model.
2. Set of objects FOE = $\{O_1, O_2, O_3,.., O_b\}$ with their names and relationships as a result of applying an ontological engine (in our case OntoExtract) on a Use Case-based system functionality. The result is represented in a part of the UO-model.
3. Set of objects FVT = $\{O_1, O_2, O_3,.., O_c\}$ with their names, relationships and functions as a result of applying an ontological engine (in our case VisualText) on a Use Case-based system functionality. The result is represented in the other part of the UO-model.
4. Set of objects BOP = $\{O_1, O_2, O_3,.., O_d\}$ with their names, relationships (including hierarchical information) and functions as a result of searching

for OBOPs in ontology libraries (in our case DAML and SHOEntity). The result is represented in the DF-model.

Fig. 16-11 shows in graphical form, although not very precise, the existing situation. Objects are within the system problem domain but, on one hand, their number is still large (this is true even for relatively simple systems) and they are defined from different perspectives (different models are used), on the other.

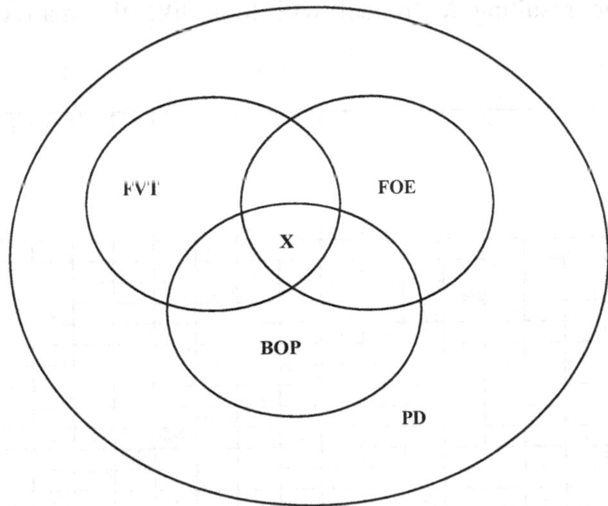

Figure 16-11. Integration procedure

Our presumption, based on a number of experiments, is that the basic objects, which will play a substantial role in ensuring the system functionality, will appear in all of the above models regardless of the perspective. This practically means that we can apply a simple integration procedure – intersection of the above sets – to identify those objects in Fig. 16-11 the resulting area is X, or

$$\mathbf{X = PD \cap FOE \cap FVT \cap BOP}$$

Applying the above procedure the developer has the opportunity to reduce the number of objects, which he/she is interested in, or to transform the full matrix model (Mf-model) to reduced matrix model (Mr-model). Along with this the developer can use another quantitative technique for reducing the number of objects using the already mentioned parameter weight, assigned to each object during the process of creating the Mf-model. This technique is based on a simple assumption, which is well supported by our experiments – an object with higher weight would play a significant role in the system and, therefore, can be identified as a separate object (ADT). At this stage of research, to determine the degree of weight as low or high we refer to our experiments, which qualitatively show that the border is somewhere about 4 or 5 as a minimum and a value above 10 should be definitely considered as high weight. For objects with low weight, there are two options, either to consider them as complementary objects, which to be included as attributes or references in other objects, or to rename and consider them as separate objects. The final decision should be taken by the developer. The resulting Mr-model will look like the matrix shown in Fig. 16-12.

		appro val	thesis	applic ation	super visor	depart ment	exami nation	degre e	permi ssion	dean	right	thesis _prop osal	thesis _rese arch	stude nt	staff_ memb er	full_ti me_r eside	final_t erm	exami nation _requi	intelle ctual_ prope	depart ment_ comm	weigh t
		o1	o2	o3	o4	o5	o6	o7	o8	o9	o10	o11	o12	o13	o14	o15	o16	o17	o18	o19	
approv	o1				×	×						×			×					×	5
thesis	o2								×	×	×	×	×	×	×				×		8
applica	o3									×				×							2
superv	o4	×										×								×	3
depart	o5	×													×					×	3
exami	o6																	×			1
degree	o7													×		×	×	×			4
permis	o8		×							×											2
dean	o9		×	×					×					×							4
right	o10		×											×					×		3
thesis_	o11	×	×		×									×						×	4
thesis_	o12		×																		1
studen	o13		×	×				×		×	×	×				×	×	×	×		10
staff_n	o14	×	×			×															3
full_tim	o15							×						×			×	×			4
final_t	o16							×						×		×		×			4
exami	o17						×	×						×		×	×				5
intelle	o18		×								×			×							3
depart	o19	×			×	×						×									4
weight		5	8	2	3	3	1	4	2	4	3	4	1	10	3	4	4	5	3	4	

Figure 16-12. Mr-model (Reduced matrix model)

4.7 C-model: Class model

The C-model is the goal of preliminary analysis of object-oriented systems. This is the well-known class hierarchy representation, including some initial but significant for the system functionality elements of objects – data and behavior (functions, operations). We stress on the word initial here to emphasize the fact that the analysis is far from over yet. The developer should continue applying the conventional analysis models, methods and techniques on the C-model, which can lead to substantial changes, including adding new objects, deleting some objects, adding or removing some elements of the included objects, etc. The C-model can be represented graphically using different tools such as Rational Rose (class diagrams), textually using either some natural language or pseudo programming language, and finally using some highly structured tag-based language.

Fig. 16-13 shows UML-based class (object) model of a part of our illustrative system in a university problem domain. This model includes working objects, identified by applying all the models discussed above, starting from the text description of the problem domain. The class model is the primary input for creating the next XML object model.

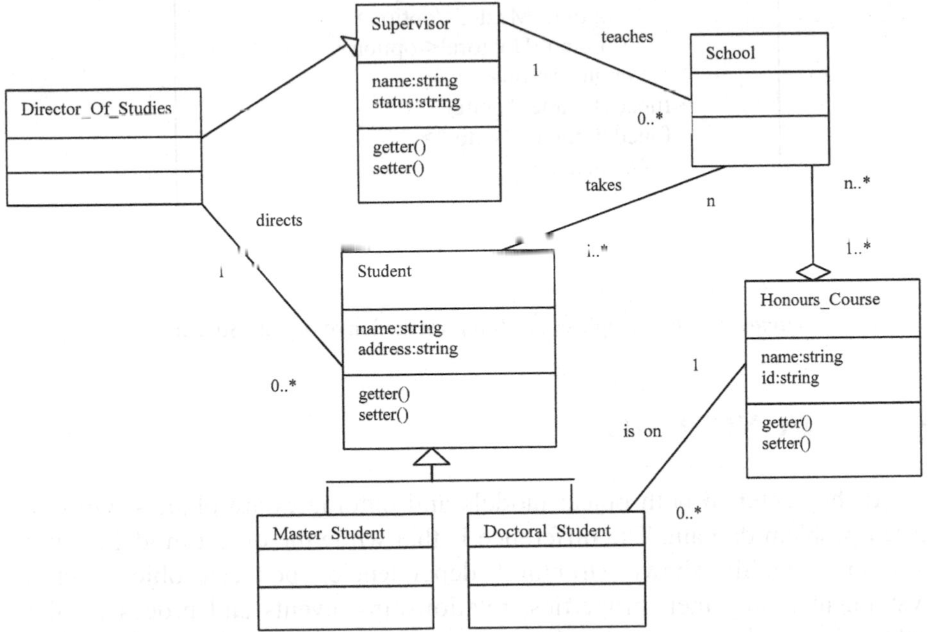

Figure 16-13. Class (object) model

4.8 XML-model: XML object model

This model is optional but extremely useful for exchanging analysis and design information through the Web for supporting collaborative work. It represents the C-model using highly structured tag-based language (the third option mentioned above) and, more specifically XML (eXtensible Markup Language) as a language-specification for computer-readable documents or a metalanguage, which can be used as a mechanism for representing other languages in a standardized way (Klein, 2001). In our case we use W3C XML Schema, which allows the highest flexibility in describing all necessary elements of any object hierarchy on one hand and the details of object model, on the other. Fig. 16-14 illustrates a part of the XML-based description of the object "student" as an ADT.

```
<elementtype name="student">
   <empty/>
   <attdef name="student name"
datatype="string"/>
   <attdef name="degree">
      <enumeration datatype="NMTOKEN">
         <option>Bachelor</option>
         <option>Master</option>
         <option>Doctoral</option>
      </enumeration>
    <funcdef name="getter">
    <funcdef name="setter">
       <required/>
       </funcdef>
    </attdef>
              </elementtype>
```

Figure 16-14. Example of XML representation of object "Student"

5. CONCLUSION

At the center of both object models and ontologies are objects within a given problem domain. The difference is that while the object model should contain explicitly shown structural dependencies between objects in a system, including their properties, relationships, events and processes, the ontologies are based on related terms only. On the other hand, the object model refers to the collection of concepts used to describe the generic characteristics of objects in object-oriented languages. Because ontology is accepted as a formal, explicit specification of a shared conceptualization, we can naturally link ontologies with object models, which represent a system-oriented map of related objects.

We believe that merging ontologies with existing methods, techniques, and tools used during the analysis phase of complex object-oriented software systems can contribute significantly to reaching better decisions with a positive effect on all the subsequent phases of the development process. This paper describes a methodology for supporting the high-level analysis phase of object-oriented software engineering using ontologies for identification of system objects. Eight models are introduced and briefly described in the paper as a part of this methodology. We believe that these models and the process of their transformation can help developers of complex object-oriented software systems to: (a) transform user requirements (represented as text description) into an object model of the system under development based on the use of ontologies; (b) improve the existing methods and techniques for creating a specific ontology from a text description of the system problem domain, which would serve as a source for identifying the objects and their respective ADTs; (c) work out implementation techniques and tools for semi-automated or automated generating and editing of ADTs for object-oriented application software development, and (d) improve the effectiveness and efficiency of the existing methodology for high-level system analysis in object-oriented software engineering.

It can be expected more research work to be done aimed to the formalization of the methods and techniques introduced so far in order to make them a part of CASE. Abstract Data Types identification is based on ontology analysis but if for a given problem domain such an ontology still does not exist, the developers should be ready to create this ontology themselves including a description of well selected ontological business object patterns. In any case we strongly believe that using ontologies has a great potential for analysis and design of complex object-oriented software systems.

REFERENCES

Angele J., Staab S., and Schurr H., 2003, Object Oriented Logics for Ontologies. *Draft Whitepaper Series*. Karlsruhe, Germany.

Batanov D. N. and Arch-int S., 2003, Towards construction of business components: an approach to development of web-based application systems, In: Peckham J and Lloyd SJ (eds) *Practicing Software Engineering in the 21st Century*. IRM Press, pp 178-194.

Bennett S., McRobb S. and Farmer R., 1999, Object-Oriented System Analysis and Design Using UML. McGraw-Hill, International Editions 2000, London.

Chandrasekaran B., Josephson J. R. and Benjamin V. R., 1999, What are ontologies, and why do we need them? *IEEE Intelligent Systems* 14(1): 20-26.

ChiMu Corporation, 2003, Object Modeling Foundations of O-R Mapping. [online] Available: http://www.chimu.com/publications/objectRelational/part0003.html.

Corcho O., Fermandez M., and Perez A. G., 2001, OntoWeb Technical Roadmap v1.0. This document is part of a research project funded by the IST Program of the Commission of the European Communities as project number IST-2000-29243.

Cranefield S. and Purvis M., 1999, UML as an Ontology Modeling Language. *Proceeding of the IJCAI-99 Workshop on Intelligent Information Integration*. Department of Information Science, University of Otago, New Zealand.

Deridder D., Wouters B., 1999, The Use of Ontologies as a Backbone for Software Engineering Tools, Programming Technology Lab, Vrije Universiteit Brussel, Brussels, Belgium.

Ding Y. and Fensel D., 2001, Ontology Library Systems: The key to successful Ontology Re-use. This document is part of a research project funded by the IST Program of the Commission of the European Communities as project number IST-2000-29243.

Engles R., 2001, Del 6: CORPORUM – OntoExtract ontology extraction tool, On-To-Knowledge: Content-driven knowledge management tools through evolving ontologies. IST project IST-1999-1032, On-To-Knowledge.

Gil Y. and Ratnakar V., 2002, A comparison of (semantic) markup languages. *Proceedings of the 15th International FLAIRS Conference*, Special Track on Semantic Web, Pensacola, FL.

Gruber T. R., 1993, A translation approaches to portable ontology specifications. *Knowledge Acquisition* 5: 199-220.

Gruber T. R., 1994, Towards Principles for the Design of Ontologies Use for Knowledge Sharing. In Proceedings of IJHCS-1994, 5 (6): 907-928.

Heflin J., Volz R. and Dale J., 2002, Requirements for a Web Ontology Language. W3C Working Draft.

Klein M., 2001, XML, RDF and relatives. *IEEE Intelligent Systems* March/April, pp 26-28.

Knublauch H., 1999, Three Patterns for the Implementation of Ontologies in Java. *Submitted to OOPSLA'99 Metadata and Active Object-Model Pattern Mining Workshop*, Research Institute for Applied Knowledge Processing (FAW), Germany.

Manola F., 1999, Technologies for a web object model. *IEEE Internet Computing* January-February, pp 38-47.

Mohan P. and Brooks C., 2003, Learning Objects on the Semantic Web. *Proceedings of International Conference on Advanced Learning Technologies.* Athens, Greece, Jul. 7 – Jul. 14.

Noy N. F., Sintek M., Decker S. et al., 2001, Creating semantic web contents with Protégé-2000. *IEEE Intelligent Systems* March/April, pp 60-61.

Studer R., Benjamins R., and Fensel D., 1998, Knowledge Engineering: Principles and Methods. *Data & Knowledge Engineering,* Vol. 25, No. 1-2, March, pp 161-197.

Swartout B., Patil R., Knight K. and Russ T., 1996, Toward Distributed Use of Large-Scale Ontologies. *Proceedings of the Tenth Knowledge Acquisition for Knowledge-Based Systems Workshop,* November 9-14. Banff, Alberta, Canada.

Swartout W., 1999, Ontologies. *IEEE Intelligent Systems* January/February, pp 18-25.

Thomason T., Sauter V., 1999, Object-Oriented Analysis Key Concepts, Benefits and Criticisms. [online] Available: http://www.umsl.edu/~sauter/analysis/ooa.html.

Volz R., Oberle D. and Studer R., 1999, Views for light-weight web ontologies. *Proceeding of SAC 2003.* Melbourne, Florida, USA.

Weiss M. A., 1993, Data Structures and Algorithm Analysis in C. Benjamin/Cummings Publishing Company, Florida International University, Redwood City, CA.

[1] http://www-ksl-svc.standford.edu:5915/
[2] http://www.isi.edu/isd/LOOM/LOOM-HOME.html
[3] http://kmi.open.ac.uk/projects/ocml/
[4] http://www.ontoprise.de/documents/tutorial_flogic.pdf
[5] http://www.w3.org/RDF/
[6] http://www.w3.org/TR/rdf-schema/
[7] http://www.cs.umd.edu/projects/plus/SHOE/
[8] http://www.ai.sri.com/~pkarp/xol/
[9] http://www.ontologos.org/OML/OML%200.3.htm
[10] http://www.ontoknowledge.org/oil/
[11] http://www.daml.org/language/
[12] http://www.w3.org/XML/
[13] http://www.w3.org/MarkUp/
[14] http://www.cyc.com/cycl.html
[15] http://www.opengalen.org/open/CRM/index.html

[16] www.adapower.net/booch/
[17] http://eldora.open.ac.uk:3000/webonto
[18] http://www.daml.org/ontologies
[19] http://www.starlab.vub.ac.be/reserach/dogma/OntologyServer.htm
[20] http://suo.ieee.org/refs.html
[21] http://ontoserver.aifb.uni-karlsruhe.de/
[22] http://saussure.irmkant.rm.cnr.it/nto/

Chapter 17

AN ONTOLOGY-BASED EXPLORATION OF KNOWLEDGE SYSTEMS FOR METAPHOR

Chu-Ren Huang, Siaw-Fong Chung and Kathleen Ahrens
Academia Sinica, No. 128, Sec. 2, Academia Road, Nankang, Taipei, Taiwan R.O.C. 115, Graduate Institute Of Linguistics, National Taiwan University, No. 1, Sec. 4, Roosevelt Road, Taipei, Taiwan R.O.C. 106

Abstract: This chapter takes the complex knowledge systems of metaphors and shows that their structured knowledge can be represented and predicted by ontology. The complex knowledge system of metaphors contains two knowledge systems, source domain and target domain, as well as the knowledge mapping between the two domains. Hence metaphors offer a test case of how structured knowledge can be manipulated in an information system. In terms of the theory of metaphor, we integrate the Conceptual Mapping Model with an ontology-based knowledge representation. We demonstrate that conceptual metaphor analysis can be restricted and eventually, automated. In terms of knowledge processing, we argue that the knowledge structure encoded in ontology, such as the Suggested Upper Merged Ontology (SUMO), is the necessary foundation for manipulating information from multi-domain and multilingual sources. We first extract source domain knowledge structure based on ontology. Next we show that the ontological account allows correct explanation of the parallel yet different use of the same source domain in two different languages. Thirdly, we showed that the restricted set of upper ontology can be combined with the open lexical knowledgebase of wordnets to provide a principled, yet robust, general coverage of language-based knowledge systems.

Key words: conceptual mapping; corpus; knowledge system; metaphor; ontology; suggested upper merged ontology, wordnet

1. BACKGROUND

Computational ontology can provide information systems with the structure to acquire and organize information. [1] Even though the programmatic nature of computational ontology is well-suited to providing a uniform platform for information integration, they also face the challenge of how to accommodate information from different and possibly conflicting conceptual systems. One difficult case involves metaphors. Since metaphors are familiar, concrete terms used to describe abstract concepts; they necessarily involve more than one conceptual system.

In this chapter, we refer to any information source with inherent conceptual coherence as a **knowledge system**. We will show that ontology are up to the challenge to represent different knowledge systems. In particular, we apply SUMO (Suggested Upper Merged Ontology) [1] to explore the complex knowledge systems involved in comprehending metaphor. We will demonstrate that, based on corpus data, ontology can be applied to discover and define the source domain knowledge in metaphors. Finally, by utilizing its inherent logical inference structure, we show that ontology allows a principled way to postulate conceptual mappings that bridge the complex knowledge systems of metaphor.

We adopt John F. Sowa's definition of ontology as 'a catalog of the types of things that are assumed to exist in a domain of interest ***D*** from the perspective of a person who uses a language ***L*** for the purpose of talking about ***D***.' [2] A computational ontology is a computational implementation of such an ontology. A computational ontology typically contains a list of atoms as well as their relations. It is important to note that in this definition, ontology is language-based and domain-specific, although it does express the shared conceptualization of that specific domain given the language.

Sowa's definition of ontology allows its use in the Semantic Web [3], where each web resource is required to have its own ontology to explicitly state the conceptual structured used in that resource. It also underlines the need to have a shared upper ontology where representations of individual ontology can be uniformly described and unified. This provides the basis for knowledge sharing.

We propose a new approach to conceptual metaphors in this chapter. The new approach incorporates two computationally trackable elements. First, the data analysis is corpus-based, following the example of MetaBank [18]. Second, the representation is ontology-based. Both elements strengthen our Conceptual Mapping and Empirical Prototype account of metaphors.

[1] Here we adopt the definition from http://www.projectauditors.com/, (omissions ours) that an information system is 'a structured, interacting, complex of persons, machines, and procedures designed to produce information … for use as a basis for decision-making ...'.

2. KNOWLEDGE SYSTEMS: MOTIVATION AND THEORETICAL PREMISES

In order to gather and use information from multiple sources, the information must be correctly aligned and uniformly represented. In addition, it must be recognized first that these pieces of information come from different knowledge systems and have their own conceptual coherence which may conflict with each other. Thus, two essential tasks are that information from compatible knowledge systems must be correctly synchronized and information from incompatible knowledge systems must be properly integrated with minimal loss of information. We also need to recognize that information must be situated in a knowledge system in order to be useful. One of the most efficient ways to situate information is to put it in a well-structured and complete knowledge representation system, such as a computational ontology. In sum, information can only contribute to a decision making process when it is correctly interpreted given the presuppositions and logical entailments encoded in the knowledge system. In what follows, we will describe the knowledge systems that are used in this study.

2.1 Corpora and WordNet: Two kinds of linguistic knowledge systems

Human beings are agents in decision making as well as important sources of information; while language is the definitive human tool for expressing and storing information. Hence, the focus of this study is on language as a knowledge system.

There are two ways to look at language as a knowledge system. The first is to look at the accumulative data of language use as a collection of knowledge with implicit structure. This is the corpus-based approach, where corpus is defined as a set of electronic texts collected under a set of design criteria. The second is to explicitly encode linguistic relations in a language resource. One typical approach is to encode the semantic relations among all words in a language. These words form a network built on a set of pre-defined logico-linguistic relations. This is the wordnet approach. It is important to note that, in either linguistic approach, the theoretical premise is that words are linguistically instantiated conceptual atoms; hence the collection of all words in a language is the shared and complete set of conceptual atoms of people using that language. Thus wordnets are the representation of a linguistically instantiated knowledge systems, while corpora are collections of instantiated instances of a knowledge system.

The first and prototypical wordnet is English WordNet.[2] WordNet is a lexical knowledgebase for English language constructed by the Cognitive Science Laboratory of Princeton University in 1990 (http://wordnet.princeton.edu/index.shtml, [4]). Its content is divided into four categories based on psycholinguistic principles: nouns, verbs, adjectives and adverbs. WordNet organizes the lexical information according to word meaning and each synset contains a set of lemmas (i.e. word forms) sharing the same sense. Notice that each lemma instantiates one or more senses. In addition, WordNet is a semantic network linking synsets with lexical semantic relations. WordNet is widely used in Natural Language Processing applications and linguistic research. The most updated version of WordNet is WordNet 2.0. We adopted WordNet 1.6, the version which is used by most applications so far.

2.2 Metaphor: A Complex Knowledge System

A metaphor is given the definition of 'a figure of speech in which an expression is used to refer to something that it does not literally denote in order to suggest a similarity' by WordNet 1.6. In use, the expression chosen is often familiar and concrete, and the figurative meaning abstract. There are two main approaches to metaphor, namely the classical approach and the cognitive approach. The classical approach goes back to as far as 1960s in which metaphor was seen philosophers such as Black [5] and Searle [6] as a violation of the literal meanings The other approach, which is the cognitive approach, is based on the groundbreaking theory of conceptual metaphor by Lakoff and Johnson [7] who described the formation of a metaphor as a mapping from a source domain (i.e. the literal expression) to a target domain (the figurative reading). By this definition, metaphors are complex knowledge systems involving two knowledge domains. In addition to this main-stream theory, there are also other theories under the cognitive paradigm. Psycholinguists such as Camac and Gluckberg [8] and Gibbs [9] deal primarily with similarity-creation between the target and source domains. Works in this direction usually concentrate on discovering the similarities between linguistic forms such as that between two ideas, or words of the same forms (usually nouns) in a string of words [8] and two semantic domains [10]. However, what these works have in common is that they try to explain metaphors through linguistic similarities found within the two domains. One famous work in this direction is Gentner's [11] structure-

[2] Following convention, WordNet (with capitalization) is a trademarked proper name referring to the Princeton English WordNet. In this chapter, the non-capitalized 'wordnet' refers to WordNet-like lexical knowledgebases that were built later, including those for languages other than English.

mapping model in which attributes in two different domains are mapped onto one another to establish the link between the domains.

Since the diversities in approaching metaphors, different terms have been suggested to describe the mapping of the abstract to the concrete ideas. Among which are Richards's [12] 'Vehicle' (the Source) and 'Topic' (the Target), and Black's [5] 'Systems' to represent both source and target domains. For the convenience of description, this chapter will adopt Lakoff and Johnson's [7] definition of source and target domains to refer to the abstract and concrete ideas respectively.

From the point of view of information systems, metaphor presents itself as a perfect case for how to uniformly representing information from two different knowledge systems. Studies which attempt to represent figurative meanings in addition to the lexical meanings in electronic sources include Lőnneker [13], Alonge and Lönneker [14] and Peters and Wilks [15]. All these works are concerned with making connection between the two knowledge systems so as when one system (such as literal one) is activated; the other system (such as the metaphorical one) will be activated as well. In this chapter, we propose an ontology based approach to the representation of information in this complex knowledge system.

The theory of metaphor by Lakoff and Johnson [7] has been the focus of study on lexical and figurative meaning for the past two decades. Are conventional conceptual metaphors a cognitive rather than a linguistic phenomenon? Work within Cognitive Linguistics would seem to say that this is the case. For example, Lakoff [16] writes with respect to the source-target domain mapping of the conventional conceptual metaphor LOVE IS A JOURNEY:

> Is there a general principle governing how these *linguistic expressions* about journeys are used to characterize love.... [Yes], but it is a *general principle* that is neither part of the grammar of English, nor the English lexicon. Rather it is *part of the conceptual system underlying English....* (Page 306, italics ours)

Thus, the onus of dealing with metaphorical meaning in the lexicon is not necessary. Metaphor may be treated at a different (i.e. higher) cognitive level.

But is it really the case that there are no general principles that can be extracted and proposed at the lexical level? The Conceptual Mapping (CM) Model [17] was proposed to constrain the Contemporary Theory of Metaphor [16]. This model analyzes the linguistic correspondences between a source and target (knowledge) domain in order to determine the underlying reason for the source-target pairings. The underlying reason is formulated in terms of a Mapping Principle. The theory also postulates a Mapping

Principle Constraint, which says that a target domain will select only source domains that involve unique mapping principles.

For example, Ahrens [17] points out that in the conceptual metaphor IDEA IS BUILDING in Mandarin, the linguistic expressions relating to the concept of foundation, stability and construction are mapped (i.e. are conventional linguistic examples) while concepts relating to position of the building, internal wiring and plumbing, the exterior of the building, windows and doors are not (and these are the concepts that are in the real world knowledge of the source domain). Thus she postulates that the target domain of IDEA uses the source domain of BUILDING in order to emphasize the concept of structure. Thus, when someone talks about ideas and want to express positive notions concerning organization, they use the source domain of BUILDING. The Mapping Principle formulated in this case was therefore the following:

(1) Mapping principle for IDEA IS BUILDING: Idea is understood as building because **buildings involve a (physical) structure and ideas involve an (abstract) structure.** [17]

When IDEA is talked about in terms of FOOD, however, the expressions that are mapped are 'ingredient', 'spoil', 'flavorless', 'full', 'taste', 'chew', 'digest' and 'absorb'. Mandarin Chinese, in contrast with English, does not have conventional expressions relating to 'cooking' or 'stewing' of ideas. Thus, the postulated Mapping Principle is: Idea is understood as food because **food involves being eaten and digested (by the body) and ideas involved being taken in and processed (by the mind)** [17].

Thus, IDEA uses the source domains of BUILDING and FOOD in Mandarin Chinese for different reasons, namely to convey information related to 'structure' or 'processing' (i.e. 'understanding') respectively. Thus, it is similar to the Contemporary Theory of Metaphor in that it supposes that there are systematic mappings between a source and target domain, but it goes a step further in postulating an underlying reason for that mapping. The CM Model predicts that conventional metaphors, novel metaphors that follow the mapping principle and novel metaphors that don't follow the mapping principle will be rated differently on interpretability and acceptability scales when other factors, such as frequency are controlled for. This model is supported in psycholinguistic experiments because it correctly predicted the processing differences involved between conventional and novel metaphors [17].

2.3 The Conceptual Mapping Model and Ontology

The CM model of metaphor presupposes structured shared source domain knowledge. For a mapping to be conventionalized and understood by speakers, the content and structure of the source domain knowledge must be *a priori* knowledge and should not have to be acquired. How to define and verify such structured knowledge is a challenge to this theory. We attempt to meet this challenge in two ways: first, by assuming that the source domain knowledge representation is instantiated by a shared upper ontology, such as SUMO. If the source domain knowledge representation is indeed ontology-based, a natural *a priori* knowledge source for a mapping principle is the inference rules encoded on a particular conceptual node of SUMO. In order to verify such hypothesis, we can take a further step of examining actual mappings of linguistic expressions in the corpora, and extracting the most frequent mappings. We hypothesize that the underlining mapping rule is instantiated by the prototypical expression involving that metaphor. We call this account the Empirical Prototype account, since the mapping is empirically verified by identifying and account for the most typical instance of that metaphor. In practice, we predict that frequency of use in a newspaper corpus can be used to predict the underlying mapping principle.

The integration of an upper ontology to the CM model has the following theoretical implications: First, the source domain knowledge representation is now pre-defined and constrained. Second, the validity of such a hypothesis will in turn support the robustness and universality of the proposed upper ontology.

3. RESOURCES

Our study concentrates on linguistic data since it offers the richest source of human-oriented information. In particular, all data are extracted from corpora, while the knowledge representation is obtained through both wordnets and ontology.

3.1 Corpora: Sinica Corpus, WSJ Corpus, and the Web

Corpora are a unique resource in knowledge engineering and central to recent developments in natural language processing. On one hand, they are attested and realistic linguistic uses and hence provide verifiable empirical foundation for research. On the other hand, they are large scale datasets that are both well-defined and sharable. Thus corpora provide the foundation for stochastic studies. In terms of information systems, corpora provide a test ground for how information can be gathered from actual and non-uniform language sources. We draw mainly on two corpora in this data. The primary source, since our study focuses on Mandarin Chinese, is the Academia Sinica Balanced Corpus of Modern Mandarin Chinese (Sinica Corpus, http://www.sinica.edu.tw/SinicaCorpus/). This is a tagged corpus of 5 million words of modern Mandarin usage in Taiwan. In our comparative work with English, we use the 1994 portion of the Wall Street Journal Corpus (WSJ Corpus). This can be accessed through the Linguistic Data Consortium (http://www.ldc.upenn.edu/ldc/online/index.html).

A new approach to corpus-based studies treats the World Wide Web directly as a corpus [21]. Since the web now is also the richest and most readily available source of information, this approach has strong implications for the constructions of future information systems. In this current study, we take the most fundamental step of supplementing data from the web when they were not attested in the corpora we use.

3.2 Princeton WordNet

The Princeton WordNet is the prototype of wordnets in the world. It is a monolingual wordnet that encodes lexical knowledge in terms of concepts and semantic relations. In WordNet 1.6., the version adopted in this study, there are 99,642 synsets. Each synset contains one or lemmas (i.e. word forms). There are in 174,007 synset to lemma mappings in total. Since a lemma can be mapped to more than one synsets and be polysemous, there are 122,864 unique lemmas in WordNet 1.6. The conceptual network of WordNet is build upon synsets as atoms and and linked with lexical semantic relations. WordNet encodes 11 different lexical semantic relations: synonymy, antonymy, hyponymy, hypernymy, troponymy, and three types of meronymy and holonymy. Synonymy is defined by members of the same synset, while hypernymy and hyponymy are encoded to form an inheritance tree. All other relations are encoded as a paradigmatic extension of the main tree. In our study, Princeton WordNet serves as a cross-lingual index of concepts as well as link to upper ontology.

3.3 Sinica BOW

The Academia Sinica Bilingual Ontological Wordnet (Sinica BOW, http://BOW.sinica.edu.tw) integrates three resources: WordNet, English-Chinese Translation Equivalents Database (ECTED), and SUMO (Suggested Upper Merged Ontology). This structure of the Sinica Bow can be seen in Figure 17-1. In this figure, the interface between the different electronic resources is shown through the connecting arrows between these resources. The three resources were originally linked in two pairs: WordNet 1.6 was manually mapped to SUMO [22] and semi-automatically to ECTED. In fact, the 122,864 unique synset-lemma pairs are mapped to 195,817 words in Chinese. ECTED encodes both equivalent pairs and their semantic relations [23], hence offers a rich bilingual knowledgebase.

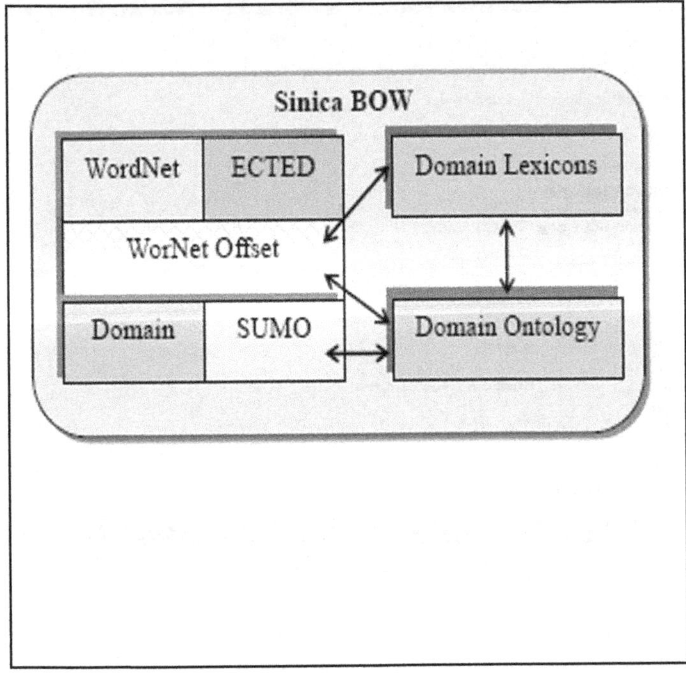

Figure 17-1. The resources and structure of Sinica BOW

With the integration of these three key resources, Sinica BOW functions both as an English-Chinese bilingual wordnet and a bilingual lexical access to SUMO. Sinica BOW allows versatile access and facilitates a combination of lexical, semantic, and ontological information. One of the new additions to Sinica BOW is a version comparison function between WordNet 1.6 and 1.7. Figure 17-2 shows a snapshot of the results yielded from the English keyword 'growth.' In Figure 17-2, the search results for 'growth' provide the WordNet senses in English as well as their translation in Chinese, with additional links to their related SUMO nodes.

It is important to note that the versatility of the Sinica BOW is built in with its bilingualism, and the lemma-based merging of multiple resources. First, either English or Chinese can be used for the query, as well as for presenting the content of the resources. Second, the user can easily access the logical structure of both the WordNet and SUMO ontology using either words or conceptual nodes. Third, multiple linguistic indexing is built in to

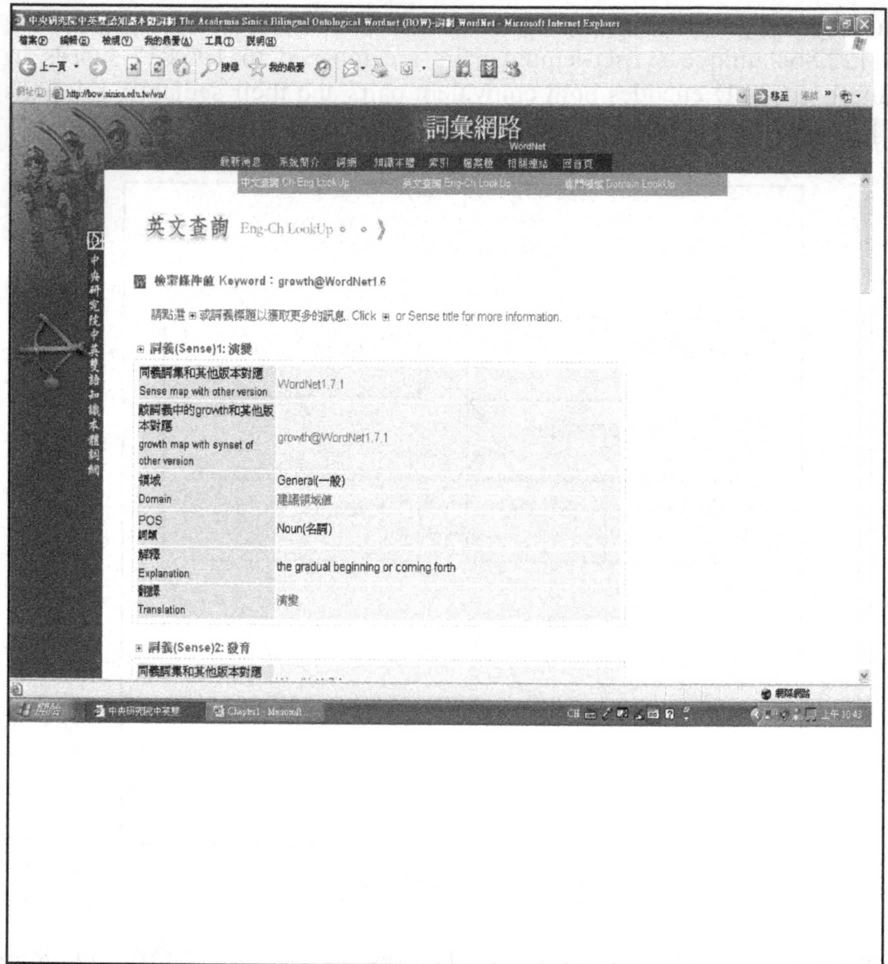

Figure 17-2. A Snapshot of the Sinica BOW

allow additional versatility. Fourth, domain information allows another dimension of knowledge manipulation. This function is crucial to our study on metaphoric systems. We use this bilingual ontological wordnet as a lexical knowledgebase to interface with the upper ontology of SUMO.

3.4 SUMO (Suggested Upper Merged Ontology)

Suggested Upper Merged Ontology (SUMO, http://www.ontologyportal.org) is a shared upper ontology developed by the IEEE Standard Upper Ontology Working Group. It is a theory in first-order logic that consists of approximately one thousand concepts and 4000 axioms. Each concept atom is well-defined and associated with a set of axioms for first-order inference.

It is well-defined with both a textual explanation for human use and a formal definition in the knowledge representation language of SUO-KIF. The axioms are also written in SUO-KIF. In is important to note that not all concept nodes have linguistic names, although linguistics names are used as mnemonics. A pair of good examples of linguistic and non-linguistic nodes is Object and CorpuscularObject, which happens to be a subclass of Object. The conceptual hierarchy of SUMO is built upon the traditional IS-A relations. However, there are two important design features that differentiate SUMO from more traditional ontology. The first is that it allows multiple inheritances to better represent human conceptualization. For instance, An Organism has two super-classes. It is both an Agent and an OrganicObject. A set of functions and relations that are considered atom and used in definition and axioms are also well-defined as part of the upper ontology. That is, SUMO is a self-contained upper ontology that is not dependent on other a prior conceptual structure.

For expansion, SUMO also contains a conformant middle level ontology (MILO) and domain ontology. Including domain ontology, SUMO contains more than 20,000 terms and more than 60,000 axioms. Its purpose is to be a shared and inter-operable upper ontology (Niles and Pease [24], Pease and Niles [25], Sevcenko [26]) Since ontology are formalized descriptions of the structure of knowledge bases, SUMO can also be viewed as a proposed representation of shared human knowledge, and thus a good candidate for mapping information about the source domain to the target domain. It can be applied to automated reasoning, information retrieval and inter-operability in E-commerce, education and NLP tasks.

The application of SUMO in knowledge engineering and in processing of lexical meaning is facilitated by its interface with WordNet.[3] Niles and Pease [12] mapped all synsets of WordNet to at least one SUMO term. This means that any word listed in WordNet is assigned a corresponding ontological location in the knowledge representation of SUMO. Through the encoded English-Chinese bilingual wordnet, Sinica BOW now allows mapping from a Chinese lexical meaning to a SUMO concept node. We use these mappings between lexical knowledge bases with ontology as tools to assign shared knowledge structure to unstructured multilingual information. It is important to note that both WordNet and SUMO are free resources. Combining the over 100,000 Enlglish WordNet and the over 20,000 conceptual terms or SUM O forms a formidable lexical knowledge resource. In addition, we have more than 150,000 Chinese translations linked to both English WordNet and SUMO.

4. FROM LINGUISTIC DATA TO SYSTEMIC KNOWLEDGE

In order to discover the knowledge system of metaphor as attested by corpus data, we first extract metaphoric uses from corpus and analyze them. We extract 2000 instances of *jingji* 'economy' from Sinica Corpus. Each of these 2000 was examined and all metaphorical instances were marked. (A metaphorical instance is defined as when an abstract concept such as 'economy' is discussed in terms of a concrete concept, such as 'building'.) All instances of concrete concepts were then grouped into source domains. All source-target domain pairings that had more than 20 instances were then examined. In Tables 17-1–17-4 below we show the source domains that were found for *jingji* 'economy' and we give the total number of instances and the number of tokens for each metaphor, as well as a proposed mapping principle based. Also note that the following mappings were manually analyzed and classified.

The most frequent mapping instance within a source domain indicates the basis of the reason for the source-target domain pairing, i.e. the mapping principle. We hypothesize that each source-target domain pairing will have a prototypical instance of mapping as evidenced by an individual lexical item that is highly frequent as compared with other mappings. In addition, we propose using an ontological-based knowledge representation, such as SUMO, to define and delimit the source domain knowledge in the CM Model. This has the advantage of using SUMO to infer knowledge through automatic reasoning, and as well as constraining the scope and falsifiablity of the conceptual metaphor.

We first note that the EP (Empirical Prototype) hypothesis holds up since in three of the four source-target domain pairings there are one or two lexical items that is/are obviously more frequent than the others (cf. Tables 17-1–17-4).

For example, for ECONOMY IS A PERSON, the mapping principle is postulated to have to do with the life cycle of a person (and not, for example, the mental health of a person) because of the frequent occurrence of the lexical item '*chengzhang*' (growth).

In the case of ECONOMY IS A BUILDING in Table 17-2 below, the mapping principle is postulated to having to do with structure, and not for example, leaky plumbing.

This is an interesting case because, as mentioned above, Ahrens [17] examined IDEA IS A BUILDING and postulated that the mapping principle also had to do with structure (i.e. the structure of a building and the structure of ideas). As Ahrens [17] points out, it is not always the case that different

Table 17-1. ECONOMY IS A PERSON (121 instances)
Mapping Principle: Economy is person because people have a life cycle and economy has growth cycle.

	Metaphor	Freq.
Entities	***chen2zhang3* (growth)**	**67**
	shuai1tui4 (regression/decay)	8
	chen2zhang3chi2 (growth period)	2
	ming4ma4i (lifeblood)	2
	bing4zhuang4 (symptoms)	1
Quality	*shuai1tui2* (weaken and degenerate)	1
Functions	*chen2zhang3* (grow)	21
	fu4shu1 (regain consciousness)	9
	[illegible]	[illegible]
	e4hua4 (deteriorate)	4
	hui1fu4 (recover)	1

Table 17-2. ECONOMY IS A BUILDING (102 instances)
Mapping Principle: Economy is building because buildings involve a (physical) structure and economy involves an (abstract) structure.

	Metaphors	Frequency
Entities	***jian4she4* (construction)**	**39**
	jie2gou4 (structure)	20
	ji1qu3 (foundation)	15
	gui1mo2 (model)	5
	gen1ji1 (foundation)	2
	zhi1chu4 (pillar)	1
	chu2xing2 (model)	1
Qualities	*wen3ding4* (stable)	8
	wen3gu4 (firm)	2
Functions	*chong2jian4* (re-build)	9

target domains use the same aspect of a source domain. For example, the source domain of FOOD is used differently for IDEAS (to express the notion of digestion and processing) as compared with LOVE which uses FOOD to compare different tastes to different feelings.

For ECONOMY IS A COMPETITION, shown in Table 17-3, the emphasis is on the strength of participant in order to defeat the opponent.

In ECONOMY IS WAR (Table 17-4), however, there is no clear-cut instance of a frequent mapping. We suggest that this is because WAR is a subset of the source domain of COMPETITION (i.e. a violent contest) in the SUMO representation, as discussed in section 5 below.

Table 17-3. ECONOMY IS A COMPETITION (40 instances)
Mapping Principle: Economy is competition because a competition involves physical and mental strength to defeat an opponent and an economy requires financial strength in order to prosper against other economies.

	Metaphors	Frequency
Entities	***shi4li4* (actual strength)**	**14**
	jing4zheng1 (competition)	12
	jing4zheng1li4 (power of competition)	3
	jing4zheng1you1shi4 (advantage in competition)	3
	ruo4zhe3 (the weak one)	2
	dou4zheng1 (a struggle)	2
	ruo4shi4 (a disadvantaged situation)	1
	qiang2guo2 (a powerful nation)	1
	tui2shi4 (a declining tendency)	1
Function	*shuai1bai4* (to lose)	1

Table 17-4. ECONOMY IS WAR (23 instances)
Mapping Principle: Economy is war because war involves a violent contest for territorial gain and the economy involves a violent contest for territorial gain and the economy involves a vigorous contest for financial gain.

	Metaphors	Frequency
Entities	*qing1lue4* (invasion)	4
	da4quan2 (immense power)	4
	zhan4 (battle)	2
	lao3bing1 (veteran)	1
	gung1fang3zhan4 (defend and attack battle)	1
	che4lue4 (tactics)	1
Qualities	*qian1chuang1bai3kong3* (one thousand boils and a hundred holes; holes all over)	1
Functions	*gua4shuai4* (to take command)	5
	quan2li4chong1chi4 (to dash with full force)	1
	(da1quan2) chao1zai4 shou3shang4 (to grasp the power)	1
	xi1sheng1 (sacrifice)	1
	xi1sheng1ping3 (victims)	1

In sum, the corpora data show that the use of metaphoric expressions is systematic. This supports the CM model's hypothesis that there is a subset of linguistic expressions within a particular source domain that map to a target domain. It is not the case that 'anything goes.' In fact, the corpora data presented above suggest an even more restricted view that there are usually one or two linguistic expressions that frequently map between the source and target domains and 'drive' the motivating relationship between them. In the next section, we look at whether or not the source domain knowledge can be defined *a priori* through an upper ontology such as SUMO.

5. STRUCTURAL REPRESENTATION OF SOURCE DOMAIN KNOWLEDGE

After showing that metaphor uses can be treated as a knowledge system governed by mapping rules, the next challenge is how to represent and verify the structured knowledge in a source domain. Since a shared upper ontology is designed to represent the shared knowledge structure of intelligent agents and allows knowledge exchange among them, we propose to adopt a shared upper ontology to represent the knowledge systems of metaphors. As mentioned earlier in this chapter, we adopt SUMO as our shared upper ontology.

In SUMO, conceptual terms are defined and situated in a tree-taxonomy. In addition, a set of first order inference rules can be attached to each conceptual node to represent the knowledge content encoded on that term. The conceptual terms of SUMO are roughly equivalent to the source domains in MP theory. Hence the well-defined SUMO conceptual terms are candidates for knowledge representation of the source domain in the MP theory of metaphor. In other words, SUMO provides a possible answer the question of how source domain knowledge is represented and how does this knowledge allows the mapping in conceptual metaphors. We examine how this might be possible by looking at two conceptual terms that are represented in SUMO and are related to our source domains – CONTEST and ORGANISM.

5.1 Economy is Contest

First, we found that what we intuitively termed as 'competition' above has a corresponding ontological node of Contest. The term Contest is documented as 'A SocialInteraction where the agent and patient are CognitiveAgents who are trying to defeat one another.' Its only axiom for inference is quoted here:

(=> (instance ?CONTEST Contest) (exists (?AGENT1 ?AGENT2 ?PURP1 ?PURP2) (and (agent ?CONTEST ?AGENT1) (agent ?CONTEST ?AGENT2) (hasPurposeForAgent ?CONTEST ?PURP1 ?AGENT1) (hasPurposeForAgent ?CONTEST ?PURP2 ?AGENT2) (not (equal ?AGENT1 ?AGENT2)) (not (equal ?PURP1 ?PURP2)))))

The knowledge inference rule stipulates that each instance of Contest is carried out by two agents and each has his own non-equal purpose. This is exactly the source knowledge needed for the metaphor mapping. When the conceptual metaphor is linguistically realized, lexical expressions are then chosen to represent the conceptual terms of both purposeful agents, as well as conflicting purposes for the agents. Notice that in contest, as in economy, it is not necessary to have only one winner. There may be multiple winners and perhaps no winners. In other words, the agents' purpose may not be conflicting. But the purposes-for-agent are definitely different for each agent.

In addition to the 40 instances of economy metaphors involving contest, there are also 23 instances of metaphors involving War. In these cases, it is interesting to observe that the central concept is still the conflicting purposes (one's gain is another's loss) of the warring party. This is confirmed by the shared ontology. In SUMO, a War is a kind of ViolentContest, which in turn is a kind of Contest.

For example, in SUMO, the term War is defined as 'A military confrontation between two or more Nations or Organizations whose members are Nations.' Moreover, the term ViolentContest is defined as 'Contest where one participant attempts to physically injure another participant.' As can be seen from the definition and the metaphoric uses involving War, the ontological source domain knowledge is not involved.

In fact, when examined more closely, it is clear that when the domain knowledge of War is used, it either further specifies the conflicting purposes by elaborating on the quality and manner of the conflict, or elaborating on the agent participants as combatants. In other words, Economy is War is not a different mapping. It is subsumed under the mapping of Economy is Contest, with added elaborations on the participants.

By carefully examining the mapping from source domain knowledge based on SUMO, we discovered not only that mappings are indeed based on a priori source domain knowledge, we also discovered that a metaphor can often involve additional and more specified terms within a domain, as in the case of 'ECONOMY IS WAR.' In these cases, no additional mapping is required. The same structured domain knowledge is used, and the subsumed terms offers only elaborations based on the same knowledge structure.

5.2 Economy is Organism

An example where the knowledge system of SUMO ontology reminded us to re-think the structure of the source domain involves Organism. We arrived at this conclusion by re-examining the examples that we generalized as Economy is a Person in the previous section. After closer examination with the help of SUMO knowledge representation, we found that the linguistic realizations of this mapping do not involve any knowledge that is specific to Human. In fact, it only involves the notion of a life cycle, which is the defining knowledge involving an Organism.

Organism is defined in SUMO as 'a living individual, including all Plants and Animals.' The crucial knowledge that is encoded in of the attached inference rules is as follows:

=> (and (instance ?ORGANISM Organism) (agent ?PROCESS ?ORGANISM)) (holdsDuring (WhenFn ?PROCESS) (attribute ?ORGANISM Living)))

The above inference rule encodes the knowledge that 'An organism is the agent of a living process that holds over duration.' In other words, having a life cycle is the defining knowledge of an Organism. This turns out to be the source domain knowledge that is involved in the mapping.

It is interesting to note that since the mapping between two source domains to the same target domain are principled and constrained, *a priori*, our theory will predict that simultaneous mapping is possible when the mappings are compatible with each other. Since the Purpose of an Organism is to prolong his own life cycle, co-existing mapping of Economy is Organism and Economy is Contest would be possible if the PurposeForAgent is an Organism. We found that in actual linguistic data, such as in *jingji jiu shi luorou qiangshi* 'Economy is the strong feeding on the weak.' In other words, these complex knowledge systems can be combined to form more complex knowledge systems given appropriate conceptual constraints.

6. PARALLEL KNOWLEDGE SYSTEMS: *ECONOMY IS A TRANSPORTATION_DEVICE* IN CHINESE AND ENGLISH

We showed in the last section how a shared upper ontology could be used to formally represent a single complex system. In particular, we showed that the SUMO ontology can be applied to precisely capture the structured source domain knowledge that is being mapped to describe the target domain. In other words, the knowledge structure transfer from one domain to the other is successfully described. In this session, we go further to show that such a methodology can also be applied to account for parallel complex knowledge systems. In particular, we attempt to account for parallel, yet non-identical, metaphors in two different languages. We will account for the parallel metaphors of **Economy is a Transportation Device** in both Mandarin Chinese and English.

We will show in this section that, different knowledge structures can be mapped from the same source domain. In terms of information systems, this clearly shows that it is often not enough to know the domain of the information source. The proper knowledge structure of the information must be presented in order for it to be useful. We first show that the source domain of TransportationDevice is used in both Chinese and English to describe economy. Both languages use the same hierarchical source knowledge structure, incorporating the parent concept of motion, daughter concept of 'Transportation,' and the related concept of 'Transportation Device,' as illustrated by (6). However, the two languages choose two different entities to instantiate the concept of TransportationDevice.

6.1 The Data

After examination of extracted data in both languages, the English data from the WSJ Corpus and Chinese from the Sinica Corpus, we identify two source domains that are related. ECONOMY IS AN AIRPLANE in Chinese and ECONOMY IS A VEHICLE in English both belong to the domain of 'Transportation'.

From Tables 17-5 and 17-6, we notice that the source domain of AIRPLANE is used prototypically in Chinese to map a 'rising action' whereas the source domain of MOVING VEHICLE is used to map the 'speed' of movement in English economy metaphors. Examples of sentences for these metaphors are given in (2) and (3):

Table 17-5. ECONOMY IS AN AIRPLANE (Mandarin Chinese)
Mapping Principle: Economy is an airplane because an airplane ascends and an economy rises.

	Metaphors	Frequency
Functions	*qi3fei1*'to take off'	8
	fei1sheng1 'ascending (while flying)'	1
	tu1fei1 'sudden ascending (while flying)'	1

Table 17-6. ECONOMY IS MOVING VEHICLE (English)
Mapping Principle: The economy is a moving vehicle because moving vehicle has speed of movement and economy has speed of development.

	Metaphor	Frequency
Entities	slowdown	3
	track	2
	slowing	1
	turn	1
	turnaround	1
	driver	1
Quality	on track	2
	slower	1
	slowing	1
Functions	to slow	11
	slow down	3
	adding fuel	2
	to race	2
	speed	1
	turns around	1
	barreling down thee highway	1

(2) ECONOMY IS AIRPLANE (Chinese)

臺灣 經 了 經濟 起飛

taiwan jingli le jingji qifei

Taiwan experience ASP economy take off

"Taiwan has experienced a rise in its economy"

(3) ECONOMY IS MOVING VEHICLE (English)

a. the **economy** is going to **slow down** ,

b. the U.S. **economy** were **barreling down the highway** at 100 miles

In order to check whether these two related conceptual metaphors (in different languages) can be captured by a single structured ontology, we searched for the key concepts in the Mapping Principles for AIRPLANE and MOVING VEHICLE.

For example, when the key concept of 'ascend' was searched for ECONOMY IS AN AIRPLANE, the results from SUMO show that the concept of 'ascend' is defined as 'travel up' and it corresponds with the node of 'Motion,' which comprises the subclasses of 'BodyMotion,' 'Direction Change,' 'Transfer,' 'Transportation' and 'Radiating' (refer to Figure 17-3).

Among these subclasses, 'Transportation' possesses the following definition in (4), which corresponds with the source domain we have identified – i.e., AIRPLANE for 'ascend.'

(4) Motion from one point to another by means of a Transportation Device.

If trans is an instance of transportation, then there exists transportation device device so that device is an instrument for trans.

From Figure 17-3, although the related subclass of 'DirectionChange' is also under the Motion node, it is not on the conceptual branch linking Motion to Transportation and then to TransportationDevice. In other words, it is not directly related to the metaphor ECONOMY IS AN AIRPLANE. The prototypical occurrences of *qifei* 'take off' do not reflect 'DirectionChange;' rather, instead it refers to the motion of the transportation device.

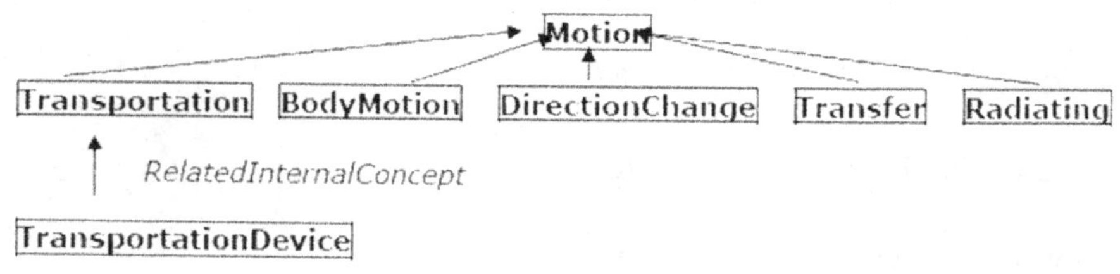

Figure 17-3. Nodes of 'Motion'

Hence, the ontological relations of the concept Transportation as referred to in the ECONOMY IS A AIRPLANE metaphor is more precisely shown in (5).

(5) Process

↑

Motion

↑

Transportation

↑ *RelatedInternalConcept*

TransportationDevice

Transportation is internally related to TransportationDevice. This relation is defined in (6) and the definition of TransportationDevice is given in (7).

(6) transportation is internally related to transportation device.

(relatedInternalConcept Transportation TransportationDevice)

(7) If *device* is an *instance* of *transportation device*, then *device* is *capable* to do *transportation* in role *instrument*.

(=> (instance ?DEVICE TransportationDevice)

(capability Transportation instrument ?DEVICE))

Therefore, the source domain of AIRPLANE in Mandarin Chinese has mappings corresponding to the node of 'TransportationDevice,' which is a lower node for 'Motion' in SUMO.

6.2 Economy is Moving Vehicle in English

We next searched for the concept of 'speed,' which is identified as the most prototypical mapping of ECONOMY IS A MOVING VEHICLE to study the knowledge domain comparison between Chinese and English economy metaphor. The concept of 'speed' is represented in SUMO as two separate linguistic functions, i.e., 'speed' as noun and verb. Their respective corresponding nodes for nominal and verbal readings are given in (8) and (9).

(8) Corresponding Nodes for Nominal 'Speed'

Motion

↑

BiologicallyActiveSubstance

↑

FunctionQuality

↑

RationalNumber

↑

SpeedFn(Function)

(9) Corresponding Nodes for Verbal 'Speed'

Motion

↑

RationalNumber

↑

Increasing

↑

NormativeAttribute

Among these nodes, 'Motion' reflects the majority linguistic expressions in Table 17-6, with the most prototypical mapping of 'slowing down.'

If the concept of 'speed' shares the similar corresponding nodes of 'Motion,' then its subclasses are predicted to be similar to the hierarchy shown in (6). Within this hierarchy, 'speed' also has a corresponding node with 'Transportation' and 'TransportationDevice.'

6.3 Implications: Inferring information from knowledge systems

In terms of the parallel metaphor 'ECONOMY IS A Transportion Device,' two different empirical prototypes are used: AIRPLANE is used in Chinese, and VEHICLE in English. They are mapped differently in Mandarin Chinese and English due to the conceptual variations between the two speech communities. The use of the car in the English speaking communities is similarly a general experience of life, which is mapped to the experience of a cyclical economy. The subsidiary function of 'Speed' represented in the metaphor can also be entailed with people's familiarity with the function of the car. Chinese speakers do not have the same relationship to cars as English-speakers. However, Chinese speakers do perceive both economy and airplane as tools towards modernization. Hence it is reasonable for them to use the more concrete image to describe the more abstract concept.

The findings discussed above have several implications: First, the source domain knowledge in a metaphor can be structured, instead of just an atomic conceptual node. This structure can be precisely captured by ontology, such as SUMO. Second, metaphors have strong conceptual motivation. Hence, even though that metaphors may be parochially realized with different terms in different languages, there is a good possibility that these terms may actually represent identical conceptual structure. This is shown in this paper with the contrast between English VEHICLE and Chinese AIRPLANE, both of which turn out to represent identically structured source knowledge. Third, while conceptual structures are shared, the choices in which subsidiary components may be instantiated may be motivated by the shared experience of the speakers of that language.

7. EXTENDING ONTOLOGY WITH WORDNET: MERGING KNOWLEDGE STRUCTURE FROM MULTIPLE SOURCES

An inherent dilemma of adopting a shared upper ontology is that it cannot cover all concepts. A shared upper ontology is designed to cover the full range of knowledge systems, and hence is restricted to these common conceptual roots. It must exclude idiosyncratic concepts and structures of individual systems. SUMO, for instance, is limited to no more than 1,000 concepts. However, the information systems that need to be captured far exceed these conceptual nodes. We propose to overcome this lack of variations by combing information from an upper ontology and a lexical ontology, such as a wordnet.

A wordnet is a semantic network consists of all lexical items from a language and linked by lexical semantic relations. The complete list of words from a language is basically a list of all the linguistically coded concepts in that language. We could take them to be the complete list of conceptual atoms used by speakers of that language. Since all things describable in that language can be reduced to a list of words as descriptive atoms, a wordnet is simply an ontology which has the widest coverage in that particular language. When a wordnet is linked to a shared upper ontology, the combined knowledge system enables comprehensive coverage of conceptual variants as well as uniform knowledge representation. The mapping between SUMO and WordNet by Niles [22] provided such an infrastructure. Further work has been done to expand this infrastructure to a bilingual one by the construction of Sinica BOW [17].

In terms of our corpus-based prediction of structure representation of the complex knowledge of metaphors, we have noted that it is often impossible to predict mapping to a SUMO node when there are not enough instances attested in the corpora. We examine two instances here that are not attested in the Sinica Corpus: LOVE IS A PLANT (Table 17-7) and LOVE IS FOOD (Table 17-8).

Table 17-7. LOVE IS PLANT Definitions from WordNet and SUMO

Items	WordNet Senses	Explanation	SUMO Category
mengya	**2: sprout**	grow sprouts, of a plant	Growth
miao	**1: seedling**	young plant or tree grown from a seed	FloweringPlant
zhang	**1: grow**	come to have, of physical features and attributes	Growth
guangai	**1: water**	pour water on	Wetting
kaihua	**1: bloom**	produce or yield flowers	Growth

Table 17-8. LOVE IS FOOD Definitions from WordNet and SUMO

Items	WordNet Senses	Explanation	SUMO Category
ziwei	**1: taste**	distinguishing a taste by means of the taste buds	Tasting
ku	**1: bitter**	one of the four basic taste sensations; sharp and disagreeable; like the taste of quinine	TasteAttribute
Weidao	**1: taste**	distinguishing a taste by means of the taste buds	Tasting
Chi	**1: eating**	the act of consuming food	Eating

Ahrens [7] proposes the following MP for LOVE IS A PLANT: “Love is understood as plant because plants involve physical growth and love involves emotional growth.” Since corpora searches do not come up with any instances of this metaphor, it is difficult to ascertain the validity of this principle. We therefore propose looking at the 1) WordNet sense, 2) the WordNet definition and the 3) SUMO node for the WordNet sense for the intuition-based examples in order to see if there are any semantic overlaps within, or between, these three types of information. Table 17-7 shows that the word “Growth” appears three times in the SUMO category, out of the five examples. “Grow” also appears three times in the sense and definition columns from WordNet. Thus, the combination of WordNet information and the SUMO representation agrees with the MP originally given.

In another example that has less than ten corpora examples, LOVE IS FOOD (Table 17-8), both the WordNet information and the SUMO information again matches up with the Mapping Principle suggested in Ahrens [17], that "Love is understood as food because food has different tastes as love involves different feelings." Table 17-8 shows that *taste* is mentioned five times in the WordNet sense and definition, and three out of four times in the SUMO category. Thus, determining the number of overlapping lexical items in WordNet definitions and SUMO categories to verify Mapping Principles seems to hold promise for instances where there are not enough examples to make a judgment based on frequency alone. This combinational approach can also be extended to economy-related metaphors (Table 17-9).

Table 17-9 shows that there are three instances of the concept of 'Invasion' found in the WN definitions, but they are all in the same definition. An alternate hypothesis is that 'ViolentContest' is the critical issue since it occurs in the SUMO nodes of two different words. In addition, in Section 5.1 (also in Ahrens et al. [28]), we noted that ECONOMY IS WAR is a subset of the ECONOMY IS CONTEST metaphor, with the MP of 'Economy is war because war involves a violent contest for territorial gain and the economy involves a vigorous contest for financial gain.' Moreover, the SUMO node of WAR is linked to ViolentContest. This example demonstrates that not only do we need to have an expansion of Sinica Bow to link to more items in WordNet, we also need to expand our notion of semantic space to include related SUMO nodes. In sum, our current analysis suggests that the previous MP was correct.

Table 17-9. ECONOMY IS WAR Definitions from WordNet and SUMO

Items	WordNet Senses	Explanation	SUMO Nodes
cinlue	**4: invasion**	the act of invading; the act of an army that invades for conquest or plunder	Violent Contest
zhan	**1: war**	the waging of armed conflict against an enemy	War
laobing	**1: veteran**	a serviceman who has seen considerable active service	SocialRole
Celue	**6: ambush**	the act of concealing yourself and lying in wait to attack by surprise	Violent Contest
xisheng	**1: sacrifice**	kill or destroy	Killing
xishengpin	**1: sacrifice**	personnel that are sacrificed (e.g., surrendered or lost in order to gain an objective)	Human

In order to further verify this point, the following discussion demonstrates that conceptual metaphors with the similar source domain of WAR show the similar mapping of the concept 'contest.' Table 17-10 gives instances of STOCK MARKET IS WAR. Although different lexical items are mapped as compared with ECONOMY IS WAR, the mapping of the concept of 'contest' is the same.

Thus, the proposed MP is the same; 'Stock market is war because war involves a violent contest for territorial gain and the stock market involves a vigorous contest for financial gain.' Note that although economy and stock market are two different *target* domains, they do have a conceptual relation. The stock market (referring to market activities) are one of the most typical and prominent processes in economy. Hence, it is a significant sub-type of the economy concept.

Table 17-10. STOCK MARKET IS WAR Definitions from WordNet and SUMO

Items	WordNet Senses	Explanation	SUMO Nodes
zhan	**1: war**	the waging of armed conflict against an enemy	War
celue	**6: ambush**	the act of concealing yourself and lying in wait to attack by surprise	Violent Contest
dilei	**1: land_mine**	an explosive mine hidden underground; explodes when stepped on or driven over	Weapon
guanka	**1: checkpoint**	a place (as at a frontier) where travellers are stopped for inspection and clearance	LandArea
fangwei	**2: defend**	be on the defensive; act against an attack	Contest
shanggong	**1: attack**	take the initiative and go on the offensive: "The Serbs attacked the village at night"	Contest
tiaozhan	**4: challenge**	a call to engage in a contest or fight	Requesting
cheli	**1: evacuation**	the act of evacuating; leaving a place in an orderly fashion; esp. for protection	Motion

8. SUMMARY AND IMPLICATIONS

In this chapter, we applied ontology to the study of the complex knowledge system of metaphors and showed that a shared upper ontology, such as SUMO, provides a framework to do formal and principled representation of the structured knowledge of the complex system. In addition, we showed that SUMO can be combined with a language wordnet to provide comprehensive coverage of all alternative conceptual variations.

The implications of such an approach can be illustrated by an example. The term 'soft landing' has recently become popular and is often collocated with China's economy. 'Hard-landing,' though not as popular, has similar distributions. Although it is possible to trace back the use of both terms to as early as Robert J. Gordon's 1985 article [29], it is also true that this expression never took root in daily English. Moreover, we only found one major dictionary, the 1996 Random House Unabridged Dictionary [30], listing the economy reading of soft-landing. However, these terms have been popular in Chinese for the past 20 years, since 1985, when the government made their first attempt to control inflation. And indeed, the term entered daily English use last year only when the Chinese premier made an announcement that China will micro-manage the economy to make sure inflation will not occur. On one hand, we can see that although the term is used quite early in English, the actual uses are restricted to very few academic papers. There is a very simple explanation for this. As we explored in the last couple sections, the metaphor mapping principle is Economy is an Airplane in Chinese, and Economy is Vehicle for English. Thus, even though the use of soft-landing can be understood both in Chinese and English, it became a frequent expression in Chinese. This is because this novel metaphor can be directly incorporated into the knowledge system of economy is an airplane. From web-based data, it is clear that when 'soft-landing' (or the less popular antonym 'hard landing') is used to describe economy in English, it highly collocates with references to the Chinese economy. For instance, 9 out of 10 highest ranked result of the Google search 'economy soft-landing' refer to China.

9. CONCLUSION

Ontology is powerful tools for building and integrating knowledge systems. Although our work is now highly dependent on manual human intervention, we can also make crucial use of computational ontology and electronic resources. We foresee construction of domain-specific ontology to be the next crucial step in this line of research. Construction of specific ontology can be semi-automated, especially with respect to the extraction of conceptual terms and their mappings to a shared upper ontology. When enough specific ontology is constructed, then a fully automatic integration of information can become a reality in the future.

REFERENCES

[1] SUMO (Suggested Upper Merged Ontology). http://www.ontologyportal.org or http://ontology.teknowledge.com.

[2] Sowa, John F. http://www.jfsowa.com/ontology/.

[3] Berners Lee, T., Hendler, J. and Lassila, O., The semantic web. *Scientific American*, 35 43 (2001).

[4] Fellbaum, C. ed., *WordNet: An Electronic Lexical Database*. Cambridge, MA: MIT Press (1998).

[5] Black, M., *Models and Metaphors*. New York: Cornell University Press (1962).

[6] Searle, J. R., Metaphor. In: Ortony A. ed. *Metaphor and Thought*, 2nd ed. Cambridge: Cambridge University Press. 92 123 (1979).

[7] Lakoff G. and Johnson, M., *Metaphors We Live By*. Chicago and London: The University of Chicago Press, (1980).

[8] Camac, M., and Glucksberg, S, Metaphors do not use associations between concepts, they are used to create them. *Journal of Psycholinguistic Research*, 13.: 443 455 (1984).

[9] Gibbs, R.W., *The Poetics of Mind*. Cambridge: Cambridge University Press. (1994).

[10] Kelly, M. and Keil, F. C., Conceptual domains and the comprehension of metaphor. *Metaphor and Symbolic Activity*, 2: 33 51 (1987).

[11] Gentner, D., Structure-Mapping: A Theoretical framework for analogy. *Cognitive Science*. 7:155 170 (1983).

[12] Richards, I. A., *The Philosophy of Rhetoric*. Oxford: Oxford University Press (1965).

[13] Lonneker, B., Is there a way to represent metaphors in WordNets? Insights from the Hamburg Metaphor Database. In the *Proceedings of the ACL Workshop on the Lexicon and Figurative Language*. 18 26. (2003).

[14] Alonge, A. and Lönneker, B., Metaphors in Wordnets: From theory to practice. In *Proceedings of the 4th International Conference on Language Resources and Evaluation, Lisbon, Portugal, 26-28 May, 2004 (LREC 2004)*. ELRA. 165 168 (2004).

[15] Peters, W. and Wilks, Y.,, Data-driven detection of figurative language use in electronic language resources." *Metaphor and Symbol*, 18(3):161 173. (2003).

[16] Lakoff, G., The Contemporary Theory of Metaphor. In: Ortony A. ed. *Metaphor and Thought*, 2nd ed. Cambridge: Cambridge University Press. 202 251 (1993).

[17] Ahrens, K., When love is not digested: Underlying reasons for source to target domain pairing in the Contemporary Theory of Metaphor. In Hsiao, Y. E. ed. *Proceeding of the First Cognitive Linguistics Conference*. Taipei: Cheng-Chi University. 273 302 (2002).

[18] Martin J., Metabank: a knowledge base of metaphoric language conventions. *Computational Intelligence*. 10:134-149 (1992).

[19] Gentner, D. and Wolff, G., Evidence for role-neutral initial processing of metaphors. *Journal of Experimental Psychology*, 26:529 541 (2000).

[20] McGlone, M. S., 996, Conceptual Metaphors and Figurative Language Interpretation: Food for Thought? *Journal of Memory and Language*. 1996; 35: 544-565.

[21] Kilgarriff, A. and Grefenstette, G., eds., *Special issue on Web as Corpus. Computational Linguistics*, 3:333–347 (2003).

[22] Niles, I., Mapping WordNet to the SUMO Ontology. *Teknowledge Technical Report* (2003).

[23] Huang, C-R, Tseng, Elanna I. J., Tsai Dylan B. S., and Murphy, B..,Cross-lingual portability of semantic relations: Bootstrapping Chinese WordNet with English WordNet relations. *Languages and Linguistics*. 4(3):509 532 (2003).

[24] Niles, I., & Pease, A. Toward a Standard Upper Ontology. *Proceedings of the Second International Conference on Formal Ontology in Information Systems (FOIS-2001)* (2001).

[25] Pease, A. & Niles, I., IEEE Standard Upper Ontology: A Progress Report. *Knowledge Engineering Review, Special Issue on Ontology and Agents*. 17 (2002).

[26] Sevcenko, M., Online presentation of an upper ontology. *Proceedings of Znalosti 2003*. Ostrava, Czech Republic (2003).

[27] Huang, C-R, Chang, R-Y and Lee, S-B., Sinica BOW (Bilingual Ontological Wordnet): Integration of Bilingual WordNet and SUMO. *Proceedings of the 4th International Conference on Language Resources and Evaluation (LREC2004)* (2004).

[28] Ahrens K., Chung, S-F. and Huang, C-R., Conceptual Metaphors: Ontology-based representation and corpora driven Mapping Principles. *Proceedings of the ACL Workshop on The Lexicon and Figurative Language*. pp. Sapporo, Japan. 53 41 (2003).

[29] Gordon, R. J.,Understanding Inflation in the 1980's. *Brookings Papers on Economic Activity*. (1985).

[30] *Random House Unabridged Dictionary*, Random House Press (1996).

ON-LINE RESOURCES

Sinica BOW: Academia Sinica Bilingual Ontological Wordnet. http://BOW.sinica.edu.tw

Sinica Corpus: Academia Sinica Balanced Corpus. http://www.sinica.edu.tw/SinicaCorpus/

SUMO: Suggested Upper Merged Ontology. http://www.ontologyportal.org or http://ontology.teknowledge.com

WordNet http://wordnet.princeton.edu/index.shtml

WSJ Corpus: The Wall Street Journal Corpus. Accessed through the Linguistic Data Consortium http://www.ldc.upenn.edu/ldc/online/index.html.

Chapter 18

THE KNOWLEDGE COLLECTIVE FRAMEWORK MAKES ONTOLOGY BASED INFORMATION ACCESSIBLE, MAINTAINABLE, AND REUSABLE

Jay A. Yusko[1] and Martha W. Evens[2]
[1]*Illinois Institute of Technology, 244 Gazebo, Lombard, IL 60148, jay.yusko@gensolco.com;*
[2]*Illinois Institute of Technology, 10 West 31st Street, Chicago, IL 60616, evens@iit.edu*

Abstract: The Knowledge Collective is a multi-layer, multi-agent framework for information reuse in an intelligent knowledge base that supports a collection of agents called MicroDroids, which provide information management capabilities through a variety of interfaces for experts, human users, and software components. This information is stored in a variety of internal structures (e.g., Java objects, rules, database structures). The main concept is that information is stored in a format that is natural to the type of information being maintained (e.g., data, metadata, ontologies, concept maps, lexicons, rules). The Knowledge Collective will make ontology based information accessible to many end users, maintainable by domain experts and reusable by many users across many applications without knowing how or where the information is stored. The Knowledge Collective's first use is in version 4 of CIRCSIM-Tutor, an Intelligent Tutoring System developed at the Illinois Institute of Technology in Chicago, IL.

Key words: Multi-Agent System (MAS); knowledge base; ontology; ontology inference engine; Intelligent Tutoring System (ITS)

1. INTRODUCTION

How can we make computers more useful? Can we really make them understand human users and carry out a conversation in applications like Intelligent Tutoring Systems (ITS)? Can they teach students about concepts in a complex domain like medicine? Human tutors can teach another person about a specific domain because they understand the domain that they are teaching. A professor of physiology can teach a first year medical student about the Baroreceptor Reflex because the professor is an expert on the topic. That same professor would probably have a hard time tutoring students about finance or electrical engineering. It would take different professors, experts in these domains, to tutor a student about these topics.

So how do we expect a dumb computer to tutor medical students about different medical domains? In fact, how can a computer even understand how to be a tutor in the first place? The computer has to understand the domain it wants to tutor the student in and it has to understand how to be a tutor in general.

The computer can only understand a domain in terms of the model it is given (Yusko, 1994; Bredeweg and Forbus, 2003; Falkenhainer and Forbus, 1988). That model is ontology. In fact, there are many models or ontologies involved in being a tutor (Khuwaja and Patel, 1996). However, it is not that simple. Just as a university needs many professors to tutor students in different domains, this computer system will need many domain experts using many different kinds of models.

How can we build a system that meets the requirements to tutor a student in one domain area like the Baroreceptor Reflex? A large ontology will not meet the needs. It might work, but it would be very difficult to maintain because we are talking about many areas of expertise combined into one. This process is much more feasible with much smaller ontology that covers the areas of expertise that are needed. This advantage has its own built-in cost: how do we make these ontologies work together and, more important, how do we maintain them in a consistent fashion?

What is needed is a university inside the computer system. All the members of this group of expert agents need to have their own ontologies and work together as a team to tutor students. The Knowledge Collective (TKC) is the realization of this vision. It is a multi-layered, multi-agent framework for developing and maintaining intelligent knowledge bases that can be used in areas like Intelligent Tutoring Systems (ITS) such as CIRCSIM-Tutor (Michael et al., 2003; Evens and Michael, in press). It is made up of many intelligent agents called MicroDroids that are capable of working together as a team to solve problems in an ITS. This is the team or virtual university that we are developing at Illinois Institute of Technology to be used by the next generation of CIRCSIM-Tutor and by other medical tutoring systems in the future. TKC is the framework, or foundation, that will allow many smaller maintainable ontologies to be used together to solve problems in areas like Qualitative Reasoning across many domains in an ITS. In fact, TKC is developed around the concept of ontologies and is controlled by ontologies and their inference engines.

1.1 Overview

The background and the domain for the research are described in Section 2. Section 3 discusses ontologies. MicroDroids are explained in Section 4. The Knowledge Collective is discussed in Section 5. Section 6 describes an example of TKC process. Section 7 brings it all together.

2. BACKGROUND AND DOMAIN

The ability of many users to reuse information across many applications is important for the success of an intelligent knowledge base. A good example is the work that is being done with Intelligent Tutoring Systems (ITS) that we developed at the Illinois Institute of Technology (IIT) in Chicago, IL. The knowledge base described in this chapter is the seventh in a series of knowledge bases that have been built from scratch to support the CIRCSIM-Tutor system (Evens and Michael, in press). Each time we interviewed the experts they have spent much time reprogramming the information in a form that the experts cannot read. We are now starting to build two new tutorials that cover much of the same material – one is a Concept Map Tutor for the Baroreceptor Reflex; the other is an intelligent tutoring system called GASP-Tutor. It is clearly time to stop tearing up knowledge bases and building new ones. Instead, it is time to plan in advance to make the knowledge reusable. Instead of starting the knowledge engineering process all over again, we decided to design a knowledge base to serve all of these different systems and to create a tool that allows the expert to define and read what is in the knowledge base. We repeat this history of the dead knowledge bases developed in the past, in the hope of avoiding reliving it.

CIRCSIM-Tutor is an intelligent tutoring system that carries on a natural language dialogue with the goal of helping first-year medical students learn how to solve problems involving the Baroreceptor Reflex, the negative feedback reflex system that acts to maintain blood pressure in the human body. The CIRCSIM-Tutor project grew out of an earlier computer-aided instruction system called CIRCSIM. It presents students with a perturbation to the blood pressure, asks them for predictions about how this situation will affect seven important physiological parameters, analyzes the patterns of errors in those predictions, and reels out one of 243 paragraphs of canned remedial text stored in the system (Rovick and Michael, 1986). CIRCSIM was and is a big success, but its builders, who are Professors of Physiology at Rush Medical College, thought that their students could learn even more from a system that could ask the students to provide explanations, understand their answers, and comment on them. We set out to build a system capable of carrying on a natural dialogue with the users.

The first version calculated the predictions for the four problem situations correctly, but it did not solve those problems in the logical order that Michael and Rovick wanted their students to use. The second version changed some of the rules to produce the answers in a logical order, but as Yuemei Zhang (Zhang, 1991; Zhang et al., 1987, 1990), who was writing the Discourse Generation portion of the system, immediately pointed out that the knowledge base still contained nothing that the system could use to guide the students through solving the problem. The third version contained a solution tree for each of the four problems then implemented, which provided a trace of the ideal solution for that problem. Zhang agreed that this was a big improvement and she started to produce code to explicate the trace, but she argued that this version was still not enough, because it did not provide support for discussing the steps in the problem-solving algorithm with the student or for generating explanations.

Nakhoon Kim (Kim, 1989) built the fourth version of the CIRCSIM-Tutor problem solver using a knowledge base that consisted of a hierarchical set of Prolog rules that described the problem-solving algorithms and used them to solve problems. At this point, he declared victory and integrated the pieces of the prototype system so that it could request predictions, analyze the predictions entered by the student, build an overlay model of the student's knowledge of the Baroreceptor Reflex, determine a set of topics to be taught, and plan how to teach them. Kim's Prolog Prototype (Kim, Evens, Michael, and Rovick, 1989) did not attempt to carry out a natural language dialogue with the student, but it performed all the other steps in the tutoring process and we learned a great deal from building it especially about knowledge representation (Kim, 1989).

In 1990-1991 Chong Woo (Woo, 1991; Woo et al., 1991) constructed a complete version of CIRCSIM-Tutor in Lisp and Zhang seized the chance to build the knowledge base of her dreams. The fifth version of the knowledge base is a collection of frames, which, with some additions as we added problems to the system, has powered the system for the last ten years. After being tested with large classes of students at Rush it is now in routine use. Woo and Zhang built a frame for every phase, every parameter, every causal relationship, as well as for other concepts that the students need to learn in order to understand negative feedback systems like "neural variable" and "regulated parameter." At Zhang's insistence, some anatomy frames were added as well. The experts did not think that anatomical concepts belonged in a physiology knowledge base, but Zhang pointed out many places where anatomy was mentioned in the human tutoring transcripts and our experts agreed that we could include anatomical references so long as we limited their use to understanding them in student inputs and responding to those inputs. The code for the problem-solving algorithms was added to the frames as well, so that the Discourse Generator could discuss the algorithms with the student. Fortunately, Lisp code can also serve as Lisp data.

The sixth version of the knowledge base was built in CLOS (the Common Lisp Object System) by Ramzan Ali Khuwaja (Khuwaja, 1994; Khuwaja et al., 1992, 1994) to support his multilevel model of the domain knowledge base. He carried out a detailed analysis of the domain knowledge in the transcripts and discovered that the experts organized it in three levels. The top level corresponds to the Concept Map that they hoped the students would internalize and make use of in problem solving. The middle level contains additional concepts that they used in devising hints and giving explanations. The bottom level contains many other concepts that were somtimes mentioned by students but not used by the expert tutors unless a student alluded to them first. Perhaps because CLOS was new and Khuwaja was new to this kind of programming, his module suffered from performance problems. We continued to use Woo and Zhang's frame knowledge base but added frames for the other two levels.

The current ideas about the knowledge base owe a great deal to the work of Reva Freedman (Freedman, 1996; Freedman and Evens, 1997; Freedman et al., 1998), who argued that much of the knowledge could and should be written in rule form. The result, she claimed, would be much easier for the experts to read and update. The experts never liked the frames. She demonstrated the feasibility of her approach by actually producing a large number of these rules in her dissertation.

Two new tutoring systems are now in the planning stage, another dialogue-based Intelligent Tutoring System called GASP-Tutor and a Concept Map Tutor. The focus of GASP-Tutor centers around two interacting negative reflex systems that control ventilation in the human body. Analysis of human tutoring transcripts shows a large overlap in language and reasoning between GASP-Tutor and CIRCSIM-Tutor. The Concept Map Tutor covers the same domain. If all three systems could use the new CIRCSIM-Tutor knowledge base, we would save a tremendous amount of time and effort both for the developers and for the experts.

Systems like the ones discussed above require models of the domain, models of tutoring, student models, and language models. These multiple models require the system to organize and store many kinds of knowledge. All these models need to be stored as individual ontologies so that:

- Many users and domain experts can access the information in the ontologies

- Domain (including Pedagogy) experts can maintain their specific ontologies
- The ontologies can be reused by many end users and across many applications
- The information from multiple ontologies can be used together to solve problems (e.g., using Qualitative Reasoning)

3. ONTOLOGIES

Ontologies are the core concept that tie information about specific domains together and make them usable. Ontologies give the MicroDroids the semantics to communicate with each other. The MicroDroids give the ontologies the ability to be shared by multiple users and applications. An Ontology Inference Engine (ONTIE) controls the reasoning about the ontological information. For this discussion, it is important to understand what ontology is in general and how they are used in TKC.

3.1 Definitions

Don Hutcheson (2003, p. 45) defines an ontology as "a list with relationships to other lists." The Foundation for Intelligent Physical Agents (FIPA) defines ontology in the following way (FIPA, 2002a, p. 34):

> Ontology provides a vocabulary for representing and communicating knowledge about some topic and a set of relationships and properties that hold for the entities denoted by that vocabulary.

Ontology is a model of a specific domain that can be used for Qualitative Reasoning (Yusko and Evens, 2004) about either structural objects and their relationships or processes using the Qualitative Process Theory of Kenneth Forbus (1985). The ontologies enable agents to communicate with each other and with an end user in an intelligent manner. FIPA has a specification for an ontology service (FIPA, 2002b). This specification assumes that the system has an ontology server. It talks about using ontology agents to make the ontology available to all agents in the system (FIPA, 2002b, pp. 1-8).

The concept of an ontology server with ontology agents does not properly fit The Knowledge Collective framework. Each time a user connects to TKC, a session is set up. This session will last until the end user has completed the desired tasks. The important issue dealing with the ontology for TKC is that each user session will dynamically build its own ontology. This is done by multiple MicroDroids being brought into the session, each one bringing their own specific domain ontology with them.

Each user session can have a different overall ontology depending on what the user is trying to accomplish.

Much ontology is stored physically in frames (FIPA, 2002b, p.16). The thought was originally to store TKC ontologies in frames (Yusko, 1984). Reasoning about frame based ontologies in agent systems is usually done using predicate logic expressed in Prolog type rules. TKC will use production rules of various kinds as an Ontology Inference Engine (ONTIE) to accomplish Qualitative Reasoning about specific domains. For this reason ontologies will be maintained as UML models which are converted to Java classes. This is explained in the discussion of the Ontology Inference Engine in Section 3.4.

3.2 Types

Much ontology is hierarchies of information typically based on the ISA relationship. If we use the FIPA definition stated above, then we can envision many types of ontologies with an unlimited number of relationships. We have to keep in mind that the purpose of using ontologies in TKC or any intelligent knowledge base is to store information and for informational semantics. We have classified some of the major types of ontologies used in TKC as follows: Artifact Based, Process Based, Concept Map Based, and Flow Based. Each of the types defines specific parts of a domain. To do Qualitative reasoning, it takes a combination of ontologies to define a specific domain.

3.2.1 Artifact Based Ontologies

Artifact based ontologies are objects and their relationships. They can be represented by a UML Class Model. The class model for a MicroDroid in Figure 18-1 is a good example of this type of ontology. In this case it is really a part/whole model of a MicroDroid.

3.2.2 Process Based Ontologies

Process based ontologies deal with process flows, which can be represented by UML Activity Models. An activity model represents how the flow of control works in a process. A good example can be seen in Figure 18-2: the process flow for CIRCSIM-Tutor (Evens and Michael, in press).

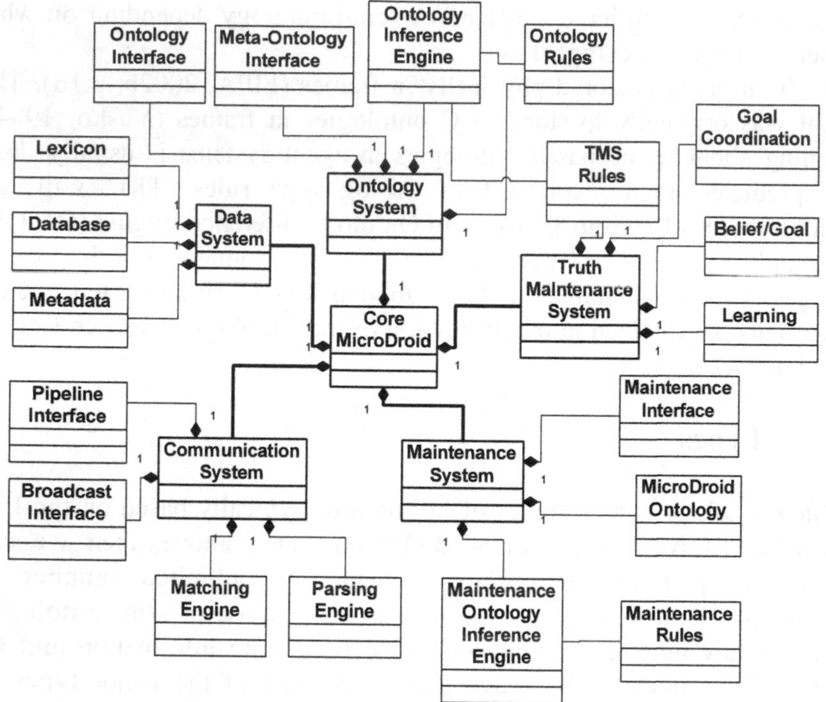

Figure 18-1. MicroDroid Ontology

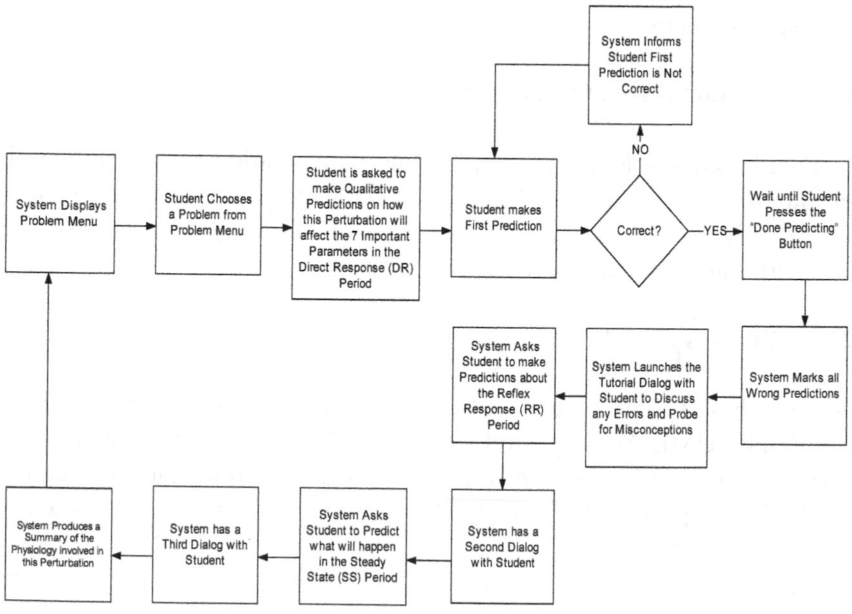

Figure 18-2. CIRCSIM-Tutor Ontology (Evens and Michael, in press)

3.2.3 Concept Map Based Ontologies

Concept Map based ontologies are concepts and their relationships. They represent how one concept affects another concept. Figure 18-3 shows a good example is the Concept Map for CIRCSIM-Tutor (Khuwaja, 1994, p. 73). This model is used to define the different concepts in CIRCSIM-Tutor and how they affect each other. This is vital to define cause and affect relationships that are used in Qualitative Reasoning.

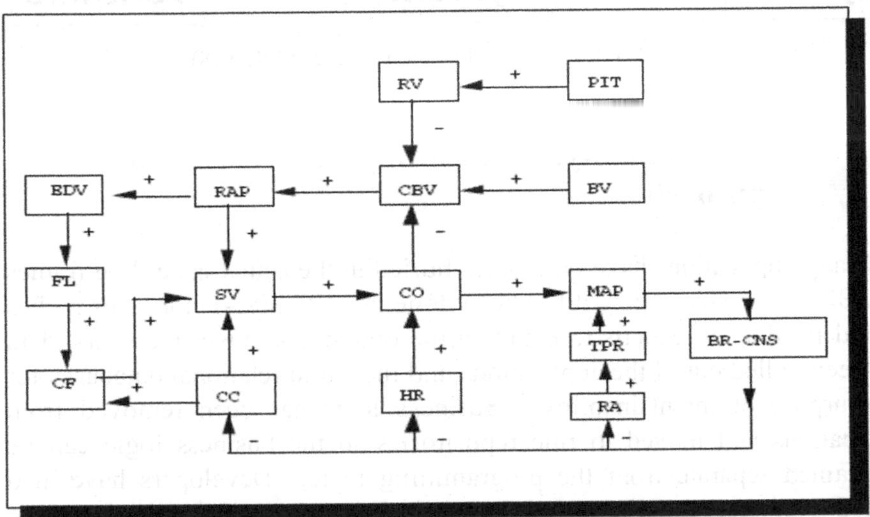

Figure 18-3. Baroreceptor Reflex Concept Map Ontology (Khuwaja, 1994, p. 73)

3.2.4 Flow Based Ontologies

Flow based ontologies are very similar to process based ontologies. However, they model the flow of something physical instead of process control. Figure 18-4 shows a good example of the blood flow in the cardiovascular system (Zhang, 1991, p.68). (Note that CIRCSIM-Tutor deliberately ignores the pulmonary circulation and the arterioles and capillaries). In the case of this ontology, the flow of blood through the circulatory system is modeled. This allows Qualitative Reasoning about the actual blood flow.

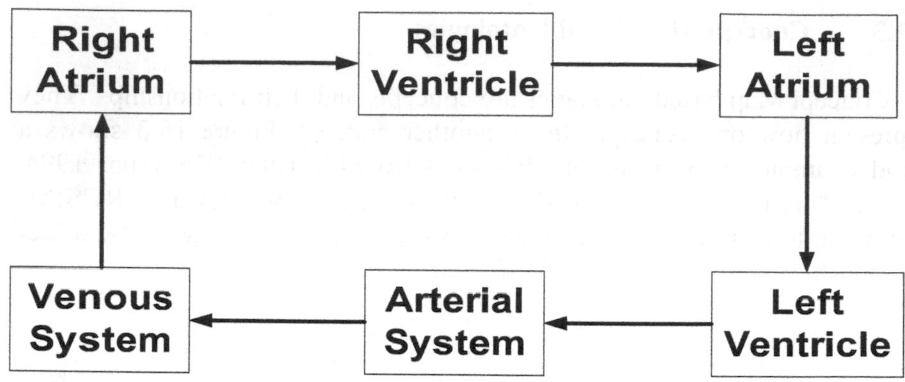

Figure 18-4. Circulatory Flow Path (Zhang, 1991, p.68)

3.3 Maintainability, Accessibility, and Reusability Approach

Many applications have ontologies buried in the actual code, like frames in LISP code. This is how it has been done in CIRCSIM-Tutor. This makes it hard for domain experts to maintain the ontologies. Over the years, data has been pulled out of the applications and moved to relational databases for the purpose of maintainability. Business logic has been removed from applications and moved to rule repositories so the business logic can be maintained separate from the programming logic. Developers have also started to move ontologies out of the applications to ontology repositories so they can be maintained separately from the programming logic. Each of these separations allows domain experts to maintain information about their specific domains and end users to access and reuse it whether it is data, business logic, or ontologies. This is a good approach, until the domain expert has to maintain all three information types at the same time.

In TKC, this is taken one step further by allowing a single MicroDroid to manage and understand all three types of information so that the domain expert only has to understand the domain, not how or where the information is stored. This framework is described in Section 5.

3.4 Ontology Inference Engine

As stated earlier, most ontology is frame based and use Prolog based logic rules to reason about the ontology. A good example of this is Protégé (Knublauch, 2005), which is a frame based ontology management system that uses an ontology repository. Algernon (Hewett, 2005) is a Prolog based logic rule inference engine that works with Protégé and is a Prolog based logic rule system. Many more examples can be found in (Gomez-Perez, Fernandez-Lopez and Corcho, 2004) and (Fensel, 2004).

We have taken a different approach to managing ontologies. TKC is geared towards accessibility, maintainability by the domain expert and reusability by many end users and across many applications. All ontology is maintained as a small domains specific unit and managed by a specific class of MicroDroid. The ONTIE architecture is show in Figure 18-5. The ontology itself is developed and maintained in a UML model using UML2 from Omando (Hussey, 2004), which is a plug-in to the Java environment called Eclipse (Gallardo, Burnett and McGovern, 2003). This model is converted in the Eclipse environment to Java classes, using the Eclipse Modeling Framework (Budinsky et al., 2004). The Java classes are then imported into the ILOG® JRules™ development environment as a Transaction Object Model (XOM). The XOM is then imported into JRules Rule Builder. The Java classes are also deployed to the MicroDroid.

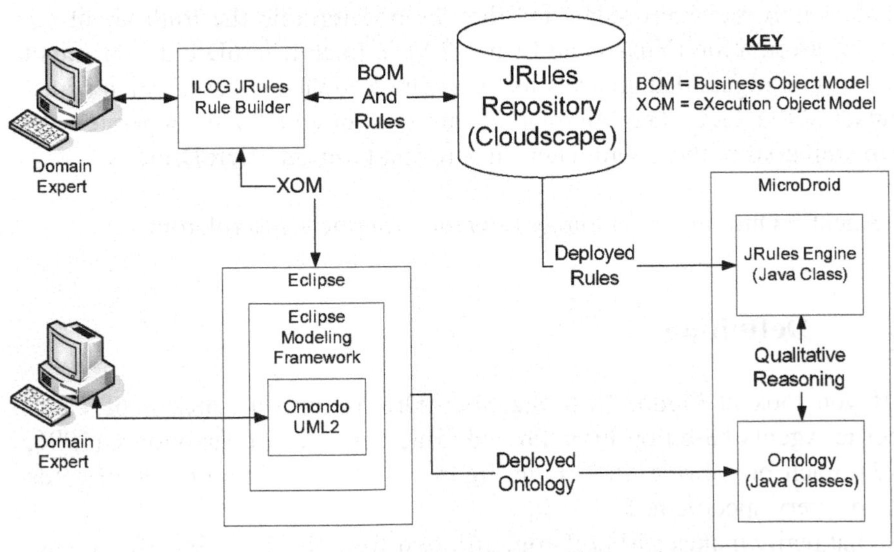

Figure 18-5. Ontology Inference Engine Architecture

JRules automatically builds a Business Object Model (BOM) from the XOM. The rules are then written against the BOM. JRules is a Business Rule Management System (BRMS) that uses production rules that understand and are integrated with the BOM and are controlled by a rule engine, which is a Java class. The rules are then deployed to the JRules rule engine in the MicroDroid. These rules are used to do Qualitative Reasoning about the ontology the MicroDroid is maintaining.

The Ontology Inference Engine (ONTIE) is based on a BRMS. BRMS differs from the basic Expert System technology. Both a BRMS and an Expert System can use production rules, be forward chaining, and use the Rete algorithm (Friedman-Hill, 2003, pp. 136-189) for conflict resolution. The real difference is the integration with an object model. An Expert System is not integrated with an object model. This integration with an object model is what makes a BRMS more useful as an Ontology Inference Engine than an Expert System.

4. MICRODROIDS

MicroDroids are a class of agents. Each MicroDroid is a pattern composed of objects that do a specific function or task. They understand how they fit into the environment and know what they can process and how to ask other MicroDroids for help. They are the navigators that translate the metadata into metaknowledge and they help determine the truth about the domain information (Yusko and Evens, 2002). Each MicroDroid is an agent and a virtual object that controls its own mini knowledge base, which is just a subset of the TKC. The MicroDroids are goal oriented and cooperate with the overall goal of the Coordinator. In simplest terms, a MicroDroid is:

Agent + Ontology + Ontology Inference Engine = MicroDroid

4.1 Definition

If you look at Figure 18-6, the MicroDroids form a subclass of Task-Specific Agents based on Franklin and Graesser's Agent Taxonomy (1996, p. 23). Each box inside of TKC in Figure 18-10 is a class of MicroDroids that do a very specific task.

What really makes a MicroDroid different from the Task-Specific Agents is the fact that MicroDroids do not depend on an ontology server or an ontology agent. Built into every MicroDroid are its own ontology, an Ontology Inference Engine, and an embedded database. This is vital since the ontology used during an end user session is built dynamically from the ontologies of each MicroDroid participating in the session. This also allows each MicroDroid to do Qualitative Reasoning about its specific domain using an ontology inference engine based on production rules using the ILOG JRules environment.

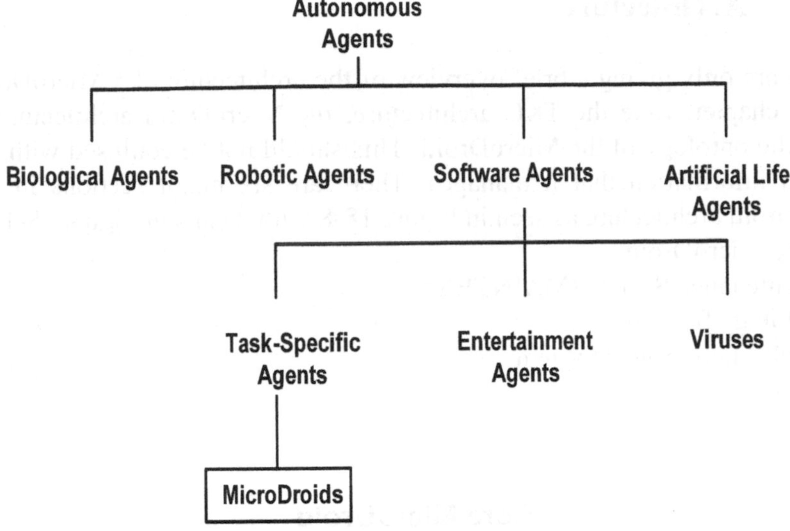

Figure 18-6. Franklin and Graesser's Agent Taxonomy (1996, p. 23)

MicroDroids belong to a class hierarchy (see Figure 18-7). The root is MicroDroid Base. There are two main subclasses: Layer MicroDroid and Special Purpose MicroDroid. There are two Layer MicroDroid classes: Application MicroDroid and Solution MicroDroid. These classes have many subclasses as seen in Figure 18-10. Each if these subclasses can have many instances. There are three Special Purpose MicroDroid classes: Coordinator MicroDroid and User Profile MicroDroid. They can each have many instances, but no subclasses.

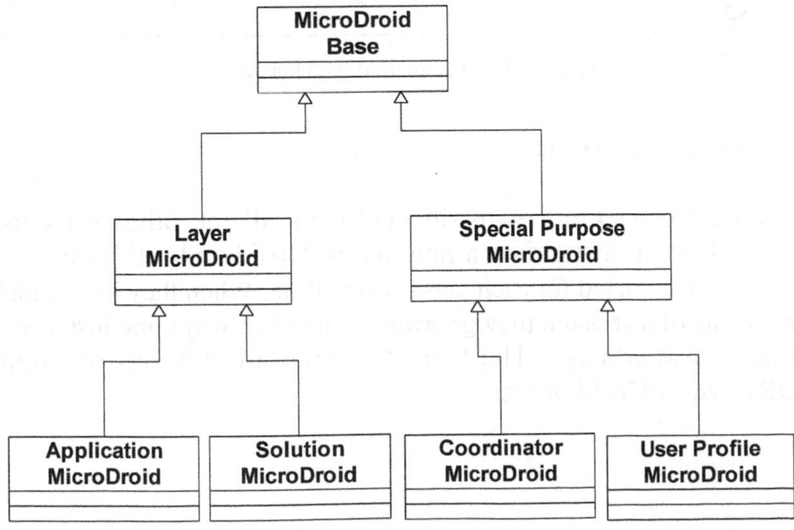

Figure 18-7. MicroDroid Hierarchy

4.2 Architecture

We are only giving a brief overview of the architecture of a MicroDroid in this chapter. Like the TKC architecture, the MicroDroid architecture is really the ontology of the MicroDroid. This should not be confused with the domain information that it manages. There are six major sections in the MicroDroid architecture as seen in Figure 18-8 with details in Figure 18-1:

1. Core MicroDroid
2. Maintenance System (MAINTEX)
3. Ontology System
4. Truth Maintenance System
5. Data System
6. Communication System

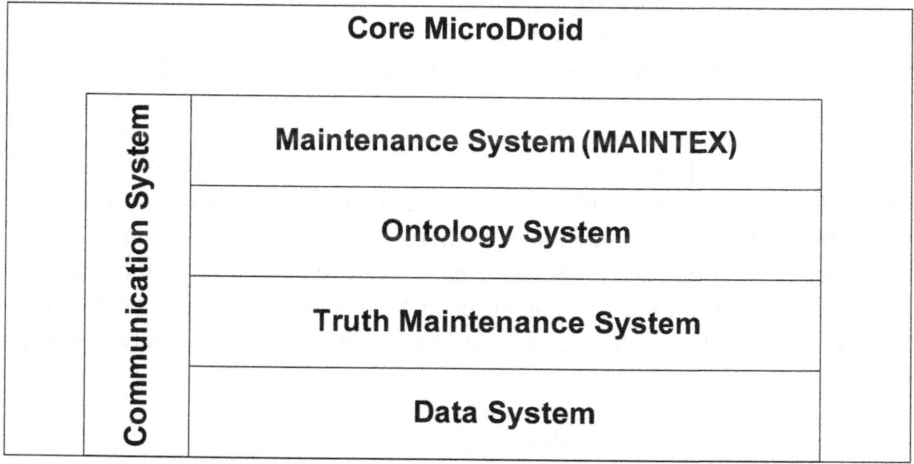

Figure 18-8. MicroDroid Architecture

4.2.1 Core MicroDroid

The core MicroDroid owns and controls all the other systems. It understand how to instantiate a new MicroDroid and retire one. There can be many instantiated for each class at one time. When they have finished serving as part of a session, they go away. There is always one instance that is waiting to answer a call. The Core MicroDroid only has one object, the CORE MicroDroid object.

4.2.2 Maintenance System

This system is the Maintenance Expert (MAINTEX) that knows how to maintain all the information that the MicroDroid manages. There are three main objects in this system. The first object is the MicroDroid Ontology, which interfaces to the ontology that defines the MicroDroid. The second object is the Maintenance Ontology Inference Engine and the Maintenance Rules, which are used to reason about the MicroDroid's own ontology. Therefore, it can reason about any part of the MicroDroid. The last part of the MicroDroid is the Maintenance Interface object. This object connects to the COORDINATOR MicroDroid and forms a portal from the Graphical User Interface Layer to MAINTEX.

4.2.3 Ontology System

This system contains the objects needed for dealing with domain specific ontologies. It has an Ontology Inference Engine (ONTIE) and a set of Ontology Rules specifically for doing Qualitative Reasoning about the ontology. It also has a Meta-Ontology Interface that deals with information about the ontology structure and how the ontology relates to other domain specific information within the MicroDroid.

This system contains the objects needed for dealing with domain specific ontologies that the MicroDroid has to manage. It has an Ontology Inference Engine for doing Qualitative Reasoning about the ontology. It also has a meta-ontology interface that deals with information about the ontology structure and how the ontology relates to other domain specific information within the MicroDroid.

4.2.4 Truth Maintenance System

The Truth Maintenance System (TMS) is for dealing with goals, beliefs and learning. MicroDroids have the ability to deal with Truth Maintenance. This Truth Maintenance System functionality comes with ILOG® JRules™ (ILOG, 2004, p. 115).

The MicroDroid learning system is part of this system. When a MicroDroid is instantiated, it has all the knowledge of the MicroDroid instances that came before it in this class. When the MicroDroid is finished with a session, it is destroyed, but all acquired knowledge is kept for future MicroDroids. This same type of learning can be used with student models since it is nothing more than a MicroDroid.

4.2.5 Data system

The Data System stores all non-active ontology information such as facts, lexicons, metadata, ontology persistence information and rules. This information is stored in files or in a database. In TKC, the Database being used is Cloudscape® (Saunders and Anderson, 2004) an open source database system from IBM. Cloudscape is being used because it was developed to be embedded in a Java application without the use of a database management system. This system has objects for dealing with different types of data: Database information, Lexicons and Metadata.

4.2.6 Communication System

The multi-agent capabilities in TKC will not use any specific agent protocols like other multi-agent systems. The communications between the MicroDroids are handled using the Java Message Service (JMS) (Haase, 2002). This is a loosely coupled peer-to-peer communication system. The messages are asynchronous and the sender has no knowledge about the receiver. The MicroDroids are just clients and the controlling server for JMS is JBoss (Taylor et al., 2004).

Messages are sent out by the sending MicroDroid in a publish/subscribe methodology. This is a broadcast message. Once another MicroDroid answers, a pipeline is setup between the two MicroDroids using a point-to-point messaging methodology. IBM® WebSphere QualityStage handles the parsing, standardization, translation, and matching of the attributes and terms in the message.

Figure 18-9 is an example of what is happening during communications. Each box is an instance of the MicroDroid class that is represented by the label. The thick lines are active and the thin lines are waiting for use. The End User has asked the COORDINATOR MicroDroid for Information. The COORDINATOR MicroDroid sends out a broadcast message. The CARDIOVASCULAR INFORMATION SYSTEM MicroDroid answers and a peer-to-peer connection is set up between them. The CARDIOVASCULAR INFORMATION SYSTEM MicroDroid then sends out a broadcast message. The CARDIOVASCULAR PHYSIOLOGY MicroDroid has not answered yet. When the CARDIOVASCULAR PHYSIOLOGY Micro Droid answers, a peer-to-peer with the CARDIOVASCULAR INFORMATION SYSTEM MicroDroid will be set up. The CIRCSIM-TUTOR Micro Droid is just waiting for a broadcast message that it is interested in answering.

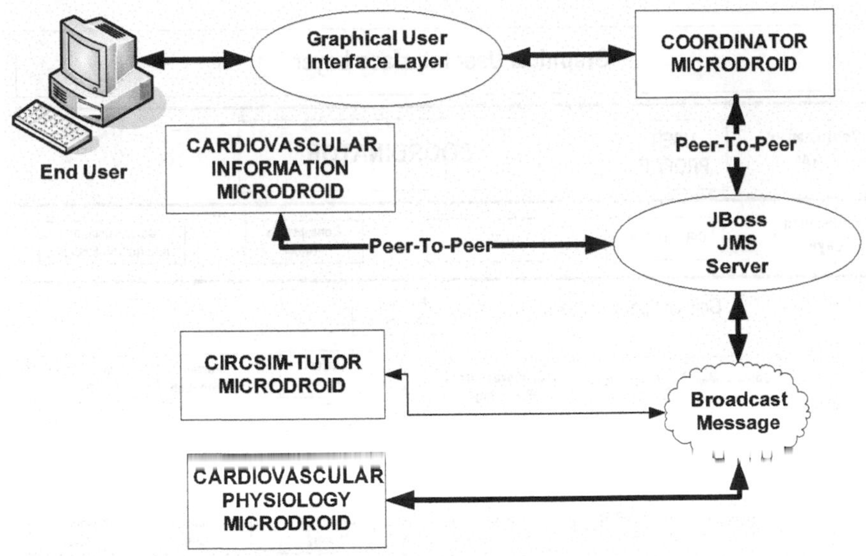

Figure 18-9. MicroDroid Architecture

5. THE KNOWLEDGE COLLECTIVE (TKC)

The Knowledge Collective is a multi-layer, multi-agent system (Ferber 1999; Weiss, 2000) composed of four layers as seen in Figure 18-10:

1. Graphical User Interface
2. Coordination
3. Application
4. Solution

These four layers make up the overall high level ontology for TKC. There is an object ontology used for doing Qualitative Reasoning about The Knowledge Collective in general. The actual ontology model is in Figure 18-11. Each layer is composed of classes of MicroDroids. Therefore, there can be many instances of each MicroDroid.

5.1 Graphical User Interface Layer

The Graphical User Interface Layer is the portal into TKC and therefore, into the actual application information. It can be composed of many screens for the end user, the developer, and the expert to input and retrieve information, data and metadata from or to TKC. It gives the end user access to application information. It gives the developer the ability to add, delete, maintain or monitor the MicroDroids in each layer. It also allows the subject matter experts to view, add and update their subject areas. It is the view into COORDINATOR MicroDroid.

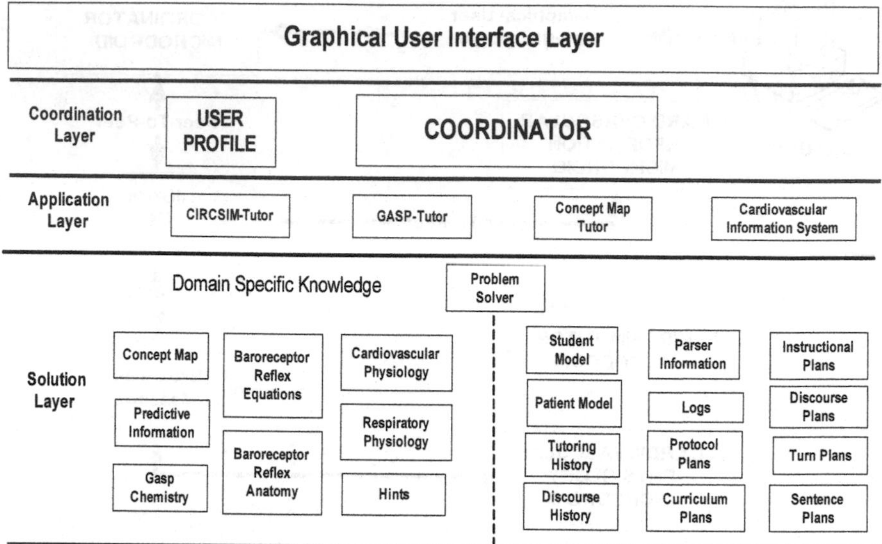

Figure 18-10. The Knowledge Collective Architecture

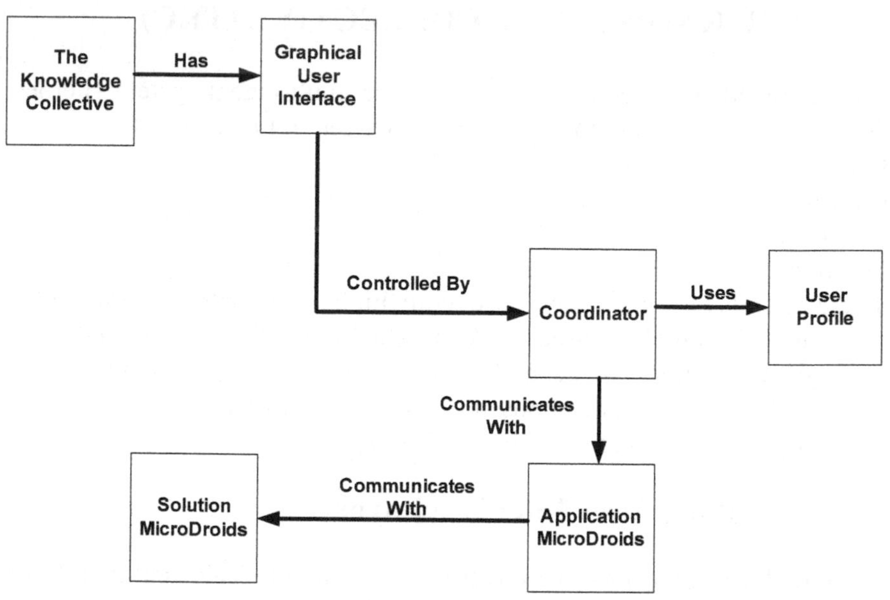

Figure 18-11. TKC Ontology

5.2 Coordinator Layer

The Coordinator Layer controls TKC. This layer always contains two specific purpose MicroDroids: COORDINATOR MicroDroid and USER PROFILE MicroDroid. The COORDINATOR MicroDroid works with the Graphical User Interface Layer to communicate with an end user, a developer, or a domain expert. The COORDINATOR MicroDroid also sets up a common goal that starts a session. The rest of the MicroDroids in TKC cooperate to satisfy this goal. The COORDINATOR MicroDroid can find out about all of the MicroDroids in TKC by asking them for information. If MicroDroids are added or deleted, or their functionality is changed, the COORDINATOR MicroDroid will know about these changes by broadcasting a message. It sends out orders along with the goals to find one or more MicroDroids in the Application Layer to solve end user problems. However, the COORDINATOR MicroDroid can interface with any MicroDroid in TKC to solve various development and maintenance problems.

The COORDINATOR MicroDroid is the keeper of the information about TKC. It has the TKC ontology (see Figure 18-10); it has the ONTIE rule set for the ontology and any other needed information about TKC. If you want to ask questions about TKC, the COORDINATOR MicroDroid is capable of answering those questions.

Another important role for the COORDINATOR MicroDroid is to help an expert (e.g., Joel Michael, Professor of Physiology at Rush Medical Center in Chicago, IL) maintain his Cardiovascular Physiology information. The COORDINATOR MicroDroid will send out a broadcast message looking for the MicroDroid that knows about the Cardiovascular Physiology System. When the CARDIOVASCULAR PHYSIOLOGY MicroDroid (see Figure 18-10) answers, a direct pipe between the COORDINATOR MicroDroid and the CARDIOVASCULAR PHYSIOLOGY MicroDroid is set up along with the proper user interface for maintenance.

A USER PROFILE MicroDroid can represent an end user, a domain expert, or a developer. It controls the information about a specific user.

5.3 Application Layer

The Application Layer contains a MicroDroid for each application in TKC. These MicroDroids get their orders from the COORDINATOR MicroDroid. They work individually to solve application problems. They use from one to many MicroDroids in the Solution. This is the only layer that is application specific. The Knowledge Collective example in Figure 18-10 is designed to support three medical tutoring systems

(CIRCSIM-Tutor, GASP-Tutor and Concept Map Tutor) and a Cardiovascular Information System.

CIRCSIM-Tutor (Michael et al., 2003) deals with the Baroreceptor Reflex, the negative feedback component of the Circulatory System that controls the blood pressure. GASP-Tutor is a new tutoring system (still being implemented) that deals with the pulmonary system with a focus on the two interacting negative feedback systems that control breathing and gas exchange in the lungs. The Concept Map Tutor helps a user manage concepts and their relationships in the Baroreceptor Reflex. The Cardiovascular Information System answers questions about cardiovascular physiology.

5.4 Solution Layer

There are many classes of MicroDroids in the Solution Layer. Each one knows how to deal with a specific domain as seen in Figure 18-10. They get their marching orders from an Application MicroDroid. They can work individually or in teams to solve an application problem.

These MicroDroids are very information specific. If you add a new Application MicroDroid that will use the same solution information, the same Solution MicroDroid will respond. If changes are made to the application data structure, these MicroDroids will not have to be modified. There are specific MicroDroids that can deal with domain specific information and others that deal with application specific information. For instance, CIRCSIM-Tutor uses all the MicroDroids in this layer except the Chemistry and Respiratory Physiology MicroDroids, which are specific to GASP-Tutor. GASP-Tutor will use all the MicroDroids in the layer except the Baroreceptor Reflex Equations and Baroreceptor Reflex Anatomy MicroDroids, as can be seen in Figure 18-10. This configuration really supports the knowledge and ontology reuse capabilities of TKC.

6. TKC PROCESS EXAMPLE

A good way of looking at TKC is that each MicroDroid has a story to tell. If an expert is a person that remembers the right story at the right time (Schank, 1990), then the right MicroDroid has to speak up at the right time thereby becoming the specific expert at that point in time.

When dealing with a student, TKC is trying to tell a story based on the input from the student. A story is based on many parts. The COORDINATOR MicroDroid sets up the storyline. Based on the storyline and the ontology, different MicroDroids fill in different parts of the overall story with there stories. Each one is an expert and tells the right story at the right time. Therefore, like a human expert, TKC remembers the right story at the right time by combining the stories of all the MicroDroids that answer.

The system only understands the environment of the session with a user by the model of the environment that it is given. This model is an ontology. TKC is a collection of ontologies. Each session with a user has its own ontology. When a user logs into TKC, the user is working through the Graphical User Interface Layer. This is the portal into the COORDINATOR MicroDroid and to a USER PROFILE MicroDroid. These two MicroDroids are a part of all sessions and supply the initial ontology for the session. Then, the session ontology grows as new MicroDroids are added to the session.

The COORDINATOR MicroDroid has to set up a subject area ontology. This is the purpose of the COORDINATOR MicroDroid to ascertain what the user wants to do. The USER PROFILE MicroDroid sets up the user ontology so that the system can understand the user. The COORDINATOR MicroDroid then ascertains what the user wants to do and sets up the subject. If the user wants to diagnose a circulation problem, then the COORDINATOR MicroDroid broadcasts the request to the Application Layer. A CARDIOVASCULAR INFORMATION SYSTEM MicroDroid would answer and a session pipeline would be set up with the COORDINATOR MicroDroid for the user. The COORDINATOR MicroDroid communicates with the user via the Graphical User Interface Layer. If the user wants to learn about the Baroreceptor Reflex, the CIRCSIM-TUTOR MicroDroid would answer and a pipeline would be set up. If the user wants to understand circulatory chemistry issues, then the COORDINATOR MicroDroid broadcasts the request to the Application Layer. The GASP-TUTOR MicroDroid answers and a session pipeline is set up with the COORDINATOR MicroDroid for the user. The COORDINATOR MicroDroid communicates with the user via the Graphical User Interface Layer. If no MicroDroid answers, a list of possible applications is given to the user.

If the CIRCSIM-TUTOR MicroDroid answers, session ontology is set up. In this case, the CIRCSIM-TUTOR MicroDroid has process ontology as shown in Figure 18-2 (Evens and Michael, in press). Every time a new MicroDroid answers, a new piece of the session ontology is produced. Each MicroDroid understands the environment it works in and adds a piece of the ontology to the session ontology. Therefore, the ontology for the session is developed dynamically as each new MicroDroid becomes part of it. When a session is complete, the MicroDroids involved drop out and take their ontologies with them. The ontology of the session grows as the session develops. A network of MicroDroids is developed with each bringing its own piece of the session ontology. As the session grows, the number of MicroDroids needed will increase.

When a session is complete, the instantiated MicroDroids save what they have learned for future MicroDroids to use. Then they eliminate themselves from the system. There is always a MicroDroid from each class waiting to server the end user.

7. CONCLUSION

To make the information in The Knowledge Collective accessible, maintainable, and reusable; the information needs to be divided into small domain specific units. Each unit is managed by a MicroDroid. End users, whether they are just using the information or are experts maintaining their specific domain information, must be able to perform the needed tasks without any knowledge where the information is stored or how it is structured. This way the information can be stored in the most efficient way possible for that particular type of information: data, metadata, ontologies, or rules.

One of the major reasons for information is to solve problems and answer questions. Applications like CIRCSIM-Tutor need both Baroreceptor Reflex information and tutoring information. The information from many different domain specific units needs to be combined to solve the total problem.

All the above describes the purpose of The Knowledge Collective framework. The implementation is unique because of the combination and use of many general commercial and open source products instead of developing specific vertical modules specific to the framework. The main idea is to have a framework that can deal with ontologies without developing yet another ontology language or application programming interface for ontologies, or worrying about how different ontologies can be mapped or merged. For a more detailed description of The Knowledge Collective, see Yusko (2005).

8. ACKNOWLEDGMENTS

We would like to thank ILOG® for supplying their JRules™ System and IBM® for supplying their WebSphere QualityStage product for this work since both are commercial products.

This work was partially supported by the Cognitive Science Program, Office of Naval Research under Grant 00014-00-1-0660 to Stanford University as well as Grants No. N00014-94-1-0338 and N00014-02-1-0442 to Illinois Institute of Technology. The content does not reflect the position or policy of the government and no official endorsement should be inferred.

REFERENCES

Bredeweg, B. and Forbus, K. D. (2003). Qualitative Modeling in Education. *AI Magazine*, Volume 24, No. 4, pp. 35-46.

Budinsky, F., Steinberg, D., Merks, E., Ellersick, R., and Grose, T. (2004). *Eclipse Modeling Framework*. Reading, MA: Addison-Wesley.

Evens, M. W., and Michael, J. A. (in press). *One on One Tutoring by Humans and Computers*. Mahwah, NJ: Lawrence Erlbaum.

Falkenhainer, B., and Forbus, K. D. (1988). Setting up Large-Scale Qualitative Models. In: *Proceedings of the American Association for Artificial Intelligence (AAAI-90)*, St. Paul MN pp. 301 301.

Fensel, D. (2004). *Ontologies: A Silver Bullet for Knowledge Management and Electronic Commerce*. Second Edition. New York, NY: Springer.

Ferber, J. (1999). *Multi-Agent Systems: An Introduction to Distributed Artificial Intelligence*. Reading, MA: Addison-Wesley.

FIPA (2002a). FIPA Abstract Architecture Specification. Foundation for Intelligent Physical Agents. Geneva, Switzerland.

FIPA (2002b). FIPA Ontology Service Specification. Foundation for Intelligent Physical Agents. Geneva, Switzerland.

Forbus, K. D. (1985). Qualitative Process Theory. In: D. Bobrow (Ed.) *Qualitative Reasoning about Physical Systems*. Cambridge, MA: The MIT Press. pp. 85–168.

Franklin, S., and Graesser, A. (1996). Is It an Agent or Just a Program? A Taxonomy for Autonomous Agents. In: *Proceedings of the Third International Workshop on Agent Theories, Architectures, and Languages*. New York: Springer-Verlag. pp. 21-35.

Freedman, R. (1996). Interaction of Discourse Planning, Instructional Planning and Dialogue Management in an Interactive Tutoring System. Ph.D. Dissertation. Dept. of Computer Science. Evanston, IL: Northwestern University.

Freedman, R., and Evens, M. W. (1997). The Use of Multiple Knowledge Types in an Intelligent Tutoring System. In: *Proceedings of the Cognitive Science Conference*. Stanford, CA. p.920.

Freedman, R., Zhou, Y., Glass, M. S., Kim, J. H., and Evens. M. W. (1998). Using Rule Induction to Assist in Rule Construction for a Natural Language-based Intelligent Tutoring System. In: *Proceedings of 20th Annual Cognitive Science Conference*. Madison, WI, August. pp. 362-367.

Friedman-Hill, E. (2003). *JESS In Action: Rule-Based Systems in Java*. Greenwich, CT: Manning Publications Co.

Gallardo, D., Burnett, E., and McGovern, R. (2003). *Eclipse in Action: A Guide for Java Developers*. Greenwich, CT: Manning Publishing Co.

Gomez-Perez, A., Fernandez-Lopez, M., and Corcho, O. (2004). *Ontological Engineering*. New York, NY: Springer.

Haase, K. (2002). *Java Message Service API Tutorial*. Palo Alto: Sun Microsystems, Inc.

Hewett, M. (2005). Algernon Overview. http://algernon-j.sourceforge.net/doc/overview.html. 1/4/2005.

Hussey, K. (2004). Getting Started with UML2. http://dev.eclipse.org/viewcvs/indextools.gi/~checkout~/uml2-home/docs/articles/Getting_Started_with_UML2/articl.html. 1/4/2005.

Hutcheson, D. S. (2003). Architecture Comes Alive for IBM. In *Enterprise Architect.* Vol. 1 No. 2. Fawcett Technical Publications Inc. Palo Alto, CA. pp. 41-45.

ILOG (2004). ILOG JRules 4.6.2 Rule Engine User's Manual. Mountain View: ILOG Inc.

Khuwaja, R. A. (1994). A Model of Tutoring: Facilitating Knowledge Integration Using Multiple Models of the Domain. Ph.D. Dissertation. Computer Science Department. Chicago, IL: Illinois Institute of Technology.

Khuwaja, R. A., and Patel, V. (1996). A Model of Tutoring Based on the Behavior of Effective Human Yutors. In: *Proceedings of the Third International Conference on Intelligent Tutoring Systems (ITS '96),* Montreal, Canada. pp. 130-138.

Khuwaja, R A., Rovick, A. A., Michael, J. A., and Evens, M. W. (1992). Knowledge Representation for an Intelligent Tutoring System Based on a Multilevel Causal Model. In: *Proceedings of ITS '92*, Berlin: Springer. pp. 217-224.

Khuwaja, R. A., Evens, M. W., Rovick, A. A., and Michael, J. A. (1994). Architecture of CIRCSIM-TUTOR (v.3): A Smart Cardiovascular Physiology Tutor. In: *Proceedings CBMS94*, Winston-Salem, NC, June 10-11. pp. 158-163

Kim, N. (1989). An Intelligent Tutoring System for Physiology, Ph.D. Dissertation, Illinois Institute of Technology, Chicago, IL.

Kim, N., Evens, M. W., Michael, J. A., and Rovick, A. A. (1989). An intelligent tutoring system for circulatory physiology. In: H. Maurer, (ed.), *Computer Assisted Learning.* Berlin: Springer-Verlag. pp. 254-266.

Knublauch, H. (2005). An AI Tool for the Real World: Knowledge Modeling with Protégé. http://www.javaworld.com/javaworld/jw-06-2003/jw-0620-protege.html. 1/28/2005.

Michael, J. A., Rovick, A. A., Glass, M.S., Zhou, Y., and Evens, M. (2003). Learning from a Computer Tutor with Natural Language Capabilities. In: *Interactive Learning Environments,* Vol. 11, No.3, *pp.* 233-262. Nov. 2003.

Rovick, A. A., and Michael, J. A. (1986). CIRCSIM: An IBM PC Computer Teaching Exercise on Blood Pressure Regulation. Paper presented at the XXX IUPS Congress, Vancouver, Canada.

Saunders, K., and Anderson, J. (2004). Cloudscape Version 10: A Technical Overview. http://www-106.ibm.com/developerworks/db2/library/techarticle/dm-0408anderson/index.html. 12/17/2004.

Schank, R. C. (1990). *Tell Me A Story: A New Look At Real and Artificial Memory.* NY. Charles Scribner's Sons.

Taylor, L. and The JBoss Group (2004). Getting Started with JBoss: J2ee applications on the JBoss 3.2.x Server. http://www.jboss.org/index.html?module=downloads&op=displayCategory&authid=b589041aeedbb907344975f1756201ac&categoryId=8. 4/23/2005.

Weiss, G. (Ed.) (2000). *Multiagent Systems: A Modern Approach to Distributed Artificial Intelligence.* Cambridge, MA: The MIT Press.

Woo, C. W. (1991). Instructional Planning in an Intelligent Tutoring System: Combining Global Lesson Plans with Local Discourse Control. Ph.D. Dissertation, Computer Science Department, Illinois Institute of Technology.

Woo, C. W., Evens, M. W., Michael, J. A., and Rovick, A. A. (1991). Dynamic Planning in an Intelligent Cardiovascular Tutoring System. In: *Proceedings of the Fourth Annual IEEE Symposium on Computer Based Medical Systems,* Baltimore, May. pp. 226-233.

Yusko, J. A. (1984). FBL: Frame Building Language. Final Project CSC580, Dept. of Computer Science. Chicago, IL: DePaul University.

Yusko, J. A. (1994). The Reality of Change. Internal white paper. Unlimited Solutions, Inc. Lombard, IL.

Yusko, J. A. (2005). The Knowledge Collective: A Multi-Layer, Multi-Agent Framework for Information Reuse in an Intelligent Knowledge Base. Ph.D. Thesis, Computer Science Department, IIT. Chicago, IL.

Yusko, J. A., and Evens, M. W. (2002). The Knowledge Collective: Using MicroDroids to Turn Meta Data into Meta Knowledge. In: *Proceedings of the Thirteenth Midwest Artificial Intelligence and Cognitive Science Conference.* Chicago, IL. pp. 56-60.

Yusko, J. A., and Evens, M. W. (2004). Dynamic Ontological Support for Qualitative Reasoning in The Knowledge Collective (TKC). In: *Workshop on Qualitative Reasoning,* Northwestern University, Evanston, IL. pp. 187-193.

Zhang, Y. (1991). Knowledge-Based Discourse Generation for an Intelligent Tutoring System. Ph.D. Dissertation, Computer Science Department. Chicago, IL: Illinois Institute of Technology.

Zhang, Y., Evens, M. W., Michael, J. A., and Rovick, A. A. (1987). Knowledge Compiler for an Expert Physiology Tutor, In: *Proceedings ESD/SMI Conference on Expert Systems,* Dearborn, June, 1987, pp. 153-169.

Zhang, Y., Evens, M. W., Michael, J. A., and Rovick, A. A. (1990). Extending a Knowledge Base to Support Explanations. In: *Proceedings of the Third IEEE Conference on Computer-Based Medical Systems,* Chapel Hill, NC, June 4-6. pp. 259-266.

Chapter 19

INFORMATION SYSTEMS ASPECTS AND THE ONTOLOGY OF HYPERMEDIA SYSTEMS

Miguel-Ángel Sicilia, Elena García-Barriocanal and Salvador Sánchez-Alonso

Computer Science Department, University of Alcalá; Ctra. Barcelona km. 33.600 – 28871, Alcalá de Henares, Madrid (Spain); {msicilia,elena.garciab,salvador.sanchez}@uah.es

Abstract: The emergence of Web technologies has made widespread the use of hypermedia systems as the underlying support for Information Systems in organizations. Hypermedia elements and their associated functionality in this context become organizational assets that are created, improved and delivered to users in an attempt to increase the overall value of the system. Semantic Web approaches to Information Systems focus on providing computational semantics to resources by means of shared meanings encoded as part of formal ontologies. These meanings in turn are intended to enable a higher degree of automation and delegation of tasks to software agents. This chapter addresses the fundamental elements of the ontological representation of hypermedia structures and their connection to the main aspects of Information Systems in the organizational context. Concretely, the integration of hypermedia concepts in a Knowledge Management framework is described, and the role of adaptiveness is characterized as a function driven by organizational value inside such framework. The resulting ontological framework provides ground for the development of ontology-based Information Systems in which hypermedia assets are managed.

Key words: Hypermedia, Information Systems, Ontology, Semantic Web, Adaptive Hypermedia, Knowledge Management

1. INTRODUCTION

Hypermedia systems have become a part of every day's work and life with the widespread adoption of the World-Wide-Web. Nonetheless, the Web as a distributed system is actually a concrete realization of the earlier concept of "hypermedia system" that traces back to the seminal writings of

Bush [4]. As a result of the evolution and growth of the Web, hypermedia systems engineering – and specially Web engineering – has flourished as a discipline encompassing specific techniques, tools and methods. Montero et al. Provide a review of outstanding methods in [19]. Since early hypermedia models can be considered as more general and richer in terms of possibilities than the Web itself [21], the use of generic hypermedia models in research provides the benefit of a higher level of abstraction. Such abstraction covers both the elements of the current Web and prospective extensions like XLink[1] or similar recommendations oriented to extending the representational constructs of the Web.

There is a large degree of overlapping between existing hypermedia meta-models[2], even though a lack of consensus on the precise definition of basic concepts like node or content, and the degree of granularity of the entities that can be represented with these models, still persists. Abstract models like Labyrinth [6] have been proposed as a framework covering existing ones, thus providing a common core of modeling constructs that can be used as a foundation for more concrete models, either technology-specific or domain-oriented. However, specific uses of hypermedia technologies still require further conceptualization efforts to come up with a general-purpose framework that could be used for interoperability and conceptual coherence between systems. A concrete case of such specialized use is that of Information Systems, understood as systems that serve an organizational purpose [8]. Such consideration introduces the dimension of organizational structure and role, and entails that hypermedia information resources and their specific usage have an associated value [5] that is contingent to the context and situation of the organization in which they are being created, updated or handled. Consequently, shared representations of Information Systems that use some sort of hypermedia technology as their information management and delivery paradigm should integrate organizational aspects with both core hypermedia concepts and specialized hypermedia assets. Particularly, learning objects [22] can be considered as hypermedia nodes that are used as resources in learning activities of any kind. Provided that the concept of value in Information Systems is closely connected with the concept of organizational learning and behavior [20], learning objects and the "learning designs" in which they participate deserve a special attention. As a matter of fact, the consideration of such kind of resources along with their temporal and process aspects is actually considered in current approaches to Information Systems [11]. The missing link between hypermedia and Information System thus appears as the connection of

1 http://www.w3.org/TR/xlink/.

2 The term meta-model is introduced here to differentiate models of concrete hypermedia applications from the modeling frameworks used to produce it.

learning resources to the fabric of hypermedia. In other words, a conceptualization is required that puts hypermedia elements in terms of Information System structure. Formal ontology is proposed in this chapter as the representational framework required to filling that gap.

Formal ontologies [1] are a vehicle for the representation of shared conceptualizations. Ontologies based on description logics [10] or related formalisms provide the added benefit of enabling certain kinds of reasoning over the terms, relations and axioms that describe the domain, and broader notions of semantics could be used to extend the formal semantics for specific purposes [25]. Hypermedia information systems equipped with an ontology of hypermedia – at design and execution time – could then be viewed as a concrete class of ontology-driven information systems [11] supporting both their user interface and its functionality and also the connection to the organizational aspects that give a teleological dynamic to resource management. A pragmatic benefit derived from the use of formal ontologies is that it is accompanied by a growing body of Semantic Web [2] tools, techniques and knowledge.

In this chapter, the integration of technical hypermedia concepts in the framework of organizational Information Systems is described. To do so, the essential elements of core hypermedia ontology are first identified, and then they is put in connection with the concepts of individual and organizational knowledge. This in turn entails that the tailoring of the hypermedia structure should be driven by organizational value. The use of current description-logics languages like OWL [9] in this conceptual framework enables a seamless integration of comprehensive organizational contexts with information resources. The ontology here described may be extended, updated or changed, since its purpose is that of serving as the basis for further research and technical developments.

The methodological approach for the development of the ontology uses some ideas in the Helix-Spindle model [17] and tailors them to the specifics of this case in two aspects. On one hand, the core elements of the hypermedia ontology are derived from the existing Labyrinth model, in a sort of literature-based process [26]. The rationale for it is that Labyrinth was actually the result of a process of bringing together elements that were found fragmentary in precedent models, and thus it can be considered as a shared conceptualization in itself. On the other hand, the specific aspects of Information Systems value are based on the recent ontology of Knowledge Management (KM) described by Holsapple and Joshi [14], in which learning and information assets are put in the context of organizational activities. The informal and structured processes for ontology engineering were yet carried out by Holsapple and Joshi, so that the remaining work was that of formally integrating general purpose and specific hypermedia concepts. The large and stable OpenCyc (http://www.opencyc.org/) commonsense knowledge base (an open source version of Cyc [18]) has been used as a framework to restrict the definitions to those specific of the domain, reusing the concepts and relations in OpenCyc. For brevity, only the main ontological definitions will be discussed.

The rest of this chapter is structured as follows. Section 2 describes the core elements of the ontology of hypermedia systems, from a technical viewpoint. Then, Section 3 provides the details of its integration with main Information System aspects. Concretely, hypermedia elements are described as knowledge assets in the context of KM. Then, adaptive hypermedia objectives are re-formulated as value-driven in that context. Finally, conclusions and future research directions are described in Section 4.

2. STRUCTURAL ELEMENTS OF THE ONTOLOGY OF HYPERMEDIA SYSTEMS

The engineering process of ontology of hypermedia needs to explicitly cover all the concepts in existing hypermedia models. In consequence, our point of departure has been an existing meta-model: the Labyrinth model [6, 7]. This particular model was selected for two reasons: due to its abstract nature as well as for the fact that it was crafted as an extension of a compendium of concepts that appeared in previous hypermedia models (see [6]). In addition, the Labyrinth hypermedia model has been recently extended to cope with imprecise information [28], which is present in any system that observes its users in search for tacit knowledge or preference elicitation [27]. For our purposes, the ontology should provide the elements to relate the hypermedia structure to issues of interest a diversity of stakeholders. At the broadest level, this focus includes the user, the design, the activities involved, and the content that is actually used and re-used [23].

From a pragmatic viewpoint, and given the importance of the Internet in our current economy and society, such ontology should explicitly cover all the elements of current Web technology, as well as a concrete realization of the hypermedia concept. This requires the inclusion of content models that reach the fine granularities that are currently addressed by XML-based Web languages like XPath[3]. The conceptual intersection of general hypermedia systems and the concrete Web technology, results in an ontology enabling several levels of descriptive detail. This is not a major issue since the current Web can be considered a restricted implementation of existing abstract hypermedia models. In addition, semantic annotations about the hypermedia

[3] http://www.w3.org/TR/xpath.

elements should be provided, using a flexible approach not constraining potential uses or applications. The rest of this section provides the basic definitions by using elements of the OntoClean framework proposed by Welty and Guarino [37].

2.1 Nodes, Contents, Links and Hyperdocuments

The concept of hyperdocument in Labyrinth is expressed in terms of "basic hyperdocuments" defined as tuples (1) with some elements and functions. The first seven elements in (1) represent users (and groups of them), nodes, contents, anchors, links, attributes and events, respectively. The last four elements are functions determining, respectively, the location of contents in a node, the list of attributes, the list of events, and the access category of an element.

$$HD^{B} = (U, N, C, A, L, B, E, lo, al, el, ac) \qquad (1)$$

Personalized hyperdocuments are considered as variants of basic hyperdocuments, but this aspect of adaptiveness will be discussed in the next section. The model of Labyrinth for that is fairly limited since it does not represent adaptive processes, but only their results.

From an ontological perspective, the definition in expression (1) does not separate the elements according to their *unity*, in the sense given in [37], since the concept of nodes, contents and anchors can be considered as a system of digital wholes, separated from the rest of the elements. In other words, the mereology (i.e. the study of the parts and aggregation relationships) of the hypermedia space can be formulated in a more coherent way. This holds even for links, which can be considered independent entities that are dependant – but not necessarily part of – nodes and contents.

Table 19-1 provides an alternative ontological definition, separating the different aspects of the static hypermedia structure, and providing the analysis of relevant terms following the methodological guidelines provided by OntoClean [37]. Dynamic aspects (E, el), as described in detail in [7], are not analyzed in this chapter.

Nodes in Labyrinth are considered as "containers of information" of different media types. This definition is closely connected with the OpenCyc notion of `InformationBearingThing` as "each instance of InformationBearingThing is an item that contains information (for an agent who knows how to interpret it).", and even with its specialization `ComputerFileCopy` if a more restrictive view on the "storage" layer [12] of hypermedia elements is considered. Surprisingly, the notion of "content" is also defined as "a piece of information". The subtle difference between the two lies in that nodes can be arbitrarily composed while contents are considered as atomic pieces of information with a specific type (audio, video, etc). This entails that contents can be considered as suppliers of identity conditions (+O), while nodes in such view have an identity derived from their parts (-I). This can be explained by the fact that contents should be locatable in some way in the "storage" layer (in terms of the original Dexter hypermedia model), e.g. some place in a file system for the case of HTML. On the contrary, some nodes may have a dynamic nature and so that it becomes hard to find a carried or supplied identity condition for them. Uniform Resource Identifiers are of course associated to every node on the Web, but this is not an essential association (redirections or other dynamic changes may occur).

Table 19-1. Main ontological aspects of hypermedia (meta-)models

Aspect	Relevant terms	Web interpretation
Hypermedia content structure (N,C, A, lo)	Content +R +O -D Node ~R –I +D +UM Anchor +R +O +D	Nodes are the units of navigable contents, e.g. HTML pages or other files that are directly navigable with a browser, while contents are their fragments or media elements embedded in them.
Hypermedia navigational structure (L)	Link +R+O+D	Links as determined by <A> or <IMG> elements
Hypermedia users (U, ac)	User +R+I Group +R-U+O-D	not applicable
General descriptive elements (B, al)	any concrete axiom or constraint inside the ontology	Descriptions in <META> tags.

Contents are also rigid and do not depend on any of the other elements. Rigidity entails that the defining term is essential to all its instances – with this regard, atomic media elements remain so in every possible world. The compositional nature of nodes precludes them for being considered as rigid, since they could always be embedded in a higher level node, thus loosing their character of units of navigation. Thus, they can be considered as anti-rigid, since every node is subject to that possible change.

In addition, the consideration of what is a node is somewhat conventional, since it is a unit of navigation of the hypermedia space, i.e. nodes are rendering units in the user agent (browser). Nodes are considered as entities that can be the destination of a link traversal and thus depend on the existence of some content. Their identification according to their structure of parts (other nodes or contents) makes them mereologically extensional (+ME), and the notion of morphology, as understood by the location of contents as part of nodes, provides them with morphological unit (+UM). It should be noted that such morphology in Labyrinth concerns both "position" and "time", giving room to the synchronization of contents that are at the essence of the multimedia concept. Since nodes that are embedded in others may not be considered as units of navigability, thus depending on the navigational structure, we have considered the concept as anti-rigid. Then the notion of *Anchor* determines the space of possible linking in the node-content mereology. Current Web specifications like XPointer[4] support the definition of anchors to virtually every element of Web content, which results in that such expressions are self-identifying (+O) and dependant (+D) on, at least, one content or node element.

The notion of *Hyperdocument* can be assimilated to that of Node, and specified in a purely conventional manner, thus being anti-rigid ~R. This ontological commitment comes from the fact that the boundaries of what hypermedia "applications" or "documents" are, becomes in many cases a matter of functional convention, that heavily depend on the uses they are given in specific contexts.

Links are first-class citizens in hypermedia models, contrary to the realization of links in the Web, where they are embedded in nodes (i.e. pages) as concrete markup elements, and restricted to unidirectional. Considering links as independent entities allows the definition of multi-directional, complex relational structures, as can be defined in XLink. In addition, links can also be used as assets in themselves, since they may embed type information [35] useful as personalized information connecting tools [29]. The description of full-fledged links can be derived from the XLink specification in terms of locators and arcs that conform graphs with edges labelled by types. Therefore, links depend on the locators they connect, i.e. they are dependant on the notion of Anchor. It should be noted that a concrete user interface related interpretation of both multi-dimensional links and link types does not exist as a common or standard convention. This fact could also be represented in the hypermedia ontology as annotations to the link-describing elements themselves.

The concept of *User* in Labyrinth encompasses both individuals and groups of individuals. This convenience definition requires a differentiation in ontological terms, since groups as considered in hypermedia provide no unity condition with respect to their constituents. In addition, individuals are considered to carry (but not to supply) identity conditions, since the identity derived from the *Person* (+O) should be clearly differentiated from the

[4] http://www.w3.org/TR/xptr/.

contingent relationship of Persons to some tasks. These can be modelled by the abstract notion of *Role*, which determines specific usages of the hypermedia space. It is relevant to point out that the concept of role is used in learning activity modelling languages like IMS LD (http://www.imsglobal.org/learningdesign/) as a differentiated activity-oriented concept.

General (meta-) descriptive elements of each of the hypermedia elements were modelled in Labyrinth as attributes in the set B. However, when describing the hypermedia models as instances in ontology, such descriptive attributes can be simply modelled by property constraints on the classes representing each element. This provides the benefit of flexibility, as well as the advantage of having available the reasoning and consistency checking tools of logic languages to act on the definitions of the hypermedia structure and description.

2.2 Semantic Annotation of Hypermedia Elements

Many existing approaches to annotating Web resources are based on extending markup elements or embedding metadata fragments in the nodes, e.g. [13]. Other approaches make use of separate metadata files that use URIs to reference the elements described (in fact, this is the approach implicit in the IEEE LOM metadata, which provides an "Identifier" category to refer to external content). A recent review of these and other annotation techniques is provided by Corcho [39].

Nevertheless, when using ontological knowledge bases to represent metadata, both approaches have the drawback of separating the representations of the resources from the element itself. While this is useful for practical purposes, this entails that hypermedia elements and their relationships are not represented as concepts and properties in the ontology, missing the opportunity of obtaining a richer level of representation. The approach described by Sicilia and Garcia [33] entails a representation of hypermedia wholes and their parts in the same ontological language as annotations, thus providing a coherent integration of both. When using Web-based ontology description languages [9], ontology instances of hypermedia elements become identified by URIs, thus coming to flexibility in producing distributed and loosely-connected annotations for public or organizational hypermedia descriptions. The approach of ontology-driven markup (i.e. annotations linked to a given ontology) could be used as an alternative, since such explicit linking enables the dynamic, on-the-fly representation of the hypermedia structure inside the ontology-based system, thus preserving the benefit of having a logics-based infrastructure for reasoning.

A company developing a project proposal for a given organization or client company, for example, could be interested in automating a task consisting of gathering hints about those elements in the proposal that were highly valued in previous proposals for the same or other target institutions. Provided that the different parts of previous proposals are structured as nodes and contents, links can be defined as connectors of the important parts of the documents with the target, typed as `valuedByTarget`. This knowledge could be later automatically or manually reused in similar proposals. Links that connect hypermedia contents to representations of organizational partners allow a form of associative corporate memory that intimately connects hypermedia to entities relevant to the organization, without a separation in the representation language between them. Other kinds of knowledge could relate hypermedia elements according to their content. For example, the detection of inconsistent policies for the choices given to the same customer could be marked as a link connecting the inconsistent parts of the document considered relevant (instances of anchors referring to node parts).

3. ASPECTS OF THE HYPERMEDIA ONTOLOGY INSIDE AN INFORMATION SYSTEMS FRAMEWORK

Hypermedia-based Information Systems use the infrastructure described above as the delivery mechanism of information resources of a diverse kind. However, the consideration of the organizational framework requires a conceptualization of the role of hyperdocuments in organizational behaviour, beyond their mere existence as information-bearing things. In this context, *Knowledge Management* provides an appropriate context in which hypermedia structures represent interconnected knowledge assets, and adaptiveness becomes a mechanism for the optimization of asset delivery to the users that requires them at each moment according to organizational needs. In the rest of this section, these issues will be briefly described.

3.1 Hypermedia resources as knowledge assets

Hypermedia in the organizational context requires a specific conceptualization that connects with the notions of *value* [5] that is considered to drive Information Systems assessment and design. The connection point can be considered as that of identifying hypermedia elements as a particular class of potential value-providing elements in a process-oriented view of organizational learning. Existing conceptualizations of Knowledge Management (KM) provide the framework in which such integration can take place.

The ontology of Holsapple and Joshi (H&S from here on) [14] describes fundamental KM concepts and axioms. Other authors also provide integrative views of the diverse perspectives on KM for specific elements. This chapter focuses on the concrete class of knowledge processes that result in learning activities, even though other kinds of activities could be modelled in a similar way. Our interest in learning is in that its enabling activities are directly related to learning processes as those that are supported by modern e-learning standardized technology, for which some OpenCyc previous integration work has also been described [30, 31]. Thc provision of knowledge representations integrating KM and e-learning standards has been pointed out as an important research direction elsewhere [33].

Recent work has provided an explicit formulation of H&S ontology in terms of OpenCyc definitions [32]. In what follows, a brief summary of these definitions is provided (references to H&S definitions appear in brackets), and the concrete aspects related to hypermedia elements are further developed to frame them properly in the KM context.

The definition of KM in H&J (Holsapple and Joshi) ontology "An entity's systematic and deliberate efforts to expand, cultivate, and apply available knowledge in ways that add value to the entity [..]"[DKMC1] requires the early definition of "entities" capable of engaging in KM, which are considered to include at least individuals, organizations, collaborating organizations and nations, as stated in [DKMC2-5]. The term `#$Organization`[5] in OpenCyc covers such entities. The concept of knowledge processor [DKMC10] as a member of an entity can be modelled through the concept of `#$IntelligentAgent`, which are by definition "capable of knowing and acting, and of employing their knowledge in their actions". Humans are, by logical definition, intelligent agents; certain software pieces may also fit this definition, since they are not restricted to not being able to know [AKMC10]. The subtype `#$MultiIndividual Agent` fits the definition of collective agents [AKMC11], which accounts for many organizational phenomena including formal organizational structure but also informal social networks.

The definition of Knowledge as "that which is conveyed by usable representations" [DKMC6] can be integrated in OpenCyc by considering usable representations [AKMC2] as information bearing things, i.e. "Each instance of `InformationBearingThing` (or "IBT") is an item that contains information (for an agent who knows how to interpret it)". The types of representations described in [AKMC1] are similar to some OpenCyc subclasses like `SoundInformationBearingThing`, and are specific of contents according to the core hypermedia model.

[5] The #$ prefix is the CycL convention for constants.

The recognizable kinds of knowledge manipulation are referred to as Knowledge Manipulation Activity (KMA) [DKMC12]. Activities in OpenCyc are represented as `#$Actions`, a collection of `#$Events` carried out (`#$doneBy`) by a "doer". This generic concept of action can be specialized to represent KMA executions by restricting them to be carried out by intelligent agents. The predicate `#$ibtUsed` can be used to represent the knowledge representations manipulated by KMAs. In addition, since KM activities are deliberate, it is probably more adequate to use the subclass `#$PurposefulAction` and the predicate `#$performedBy`.

The definitions just described provide three main integration points with the core ontology of hypermedia described above:

1. `#$IntelligentAgent` includes the definitions of User and Group. The inclusion of the predicates defined as `#$Roles` (roles can be defined for specific kinds of actions with particular restrictions) resolves the issue of different kinds of involvement that were implicit in Labyrinth's model of hypermedia.
2. `#$IBT` as a subsumer of Node and Content provides the characterization of hypermedia elements as knowledge assets. It is important to highlight here that Links should also be considered as stand-alone `#$IBTs` (as considered in [29]). Axioms to represent the fact that nodes are atomic while nodes are not should be provided. Further, anchors could be defined simply as locators to parts of contents and nodes. Since this is specific of the media and technology (e.g. video in specific formats), the only general restriction is that anchors can be "resolved", and thus used for the purpose of linking.
3. `#$PurposefulActions` allows the introduction of the notion of value yet mentioned. The static hypermedia elements require purposeful efforts to obtain a timely and targeted delivery of information [8] that produces an effect in the organization as a whole.

In the H&J ontology, learning is defined as "a process whereby KRs are modified; an outcome of a KME involving changes in the state of an entity's knowledge" [DKMC17] (KME are episodes involving KMAs). Current approaches to Web-based learning are based on the concept of learning object, for which several definitions have been proposed. Reusability is considered to be an essential characteristic of the concept of learning object as the central notion for modern digital learning content design. For example, Polsani [22] includes reuse in his definition of learning object as "an independent and self-standing unit of learning content that is predisposed to reuse in multiple instructional contexts". Wiley [38] also mentions the term in his learning object definition "any digital resource that can be reused to support learning". Existing work has dealt with the integration of that concept in OpenCyc [30][31]. Learning objects are currently centred on Web technology, and thus, the hypermedia ontology described above is a generalization of those definitions. The main difference is that the concept of LearningObject should be considered as anti-rigid (~R) because those hypermedia structures are considered learning objects by virtue of their use (or by a consideration of their potential utility) in specific learning contexts [40, 41]. Thus, learning objects are so by extrinsic determination, e.g. by the selection of a part of a hypermedia whole as a resource which is adequate for a coming learning need. Links as independent learning assets were described in [29], so that they can be assimilated also to the same definition.

Following the mapping of learning objects, IMS LD learning activities and associated higher level wholes of activities (methods, plays, acts) can be considered as templates of actual `#$PurposefulActions`. This allows a seamless mapping of KM concepts to common learning technology practice.

A final but important issue to be considered in the mapping of hypermedia to KM is that value is not an intrinsic property of hypermedia elements, but a function of temporal conditions that depends on several dimensions. Figure 19-1 depicts these overall aspects.

Value assessment is therefore attached to the actual activities that disseminate the IBTs (be there nodes, contents or links). A hypermedia element can be indirectly assessed as a stand-alone resource, hence summarizing the assessment of the activities in which it was involved. In addition, some value notion(s) must be considered in the assessment process, and consequently be part of the overall ontology. For example, a straightforward notion of cost-benefit analysis could be considered, where costs are defined as the acquisition of the required knowledge assets plus the costs of designing and carrying out the purposeful activity. However, much work is still required in formalizing and comparing value assessment models that use the kind of comprehensive knowledge bases described herein. Both the previous background and competency of users in the activity, and the alignment with organizational objectives should also be considered. To this respect, knowledge gap analysis based on ontologies of competencies could be used as a starting point [34].

3.2 Adaptive hypermedia as a value carrier

Adaptive hypermedia systems [3] extend hypermedia with the capability of tailoring contents, links and navigation to the diverse preferences, knowledge or objectives of users or groups. The use of an ontological account of adaptive hypermedia would eventually enable the interchange of semantic user model data (enhancing user model servers [16]) and even that of adaptive behaviours. Additionally, it would provide a reference framework to evaluate the appropriateness of concrete adaptive technologies with regards to concrete contexts of use.

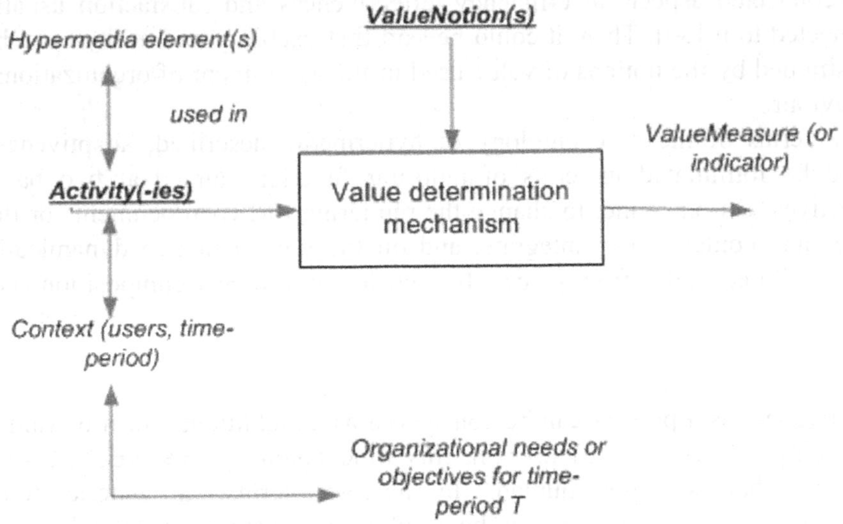

Figure 19-1. Elements in the assessment of value

Existing knowledge representation of adaptive hypermedia systems can be expressed, in many cases, in terms of ontologies with an added support for reasoning. In systems that consider uncertainty or imprecision explicitly, the use of recent advances in fuzzy description logics could add a flexible numerical representation of imperfect information [27]. The main technical elements of such integration are the representation of vague categories and modes of inference [28]. Examples of such vagueness handling in the context just described are the expression of competencies in vague terms and the expression of links between hypermedia elements (links between nodes) among others as fuzzy time intervals. For example, delivering learning activities to the employees that are **closer to** the target required profile for an upcoming project entails the determination of closeness between profiles, which is a soft concept with no clearly defined boundaries. Another example may be that of defining internal reports that **refute** or **confirm** the knowledge provided in others – a typical case of fuzzy link [29]. Further, employee categories as "Knowledge Brokers" or fuzzy groups – e.g. people "**interested in**" quality – are typical examples of vague categories as applied to users and groups of the hypermedia space.

The integration of an ontological representation of hypermedia within the KM framework, as described above, results in a reformulation of common evaluation criteria for adaptive systems. Research in adaptive hypermedia often considers usability as the main objective of introducing adaptivity [15]. The reformulation consists in putting the usability criteria under the constraint of organizational needs and objectives, while retaining the interconnected aspects of efficiency, effectiveness and satisfaction usually connected to it [36]. Then, it could be said that usability and utility must be constrained by the notions of value used in the assessment of organizational behaviour.

In terms of the core ontology of hypermedia described, adaptiveness could be formulated in terms of tailoring functions aimed at two basic objectives. On one hand, to change the rendering of hyperdocuments or the nodes and contents they integrate, and on the other hand, to dynamically create tailored nodes from pieces. In fact, learning object composition (i.e. the aggregation of learning objects to form a higher level unit of instructions, let's say, combining units into a course) and adaptive linking as well as adaptive content technologies [3] fall under the latter category. Nevertheless, adaptiveness as a process can be considered as an additional form of value-producing `#$PurposefulAction`, this time taken by `#$IntelligentAgents` that are not human. In abstract terms, a generic term `AdaptiveCreationAgent` can be used as a subsumer or any kind of adaptive functionality. Such agents have some differentiated characteristics:

- They have knowledge of some value notion(s), as described in Figure 19-1.
- They are organization-specific, and thus they have knowledge of some or part of the ontology that describes the organization.
- They have knowledge about at least some of the characteristics of users and/or groups.
- They manipulate and join together existing instances of Node, Content, Anchor and Link with a purpose related to the preceding elements, or alternatively, to modify some of their properties to come up with personalized versions.

Knowledge about the various elements described could be expressed in terms of statements, which may additionally include any kind of domain ontology describing part of the organization or its context. Such statements are in reality the semantic annotations of the hypermedia elements as described before in this chapter. The selection of which classes of statements are to be used and the decision procedures to tailor them are the determinants of each concrete adaptation technique. It should be noted that this generalist approach provides a broader and more integrated view to "semantic adaptive systems" compared to other frameworks.

The above characterization offers a framework to compare and classify existing approaches to personalization. For example, pure social filtering techniques as that of the original GroupLens [24] are only aware of statements in the form rating (user, item, value), where the items are contents describing commercial products or any other information, and the decision procedures are based on using those statements to build models of similarity between users.

4. CONCLUSIONS AND FUTURE WORK

Hypermedia models as a generalization of Web technology are an important element in ontological approaches to Information Systems. Existing integrative hypermedia models can be used as the basis for a core ontology of hypermedia elements, and Knowledge Management and organizational learning artefacts can be expressed as concrete realizations of such elements. In this context, adaptive hypermedia becomes a function oriented to increase organizational value by tailoring hypermedia nodes to the characteristics of users or groups in the context of concrete organizational activities.

The work presented here is intended as a basis for an integrated approach to Ontology-based Information Systems with hypermedia characteristics. The ontological definitions described in the paper are not intended to be definitive or close-ended. On the contrary, they are posed as an initial definition to motivate further engineering in both the formal and the conceptual aspects of organizational learning. Future work should refine and extend the ontological framework sketched by introducing additional elements related to the organizational context, as well as more specific notions of value for information assets.

REFERENCES

Baader, F., Calvanese, D., McGuinness, D., Nardi, D., Patel-Schneider, P. (eds.). (2003). The Description Logic Handbook. Theory, Implementation and Applications, Cambridge.

Berners-Lee, T., Hendler, J., Lassila, O. (2001). The Semantic Web. Scientific American, 284(5), 34-43.

Brusilovsky, P. (2001) Adaptive hypermedia. User Modeling and User Adapted Interaction, 11 (1/2), pp. 87-110.

Bush, V. As We May Think. Atlantic Monthly 1945.

Cronk, M.C. and Fitzgerald, E.P. (1999). Understanding "IS business value": derivation of dimensions. Logistics Information Management, 12(1/2), 40-49.

Diaz, P., Aedo, I., Panetsos, F. (1997). Labyrinth, an abstract model for hypermedia applications. Description of its static components. Information Systems, 22(8), 447-464.

Diaz P., Aedo I. y Panetsos F. (2000). Modeling the Dynamic Behavior of Hypermedia Applications. IEEE Transactions on Software Engineering, 27 (6). 550-572.

Falkenberg, E.D. et. al. (1998). FRISCO - A Framework of Information System Concepts - The FRISCO Report. IFIP WG 8.1 Task Group FRISCO.

Fensel, D. (2002). Language Standardization for the Semantic Web: The Long Way from OIL to OWL. Proc. of the 4th International Workshop on Distributed Communities on the Web, DCW 2002: 215-227

Gruber T. (1995). Towards principles for the design of ontologies used for knowledge sharing. International Journal of Human-Computer studies, 43 (5/6), 907 - 928.

Guarino, N. (ed.) (1998). Formal Ontology in Information Systems. In Proceedings of FOIS'98, Trento, Italy, 6-8 June 1998. Amsterdam, IOS Press, pp. 3-15.

Halasz, F. and Schwartz, M. (1994). The Dexter hypertext reference model. Communications of the ACM, 37(2):30=39

Heflin JD, Hendler JA (2001) A Portrait of the Semantic Web in Action. IEEE Intelligent Systems and their applications 16(2): 54-59

Holsapple, C.W. and Joshi, K.D. A formal knowledge management ontology: Conduct, activities, resources, and in°uences. Journal of the American Society for Information Science and Technology, 55(7): 593{612 (2004).

Höök, K. (1998) Evaluating the Utility and Usability of an Adaptive Hypermedia System, in Journal of Knowledge Based Systems, Volume 10, issue 5, 1998.

Kay, J., Kummerfeld, B. and Lauder, P. (2002). Personis: A Server for User Models. In Proceedinfs of the Adaptive Hypermedia and Adaptive Web-Based Systems Conference, 203-212.

Kishore, R., Zhang, H. and Ramesh, R. (2004). A Helix-Spindle model for ontological engineering. Commun. ACM 47(2): 69-75.

Lenat, D. B. Cyc: A Large-Scale Investment in Knowledge Infrastructure. Communications of the ACM 38(11): 33{38 (1995).

Montero, S. Diaz, P., Aedo, I (2002). Requirements for Hypermedia Development Methods: A Survey of Outstanding Methods. In Proceedings of the 14th International Conference in Advanced Information Systems Engineering, CAiSE 2002, 747-751.

Örtenblad, A. (2001). On di®erences between organizational learning and learning organization. The Learning Organization, 8(3), pp. 125-133.

Pam, A. and Vermeer, A. (1995). A Comparison ofWWWand Hyper-G. Journal of the Universal Computer Science 1(11),744-750.

Polsani, P. R. (2003). Use and Abuse of Reusable Learning Objects. Journal of Digital information, 3(4).

Rapp, D.N., Taylor, H. and Crane, G. (2003). The impact of digital libraries on cognitive processes: psychological issues of hypermedia. Computers in Human Behavior, 19(5), 609-628.

Resnick, P., Iacovou, N., Suchak, M., Bergstrom, P., and Riedl, J. (1994). GroupLens: An Open Architecture for Collaborative Filtering of Netnews. In Proceedings of CSCW 94 Conference on Computer Supported Cooperative Work, New York: ACM. 175-186.

Seth, A. et al.(2005). Semantics for the Semantic Web: The Implicit, the Formal and the Powerful. Intl. Journal on Semantic Web and Information Systems 1(1), 1-18.

Sicilia, M.A., Garcia, E., Aedo, I. and Diaz, P. (2003). A literature-based approach to annotation and browsing ofWeb resources. Information Research 8(2).

Sicilia, M.A. Observing Web Users: Conjecturing and Refutation on Partial Evidence. In: Proceedings of the North American Fuzzy Information Processing Society (2003):530-535.

Sicilia, M.A. The Role of Vague Categories in Semantic and Adaptive Web Interfaces. Proc. of the Workshop on Human Computer Interface for Semantic Web and Web Applications, Springer Lecture Notes in Computer Science 2889, 210-222 (2003).

Sicilia, M.A., Garcia, E., Aedo, I. and Diaz, P. (2004). Using links to describe imprecise relationships in educational contents, International Journal of Continuing Engineering Education and Lifelong Learning 14(3), 260 - 275.

Sicilia, M. A., García, E. and Sánchez, S. On integrating learning object metadata inside the OpenCyc knowledge base. In Proceedings of the 4th IEEE International Conference on Advanced Learning Technologies - ICALT 2004. Joensuu, Finland.

Sicilia, M.A., García, E., Sánchez, S. and Rodríguez, E. Describing learning object types in ontological structures: towards specialized pedagogical selection. In Proceedings of ED-MEDIA 2004 - World conference on educational multimedia ,hypermedia and telecommunications. Lugano, Switzerland (2004).

Sicilia, M.A. and Lytras, M. (2005). Integrating Descriptions of Knowledge Management Learning Activities into Large Ontological Structures: A Case Study. Data and Knowledge Engineering, Elsevier (to appear).

Sicilia, M.A., García, E. (2005) On the Convergence of Formal Ontologies and Standardized e-Learning. Journal of Distance Education Technologies 3(2), 13-29.

Sicilia, M.A. (2005). Ontology-Based Competency Management: Infrastructures for the Knowledge-intensive Learning Organization. In: Lytras and Naeve (Eds.): Intelligent Learning Infrastructures in Knowledge Intensive Organizations: A Semantic Web perspective. IDEA, USA, pp. 302-324.

Trigg, R. H. and Weiser, M. "TEXTNET: A Network-Based Approach to Text Handling". ACM Transactions on Office Information Systems, 4(1), 1986, p.1-23.

Van Welie, M., van der Veer, G.C. & Eliëns, A. (1999), Breaking down usability, Proc. of Interact'99. 613-620.

Welty, C. and Guarino, N. Supporting ontological analysis of taxonomic relationships. Data and Knowledge Engineering 39(1), 2001, pp. 51-74.

Wiley, D. A. (2001). The Instructional Use of Learning Objects. Association for Educational Communications and Technology, Bloomington.

Corcho, O. (2005) Ontology-based document annotation: trends and open research problems. International Journal on Metadata, Semantics and Ontologies 1(1).

Sicilia, M. A., Sánchez-Alonso, S. and Soto, J. 2005. Resource descriptions for semantic element repositories: addressing flexibility. In Proceedings of m-ICTE 2005 - Third International Conference on Multimedia and Information & Communication Technologies in Education, pp. 1045-1049.

McGreal, R. Learning Objects: A Practical definition. International Journal of Instructional Technology and Distance Learning 1(9) (2004).

Chapter 20

ONTOLOGY-ENABLED DATABASE MANAGEMENT SYSTEMS

N.L. Sarda
Indian Institute of Technology, Bombay, Mumbai, 400076 India

Abstract: Many large organizations have their data and processing spread across multiple independent database applications. These data sources, with their own schemas, need to inter-operate to meet new requirements, both within and across organizations. In this paper, we propose a vision of an ontology-enabled database management systems (called OeDBMS) so that the end users can co-relate and integrate ontologies associated with individual sources and extract, co-relate and integrate data from different sources. We propose the architecture and ontology model for OeDBMS. We propose many useful extensions to the RDF/S-based ontology models that are emerging as standards, and provide a graph-based abstraction for the model. This becomes a basis for defining many useful ontology operators and an ontology query language for browsing, searching, matching and maintaining ontologies. We also address the need for ontology evolution by providing temporal support for ontology.

Key words: conceptual modeling; database systems; inter-operability; ontology integration; ontology management; ontology-metadata mapping

1. INTRODUCTION

Most organizations have their operational data stored in and maintained by relational database management systems (RDBMS). RDBMS allows the logical structure of data to be described in a schema using modeling primitives like tables (relations), attributes, domains, and integrity specifications in terms of keys and assertions. The tables are designed to support efficient processing of data. Consequently, the users of database must explicitly understand the meaning of data from the structure of the stored data in order to write queries for extracting the required information.

This is often a challenging task. Often, even the names of tables and columns are quite cryptic, and tables are 'de-normalized' for efficient processing, making it hard for users to associate clear meanings with the database tables. One can easily visualize the challenge faced by users with large and complex databases containing hundreds of tables and thousands of columns.

The above situation becomes more complicated when we consider the following issues:

1. An organization may have multiple databases, each serving domain-specific applications. However, it often becomes necessary to co-relate data across these independent databases. In order to do this, we need to precisely understand the meaning and structure of data. The problems of identifying and resolving semantic and syntactic 'heterogeneity' and construction of 'integrated' schema have received considerable attention [4] in the past, but there are no simple or automatic solutions for this critical problem.
2. The application requirements evolve over time, requiring changes to database schema and application programs. To make changes, it is important to understand the current database contents and the processing semantics as embedded in the application code.
3. A database application is often much more than just the schema. It contains definitions of views, triggers, forms, report specifications, and stored procedures (modules). Each of them embodies some meaning or business rule, essential for understanding the stored data. Moreover, each of them may evolve over time, and it is essential to manage all these application components [21] than just the database.

To address the above problems, efforts were made to develop standards for metadata. repositories. The standards, such as [15], have primarily addressed technical metadata useful to designers, developers and administrators. The end-users, however, need business metadata that explain data and processing in terms of business concepts, rules and processes. There are no standards for business metadata (although efforts in specific domains such as finance [19] exist). Approaches to integration have ranged from writing specific 'adapters', storing metadata and their inter-relationships [9] to mediations based on ontologies in specific domains [8] where business metadata standards exist.

The work in conceptual modeling [13][20] is addressed towards capturing data semantics and structure during requirements analysis, covering both the static and dynamic aspects of information processing. A conceptual model is application focused, where as an ontology would be more generic (and, hence, more open to sharing). The ubiquitous Entity-Relationship (ER) model focused on the static aspects of the real-world. The object-oriented conceptual models (e.g., the model in [20] and Telos [13]) also captured the 'usage world' (i.e., 'behavior') consisting of tasks, activities, users, and user interfaces. Telos, in fact, is an extendible model that allows new modeling primitives to be defined. It may be emphasized here that all this knowledge captured in the conceptual schema is relevant during initial development, and also during later maintenance and use [13]. In fact, Papazoglou [20] identifies querying the conceptual schema as an important requirement for end-users.

The world wide web (www) has become a very large repository of documents with diverse content and structure. A large number of people use www as a first source of information (through search engines). However, due to lack of any organization and standards, users find it difficult to access information and co-relate it across sources. Semantic Web [23] is a vision for the future of web, which will allow documents to be associated with metadata [5] so that user applications (or, 'agents') can access and co-relate the relevant documents. The semantic web vision consists of defining ontologies for formally describing contents of web documents. Lot of effort has been directed towards creating markup languages for ontology specifications, starting from XML(Schema), RDF/S [5], DAML+OIL [26] (for their comparison, see [7]). OWL [18] is the new standard proposed by W3C for capturing the semantics of documents on the web. Most of these use object-oriented paradigm, offering concepts of classes, properties, inheritance and instances. Martin [12] brings out challenges in defining and sharing ontologies for natural language documents.

The www situation described above also prevails in many large organizations, which have hundreds of database applications. Here also, we have a need for integration, inter-operability, and flexible data access across multiple sources. There have been many efforts towards semantic integration of heterogeneous data sources [4] [13], where conceptual models for data sources are sought to be integrated semi-automatically. Bernstein et al. [3] have recognized management of models as a core requirement for building new and managing existing applications. They propose an object-oriented approach both for modeling and mapping (between models), and a set of high-level algebra operations on the models, such as matching, merging, differencing, inversion, etc.

Recently, Barrett et al. [2] have proposed an RDF-based ontology and metadata representation for integrating data sources. The schema-level metadata (tables and their columns) are mapped on a single shared ontology. Some implementation-specific information about the source (called 'infrastructure' ontology) is also defined to facilitate query processing. They permit browsing of the ontology, schema information, and also the data. Sugumaron and Storey [24] describe a methodology and tool for creating and managing ontologies. Suwan Manee et al. [25] describe integration using OWL where OWL itself is used to define mappings across ontologies.

Providing key-word based access to databases (quite like that permitted by search engines) has emerged as an important research area [22]. It becomes a brute-force exhaustive process (when the given keywords are looked up as values under all possible columns of various tables in a database). Ontology-based access allows users to form meaningful queries using keywords that represent concepts in the ontology and get understandable answers (this is demonstrated to some extent in [22]).

RDF/Schema (or, DAML+OIL and OWL which are closely-related to RDF/Schema) based ontologies are gaining popularity due to their flexibility. We also require a powerful query language to access the ontologies and the resources they describe. RQL [10] is one significant effort in this direction. It allows storage of large volumes of RDF schemas and resources, and enables querying them (individually as well as collectively) using SQL-like syntax.

In this chapter, we describe our approach and the ongoing research work for inter-operability and integration of multiple database sources based on defining and sharing ontologies and creating mappings between them. We extend the ontology models to describe not only the data domain, but also to specify tasks, activities and evolution. The motivation for the latter is that an ontology should capture both the 'subject world' and 'usage world' [13] of the application domain. Our main proposal is to extend today's database management systems so that they support maintenance and sharing of ontologies of application domains besides providing efficient storage and retrieval of data and supporting transactions. We claim that this increment in the DBMS technology will address the issue of inter-operability at the very root of the problem, and will fundamentally change the way we build database application. In Sec. 2, we briefly review approaches to integration. In Sec. 3, we give as an example the recent efforts of OGC [17] to achieve similar goals of inter-operability among data sources containing geographic data. In Sec. 4, we present the overall architecture of an Ontology-enabled DBMS (called OeDBMS). In Sec. 5, we propose extensions for ontology specifications languages to define the metadata and ontology associated with database applications and their mappings from one application to another. In. Sec. 6, we propose a graph model for the ontology, and propose a set of ontology operators that become basis for querying, matching, merging, etc. to facilitate the desired inter-operability and integration. Finally, in Sec. 7, we conclude and discuss future work.

The code and specification examples given in the paper are illustrative. They have been highly simplified (with liberties taken with the syntax of specification languages) for presentation and understanding.

2. APPROACHES TO INTEGRATION

Ontology-based integration of multiple data sources may be approached in fundamentally two different ways. A typical data source has components as shown in Fig. 20-1. The database schema defines how the data in the database is structured (say, in tables, columns, etc.) for storage. The meaning of data is captured in the conceptual model or the ontology, which is generally prepared at the analysis and design stage of the application development. In the conventional database systems, the ontology is not explicitly captured, and hence the conceptual model and its mapping with the metadata (i.e., the schema) is not available to the users.

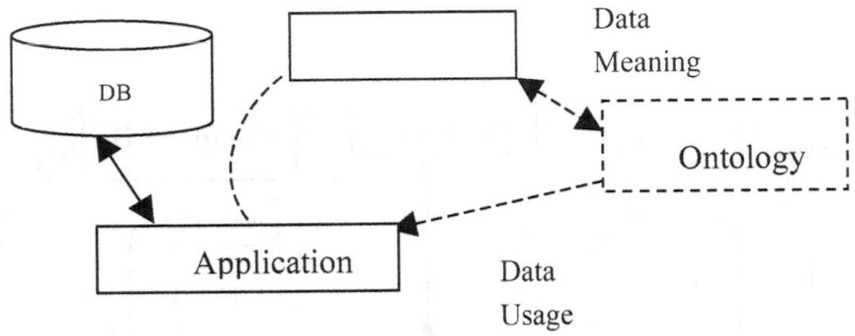

Figure 20-1. Components of typical DB application (Ontology component usually does not exist explicitly)

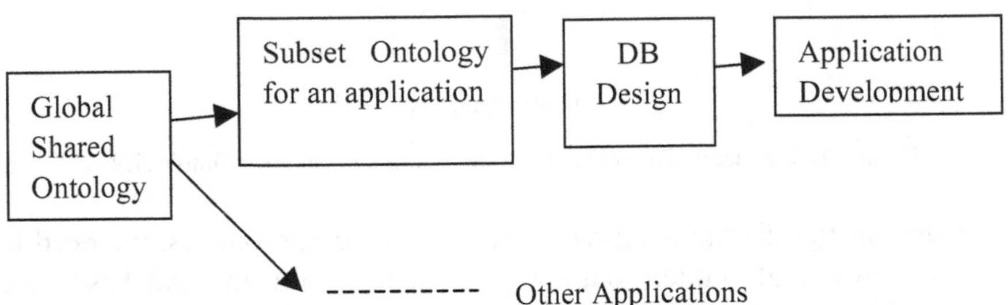

Figure 20-2. Top-Down development approach that begins with global (organization-wide) ontology

Fig. 20-2 depicts the 'top-down' approach to development where the applications are designed and built in the context of a global shared ontology. Each application refers to a subset of this global ontology. Correlating data across applications is relatively straight forward as data can be mapped to the global entities and attributes. However, this is an idealistic situation. Creating and maintaining global ontologies is a major challenge, and business data processing needs are often handled independently, leading to development of applications individually with little or no coordination among them for standardizing data semantics and structure.

Fig. 20-3 outlines a more practical strategy where we can build a 'federation' of independent data sources through their ontologies. We can begin here by first defining ontologies for the existing applications. We can next define mapping between the ontologies so that concepts and properties can be related across the data sources. We may also identify common ontology to minimize the extent of source-to-source mappings.

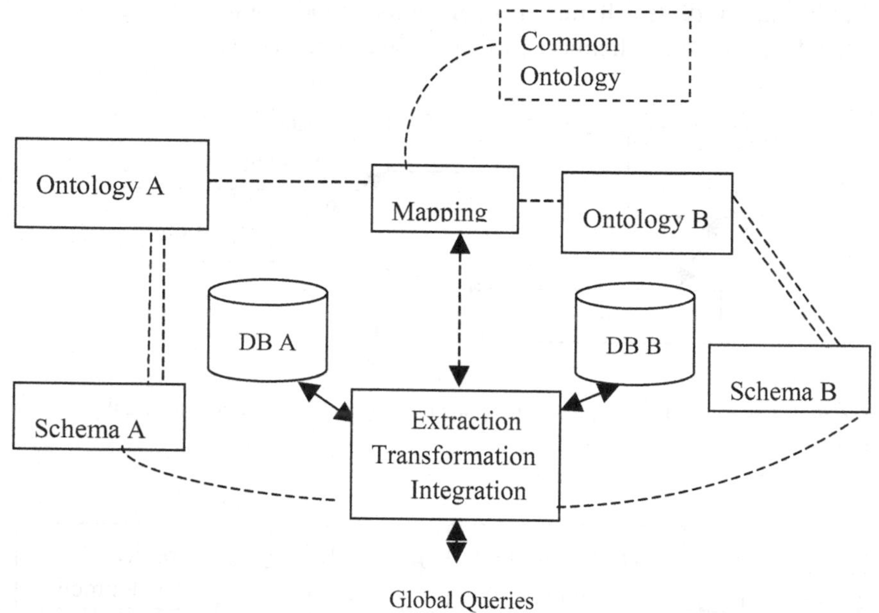

Figure 20-3. Federated approach based on mappings between Ontologies

As seen in the diagrams representing the above approaches, we need to define a conceptual model (ontology), a schema for the database, and mappings between the ontology and schema on one hand (represented by double-dashed lines in Fig. 20-3) and ontology to ontology (represented by simple dashed lines) on the other. These mappings become the basis for inter-relating the data across the sources, based on which the data can be extracted, transformed and integrated to answer multiple-source queries. The architecture of QeDBMS proposed in the next section identifies components and capabilities to support both the approaches to inter-operability given above.

Ontology area and tools and methodologies for creating and maintaining ontologies have received a lot of attention in the recent past (for example, see [16]). Tools will also be devised to facilitate schema-ontology and ontology-ontology mappings. However, we believe that a considerable amount of domain-specific human expertise will be required to define the ontologies as well as mappings.

3. INTER-OPERABILITY STANDARDS FOR GEOGRAPHIC DATA

In this section, we discuss the approach and the emerging standards for sharing and inter-operability of geographical data. In most countries, to support planning as well as to handle emergency situations, large volumes of spatially referenced data and information related to many domains (such as population, hydrology, land-use, climate, soils, etc) are being collected, and stored and processed in digital form. Most countries (see [14] for India's initiative) are creating a National Spatial Data Infrastructure to share the geo-spatial data that are often collected over long periods of time by various governmental and private agencies (in India, some of these agencies are Survey of India, Indian Space Research Organization, Geological Survey of India, and Indian Census). The geo-spatial data exists in various proprietary formats on different computing platforms using a variety of GIS products.

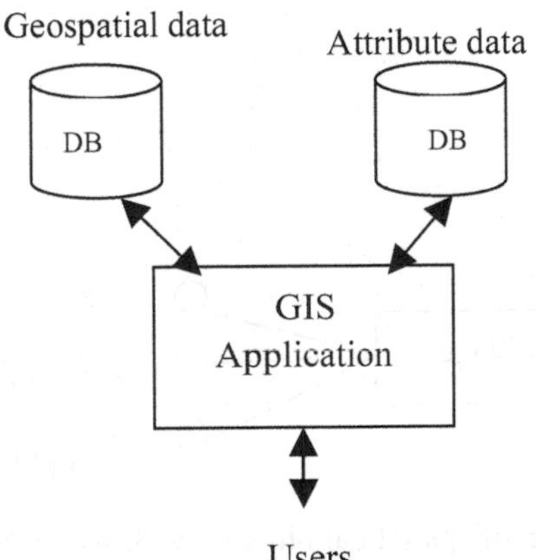

Figure 20-4. A typical source

To facilitate standardization for inter-operability, the Open GIS Consortium (OGC) (www.opengis.org) was setup with a mission to define modeling, representation, and interface standards for global use. We review their approach as a model case for inter-operability that can be generalized into a framework for sharing and inter-operability in other domains, and which motivates our goal as well as our proposed architecture for an ontology-aware database management system.

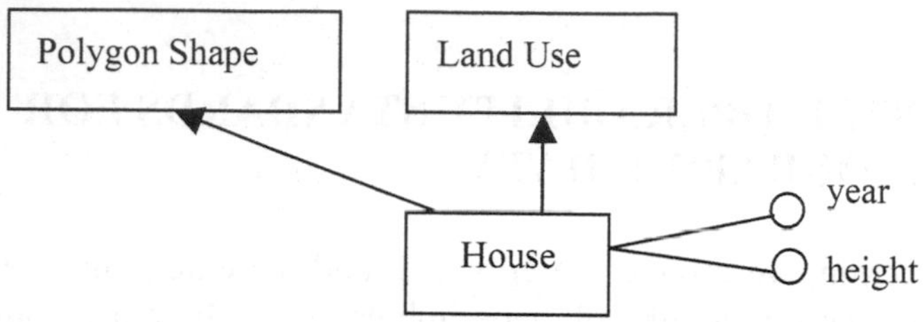

(a) geo-spatial feature in source 1

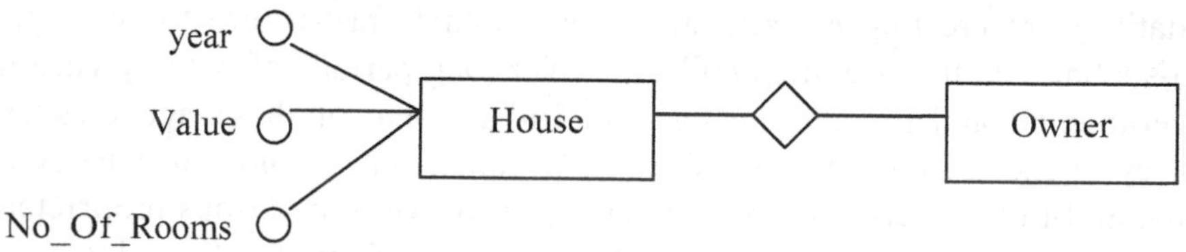

(b) Same feature with additional attributes in source 2

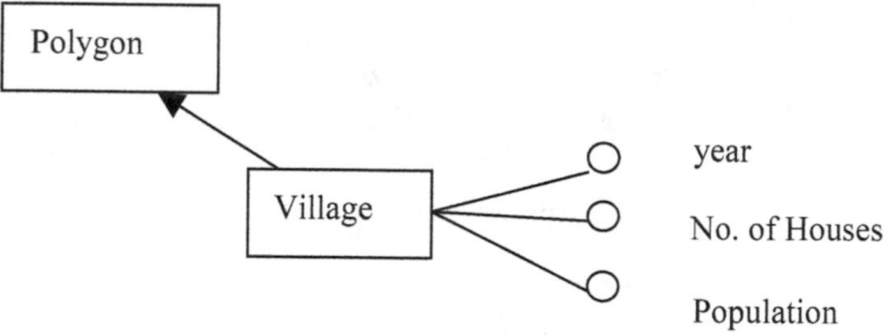

(c) Aggregation of spatial data in source 3, where Village aggregates data about various geo-spatial objects in its own boundary.

Figure 20-5. Geospatial features stored in different sources

Fig. 20-4 shows a typical GIS of an agency. It stores time-varying attribute data for various geo-spatial objects. Fig. 20-5 describes how two sources may contain different data about the same geographical object. We see in Fig. 20-5(a) and 20-5(b) that a house is described with different attributes in the two different sources. Fig 20-5(c) gives another example of data overlap due to spatial aggregation. The 'Village' is a coarser object which spatially covers many finer-granularity objects such as 'house' within its boundary. We may have applications requiring exchange of data across such sources for a given geographical area.

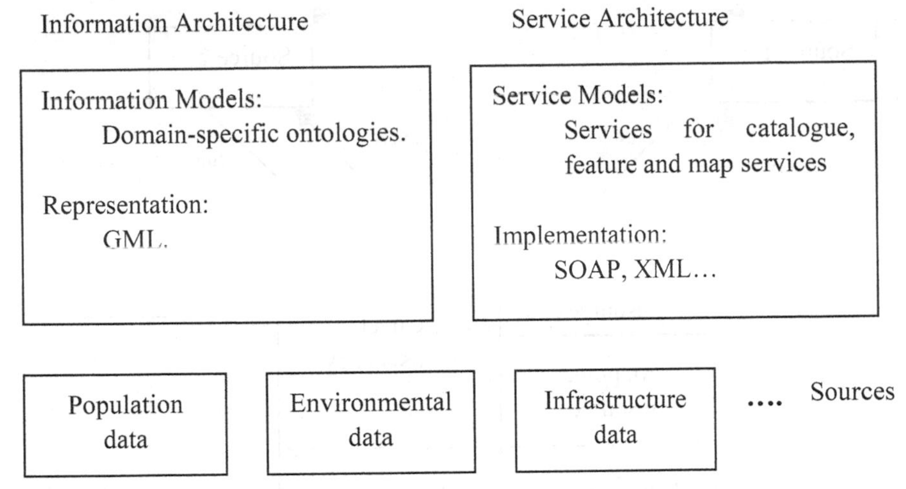

Figure 20-6. Enabling inter-operability through information models and web services as envisaged by OGC (Open GIS consortium)

OGC [17] has defined a framework for inter-operability as summarized in Fig. 20-6. The Information Architecture defines abstract (at base or common level) and domain-specific application models using the Geography Markup Language (GML) [11] for representation and exchange of data. The various sources such as population may exist as independent data sources. OGC defines a service architecture for permitting access to the models (i.e., the ontologies) as well as data. The emerging web services technology based on XML, SOAP and other www standards is used to define standard interfaces for accessing definitions (Catalogue Service), retrieving data objects (Feature Service) and preparing maps (Map Service).

Fig. 20-7 gives a possible implementation architecture for the OGC vision. The reference ontology could be the GML base schemas and shared application schemas. The ontologies associated with individual sources may extend features (objects) in the reference schema, add new features, or create derived (e.g., coarse granularity) features. User queries need to be mapped onto the individual sources based on what they contain, then translated with respect to the metadata at local sources (which give how the data is physically stored) and operations supported by them, executed to extract the required data form those sources, and finally the results form sources validated (e.g., for temporal consistency) and integrated before presenting them to the user.

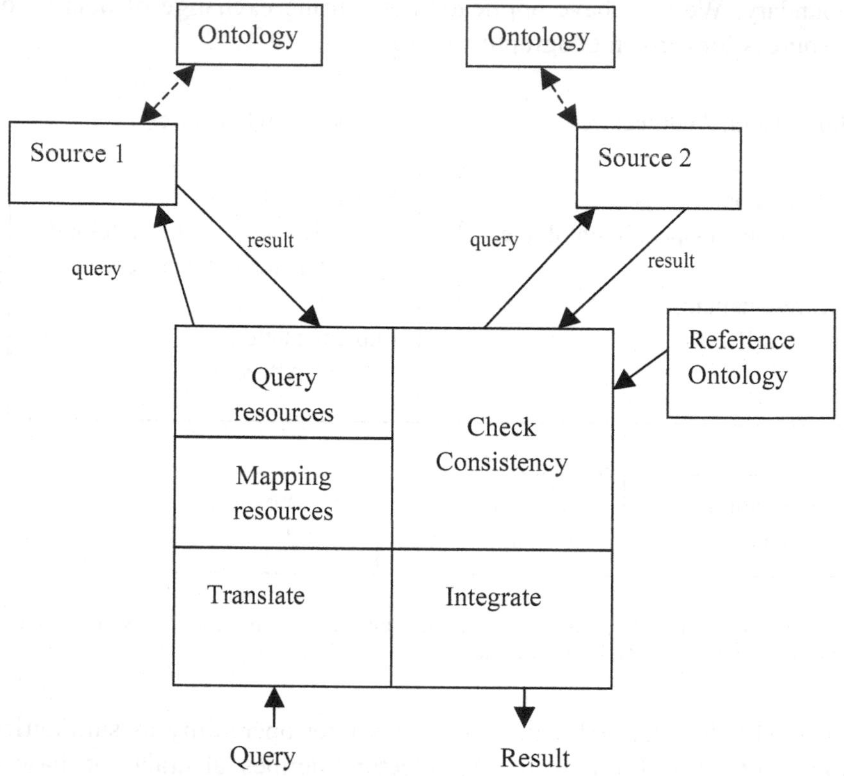

Figure 20-7. Ontology-driven inter-operability environment

We believe that the approach and the framework defined by OGC are ideal to address the difficult problem of inter-operability, which can be further eased considerably by ontology-enabled database systems.

4. ONTOLOGY-ENABLED DBMS (OEDBMS): AN OVERVIEW

Fig. 20-8 shows the overall architecture for the proposed ontology-enabled DBMS. It subsumes the conventional data management component. It has a new Ontology Management Sub-System (OMS) with the following capabilities:

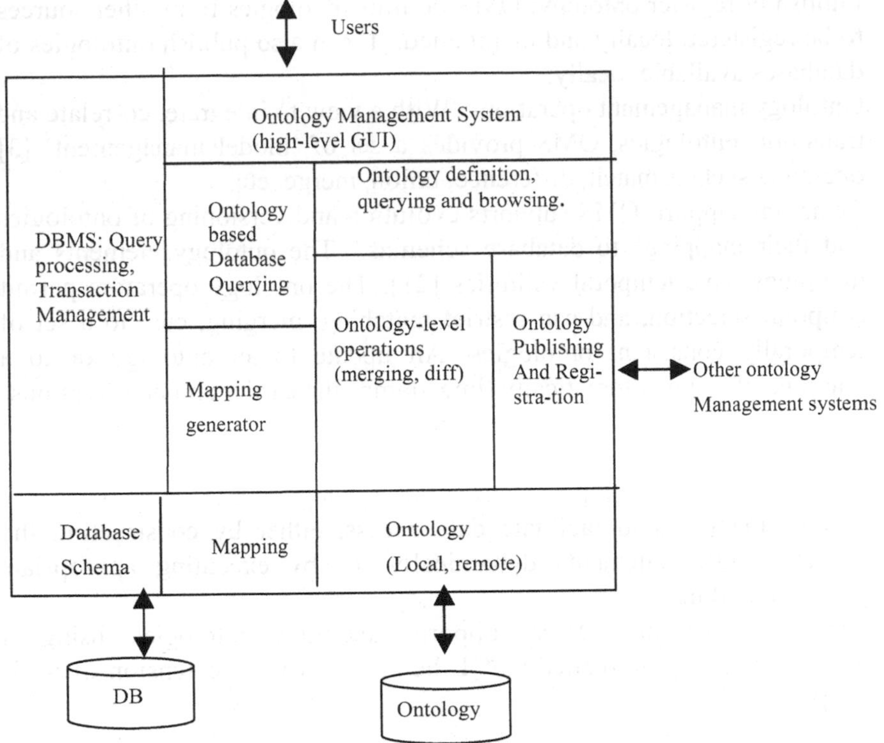

Figure 20-8. Database management system extended for ontology management

1. Ontology creation: using the extended RDF-based ontology specification language (described in Sec. 3), ontologies can be created and edited. Multiple tools may be provided to facilitate automatic generation of verbose RDF specifications from high-level diagramming tools (based on UML or ER models).
2. Register a database source and prepare its mapping with appropriate ontology: this component provides assistance in creating a mapping between an ontology and a database schema.
3. Ontology validation: there are many standardization efforts for XML-based specification of business directories to facilitate Business-to-Business e-commerce (often in specific domains such as finance). ebXML (see http://www.ebxml.org/) is one such example. There are also extensive language resources (such as Wordnet, see http://www.cogsci.princeton.edu/~wn/), which define words and relationships (e.g., synonymy) between them. These resources can be used to validate ontology definitions for consistency, completeness, and adherence to standards.

4. Publish or register ontology: OMS permits ontologies from other sources to be registered locally and maintained. It can also publish ontologies of databases available locally.
5. Ontology management operations: With a view to integrate, co-relate and transform ontologies, OMS provides a set of 'model management' [3] operators such as match, difference, union, merge, etc.
6. Temporal support: OMS supports evolution and versioning of ontologies and their mappings to database schemas. The ontology elements and mappings have temporal validities [21]. The ontology operators permit temporal selection, and can restrict matching, merging, etc., to a set of temporally consistent ontologies. An update to an ontology or to a mapping element automatically time-stamps the earlier and new versions.
7. Data access: Data stored in the DBMS may be browsed through the ontology elements, either through a declarative query language or through a graphical representation of ontology. OMS uses ontology-schema mappings to facilitate data access, either by constructing the required SQL statements dynamically, or by executing appropriate program modules.
8. Ontology querying: OMS supports querying ontologies using a declarative language (called OnQL here, which is an extension of RQL [10]).

5. ONTOLOGY AND MAPPING SPECIFICATIONS

Models based on ER and UML have been used popularly for conceptual modeling. These models use concepts like Class (Entity), Attributes (Property), and Association (Relationship) at data modeling level, and activities and state transitions for behavior (or, dynamic) modeling.

The recent ontology languages [18] based on RDF [5] use Classes and Properties. Classes define concept categories, and their instances are resources without any inherent value or state. Properties associate values or other resources with a given resource. Properties have a domain and range. Sub-classes and sub-properties can be used to further restrain a class or property (thus, a property is a 'first class' ontology element). The flexibility provided by RDF is useful for resources on the web (where, for example, two resources defined by a Class may have quite different properties).

Our primary aim is to model database applications. However, we also want our ontology specification to closely follow the Semantic Web initiative, so that web-based 'agents' may also be able to query database sources. Hence, our ontology specification is based on extended RDF. We propose a high-level UML-like modeling interface (and derive verbose RDF descriptions from these models), and also propose a few important extensions to RDF/Schema for modeling complex structures (such as aggregations) and behavior. The extensions are as follows:

1. The ontology definitions do not contain instances. The instances are stored in a database (using a relational schema) separately. The schema defines the metadata whereas the ontology defines data meaning. Extension is required to specify ontology-metadata mappings.
2. An object property p_1 itself may be a domain of another property p_2, which may be a data property or object property. Further, a property p_1 can be 'inverse' of another property p2, allowing us to capture bi-directional nature of real-world relationships [6].
3. We provide ontology elements for defining states and state transitions of the real-world entities modeled in a database. We can specify activities as state-change agents and capture dynamics of an application at a high level. The activities are like services available from the application. They may be defined as web services with action semantics captured using DAML-S [1].

We illustrate our UML-like diagramming notation in Fig. 20-9. The Student class has attributes, methods and an association. The association Study has an attribute called grade. A student instance can be considered to have states: created, registered (for a course), and deleted. We can translate the model in Fig. 20-9 into RDF-like ontology as follows (using standard namespaces and our extension namespace 'extn'). We only show the specification in a skeleton form. Note that Grade is defined as a property of Study (which itself is an object property), and Register is an activity performed on Student to take it from Created state to Registered state.

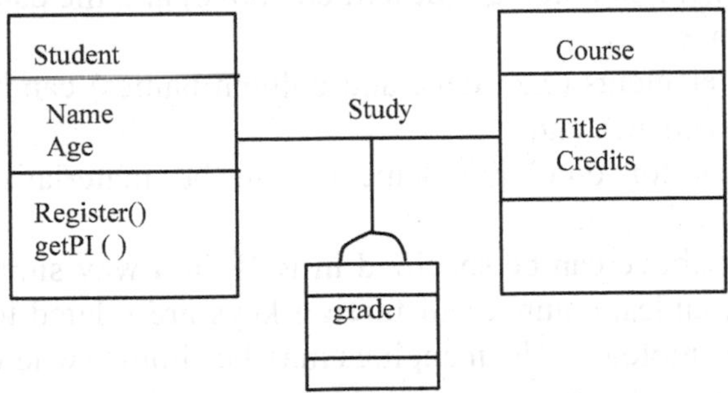

Figure 20-9. An application model in UML

```
<daml:Class rdf:ID = "Student">   ...
</daml:Class>
<daml:DatatypeProperty  rdf:ID = "name">
   ...
```

```
  <rdfs:domain  rdf:resource = "#Student"/>
  <rdfs:range     rdf:resource = "http://www.w3.org/2000/10/
                              XMLSchema#String "/>
 </daml:DatatypeProperty>
     ...
 <daml:ObjectProperty   rdf:ID = "Study">
       <rdfs:domain rdf:resource = "#Student"/>
       <rdfs:range rdf:resource = "#Course"/>
       <extn:inverse rdf:resource = "#Studied-by"/>
</daml:ObjectProperty>
<extn:PropAttribute       rdf:ID = "Grade">
        ...
     <extn:domain  extn:prop Resource = "# Study">
     <rdfs:range      rdf:resource= "..... XMLSchema#decimal"/>
</extn:PropAttribute>
<extn:ObjState  rdf:ID = "# Student">
      <daml:oneOf    rdf:parseType = "daml:collection">
             <daml:Thing     rdf:ID = "Created "/>
             <daml:Thing     rdf:ID = "Registered "/>
              ...
     </daml:oneOf>
</extn:objState>
<extn:ObjActivity    rdf:ID = "Register ">
          <extn:forObject      rdf:ID = "#Student "/>
          <extn:domainState   rdf:ID = "#Created "/>
          <extn:rangeState     rdf:ID = "#Registered "/>    ...
</extn:ObjActivity>
```

The database schema for the application modeled in Fig. 20-9 may contain 3 tables (viz., Student, Course, Study) and many stored program modules including those for the shown methods. The mapping specifications between the application ontology (described above) and the database schema essentially indicates

1. how schema elements (e.g., table and column names) can be interpreted as ontology elements, and
2. how instances for ontology elements can be materialized from the database.

The first part above can be specified in RDF in a way similar to Barrett et al. [2], where tables, column and foreign keys are related to classes and properties in the ontology. The mappings may be simple (where one class in the ontology maps onto one database table) or complex (where a class may be mapped into two or more tables and vice-versa). The program modules can be related to the activities defined in the ontology (e.g., the activity Register above maps directly to program module "register.c", which may be a function in language C). We show a sample ontology-metadata mapping specification below where the class Student in 'acad' is completely mapped onto a table StdTab in the acadDB schema in an RDBMS. We also show how property-to-column and activity-to-module mappings can be defined.

```
<map:Class-to-Table mapping = complete>
   <map:Class rdf:resource = "&acad:Student">
   <map:Table  rdf:resource = "&acadDB:StdTab">
</map: Class-to-Table>
<map:Property-to-Column mapping = simple>
   <map:Property rdf:resource = "&acad:Roll-number">
   <map:Column  rdf:resource = "&acadDB:rno">
</map:Property-to-Column>
<map:Activity-to-Module>
   <map:Activity  rdf:resource = "&acad:Register">
   <map:Module  rdf:resource = "&acadDB:register.c">
</map:Activity-to-Module>
```

The second part of mapping indicated above will be used for data browsing and data retrieval (by end-users or autonomous web agents). We indicate materialization of instances by SQL queries or by program modules (if available). In RDF documents, the instances have unique identifiers, whereas in relational databases, the instances may be identified by some key attribute. If 'rno' (for roll-number) in StdTab (for student table) is the primary key in the schema, we can designate it for materializations of Student class instances as follows:

```
<extn:instances    rdf:ID = "#Student">
  <extn:usingSQL    extn:Query = "Select rno from StdTab"/>
</extn:instances>
```

Similarly, the property instances can be obtained from a database by retrieving appropriate attributes from one or more tables.

The ontology mappings across sources can also be specified in a similar manner. Here also, mappings could be simple or complex. The mappings may further indicate whether instances (data) in the sources overlap or are disjoint. Since the instances are managed by DBMS, where the schemas define local-level keys (that may act as object identifiers), it is essential to indicate explicitly how instances across databases may be matched. By default, we take instances in different databases to be independent (e.g., a student with roll-number 1234 in database of School A is different from a student with same roll number 1234 in another School B).

Let us consider an example of how semantics and data mappings among data stored in two databases can be captured. Fig. 20-10 shows an example with overlaps at both the conceptual and data levels, to be captured by defining mappings at ontology as well as at instance (database) levels. We

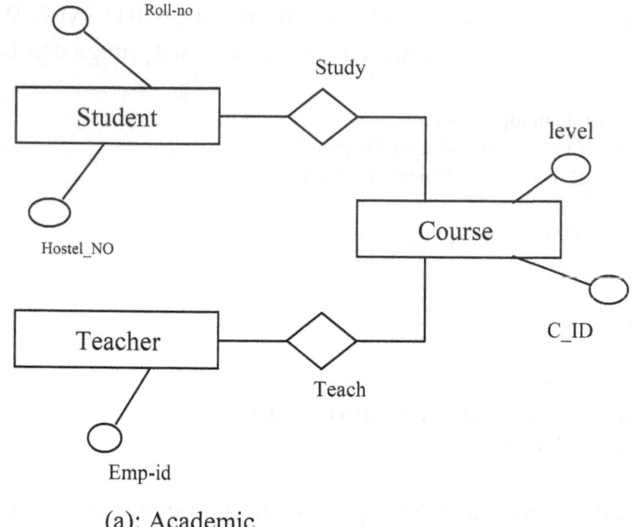

(a): Academic

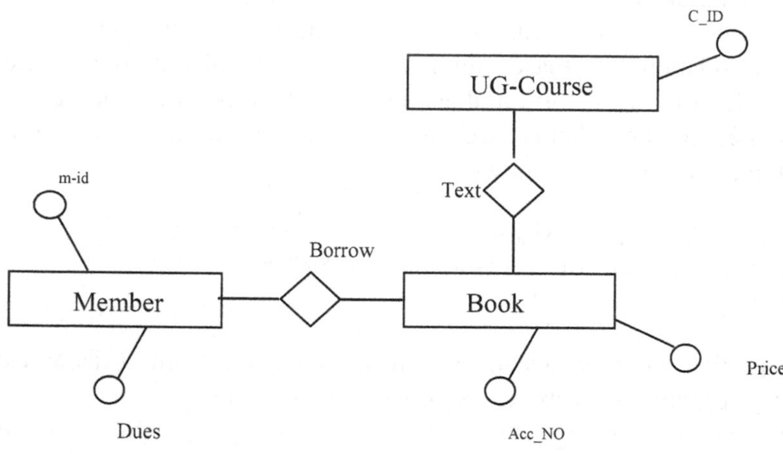

(b): Library

Figure 20-10. Two database applications with schema-level and database-level overlaps

should be able to define mappings at class, property and instance levels as per the examples illustrated below:

1. Student and Teacher are subset of Member. All students and teachers are members
2. UG-course is a Course with level less than 4
3. m-id (member-id) is same as roll-no for student members
4. Some attributes of the common entities are specific to individual applications in spite of the above correspondences

5. attribute relationships are specified using extended constraint or computational specifications (e.g., attribute A in DB1 may be equal to B+C in DB2 for some related entities).

Some of the above mappings may be captured as follows (assume 'acad' and 'lib' are namespaces containing ontology definitions for the two databases of Fig. 20-10). Suwan Manee et al. [25] describe similar approach for defining mappings between ontologies.

```
<map: Class-to-Class  rdf:about = "&acad:Student">
   <map:subsetOf  rdf:resource = "&lib:Member">
</map: Class-to-Class>
<map: Propert-to-Property  rdf:about = "&acad:rollno">
   <map: EqvProperty  rdf:resource = "&lib:m-id">
</map: Propert-to-Property>
<map: Class-to-Class  rdf:about = "&lib.UG-Course">
   <map: EqvClass>
      <map:RestrictionCondition>
         <map:condition  map:CondString = "< 4">
         <map:forProperty  rdf:resource = "&acad:level">
      </map:RestrictionCondition>
   </map: EqvClass>
</map: Class-to-Class>
```

As mentioned earlier, we permit temporal modeling of classes and properties by time-stamping them with intervals during which they are valid. We can achieve this by using subclass and property attribute features as in GML [11] where temporal attributes can be inherited by classes from an abstract type.

6. ONTOLOGY OPERATIONS AND QUERYING

In this section, we describe the main features of the Ontology Query Language (OnQL). It is based on a set of operators for querying and updating ontologies, and for querying instances stored in a database schema. We focus on these operators rather than giving syntax of OnQL.

An ontology may be represented as a directed graph where nodes represent class or property elements, and edges represent subclass, sub-property, or domain/range links. A simple example is shown in Fig. 20-11. This representation (unlike that in [10]) allows us to represent sub-properties and property-attributes in a proper graph form (whereas [10] requires *linking of edges* for sub-properties). Activities are also represented as nodes, with links to classes used/affected by them.

An ontology O is basically a tuple <N, E> where N is a set of nodes (each with node-type and label as associated data) and E is a set of edges. The label of an edge may be one of {domain, range, is-a, type, affects}. This graph may be traversed by following one or more types of edges, and visiting all or specific type of nodes. For instance, one may find all derived classes of a node n_1 by following is-a edges from n_1 and visiting nodes of type class. Note that directed edges may be traversed in opposite direction for the inverse of the meaning represented by it.

We define various types of ontology operators for use in searching, comparing, updating, or extracting (parts of) of ontologies. They can be easily understood in terms of the graph model. We describe below the main operators:

1. <u>during</u> (O_1, I): returns ontology O_2 containing only those elements of O_1 that are valid during time interval I. The graph corresponding to the result O_2 may or may not be connected.
2. <u>intersect</u> (O_1, O_2): returns O_3 whose elements are present in both O_1 and O_2.
3. <u>difference</u> (O_1, O_2): returns O_3 (a subset of O_1) containing elements of O_1 that are not present in O_2.
4. <u>addNode</u> (O_1, n_1): the node element, possibly representing a new class, is added to O_1 (with NOW..∞ as valid time stamp on the new node n_1).
5. <u>connect</u> (O_1, n_1, n_2, label): this operation connects nodes n_1 and n_2 in O_1 by an edge labeled with the given label.
6. <u>select</u> (O_1, p): allows to select O_1 elements which satisfy predicate p into result O_2. p may simply be a node n_1 (with desired type and label), or may specify specific traversals from some node n_1. Some examples of selections (omitting syntax details) are given below:
   a) select classes whose labels contain the string "student,"
   b) select all properties whose domain is the "student" node
   c) select direct subclasses of "student" or all transitive subclasses of "student"
   d) select sub graph that connects nodes n_1 and n_2

The graph model and the basic ontology operations described above give us a strong foundation for analyzing, transforming and integrating ontologies. Ontology transformations are based on both the structure and the meaning. A good domain understanding is necessary to carry out the transformations and integration. These challenging tasks can be done semi-automatically using the above operations and supported by a user-friendly interface.

To permit step-by-step analysis and matching of elements in two ontologies O_1 and O_2, we permit establishing 'matches' links between nodes of O1 and O_2. For example, we may define the 'matches' link between

Student and Member classes (see Fig. 20-10). A probability q can be associated with 'matches' links, indicating analyst's confidence in the match. Probabilistic matches must ultimately be resolved by application administrators.

The analysis for matching is based on names, descriptions (if supplied), and structure (type or permitted values) of the classes (properties). Two properties are matched based on their names/descriptions using Wordnet. Classes are matched based on their names/descriptions and existence of a matching unique (key) property. Probabilities may be associated to reflect some 'distance' between the words. Given such 'matches' links between O_1 and O_2, we provide another useful (heuristic-based) operator propagate (O_1, O_2) to further propagate matches between O_1 and O_2. At present, we include the following heuristics:

1. Class-to-Property propagation: if n_{11} (in O_1) and n_{21} (in O_2) are class nodes and they match with probability q, and they are domains of property nodes n_{12} and n_{22} whose labels are similar and/or whose types are similar, then n_{12} and n_{22} also match with probability q (or a fraction of q in case labels are not 'close' or types do not match perfectly).
2. Property-to-Property propagation: if n_{11} and n_{21} match with probability q_1, n_{12} and n_{22} match with probability q_2, and n_{11} and n_{12} are linked (as domain and range) to node n_{13} whereas n_{21} and n_{22} are linked similarly to node n_{23} that has label similar to n_{13}, then nodes n_{13} and n_{23} match with probability $q_1 x q_2$.
3. Property-to-Class propagation: if two classes (n_{11} in O_1 and n_{21} in O_2) have many matching properties (including those which are unique), then the classes also match (with probability derived from those of property match probabilities).

In fact, we plan to make the propagate operation rule-based, so that the ontology integration module may turn the rules on or off, or add new rules. This module gives initial analysis of potential matches, which are reviewed and finalized by the human experts.

Finally, we provide getData (O_1, n_1) operator on node n_1 of the ontology O_1. Assuming that a mapping between that node and the database schema of O_1 is already available, it executes the mapping (typically an SQL query) to get data from the database.

While we expect the above operators to be used directly through a suitable interactive interface, we provide a declarative query language where ontologies can be selected, path expressions can be specified, and nodes can be selected (based on their type and label) and displayed. To illustrate, the following OnQL query gets all properties and their ranges for class Student in Ontology O_1:

```
select $P, range($P)
from O1.$C, O1.$P
where $C = "Student" and $C = domain($P)
```

Here, $C and $P are variables which range over all class nodes and property nodes in O_1. We select only those nodes and edges (connecting class and property nodes) which satisfy the *where* condition, and print property names and their ranges (printing a node is equivalent to printing its label).

7. CONCLUSIONS

The primary objective of this chapter is to propose an ontology-enabled database management system (OeDBMS), which acts as an integrated platform to develop and store ontology, to design and implement database applications, and to support inter-operability and integration of multiple database sources by co-relating and integrating their ontologies. We motivated this need, and proposed that ontologies be specified using the emerging RDF/OWL based standards so that the futuristic software agents on the web can access these ontologies and also the corresponding data in the databases. We have identified the architecture and important functionalities for OeDBMS.

Our objective is to enable inter-operability/integration of existing database applications through shared ontologies. While some tools can be devised to facilitate identification of schema-ontology and ontology-ontology mappings, we expect that a considerable amount of human domain-expertise will be required to define them.

We have also identified the need to extend the scope of ontology models, and to align them with the modeling capabilities of the well-established models (such as ER and UML) so that the ontologies capture the structure, meaning and usage of the data in a database application. We have proposed the required extensions towards this goal. We have formalized the extended-ontology model as a graph model, and have made that a basis for proposing a set of powerful ontology operators. These operators provide a systematic support for various tasks such as browsing, querying, analysis, comparing, matching, match propagation, and integration of ontologies. They provide a strong support to domain experts in achieving the goals of inter-operability and integration across multiple database sources. The extended scope of our ontology model also provides for specification of activities (i.e., processing), and for specification of mappings between ontologies and database schemas.

The OeDBMS vision may appear to be very ambitious considering its proposed scope and the implicit challenges. However, we see that the required components are already in place. These include ontology languages, metadata standards, web services, and the frameworks such as the one visualized by OGC. When put together as proposed in OeDBMS, the whole will be much bigger than the parts and will meet the much desired goal of inter-operability.

We see many challenges and opportunities for further work in this area. The challenges we plan to address in future include: validation of ontologies (using web-based resources such as Wordnet, ebXML), using the graph-based model to capture integrity constraints (as in the Telos model [13]), rule-based and heuristic-driven implementation for propagation of matching across ontologies, and optimization of ontology queries.

REFERENCES

1. Anupriya Ankolekar et al., 'DAML-S: Semantic Markup for Web Services', Proc. of SWWS'01, the First semantic web working symposium, Stanford University, California, USA, 2001.
2. Barett T., Jones D., Yuan J., Sawaya J., Usehold M., Adams T., and Folger D., 'RDF Representation of Metadata for Semantic Integration of Corporate Information Resources', Prof. of WWW2002 Workshop on Real World RDF and SemanticWeb Applications, Hawaii, USA, May 2002, pp. 20-28.
3. Bernstein P.A., Levy A.Y. and Pottinger R.A., 'A Vision for Management of Complex Models', Technical Report MSR-TR-2000-53, Microsoft Research, Microsoft Corporation (www.research.microsoft.com).
4. Calvanese D. et al., 'Towards a Comprehensive Methodological Framework for Semantic Integration of Heterogeneous Data Sources', Proc. of 8th Intl. Workshop on Knowledge Representation meets Databases (KRDB 2001), 2001 (http://ceur-ws.org/vol-45/).
5. Candan K.S., Liu H., and Suvarna R., 'Resource Description Framework: Metadata and its Applications', SIGKDD Explorations, Vol.3, Issue 1, July 2001, pp. 6-19.
6. Corby O., Faron-Zucker C., 'Corese: a Corporate Semantic Web Engine'; Proc. of. WWW2002 workshop on Real World RDF and Semantic Web Applications, Hawai, USA, May 7, 2002.
7. Gil Y. and Ratnakar V., 'Markup Languages: Comparison and Examples' available at http://trellis.semanticweb.org/expect/web/semanticweb/comparison.html.
8. Jayasena S., Bressan S., Madnick S., 'Financial Information Mediation – A Case Study for Standards Integration for Electronic Hill Presentment and Payment using the CION Mediation Technology', in Proc. of 5th Intl. Workshop on Technology For E-Services, M. Shan et al. (eds.), Lecture Notes in Computer Science, 3324, Springer Verlag 2005.
9. Jeong-Oog Lee et al., 'The Roles of Ontology and Metadata Registry for Interoperable Databases', Proc. of ICDCIT – 2004 Intl. conf – on Distributed Computing and Internet Technologies, Bhubhaneshwar, India, Dec – 2004, R. K. Ghosh, H. Mohanty (eds.), Lecture Notes in Computer Science, 3347, Springer 2004.
10. Karvounarakis G., Alexaki S., Christophides V., Plexousakis D. and Scholl M., 'RQL: A Declarative Query Language for RDF', Prof. of WWW2002, May 7-11, 2002, Hawaii, USA.

11. Lake R. et al., 'Geography Mark-up Language (GML)', John Wiley, 2004.
12. Martin P., 'Knowledge Representation, Sharing, and Retrieval on the Web', in Web Intelligence, Ning Zhong et al. (eds.), Springer-Verlag, 2003.
13. Mylopoulos J., 'Conceptual Modeling and Telos', in Conceptual Modeling, Databases and CASE, P. Loucopoulos and R. Zicari (eds.), John Wiley, 1992, pp. 49-68.
14. National Spatial Data Infrastructure, India's road map for the future, http://www.nsdiindia.org.
15. Object Management Group, 'Common Warehouse Metamodel Specification', at http://www.omg.org/cwm/
16. OntoWeb, 'A Survey of Ontology Tools' (Deliverable 1.3), 31 May 2002, http://www.ontoweb.org (also see Proc. of Intl Conf on Knowledge Eng and Knowledge Mana available at http://ceur-ws.org/vol-62).
17. Open GIS Consortium, http://www.opengeospatial.org/.
18. OWL Web Ontology Guide, March 2003, available at http://www.w3.org.
19. Open Financial Exchange Specification OFX 2.0.2, Open Financial Exchange, http://www.ofx.net/ofx/.
20. Papazoglou M. P., 'Unraveling the Semantics of Conceptual Schemas', Comm. of ACM, 9(58), Sept. 1995, pp. 80-94.
21. Sarda N.L., 'A Framework for Application Evolution Management', Prof. of 10th Australasian Database Conf. (ADC '99), Univ. of Auckland, New Zealand, Jan. '99.
22. Sarda N.L., and Jain A., 'A System for Keyword-based Searching in Databases', http://arXiv.org/abs/cs/0110052, Octo. 2001.
23. Semantic Web Organization, http://www.semanticweb.org/.
24. Sugumaran V. and Storey V.C., 'Ontologies for Conceptual Modeling: their creation, use, and management', Data & Knowledge Engineering, 42(2002), pp.251-277.
25. Suwan Manee S., Benslimane D., Thiran P., 'Semantic Integration with OWL', Proc. of Intl. conf. on management of Data (COMAD) 2005, Goa, India, Jan. 2005.
26. van Harmelen F., Patel-Schneider P.F., and Horrocks I. (ed.), 'Reference Description of the DAML+OIL (March 2001) ontology markup language', available at http://www.daml.org/.

Chapter 21

ENHANCING INTEROPERABILITY AND WEB SERVICES STANDARDS THROUGH ONTOLOGICAL ANALYSIS

Peter Green[1], Michael Rosemann[2] and Marta Indulska[1]
[1]UQ Business School, The University of Queensland, Ipswich QLD 4305, Australia; [2]Faculty of Information Technology, Queensland University of Technology, Brisbane QLD 4000, Australia

Abstract: A web service choreography standard enables a standardized description of business processes that allows not only a clear specification of the control flow, but also it forms the basis for the actual process execution. Such standards are part of the Web Services stack and facilitate Enterprise Systems interoperability. A simple indication of the rapid growth of this area is the number of new and existing standards. While the need for the theoretical evaluation and comparison of these standards is being addressed, regardless of the results of such evaluations and comparisons, the interoperability enabled by such standards is still limited. This limitation stems from a number of shortcomings. First, there is a lack of agreement on a general ontology that can be used to describe any type of phenomena in the world. Second, there is limited agreement on the actual set of phenomena that is being modeled in the Enterprise Systems interoperability domain. Third, interoperability is limited by the lack of agreement on the mapping of such phenomena to the chosen general ontology. Last, a means for replicating the constructivist processes that humans use to ascribe meaning to phenomena is lacking. In this paper, we address each of these limitations. We argue that the BWW representation model is a good choice of a general ontology to be used in this domain. Utilizing this ontology for the purposes of analysis, we present the unique set of phenomena that is currently being modeled by the collective of the four leading Enterprise Systems interoperability standards, *viz.* ebXML BPSS, BPML, BPEL4WS, and, WSCI, and the mappings of these phenomena to the chosen general ontology. Further, we discuss the problems in true interoperability of being able to negotiate and ascribe meaning to constructs.

Key words: BWW model; ontology; enterprise interoperability standards; ebXML; BPML; BPEL4WS; WSCI

1. INTRODUCTION

Enterprise Systems and other software packages, together with middleware solutions such as workflow management and Enterprise Application integration, have facilitated the integration of functions and data within many organizations. After more than a decade of such integration initiatives, an extension of the scope of integration management is apparent. The integration of business processes *between* organizations now becomes a major focus. The interoperability of Enterprise Systems or the integration of cross-organizational business processes in general, requires a clear and independent specification of the information flow between the participating business partners. The extensible mark-up language, XML, provided a new approach to describe such standardized documents and systems. It also allowed the development of autonomous and modular solutions that can be published, identified, and accessed independently from the technological platform. This set of solutions is commonly termed Web Services.

Various XML-based standards have been developed and proposed for the area of Enterprise Systems interoperability (ESI) and Web Services. These standards cover different layers of the Web Services stack and range from very technical specifications to languages for executable business processes. However, underlying all of these standards is the fact that they are attempting to emulate real-world entities as well as the ways they interact to perform such useful tasks as business processes (sales, purchasing, and fulfillment) through computer systems interoperation. Accordingly, all of these standards are based on some model of how the real-world entities and processes are expected to operate.

With the rapid increase in the number of such 'standards', there is now a need for an objective basis on which to compare and evaluate them. This situation can be compared with the traditional area of Information Systems Analysis and Design (ISAD) techniques. Many modeling techniques have been developed for the description of data, functions, objects, processes, and the like. The development, evaluation, and selection of these techniques, however, have been difficult due to the lack of a generally accepted theoretical foundation that could serve as a benchmark. One promising benchmark for the analysis of ISAD grammars has been the collection of ontological models developed by Bunge, Wand and Weber (BWW) (1990, 1993, 1995). Based on sound philosophical foundations, these models provide a well-defined list of constructs and interrelationships that are perceived as relevant and that can be used as a platform for the analysis of such grammars. The extent to which a grammar does not cover all BWW constructs and the extent to which the elements of a grammar go beyond the BWW models provide valuable insights into the potential shortcomings of that grammar. The popularity of using ontologies for the analysis of techniques that purport to assist analysts to develop models that emulate portions of the real world has been growing steadily. The Bunge-Wand-Weber (1997) ontological models, for example, have been applied extensively in the context of the analysis of many of the most popular modeling techniques over the years. Most recently, Green *et al.* (2005) and Green, Rosemann and Indulska (2005) have extended the use of this evaluative base into the area of enterprise systems interoperability using business process modeling languages like ebXML, BPML, BPEL4WS, and WSCI.

Green *et al.* (2003) note however, that, regardless of the results of such analyses, the level of interoperability afforded by these standards is limited and relies on *a priori* agreement on, not only a particular standard, but also the constructs that form the standard. It is proposed that in order to achieve the goal of *full* interoperability, four fundamental problems must be resolved. First, an agreement must be reached on a general ontology that can be used to describe any type of phenomena that occurs in the world. Second, an agreement must be achieved on the phenomena that exist within a specific domain and the meaning of those phenomena. Third, an agreement must also be obtained on the mapping of the various phenomena within the domain to the chosen general ontology. Last, in order to achieve transparent interoperability, a means of replicating the constructivist process that humans use to ascribe meaning to new or existing phenomena of the specific domain must be developed.

Accordingly, the main objective of this paper is to address these four fundamental problems in the light of the dominating web services standards, *viz.*, ebXML, BPML, BPEL4WS and WSCI. There are several contributions that we aim to make. First, we argue that the BWW representation model is a good choice for a general ontology that can be used to describe any type of phenomena that occurs in the world. Second, we examine each of the four selected web services standards in order to identify non-redundant unique phenomena that are being represented across the four standards. Logically, such a set of phenomena defines the *domain of interoperability* that the collective of authors, researchers, and developers of such standards is attempting to represent and explain. Third, we present the BWW representation model mapping of the phenomena in this domain. This analysis also identifies those ontological constructs for which there are no representations in the overall target domain. Last, we examine the notion of the need for constructivist processes. We posit that it is these *excess* constructs that most require negotiations by the interacting parties to assign meaning to these constructs. In order to achieve interoperability, all constructs used must have the same meaning for *all* interacting parties.

Accordingly, there must be some mechanism(s) that allows meaning to be *negotiated* and assigned to these ontologically meaningless constructs – *excess* constructs.

This chapter is structured as follows. Section 2 gives a brief introduction to the BWW representation model and provides the argument for using the BWW representation model as the ontology of choice for describing the phenomena that occur within the Enterprise Systems interoperability domain. Section 3 outlines some related research. In Section 4, we present the research methodology utilized. Section 5 presents the general phenomena which are found to be missing across the four standards, as well as the set of non-redundant unique phenomena that are modeled via the collective of these standards. In Section 6 we present the mapping of these phenomena to the chosen general ontology. Section 7 discusses some of the problems faced as a result of the *excess* constructs. Section 8 concludes the chapter with a summary of outcomes, future directions, and some limitations of the presented work.

2. THE BUNGE-WAND-WEBER ONTOLOGICAL MODEL

Wand and Weber (1989a, 1989b, 1990a, 1990b, 1991, 1993, 1995) have investigated the branch of philosophy known as ontology (or meta-physics) as a foundation for understanding the process in developing an information system. Ontology is a well-established theoretical domain within philosophy dealing with models of reality. Today, however, interest in, and applicability of ontologies, extends to areas far beyond meta-physics. As Gruninger and Lee (2002) point out, "…a Web search engine will return over 64,000 pages given 'ontology' as a keyword…the first few pages are phrases such as "enabling virtual business", "gene ontology consortium, and "enterprise ontology"." It should be noted that a more recent Google search (July 2005) returned 4.4 million hits. The usefulness of ontology as a theoretical foundation for knowledge representation and natural language processing has been a fervently debated topic in the artificial intelligence research community (2002). Holsapple and Joshi (2002) for example, argue the importance of ontologies in the emergent era of knowledge-based organizations and the conduct of knowledge management in those organizations. Kim (2002) shows how ontologies can be engineered to support the first phase of the evolution of the 'semantic Web'.

Wand and Weber (1989a, 1989b, 1990a, 1990b, 1993, 1995) and Weber (1997) have taken, and extended, an ontology presented by Bunge (1977) and applied it to the modeling of information systems. Their fundamental premise is that any ISAD modeling grammar must be able to represent all things in the real world that might be of interest to users of information systems; otherwise, the resultant model is incomplete. If the model is incomplete, the analyst/designer will somehow have to augment the model(s) to ensure that the final computerized information system adequately reflects that portion of the real world it is intended to support. The Bunge-Wand-Weber (BWW) models (1989a, 1989b, 1990a, 1990b, 1993, 1995) consist of the representation model, the state-tracking model, and the good decomposition model. This work focuses on the representation model. The representation model defines a set of constructs that, at this time, is thought by the researchers to be necessary and sufficient to describe the structure and behavior of the real world. This model can, therefore, be used as a benchmark for the evaluation of ISAD grammars.

Weber (1997) clarifies the two cases that may occur when an ISAD grammar is analyzed according to the representation model. After a particular ISAD grammar has been analyzed, predictions on the modeling strengths and weaknesses of the grammar can be made according to whether some or any of these situations arise out of the analysis.

1. *Ontological Incompleteness (or Construct Deficit)* exists unless there is at least one ISAD grammatical construct for each ontological construct.
2. *Ontological Clarity* is determined by the extent to which the grammar does not exhibit one or more of the following deficiencies:
   – *Construct Overload* exists in an ISAD grammar if at least one ISAD grammatical construct represents more than one ontological construct.
   – *Construct Redundancy* exists if more than one ISAD grammatical construct represents the same ontological construct.
   – *Construct Excess* exists in an ISAD grammar when an ISAD grammatical construct is present that does not map into any ontological construct.

Table 21-1 presents plain English definitions of the constructs of the BWW representation model (from Wand & Weber (1993) and Weber (1997) with minor modifications). (Fundamental and core ontological constructs are identified by a '*'.)

Green *et al.* (2003) argue that, in order to achieve a better degree of interoperability, there is a need for an agreement on a general ontology that can be used to describe any type of phenomena that occurs within the ESI domain. A general ontology is a theory that describes the structure and dynamics of the world *in general*. It should, therefore, be capable of describing any phenomenon in the world. On the one hand, a general ontology is a taxonomic tool. It provides a means of precisely classifying phenomena in the world. On the other hand, it is a predictive tool. It allows the existence of certain kinds of phenomena and relationships among certain kinds of phenomena to be anticipated. For instance, Bunge's ontology (1977) describes the world as being made of things, properties of things, states of things, events that occur to things, laws, transformations, couplings, systems, and so on. Anything in the world is an instance of one of these constructs. Bunge's ontology also predicts the existence of certain types of phenomena when other types of phenomena exist. For instance, if two things in the world are coupled, the composite thing comprising the two things that are coupled will have at least one emergent property (a property not possessed by the individual things in the coupling).

Table 21-1. Ontological constructs in the BWW representation model

Ontological Construct	Explanation
THING*	A thing is the elementary unit in the BWW ontological model. The real world is made up of things. Two or more things (composite or simple) can be associated into a composite thing.
PROPERTY*: IN GENERAL IN PARTICULAR HEREDITARY EMERGENT INTRINSIC NON-BINDING MUTUAL BINDING MUTUAL	Things possess properties. A property is modeled via a function that maps the thing into some value. For example, the attribute "weight" represents a property that all humans possess. In this regard, weight is an attribute standing for a property in general. If we focus on the weight of a specific individual, however, we would be concerned with a property in particular. A property of a composite thing that belongs to a component thing is called an hereditary property. Otherwise it is called an emergent property. Some properties are inherent properties of individual things. Such properties are called intrinsic. Other properties are properties of pairs or many things. Such properties are called mutual. Non-binding mutual properties are those properties shared by two or more things that do not "make a difference" to the things involved; for example, order relations or equivalence relations. By contrast, binding mutual properties are those properties shared by two or more things that do "make a difference" to the things involved.
ATTRIBUTES	Attributes are the names that we use to represent properties of things.
CLASS	A class is a set of things that can be defined via their possessing a single property.
KIND	A kind is a set of things that can be defined only via their possessing two or more common properties.
STATE*	The vector of values for all property functions of a thing is the state of the thing.
CONCEIVABLE STATE SPACE	The set of all states that the thing might ever assume is the conceivable state space of the thing.
STATE LAW	A state law restricts the values of the properties of a thing to a subset that is deemed lawful because of natural laws or human laws.
LAWFUL STATE SPACE	The lawful state space is the set of states of a thing that comply with the state laws of the thing. The lawful state space is usually a proper subset of the conceivable state space.

Ontological Construct	Explanation
EVENT	A change in state of a thing is an event.
CONCEIVABLE EVENT SPACE	The event space of a thing is the set of all possible events that can occur in the thing.
TRANSFORMATION*	A transformation is a mapping from one state to another state.
LAWFUL TRANSFORMATION	A lawful transformation defines which events in a thing are lawful.
LAWFUL EVENT SPACE	The lawful event space is the set of all events in a thing that are lawful.
HISTORY	The chronologically-ordered states that a thing traverses in time are the history of the thing.
ACTS ON	A thing acts on another thing if its existence affects the history of the other thing.
COUPLING: BINDING MUTUAL PROPERTY	Two things are said to be coupled (or interact) if one thing acts on the other. Furthermore, those two things are said to share a binding mutual property (or relation); that is, they participate in a relation that "makes a difference" to the things.
SYSTEM	A set of things is a system if, for any bi-partitioning of the set, couplings exist among things in the two subsets.
SYSTEM COMPOSITION	The things in the system are its composition.
SYSTEM ENVIRONMENT	Things that are not in the system but interact with things in the system are called the environment of the system.
SYSTEM STRUCTURE	The set of couplings that exist among things within the system, and among things in the environment of the system and things in the system is called the structure.
SUBSYSTEM	A subsystem is a system whose composition and structure are subsets of the composition and structure of another system.
SYSTEM DECOMPOSITION	A decomposition of a system is a set of subsystems such that every component in the system is either one of the subsystems in the decomposition or is included in the composition of one of the subsystems in the decomposition.
LEVEL STRUCTURE	A level structure defines a partial order over the subsystems in a decomposition to show which subsystems are components of other subsystems or the system itself.
EXTERNAL EVENT	An external event is an event that arises in a thing, subsystem, or system by virtue of the action of some thing in the environment on the thing, subsystem, or system.
STABLE STATE*	A stable state is a state in which a thing, subsystem, or system will remain unless forced to change by virtue of the action of a thing in the environment (an external event).
UNSTABLE STATE	An unstable state is a state that will be changed into another state by virtue of the action of transformations in the system.
INTERNAL EVENT	An internal event is an event that arises in a thing, subsystem, or system by virtue of lawful transformations in the thing, subsystem, or system.
WELL-DEFINED EVENT	A well-defined event is an event in which the subsequent state can always be predicted given that the prior state is known.
POORLY-DEFINED EVENT	A poorly-defined event is an event in which the subsequent state cannot be predicted given that the prior state is known.

In terms of interoperability, unless the domain phenomena represented by two standards are based upon a common general ontology, interoperability will be limited because of a lack of shared understanding or conceptualization of the relevant real-world constructs. For example, consider a general ontology that distinguishes between things and properties of things in the world and another general ontology that makes no such distinction (the world is only made up of things or objects). In the context of conceptual modeling, the former general ontology is the underpinning for grammars like the entity-relationship grammar (Chen, 1976) and various object-oriented grammars (Opdahl & Henderson-Sellers, 2001). The latter ontology is the underpinning for the object-role grammar (Halpin, 2001).

We argue that the well established representation model in the Bunge-Wand-Weber (BWW) suite of models is a good choice of general ontology for a number of reasons. The BWW representation model appears to be relatively complete and general (*c.f.* the ontologies of Edmund Husserl and Achille Varzi – partial ontologies) and its constructs are clearly and rigorously defined using set-theoretic language. The representation model also has much overlap with existing concepts in the Information Systems modeling world. It contains all constructs currently thought necessary to model things and interactions between things in the real world. In various conceptual modeling grammars and enterprise systems interoperability standards we seek to represent such things and interactions between them. It then follows that these grammars and standards should have a representation for each of the constructs in the BWW representation model. Further, we, and other researchers, have shown the usefulness of the BWW representation model for analyzing, evaluating, and engineering techniques in the areas of traditional and structured systems analysis, object-oriented modeling, and process modeling (see Section 3).

3. RELATED RESEARCH

To date, the related work utilizing the BWW models has almost exclusively been focused on business analysis modeling techniques such as DFDs, ER diagrams, object-oriented schemas, and process modeling grammars such as ARIS. Table 21-2 summarizes several important items of related BWW work. Only BWW work relevant process modeling and Enterprise Systems interoperability is discussed in more detail. For detailed analysis of the other existing BWW related research the reader can refer to Green and Rosemann (2002) and Green, Rosemann and Indulska (2005).

Table 21-2. Related work using the BWW models

	Business Systems Analysis Grammar					Ontological			Other
Study	Traditional	Structured	Data Centered	O-O	Process	Completeness	Clarity	Good Decomposition	
Wand & Weber (1989b)		✓	✓			✓			
Wand & Weber (1993, 1995)			✓			✓			
Weber (1997)			✓			✓	✓		
Weber & Zhang (1996)			✓			✓	✓		
Green (1997)	✓	✓	✓			✓	✓		
Parsons & Wand (1997)				✓		✓	✓		
Wand, Storey & Weber (1999)			✓				✓		
Rosemann & Green (2000)						✓	✓		✓
Green & Rosemann (2000)					✓	✓	✓		
Bodart *et al.* (2001)			✓				✓		
Opdahl & Henderson-Sellers (2001)				✓			✓		
Soffer *et al.* (2001)				✓	✓	✓	✓		✓
Evermann & Wand (2001)				✓					
Green & Rosemann (2002a)					✓	✓	✓		
Green & Rosemann (2002b)						✓	✓		✓
Sia & Soh (2002)						✓			✓
Burton-Jones & Meso (2002)				✓				✓	
Shanks *et al.* (2003)			✓	✓			✓		
Opdahl & Henderson-Sellers (2002)				✓		✓	✓		
Rosemann & Green (2002)				✓	✓	✓	✓		
Davies, Green & Rosemann (2002)						✓	✓		✓
Davies *et al.* (2003)						✓	✓		✓
Davies, Rosemann, Green (2004)					✓	✓	✓		
Fettke & Loos (2003)						✓	✓		✓
Green, Rosemann & Indulska (2005)						✓	✓		✓
Green *et al.* (2005)						✓	✓		✓

Green and Rosemann (2002b), Green, Rosemann and Indulska (2005) and, Green *et al.* (2005) extend the application of the BWW models into the domain of Enterprise Systems interoperability. Their work utilizes the BWW representation model for the purpose of analysis of leading Enterprise Systems interoperability grammars, *viz.* ebXML, BPEL4WS, BPML, and WSCI. The results of the analysis indicate a number of potential shortcomings of the individual grammars, as well as some shortcomings of the four leading standards as a whole.

Soffer *et al.* (2001) propose an ontology-based model for the evaluation of off-the-shelf information systems requirements (OISR) specifications. The work uses the BWW model as a basis for the formulation of a specialized evaluation framework for OISR. The developed framework is demonstrated through its application to the Object-Process Methodology (OPM), resulting in the identification of deficiencies in ontological clarity of OPM, while finding that OPM is ontologically complete (with respect to the specialized framework). Furthermore, the authors go on to perform an ontological comparison of OPM and ARIS, finding that OPM is superior to ARIS for the purposes of OISR modeling. These findings, however, are not followed up by an empirical study.

Green and Rosemann (2000) have extended the analytical work into the area of integrated process modeling based on the techniques presented in Scheer (2000). This analysis identified omissions in not just the individual views (data, function, organization, process, and output) but when the views are used in combination also. For example, even across the four views, no representations exist for *conceivable state space, lawful state space, conceivable event space*, or *lawful event space*. Accordingly, it is hypothesized that a sufficient focus to identify all-important state and transformation laws may not be present during modeling. Hence, problems will be encountered in capturing all the potentially important business rules of the situation. Furthermore, Green and Rosemann (2002a) attempted to test the propositions of Green and Rosemann (2000) with postgraduate students who were involved in process modeling projects in industry. Essentially, they found support for their propositions with regard to the modeling of necessary business rules, the scope and boundary of systems, and the decomposition of systems. Unfortunately, their study was limited in terms of the sample size.

As shown in Table 21-2, of the listed twenty-six works that utilize the BWW models, one has applied the model for the purpose of analyzing traditional ISAD grammars. Structured ISAD grammars have been analyzed in two of the listed works, while data-centered and object-oriented grammars were analyzed in eight of the works respectively. Five publications have also focused on the process modeling domain, while nine have applied the BWW models for other purposes, e.g. activity based costing or off-the-shelf information systems requirements modeling. Of those nine, three focus on Enterprise Systems interoperability. Of all the listed publications, twenty have to some degree focused on the concept of ontological completeness with respect to the BWW model; twenty-one have considered ontological clarity, while one has considered good decomposition.

4. RESEARCH METHODOLOGY

The research presented in this paper can be divided into two distinct stages. The first stage involves the BWW representation mapping analysis of each of the standards in question; ebXML BPSS, BPML, BPEL4WS and WSCI. The second stage involves an analysis of the mapped grammatical constructs in order to identify a set of unique constructs in the domain of ESI.

4.1 BWW representation mapping analysis

The current practice of ontological analysis is not without its criticisms (see *e.g.*, Green & Rosemann, 2002a, 2002b; Rosemann, Green & Indulska, 2004). Being mindful on these criticisms, we extended the current practice and a research methodology was developed and employed that improved the internal and external validities (Rosemann, Green & Indulska, 2004). This process was achieved through the undertaking of individual analyses by at least two members of the research team, followed by consensus as to the final analysis by the entire group of researchers. Each of the candidate standards was dealt with separately using this methodology. ebXML BPSS 1.01 (2001) was the first for analysis, followed by BPML 1.0 (2002), BPEL4WS 1.1 (2003) and WSCI 1.0 (2002). In the analysis of each of these protocols, four distinct steps were taken to arrive at the final representation modeling analysis. A deeper discussion of the entire process of ontological analysis can be found in Rosemann, Green & Indulska (2004).

Step 1: Using the specification of the candidate standard, two of the researchers separately read the specification and interpreted, selected and mapped the BWW ontological constructs to candidate grammatical constructs to create individual first drafts of the analysis.

Step 2: These two researchers met to discuss and defend their interpretations of the representation modeling analysis. This meeting led to an agreed second draft version of the analysis that incorporated elements of both researchers' first draft analyses. In order to assess the degree to which both researchers' first draft analyses agreed, a ratio of the total number of agreed construct mappings to the total number of identified constructs from the specification (by both researchers) expressed as a percentage of mapping agreement was recorded.

Step 3: The second draft version of the analysis for each of the interoperability candidate standards was then used as a basis for defense and discussion in a meeting between the first two researchers and the remaining researchers. Each of the standards was dealt with individually in separate meetings as each of the second draft analyses was finalized. The outcomes of these meetings were the final results for each of these standards.

Step 4: The final analysis for each of the candidate standards became the basis for the second phase of the research, in which a unique set of grammatical constructs was identified.

4.2 Grammatical Construct Overlap Analysis

Once the individual representation modeling analyses were completed for all four of the candidate interoperability standards, the mapped grammatical constructs were analyzed in order to arrive at a set of *unique* grammatical constructs in the domain of ESI. This process was achieved through the undertaking of a systematic grammatical construct comparison that was carried out between grammatical constructs that have been mapped to the *same* ontological construct. For example, taking the set of all grammatical constructs (across the four standards) that have been mapped to the ontological construct *event*, we compared the definitions of the constructs and eliminated any duplicate constructs arriving at a set of unique grammatical constructs that represents an *event* in this domain.

This analysis was performed in the same order as analysis at stage one, *i.e.* given a set of constructs that have been found to map to a specific ontological construct, ebXML BPSS (2001) constructs were considered first, followed by the analysis and elimination of equivalent BPML (2002) constructs, then followed by the analysis and elimination of equivalent BPEL4WS (2003) constructs, and, finally, followed by the analysis and elimination of equivalent WSCI (2002) constructs. Adopting this process may result in a situation in which, having had a different starting point, the set of unique grammatical constructs found across the four standards may be slightly different as constructs representing the same phenomenon may have different names across the specifications. This situation, however, is not considered to be problematic as the *meaning* of the constructs is the same, regardless of the construct name chosen by the specification's authors.

5. PHENOMENA WITHIN THE ENTERPRISE SYSTEMS INTEROPERABILITY DOMAIN

Green *et al.* (2003) argue that one of the requirements of achieving full interoperability is the *a priori* agreement on the set of phenomena that exist within the domain being modeled. In answer to this requirement, one of the motivations of our research was to analyze, using the BWW representation model, the leading standards in the ESI domain in order to be able to provide practitioners and the authors of these standards with a clearer picture of the perceived requirements of Enterprise System interoperability.

The analysis of these standards has shown that there exist six ontological constructs with no representation in *any* of the four standards (Green *et al.*, 2005). These are *thing, kind, conceivable event space, system environment, system decomposition* and *level structure.* From the results of this analysis we can deduce that there will be some weaknesses or problems when these standards are used in their current versions. Each case of a missing representation for an ontological construct implies that the standard in question is unable to model some type of phenomena in the real world. For example, the lack of representation for the *kind* ontological construct limits the specification in its ability to model subtypes. At this stage, it is unclear if representation for these ontological constructs is perhaps not required in the domain of ESI or if it is erroneously missing. Empirical testing is required in order to ascertain the need for the existence of grammatical constructs in this domain that allow representation of the missing ontological constructs.

The analysis has also shown that, while there is an overlap between these standards, each standard adds additional constructs for the purpose of facilitating interoperability (Green *et al.,* 2005). From this analysis we can deduce the set of unique constructs required for the enterprise systems interoperability domain, as represented by the four leading standards *viz.* ebXML, BPEL4WS, BPML, and WSCI.

After the initial identification of missing ontological constructs, we concentrate on the remaining twenty-six ontological constructs for which a mapping does exist in one or more of the ESI standards. Correspondingly, the representation mapping results have been further analyzed in order to eliminate any overlapping constructs across the four standards. We consider such a set of unique grammatical constructs found to have a mapping to the BWW representation model, to be a good representation of the domain of ESI as currently accepted by the collective of the authors of these standards. Table 21-3 lists the obtained set of constructs, while differentiating them by the standard from which they derive (as per research methodology outlined).

Table 21-3. Set of unique grammatical constructs across the four ESI standards

ebXML	BPEL4WS	BPML	WSCI
-Business Partner Role	-Correlation Set	-Property	-Set of properties
-Authorized Role	-Partner	-Property Instance	-One-Way Action
-Attribute Definitions	-Set of variables	-Names of Properties	-Request-Response Action
-Business Document	-Reply	-Signal	-Notification Action
-Document Envelope	-Create Instance (on Activity)	-Message	-Solicit-Response Action
-Attachment	-Wait	-Event (Process Defn.)	-Instantiation (Process)
-Start	-Event Handler	-Instant(Schedule Defn.)	-Delay
-Success	-Receive	-Action	-On Timeout
-Failure	-Throw	-Assign	-On Fault
-Fork	-Terminate	-Fault	-Model
-Join	-Alarm Event (onAlarm)	-Raise	
-Wellformedness Rules	-Message Event (onMessage)	-Compensate	
-RequestingBusinessActivity	-Pick	-Compensation Process	
-RespondingBusiness-Activity	-Role	-Exception Process	
-Business Transaction	-Service Link	-Process	
-<preCondition> and <postCondition> on Business Transaction & Binary Collaboration	-Business Process Instance	-Fault Handler	
-Transition	-Partners	-Schedule	
-Transition obeying Wellformedness rules		-Transaction	
-Choreography		-While	
-BusinessTransaction-Activity		-Until	
-CollaborationActivity		-Switch	
-Binary Collaboration		-Condition	
-Multi-Party Collaboration			

While this derived set of constructs can serve as the description of the currently assumed modeling requirements of ESI, agreement on this set alone is not enough to facilitate a greater extent of interoperability. In order to increase such capability, there must also be an agreement on the mapping of these phenomena, or grammatical constructs, to the chosen general ontology. If such an agreement does not exist, interoperability will be hampered by assumptions of construct equivalence where none exists. Essentially, even if two machines use the same general ontology to represent domain phenomena, they must also use the same mapping between domain phenomena and the general ontology if interoperability is not to be limited (Green *et al.,* 2003).

6. MAPPING TO THE GENERAL ONTOLOGY

In this section we present the mapping of the unique set of constructs to the BWW representation model – our chosen general ontology. The mapping was obtained by the application of the BWW representation analysis methodology described in Section 4. The results of the mapping are summarized in Table 21-4. Due to space constraints we are unable to present the reasoning behind the mapping of each of the unique constructs. Instead, we present, for demonstration, the reasoning behind the results of the mapping for a number of chosen ontological constructs, *viz. state law, lawful state space, history, acts on, system, system structure*, and, *sub-system*. Detailed explanations of the results of the representation mapping of each of the standards are presented in Green, Rosemann & Indulska (2005) and Green *et al.* (2005).

Table 21-4. Summary of identified mappings for non-redundant constructs

Ontological Construct	Specification Constructs
THING	
PROPERTY	
IN GENERAL	Property
IN PARTICULAR	Property Instance
HEREDITARY	
EMERGENT	Business Partner Role, Authorized Role, Correlation Set
INTRINSIC	
MUTUAL NON-BINDING	
MUTUAL BINDING	BusinessTransactionActivity, CollaborationActivity, Service Link
ATTRIBUTES	Attribute Definitions, Names of Properties
CLASS	Business Document, Document Envelope, Attachment, Partner
KIND	
STATE	Start, Success, Failure, Fork, Join, Signal, Set of variables/properties
CONCEIVABLE STATE SPACE	Set of all states identified in State
STATE LAW	Wellformedness Rules
LAWFUL STATE SPACE	Set of all states conforming to all Wellformedness Rules
EVENT	RequestingBusinessActivity, RespondingBusinessActivity, Business Transaction, Message, Event (Process Definition), Instant (Schedule Definition), Reply, Create Instance (on Activity), Wait, One-Way Action, Request-Response Action, Notification Action, Solicit-Response Action, Instantiation (Process)

Ontological Construct	Specification Constructs
CONCEIVABLE EVENT SPACE	Set of all events identified above
LAWFUL EVENT SPACE	All events satisfying the Wellformedness Rules, <preCondition,postCondition> on Business Transaction & Binary Collaboration
TRANSFORMATION	Transition, Action, Assign, Fault, Raise, Compensate, Compensation Process, Exception Process, Process, Fault Handler, Schedule, Event Handler, Receive, Throw, Terminate, Alarm Event (onAlarm), Message Event (onMessage), Delay, On Timeout, On Fault
LAWFUL TRANSFORMATION	A Transition which obeys all Wellformedness rules, Transaction, While, Until, Switch, Pick
STABILITY CONDITION	Condition
HISTORY	Choreography
ACTS ON	Role
COUPLING: BINDING MUTUAL PROPERTY	BusinessTransactionActivity, CollaborationActivity, Service Link
SYSTEM	Binary Collaboration, Multi-Party Collaboration, Business Process Instance, Model
SYSTEM COMPOSITION	Partners
SYSTEM ENVIRONMENT	
SYSTEM STRUCTURE	Partners
SUBSYSTEM	Binary Collaboration
SYSTEM DECOMPOSITION	
LEVEL STRUCTURE	
STABLE STATE	Start, Fork, Join, Success
UNSTABLE STATE	Failure
EXTERNAL EVENT	Requesting Business Activity, <BeginsWhen> on Binary Collaboration & Business Transaction, <EndsWhen> on Binary Collaboration, Message, Event (Process Definition), One-Way Action, Request-Response Action, Instantiation (Process)
INTERNAL EVENT	Business Transaction, Responding Business Activity, <EndsWhen> on Business Transaction, Instant (Schedule Definition), Reply, Create Instance (on Activity), Wait, Notification Action, Solicit-Response Action, Fault
WELL-DEFINED EVENT	RequestingBusinessActivity, Event (Process Definition), Instant (Schedule Definition), Create Instance (on Activity), Instantiation (Process), Fault
POORLY-DEFINED EVENT	Business Transaction, Responding Business Activity, Message, Reply, One-Way Action, Request-Response Action, Notification Action, Solicit-Response Action

The ontological construct *state law* has been found to have a representation only in ebXML. There exists a clear mapping of *state law* to an ebXML Wellformedness Rule (specified as a textual constraint in the specification). There is no actual construct to represent the *lawful state space*. However, we can identify the scope of the *lawful state space* construct as the set of all states that conform to the set of all Wellformedness Rules despite the lack of construct mapping. The lack of such constructs, however, impacts on the ability to achieve in-depth understanding of a system as the user is not aware of all states that a system might enter.

The ontological construct *history* has been found to only have representation in the ebXML specification. There is an unambiguous mapping between *history* and the ebXML construct Choreography. Choreography lists the chronological transitions of states of the system. This definition fits neatly with the definition of a *history* ontological construct. However, it is unclear from the specification how the construct is used or where such a choreography is stored.

The ontological construct *acts on* has also been found to be represented solely by one of the four chosen standards. A *thing* is said to *act-on* another *thing* if its existence affects the history of the other *thing*. The BPEL4WS Role construct specifies how one partner acts on another partner by specifying the roles the partners play in an interaction.

The ontological construct *system* has been found to have a mapping to ebXML, BPEL4WS and WSCI constructs. *System* is comparable to the BinaryCollaboration and MultiPartyCollaboration ebXML constructs. A BinaryCollaboration is a protocol of interaction between two roles that cannot be broken up further into two sets with no couplings. Furthermore, MultiPartyCollaboration is partitioned into subsystems. However, couplings exist between the subsystems; therefore MultiPartyCollaboration is itself a system. From the definition of a MultiPartyCollaboration, "a synthesis of BinaryCollaborations", it is clear that BinaryCollaboration is itself a *sub-system*. A Business Process Instance in BPEL4WS involves a number of partners (no restriction on the actual number of participants) interacting with each other to accomplish a common goal – again, a *system*. For example, an instance of a ticket booking business process involves a traveler, a travel agent and the airline, working together in order to obtain a ticket booking that meets the traveler's requirements. Such a scenario fits in with the BWW definition of a system being a set of things coupled together. Additionally, the WSCI Model construct describes the message exchange view of a process in terms of participants and links between operations of communicating participants. These links indicate direct message flow between the linked operations and therefore represent the couplings between things in the system.

The ontological construct *system structure* has been found to have a mapping to the BPEL4WS Partners construct (differentiated from the BPEL4WS Partner construct). The Partners construct defines *all* the partners that are taking part in a particular business process instance, thus defining all *things* within the system (*system composition*). It also defines what the roles of the individual partners are, therefore also modeling the couplings that exist among the things in the system (*system structure*).

7. TOWARDS REPLICATING HUMAN CONSTRUCTIVIST PROCESSES

We argue that the fourth and final step for true interoperability to be achieved is a process that, where confusion has occurred, allows meaning to be negotiated and assigned to constructs by the interacting parties. This process would be akin to the situation when two humans are attempting to communicate and interoperate. Even though the syntax of the language used for the communication is correct between the interacting parties, there usually will be confusion over the ascribed meaning for one or more of the language constructs used. In such circumstances, the confused party initiates a human constructivist process of negotiating and assigning meaning to the construct(s) in question. The confused party asks, "What do you mean by….?" In a similar manner, for true interoperability to occur, interacting systems need to be able to complete a similar constructivist process. The systems need to be able to ask, "What do you mean by this construct(s)?"

In Green *et al.* (2003), we proposed that this step, at the present point in time, significantly limits full interoperability. Indeed, information systems of today generally lack the ability to replicate the constructivist process that humans use to ascribe meaning to new or existing phenomena. Essentially, computers do not have the same ability to reason as humans do. Until they do, they will not be able to negotiate automatically interactions with each other – this limitation appears to persist well into the foreseeable future. However, we argue that, having accomplished our steps 1-3, this problem of limited constructivist ability can be mitigated.

Having performed our steps 1-3, we have identified the *common* grammar for the context or domain of interoperating information systems. We have ascribed real-world meaning to these grammatical constructs within the domain of systems interoperability by mapping them to underlying real-world ontology. If a construct is used during interoperation and one of the participating parties does not understand how to interpret the construct, the meaning of the construct(s) may be able to be deduced through AI-based systems tailored to the domain of understanding – Enterprise Systems interoperability.

In terms of our analysis of the four competing standards for interoperability, we found many constructs to exhibit excess (e.g. DocumentSecurity (ebXML), Performs (ebXML), Empty (BPML), Message Definitions (BPEL4WS), Selector (WSCI)) – that is, they had no apparent real-world meaning.

We suspect that, when a company uses one or more of these constructs in an implementation of interoperability for its information system, the implementer(s) usually will have a different understanding of some of the constructs from those used by implementer(s) at another company. This situation would be particularly exacerbated with constructs deemed as *excess*. Interoperability implementers at different companies may well ascribe totally different meanings to *excess* constructs, even though they are using the same syntax of the standards across different companies' systems. Although limited in its use, an AI-based system sensitive to the *domain-focused* ontology of Enterprise Systems interoperability can help to deduce (-partially negotiate) and ascribe consensual meaning for those *excess* constructs. In this way, our steps 1-3 can provide a basis on which to mitigate the current problem for systems interoperability of implementing the equivalent of a human constructivist process to ascribe meaning.

8. CONCLUSIONS AND FUTURE WORK

While this paper demonstrates the wide application of the BWW model from the evaluation and comparison of Information Systems Analysis and Design techniques to the area of ESI standards, its main purpose and contribution lies in addressing the four fundamental problems currently thought to be limiting interoperability (as identified by Green *et al.* (2003)). These problems include the lack of agreement on a general ontology, lack of agreement on a set of phenomena within a considered domain, lack of agreement on the mapping of the phenomena to the general ontology, and, finally, lack of capability for replicating the constructivist process that humans use to ascribe meaning to these phenomena. Accordingly, and in the light of the dominating web services standards, *viz.*, ebXML, BPML, BPEL4WS and WSCI, we address the aforementioned problems in the domain of enterprise systems interoperability.

We propose that the BWW representation model is suitable as a general ontology for ESI standards due to its ability to represent all *things* in the real world, and the interactions between those *things*, as well as due to its rigorous definition. We further examine the four leading ESI standards in order to derive the set of phenomena and their mappings to the general ontology that is thought currently to be required in modeling this domain. Last, we discuss the problem in true interoperability of being able to negotiate and ascribe meaning to constructs. In other words, when implementers in one system ascribe meaning and use constructs in the interoperability language in a different way from what implementers in another system might be expecting, we discuss a possible mechanism to mitigate this problem by facilitating the systems being able to ask partially the human constructivist question, "What do you mean by…?"

While we have made every effort to increase the validity of our analysis, *viz.*, using independent analyzers and then using different levels of review of the analysis, limitations in the work remain. Most notably, the level of granularity in the definition of certain constructs in the standards was significantly different from that of the ontological constructs. So, while two or more constructs (across different standards) might be representing the same ontological construct generally, the manner in which they were intended to be used or executed obviously was not the same. The implications of the difference between ontological meaning, and use or execution, will be investigated further in subsequent work into refining the research methodology.

Future work in this area will involve empirical validation of our analyses of the four enterprise interoperability standards, as well as further research into ontological analysis methodologies and fine-tuning the BWW representation model specifically for the ESI domain. Work on a scoring model that allows for easier comparison of ontological analyses of various grammars is also underway.

REFERENCES

BEA Systems, International Business Machines Corporation, Microsoft Corporation, SAP AG, and Siebel Systems, 2003, *Business Process Execution Language for Web Services v1.1*

Bodart, F., Patel, A., Sim, M., and Weber, R., 2001, Should Optional Properties be used in Conceptual Modeling? A Theory and Three Empirical Tests, *Information Systems Research,* **12**(4):384 405.

BPMI.org, 2002, *Business Process Modeling Language.*

Bunge, M., 1977, *Treatise on Basic Philosophy: Volume 3: Ontology I: The Furniture of the World*, Reidel, Boston.

Burton-Jones, A. and Meso, P., 2002, How good are these UML diagrams? An empirical test of the Wand and Weber good decomposition model, in: *23rd International Conference on Information Systems*, Barcelona.

Chen, P.P.S., 1976, The Entity-Relationship Model – Toward a Unified View of Data, *ACM Transactions on Database Systems*, **1**(1): 9 36.

Davies, I., Green, P., Milton, S., and Rosemann, M., 2003, Using Meta Models for the Comparison of Ontologies, in: *Evaluation of Modeling Methods in Systems Analysis and Design Workshop*, Klagenfurt.

Davies, I., Green, P., and Rosemann, M., 2002, Facilitating an Ontological Foundation of Information Systems with Meta Models, in: *13th Australasian Conference on Information Systems*, Melbourne.

Davies, I., Rosemann, M., and Green, P., 2004, Exploring Proposed Ontological Issues of ARIS with Different Categories of Modellers, in: *15th Australasian Conference on Information Systems*, Hobart.

Evermann, J. and Wand, Y., 2001, Towards Ontologically Based Semantics for UML Constructs, in: *20th International Conference on Conceptual Modeling (ER)*, Yokohama,

Fettke, P. and Loos, P., 2003, Ontological evaluation of reference models using the Bunge-Wand-Weber-Model, in: *9th Americas Conference on Information Systems,* Tampa.

Green, P., Indulska, M., Rosemann, M., and Weber, R., 2003, Will XML technologies and web services solve the interoperability problem?, in: *International Workshop on Utility, Usability and Complexity of Emergent IS*, Namur.

Green, P., Rosemann, M., and Indulska, M., 2005, Ontological evaluation of enterprise systems interoperability using ebXML. *IEEE Transactions on Knowledge and Data Engineering*, **17**(5):713 725.

Green, P., Rosemann, M., Indulska, M., and Manning, C., 2005, Candidate Interoperability Standards: An Ontological Overlap Analysis, *UQ Business School Report*, The University of Queensland, Brisbane.

Green, P.F., 1997, Use of Information Systems Analysis and Design (ISAD) Grammars in Combination in Upper CASE Tools - An Ontological Evaluation, in: *2nd CaiSE/IFIP8.1 International Workshop on the Evaluation of Modeling Methods in Systems Analysis and Design*, Barcelona.

Green, P.F. and Rosemann, M., 2000, Integrated process modeling: An ontological evaluation, *Information Systems*, **25**(2):73 87.

Green, P.F. and Rosemann, M., 2002a, Perceived ontological weaknesses of process modeling techniques: Further evidence, in: *10th European Conference on Information Systems*, Poland.

Green, P.F. and Rosemann, M., 2002b, Usefulness of the BWW Ontological Models as a "Core" Theory of Information Systems, in: *Information Systems Foundations: Building the Theoretical Base*, Canberra.

Gruninger, M. and Lee, J., 2002, Ontology: Applications and design, *Communications of the ACM*, **45**(2):39 41.

Halpin, T., 2001, *Information Modeling and Relational Databases: From Conceptual Analysis to Logical Design*, Morgan Kaufmann, San Francisco.

Holsapple, C.W. and Joshi, K.D., 2002, A Collaborative Approach to Ontology Design, *Communications of the ACM*, **45**(2):42 47.

Kim, H.M., 2002, Predicting how the Semantic Web will evolve, *Communications of the ACM*, **45**(2):48 54.

Opdahl, A.L. and Henderson-Sellers, B., 2001, Grounding the OML metamodel in ontology, *Journal of Systems and Software*, **57**(2):119 143.

Opdahl, A.L. and Henderson-Sellers, B., 2002, Ontological evaluation of the UML using the Bunge-Wand-Weber Model, *Software and Systems Modeling*, **1**(1):43 67.

Parsons, J. and Wand, W., 1997, Using objects in systems analysis, *Communications of the ACM*, **40**(12):104 110.

Rosemann, M. and Green, P., 2002, Developing a meta model for the Bunge-Wand-Weber ontological constructs, *Information Systems*, **27**(2):75 91.

Rosemann, M., Green, P., and Indulska, M., 2004, A Reference Methodology for Conducting Ontological Analyses, in: *International Conference on Conceptual Modeling (ER)*, Shanghai.

Rosemann, M. and Green, P.F., 2000, Integrating Multi-Perspectives into Ontologies, in: *21st International Conference on Information Systems*, Brisbane.

Rosemann, M., Vessey, I., and Weber, R., 2004, Alignment in enterprise systems implementations: The role of ontological distance, in: *25th International Conference on Information Systems*, Washington D.C..

Scheer, A.-W., 2000, *ARIS - Business Process Modeling*. 3 ed., Springer, Berlin.

Shanks, G., Tansley, E., and Weber, R., 2003, Using ontology to validate conceptual models, *Communications of the ACM*, **46**(10):85 89.

Sia, S.K. and Soh, C., 2002, Severity assessment of ERP-organization misalignment: Honing in on ontological structure and context specificity, in: *23rd International Conference on Information Systems*, Barcelona.

Soffer, P., Boaz, G., Dori, D., and Wand, Y., 2001, Modeling off-the-shelf information systems requirements: An ontological approach, *Requirements Engineering*, **6**:183 199.

UN/CEFACT and OASIS, 2001, *ebXML Business Process Specification Schema.*

W3C, 2002, *Web Service Choreography Interface*.

Wand, Y., Storey, V.C., and Weber, R., 1999, An ontological analysis of the relationship construct in conceptual modeling, *ACM Journal*, **24**(4):494 528.

Wand, Y. and Weber, R., 1989a, A model of control and audit procedure change in evolving data processing systems, *The Accounting Review*, **LXIV**(1):87 107.

Wand, Y. and Weber, R., 1989b, An ontological evaluation of systems analysis and design methods, in: *Information System Concepts: An In-depth Analysis*, E.D. Falkenberg and P. Lindgreen, eds., North-Holland, pp. 79 107.

Wand, Y. and Weber, R., 1990a, Mario Bunge's Ontology as a formal foundation for information systems concepts, in *Studies on Mario Bunge's Treatise*, P. Weingartner and G.J.W. Dorn, eds., Rodopi, Atlanta. pp. 123 149.

Wand, Y. and Weber, R., 1990b, An ontological model of an information system, *IEEE Transactions on Software Engineering*, **16**(11):1281 1291.

Wand, Y. and Weber, R., 1991, A unified model of software and data decomposition, in: *12th International Conference on Information Systems*, New York.

Wand, Y. and Weber, R., 1993, On the ontological expressiveness of information systems analysis and design grammars, *Journal of Information Systems*, **3**(4):217 237.

Wand, Y. and Weber, R., 1995, On the deep structure of information systems, *Information Systems Journal*, **5**:203 223.

Weber, R., 1997, *Ontological Foundations of Information Systems*. Coopers & Lybrand Accounting Research Methodology, Monograph No. 4, Melbourne.

Weber, R. and Zhang, Y., 1996, An analytical evaluation of NIAM's grammar for conceptual schema diagrams, *Information Systems Journal*, **6**(2):147 170.

Chapter 22

CONTEXT-AWARE ONTOLOGY SELECTION FRAMEWORK

Simone A. Ludwig[1] and S.M.S. Reyhani[2]

[1]*School of Computer Science, Cardiff University, Cardiff CF24 3AA, UK;* [2]*Department of Information Systems and Computing, Brunel University, Uxbridge, Middlesex UB8 3PH, UK*

Abstract: Automatic discovery of services is a crucial task for the e-Science and e-Business communities. Finding a suitable way to address this issue has become one of the key points to convert the Web in a distributed source of computation, as it enables the location of distributed services to perform a required functionality. To provide such an automatic location, the discovery process should be based on the semantic match between a declarative description of the service being sought and a description being offered. This problem requires not only an algorithm to match these descriptions, but also a language to declaratively express the capabilities of services. This section presents a context-aware ontology selection framework, which allows an increase in precision of the retrieved results by taking the contextual information into account.

Key words: Context information; semantic service discovery; web services

1. INTRODUCTION

Recently, more and more organizations are implementing IT systems across different departments. The challenge is to find a solution that is extensible, flexible and fits well with the existing legacy systems. Replacing legacy systems to cope with the new architecture is not only costly but also introduces a risk to fail. In this context, the traditional software architectures prove ineffective in providing the right level of cost effective and extensible Information systems across the organization boundaries. Service Oriented Architecture (SOA) [1] provides a relatively cheap and more cost-effective solution addressing these problems and challenges.

One important factor in defining a new model of Software Architecture is the ever-changing business model. Modern day business constantly needs to adapt to new customer bases. The ability to quickly adapt to the new customer base and new business partners is the key to success. Sharing IT systems with other organizations is a new trend in the business. For example, businesses like online auctions are opening their systems to third party organization in an effort to better reach their customer base. In this context, SOA offers benefit and cost-effectiveness to the business. The process of adapting to the changing business model is not an easy task. There are many legacy systems, which are difficult to make available to the new business partners. These legacy systems might need to change to support the new business functions and integrate to the newly developed IT systems or integrate to the IT systems of its partners'. The complexity of this on the whole is what makes it a constant challenge to organizations.

Dynamic discovery is an important component of SOA. At a high level, SOA is composed of three core components: service providers, service consumers and the directory service. The directory service is an intermediary between providers and consumers. Providers register with the directory service and consumers query the directory service to find service providers. Most directory services typically organize services based on criteria and categorize them. Consumers can then use the directory services' search capabilities to find providers. Embedding a directory service within SOA accomplishes the following:

- Scalability of services
- Decoupling consumers from providers
- Allowing updates of services
- Providing a look-up service for consumers
- Allowing consumers to choose between providers at runtime rather than hard-coding a single provider.

Although the concepts behind SOA were established long before web services came along, web services play a major role in SOA. This is because web services are built on top of well-known and platform-independent protocols (HTTP (Hypertext Transfer Protocol) [2], XML (Extensible Markup Language) [3], UDDI (Universal Description, Discovery and Integration) [4], WSDL (Web Service Description Language) [5] and SOAP (Simple Object Access Protocol) [6]). It is the combination of these protocols that make web services so attractive. Moreover, it is these protocols that fulfil the key requirements of a SOA. That is, a SOA requires that a service be dynamically discoverable and invokeable. This requirement is fulfilled by UDDI, WSDL and SOAP.

However, SOA in its current form only performs service discovery based on particular keyword queries from the user. This, in majority of the cases leads to low recall and low precision of the retrieved services. The reason might be that the query keywords are semantically similar but syntactically different from the terms in service descriptions. Another reason is that the query keywords might be syntactically equivalent but semantically different from the terms in the service description. Another problem with keyword-based service discovery approaches is that they cannot completely capture the semantics of a user's query because they do not consider the relations between the keywords. One possible solution for this problem is to use ontology-based retrieval.

In this approach, ontology is used for classification of the services based on their properties. This enables retrieval based on service types rather than keywords. This approach uses context information to discover services using context and service descriptions defined in ontology.

2. BACKGROUND TO ONTOLOGIES

When two or more parties seek a common understanding of something, they must work together to ensure that there is a high degree of correlation and similarity between the details of their respective descriptions and definitions of what they are trying to agree on [7]. This implies that shared understanding requires shared definitions. For example, day-to-day human interactions are made possible by the fact that our society's members share common knowledge and common values. This sharing of common understanding is categorized as the science of ontology, which involves the study of the general concepts and abstractions that make up the fundamental aspects of our world.

Until the 20th century, ontology was considered a sub-field of philosophy. Since the early 1990s, an ontology is also a way to model things in computer science and artificial intelligence. The meaning of the term *ontology* has evolved over the years, and its definition has been slightly blurred when applied to different areas of computing and cybernetics.

Despite certain claims, the term *ontology* is used in a radically different sense in artificial intelligence. This term first appeared in the artificial intelligence literature in 1992 in a paper by Gruber, who stated that "an ontology is a set of definitions of content-specific knowledge representation primitives: classes, relations, functions, and object constants" [8]. With this definition, ontology is both human and machine readable. Ontology, together with a syntax and semantics, provides the language by which knowledge-based systems can interoperate at the knowledge-level by exchanging assertions, queries and answers.

For Gruber, ontology is the term used to the shared understanding of some domain of interest. It necessarily entails or embodies some sort of world view with respect to a given domain. The world view is often conceived as a set of concepts (e.g., entities, attributes, and processes), their definitions and their inter-relationships; this is referred to as a *conceptualization*. Such a conceptualization may be implicit, e.g. existing only in someone's head, or embodied in a piece of software. For example, an accounting package presumes some world view encompassing such concepts as invoice, and a department in an organization. The word ontology is sometimes used to refer to this implicit conceptualization. However, the more standard use is that the ontology is an explicit account or representation of a conceptualization [9].

Depending on who you talk to, the purpose of ontology can range from a mere vocabulary of terms to a strict formal logic. To understand the terminology used, let us consider the example of an auction. Auction ontology would have to define sellers, buyers, bids, etc. In particular, the following aspects could be found [10]:

- *Taxonomy of concepts:*
  Both buyers and sellers could be considered agents; as a result, agent is the super-concept of the concepts buyer and seller.
- *Relationships between the concepts:*
  Sellers offer goods or buyers make bids.
- *Facts:*
  A fact could be that eBay is a marketplace.
- *Rules:*
  If a buyer makes a bid, then include him in the marketing category "parent".
- *Constraints:*
  A later bid for the same offer must be higher.

In this example, the ontology would contain the taxonomy of the concepts in a domain and would define the relationships between these concepts. The facts, rules and constraints defined could then be applied to the ontology in order to reason about the knowledge.

3. RELATED RESEARCH

The Web Services Description Language (WSDL) is an XML-based language used to describe a Web service. This description allows an application to dynamically determine a Web service's capabilities, which are for example, the operations it provides, their parameters, return values, etc. A UDDI repository is a searchable directory of Web services that Web service requestors can use to search for Web services and obtain their WSDL documents. WSDL documents, however, do not need to be published in a repository for consumers to take advantage of them. They are also obtainable through a Web page or an email message.

The Universal, Description Discovery and Integration Extension (UDDIe) [11], takes an approach that relies upon a distributed registry of businesses and their service descriptions implemented in a common XML format. UDDIe specifications consist of an XML schema for SOAP messages, and a description of the UDDIe API specification. Together, these form a base information model and interaction framework that provides the ability to publish information about a broad array of Web services. It follows the same specification and standards for the registry data structure and API specification for inquiring and publishing service from the registry. However, there are slight changes and extensions in the data structure and the API to improve and maximize the use of the registry. UDDIe defines four core types of information that provide the kinds of information that a technical person would need to know in order to use a partner's Web services. These are: business information; service information; binding information; and information about specifications for services. Further, this information can be discovered by discovery calls based on the later data types.

The Web Service Modeling Ontology (WSMO) [12] provides the conceptual framework for semantically describing web services and their specific properties. The Web Modeling Language (WSDL) is a formal language for annotating web services with semantic information, which is based on the WSMO conceptual framework. WSMO aims to create ontology for describing various aspects related to Semantic Web Services, with the defined focus of solving the integration problem. WSMO also takes into account specific application domains (e-Commerce and e-Work) to ensure the applicability of the ontology for these areas.

Mandel and Sheila [13] automated web service discovery by using a semantic translation within a semantic discovery service. The approach uses a recursive back-chaining algorithm to determine a sequence of service invocations, or service chain, which takes the input, supplied by BPWS4J and produces the output desired by BPWS4J. The translation axioms are encoded into translation programs exposed as web services. The algorithm invokes the DQL (DAML Query Language) [14] service to discover services that produce the desired outputs. If the semantic discovery service does not have a required input, the algorithm searches for a translator service that outputs the required input and adds it to the service chain. As the process is recursive it terminates when it successfully constructs a service chain, or the profiles in the knowledge base are exhausted.

Semantically enhanced service discovery has also been introduced in the area of Mobile Computing. DReggie [15] is a dynamic service discovery infrastructure targeted at mobile commerce applications that besides performing syntactical matching exploits semantic matching using DAML (DARPA Agent Markup Language) to describe services and uses a Prolog reasoning engine for inference. A DReggie Lookup Server to which DReggie Clients submit their services performs the matching process and returns information about matches back to the clients.

The UUID-based description and matching of services mechanism of Bluetooth was enhanced using semantic information associated with services rather than simple UUIDs in hotspot environments [16]. This includes priorities, expected values or service attributes and some index of a match's closeness. To support this matching mechanism and allow more efficient service discovery, a service ontology described in a semantic language and a Prolog-based reasoning engine that uses the ontology was introduced.

Similar research in the Grid area was addressed by Deelman et al. [17] with their workflow generator and Tangmurarunkit et al. [18] with their resource selector. The workflow generator addresses the problem of automatically generating job workflows for the Grid. They have developed two workflow generators. The first one maps an abstract workflow defined in terms of application-level components to the set of available Grid resources. The second generator takes a wider perspective and not only performs the abstract to concrete mapping but also enables the construction of the abstract workflow based on the available components. The system operates in the application domain and chooses application components based on the application metadata attributes.

The ontology-based resource selector exploits ontologies, background knowledge, and rules for solving resource matching in the Grid to overcome the restrictions and constraints of resource descriptions in the Grid. In order to make the matchmaking more flexible and also to consider the structure of VOs the framework consists of ontology-based matchmakers, resource providers and resource consumers or requesters. Resource providers periodically advertise their resources and capabilities to one or more matchmakers using advertisement messages. The user can then activate the matchmaker by submitting a query asking for resources that satisfy the request specification. The query is then processed by the TRIPLE/XSB deductive database system [19] using matchmaking rules, in combination with background knowledge and ontologies to find the best match for the request.

4. CONTEXT-AWARE ONTOLOGY SELECTION FRAMEWORK

As seen from the existing approaches the need for more expressiveness of service descriptions was stated revealing the limitation of a syntactic approach to service discovery. To follow these movements proposed by the related work towards a semantic based approach for service discovery the context-aware ontology selection framework is proposed. This approach supplements the current approaches by taking context attributes for the service discovery process into account. Additional requirements have driven this framework towards a context-aware ontology selection framework.

4.1 Need for "Context-Awareness"

Definition of context and "context-awareness" is challenging and is done in many research areas such as artificial intelligence, human-computer interaction, ubiquitous computing etc. In the past, context has been left out in computer science [20]. The computer science field has strived for context-independence for simplicity reasons. By improving the computer's access to context, thereby introducing context-independence, the richness of communications in human-computer interactions can be improved and more useful computational services can be created [21]. For instance, consider the following example of an e-shopping service, where the e-services can be selected depending on the shopping context. This incorporation of contextual information for the matchmaking process should provide a higher precision and recall of service matches.

4.2 Framework Requirements

An advertisement matches a request, when the advertisement describes a service that is sufficiently similar to the service requested [22]. The problem of this definition is to specify what "sufficiently similar" means. Basically, it means that an advertisement and a request are "sufficiently similar" when they describe exactly the same service. This definition is too restrictive, because providers and requesters have no prior agreement on how a service is represented and additionally, they have very different objectives. A restrictive criterion on matching is therefore bound to fail to recognize similarities between advertisements and requests.

Specific requirements for the context-aware ontology selection framework are as follows:

1. Specification of context descriptions: Enabling the selection of services via the context descriptions.

2. High degree of flexibility and expressiveness: The advertiser must have total freedom to describe their services. Different advertisers want to describe their services with different degrees of complexity and completeness. The description tool or language must be adaptable to these needs. An advertisement may be very descriptive in some points, but leave others less specified. Therefore, the ability to express semi-structured data is required.
3. Support for subsumption: Matching should not be restricted to simple service name comparison. A type system with subsumption relationships is required, so more complex matches can be provided based on these relationships.
4. Support for data types: Attributes such as quantities and dates will be part of the service descriptions. The best way to express and compare this information is by means of data types.
5. Matching process should be efficient: The matching process should be efficient which means that it should not burden the requester with excessive delays that would prevent its effectiveness.
6. Flexible and modular structure: The framework should be flexible enough to Web applications to describe their context semantics in a modular manner.
7. Lookup of matched services: The framework should provide a mechanism to allow the lookup and invocation of matched services.

4.3 Architecture

The architecture shown in Figure 22-1 comprises of clients, matchmaker, context and service ontology, registries and web servers which host the web services.

The components are now explained in more detail:

1. Clients provide an interface for the users to describe their service requests. The interface also lists the matches and provides a facility to call the web services retrieved.
2. Registries contain the service information storing all service data. Service descriptions are in the form of service name, service attributes (inputs and outputs), service description and metadata information.
3. Web Servers host the web services.
4. Matchmaker consists of the matching module including the matching algorithm and a reasoner for the ontology matching part. The matching algorithm is explained in further detail in the following section.
5. Ontology (context and services) describes the domain knowledge such as book shop services and provide a shared understanding of the concepts used to describe services. Contextual information is crucial to ensure a high quality service discovery process [8].

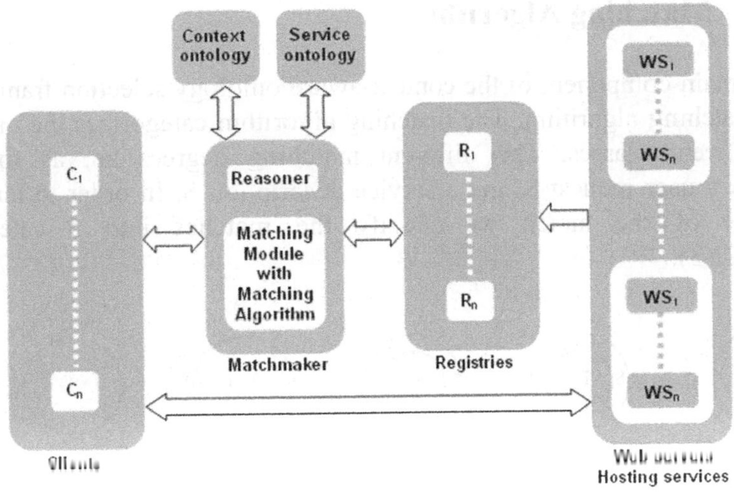

Figure 22-1. Matching Architecture

The sequence diagram in Figure 22-2 shows the interactions of a service request. The user contacts the matchmaker where the matching algorithm is stored (1). The matchmaker contacts the context ontology (2 and 3) and reasons depending on a set of rules defined. The same is done for the services ontology (4 and 5). Having additional match values the registry is then queried (6) to retrieve service descriptions which match the request and returns the service details to the user via the matchmaker (7). The parameters stored in the registry are service name, service attributes, service description, metadata information and contact details. Having the URL of the service the user can then call the web service (8) and interact (9) with it.

Three steps are necessary to perform the request. First the service request is matched semantically within the context specified which provides further attributes for the service matching where services are matched semantically within their service domain and finally a lookup with the registry is done to return the matched service details.

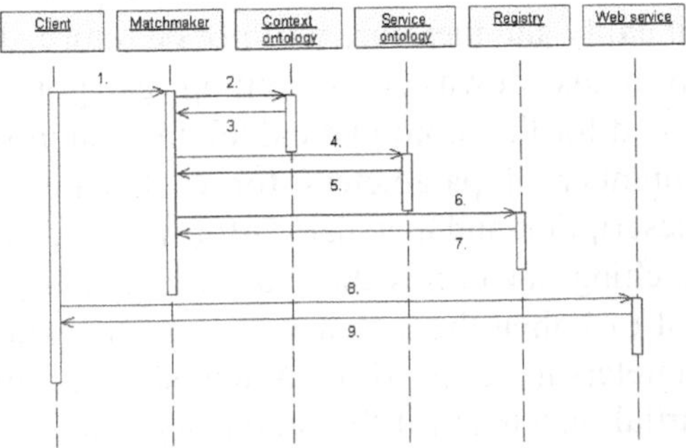

Figure 22-2. Interaction Diagram

4.4 Matching Algorithm

The main component of the context-aware ontology selection framework is the matching algorithm. The matching algorithm categorizes the matches into different classes. The different matching degrees are as follows. Consider a user request R and a service description S. In order to rank the relevance of the match we classify the matches into 5 categories (Figure 22-3).

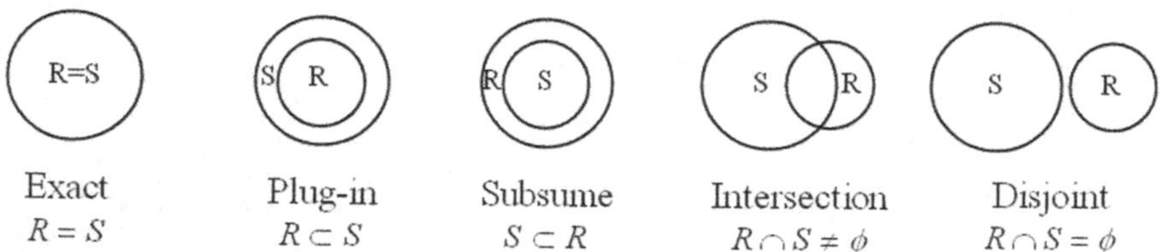

Figure 22-3. Matching Categories

These are:

1. *Exact match* $R = S$: The request matches the service exactly, i.e. all properties are a match.
2. *Plug-in match* $R \subset S$: The service allows more than the requester wants.
3. *Subsume match* $S \subset R$: A subset of the request is fulfilled.
4. *Intersection match* $R \cap S \neq \phi$: The request is partially fulfilled.
5. *Disjoint match* $R \cap S = \phi$: The request and the service do not share any properties.

Three categories can be derived from classifying the types of matches that are useful for the user. These are:

1. *Precise match*: Exact and Plug-in match. The service provides the requested functionality or more.
2. *Partial match*: Subsume and intersection match. The service is capable of providing part of the requested functionality.
3. *Mismatch*: Disjoint match. The service is not capable of providing the requested functionality and therefore will not be returned to the user.

Furthermore, to break down the matching categories, the matching algorithm implemented for the prototype calculates match scores taking into consideration the number of parameters for each category type (service attributes, service description and metadata information). To relate the match scores with the matching categories the classification is as follows. If the match score is equal to 1 then the match was a precise match which means that all service parameters matched. If the match score is smaller than 1 then the match was a partial match and if the match score returns 0 then it was a mismatch.

```
SNR: Service name from request
SAR: Service attributes from request
SDR: Service description from request
SMR: Service metadata information from request
SN:  Service name from registry
SA:  Service attributes from registry
SD:  Service descriptions from registry
SM:  Service metadata information from registry
MV:  Match value
MS:  Match score
MD:  Match details of service

SNR, SAR, SDR, SMR ← read_service_request_from_GUI()
SN, SA, SD, SM ← load_service_descriptions()
for all service_descriptions_in registry do
     if SNR equals SN
          MS = 1
     else
          ontology_search_of_context_and_services()
          check_SAR_with_SA()
          MV ← calculate_match_value()
          check_SDR_with_SD()
          MV ← calculate_match_value()
          check_SMR_with_SM()
          MV ← calculate_match_value()
          MS ← calculate_match_score()
     end if
     MD ← store_service_match_details()
end for
```

Figure 22-4. Matching Algorithm

The matching algorithm (Figure 22-4) is defined taking the classification and match categories into consideration. The algorithm reads the service request parameters from the GUI first. Then a connection to the registry is made in order to search and read the service parameters. In a "for loop" considering all services stored in the registry, first the service name of the service is compared with the service name of the request. If they are "equal" (assuming that the user knows the name of the service) the match score is set to 1 and no further steps are necessary. If "not" then the following steps need to be performed. The context and service ontology parameters are read, then the registry is queried using the service request and ontology parameters. If matches are found, then the match values are calculated for all three categories (service attributes, service description and service metadata). Afterwards the overall match score for a particular service is calculated and the service details are retrieved which are then stored and returned.

The overall consideration within the matchmaking approach for the calculation of the match score is to get a match score returned which should be between 0 and 1, where 0 represents a "mismatch", 1 represents a "precise match" and a value in-between represents a "partial match". The overall match score consists of the match score for service attributes, service description and service metadata respectively:

$$M_O = \frac{M_A + M_D + M_M}{3} \tag{1}$$

where $M_O, M_A, M_D,$ M_M are the overall, attribute, description and metadata match scores respectively.

Looking at the service attributes first, it is necessary to determine the ratio of the number of service attributes given in the query in relation to the number given by the actual service. To make sure that this ratio does not exceed 1, normalization is performed with the inverse of the sum of both values. This is multiplied by the sum of the number of service attributes matches divided by the number of actual service attributes (2a). Similar equations (2b) and (2c) were derived for service descriptions and service metadata respectively. The importance of service attributes, description and metadata in relation to each other is reflected in the weight values.

$$M_A = \frac{w_A}{(n_{AQ} + n_{AS})} \cdot \frac{n_{AQ}}{n_{AS}} \cdot \frac{n_{MA}}{n_{AS}} \tag{2a}$$

$$M_D = \frac{w_D}{(n_{DQ} + n_{DS})} \cdot \frac{n_{DQ}}{n_{DS}} \cdot \frac{n_{MD}}{n_{DS}} \tag{2b}$$

$$M_M = \frac{w_M}{(n_{MQ} + n_{MS})} \cdot \frac{n_{MQ}}{n_{MS}} \cdot \frac{n_{MM}}{n_{MS}} \tag{2c}$$

where w_A, w_D and w_M are the weights for attributes, description and metadata respectively; n_{AQ}, n_{AS} and n_{MA} are the number of query attributes, service attributes and service attribute matches respectively; n_{DQ}, n_{DS} and n_{MD} are the number of query descriptions, service descriptions and service description matches respectively; n_{MQ}, n_{MS} and n_{MM} are the number of query metadata, service metadata and service metadata matches respectively.

4.5 How does the Architecture fulfill the Requirements?

This framework is based on semantic service descriptions and it fulfils the seven requirements specified in section 4.2 as follows. Requirement 1 is satisfied with the context selection stage. Requirement 2 to 5 are fulfilled by the use of a shared ontology and a reasoning engine to achieve semantic matchmaking. Shared ontologies are needed to ensure that terms have clear and consistent semantics. Otherwise, a match may be found or missed based on an incorrect interpretation of the request. The matchmaking engine should encourage providers and requesters to be precise with their descriptions. To achieve this, the service provider follows an XML-based description, which is the ontology language OWL. To advertise and register its services the service requester generates a description in the specified OWL format. Defining the ontologies precisely allows the matchmaking process to be efficient. The advertisements and requests refer to OWL concepts and the associated semantics. By using OWL, the matchmaking process can perform implications on the subsumption hierarchy leading to the recognition of semantic matches despite their syntactical differences between advertisements and requests. The use of OWL also supports accuracy, which means that no matching is recognised when the relation between the advertisement and the request does not derive from the OWL ontologies. Complex reasoning needs to be restricted in order to allow the matching process to be efficient. Requirement 6 is fulfilled as the framework supports flexible semantic matchmaking between advertisements and requests based on the ontologies defined. Minimising false positives and false negatives is achieved with the selection process, where the request is matched within the appropriate application context. The context and semantic selection stages could have been integrated into one, however having context and services ontologies separately allows a modular design as it encapsulates the context knowledge from the services knowledge. This allows other applications to specify their service semantics separate from the context semantics and furthermore allows the context selection e.g. been inplemented and searched for via database queries. Requirement 7 is fulfilled by the use of a registry service. The registry service allows the lookup of service details to provide the user with the service URL.

5. IMPLEMENTATION OF PROTOTYPE

The prototype implementation is shown in Figure 22-5. The implementation is centred around the context and services ontologies that structure knowledge about the domain for the purposes of presentation and searching of services. The matchmaking engine performs the semantic match of the requested service with the provided services. This allows close and flexible matches of the matchmaking process. This prototype is based on Web services technology standards. The user interface is developed with Java Server Pages (JSPs). The communication from the JSPs with the underlying process is done with JavaBeans. The implementation of the Web services was done in Java using WSDL, XML and SOAP. The UDDI registry is used for the final selection stage which is the registry selection. The actual service is matched with the service request depending on the ontologies loaded.

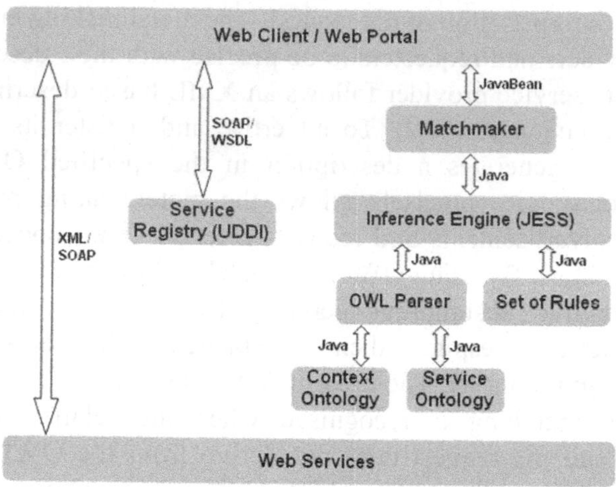

Figure 22-5. Prototype Implementation

The heart of the portal implementation is the semantic matchmaking. The OWL parser parses the context and services ontologies. With a defined set of rules the inference engine reasons about the ontologies and with the matched results a lookup in the UDDI registry is performed. The services get then displayed in the user portal, where the user can select the appropriate service from the list.

For the context and services ontologies OWL was chosen as it provides a representative notion of semantics for describing the context and services. OWL allows subsumption reasoning on concept taxonomies. Furthermore, OWL permits the definition of relations between concepts. For the inference engine rules were defined using the JESS (Java Expert Systems Shell) language [23]. The JESS API (Application Programming Interface) is intended to facilitate interpretation of information of OWL files, and it allows users to query on that information. It leverages the existing RDF API to read in the OWL file as a collection of RDF triples.

JESS was chosen as a rule-based language for the prototype as it provides the functionality for defining rules and queries in order to reason about the ontologies specified. JESS is an expert system shell and scripting language written entirely in the Java language. JESS supports the development of rule-based expert systems which can be tightly coupled to code written in the portable Java language. JESS is a forward chaining production system that uses the Rete algorithm [24]. The Rete algorithm is intended to improve the speed of forward-chained rule systems by limiting the effort required to recompute the conflict set after a rule is fired. Its drawback is that it has high memory space requirements. In the prototype implementation, queries depending on the specified ontology and service definition structure are specified. These get called whenever a search request is performed by the user. The search request is given by search parameters the user specifies. If datatypes, in JESS syntax `PropertyValue`, of a defined class should be found then the `defquery` in Figure 22-6 is invoked.

```
(defquery query-for-class-of-a-given-property
"Find the class to a given property."
  (declare (variables ?class))
  (triple
    (predicate "http://www.w3.org/2000/01/rdf-schema  #domain")
    (subject ?class)
    (object ?x)
  )
)
```

Figure 22-6. JESS Rule

With such queries, reasoning about classes of the ontology is achieved with the matching modules and works as follows. The context ontology is parsed by a OWL parser. The attributes and classes of OWL describe the concept of the ontology. The service request is being matched semantically by parsing the context and services ontology and the application of the rules defined. The OWL code facilitates effective parsing of service capabilities through its use of generic RDF(S) symbols compared with OWL specific symbols. With a defined set of rules an inference engine reasons about the value parameters parsed from the ontology. Other rules implemented include sub-classing, datatype, object and functional properties.

6. APPLICATION EXAMPLE

An application scenario was chosen to demonstrate the usability of the approach. It is assumed that many e-shopping web services are available on the Web. These can be any kind of services e.g. Amazon, eBay, etc., wrapped as web services offering different goods to buy such as *Books*, *Bikes* and *CDs*. It is furthermore assumed that in most cases a client searches for a service not knowing the service name. The user only specifies a service request with a few keywords describing the service needs. For this scenario a context ontology was created supplying the categories of services for e-shopping.

This ontology, shown in Figure 22-7, lists the contexts chosen which represent *Food*, *Clothes*, *Bikes*, *Cars*, *Shoes*, *Books* and *CDs*. The underlying classes show many associative links to the different categories. These are normally linked directly with the category class, however for the ease of the reader this single-structured hierarchy was used. In addition, it only shows the classes of the context hierarchy but not the attributes.

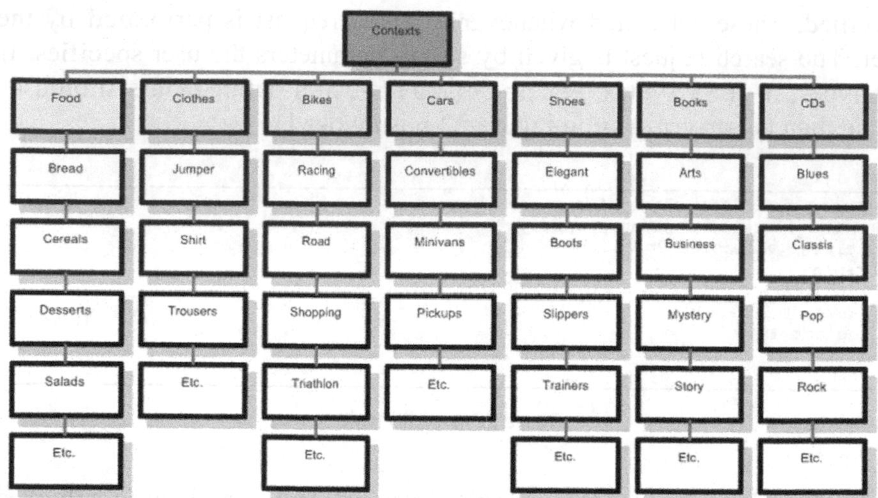

Figure 22-7. Context Hierarchy

Each of the classes belonging to one of the categories contains attributes describing the class further. E.g. class *Business* contains the attributes *computing, reading*, etc. For a special application domain the two identical attributes in more than one class could be eliminated. However, if context ontologies would be reused from other sources this can not be disqualified. The prototype implementation solves the problem by taking the additional context parameters into account to eliminate the "wrong" context. If the user only specifies one context parameter which matches two categories then the prototype returns a mismatch statement.

Figure 22-8 shows the fragment of the OWL description of the context ontology showing class (`<owl:Class rdf:ID="Services"/>`) and subclass (`<owl:Class rdf:ID="Services"/>`) relationships. An OWL ontology is made up of several components, some of which are optional, and some of which may be repeated. OWL constructs are presented in a structured format including RDF triples as shown below.

In Figure 22-9, the structure of the e-shopping services ontology is shown. The first level contains the corresponding categories of the context ontology. The second level represents the actual service implementation with the attributes below. Given in this hierarchy is only one service specification outlining the *Books* web service. Different service implementations are *BookBuy*, *Bookshop*, *BuyBooks*, *Books* and *BookSale*.

```
<?xml version="1.0"?>
<rdf:RDF
    xmlns:rdf="http://www.w3.org/1999/02/22-rdf-syntax-ns#"
    xmlns:rdfs="http://www.w3.org/2000/01/rdf-schema#"
    xmlns:owl="http://www.w3.org/2002/07/owl#"
    xmlns="http://www.cs.cardiff.ac.uk/ontologies/context.owl#"
  xml:base="http://www.cs.cardiff.ac.uk/ontologies/context.owl">
  <owl:Ontology rdf:about=""/>
  <owl:Class rdf:ID="Context"/>
  <owl:Class rdf:ID="Road"><rdfs:subClassOf><owl:Class rdf:ID="Bikes"/>
     </rdfs:subClassOf></owl:Class>
  <owl:Class rdf:ID="Books"><rdfs:subClassOf
     rdf:resource="#Context"/></owl:Class>
  <owl:Class rdf:ID="Triathlon"><rdfs:subClassOf><owl:Class
     rdf:about="#Bikes"/></rdfs:subClassOf></owl:Class>
  <owl:Class rdf:ID="Bikes"><rdfs:subClassOf
     rdf:resource="#Context"/></owl:Class>
  <owl:Class rdf:ID="Racing"><rdfs:subClassOf
     rdf:resource="#Bikes"/></owl:Class>
  <owl:Class rdf:ID="Food"><rdfs:subClassOf
     rdf:resource="#Context"/></owl:Class>
  <owl:Class rdf:ID="Shopping"><rdfs:subClassOf
     rdf:resource="#Bikes"/></owl:Class>
...
</rdf:RDF>
```

Figure 22-8. Fragment of OWL Context Ontology

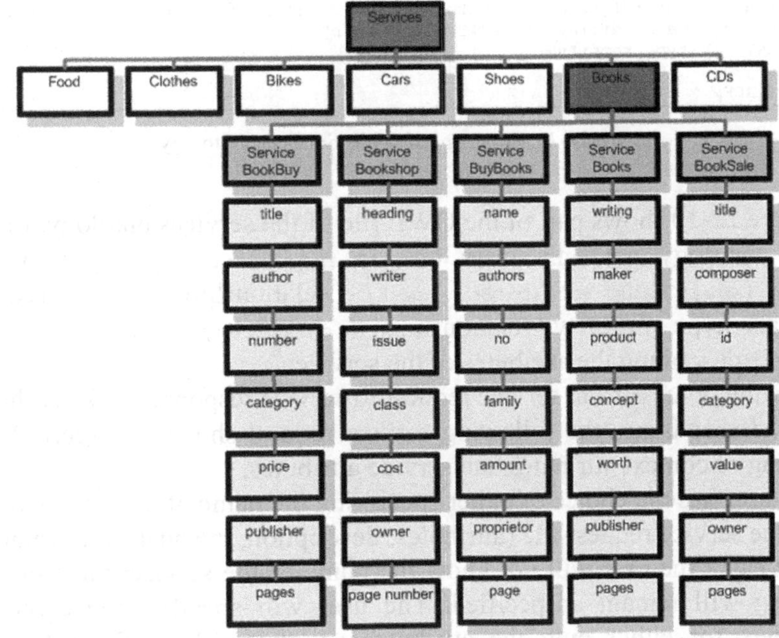

Figure 22-9. Services Hierarchy

```
<?xml version="1.0"?>
<rdf:RDF
    xmlns:rdf="http://www.w3.org/1999/02/22-rdf-syntax-ns#"
    xmlns:rdfs="http://www.w3.org/2000/01/rdf-schema#"
    xmlns:owl="http://www.w3.org/2002/07/owl#"
    xmlns="http://www.cs.cardiff.ac.uk/ontologies/services.owl#"
  xml:base="http://www.cs.cardiff.ac.uk/ontologies/services.owl">
  <owl:Ontology rdf:about=""/>
  <owl:Class rdf:ID="Services"/>
  <owl:Class rdf:ID="Cars"><rdfs:subClassOf
    rdf:resource="#Services"/></owl:Class>
  <owl:Class rdf:ID="ServiceRacer"><rdfs:subClassOf><owl:Class
    rdf:ID="Bikes"/></rdfs:subClassOf></owl:Class>
  <owl:Class rdf:ID="Books"><rdfs:subClassOf
    rdf:resource="#Services"/></owl:Class>
  <owl:Class rdf:about="#Bikes<owl:Class rdf:ID="Services"/></owl:Class>
  <owl:Class rdf:ID="Food"><rdfs:subClassOf rdf:resource="#Services"/>
  </owl:Class>
  <owl:Class rdf:ID="CDs"><rdfs:subClassOf rdf:resource="#Services"/>
  </owl:Class>
  <owl:DatatypeProperty rdf:ID="Price">
    <rdfs:domain rdf:resource="#ServiceRacer"/>
    <rdfs:range rdf:resource="http://www.w3.org/2001/XMLSchema#string"/>
  </owl:DatatypeProperty>
  <owl:DatatypeProperty rdf:ID="CatalogueNumber">
    <rdfs:range rdf:resource="http://www.w3.org/2001/XMLSchema#string"/>
    <rdfs:domain rdf:resource="#ServiceRacer"/>
  </owl:DatatypeProperty>
  <owl:DatatypeProperty rdf:ID="NumberOfGears">
    <rdfs:range rdf:resource="http://www.w3.org/2001/XMLSchema#string"/>
    <rdfs:domain rdf:resource="#ServiceRacer"/>
  </owl:DatatypeProperty>
  <owl:DatatypeProperty rdf:ID="WheelSize">
    <rdfs:range rdf:resource="http://www.w3.org/2001/XMLSchema#string"/>
    <rdfs:domain rdf:resource="#ServiceRacer"/>
  </owl:DatatypeProperty>
  <owl:DatatypeProperty rdf:ID="FrameSize">
    <rdfs:range rdf:resource="http://www.w3.org/2001/XMLSchema#string"/>
    <rdfs:domain rdf:resource="#ServiceRacer"/>
  </owl:DatatypeProperty>
...
</rdf:RDF>
```

Figure 22-10. Fragment of OWL Services Ontology

Figure 22-10 shows part of the OWL file of the services ontology. In this service ontology not only class (`<owl:Class rdf:ID="Services"/>`) and subclass (`<owl:Class rdf:ID="Services"/>`) relationships are declared but also data type property relationships (`<owl:DatatypeProperty rdf:ID="Price">`) describing the attributes of the service.

How the process from service request to service response works is shown next. The user issues the following service request shown in Figure 22-11 consisting of context attributes and service attributes.

The user has the choice of either specifying the name of the service or the rest of the service request file (attributes, description, metadata and weights). In most cases the user will not know the name of the service; therefore the name tag will remain unspecified. The user will specify service request parameters for either only the attribute section or all of the categories

```
<ServiceRequest>

    <Name>                                                    EITHER
        <parameter name="" value="">
    </Name>

    <Attributes>                                                  OR
        <ContextAttributes>
          <parameter name="computer" value="">
          <parameter name="reading" value="">
        </ContextAttributes>
        <ServiceAttributes>
          <parameter name="title" value="">
          <parameter name="author" value="">
          <parameter name="isbn" value="">
          <parameter name="category" value="">
          <parameter name="price" value="">
          <parameter name="pages" value="">
        </ServiceAttributes>
    </Attributes>

    <Description>
        <parameter name="description" value="This guide discusses Information
        Retrieval data structures and algorithms">
    </Description>

    <Metadata>
        <parameter name="attribute1"
         value="http://www.amazon.com/exec/obidos/tg/detail/-
         /0134638379/102-2173778-1724124?v=glance">
        <parameter name="attribute2"
         value="http://www.amazon.com/gp/reader/0134638379/
                    ref=sib_dp_pt/102-2173778-1724124#reader-link">
    </Metadata>

    <Weights>
          <parameter name="attributes" value="0.5">
          <parameter name="description" value="0.3"
          <parameter name="metadata" value="0.2">
    </Weights>

 </ServiceRequest>
```

Figure 22-11. Example of Service Request

attributes, description and metadata. The weight values can be defined according to the user's preference. The context attributes are first taken and the context ontology is queried using these search attributes resulting in the context keyword *Books* which is used for the service search part. The services ontology is then reasoned by using the context keyword and the service attributes specified in the service request query. All the retrieved services (*BookBuy*, *Bookshop*, *BuyBooks*, *Books* and *BookSale*) are then calculated using the match score metric, in order to identify the ranking of the service result set. After these services are matched the service details are retrieved from the registry and returned to the user.

7. EVALUATION OF PROTOTYPE

The purpose of this section is to show that the prototype implementation satisfies the performance requirements as applied in real-world applications and most importantly to show the quality improvement of the matches. Three different set of evaluation measures were carried out. These are performance measurements, precision and recall measurements and match score measurements.

7.1 Performance Measurements

Measurements were carried out to investigate the performance of the prototype. Ten measurements were taken to quantify the time needed to fulfill a service request. Only the service discovery process was measured (without an actual service call) as the primary focus was the matchmaking.

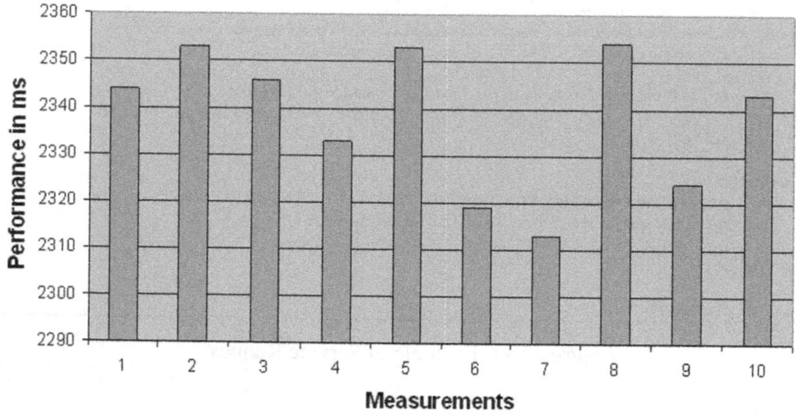

Figure 22-12. Performance Measurements

Figure 22-12 shows that the average time of a search request to be matched is 2338ms. The distribution shows a variation of ± 21ms of the average result. This is a quite acceptable performance outcome in comparison to real-world applications. However, the ontology size might be much bigger for real-world applications which need to be investigated next.

Another set of performance measurements of the prototype were conducted in order to see how the behaviour of the performance over the complexity of an ontology varies. Only the services ontology was enabled having the context ontology part disabled providing the search request with the context attribute. The measurement setting had the following conditions. All nine ontologies of different complexity levels were placed on the Internet and retrievable by a URL, so that real world measurements could be conducted. The complexity of 1 of the ontology is defined as having 112 elements, thereof 47 classes and 65 data type properties. Complexity 2 is the double amount of elements. Having complexity 16 results in 1792 elements, where 752 are classes and 1040 are data type properties.

Figure 22-13 shows the performance measurements of the prototype with respect to ontology complexity. The graph shows a linear distribution. The regression line shows an average increase of about 700ms per increase of complexity of the ontology. There is an offset of about 2000ms which is due to the instantiation and resetting of the reasoning engine and the rules and queries applied. As expected, the flexible and powerful matchmaker has a disadvantage which is a reduced performance, in particular for large ontologies. The results highlight the linear degradation in performance exhibited by the search. If only a keyword based approach was desired the performance would be better. However, for small and medium size ontologies (up to 1000 elements) the evaluation shows an acceptable performance.

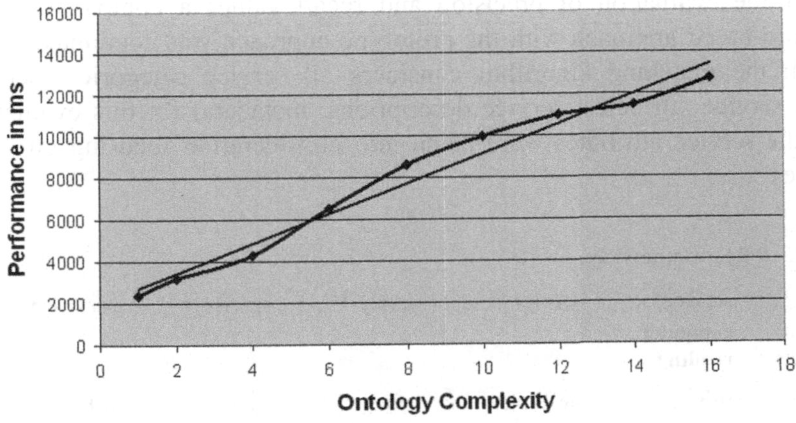

Figure 22-13. Performance versus Ontology Complexity

As expected, the additional functionality results in a lower performance shown in the linear performance decrease by an increase in complexity of the ontology. However, the prototype approach achieves an increase in the quality of service matches. Therefore, precision and recall measurements were taken to show the quality improvement for this semantic approach.

7.2 Precision and Recall Measurements

The evaluation is done by calculating precision and recall rates. Consider a set of relevant services (R) within a set of advertised services (A). Ra is the number of services in the intersection of the sets R and A .

Precision is the fraction of advertised services which are relevant i.e., $PRECISION = \frac{|Ra|}{|A|}$. The highest number is returned when only relevant services are retrieved.

Recall is the fraction of relevant services which have been retrieved i.e., $RECALL = \frac{|Ra|}{|R|}$. The highest number is returned when all relevant services are retrieved.

For the evaluation of precision and recall values a comparison of a keyword-based approach with the prototype approach was conducted. Even though the matching algorithm considers all service categories (service name, service attributes, service descriptions, metadata) for this evaluation only the service attributes were taken into consideration focusing on book services.

Table 22-1. Relevant services

	service 1	service 2	service 3	service 4	service 5
context attributes	**computer reading**				
service attributes	**title**	**heading**	name	writing	**title**
	author	writer	**authors**	maker	**composer**
	number	issue	no	product	**id**
	category	class	**family**	concept	**category**
	price	cost	**amount**	worth	**value**
	publisher	owner	**proprietor**	**publisher**	owner
	pages	**page number**	**page**	**pages**	**pages**

Table 22-1 shows the relevant services. All attributes shown in the table are the service attribute parameters used for this evaluation. Matches are indicated in bold.

Table 22-2. Irrelevant Services

	service 6	service 7	service 8	service 9	service 10
context attributes	graph picture				
service attributes	**title**	**issue**	**name**	**product**	**composer**
	number	owner	**proprietor**	**pages**	**id**
	price	isbn	issn	book	**value**
	pages	drink	shop	meal	**pages**
	book	pixel	colour	point	book
	shop	font	paragraph	space	food
	colour	space	bold	font	colour

Table 22-2 shows the irrelevant services. The attributes indicated in bold match with the extended context ontology taken for this experiment; however the context parameters do not match the Book category. The number of service attributes is the same for relevant and irrelevant services.

The service requests are similar to the one shown in Figure 22-11. The context parameters define the category of the service request which results in the split of the two tables (Table 22-1 and 22-2) being relevant services and irrelevant services. The user wants to find Book shop services and specifies a service request 1 with the parameters as stated in Figure 22-12 which are exactly the parameters specified for service 1 in Table 22-1. Service request 2 is specified with the parameter of service 2 (Table 22-1) and so on. The context parameters are always the same as defined in Figure 22-11.

Table 22-3. Request and matches

	Number of relevant services	Keyword-based approach	Prototype implementation
Request 1	5	3 relevant 3 irrelevant	5 relevant
Request 2	5	2 relevant 1 irrelevant	5 relevant
Request 3	5	1 relevant 1 irrelevant	5 relevant
Request 4	5	3 relevant 3 irrelevant	5 relevant
Request 5	5	3 relevant 4 irrelevant	5 relevant

Table 22-3 shows the request and the matches comparing the keyword-based approach with the prototype approach. It shows that only the keyword-based approach returns irrelevant matches as the prototype was customized. Figure 22-14 shows the results of the precision and recall values. The precision and recall results of the keyword-based approach range between 20% and 70%, whereby the prototype approach achieved a precision and retrieval rate of 100% in this experimental setup. As the recall and precision rates from the prototype show higher values than the rates from the keyword-based approach, it shows that the user receives a better subset of services that are relevant and in addition, the user receives fewer services that are irrelevant.

Due to the fact that this research is conducted in a limited application domain, the set of advertised services, query and ontology arc highly adapted and therefore a result of 100% is retrieved. In a real-world application scenario this correlation might not always be that high, especially if the context ontology is used from third-parties.

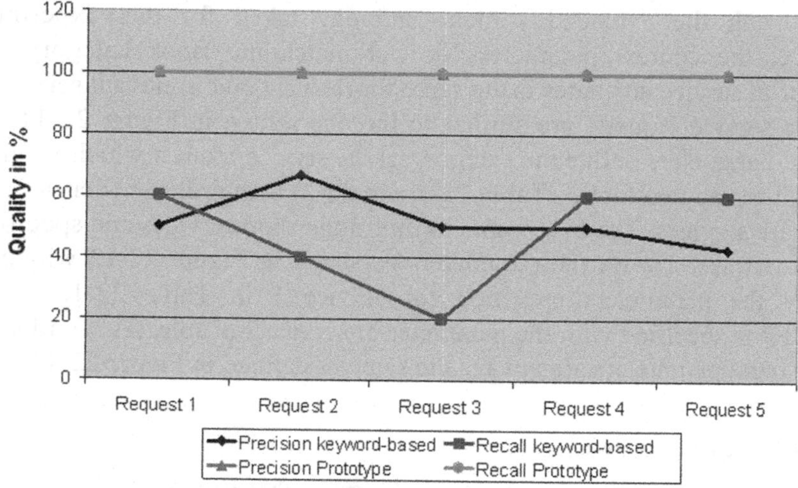

Figure 22-14. Evaluation of Precision and Recall Values

The accomplished result of service matches does not state that in every application scenario always values of 100% are achieved but it indicates the improvement in quality of service discovery results using this semantic approach.

7.3 Match Score Measurements

The precision and recall measurements showed that the quality of the return of service matches is increased. However, to ensure a ranking process to indicate which returned services match best, the match score values were introduced. The service requests were the same as the ones from the precision and recall measurements (Figure 22-11) with the additional parameters for description and metadata. The weight values were set to 1/3 for service attributes, service descriptions and metadata information respectively. Table 22-4 shows the match scores for the five service requests.

Table 22-4. Match Scores

Request	M_A	M_D	M_M	M_O
1	0.543	0.621	0.234	0.466
2	0.285	0.477	1	0.587
3	0.482	0.286	0.425	0.397
4	0.318	0.419	0.527	0.421
5	0.424	0.539	0.611	0.524

The match scores are vital in a matching system where due to the semantic matching process the quality of service matches is increased but whereby the user needs to be given a ranked service result set in order to indicate the best matches. Best matches are those with the highest similarity in comparison to the service request.

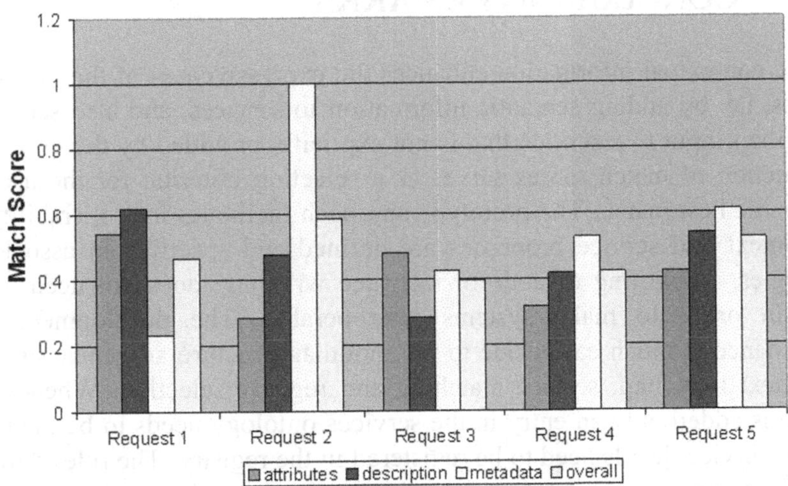

Figure 22-15. Match Scores Diagram

Figure 22-15 shows the distribution of match scores for the five service requests. The average match score is 0.479. This shows that providing the user with three categories (service attributes, service description and metadata information) allows specifying the service request more flexibly. The weight values can be specified by the user as a confidence value indicating which of the three categories are more important than the others.

7.4 Summary

As seen by the performance measurements the additional semantic feature results in a lower performance, however a higher precision for service matches is achieved. In particular, an acceptable performance is achieved for small and medium sized ontology. The fact of the linear decrease of performance for growing ontology needs to be considered carefully at design time. The choice of a "faster" reasoning engine might improve the matchmaking speed. Precision and recall measures showed the increase of quality of service matches, which was achieved by the customization and use of the context and services ontology. The only problem is that the user might be overwhelmed by the number of service responses, therefore the match score values are vital. The match score values are a good measure to firstly rank the service responses and secondly restrict matches where the match score is smaller than a certain threshold value. The evaluation of the prototype showed a significantly improved precision of service matches.

8. CONCLUDING REMARKS

The contextual information enhances the expressiveness of the matching process, i.e. by adding semantic information to services, and also serves as an implicit input to a service that is not explicitly provided by the user. The introduction of match scores serves as a selection criterion for the user to choose the best match. The prototype approach facilitates interoperability as the context and service properties are defined and specified in associated ontologies. Re-writing of code or interface wrapping does not need to be done in order to make systems interoperable. The development and maintenance is much easier due to the modular structure and encapsulation of context matching, service matching and registry selection. Whenever a service is added only an entry in the services ontology needs to be included and the service details need to be registered in the registry. The rules defined in the reasoning engine do not need to be modified and the service discovery process is not affected at all when adding services. This is a very important feature for modern information systems, and especially for Web services, where interoperability is a major issue. A drawback of this approach is that users registering services need to know the category their services belong to. Cases where a service falls into more than one category need to be registricted in order to allow an automatic and precise discovery and selection of service matches.

REFERENCES

1. J. McGovern, S. Tyagi, M. Stevens, S. Mathew, The Java Series Books - Java Web Services Architecture, Chapter 2, Service Oriented Architecture, 2003.
2. HTTP - Hypertext Transfer Protocol, W3C, 2004. http://www.w3.org/Protocols/.
3. Extensible Markup Language (XML), W3C, 2004. http://www.w3.org/XML/.
4. UDDI Technical White Paper. http://www.uddi.org/pubs/Iru_UDDI_Technical_White_Paper.pdf.
5. Web Services Description Language (WSDL) 1.1, W3C, 2004. http://www.w3.org/TR/wsdl.
6. SOAP Version 1.2, W3C, 2004. http://www.w3.org/TR/soap/.
7. W3C Working Draft, "Requirements for a Web Ontology Language". http://www.w3.org/TR/webont-req/.
8. T.R. Gruber, ONTOLINGUA: A Mechanism to Support Portable Ontologies, Version 3.0, Technical Report KSL 91-66, Knowledge Systems Laboratory, Department of Computer Science, Stanford University, 1992.
9. M. Uschold, M. Gruninger, Ontologies: Principles, Methods and Applications, Knowledge Engineering Review, 1996, 11-2.
10. S.A. Ludwig, A Semantic Approach To Service Discovery In A Grid Environment, Ph.D. Thesis, Brunel University, UK, 2004.
11. A. ShaikhAli, O. Rana, R. Al-Ali, D.W. Walker, UDDIe: An Extended Registry for Web Services, *Proceedings of the Service Oriented Computing: Models, Architectures and Applications*, SAINT-2003, Orlando, USA, 2003.
12. U. Keller, R. Lara, A. Polleres, I. Toma, M. Kifer, D. Fensel, WSML Deliverable – WSMO Web Service Discovery, WSML Working Draft, 2004.
13. D.J. Mandell, S.A. McIlraith, A Bottom-Up Approach to Automating Web Service Discovery, Customization, and Semantic Translation, *Proceedings of the 12th International World Wide Web Conference*, Workshop on E-Services and the Semantic Web(ESSW'03), Budapest, 2003.
14. R. Fikes, P. Hayes, I. Horrocks, DAML Query Language, Abstract Specification, 2002. D. Chakraborty, F. Perich, S. Avancha, and A. Joshi, Dreggie: Semantic service discovery for m-commerce applications, *Workshop on Reliable and Secure Applications in Mobile Environment*, 20th Symposium on Reliable Distributed Systems, New Orleans, LA, October 2001.
15. S. Avancha, A. Joshi, T.W. Finin, Enhanced Service Discovery in Bluetooth, IEEE Computer 35(6): 96-99, 2002.
16. E. Deelman, J. Blythe, Y. Gil, C. Kesselman, G. Mehta, K. Vahi, A. Lazzarini, A. Arbree, R. Cavanaugh, S. Koranda, Mapping Abstract Complex Workflows onto Grid Environments, *Journal of Grid Computing*, Vol. 1, No. 1, pp 9--23, 2003.
17. H. Tangmunarunkit, S. Decker, C. Kesselman, Ontology-based Resource Matching in the Grid - The Grid meets the Semantic Web, *Proceedings of the First Workshop on Semantics in Peer-to-Peer and Grid Computing (SemPG03)*, In conjunction with the Twelfth International World Wide Web Conference 2003, Budapest, Hungary, May 2003.
18. The XSB Research Group. http://xsb.sourceforge.net.
19. H. Lieberman et al. Out of context: Computer systems that adapt to, and learn from, context, *IBM system journal*, Volume 39, Numbers 3 & 4, MIT Media Laboratory, 2000.
20. A. Dey, Providing Architectural Support for Context-Aware applications, Thesis, Georgia Institute of Technology, November 2000.

21. M. Paolucci, T. Kawamura, T.R. Payne, K. Sycara, Semantic Matching of Web Services Capabilities, *Proceedings International Semantic Web Conference (ISWC 02)*, 2002.
22. JESS, Java Expert Systems Shell. http://herzberg.ca.sandia.gov/jess/docs/61/index.html.
23. C.L. Forgy, Rete: A Fast Algorithm for the Many Pattern/Many Object Pattern Match Problem, *Journal of Artificial Intelligence* 1982, 19-17-37.

Chapter 23

ONTOLOGY-BASED USER MODELING

for Knowledge Management Systems

Liana Razmerita

INRIA Sophia-Antipolis, Project Acacia 2004, route des Luciole, BP 93 06902, Sophia Antipolis Cedex, razmerital@wanadoo.fr

Abstract: What are the key success factors for a knowledge management system (KMS), and how to design and implement successful knowledge management systems, are topical research areas. We argue that designing effective knowledge management systems requires not only a focused view, which is achieved by considering organizational imperatives and technological solutions, but it also benefits from a larger perspective that considers a user-centered design, the individual needs of the users (e.g. work tasks, responsibilities), individual motivational drivers, usability and ergonomics issues. This article emphasizes the role of user models and user modeling within Ontology-based Knowledge Management System (OKMS), integrating a highly interdisciplinary approach. It shows how user models, models of the knowledge workers and user modeling processes can be applied in the context of knowledge management systems. An ontology-based user modeling approach is proposed and concrete examples of how ontology-based inferences can be used for expertise modeling are provided. This chapter emphasizes the importance of using ontology-based representations for modeling the users and providing enhanced user support and advanced features in KMSs.

Key words: Ontology-based User Modeling; User profiles; Knowledge Management Systems; Agents; Semantic Web Services; Personalization; Skill Management; Networking; Collaboration

1. INTRODUCTION

The knowledge-based and organizational theories of the firm suggest that knowledge is the organizational asset that enables sustainable competitive advantage in very dynamic and competitive markets. (Davenport and Prusak, 1998; Nonaka and Hirotaka, 1995, etc.). Therefore in the last few years, many organizations have perceived the need to become more “knowledge-oriented” or “learning” organizations. KMSs are information systems dedicated to manage knowledge processes and represent a key element for knowledge-oriented organizations.

Knowledge Management Systems (KMSs) are designed to allow users to access and utilize the rich sources of data, information and knowledge stored in different forms. They also support knowledge creation, knowledge transfer and continuous learning for the knowledge workers. Knowledge Management Systems contain both explicit and implicit or tacit knowledge. *Explicit knowledge* is the most visible form of knowledge and the one we are most familiar with. It is easily written down and includes artifacts and data stored in documents, reports that are available within and outside the organization, and software. But, Knowledge Management Systems can, to some extent, address the management of *tacit knowledge.* Tacit Knowledge is more difficult to articulate, and includes the experience, know-how, skills, knacks and the expertise of the people. According to Nonaka and Takeuchi (1995) *“[..The] more important kind of knowledge is tacit knowledge*.”

This chapter puts forward the arguments for integrating user modeling in KMSs. It emphasizes the role of user modeling within Ontology-based Knowledge Management System (OKMS). A user model is a key component for providing enhanced features such as: personalization, expertise discovery, networking, collaboration and learning (Razmerita et al., 2003). More particularly, an ontology-based user modeling approach is proposed and concrete examples of how ontology-based inferences can be used for expertise modeling are provided. The chapter shows the importance of using ontology-based representations for modeling the users and it pinpoints future work directions.

The integration of user models in KMSs opens a large number of research questions some of these are common to the general objectives of user modeling, others are more specific to the Human-Computer Interaction and to Knowledge Management whilst others are related to the use of ontology for representing user models. The problem of user modeling addresses two important user needs: a need for enhanced support for filtering and retrieving the knowledge available in the system, and a need to better manage the tacit knowledge. The management of the tacit knowledge includes a need to access the qualification and experience of peer knowledge workers in the company. In Knowledge Management Systems, user models or user profiles have frequently been created to represent user competences or preferences. This view is extended by including other characteristics of the users. For example the *Behavior* concept models some characteristics of users interacting with a KMS (e.g., type of activity, level of activity, level of knowledge sharing). These characteristics are inferred based on the user activity in the system. The proposed user model is conceptualized based on the Information Management System Learning Information Package specifications and is defined as user ontology, using Semantic Web technologies.

The chapter is organized as follows. The second section introduces some of the challenges associated with the development of a next generation of KMSs. Section 3 discusses the role of user modeling in an OKMS. Section 4 presents the process of building the user ontology and proposes a set of user modeling mechanisms for modeling the user's behavior in a KMS. Section 5 presents an integrated architecture of an OKMS emphasizing points of entry for the user modeling module. Finally, the last section concludes with a discussion on the user modeling and ontology-based modeling and indicates to future work directions.

2. TOWARDS A NEXT GENERATION OF KNOWLEDGE MANAGEMENT SYSTEMS

2.1 The Knowledge Management Challenges

KMSs have been defined in a number of different ways. "Knowledge Management Systems (KMSs) refer to a class of information systems applied to managing organizational knowledge"(Leidner and Alavi, 2001). Many of the current KMSs integrate knowledge processes from an organizational perspective focused on technological solutions. From this technological perspective, the main objective of KMSs is to provide uniform and seamless access to any relevant information for a task to be undertaken. Thus, KMSs can be defined as: "the process of capturing, organizing and retrieving information based on notions like databases, documents, query languages and knowledge mining." (Thomas and Kellogg, 2001)

Nowadays, KMSs are challenged to integrate complex knowledge-oriented processes which facilitate work processes, knowledge creation, knowledge transfer and continuous learning for the knowledge workers. Schutt (2001) emphasizes that the challenge of actual KMSs is to foster knowledge management processes with the final goal to increase the productivity of their employees. The complexity of business processes implies that KMSs capture, store and deploy a critical mass of knowledge in various forms. Large, distributed organizations, such as Indra, do not necessarily have an integrated solution for knowledge management. Generally, large organizations use a portfolio of tools such as enterprise portals, databases, different collaboration tools, forums, threaded discussions or shared spaces, etc. In certain cases, each division creates its own application for managing knowledge and accumulates valuable information there. Furthermore, there is usually little or no integration of the various knowledge management tools, databases, and portals. Knowledge resources are not centralized and the amount of distributed knowledge sources available can constitute an obstacle for finding and retrieving the relevant knowledge. Moreover this critical mass of corporate resources is also a factor which contributes to an information overload process for its users. As a result knowledge workers waste time searching for the necessary corporate resources to perform work tasks efficiently.

2.2 Perceived Needs of the User

Some important issues that need to be addressed by the next generation of KMSs have been identified by surveying the opinion of the knowledge workers of two large, geographically-distributed Spanish companies from information technology sector: Indra and Meta4. These surveys pointed out important issues which need to be taken into account in the design of a next generation of KMSs. Amongst these issues are:

- a need to better organize the content of the KMSs;
- a need for enhanced user support for filtering and retrieving the knowledge available in the system;
- a need to access the qualifications and experience of peer knowledge workers in the company.

The integration of complex business processes requires more functionality to be integrated and knowledge management solutions become implicitly high functionality applications. However, in an extended survey of the vision of the executives impressions on KMSs (Knowings enquete, 2003) keywords such as: utility, simplicity, conviviality, adaptability to the needs and specificity of the enterprise were emphasized. Additionally, in this survey personalization is associated with the access to the knowledge assets and with the simplicity of use of the system. The problem of user modeling relates to the aforementioned issues, namely the information overload issue, the need for enhanced user support, personalization and the need to better manage the tacit knowledge. The need for enhanced user support is expressed as "to not get lost" amongst hundreds of documents and to filter "information and noise". Research on personalization, semantic web technologies, adaptive hypermedia and user modelling is the basis for implementing novel mechanisms for filtering and retrieving the knowledge available in the system.

2.3 Employing Ontologies in KMSs

Semantic web technology, ontology, service-oriented architectures including: software agents, web services or grid services and user modelling are emerging technologies to be integrated in the design of a next generation of KMSs. Integrated architectures using emerging technologies such as: web services, ontology, and agent components for user-centric, smart office task automation have been recently prototyped (Tsai et al. 2003, Razmerita et al. 2003, Gandon et al., 2002).

2.3.1 Ontology for KMS

Ontology is approached with different senses in different communities. Often ontology is just a fancy name denoting a simple taxonomy, or a set of activities performed according to a standardized methodology, or a certain conceptual analysis used to model the domain knowledge. Several definitions for ontology in artificial intelligence have been proposed. Hendler (2001) defines ontology as: "a set of knowledge terms, including the vocabulary, the semantic interconnections and some simple rule of inference and logic for some particular topic." The use of ontology has become popular in many application domains including: knowledge engineering, natural language processing, knowledge representation, intelligent information integration and knowledge management. The ontology represents and structures the different knowledge sources in its business domain (O'Leary, 1998, Abecker et al., 2000, Stojanovic et al., 2001). Existing knowledge sources (documents, reports, videos, etc.) are mapped into the domain ontology and semantically enriched. This semantically enriched information enables better knowledge indexing and searching processes and implicitly a better management of knowledge. According to Kim et al. (2004) an ontology-based system can be used not only to improve precision but also to reduce search time. Due to these reasons, ontology-based approaches will likely be the core technology for the development of a next generation of Knowledge Management Systems (KMSs).

However bringing ontology to real world enterprise application is still a challenge. Maedche et al. (2003) explains why ontology-based representations and Semantic Web technology are still in early stages for enterprise OKMS. One reason would be that ontology-based conceptual representations lack certain features which are important for classical database driven information systems. Features such as scalability, persistency, reliability, and transactions standardized in classical data-base driven applications are typically not available in ontology-based systems. Another reason is that a large amount of information in an enterprise exists outside classical KMSs, in applications such as: groupware, databases or other applications that have been used regularly within organizations.

2.3.2 Ontology-based Knowledge Modeling

"Ontology entails or embodies some sort of world view with respect to a given domain. The world view is often conceived as a set of concepts (e.g. entities, attributes, and processes), their definitions and their inter-relationships; this is referred to as a conceptualization." (Uschold and Gruninger, 1996)

Ontology-based modeling has rapidly developed as a new approach for modeling knowledge, in the last few years. Consequently, the term ontology engineering has emerged. "The goal of so called ontological engineering is to develop theories, methodologies and tools suitable to elicit and organize domain knowledge in a reusable and transparent way." (Guarino, 1997)

Amongst the technological challenges ontology engineering tools needs to provide reliable solutions for: managing multiple ontologies, evolving ontologies, scalability. (Maedche et al., 2003).

Guarino et al. (1994) emphasize the fact that: "rigorous ontological foundation for knowledge representation can result in better methodologies for conceptual design of data and knowledge bases, facilitating knowledge sharing and reuse."

Noy et al. (2001) have highlighted several reasons for developing ontologies: 1) to share common understanding of the structure of information among people or software agents; 2) to enable reuse of the domain knowledge; 3) to make domain assumptions explicit; 4) to separate domain knowledge from the operational knowledge; 5) to analyze domain knowledge.

Different methodologies for development of ontology-based Knowledge Management Applications have been recently proposed. (Sure et al., 2003, Dieng et al., 1999, 2004).

We agree with Studer et al. (1998) who emphasizes that building ontology for a particular domain requires a profound analysis, revealing the relevant concepts, attributes, relations, constraints, instances and axioms of that domain. Such knowledge analysis typically results in hierarchy of concepts with their attributes, values and relations. Further, this knowledge analysis phase is followed by an implementation stage. Implementing the designed ontology in a formal language enables to make it a machine processable model.

Similar somehow to a software engineering process, Uschold and Gruninger [1996] define a skeletal methodology for building ontology. The process of building ontology is divided into three basic steps: capturing, coding, and integrating with existing ontology.

The process of ontology capture comprises:

- Identification of the key concepts and relationships in the domain of interest;
- Production of unambiguous text definitions for the concepts and their relationships;
- Identification of the terms to refer to such concepts and relationships Ontology capture corresponds to a specification phase in software engineering.

The process of coding implies the representation of the ontology in some formal language. This implies a decision on the representation formalism, namely the ontology representation language, to be used. A set of ontology languages such as: OWL, KAON, extending Resource Description Framework /Schema (RDF/RDFS), recommended by the World Wide Web Consortium facilitate the implementation of ontology-based applications. These languages enable expression and implementation of ontology-based conceptual models in a computational form.

The process of integrating with existing ontology During this phase the problem of interoperability with other existing ontology must be clarified. Major problems may arise if similar concepts are already defined in existing ontology or if different representational ontology languages are used.

Bachimont (2000) views the ontology modelling process as a three step process but from another perspective. The first step implies specifying the linguistic meaning of the concepts which correspond to a semantic commitment. The second step is an ontological commitment by specifying the formal meaning of the ontology. In a third step, ontology achieves computational commitment by being integrated in a system.

2.3.3 Semantic Services for the Users

The distributive nature of tasks to be handled in a KMS determines a natural choice for multi-agent or service-oriented architectures. Moreover, service-oriented architectures are viewed as an attractive solution for enterprise application integration, business process management and the design of advanced information systems. The core technology for service oriented architectures is web services. Web services are software applications that can be discovered, described and accessed based on XML and standard Web protocols over intranets, extranets and the Internet (Daconta et al., 2003). Initially the web service efforts focused on interoperability, standards and protocols for performing business to business transactions. Web services are a key technology providing solutions for data integration issues. Basic web service technologies are: SOAP (Simple Object Access Protocol), WSDL (Web Service Description Language) and UDDI (Universal Description Discovery & Integration).

Semantic Web services are extensions of web services, providing a richer semantic description for services. They are implemented using languages such as: Web Ontology Language for Services OWL_S (OWL_S, 2004), Web Services Modeling Ontology WSMO (WSMO, 2005) and Internet Reasoning Service Framework IRS (IRS, 2004). The associated semantic description of services will facilitate the discovery, the comparison or the composition of simple services by other software entities or by humans. Ontology constitutes basic vocabularies facilitating the communication, the composition and the interoperability of semantic services and agents.

Web services can also be seen as independent agents that produce and consume information, enabling automated business transactions (Paolucci and Sycara, 2003). Societies of agents can act with the purpose of helping the user or solving problems on behalf of the users. Specialized agents can cooperate, negotiate, and communicate in order to achieve various functions such as: discovery and classification of new knowledge, search and retrieval of information, the automatic evolution of the domain ontology, etc. The following section puts forward the arguments for user modelling processes in KMS.

3. USER MODELLING IN KNOWLEDGE MANAGEMENT SYSTEMS

In order to support personalized interaction with the users, information systems need to construct or access and maintain a user model. Moreover, knowledge workers are the most valuable resource of corporate memory and the key element in the management of tacit knowledge. Making the experience of people more visible in organization and capitalizing the knowledge of the employees is important for companies. Organizations are more and more concerned with aspects related to how to capitalize and manage the individual knowledge. On the one hand, user modeling processes support the acquisition of competencies, qualifications, and work experience explicitly or implicitly. On the other hand, the implicit complexity of KMSs doesn't necessarily fit the need of the users to have simple systems: systems adapted to their specific needs. The knowledge workers of Indra, a Spanish company, the end-users of the Ontologging system, suggested: "to include mechanisms in order to acquire knowledge about user profile and filter information and noise" and to "adapt the tools to each company or sector".

The heterogeneity of users, differences in users' responsibilities, different domains of interests, different competencies, and work tasks to be handled in a KMS drives a need to focus on the users, on the user needs and variability in KMS design. Characteristics of the users integrated in the user models are the basis for personalization of the user interaction with the system. Moreover, the adoption of KMSs also might require a change process of the current work practices of the knowledge workers and implicit changes at the organizational level. For example, the issue of how to motivate people to share their knowledge is not simply solved by offering people tools for doing this. Consequently, some incentives for the adoption of knowledge sharing practices might need to be introduced at the whole organizational level. User modeling mechanisms can be used to determine a behavioural model of a user interacting with a KMS, and to provide adapted feedback or rewards to the users (Razmerita, 2003). Organizations need to create the enabling factors for the knowledge workers: to be creative, to submit knowledge assets in the system and to diffuse their knowledge. For example, knowledge workers might not be intrinsically motivated to spend time sharing knowledge or to submit knowledge to the system, especially if it requires extra work.

3.1 Personalization

An important strand of research in user modeling aims to enhance the interaction between the users and the systems. The goal of this research is to make complex systems more usable, to speed-up and simplify interactions (Kay, 2000). Fischer (2001) provides some insights in the design of human-centred systems supported by user modeling techniques. He emphasizes that high functionality applications must address three problems: (1) the unused functionality must not get in the way; (2) unknown existing functionality must be accessible or delivered at times when it is needed; and (3) commonly used functionality should be not too difficult to be learned, used and remembered. However there clearly exist adaptation methods and personalization techniques that are specific to KMSs. These adaptation methods and personalization techniques relate to specific objectives of KMSs. Amongst these specific objectives are:

- how to motivate people to create knowledge and submit new knowledge assets in the system;
- how to stimulate collaboration and knowledge sharing between knowledge workers irrespective of their location;
- how to alleviate information overload, how to simplify business processes and work tasks, and so forth.

Personalization techniques rely on the user's characteristics captured in user models or user profiles. User's characteristics can be used for providing different types of adaptations and personalised services. Personalisation of a KMS is the process that enables interface customization, adaptations of the functionality, structure, content and modality in order to increase its relevance for its individual users (Razmerita, 2005).

Personalization can be achieved in two different ways: based on the agent's intervention such as synthetic characters or information filtering agents, or based on various types of intelligent services that are transparent to the users, also addressed as adaptive techniques in the user modeling literature.

Such personalization mechanisms are based on the user's characteristics and they could include:

- direct access to customized relevant knowledge assets;
- provide unobtrusive assistance;
- help to find/to recall information needed for a task;
- offer to automate certain tasks through implicit or explicit interventions.

The adaptation techniques, at the level of the user interface, can be classified into three categories: adaptation of structure, adaptation of content, adaptation of modality and presentation. For instance, in the range of adaptation of structure, the system can offer personalised views of corporate knowledge based on interest areas and the knowledge of the users or based on the role and competencies of the users. "Personalised views are a way to organise an electronic workplace for the users who need an access to a reasonably small part of a hyperspace for their everyday work." (Brusilovsky, 1998)

Adaptation of content refers to the process of dynamically tailoring the information that is presented to the different users according to their specific profiles (needs, interests, level of expertise, etc.). The adaptation of content facilitates the process of filtering and retrieval of relevant information. In KMS recommender systems, information filtering agents and collaborative filtering techniques can be applied with the purpose of adaptation of content. The adaptation of presentation empowers the users to choose between different presentations styles, such as different layouts, skins, or fonts. Other preferences can include the presence or absence of anthropomorphic interface agents, the preferred languages, and so forth. Different types of sorting, bookmarks, and shortcuts can also be included in a high functional system. Adaptation of presentation overlaps to a certain extent with interface customisation. The adaptation of modality enables changes from text to other types of media to present the information to the user (text, video, animations, or audio) if they are available in the system. In modern adaptive hypermedia, user can select different types of media.

These personalisation mechanisms are described and exemplified with details in Razmerita (2005).

Recently, the concept of contextualization of knowledge goes beyond personalization. Dzbor et al. (2004) propose to bring the knowledge to the user through 'personal portals' taking into account timely and situational issues and using a wider variety of interaction modalities.

Baumgartner et al. (2005) proposes mechanisms for reasoning on the Semantic Web in order to achieve personalized views on the data. Semantic Web enabled information systems will extract relevant information from the Web, process and combine different pieces of distributed information in such a way that the content selection and presentation fits to the individual needs of the user. (Baumgartner et al., 2005)

3.2 Learning and Change

The role of user models, addressed as student/learner models in the context of learning environments, has been emphasized by the whole body of research dedicated to e-learning, intelligent tutoring systems, interactive learning environments, computer based learning, etc. The student/learner model is often associated with cognitive diagnosis. The student modelling process or the cognitive diagnosis involves an assessment of what the student knows or/and what the student doesn't know (knowledge gap, his/her misconceptions) or/and his/her learning style, etc. These individual characteristics are used to tailor the learning processes, to adapt the content of the lessons, to adapt the agents' interventions to the specific needs of the learner.

In the context of KMSs, we approach learning from a change management perspective. In our view learning is not only a process of acquiring new pieces of knowledge but it often involves a behavioral change for the user. Learning is seen as a continuous process, taking place at individual and social level that includes the acquisition of knowledge as well as the contextual use of the knowledge acquired. From this perspective a system can also criticize, provide feedback and stimulus for behavioral change at the individual level (Angehrn, 1993).

A KMS facilitates storing, searching and retrieving of knowledge assets but it also aims at fostering the users' participation in knowledge sharing and knowledge creation-the adoption of knowledge management behaviors. Through user modeling processes we track the user's level of knowledge sharing and his/her level of activity, his/her predominant type of activity.

By modeling the user's behavior different types of stimulus agents can intervene or provide feedback to stimulate the user towards learning and change. The adoption of knowledge management behaviors involves learning and a change process. It can be facilitated by different intervention strategies acting at the cognitive, cultural and social level. On the one hand, these inferred characteristics make aware the user about his/her behavior in the system. On the other hand, the identified behaviors are used to motivate the user to be active in the system: to share and to create knowledge. Thus the system can provide rewards, recognition mechanisms or other motivational mechanisms. For instance, the system can offer virtual money or it can acknowledge the "knowledge champions" as a mechanism for motivating the users.

3.3 Networking and Collaboration

The dichotomy of knowledge as tacit and explicit knowledge implies a requisite for sharing knowledge, collaboration and networking. Much progress has been witnessed in computer mediated collaboration or computer supported collaborative work in recent years. Different types of communication systems from email to more advanced groupware systems (e.g. shared workspaces, discussion forums, chat systems, instant messaging systems, video-conferences, etc.) enable virtual interactions, knowledge exchanges, collaboration and learning in distributed working environments.

"Collaboration is a social structure in which two or more people interact with each other and in some circumstances, some types of interaction occur that have a positive effect." (Dillenbourg et al., 1996)

Aspects on how to help people collaborate and facilitate the exchange of their knowledge enabling learning and thus supporting the achievement of individual and collective goals has been the target of innumerable theoretical research and practical projects. (DeSanctis & et al. 2001; Gongla and Rizzuto 2001; Lesser and Storck 2001).

In the context of learning environments, Dillenbourg and Self (1995) have emphasized that "*collaborative style depends on many factors: the learners' characteristics, their relationship, the nature of the task or the context.*"

For example, the process of grouping people based on domain of interests, roles support building *communities of practice* or *communities of interests*. In certain systems like Knowledge Pump or CWall, communities are built based on the user's domain of interests. (Snowdon and Grasso, 2002) A community of practice is a term introduced by Xerox research, and: "*it refers to a group of people who are peers in the execution of real work*" (Skyrme, 1999).

Greer et al. (1998) have shown how user model can be used to support peer help and collaboration in distributed workplace environments. Peer Help System (PHelpS) finds peers, knowledge workers which can help with various work related tasks. In certain systems collaboration is aided with matchmakers. Matchmaker agents can establish connections between users with similar domains of interests and expertise. (Chen et al., 1998)

The result of the networking is the construction of a social network. The user's social network represents the relationships of one community member with others and with individuals and communities external to the one considered. Included in the social network are: (1) the personal network composed of friends and acquaintances; (2) the affiliation to sub-communities, and (3) the organizational network, such as the boss, the colleagues, and the work acquaintances. The importance of social networks in innovation diffusion, business processes and economics is very well recognized, some of the studies include (Deroïan 2002, Janssen and Jager 2001). More recently, an important strand of research for social networks, collaboration or communities are associated with Semantic Web technology and simple Friend of a Friend (FOAF) type of user ontology.

3.4 Expertise Discovery or Skill Management

The problems of expertise discovery, expert finding, and skill mining or intellectual capital management have been widely discussed in the knowledge management literature. The literature on knowledge management emphasizes the importance of tacit knowledge. Making the competencies, the qualifications and the users' domains of interests explicit enables location of domain experts and an improved skill management. A survey of the different expert finder systems and the associated expertise modeling techniques can be found in Yimam and Kobsa (2000). A number of commercial applications incorporate expert finding capabilities: (e.g., *Knowledge Server*TM from Autonomy[1], Inc.; *KnowledgeMail* from Tacit Knowledge Systems[2], *Organik*® from Orbital Software[3]; *Raven* from Lotus Development Corp[4]). Benjamins et al. (2002) points out the importance of possibility to manage and monitor the skills by the employees. They argue that this enables the calculations of the knowledge gaps between current and desired position and this will likely improve involvement and motivation. This is also a valuable option not only for the knowledge workers who need to complete different job related tasks but also for human resource management units especially for big, distributed organizations. Ontology-based frameworks for skill management based on description logic (Colucci et al., 2003) or for group competencies (Vasconcelos et al., 2003) have recently been proposed.

1 http://www.autonomy.com/.
2 http://www.tacit.com/.
3 http://www.orbitalsw.com/.
4 http://www.lotus.com/home.nsf/welcome/km.

4. ONTOLOGY-BASED USER MODELING

4.1 Building the User Ontology

This section describes the process of building the user ontology, based on ontology engineering principles overviewed in section 2.3.2, along with associated user modeling processes. One of the major tasks associated with the definition of user ontology has been the definition of a vocabulary, as an agreed conceptualization. In order to guarantee a shared vision of the conceptualization of the user model, the proposed user ontology relies on Information Management Systems Learner Information Package specifications (IMS LIP) specifications, as an upper level ontology. The IMS LIP package (IMS LIP, 2001) is structured in eleven groupings including: Identification, Goal, QCL (Qualifications, Certification and Licenses), Accessibility, Activity, Competence, Interest, Affiliation, Security Key and Relationship. The user ontology has been developed based on a top down approach starting from IMS LIP specification, based on Ushold and Gruninger methodology (1996). The user ontology has been specified taking into consideration: end-user requirements (provided INDRA), KnowNet user model (provided by Meta4) and research conducted at CALT/ INSEAD.

The definition of the user ontology captures rich metadata about the employee's profile including characteristics such as: identity, email, address, competencies, cognitive style, preferences, etc. but also a behavioral profile as described in the next section. The user model comprises an implicit part, acquired based on the user interaction with the system, and an explicit part, gathering data explicitly through the user profile editor (Figure 23-1).

The user model implemented as a user ontology using KAON captures all aspect identified as relevant for the KMS and for the users. KAON – Karlsruhe Ontology and Semantic Web (Maedche et al., 2003) framework is a toolsuite for managing ontology. As a web ontology language, KAON extends Resource Description Framework RDF/RDFS language, a recommendation of W3C.

The specification and implementation of the ontology is generic enough to allow the ontology to be adapted to different application domains.

4.2 Modeling Users' Behavior in KMSs

KMSs need to encourage people to codify their experience, to share their knowledge and to develop an "active" attitude in using the system. For this purpose we have extended the IMS LIP groupings with the Behavior concept. The Behavior concept and its sub-concepts were introduced to "measure" two processes that are important for the effectiveness of a KMS, namely knowledge sharing and knowledge creation.

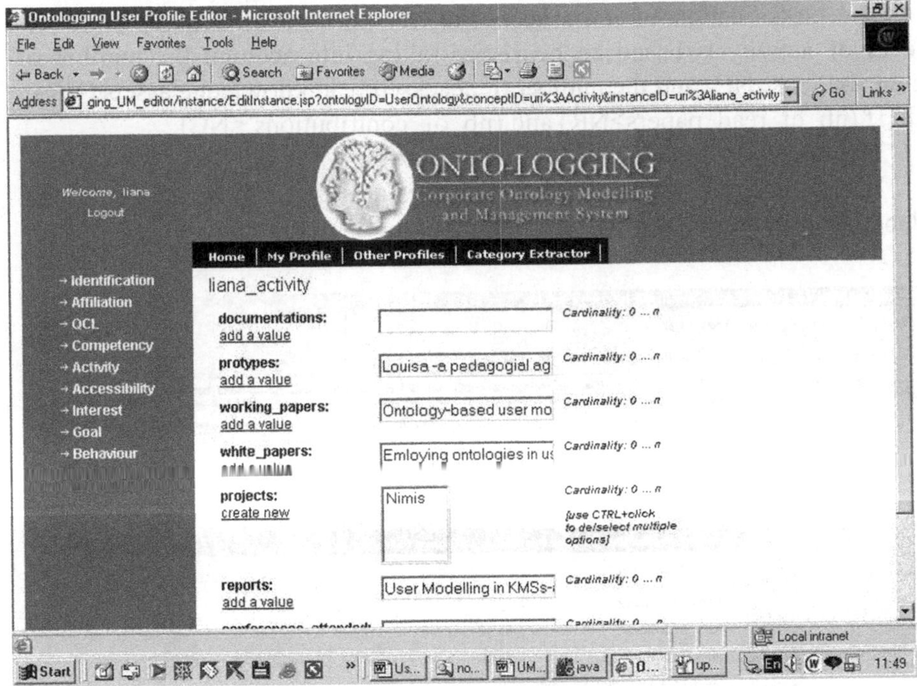

Figure 23-1. User Profile Editor, in the edit mode

The Behavior concept, see Figure 23-2, describes characteristics of users interacting with a KMS such as: level_of_activity, type_of_activity, level_of_knowledge_sharing, etc. Based on their activity in the system, namely the number of contributions to the system and the number of the documents read the user modeling system classifies the users into three stereotypes: readers, writers or lurkers. These categories are properties of the type_of_activity concept. The level_of_activity comprises four attributes that can be associated with the users: very active, active, passive or inactive. The classification of the users according to the type_of_activity or level_of_activity is based on heuristics. For example a lurker is defined as somebody who doesn't contribute and who reads/accesses very few knowledge assets in the system.

Whenever a user contributes a knowledge asset to the system an associated variable nb_of_contributions is incremented. Similar it happens when the user reads, query or comments papers.

∀x ProvideResource -> increase(nb_of_contributions(x))

∀x ReadResource -> increase (nb_of_read_papers(x))

∀x ProvideMetadata -> increase(nb_of_read_papers(x))

∀x Query -> increase(nb_of_query(x))

The classification of users according to the type_of_activity or to the level_of_activity is based on heuristics taking into account the number of contributions (NC) and the number of accessed/read knowledge assets (NR).

If (nb_of_read_papers>NR) and (nb_of_contributions <NC)

Then user(x) ="reader" (during timeframe)

Where, NR, NC and timeframe are constants that can be parameterized depending on the activity in the system.

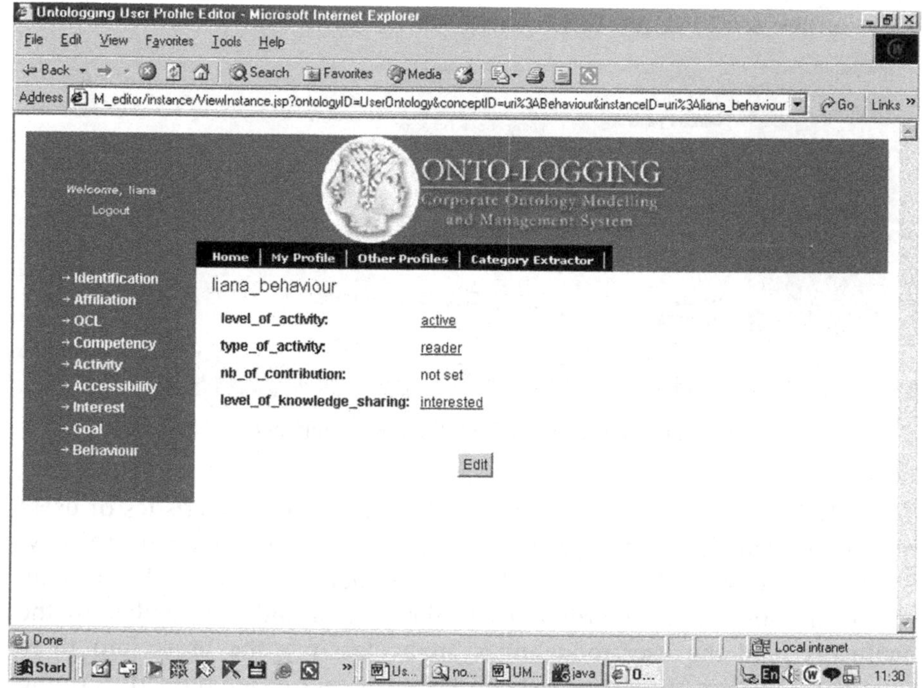

Figure 23-2. User Profile Editor – the Behavior concept

The **level of activity** captures if a user is very active, active, visitor or inactive. We define a **very active** user as somebody who reads/accesses and contributes with knowledge assets. An **active** user has less activity in the system then a very active user. A **visitor** is somebody who rarely uses the system while the person classified as **inactive** has no activity in the system. An example of inference rule for classifying the users based on their level of activity is:

If (nb_of_read_papers > NR) and (nb_of_contributions >=NC+1)

Then user(x) = "very active" (during timeframe)

Through the level_of_knowledge_sharing we are capturing the level of adoption of knowledge sharing practices. The system uses the principle of fuzzy classifier systems to assign the users in a certain category according to their level of knowledge sharing. The user's states in relation with the level of knowledge sharing are: unaware, aware, interested, trial and adopter. Users are assigned into a certain category according to their level of knowledge sharing. Fuzzy logic is often used to model various types of commonsense reasoning (Dubois and Prade, 1995). Fuzzy logic research concentrates on approximate reasoning and reasoning under uncertainty issues. "*Fuzzy logic aimed at a formalization of models of reasoning that are approximate rather than exact.*" (Zadeh, 1995) It has been applied in various application domains like: knowledge based systems, knowledge acquisition, control systems etc. We use the principle of fuzzy classifier systems in order to assign the users in different categories according to their level of knowledge sharing.

Fuzzy classifier systems imply a two steps process:

- create a fine grained fuzzy partition;
- generate fuzzy rules and calculate membership function or degree of membership;

Through the *level_of_knowledge_sharing* we are capturing the level of adoption of knowledge sharing practices based on two fuzzy sets. We use the type of activity and the level of activity to codify the membership value of a user to a certain category. We calculate the membership of a candidate X in a category as a function $Y=f(x_1, x_2)$ where:

Y – the level of knowledge sharing is fuzzified as:

[very high, high, medium, low, very low] they can be mapped into the stereotypes:

[adopter, trial, interested, aware, unaware]

x_1 is the type of activity is fuzzified as: [high, medium, low] which can be mapped into the stereotypes [writer, reader, lurker]

x_2 is the level of activity is fuzzified as: [high, medium, low, very low] which corresponds to the categories [very active, active, visitor, inactive]

Table 23-1. The calculus of the level of knowledge sharing

$Y=f(x_1, x_2)$	high	medium	low	very low
high	very high	very high	medium	
medium	high	medium	low	
low			very low	very low

We have created a table with the columns corresponding to the linguistic variables for the level of activity and with the rows corresponding to the linguistic variables for the type of activity. The rules are defined similar to a fuzzy controller. No valid rules are applied for the grey cells.

Translated from the table, the classifier system uses the following rules:

If x_1 is high and x_2 is high then Y is very high
If x_1 is high and x_2 is medium then Y is very high
If x_1 is high and x_2 is low then Y is medium
If x_1 is medium and x_2 is high then Y is high
If x_1 is medium and x_2 is medium then Y is medium
If x_1 is medium and x_2 is low then Y is low
If x_1 is low and x_2 low then Y is very low
If x_1 is low and x_2 is very low then Y is very low

By "defuzzifing" the rules above we obtain the following rules using the initial linguistic variables associated with the level of knowledge sharing, the type of activity and the level of activity.

The user states in relation to the level of knowledge sharing are defined as: unaware, aware, interested, trial and adopter using Roger's terminology related to the attitude of people towards innovation (Angehrn and Nabeth, 1997). Based on the identified characteristics, the system provides feedback, virtual reward or adapted interventions for a behavioural change (e.g. for adoption of knowledge sharing behaviour).

4.3 Exploiting Metadata and User Modeling

Let's have a look at a more concrete example of applying ontology-based user modeling for inferring domains of interests or expertise finding in the context of KMSs. It has been shown previously that the user ontology describes various properties and concepts relevant for the user model. The concepts of the user ontology are bridged with the concepts of the domain ontology through properties.

Figure 23-3 depicts a part of the user ontology in a graph-based representation. Concepts are represented with green ovals, darker colour, while properties of the concepts are represented with orange ovals. These properties of concepts, such as: "works_at", "works_on", "cooperates_with", associated with ontology language specific reasoning mechanisms facilitate further inferences. For instance, the fact that: "Smith works_on Ontologging project". Given the fact that, the range of the property "works_on" is restricted to concept Project and Ontologging is described as a project about: knowledge management, user modeling and ontology. Based on these facts an ontology-based system can automatically infer that Smith might be interested in or has expertise in: ontology, knowledge management and user modeling.

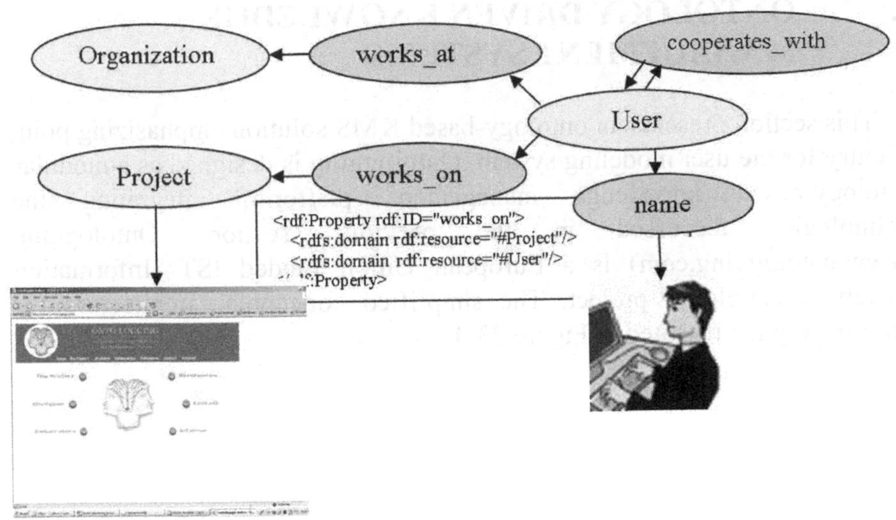

Figure 23-3. Application scenario of the user ontology

(User, works_on, Project)
(Project, related_to, Topic)
In our examples the previous RDFS tuples are instantiated as following:
(Smith, works_on, Ontologging)
(Ontologging, related_to, Knowledge Management)
(Ontologging, related_to, Ontology)
(Ontologging, related_to, User modeling)

Ontology languages offer associated reasoning mechanisms such as description logic or F-logic (Kifer, 1995). Using inferences implemented in F-logic an ontology-based KMS can deduce that Smith might be an expert in Knowledge Management, Ontology and User modeling. An Ontobroker (Decker et al., 1999) specific syntax written in F-logic to query all the people working in Knowledge Management looks like:

FORALL Y,Z <- Y:User [works_on ->>Z] and Z: Project [related_to->>KnowledgeManagement]

Thus, without requiring people to constantly update their profiles (their expertise, interests), an ontology-based KMS could facilitate finding the experts, knowledgeable persons in a domain or domains of interests for the users. This example shows how semantic-enriched knowledge assets and associated reasoning mechanisms can be used for inferring new knowledge in semantic web enabled information systems.

5. ONTOLOGY-DRIVEN KNOWLEDGE MANAGEMENT SYSTEMS

This section presents an ontology-based KMS solution emphasizing point of entry for the user modeling system. Ontologging is designed as a modular ontology-based knowledge management platform, integrating the technologies discussed in the previous section. Ontologging (www.ontologging.com) is a European Union funded IST (Information Society Technology) project. The simplified conceptual architecture for Ontologging is presented in Figure 23-4.

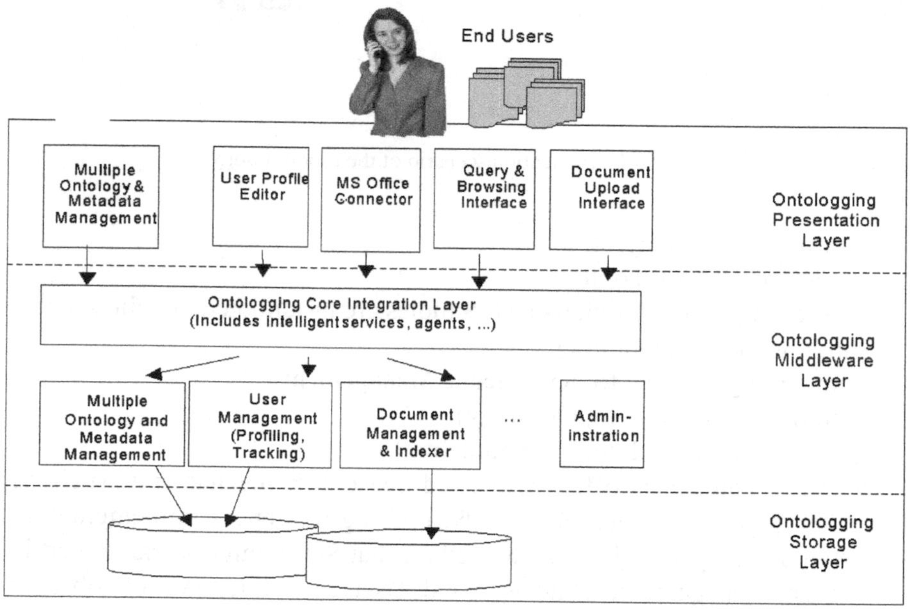

Figure 23-4. Ontologging conceptual layered architecture

Ontologging has a three-tiered architecture, integrating Karlsruhe Ontology and Semantic Web framework (KAON[5]) as a tool suite for managing ontology. KAON is "an open-source ontology management infrastructure targeted for semantic driven business applications" (Maedche et al., 2002). The Distributed User Interface (DUI) provides an integrated platform for the different knowledge management tools available for the end users. The distributed user interface of Ontologging system is designed using XML-driven components. The interface includes a 'template mechanism' to customise a personalised view. Through this template mechanism the

[5] http://kaon.semanticweb.org.

different work units can personalise their view of the organisational memory, or select parts of it that are related to their expertise, interests, and so forth. The DUI includes two main layers: the user interface layer and the component layer. The user interface layer consists of: search interface, browse interface, property edition and upload, result presentation interface, document download' and an agent management interface.

The three layers making up the Ontologging architecture are described briefly below:

- The presentation layer includes different modules which enable the end-users to have access to the functionality of the KMS (e.g. Query, Browsing and Editing, User Profile Editor, etc.). The end-users access the system via different clients, e.g. a Web-based browsing and querying interface (see Figure 23-5) or a Ms Office-based connector.
- The middleware layer is made up of Core Integration Layer (CIL) and different APIs which provide the core functions of the system. (e.g. multiple ontology and metadata management, user management, document management and indexer, administration etc.) KAON is at the core of the middleware layer. CIL coordinates the interaction of various components in the system and hosts a set of intelligent services and agents. The role of intelligent services and agents is to improve the user interaction with the system based on the user's characteristics. The user's characteristics are inferred by the user modeling processes or provided the user through the user profile editor. The user profile editor enables also to have access to the other' knowledge workers profile. The system uses web services (using Microsoft .Net framework) to interconnect different application systems and technologies. A certain numbers of wrappers have been implemented with the role of lifting applications at the ontology level. Knowledge edition tools are used for providing metadata, or uploading corporate resources into the system (see Figure 23-6).
- The storage layer consists of data repositories for the KMS. It consists mainly of relational database technology.

The front-end of the system is organized into several applications including: User Profile Editor (Figure 23-1, 23-2), Query, Browsing, (Figure 23-5) and Knowledge Editing (Figure 23-6), and Ontology management tools. End-users will access the system via different clients, e.g. a MS Office-based connector and a Web-based browsing and querying interface.

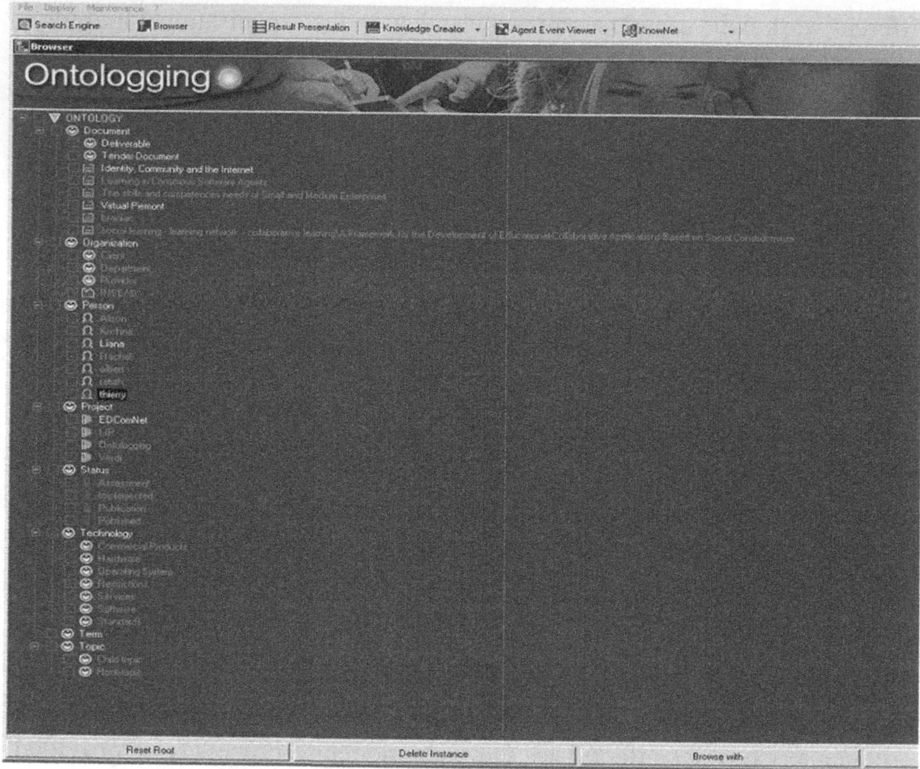

Figure 23-5. Ontologging system: Browsing mode in a classical tree like representation

Presentation clients access the back-end system via an integrated SOAP-based service interface. Dedicated query and browsing tools are employed for search and navigation through the different knowledge bases. The knowledge editing tools enable to upload documents and add new knowledge assets into the system. Ontology management tools facilitate the set-up and the evolution of ontology based on user friendly graph-based representation. These tools are mainly dedicated for ontology engineers or for knowledge managers. They include ontology editors (e.g. OntoMat-SOEP, OIModeler) which enable manual ontology engineering but they also include mechanisms for automatic ontology augmentation. (Motik et al., 2002).

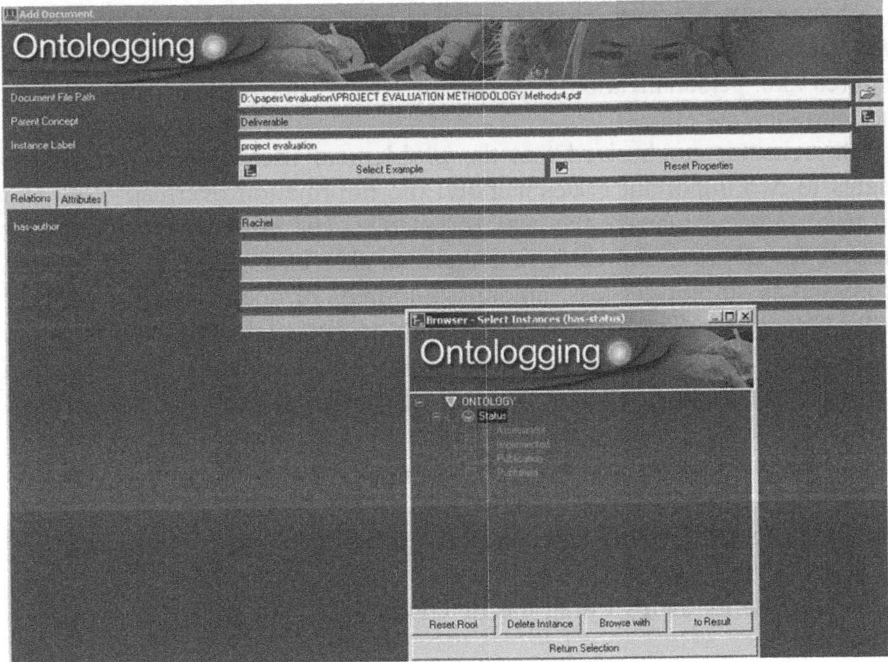

Figure 23-6. Ontologging system: the knowledge edition tools

6. DISCUSSION

In the last few years the current vision and goals of KMSs have broadened. Unlike databases, KMSs aim to go beyond the mere administration of data; they need to support a better management of the tacit knowledge, learning processes, knowledge creation, knowledge sharing and collaboration between employees irrespective of their location. Semantic Web technology enables to go beyond a traditional document-centred knowledge management system. It becomes possible to support more complex knowledge oriented processes by exploiting the metadata and the relationships between the concepts. The next generation of information systems needs to overcome technological challenges associated with the use of emerging technologies, but it also needs to integrate a highly multidisciplinary approach. Such a multidisciplinary approach for designing effective KMS requires not only a focused view which is achieved by considering organizational imperatives and technological solutions, but can also benefit from a user-centred solution. A user-centered solution considers the individual needs of the users, individual motivational drivers, and usability and ergonomics issues.

This chapter has presented the role of user modeling in a KMS. It has been showed that user model is a key component for providing enhanced features like: personalization, expertise discovery, networking, collaboration and learning.

This chapter emphasized that the problem of user modeling in KMSs relates to two important issues namely: the information overload issue and the need to better manage the tacit knowledge. The need for enhanced user support for filtering and retrieving the available knowledge in the system expressed as "to not get lost" amongst hundreds of documents and to filter "information and noise" relates to research on personalization and adaptive hypermedia. User modeling techniques for personalized interaction facilitates the building of systems that adapt to the user's characteristics. Knowledge workers want convivial, simple systems adapted to their specific needs. Personalisation and adaptive features for KMSs are becoming inescapable features of the current KMSs. Personalisation has a utility function and a conviviality function (Razmerita, 2005).

From the utility perspective:

- personalisation helps fitting the functionality of the system to the user's needs;
- personalisation reduces the information overflow by providing users with the most relevant information.

From the conviviality perspective:

- personalisation helps to bridge the gap between the 'designer's view of the system' and the end-user's view of the system, and to take into account the user's preferences.

This chapter presents a set of user modeling processes specific to KMSs. The user modeling system assesses the activity of the users in order to provide feedback or reflection. The behaviour of the users in the system can be associated with incentives provided to the users to share their knowledge and be active in the system. Of course the issue of sharing knowledge and contributions to the system is complex and it should not be limited to simple incentives. It might imply changes of the current work practices and it can be associated with other managerial interventions.

Ontology-driven KMSs open up new perspectives to manage business processes in a KMS. The evaluation of the Ontologging system emphasized that concept-based navigation and enhanced search capabilities are two enhanced features of OKMS. The main advantage is the power of the relationships which enables users to navigate from one concept (and its instances) to another concept (and its instances) easily. Relationships between concepts allow to navigation from one concept and its instances to another related concept and its instances. Metadata and ontology-based representations connect knowledge assets with people. In the user ontology, people are modeled as authors of the documents or contributors, through relationships such as: “is_author”, “has_contributor”. People are connected with other people through “collaborates_ with” and “works_with” type of relationships. These relationships constitute contextual links among the various chunks of content. Future work would involve making better use of the associated semantic of knowledge through rules and logic. A rule can specify an action if certain conditions are met. Integration of associated reasoning mechanisms can open up the possibility of making knowledge assets intelligently accessible and associate various types of intelligent services, such as personalized services. Semantic-enriched resources and ontology can support the development of a new range of services to enhance the user support. According to user’s profile, such services can semantically classify knowledge assets, personalize the content, structure or change the modality of interaction with the system, retrieve appropriate and semantically relevant knowledge, foster collaboration between knowledge workers, model social networking processes, support the formation of communities of practices, and so forth.

In the last few years the current vision and goals of KMSs has broadened. Unlike databases, KMSs aim to go beyond the mere administration of data; they need to support a better management of the tacit knowledge, learning processes, knowledge creation, knowledge sharing and collaboration between employees irrespective of their location. Semantic Web technology enables to go beyond a traditional document-centred knowledge management system. It becomes possible to support more complex knowledge oriented processes by exploiting the metadata and the relationships between the concepts. The next generation of information systems needs to overcome technological challenges associated with the use of emerging technologies, but it also needs to integrate a highly multidisciplinary approach. Such a multidisciplinary approach for designing effective KMS requires not only a focused view which is achieved by considering organizational imperatives and technological solutions, but can also benefit from a user-centred solution. A user-centered solution considers the individual needs of the users, individual motivational drivers, and usability and ergonomics issues.

This chapter has presented the role of user modeling in a KMS. It has been showed that user model is a key component for providing enhanced features like: personalization, expertise discovery, networking, collaboration and learning.

The chapter emphasized that the problem of user modeling in KMSs relates to two important issues namely: the information overload issue and the need to better manage the tacit knowledge. The need for enhanced user support for filtering and retrieving the available knowledge in the system expressed as "to not get lost" amongst hundreds of documents and to filter "information and noise" relates to research on personalization and adaptive hypermedia. User modeling techniques for personalized interaction facilitates the building of systems that adapt to the user's characteristics. Knowledge workers want convivial, simple systems adapted to their specific needs. Personalisation and adaptive features for KMSs are becoming inescapable features of the current KMSs. Personalisation has a utility function and a conviviality function (Razmerita, 2005).

From the utility perspective:

- personalisation helps fitting the functionality of the system to the user's needs;
- personalisation reduces the information overflow by providing users with the most relevant information.

From the conviviality perspective:

- personalisation helps to bridge the gap between the 'designer's view of the system' and the end-user's view of the system, and to take into account the user's preferences.

The chapter presents a set of user modeling processes specific to KMSs. The user modeling system assesses the activity of the users in order to provide feedback or reflection. The behaviour of the users in the system can be associated with incentives provided to the users to share their knowledge and be active in the system. Of course the issue of sharing knowledge and contributions to the system is complex and it should not be limited to simple incentives. It might imply changes of the current work practices and it can be associated with other managerial interventions.

Ontology-driven KMSs open up new perspectives to manage business processes in a KMS. The evaluation of the Ontologging system emphasized that concept-based navigation and enhanced search capabilities are two enhanced features of OKMS. The main advantage is the power of the relationships which enables users to navigate from one concept (and its instances) to another concept (and its instances) easily. Relationships between concepts allow to navigation from one concept and its instances to another related concept and its instances. Metadata and ontology-based representations connect knowledge assets with people. In the user ontology, people are modeled as authors of the documents or contributors, through relationships such as: "is_author", "has_contributor". People are connected with other people through "collaborates_ with" and "works_with" type of relationships. These relationships constitute contextual links among the various chunks of content. Future work would involve making better use of the associated semantic of knowledge through rules and logic. A rule can specify an action if certain conditions are met. Integration of associated reasoning mechanisms can open up the possibility of making knowledge assets intelligently accessible and associate various types of intelligent services, such as personalized services. Semantic-enriched resources and ontology can support the development of a new range of services to enhance the user support. According to user's profile, such services can semantically classify knowledge assets, personalize the content, structure or change the modality of interaction with the system, retrieve appropriate and semantically relevant knowledge, foster collaboration between knowledge workers, model social networking processes, support the formation of communities of practices, and so forth.

ACKNOWLEDGMENT

The work reported in this paper was done in the context of the Ontologging project, an EU funded project, and it has been continued during a postdoctoral position within Acacia project. Ontologging system has been developed by Ontologging consortium: CALT (Center of Advanced Learning Technologies), INSEAD, France, INDRA and Meta4, Spain, Archetypon, Greece, FZI, Germany and Deltatec, Belgium. Thanks are due to Thierry Nabeth and Camille Wormser for providing me feedback on this paper.

REFERENCES

Angehrn, A., Nabeth, T., Leveraging Emerging Technologies in Management-Education: Research and Experiences, *European Management Journal*, Elsevier, 15, pp. 275-285, 1997.

Abecker A., Bernardi A., Hinkelmann K., Kühn O., and Sintek M., Context-Aware, Proactive Delivery of Task-Specific Knowledge: The KnowMore Project. Int. Journal on Information Systems Frontiers (ISF) 2(3/4):139-162, Special Issue on Knowledge Management and Organizational Memory, Kluwer, 2000.

Baumgartner, R., Enzi, C., Henze, N., Herrlich, M., Herzog, M., Kriesell, M., and Tomaschewski, K.: Semantic Web enabled Information Systems: Personalized Views on Web Data. International Ubiquitous Web Systems and Intelligence Workshop (UWSI 2005), Co-located with ICCSA 2005, Suntec Singapore, 9-12 May 2005.

Bachimont, B., "Engagement sémantique et engagement ontologique: conception et réalisation d'ontologies en ingénierie des connaissances", in *Ingénierie des connaissances, Evolutions récentes et nouveaux défis*, éd. par Jean Charlet et al. , Paris: Eyrolles, pp. 305-325, 2000.

Benjamins V. R., Cobo, J., M., L., Contreras, J., Casillas J., Blasco J., de Otto B., García J., Blázquez M., Dodero J. M. (2002): Skills Management in Knowledge-Intensive Organizations. EKAW 2002: pp. 80-95.

Brusilovsky, P. (1998). Adaptive educational systems on the World Wide Web: A review of available technologies. *Proceedings of the 4th International Conference in Intelligent Tutoring Systems,* San Antonio, TX.

Chen, J., R., Mathe, N., and Wolfe S., (1998), Collaborative Information Agents on the World Wide Web, In ACM DL, pages 279–280.

Colucci, S., Di Noia, T., Di Sciascio, E., Donini, F.M., Mongiello, M., Piscitelli, G., Semantic-based Approach to Task Assignment of Individual Profiles. In Proc. of I-Know '04, pp. 285-292, Springer, 2004.

Davenport, T., H., Prusak L., (1998), Working Knowledge: How Organizations Manage What They Know, Harvard Business School Press.

Dillenbourg, P., and Self, J., (1992), A framework for learner modeling. *Interactive Learning Environments*, 2 (2), 111-137.

Deroïan, F., (2002), *Formation of social networks and diffusion of innovations*, Research Policy, Volume 31, Issue 5, July 2002, Pages 835-846.

Dore, L., (2001), Winning through Knowledge: How to Succeed in the Knowledge Economy, Special Report by the Financial World, The Chartered Institute of Bankers in association with Xerox. London: March, 2001.

DeSanctis, G., Wright, M., Jiang, L., (2001), Building a Global Learning Community, CACM, Issue: Global Applications of Collaborative Technology, Vol. 44, No. 12 December, 2001.

Daconta, M, C., Obrst, L, J., Smith, K, T., 2003 The Semantic Web: A guide to the future of XML, Web Services and Knowledge Management, Wiley Publishing Inc. Indiana

D. O'Leary. Using Artificial Intelligence in knowledge management: Knowledge bases and ontologies. *IEEE Intelligent Systems*, 13(3):34–39, May/June 1998.

Dzbor, M., Motta, E., Uren, V., Lei, Y., Reflection on the future of knowledge portals. AIS SIGSEMIS Bulletin 1(2), pp. 32-35, July 2004.

Dieng, R., Corby, O., Giboin, A., Ribière, M., Methods and Tools for Corporate Knowledge Management. S. Decker and F. Maurer eds, *International Journal of Human-Computer Studies, special issue on knowledge Management,* vol. 51, pp. 567-598, 1999. Academic Press.

Dieng-Kuntz, R., Corby, O., Gandon, F., Golebiowska, J. *Ontologies pour un Web sémantique d'entreprise.* Chapitre 1 de Gestion Dynamique des Connaissances Industrielles, Benoît Meynard, Muriel Lombard, Nada Matta, Jean Renaud, éds, Hermès, 2004.

Gandon, F., Dieng-Kuntz, R., Corby, O., Giboin, A., Semantic Web and Multi-Agents Approach to Corporate Memory Management, 17th IFIP World Computer Congress IIP Track – Intelligent Information Processing, p. 103-115, August 25-30, 2002, Montréal, Canada.

Greer, J., McCalla, G., Collins, J., Kumar, V., Meagher, P., and Vassileva, J.,(1998): *Supporting Peer Help and Collaboration in Distributed Workplace Environments.* International Journal of Artificial Intelligence in Education 9, 1998, pp. 159-177

Guarino, N., 1997, "*Understanding, building, and using ontologies: A commentary to* "Using Explicit Ontologies in KBS Development", by van Heijst, Schreiber, and Wielinga." International Journal of Human and Computer Studies 46: 293-310.

Guarino, N., Carrara, M., Giaretta, P., *An ontology of meta-level categories*, in: Sandewall, D., J., E., Torasso, P., (Eds.), Principles of Knowledge Representation and Reasoning: Proceedings of the Fourth International Conference (KR94), Morgan Kaufmann, San Mateo, CA, 1994, pp. 270-280.

IMS LIP, 2001, IMS Learner Information Package http://www.imsproject.org/aboutims.html, 2001.

IRS, 2004, Internet Reasoning Service Framework, http://kmi.**open**.ac.uk/projects/**irs**/.

Janssen, M.,A., and Jager, W., (2001),Fashions, habits and changing preferences: Simulation of psychological factors affecting market dynamics, Journal of Economic Psychology, Volume 22, Issue 6, December, Pages 745-772.

Kay, J, (2000), User modeling for adaptation, in *User Interfaces for All*, Stephanidis (ed), C, Salvendy, G, (General Editor), Human Factors Series, Lawrence Erlbaum Associates, 271—294.

Kim, H. Y., Rieh, S. Y., Ahn, T.K., & Chang, W. K., Implementing an ontology based knowledge management system in the Korean financial firm environment. Proceedings of the 67th Annual Meeting of the American Society for Information Science and Technology. Medford, N.J. Information Today.

OWL_S, 2004, W3C, Web services activity OWL-S submission, http://www.w3.org/Submission/2004/SUBM-OWL-S-20041122/.

Paolucci, M., Sycara, K., Autonomous Semantic Web services, Internet Computing, IEEE, Volume: 7, Issue: 5, Sept.-Oct. 2003, Pages: 34 – 41.

Maedche, A., Motik, B., Stojanovic, L., Studer, R. and Volz, R., Ontologies for Enterprise Knowledge Management, *IEEE Intelligent Systems*, November/December, 2002.

Malhotra, Y., Integrating Knowledge Management Technologies in Organizational Business Processes: Getting Real Time Enterprises to Deliver Real Business Performance, *Journal of Knowledge Management*, Special Issue on Knowledge Management and Technology, Q4, 2004.

Motik, B., Maedche, A. and Volz, R.,: A Conceptual Modeling Approach for building semantics-driven enterprise applications, Proceedings of the First International Conference on Ontologies, Databases and Application of Semantics (ODBASE-2002), Springer, California, USA, 2002.

Maedche, A., Motik, B., Stojanovic, L., Studer, R. and Volz, R., Ontologies for Enterprise Knowledge Management, *IEEE Intelligent Systems*, November/December, 2002.

Nonaka, I. and Hirotaka T., (1995), The Knowledge-Creating Company, Oxford University Press.

Noy N., F., Sintek M., Decker S., Crubezy, M., Fergerson, R., W., &. Musen, M. A., 2001, Creating Semantic Web Contents with Protege-2000. *IEEE Intelligent Systems* 16(2):60-71.

Razmerita, L., Angehrn A., Maedche, A., Ontology-based user modeling for Knowledge Management Systems, in Proceedings of "UM2003 User Modeling: Proceedings of the Ninth International Conference", Pittsburgh, USA, Springer Verlag, pp.213-217, 2003.

Razmerita, L, 2003, "User Model and User Modeling in Knowledge Management Systems: An Ontology-based Approach", PhD thesis, University of Toulouse, France, 2003.

Razmerita, L., User modeling and personalization of the Knowledge Management Systems, book chapter in Adaptable and Adaptive Hypermedia, edited by Sherry Chen and George Magoulas, to be published by Idea Group Publishing, 2005.

Stojanovic, L., Maedche, A., Motik, B., Stojanovic, N., (2002): User-Driven Ontology Evolution Management, Proceedings of the 13th European Conference on Knowledge Engineering and Management, EKAW-2002, Springer, LNAI, Madrid, Spain.

Snowdon, D. Grasso, A., (2002), Diffusing information in organizational settings: learning from experience, Conference on Human Factors and Computing Systems, Minnesota, pp. 331 – 338.

Skyrme, J, (1999), Knowledge Networking, Creating the Collaborative Enterprise, Butterworth-Heinemann.

Sure, Y., Staab, S., Studer, R., Methodology for development and employment of ontology based knowledge management applications, ACM, Volume 31, Issue 4 (December 2002).

Staab S., Domingos P., Mika P., Golbeck P, Ding L, Finin, T., Joshi, A., Nowak, A., Vallacher, R.. "Social Networks Applied," *IEEE Intelligent Systems*, vol. 20, no. 1, pp. 80-93, January/February 2005.

Tsai T., Yu H., Shih H., Liao P., Yang R., Chou, S., T: Ontology-Mediated Integration of Intranet Web Services, IEEE Computer 36(10): 63-71 (2003).

Uschold, M. and Gruninger, M., "Ontologies: principles, methods, and applications", *Knowledge Engineering Review*, volume 11, number 2, pages 93–155, 1996.

Vasconcelos, J., Kimble, C., Rocha, A., Ontologies and the Dynamics of Organisational Environments: An Example of a Group Memory System for the Management of Group Competencies, Proceedings of I-Know'03, Graz, Austria, 2003.

WSMO, 2005, Web Service Modeling Ontology Project, http://www.wsmo.org/2004/d7/v1/index.html.

Chapter 24

ONTOLOGY-BASED USER PROFILES FOR PERSONALIZED SEARCH

Susan Gauch[1], Mirco Speretta[1] and Alexander Pretschner[2]

[1]University of Kansas; [2]ETH-Zurich

Abstract: As the number of Internet users and the number of accessible Web pages grows, it is becoming increasingly difficult for users to find documents that are relevant to their particular needs. Users who submit a query to a publicly available search engine must wade through hundreds of results, most of them irrelevant. The core of the problem is that, whether they are an eighth grade student or a Nobel Prize winner, the identical Web pages are selected and they are presented in the same way. In this chapter, we report on research that is aimed at providing search results tailored to individual users. In order to provide these personalized search results, the search engine exploits information about the user captured in automatically created user profiles. We compare a variety of mechanisms for automatically creating the user profiles, and discuss open issues in user profile creation, representation, and use.

Key words: ontology; personalization; user profiles; Web search

1. INTRODUCTION

The World Wide Web has experienced continuous, exponential growth since its creation. As the number of Internet users and the number of accessible Web pages grows, it is becoming increasingly difficult for users to find documents that are relevant to their particular needs. The primary way that users of the Internet find the information for which they are looking is to submit a query to a search engine and peruse the collection of urls returned. As of February 2005, Google [Google 2005] reports 8.1 billion indexed pages in its database, yet a recent analysis reveals that the average query continues to be only 2.2 words long [Beitzel 04, Jansen 00]. It is not surprising that, when search engines are asked to select the best 10 documents out of billions, approximately one half of the documents on the first page are irrelevant [Casasola 98, Pretschner 99a]. One of the main reasons for obtaining poor search results is that many words have multiple meanings [Krovetz 92]. For instance, two people searching for "wildcats" may be looking for two completely different things (wild animals and sports teams), yet they will get exactly the same results. It is highly unlikely that the millions of users with access to the Internet are so similar in their interests that one set of results fits all needs. What is needed is a solution that will personalize the information selection and presentation for each user.

This paper explores the use of ontology-based user profiles to provide personalized search results. In this work, we use ontology that consists of hierarchies of concepts in which each concept is defined by a set of documents, and hierarchy is induced by an informal specialization relationship. In essence, user profiles consist of weighted ontology. We review a variety of sources of information from which the ontology-based profiles can be created, and describe improvements in accuracy achieved when the user profiles are used to select search results. Section 2 provides an introduction to some related work and, in Section 3, we describe how user profiles can be created from user's browsing behavior. In Section 4, we show how these profiles can be used to improve search results. Section 5 presents an alternative approach to user profile creation, one that focuses on user interactions with the search engine itself that shows significant improvement in search accuracy. Finally, Section 6 concludes the chapter with a summary of the results of these investigations and discusses our current focus on conceptual, personalized search.

2. RELATED WORK

The following section presents related work on personalization, and, in particular, ontology-based personalization.

2.1 Text Classification

Since we create our user profiles automatically using text classification techniques, we start by briefly reviewing research in this area. Classification is one approach to handling large volumes of data. It attempts to organize information by classifying documents into the best matching concept(s) from a predefined set of concepts. Several methods for text classification have been developed, each with a different approach for comparing the new documents to the reference set. These include comparisons between a variety of frequently-used vector representations of the documents (Support

Vector Machines, k-nearest neighbor, linear least-squares fit, tf * idf); use of the joint probabilities of the words being in the same document (Naive Bayesian); decision trees; and neural networks. Surveys and comparisons of such methods are presented in [Sebastiani 02, Yang 99, Pazzani 96, Ruiz 99].

2.2 Personalization

Personalization is a broad field of active research. Applications include personalized access to online information such as personalized "portals" to the Web, filtering/rating systems for electronic newspapers [Chesnais 95], Usenet news filtering, and recommendation services for browsing, navigation, and search. Usenet news filtering systems include *GroupLens* [Konstan 97], *PSUN* [Sorensen 95], *NewT* [Sheth 94], *Alipes* [Mladenic 98], and *SIFT* [Yan 95]. *SiteIF* [Stefani 98] and *ifWeb* [Asnicar 97] aim to provide personalized search and navigation support. *InformationLens* [Malone 87] is a tool for filtering and ranking e-mails. Implicit rating and filtering are, among other topics, discussed in [Nichols 97, Oard 96]. Finally, [Vivacqua 99] describes a system for expertise location in Java source code. [Pretschner 99a] describes approximately 45 personalization systems and contains a detailed bibliography.

Personalized search is addressed by a number of systems. *Persona* [Tanudjaja 02] uses explicit relevant feedback to update user profiles that are represented by means of weighted open directory project taxonomy [ODP 04]. These profiles are used to filter search results. Personalized variants of PageRank, as found in PersonalizedGoogle or the Outride Personalized Search System [Pitkow 02], are also discussed in [Haveliwala 02, Richardson 02, Jeh 03, Aktas 04]. *Persival* [McKeown 03] re-ranks the search results of queries for medical articles w.r.t. profiles—keywords, associated concepts, and weights—generated from an electronic patient record. [Liu 02] filters search results on the grounds of user profiles obtained from earlier queries. These profiles consist of a set of categories, and weighted terms associated with each category. In their work on personalizing search results, [Sugiyama 04] distinguish between long-term and short-term interests. While aiming at personalization in a broader sense, [Almeida 04, Joachims 02] use click-through data to increase the performance of search results.

Many personalization projects have focused on navigation. *Syskill & Webert* [Pazzani 96] recommends interesting Web pages using explicit feedback. If the user rates some links on a page, *Syskill & Webert* can recommend other links on the page in which they might be interested. In addition, the system can construct a Lycos query and retrieve pages that might match a user's interest. *Wisconsin Adaptive Web Assistant* (WAWA) [Shavlik 98, Shavlik 99] also uses explicit user feedback to train neural networks to assist users during browsing.

Personal WebWatcher [Mladenic 98] is an individual system that is based on *WebWatcher* [Armstrong 95, Joachims 97]. It "watches over the user's shoulder," but it avoids involving the user in its learning process because it does not ask the user for keywords or opinions about pages. *Letizia* [Lieberman 95, Lieberman 97] is a similar individual system that assists a user when browsing by suggesting links that might be of interest and are related to the page the user is currently visiting. The system relies on implicit feedback including links followed by the user or pages and/or bookmarked pages. *WebMate* [Chen 98] is an individual system based on a stand-alone proxy that can monitor a user's actions to automatically create a user profile. Then, the user can enter an URL and *WebMate* will download the page, check for similarity with the user's profile, and recommend any similar pages. *Amalthaea* [Moukas 96] is a server-based system that employs genetic algorithms to also try to identify Web pages of interest to users.

Most personalization systems are based on some type of user profile, most commonly a set of weighted keywords. Systems that use structured information rather than simple lists of keywords include *PEA* [Montebello 98] and *SiteSeer* [Rucker 97], both of which use bookmark information, *PSUN* [Sorensen 95] which uses K-lines, and *SiteIF* [Stefani 98] which uses semantic networks. Like [Sugiyama 04], by incorporating temporal information, [Widyantoro 01] uses an extended user profile model that distinguishes between a user's short term and long term interests. *SmartPush* [Kurki 99] uses concept hierarchies for user profiles. As discussed above, *Persona* [Tanudjaja 02] and the Outride Personalized Search System [Pitkow 02] rely on the open directory project ontology to store user profiles.

2.3 User Profiles and Ontologies

In order to build a user profile, some source of information about the user must be collected. Commercial systems, e.g., MyYahoo, explicitly ask the user to provide personal information that is simply stored to create a profile. Explicit profile creation is not recommended because it places an additional burden on the user, the user may not accurately report their own interests, and the profile remains static whereas the user's interests may change over time. Thus, implicit profile creation based on observations of the user's actions is used in most recent projects. [Chan 00] describes the types of information available. His model considers the frequency of visits to a page, the amount of time spent on the page, how recently a page was visited and whether or not the page was bookmarked. Similar to our research, the user's surfing behavior is used to create the user profiles in *Anatagonomy* [Sakagami 97], *Letizia* [Lieberman 95, Lieberman 97], *Krakatoa* [Kamba 95], *Personal WebWatcher* [Mladenic 98], and *WBI* [Barrett 97], and the system described in [Sugiyama 04].

Our user profiling technique [Pretschner 99b, Chaffee 00, Gauch 03, Trajkova 04] focuses on automatically creating user profiles based on ontology. Besides the obvious similarities with [Tanudjaja 02] and [Pitkow 02], in our use of ontology, we overlap somewhat with initiatives aimed at creating a Semantic Web [Berners-Lee 01]. In the Semantic Web approach, the information encoded is given a well-defined meaning using predefined ontology. The predefined ontology, on the other hand, consists of term descriptions and their interrelationships that allow making inferences and retrieving more relevant information that the keyword-based search. Systems such as *Ontogator* [Hyvonen 03], ontology-based image retrieval and recommendation browser, *Ontobroker* [Fensel 99], a hyperbolic browsing tool that uses ontology to annotate Web documents and answer queries, and *OntoRama* [Eklund 02], a generic ontology viewer, make use of the latest tools and ontology representation formats. However, these proposals tend to focus on encoding semantics into the Web pages to describe their content, whereas we use classification techniques to automatically create profiles for users and/or Web sites. The Semantic Web approaches also differ in that they provide a mechanism for representing a wide variety of link types and/or link labels between concepts whereas our hierarchies are simpler since they handle only unlabelled links (assumed to represent parent-child relationships) between concepts.

In the Semantic Web, ontology is modeled using ontology representation languages such as the *Extensible Markup Language* (XML), the *Resource Description Framework* (RDF), *RDF Schema*, *DAML+OIL*, or the *Web Ontology Language* (OWL) [W3C 04]. Although using representation languages to define ontology and then annotating the pages initially requires a significant investment in manual encoding, it facilitates reasoning and inference on the defined information and promises to improve searching and browsing the Semantic Web. In future, our work may inter-operate with Semantic Web approaches by automatically classifying documents (or users) with respect to concepts within ontology, helping to automate the ontological markup of web pages or the creation of ontologically-based user profiles.

Another IR system that structures information through the use of ontology is *OntoSeek* [Guarino 99], which is designed for content-based information retrieval from online yellow pages and product catalogs. OntoSeek uses simple conceptual graphs to represent queries and resource descriptions. The system uses the *Sensus* ontology [Knight 99], which comprises a simple taxonomic structure of approximately 70,000 nodes. The system presented in [Labrou 99] uses *Yahoo!* [Yahoo 05] as ontology. The system semantically annotates Web pages via the use of Yahoo! categories as descriptors of their content. This system uses *Telltale* [Chower 96a, Chower 96b, Pearce 97] as its classifier. Telltale computes the similarity between documents using *n*-grams as index terms.

The ontology used in the above examples use simple structured links between concepts. A richer and more powerful representation is provided by *SHOE* [Heflin 99, Luke 97]. SHOE is a set of Simple HTML Ontology Extensions that allow WWW authors to annotate their pages with semantic content expressed in terms of ontology. SHOE provides the ability to define ontology, create new ontology which extend existing ontology, and classify entities under an "is a" classification scheme.

The research reported here builds on many ideas presented above, however, the combination of automatic profile creation on the grounds of browsing/searching histories, the representation of user profiles as weighted ontology, the application in web search and processing on both server and client sides seem to be unique.

3. USER PROFILING

Any personalized system relies on the use of some form of user profile. The user profile may be created explicitly, by users filling in online forms, or implicitly from information gathered from users as they use the system. It may reside on the client machine or at the server. It may be temporary, created for each user session, or persistent, stored and reused over many sessions. Finally, the user profiles may be represented as a set of attribute values stored in databases, keyword vectors, or ontology.

In our research, we focus on creating the user profile automatically and implicitly while the users engage in their normal tasks. By creating the profiles implicitly, no additional burden is placed upon the user. They get the advantages of personalized results with no additional cost in terms of effort. Another advantage of implicitly creating a profile is that the profile has the ability to change over time as user's interest change. Explicitly created profiles run the risk of becoming inaccurate over time as users shift interests but fail to update their profiles.

Our user profile is essentially a reference ontology in which each concept has a weight indicating the user's perceived interest in that concept. Profiles are generated by classifying text representative of the user's interests into the concepts contained in the reference ontology and the results of the classification are accumulated. Thus, the concepts in the reference ontology receive weights based on the amount of text collected from the user related to that concept. No explicit user feedback is necessary. Section 4 explores the use of Web pages that reflect user browsing histories. Section 5 discusses profiles built from queries submitted and/or snippets examined during searching. The remainder of this section discusses the creation of the user profiles, regardless of the source of the representative text.

3.1 Reference Ontology

Since our user profile is essentially a weighted ontology, our first goal was to locate or create reference ontology on which to base our user profile. Rather than create our own ontology, a time consuming process, we chose to base our ontology on already existing subject hierarchies. Online portals such as *Yahoo.com* [Yahoo 2005] and *About.com* [About 2005] provide manually-created online subject hierarchies and a set of Web pages manually associated with each subject designed to organize Web content for easy browsing by end-users.

One of the advantages of our approach is that our system can work with a reference ontology created from any subject hierarchy that has associated textual information. To date, we have based our reference ontology on subject hierarchies and associated Web pages from Yahoo!, Magellan, Lycos, and the Open Directory Project. Since most subject hierarchies allow a given subject to have more than one parent, the subject "hierarchy" is actually a directed acyclic graph (DAG). We implemented the DAG by replicating the subject (and associated Web pages) in each location to which it is linked. The subject hierarchies typically contain well over 100,000 subjects arranged in a DAG with a depth exceeding 10. Since we wish to create a relatively concise user profile that identifies the general areas of a user's interests, we create our reference ontology by using concepts from only the top few levels of the subject hierarchy. In addition, since we want concepts that are related by a generalization-specialization relationship, we remove subjects that were linked based on other criteria, e.g., alphabetic or geographic associations.

The automatic profile creation described in the next section is based upon text classification algorithms. In order to classify the user's representative text into concepts in the reference ontology, the classifier requires a collection of associated Web pages to be used as training data for each concept. Thus, we exclude concepts from the reference ontology if there are too few Web pages to adequately train the classifier.

For the experiments on personalized search based on browsing histories described in Section 4, the reference ontology on which the user profile is based consisted of the 4,417 concepts from the top four levels of the subject hierarchy created by Magellan that had adequate training data. After this study was concluded, Magellan ceased to exist as a directory site. Because their directory was being made freely available, the Open Directory Project was chosen as a replacement. Therefore, for the experiments in personalized search based on search activity described in Section 5, the reference ontology contained 1,869 concepts from the top 3 levels of the Open Directory Project's [ODP 04] subject hierarchy. To create all reference ontology, we created a local copy of their subject hierarchy by spidering or ftp. We then parsed each subject page to locate the content Web pages linked for each subject that were then downloaded to be used for training the classifier.

3.2 User Profile Creation

The user profiles creation consists of two phases: training the classifier and classifying user-sample texts representative of the user's interests.

3.2.1 Training the Classifier

During classifier training, a fixed number of sample documents for each concept are collected and used as examples for the concept. These are the Web pages that are associated with a node in the subject hierarchy, and they form the training set. We employ a vector space classifier in which each concept is represented by a vector of weighted terms. The terms are extracted from the training set and weighted using a variation of the vector space term weighting formula. As shown in Equation (1), the weight of term *i* in concept *j* is calculated as:

$$wt_{ij} = tf_{ij} * icf_i * cdf_{ij} \quad (1)$$

where

tf_{ij} = the total frequency of term *i* in all training documents for concept *j*

icf_i = the inverse concept frequency

= log (TotalConcepts/NumConcepts containing term *i*)

cdf_{ij} = the concept document frequency

= log (NumTrainingDoct for concept *j* containing term *i*)/(Total TrainingDoct for concept *j*)

The first two factors weight a term based on its total frequency in the training set for a concept and the rarity of the term in the training sets for other concepts. Essentially, icf_i is equivalent to the traditional idf_i calculated per concept rather than per document. Note that we use an extra factor, the *cdf* (concept document frequency) in addition to the traditional *tf * idf*. Earlier experiments [Gauch 04] found a significant improvement in classifier accuracy when the *cdf*, a measure of how many of the individual training documents in the training set contain the term, was also used to weight the importance of a term as a representative of a concept.

Because not all training documents are the same length, the concepts vary somewhat in the amount of training data. To compensate for this, the term weights in each concept vector are normalized by the vector magnitude, creating unit length vectors. Equation (2) shows the calculation of nwt_{ij}, the normalized weight of term *i* in concept *j*.

$$\mathrm{nwt}_{ij} = (\mathrm{wt}_{ij} / \mathrm{vector - length}_j) \tag{2}$$

where

$$\mathrm{vector} - \mathrm{length}_j = \sum \mathrm{wt}_{ij}$$

The dimensionality of the concept vectors is very large, one dimension for every word used in any document in the collection. This dimensionality is somewhat reduced by removing stop words and further reduced by stemming. However, since the training set for each concept contains only a small fraction of the possible words, and absent terms receive a weight of 0, these concept vectors are very sparse. Thus, for fast access during classification, our classifier stores the mappings from terms to concept weights calculated during training in a traditional inverted file.

We have trained the classifier with a wide variety of Web pages per concept and have found that the classification algorithm is not particularly sensitive to the amount of training data. Using a variety of subject hierarchies, we found that anywhere from 5 pages to 60 pages per concept can provide reasonably accurate classification [Gauch 04]. When trained with 30 documents per category for 1,484 ODP concepts in the top 3 levels, the correct concept for a document was the top-ranked concept 46% of the time and occurred among the top 5 ranked concepts 79% of the time.

We have used a vector space classifier; however other classification algorithms would be equally appropriate. When compared to a Naïve-Bayes classifier [Zhu 99], we found that our classifier was significantly more accurate. Recently, we found that hierarchical classification, classifying documents into the best top level category and then "walking" the document down the subject hierarchy by classifying the document into sub concepts of that concept only provided a large increase in the accuracy of the highest matching concept (70% versus 46%) [Pulijala 04], so we are modifying our profile creation to incorporate these new results. Finally, several studies such as [Joachims 98] suggest that Support Vector Machine (SVM) classifiers are more accurate than vector-space classifiers, so we are conducting experiments to confirm these results in our large concept space.

3.2.2 Building the User Profile

The representative text collected for each user is periodically classified into the appropriate concept(s) in the reference ontology. For each of the text samples, a document vector is calculated using the same formulae used for the concept vectors. The similarity between the vector for sample *k*, d_k, and the vector associated with concept *j*, c_j, was calculated using the cosine similarity measure (see Equation 3). The concepts with the highest similarity values were assumed to be those most related to the sample text.

$$similarity(d_k, c_j) = \frac{\sum_{i=1}^{n} (ntd_{ik} * ntc_{ij})}{\sqrt{\sum_{i=1}^{n} ntd_{ik}^2 * \sum_{i=1}^{n} ntc_{ij}^2}} \tag{3}$$

where

ntd_{ik} = the normalized weight of term *i* in document k

ntc_{ij} = the normalized weight of term *i* in concept *j*

n = the number of unique terms in the document collection *D*

Initially, a user's profile starts off with all concepts in the ontology having a weight of zero. As sample texts are classified with respect to the reference ontology, the values reported by the classifier are added to the top five concept's weights, i.e., the user profile. Over time, as more and more text is classified, the weights are accumulated. Concepts into which many representative texts are classified continue to increase in weight, and it is our hypothesis that higher weighted concepts represent concepts of greater user interest.

4. PERSONALIZING SEARCH BASED ON BROWSING HISTORIES

Our initial investigations into personalized search built user profiles from browsing histories. For our experiments, users shared with us the urls they visited over a period of several weeks by periodically emailing us their browser caches. In a deployed system, this information would need to be collected at the desktop or by a proxy server and either shared with the search engine or, alternatively, a desktop search bot could use the profile to re-rank the results locally. The advantage to the last architecture is that the user's browsing history would be collected, processed, and used entirely by their desktop computer, addressing the privacy concerns that arise when user profiles are created and shared.

Each url in the user's browsing history is spidered to collect a local copy and these Web pages are used as the representative text for the user. Each page is classified and the results are added to the profile. Since the classifier returns a list of matching concepts in decreasing order of weight, one factor to consider is how much of this list to use when adding to the profile. For these experiments, we used the top matching 5 concepts for each web page. This decision is based on our analysis the results of classifying Web pages. The correct concept occurs in the top 5 categories 80% of the time, and the classifier accuracy falls off dramatically as we progress further down the list.

We also investigated the influence of two other factors in the page-concept similarity calculation used when building the user profile: the duration of the visit and the page length. Intuitively, if a user spends a long time on the page, their interest value in that page should be increased. However, if the page is long, the influence of the time factor should possibly be decreased since the increased time may be due to the amount of information presented, not the level of interest. We used four different formulae (shown in Equation (4)) to combine the time and page length factors to adjust the weight of a concept c_j in a user profile. This happens on the grounds of a previously visited document d_k classified into c_j.

$$update(d_k, c_j) = timelengthfactor * similarity(d_k, c_j) \quad (4)$$

where

timelengthfactor is calculated in one of four ways:

$$\frac{time}{length} \quad \text{(i)}$$

$$\log\frac{time}{length} \qquad \text{(ii)}$$

$$\log\frac{time}{\log length} \qquad \text{(iii)}$$

$$\log\frac{time}{\log\log length} \qquad \text{(iv)}$$

time = the amount of time the user spent visiting the page in seconds
length = the length of the page in bytes

The first two *timelength* factor formulas, (i) and (ii), are straightforward normalizations of the time spent browsing the page by the length of the page. For formulae (iii) through (iv), the importance of length as a normalizing factor on time is decreased by first logging and then log-logging the length component The evaluation of our user profile creation algorithm consisted of two parts [Pretschner 99b]. First, we tested our profile creation algorithm to determine whether or not it was able to create a stable user profile. The second experiment validated our automatically generated user profiles against actual user interests.

4.1 Profile Convergence

One would assume that each person has a relatively stable collection of interests that may change over time [Lam 96]. We wished to determine how long it takes our system to identify this core set of interests. In our work, a user profile is said to be convergent if the number of concepts with non-zero interest values converges over time. Users varied in the number of categories to which their profiles converged, most containing between 50 and 200 concepts that account for 95% of the total accumulated profile weight. Low-weighted concepts were ignored to filter "noise" introduced by text classification and/or user navigation errors.

For the experiments, a group of sixteen users were monitored for 26 days. These sixteen users together surfed 7,664 documents. The users spent a mean of 54.6 seconds per page, with a standard deviation of 93.4 seconds. 20% of all pages were visited for less than 5 seconds. All profiles showed a tendency to converge after roughly 320 pages, or 17 days, of surfing when the document-concept similarity values were adjusted by the *timelength* formulae (iii) and (iv). These are the formulae that minimize the effect of the length of the page on the document/concept similarity calculation. On the other hand, when we used *timelength* formulae (i) and (ii), the profiles did not converge. This indicates that the length of a surfed page is not an important factor when calculating the user's interest in a particular page (and thus their interest in the page's associated concepts). Thus, it seems that users can tell at a glance that a page is irrelevant and, in general, reject it quickly regardless of its length.

4.2 Comparison with Actual User Interests

Although convergence is a desirable property, it does not measure the accuracy of the generated profiles. Thus, the sixteen users were shown the top twenty concepts in their profiles in random order and asked how appropriately these inferred concepts reflected their true interests. For both the top ten and top twenty concepts, approximately one half of the concepts represented actual interests (5.2 and 10.5 respectively), one quarter represented errors and the remaining quarter represented topics of marginal interest. Bearing in mind that the "good" concepts have been chosen out of 4,400 concepts, this result is encouragingly accurate. 75% of the twenty categories chosen reflect actual interests even though these represent only 0.5% of all possible concepts.

Because queries are so short, search engines generally do not receive enough detail about the user's information need. As a result, many retrieved documents are irrelevant. Although the profiles created as described in Section 3 were not perfect, we hypothesized that they were accurate enough to allow a search engine to provide personalized search. We evaluated the use of our automatically created user profiles for personalized search using two different approaches:

1. <u>Re-ranking</u> Re-ranking algorithms apply a function to the document-query match values and/or the rank orders returned by the search engine. If that function is well chosen, it should move relevant documents higher in the list and demote non-relevant documents.
2. <u>Filtering</u> Filtering systems determine which documents in the result sets are relevant and which are not. Good filters remove many non-relevant documents and preserve the relevant ones in the results set.

4.3 Evaluation

For a given query, re-ranking was done by modifying the ranking that was returned by the ProFusion meta-search engine [ProFusion 02]. We classified each of the documents in the result set into the categories of the reference ontology. Rather than using the full documents, which would require a serious delay while the documents were fetched, we classified only the titles and summaries shown on the search engine result page. These, according to [Casasola 98] and [Pazzani 96], are sufficient for accurate classification. We then wanted to estimate the user's interest in a document by examining the user's interests in the concepts to which the document belonged. This was done by averaging the user profile's values for the four concepts identified as being the most similar to the document.

Once we had an estimate for the user's interest in the document's concepts, we re-calculated the match values between the query and the documents. For each search engine result r, we calculated new match values, new_wt_r, based on the match value returned by the search engine, the similarity between the result and its top concepts, and the level of user interest in the top concepts. Equation (5) shows the recalculation of the document/query match weight:

$$new\_wt_r = wt_r * (0.5 + \frac{1}{4}\sum_{l=1}^{4} u_{crl}) \tag{5}$$

where

wt_r is the weight returned by the search engine for result r
u_{crl} is the user's interest in concept c_{rl} (from their profile)
c_{rl} is the lth most highly weighted concept for result r

To compare the results produced by the different re-ranking formulae, we used the eleven point precision average [Harman 96]. The eleven point precision average evaluates ranking performance in terms of *recall* and *precision*. Recall is a measure of the ability of the system to present all relevant items (i.e., it is the percentage of relevant documents retrieved), and precision is a measure of the ability of a system to present only relevant items (i.e., it is the percentage of retrieved document that are relevant).

Sixteen users were each asked to submit three queries (48 total). Two queries per user were used for training (32 total) and the third query was reserved for evaluation (16 total). The results were presented in random order, and the users were asked to judge each result as being "relevant" or "non-relevant."

On average, before re-ranking, only 8.7 of the twenty retrieved pages were considered to be relevant. This is consistent with the findings in [Casasola 98] which reports that roughly 50% of documents retrieved by search engines are irrelevant. The reranking of documents by promoting those that classify into concepts of high interest to the user produced an overall performance increase of 8% (see Figure 24-1). In particular, the biggest improvement occurs within the most highly-ranked documents (recall<.3). Since the top documents are those most likely to be examined by a user, improvement at the top of the list is encouraging.

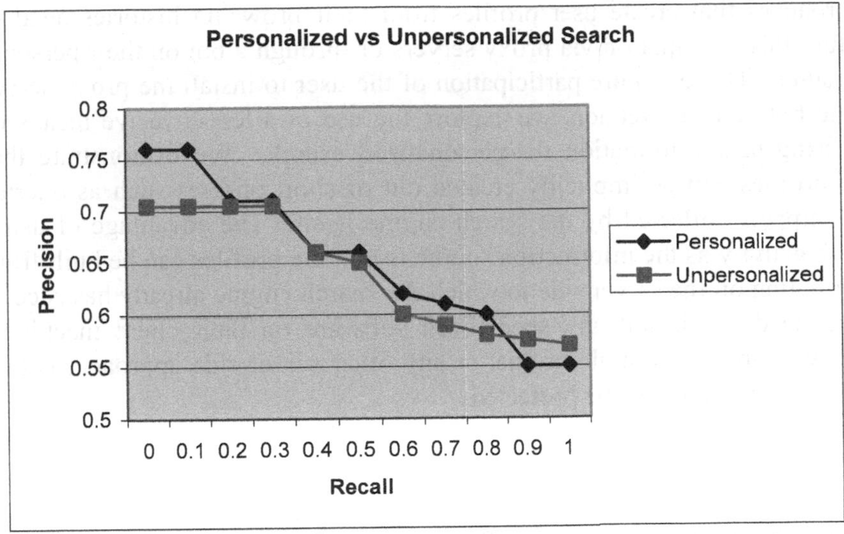

Figure 24-1. Recall and Precision with and without Personalized Reranking

We also evaluated the ability of the user profile to filter documents from the result set. After calculating personalized match values (see Formula 7), we excluded documents whose revised match values fell below a threshold. We evaluated a variety of threshold values and achieved approximately a 2:1 ratio of irrelevant documents removed to relevant documents removed at all values of the threshold. Clearly, as the threshold was raised, more documents of both types were removed.

4.4 Discussion

We were able to create large, structured, user profiles entirely automatically by classifying content from the user's browsing cache into concepts in reference ontology. These profiles were shown to converge and to reflect actual user interests quite well. To evaluate their usability, two applications have been investigated: re-ranking and filtering search results. In terms of re-ranking, performance increases of up to 8% were achieved. In terms of filtering, roughly a 2:1 ratio of irrelevant documents to relevant documents was removed.

5. PERSONALIZING SEARCH BASED ON SEARCHING HISTORIES

As a comparison to building user profiles based on browsing activity, we explored the construction of the user profiles based on user search activity.

Approaches that create user profiles from their browsing histories need to capture this information via proxy servers or through a bot on their personal computer. These require participation of the user to install the proxy server or the bot. In this section, we explore the use of a less-invasive means of gathering user information for personalized search. We demonstrate that user profiles can be implicitly created out of short phrases such as queries and snippets collected by the search engine itself. The advantage of using search activity as the information source is that the profiles can be built from information on the server side to which the search engine already has access. Users need not install any specialized software on their client machines. However, one concern about this, or any other server-side approach, is that the users' privacy must be protected.

5.1 Approach

In order to investigate the effectiveness of personalized search based upon user search histories, we implemented *GoogleWrapper*: a server-side wrapper around the Google search engine, that logs the queries, search results (titles, snippets, and rank), and Web pages selected from the result set. Similar to the browsing history based user profiles, this per-user search information is classified into a concept hierarchy based upon the Open Directory Project [ODP 04], producing conceptual user profiles. Search results are also classified into the same concept hierarchy, and the match between the user profile concepts and result concepts are used to re-rank search results, providing personalized results.

The architecture of our system consists of two modules:

1. GoogleWrapper: a wrapper for Google that implicitly collects information from users. Google APIs [Google APIs] and nusoap library [NuSOAP] were used for the implementation. Users register with their email addresses in order to create a cookie to store and upload their userID on their local machines. If the cookie was lost, GoogleWrapper notified the user and they could login to reset the cookie. When queries are submitted by users, GoogleWrapper logs the query and the userID and then forwards the query to the Google search engine. It intercepts the search engine results, logs them, re-ranks them, and then displays them to the user. When users click on a result, GoogleWrapper logs the selected document along with the user ID before redirecting the browser to the appropriate Web page.
2. The classifier from KeyConcept [KeyConcept 03], a conceptual search engine, is used to classify queries, snippets for each user as well as the search engine results. This vector space model classifier implements a k nearest neighbors algorithm.

We conducted a controlled study to determine the effectiveness of using search-history based user profiles for personalized search. The study was conducted through three phases:

1. collecting information from users. All searches for which at least one of the results was clicked were logged.
2. creation of user profiles. Two different sources of information were identified for this purpose: all queries submitted for which at least one of the results was visited, and all snippets visited. Profiles were created by classifying each query in turn, and accumulating the concept scores, or by apply the same process to the selected snippets one by one.
3. evaluation: the profiles created were used to calculate a new rank of results browsed by users. This rank was compared with Google's rank.

When a user submits a query to the search engine, the titles, summaries and ranking results are obtained. The top 10 results are re-ranked using a combination of their original rank and their conceptual similarity to the user's profile. The search result titles and summaries are classified to create a document profile in the same format as the user profile. The document profile is then compared to the user profile to calculate the conceptual similarity between each document and the user's interests. The conceptual match between the document profile and the user profile is calculated using the cosine similarity function.

$$conceptual\_match(user_i, doc_j) = \sum_{k=1}^{N} cwt_{ik} * cwt_{jk} \tag{6}$$

where

cwt_{ik} = Weight of Concept_k in UserProfile_i
cwt_{jk} = Weight of Concept_k in DocumentProfile_j
N = Number of Concepts

The documents are re-ranked by their conceptual match to produce their conceptual rank. The final rank of the document is calculated by combining the conceptual rank with Google's original rank using the following weighting scheme:

$$\text{FinalRank} = \alpha * \text{ConceptualRank} + (1-\alpha) * \text{GoogleRank} \tag{7}$$

α has a value between 0 and 1. When α has a value of 0, conceptual rank is not given any weight, and FinalRank is equivalent to the original rank assigned by Google. If α has a value of 1, the search engine ranking is ignored and pure conceptual rank is considered. The conceptual and search engine based rankings can be blended in different proportions by varying the value of α.

5.2 Experimental Setup

GoogleWrapper was used by six volunteers for a period of almost 6 months. These users included faculty members and graduate students from Computer Science, Mathematics, and Pharmaceutical Chemistry. They were asked to use GoogleWrapper instead of their regular search engine and all the queries submitted, and the results selected, were recorded.

5.2.1 Studying User Behavior

Our first version of *GoogleWrapper* showed all results retrieved from Google, displaying ten results per page, presented in the original order. We used this version to collect data about how users normally interact with a search engine. After collecting 576 queries for which at least one result was selected, we randomly picked a sample set of 100 queries for further analysis. From this sample, we found that 94% of the user-selected results occurred in the first 3 Google-ranked results, and no result after the tenth result, i.e., on the second page, was ever selected. The top-ranked result was by far the most frequently selected (60%), followed by the second result (20%), and the third (14%). These results lead us to the conclusion that users tend to find the answer they seek on the first page of results. Thus, for our later experiments, we only categorize and re-rank the top 10 results from Google since, in every one of our successful queries, the result the user selected was within that set.

Our second conclusion was that users may be influenced by the rank-order of the result presentation. To verify this hypothesis, we modified GoogleWrapper so that it displayed the top ten results from Google in random order. We randomly selected another sample set of 100 queries and we performed the same analysis. This time, the original rank of the user-selected result was more uniformly distributed across the 10 results displayed. The top three results from Google accounted for 46% when they are presented in random order versus 94% when they are shown in the original order. Google's top result was selected only 15% of the time when it was shown in a random position versus 60% when it is presented at the top of the page. From this, we concluded that user judgments are affected by presentation order, so we continued to randomize the search engine results before presenting them to the user in later experiments.

5.2.2 Collecting Sample Data for Personalization Study

The final version of *GoogleWrapper*, used to collect the user information for our study of personalized search, presented the top 10 results for each query in random order. Using this system, we collected 609 queries for which at least one result was selected. We removed duplicate queries per each user and, from this collection, we selected and distributed 282 submitted queries (47 per user) into the following sets:

- 240 (40 per user) queries were used for training the user profiles;
- 30 (5 per user) queries were used for testing personalized search parameters;
- 12 (2 per user) queries were used for validating the selected parameters.

The search engine has two sources of information from which it could construct a user profile: the queries submitted and the snippets from user-selected results. In the following section, we present four experiments in which we investigated the effects of user profiles built out of queries and snippets. We measured the accuracy of such profiles by comparing, for user selected results, Google's original rank with the conceptual rank based on the profile. Because our goal was to evaluate the quality of the user profiles, not produce the best possible search results, we set α to 1 so that Google's original rank did not affect the FinalRank. Once the best conceptual match was determined, we conducted further experiments to evaluate the effect of varying α on the final results.

5.3 Building a profile from queries

The user profile was created by categorizing the queries selected for training and accumulating the returned concepts and weights. One question that needed to be resolved was, since the categorizer returns a weighted list of concepts and weights, how many of these concepts per query should be used to update to the profile. To answer this, we randomly selected 30 queries (5 per user) and performed a detailed analysis of the classification results. For each query, the top 10 concepts returned by the classifier were manually judged as relevant or not. From this, we found that the top 4 concepts assigned per query were relevant 78% of the time, and that the accuracy dropped dramatically further down the list. Thus, in the experiments that follow, we built the query-based profiles from the top 4 classification results per query.

5.4 Building a profile from snippets

In this case, user-selected snippets (titles and summaries) were used to build the user profiles. As with query-based profiles, we needed to determine the number of classification results to add to the user profile. Once again, we performed an analysis of the classifier accuracy on 30 randomly chosen user-selected snippets (5 per user). Since the snippets contain more text than an average query, the classifier seems to be able to identify more valid concepts per snippet. Compared to the query classification results, the accuracy does not drop as precipitously. Overall, the top 5 classified results are accurate 71% of the time and, further down the list, the accuracy begins to steadily decrease. Based on these results, the snippet-based profiles reported in this study were built using the top 5 concepts returned from the classifier.

5.5 Using a query-based profile for personalized search

The first variable we investigated was the number of training queries necessary to create a useful user profile. As mentioned in Section 5.4, we used the top 4 concepts returned by the classifier for each training query. We evaluated user profiles created using training sets of 5, 10, 20, 30 and 40 queries. When the search result snippets are classified, the classifier returns an ordered list of matching categories and the weight of that match. As with the training data, we need to decide how many of these weighted categories to use to represent the search result. Based on earlier experiments [Challam 04] that evaluated the effect of the number of snippet categories on the accuracy of the conceptual match, we used the top 7 concepts returned by the classifier for each search result (snippet and title). The final variable we studied was the number of concepts from the user profile to use when calculating the conceptual match between the profile and the search results. We varied the number of profile concepts used from 1 to 20.

The resulting profiles were evaluated based upon the rank of the user-selected result produced by the concept ranking algorithm alone, without any contribution from Google's original ranking. This conceptual rank was compared to Google's original rank of the selected result to see if there was any improvement. The rank of the selected result was averaged over all queries, and the average rank of the user-selected result was compared. In general, the lower the average rank, the more highly ranked the selected result and the better the system. With a perfect search engine, the result presented at the top of the list would be the one the user selected, i.e., it produce an average rank of 1.

Table 24-1. The effect of number of training queries on the conceptual rank of user-selected results

# Training Queries	Avg. Rank	Improvement	# Profile Concepts Used
0 (Google)	4.4	–	–
5	3.7	16%	4
10	3.3	24%	10
20	3.1	29%	5
30	2.9	33%	4
40	3.0	31%	5

Table 24-1 shows the average rank of the user-selected result for different numbers of training queries per user. We conducted a series of test runs varying the number of user profile concepts used from 1 through 20. The results for the 30 testing queries (5 per user) were averaged for each test run, and the best results are shown. The average original Google rank for the 30 testing queries is 4.4. In contrast, when 30 training queries are used to build the profile, and 4 concepts from that profile are used during conceptual match, the average conceptual rank is 2.9. Thus, on average, the personalized search engine moved the user-selected result up the list 1.5 spots, from an average of 4.4 to 2.9, in the best case. Using a paired, two-tailed t-test, this improvement of 33% was found to be statistically significant ($p = 0.002$).

5.6 Using a snippet-based profile for personalized search

This experiment repeats the one described in the previous section with profiles built using snippets rather than queries. As mentioned in Section 5.4, we used the top 5 concepts returned by the classifier for each training snippet. We evaluated user profiles created using training sets of 5, 10, 20, 30 and 40 snippets and conceptual match using 1 through 20 profile concepts using the same 30 test queries. As before, search results were represented by the top 7 concepts returned by the classifier.

Table 24-2. The effect of number of training snippets on the conceptual rank of user-selected results

#Training Snippets	Avg. Rank	Improvement	# Profile Concepts used
0 (Google)	4.4	–	–
5	3.2	27%	5
10	3.2	27%	9
20	3.1	29%	7
30	2.9	34%	20
40	3.0	31%	18

Table 24-2 shows the rank of the user-selected result for different number of training snippets per user. We conducted a series of test runs varying the number of user profile concepts used from 1 through 20. The average original Google rank for the 30 testing queries is 4.4. In contrast, when 30 training snippets are used to build the profile, and 20 concepts from the profile are used during conceptual match, the average conceptual rank of the selected result is 2.9. Once again, the personalized system was able to move the user's choice closer to the top of the list. Using a paired, two-tailed t-test, this improvement of 34% was found to be statistically significant ($p = 0.007$).

5.7 Discussion

To better understand the effect of the number of concepts used from the user profile on the quality of the conceptual match, we focused our attention on the best query and snippet based profiles. These occurred when 30 queries and 30 snippets, respectively, were used for training.

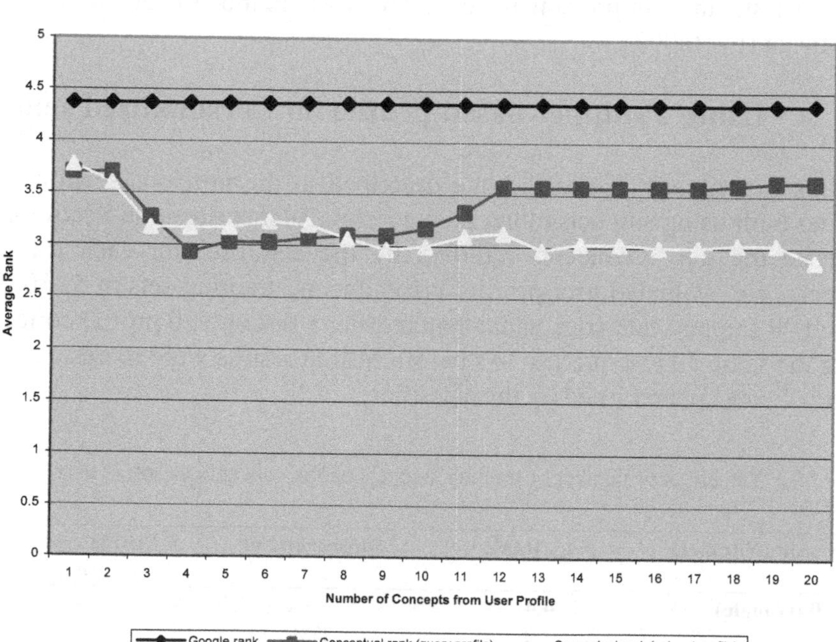

Figure 24-2. Effect of the number of user profile concepts used during conceptual match on conceptual rank (30 training queries/snippets)

From Figure 24-2, we observe that using even a single concept from the user profile provide improved results. As more profile concepts are used, this improvement increases. With query-based profiles, the best results are seen when 4 concepts are used, after which there is a plateau, but when more than 10 concepts are used, we see a decrease in performance to another plateau. So, although all numbers of tested profile concepts show improvement, the best results occur with between 4 and 10 concepts. In contrast, with snippet-based profiles, the improvement remains constant or slightly increases as more concepts are added. We attribute this difference to the fact that, compared to queries, the snippets contain more text and thus create profiles that are more complete and contain more valid concepts. However, the overall improvement achievable with either profile is comparable.

We also examined the results to investigate their effect on the individual testing queries. The query-based profile improved the ranking for 13 queries, hurt the ranking for 3, and left 14 unchanged. In comparison, the snippet-based profile improved the ranking for 11 queries, hurt 4, and left 15 unchanged. They both helped far more queries than they hurt, a promising result.

To validate that the user profiles created above are able improve queries that were not used to tune the profile creation algorithms; we conducted a validation experiment with 12 new queries (2 per user).

Table 24-3. Conceptual rank of user-selected results for the set of 12 validation queries

Ranking Algorithm	Avg. Rank	Improvement	#Training Queries/ Snippets	#Profile Concepts Used
Google (Original)	4.8	–	–	–
Query-based	1.8	37%	30	4
Snippet-based	3.5	27%	30	20

Table 24-3 summarizes these results and we notice comparable improvements for the validation queries as observed for the original test queries used to tune the profile creation algorithms. For these queries, the result the user chose was ranked 4.8 (on average) by Google, 3.5 based on conceptual match with the snippet-based profile, and 1.8 when the query-based profile was used. The query-based profile produced a 37% improvement (versus 33% for the testing queries) and the snippet-based profile produced a 27% improvement (versus 34% for the testing queries). Given how short queries are, it is surprising that they perform as well, or better, than snippets in representing user interests.

Our final set of experiments looked at combining the conceptual rank with Google's original rank to produce a final rank for the results. By varying α from 0 to 1.0 in steps of 0.1, we varied the relative contributions of the two rankings. Our best results occurred when α was 1.0 (i.e., the final rank was entirely determined by the conceptual rank, with no contribution from Google's original rank). We explain this result by noting that the top 10 results from the search engine are all very good matches for the keywords in the query and that the important distinguishing feature between them is how well they match the user's interest.

6. CONCLUSIONS AND FUTURE WORK

Our research goal is to provide personalized search results based upon user profiles built from implicit user feedback. The profiles are represented as weighted concept hierarchies whose weights are determined by classifying representative text from a variety of sources: browsing histories, search engine queries, and the snippets of selected search results.

When building profiles by classifying the contents of a user's browsing history, we found that the user profiles converged to a stable set of 50 to 100 concepts after approximately 320 browsed pages. We found that incorporating a small contribution from the time spent browsing the page into the classification formula lead to profile convergence, but that the size of the page was not an important factor. We were able to demonstrate that the user profiles were reasonably accurate in that 75% of the concepts identified were judged by the users to accurately reflect their actual interests.

We created a personalized search system that made use of the browsing-history based user profiles. Documents in the result set of an Internet search engine were classified based on their titles and summaries. Those documents that were classified into concepts that were highly weighted in the user's profile were promoted by a re-ranking algorithm. Overall, an 8% improvement in the top 20 precision resulted from this personalized re-ranking, with the biggest improvement seen in the top-ranked results.

Because there are barriers to securely collecting and using browser histories, we explored the creation of user profiles from information directly available to the search engine itself – the user queries and selected search results. We were able to demonstrate that information readily available to the search engine server is sufficient to provide significantly improved personalized rankings. We found that using a profile built from 30 queries produced an improvement of 33% in the rank of the selected result and that a user profile built from snippets of 30 user-selected results showed an equivalent improvement of 34%. Our best results occurred when conceptual ranking considered only 4 concepts from the query-based profile, and all 20 concepts from the snippet-based profile. The ranking improvements hold fairly steady across the evaluated range of 1 – 20 concepts used, especially in the case snippet-based profiles are used.

The personalized search improvements were greater for profiles built from search interactions than when profiles were built from browsing histories (27% – 37% improvement versus 8%). Since the browsing experiments used a somewhat different ontology (Magellan versus ODP), the numbers cannot be directly compared. However, this was a somewhat surprising result. Because Web pages contain more representative text than queries and/or snippets, we expected that classifying the browsing histories would lead to more accurate user profiles. In fact, the opposite seems to be true. In retrospect, we believe that this result is due to the increased noise added when entire Web pages are classified rather than queries/snippets. The text collected by the search engines directly may be much smaller, but they are a more focused, direct representation of the user interests. Thus, they provide a clearer indication of user interests than entire Web pages of which only a small portion may be of interest to a given user.

We are currently exploring a variety of extensions to our personalized search approach. The user profiles we used to build were based on a three-level deep concept hierarchy. We would like to examine the effect of using fewer or more levels of the ODP [ODP 04] hierarchy as our profile representation. Also, the current concept hierarchy is static, and we would like to evaluate algorithms to dynamically adapt the hierarchy for specific users by merging and/or splitting concepts based upon the amount of user interest. Finally, we would like to combine the user profiles with the document selection process, not just the document re-ranking, to provide a wider set of relevant results to the user rather than just reorganizing the existing results. This is the goal of KeyConcept [KeyConcept 03], a conceptual search engine that incorporates document classification during indexing. Our next step is to merge the automatically created user profiles with KeyConcept so that the user profile is implicitly submitted along with the query terms. Documents that match the supplied keywords and also the concepts in the user profile will be preferentially retrieved. It is our hope that we will thereby make a major step towards truly personalized search.

REFERENCES

[About 2005] About. http://www.about.com.

[Aktas 04] Aktas M.S., Nacar M.A., Menczer F. Personalizing PageRank Based on Domain Profiles. *In Proceedings 6th SIGKDD Workshop on Web Mining and Web Usage Analysis* 2004.

[Almeida 04] Almeida R., Almeida V. A Community-Aware Search Engine. *In Proceedings of the 13th International Conference on the World Wide Web*, May 2004

[Armstrong 95] Armstrong R., Freitag D., Joachims T., Mitchell T. WebWatcher: A Learning Apprentice For The World Wide Web. *In Proceedings of the AAAI Spring Symposium On Information Gathering* 1995; 6-12.

[Asnicar 97] Asnicar F., Tasso C. ifWeb: A Protoype of User Model-Based Intelligent Agent for Documentation Filtering and Navigation in the World Wide Web. *In Proceedings of the 6th International Conference on User Modeling* June 1997.

[Barrett 97] Barrett R., Maglio P., Kellem D. How to Personalize the Web. *In Proceedings of ACM CHI'97*, Atlanta, USA, 1997.

[Beitzel 04] Beitzel S., Jensen E., Chowdhury A., Grossman A., Frieder O.: Hourly Analysis of a Very Large Topically Categorized Web Query Log. In Proceedings of the 27th Annual International ACM SIGIR Conference, Sheffield, July 2004.

[Berners-Lee 01] Berners-Lee T., Hendler J., Lassila O. The Semantic Web. *Scientific American* May, 2001; 284(5): 34 – 43.

[Casasola 98] Casasola E. ProFusion Personal Assistant: An Agent for Personalized Information Filtering on the WWW. *Master's thesis*. The University of Kansas, 1998.

[Chaffee 00] Chaffee J., Gauch S. Personal Ontologies For Web Navigation. *In Proceedings of the 9th International Conference On Information Knowledge Management (CIKM)* 2000; 227-234.

[Challam 04] Challam V. Ontology-Based User Profiles for Contextual Search. *Master's thesis*. The University of Kansas, 2004.

[Chan 00] Chan P. Constructing Web User Profiles: A Non-Invasive Learning Approach. In: *Web Usage Analysis and User Profiling*, LNAI 1836, Springer-Verlag, 2000: 39-55.

[Chen 98] Chen L., Sycara K. A Personal Agent for Browsing and Searching. *In Proceedings of the 2nd International Conference on Autonomous Agents* 1998; 132-139.

[Chesnais 95] Chesnais P., Mucklo M., Sheena J. The Fishwrap Personalized News System. *In Proceedings of IEEE 2nd International Workshop on Community Networking: Integrating Multimedia Services to the Home* June 1995.

[Chower 96a] Chower G., Nicholas C. Resource Selection in Café: an Architecture for Networked Information Retrieval. *In Proceedings of SIGIR'96 Workshop on Networked Information Retrieval.* Zurich, 1996.

[Chower 96b] Chower G., Nicholas C. Meta-Data for Distributed Text Retrieval. *In Proceedings of First IEEE Metadata Conference* 1996.

[Eklund02] Eklund P., Green S., Roberts N., Ontorama: Browsing an RDF ontology using a hyperbolic-like browser. In: *The First International Symposium on CyberWorlds (CW2002).* Theory and Pracitces,IEEE Press, November 2002.

[Fensel99] Decker S., Erdmann M., Fensel D., Studer R. Ontobroker: Ontology Based Access to Distributed and Semi-Structured Information. In: R. Meersman et al., editors, *Database Semantics: Semantic Issues in Multimedia Systems*. Kluwer Academic Publisher, 1999; 351-369.

[Gauch 03] Gauch S., Chaffee J., Pretschner A. Ontology-Based User Profiles for Search and Browsing. *Web Intelligence and Agent Systems* 2003; 1(3-4):219-234.

[Gauch 04] Gauch S., Madrid, J., Induri, S., Ravindran, D., and Chadlavada, S. KeyConcept: A Conceptual Search Engine, *Information and Telecommunication Technology Center Technical Report,* ITTC-FY2004-TR-8646-37, University of Kansas, 2004.

[Google 2005] Google Search Engine. http://www.google.com.

[Google APIs] Google Web API's. http://www.google.com/apis/.

[Gövér 99] Göver N., Lalmas M., Fuhr N. A Probabilistic Description-Oriented Approach for Categorising Web Documents. *In Proceedings of the 8th International Conference on Information and Knowledge Management* 1999; 475-482.

[Guarino 99] Guarino N., Masolo C., Vetere G., OntoSeek: Content-Based Access to the Web. *IEEE Intelligent Systems*, May 1999; 14(3):70-80.

[Harman 96] Harman D. Evaluation Techniques and Measures. *In Proceedings of the 4th Text REtrieval Conference (TREC-4)* 1996; A6-A14.

[Haveliwala 02] Haveliwala T. Topic-sensitive PageRank. In: Lassner, D., De Roure, D., Iyengar, A., eds.: *In Proceedings 11th International World Wide Web Conference,* ACM Press, 2002.

[Heflin 99] Heflin J., Hendler J., Luke S. SHOE: A Knowledge Representation Language for Internet Applications. *Technical Report CS-TR-4078 (UMIACS TR-99-71)*, University of Maryland at College Park, 1999 http://www.cs.umd.edu/projects/plus/SHOE/pubs/techrpt99.pdf.

[Hsu 99] Hsu W., Lang S. Classification Algorithms for NETNEWS Articles. *In Proceedings of the 8th International Conference on Information and Knowledge Management* 1999; 114-121.

[Hyvönen] Hyvönen E., Saarela S., Viljanen K. Intelligent Image Retrieval and Browsing Using Semantic Web Techniques. *A Case Study. Presented at the International SEPIA Conference at the Finnish Museum of Photography*, Helsinki, September 2003.

[Jansen 00] Jansen B.J., Spink A., Saracevic T. Real life, real users, and real needs: a study and analysis of user queries on the web. *Information Processing and Management* 2000; 36(2):207-227.

[Jeh 03] Jeh G., Widom J. Scaling personalized Web search. *In Proceedings 12 th International World Wide Web Conference* 2003.

[Joachims 97] Joachims T., Freitag D., Mitchell T. WebWatcher: A Tour Guide for the World Wide Web. *In Proceedings of IJCAI'97* August 1997.

[Joachims 98] Joachims T. Text Catehorization with Support Vector Machines: Learning with Many Relevant Features. *In Proceedings of the European Conference on Machine Learning*, Springer, 1998.

[Joachims 02] Joachims T.: Optimizing Search Engines using Clickthrough Data. *In Proceedings of the ACM Conference on Knowledge Discovery and Data Mining (KDD)*, ACM, 2002.

[Kamba 95] Kamba T., Bharat K., Albers M. The Krakatoa Chronicle – An Interactive, Personalized Newspaper on the Web. *In Proceedings of the 4th International WWW Conference* 1995; 159-170.

[KeyConcept 03] KeyConcept Project. http://www.ittc.ku.edu/keyconcept.

[Knight 99] Knight K., Luk S. Building a Large Knowledge Base for Machine Translation. *In Proceedings of American Association of Artificial Intelligence Conference (AAAI)* 1999; 773-778.

[Konstan 97] Konstan J., Miller B., Maltz D., Herlocker J., Gordon L., Riedl J. GroupLens: Applying Collaborative Filtering To Usenet News. *Communications of the ACM* 1997; 40(3): 77-87.

[Krovetz 92] Krovetz R., Croft B. W. Lexical Ambiguity and Information Retrieval. *ACM Transactions on Information Systems* 1992; 10(2):115-141.

[Kurki 99] Kurki T., Jokela S., Sulonen R., Turpeinen M. Agents in Delivering Personalized Content Based on Semantic Metadata. *In Proceedings of the 1999 AAAI Spring Symposium Workshop on Intelligent Agents in Cyberspace* 1999; 84-93.

[Labrou 99] Labrou Y, Finin T. Yahoo! As An Ontology – Using Yahoo! Categories To Describe Documents. *In Proceedings of the 8th International Conference On Information Knowledge Management (CIKM)* 1999; 180-187.

[Lam 96] Lam W., Mukhopadhyay S., Mostafa J., Palakal M. Detection of Shifts in User Interests for Personalized Information Filtering. *In Proceedings of ACM SIGIR'96*, Zurich, Switzerland, 1996.

[Larkey 98] Larkey L. S. Automatic Essay Grading Using Text Categorization Techniques. *In Proceedings of the 21st Annual International ACM SIGIR Conference on Research and Development in Information Retrieval* 1998; 90-95.

[Lieberman 95] Lieberman H. Letizia: An Agent That Assists Web Browsing. *In Proceedings of the 14th International Joint Conference On Artificial Intelligence* 1995; 924-929.

[Lieberman 97] Lieberman H. Autonomous Interface Agents. *In Proceedings of the ACM Conference on Computers and Human Interaction (CHI'97)* May 1997.

[Liu 02] Liu F., Yu C., Meng W. Personalized web search by mapping user queries to categories. In Proceedings CIKM'02 2002; 558-565.

[Luke 97] Luke S., Spector L., Rager D., Hendler J. Ontology-Based Web Agents. *In Proceedings of the First International Conference on Autonomous Agents (AA'97)* 1997.

[Lycos 02] Lycos. http://www.lycos.com.

[Malone 87] Malone T., Grant K., Turbak F., Brobst S., Cohen M. Intelligent Information Sharing Systems. *Communications of the ACM* 1987; (30): 390-402.

[McKeown 03] McKeown K., Elhadad N., Hatzivassiloglou V. Leveraging a common representation for personalized search and summarization in a medical digital library. *In Proceedings of the 3rd ACM/IEEE-CS joint conference on Digital libraries* 2003; 159-170.

[Mladenic 98] Mladenić D. Personal WebWatcher: Design and Implementation. *Technical Report IJS-DP-7472*, J. Stefan Institute, Department for Intelligent Systems, Ljubljana, Slovenia, 1998.

[Montebello 98] Montebello M., Gray W., Hurley S. A Personable Evolvable Advisor for WWW Knowledge-Based Systems. *In Proceedings of the 1998 International Database Engineering and Application Symposium (IDEAS'98)* July 1998; 224-233.

[Moukas 96] Moukas A. Amalthaea: Information Discovery And Filtering Using A Multiagent Evolving Ecosystem. *In Proceedings of the Conference on the Practical Application of Intelligent Agents and MultiAgent Technology* 1996: http://moux.www.media.mit.edu/people/moux/papers/PAAM96.

[Nichols 97] Nichols D. Implicit Rating and Filtering. *In Proceedings of the 5th DELOS Workshop on Filtering and Collaborative Filtering* November 1997.

[NuSOAP] NuSOAP Library. http://dietrich.ganx4.com/nusoap.

[Oard 96] Oard D., Marchionini G. A Conceptual Framework for Text Filtering. *Technical Report EE-TR-96-25 CAR-TR-830 CLIS-TR-9602 CS-TR-3643*. University of Maryland, May 1996.

[ODP 04] The Open Directory Project (ODP). http://dmoz.org.

[Pazzani 96] Pazzani M., Muramatsu J., Billsus D. Syskill & Webert: Identifying Interesting Web Sites. *In Proceedings of the 13th National Conference On Artificial Intelligence* 1996; 54-61.

[Pearce 97] Pearce C., Miller E. The TellTale dynamic hypertext environment: Approaches to scalability. In: *Advances in Intelligent Hypertext, Lecture Notes in Computer Science.* Springer-Verlag, 1997.

[Pitkow 02] Pitkow J., Schütze H., Cass T. et all. Personalized search. *CACM* 2002; 45(9):50-55.

[ProFusion 02] ProFusion. http://www.profusion.com.

[Pretschner 99a] Pretschner A.. Ontology Based Personalized Search. *Master's thesis.* University of Kansas, June 1999.

[Pretschner 99b] Pretschner A., Gauch S. Ontology Based Personalized Search. *In Proceedings of the 11th IEEE International Conference on Tools with Artificial Intelligence (ICTAI)* November 1999; 391-398.

[Pulijala 04] Pulijala A., Gauch S. Hierarchical Text Classification. *International Conference on Cybernetics and Information Technologies, Systems and Applications: CITSA 2004* Orlando, FL, July 21 - 25, 2004.

[Richardson 02] Richardson M., Domingos P. The intelligent surfer: Probabilistic combination of link and content information in PageRank. In: *Advances in Neural Information Processing Systems* 14, Cambridge, MA, MIT Press 2002; 1441–1448.

[Rucker 97] Rucker J., Polanco M. J. Siteseer: Personalized Navigation For The Web. *Communications of the ACM* 1997; 40(3): 73-75.

[Ruiz 99] Ruiz M., Srinivasan P. Hierarchical Neural Networks For Text Categorization. *In Proceedings of the 22nd Annual International ACM SIGIR Conference on Research and Development in Information Retrieval* August 1999; 281-282.

[Sakagami 97] Sakagami H., Kamba T. Learning Personal Preferences on Online Newspaper Articles From User Behaviors. *In Proceedings of the 6th International WWW Conference* 1997; 291-300.

[Salton 89] G. Salton. Automatic Text Processing. Addison-Wesley, 1989. ISBN 0-201-12227-8.

[Sebastiani 02] Sebastiani F. Machine Learning in Automated Text Categorization. *ACM Computing Surveys* 2002; 34(1):1–47.

[Shavlik 98] Shavlik J., Eliassi-Rad T. Intelligent Agents for Web-Based Tasks: An Advice-Taking Approach. *In Working Notes of the AAAI/ICML-98 Workshop on Learning for text categorization.* Madison, WI, 1998.

[Shavlik 99] Shavlik J., Calcari S., Eliassi-Rad T., Solock J. An Instructable, Adaptive Interface for Discovering and Monitoring Information on the World Wide Web. *In Proceedings of the 1999 International Conference on Intelligent User Interfaces.* Redondo Beach, CA, 1999.

[Sheth 94] Sheth B. A Learning Approach to Personalized Information Filtering. *Master's thesis*. Massachusetts Institute of Technology, 1994.

[Sorensen 95] Sorensen H., McElligott M. PSUN: A Profiling System for Usenet News. *In Proceedings of CIKM'95 Workshop on Intelligent Information Agents* December 1995.

[Stefani 98] Stefani A., Strappavara C. Personalizing Access to Web Sites: The SiteIF Project. *In Proceedings of the 2nd Workshop on Adaptive Hypertext and Hypermedia HYPERTEXT'98* June 1998.

[Sugiyama 04] Sugiyama K., Hatano K., Yoshikawa M. Adaptive web search based on user profile constructed without any effort from users. *In Proceedings 13th Intl. Conf. on World Wide Web* 2004; 675-684.

[Tanudjaja 02] Tanudjaja F., Mui L. *Persona*: A Contextualized and Personalized Web Search. *Proc 35th Hawaii Intl. Conf. on System Sciences* 2002.

[Trajkova 04] Trajkova J., Gauch S. Improving Ontology-Based User Profiles. *In Proceedings of RIAO 2004*, University of Avignon (Vaucluse), France, April 26-28, 2004; 380-389.

[Vivacqua 99] Vivacqua A. Agents for Expertise Location. *In Proceedings of the 1999 AAAI Spring Symposium Workshop on Intelligent Agents in Cyberspace* 1999; 9-13.

[W3C 04] Web-Ontology (WebOnt) Working Group. http://www.w3.org/2001/sw/WebOnt/ 2004.

[Widyantoro 01] Widyantoro D. H., Ioerger T. R., Yen J. Learning User Interest Dynamics with a Three-Descriptor Representation. *Journal of the American Society of Information Science and Technology (JASIST)* 2001; 52(3):212-225.

[Yan 95] Yan T., García-Molina H. SIFT – A Tool for Wide-Area Information Dissemination. *In Proceedings of USENIX Technical Conference* 1995; 177-186.

[Yang 99] Yang Y., Liu X. A Re-Examination Of Text Categorization Methods. *In Proceedings of the 22nd Annual International ACM SIGIR Conference on Research and Development in Information Retrieval* August 1999; 42-49.

[Yahoo 2005] Yahoo! Search Engine. http://www.yahoo.com.

[Zhu 99] Zhu X, Gauch S., Gerhard L., Kral N., Pretschner A. Ontology-Based Web Site Mapping For Information Exploration. *In Proceedings of the 8th International Conference On Information Knowledge Management (CIKM)* 1999; 188-194.

ODIS Applications

Chapter 25

ONTOLOGY-DRIVEN INFORMATION SYSTEM FOR SUPPLY CHAIN MANAGEMENT

Charu Chandra and Armen Tumanyan

Industrial and Manufacturing Systems Engineering Department, University of Michigan – Dearborn, 2340 Engineering Complex, 4901 Evergreen Road, Dearborn, MI 48128

Abstract: Information system design for a supply chain with its complex organizational dynamics and operational uncertainty is a challenging task. The problem assumes greater significance due to the necessity of integrating largely distributed and diverse information system implementations. A framework to address these issues is proposed. Its implementation is a semantic application that is deployed on the Web and managed by agents. This chapter describes the usefulness of separating domain knowledge from information system solutions and developing models in the form of ontologies. An ontology-driven information system for supply chain management incorporating various forms of modeling in decision-making is described. Ontology is proposed as a separate component in information system architecture that effectively complements its three other constituents, viz., interface, management, and gathering. We demonstrate how ontology development is becoming a critical aspect of the information system design. The object-oriented system development life cycle is utilized for this purpose. The role of ontology in information system's two temporal dimensions is demonstrated. At development time, ontology replaces the information system analysis completely and the design stage partly. At run time, ontology separates the domain knowledge from other components and delivers it to them upon request, thus ensuring the compatibility of information support with organizational dynamics, and its adaptability to the rapidly changing environment.

Key words: ontology; information support; ontology-driven information system; supply chain modeling

1. SUPPLY CHAIN AND ITS INFORMATION NEEDS

Supply chain (SC) is a logistics network of manufacturing, plant operations, distribution and warehousing facilities utilized to effectively integrate plans and actions of suppliers, manufacturers, and distributors through performing functions of procurement of materials, transformation of these materials into intermediate and finished products, and their distribution to customers in the right quantities, to the right locations, and at the right time, in order to meet required service level with minimal cost. It is an extended enterprise with complex organizational structure. SC is not a monolithic organism and is configured as a union of independent units with distinct objectives and policies. These units can be separate organizations, or sub-units of a larger organization.

Information system for supply chain must reflect its evolving structure so as to provide an information platform, whereby members can communicate with each other and solve problems efficiently. One of the primary problems of SC information system (IS) organization is the integration of information in an environment where it is distributed to a large and diverse network with different and sometimes-incompatible information representations. Among the primary information requirements for this complex system are the necessity of standardization, unified information representation, and scalability of information dissemination.

Issues in managing supply chain: The lack of information sharing and synchronization across SC creates the so called "bullwhip effect", wherein demand variability upstream the SC is magnified causing increased inventory level, stock-out at certain times despite overstocking, and increased operational costs (Lee et al., 1997). While, it is not feasible to eliminate the bullwhip effect; however, identifying issues and problems that cause it and solving them systematically can alleviate its impact on the SC.

Information needs for supply chain management: Li et al. (2001) propose an information-sharing environment for tackling the bullwhip effect, whereby four types of information are considered for sharing across SC, viz., order, demand forecasting, inventory management, and shipment. The SC informational specifics require not only sharing data, but also integrating decision-making processes. A typical IS for SC offers a collaborative environment, wherein its members work together on common problems that will make SC processes streamlined and effectively managed. In this environment, members also need to share their objectives, which can be formulated as constraints to be satisfied. SC IS should be compatible with its organizational structure, which can be dynamic with uncertain operational specifics. An adequate information support is required for such an organization.

Role of ontology in supply chain management: In consideration of its complex internal and external relationships such as described above, SC is considered as a network of distributed functions with integrated business processes. Hence, designing IS to facilitate decision-making in SC entails designing information and developing solutions for specialized functions in an integrated environment. Fox et al. (2000) have adopted this approach while considering SC as composed of a set of intelligent software agents, each responsible for one or more activities in the SC pertaining to various functions and interacting with other agents in the planning and execution of their responsibilities. An agent employs a goal oriented software process, where knowledge can be either hard-coded into its logic or separated from the latter and delivered to the agent on as needed basis. It is in this context, that we advocate a pivotal role for ontology in addressing information needs of decision-making for issues and problems encountered by a SC. The approach proposed in this chapter is to build a problem-oriented ontology-driven information system (ODIS) for decision-making in SC. The goal is to create a framework for SC modeling and integration through intelligent information sharing. Developing ODIS is a trend in current research, where domain experts, knowledge and software engineers work collaboratively in identifying domain, general and specific ontologies to support decision modeling for organizational processes (Guarino, 1998) and building the IS infrastructure based on developed ontologies.

Ontology and ontology-driven information systems for supply chain management: The notion of ontology is used to explain the nature of reality (Vasconcelos et al., 2002), and systematically represent its existence. Sowa (2000) defines ontology as the study of categories of things that exist or may exist in some domain. The purpose of using ontologies in the SC domain is to support its decision-making capabilities for various categories of encountered issues and related problems. Two main functions are supported by ontologies, viz., transparent access to largely distributed data resources and delivering problem-specific knowledge. The primary function of an ODIS is identifying problems, building suitable ontologies for them, organizing an environment for maintaining ontologies, and providing access to them.

The framework proposed in this chapter has ontology creation as an integral part of IS development and presents the pivotal role of ontologies in IS architectural components, viz., interfaces, management, and gathering. The role of ontology in development time is to separate the domain analysis from its development stage, and consequently domain knowledge from its implementation. As a result, ontologies are built explicitly representing domain specific knowledge that can be used and reused for different IS implementations. If domain knowledge is updated, ontologies reflect a change in the implemented IS. An example with SC inventory control problem illustrates this assertion. The inventory level constraint as more than the forecasted demand is not hard-coded into software application, but is a standalone construct in the form of an axiom. The application finds this axiom (rule); uses it and follows instructions described therein. The usefulness of separating the domain knowledge from particular IS implementation is twofold. Firstly, the synchronization of IS development efforts among SC members, where they share their domain knowledge is practically difficult, if not feasible. Secondly, due to dynamic and uncertain nature of SC organization, domain knowledge is also susceptible to change. When it is changed, ontologies reflect these changes, and software applications react to them transparently, e.g., if service level now is not 100 percent, the inventory is not necessarily equal to or more than the demand.

The *objective* of this chapter is to describe the important role of ontology in IS design for decision-making in SC management.

The *contribution* of this chapter is to propose an ontology-driven information system that is closely aligned to the supply chain modeling process. This approach offers the promise of mapping information needs of quantitative and qualitative problem-solving techniques and decision-making criteria employed for supply chain management.

The roadmap for ontology-driven information system in supply chain management: In this chapter, we focus mainly on the ontology modeling for a supply chain information system. Figure 25-1 depicts primary building blocks for system development. SC IS fundamentals integrate concepts, techniques, and technologies for syntactic and semantic approaches to design and development of systems, as described in section 2. Among the prominent challenges to SC IS design are system – dynamics, uncertainty, and legacy, primarily due to the real-time decision-making environment prevalent in a SC as described in section 3. This discussion on SC IS fundamentals and challenges guide and motivate design and development of these systems. In section 4, the rationale and a blueprint of ODIS for supply chain management is described. In section 5, real-time implications of ODIS are highlighted and extending the traditional information system architectures to deal with such an environment in SC is discussed. In section 6, ontology development for supply chain management is described as it relates to various modeling needs for supply chain decision-making in the system development life cycle. The last section offers a summary of concepts enunciated in this chapter and provides some ideas for future research in use of ontology in IS design for complex systems, such as SC.

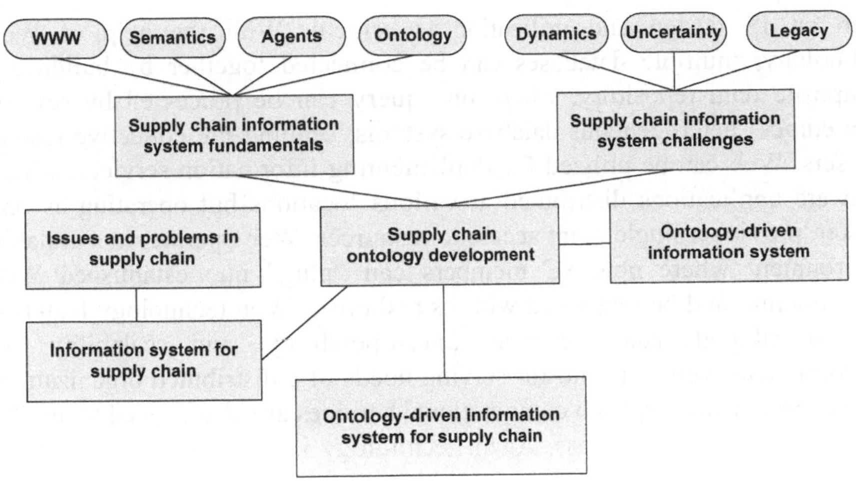

Figure 25-1. Ontology-driven information system for supply chain development - a roadmap

2. SUPPLY CHAIN INFORMATION SYSTEM FUNDAMENTALS

Supply chain – a non-traditional organization: For a traditional organization, generally IS design starts when all requirements are known and collected a priori since it is usually built to support functional requirements of a specific organization. SC is not a typical standard organization, but an extended enterprise with dynamically changing organizational and functional structure, required to meet an evolutionary business environment. Applying traditional methods for IS design cannot normally satisfy needs of SC. These methods address two main issues, viz., 1) structured data requirements, and 2) process functions within the organization. The former provides input for design of database management tools, while the latter offers input for designing software application with functional capabilities to meet process requirements. Other traditional solutions are based on analytical tools that are sometimes difficult to implement because of changing requirements and integration with existing practices and legacy systems.

Designing IS for SC requires an amalgamation of methodologies and technologies that offer inter-operability, scalability, and distributed information content; capable of supporting qualitative and quantitative analysis techniques applied to problem-solving in SC decision-making. Some of these are discussed below.

World Wide Web (or Web) offers a distinct advantage to SC partners by linking them together in an on-line interoperable mode. The impact of

Web on IS design and utilization is critical. With the help of Web technology, multiple databases can be connected together by building a composite data repository, where one query can be processed by several (sometimes) heterogeneous database systems, sending the collective results to users. Web can be utilized for implementing information services, where software applications distributed at various locations but operating as one cluster, provide a single point access to resources. Web operates in a scalable environment where new SC members can "plug" into established Web infrastructure and be integrated with its resources. Web technology features, viz., distributed data exchange, inter-operability, and scalability are appropriate as well as useful for serving needs of a distributed organization, such as SC. However, Web computational services are also needed to aid the SC decision-making process. Agent technology is suggested as one of the solutions for providing these services (Aldea et. al., 2004; Jennings, 2000).

Agent technology provides problem-solving capabilities to networked organizations, such as SC. A software agent is designed for a particular purpose, viz., to achieve a specific problem-solving goal. These software entities communicate with each other by sending messages, searching in the information space for necessary information autonomously, with or without human interference. Agents do not necessarily know how other agents are built and function; only thing they are concerned about is the communication protocol, which assumes shared information representation formalism achieved by applying either syntactical or semantical approaches. The former assumes the existence of shared vocabulary, while the latter allows different interpretations of same terms, but requires taxonomic linkages between these interpretations. Information semantics can be controlled centrally by a common ontology, or in a distributed manner by clustering different ontologies. The communication problem is only one aspect of an agent's existence and functionality. Another useful feature of ontologies in these domains is the fact that agents require specialized knowledge, viz., 1) the heuristics of finding required information, and 2) their processing logic. As presented later in this chapter, ontologies are capable of capturing and delivering this knowledge to software agents.

Semantics is touted as key ingredient in the next generation of information system applications (Sheth and Ramakrishnan 2003). It facilitates interoperability of SC members and is also a technique for coping with heterogeneity and the dynamic nature of SC information resources. Without explicit semantics, software agents, in order to communicate would require direct translation from one system to another. While the physical level of interoperability, distributed computing, and Internet provides scalability, the logical level is provided by semantics of knowledge representation. Traditional IS component, such as database provides very little semantics. Semantics used at database development time, such as entity-relationship-models (ERM) or Unified Modeling Language (UML) diagrams are lost in the translation into physical database schema and thus are unavailable, once the system is implemented. Ontologies, in contrast to database schemas are logical contracts and incorporate semantics. In this chapter, a SC IS is proposed as a semantic application rooted in ontology creation as its main enabler.

Ontology: Early research in ontology was limited to semantic network of the domain, which is related to identifying domain concepts and their relationships (Guarino, 1995; Gruber, 1993). The focus of this research was on defining ontology, and how ideas from philosophy and artificial intelligence disciplines can be incorporated in the information technology field. Current research in ontology broadens its scope and comprises other aspects of the domain, such as description of situations and events (Matheus et al., 2003), the logic of processes (Gruninger and Menzel, 2003), and representation of tasks and problems (Chandrasekaran et al., 1998). The description of situations in SC is representation of various relationships among domain concepts, and what triggers their change, e.g., "the resource is to be reloaded from a product without order, to a product with order". SC process descriptions are explicit representations documenting the flow of a particular process. An example of a SC process is description of a high level "order fulfillment process", or a low level "product shipment scheduling process". Utilization of ontologies in tasks and problems representation is for the purpose of simplifying the complex SC domain by building a hierarchy of tasks with high-level abstraction at the top level and practical tangible issues at the bottom level.

In agent technology domain, ontology provides the format of messages exchanged among agents (Jones, 1998). This format can be primitive when agents are using shared vocabulary or non-primitive when agents are interacting at a semantic layer. The latter is much more complex and requires ontology to support inference function to map different interpretations of the same object. There are many definitions of ontology, but the common one is that ontology conceptualizes the domain by explicitly defining all primitives, concepts, and constraints and represents it with a formal language that can be processed by computers. But the question "what the domain is?" still remains open. What aspects of the domain are supposed to be covered by ontology? Chandra and Tumanyan (2004c) distinguish two features in any domain: static and dynamic. Accordingly, they propose an ontology reference model to reflect these aspects. Through this approach it is shown how static and dynamic natures of the domain can be captured and embedded into information system. A reference model is enumerated to formally represent functional requirements of ontologies to be designed.

Ontology provides the structure and the content of knowledge at a level independent of particular implementations through syntactic and semantic terms for describing knowledge about a domain (Benjamins et al., 1998; Vasconcelos et al., 2002) and capture object features, viz., domain consisting of objects, objects that relate to each other, object possessing attributes, object participating in processes, object that may have one or more states or situations defining values of its attributes, object reacting to events triggering the change of its state, and object containing other objects.

In the context of this chapter, SC ontology modeling is a process whereby ontologies are built as object representation of SC domain at a logical level, capturing various aspects of above itemized features.

The SC IS framework proposed in this chapter offers a collection of semantic applications enabled by ontologies and deployed on a Web environment (such as Semantic Web services) and managed by a set of software agents; designed for problem solving in SC.

3. SUPPLY CHAIN INFORMATION SYSTEM DESIGN CHALLENGES

Among the main issues addressed by SC IS design process are organizational and technological changes. SC poses technological challenges to IS design since they are created for a specific purpose and have finite useful lifetime. These systems have to be designed to reflect dynamic and uncertain nature of the market (Muckstadt et al., 2001).

The *first* challenge is dealing with organizational structural change problem. Theoretically, for each commodity a separate SC can be designed and thus, a separate IS solution could be required.

The *second* challenge posed to SC IS design process is the operational uncertainty attributed to customer demand variability. Variability and uncertainty erode SC efficiency and profitability. An IS design solution that captures information capable of supporting solutions to manage fluctuations in demand (the bullwhip effect) is required. To address the bullwhip effect, many techniques are employed to manage various supply chain processes, such as order information sharing, demand forecasting, inventory management, and shipment scheduling (Li et al., 2001). These and other supply chain management issues have implications beyond SC organizational boundaries (Lambert and Cooper, 2000) and all or most of SC members are engaged in each of the above-mentioned SC process.

The *third* challenge is related to existence of legacy systems. SC organization does not emerge as a new entity, but rather as a collection of already existing companies with different, sometimes incompatible IS implementations. Integration of these different IS solutions is the task of SC IS serving as an umbrella, under which all stand alone systems may coexist, operate independently for solving internal problems, and collaborate across organizational boundaries with other systems on common problems for achieving shared goals.

The above-mentioned challenges are central to defining a new vision of SC IS design. Table 25-1 summarizes causes, challenges and solutions for the SC IS design process. We briefly discuss these dimensions below.

Table 25-1. Dimensions of supply chain information system design process

Causes	Challenges	Solutions
Dynamics	Organizational change	Organization ontology
Uncertainty	Collaboration	Problem Ontology
Legacy	Integration of existing systems	Internet, Semantics, Agents, Ontology

Organization issues are concerned with organizational structures such as goal, administration, product, process, project, resource etc. Organizational structures are areas, where domain requirements and specifications originate. Consequently, organization knowledge is captured and represented in IS. To support organizational functions, information support should be compatible with its structure. This is the most challenging issue of SC IS design, since structures are subject to change frequently and sometimes unexpectedly. The approach proposed in this chapter suggests building a knowledge repository of organizational knowledge presented in the form of organization ontology. It is not linked to any particular IS implementation, but is rather an independent process that can be used in temporal dimensions, viz., development and run-time. Its usefulness is particularly demonstrated in the latter case where change management is brought to a change of organization ontologies to reflect the reality. It can be a new objective dictated by new customer demand, or adding a new member to the SC. The existing IS infrastructure does not need to be revised, but rather reflects changes in ontology and acts according to new requirements.

The second dimension listed in Table 25-1 is collaboration. For supply chain members to work collaboratively, they must do more than merely cooperate. Working jointly, they have to decide how capacities should be created throughout the SC system. They have to decide quantities of products stored, and policies for inventory replenishment. They have to identify actions required when an unexpected event occurs. Strategic, tactical, and operational plans must be developed collaboratively to achieve maximum efficiency and effectiveness. Problem ontology provides means to represent such problems that are common to SC members and where they share common view to processes, which can be either syntactic or semantic. Problem ontologies capture meaning of the problem and represent it in a formal language. These are computational representations carrying knowledge about problems: concepts (setup cost, inventory holding cost, etc., their relationships (setup cost is related to production of product P on resource R at a specific point of time T), and problem solving methods. The latter is concerned with capturing all necessary knowledge for solving the problem. An example is the step-by-step procedure that brings up a solution (check inventory level; if it is lower than L, place an order equal to O for its replenishment).

The SC IS design process elaborated in this chapter supports an integrated decision-making environment by proposing close coupling between the decision-making problem and its causes, emergent challenges and opportunities, and solutions devised for problem solving in a specific domain. The implementation of this design is a semantic application supported by organization and problem ontologies.

4. ONTOLOGY-DRIVEN INFORMATION SYSTEM DESIGN FOR SUPPLY CHAIN MANAGEMENT

Traditionally, IS architecture (ISA) can be divided into three layers or components (Guarino, 1998; Xu, 2000; Kerschberg and Weishar, 2000). These are:

1. *Interface*: users perceive available information through browsing and making queries. This layer must support scalable organizing, browsing, and search.
2. *Management*: responsible for integration and distribution of information and processing logic organization. Application programs belong to this layer.
3. *Gathering*: responsible for collecting, and storing information in a persistent way. Database systems and data repositories are these types of components.

In the domain of ontology application in ISA, two directions can be distinguished: ontology aware, and ontology-driven IS. In the first case, IS is aware of existence of ontologies and can use it for whatever specific application purpose it is needed. In the second case, ontology is another component of IS. ODIS is a trend in current research that envisions utilization of its fourth component ontologies in the development and utilization of first three components of IS (Guarino, 1998; Fonseca et al., 2003; Sheth and Ramakrishan 2003). In this section, the development aspect of ontology is presented. Each of the three components can use ontologies in their specific way.

The most obvious use of ontology is in connection with the database component. In fact, ontology (data model) can be compared with the schema component of a database. Both are logical systems expressing domain knowledge with semantics. Database system management is central to SC management since it captures and stores data necessary for business operations. A number of techniques have been developed (Sugumaran and Storey, 2002) for automating database design but these systems do not contain knowledge about the domain and how it operates. The necessity of applying knowledge-based systems emerges, which can be classified as simplified view of system's environment, labeled as conceptualization. For the purpose of making database design systematically organized, we have to develop an inference mechanism to understand what different terms mean and how they are related semantically. These issues can be addressed by the use of organization ontology. By providing the domain semantic network, organization ontologies support and guide the creation of database conceptual schemas. A useful discussion on application of ontologies in database designs in particular and IS design in general can be found in Fonseca et al. (2003) and Storey et al., (1998).

Another aspect of ontology application in ***gathering*** component is the integration of various legacy systems. Taxonomic links between various interpretations of same terms and definitions help to overcome differences in vocabulary. This can be accomplished through semantic annotations assigned to terms deployed in different systems. SC organization ontology application as a common guideline can facilitate the generation of these annotations.

Maybe not so obvious, but nevertheless very important is the use of an ontology in connection with the user ***interface*** component. In this perspective, ontologies are becoming an important aspect in developing Web applications, especially for building the Semantic Web (Berners-Lee et al., 2001). This is due to the fact that the description languages proposed (Fensel, 2002; Fensel et al., 2001) are represented in XML format, and deployed on the Web. Ontologies can be used in interface component in several ways. One of those is to implement an interface as a query where the user types the term and ontology is used for expanding queries (Ontoquery, (Andreasen et al., 2000)). This approach is based on the assumption that Web resources are annotated and linked to common ontologies. The query formation process involves a search and navigation in knowledge repository stored in ontologies. Relationships among concepts in ontologies are used to build a graph of possible paths that guide users to knowledge. Another possible way of interface implementation is hard coding of ontologies into user interfaces. Ontologies embody semantic information on constraints imposed on classes and relationships, used to model a given domain and task. This concept has been successfully used in the Protégé project to generate form-based interfaces that check for constraints violation (protege. stanford.edu).

Application programs are still an important part of many IS. These usually contain domain knowledge, which for various reasons is not explicitly stored in the database. Some parts of this knowledge are encoded in the static part of the program in the form of type or class declarations; other parts e.g., business rules are implicitly stored in the (sometimes obscure) procedural part of the program. Two forms of embedment of ontologies into information system ***management*** component are considered. The first form is development of conventional software applications, where all functionalities are gathered under one umbrella, and work with central, or distributed data storage systems. Ontology data model consisting of domain concepts and their relationships is turned into class diagram of software application. Functionalities are added to classes from ontology axioms, where constraints, heuristics, and problem solving methods are formally presented. The second form of ontology application into management components is related to agent technology. Organization ontology provides structure of SC domain, the environment where agents are deployed and operate. Problem ontology provides functionalities and properties to each agent.

Facing the problem of largely distributed systems integration and the necessity of SC member's close collaboration in a dynamically changing environment as described in the previous sections, ontologies are proposed as key enablers for implementing a Web-based, agent managed application, where information and data are distributed and shared at a semantic level.

5. ONTOLOGY AT RUN-TIME: AN EXTENSION TO EXISTING INFORMATION SYSTEM ARCHITECTURE FOR SUPPLY CHAIN MANAGEMENT

In the ISA of a knowledge intensive organization, such as SC, ontologies are proposed to be the fourth component in addition to three components described in the previous section, thus emphasizing the importance and significance of the essential role that ontologies play in making information system ontology-driven. The main idea of ontology utilization at run time is to separate domain inherent knowledge from the previously described three components of IS, conceptualize as a separate entity and provide an environment where those components can use and reuse coded knowledge whenever there is a need for it.

The IS proposed for SC consisting of four components is depicted in Figure 25-2.

1. *Management* component is implemented through software agents.
2. *Interface* component is implemented with Semantic Web and Semantic Web services.
3. *Ontology* component is the library and the ontology server to support their capture, assembly, storage and dissemination.
4. *Gathering* components is the same as in traditional IS, but with taxonomic link to common ontologies.

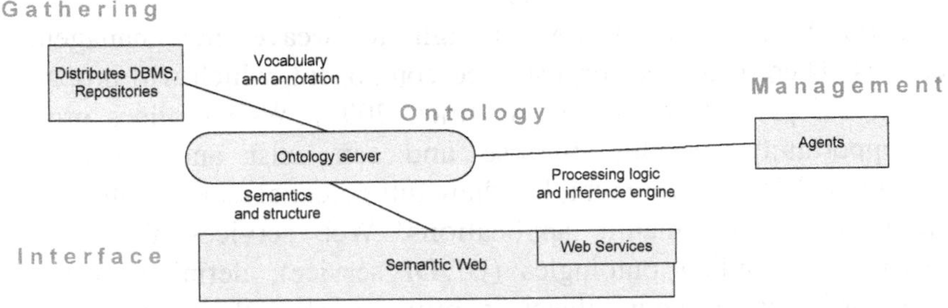

Figure 25-2. Ontology-driven information system components

We discuss each of these components in the following sub-sections.

5.1 Interface – Semantic Web: an environment for supply chain collaboration

The Semantic Web is an extension of the current Web in which information is given well-defined meaning, enabling computers and people to work cooperatively. It has machine-understandable semantics of information and distributed reasoning services that support task management. Two aspects are distinguished in Semantic Web viz. the description of things, or in other words structure of available resources or problem representations (the second requirement, represented by Eq. (7) in section 6.2) and their content (the first requirement, Eq. (1) in section 6.2). This chapter is concerned with the second aspect, leaving domain structure representation as future work. The idea of resource standardization is partially covered in Chandra and Tumanyan (2004b). The problem content is captured and represented by ontologies, which are deployed on Semantic Web usually as XML documents.

In early works, the role of ontology in Web applications (Berners-Lee et al., 2001) was limited to adding pointers from terms used in Web sites to common ontology, i.e., as a syntactical rather than semantic convention. The approach advocated in this chapter is to give more proactive role to ontologies, which serve as a common interface for knowledge searching, navigating, and browsing.

As an interface component, ontologies provide two functionalities implemented and deployed on the semantic Web: (1) structure of domain, and (2) reasoning support. The domain can be organizational or problem-oriented, whose structure is represented by data model (Eq. (4) in section 6.2). Reasoning support provides query answering services, as well as maps with other ontologies or term interpretations. Formally, Eq. (2) in section 6.2 can capture reasoning functions.

Semantic Web alone is not enough to weave SC management applications. There is a need for a service component, which will propagate ontologies and promote their use (Systinet, 2003). Web services provide unique opportunity for this purpose and can exist and function in "conventional" Web environment, but their full potential can be utilized only in conjunction with semantic applications. Web services also provide mechanisms for finding ontologies (UDDI service); defining locations, where a particular ontology object is built up (WSDL service), and a message layout that defines a uniform way of passing XML encoded ontologies (SOAP service). "Once a Web service is deployed, other applications (and other Web services) can discover and invoke the deployed service" (Bussler, 2004).

5.2 Management – Software agents as facilitators of supply chain collaboration

The main difference between semantics and "conventional Web" is content representation, which is machine-process able. By machine, we mean software agents, which use semantic Web services to find and invoke necessary knowledge for implementing their tasks. Software agents are the most effective technology for coping with dynamics of SC system. Agents are interfaces through which SC members advertise their services, searching for services provided by other SC members, accepting requests by other agents, and delivering services. Ontologies provide means for agents to collaborate. Four main services delivered by ontologies to agents build up the management component, viz., (1) communication language, (2) data query engine, (3) data representation structure, and (4) problem solving methods.

As the communication language, ontologies provide a common vocabulary of terms and definitions in case there is only one ontology. If there is more than one ontology, which most probably is the case, there should be ontology mappings between different ontologies through annotations. As the data query engine, ontologies commit to data storage systems, linking terms and definitions identified in vocabulary with variables, values and delivering ontology objects (these are ontology instances, described in Chandra and Tumanyan, 2004a) to software agents. Since agents are autonomous software pieces, they require data to be structured to ensure their unambiguous consumption. Data representation structure is defined by SC ontology, which is discussed later in the chapter.

Representing problem solving principles in knowledge design involves separating the problem solving logic from software application development and store it as ontologies. Agents need to be closely aligned with SC ontology in order to be able to extract problem solving knowledge and follow the required steps.

Problem solving methods consist of a concept or a group of concepts gathered in relationship to present one specific aspect of dynamics of the problem that ontology is built for. An example of problem solving method is description of the process when an order is to be placed. Inventory replenishment algorithm assumes checking the inventory level periodically; if it is less than a predefined level, an order equal to a specified value is placed. This narrative knowledge can be formalized using ontology calculus as follows:

$$Poss(do((L * AVG + z * STD) = s) > Il) \equiv MakeOrder(s - Il)$$

Where, s is the reorder level, L is lead-time, AVG, STD are forecasted demand means and standard deviation respectively, and z is customer service indicator. If inventory level (IL) is less than the calculated reorder level, an order is placed (Order), which is equal to the difference of reorder and inventory levels.

5.3 Gathering – databases with ontological links

One of the challenges of SC IS organization is the integration of existing legacy systems. This is mostly related to the gathering component. Different database systems, platforms, and interpretations of same concepts are some but not the full list of issues that ontology has to cope with. In order to make these different systems to work together and to understand each other's definitions, an additional layer is proposed to be implemented, viz., ontology inference engine. Before a query reaches the database tables, it is checked for meaning of terms used in it. Chandra and Tumanyan (2004c) describe this process as ontological commitment, where abstract terms are linked with variables (see Eq. (5) in section 6.2). Ontology inference engine finds terms used in specific database implementations and translates the query into another query, understandable by the particular system. For the simplest case, when there is only one common ontology, the inference engine has a flat structure, one engine for one database. For complex cases, where there is more than one ontology, the engine may have a hierarchical structure implemented in a distributed environment, partly on ontology server, and partly on database systems.

6. ONTOLOGY DEVELOPMENT FOR SUPPLY CHAIN MANAGEMENT

The ODIS for SC described in this section is aimed at supporting various types of modeling that are necessary in supply chain management tasks. A full complement of complex modeling techniques that enable both qualitative and quantitative analysis are employed for supply chain management. These techniques employ syntactic and semantic forms in modeling supply chain problems. For instance, symbolic models are utilized to extrapolate abstraction from the narrative description of supply chain problems using symbols, to which specific "meanings" are assigned, including operational transformations. These abstractions may represent supply chain at the system level, or a process/activity level as an overall process model. These symbolic models of supply chain are transformed to computational models by reduction of the symbolic model to a form that permits computation, by assigning specific values to parameters, and performing indicated operations. Computational models are applied to explore "what if" questions related to supply chain problems by varying parameter values, seeking "optimum" values, or otherwise exploring alternatives.

In designing the above supply chain modeling techniques, various types of knowledge are enumerated, viz., business and organizational knowledge, analytical modeling knowledge, decision theory knowledge, and experience domain knowledge. This knowledge set has both macro as well as micro dimensions, from very general to highly specific. In designing ontology for supply chain management, this fact is extremely important to recognize. Figure 25-3 depicts various stages of modeling utilized in supply chain management problems, where labels on the left hand side of the figure depict various modeling stages in the supply chain decision-making process life-cycle, while those on the right hand side depict suggested methodologies and approaches that may be undertaken for implementing these stages.

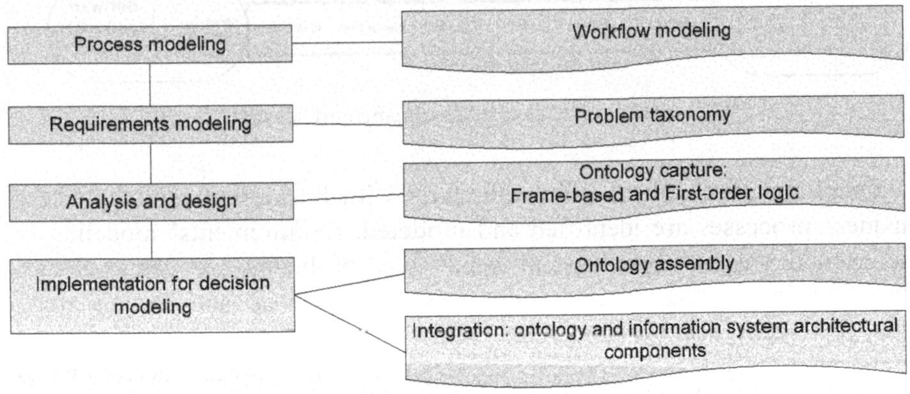

Figure 25-3. Ontology development modeling life cycle for supply chain management

Other methodologies applied to ontology development only partly cover the modeling life cycle. Well-accepted stages in ontology development are specification, conceptualization, formalization, implementation, and maintenance (Pinto and Martins, 2004). Specification stage defines the purpose of designed ontology. Conceptualization stage deals with building conceptual models consisting of concepts and their relationships. During the formalization stage concepts are defined through axioms with intentional meaning of these concepts and possible interpretation. Implementation stage is concerned with writing down conceptual descriptions and axioms in a knowledge representation language. Maintenance is a process for updating and correcting developed ontologies. Throughout this process ontology evaluation is carried out. With the approach proposed in this chapter, ontology development starts with modeling the SC domain, documenting its static and dynamic aspects and based on explicit domain models designing the domain knowledge in the form of ontologies, which will be utilized for information support. The difference between this approach and the standard life cycle is depicted in Figure 25-4. It enhances ontology development process with (1) bringing business process modeling and system requirement identification tasks into the ontology development picture as a part of domain analysis and modeling, and (2) developing computational models for ontologies that can be used directly in IS components at run time. These advances are attributed to the fact that ontologies could play a central role in

IS design and utilization; hence they reflect all aspects of SC domain, which could not be accomplished without systematic approaches and methods.

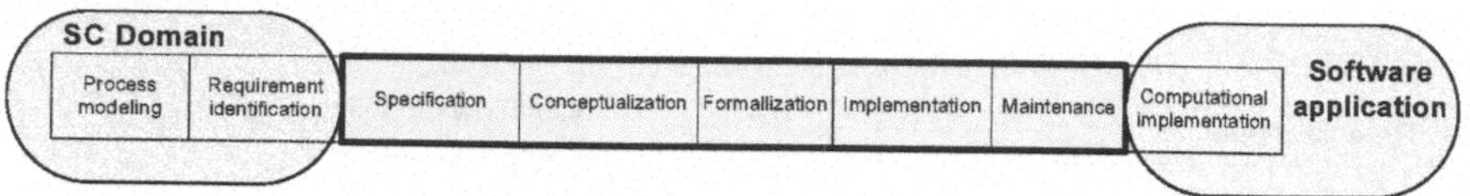

Figure 25-4. Ontology development life cycle

Ontology development life cycle starts with business modeling, where business processes are identified and modeled. Requirements' modeling is the second stage, where system needs and problems are captured and classified in relation to each other. System analysis and design stage identifies candidate architectures and solutions to meet functional requirements. System components are designed and synthesis performed to prove the proposed concepts. The implementation stage assembles designed elements in an integrated environment and builds the system. Test and evaluation stage defines the criteria upon which the developed ontologies are verified and validated.

6.1 Process modeling

Process modeling is applied to capture the complexity of an organizational system. It involves abstractions of complex realities to capture business functions. Just as in software engineering, where designers have created standards for common situations to promote component reusability; similarly SC organizational engineering needs to capture patterns of common processes adopted by its members. A well-known example of business process modeling is the "MIT Process Handbook Project" (Malone et al., 1999) intended to help managers in redesigning organizational processes, adding new processes, and sharing knowledge about organizational structure. Organizational processes are studied at different levels of abstraction and similarities and differences identified. By applying coordination theory from Computer Science, relationships among processes are drawn. The primary contribution of research performed in this project is that it allows to explicitly representing similarities of business processes based on which different alternatives can be generated for performing the given process.

The methodology for process modeling is similar to the one used in software engineering with subtle differences. Using software engineering concepts, a hierarchy of objects with associated properties and methods are designed. Process modeling yields a hierarchy of activities with associated objects. For modeling processes, a combined methodology is proposed by adopting two well accepted methods for process decomposition: (1) supply chain operation reference-model (SCOR) (Stewart, 1997) as a framework for capturing processes at higher level of abstraction, and (2) integrated definition (IDEF) (Lin et al., 2002) methods for representing processes at lower level, viz., task and activity.

SCOR integrates business processes, benchmarking, and best practices into a cross-functional framework. SCOR model builds a hierarchy of SC processes, which can be divided into three levels: process type, process category, and process element. Process type defines five basic management processes in SC (Plan, Source, Make, Deliver, Return) that provide the organizational structure of the SCOR model. The second level defines three process categories: planning, execution, and enable. A planning element is a process that aligns expected resources to meet anticipated demands. Execution processes are triggered by planned or actual demand that changes the state of products. They include scheduling and sequencing, transforming materials and services, and moving product. Enable processes prepare, maintain, and manage information or relationships upon which planning and execution processes rely. The SCOR second level also defines criteria for process classification, e.g., for Make process type, three categories are identified in SCOR: M1 make-to-stock, M2 make-to-order, and M3 engineer-to-order. The third level presents detailed process elements' information on each process category described at the second level, particularly process input, process output, process flows, performance attributes, and best practices for their implementation.

The implementation level is out of scope of SCOR; hence this level is defined using IDEF methods. Process modeling at this level aims to represent processes specified in SCOR third level as a collection of tasks executed by various resources within a SC. Each process transforms inputs into a specific set of outputs to achieve some functional goals. In comparing various business process modeling methods provided by Lin et al. (2002), three methods have been selected: IDEF0, IDEF1, and IDEF3. IDEF0 method is designed to model decisions, actions, and activities of a SC targeted to analyze its functional perspectives. IDEF1 is an information modeling method used in identifying 1) information collected, stored, and managed by a SC, 2) rules governing the management of information, 3) logical relationships within enterprise reflected in information, and 4) problems resulting from lack of good information modeling (Mayer et al., 1995). IDEF3 describes processes as sequence of events and activities. It is a scenario-driven process modeling technique based on precedence and causal relationships between events and situations. IDEF3 model provides the method for expressing and documenting SC domain experts' knowledge about how a particular process works, in contrast to IDEF0, which is concerned with activities that a SC performs.

The proposed process-modeling framework can be represented as a hierarchy of SC processes, where higher-level representations are for representing more generic issues, such as tactical planning and coordination, whereas lower levels are for representing specific issues, such as operational planning and execution. The taxonomy of SC processes and problems associated with them are depicted in Figure 25-5.

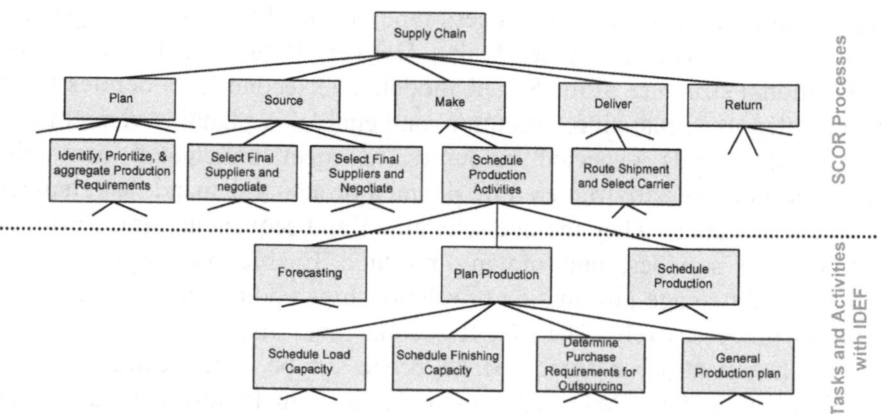

Figure 25-5. A supply chain process model hierarchy

6.2 Requirements modeling

Each level depicted in Figure 25-5 defines the level of information generalization that process models capture. Analyzing problem-oriented nature of activities and processes in SC, IS requirements can be formulated as follows:

1. Necessity of knowledge modules that carry information about processes and problems identified above. Knowledge requirements comprises following issues for each process to be defined (Chandra and Tumanyan 2004a):
   - Entities and their properties
   - Relationships “within” problem and “between” problems
   - Constraints
   - Behaviors
2. Systematic representation of processes and problems. The process model hierarchy depicted in Figure 25-5 serves as a guideline for building problem taxonomy by applying classification taxonomic schemas (Chandra and Tumanyan 2004b).

Ontologies are intended to meet both requirements. In accordance with the first requirement, ontologies could be developed as knowledge modules that comprise data necessary for modeling the problem and rules that relate data elements to each other. In accordance with the second requirement, ontologies are classified as a hierarchy, where higher-level modules describe more generic problems, whereas lower levels are knowledge modules about more specific practical issues. Chandra and Tumanyan (2004c) have developed a reference model for ontology development, whose formalisms are used herein for requirements representation.

Formally, the first requirement can be formulated as:

$$O = (M, \mathrm{C}, \mathrm{H}) \tag{1}$$

Where, O is the target ontology, M is the problem or process data model, C is a set of axioms formalizing constraints placed on entities, H is a set of algorithm's axioms formally representing problem behavior.

Constraints can be identified through studying situations where processes occur. More the number of situations (observation channels), more are chances that all possible constraints are studied.

$$C = (C \rightarrow V \cup \mathrm{B}_C) \tag{2}$$

Where, B_C is the set of observation channels (Guarino, 1998), through which constraint C is assigned to variables V.

Algorithm captures conceptualized knowledge related to problem solving methods. Observation channels B_H are required to define algorithm H, which utilizes data model M to solve the problem.

$$H = (H \rightarrow M \cup \mathrm{B}_H) \tag{3}$$

Problem data model consists of problem representation and its commitments to existing IS infrastructures. Eq. (1) is a generic model representation. Starting from this point, models are represented for a specific problem w. Data model can be formally represented as:

$$M_w = (S_w, \mathrm{I}) \tag{4}$$

Where, S_w is a problem representation and I are ontological commitments that link ontology vocabulary with the terminology adopted and used by existing IS. Problem representation S_w is a collection of entities, their properties, and relationships between properties as well as relationships with other problem properties:

$$S_w = (T_w, \mathrm{R}_w) \tag{5}$$

Where, T_w is a set of entities (in System Science these are called things) pertinent to problem w, T_w are entities participating in this process, R_w are relationships among entities. Entities possess attributes:

$$T_w = \{a_i \mid a_i \subseteq A\} \tag{6}$$

Where, a_i is a set a properties or attributes relevant to problem w, and is a subset of the entire collection of attributes A, describing SC domain.

The first requirement presented by Eq. (1) is concerned with defining components and features of a domain related to one problem. The second requirement presented by Eq. (7) defines relationships among problems themselves. Thus, the SC domain can be represented as a set of problems related to each other:

$$S = \{S_w, F_w \mid w \in W\} \tag{7}$$

Where, W is the number of all SC problems, and F_w defines hierarchical relationships among problems and can be formally presented as:

$$F_{w1}(S_{w1}, S_{w2}) = \{(x, y) : y \in \{S_{w1}\} \wedge x = \{S_{w2}\} \wedge \forall x \mapsto y \mid w1, w2 \in W\} \tag{8}$$

In each relationship, there is only one y, which is an element of a set S_{w1}; x is a set of attributes of component S_{w2}, and each x is designed to describe the element y.

6.3 Analysis and design

This stage of ontology development is for analyzing and designing information support constructs for SC problems. UML can be utilized for representing complex business processes. The advantage of using process models is that use case diagrams can be applied to conceptually closed systems (Bowler, 1981) viz., particular problems. Process model defines scope of the “closed” system and equations specified as requirements define elements needed to be identified.

SC as any other system has static and dynamic features. SC problem analysis considers these two aspects. Ontology data model (Eq. (4) in section 6.2) is the static aspect and can be represented as semantic network consisting of concepts and their relationships. Ontology axioms constitute the dynamic aspect and are expressed through algebraic formulas.

6.3.1 Ontology data model

UML class diagrams are utilized for representing problem semantic network. The process of building the semantic network (or frame-based system representation) starts with studying the problem documented using SCOR formalisms together with IDEF methods. One of the issues that arise is how to make data models designed for problems to be compatible with each other (Eqs. (2)-(3); in section 6.2).

Chandra and Tumanyan (2004b) propose principles of system taxonomy as a common source for concepts and structure of semantic network representation. The idea of system taxonomy arises from the necessity of having information representation standardized, which assumes shared vocabulary and unified information format / knowledge representation. System taxonomy is designed for the entire SC and comprises practically all aspects of SC domain. For this purpose, elements of system theory are utilized. SC is considered as a holistic, open, complex, and managerial system. The holistic facet is ensured by presenting SC as consisting of seven components: input, output, environment, function, process, agent, and mechanism. As a complex system, SC is a set of components, which can be decomposed into subcomponents. As an open system, SC is in continuous interaction with its environment. Incorporating issues related to mechanisms for planning and controlling processes reflects the managerial facet and problem in SC at three managerial levels, viz., strategic, tactical and operational. The overall structure of system taxonomy is depicted in Figure 25-6.

System taxonomy is built using a classification schema, according to which SC characteristics are classified based on their relevance to seven system components, which are implemented as packages. Further decomposition of these packages and grouping characteristics into new sub-packages yields a hierarchy of SC issues labeled as system taxonomy. The input package contains system requirements, resources, and customer needs, etc. In the output package, product and services produced by the SC system are described. The environment package is concerned with the organizational behavior, market conditions, and constraints imposed on SC as a whole and on its components. Agents are catalysts, which may bring about a change in the system, viz., SC members, their roles, etc. In the function package, goals and objectives are presented as well as means for achieving them. Mechanism package provides methodologies, strategies, and tools necessary for managing the SC system. Process package captures details about different types of flows, viz., material, demand, information, etc.

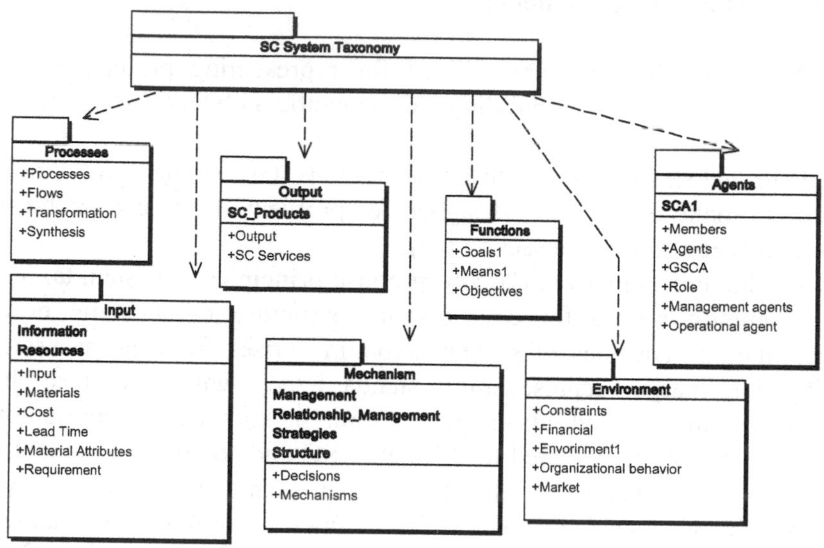

Figure 25-6. Supply chain system taxonomy

The Ontology data model analysis and design consists of following steps:

1. Find the set of involved attributes through studying a process model,
2. Find in system taxonomy these attributes and mark classes that they belong to, and
3. Project system taxonomy into problem structure by selecting only marked classes.

The first step is a study of finding characteristics related to problem, e.g. for inventory control problem following parameters are involved: service level, backorder cost, required inventory level, maximum inventory level, inventory holding cost, etc. The second step is a search of characteristics found in system taxonomy hierarchy depicted in Figure 25-6. Obviously, this figure reflects only the top level representation of a SC. Every package consists of classes, parameters, and other packages. Characteristics listed above are located mostly in input and output packages. As a result of applying the third step, a new diagram is depicted containing only specified characteristics and having the same structure as the system taxonomy. An inventory problem model is depicted in Figure 25-7. Service level and backorder cost parameters reside in the input package. Other parameters describing the product features, such as demand, inventory holding cost, etc.

reside in the output package. As can be seen, new groupings, such as "Demand", "ProductCost" is formed to make the information representation more accurate.

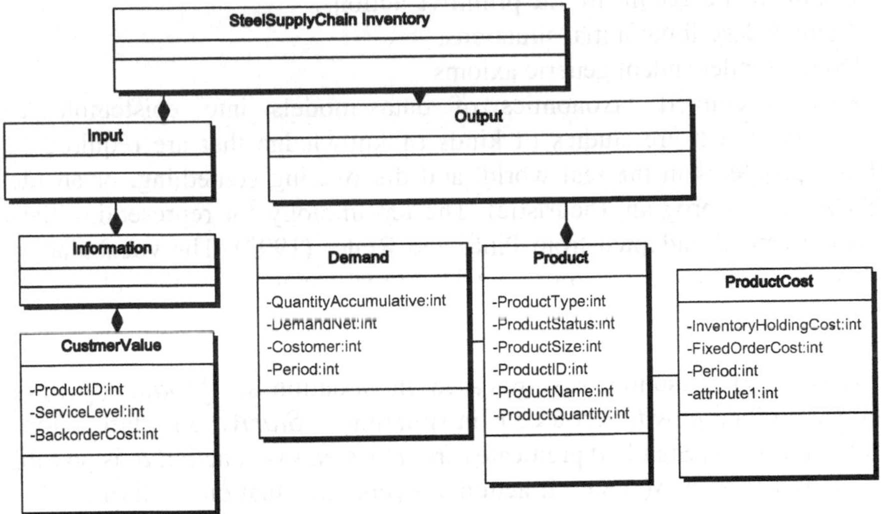

Figure 25-7. Inventory control problem data model

6.3.2 Ontology axioms and problem solving methods

The process of axioms and problem solving methods analysis and design is the search for rules relevant to the problem for which ontology is to be built. Rules capture relationships among attributes included in the data model. The theory of axioms representation is based on situation calculus, a set of algebraic expressions designed to capture system dynamics. Situation calculus (Lesperance et al., 1995) as a tool for first-order logic representation has been adopted to provide semantics to SC ontology axioms. In situation calculus, the sequence of actions is represented with first order term called situation. These representations are carried out with the help of symbols denoting an action or a predicate. Thus, the symbol $Do(x, s)$ represents a new state s_1, which is a result of an action applied in situation s. Situations, whose true values vary from situation to situation, are called functional fluents. These take the situation s as the last argument, which serves as a precondition. $Delivering(airfare, product, s)$, statement is a fluent, meaning that the product is delivered by airfare only in situation s. Actions have preconditions identifying when these are physically possible. An example of a precondition can be $Poss(Demand, Seasonal) \equiv Apply(Time\_Series, method)$, where time-series method can be applied only when the demand is seasonal. In general, applying a set of axioms captures the dynamics of the domain of interest:

1. Action precondition axiom for each primitive action.
2. Successor state axioms for each fluent.
3. Unique name axioms for the primitive actions.
4. Axioms describing initial situations.
5. Domain independent generic axioms.

Axioms convert taxonomies of data models into epistemological constructs, which are studies of kinds of knowledge that are required for solving problems in the real world, and discovering something, or an idea embedded in a program (heuristic). The terminology for representing these axioms is mostly adopted from Pinto and Reiter (1993). The vocabulary of statements and predicates to present SC domain specifics is the subject of a separate research. Standard statements are: $Do(a,s)$ perform action a in situation s, $Consume(p,s)$ - product p is consumed in situation s, $\mathrm{Re}lease(r,s)$ - resource r is released in situation s, $\mathrm{Pr}oduce(p,r,s)$ - produce product p, with resource r, in situation s, $Start(a,s)$ - start action a in situation s, etc. Standard predicates are $Poss(a,s)$ - if action a, is possible in situation s, $Occurs(a,s)$ - if action a, occurs in situation s, $Actual(s)$ - if situation s exists, $Holds(f,t)$ - if function f is held during time t, $During(t,s)$ - is situation s exists during time t, $Enables(a,s)$ - if action a is enabled in situation s, etc.

Extended terminology can be added to express specific activities that are involved in SC. The sequence of these statements and predicates can be used to present new actions, such as sequences of letters make words, thus trying to conceptualize any activities that may occur in SC.

6.4 Implementation for decision modeling

The implementation is concerned with representation of knowledge captured during the design stage in ontological constructs, which comprises: 1) committing to basic terms that will be used to specify ontology, 2) choosing a representation language, and 3) writing the code. It simply has to do with writing down in some language or communicative medium, descriptions or pictures that correspond in some salient way to the world or a state of the world of structured data.

For ontology representation, different programming languages and standards have been utilized. Ontolingua (Farquhar et al., 1997) adds primitives to defined classes, functions, and instances. Ontolingua is not a representation system, but rather a mechanism for translating from standard syntax to multiple representation systems. OIL (Ontology Interchange Language) (Fensel et al., 2001) fuses two paradigms: frame-based modeling with semantics based on description logic, and syntax based on web standards such as, Extensible Markup Language (XML) schema and resource description framework (RDF) schema. Both, Ontolingua and OIL, are frame-based languages that do not provide formalism for first-order logic.

XML formalism presents new opportunities for knowledge representation and acquisition and has two aspects. First, XML documents can be easily translated into knowledge representation format and parsed by problem solving environments or domains. Second, XML can directly connect with data storage repositories (RDBMS or ERP systems), thus providing database queries to be more expressive, accurate and powerful. The two objectives can be achieved by enhancing semantic expressiveness of XML, especially XML data schemas (XSD). Complementary to the ODIS framework described in this chapter, this research effort proposes SC ontology language, which consists of two parts: extended situation calculus presented in the previous section and SCML for presenting knowledge about SC in a computational language that can be utilized by software applications, particularly software agents. The specification of SCML is formulated as a XSD data schema depicted in Figure 25-8. It reflects system representation formalism presented in system taxonomy, viz. at the top level there are seven groupings: input, output, functions, environment, processes, and mechanisms. Each grouping is a container, which consists of subclasses.

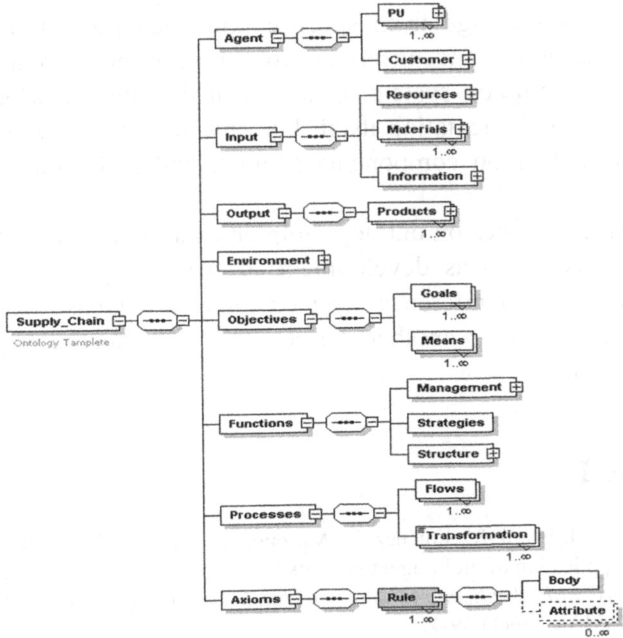

Figure 25-8. Data schema for supply chain markup language (a snapshot captured using XMLSpy software tool)

First seven elements (relative to root "Supply_Chain" element) correspond to ontology data model and constitute the problem semantic network. The eighth element is designed to represent axioms, the dynamic aspect of the problem. The latter is a set of rules, which may have attributes and the body, where relationships among attributes are presented.

7. CONCLUSIONS AND FUTURE RESEARCH

The complexity of SC organization and its needs suggest that traditional IS solutions could not adequately meet requirements of SC process integration and shared problem solving. The main ingredients of SC informational challenges are its dynamic and uncertain nature as well as the existence of legacy systems and an adequate IS solution is required to deal with these aspects. The proposed approach is based on ontological modeling of domain knowledge for SC, which can be used either at development or run time of IS. The usefulness of applying ontologies at development time is the separation of system analysis from other components of IS development life cycle, and their representation with formal models. This provides unambiguous interpretation of system features, which are used and reused for various purposes, such as resolving one specific problem, or designing enterprise IS architecture. The usefulness of ontology application at run time is separation of knowledge from specific implementation, thus providing adaptability to changing and uncertain environment and compatibility with dynamics of SC complex system. Changes in domain knowledge do not yield changes in implementation itself, but only in ontologies. IS database, interface, and application components adapt to these changes by utilizing ontologies.

A wide range of issues on ontology implementation into IS infrastructure remain unresolved, such as development of search algorithms as part of interface component, or inference layer on top of a database for translating queries from one system to another. These issues will lead the way for future research on ODIS.

REFERENCES

Aldea, A., Bañares-Alcántara, R., Jiménez, L., Moreno, A., Martínez, J., and Riaño, D., 2004, The scope of application of multi-agent systems in the process industry: three case studies, *Expert Systems with Applications Journal, Intelligent Computing in the Petroleum Industry special issue.* **26**(1):39-47.

Andreasen, T., Fischer-Nilsson, J., and Erdman-Thomsen, H., 2000, Ontology-based querying. In: Larsem, H.L. et al. (eds.) *Flexible Query Answering Systems, Recent Advances*, Physica-Verlag, Springer, 15–26.

Berners-Lee, T., Hendler, J., and Lassila, O., 2001, The semantic Web. *Scientific American.* **284**(5):34–43.

Benjamins, V., Fensel, D., and Gómez Pérez, A., 1998, Knowledge management through ontologies, *Proceedings of the 2nd International Conference on Practical Aspects of Knowledge Management (PAKM 98)*, Basel, Switzerland.

Bowler, T.D., 1981, *General System Thinking its Scope and Applicability*, Elsevier North Holland, Amsterdam, The Netherlands.

Bussler, C., 2004, Semantic Web services, *ICWE 2004*, Munich, July 27.

Chandra, C., and Tumanyan A., 2004a, Supply chain system analysis and modeling using ontology engineering, *Americas Conference on Information Systems AMCIS'04, New York, NY.*

Chandra C., and Tumanyan A., 2004b, Information modeling to manage supply chain: problems taxonomy, *Proceedings of the 13th Annual Industrial Engineering Research Conference IERC-2004*, Houston, Texas USA.

Chandra C., and Tumanyan A., 2004c, Ontology driven knowledge design and development for supply chain management, *Proceedings of the 13th Annual Industrial Engineering Research Conference IERC-2004*, Houston, Texas USA.

Chandrasekaran, B., Josephson, B., Richard, J.R., and Benjamins, V., 1998, Ontology of tasks and methods, *Extension to 1997 AAAI Spring Symposium and the 1998 Banff Knowledge Acquisition Workshop.*

Farquhar, A., Fikes, R., and Rice, J., 1997, The Ontolingua server: a tool for collaborative ontology construction, *International Journal of Human-Computer Studies*. **46**(6):707—727.

Fensel, D., Harmelen, F., Horrocks, I., McGuinness, D.L., and Patel-Schneider, P. F., 2001, OIL: An ontology infrastructure for semantic Web, *IEEE Intelligent systems*. March/April, 38-45.

Fensel, D., 2002, Language standardization for the semantic Web: the long way from OIL to OWL. *Proceedings of the 4th International Workshop on Distributed Communities on the Web*, Lecture Notes in Computer Science. **2468**:215–227.

Fonseca, F., Davis, C., and Camara, G., 2003, Bridging ontologies and conceptual schemas is geographic information integration, *GeoInformatics*. **7**(4):355-375.

Fox, M., Barbuceanu, M., and Teigen, R., 2000, Agent-oriented supply-chain management, *The International Journal of Flexible Manufacturing Systems.* **12**:165–188.

Gruber, T., 1993, A translation approach to portable ontology specifications, *International Journal of Knowledge Acquisition for Knowledge-Based Systems*. **2**(5):199-220.

Grüninger, M., and Menzel, C., 2003, The process specification language (PSL): theory and application, *AI Magazine*. 63-74.

Guarino, N., 1995, Formal ontology, conceptual analysis and knowledge representation, *International Journal of Human and Computer Studies, special issue on The Role of Formal Ontology in the Information Technology*. **43**:5/6.

Guarino, N., 1998, Formal ontology and information systems, *Proceedings of FOIS'98*, Amsterdam, IOS Press.

Jennings, N.R., 2000, On agent-based software engineering, *Artificial Intelligence*. **117**:277–296.

Jones, D., 1998, Developing shared ontologies in multi-agent systems, *In International Workshop on Intelligent Information Integration (ECAI-98)*, Brighton, UK.

Kerschberg, L., and Weishar, D. J., 2000, Conceptual models and architectures for advanced information systems, *Applied Intelligence*. **13**:149-164

Lambert, D.M., and Cooper, M.C., 2000, Issues in supply chain management, *Industrial Marketing Management*. **29**:65–83.

Lee, H.L., Padmanabhan, V., and Whang, S., 1997, The bullwhip effect in supply chains, *Sloan Management review*. **38**(3):93-102.

Lesperance, Y., Levesque, H.J., Lin, F., and Scherl R. B., 1995, Ability and knowing how in the situation calculus. *Studia Logica*. **66**(1):165-186.

Li, J., Shaw, M.J., and Sikora, R.T., 2001, The effects of information sharing strategies on supply chain performance, Technical Report.

Lin, F., Yang, M., and Pai, Y., 2002, A generic structure for business process modeling, *Business Process Management Journal*. **8**(1):19-41.

Malone, T., Crowston, K., Lee, J., Pentland, B., and O'Donnell, E., 1999, Tools for inventing organizations: toward a handbook of organizational processes, *Management Science*. **45**(3):425-443.

Matheus, C.J., Kokar, M.M., and Baclawski, K., 2003, A core ontology for situation awareness, *In Proceedings of Sixth International Conference on Information Fusion*, Cairns, Australia, July, 545-552.

Mayer, R.J., Benjamin, P., Caraway, B.E., and Painter, M.K., 1995, A framework and a suite of methods for business process reengineering, in B. Kettinger & V. Grover (Eds.), *Business Process Reengineering: A Managerial Perspective*, 245-90.

Muckstadt, J.A., Murray, D.H., Rappold, J.A., and Collins, D.E., 2001, Guidelines for collaborative supply chain system design and operation, *Information Systems Frontiers*. **3**(4):427–453.

Pinto, J., and Reiter, R., 1993, Temporal reasoning in logic programming: a case for the situation calculus. *ICLP*. 203-221

Pinto, H.S., and Martins J.P., 2004, Ontologies: how can they be Built? *Knowledge and Information Systems*. **6**:441–464.

Sheth, A., Ramakrishnan, C., 2003, Semantic (Web) technology in action: ontology driven information systems or search, integration and analysis, *IEEE Data Engineering Bulletin, Special issue on Making the Semantic Web Real*. December.

Sowa, J., 2000, Ontology, Metadata, and Semiotics. International Conference on Conceptual Structures, *ICCS'2000*, Darmstadt, Germany, August, 4-18.

Stewart, G., 1997, Supply-chain operations reference model (SCOR): the first cross-industry framework for integrated supply-chain management, *Logistics Information Management*. **10**(2):62–67.

Storey, V.C., Dey, D., Ullrich, H., and Sundaresan, S., 1998, An ontology-based expert system for database design, *Data & Knowledge engineering*. **28**:31-46.

Sugumaran, V., and Storey, V. C., 2002, Ontologies for conceptual modeling: their creation, use, and management, *Data Knowledge Engineering*. **42**(3):251-271.

Systinet, 2003, Web Services: a practical introduction to SOAP Web services, Information Weeks White Papers.

Vasconcelos, J., Gouveia, F., and Kimble, C., 2002, An organizational memory information system using ontologies, *Proceedings of the 3rd Conference of the Associação Portuguesa de Sistemas de Informação University of Coimbra*, Portugal, November.

Xu, L.D., 2000, The contribution of system science to information system research, *Systems Research and Behavioral Science*. **17**:105-116.

Chapter 26

FRAMEWORK FOR ENHANCED INTEROPERABILITY

Through ontological harmonization of enterprise product models

Ricardo Jardim-Goncalves[1], João P.M.A. Silva[2], António A.C. Monteiro[2] and Adolfo Steiger-Garção[1]

[1]*Dep. Eng. Electrotécnica, Universidade Nova de Lisboa, Caparica, UNINOVA, PORTUGAL, rg@uninova.pt, http://www.uninova.pt;* [2]*Departamento de Eng. Mecânica, Universidade do Minho, Campus de Azurém, Guimarães, PORTUGAL, jpmas@dem.uminho.pt, http://www.dem.uminho.pt*

Abstract: Today, enterprises have information technology that could fulfill their requirements in each operational phase and with external partners, e.g., suppliers. For instance, in industrial environment, many applications are available to support operating their Product Life Cycle stages. However, organizations typically acquire them aiming to solve focused needs, without an overall view of the global enterprise's system integration. Even when enterprise models are interoperable, very often difficulties arise with respect to data semantics when information has to be exchanged, though common semantic models are not in place. Researchers have proposed methodologies and platforms to assist the integration of applications and data. However, implementing new technology in organizations is a complex task, and the advent of continuous technological evolution makes organizations unable to be constantly updated. Such dynamics has a recognized impact in costs and work environment that companies cannot afford, and most of such proposals do not go beyond the research phase. This chapter proposes a methodology to enhance enterprise's interoperability, keeping the same organization's technical and operational environment, improving its methods of work and the usability of the installed technology through ontological harmonization of the enterprise product models in use. The presented work was developed and has been applied in the scope of the Intelligent Manufacturing Systems (IMS) SMART-fm program (www.ims.org) and European ATHENA project (www.athena-ip.org), under real industrial environments.

Key words: Enterprise Modeling; Product Modeling; Ontology; Reusability and Interoperability

1. INTRODUCTION

During the last years industry has observed the evolution of the Product Life Cycle (PLC) concept. The conventional way of developing a product in sequential stages, has been substituted by concurrent and collaborative engineering[1,2]. This innovative environment revealed to be decisive in certain industries, from the biggest like automotive and aeronautic, to those strongly involving SMEs, like furniture or building and construction[3,4,5].

Indeed, the exigency to reduce manufacturing time and increase product quality is growing day by day. Consumers are requesting more features, looking for customized products in shorter time. Such evolution implies thousands of parts correctly ordered, manufactured and assembled, and requires the involvement of complementary activities and experts from a wide range of disciplines[6].

In this scenario, precise data exchange between internal and external production agents plays a key role, where an initial product data model must be instantiated during the early design and tooling phases, being updated along the PLC.

To have this data flow accurate, data models and processes need to be interoperable. However, this situation has been identified difficult to achieve, because typically there are many different software applications in use, each one adopting its own data structure and semantics[7-10].

Additionally, when developing a product each participant team normally has its specific method of work and self-containing language. This fact does not result in a flawless interaction with others. For example, it is frequent to find the situation where in different PLC stages the use of dissimilar vocabulary addresses exactly the same component[11].

It results that, in general, the information managed in each PLC stage regards to different classifications, levels of access and detail. For example, the design team may entitle a bolt using one expression that, to prevent design errors, needs accurate information regarding the component. However, such detailed information may be valueless to the maintenance team, which for a successful part replacement, only needs the reference and the component genre identification. This means that design team "views" the same information in a distinct manner and with a different level of detail than the maintenance team.

Figure 26-1 depicts this circumstance along some principal PLC stages, where different "views" are identified on top of a same taxonomy, highlighting different viewpoints on the same class of information, e.g., with semantic and vocabulary variants. Although not represented in this figure, additional "views" show up when considering external agents, e.g., suppliers, when bringing their own taxonomies into the system. Thus, the scenario of different taxonomies identified within and across the PLC stages, internally and externally to the organizations, makes this problem complex.

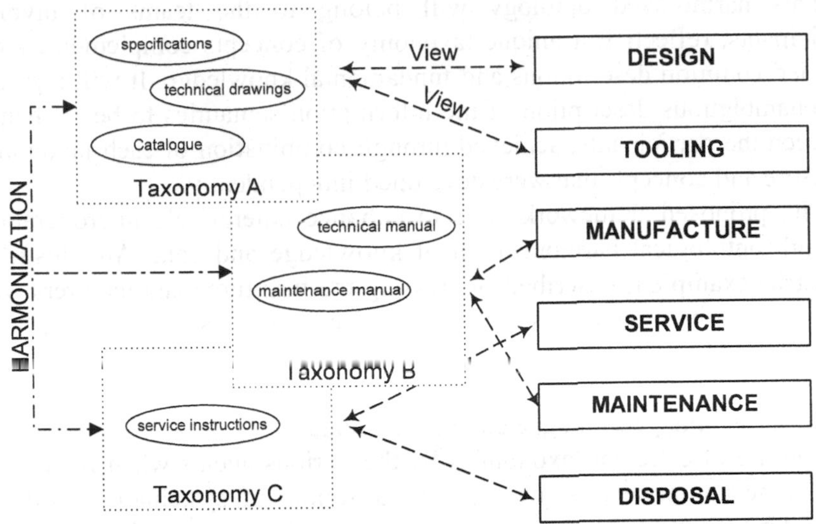

Figure 26-1. "Views" according to the different taxonomies in use by PLC stages

To assist solving this sort of problems, Radeke[12], Davulcu[13] and Erwan Berton[14] point towards the use of a single ontology framework. However, in the presented situation of broad heterogeneity, where many taxonomies and semantics can be found within the product life cycle, to achieve seamless interoperability within and between its stages it will require a common agreement of the complete system's information structure and semantics. Only in this way it will be possible to unambiguously describe the meaning of the whole data instantiated in the enterprise models, and exchanged between the applications along the PLC stages.

Kishore, Zhang and Ramesh[15] divided the scope of the ontology in three abstraction levels, i.e. 1) the universe of discourse, 2) a domain of interest, and 3) an instance of the domain of interest. These three levels are focused respectively on the 1) general purpose ontology, on the 2) underlying frameworks and on 3) particular company's systems.

Also, Noy[16,17], McGuinness[18], Mitra[19] and Klein[20] propose a set of methodologies and software tools to support the development and harmonization of ontology, essentially when its use becomes more prevalent. Three perspectives have been identified to manage such harmonization by means of 1) merging[21,22], 2) aligning[23] and 3) integrating[21] procedures.

The work presented in this chapter addresses applied research in the underlying frameworks and respective instantiation on particular company's systems. It proposes and develops the combination of the many ontological worlds towards a harmonized one to get enhanced stage of global common understanding.

This harmonized ontology will belong to the teams of involved participants, reflecting a unique taxonomy of concepts complemented with detailed common descriptions and fundamental knowledge. It will represent the unambiguous description of the information semantics to be exchanged between the participants, achieved through combination of each taxonomies structure and concepts that were developed independently.

The proposed framework aims to enhance enterprise's interoperability through ontological harmonization of knowledge and data. An illustrative industrial example is described, addressing the furniture manufacturers when exploring different suppliers of mechanical components. The complexity of the problem is noticed when singular difficulties arise in the moment that clients and suppliers with different qualified profile and background attempt to use and exchange catalogue components data.

The use of different taxonomies by the various agents when referencing to a same component is identified as a source of systematic errors and misunderstandings. The framework proposed in this chapter assists organizations to solve this problem in nowadays traditional industrial working procedures, anticipating the use of web tools to support the implementation of the proposed framework, whilst preserving manufacturer's departments' culture and suppliers' independence.

Having manufacturers and suppliers this problem solved, they can save costs (e.g., buying cheaper a same component), additional work (e.g., easier procedure to identify one component) and time schedule delays (e.g., faster to get a solution), and set their business open to new opportunities (e.g., catalogues are universally understood). The presented work was developed, applied and under experimentation in the scope of the IMS SMART-fm and European ATHENA projects.

2. A STUDY USING A CLASSIC MECHANICAL BOLT

Along the PLC phases, several stages can be identified where the search for products in catalogues is necessary. A typical situation is whenever it is needed the substitution of a component during manufacturing or maintenance. As well, when designers intend to provide alternative solutions, preventing single supplier dependency and reduce the manufacturing costs, the inclusion of alternative parts in the design of a product is a wise approach of management requiring the handling of a range of catalogues.

The necessary incorporation of different brought-in parts requires detailed data check and update by different teams, to keep valid the initial design conditions and maintain the product assembly consistency. This task is often facilitated with computational tools, and the components' data representation should be of common understanding, to reduce re-work and time consuming during catalogue examination.

Considering the specific example of searching for a classic mechanical bolt, many catalogues in paper or in digital format can be found. Nowadays, with the Internet browsing potentialities, a popular engine like *Google* can immediately find a large number of links for on-line catalogues of hexagonal head type bolts.

Amazingly, although all these catalogues reference to the same type of physical component, each one usually represents their specifications in different formats and with heterogeneous contents and classification. In fact, different catalogues tend to adopt different variables, unlike coding fields (though equivalent) or widespread designations, most of them diverging from available advisory ISO standard designations.

In practice, the International Standard *ISO 1891:1979 Bolts, screws, nuts and accessories – Terminology and nomenclature*[24], *ISO 225:1983 Fasteners – Bolts, screws, studs and nuts –Symbols and designations of dimensions*[25] and the *ISO 4017:1999 Hexagon head screws*[26] specify terms, dimensions, tolerances and material requirements, including metric coarse threads and diameters for hexagon head screws. These standards represent a first worldwide attempt to uniform variables, structure and designation of fastener's components and hexagon head screws. However, they describe them in a glossary style, complemented with some illustrative figures, without any ontological principles underneath. An extract of ISO 225 standard is depicted in Figure 26-2.

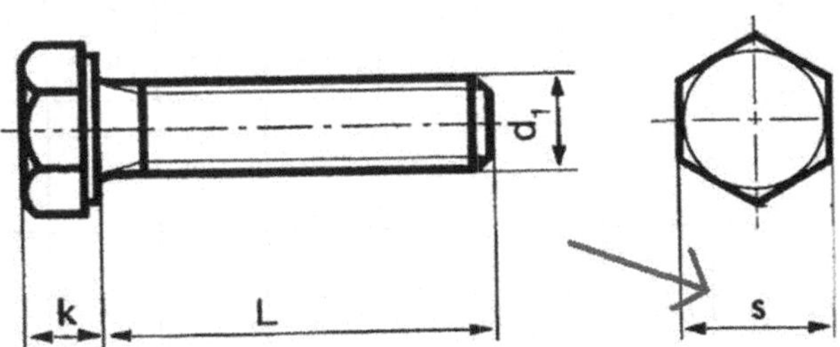

Figure 26-2. Main bolt variables definition according ISO 225[25]

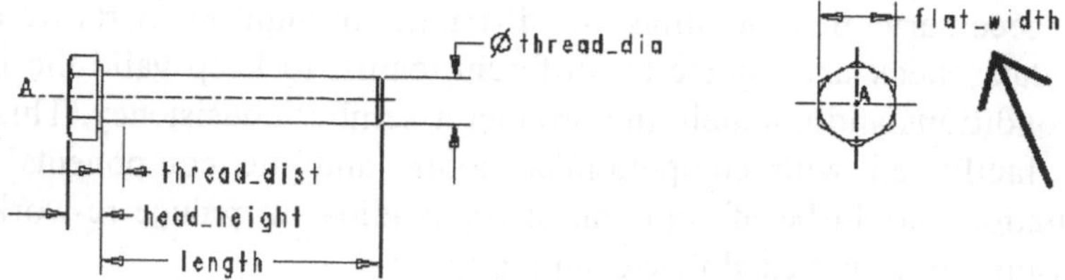

Figure 26-3. Variables' specification in a fastener's catalogue for an ISO 4017 Hexagonal head bolt

However, despite these advisory international standard guidelines, very often the supplier's catalogue codification and properties list are delivered not compliant with the standard. Figures 26-3, 26-4 and 26-5 are snapshots from three different suppliers' catalogues showing the properties of an ISO 4017 hexagon head bolt. Different terminology and classifications can be clearly identified referring to the same nominal parameters, and all divergent from the standard guidelines.

Section 1
Threaded Fasteners

FULL THREAD HEXAGON HEAD SCREWS # 933

Ref: DIN 933/ISO 4017/EN 24017 (Similar to ANSI B 18.2.3.1 M)

To obtain detailed dimensional and tolerance information for all diameters, please refer to the master dimensional chart on page 1-2.
For information about material grades, property classes, tensile strengths and tightening torque values, etc., please refer to Useful Information Section 10.

NOM. SIZE	# 933 8.8 Black	# 933 ZP 8.8 Zinc	# 933 ZY 8.8 Zinc Yellow	# 933 10 10.9 Black	# 933-10 ZP* 10.9 Zinc	# 933 A2 304 Stainless	# 933 A4 316 Stainless	# 933 BR Brass	# 933 PL Plastic Polyamide 6.6	# 933 AL Aluminum
3 x 5	x	x	-	-	-	-	x	-	x	-
3 x 6	x	x	x	-	-	x	x	x	x	-
3 x 8	x	x	x	-	-	x	x	x	x	-
3 x 10	x	x	x	-	-	x	x	x	x	-
3 x 12	x	x	x	-	-	x	x	x	x	-
3 x 14	x	x	-	-	-	x	-	-	-	-
3 x 16	x	x	x	-	-	x	x	x	x	-
3 x 18	x	x	-	-	-	x	-	-	-	-
3 x 20	x	x	x	-	-	x	x	x	x	-
3 x 25	x	x	x	-	-	x	x	x	x	-
3 x 30	x	x	-	-	-	x	x	x	-	-

Figure 26-4. Another supplier's catalogue page for the same component

BOLT SPECIFICATIONS

DIMENSIONS

The diameter specifies the shank and threaded outside size i.e. 1/4" BSF bolt is 1/4" dia. The length of the bolt is always measured from beneath the head.

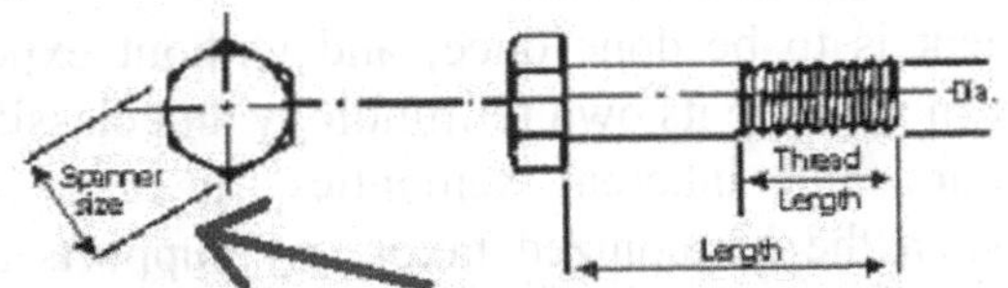

Thread lengths vary over the size ranges but are generally 3/4" to 1". UNF bolts are often referred to by their spanner size rather than diameter i.e. 1/2" AF (across flats) - 5/16" dia.

Spanner Sizes and Threads

Metric

SIZE	THREAD PITCH	SPANNER SIZE
M6 (6mm)	1.00mm	10mm
M8 (8mm)	1.25mm	13mm
M10 (10mm)	1.50mm	17mm
M12 (12mm)	1.75mm	19mm

Tensile Strength

Grade 'R'	45-50 Tons/Inch²
Grade 'S'	50-55 Tons/Inch²
Grade '8.8'	50-55 Tons/Inch²

Figure 26-5. Characteristics and variables definition in another catalogue for the same hexagonal head bolt

In these catalogues, the diameter of bolt's head is labeled by *flat width* (Figure 26-3) or *spanner size* (Figure 26-5), whereas the standardized variable designation is *s* (Figure 26-2). Figure 26-4 exemplifies yet another supplier's catalogue, where different table entries are adopted for the same bolt. This succinct real example, that is part of the day by day PLC teams' modus-operandi, demonstrates the extension of the problem and the need for a methodology to contribute to solve it.

Due to the worldwide number of existing catalogue components and diversity of teams' culture, only in very specific situations one supplier would adopt the terminology and classification of a manufacturer or vice-versa. To impose a unique terminology and classification would be a solution. However, those suppliers not adhering to it most probably would be ignored, and this is not a favorable business situation, not permitting for instance an open selection of the supplier.

For that reason, to envisage forcing manufacturers or suppliers to adopt a specific ontology, even if it is based on the standards, does not work in most of the cases, especially when the involved organizations are SMEs. Thus, an advantageous solution would be to keep the terminology and classification in use by each one, and adopt a harmonized ontology to communicate between them. In this case, each team has to develop its own translator between its particular ontology and the harmonized.

This development is to be done once, and without expected difficulty thought they know in advance its own terminology and classification and the harmonized structure and inherent semantics. In case of a required expansion, e.g., when the harmonized taxonomy supports a new supplier with extended properties, the respective translators would be updated accordingly to support them.

3. ONTOLOGICAL APPROACH

Ontology is the study of the categories of things within a domain and reflects a view of a segment of the reality. Its definition comes from philosophy and provides a logical framework for research on knowledge representation, embracing definition, classification and relationships of concepts[27].

In this context, two or more communities (e.g., organizations, teams), operating in the same domain may use different terminologies and have different views on the same concept, leading to different underlying ontology, and consequently conducting to problems of interoperability. At a first level this problem comes out in the communication between humans, then between humans and computer systems, and finally between computer systems[28,29].

For example, in the study presented in section 2, when a client talks with suppliers searching for a specific component, they need all to understand each other. If for any reason this is not the case, humans are able to reasoning and combine their knowledge attempting to converge to a common understanding, and hence communicate.

In opposition to this interactive and intelligent human to human process, computer systems communicate under a well established syntax, through rigid communication protocols. However, the inclusion of semantics in the communication protocol under a well established classification mechanism, making use of knowledge modeling components described according established semantic representation paradigms, complements the information exchanged contributing for an enhanced understanding between the systems[30].

Therefore, an interoperable system that seamlessly communicates and understands each other requires the comprehensive understanding of the meaning of the data exchanged within the domains involved. This can be realized, if the communication process is supported by an ontology developed under global consensus[31,32,33].

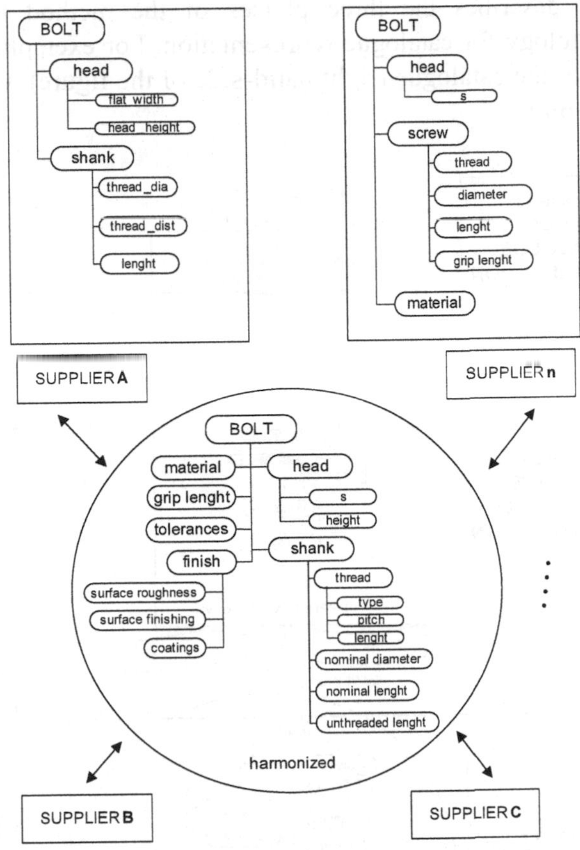

Figure 26-6. Example of a scenario for harmonized classification

3.1 Converging by means of harmonization

To obtain this consensual model, it is necessary to classify and merge the concepts from the different sources within the domain of applicability, describing them in a unique harmonized structure of classes, attributes, relationships, knowledge components and definitions[30].

However, as exemplified in Figure 26-6, the classification of *Bolt*'s properties of *Supplier A* differs from a *Supplier n*. Also, the attributes' definition are different for the same *Bolt* property addressed, i.e., both bolt head properties *flat_width* or *s*, respectively in taxonomy of *Supplier A* and *Supplier n*, specify exactly the same bolt head dimension. Other similar occurrences can be identified within this same example.

Through a combining procedure, the harmonized classification is defined, structuring the various suppliers' information from different sources and for diverse product categories[34,35].

Figure 26-7 describes the three phases of the method to achieve a harmonized ontology for catalogue representation. For exemplification, it is used a sub-set of the catalogue (right hand-side of the figure), with focus on the component *Bolt*.

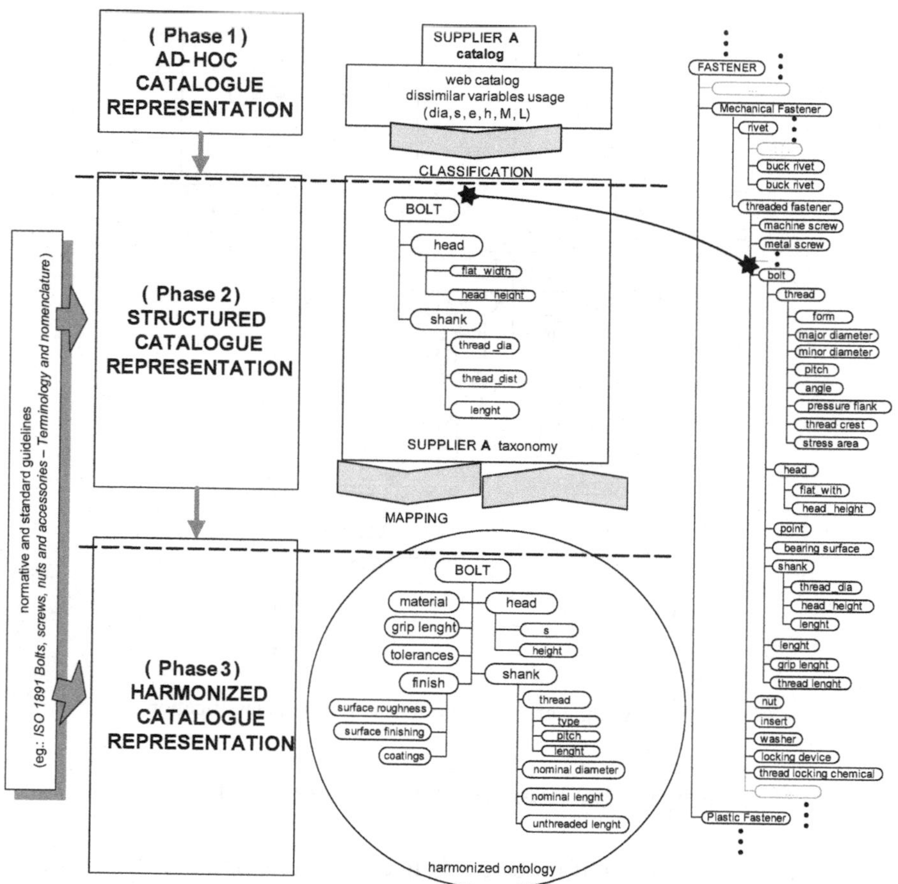

Figure 26-7. Phases to achieve a harmonized catalogue representation – focus on "*Bolt*"

The first phase, identified as *ad-hoc catalogue representation*, refers to the representation of catalogues as they are usually found in the market. Here, the definition of catalogue has casual categorization or nomenclature, belonging to an incipient phase of a taxonomy development which terminology typically does not follow the standards.

In the *structured catalogue representation* phase, catalogue's components are classified and organized, conferring logical structure and semantic contents to the catalogue representation. The adoption of standard-based, versus proprietary, specifications should be encouraged to be taken on this phase.

In the case of catalogues of *Bolts* it is recommended to be used as a reference the standard previously defined and developed by ISO (e.g., *ISO 225:1983 Fasteners – Bolts, screws, studs and nuts – Symbols and designations of dimensions*). However, although this facilitates the harmonization of the catalogues, companies typically react to change its own culture and methods of work, and refrain to adopt the standard in favor of developing a proprietary structured catalogue. Nevertheless, to achieve a structured representation is a major advance in the representation of their catalogues, offering novel possibilities for search and analysis of its components.

During the third and last phase, identified as *harmonized catalogue representation*, it is developed an agreement among other agents in the domain of application. Thus, catalogues' representation are harmonized and complemented with semantics, towards a consensual common ontology. The methodology proposed to develop this harmonization is described in next sub-section.

The lost of supplier's organizational identity could be a concern when developing the *harmonized catalogue representation.* However, this is not the case, thought each catalogue's owner should keep bidirectional mapping rules between its own structure and the harmonized one, enabling organizations to keep using its own practices.

3.2 Methodology for harmonization of ontology

The proposal for a methodology to develop harmonized ontology is depicted in Figure 26-8. This methodology supports the progress from the phase 2 to the phase 3 (Figure 26-7 above) to complete the harmonization for representation of catalogues.

The entry point for this methodology is the identification of the domain and scope of the ontology to harmonize. Each supplier takes the catalogues in such range, and develops the respective taxonomy and inherent semantics according to the procedures explained in section 3.1 (Phases 1 and 2).

The choice of the taxonomy's scope and the subdivision of subjects rely on the market itself, with influence of the pre-existing catalogues and standardization initiatives. The development of each own supplier's ontology, can be done based on the method proposed by (Noy, 2002)[16].

Having the set of ontology available (Phase 2), the harmonization process can start.

Ontology reconciliation is a human-mediated process, supported by specialized software tools, addressing the merging, aligning and integrating procedures for ontology harmonization[36]. The management of ontology reconciliation and the resolution of most of the ontological mismatches require direct human involvement to identify, for instance, unique concepts and concepts that are similar in meaning but have different names or structures.

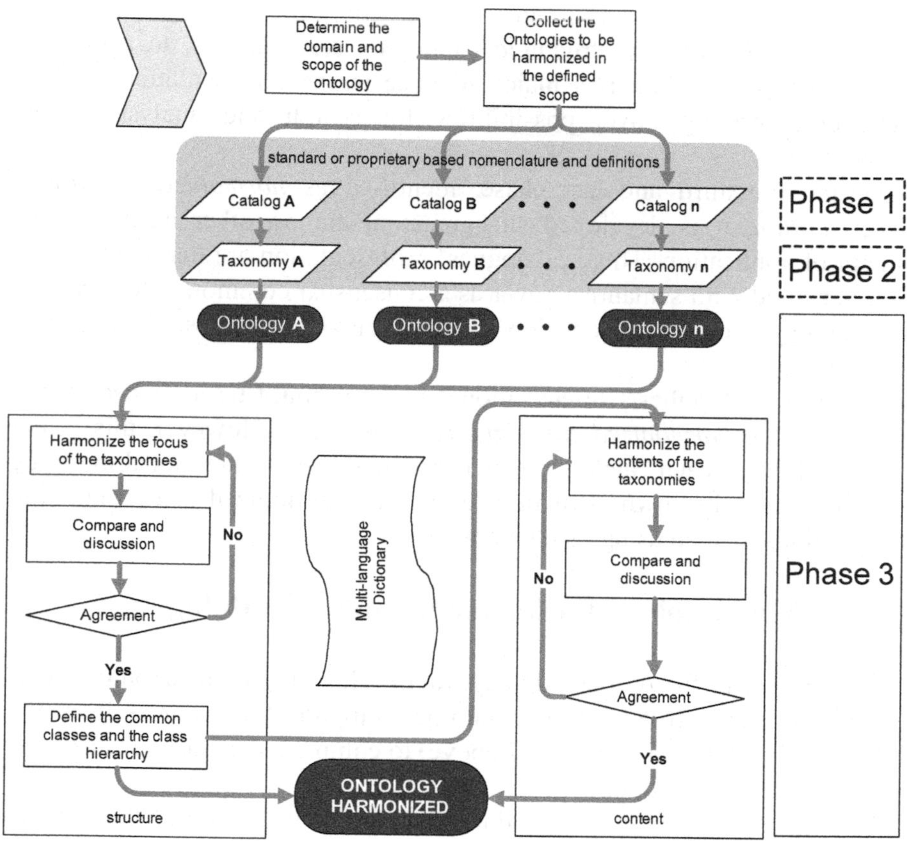

Figure 26-8. Methodology for harmonization of ontologies

Indeed, mismatches between individual ontology can take place at conceptual, terminological, taxonomical, definitional, or even, at syntactic level. Thus, correspondences, i.e., mapping, between concepts and knowledge have to be established, identified gaps bridged, and acknowledged overlaps matched.

Phase 3 is divided in two sequential procedures, to be mediated by humans and assisted by software tools for ontology reconciliation, e.g., Prompt[17], Chimaera[18], ONION [19], OntoView[20], GLUE[37], OBSERVER[38].

Initially, this phase works towards an agreement on the ontology's common structure, i.e., hierarchy and relationship between classes (left-hand side of Figure 26-8), and later on its contents, i.e., knowledge modeling components for semantic analysis and reasoning support (right hand side of Figure 26-8). Along Phase 3, the reconciliation tools are used to support the human decisions towards the harmonized ontology. Because it is unlikely that one single tool adequately handles all aspects of ontology harmonization, the Hameed's workbench should be evaluated for the appropriate tool selection in each stage of the reconciliation process[39].

With the boundaries of each taxonomy on hand identified, they are discussed in workshops until the harmonizing team reaches a common agreement on the focus for the foreseen combined taxonomy. The definition of the harmonized taxonomy's scope and the subdivision of subjects should be leaded by the users, and guided by the market itself with influence of the pre-existing catalogues, standards and expertise of the involved agents. Concentrated on the agreed focus, the common classes and respective classification are defined, and the structure of the harmonized ontology established.

In the specific case of the furniture industry the CEN-ISSS (CEN/ISSS – European Committee for Standardization/Information Society Standardization System, http://www.cenorm.be), did setup up the funStep Workshop, where an internet forum was established and physical meetings occur 4 times per year. Due to the real business interests behind this harmonization activity, this workshop has produced agreements that have been reported in CWAs (CEN Workshop Agreements). Another example refers to the workshops organized by the International Alliance for Interoperability (IAI), working in the scope of the building and construction industry.

Following a similar procedure, and guided by the established harmonized structure, the knowledge modeling components in place are compared and discussed until agreement how they might be combined and incorporated. When accomplished, the harmonized ontology is thus established together with the mapping tables describing the ontological relationships between the harmonized and each one of the individual ontology.

Semantic difficulties related to the natural language of the potential users of the harmonized ontology likely happen. To assist on it, the ontology is complemented with a multi-language dictionary where a set of normalized tokens gives the reference to the corresponding concepts and definitions in different native languages[40,41].

Figure 26-9 exemplifies one harmonization of individual ontology between two suppliers, with focus on *Bolt*. In this case, the terminology, concepts and knowledge modeling components of each individual ontology were harmonized through inter-partners consensual procedure, according to the proposed methodology.

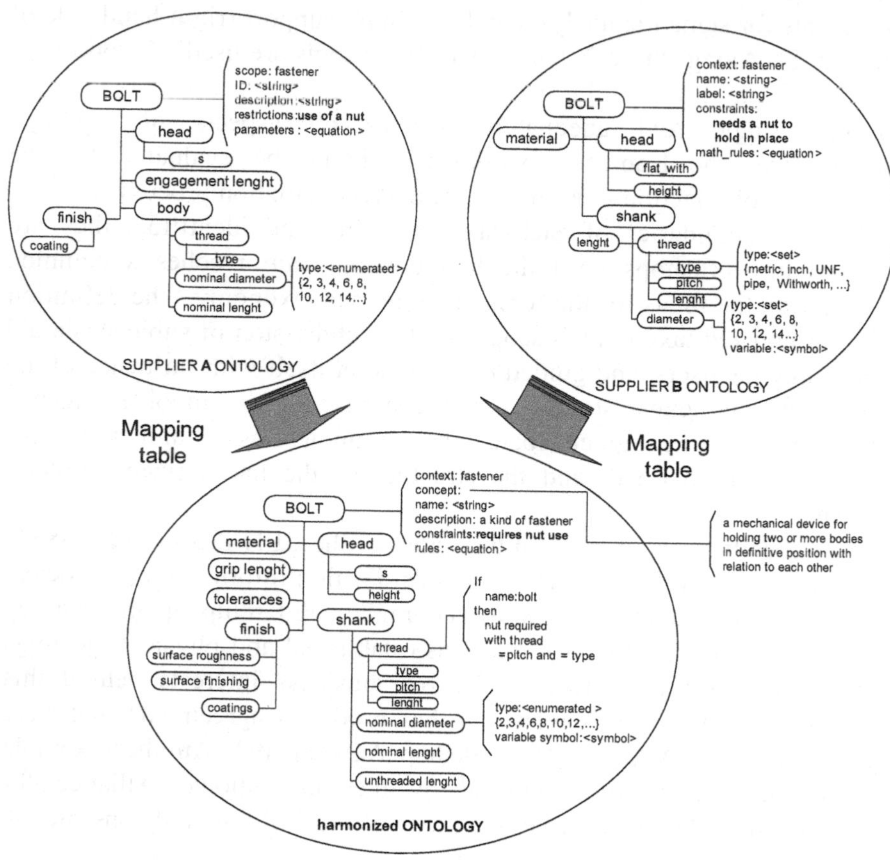

Figure 26-9. Example of harmonization between suppliers

In this example, it is illustrated that Supplier A's nominal diameter (enumerated: 2,3,4,...) is harmonized with the Supplier B's diameter (set: 2,3,4,...), resulting in the nominal diameter (enumerated:2,3,4,...) representation. Also, the Supplier A's restriction (use of a nut) is harmonized with the Supplier B's constraint (needs a nut to hold in place), resulting in the constraint (requires nut use). As well, a new rule was added to the harmonized ontology, stating that a bolt always requires a nut with equal thread's pitch and thread's type.

The dimension of the resultant ontology, as a harmonization of different ontology, will not necessary reflect the arithmetic sum of the defined concepts in each of the individual inputs. Although most probably it will be larger than the most complete individual one, thought it could be expanded with new concepts and content richness, very often it is essentially the same considering it is defined to operate in the same scope and only direct mapping between concepts is needed to be established.

As well, each supplier's ontology will not get expanded after harmonization, having in the mapping table the characterization of the ontological relationships with the harmonized one.

The harmonized ontology, when established and accepted by a substantial critical mass of users, shall result in a standard. Industrial associations, business consortia and users' groups shall assume the leadership to maintain and keep it updated, and work close to the standardization bodies to develop the necessary normalization activities. The funStep IG (hhtp://www.funstep.org) is the example of a user's group that has been working for the furniture industry in this way.

4. SCENARIO EXPERIMENTED

To validate the framework proposed by the authors, the experimented industrial scenario addresses the interoperability problem between furniture manufacturers and suppliers of components, when they face communication difficulties generally resulting from the lack of knowledge regarding data representation and semantics of the other interlocutor.

Many characteristic situations were identified where this problem exists along the manufacture chain and product life cycle. For example, whenever it is needed to search for information about a component during product design or maintenance, and the potential suppliers do not use the same catalogue's designation or classification.

Remarkably, although many of these organizations already use information technology to support the supply chain management, in the current manufacturing environments and particularly in the SME segment, the search in catalogues and exchange of information is mostly paper based, and the described interoperability problem is well recognized even at a primary level, where the interlocutors are both humans.

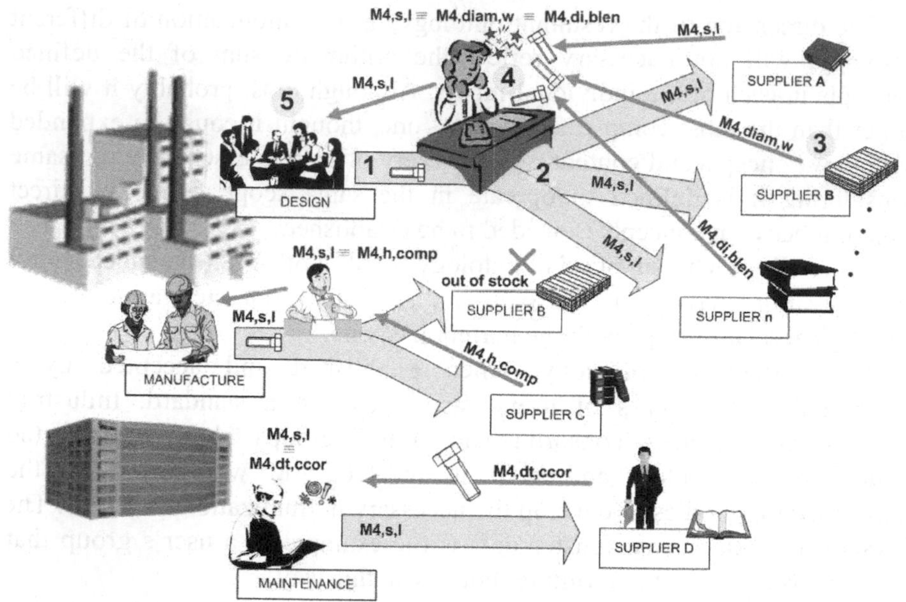

Figure 26-10. The scenario experimented

Figure 26-10 illustrates the scenario, describing phase by phase one of the typical situations where furniture manufacturers find difficulties to select and obtain specific mechanical components for design and production. For simplicity of reference in the text, the phases (1-5) described are numbered and identified in the figure. Also, the language adopted to explain it is the one in practice by the industry.

The first phase starts when the design team demands to search for a specific mechanical hexagonal bolt. The required characteristics of the component are communicated to the procurement department (phase 2), responsible to identify and query candidate suppliers. The search is made by a mediator consulting the catalogues available in house, and making phone calls or sending a fax to directly contact the suppliers.

Suppliers respond (phase 3) verbally or sending their leaflets and catalogues with information about the component. However, each one is using different nomenclature and variables names (most proprietary) to describe the same physical component. Thus, a dialog with the supplier is started, to validate the compliance between required properties and characteristics of candidate parts, and clarify definitions and redundancies between nomenclatures.

Next phase (4 in the picture) is a manual job and a mental challenge, where it is necessary to identify and establish the correspondence, i.e. mapping, between the different supplier's nomenclatures and the one in use by the design team. Then, the component's reference code is delivered to the design team (phase 5).

In addition, Figure 26-10 illustrates two other typical situations where similar problems occur: one involving the manufacturing department, and the other the maintenance team. In these two situations, the chosen supplier runs out of stock or founds discontinued the searching component. Consequently, both situations require a new try to find another equivalent component, following the searching procedure as described before.

The introduction of the proposed methodology in this scenario was recognized advantageous by the participating users. When the method was applied to combine a set of selected catalogues of components, it resulted in a harmonized ontology defined along with the mapping table describing the relationships between the manufacturer's component classification and those defined by each supplier's[42].

Using this result, the mediator can manage the harmonized ontology together with the table with the mapping rules between the manufacturer's and the suppliers' schemes to describe the components in search. This is of valuable help to the mediator, because in a glance he can have a systematic and immediate understanding about the components he is managing, enabling him to actuate faster and more accurately.

Over time, the interoperability under this scenario is improved whenever more and more catalogues are combined by the manufacturer and the respective mapping table updated. Nevertheless, if for any reason the harmonization of a new catalogue does not take place, the components described in it can still be chosen. However, in this case the mediator can not take advantage of the available mapping guidelines, and should proceed as habitually did before.

Figure 26-11 illustrates the framework for the use of the harmonized ontology and mapping table in the context of the experimented scenario.

This Figure 26-11 is divided in two parts. The upper side depicts the use of the framework when applied to the manufacturing environment as it was found when the study started. However, in the advent of the internet and networked organizations opportunities, these organizations aim to start using more and more computational systems to manage these activities, and the web to communicate between them.

In this envisaged scenario, the harmonized ontology and mapping table is implemented in a proper software platform. This platform is generic and open, providing web-based functionalities. With it, the mediator is assisted getting a transparent interface between the information from the users (e.g., manufacturer's design team) and suppliers' catalogues.

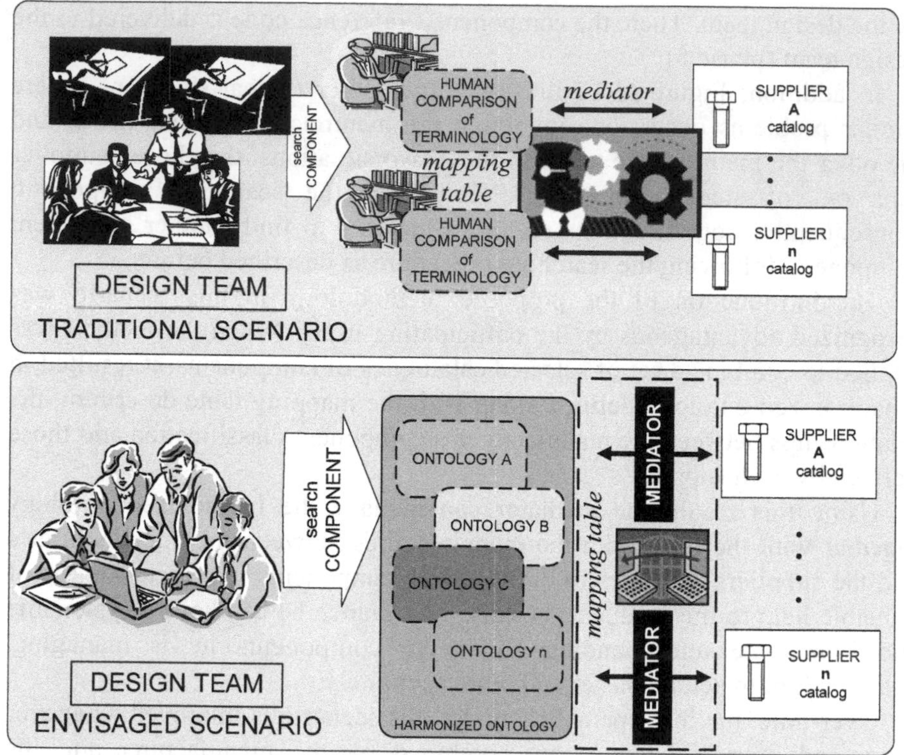

Figure 26-11. Framework for the use of the harmonized ontology and mapping table

A prototype was developed, and the platform has been experimented under the scenario described. Software for design, an ERP and a marketplace representing many suppliers have been involved in the conducting tests, reporting encouraging results[43].

In this moment, the motivation is to extend the prototype, and move towards a complete automatic scenario where the search and selection of components would be directly executed by the involved parties through a *computational mediator*, completely automated and embedded in a web application.

Protégé-2000 is a well known and widely recognized ontology and knowledge-base editor developed at Stanford University. It is an open-source Java tool that provides an extensible architecture for the creation of customized knowledge-based applications[44].

As well, web services have been recognized as "XML-enabled standards to allow publishing of applications to other parties across platforms"[45]. The use of web services is expanding rapidly. During the recent years the web services have turned into the greatest development craze, as they provide independently of the platforms running, a standard means of communication among different software applications in networked environments.

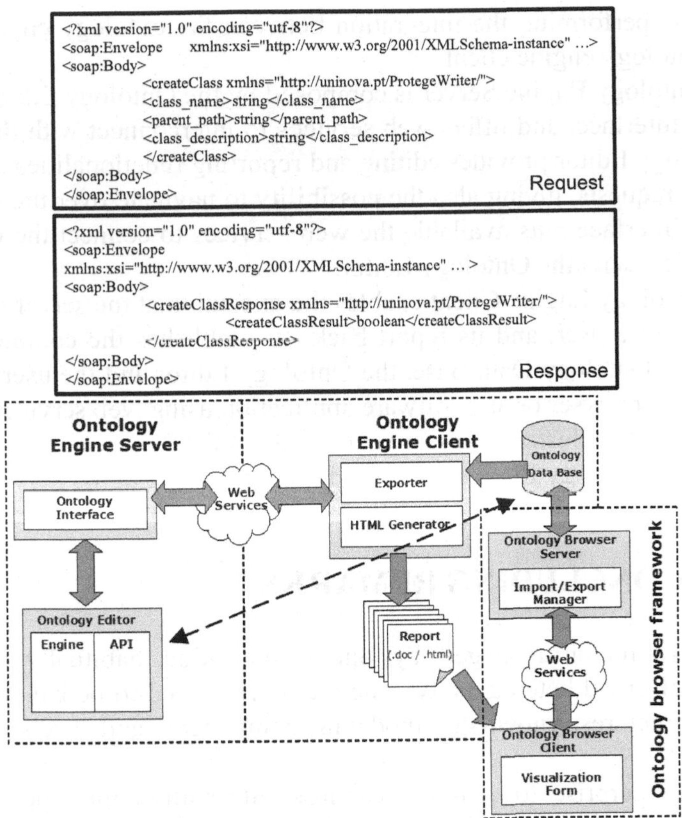

Figure 26-12. Architecture of the platform and an example of a Request/Response SOAP web service message

Web services are based on the potential of the combination of XML (Extensible Markup Language), a service-oriented architecture (the Web Services Description Language, or WSDL), registration through a UDDI (Universal Description, Discovery and Integration) repository, and communication encoded using SOAP (the Simple Object Access Protocol)[46].

A web service is a software mechanism identified by a Universal Resource Identifier (URI), whose public interfaces and bindings are defined and described using XML. The characterization of a web service can be discovered by any software system, throughout standardized procedures over the internet.

The platform developed (Figure 26-12) uses Java technology to extend the Portégé-2000 editor, and adopts a recognized open mechanism for implementation of web-enabled services[47].

The Ontology Engine establishes the connection between the Ontology Data Base and the Ontology Editor. They communicate using web services technology, performing the integration between the ontology engine server and the ontology engine client.

The Ontology Engine Server is composed by the Ontology Editor and the Ontology Interface, and offers web services to interconnect with the Editor. The Ontology Editor provides editing and reporting functionalities as a result of client's requests, giving also the possibility to navigate over the data. The Ontology Interface puts available the web services to connect the Ontology Engine Client with the Ontology Editor.

The Ontology Engine Client enables the execution at the server of service requests from a user, and its report back. It establishes the communication between the Ontology Data Base, the Ontology Editor and the user, through the Ontology browser or any software application using web services.

Figure 26-12 illustrates an extract of the SOAP messages exchanged between the Ontology Engine Client and the Ontology Engine Server[48].

5. CONCLUDING REMARKS

The information managed by one organization habitually embraces situations of broad heterogeneity, where concepts need to be handled under different structures, knowledge modeling components and levels of access and detail.

For an enterprise to achieve seamless information interoperability, it requires a common agreement of the global information system's structure and semantics. Only in this way it will be possible to unambiguously describe, internally and externally to the organization, the complete meaning of the data instantiated and exchanged through the enterprise models.

To contribute to get such stage of global common understanding, this chapter proposes a methodology that combines the many ontological worlds in place, i.e., the instances of domain, developing a harmonized ontology aiming to represent a domain of discourse. To obtain this consensual model, it is necessary to classify and combine the concepts from the different sources within the domain of applicability, describing them in a unique harmonized hierarchal structure of classes and definitions. This situation of common understanding enforces the business relationships between organizations, and facilitates the internal communication between the different organization's departments and services.

To validate the methodology, real industrial scenarios have been experimented addressing the interoperability problem between furniture manufacturers and suppliers of components, when they face communication difficulties generally resulting from the lack of knowledge regarding data representation and semantics of the other interlocutor.

When the methodology was applied to combine a set of selected catalogues of components, it resulted in a harmonized ontology described along with the definition of the relationships between the manufacturer's component classification and those defined by each supplier's.

The harmonized ontology was implemented in a proper software platform. This platform is generic and open, providing web-based functionalities. With it, the mediator got a computer based interface between the information from the users (e.g., manufacturer's design team) and suppliers' catalogues.

The platform was experimented with encouraging results under the scenarios described, and the proposed framework was recognized innovative and of economical relevance for the participating users, as an enabler for new opportunities to identify and select components, and for the implementation of faster and more accurate management procedures.

Lassila and McGuinness[49] classify ontologies according to the information the ontology needs to express the richness of its internal structure. Considering the industrial scenarios addressed in this chapter, the typical current situation for representation of industrial catalogues of components falls in the Terms/Glossary category.

With the contribution of the work presented, the envisaged scenario is the one where the catalogues will be represented by ontologies that may place restrictions, expressing general logical constraints. Figure 26-13 depicts the identified impact of the chapter's contribution, according to the Lassila and McGuinness categorization.

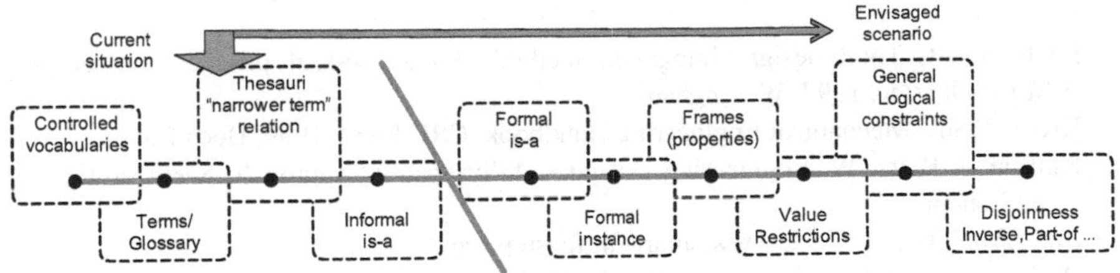

Figure 26-13. Impact of the chapter's contribution, according to the Lassila and McGuinness categorization

The presented work was developed in the scope of the Intelligent Manufacturing Systems (IMS) SMART-fm program (www.ims.org) and European ATHENA project (www.athena-ip.org), under real industrial environments. In this moment the funStep IG, a group with more than 250 furniture related companies, is taking these results to recommend them to be adopted by its members as a basis for their business and manufacturing activities, whenever a harmonized ontology for the representation of catalogues of furniture products and parts has to be developed.

The problem addressed is not specific from the furniture industry. The presented framework can be adapted to any situation where the harmonization of ontologies can be envisaged as a contribution to improve interoperability. In the ATHENA project, proposals to contribute to solve the same class of problems are in study to be applied in the automotive, aeronautics and telecommunication industries, considering as a basis the framework presented.

ACKNOWLEDGEMENTS

The presented work is partly funded by the European Commission through the IMS SMART-fm and IST ATHENA IP research projects, and endorsed by the Intelligent Manufacturing Systems program. It does not represent the view of the E.C. or IMS, and authors are responsible for the content. IMS SMART-fm is funded by the European Commission, under the 5th Framework R&D Program, contract n° IST-2001-52224. ATHENA IP is funded by the European Commission, under the 6th Framework R&D Program, contract n° 507849. The authors thank and acknowledge the members of the SMART-fm and ATHENA consortium.

REFERENCES

1. Ulrich, K.T. & Eppinger, S.D., *Product Design and Development*, McGraw-Hill, 2000, New York.
2. Pugh, Stuart, Total design: integrated methods for successful product engineering, *Adddison-Wesley*, 1997, Wokingham.
3. Kreith, Frank, Mechanical Engineering Handbook, CRC Press, 1999, Boca Raton.
4. Pahl, G. & Beitz, W. Engineering Design – A Systematic Approach, *Springer-Verlag*, 1996, London,
5. IMS SMART-fm project, www.smart-fm.funstep.org.
6. Drejer, A.; Gudmundsson, Agnar Exploring the concept of multiple product development via an action research project, *Integrated Manufacturing Systems,* 2003, Vol. 14, Number 3, pp. 208-220.
7. Clements, P. Standard support for the virtual enterprise, *Int. Conf. on Enterprise Integration Modeling Technology – ICEIMT'97*, 1997, Italy.
8. Lazcano et al. The wise approach to electronic commerce, *International Journal of Computer Systems Science & Engineering*, 2000, Vol. 15, No. 5.
9. Poole, John D. Model-Driven Architecture: Vision, Standards And Emerging Technologies, *ECOOP 2001,* 2001, Hungary, University of California.
10. Nagi, L. Design and Implementation of a Virtual Information System for Agile Manufacturing, *IIE Transactions on Design and Manufacturing*, 1997, Vol. 29(10), pp. 839-857.

11. Jardim-Gonçalves, R. and Steiger-Garção, A. Implicit multi-level modelling for integration and interoperability in flexible business environments, submitted to *Communications of ACM*, special issue on Enterprise Components 2002.
12. Radeke, E. et al. Distributed information management in virtual engineering enterprises by *GEN. RIDE-VE'99* IEEE Computer Society, 1999 pages 36–43.
13. Davulcu, H. Modeling and analysis of interactions in virtual enterprises. *IT for Virtual Enterprises*, IEEE Computer Society 1999, pages 12–18.
14. Erwan Breton, Jean Bézivin Using Meta-Model Technologies to Organize Functionalities for Active System Schemes, *5th International Conference on Autonomous Agents,* 2001, Canada.
15. Kishore, R, Zhang, H, Ramesh, R., A Helix-spindle model for ontological engineering, *Communications of the ACM,* February 2004; vol.47, n.o2, pp 69-75.
16. Noy, Natalya and McGuinness, Deborah, Ontology development 101: A Guide to Creating Your First Ontology, *Stanford Knowledge Systems Laboratory Technical Report KSL-01-05 and Stanford Medical Informatics Technical Report SMI-2001-0880*, 2002.
17. Noy, N F, Musen, M A (2001) Anchor-PROMPT: Using Non-Local Context for Semantic Matching. In Workshop on Ontologies and Information Sharing at the 17th International Joint Conference in Artificial Intelligence (IJCAI-2001), Seattle, USA.
18. McGuineness D L, Fikes, R, Rice, J, Wilder, S (2000) An Environment for Merging and Testing Large Ontologies. In Cohn, A, Giunchiglia, F, and Selman B (eds), KR2000: *Principles of knowledge representation and reasoning, pp 483-493*.
19. Mitra, P, Kersten, M. Wiederhold, G (2000) Graph-Oriented Model for Articulation of Ontology nterdependencies. *In Proceedings of the 7th International Conference on Extending Database Technology*, Spriger-Verlag.
20. Klein, M, Kiryakov, W, Ognyanov, D, Fensel, D (2002) Ontology Versioning and Change Detection on the Web. *In 13th International Conference on Knowledge Engineering and Knowledge Management (EKAW02),* Siguenza, Spain.
21. Pinto, H S, Martins, J P A, Methodology for Ontology Integration, *in Proceedings of the First International conference on knowledge Capture (K-CAP 2001)*, ACM Press, 2001.
22. Stumme, G, Maedche, A Ontology Merging for Federated Ontologies on the Semantic Web, *IJCAI-01 Workshop on Ontologies and Information Sharing*, 2001, pp. 91-99.
23. Noy, N F, Musen M A, PROMPT:Algoritm and Tool for Automated Ontology Merging and Alignment, *IJCAI-01 Workshop on Ontologies and Information Sharing* , 2000, pp 63-70.
24. ISO 1891:1979 Bolts, screws, nuts and accessories – Terminology and nomenclature, International Standard Organization.
25. ISO 225:1983 Fasteners – Bolts, screws, studs and nuts –Symbols and designations of dimensions, International Standard Organization.
26. ISO 4017:1999 Hexagon head screws – Product grades A and B, International Standard organization.
27. Steven Willmott, et.al Multilingual Agents: Ontologies, Languages and Abstractions, *5th Int. Conference on Autonomous Agents*, 2001, Canada.
28. Uschold, M. and Gruninger, M. Ontologies: Principles, *Methods and Applications Knowledge Engineering Review*, 1996, Volume 11 Number 2, June 1996.
29. Fox, M.S. and Gruninger, M. Ontologies for Enterprise Modelling, *Proceedings of ICEMT'97*, 1997, Italy.
30. Gomez-Perez, A, et.al, (2004), Ontological Engineering, with examples from the areas of Knowledge Management, e-Commerce and the Semantic Web, Springer-Verlag, ISBN 1-85233-551-3.

31. Gruninger, M. Using Ontologies to Evaluate Knowledge-based Systems, *PerMIS USA*, (2002).
32. Léger, Alain, et.al. OntoWeb, IST-2000-29243, *Successful Scenarios for Ontology-based Applications*, 2002.
33. Shen, W., Norrie, D.H. & Barthès, J.P; Multi-Agent Design Systems for Concurrent Intelligent Design and Manufacturing. 2001, *Taylor & Francis*, London.
34. Gruber, Thomas, A translation Approach to portable Ontologies. *Knowledge Acquisition, Elsevier*, 1993, Vol. 5, Issue 2, pp 199-220.
35. Xexéo, Geraldo, et al, Peer-to-Peer Collaborative Editing of Ontologies, Rio de Janeiro, Brazil.
36. Staab, S and Studer, R, (2004), Handbook on Ontologies, Springer-Verlag, ISBN 3-540-40834-7.
37. Doan, A, et.al, (2002), Learning to map between ontologies on the semantic web. *In the Eleventh International WWW Conference*, Hawaii, US.
38. Mena, E, et.al, (2000), OBSERVER: An approach for query processing in global information systems based on interoperation across pre-existing ontologies, *Distributed and parallel databases – An international journal, 8(2)*.
39. Hammed, A, Sleeman, D H, Preece, A, (2002), OntoManager, A workbench Environmet to facilitate Ontology Management and Interoperability. In *EON-2002: EKAW-2002 Workshop on Evaluation of Ontology-based tools*.
40. Heflin, Jeff and Hendler, James (2000). Semantic Interoperability on the Web, Proceedings of Extreme Markup Languages. *Graphic Communications Association*, 2000. pp. 111-120.
41. Malo, P., et al. Multilingual on-line dictionary: Breaking the language barriers in the advent of open markets, IEEE International Conference Intelligent Systems. Session: Intelligent Infrastructures for advanced Interoperable Organizations, 2004, Varna, Bulgaria.
42. Kohler, S. et al. Harmonized taxonomies for furniture classification, SMART-fm, www.smartfm.funstep.org (2004).
43. Nunez, M. J., Definition of the SMART-fm pilot demonstrators, SMART-fm, www.smartfm.funstep.org, 2003.
44. Protege (2003). http://protege.stanford.edu/.
45. Brown, D. H., Associates, Inc. 2003, http://dhbrown.com.
46. W3C Web Services Architecture Requirements, 2003, www.w3.org/2002/ws/.
47. Jardim-Goncalves, R., Sarraipa, J., Internet-based cooperative environment for the development of the taxonomy and terminology, in *Taxonomy and Glossary for interoperability, IDEAS Roadmap*, www.ideas-roadmap.net, 2003, pp. 104-116.
48. Jardim-Goncalves, R., et.al. (2004), Ontology-based framework for advanced networked industrial environments, *INCOM2004, 11th IFAC Symposium on Information Control Problems in manufacturing*, April 2004, Salvador, Brazil.
49. Lassila, O, McGuiness, D, The role of frame-based representation on the semantic web. Report KSL-01-02. Knowledge Systems Laboratory. Stanford University (CA, USA), 2001.

Corresponding author. Ricardo Jardim-Goncalves Current address: UNINOVA, Depart. de Engenharia Electrotécnica, Faculdade de Ciências e Tecnologia, Monte de Caparica, PORTUGAL. Tel.: +351 21 2948527; fax: +351 21 2941253; email: rg@uninova.pt

Chapter 27

FOUNDATIONS FOR A CORE ONTOLOGY OF MANUFACTURING

Stefano Borgo[1] and Paulo Leitão[2]
[1]Laboratory for Applied Ontology, ISTC-CNR, via Solteri 38,38100 Trento, Italy, borgo@loa-cnr.it; [2]Polytechnic Institute of Bragança, Quinta Sta Apolónia, Apartado 1134, 5301-857 Bragança, Portugal, pleitao@ipb.pt

Abstract: An initial fragment of a core ontology for the manufacturing domain is presented and motivated. It consists of an ontological classification of ADACOR concepts according to the DOLCE foundational ontology. The ontology is conceptually transparent and semantically explicit thus suitable for information communication, sharing, and retrieval. The system here described considers entities performing the manufacturing scheduling and control operations only.

Key words: Foundational Ontologies; Manufacturing Control Systems

1. INTRODUCTION

If "communication age" and "information era" are popular terms highlighting the characteristics of the time we are living, the struggle for mutual and reliable understanding that is nowadays recognizable across all application domains suggests that a more appropriate term to capture the trend in today and the near future research could be "the semantic period".

This special nature of our time can be seen in application domains as well and the popularity of the term "ontology" in manufacturing is an example. Generally speaking, this term refers to knowledge engineering artifacts that are constituted by a natural or formal language plus a set of assumptions and constraints (Guarino, 1998).

The development of ontology may take from a few hours up to months or even years depending on the choice of the language, the covered topics, and the level of formality and precision. The ultimate goal is the unambiguous description of a certain "reality" of interest. The type of application or the sought generality leads to the choice of a construction methodology which, in turn, guarantees the reliability of the resulting ontology. There are several possible ways to evaluate an ontology among which the expressivity of the adopted language (glossaries, controlled/natural/formal languages), the purpose of the ontology (knowledge sharing, domain modeling, information retrieval, natural language processing,...), the domain covered (management, business, law, medicine, digital libraries...), the structural complexity of the system (tangledness of the taxonomy, degree of branching, depth of the hierarchy, modularity,...) and so on.

Taking semantics at face value, one can roughly divide ontological systems in classes starting from those with weak semantics like glossaries, thesauri, and taxonomies (*terminological ontologies*) and ending with rich logical theories (*formal ontologies*). The first type of ontologies, like WordNet (Fellbaum, 1998), is helpful in organizing catalogs, databases and protocols where only terminological services are needed. When looking for conceptually transparent and semantically robust systems, sophisticated knowledge structures like formal ontologies need to be used. Formal ontologies can be very general (*foundational*) or domain dependent (*core*). Generally, core ontology is aligned to a foundational one to guarantee interoperability in open and evolving environments.

Nowadays only a few projects have produced widespread formal ontologies, e.g. the GALEN project[1] in the medical field. There are several reasons for this. Formal ontologies are relatively new and only in the last few years reliable methodologies have been introduced and consistently applied (Oltramari et al., 2002). Moreover, the development of applications based on these ontologies is sometimes demanding so that often research concentrates on smaller projects, e.g. (Bertolazzi et al., 2001), whose results are unfortunately hardly generalizable.

This paper starts from a widely used foundational ontology and develops a formal ontology for manufacturing scheduling and control environments. The aim is to extend this approach the other aspects of the manufacturing domain in order to build a core ontology for this domain that guarantees: (1) integration with a well organized and accepted foundational ontology; (2) accessibility to agents in the manufacturing domain; and (3) suitability for product and process modeling as well as for information sharing, exchange and retrieval.

It is important to understand that the adoption of foundational ontologies does not force to change the production nor the production organization. If ontological considerations will likely suggest changes in the overall enterprise information system to optimize knowledge management and to

[1] http://www.opengalen.org/.

guarantee data consistency, the very fact that a foundational ontology focuses on data *content* and *description* should make clear that the production and its organization do not concern the ontology itself. Indeed, foundational ontologies are independent from the type of products or the number of their variants, their functionalities, qualities or else. Actually, foundational ontologies can improve the product quality by giving a tool to handle non-functional requirements (security, reliability) which are hard to consider within standard architecture languages.

This paper is organized as follows. In section 2 the application domain is introduced and specific concepts are highlighted. Section 3 gives a general overview of important projects that bring the ontological perspective into the manufacturing area. The next section describes the chosen domain architecture and, in section 5, the DOLCE foundational ontology is presented. The core of the paper is section 6 where the alignment between the domain architecture and the formal ontology is motivated and carried out. A few examples show how to express relevant information in the resulting formal language. The last section briefly discusses the use of the proposed manufacturing ontology in applications, adds some final considerations, and lists future steps to be carried out.

2. SCHEDULING AND CONTROL PROBLEM DESCRIPTION

The manufacturing domain is and will be in the future one of the main wealth generators in Europe. Nowadays it represents approximately 22% of the GNP of the EU and 70% of the employment (European Commission, 2004). The development of adaptive, digital, networked and knowledge-based manufacturing processes is the key factor for the competitiveness and success of a manufacturing enterprise.

This study applies to manufacturing scheduling and control systems: it considers a manufacturing enterprise that produces discrete items and models components of the factory plant as well as aspects of the scheduling, monitoring, and execution processes.

2.1 Manufacturing System Description

A manufacturing enterprise *produces* products which are offered to the market. Within the enterprise, the products are described by the *product model*, which contains all technical data and describes the structure of a product (list of sub-products or parts that assembled constitutes the product), and by the *process model*, which defines how to produce the product.

The process model specifies the *process plan*, that is, a list of operations necessary to produce a part. In this context, an *operation* is a job to be executed in order to produce the product and is characterized by a set of information, such as estimated processing time, description, precedence, and requirements. Assembly, storage, transportation, manipulation, maintenance and inspection, are examples of operations.

A customer interacts with a company to order one of the available products or a new product. This order, known as *customer order*, must include reference to a product, a quantity, a deliver date, and a price. Additionally, the enterprise management system creates *forecast orders* to anticipate the market demands. The manufacturing planning convert the customer and forecast orders into *production orders*, aggregating if possible several customer and forecast orders into a production order, to obtain volume and transport advantages. A production order is indexed to a product object and comprises a list of work orders. A *work order* is the description of an operation (a job) and thus is a part of a process plan. Work orders are intended to be executed by *resources* such as movers, transporters, drilling machines, milling machines, turning machines and tools. Each resource is an entity that can execute a certain range of jobs, when it is available, as long as its capacity is not exceeded.

The *shop floor* consists of a group of resources with different characteristics (spindle speed, list of tools and grippers, payload, time autonomy, work volume, repeatability, etc.), whose combined features allow to execute the products. The *factory model* describes each individual shop floor's resource as well the logical and physical organization of these resources. The availability of a resource is represented by an *agenda* that indicates the list of work orders allocated to the resource over the time. In particular, the agenda comprises time slots where the resource is: free, allocated to execute orders, temporarily out of service (e.g. due to maintenance) and out of service (e.g. due to a break in the provision of needed elements like water or electric power).

2.2 Manufacturing Control Description

The main functions that a *manufacturing control system* (*MCS* for short) fulfills are process planning, resource allocation planning (scheduling), plan execution, and pathological state handling.

The production of a product involves the execution (according to a precedence diagram) of the steps defined in the process plan. At the *process planning* level, the *MCS* launches the production orders to the shop floor together with a process plan. The latter provides the required sequence of operations and the required machine type for each operation. Based on the available resources, it is possible to create alternative process sequences (aiming to achieve flexibility), each one indicating the exact resource that should execute each operation.

Through the *resource allocation planning*, the *MCS* schedules the necessary operations to produce the parts (including processing, transport, maintenance and set-up operations) taking into account the process plans, the constraints and resources capacity. The goal is to produce the products while minimizing the costs and increasing the productivity. Also, at this level the *MCS* considers possible reorganizations of the production unit (in general by varying the resource allocations) if a modification in demand or machine failure makes it necessary.

The *plan execution functions* of the *MCS* take care of the physical implementation of the schedule into the factory. The scheduled orders are dispatched to the manufacturing plant, i.e. the resources, and a monitoring activity of the production progress takes place. The reaction to disturbances is first considered by the *MCS* at the level of the plan execution but may imply re-scheduling of the operations to minimize the effects of the disturbance and, in some cases, the interruption of the production process.

The *pathological state handling* level intends to keep the system in a safe state, in order to avoid and/or recover from undesirable system states, such as deadlock.

3. ONTOLOGIES AND THE MANUFACTURING DOMAIN

In order to improve agility and flexibility, nowadays one uses distributed approaches in developing manufacturing control applications. These are built upon autonomous and cooperative entities, such as those based on multi-agent and holonic systems. Holonic Manufacturing System (HMS)[2] translates to the manufacturing world the concepts developed by Arthur Koestler for living organisms and social organizations (Koestler, 1969). Holonic manufacturing is characterized by holarchies of holons (i.e., autonomous and cooperative entities), which represent the entire range of manufacturing entities. A holon is a part of a (manufacturing) system that has a unique identifier, may be made up of subordinate parts and, in turn, can be part of a larger whole.

2 http://hms.ifw.uni-hannover.de/.

3.1 Manufacturing Interoperability

In distributed manufacturing environments (with autonomous entities representing machines, cells, factories or even enterprises) it is important to guarantee the compatibility between the distributed entities or applications (i.e. issues related to interfaces and protocols) and to verify that the semantic content is preserved during the exchange of messages between distributed entities. Thus, interoperability in distributed platforms increases the need for shared ontologies. Specifically, the term 'manufacturing interoperability' is related to the ability to share technical and business information throughout a distributed factory plant or even an extended or virtual manufacturing enterprise. A study commissioned by NIST (National Institute of Standards and Technology) (Brunnermeier and Martin, 1999) reported that the U.S. automotive sector alone expends one billion dollars per year to solve interoperability problems.

The ontologies currently used in the manufacturing domain are the result of non-coordinated efforts and relinquish the interoperability with other agents communities. Indeed, proprietary manufacturing ontologies have been developed to support the interoperability between distributed entities belonging to the same platform only. The lack of interoperability between different agent-based or holonic manufacturing control platforms pushes for a common manufacturing ontology capable of merging (or at least of communicating adequately with) these.

3.2 Toward Standard Manufacturing Ontologies

Since interoperability has become a central issue in the manufacturing domain, several efforts have been undertaken to develop standard mechanisms for the unambiguous exchange of information in this area. This section reviews some of these efforts and highlights important aspects for a general manufacturing ontology.

The EDI (Electronic Data Interchange) is a standard suitable for applications that want to exchange data through standard formats. EDI is limited to business data only, thus those applications that need to manage engineering and technological information have to resort to other standards targeting more closely the exchange of product data.

Several proposals have been presented for this goal. The IGES (Initial Graphics Exchange Specification) and SET (Standard d'change et de Transfert) have been important stimuli for the data exchange standardization but they fall short of solving the entire problem because the proposed standardization considers the information at the geometrical level and disregards the technological data. STEP, Standard for the Exchange of

Product Model Data developed by the International Organization for Standardization (ISO), defines a standard data format for exchanging a complete product specification (e.g. geometry and production process) between heterogeneous CAD/CAM systems or entities belonging to a supply chain. ISO developed also Plib, Parts Library (http://www.tc184-sc4.org/), which is a computer-interpretable representation of parts library data to enable a full digital information exchange between suppliers and users. Plib and STEP share a common technology basis and is completely interoperable, one focusing on product data, the other on libraries of parts. However, since STEP refers to the product information only and Plib to representation and exchange of part library data, the process and enterprise engineering information are out of their scope.

Another set of initiatives seek to fulfill the gaps. The Process Specification Language project (PSL) (Schlenoff et al., 1996) aims to develop a general ontology for representing manufacturing processes to serve as an interlingua to integrate multiple process-related applications throughout the manufacturing life cycle. A Language for Process Specification (ALPS) (Catron and Ray, 1991) identifies information models to facilitate process specification and to transfer this information to process control. The TOVE, Toronto Virtual Enterprise project (Fadel et al., 1994), defines a domain-specific formal ontology for enterprise modeling which is not connected to foundational ontologies. The Enterprise Ontology provides "a collection of terms and definitions relevant to business enterprises to enable coping with a fast changing environment through improved business planning, greater flexibility, more effective communication and integration" (Uschold et al., 1998). The goal of the Process Interchange Format project (PIF) (Lee et al., 1998) is to support the exchange of business process models across different formats and schemas. Finally, the Plinius project (van der Vet et al., 1994) aims to define a domain-specific ontology for mechanical properties of ceramic material.

In spite of the referred efforts to develop ontologies in areas related to manufacturing, as of today no formal ontology is available in the manufacturing domain. Nonetheless, it is recognized that the application of formal ontologies to support the interoperability between agent-based and holonic manufacturing control applications could provide a reliable and durable solution to this problem. The ongoing activity of the holonic manufacturing community within FIPA (Foundation for Intelligent Physical Agents) to adequate the FIPA specifications to the manufacturing requirements would benefit as well from the adoption of well-justified and organized formal ontologies, that is, ontologies furnished with a deep logical characterization.

3.3 Foundational Ontologies

As anticipated in section 1, foundational ontologies are formal ontologies devoted to facilitate mutual understanding in the large and are developed independently of specific domains. Because of this approach, they comprise only general concepts and relations, and to be applied they need to be populated with notions specific to the domain of interest. Indeed, these ontologies aim at setting a general framework that can be tailored to any application domain; in this way they furnish a reliable tool for information sharing and exchange in all areas. In short, foundational ontologies are characterized by the following crucial properties: they are *general* in the sense that they limit themselves to the most reusable and widely applicable concepts leaving to the user the population of the ontology with more specific concepts; they are *reliable* since they are logical theories with rich axiomatizations and with careful analysis of their formal consequences (theorems); and they are *well organized* because the construction of a foundational ontology is based on philosophical principles whose choice is explicitly motivated.

Just a few foundational ontologies have been developed to a satisfactory level in the literature: DOLCE, the Descriptive Ontology for Linguistic and Cognitive Engineering (Masolo et al., 2003) http://www.loa-cnr.it/DOLCE.html; GFO, the General Formal Ontology (Heller and Herre, 2003) http://www.onto-med.de; OCHRE, the Object-Centered High-level Reference Ontology (Masolo et al., 2003); and, although still in a preliminary form, BFO, the Basic Formal Ontology (Masolo et al., 2003), http://www.ifomis.de. Two other systems are sometimes considered in the literature although they are not, strictly speaking, foundational ontologies. These are OPENCYC (http://www.opencyc.com) and SUMO (http://www.ontologyportal.org).

Two issues should be carefully analyzed in choosing a foundational ontology for applications: the ontology must include a set of conceptual distinctions sufficient for that domain (e.g. the distinction between abstract and concrete, agentive and non-agentive, etc.), and all the relevant entities should be clearly characterizable within the ontology (e.g. orders, resources, sensors, measurable qualities, etc.).

4. THE ADACOR MANUFACTURING ONTOLOGY

In the manufacturing domain, manufacturing control approaches are implemented and improved continuously. To ground the discussion, this paper selects architecture and provides an ontological assessment of its concepts. That is, the notions of this architecture are analyzed for their ontological commitment (Guarino, 1998), classified following a foundational ontology, and formalized accordingly. The result of this process is a formal system comprising the architecture notions and their ontological organization, that is, a system that can be taken as *core ontology* for the manufacturing domain. This system is not limited to the chosen architecture. New concepts can be added from other architectures by following the methodology (see section 6) and other systems can openly and safely communicate with any aligned architecture (if they can manage the language of the ontology) even without being aligned themselves.

ADACOR (ADAptive holonic COntrol aRchitecture for distributed manufacturing systems) (Leitão et al., 2005) is the architecture here analyzed. Based in the HMS paradigm, it addresses the agile reaction to disturbances at the shop floor level in volatile environments and it is built upon a set of autonomous and cooperative holons, each one being a representation of a manufacturing component, i.e., a physical resource (numerical control machines, robots, etc.) or a logic entity (orders, etc.).

ADACOR defines its own proprietary manufacturing ontology, expressed in an object-oriented frame-based manner as recommended in the FIPA Ontology Service Recommendations (http://www.fipa.org/). It uses classes to describe concepts and predicates and fixes them as part of the application ontology. In this way, ontology is quickly generated with an immediate underlying implementation.

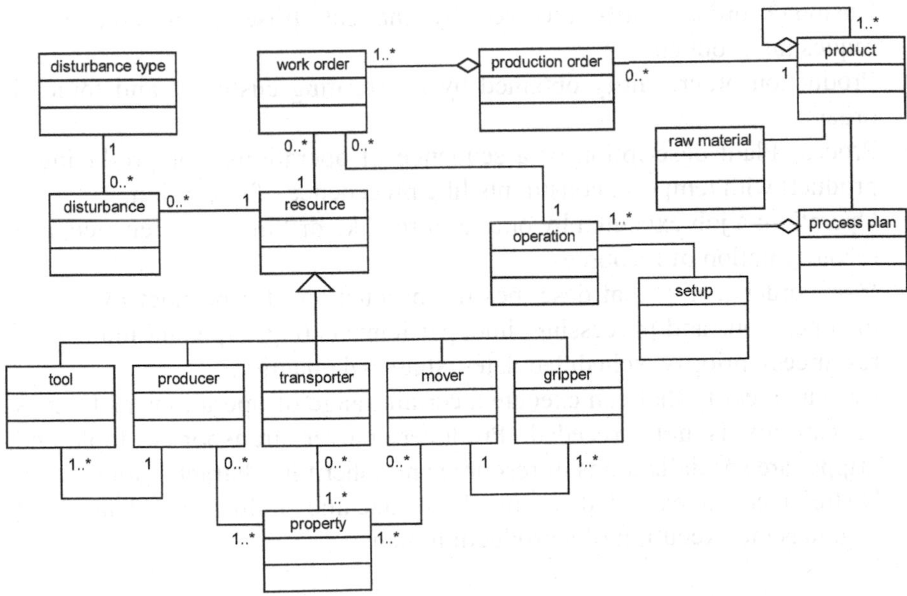

Figure 27-1. Manufacturing Ontology in the ADACOR Architecture

The manufacturing ontology used in ADACOR is developed through the definition of a taxonomy of manufacturing components, which contributes to the analysis and formalization of the manufacturing problem (these components are mapped into a set of objects, illustrated in the UML class diagram of). For this, one must fix the vocabulary used by the distributed entities over the ADACOR platform, isolate the ADACOR-concepts, the ADACOR-predicates and -relations, the ADACOR-attributes of the classes, and the meaning of each term. Note that not all ADACOR concepts find a place in Figure 27-1. The diagram is restricted to the relationships between simple manufacturing components used by the manufacturing control system. For example, a production order may index one customer order or an aggregation of these although this relationship and the latter concept are not shown.

4.1 ADACOR Concepts

ADACOR-concepts are expressions that hold for complex entities whose structure can be defined in terms of classes or objects. The main concepts in the ADACOR architecture, Figure 27-1, are informally described as follows:

- Product: entity produced by the enterprise (it includes sub-products).
- Raw-material: entity acquired outside the enterprise and used during the production process, e.g. blocks of steel, nuts and bolds (unless produced internally).
- Customer order: entity received by the enterprise from a customer requesting products.
- Production order: entity obtained by aggregating customer and forecast orders.
- Process Plan: description of a sequence of operations (for producing a product) with temporal constraints like precedence of execution.
- Operation: a job executed by one resource like drilling, maintenance, and reconfiguration of resources.
- Work order: entity that describes the production of a product by listing the operations and processing time, participants (e.g. type and number of resources), priority, scheduled dates, state and quantity.
- Resource: entity that can execute a certain range of operations as long as its capacity is not exceeded. Producer, mover, transporter, tool, and gripper are specializations of resource and inherit its characteristics[3].
- Disturbance: unexpected event, like machine failure or delay that degrades the execution of a production plan.

[3] Here human operators are not considered among the resources of the system.

- Setup: set of actions that it is necessary to execute in order to prepare a manufacturing resource for the execution of a range of operations.
- Property: an attribute that characterizes a resource or that a resource should satisfy to execute an operation.

In agent-based or holonic manufacturing control approaches, the control is achieved by the interaction between distributed entities, i.e. the agents or the holons. An agent or holon in ADACOR is an entity that represents manufacturing components like resources, products or orders.

4.2 ADACOR Predicates

Predicates establish relationships among concepts, for instance:

- ComponentOf(x,y): product x is a component of product y.
- Allocated(x,y,t): operation x is allocated to resource y at time t.
- Available(x,y,t): resource x is available at time t for operation y.
- RequiresTool(x,y): execution of operation x requires tool y.
- HasTool(x,y,t): resource x has tool y available in its magazine at t.
- HasSkill(x,y): resource x has property (skill) y.
- HasFailure(x,y,t): a disturbance x occurred in resource y at time t.
- Proposal(x,y,w,z,u): the entity x proposes to the entity y the execution of the work order w with location u and charging the price z.
- Precedence(x,y): operation x requires previous execution of y.
- UsesRawMaterial(x,y): production order x uses raw material y.
- RequestSetup(x,y): operation x needs the execution of setup y.
- HasProcessPlan(x,y): production of x requires process plan y.
- OrderExecution(u,x,w,y): operation u is listed in process plan w (describing production of y) for production order x.
- HasRequirement(x,y): operation x requires property y.
- HasGripper(x,y,t): resource x has gripper y in its magazine at time t.
- ExecutesOperation(x,y): work order x includes operation y.

If these predicates are available, an *agenda* can be defined as a set of Allocated(x,y,i) and Available(x,y,t) predicates.

4.3 Attributes of ADACOR Concepts

Attributes are values relative to properties of concepts. Here is a list of properties (in brackets an example of measure units) associated with the skills of a resource or the requirements of an operation:

- Axes: a non-negative integer, e.g. the number of axes of a machine.
- ProcessingType: a type of processing e.g. turning, milling, or drilling.
- Repeatability: a non-negative integer, it gives an indication about the precision of the machine (expressed in mm).

- FeedRate: a positive rational number, it gives the feed rate of a specific axis (expressed in mm/rot).
- SpindleSpeed: a range of non-negative integers, it gives the spindle speed in the form [min, max] (expressed in rpm).
- CuttingSpeed: a positive rational number, it gives the cutting speed (expressed in mm/s).
- Tailstock: a range of non-negative integers, it gives the size in form [min,max] of pieces that the machine can process (expressed in mm).
- Payload: positive integer, it gives the maximum load of the robot that guarantees the repeatability (expressed in kg).
- MaxReachability: positive integer, it gives the work volume of the robot (expressed in mm).
- Autonomy: non-negative integer, it gives the amount of time that an autonomous vehicle can work without the need to re-fill its batteries (expressed in hours).
- MagazineCapacity: non-negative integer, it gives the number of tools or grippers that the magazine of a machine or robot can store.

5. THE DOLCE FORMAL ONTOLOGY

In section 3.3, a number of foundational ontologies have been introduced. This section focuses on the DOLCE ontology and presents those features that are most relevant for manufacturing core ontology. The interested reader can find in (Masolo et al., 2003) the motivations for this ontology and a throughout discussion of technical aspects.

5.1 DOLCE from the Manufacturing Perspective

The Descriptive Ontology for Linguistic and Cognitive Engineering, DOLCE, concentrates on *particulars*, that is, roughly speaking, objects (physical or abstract), events, and qualities. The ontology does not attempt to provide taxonomy of properties and relations and these are included in the system only if crucial in characterizing particulars.

The DOLCE ontology provides a good framework for the manufacturing area: it adopts the distinction between objects like products and events like operations; it includes a useful differentiation among individual qualities, quality types, quality spaces, and quality values; it allows for fine descriptions of properties and capacities; and it relies on a very expressive language, namely first-order modal logic. Because of these features, the formalization of categories like physical object, agent, and process can be done following the corresponding notions as used in the manufacturing domain. Furthermore, in DOLCE the user can choose and characterize the qualities needed in the application which provides a great level of freedom and facilitates update and maintenance. From the implementation viewpoint, lightweight versions of DOLCE are available in LOOM, DAML+OIL, RDFS, and OWL and the full system is implemented in CASL (see http://www.brics.dk/Projects/CoFI/CASL.html) with connections to theorem provers and graphical tools.

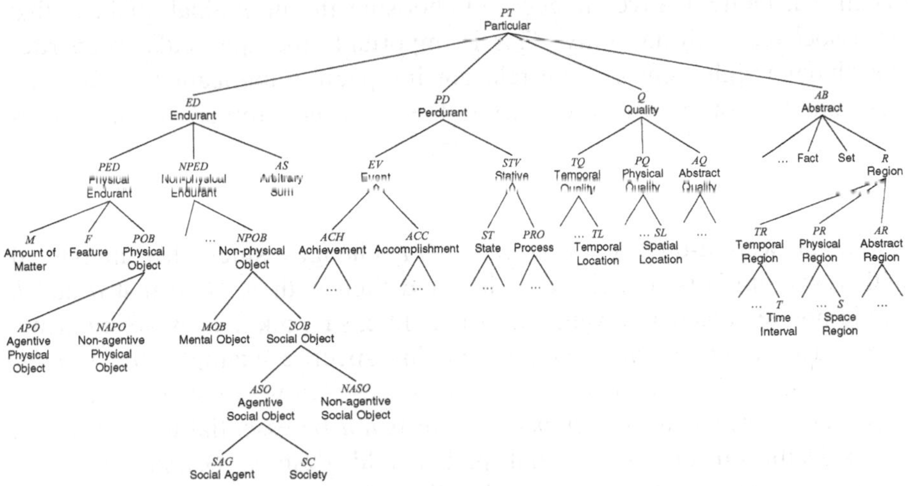

Figure 27-2. Taxonomy of DOLCE basic categories (Masolo et al., 2003)

The development of DOLCE has been explicitly influenced by natural language and cognitive considerations. This explains in part the adoption of a *multiplicative approach*, that is, the assumption that different entities can be co-localized in the same space-time. For example, a drilling machine and the amount of matter that forms it are captured in DOLCE as two distinct entities (as opposed to different aspects of the same entity). The reason lies on the different set of properties that these entities enjoy: the drilling machine ceases to exist if a radical change of shape occurs (e.g., when it is crashed and it cannot be repaired) while its amount of matter is not affected.

The ontology uses *endurant* for objects like "gripper" or "plastic", and *perdurant* for events like "making a hole", "moving a steel block" and the like. The term 'object' is used in the ontology to capture a notion of unity as suggested by the partition of the class "physical endurant" into classes "amount of matter", "feature", and "physical objects" (Figure 27-2). Both endurants and perdurants are associated with a bunch of *qualities*; the list of qualities may depend on the entity: shape and weight are usually taken as qualities of endurants, duration and direction as qualities of perdurants.

Roughly speaking, in DOLCE an *individual quality* is a quality associated with *one and only one* entity; it can be understood as the particular way in which that entity instantiates the corresponding property. For example, in DOLCE the endurant *Gripper_321* (a physical machine) has its own individual instantiation of property "having weight". This instantiation is the *individual weight-quality* of *Gripper_321*. *Gripper_321* may have several individual qualities, each related to a different property: the individual weight-quality, the individual shape-quality, the individual color-quality, etc. Recall that DOLCE gives freedom in choosing the individual qualities that are associated with an entity. This is important since particular properties like "having light sensors" are relevant in specific applications only. Yet, they should not be ruled out from the start nor forced to be always considered. The change of an endurant in time is explained through the change of some of its individual qualities. For example, with the substitution of a component, *Gripper_321* may increase its weight from a to b, then the individual weight-quality of *Gripper_321* changes since that individual quality was initially associated with a and then with b. Note that a and b should not be considered weight measures like, say, 5 kg. They are elements of a space called *quality space* or, in this specific example, the *weight-quality space*. We will discuss quality spaces below. First, note that the substituted component of *Gripper_321* must *not* be essential to the gripper. The substitution of an essential part would destroy *Gripper_321* and generate a new one. Finally, note that the gripper cannot exist without its individual qualities: DOLCE forces a strict existential dependence between individual qualities and their hosts.

The example of the gripper makes clear that the "position in the quality space" of an individual quality can change over time. DOLCE calls such positions *qualia* (*quale* in singular form). A *quality space* for a property is the collection of all possible qualia (positions) that an individual quality can assume. Suppose that in an application an endurant is either heavier, equal, or lighter than another endurant α. Then, an admissible weight-quality space for that application has *at least* three distinguished positions: one is the position taken by the individual weight-qualities of endurants lighter than α, a second position is taken by the individual weight-qualities not distinguishable from the individual weight-quality of α, and the third is the position of the individual weight-qualities of the heavier endurants. If other considerations seem to require a different system, one can assume that the quality space (the set of positions) is more complex, for instance the set of non-negative real numbers. This latter case can be described in DOLCE by positioning the individual weight-quality of α at some positive real x and the individual quality of an endurant lighter than α to the sub-region $\{z \in \Re^+ \mid z < x\}$. (Here the position is the whole region, not just a point in it.

Mereological principles are used to map between regions and points when needed.) Similarly, the individual quality of an endurant heavier than α is positioned at the sub-region $\{z \in \Re^+ \mid z > x\}$. The mapping between the two weight-quality spaces just described is trivial. Note that neither measurement methods nor units have been used, these must be introduced explicitly.

Finally, DOLCE is actively compared to other foundational ontologies at different levels of formality (Masolo et al., 2003; Martin, 2003). Since DOLCE is included in merging initiatives, the core ontology here proposed is likely to be automatically connected to any other manufacturing ontology developed for interoperability.

5.2 Categories and Relations in DOLCE

The categories of Figure 27-2 relevant to our work are here introduced.

ED(x), *PED(x)* stand for "*x* is an endurant" and "*x* is a physical endurant", respectively, with the latter is a subclass of the first.

- *NAPO(x)* stands for "*x* is a non-agentive physical object", i.e., endurants that have spatial and temporal location but not intentions, believes, or desires, like "products" and "production orders".

In the manufacturing domain, one needs to deal with a variety of operations (jobs). First, note that here an operation is a precise event or happening, that is a precise perdurant, and not a type of perdurants. (Types are introduced through the use of descriptions. This crucial distinction will be developed at another stage of this work. See also section 6). An operation in DOLCE is said to be *homeomeric* if every temporal part of it is itself an operation of the same "type". For instance, a "milling" operation during interval *t* is homeomeric since if one divides this interval in two parts, say, *t_1* and *t_2*, the sub-operation during *t_1* is still a milling operation and so is the sub-operation during *t_2*. This does not hold for "setup" operations. A setup operation requires the completion of a process which is obtained once a specific state is reached. If this does not happen, the setup does not occur. Thus, if a setup operation is divided in two temporal parts as before, only one of the two sub-operations (if any) can be considered a setup operation. This and similar distinctions drive the ontological classification of the ADACOR notions and are captured by the DOLCE predicates below.

- *PD(x)* stands for "*x* is a perdurant".
- *ACH(x)* stands for "*x* is an achievement", i.e., perdurants that are *anti-cumulative* (summing two achievements one does not obtain an achievement) and *atomic* (they do not have temporal parts). E.g., the "completion of a reconfiguration"[4].

[4] Note the distinction between "completion of a reconfiguration" and "reconfiguration". Only the first is an achievement.

- *ACC(x)* stands for "*x* is an accomplishment". These are *non-atomic* perdurants since they have temporal parts. E.g. "machine reconfiguration". The fact that the sum of two "machine reconfigurations" is not a "machine reconfiguration" itself shows that accomplishments are *anti-cumulative*.
- *ST(x)* stands for "*x* is a state", i.e., *cumulative* perdurants like "drilling" (the sum of two drilling operations is again a drilling operation). These perdurants are also *homeomeric*.
- *qt(q,x)* stands for "q is an individual quality of x".
- *ql(r, q)*, *ql(r,q,t)* stand for "*r* is the quale of the perdurant's quality *q*", "*r* is the quale of the endurant's quality *q* during time *t*", respectively.

6. THE ALIGNMENT ADACOR – DOLCE

DOLCE provides a distinct category for each type of entity in ADACOR. Beside the distinction between endurants and perdurants, descriptions are modeled explicitly as abstract entities, and properties are rendered through the associated qualities. In this section the ADACOR concepts, predicates and attributes are checked from an ontological perspective and classified in DOLCE. For lack of space, not all the notions of section 4 are included. Nonetheless, the overall framework should be clear from the cases below.

6.1 ADACOR – DOLCE: Endurants

A crucial point is the distinction between endurants and their descriptions. An example is given by the concept of "order", let it be "customer order", "production order" or "work order". In the manufacturing enterprise "order" is at the same time the physical support for some data (a physical object like a sheet of paper or a part of a computer device) and the description of an entity or event (the description of an operation that must be executed or of a product that must be produced). Since "order as a physical object" and "order as a description" have different properties (if one can take a physical object from one office to another, it makes no sense to take an abstract entity from an office to another; likewise a product can conform to a description but not to a paper)[5], it is necessary to make sure that the formalization keeps them distinct.

[5] Here one should refrain from exploiting the ambiguities of natural language (one of the reasons for employing formal ontology). In a given context one finds meaning even for sentences like "take this description to the management office" or "this bolt conforms to the paper they gave me". If sentences are interpreted contextually, the communication cannot be reliable unless there is only one context.

For each ambiguous ADACOR concept, two predicates are introduced in DOLCE; one referring to endurants (in this case the very same expression is used), the other referring to descriptions (in this case the superscript '*D*' is added). Here it is assumed that a description is considered as long as recorded in some physical object, e.g. in a document about product specifications. (The study of descriptions is not presented here except for one minor case.)

Products, resources and orders (as physical endurants) are non-agentive entities, thus they are naturally classified as *NAPO*

$$(Product(x) \vee Resource(x) \vee Order(x)) \rightarrow NAPO(x)$$

At the level of descriptions,

$$\left(Product^{D}(x) \vee Resource^{D}(x) \vee Order^{D}(x)\right) \rightarrow AB(x)$$

where *AB* is the predicate that characterizes abstract entities in DOLCE (entities neither in space nor in time).

Since raw-material may refer to physical objects (bolts, lenses, etc.) as well as to amounts of matter (water, sand or gasoline), this concept is mapped to the category *PED* which includes both

$$Raw\_material(x) \rightarrow PED(x)$$

The constraint $Raw\_material(x) \rightarrow (POB(x) \vee M(x))$ would be too restrictive since it requires any raw-material to be either a physical object or an amount of matter (the two class are disjoint in DOLCE). That would exclude raw-material composed of physical objects and some amount of matter. Instead, it is necessary to add the restriction that features are not raw-material

$$Raw\_material(x) \rightarrow \neg F(x)$$

Note that the notion of raw material is not ontological. A company that produces clothes and that buys buttons from another producer classifies the buttons as raw-material. Indeed, buttons are here parts of the produced items without being products themselves. However, the very same items are products for the button producer. This discrepancy is only apparent since ontologically the items (call them raw-material or products) have the same individual qualities in all contexts.

Some ADACOR concepts, like "Order" or "Resource", are totally determined in terms of more specialized entities also in ADACOR. In these cases, the formalization lists which entities these concepts subsume. In particular, the "Order" and "Resource" are partitioned as follows

$$Order(x) \leftrightarrow (Production\_order(x) \vee Customer\_order(x) \vee Work\_order(x))$$

$$Resource(x) \leftrightarrow (Producer(x) \vee Mover(x) \vee Transporter(x) \vee Tool(x) \vee Gripper(x))$$

6.2 ADACOR – DOLCE: Perdurants

Most of the entities in ADACOR are perdurants (or descriptions of perdurants) since they identify activities or states. If the classification of "Operation" as generic perdurant is immediate, the notion of "Disturbance" is more involved and will be discussed below together with "Delay" and "Failure". As for "Completion", it marks the end of an event and thus it is an achievement. The remaining operations are divided in two groups: stative perdurants and accomplishment perdurants.

$$Operation(x) \rightarrow PD(x)$$

$$Disturbance(x) \rightarrow ACH(x)$$

$$(Transportation(x) \vee Turning(x) \vee Drilling(x) \vee Milling(x)) \rightarrow ST(x)$$

$$(Setup(x) \vee Reconfiguration(x) \vee Inspection(x) \vee Maintenance(x) \vee Assembly(x) \vee Production(x)) \rightarrow ACC(x)$$

It is natural to consider "transportation" as a state: since all the temporal parts of a transportation event can be classified as transportations themselves, this type of event falls in the class of stative perdurants (*ST*). A similar argument holds for "turning", "drilling", and "milling" since these are relatively simple perdurants. More specialized operations, for instance operations where it is necessary to distinguish explicitly different phases of execution (say, to resume properly after a failure event), may require the notion of process. As of now, this kind of operations is not present in ADACOR. The remaining operations are all implicitly characterized by a notion of "final state" and, consequently, classified as accomplishments.

"Operation", "Disturbance", and "Reconfiguration" are characterized by more specialized notions as follows

$$Disturbance(x) \leftrightarrow (Failure(x) \vee Delay(x))$$

$$\begin{aligned} Operation(x) \leftrightarrow (&Completation\_of\_setup(x) \vee Reconfiguration(x) \vee \\ &\vee Inspection(x) \vee Setup(x) \vee Maintenance(x) \vee Turning(x) \vee \\ &\vee Production(x) \vee Milling(x) \vee Transportation(x) \vee \\ &\vee Assembly(x) \vee Drilling(x)) \end{aligned}$$

$$\begin{aligned} Reconfiguration(x) \leftrightarrow (&Addition\_of\_new\_resource(x) \vee \\ &\vee Change\_of\_layout(x) \vee \\ &\vee Removal\_of\_resource(x) \vee \\ &\vee Change\_of\_resource\_capability(x)) \end{aligned}$$

Correctly, ADACOR considers "Operation" and "Disturbance" as disjoint notions, that is, no entity is both an operation and a disturbance.

$$Operation(x) \rightarrow \neg Disturbance(x)$$

There is a misalignment between the notion of "setup" as an operation (above) and the concept of "setup" shown in Figure 27-1. In some cases, "setup" is seen as a requirement for other operations and this justifies its addition as a separate entry in Figure 27-1. The status of "being a requirement" can be captured ontologically through a standard *precedence* relation.

"Delay", "Disturbance", and "Failure" are special kind of events in ADACOR. A disturbance is an unexpected event: machine failure or machine delays are the only examples of disturbances considered. These events affect the scheduled production plan. When an operation is being executed, several different scenarios can be expected: (1) the resource finishes the execution of the operation within the estimated time interval, (2) the resource fails and it cannot finish the operation (a failure has occurred) or (3) the operation is delayed (a delay has occurred). Thus, failures and delays are perdurants and machines participate in them. Clearly, a failure is a kind of achievement (the event at which a production plan rescheduling is requested). The classification of "Delay" is similar although it might be less obvious. First it is important to understand that not all holdups are delays. For a delay to occur, it is not enough to have an operation postponed or retarded. What matters is the satisfaction of the temporal constraints set by the production plan. A delay occurs only when it is acknowledge that the production plan cannot be satisfied. Thus, it marks a state where a production plan rescheduling is requested and so it is an achievement. In short, the distinction between "Failure" and "Delay" is based on the cause that brought to the rescheduling request, not on the type of perdurant these notions refer to. For the sake of completeness, regarding the anti-cumulativeness property note that the sum of two delays is not itself a delay since it does not correspond to a "single" rescheduling request.

6.3 ADACOR – DOLCE: Qualities

In the terminology of DOLCE, skills are qualities of endurants. For each type of skill it is introduced a quality space and, for each endurant that has that skill, an individual quality specific to that entity. The quale gives a classification of that endurant with respect to the given skill. Since skills require the introduction of all these different elements, details about the ontological analysis of skills will be presented in a dedicated paper. Here it suffices to give a guiding example through the attribute "Autonomy".

First, note that kills are not necessarily *ontological* qualities. The notion of "Autonomy" is important in the manufacturing area and it is considered as an independent property in ADACOR. Thus, it is included in the proposed manufacturing ontology. However, in other applications it might be given as a derived property (depending on, say, batteries power and energy consumption). DOLCE can deal with both cases and it furnishes the tools to coherently relate the different characterizations.

The autonomy of a resource measures how long it can work without the need to re-fill its batteries. If *AutL* is the class of individual autonomy-qualities, then the following constraint says that "Autonomy" is a quality defined for resources only

$$AutL(q) \rightarrow \exists x(qt(q,x) \wedge Resource(x))$$

Literally the formula states that each individual autonomy-quality is a quality of a resource. The uniqueness of the resource is derived from the formalization of DOLCE itself.

The specific relations "q is the autonomy-quality of resource x" and "resource x has autonomy-quale d at time t" are not part of the language and can be defined as follows

$$Autonomy(q,x) =_{def} Resource(x) \wedge AutL(q) \wedge qt(q,x)$$

$$Autonomy(d,x,t) =_{def} Resource(x) \wedge \exists q(Autonomy(q,x) \wedge ql(d,q,t))$$

Assume now that f is a function from the autonomy-quality space to the non-negative integers obtained by fixing some standard measurement method and unit for this property. Also, assume autonomy is expressed in hours and that relation *Executes(x,y,t)*, which reads "resource *x* starts executing operation *y* at time *t*", is given (see for instance (Borgo and Leitão, 2004)). Then, the language allows us to put constraints on the autonomy capacity of a resource by

$$Operation\_requires\_autonomy(x,y) =_{def}$$
$$Operation(x) \wedge \forall z,t,d(Executes(z,x,t) \wedge Autonomy(d,z,t) \rightarrow f(d) \geq y)$$

$$Operation\_requires\_autonomy(milling_{\alpha},3)$$

From the definition *x* is an operation that requires autonomy of at least *y* to be executed, and the other formula constrains operation $milling_{\alpha}$ to be executed by resources with at least 3 hours autonomy.

6.4 The ADACOR – DOLCE Notion of Component

This part focuses on the ADACOR concept "ComponentOf" (see section 4.2) and the notion of process plan.

From section 2.1, the structure of a product is included in the product model. Assume that the production of a product consists simply in assembling its components. A component may be complex, i.e., itself decomposable into simpler components, or atomic. The idea is that all the elements that are assembled at some point of the production process are components of the product itself. The ADACOR notion "ComponentOf" is needed to provide this composition-hierarchy in the product model. The goal is to capture this informal description from an ontological viewpoint in order to avoid misinterpretations of the product model. For this, the predicate *Component_of* is introduced in DOLCE

$$Component\_of(x,y) \rightarrow ((Product(x) \vee raw\_material(x)) \wedge Product(y))$$

$$Component\_of(x,y) \rightarrow \neg Component\_of(y,x) \quad (anti-symmetric)$$

$$Component\_of(x,y) \wedge Component\_of(y,z) \rightarrow$$
$$\rightarrow Component\_of(x,z) \qquad (transitive)$$

$$\forall x \exists y(Product(x) \wedge \neg raw\_material(x)) \rightarrow Component\_of(y,x)$$
$$(if\ x\ is\ a\ produced\ product,\ then\ it\ has\ components)$$

The first condition says that if x composes y, then x is either a product or raw material while y is a product. The second condition implies that a component cannot be a component of itself. The next formula states transitivity: a component of a component of z is also a component of z. Finally, a constraint is added to the effect that only products which are also raw material have no component. The inverse relation "x has component y", call it *Has_component*, is given by

$$Has\_component(x, y) \leftrightarrow Component\_of(y, x)$$

Regarding the notion of process plan, a graphical and mathematical representation of process planning information can be done using standard graph theory as in (Cho and Wysk, 1995). This allows us to represent processing precedence, alternative sequences and parallel actions. (Cho and Wysk, 1995) introduces an AND/OR based graph to represent the operations and their precedence relationship (Figure 27-3).

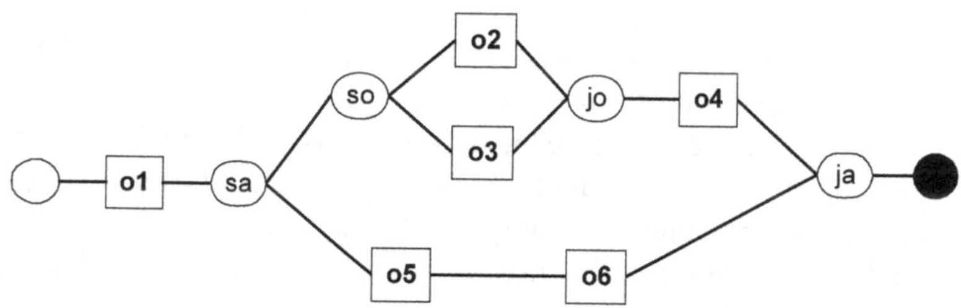

Figure 27-3. A Process plan representation example.

There are five types of nodes: *operation*, *split-or*, *split-and*, *joint-or*, and *joint-and*. All paths following a *split-and* type node must be processed since they are always necessary for the production. A *joint-and* type node brings multiple paths back together after a *split-and* type node. Only one path following a *split-or* type node must be selected for execution. In this way, one can represent operations alternatives. A *joint-or* type node is required to bring multiple paths together after a *split-or* type node. Figure 27-3 exemplifies an AND/OR based graph, where the process plan comprises the execution of operation **o1** and the execution of one of two alternative set of operations: the first one comprises the execution of operation **o2** or **o3** followed by the execution of **o4**, and the second one comprises the execution of operations **o5** and **o6**.

Below a representation in DOLCE of the temporal sequence of operations in Figure 27-3 is given. To keep the formula simple, the "disjoint or" connective (indicated by symbol $\dot{\vee}$) is used: a formula of form $\alpha \dot{\vee} \beta$

reads "either α or β is true but not both". Among the nodes, only operations need to occur in the formalization. Terms $o_1,\ldots, o_6$ refer to **o1**,..., **o6**, respectively as occurring in Figure 27-3. Recall that the relation *Executes(x,y,t)* stands for "resource *x* executes operation *y* at time *t*". In the formula, x_i stands for a resource (say, a machine) and t_i for the initial time of the execution[6].

$$
\begin{aligned}
&\exists x_1,\ldots, x_6, t_1,\ldots, t_6 \\
&\quad (t_1 < t_2, t_3, t_5 \wedge t_2, t_3 < t_4 \wedge t_5 < t_6 \wedge t_2 = t_3) && (\textit{temporal constraints}) \\
&\quad \wedge [Executes(x_1, o_1, t_1) && (\textit{starting condition}) \\
&\quad\quad \wedge (Executes(x_2, o_2, t_2) \dot{\vee} Executes(x_3, o_3, t_3)) && (\textit{do either } o_2 \textit{ or } o_3) \\
&\quad\quad \wedge Executes(x_4, o_4, t_4) \wedge Executes(x_5, o_5, t_5) \wedge Executes(x_6, o_6, t_6)]
\end{aligned}
$$

7. CONCLUSIONS AND FUTURE WORK

The ADACOR manufacturing ontology, described in the section 4, was implemented as part of a multi-agent manufacturing control system by using the JADE (Java Agent Development Framework) framework. The experience gained during the development phase, highlighted the difficulties to build, maintain and modify proprietary ontologies to be used by heterogeneous manufacturing control applications, especially those built upon distributed approaches such as multi-agent systems. This problem pushed for new approaches in the development of manufacturing ontologies to simplify the effort to build, maintain and modify the ontologies. The adoption of an established foundational ontology was suggested to overcome this problem and to improve the consistency of the overall system.

In this paper, a classification of ADACOR concepts according to the DOLCE foundational ontology has been proposed resulting in the core ontology of section 6. This ontology improves and extends (Borgo and Leitão, 2004) and can be used within actual implementations of ADACOR and adapted to other architectures. The formal expressions generated by this ontology can be furnished together with the data exchanged among the agents and holons in this way guaranteeing the correct interpretation of the data. The formal expressions can be obtained either at development time (for general data) or at run-time throughout the available lightweight versions of DOLCE. A quick check through the same lightweight version of the system ensures the correct meaning of the data is understood by the receiver.

6 One can restate the formula using time intervals or adding more time constraints by taking into account the duration of the different operations.

Roughly, every time a term or a set of data are ontologically ambiguous, a flag is set to mark the data; both the sender and receiver can check the possible meanings and start a negotiation process if needed.

When the ontology is completed to cover all the concepts and relations of ADACOR, a series of tests will be executed to evaluate in real applications the reliability of the core ontology as well as its usefulness in the manufacturing area. In spite of some efforts to develop ontologies in areas related to manufacturing, as of today no available (or even proposed) formal ontology sccms capable to cover the all domain.

The core ontology presented in this paper is well-founded because built according to a foundational ontology (DOLCE), because adopting formal semantics, and because following the methodology of formal ontology. This fact makes the proposed core ontology conceptually transparent and semantically explicit, two conditions crucial for information communication, sharing, and retrieval. However, this system is only an initial step in the realization of our goal since only entities performing the manufacturing scheduling and control operations have been considered and no test in real applications has been carried out yet. Also, specifications of additional information beyond process data, for instance resource commitments, costs, delivery times and machine failures need to be investigated further.

Manufacturing enterprises normally suffer for lack of generality, reliable intra/inter communications and re-usability of their systems. Since the proposed here approach presents some innovations, such as formal specification, independence from implementation and platforms, generality and re-usability, if successful it will support the development of heterogeneous and distributed manufacturing scheduling and control systems, allowing a later integration of information systems at intra-enterprise and inter-enterprise levels.

ACKNOWLEDGEMENTS

The Provincia Autonoma di Trento (IT) funded one author through the projects “Logical Instruments for Ontology Analysis” and “Mostro”.

REFERENCES

Bertolazzi, P. Krusich, C. and Missikoff, M., 2001, An Approach to the Definition of a Core Enterprise Ontology: CEO, OES-SEO 2001, International Workshop on Open Enterprise Solutions: Systems, Experiences, and Organizations, Rome, September.

Borgo, S. and Leitão, P., 2004, The role of Foundational Ontologies in Manufacturing Domain Applications, in R. Meersman and Z. Tari (eds.), OTM Confederated International Conferences, ODBASE 2004, LNCS 3290, Springer, pp. 670–688.

Brunnermeier, S. B. and Martin, S. A., 1999, Interoperability Cost Analysis of the U.S. Automotive Supply Chain (Planning Report #99-1), Technical report, NIST, Research Triangel Institute (also available at http://www.nist.gov/director/progofc/ report99-1.pdf).

Catron, B. and Ray, S., 1991, ALPS: A Language for Process Specification, *International Journal of Computer Integrated Manufacturing*, **4**(2): 105–113.

Cho, H. and Wysk, R., 1995, Intelligent Workstation Controller for Computer Integrated Manufacturing: Problems and Models, *Journal of Manufacturing Systems*, **14**(4):252–263.

European Commission, Manufuture, 2004, A Vision for 2020, Assuring the Future of Manufacturing in Europe, Report of the High-level Group.

Fadel, F., Fox, M. and Gruninger, M., 1994, A Generic Enterprise Resource Ontology, In 3rd IEEE Workshop on Enabling Technologies: Infrastructures for Collaborative Enterprises.

Fellbaum, C. (ed.),1998, *WordNet An Electronic Lexical Database*, Bradford Book.

Guarino, N., 1998, Formal ontology in information systems, In N. Guarino (ed.), Proceedings of the 1st Intern. Conf. on Formal Ontology in Information Systems, IOS Press, pp. 3-15.

Heller, B. and Herre, H., 2003, Ontological Categories in GOL, *Axiomathes*, (**14**)1:57–76.

Koestler, A., 1969, *The Ghost in the Machine*, Arkana Books, London.

Lee, J., Gruninger, M., Jin, Y., Malone, T., Tate, A. and Yost, G., 1998, The PIF Process Interchange Format and Framework, *Knowledge Engineering Review*, **13**(1):91–120.

Leitão, P., Colombo, A. and Restivo, F., 2005, ADACOR, A Collaborative Production Automation and Control Architecture, *IEEE Intelligent Systems*, **20**(1):58-66.

Martin, P., 2003, Correction and Extension of WordNet 1.7, Proceedings of the 11th Intern. Conf. on Conceptual Structures, LNAI 2746, Springer, pp. 160–173.

Masolo, C., Borgo, S., Gangemi, A., Guarino, N. and Oltramari, A., 2003, Ontology Library (Wonder-Web Deliverable D18), Technical report, Laboratory for Applied Ontology, ISTC-CNR, (also at http://wonderweb.semanticweb.org/deliverables/documents/D18.pdf).

Oltramari, A., Gangemi, A., Guarino, N., and Masolo, C., Restructuring WordNet's Top-Level: The OntoClean approach, Workshop Proceedings of OntoLex 02, Ontologies and Lexical Knowledge Bases, LREC2002, May 27, 2002, pp. 17-26.

Schlenoff, C., Knutilla, A. and Ray, S., 1996, Unified Process Specification Language: Requirements for Modeling Process, In NIST, Interagency Report 5910, Gaithersburg MD.

Uschold, M., King, M., Moralee, S. and Zorgios, Y., 1998, The Enterprise Ontology, *Knowledge Engineering Review, Special Issue on Putting Ontologies to Use*, **13**(1):31–89.

van der Vet, P., Speel, P.-H. and Mars, N., 1994, The PLINIUS Ontology of Ceramic Materials, In ECAI'94, Workshop on Comparison of Implemented Ontologies.

Chapter 28

ENGINEERING A DEVELOPMENT PLATFORM FOR ONTOLOGY-ENHANCED KNOWLEDGE APPLICATIONS

Gary H. Merrill

Analysis Applications, Research, and Technologies (A^2RT), GlaxoSmithKline Inc., Research and Development, Research Triangle Park, North Carolina

Key words: Data mining, machine learning, ontology-driven, ontology-enhanced, biomedical ontologies, knowledge discovery, XML Topic Maps

1. INTRODUCTION

Babylon Knowledge Explorer (BKE) is an integrated suite of tools and information sources being developed in GlaxoSmithKline's A^2RT to support the prototyping and implementation of ontology-driven information systems and ontology-enhanced knowledge applications. In this paper we describe the current state of BKE development and focus on some of its distinctive or novel approaches, highlighting

- How BKE makes use of multiple large pre-existing ontologies in support of text and data mining.
- The methodology employed for importing an ontology and making it immediately accessible to BKE's tools, interfaces, and API.
- A formal description of BKE's ontology-based fact model and how this is employed in implementing information retrieval and data mining capabilities.
- A sample application built on BKE that illustrates an ontology-enhanced machine learning tool.

1.1 An Engineering Perspective

The best is the enemy of the good enough.
– *Old Russian proverb*

All that is useful is simple
– *Mikhail Kalashnikov*

Ontologies can be complex structures, and any attempt to handle ontologies in full generality – to develop them, edit them, maintain them, manage them, and apply them – can become entangled in an even more complex set of issues pertaining to representation, languages, tools and management systems. We attempt to avoid as many of those complexities as possible by taking a fundamentally engineering approach to the use of ontologies in providing solutions to problems of data mining and knowledge exploration in several scientific domains. Throughout, our emphasis will be less on theoretical issues (though these will be discussed when appropriate) and more on the practical aspects and engineering challenges in making use of multiple large domain ontologies in providing a basis and framework for developing real-world applications using those ontologies in effective ways.

The quotations beginning this section reflect our fundamental engineering orientation and should be kept in mind as details of our approach, design, and implementation unfold. We do not embrace Kalashnikov's aphorism without reservation, particularly since there are any number of things that are useful but not simple. But in the area of ontologies there is a danger in trying to do too much – to build systems that are too sweeping and powerful, and thus to fall short of otherwise reachable practical goals.

Complexity is not in itself useful or beneficial, and it is often the enemy of accomplishment and success. It should (following Ockham and others) always be justified in terms of goals, results, and alternatives. Often, however, a justification is offered in terms of generality and scope. Generality, as well as the attendant elegance that should accompany it, has much to be said for it. But unless the generality is *needed* and *useful*, it is difficult to justify its pursuit on principled grounds; and if it is not constrained by well-defined goals and criteria of adequacy, its pursuit may contribute only to an unusable result. From the start, one of the high-level goals of BKE development has been to see how far we could get with an initially simple approach – but one that might be extended as required by additional practical goals and needs. This approach and attitude will be seen repeatedly in the choices we have made in such areas as ontology representation, implementation technology and methodology, and how we apply ontologies to our data and textual sources.

We begin by describing the history of BKE's conceptual development; the goals and motivations driving its creation, design, and implementation; and the choices and challenges encountered in pursuing its vision. This is followed by discussions of the representation of ontologies within BKE, the model of ontology-based "facts" that underlies much of our ontology use, and how each of these result from addressing the goals and needs of our environment. We then consider an explicit example of employing BKE to develop an ontology-enhanced knowledge application, and finally discuss what we have learned and our plans for future work.

1.2 Ontology-Driven and Ontology-Enhanced Systems

In order to facilitate our future discussions – particularly those pertaining to goals, motivations, and features – we will employ a distinction between ontology-*driven* systems and ontology-*enhanced* systems. This distinction is based on the role that ontologies play in the system under consideration.

We take an *ontology-driven system* (application, algorithm, product, implementation, etc.) to be a system in which one or more ontologies serve as essential components of the fundamental function or methodology of the system. The active connotation of 'driven' is critical here, and in discussing ontology-driven systems authors typically use such phrases as "based on [one or more ontologies]", "[the ontology] serves as the basis for", or "the ontology determines ...". The test for ontology-driveness is "What would be left if you took the ontology (ontologies) away?" If the answer is "Not much" or "Virtually nothing" or "Nothing useful", then the system in question is ontology-driven.

In contrast, an *ontology-enhanced system* is one in which some capability, increased precision, scope, or functionality is *added to* an existing system (application, algorithm, product, implementation, etc.). In discussing ontology-enhanced systems, such phrases as "improved by [the addition of ontologies]", "extended by", and "enhanced by" are typically used. Thus we see references to "ontology-enhanced search engines" or "ontology-enhanced information extraction" applications. Here, in answer to "What would be left if you took the ontology away?" the answer is "The underlying method (algorithm, system, etc.) that is being improved through use of the ontology."

2. THE PATH TO DEVELOPMENT

BKE was originally conceived primarily as a knowledge exploration environment for text mining and analysis applications, and as a response to frustrations with a variety of other products and technologies of that sort. It was also originally intended to be a platform that could be put directly into the hands of (admittedly somewhat sophisticated) users, or at least one having components that could easily be employed by a wide range of users faced with tasks of information retrieval, information extraction, and text or data analysis in various scientific or other domains related to drug discovery, development, and marketing. Indeed, a precursor project to BKE ([12]) clearly emphasized this text mining orientation and the primary role of ontologies as an efficient and economical way to achieve a certain level of enhanced information retrieval and information extraction capabilities that would otherwise require more powerful techniques of computational linguistics.

However, although BKE is still at a prototypical stage, its initial application in some simple projects, coupled with what others have come to see as its strengths and potential uses, has forced us to reevaluate our original goals, reconsider our overall model of BKE as an ontology-based data exploration environment, and reexamine the central role of ontologies within the system. What has emerged – in fact, what is still emerging – is a model of BKE according to which it is an *ontology-driven information system* serving as a *platform* for developing *ontology-enhanced applications* or other ontology-driven systems. In order to understand the role of BKE, its current content and architecture, and decisions that have been made in its design and development, we must consider some of this history and the context within which BKE is being used.

2.1 The BKE Application Environment

The design of BKE within GSK's Data Exploration Sciences is driven by our environment of data exploration and knowledge discovery, and by the requirements we face in delivering exploratory and analytical results. Although virtually all of our work can be seen as taking place within the broad areas of biology, medicine, and pharmaceuticals, closer attention reveals that there are actually a number of fairly distinct sub-areas within which projects typically take place.

Some of our projects, for example, focus in the area of adverse drug events (referred to as "safety" or "pharmacovigilence" within the pharmaceutical industry). Here the objects of interest are drugs, drug names, chemical compounds, medical diagnoses, conditions, and treatments. The ontologies of interest and value in these areas then include such examples as the WHO Drug Dictionary and MedDRA.[1] Other projects involve microarray analyses and proteins, epidemiological studies and disease, biomarkers and genes, models of disease and treatment, and prescribing patterns for off-label use of our pharmaceutical products. Ontologies of interest in these areas may include such examples as a BioWisdom ([2]) protein ontology, the Gene Ontology ([7]), or ontologies based on one or more internally developed dictionaries or thesauri. A set of publicly available ontologies in the biological domain may be found in the Open Biological Ontologies project ([16]).

[1] In informal discussion we will tend to gloss the distinctions among dictionaries, thesauri, taxonomies, and ontologies. For more details on this distinction see, for example, [12] and [13]. In general, when we refer to a dictionary or thesaurus as an "ontology" we intend to refer to the (or an) ontology associated with (or derived from) that dictionary or thesaurus.

In addition to providing us with opportunities and requirements to use a number of ontologies, our projects impose time constraints as well. We are not an information technology organization, but are rather a scientific and analytical organization, and so our projects do not follow a common IT scenario of planning, design, implementation, and finally a "roll out" of an application to a large user group – a process that typically takes a significant number of months or even years. Instead, we must respond relatively quickly to the need for enhanced information, analysis, or modeling as part of the drug discovery, development, or post-marketing processes. While we do have some longer term research projects, most of our critical path projects require results within several months, several weeks, or even just a few days.

Likewise, we are not an ontology research, development, or maintenance organization. Sister organizations fulfill these roles, and many ontologies of value and interest are available in the public domain. One of the strongest motivating factors behind the development of BKE was the desire (and need) to take advantage of pre-existing ontologies, and to do so in a context where we cannot afford to wait on what might be perceived as ontology improvements or refinements. Our environment and business goals make it necessary to take advantage of what ontologies are available now – regardless of the fact that they may be imperfect or flawed in certain respects. This puts our use and approach to ontologies squarely in the domain of engineering rather than the domain of theory or research. It may be well-known, for example, that from a formal, conceptual, and computational point of view the Gene Ontology is flawed ([26]). And the same may be said of a variety of other ontologies as well (see, for example, some of the difficulties in using the WHO Drug Dictionary described in [13]). But our response to this cannot be to devote time and effort to repairing such flaws in a systematic manner. Instead, it is to work with what is available or (perhaps more accurately at times) to make what is available work. It is this goal, more than any other, that has driven BKE's approach to ontology representation and use.

Finally, we are not a "service organization" which applies standard and well-known methods to problems in standard and well-known ways. Our role is often to bring new methods to bear on the problems that confront us, to apply old methods in novel ways, or to combine a number of (sometimes disparate) methodologies in achieving our goals. These methodologies may include, for example, classical statistics, clustering, knowledge representation, information retrieval and extraction, and various approaches to machine learning such as association rule induction, market basket analysis, support vector machines, decision trees, and genetic algorithms.

An additional constraint intrudes if we wish to make use of ontologies in a way that is not totally transparent to our clients and users. The very concept of an ontology, and indeed the term 'ontology' itself, is completely foreign to these groups – to the degree that in initial presentations and conversations they often mistake it for 'oncology' or 'ontogeny'. They are, on the other hand, intimately familiar with a wide variety of *dictionaries* or *thesauri* which they expect to be presented in tree-structured (or "outline") formats, and several groups are devoted to the creation, adaptation, maintenance, and updating of business-related dictionaries and thesauri. As we shall see in a later section, these considerations can have an effect on how we present ontologies or certain ontological structures to users in so far as this is necessary.

Our application environment is then characterized by the following features:

- Projects range across several domains (predominantly technical or scientific in nature).
- These domains have associated with them one or more large and complex ontologies, though clients and potential users typically think of these in terms of dictionaries and thesauri.
- Our response to problems and the delivery of our results must be relatively rapid.
- Our ability to make use of ontologies and to integrate this with a variety of knowledge exploration, data mining, information retrieval, and related technologies, methods, and products must be flexible and under our full control.

Against this background we can now consider the fundamental questions of why BKE has been developed and what has guided its architecture, design, and implementation.

2.2 Buy or Build?

Over a period of several years we have had a number of opportunities for experimenting with a range of products and technologies oriented towards intelligent information retrieval, information extraction, text mining, and data mining.

Projects and experience in these areas include:

- A prototype web-delivered "function database" in the area of genes, proteins and biological function based on the Cyc ([5]) knowledge base techology and an ontology constructed in an automated manner from the SwissProt protein database.
- A pilot information extraction project in the domain of pharmacokinetics using Celi's Sophia ([4]) system.
- Experimentation with the Temis Insight Discoverer ([28]) and protein ontologies in conjunction with Novartis Knowledge Miner ([31]).
- Support and use of GlaxoSmithKline's Thesaurus Manager (a Cyc-based application) in enhanced information retrieval projects.

- A prototype concept-enhanced information retrieval system using the Verity search engine and Verity's support for taxonomies and knowledge trees ([12], [32]).

In addition, we have evaluated or piloted a number of other commercial and academic text/data mining systems, but never progressed much beyond the pilot stage with any of these. There are a number of reasons for this.

Cyc, for example, tries to be everything to everyone – a universally intelligent system with "common sense". The result is an ambitious system that is large, complex, unfocused, and somewhat cumbersome to use. It has great power, but harnessing that power in both a timely and economically feasible way is quite challenging. And as is quite often the case in large, general, and comprehensive systems, problems of adequate performance (particularly for interactive applications) readily arise. Novartis Knowledge Miner, though widely deployed, is based in large part on underlying commercial search engine technology, and is too closely tied to an information retrieval paradigm – as in fact is the author's system described in [12]. Such systems lack scope, flexibility and extensibility. Other applications (Celi's Sophia and the Temis Insight Discoverer) focus on a paradigm appropriate to information extraction from text – and likewise tend to lack a certain flexibility and extensibility. Each of these systems has something (often quite a bit) to recommend it, and yet none of them seem to address well a set of needs that we constantly encounter in our scientific and industrial context. This is in part because they are technology-focused rather than problem-focused.

What we tend to encounter, again and again as a result of such experiments, is the same set of sobering realizations:

- Any commercial product in this arena is quite expensive. It must be of demonstrated value in order to acquire it, and demonstrating that value in itself requires the expenditure of substantial effort and funds.
- Academic systems are not without their own expense, the quality of their engineering is almost invariably low, adaptation and maintenance is costly, they typically lack any degree of support, and they do not scale well.
- Even if such a system (commercial or academic) is acquired, substantial additional effort, time, and funding is necessary to *apply* it to any given problem. And this is perhaps the single most common source of the failure to sustain such projects beyond the pilot phase as the cost, effort, and required skill set are easily underestimated.
- Applying any system of this sort to a specific problem always requires some modification to the system. For example, application to a particular domain, corpus, or data set may require a different or modified lexicon, lexical analyzer, parser, query mechanism or interface, ontology, or underlying algorithms or databases. These modifications must be performed by the product

developers, and this involves a process of requirements, negotiation, development, and testing that is both lengthy and expensive.

- In so far as our needs in applying the system deviate to any degree from the designers' and marketers' views for their product, they are disinclined to give our needs the priority we require. After all, they are providing a product to a (hopefully) large number of clients and cannot afford to devote their resources to serving only one in the short term. Again, the result is a slow and expensive response to needed changes – or worse, an inability to even address such changes.

An excellent illustration of this last point is to be found in the system described in [12]. There it was hoped to use a powerful and well-tested commercial product that supported taxonomies and sophisticated information retrieval capabilities, first, to create an ontology-driven enhanced information retrieval system, and then to extend this to an information extraction system where information would be retrieved at the granularity of "facts" rather than entire documents. While the Verity product had the required capabilities in terms of representing the necessary ontologies, and while it possesses superior query and information retrieval capabilities, it was not capable of returning the very fine-grained information (such as exact positions of tokens in the text corpora) needed to support our goal of information extraction. Modifying the product to provide such information would have required significant reimplementation, perhaps significant redesign, and would have destabilized the product for all users for an indeterminate amount of time. This is not something that a vendor can reasonably be expected to do.

At precisely this point the project of [12] was abandoned and work on BKE was begun. In the end, experience and a bit of thought suffices to show that the question is rarely "Buy or build?" but "How much to buy and how much to build?" It is virtually impossible to buy exactly what you need in the way of sophisticated software systems, and as what you need approaches more closely the boundaries of new and advanced technologies, the chance of buying it becomes even more remote. Even if you do buy a "solution", you still face difficult challenges of applying or adapting it. There is no solution until that is accomplished, and you are involved in additional dependencies and additional expense. It had become clear that our requirements for flexibility, adaptability, integration with other (internal and external) systems, and the need for rapid development and response demanded that we construct our own system to serve at least as a framework for developing the basic building blocks we needed as well as fundamental capabilities enabling integration of these with other applications and technologies.

2.3 The Development Environment for BKE

Once the commitment to build rather than buy had been made, and with experience gained from the variety of projects mentioned above, a number of decisions needed to be made. These were guided by the principles and requirements in Table 28-1.

Table 28-1. Development environment principles and requirements

Performance: A primary goal both for the environment being developed and for any subsequent applications based on it was relatively high performance.

Development Speed: Development was expected to proceed quickly, especially through an initial prototyping phase.

Flexibility: The resulting development platform had to be flexible in the sense that it should be easily and quickly modifiable, allowing for new additions and changes in implementation. It must provide us with the capability of quickly responding to new or unanticipated needs.

Cost: Cost of development tools and of runtime deployment of any applications was to be minimized.

Performance was a concern for several reasons. First we had a vision from the beginning of being able to provide highly interactive and responsive knowledge applications. We also anticipated (and still do) adding more sophisticated computational linguistics capabilities as our environment and applications evolved. And we expected that our applications would need to deal with very large amounts of data – transforming or analyzing it in various ways – as well as with large ontologies.

Development speed was an issue because the project was not well-staffed (one full-time developer – the author – and an undergraduate part-time assistant) and because we could not afford to make it an open-ended research project. Our fundamental goal was to bring ontology-based technology to bear on our business problems, and to do so in a flexible and timely manner.

Cost, of course, is always an issue. But since this project was at least in part an advanced technology research project (though with very definite application-oriented goals), we were committed to not spending any more than was absolutely necessary in order to establish and maintain our development environment.

The first major decision that needed to be made was then what the fundamental development environment should be, what programming language (or languages) should be adopted, and what tools should be acquired and employed. Three possibilities were considered: Java, C, and Python.

Although Java offers several advantages in an environment where applications are intended (or required) to be web-delivered, for our purposes this was not of significant concern. For this and other reasons pertaining largely to performance and ease of deployment, we decided against Java.

In terms of performance, C (or C++) was the clear choice. Somewhat surprisingly, perhaps, portability turns out not to be much of an issue here since there are a number of libraries now available for creating highly portable C/C++ applications – including ones with sophisticated graphical user interfaces. But although using C/C++ would have met our criterion of performance, it would have a serious impact on our criterion of development speed (where Java again would have offered some advantage). Even with (or perhaps because of) a couple of decades of experience behind us in developing C applications and C tools, we were reluctant to adopt a C/C++ development approach because of the obvious impact we knew this would have on our pace of development and our ability at a later time to modify or expand rapidly both BKE and applications built by using it.

This left Python, which in effect gave us the benefits of C as well. Python, like Java, runs on a "virtual machine". But its underlying run-time engine is C-based, and it bears an intimate relationship to C in that it is quite straightforward to code "C extensions" and thereby achieve the performance of a C implementation except for those portions of the code that remain directly in Python. The accepted technique in circumstances where performance is important is to create a prototype in Python and then to rewrite performance-critical portions of it in C as necessary. While pure Python applications are known to be much slower than C applications and slower than Java applications, no "real" Python applications are pure but instead rely heavily on modules or libraries coded in C that have a Python "wrapper". In addition, even a pure Python application having a significant amount of Python code can be given a substantial performance improvement (up to approximately 30%) through the use of the Psyco run-time Python optimizer ([21]).

Python has a number of built-in features and data structures that make it very attractive for rapid development, and it has a huge standard library supporting all the capabilities we would need. Moreover, a number of powerful, portable, and high-performance packages of just the sort we would need are available with Python wrappers or Python interfaces. We also were aware that a number of research groups were in the process of rewriting their libraries and applications in Python (often having originally implemented them in Perl or Lisp), and that it was becoming commonplace for applications and libraries to provide a Python wrapper for developers. For these reasons we chose Python as our fundamental development environment, and added the following components:

- WxPython ([36]), the Python rendition of the wxWidgets C++ GUI development framework.

- BSDDB ([1]), the Berkeley database library which we use for our low-level implementation of ontologies.
- The Metakit ([14]) database library that we use quite extensively for term indices, onto-indices, search results, and to hold temporary and intermediate representations of data.
- Plex ([19]), the Python variant of the Lex lexical analyzer generator that we use for our tokenizers.
- The Orange machine learning library ([9]).
- Psyco ([21]), the Python run-time optimizer.

The only development tools we subsequently acquired were the Wing IDE ([34]) development environment, wxDesigner ([35]) to help with GUI development, and Microsoft's SourceSafe for source control. For two developers, the total cost of our development environment has been less than US$1,500. It is possible even to eliminate this minor cost by using available open source development environments and source code control systems, but our experiments with these were not wholely satisfactory. BKE is now a bit over 20,000 lines of Python code, and we continue to regard our choice as a wise one. It has provided us with a low cost, powerful, and flexible development environment. This environment is almost wholly open source, and BKE itself relies only on open source technology.

3. ONTOLOGIES IN BKE

From the beginning we envisioned using ontologies in two fundamental ways. First, of course, we saw the obvious uses of ontologies to enhance information retrieval and to accomplish some degree of information extraction – particularly from textual sources. Second, we sensed a significant potential for using ontologies in a role to enhance a variety of techniques of data mining ranging from the application of standard statistical methods to sophisticated methods of machine learning. As our development progressed and the nature and possible uses of ontologies became more familiar to our broader research group, this second application of ontologies began to receive more attention and to dominate our thinking. In turn, this has resulted in a shift in emphasis within BKE from the original primarily text-oriented stance to placing more emphasis on applications to structured and semi-structured data. In our environment it turns out that while substantial lip service may be given to the need for text mining, there is a much more pronounced and immediate need for analyzing structured data because this is the type of data yielded by gene expression experiments, marketing and epidemiological studies, and clinical trials. Consequently, some of the original (text-oriented) design goals of BKE have been delayed in implementation in favor of work directed towards supporting the analysis of structured data.

3.1 Source and Ontology Characteristics

As we mentioned briefly in Section 2.1, the data sources with which we deal almost universally pertain to scientific domains and the ontologies of interest in analyzing these domains are therefore large and fairly rigorously constructed scientific ontologies. Our view of these ontologies is that they encode some of the fundamental semantic or nomic relations among entities in those domains and thereby provide us with a concise and computationally useful representation of the underlying science. Moreover, these ontologies are widely recognized, trusted, and used in a number of contexts.

Our sources are likewise most often the results of careful scientific observation or the collection of data. This may involve laboratory experiments resulting in gene expression data, data relating diets in diabetic and non-diabetic mice to levels of protein products in their cells, the effects of different drugs on such mice, reports from a variety of sources pertaining to adverse drug events, clinical trials data, massive amounts of data concerning prescriptions of our drugs for a variety of conditions, and so on. In addition, the terms used in these sources to describe or categorize the data are in fact drawn from various commonly accepted systems of nomenclature or controlled vocabularies. That is, *the terms characterizing the data are terms drawn from (or appearing in) the large scientific ontologies we would use to analyze the data.* At times, such a correspondence is even tacitly or explicitly mandated by regulatory agencies.

It was clear, then, that we would need to make use of multiple large ontologies and to use these in enhancing a variety of analytical techniques. We wanted our analytical and knowledge exploration tools to serve as a "back end" to any specific ontologies and data sources that we might need to use, and so an initial goal became the development of a *canonical ontology representation* that could be assumed by these back-end tools.

3.2 Criteria for an Ontology Representation Formalism

A number of ontology representation schemes or ontology representation languages exist and some are in wide use. These include CycL ([5]), RDF, and OWL ([17]). But our concern with adopting one of these was that it would be "too much", and that our progress would likely be inhibited through dealing with complexity that would not contribute to our specific engineering goals – thus violating the development philosophy and principles described in Sections 1 and 2.3. Examining our data sources, the set of ontologies we would likely use, and considering how we would most effectively use them, led us to some realizations that guided our approach to ontology representation in BKE.

For the most part, the valuable information in these ontologies resided within their *hierarchical relations*. Examples of these are the `is-a` and `part-of` relations in the Gene Ontology, relations of `in-pharmaceutical-class` and in-therapeutic-class in a GSK Thesaurus ontology, the subordination hierarchy in MedDRA, and the ATC (Anatomical-Therapeutical-Chemical) and ingredients hierarchies in the WHO Drug Dictionary. This view of the central significance of hierarchical relations in enhancing data mining methodologies and in allowing knowledge exploration of data at different "levels of abstraction" is also evident in [10], [27], and [38]. Certainly the predominant use of ontologies in real-world data mining is the role they play in generalizing data from one level of abstraction to a higher level or (in information retrieval) in expanding an ontological category in terms of its subsumed categories or instances. Consequently, we sought a canonical ontology representation that would provide a firm basis for navigating and using hierarchical relations in our ontologies.

But not all interesting or useful ontology relations are hierarchical. Among other interesting relations are equivalence relations such as isbiologically-equivalent-to or is-interchangeable-with. And finally there are interesting non-hierarchical and non-equivalence relations. For example, consider relations such as is-a-competitor-of as in "Zantac is a competitor of Pepcid" or is-marketed-in as in "Aapri is marketed in the United Kingdom". We want our ontology representation scheme to be able to represent such relations as well. On the other hand, given our practical goals for data mining with ontologies and the fact that we do not want to pursue a full-featured knowledge-based system at this point, there is no compelling reason to make our representation more complex than necessary. In fact, while our representation scheme does support such non-hierarchical relations we have not at this point had any occasion to make use of this capability.[2]

Taylor, Stoffel, and Hendler ([27]) also observe that "ontologies are only useful if they can be repeatedly queried efficiently and quickly," and our own prior experience with complex knowledge-based systems bears this out. The danger of creating a system that is too general is that it becomes unusable in practical contexts – and we are very focused on practical contexts.

Again, one of our fundamental requirements is the ability to make use of at least the "important features" of an arbitrary ontology. Given typical time constraints, we must be able to do this without it requiring excessive time and effort. And the resulting ontology representations must allow us to implement highly efficient ways of accessing and using the ontologies. These requirements are summarized in Table 28-2. We also wanted our ontology representations to be as simple as possible, given the requirements. On the basis of these guidelines – and in accord with the guiding aphorisms of Section 1 – we decided to avoid the more general and powerful (but quite complex) ontol-

[2] We are, however, starting to expand our use of ontologies and non-hierarchical relations as we begin to make use of the Gene Ontology to mine for drug discovery purposes.

Table 28-2. Development environment principles and requirements

Sufficient Generality: The scheme (or format) must support the representation of hierarchical, equivalence, and arbitrary n-ary relations.

Ease of Re-representation: It must in general be relatively straightforward to "re-represent" the important features of an arbitrary external ontology in this format.

Efficiency: The format must permit a highly efficient implementation for navigating and "computing over" the ontology, particularly in the case of hierarchical relations.

ogy representation schemes and languages, and instead to formulate our own scheme that would meet our specific criteria.

Our requirement of *Efficiency* means that ultimately our ontologies will find realization in some kind of high-performance database implementation. We need this in order to create an effective API that can be used to support interactive ontology-enhanced applications. But if this was to be the case, why not simply decide on such a low-level data-base-bound representation at the outset and use that as our canonical ontology representation? There were several reasons for not pursuing such an approach.

To begin, it was of critical importance to be able to import an existing, large, and potentially complex ontology into our system with as little effort as possible. BKE was to be a system to support the development of ontology-enhanced applications in multiple domains, and we anticipated making use of a number of distinct ontologies, each of which would be provided in its own peculiar format or representation. Attempting to map such an ontology directly into a low-level database representation (involving specific record formats, fields, table schemata, etc.) would be a complex and error-prone task. It would be difficult to "debug" the resulting low-level representation, and development time for applications would consequently be affected.

This situation is similar to one encountered in writing compilers for programming languages. There, a highly efficient final representation of a program (a machine language version of the program for the target machine) is generated by the compiler from the high-level source program. But this is not accomplished through an immediate translation of the high-level language program directly to machine code. That process is too complex, error prone, and lacking in generality. Rather, the high-level program is translated into an *intermediate representation* for an "abstract machine", and then the intermediate representation is translated to machine code. This process allows for decoupling the "front end" of the compiler (the part that translates to intermediate code) from the "back end" (the part that translates from intermediate code to machine code), and provides for a more modular and testable development of each. It also allows for an easier substitution for either of these implementations at a later stage of development – such as re-targeting the compiler for different machines or using the same back-end code generators for different high-level languages. The advantages of this approach are well-known in the compiler development community, and these advantages can be had as well in making use of ontologies in the ways we envisioned since transforming a high-level and human-readable ontology representation to a computationally efficient representation is precisely analogous to compiling a program from source code.

In addition, we anticipated the likelihood of ontologies being developed by groups not technically skilled in the details underlying BKE's implementation, but capable of creating a translator from an existing ontology to a relatively high-level representation that could be imported directly into BKE – and hence made immediately available to BKE's user interfaces, analytical tools, and API. In such a case, again, this representation should be as simple as possible in order to conform to our *Ease of Re-representation* criterion, and it should be amenable to examination and testing with tools that are either widely available or straightforward to develop.

These considerations led us, first, to a conceptual model for ontology representation within BKE and, then, to a formal realization of this conceptual model.

3.3 Babylon Topic Maps: A Canonical Ontology Representation

The representation of ontologies in BKE is treated in detail elsewhere, and we will not repeat those details here. Instead, we provide a sketch of the fundamental features of this approach and some illustrative examples. The full discussion of ontology representation in BKE may be found in [13]. Our representations of ontologies rest on a conceptual model comprised of seven fundamental components which appear in Table 28-3.

We do not, as is often the case (particularly in computer science or information science contexts) construe an ontology as a "sign system" ([10]), a "representation language", or a "controlled vocabulary", but rather as a formal structure characterizing relations among *things* as opposed to (in the case of dictionaries and thesauri) relations among *words*. It may be correct to say, for example, that the mitral valve is part of the heart but not that 'mitral valve' is part of 'heart', though it may be true to say that 'heart' is a broader term than 'mitral valve'. Likewise, it is true that Zantac and Prevacid are competitors (for treating the condition of acid stomach), but not that the words 'Zantac' and 'Prevacid' are competitors (they are not, for example, in competition to name the same chemical substance or structure).

Table 28-3. Components of BKE's conceptual model of ontologies

Topics: Topics are sometimes referred to as *categories* or *concepts* of an ontology. For a variety of reasons we prefer the more neutral "topic" terminology.

Basenames: Each topic should have associated with it a basename (often elsewhere referred to as a *preferred term* or *preferred name* for the topic).

Variants: A variant is an alternative name for the topic.

Variant Type: Each variant belongs to a variant type (representing the type of name it is with respect to the topic). A variant type is itself represented as a topic.

Hierarchical Relations: A hierarchical relation imposes a partial order on (a subset of) the ontology topics.

Equivalence Relations: Ontology topics may be related by a variety of equivalence relations. Equivalence relations are reflexive, symmetric, and transitive, and support interchange principles in at least some contexts.

N-ary Relations: Other relations are relegated to this category of arbitrary n-place relations.

This long-recognized and critical distinction between the *use* and *mention* of a term is discussed in more detail in [13], and we remark on it here largely to guard against misinterpretations. In addition, failure to enforce such a distinction can lead to confusing or non-sensical inferences, and this is a particular danger when attempting to make use of ontologies that are based on dictionaries and thesauri, as we often must. Problems arise, for example, when multiple distinct topics within the same ontology are referred to by the same name. This should not, of course, happen in the ideal case, but it is an unfortunate feature of some ontologies or of some dictionaries or controlled vocabularies from which we wish to abstract ontologies. An example concerning the term 'TETRACYCLINES' is detailed in [13], and in fact the WHO Drug Dictionary exhibits many such examples. Similar problems arise when dealing with multiple ontologies where the same term is used as a preferred term for topics in different ontologies. It is important not to confuse things with their names.

According to our conceptual model, an ontology is composed of topics which enter various relations (hierarchical, equivalence, or n-ary). In addition, and for purposes of applying the ontology to real-world problems of text and data, topics have associated with them (are designated by) basenames or variants. Moreover, each variant belongs to one or more variant types.[3]

---

[3]This model of ontology structure is similar to that adopted by MedDRA ([11]). Our use of *variants* is similar to the role of *evidence topics* in Verity ([32]). See also the very well-designed and general approach taken by the UMLS ([29]).

It must be admitted that including basenames and variants as elements of our ontologies renders the ontologies impure to some degree since it appears to conflate metaphysics with semantics and invite the sort of name/thing confusion we have just warned against. The ontologies are, after all, supposed to be about *things* and not *words*. But now we have included words in them as well. The pure approach would be to define an ontology as a completely abstract (algebraic or model-theoretic) object and then associate with this object a set of symbols (names or designators of the objects in the ontology). This is the approach taken by Cyc. But, having already made the appropriate use/mention distinction, this degree of semantic purity gains us nothing in practice; and would simply complicate our use of ontologies in computational contexts.[4] We therefore decide against the purist approach – invoking our engineering prerogative, our previously accepted Ockhamist guidelines, and a nominalistic argument that in the end words are all we ever have, to justify (carefully) including basenames and variants in our ontologies.

Figure 28-1 illustrates fragments of the WHO Drug Dictionary and MedDRA ontology as we have imported them into BKE and displayed them within BKE's hierarchy browser, which displays topics by using their basenames. Thus in Figure 28-1a, the topics for `Simvastatin`, `Pravastatin`, `Lovastatin`, etc. are displayed via the basenames 'SIMVASTATIN', 'PRAVASTATIN', 'LOVASTATIN', etc. The symbol [V] indicates a variant, and we can see that in Figure 28-1a variants of type `Use for` and `CAS registry number` are displayed for the topic `Lovastatin` while in Figure 28-1b a variant of type `ICD-9(Not current)` is displayed for the topic `Malaise`.[5]

This conceptual model finds formal expression in our implementation of *Babylon Topic Maps*. A Babylon Topic Map (BTM) is an *XML Topic Map* conforming to a set of constraints described in [13]. Figure 28-2 is a portion

[4]Should we for some reason wish to do this, Babylon Topic Maps provide us with such a capability. It is necessary only to introduce a topic of *Term*, and then to introduce each term itself as a topic that is an instance of the *Term* topic. Then, unfortunately, it becomes necessary also to introduce topics for relations between *Terms* and other *Terms* (such as a relation of synonymy) and between *Terms* and other ontology topics (such as relations of denotation or extension). That is, we end up creating an ontology of terms and an ontology of semantic relations as well. This leads to a high degree of complexity and a resulting substantial decrease in efficiency as we are then required to use such relations in computational contexts. For our purposes this gains us nothing and is precisely the useless kind of complexity and generality we are striving to avoid.

[5]In order to avoid excessive pedantry, we will often not be absolutely precise in distinguishing the informal entity or concept of which we are speaking (e.g., the drug atorvastatin) from the topic used to represent it in an ontology (e.g., `Drug_atorvastatin`), and similarly for such variant types as (informally) *use-for* or (ontology topic identifier) `use-for`. In general, we will use *italics* when speaking about the informal or common-sense item or concept and use **`bold monospaced`** font when speaking of how this appears in our BTM representations. Otherwise, we will depend on context to disambiguate such references. We will also often not distinguish among term forms that differ only in case since for the most part in information retrieval and data mining contexts we will ignore case differences.

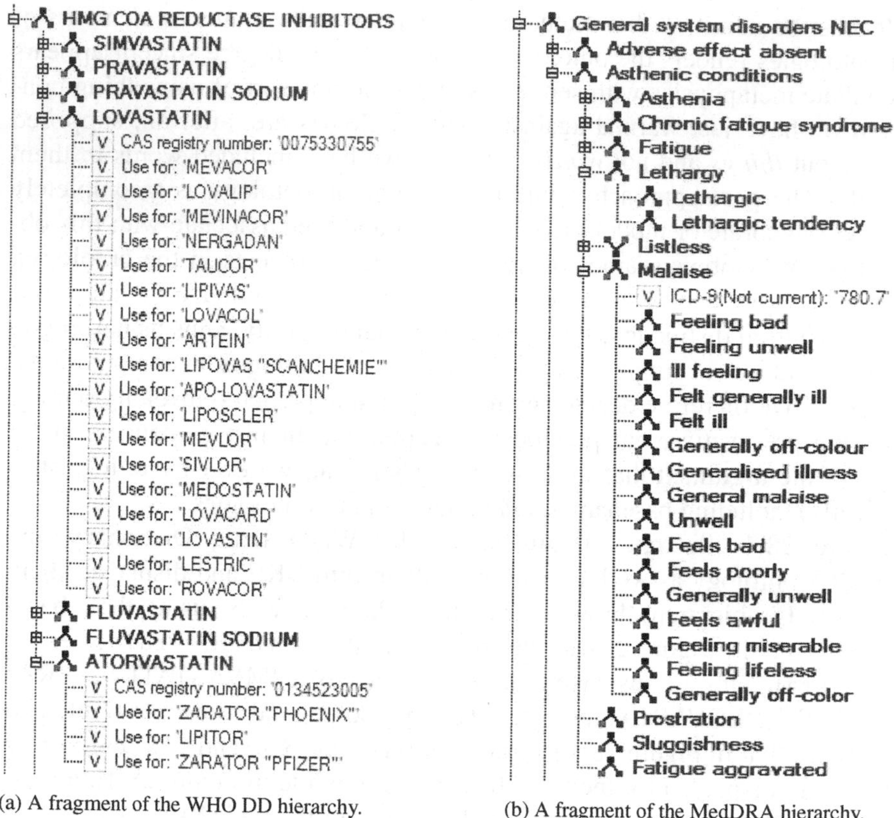

(a) A fragment of the WHO DD hierarchy.

(b) A fragment of the MedDRA hierarchy.

Figure 28-1. Fragments of the WHO DD and MedDRA ontologies.

of our Babylon Topic Map for the WHO Drug Dictionary, illustrating parts of the ontology displayed in Figure 28-1a.

Note in particular that each topic has a unique topic identifier which is different from its basename. It is possible for two distinct topics to have the same basename, and in fact this happens in our representation of the WHO Drug Dictionary ontology.

The drug whose topic identifier (`id`) is '`Drug_atorvastatin`' has the four variants mentioned above, and these are defined through the `<parameters>` and `<variantName>` tags within a `<variant>` context. The `<parameter>` element is used to describe what *type* of variant is defined. Note that each variant type is itself a topic. In the illustration we have included the topic definition for the `use-for` variant topic but have omitted the definition for the `cas-number` topic.

Figures 28-1 and 28-2 nicely illustrate the variety of names and identifiers pertaining to topics and how these are distinct from one another:

> 'Drug_atorvastatin' is the topic identifier (topic id) for the drug we commonly refer to as 'atorvastatin'. In the context of our representation, it can be thought of as a term in the metalanguage of Babylon Topic Maps and we do not expect such a term to appear in our text or data sources. We could as easily use a unique numeric identifier for such topic identifiers (and in fact do so when our BTM format is transformed into our low-level database representation), but using the more meaningful form in our intermediate representation renders Babylon Topic Maps more readable and easier to debug.
>
> 'ATORVASTATIN' is the basename for this topic. We expect such a term to appear in our sources and to thereby allow us to associate elements of the sources with topics in our ontologies. It would not be incorrect to say in this context that (the term) 'ATORVASTATIN' *stands for* (the topic) Drug_atorvastatin.
>
> 'Lipitor' is a variant of 'ATORVASTATIN'. In particular, it is a `use-for` variant of this basename whereas '0134523005' is a `cas-number` variant of the basename. Thus we can say that both 'Lipitor' and '0134523005' also stand for Drug_atorvastatin.

The hierarchical relation itself is defined through the use of `<association>` elements, and `<roleSpec>` elements are used to define the roles of the different members of the association. Non-hierarchical relations can be defined in similar ways within the BTM formalism. For more details concerning XML topic maps see [30] and [37], and for additional illustrations and details of Babylon Topic Maps, see [13].

In addition to the topics that can be thought of as comprising the "proper content" (i.e., the domain topics) of a particular ontology, each Babylon Topic Map begins with a set of standard elements defining such topics as `hierarchical-relation`, `non-hierarchical-relation`, `equivalence-relation`, `n-ary-relation`, `subsumer`, `subsumed`, and `subject-of-relation`. These in turn are used in the definitions of topics and associations for the particular ontology being represented by the BTM. And all of BKE's tools and interfaces then make use of these standard topics and relations in displaying or navigating an ontology. For example, every hierarchical relation is represented by means of associations making use of the subsumer/subsumed topics to structure that particular hierarchy. Once a relation is known to be hierarchical, BKE's tools and API know that it can be navigated by following its subsumer/subsumed chains, and this provides a seamless interface between ontology, tools, and API once an ontology has been imported using this canonical representation. We will explore some more details of this feature in a later section.

The BTM formalism is both simple and flexible, and it has so far satisfied all of our needs for representing particular ontologies within BKE. Some reflection should suffice to show that this approach is in fact very general due to the capability of representing n-ary relations and to certain abusive liberties one may take with the variant relation. Thus Babylon Topic Maps satisfy our criterion of *Sufficient Generality*.

```
<topic id="ATC_c10aa">
 <baseName>
   <baseNameString>HMG COA REDUCTASE INHIBITORS</baseNameString>
 </baseName>
</topic>

<topic id="use-for">
 <baseName>
   <baseNameString>Use for</baseNameString>
 </baseName>
</topic>

<topic id="Drug_atorvastatin">
 <baseName>
   <baseNameString>ATORVASTATIN</baseNameString>
   <variant>
       <parameters><topicRef xlink:href="#use-for"/></parameters>
       <variantName><resourceData>LIPITOR</resourceData>
</variantName>
   </variant>
   <variant>
       <parameters><topicRef xlink:href="#use-for"/></parameters>
       <variantName><resourceData>ZARATOR "PFIZER"</resourceData>
</variantName>
   </variant>
   <variant>
       <parameters><topicRef xlink:href="#use-for"/></parameters>
       <variantName><resourceData>ZARATOR "PHOENIX"</resourceData>
</variantName>
   </variant>
   <variant>
       <parameters><topicRef xlink:href="#cas-number"/></parameters>
       <variantName><resourceData>0134523005</resourceData>
</variantName>
   </variant>
 </baseName>
</topic>

<association>
 <instanceOf><topicRef xlink:href="#subsumes"/></instanceOf>
 <member>
   <roleSpec><topicRef xlink:href="#subsumer"/></roleSpec>
   <topicRef xlink:href="#ATC_c10aa"/>
 </member>
 <member>
   <roleSpec><topicRef xlink:href="#subsumed"/></roleSpec>
   <topicRef xlink:href="#Drug_simvastatin"/>
 </member>
 <member>
   <roleSpec><topicRef xlink:href="#subsumed"/></roleSpec>
   <topicRef xlink:href="#Drug_pravastatin"/>
 </member>

 <-- Other members elided for this illustration -->

 <member>
   <roleSpec><topicRef xlink:href="#subsumed"/></roleSpec>
   <topicRef xlink:href="#Drug_atorvastatin"/>
 </member>

 <-- Other members elided for this illustration -->
</association>
```

Figure 28-2. BTM element examples from the WHO Drug Dictionary

3.4 Importing Ontologies

Importing an ontology into BKE is a two-stage process. The first of these stages we refer to as *re-representation* since it requires us to transform a pre-existing representation which may appear in a variety of formats. Re-representing an ontology requires us to write a *re-representation translator* which takes as input the original ontology (dictionary, thesaurus, taxonomy, etc.) and creates as output the corresponding BTM file.

MedDRA, for example, is distributed as a set of twelve record-oriented ASCII files, each of which basically describes one of the "levels" of the MedDRA ontology and associations among the objects in the ontology (construed as a system of terms): systems and organ classes, preferred terms, low-level terms, high-level terms, and high-level group terms. Records contain various codes linking the terms and records, and refer to other systems of classification such as the Hoechst Adverse Reaction Terminology System (HARTS), the World Health Organization Adverse Reaction Terminology (WHO-ART), and ICD-9. Currently we do not make use of some of this additional information, though we have made fruitful use of the ICD-9 categories in enhancing a market-basket analysis of some large observational databases.

MedDRA is well-organized and well-documented. Our re-representation translator for it consists of approximately 200 (non-commentary) lines of Python,[6] and we have found Python especially well-suited for writing these types of translators. The resulting BTM file consists of approximately 600,000 lines of XML code, containing over 50,000 topic definitions and almost 19,000 occurrences of variants.

The WHO Drug Dictionary consists of eight record-oriented ASCII files containing information about drugs (drug names) and ingredients. It is well-documented, though not as rationally or flexibly designed as MedDRA; but our re-representation translator for it still consists of only about 150 lines of Python code. It's BTM file is approximately 500,000 lines of XML code, containing about 17,000 topic definitions and 76,000 variant occurrences.[7]

We have also at this point imported several other ontologies, including a BioWisdom protein ontology, a GSK Therapy ontology (similar to the WHO Drug Dictionary), an ontology containing two separate hierarchies (pharmaceutical and therapeutic class) from the GSK Thesaurus, and the three hierarchies of the Gene Ontology in different configurations. In each case we have discovered that size and complexity of the re-representation translator is approximately the same and it takes us from one to five days to complete and

[6]Each translator also makes use of a small 200-line library of support objects and functions as well.

[7]Figure 28-1 provides an indication of the difference in the density of variants in our WHO and MedDRA hierarchies.

test such a translator. The discrepancy among these development times is a function of the form and complexity of the original ontology (or dictionary) representation, and most of our time is devoted to first understanding fully the nature of the ontology being imported.

We have found repeatedly that the simplicity of the BTM format makes such re-representations both conceptually and technically straightforward, providing us with the rapid response capability we were striving for, and meeting our criteria for *Development Speed* and *Flexibility* described in Section 2.3 (Table 28-1). One point worth emphasizing here is that in importing ontologies with hierarchical relations, *every* hierarchical relation is represented by means of our subsumer/subsumed relation as this is illustrated in Section 3.3 and Figure 28-2. This simplifies the re-representation process for such relations and provides a standard representation for them that makes them immediately accessible to BKE's tools and API. In general, we also do not distinguish between a subsumption (or inclusion) relation in the ontology being re-represented and an *is-a*or *has-a* relation having the sense of *instantiation* rather than subsumption. There are cases in which this difference is significant (even critical), but for the most part we have discovered that – for our purposes – only added complexity without additional benefit results from enforcing the distinction.

The second stage of importing an ontology we refer to simply as *importation.* Here the BTM file is read and transformed into a high-performance and efficient representation within BSDDB databases. This operation is handled by BKE's Ontology Manager, which for reasons of space we will not illustrate here, but which presents a graphical interface for specifying the BTM file to import and how the imported ontology should be named – along with such capabilities as renaming or deleting (imported) ontologies.

Figure 28-3 shows the Hierarchy Browser as it might be used to explore an ontology to determine what level to specify for ontological generalization in the Ontology-Driven Rule Inducer (Section 6). (Levels are numbered "downward" beginning with the root as level 0 since this allows a universal and invariable number scheme for levels in any hierarchy, no matter what its full depth.) In this case the Hierarchy Browser displays a portion of the subsumption hierarchy for the WHO Drug Dictionary. Looking at the right side of the Hierarchy Browser window we can see that a search has been done for topics that start with 'tetracycline', and a number of these have been found. One of these topics is `TETRACYCLINE` itself, and the symbol **Y** indicates that it has multiple parents – which are listed in an "inverted tree" below it. We have selected its occurrence under `ANTIBIOTICS` and then clicked the `Go through` button at the lower right to navigate to that entry for `TETRACYCLINE` (at level 5) in the hierarchy display window to the left. There again, we see that this topic has multiple parents and right clicking on it pops up the dialog titled

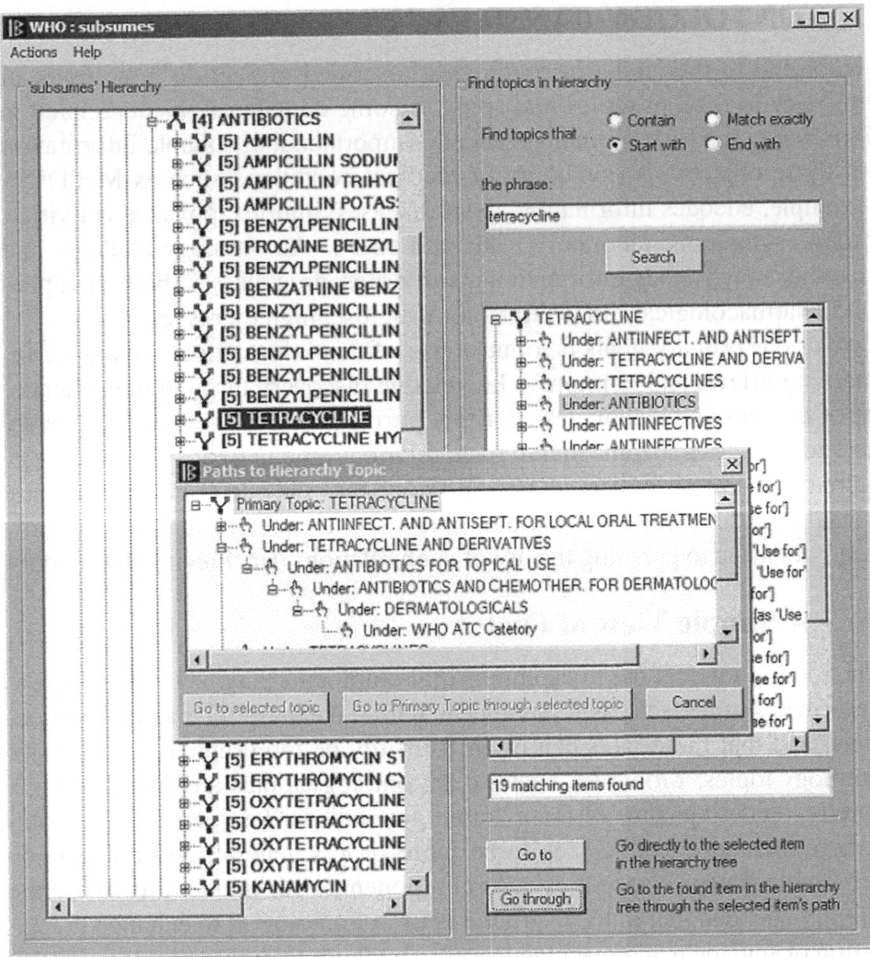

Figure 28-3. The Hierarchy Browser

"Paths to Hierarchy Topic" where we have explored the ancestral tree for this `TETRACYCLINE` topic.

In BKE's Hierarchy Browser, the symbol indicates a topic having a unique parent, and in inverted trees the symbol indicates that there is a unique path to the topic (or variant) and that you can therefore "go to" it in the browser. Using indicators and inverted trees in this manner we can present a complex hierarchy (which in reality is in the form of a directed acyclic graph) to our users as though it is the kind of tree structure with which they are familiar. And once an external ontology has been first re-represented in BTM format and then imported into our efficient database representation, it becomes automatically accessible to the Hierarchy Browser (and other tools).

4. ONTOLOGY-BASED FACTS

According to the model of ontologies described in Section 3 we think of an ontology as a set of topics that apply to some domain of objects related in various ways, and whose relations encode important and valuable information about those objects. An ontology of medical conditions such as MedDRA, for example, encodes information about diseases, injuries, physical activities, disorders, symptoms, laboratory tests, and so on. An ontology of drugs and compounds may encode information about drugs, drug classes (both therapeutic and pharmacological), indications for drug use, ingredients, etc.

One of our primary goals is to make use of this information to enhance information retrieval and to improve knowledge discovery through the enhancement of data mining techniques. For this purpose, and as we have previously remarked in Section 3.2, the hierarchical relations among topics in an ontology are often of the most immediate benefit (since they encode nomic or semantic universal generalizations relating the topics to one another), and we will now turn our attention to pursuing the use of such relations in achieving these goals.

4.1 A Simple View of Facts

The intuition we set out to capture is that ontologies may be used to express or describe "simple facts"as these appear within database records or text documents, and that these facts can often fruitfully be represented as sequences of ontology topics. Moreover, because the ontology topics are embedded in a hierarchy, rendering some of them "more general" or "less general" than others, these facts also can be seen to be more or less general, depending upon which ontology topics appear as their components. Our intention is to use the efficiently encoded hierarchical structures of our ontologies to enhance the application of statistical and machine learning methods to data, and this approach rests on a formal model of *ontology-based fact* which we shall briefly describe here before proceeding to an illustration of its implementation and use within BKE.

Consider the statement

Source 4.1: The patient felt that taking Lipitor was directly related to her feeling unwell.[8]

Here, there is a simple fact relating a drug (Lipitor) and a physical condition (feeling unwell). Such a fact can be thought of as being represented by a triple (or 3-term sequence) of *terms* occurring in the text:[9]

[8] The examples here are contrived (primarily for the sake of brevity), but are drawn from the results of queries on the web at large, or in Medline. The relation of statins (used in treating conditions of high cholesterol) to fatigue and related symptoms is now widely documented and accepted.

[9] Cf. the treatment of *concept-relation-concept* triples in [18].

Table 28-4. Facts based on an "explicit fact" and ontologies

DRUG	RELATION	CONDITION
Lipitor Atorvastatin HMG Coa Reductase Inhibitors	directly related to	Feeling unwell Fatigue Asthenic condition

Sequence 4.1: ⟨'Lipitor', 'directly related to', 'feeling unwell'⟩

And assuming that we have available to us three ontologies (one of drugs, one of relations, and one of physical conditions), then this sequence of terms can also be seen as corresponding to a sequence of *topics* drawn from those ontologies (and which are designated by those terms):

Sequence 4.2: $\langle Lipitor,\ directly-related-to,\ feeling-unwell\rangle$

In Figure 28-1b we can see that *Feeling unwell* occurs as a topic subsumed by *Fatigue*, which in turn is subsumed by *Asthenic conditions*. And Figure 28-1a illustrates the topic *Lipitor* under its parent *Atorvastatin* which is subsumed by *HMG Coa reductase inhibitors*.

These figures and the example also illustrate that (within the context of viewing information through ontologies) a single *explicit* fact may contain a wealth of implicit information. Clearly, on the basis of the two ontology fragments and Source 4.1, each of the nine relationships in Table 28-4 is also a fact. If we in addition had a relational ontology containing *directly related to* (perhaps subsumed by a *related to* or *associated with* topic), then even more implicit facts would emerge from Source 4.1.

An extension of this example illustrates that a number of apparently disparate facts may (again within the context of being viewed through ontologies) "converge"to a more general and potentially much more interesting fact. Note that the facts represented in Table 28-4 increase in generality from top to bottom.

Now suppose that our database or document corpus also contains explicit facts such as:

Source 4.2: This patient complained of listlessness after taking Zocor for several weeks.

Source 4.3: After starting a course of Mevacor, Mr. X reported feeling lethargic.

Source 4.4: Ms. Y began taking Pravachol to treat her high chlolesterol and has been describing a continuing feeling of sluggishness.

Here we have a number of basic facts that may well appear unrelated *until* looked at from the perspective of our ontologies. A set of individual reports about individual drugs being perhaps associated with several different (or at least differently described) conditions may not trigger any concern or interest at all. But once viewed through knowledge represented in our ontologies, it becomes clear that not only do we have four reports about four *different drugs* and four *different conditions*, but in addition we have four reports about a single *class of drug* and a single *type of condition*:

> *Generalized Fact:*
> HMG Coa reductase inhibitors are related to asthenic conditions.

And this is a genuine discovery.

Our informal model of knowledge exploration and discovery using ontology-based (or ontology-characterized) facts then exhibits the following features:

- There is a set of *sources* that contain information and knowledge of interest to us.
- These sources may be text documents, database records, databases, or virtually any other "information sources".
- We have available to us a set of *ontologies* whose *topics* are arranged in subsumption hierarchies.
- The sources contain explicit *occurrences* of facts that can be characterized by means of *fact templates* which are sequences of topics (the fact template *components*) drawn from our ontologies.
- Facts are fact templates that are "about"(or are *exemplified by*) occurrences in the sources.
- Some fact templates don't correspond to facts. They are not exemplified in the sources.
- Some fact templates are more general than others in virtue of the positions of their respective components in the ontology hierarchies.
- There are similarities among facts (in virtue of their topics and the orders within the ontologies), and there is a generalization hierarchy among facts that reflects the generalization hierarchies of the ontologies.
- A general fact template may be exemplified (indirectly) in a source because a more specific "instance"of it has an explicit occurrence in the source.

4.2 Simple Fact Models

We now proceed to formalizing the conceptual scheme of the preceding section.

DEFINITION 28.1 $\langle T, \prec \rangle$ *is a* hierarchical ontology *if and only if:*
1 T is a finite set (the set of topics *or* categories *of the ontology)*
2 $\prec$ is a strict order on T (the subsumption relation *among the topics)*

This is a rather minimal notion of ontology (simply as a set of topics conforming to a strict order), but it will serve our limited purposes here. Without loss of generality, and with some convenience, we may assume that such an ontology is a lattice with a supremum.[10] In addition, we will often refer to hierarchical ontologies more simply as "ontologies" in contexts where confusion is unlikely to arise.

We will employ several notational conventions in subsequent definitions and statements: If f is a function, we often will write f_x rather than $f(x)$. We will use $(x_0, \ldots, x_{n-1})$ as an ordered n-tuple, and $\langle x_0, \ldots, x_{n-1} \rangle$ for an n-term sequence (function whose domain is the natural number n). If $O = \langle \langle T_0, \prec_0 \rangle, \ldots, \langle T_{n-1}, \prec_{n-1} \rangle \rangle$ is a sequence of ontologies, we will refer to the respective sets of topics and subsumption relations as O_{T_i} and $O_{\prec_i}$, and to the set of all topics in those ontologies (i.e., $\bigcup_{i<n} T_i$) as T_O. The set $\{\tau^n : \forall_{i<n}\, \tau_i \in T_{O_i}\}$ of sequences of topics drawn respectively from the ontologies will be abbreviated as T_O^n. Finally, in unambiguous contexts we will often use τ^n to refer to an arbitrary member of T_O^n.

We next introduce the formal characterization of the *ontological generalization* of a topic, the generalization of an ontology-based fact, and the *closure* of a set of facts under the operation of ontological generalization.

DEFINITION 28.2 *If O is an n-term sequence of hierarchical ontologies and τ^n and η^n are sequences of topics drawn from O, then we say that*

- τ_i is an ontological generalization of η_i *(with respect to O) if $\eta_i \prec_i \tau_i$.*
- τ^n is an ontological generalization of η^n *(with respect to O) if for every $i < n$,*
  1. *either $\tau_i = \eta_i$ or τ_i is an ontological generalization of η_i, and*
  2. *for some $i < n$, τ_i is an ontological generalization of η_i.*

Informally, one sequence of topics is ontologically more general than another if one or more of its topics are more general than corresponding ones and none are less general. Note that a consequence of this is that not all sequences of topics drawn from the same ontology sequence are commensurate with respect to their generality.

DEFINITION 28.3 *Suppose that O is an n-term sequence of hierarchical ontologies and $X \subseteq T_O^n$. Then X is* closed under ontological generalization *(with respect to O) if every ontological generalization of each member of X is also in X.*

Informally, the idea of closure under ontological generalization is intended to specifically capture the set of all facts that are generalizations (relative to the hierarchies in question) of a given "base" or explicit fact.

The next three definitions formalize the notion of an *ontology-based simple fact model*, *exemplars* of topics (and more generally the relation of exemplification between ontology topics and objects "in the world"), *ground facts* (as

[10] For more detailed treatments of ontologies as lattices, see [8] and [6].

compared to generalized facts), and *occurrences* of facts. Following the definitions, we offer English renderings that will provide a more intuitive basis for the concepts being formally defined, and in the following section we illustrate how this model of ontology-based facts is implemented within BKE and serves as a basis for our use of ontologies in enhancing data mining methodologies.

DEFINITION 28.4 *For any natural number n, an* n-ary ontology-based simple fact model (OBSF-model) *is a sequence* $\mathfrak{M} = \langle U, O, E, G, F \rangle$ *where*

1 *U is a non-empty finite set (the* universe*) of non-empty finite sets (the* sources*)*
2 *O is an n-term sequence of hierarchical ontologies.*
3 *E is a function (the* exemplification assignment *of* $\mathfrak{M}$*) whose domain is U and such that for any* $S \in U$*,* E_S *is a function where*
   (a) $\mathcal{D}E_S = T_O$
   (b) *For any* $t \in T_O$*,* $E_S(t) \subseteq S$
4 *G is a function (the* ground fact assignment of $\mathfrak{M}$*) whose domain is U and for* $S \in U$*,* G_S *is a function such that*
   (a) $\mathcal{D}G_S \subseteq T_O^n$
   (b) *For any* $\tau^n \in \mathcal{D}G_S$*,* $G_S(\tau^n) \subseteq \{x^n : \forall_{i<n}\, x_i \in E_S(\tau_i)\}$
5 *F is a function (the* fact assignment of $\mathfrak{M}$*) whose domain is U and such that for each* $S \in U$*,* F_S *is the set of pairs* (τ^n, x^n) *where either:*
   (a) $x^n \in G_S(\tau^n)$*, or*
   (b) *there is an* η^n *such that* $(\eta^n, x^n) \in F_S$ *and* τ^n *is an ontological generalization of* η^n *with respect to O.*

Typically n will be greater than 1 and so the model will represent relations of some degree.

DEFINITION 28.5 *If* $\mathfrak{M} = \langle U, O, E, G, F \rangle$ *is an OBSF-model,* $S \in U$*, and* $\tau^n \in \mathcal{D}G_S$*, then*

1 τ^n *is a* ground fact in S of $\mathfrak{M}$. *(And hence* $\mathcal{D}G_S$ *is the* ground facts in S of $\mathfrak{M}$.*)*
2 $\bigcup_{S \in U} \mathcal{D}G_S$ *is the* ground facts of $\mathfrak{M}$.

The next definition begins to associate our formal OBSF-models with the informal concepts of ontologies, topics, facts, and sources.

DEFINITION 28.6 *If* $\mathfrak{M} = \langle U, O, E, G, F \rangle$ *is an OBSF-model,* $S \in U$*,* $x \in S$*, and* $t \in T_O$*, then*

1 x immediately exemplifies t in S *(or* x is an immediate exemplar of t in S*) just in case* $x \in E_S(t)$*. Note that* $E_S(t)$ *may be empty, in which case we say that* t is not exemplified in S.
   By extension, x^n *is an* immediate exemplar of τ^n *if* $x^n \in G_S(\tau^n)$.
2 x exemplifies t in S *(or* x is an exemplar of t in S*) just in case either x immediately exemplifies t in S or there is a t′ such that:*

(a) *x is an immediate exemplar of t′ and*
(b) *t is an ontological generalization of t′.*
By extension, x^n exemplifies τ^n *if either it immediately exemplifies* τ^n *or there is some* η^n *such that:*
(a) x^n *immediately exemplifies* η^n *and*
(b) τ^n *is an ontological generalization of* η^n.

3 f *is a* fact occurrence in *S just in case* $f \in F_S$. *And* f *is a* fact occurrence in $\mathfrak{M}$ *just in case for some S, it is a fact occurrence in S.*

The following theorems assume that $\mathfrak{M} = \langle U, O, E, G, F \rangle$ is an n-ary OBSF-model. They support our English renderings and the conformance of our formal model to our pre-systematic intuitions.

THEOREM 28.7 *If* τ^n *and* η^n *are fact templates and* τ^n *is an ontological generalization of* η^n*, then every exemplar of* η^n *is an exemplar of* τ^n.

Informally: Every ontological generalization of a fact is exemplified by all the exemplars of that fact.

THEOREM 28.8 *If* τ^n *is a fact (i.e., is a member of* $\mathcal{D}F_S$ *for some* $S \in U$*), then either:*
1 τ^n *is a ground fact, or*
2 There is a ground fact η^n *such that* τ^n *is an ontological generalization of* η^n.

Informally: Every fact is “grounded”: it is either a ground fact or an ontological generalization of a ground fact.

It is now possible to provide English renderings of some of these definitional clauses and their consequences, and exhibit how our formal model satisfies the pre-systematic characterization of facts in Section 4.1.

- Objects in sources *exemplify* ontology topics, and sequences of such objects *exemplify* sequences of topics. For example, in Source 4.1, the occurrence of the term ‘Lipitor’ exemplifies the topic *Atorvastatin* in the WHO Drug Dictionary ontology and the occurrence of the term ‘feeling unwell’ exemplifies the topic of *Malaise* in the MedDRA ontology. Further, the sequence of terms Sequence 4.1 exemplifies the sequence of topics (i.e., the fact) Sequence 4.1.
- We construe a *fact template* as a sequence of topics (in which case each topic in the template is said to be a *component* of the template).
- A *fact* is construed as a fact template that has an exemplar, which is an occurrence in a source. Facts are “about” their exemplars.
- A ground fact is a fact that has an immediate exemplar. Other facts may be thought of as *derived* or *generalized* facts since they come from ground facts by ontological generalization. Table 28-4 displays one ground fact

(that represented by Sequence 4.1 and eight other generalized facts based on that ground fact.

- Some facts have no exemplars. Other facts may have multiple exemplars. And an exemplar may exemplify multiple facts. The single exemplar of Sequence 4.1 exemplifies each of the facts represented in Table 28-4.
- F_S is the set of fact/exemplar pairs (or *fact instances*) in S (according to the OBSF-model $\mathfrak{M}$), and as such is the generalized exemplification relation for S in $\mathfrak{M}$. Note that the domain of this relation is closed under ontological generalization which is the generalization hierarchy for facts based on the hierarchies of the ontologies.
- The *set of facts in* $\mathfrak{M}$ is the set of all τ^n such that for some $S \in U$, $\tau^n \in \mathcal{D}F_S$. That is, the set of facts in a model is the set of fact templates which have exemplars. Again, Table 28-4 represents the set of facts exemplified by Sequence 4.1 (and hence by Source 4.1).

This establishes the adequacy of the simple fact model with respect to our initial concept of ontology-based facts described in Section 4.1, and we now go on to show how this model, coupled with the representation of ontologies presented in Section 3, is used within BKE to support the development of ontology-enhanced applications for text mining and data mining.

5. APPLYING ONTOLOGIES TO THE WORLD

Once we have a clear idea of what an ontology is, how ontologies are to be represented formally, and how they might be employed in the representation of relations, associations, or facts, there yet remains the problem of exactly how they are to be applied to actual sources of text and data. How do we "match up" topics in our ontologies with items of data or portions of text? This is, of course, an extraordinarily general and broad question which almost certainly lacks a single meaningful answer. But in our case, as we have seen in Sections 3.1 and 4, we have some constraints that allow us to approach an answer with some degree of efficiency.[11]

We know that our sources (whether text or structured data) are formulated to a significant degree in terms of the vocabularies associated with our ontologies – or in terms of the controlled vocabularies, thesauri, or dictionaries on which our ontologies are based. We know, for example, that our adverse event reports will use the terms in MedDRA to describe medical conditions and use the terms in the WHO Drug Dictionary to describe drugs and treatments. We know that our gene and protein data will use HUGO, SwissProt, GenBank, or other

[11] For another approach to the often overlooked issue of applying large ontologies to real-world situations, see the lexical tools provided with the UMLS Metathesaurus ([29]).

similar identifiers. And as a result, we do not face the unconstrained problem of analyzing arbitrary text or data, and the difficulty of "matching up" our text and data to these ontologies is much reduced. In fact, this was one of the original insights that drove the creation of BKE and its use of large and widely accepted ontologies in an attempt to avoid the need to implement more sophisticated techniques of entity identification, parsing, and information extraction.

BKE's approach to applying ontologies to the world (or at least to text and data sources that represent the world) rests on the three operations of tokenization, normalization, and indexing. The most straightforward way to see how this works is by looking at BKE from the perspective of its user interface.

5.1 Tokenizing, Normalizing, and Indexing

A fundamental concept within BKE is that of a *knowledge bank*. BKE's Knowledge Bank Manager provides the capability of defining and configuring a *knowledge bank*, which is conceived of as a set of *knowledge* (or *data*) *sources* to which various knowledge operations (indexing, information retrieval, information extraction, association discovery, etc.) may be applied. The Knowledge Bank Manager allows the BKE user to create, delete, rename, and clone knowledge banks. From the Knowledge Bank Manager, access is provided to interfaces for indexing a knowledge bank, viewing an indexed knowledge bank through the OntoScope, or exploring the knowledge bank with the FactFinder. Figure 28-4 shows the Index Manager interface for a knowledge bank consisting of a number of adverse events reports constructed from Canada's Adverse Drug Event Database ([3]), one of which appears in Figure 28-5.[12]

Each knowledge bank has associated with it a set of ontologies (in terms of which it is to be indexed), a tokenizer (used in indexing and matching operations), and possibly a normalizer (such as a part-of-speech stemmer) to be used in indexing and matching operations as well. Our approach to indexing and searching is that, first, every source must be indexed based on a tokenizer/normalizer combination. This produces a *term index* recording the positions of terms (identified through the tokenization/normalization process) in the sources. In order to search for ontology topics in the sources, the ontology to be used in the source must also be indexed *using the same tokenizer/normalizer combination.* Otherwise the concept of *term* relative to the sources will not match the concept of *term* relative to the ontology because what makes a sequence of characters a *term* is that it has been identified as a token by the tokenizer and normalizer. This indexing of the ontology re-

[12]The data on which these examples and later ones are based has been extracted from CADRIS, but the sample textual sources such as Figure 28-5 have been artificially reconstructed from this data. Though they accurately reflect the general form and content of adverse event reports, they are not taken directly from CADRIS and do no accurately represent its contents.

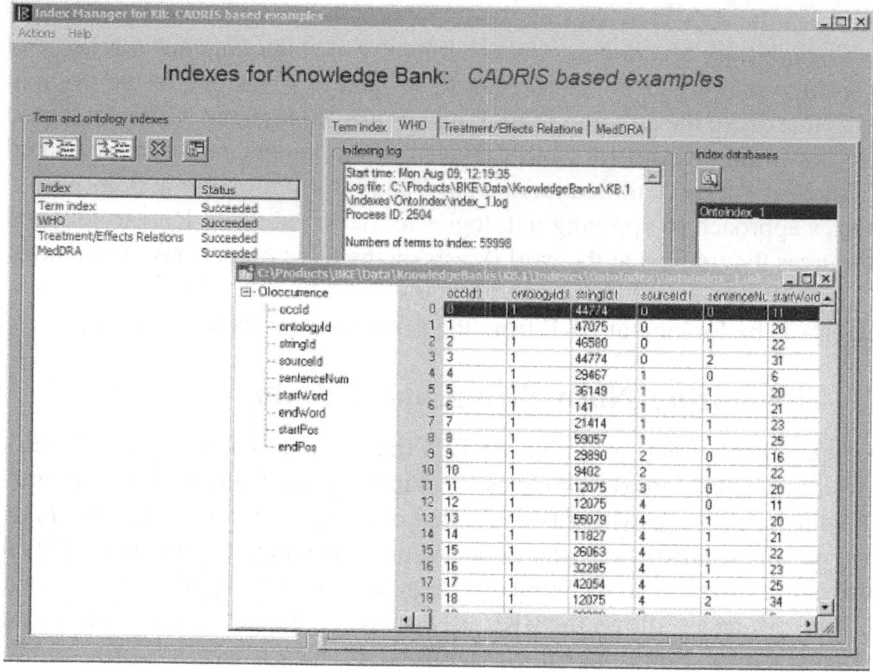

Figure 28-4. The Knowledge Bank Indexer

```
129449

"A female consumer of unknown age reported that she received Lescol
of unreported dosage once daily. She was receiving Atenolol,
Betaseron, Glyburide, Cimetidine, and Captopril concurrently.
Patient reported that after one month of Lescol treatment she
suffered from dry mouth, muscle pain, and weakness."
```

Figure 28-5. An example text source

sults in what we call an *onto-index* of the source, recording the positions of the *ontology terms* (terms representing ontology topics) in that source.

Figure 28-4 shows that the knowledge bank *CADRIS based examples* has associated with it a Term index (which records the position of each token in each of the knowledge bank's sources), and one index for each of the ontologies that have been associated with this knowledge bank. Overlaying the Index Manager in Figure 28-4 is a window showing the contents of the onto-index for the WHO ontology,[13] and it can be seen that such an onto-index records (for each occurrence of an ontology topic in a source) the ontology id (an internal

[13] This window is displayed by the KitViewer utility provided by Jean-Claude Whippler in conjunction with his Metakit ([14]) database engine.

identifier), the string id of the ontology topic basename or variant, the source id, and information pertaining to the position in the source of that occurrence of the topic identifier.

Notice that no strings appear anywhere in the onto-indexes. All string mapping is done in the Term Index (implemented as a hashed database) where each token is assigned a unique numeric representative. Once past the point of tokenization, all matching and lookup is done using the numeric representatives and this is consequently very fast. Such an approach, given the constraints that we can assume about our sources and ontologies, allows us to implement a fast query, matching, and retrieval process that avoids more complicated approaches such as regular expression matching or various kinds of parsing.

We have adopted an approach to matching ontology topics to text and data that is heavily dependent upon tokenization. In fact, each knowledge bank *must* have associated with it a particular tokenizer in terms of which its term index and onto-indexes are generated, and the Knowledge Bank Manager enforces this requirement when defining a knowledge bank. The tokenizers themselves are defined by means of BKE's Tokenizer Manager shown in Figure 28-6.[14]

Each domain (e.g., pharmacokinetics, stellar astrophysics, terrorist actions and movements, construction hardware, etc.) has its own peculiar vocabulary (and ontologies), and even the forms of words appropriate to different domains may vary widely. In many cases, for example, punctuation is not significant or important. In a domain of software, 're-implementation' and 'reimplementation' may be used interchangeably. But in other domains, such as those involving chemical compound names, even minor punctuation can be critical. It is therefore a fundamental requirement to have control over the creation and modification of tokenizers in performing any kind of linguistic analysis or named entity identification; and this is one way in which a number of text analysis products fail a criterion of flexibility in that they do not provide to the user (or developer) the ability to alter how tokenization is done. As Figure 28-6 illustrates, BKE's Tokenizer Manager allows us to easily define or modify tokenizers, which are generated from these definitions by means of the Plex lexical analyzer generator ([19]). It also has a test capability that allows us to quickly and easily test a tokenizer on samples of our sources, correcting the tokenizer and retesting as necessary. Figure 28-6 exhibits a very simple tokenizer for our sample adverse events reports which recognizes simple word forms, ends of sentences, different types of numbers, the identifier line of a report, and punctuation.

We think of normalization as a post-tokenization step in which the token can be further modified in one or more ways. One obvious type of modification

[14]The BKE Tokenizer Manager was designed and written by Natalie L. Doe of A^2RT.

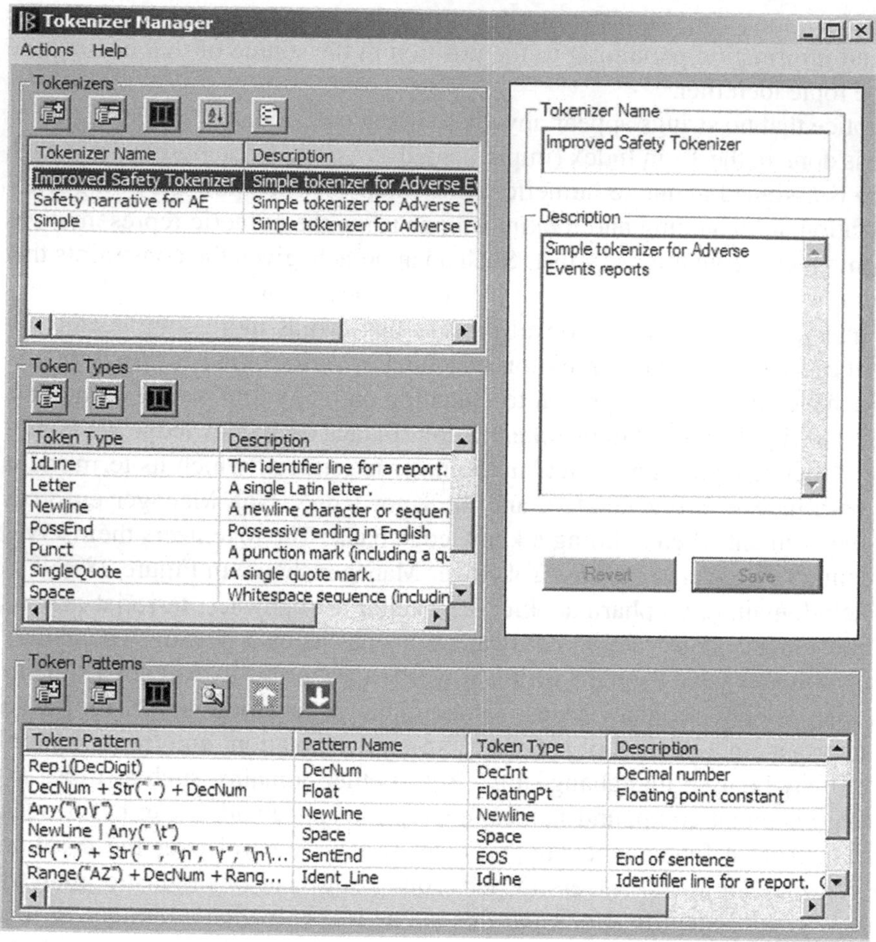

Figure 28-6. The Tokenizer Manager

involves stemming, and BKE currently can make use of the Porter Stemmer ([20]), though in most applications we have discovered that stemming does not yield improved results. Another type of normalization might be normalization to a standard spelling style (such as British English rather than American or Canadian English); or, in the case of medical contexts, we might choose to normalize some terms by replacing 'NOS' (Not Otherwise Specified) with 'NEC' (Not Elsewhere Clasified), or by eliminating these token fragments entirely.

Focusing on text sources (such as journal abstracts, articles, adverse event reports, web pages, etc.) for the purpose of illustration, we can now see how BKE matches its ontologies to "the world". The sources are first read and a general index of terms (tokens) is produced. This *term index* is then used to produce *onto-indexes* (one per ontology) of the sources in terms of the ontology

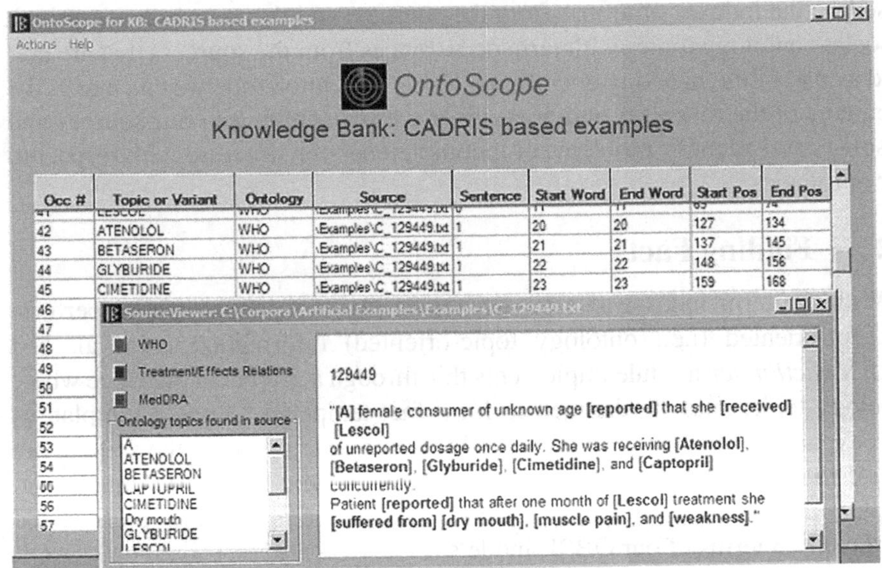

Figure 28-7. The OntoScope

topics. An onto-index associates with each of its ontology topics (zero or more) occurrences within each source. Currently, a simple approach is taken wherein the names of the ontology topics (from the embedded ontology databases) are used as "indicators" of topic occurrences in the text.[15] In practice this works well, given the large and fairly comprehensive nature of the ontologies with which we are working. Different domains and different ontologies might require a more sophisticated or complicated approach to such onto-indexing.

Figure 28-7 shows BKE's OntoScope overlayed by a SourceViewer window for one of the sources. The OntoScope allows us to examine how well our tokenizers, normalizers, and indexers are working in identifying ontology topics that occur in our sources and document corpora.

Each row in the OntoScope display indicates that a particular topic or variant has been found at a particular position in a particular source. In the example of Figure 28-7, we can see that the topic *ATENOLOL* from the WHO ontology has been identified as occurring as the 20-th word in the source (0-based from the beginning, including the numeric title designation), starting at position 127 and ending at position 134. In the SourceViewer, this is represented by color-coded brackets enclosing the term (not visible in the grayscale images used here), indicating what ontology (or ontologies, in the case of a topic occurring in more than one) that topic comes from. The OntoScope displays all this information

[15] *Cf.* the treatment of *evidence topics* in Verity®([32]). Verity is a registered trademark of Verity, Inc.

based on the indexes of terms (from the sources) and the onto-indexes (which associate ontology topics with term occurrences from the sources) that are created as part of the indexing operations. Using the OntoScope we can assess the adequacy of the tokenizer and normalizer we are applying to our sources and in some cases identify problems of incompleteness or structure with respect to our ontologies.

5.2 Finding Facts

With the term index and onto-indexes in place, it is possible to perform concept-oriented (i.e., ontology topic-oriented) information retrieval, and BKE's *FactFinder* module implements this through a graphical interface where ontology topics may be dragged to form fact templates. Such a template is then expanded into a query in terms of indicators, exemplars in the sources are bound to topics to form ground fact bindings, and the list of ground fact exemplars matching the query (exemplifying the fact template) are returned and displayed. In terms of our OBSF-models,

- The ontologies of *Definition* 1 are implemented as structured databases.
- The text corpus to be explored and mined becomes the universe U of the OBSF-model in *Definition* 4.
- This universe is then indexed in terms of the ontologies O, which results in an implementation of the exemplification assignment E.
- A topic template query is formed as a sequence τ^n of topics from T_O^n, and a procedure then implements the ground fact assignment G by binding exemplars from each $S \in U$ to this template through binding them to the template's ground facts.
- From the set of ground facts and the ontology databases, it is then straightforward to form the ontological closure of the ground fact sets and generate the exemplification relations F_S for the topic template query.

In this way a fact template (which may be of any degree of generality) is employed to discover a set of ground facts and their exemplars that may then serve as the basis for further exploration and analysis.

The Factfinder currently implements some rudimentary information retrieval and information extraction capabilities. Figure 28-8 shows the FactFinder being used to find "facts" that assert a relationship among *cholesterol and triglyceride reducers* (from the WHO ontology), any *treatment/effects relation* (from the Treatment/Effects Relations ontology), and *musculoskeletal and connective tissue disorders* (from the MedDRA ontology). The results of this query are shown in the FactFollower display of Figure 28-9 which lists some of the specific facts found. From the FactFollower, these results may be exported in various formats or used as input to analytical tools such as the rule inducer discussed in Section 6.

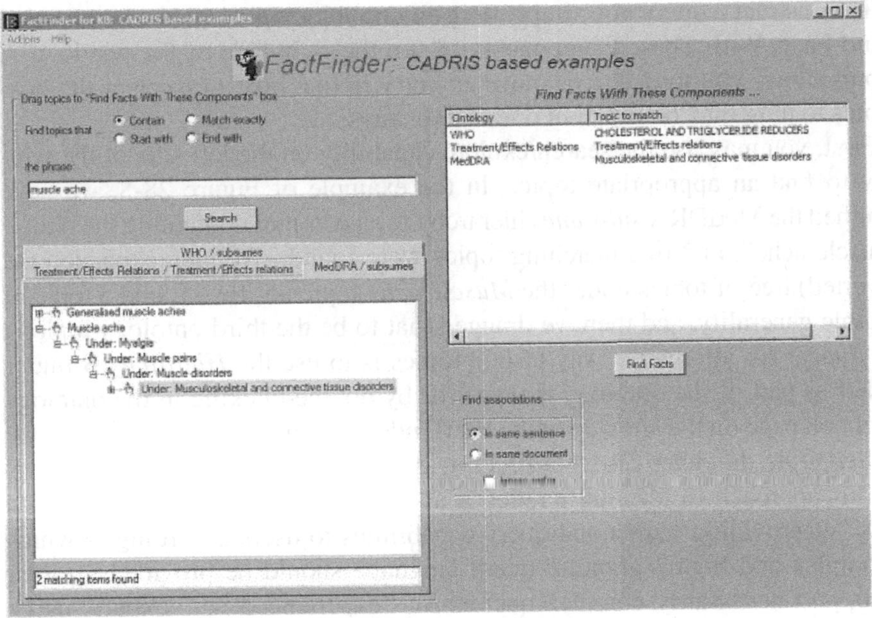

Figure 28-8. The FactFinder

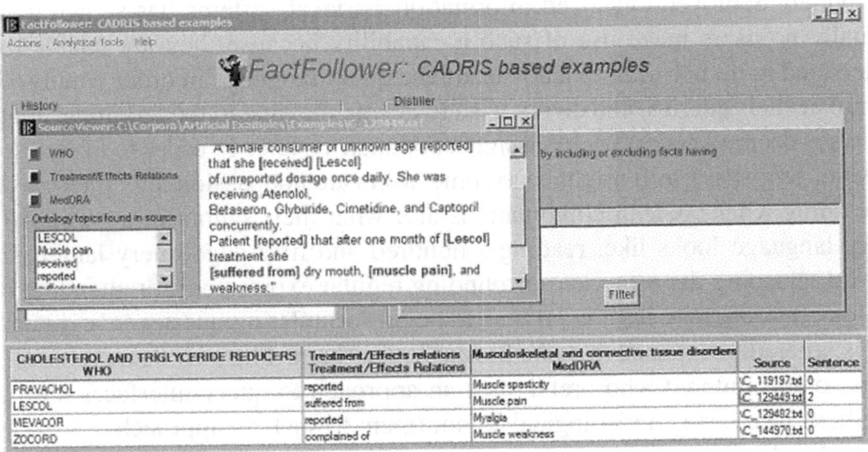

Figure 28-9. The FactFollower

The FactFinder is a fully ontology-driven query methodology and interface based on the concept of *ontology-based fact* described formally in Section 4. There is no complex query language for the user to learn and grapple with. There is no query syntax. A query is simply a sequence of ontology categories which is then matched to occurrences of those categories (occurring in that sequence) in the sources of the target corpus.

To construct a query you simply drag an ontology topic into the box labeled "Find Facts With These Components ..." on the right side of the window. A popup allows you to delete or move an entry in that box, or to clear the box. Topics to drag may be found in one of two ways.

First, you may use the search/explore capability on the left side of the window to find an appropriate topic. In the example of Figure 28-8, we have searched the MedDRA *subsumes* hierarchy for any topics containing the phrase "muscle ache", and two matching topics were found. We then expanded the (inverted) tree of topics under the *Muscle ache* topic until we found a topic of suitable generality, and then we dragged that to be the third ontology topic in our query. An alternative way to find topics is to use the *Hierarchy Browser* (either as part of the ontology manager or by double-clicking in the ontology notebook page on the left side of the FactFinder) to search for or navigate to the desired topic. In either case, constructing queries is simple, fast, and effective.

This approach to forming queries is at odds with a widely held "received view" of providing search and query capabilities to users according to which a complex and highly granular query language should be provided in order to support necessarily complex queries for "experienced" or "expert" users, and to enable users to craft the best and most precise query to achieve their information retrieval goal. However, our experience with several large-scale and widely deployed enhanced information retrieval systems has shown that virtually no users make use of such a capability because they are unable to understand it, do not want to learn an arcane query language in order simply to formulate their queries, and do not wish to devote the time to the "training" that is always deemed necessary by designers of such systems in order to make use of them. Surprising as it might be to some, users are not passionately interested in learning what boolean combinations are, what their syntax in a particular query language looks like, reading a hundred and fifty page query language manual, grasping the esoterica surrounding regular expressions, or attending a half-day introductory session on how to begin formulating queries in a system that is, after all, supposed to make life easier for them. The only "expert users" we have encountered who prefer such an approach to query interfaces are in fact those who have an ideological commitment to such an approach.

The FactFinder interface is an attempt to avoid the difficulties encountered with traditional formal query language approaches while also avoiding the difficulties and complexities of a "natural language" interface. Our ability to rely on ontologies to lend meaning and context to our queries enables us to create such an effective and easy to use interface.

6. ONTOLOGY-ENHANCED TEXT AND DATA MINING

In this Section we will provide a simple example illustrating how our implementation of ontologies, ontology-based fact models, and ontological generalization can be used to enhance a classical machine learning methodology to yield improved knowledge discovery and knowledge exploration capabilities. Our sample case is based on a data set of over 15,000 records culled from the CADRIS ([3]) database and pertaining to adverse event reports involving drugs for treating conditions of high cholesterol. We make use of the Orange ([9]) association rule generation capabilities which are easily accessed from BKE through Orange's Python wrapper API.

Figure 28-10 illustrates BKE's *Ontology-Driven Rule Inducer* graphical user interface. This allows us to load a data file, and a portion of our loaded data is displayed in Figure 28-11. The data consists of records of four fields: a report identifier, a drug name, an adverse event (medical condition), and another drug that was taken concommitently. For our purposes we will focus only on the drug names and the associated adverse events, and this is evident in the *Include attribures* window of Figure 28-10 where these fields are checked. Note

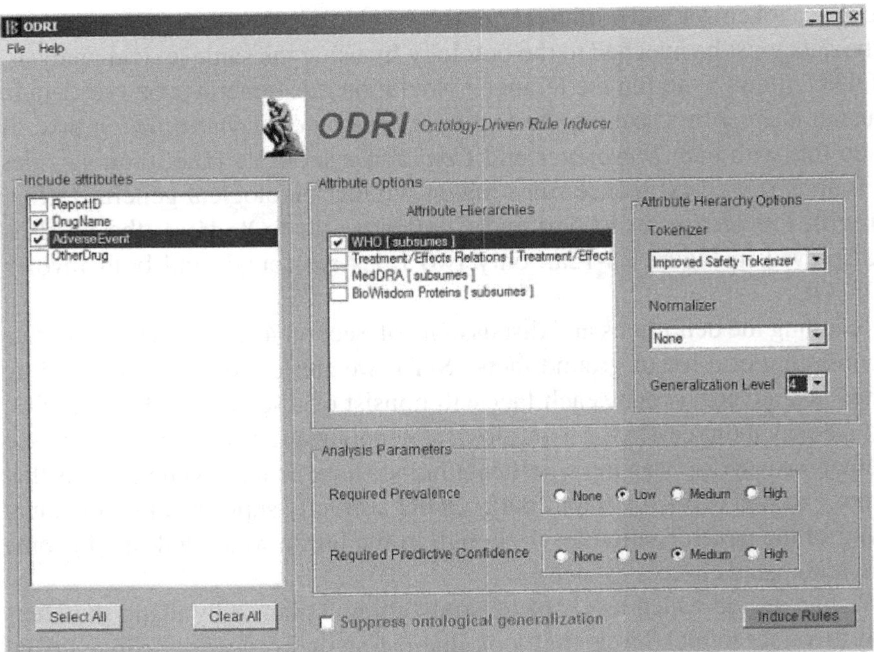

Figure 28-10. ODRI: The Ontology-Driven Rule Inducer

ODRI Data Display: drugData

File Help

	ReportID	DrugName	AdverseEvent	OtherDrug
12	122837	MEVACOR	JOINT PAIN	GRAPEFRUIT JUICE
12	122837	MEVACOR	JOINT STIFFNESS	GRAPEFRUIT JUICE
12	145687	MEVACOR	ERUPTION	PAROXETINE
12	145675	MEVACOR	HAIR LOSS	DYAZIDE
12	145675	MEVACOR	HAIR LOSS	SLOW-K
12	129482	MEVACOR	CREATINE KINASE INCREASED	ACETYLSALICYLIC ACID
12	129482	MEVACOR	CREATININE BLOOD INCREASED	ACETYLSALICYLIC ACID
12	129482	MEVACOR	MYALGIA	ACETYLSALICYLIC ACID
12	129482	MEVACOR	RHABDOMYOLYSIS	ACETYLSALICYLIC ACID
12	129482	MEVACOR	CREATINE KINASE INCREASED	METOPROLOL
12	129482	MEVACOR	CREATININE BLOOD INCREASED	METOPROLOL
12	129482	MEVACOR	MYALGIA	METOPROLOL
12	129482	MEVACOR	RHABDOMYOLYSIS	METOPROLOL
12	160510	NIACIN	FATIGUE	FLUIDS
12	160510	NIACIN	HEPATIC ENZYMES INCREASED	FLUIDS
12	160510	NIACIN	HEPATITIS	FLUIDS
12	160510	NIACIN	NAUSEA	FLUIDS

Figure 28-11. Sample data for ODRI

also that a tokenizer and normalizer must be selected since the terms occurring in the data must be matched to the ontology by using the same lexical analysis.

ODRI allows us to run the Orange association rule generator on our data in its usual manner by checking the *Suppress ontological generalization* box. If we do this with both *Prevalence* and *Confidence* set to `Medium`, then *no* rules are found. If we next induce rules (again without ontological generalization) and with *Prevalence* set to `Low` and *Confidence* set to `Medium`, the result is as displayed in Figure 28-12a: only two rules are found, and both involve BAYCOL.

Recalling the definitions and discussions of Section 4, we can view our data as consisting of a list of ground facts. Since we are looking only at the drug names and adverse events, each fact will consist of a sequence of two topics. And we may then seek to form ontological generalizations of those facts to see whether we can discover any significant higher-level or more general facts that are not exposed explicitly in our data. ODRI currently supports only a manual setting of the generalization level, though in the future we intend to add some more automated choices as well.

We can decide which levels of generalization to choose by using the Hierarchy Browser to pick levels that look interesting or worthwhile. Since ODRI runs very quickly (as a result of BKE's highly efficient underlying indexed ontologies and databases), it is feasible to make one choice and then follow

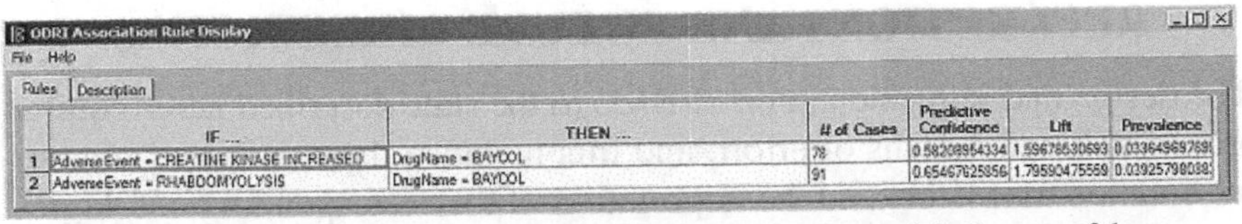

	IF ...	THEN ...	# of Cases	Predictive Confidence	Lift	Prevalence
1	AdverseEvent = CREATINE KINASE INCREASED	DrugName = BAYCOL	78	0.58208954334	1.59678530693	0.03364969769
2	AdverseEvent = RHABDOMYOLYSIS	DrugName = BAYCOL	91	0.65467625856	1.79590475569	0.03925798088

(a) Rules with no ontological generalization; Low prevalence; Medium confidence.

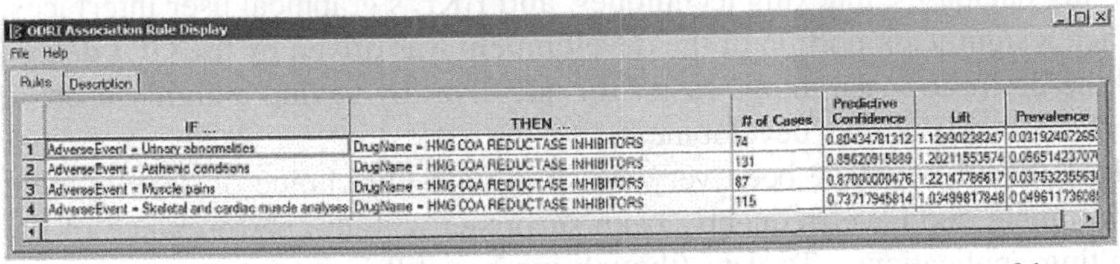

	IF ...	THEN ...	# of Cases	Predictive Confidence	Lift	Prevalence
1	AdverseEvent = Urinary abnormalities	DrugName = HMG COA REDUCTASE INHIBITORS	74	0.80434781312	1.12930238247	0.03192407265
2	AdverseEvent = Asthenic conditions	DrugName = HMG COA REDUCTASE INHIBITORS	131	0.85620915889	1.20211553574	0.05651423707
3	AdverseEvent = Muscle pains	DrugName = HMG COA REDUCTASE INHIBITORS	87	0.87000000476	1.22147786617	0.03753235563
4	AdverseEvent = Skeletal and cardiac muscle analyses	DrugName = HMG COA REDUCTASE INHIBITORS	115	0.73717945814	1.03499817848	0.04961173608

(b) Rules for WHO level = 4, MedDRA level = 3; Low prevalence; Medium confidence.

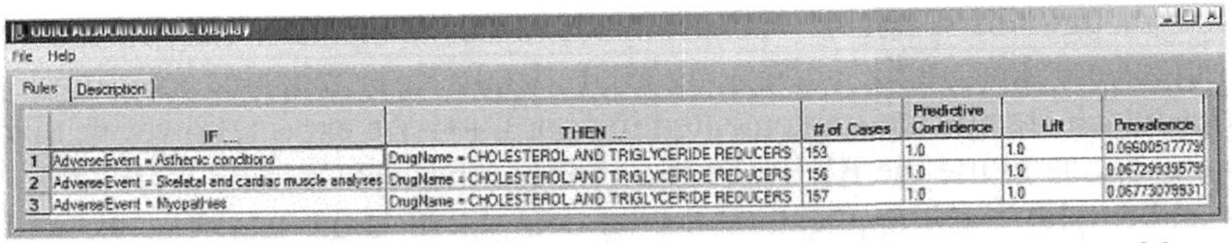

	IF ...	THEN ...	# of Cases	Predictive Confidence	Lift	Prevalence
1	AdverseEvent = Asthenic conditions	DrugName = CHOLESTEROL AND TRIGLYCERIDE REDUCERS	153	1.0	1.0	0.06600517779
2	AdverseEvent = Skeletal and cardiac muscle analyses	DrugName = CHOLESTEROL AND TRIGLYCERIDE REDUCERS	156	1.0	1.0	0.06729939579
3	AdverseEvent = Myopathies	DrugName = CHOLESTEROL AND TRIGLYCERIDE REDUCERS	157	1.0	1.0	0.06773079931

(c) Rules for WHO level = 3, MedDRA level = 3; Medium prevalence; Medium confidence.

Figure 28-12. Rules induced by ODRI

this with others, comparing the results. In fact, this is just the type of highly interactive data exploration we are striving for with BKE.

Simply double-clicking on a hierarchy in ODRI's *Attribute Hierarchies* window will pop up the Hierarchy Browser for that hierarchy, we can explore it as we did in Figure 28-3, and the levels are displayed beside the topic names. If we do this, we will see that level 3 of both MedDRA and WHO looks promising, as does level 4 of WHO. If we make such choices and switch off suppression of ontological generalization, we get the results of Figures 28-12b and 28-12c. What ODRI does, of course, is to implement the formal description of ontological generalization of Section 4, generalizing each original record appropriately and then running the association rule generator on the resulting generalized data.

Figures 28-12b and 28-12c illustrate the discovery of significant associations between *kinds of drugs* (*HMG Coa reductase inhibitors* or *cholesterol and triglyceride reducers*) and *kinds of conditions*. These associations are not explicit in the original data – the higher-level topics do not even appear in the data – and can be seen only in virtue of our (or BKE's) knowledge of the hierarchical relationships among topics in the ontologies. If we take away the ontologies, we lose these discoveries – and this matches precisely our characterization of *ontology-enhanced systems* in Section 1.2.

7. REFLECTIONS AND FUTURE DIRECTIONS

The design and implementation of BKE to the state described here required approximately ten months of effort, and this included the creation of nine re-representation translators and the importation of the corresponding ontologies. Most of this effort was devoted to the design and implementation of the underlying databases, indexing techniques, and BKE's graphical user interfaces. In fact, a significant portion of the development was driven by the GUI design and the desire to make things easier for ourselves by having a highly useable interface to aid our own development.

Throughout, we have been very satisfied with our choice of development environment and have frequently been surprised with the performance of the resulting applications. To date (though we are still in a prototypical stage), there has been no need to code any C extensions in order to enhance performance, though this is largely because most of our computationally intensive operations are done in the underlying GUI, database, or machine learning libraries which are already implemented in C or C++. We expect, however, that as we continue to use the BKE API to enhance other data mining methodologies and employ those applications in the analysis of large data sets, we will need to optimize how the API navigates the hierarchies and other relations of our ontologies. But overall, our goals of performance, development speed, flexibility, and cost have been met as we had hoped.

As we began to use BKE in some sample test projects, and as we began to demonstrate its capabilities to potential user groups, we were forced to reconsider some of our original vision concerning the role of BKE and precisely how it would be used. Two points quickly became apparent: first, that our vision of BKE's being used directly by groups interested in text and data mining was unrealistic; and second, that the original emphasis on the development of text mining capabilities was misplaced.

The first of these realizations compelled us to confront more carefully the question of who would use BKE and how it would be used; and as a consequence we have abandoned the original vision of providing BKE itself as an application to end users. The set of skills required to use BKE includes at least the ability to understand the structure and content of large and potentially complex pre-existing ontologies (dictionaries, thesauri, etc.), and to design and implement re-representations into BTM format. And these skills are simply not found in the groups which need to benefit directly from the capabilities that BKE can provide.

Consequently we have come more fully to see BKE as essentially a development *platform* from which we can create applications that such users *can* work with. In addition to using BKE to create ontology-enhanced applications we also see a role for our own use of it in what we might call *BKE-supported projects*. These are situations where we might not wish to embark on the development of a complete and deployable BKE-based application, but simply make use of BKE's ontology-based capabilities to contribute to the analysis of data for some relatively short-term goal: a kind of "mini-application". And this use is, after all, quite compatible with the description of our application environment provided in Section 2.1.

The second realization – that in our situation more benefit is to be had by concentrating on structured data rather than text – was originally something of a disappointment, but it opens a number of exciting opportunities for the fruitful direct application of multiple large ontologies to challenging problems in scientific domains. What it means in the short term is that we delay further work on text-oriented knowledge banks, the FactFinder, and the FactFollower, concentrating more on applications such as ODRI and on how ontologies can be used to enhance more sophisticated machine learning and data analysis methodologies.

In the immediate future, one area of concentration will be the use of the Gene Ontology and associated information for improving knowledge discovery in areas related to biomarker detection and gene expression. This will almost certainly involve us in a more careful representation and use of n-ary relations and how these relate to ontological hierarchies. Moreover, it also seems likely that we will want to revisit the notion of *variants* in connection with this work and perhaps replace it with a more flexible concept (one not so tightly bound to variants as *names*).

Finally, while our ontology-based fact model is reasonable and adequate for the information retrieval and information extraction contexts in terms of which it was originally conceived, it does not provide a good formal representation of facts on which to base an efficient computationally intensive approach to the use of hierarchies in enhancing the application of statistical and other analytical methods to large data sets. And there are a number of questions that must be addressed concerning how continuous-valued data should be handled, particularly in the presence of ontology topics having multiple parents within a hierarchy. We have some definite ideas about solutions to these problems, but the details remain to be worked out and will require an extension of the OBSF concept.

Looking to the future, then, there is much work to be done. But the work fits coherently within the conceptual framework supporting BKE, and we have confidence that BKE provides the foundation for advancing in these directions.

Note added in proof (June, 2005): The picture of BKE drawn here reflects its status at a point approximately a full year prior to the publication of this article – and in an industrial environment that can be a veritable eternity. In the interim we have learned additional lessons, been confronted with new challenges, and made changes in our focus and priorities in response to these.

To begin, the value of using large formal ontologies in a variety of analytical scenarios within GSK's Biomedical Data Sciences has been more widely recognized, and we have applied some of our capabilities in support of pharmacogenomics analyses using the Gene Ontology. At that point we encountered the first case in which performance of a Python program was inadequate: forming the transitive closure of the "parent of" relation in the Gene Ontology. However, as expected, it was straightforward to recode this in C, and we are able to treat this as a Python extension.

In addition, the past several months have seen some highly publicized developments pertaining to adverse events linked to Cox-2 inhibitors (though not involving GSK products), and this has compelled the FDA and pharmaceutical companies to seek improved methodologies for detecting and evaluating adverse event "signals". We have embarked on a project that will employ large ontologies to assist in mining and exploring multiple data sources (including very large observational databases of prescription and medical history information) in ways that have not previously been attempted. We have also turned our attention more carefully to the UMLS Metathesaurus as a rich resource of ontological information that can fruitfully be applied to these data sources. Overall, this project fits well with our conception of BKE as an ontology-based development platform for use in creating ontology-driven knowledge applications.

Finally, while retaining our use of Python for prototyping and potential delivery of end-user applications, we have decided to abandon wxPython (and wxWidgets) in favor of the commercial Qt and PyQt products ([24, 22]) for our user interface and graphics components. We made this decision somewhat reluctantly, but driven by the need to satisfy our criteria of *Performance*, *Development Speed*, and *Flexibility*. The consequence is that BKE will no longer be built on a wholly open source base (though its underlying machinery continues to be), but we felt compelled to make this move in order to ensure the production of high-quality and reliable applications.

REFERENCES

[1] Berkeley DB embedded database library. See http://www.sleepycat.com/ and (for the Python bsddb module) http://pybsddb.sourceforge.net/.

[2] BioWisdom ontologies page, `http://www.biowisdom.com/products/content.htm`.

[3] Canada's Adverse Drug Event Database, CBC online version, `http://www.cbc.ca/news/adr/database/`.

[4] Celi home page: `http://www.celi.it`.

[5] Cycorp home page: `http://www.cyc.com`.

[6] Bernhard Ganter and Rudolf Wille, Formal Concept Analysis: Mathematical Foundations, Springer, Berlin, 1999.

[7] The Gene Ontology Consortium, `http://www.geneontology.org`.

[8] B. A. Davey and H. A. Priestley, *Introduction to Lattices and Order*, Cambridge University Press, Second, Cambridge, 2002.
[9] J. Demsar and B. Zupin, *Orange: From Experimental Machine Learning to Interactive Data Mining*, Faculty of Computer and Information Science, University of Ljubljana, 2004, `http://magix.fri.uni-lj.si/orange/doc/wp/orange.pdf`.
[10] J. Liu, W. Wang, and J. Yang, *A Framework for Ontology-Driven Subspace Clustering*, In: Proceedings of the Tenth ACM SIGKDD International Conference on Knowledge Discovery and Data Mining, pp. 623-628, August, 2004, Seattle, Washington
[11] MedDRA home page, `http://www.meddramsso.com/NewWeb2003/index.htm`.
[12] G. H. Merrill, *The Babylon Project: Toward an Extensible Text-Mining Platform*, IT Professional, IEEE Computer Society, pp. 23-30, March/April, 2003.
[13] G. H. Merrill, *A Practical Multi-Ontology Approach to Knowledge Exploration.* In: Proceedings of Technology for Life (NC Symposium on Biotechnology & Bioinformatics), Raleigh, NC, 2004.
[14] Metakit embedded database library, `http://www.equi4.com/metakit.html`.
[15] National Center for Health Statistics, Classifications of Diseases and Functioning & Disability, `http://www.cdc.gov/nchs/icd9.htm`.
[16] Open Biological Ontologies, `http://obo.sourceforge.net`.
[17] OWL Web Ontology Language: `http://www.w3.org/TR/owl-ref/`.
[18] W. Paik, E. D. Liddy, E. Allen, E. Brown, A. Farris, R. Irwin, J. H. Liddy, I. Niles, *Applying Link Analysis to Automatically Extracted Information from Texts Using KNOW-IT*, Proceedings of the AAAI Symposium on Artificial Intelligence on Link Analysis, October, 1998, pp. 520-529.
[19] Greg Ewing's Plex lexical analysis module for Python. `http://www.cosc.canterbury.ac.nz/\~greg/python/Plex/`.
[20] Porter stemming algorithm home page: `http://www.tartarus.org/~martin/PorterStemmer/`.
[21] SourceForge home page for the Psyco Python optimizer: `http://sourceforge.net/projects/psyco`.
[22] The PyQt bindings for the Qt toolkit: `http://www.riverbankcomputing.co.uk/pyqt/`.
[23] Python home page: `http://python.org`.
[24] The Qt application development framework: `http://www.trolltech.com/products/qt/`.
[25] W. V. O. Quine, *Mathematical Logic*, Harvard University Press, Revised Edition, 1979.
[26] Barry Smith, Jacob Köhler, and Anand Kumar, *On the Application of Formal Principles to Life Science Data: A Case Study in the Gene Ontology*, forthcoming in E. Rahm (ed.), *Database Integration in the Life Sciences* (DILS 2004), Springer, Berlin, 2004.
[27] Merwyn G. Taylor, Killian Stoffel, and James A. Hendler, *Ontology-based Induction of High Level Classification Rules*, Proceedings of the SIGMOD Data Mining and Knowledge Discovery workshop, Tuscon, Arizona, 1997.
[28] Temis-Group home page: `http://www.temis-group.com`.
[29] The Unified Medical Language System (UMLS), U.S. National Library of Medicine: `http://www.nlm.nih.gov/research/umls`.
[30] Jack Park and Sam Hunting, Editors, *XML Topic Maps: Creating and Using Topic Maps for the Web*, Addison-Wesley, Boston, 2003.
[31] Therese Vachon, Nicolas Grandjean and Pierre Parisot, *Interactive Exploration< of Patent Data for Competitive Intelligence: Applications in Ulix (Novartis Knowledge Miner).* In: Proceedings of the International Chemical Informatics Conference. Nimes, France, 2001.
[32] Verity Inc., *Verity K2 Enterprise Intelligent Classification Guide V4.5*, Sunnyvale, 2002.

[33] The World Health Organization Drug Dictionary (WHO DD), `http://www.who-umc.org/faqs/faqdd.html`.
[34] The Wing IDE (integrated development environment) for Python, `http://www.wingide.com`.
[35] The wxDesigner GUI design tool, `http://www.roebling.de`.
[36] WxPython Python wrapper for the wxWidgets C++ GUI library. `http://wxpython.org/`
[37] The XML Topics Maps specification, `http://www.topicmaps.org/xtm/index.html`.
[38] Jun Zhang, Adrian Silvescu, and Vasant Honavar, *Ontology-Driven Induction of Decision Trees at Multiple Levels of Abstraction*. In: Proceedings of the Symposium on Abstraction, Reformulation, and Approximation (SARA-2002). Kananaskis, Alberta, Canada pp. 316-323.

Chapter 29

INDUCTIVE DESIGN AND TESTING OF A PERFORMANCE ONTOLOGY FOR MOBILE EMERGENCY MEDICAL SERVICES

Thomas Horan, Ugur Kaplancali, Richard Burkhard, and Benjamin Schooley
Claremont Graduate University

Abstract: Ontology provides an overarching framework and vocabulary for describing system components and relationships. As such, they represent a means to devise, analyze and compare information systems. This research investigates the development of a software-based ontology within the context of a rural wireless emergency medical (EMS) services. Wireless EMS has developed in response to the unprecedented growth of wireless as a means to communicate in emergency situations. Using an inductive, field-based approach, this study devises and tests a new ontology-based framework for wireless emergency response in rural Minnesota. The ontology is developed by integrating concepts and findings from in-depth field reviews in Minnesota into an ontological software originating out of bioinformatics. This software, Protégé 2000, is an open source ontological software system developed by Stanford University's Medical Informatics group. Using Protégé 2000, the authors developed a wireless EMS ontological framework populated by the real data gathered from field interviews and related data collection. This EMS framework distinguishes between classes of systems, instances within the classes, and the relationships among classes and instances. The next step in the research involved conducting a simulation of performance using a sample of case study data and demonstrated important linkages among system classes. It is expected that use of such performance ontology will assist researchers and program managers with identifying basic problems in terms of technical and non-technical rural EMS issues, as well as possible patterns of inconsistency or discrepancies across EMS deployments.

Key words: Web-based Ontology Development; Emergent Systems; Wireless Emergency Medical Services; Rural Mayday; Enhanced 911; Simulation

1. INTRODUCTION

Ontology is of increasing interest to Information Science researchers and professionals (McGuinness, 2002). This interest stems from both their conceptual use of organizing information and their practical use in communicating about system characteristics (Jurisica et al., 1999). Many ontological frameworks have already been developed by academic disciplines such as computer science and bio-informatics and applied to broad variety of businesses from high-tech industries to agricultural sectors (Noy et al., 2000). Within the field of IS, attention to "ontology driven information systems" is now on the rise because the concept of ontology promises a framework for communicating among architectures and domain areas (Smith, 2003).

In general, ontology refers to explicit specification of a conceptualization (Gruber, 1993). Ontology development and use of supporting tools offer an opportunity to utilize a unifying framework that embodies objects and concepts, their definitions and relationships between them. Ontology also makes representative content available for knowledge sharing by providing a set of "consistent vocabularies and world representations necessary for clear communication within knowledge domains" (Leroy et al., 1999). Three main uses of ontology are for communication, for computational inference and reuse of knowledge (Gruninger and Lee, 2002).

This study is motivated by all three uses of ontology and specifically develops a software-based ontology-driven system to tackle the complexity of wireless EMS and its end-to-end performance. This research takes an inductive approach to ontology system development and applies it within a framework to clarify the domain's (wireless EMS) structure of knowledge.

2. EMERGENCY MEDICAL SERVICES

There is increasing pressure to use mobile wireless communications for medical emergencies, yet little is known about its functionality and performance dimensions. Conditions driving the problem include rapid growth of cellular phone use for mayday, strong policy interest in "first-responder" Mayday as a consequence of 9/11, and policy regulations toward enhanced 911 (E-911) capabilities throughout the US. Statistics about system growth document this rise: Wireless 911 calls have grown from 22,000 per day in 1991 to 155,000 per day in 2001, and represent over 50% of emergency calls made (CTIA, 2002). In short, the mobile (cellular) phone has become the de facto safety lifeline, particularly for mobile travelers and especially in rural areas.

While there are several policies, market, and technological pressures leading to emergency medical services growth, the full system is quite dynamic and still unfolding—hence, it is not very well understood. There has been a substantial amount of emergency response and crisis management research and literature aimed at improving the effectiveness of the emergency response infrastructure (Davis, 2002; Hale, 1997; Perrow, 2000). Effective response to "unexpected events" (health emergencies, crises) is highly dependent upon timely and accurate information to and from all participating organizations (Arens and Rosenbloom, 2002; Turoff et. al., 2004). Moreover, the need to improve EMS services is especially true for rural areas where approximately 60 percent of all vehicle fatalities in the United States occur and the average EMS response time between a rural crash and the arrival of the victim to a hospital is 52 minutes, compared to 34 minutes for an urban crash victim (NCSA, 2002).

3. METHOD

3.1 Inductive approach

The ontology development methodology used in this study is a case-based approach applying *inductive* methods (Holsapple and Joshi, 2002). Development techniques ascribing to this approach require observing, examining, and analyzing a specific case in the domain in a non-static fashion. Inductive methods use case studies as references for ontology design and then the ontology is refined by evolving toward a more generalized ontology. The inductive approach to ontology design fits perfectly with our purpose to both contribute to and validate the conceptual framework for capturing EMS performance.

This bottoms-up approach is particularly appropriate because of the emergent nature of wireless EMS services—that is, the system is growing rapidly and very dynamically due to a number of market, and technology considerations. As advanced by Markus, Majchrzak, and Gasser (2002) such a context lends itself to a design theory approach whereby the system is captured at a point in time, while its eventual functioning may be undetermined. Knowing this, it is our intention to focus on wireless emergency response management implementation with particular attention to "on the ground" performance.

In this case, the "on the ground" dimension rural deployment in Minnesota has a distinctive approach for delivering emergency services to rural areas as compared to other states. The wireless EMS is not limited to E-911 infrastructure where PSAPs (Public Safety Answering Point) were established called TOCCs (Transportation Operation Communications Center), in different counties to aid emergency response agencies and incident management dispatches. Our fieldwork involved in-depth field interviews and site visits to Brainerd, Minnesota.[1] These interviews were focused on a local EMS services and data use therein. (The research team had previously performed a more global statewide set of interviews).[2] The findings and concepts from these field reviews were then integrated into the ontological software (Protégé) that includes its knowledgebase populated with collected data. Finally, these data were subjected to simulation analysis utilizing a business software simulation program (ARENA).

3.2 Ontology Design Using Protégé 2000

The ontological-development task is to review field interviews and data, and devise an ontology using a platform-independent ontological software product. Specific steps in the process included: local field interviews, conceptual version of the ontology, application of data to ontology (Factual Ontology), and use of ontology software (Protégé) to specify conceptual and factual ontology for EMS.

The EMS ontology was developed using Protégé knowledge acquisition software. Protégé 2000 is developed by Stanford University's Medical Informatics Group as an ontology editor and knowledgebase editor (Grosso et al., 1999). It is a java-based, platform-independent tool for developing ontology and knowledge bases.

As an ontological knowledgebase editor, Protégé 2000 has its own knowledge acquisition features similar to available database solutions in the market. The factual wireless EMS ontology and knowledgebase were constructed assuming that data from other rural Minnesota areas in addition to Brainerd will be integrated later when it is available. The only constraint for a future expansion of the knowledgebase is the limited available memory of the Protégé software in the absence of a database running as a back-end. However, since this study is focusing on aggregate EMS data rather than event-specific data the usable memory space is adequate.

Because of its graphical user-friendly interface, Protégé 2000 makes it easy to portray and modify the ontological classification of EMS systems in a visually oriented and structured manner.[3] Moreover, web publishing of the outcome in the form of an ontology and knowledgebase can increase the accessibility to the domain knowledge. Protégé capabilities in this regard will allow researchers to browse EMS ontology and knowledge bases rather

1 A more detailed accounting of the field interviews and related EMS data acquisition effort can be found in Horan et al., (2005).

2 This preliminary review is summarized in Horan and Schooley (2005). It resulting in the global framework presented in Figure 29-1 and discussed below under findings.

3 For a more complete description on Protégé, see http://protege.stanford.edu/.

than scanning hundreds of pages of technical consultancy papers and documents to quickly find and navigate domain specific knowledge.

The research team made two local site visits, interviewing representatives at each site (PSAP, TOCC). During each meeting, the research team provided an overview of the study objectives and asked each interviewee to comment on the organization's role in each step of the process and the availability of data for documenting the performance of their activity in each relevant step. Four sources were identified for use in creating a factual ontology: the Fatality Analysis Reporting System (FARS), Minnesota FARS, the Baxter Transportation and Operation Communication Center (TOCC), and the Crow Wing County PSAP. The year 2002 was identified as the most recent year with complete data at the time of the review (mid-late 2003).

3.3 Ontology Testing Using ARENA Simulation

EMS is an integrated system and, as such, a dynamic systems approach suggests the utility of *portraying* a system as an important conceptual step toward understanding how the system operates and evolves (Sussman, 2002). Included in this portrayal is the need to examine *links* across the various classes in the ontology. A means to portray and understand a system is to model and simulate its performance. Traditionally, it has been used as a technical systems and operations research tool (Sterman, 2000), but it has recently been used to understand more dynamic inter-organizational interactions (Black et. al., 2003). The ARENA simulation package was used by the research team for such as simulation because it is a robust, visually oriented software system that is well suited to processes such as call centers and emergency medical response (Kelton et al., 2004).

Drawing from this factual ontology, a preliminary simulation was conducted for rural EMS performance. A judgmental sample of emergency response cases (called "ICRs") was extracted from the raw data for 2002 with 36 days sampled at 10-day intervals.[4] In order to fully capture the expected range of daily call frequencies, data from several days with expected high emergency activity (e.g., December 31, July 4) were included in the sample. The final sample of 40 days yielded a range of eight to thirty-four incidents per day, with a mean of approximately 14 incidents per day. The distribution of call times was examined for the entire data set of 7,215 incidents, yielding an approximately uniform distribution of calls throughout the day, with the exception of markedly decreased incidence from approximately 3:00 a.m. to 6:00 a.m.

[4] The data sampling interval period of 10 days across the 2002 data was chosen to ensure a range of weekdays and weekend days would be included in the final sample of 36 days.

4. FINDINGS

4.1 A Socio-technical framework for EMS

Figure 29-1 provides a high-level overview of EMS systems in rural Minnesota. The framework helps to define the EMS system along several key strata: organizations, technology, and policy.[5] A brief summary of each layer of the framework follows.

- Organizations – The framework illustrates some of the public and private organizations involved in the Minnesota EMS and the general interorganizational relationships between these organizations.
- Technology – The top layer of the framework illustrates some of the essential networks and communications technologies used by Minnesota EMS organizations to carry out their individual and interorganizational functions.
- Policy – In order for EMS interorganizational relationships (i.e. partnerships, joint ventures, etc…) to succeed, policies need to be developed that facilitate the interorganizational use of new and existing communications technologies. The overarching EMS technology-related policies currently under development in the state are illustrated (e911, 800 Mhz radio).

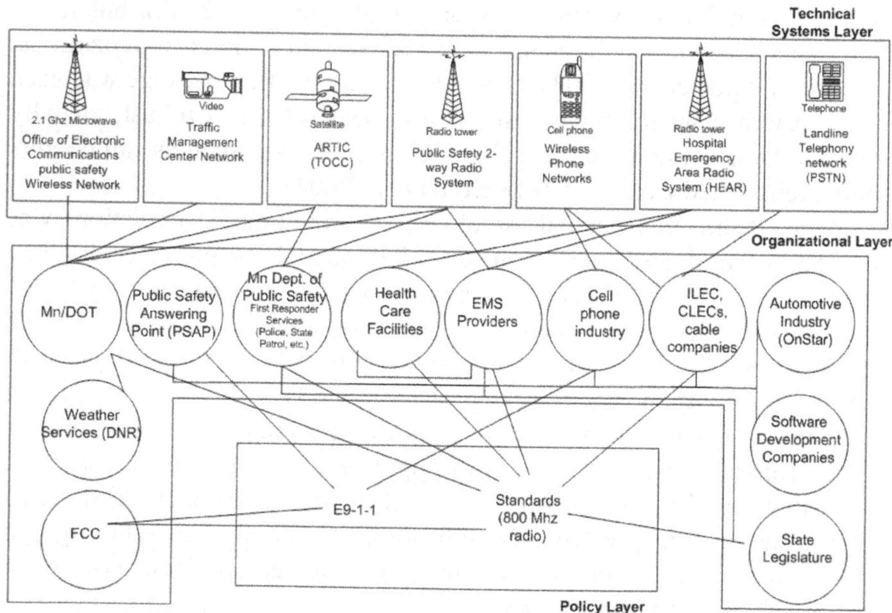

Figure 29-1. EMS in Rural Minnesota

[5] For more detail on state-wide EMS framework, see Horan and Schooley (2005).

4.2 Wireless Emergency Call Routing

While this general system architecture is useful in defining system strata, for the purposes of developing the ontology, it was necessary to translate the overall EMS system architectures into a process that traces the information flows across the EMS system. Such an evaluation occurred through the process of interviewing representatives in Brainerd, Minnesota. Figure 29-2 below shows the wireless mayday call routing procedure in rural Minnesota designed for use in the preliminary design phase of the ontology. The information flow is charted from the originating emergency call to the 911 center (PSAP) and out to various emergency service providers. The linkages of this procedure to the ensuing conceptual and factual ontology are outlined below.

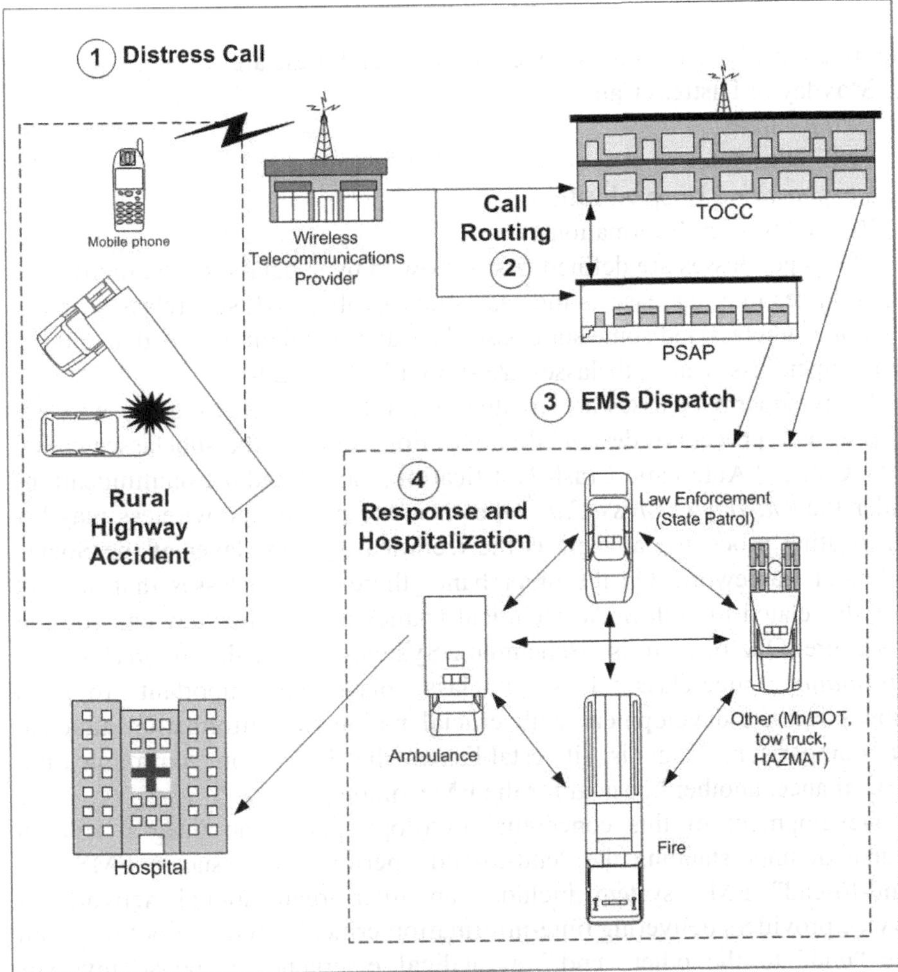

Figure 29-2. Wireless Mayday Call Routing Procedure in Rural Minnesota

4.3 Conceptual Ontology for Rural EMS

The socio-technical framework and the wireless mayday call routing procedure described above represents an architectural blueprint for conceptual EMS ontology. All or some of the components and their relationships in this architecture can be translated into an ontological framework. Figures 29-1 and 29-2 are used as the input for the development of the conceptual ontology for EMS using Protégé 2000. At the highest level, this conceptual EMS ontology provides a simple visual representation of the complex and inter-organizational EMS process through its superclass/subclass schema. Further defining subclasses for the knowledgebase implementation where instances (data) are linked with classes produced a comprehensive class hierarchy.

The first step in developing the ontology is to establish classes. As a general proposition, these classes followed the process identified in Figure 29-2. Five super-classes were defined and these are:

1. Mayday or Distress Call,
2. Call Routing,
3. EMS Dispatch,
4. Response and Hospitalization,
5. Related System Information.

The superclasses are defined first followed by subclasses. The number of superclasses may increase as the case study evolves. All superclasses had at least one subclass and some subclasses had additional classes. A detailed list of all superclasses and subclasses are shown in Table 29-1.

Many super/subclasses are created as a manifestation from the wireless mayday call procedure described above. For example, the subclasses called "911 Calls," "Automatic Crash Notification," and "Radio Communication" under the *Mayday/Distress Call* superclass are part of the wireless mayday call routing procedure as well as the technical systems layer of the Socio-technical framework. On the other hand, there are subclasses that are not directly related to both Socio-technical framework and mayday call routing procedure. One of them is "Benchmark Systems" under the *Related System Information* superclass. This subclass plays an important role in knowledgebase development with crucial nationwide information attached for comparison. That is, it establishes the basis for communicating performance, another key goal for the EMS ontology.

Development of this conceptual ontology played an integral role in course of understanding the "end-to-end" performance issue in EMS. An "end-to-end" EMS system includes an inter-organizational network of service providers delivering time-information critical services. Looking from one "end" to the other "end," a medical emergency response involves multiple government agencies and non-government organizations, from the time an emergency communication (911 phone call) is made, answered by a PSAP, dispatched to public agency resource (fire, police, ambulance), and treated at the scene and/or ambulanced to a hospital. This conceptual ontology codifies this "end-to-end" perspective and facilitates testing a performance-based ontology, through both its factual instantiation as well as fact-based simulation.

Table 29-1. Rural Minnesota Wireless EMS Classes

Superclass	Subclass (1st level)	Subclass (2nd level)
Mayday/Distress Call	*Cellular Phone Call*	*Accidental Calls*
		Dropped Calls
		Emergency Calls
	Automatic Crash Notification	-
	Radio Communication	-
Call Routing	*Network Routing*	-
	Routing (Forwarding) Between Dispatching Agencies	-
EMS Dispatch	*PSAP Dispatch*	-
	TOCC Dispatch	-
	Other Dispatchers	-
Response & Hospitalization	*Response Coordination and Hospitalization*	*Assigning EMS Dispatch*
		Arrival to Scene
		Clearing Emergency/Hospitalization
	FARS Data	*Accidents Data*
		Injury Data
		Fatality Data
Related System Information	*Technology Deployment*	*Benchmark Systems*
		Wireless Network Coverage
		Wireless E9-1-1 Deployment
	Data Management	*Data*
		IT Management

4.4 EMS Ontology Instances

Following the formation of ontology class schema, data obtained through field interviews and subsequent analysis were entered into the knowledge base. For some classes, data were not available and no instances are recorded. Nevertheless, since the ontological construction of Protégé is in place, data may be entered at any time. The collected data is then integrated and matched with the class schema of the conceptual ontology. The result was a factual ontology, shown in Table 29-2, that also shows some of the

Table 29-2. Conceptual and Factual Wireless EMS System Ontology

Wireless EMS Process	Conceptual Wireless EMS Ontology	Factual Ontology Brainerd, 2002
Mayday Call	➢ Mayday Call o *Cellular phone call* o *Automatic crash notification* o *Radio communication*	Around 21,745 wireless calls in 2002 at Brainerd (Baxter) TOCC
Call Routing	➢ Call Routing to EMS Dispatcher o *Routing delay* o *Third party routing (GM OnStar)*	Two of seven PSAPs in Brainerd (MSP-D2800) accept all local wireless 911 calls
EMS Dispatch	o Mayday Call Response o *Response delay* o Dispatch o Data Management	Brainerd PSAP made 36,488 dispatches; TOCC made 7,215 dispatches
Response & Hospitalization	➢ Response to Incident o *Response delay* ➢ Response Coordination ➢ Hospitalization ➢ Fatalities	71 Fatalities in Brainerd (MSP District 2800).
Related System Information	➢ E-911 Technology o *Network based* o *Satellite based* ➢ Wireless Coverage ➢ E-911 Deployment	Phase I – 100% complete Phase II – 33% complete

data elements of constructed knowledgebase. In this case, the factual ontology pertains to the TOCC activities located in Brainerd, Minnesota.

The process of data and/or knowledge entry is based on the previously defined slots and slot-value restrictions, relationships between classes, and properties of these relationships. Protégé 2000 uses its *Slots* and *Forms* tabs to enforce such restrictions and relationships. These tabs provide a default layout for capturing and storing data within the knowledgebase and during factual ontology development, and the research team based on the characteristics and applicability of the data at hand formulates them. Data findings used in knowledgebase are explained below.

4.5 Building a Knowledge Base

Protégé software enabled researchers to incorporate both conceptual and factual ontology of rural Minnesota wireless EMS under one ontological knowledgebase. The Protégé system created is called Minnesota Rural EMS. This system allowed researchers to explore conceptual aspects of the actual EMS process (See ontological class schema in Figure 29-3) and extract factual data reports (See Figure 29-4 presenting an instance from the knowledge base) when needed.

A factual ontology is an inclusive reflection of the knowledge, which is populated by recording the statistical and qualitative data under instances. Such knowledgebase data includes, for example, FARS data providing the official fatality statistics for accidents, wireless enhanced 9-1-1 deployments in seven MSP districts, and EMS response times measured in minutes. Moreover, this data provided the basis for a simulation of end-to-end performance using ARENA.

At the end of the knowledgebase development process, HTML files for the Minnesota Rural EMS ontology created by using Protege's HTML generator[6]. This files were posted on the Web to make the results of the ontological–knowledge base accessible to all interested parties and available for future research enquiries.

4.6 Using Ontology to Simulate Performance

Figure 29-5 provides an overview of the ARENA simulation model that was constructed using a sample of the data from the Brainerd Factual Ontology. Each of the regional PSAPs will directly dispatch ambulance, fire, city police, or tow trucks, following the same rules employed by the TOCC emergency services. During the typical scenario, events and calls are generated according to the rules in the preceding discussion of the typical

6 Samples of HTML files generated by Protégé can be found at: http://www.cgu.edu/pages/1534.asp.

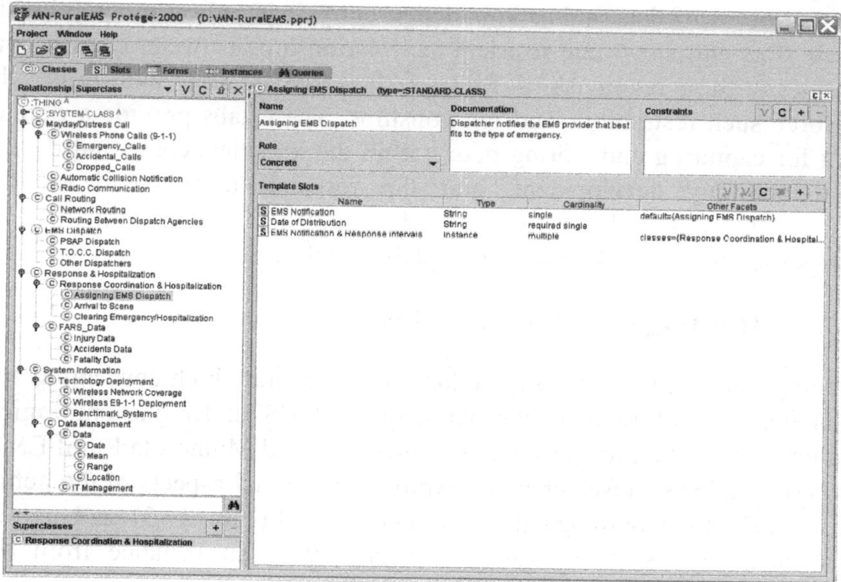

Figure 29-3. Protege 2000 interface showing classes of the ontology

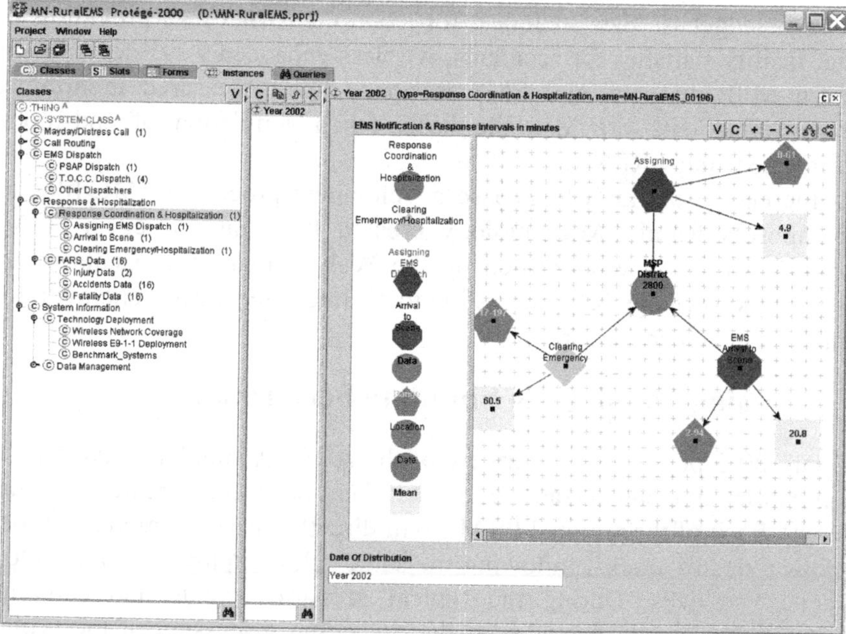

Figure 29-4. A knowledge base instance for Response & Hospitalization class

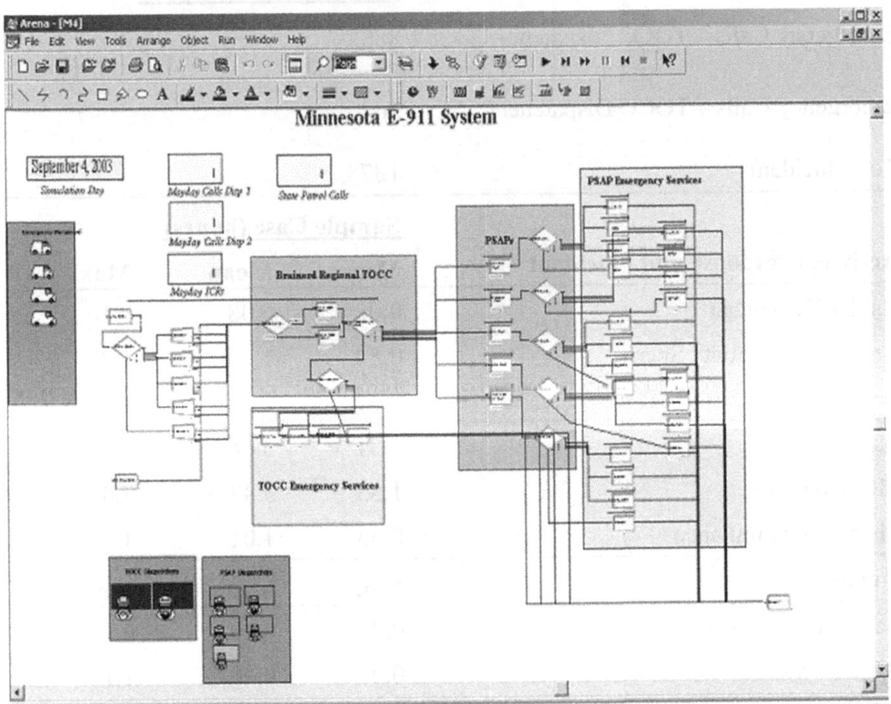

Figure 29-5. Overview of ARENA modeling parameters for factual data simulation

case. Key results of the 14-day run of this simulation scenario are included in Table 29-3.

Several observations can be drawn from these results. First, a number of system bottlenecks can be clearly identified. In the model, TOCC dispatchers spend a minimum of 1.2 minutes handling a dispatch, and an average of 4.8 minutes per dispatch. The Brainerd TOCC dispatcher may be able to begin dispatching the necessary services immediately, but the *Sample Case* may take nearly an hour to dispatch the needed services. Moreover, in the visual model, it becomes clear that this dispatching event is tightly coupled with response service, as demonstrated by subsequent queues in Morrison Ambulance. Conversely, the long queues in dispatching Department of Transportation vehicles (MN/DOT) are not coupled to any subsequent events.

Table 29-3. Representative outcomes of sample case

	Sample Case – 14 days		
Emergency Calls – TOCC Dispatcher 1	883		
Emergency Calls – TOCC Dispatcher 2	264		
Total Incidents	187		
	Sample Case (hours)		
Activity / response unit / incident	**Min**	**Mean**	**Max**
Baxter Dispatcher 1	0.02	0.08	0.16
Crow Wing County Sheriff	0.54	1.16	1.90
Baxter Tow	0.61	1.18	1.95
Mn/DOT	1.31	3.64	7.61
Morrison Fire	1.83	3.47	7.09
Morrison Ambulance	0.63	1.01	1.56
Queue	**Min**	**Mean**	**Max**
Baxter Dispatcher 1	0.0	0.20	0.92
Baxter Tow	0.0	0.06	1.18
Crow Wing County Sheriff	0.0	0.11	2.19
Mn/DOT	0.0	0.15	3.54

5. DISCUSSION

The ultimate goal of this research is to create a new means to measure, improve, and communicate about the performance of systems such as emergency medical services (EMS). Such an ontology seems particularly timely, as interest in EMS services continues to grow. With several hundred million dollars identified for building local emergency response capability (FHWA, 2002), an ontology can play an important role in organizing, documenting and communicating about system performance using a web-based, visually oriented system. Further, reporting is typically recorded in various types of paper or computer forms by individual agencies. Though there are recent national efforts to construct formalized methods and standards for emergency response reporting into a centralized database using XML and Internet protocols (see NEMSIS, 2004), there is much work to be done at the local level in terms of accepting and implementing such new systems.

This study can aid such an effort by demonstrating the use of ontological-knowledge bases to aggregate performance data from multiple organizations and to aid in diagnosing the existence or non-existence of key data elements in each step of the rural wireless EMS process. Such a system could be a useful step to designing an integrated approach to EMS performance reporting. While there are a variety of approaches available for instantiating ontology, this project demonstrated the utility of platform-independent approaches such as Protégé. Protégé was effective during this creation of a customized domain knowledge-based system because of its ease of use. Protégé capabilities for web posting also attend to the need for communicating the end results. Although Protégé supports a more text-based web appearance, the ability to provide a web-based posting of conceptual and factual ontology can facilitate discussions for further modifications to ontology that will lead to the reuse of the system and the knowledge it already contains.

Finally, this provides demonstration of how an ontology-knowledgebase can be used to track and simulate end-to-end performance. While governmental evaluations traditionally involve extensive summative assessments, such an approach brings the performance information into the organizational information system. Such an approach represents an innovation in information systems to improve governmental processes; especially those that transcend traditional organizational boundaries. While several crises management simulation developments are underway (see Jain and McLean, 2003), our endeavor is noteworthy in its use of "off-the-shelf" ontology and business process software as a platform for looking EMS performance, both extant and simulated. The research team continues to evolve this research, including conduct of additional simulation performance under various scenarios (included typical and crises) and calibration with on the ground performance. It is hoped that such an approach will lead to a robust understanding of EMS performance, and position the ontology to play an important role in organizing, documenting and communicating about results.

ACKNOWLEDGEMENTS

The authors gratefully acknowledge the support provided by the U.S. Department of Transportation, the Minnesota Department of Transportation, and the ITS Institute at the Center for Transportation Studies, University of Minnesota. Our research would not have been possible without their research and support. Earlier version of this research was presented at AMCIS 2004. Related findings on the EMS architecture and case study analysis were published in Horan and Schooley (2005) and Horan et al. (2005).

REFERENCES

Arens, Y., and Rosenbloom, P., October 2002, Responding to the Unexpected, A Report of the Feb.27-March 1, 2002, workshop in New York, NY.

Black, L.J., Cresswell, A.M., Pardo, T.A., Thompson, F., Canestraro, D.S., Cook, M., Luna, L.F., Marinez, I.J., Andersen, D.F., Richardson, G.P., 2003, A Dynamic Theory of Collaboration: A Structural Approach to Facilitating Intergovernmental Use of Information Technology, *Proceedings of the 36th Hawaii International Conference on System Science,* Kona, Hawaii.

CTIA wirclcss 911 call stats, 2002, http://www.wow-com.com/industry/stats/e911/.

Davis, S., 2002, Virtual emergency operations, *Risk Management*. 49(7):46-52.

Department of Administration, Minnesota Statewide 911 Program, 2003, "Statewide 911 Emergency Telephone Service Program Report".

Federal Highway Administration, 2002, http://www.fhwa.dot.gov/pressroom/test020207.htm.

Grosso, W.E., Eriksson, H., Fergerson, R.W., Gennari, J.H., Tu, S.W., and Musen, M.A., 1999, Knowledge Modeling at the Millennium: The Design and Evolution of Protégé 2000, in: *12th Workshop on Knowledge Acquisition, Modeling, and Management*, Banff, Alberta.

Gruber, T., 1993, A translation approach to portable ontology specifications, *Knowledge Acquisition,* 5(2):199-220.

Gruninger, M., and Lee J., 2002, Ontology applications and design, *CACM.* 45(2):39-41.

Hale, J., 1997, A layered communication architecture for the support of crisis response, *JMIS,* 14(1):235-255.

Holsapple, C., and Joshi, K., 2002, A collaborative approach to ontology design, *CACM,* 45(2):42-47.

Horan, T., McCabe, D., Burkhard, R., and Schooley B., 2005, Performance information systems for emergency response: Field examination and simulation of end-to-end rural response systems, *JHSEM,* 2(1): Article 4. http://www.bepress.com/jhsem/vol2/iss1/4.

Horan, T. and Schooley, B., 2005, Interorganizational emergency medical services: Case study of rural wireless deployment and management, *ISF*, 7(2):2005 forthcoming.

Jain, S., and McLean, C., 2003, "Modeling and Simulation for Emergency Response: Workshop Report, Standards, and Tools." Washington D.C.: U.S. Department of Commerce.

Jurisica, I. J. and Mylopoulos, E.Y., 1999, Using ontologies for knowledge management: A computational perspective, presented at *Annual Conference of the American Society for Information Science,* Washington, DC, 482-496.

Kelton, W.D., Sadowski, R.P., and Sturrock, D.T., 2004, *Simulation with Aren,* 3rd ed., McGraw Hill, New York, NY.

Leroy, G., Tolle, K. M. and Chen, H., 1999, Customizable and Ontology-Enhanced Medical Information Retrieval Interfaces, paper presented at the *IMIA WG6 Triennial Conference on Natural Language and Medical Concept Representation*, Phoenix, Arizona.

Markus, M.L., Majchrzak, A., and Gasser, L., 2002, A design theory for systems that support emergent knowledge processes, *MISQ*, 26(3):179-212.

McGuinness, D. L., 2002, Ontologies Come of Age, in D. Fensel, J.Hendler, H. Lieberman, and W. Wahlster (Eds.), *Spinning the Semantic Web: Bringing the World Wide Web to Its Full Potential,* Cambridge, MA.: MIT Press.

National Center for Statistics and Analysis (NCSA), 2002, U.S. Department of Transportation, National Center for Statistics and Analysis Fatality Analysis Reporting System (FARS) Web-Based Encyclopedia, http://www-fars.nhtsa.dot.gov.

National Emergency Medical Services Information System (NEMSIS), 2004, NEMSIS General Fact Sheet, , http://www.nemsis.org/PDFs/factsheetfinal.pdf.

Noy, N.F., W. Grosso, W., and M. Musen, 2000, Knowledge-Acquisition Interfaces for Domain Experts: An Empirical Evaluation of Protege-2000, paper presented at *Twelfth International Conference on Software Engineering and Knowledge Engineering* (SEKE2000), Chicago, Illinois.

Perrow, C., 2000, Extreme Events: A Framework for Organizing, Integrating and Ensuring The Public Value of Research, paper prepared for *Extreme Events: Developing a Research Agenda for the 21st Century*, Boulder, Colorado.

Protégé 2000 website http://protege.stanford.edu/.

Smith, B., 2003, Ontology and information systems, forthcoming in *Stanford Encyclopedia of Philosophy*, http://ontology.buffalo.edu/ontology(PIC).pdf.

Sterman, J., 2000, *Business Dynamics: Systems Thinking and Modeling for a Complex World*, McGraw-Hill/Irwin.

Sussman, J. M., 2002, Representing the transportation/environmental system in Mexico City as a CLIOS. paper presented at the *5th Annual US-Mexico Workshop on Air Quality*, Ixtapan de la Sal, Mexico.

Turoff, M., Chumer, M., Van de Walle, B., and Yao, X., 2004, The design of a dynamic emergency response management information System (DERMIS), *JITTA*, 5(4):1-36.

Chapter 30

DEVELOPMENT OF AN ONTOLOGY-BASED SMART CARD SYSTEM REFERENCE ARCHITECTURE

Interoperability based on ontology concept

István Mezgár and Zoltán Kincses
Computer and Automation Research Institute,Hungarian Academy of Sciences, Budapest, 1111 Kende u. 13-17, Hungary. E-mail: {mezgar, kincses}@sztaki.hu

Abstract: In the information society the security of information during access and communication has of basic importance. Smart cards (SC) can integrate security services and the actual application functions, so they are perfect tool to fulfill the role of the key of information society. As there is extremely high number of different smart card applications developed individually, connecting these systems, their interoperability is a growing problem. An additional problem is that the combination of functions on one card needs the thorough configuration of the smart card software. Because of the frequent changes in the SC applications during the life cycle of the card, there is a more frequent need for the reconfiguration of the card software as well. A structured, general description, reference architecture of the smart card system elements and the possible relations among them could support the interoperability and configuration/reconfiguration in a great extent. The chapter gives a short overview on smart card systems and applications, and introduces ontology – based smart card reference architecture and an smart card attack tree.

Key words: Attack tree; ontology; reference architecture; smart cards

1. INTRODUCTION

All information systems are based on human beings (users), therefore taking into consideration basic human aspects while approaching the information management, has of vital importance. Trust and confidence are essential for the users of the network-connected systems, for the Information and Knowledge Society. The lack of trustworthy security services is a major obstacle to the use of electronic and mobile technologies (e&mTechnologies) in private, in business (B2B) as well as in public services. Trust is intimately linked to consumers' rights, like security, identification, authentication, privacy, and confidentiality.

There is a strong need for a secure tool that can fulfill the above listed functions connected to trustworthy services. Smart card (SC) technology can offer a solution for current problems of secure communication and data handling with a reasonable privacy by fulfilling simultaneously the main demands of identification, security and authenticity besides the functions of the actual application.

The different practical application possibilities, the continuously growing user demands generated many of different smart card system philosophies and realizations. The needed software and hardware configuration and reconfiguration (in the future on-line, real-time SW reconfiguration) requirements, the interoperability demands among these systems, and the standardization efforts supporting the previous two demands became one of the most important issues for smart card manufacturers, providers and users.

The chapter gives an overview of the research work that aims to develop the General Reference Architecture for Smart Card systems (GRASC) that can help the work to solve the problems in the fields of configuration/reconfiguration, interoperability and standardization of smart card systems. In order to explain the complexity of the problem, first the main characteristics of smart cards systems are introduced. The challenge of interoperability is presented as well. In the next part the prototype ontology development is described. As the final step the introduction of the reference architecture is presented.

This General Reference Architecture for Smart Card systems is an ontology-based multi-view, multi-layer, and multi-element description of SC functions, SW and HW systems and applications. This representation will be integrated, unified, consistent, and - what is very important - dynamic, as it will also describe the logic connections among the elements.

2. BASICS OF SMART CARDS

2.1 Smart Card Hardware and Software

The basic idea was patented in 1974 and during the last 30 years smart cards became important elements for many fields of security and communication systems. Smart card is an integrated circuit containing a microprocessor, volatile and non-volatile memory, and associated software, packaged and embedded in a carrier. The integrated circuit is a single chip incorporating CPU, RAM, ROM, and programmable non-volatile memory (usually EEPROM). The carrier is typically made of plastic and usually conforms to ISO 7810 and 7813 – Identification Cards, but may have the smaller size of a GSM (global system for mobile communications) subscriber identification module (SIM). The chip is embedded in a module incorporating the communication channels (with contacts in accordance with ISO 7816 or contactless in accordance with ISO 14443). The requirements cover the smart card's integrated circuit and operating software, but do not include specific applications. So, smart card itself is a complex tool as it can be defined as a little computer with memory, CPU, different interfaces and operation system.

The physical shape of the smart card can be various, but the functionality and transaction-flow possibilities of the tool determines its role in a system and the possibility of integral and consistent description of the relations with other elements of the system.

2.2 Types of Smart Cards

Smart cards can be classified from different aspects, like operation mode of the card, number of functions, etc. The basic types of smart cards are the following ones:

- Memory card,
- Microprocessor card,
- Multifunctional card,
- Hybrid card (magnetic stripe + chip),
- Contactless card,
- Combi-cards (contact and contactless card),
- Optical card.

Multi-functional cards can integrate different applications and different functions as well. The SIM card in the mobile phones has also data storage and in some cases a secure communication role through encryption keys (WIM, Wireless Identity Module), generated and stored in the internal memory of the integrated circuit.

2.3 Elements of Smart Card Systems

The characteristics of these elements can be combined in many versions, and as an addition the application software have nearly "infinite" versions. Smart cards are only the most spectacular part of the whole system; the field system contains the different smart card readers, devices, and the background elements for communication, operation and storage (computers, different software and databases). There are different versions of co-operative operation of the system elements, e.g. there are special readers, which can accept more than one card simultaneously.

2.4 Application of Smart Cards

According to the original smart card concept the smart card, can store data (e.g. profiles, balances, personal data), provides cryptographic services (e.g. authentication, confidentiality, integrity), is a microcomputer, is small and personal, is a secure device.

From the above list it is obvious that there must be very broad field of applications of such a device. In the followings a reduced list of application is given, grouped according to the main fields, but of course there are far more possibilities to use smart cards. Some existing main fields of smart card applications: communication – GSM, payphones; transportation – public traffic, parking; retail – sale of goods using electronic purses, credit / debit, vending machines, loyalty programs; e-commerce – sale of information, sale of products, sale of tickets, reservations, e-banking – access to accounts, to do transactions, shares; healthcare – insurance data, personal data, personal file, government – identification, passport, driving license, office – physical access, network access, time registration; secure e-mail & Web applications.

One of the most important and complex application is using the smart card as security card. Smart cards provide opportunities for improving security of critical infrastructures, both from a physical and logical perspective. Because they are capable of performing cryptographic functions, they can perform important security services such as securely storing digital signatures, holding public key credentials, and authenticating a claimed identity based on biometric data. As such, smart cards are a crucial element in a range of current and expected critical applications and programs.

The three main threats that a security card has to prevent are the following:

- *Confidentiality*: unauthorized disclosure of information.
- *Integrity*: unauthorized modification of information.
- *Availability*: denial of service.

There are additional threats also, like:

- *Authenticity*: unauthorized use of service.
- *Non-repudiation*: replay attack.

The three main threats are usually mentioned as CIA. In Table 30-1 the threats and controls have been summarized in a structured way.

The main benefits of smart card in the different applications are that offers security access and communication defends personal rights – privacy, decreases administration, it is flexible, user-friendly, portable.

2.5 Life-Cycle of Smart Cards

The lifecycle model of smart cards is in brief as follows: Chip manufacturer → Card manufacturer (chip embossing) → Raw cards (initialization) → Initialized cards (load data) → Issued Cards (logos, printing, personal data) → Personalized cards (loading applications) → End user → Card SW reconfiguration according to the actual application. The possible connections and the lifecycle of the data and information are extremely complex.

2.5.1 Configuration

As it can be seen from the previous subchapters, the structure/configuration of a multi-function smart card can be really complex. Configuration means an arrangement of functional units according to their nature, number, and main characteristics. The elements of hardware, software both of the card and the card reader belong to the configuration. The configuration affects system performance in a great extent.

The very broad field covered by the different applications needs different solutions for the expected functions of SCs. The way of identification (able bodied, or handicapped), the different encrypting algorithms (strong, weak encryption) need different HW and SW solutions/configurations of the SC, the methods that are applied for the same function can be very different, that can resulted big number of combinations for a complex solution.

From this complex space of solutions has to be selected/configured the actual smart card, taking into consideration of the different aspects (memory and speed limitations, etc.). It is easy to imagine the complexity of a card can be used as health card, passport, bankcard, entry card, log-in card, etc.

To be able to handle this very complex configuration task it is needed a good classification both of the HW, SW elements, and the functions, the applications and the life-cycle-phases, describing the connections and limitations among them. Another demand is to have standardized interfaces to handle the different application software (interoperability), and standardized HW building blocks.

The provider of the SC application does basic configuration (initialization) of the SC the first and the card issuer accomplishes the personalization.

2.5.2 Reconfiguration

As an additional problem the set of applications of a smart card can alter during its life cycle, so the configuration has to be modified. In these cases applications have to be added or removed, namely the smart card has to be reconfigured probably several times. While talking about reconfiguration it is meant always software reconfiguration, in most cases for multifunction cards.

From customer's viewpoint the ideal solution would be such a multi-application smart card that can be used for identification, communication, for secure access of physical or binary entities and elements of different databases. While using a multi-application card there can be many reasons of reconfiguration e.g. the owner wants to use a stronger encryption, the user intends to add a new application, or simple wants to update a SW.

The user could do these reconfigurations itself on his/her PC at home, or at a bank terminal, to avoid long administrative processes. Of course the appropriate security measures should have be done for this process. As GSM telephones use smart cards called SIM cards to store subscriber and account information, the functions of this card could be extended and the phones could be used as mobile personal terminals. In this case the reconfiguration could be even faster.

For this very high level flexibility the SC structures have to be very clear, and the whole system has to work very reliable. The way out from this problematic situation is to develop the flexible reconfiguration possibility supported by reference architecture with common standards in the background.

2.6 Security of Smart Cards

Based on the literature it is possible to enumerate and understand the attacks on smart cards. These attacks can be represented in a tree based on the three main threats against confidentiality, integrity and availability. As a next step the threats can be matched with the security controls (preventive, detective, corrective) to produce a PreDeCo/CIA matrix. Security auditors use this matrix and a smart card system can be audited by using such a concept as well, to discover whether there is any lack of control of main threats. A general matrix is shown below on Table 30-1.

Table 30-1. PreDeCo/CIA matrix of smartcards

Threats / Controls	Confidentiality Unauthorized access of sensitive information	Integrity Manipulation, replacement of data or application	Availability Denial of service, blocking, damage
Preventive	Set access rights, encryption (encoding)	Encryption (hash, digital signature)	Multiplied resources, Reserves (stock)
Detective	Monitoring the access rights, analyzing access logs (accountability)	Integrity checker, Data format and interpretation standards	Sensors
Corrective	Preventive controls for the future (near nothing for the past)	Rollback, Use of backup	New resources, Exclusion of illegal communication

2.7 The Interoperability Problem

It is difficult to deploy large-scale smart card systems due to a lack of interoperability among different types of smart cards and without assurances of interoperability, owners of the systems would be "locked" into a single vendor. Thus, the issue of interoperability had to be addressed before significant investments are made. Additionally, smart card systems have historically been driven by requirements arising from specific application domains such as banking, telecommunications, and health care. This has led to the development of smart cards that are customized to the specific application requirements of each domain, with little interoperability between domains. These vertically-structured smart card systems are expensive, difficult to maintain, and often based on proprietary technology.

The configuration and the interoperability of such complex systems set up a very high demand from the system developer aspect. There are three big interoperability projects for smart cards each with the same basic goal, but with different approaches. In Europe the "Open Smart Card Infrastructure for Europe" (OSCIE) project, in Japan the "NICSS-Framework Scheme", and in the USA the "Government Smart Card Interoperability Specification" (GSC-IS). In the followings a very short summary of the listed projects is given, just to place the work the chapter is dealing with.

2.7.1 Open Smart Card Infrastructure for Europe

In Europe the interoperability efforts for smart cards are going on in the "Open Smart Card Infrastructure for Europe" project (2003, 2005). Inside this project the "Global Interoperability Framework" (GIF) part focuses on the interoperability framework.

The primary objective of the GIF is to deal with interoperability at the level of e-Identification, e-Authentication and e-Signature (IAS) between different smart card schemes in Europe. It provides both smart card schemes and e-service providers with necessary concepts and guidance. Topics covered by the GIF include all tools required for access to different e-services and securing transactions over different networks (including over the Internet), implementation of the special "high-end" security requirements, preparing information systems to exchange messages and organizing the operation of this IAS interoperability.

The following elements are out of the scope of this framework:

- Application level services that use IAS services,
- Interoperability at application service level (i.e. between services),
- Encryption using the card holder's security keys, for data confidentiality,
- Integration with services that do not use the IAS services.

Because the framework is open, not all the possibilities resulting from the higher levels of the models introduced are worked through into proposed implementations. At intervals throughout the framework, restrictions are therefore introduced before proceeding further.

The security requirement for the GIF is that security is to be 'high level', i.e. strong, in order to be able to deliver strong IAS services to service providers in both e-government and e-business sectors. The framework does not deliver explicit rules for security, first because other groups are active in this area, and second because the work on interoperability specifications will automatically bring about a leveling up of scheme security.

The interfaces to these IAS services are part of the framework. Both the internal interfaces within each scheme and the interoperability interfaces between schemes are included. However, this framework does not include detailed interface specifications, as they are the responsibility of the schemes.

2.7.2 NICSS-Framework Scheme

In Japan the interoperability activities on smart cards are going on in the NICSS (2005) group (The Next generation IC Card System Study). The Essence of NICSS-Framework Scheme is the common specification to integrate multi-application Smart Card system independently of card type / card operating system (NMDA, MULTOS, VOP (JAVA), etc.).

Main goals of NICSS are:

1. To distribute Services (Application) via the network securely after issuing a card.
2. To realize Card Service (Business) easily without a service provider have to issue a card.
3. To have a mechanism where a card issuer shares the cost of issue/operation with users.

Preconditions of NICSS:

1. To be able to apply to public services such as a residential service.
2. Regardless of area and system mounting, a public service can be run.
3. To provide consistency with card platforms recognized as de facto.
4. Contactless card use (including combination type card).
5. To support PKI.
6. To separate a card issuer's role from a service provider's and stipulate unified operation between both.

2.7.3 Government Smart Card Interoperability Specification

The National Institute of Standards and Technology (NIST) have been dealing with smart cards technology standardization in the USA for more then 15 years. NIST has already launched several studies and different other materials on smart card interoperability as the importance of data exchange among different government SC systems became necessary. NIST has also published an analysis of existing biometric and smart card interoperability standards with respect to their ability to support integrated smart card-biometric systems. As a further need the standards for additional technologies – such as contactless, biometrics, and optical stripe media – as well as integration with PKI have been arisen, to ensure broad interoperability among Federal SC systems.

NIST (2005) published the GSC-IS, Version 2.1 in July 2003 as NISTIR 6887, 2003 Edition. This document contains already the latest development as provide support for biometrics, contactless smart card technology, and Public Key Infrastructure.

The Government Smart Card Interoperability Specification has limited scope and applicability range. The GSC-IS specification defines an architectural model for interoperable smart card service provider modules, compatible with both file system cards and virtual machine cards. The GSC-IS includes a Basic Services Interface (BSI), which addresses interoperability of a core set of smart card services at the interface layer between client applications and smart card service provider modules. The GSC-IS also defines a mechanism at the card edge layer for interoperation with smart cards that use a wide variety of APDU (Application Programming Data Unit) sets, including both file system cards and virtual machine cards.

Interoperability is not addressed for the following areas:

- Smart card initialization
- Cryptographic key management
- Communications between smart cards and card readers
- Communications between smart card readers and host computer systems.

3. RESEARCH GOALS AND BACKGROUND

The main goal of the research was to develop a reference architecture for smart card systems to give a complete and well-defined general frame (applying the standards, the ready-to-use of new technologies) for the practical applications. By using the reference architecture the actual individual architectures can be configured and/or reconfigured easily, and through the applied technologies and communication protocols they are platform independent.

The reconfiguration adds to this challenge an additional layer. An ontology based reference architecture, or framework of smart card systems can help to generate a good overview of the problems and what is more important, a good structure of solutions.

Smart card related framework developments concentrate on the applications. In order to develop a harmonized, a well-balanced smart card system it would be good to take into consideration all aspects of possibilities (HW, SW, security, etc.). Talking about a "balanced" system means that the needed functions of the actual application are realized with the optimal HW and SW tools and services. "Optimal" means to select the proper technical parameters with a combination of an economic financial solution. As an example; a certain optimal security level is needed for the functions to be realized in an application. This defines several technical parameters (e.g. the type of the smart card and the reader), the internal process of the service and several additional parameters.

In case of defining more parameters of a smart card system at the same time, to find a technical and financial optimal solution is a real complex task. The process can be represented by a graph in which each node describes a possible solution of a requirement. Walking along the edges of the graph the nodes on the route will define the full smart card system configuration. As there are many possible routes, rather solutions, the selection of the parameters and elements needs a deeper decision process, so it has to be supported theoretically.

The elaboration of the general reference architecture of smart cards has two basic steps:

- development of a smart card system ontology,
- based on the ontology the general reference architecture and the reference model can be developed.

3.1 Direct Reasons of Reference Architecture Development

The broad field covered by the different applications needs different solutions for the expected functions of smart cards. The way of identification (both able-bodied and handicapped), the different encrypting algorithms (protocols and key lengths) need different HW and SW solutions/configurations and data content of the smart card. The set of applications of a smart card can alter during its life cycle several times, and in these cases the SW configuration has to be modified. Applications have to be added or removed, namely, the software of the smart card has to be reconfigured in these cases. Another demand is to have standardized interfaces to handle the different application software (interoperability), and standardized HW building blocks. The representation structure can be a reference architecture that has its theoretical base. All of these will help the "write once, run everywhere" interoperability efforts as well.

3.2 Ontology Development Reasons

In philosophy the original meaning of ontology is "the branch of metaphysical enquiry concerned with the study of existence itself". Recently the term ontology is used in artificial intelligence, in the context "an ontology is an explicit specification of a conceptualization" (Gruber, 1993). The development of engineering ontologies has a practical goal, to describe the knowledge about the selected field in a structured way taking into consideration the knowledge levels and the possible connections among the knowledge elements (Jones, D. et al., 1998). The ontology also can help in identifying requirements and defining a specification for any type of information system.

Ontology has been selected as a conceptual modeling technique in order to be able to connect to other smart card system related ontology and knowledge based systems that have been developed to solve sub-problems of configuration/reconfiguration.

There are different methodologies and tools available on the market for building ontologies. Some of them provide a complete set for building, maintaining and utilizing ontology, these are the suites. Others have open source and there are tools that can be deployed onto Java J2EE architecture, which makes an ontology -based system more robust and flexible. Every ontology tool has its own characteristics and advantages (Karlsruhe, 2005; OntoEdit, 2005; Ontopia KS, 2005; OilED, 2005). Description of ontology methodologies are introduced e.g. in (Jones, D. et al., 1998).

4. ONTOLOGY DEVELOPMENT

4.1 Basics of Smart Card Ontology

The smart card ontology, this special structured representation is the guarantee for the full description of entities (applications and system elements), their levels and the logical connections between the levels and the entities. The steps of developing the smart card ontology are the followings:

The analysis of a problem space with the goal of ontology development is not a closed and fully defined process. The IDEF5 method has been selected as a main line to assist in the creation, modification and maintenance of the ontology (KBSI, 1994) as it is a general procedure with a set of guidelines.

The main steps of the development methodology are:

- Definition of goals and organization give the purpose, the viewpoint, and context for the ontology development project. The goal defines the limits of the ontology and specifies parts of the systems that must be included or excluded.
- Knowledge, information and data collection mean that the basic data needed for ontology development are collected using different techniques including protocol analysis and expert interview.
- Analysis of collected materials in order to build the ontology is extracted from the results of data collection. First, the objects of interest in the domain are listed, followed by identification of objects on the boundaries of the ontology. Next, internal systems within the boundary of the description can be identified.
- Initial ontology development means that a preliminary ontology is developed, a quasi prototype ontology containing i.e. initial descriptions of kinds, relations and properties.
- Finalization and validation of ontology is the last phase when the prototype is refined and tested in an iterative way.

The KBSI IDEF5 methodology is essentially a deductive validation procedure as ontology structures are "instantiated" with actual data, and the result of the instantiation is compared with the ontology structure.

This methodology is based on refinement of the outputs produced, even with regard to the initial scope and level of detail, until a prototype model has been developed.

The main characteristics of the smart card ontology are:

- level of formalization: structured informal, formal,
- purpose of application: interoperability among systems, system-engineering benefits.
- subject matter: domain ontology (smart card systems),

4.2 Development of the Ontology for SC Systems

As the description of the SC ontology would well extend the given extent of this paper, only the main structure will be introduced.

The rough structure of the smart card ontology looks like:

a) Meta-ontology

- The meta-ontology defines the basic terms of the ontology. Listing a few of them:
- ENTITY, RELATIONSHIP, ROLE, ATTRIBUTE, ACTOR, TIME POINT, etc.
- Some term definition;
- ENTITY: a fundamental element modeled in the domain e.g. RSA crypto algorithm, key size

- RELATIONSHIP: the way that two or more ENTITIES can be associated with each other

b) Activities
c) Functions
d) Architectures and building blocks
e) Applications
f) Standards
g) Legal regulations
h) Life cycle phase

There are further subgroups, numerous terms and definitions completing the ontology. Part of the ontology is shown on Figure 30-1. The full smart card ontology is the base for constructing the reference architecture.

```
Functions
   Communication
      insecure
      secure
   Data storage
      write once
      write many
      emergency handling
   Identification
      Knowledge
         PIN
         Password
         Memory (e.g.: images)
      Possession
         Token
      Biometry
         Fingerprint
         Voice
         iris, palm, face
   Authentication
      one-to-one
      one-to-many
   Authorization
      management rights
      user rights
      group rights and other levels
   Encryption
      symmetric
      asymmetric
      challenge-response
   Calculation
      arithmetical
      generation of Ě (e.g. random)
   File management (e.g. move, copy also done by these)
      read
      write
      append
      delete
 System architectures
   Card environment
      Equipment for personalization
```

    - Gateway
    - Card acceptance device (CAD)
      - Contactless
        - Radio Frequency
        - Microwave
        - Capacitive
        - IrDA
        - Infra (BlueTooth)
      - Contact
        - ISO 7816
        - Laser
        - Mobile / Personal Trusted Device
      - Other
        - Barcode
        - Magnetic stripe (+ Magneprint)
        - 2D code
  - Card architectures
    - HW
      - Processor
        - 8 bit
        - 16 bit
        - 32 bit
        - 64 bit
        - crypto
      - Memory
        - RAM
        - ROM
        - EEPROM
        - other advanced technology (e.g. FLASH)
      - Shape
        - ISO 7816
        - Ring
        - USB - token
        - SIM / WIM
        - Mini SIM
      - Other
        - Display
        - Keyboard
        - Multimedia
    - SW
      - Virtual machine
        - JAVA
        - Basic
        - Multos
      - OP system
        - JAVA
        - Multos
        - Windows for Smart Cards
      - Enhanced SW tools
        - OTA / Smart Messaging
        - Dynamic download (initiate by user or operator)
    - Communication
      - See CAD
- Security equipment
  - Personal
    - One time password
    - PTD //still exists?
  - Complementary Required Module
    - SAM module
    - Master / slave relation
    - Equal level

```
      Third-party
         Racal sec. module
         AES box
         RSA SecurID
Applications
   ID/Government (inclusive local authorities)
      Passport
      Driving license
      ID card
      Social aid
         Government
         Local government systems
         Cross border systems
      Access rights card
         Digital signature
         Access Control
            Physical
            Logical
   Banking
      debit
      credit
      e-purse
   Commerce
      on-line comm.
      off-line comm.
      loyalty
   Health
      insurance (incl. pharmacy, social aid)
      emergency
      treatment history
   Traffic
      parking
      public transport
   Travel
      highway
      booking
   Industry
      control
      Intelligent Manufacturing (distributed systems too)
   Telecommunication
      SIM card
      WIM card
      TCP communication
         log-in
         crypto communication
   Disabled
      master-slave
      special/additional solutions
         elderly
         physically disabled
         mentally disabled
```

Figure 30-1. Basic entities of the smart card system ontology

4.3 Contact points with other ontologies

Smart cards are components of complex information systems. In such systems components must have well defined contact (communication) points with other elements, and subsystems like cryptographic- or biometry subsystems, as smart cards are the most frequently used elements of the system.

The proof of this approach is a smart card with biometric recognition capability (embedded in the body of the card → solution integrated in the chip module). Considering biometrical recognition systems the main solutions can be collected in a common classification scheme where the classification parameters are the language components of the ontology (of biometry).

5. APPLICATION OF THE ONTOLOGY

5.1 Attack Trees

One of the applications of the smart card ontology is building an attack tree for smart cards. The tree is developed based on the three main threats (CIA) and the root node is "smart card compromise". Sub-trees and different paths can be discovered in the whole tree depending on the parameters given to the search process. The basic attack types (the leaves of the tree) can be reconstructed if the tree-building concept differs from our one. For example the attacks can be classified as hardware-software, logical-physical, card related or environment related (PC, Card Acceptance Device, etc.) attacks (Terrance, 2004). The tree can be handled in text format (more compact) or in graphical format (more visual). Details about attack tree construction can be found in (Bruce, 1999). The three is introduced in the followings both in text (Figure 30-2) and graphical format (Figure 30-3).

```
1 <OR> Confidentiality
  1.1 <OR> Get PIN
   1.1.1 <OR> User Behavior
     1.1.1.1  Written down
     1.1.1.2  Search & find
   1.1.2 <OR> Human Eng.
     1.1.2.1  Personal (online)
     1.1.2.2  Virtual (offline)
   1.1.3 <OR> Guess (trial)
     1.1.3.1  Field test
     1.1.3.2  Luck
  1.2 <OR> Dump communication
   1.2.1  Analyze data
   1.2.2  Sniff data
  1.3 <OR> Unauthorized access
```

```
    1.3.1  Bad ACL settings
    1.3.2  Plain data
    1.3.3  Built-in code...
2 <OR> Integrity
  2.1 <OR> Application/algorithm
    2.1.1  Bad RND
    2.1.2 <OR> Bad concept/development
      2.1.2.1  Bad RND
      2.1.2.2  Test code
      2.1.2.3  Bad code
    2.1.3 <OR> External influence
      2.1.3.1 <OR> HW + OS + silicon
        2.1.3.1.1  Differential Analysis
        2.1.3.1.2  Frequency manipulations
        2.1.3.1.3  Light attacks
        2.1.3.1.4  Cryptanalysis
      2.1.3.2 <OR> Reverse engineering
        2.1.3.2.1  Chip detach
        2.1.3.2.2  Optical analysis
      2.1.3.3  Fake CAD
  2.2 <OR> Data
    2.2.1  Bad ACL settings
    2.2.2  Bad codepage
    2.2.3  Cryptanalysis
  2.3 <OR> Protocol(s)
    2.3.1  Bad algorithm
    2.3.2  Bad design
    2.3.3  Bad implementation
3 <OR> Availability
  3.1 <AND> Block access
    3.1.1  Block PIN
    3.1.2  Block PIN2/PUK
  3.2 <OR> Denial of Service
    3.2.1  Extreme communication
  3.3 <OR> HW damage
    3.3.1 <OR> Card damage
      3.3.1.1  Physical damage
      3.3.1.2  Logical
    3.3.2 <OR> CAD damage
      3.3.2.1  Physical
      3.3.2.2  Logical
    3.3.3  CAD-holder damage
```

Figure 30-2. Attack tree of smart card (text version)

Such an attack tree has many contact points with other attack trees like the one of PGP or biometry or even with the attack tree of the operating system of the computer into which the card reader is connected.

The tree was designed in the SecurITree software of Amenaza Ltd., and the next figure shows a part of the image version.

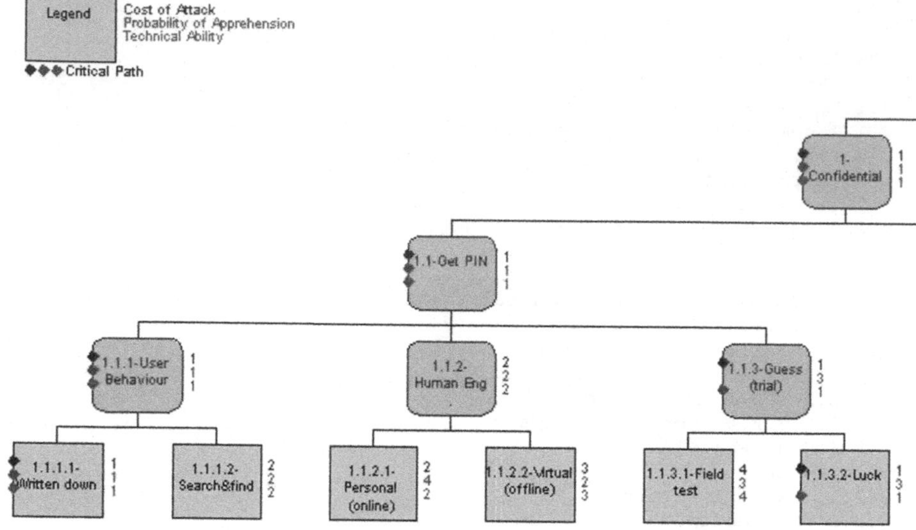

Figure 30-3. Smart card attack tree (part of the image version)

5.2 Building the Reference Architecture

An architecture can be defined as the collection of design principles, physical configuration, functional organization, operational procedures, and data formats used as the bases for the design, construction, modification, and operation of a system. Reference architecture (RA) is a combination and arrangement of functional groups and reference points that reflect all logically possible system architectures in a structured, flexible and modular way. Reference architecture gives the general representation of the architecture from which all individual architectures can be derived. A RA can contain reference models (RM) on lower levels, or it can be built on a coherent set of RMs as well.

Based on the ontology the number and content of the dimensions of the reference architecture can be defined. Based on the RA the discrete reference models can be allocated as a second step. This definition is not a one-step action, rather a limited iterative process, as the RA has direct effects on the RM set, but the RMs also can influence the structure of the RA in the development phase.

On the bases of the content of RA dimensions the set of the reference models will be defined. It can be done based on the elements of the ontology taking into consideration the logical, the functional and the derivative connections. Each RM is in a close, strict functional/logical contact with the neighboring reference models. This results that the boundary communication between the RMs and the logic (I/O dataflow) of this communication can be defined exactly. Based on this knowledge exact protocols can be determined.

As a first step a 3D model is used for demonstrate the idea and the relations among the elements. A sample system can be seen on Figure 30-4. The parameters are forming intervals, which can be divided into sub-parts. Each interval is open from left and from right.

The (x, y, z) = (0, 0, 0) is the starting point. In general there is no case of one or two axis parameter being selected to be zero. It can be useful to talk about just two axes, not taking in consideration the third one, but the physical products are determined with three axes.

When the related systems (SAM cards, readers, PCs, mobiles with dual slot) are analyzed then is interesting the contact between these systems. This maybe a further research topic ("Relations between SMC related 3D models"), but this is out of the scope of this paper.

The cube illustration does not disclose the concept of a multidimensional model, which could be described by formal logic rules. The 3D model is simple better for visual presentations.

On the axes there are elements, which determine small cubes or group of cubes. The group of cubes means sub-cubes where is possible one side, one edge or just one point to be the contact surface with another sub-cube. There is no case of a system with gap, because the rows can be changed like in a matrix, therefore the end result will be always a group of cubes with surface contact at least in one point with one another cube. The requirements are chosen on the axes, and the selected ones define the formation. There will be no cube "alone" in the system without at least one corner in contact with another cube.

If two cubes have one common side, then this is a strong requirement for a standard, which describes this contact surface. The two cubes could be unified depending on the situation of other cubes, and can create one bigger formation for example a rectangle.

Now the research work is in the first phase on finding the optimal set for axes and the optimal order between parameters of axes. How the multi-application cards will spread, the formations will be bigger sub-formations of united cubes. In such a system there is a need of a description methodology, which helps in handling the unions and separations, integration of elements in a complex system and also derivation of sub-formation from a complex system. The design has been done top-down, the realizations goes on based on the bottom-up methodology, which is also better in security field: revoke all the rights, and give just what is needed. There are some special cases where no parameters are taken from at most one axis. In these cases this "configurations" are rather live and running SMC applications.

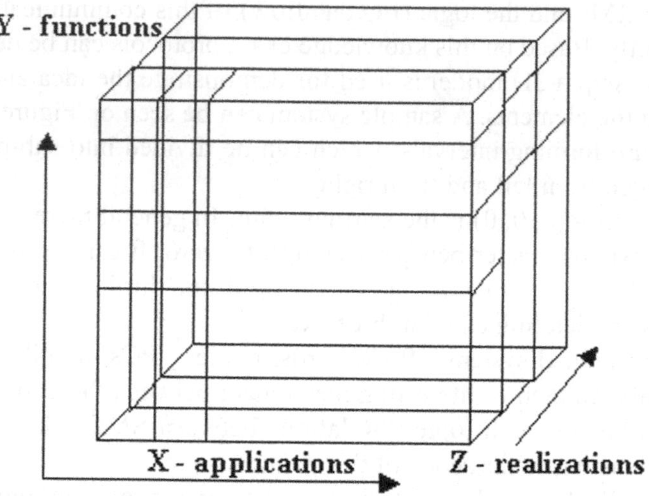

Figure 30-4. Global 3D model and the axes (example)

In order to get an easy to use, theoretically well-established and consistent GRASC, several iteration steps have to be done. The ontology defines a pretty stable RA, the modifications can be done in the order/place of the reference models inside the RA and in the taxonomies of the RMs.

As it was mentioned, the three different contact types are: a side (e.g. green contact, the two parameter can be considered one application), an edge (e.g. red contact, the applications are separated but they communicate) or a point (e.g. yellow point, there is no communication, moreover there is a security protection against any type of communication) as shown in (Figure 30-5).

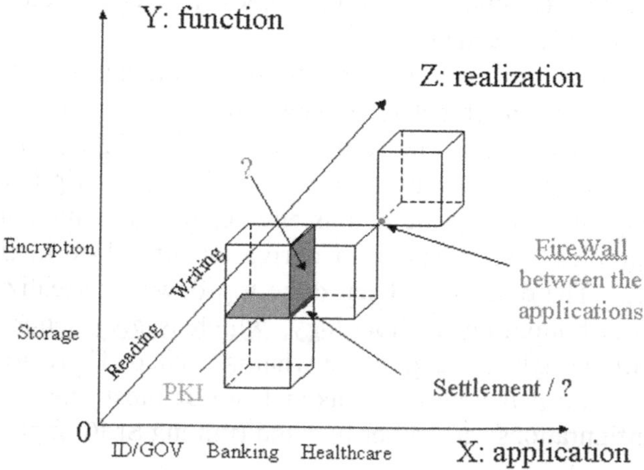

Figure 30-5. Example with firewall application

Based on the entities on the axes it can be constructed other 3D models and is also possible to create models in higher dimensions. The problem is how to handle such models, because the visualization is not so easy, although mathematically is possible to create formalism based on the indexes of the elements. The solution is the application of a fin & leading axe, where the most common axe is the leading one (in our case it is Y, the axe of functions) and the other axes are in a plain (see Figure 30-6).

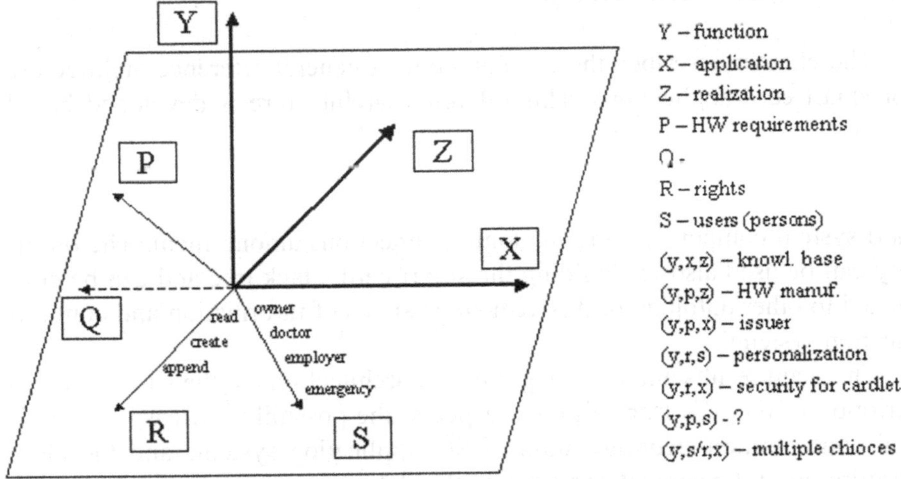

Figure 30-6. Leading axe and fin (plain of axes)

Thanks to this concept a multidimensional system can be handled by decomposition to a basic 3D system and the remaining axes are part of the plain. By changing one axe the user can cross in one or more steps between any 3D systems.

5.3 Expected Results and Future Plans

The expected results of General Reference Architecture of Smart Cards are the followings:

1. A structured description of smart card systems from different aspects.
2. Easy configuration/reconfiguration possibilities of SCs for different (multi) applications.
3. Content and form of communication can be clearly described in case of different functions/applications.

4. Generation of new research directions.
5. These expected benefits of the GRASC can support the SC system standardization activities (and all SC applications) in a great extend.

According to the first results there will be the possibility to make practical use of the descriptions of the inter-reference model communication as well.

6. CONCLUSIONS

The chapter described the development of general reference architecture for smart card applications. This reference architecture is developed based on smart card system ontology, uses several taxonomies and knowledge based technologies. The ontology provides the base for the construction of the reference architecture through the systematic description of the smart card system components and the logic connections among them. The ontology can be used also for building the smart card attack tree and can be connected to other ontology of different subsystems of information and communication systems.

The main results and advantages of the architecture are the structured description of the SCs from different aspects, the possibility of easy and optimal configuration/reconfiguration of SC application systems and the clear description of the content and form of the data exchange in case of different functions/applications. The smart card system ontology can help to develop a more consistent and flexible reference architecture.

The interoperability requirements can be supported by the architecture as well, and it can also help in standardization activities. The ontology itself can serve as a common description, which can be extended or connected to other ontology in the future.

ACKNOWLEDGEMENT

The work included in this paper has been done with the support of the OTKA (Hungarian Scientific Research Fund) project with the title "The Theoretical Elaboration of a General Reference Architecture for Smart Cards" (Grant No.: T 030 277).

ACRONYMS

B2B – business to business
CPU – Central Processor Unit
EEPROM – Electronically Erasable Programmable Memory
IAS – Identification, Authentication and Signature
ISO – International Organization for Standardization
GIF – Global Interoperability Framework
GRASC – General Reference Architecture for SC
GSC-IS – Government Smart Card Interoperability Specification
GSM – Groupe Speciale Mobile (aka Global System for Mobile Communications)
HW – hardware
NIST – National Institute of Standards and Technology
PC – personal computer
RA – reference architecture
RAM – Random Access Memory
RM – reference model
ROM – Read Only Memory
SIM – Subscriber Identity Module
SW – software
SC – smart card
WIM – Wireless Identity Module

REFERENCES

Bruce Schneier: Attack Trees – Modeling security threats. Dr. Dobb's Journal, December 1999. pp. 318-333, (February 17, 2005); http://www.schneier.com/paper-attacktrees-ddj-ft.html.

Denny Michael, Ontology Building: A Survey of Editing Tools, (February 17, 2005); http://www.xml.com/pub/a/2002/11/06/ontologies.html.

Gruber, T. R., A translation approach to portable ontologies. Knowledge Acquisition, 5(2):199-220, 1993.

Jones, D., Bench-Capon, T., and Visser, P. Methodologies for ontology development, XV. IFIP World Computer Congress, Vienna/Austria and Budapest/Hungary, 31 August – 4 September, 1998, CD-ROM Edition.

KBSI 1994, The IDEF5 Ontology Description Capture Method Overview, KBSI Report, Texas.

NICSS group, NICSS-Framework Scheme, (February 17, 2005); http://www.nicss.gr.jp/.

NIST, Government Smart Card Interoperability Specification (GSC-IS), Version 2.1, Interagency Report 6887 – 2003 Edition, July 16, 2003, (February 17, 2005); http://www.incits.org/tc_home/m1htm/docs/m1030398.pdf.

OilED, (February 17, 2005); http://oiled.man.ac.uk/.

OntoEdit, (February 17, 2005); http://www.ontoprise.com.

Open Smart Card Infrastructure for Europe, V2, Volume 3: Global Interoperability Framework for identification, authentication and electronic signature (IAS) with smart cards, Part 1: Contextual and Conceptual Modeling, Authors: eESC GIF Expert Group, OSCIE Volume 3 Part 1 (March 2003), (February 17, 2005); http://www.eeurope-smartcards.org/Download/03-1.PDF.

Terrance R. Ingoldsby: Understanding Risk Through Attack Tree Analysis, CSI Computer Security Journal, Spring 2004, Volume XX, Number 2. pp 33-59, (February 17, 2005); http://www.amenaza.com/request_methodology.html.

The Ontopia Knowledge Suite, (February 17, 2005); http://www.ontopia.net.

University of Karlsruhe, Karlsruhe Ontology (KAON) Tool Suite, (February 17, 2005); http://kaon.semanticweb.org.

Chapter 31

USING ONTOLOGIES IN MOBILE SURVEYOR

Xin Zheng and Delbert Hart
Computer Science Department, University of Alabama in Huntsville, Huntsville, AL 35899, USA

Abstract: Monitoring is not simply the collection and enumeration of data points but the discovery of information and knowledge inherent within a system under study. Mobile Surveyor, a model-based monitoring system, provides a new perspective and approach to software monitoring by incorporating data models throughout the monitoring process. This paper presents the construction and usage of ontology in Mobile Surveyor, attempting to capture the conceptual structure that offers semantic terms to model the system and build a generic application-independent monitoring tool. Ontology enables the information and knowledge in Mobile Surveyor to be accessible, sharable, reusable and transformable to the heterogeneous systems and applications that use Mobile Surveyor. The Ontolingua Server with OKBC is used to provide an environment for ontology development and knowledge base query and manipulation. The performance of Mobile Surveyor and the role ontology play in it are demonstrated by using a mobile application as the case study.

Key words: Application of Ontology; Ontology Design; Knowledge Reuse and Sharing; Model-based Monitoring

1. INTRODUCTION

1.1 Motivation

Software monitoring is a process of data collection and analysis, seeking to provide insight into the states and behaviors of an application for the purpose of testing, debugging, detecting, visualizing, and steering. Typically, a large volume of data is generated even from monitoring relatively trivial programs. Simply collecting raw data and making it available to users is the focus of most monitoring systems. The task of analysis falls to the end user via a visualization process, or programs are used to test specific hypotheses on an ad-hoc basis. In either case, higher level information or knowledge about an application is viewed as a derived product rather than an integral part of the process.

Model-based monitoring's incorporation of knowledge artifacts throughout the data collection and analysis process is what distinguishes it from other monitoring paradigms. Model-based monitoring maintains both a perceived model (for description) and a monitoring model (for prediction) for an attribute being monitored, where description and prediction are integral functionalities of data mining[1]. Perceived models summarize different aspects of what is currently known, while monitoring models are used as the basis of future data collection.

Mobile Surveyor[2] is a software monitoring tool based on the model-based monitoring approach. The principle motivation for Mobile Surveyor is to address the challenges of monitoring in mobile systems, which are limited resources and disconnected operation. By dynamically making decisions in real time of what data to collect and what to drop based on a monitoring model, the amount of memory used in data collection and network bandwidth needed in data transmission can be significantly reduced. The use of more complicated algorithms to perform model-based monitoring may not necessarily incur higher CPU usage than the simple raw data collection[3].

The scope of model-based monitoring does not have to be restricted to mobile systems. Being demonstrated by the case study on a mobile application, the success of Mobile Surveyor in achieving resource savings effectively under the condition of satisfying the user's monitoring requirements encourages us to take a further step. We seek to develop Mobile Surveyor into an application-independent software monitoring tool for all computing platforms, make it compatible to other software tools, and realize knowledge sharing. To achieve the goal of communication and interoperation in heterogeneous systems, a common shared conceptualization of the domain is needed. Mobile Surveyor explores the way for its information and knowledge management from the use of ontology.

1.2 Roles of Ontology

Classification of information systems falls into two broad categories based on either the mechanism or the content[4]. Mechanisms are proposed to solve the problem of how one would like to do the computations, that is, how to operate on the information or data. This includes works such as rule systems, neural networks, decision tree structures, probability theory, fuzzy logic, and generic abstraction dimensions. However, no matter how good a mechanism is, it has to work on a concrete domain that is represented based on a content theory. The content theory, defining the fundamental structure of a domain, is about "the sorts of objects, properties of objects, and relations between objects that are possible in a specified domain of knowledge"[4]. It attempts to capture the conceptual structure that offers semantic terms to model a domain. The identification of proper concepts for the modeling is known as *ontology*.

Ontology clarifies the structure of what things exist and enables knowledge sharing and reuse. This sharing and reuse can be at both the knowledge structure and representation levels. Weak domain analysis may lead to an incoherent knowledge base, whereas effective semantic analysis guarantees that the knowledge translation between different viewpoints and languages does not change the intrinsic knowledge structure conceptually. For instance, ontology may be transformed into forms such as W3C XML schemas, RDF schemas, database schemas and UML diagrams to realize incorporation with other existing enterprise applications. A language such as Ontolingua[5] can be serialized in a number of representations including DAML+OIL[6], Loom[7], Prolog[8] and CLIPS[9]. In building knowledge representations based on ontology, the representation language used for the encoding, the vocabulary and syntax associated with concepts and relations can be all sharable and reusable so as to eliminate the possible duplicated effort on the domain-specific knowledge representation process.

One class of applications in knowledge sharing and reuse is to include, translate, or merge existing ontology in building the new ones[10, 11]. Another class is to allow applications to query ontology to learn about the vocabulary in a domain and ask about the relations between terms for further inference and reasoning[12, 13]. Querying at the ontology level, the meta-structure of knowledge can be interpreted without having to know the low-level information.

1.3 Using Ontology in Mobile Surveyor

The goal of using ontology in Mobile Surveyor is to realize knowledge sharing and reuse in heterogeneous systems, which can be summarized in four ways. First, the ontology can be included by other ontology for the reuse of terms and relations that have already been defined, for example, in case of visualization systems that need Mobile Surveyor as a preceding tool or subsystem, and other monitoring systems that find Mobile Surveyor useful to collaborate with. Second, the ontology embodies the application-independent feature of Mobile Surveyor so that it can be applied to the monitoring of software applications generically with easy extension. Third, the ontology can be translated or mapped to other languages/forms to achieve the information transformation among heterogeneous systems without changing the semantic structure conceptually, which in this paper is the database schema mapping. Last, the ontology format enables us to perform queries based on logical relations of the knowledge base built on the ontology so as to utilize knowledge of the domain for model building and any other requests of knowledge discovery.

There is much current ontology editing tools[14]. We chose Ontolingua for the development of Mobile Surveyor ontology. Conforming to OKBC[15] model with full KIF[16] axioms, Ontolingua Server[5] provides a distributed collaborative environment to create, browse, edit, query, and modify ontology. As a pure specification language, KIF does not include commands for knowledge base query or other operations. OKBC provides complementary support to knowledge sharing in this aspect. The development of Mobile Surveyor ontology publishes a new class of ontology in Ontolingua Server that supports a shared ontology library for geographically distributed groups, providing a possibility for knowledge reuse and sharing in the area of software monitoring tools.

To better build the ontology, it is necessary to understand how Mobile Surveyor conducts model-based monitoring. An overview of Mobile Surveyor can be found in Section 2. Section 3 covers the domain analysis and conceptual design of ontology construction. The use of ontology in Mobile Surveyor is described in Section 4, including the knowledge base querying and ontology mapping.

2. MOBILE SURVEYOR

As ubiquitous computing matures, mobile devices have become an important computing platform. From the research use of environment exploration systems in hydrologic survey and geological prospecting, the civil application of navigation systems in vehicles, to the pervasive use of handhelds, software applications on mobile devices have been booming in recent years. However, monitoring and understanding the operation of software on mobile devices is difficult because traditional monitoring tools do not adequately address the challenges of disconnected operation and limited resources in mobile systems.

Disconnected operation distinguishes monitoring mobile software from other forms of distributed software by restricting monitoring to use a post-mortem form of data collection. Postmortem collections buffer the data until a time when the mobile entity is connected to the network and the information can be transmitted to a central data processing tool. Postmortem data collection is difficult due to the limited storage space available in mobile systems. Even when the mobile system is connected to the network, bandwidth may be scarce and needed by the main application, leaving little (if any) bandwidth for the monitoring task. Another drawback of disconnected operation is that it prevents users from sending new instructions to direct the monitoring in real time.

The scarcity of resources that include memory, processing time, network bandwidth, and network connectivity encourages sophisticated techniques over brute force approaches to mobile monitoring.

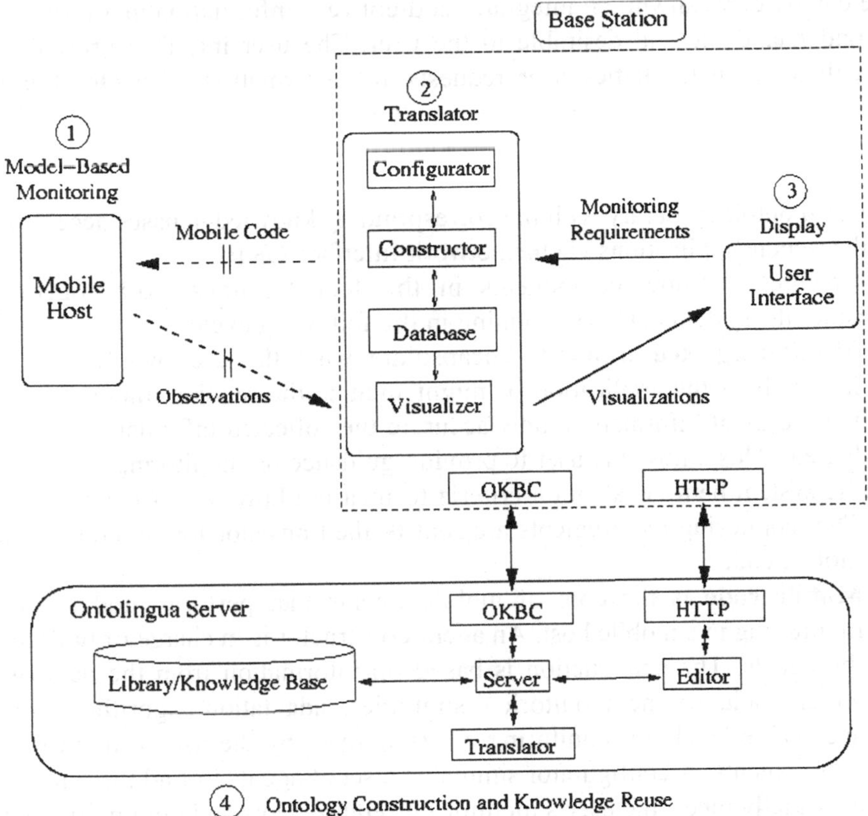

Figure 31-1. Overview of Mobile Surveyor's architecture: The solid and dashed arrows represent permanent and transient communication channels, respectively. Mobile Surveyor employs Ontolingua Server (OS) for its ontology development and knowledge reuse and sharing

2.1 System Overview

Mobile Surveyor consists of components in four locations: 1) the mobile host, 2) the translator, 3) the user interface, and 4) the Ontolingua Server (Figure 31-1). The translator and the user interface may be co-located on a special node in the system, which we call the base station, although they are logically distinct. The components on the mobile host are responsible for managing the local resources available for monitoring and for providing an execution environment for the mobile code to perform model-based monitoring. This environment is called a milieu. More detailed information of how the mobile agents interact with milieu to share the limited resources and how they operate monitoring can be found in[2]. The translator acts as a bridge between the user and the mobile host. It creates a set of mobile agents for monitoring based on the user requirements and information provided by the database. Meanwhile it integrates and conveys information in a form that is understandable and desirable to the user. The user interface provides a visualization that satisfies user requests for information. The Ontolingua Server interacts with the remote distributed application (that in this case is Mobile Surveyor) through HTTP to allow browsing, building, and editing ontology that are stored at the server. The Ontolingua Server also maintains a shared ontology library with the corresponding knowledge bases accessible to the remote applications via the network interface OKBC.

To illustrate how components in the four locations work together, consider the system data flow running in the following cycle.

1. **Monitoring Requirements** encapsulate what the user would like to know about the application. It might include the relative importance of the pieces of information, how accurate the collected information should be, etc. This allows the user to provide guidance on monitoring and gives the system better evaluation criteria to measure how well it is operating. The monitoring requirements are sent to the translator for generating the mobile code.
2. **Mobile code** is the core of mobile agents that perform model-based monitoring in a mobile host. An agent constructor is in charge of building the agents. The construction is based on information from the database which includes the monitoring strategies, adaptation algorithms, and acceptable levels of monitoring errors defined by the user's monitoring requirements. A configurator simulates a set of agents to find the one that maximally meets the user's monitoring requirements and minimally takes up system resources[17]. The chosen agent is dispatched to the mobile host the next time it is connected to the network.
3. **Observation** is the information about a set of variables obtained from monitoring. It may or may not contain actual data points of a variable over time, but it must represent the variable at a certain level of abstraction, for instance, the model that is used to monitor this variable or the parameters of the model. When querying on a variable at a particular time, it will return a value along with other information such as a certainty level. Observations based on the monitoring models are sent

back to the base station when network conditions permit. Observations can also come from user input and source code analysis.
4. **Visualization** of the data is presented to the user. The analysis of the collected information refines it for graphical display. The analysis considers both raw data and relevant meta-data, such as certainty and accuracy for the visualization.
5. **Monitoring Requirements** are specified by the user who has new requests for querying the running application. A new monitoring cycle starts from 1.

Mobile Surveyor employs the Ontolingua Server to accomplish its ontology construction and to realize knowledge reuse and sharing. The detailed discussion of using Ontolingua Server can be found in Section 4.

2.2 Technical Challenges

Technical challenges exist in each part of Mobile Surveyor development. This includes the design of milieu in mobile host, the approach to model building, agent construction, and configuration, the understanding and handling of user's monitoring requirements (QoS), the uncertainty analysis of information from various sources. This paper focuses on the use of ontology in Mobile Surveyor. It addresses this from the viewpoint of ontology construction and manipulation in the effort to provide an application-independent ontology design for knowledge reuse and sharing.

3. ONTOLOGY IN MOBILE SURVEYOR

3.1 Ontology Construction

Mobile Surveyor aims to provide a general monitoring tool for all software applications in all computing platforms. Therefore, the data collection may vary from program level events, the utilization and contention with system resources, to the behavior of operating systems. The user requirements of monitoring can be custom or general, from the coarse to fine granularity. The applications to be monitored may be running on heterogeneous systems. This variety of data sources makes it essential to employ an application-independent approach to ontology construction in Mobile Surveyor.

To represent a domain using ontology, it is important to clarify the structure of information of the domain. Ontology may vary not only in their contents, but also in the structures. The same domain may have different ontology to represent the different viewpoints or satisfy the different abstraction needs. The differences range from the dividing of concepts and instances, classes and subclasses, to the recognizing of relations between the re-organized information. The ontology construction in Mobile Surveyor will formally deal with these semantic representations and make effective use of meta-descriptions in operating on the structures.

Mobile Surveyor not only integrates the high level abstraction and knowledge discovery throughout the whole process of data collection and analysis, but turns the user from a passive receiver of information to a proactive one that participates in monitoring. It captures a user's monitoring requirements as a set of quality of service (QoS) specifications and embeds them in mobile agents. The user may also give any heuristics and assertions of the attributes to be monitored. The ontology construction in Mobile Surveyor is expected to reflect this user interaction in monitoring.

Since the model building process in Mobile Surveyor covers the use and analysis of information from various data sources, the uncertainty lying in these different levels of information and knowledge makes model building challenging. The ontology construction is also responsible for representing the propositional attitude to the information and inferences of a domain, such as beliefs, hypotheses, assertions, and predictions.

To sum up, Mobile Surveyor applies ontology to enhance its model building and knowledge management activities by considering the ontology construction from the following aspects: levels of abstraction, QoS specification, propositional attitude, and relationship identification.

3.1.1 Data Source

We look into the structure of information in Mobile Surveyor starting from the understanding of where data comes from. Data sources in Mobile Surveyor fall into three categories:

- **Observer:** Observers only provide raw data. Most observations are from monitoring agents with data represented as a set of value-timestamp pairs along with meta data associated with those points. Observations may also come from user inputs and source code analysis.
- **Estimator:** Estimators interpret data from observers. The estimations may be a sequence of data values recreated for visualization, or a judgment regarding which model might be suitable for future monitoring of a variable.
- **Transformer:** Transformers provide data items derived from observers and estimators. The transformer creates new computed values and derives new variables.

3.1.2 Levels of Abstraction

The construction of ontology ranges in abstraction, from very general terms to the terms that are bound to specific domains. Aiming to provide a general monitoring tool, the domain that Mobile Surveyor studies is a category of all software applications and the vocabularies it uses should be the application-independent terms that identify the fundamental descriptions of all applications. Mobile Surveyor is concerned with the overall representation of how software is running and what attributes are monitored.

A group of general entities are identified in Mobile Surveyor, such as *Application*, *Attribute, Model, QoS*, and etc. *Application* is a class of all software applications that Mobile Surveyor works on and it takes any of these applications as a subclass. Usually, each application has a different set of attributes to be monitored. There is more than one way to handle these attributes. We use *Attribute* as a superclass of any attribute sets so that each individual application holds a "has" relation with a particular set of attributes (Figure 31-2, solid line with the arrow). An alternative that seems simpler to build this ontology is to get rid of the layer of attribute sets and make the instances straightly the leaf nodes of *Attribute*. But a problem of this approach is that each individual application will "has" the higher level concept *Attribute* that covers all the attributes but not all of them belong to a specific application (Figure 31-2, dashed line with the arrow). To improve the design, there has to be axioms defined to specify the relations and restrictions between the instance attributes and the applications. There is the same concern of abstraction for the entities *Model* and *QoS* that we will cope with next.

3.1.3 Models and QoS

The goal of Mobile Surveyor is to achieve data collection efficiently by using data models through out the monitoring and analysis process. As introduced in section 2, there are two types of models in Mobile Surveyor, monitoring models and perceived models. Both types of models have a strategy associated, which ranges from very generic (e.g., periodic sampling) to attribute specific (e.g., modeling a data sequence as a set of triangle waveforms). But there are some other particular features of monitoring models.

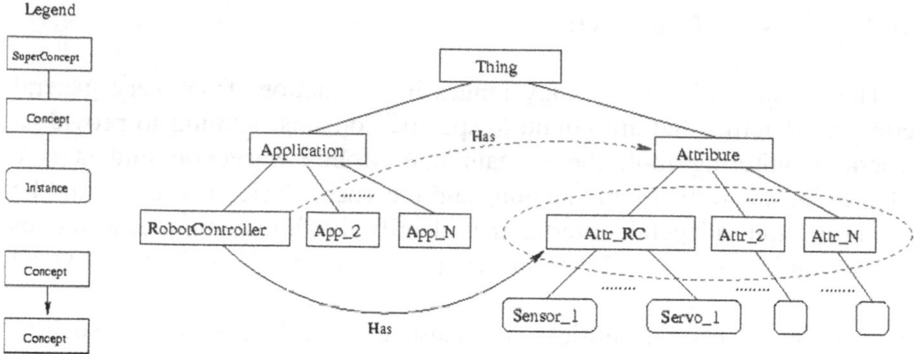

Figure 31-2. Levels of abstraction (1): Applications and Attributes. The dashed lines illustrate a possible alternative approach to the ontology design

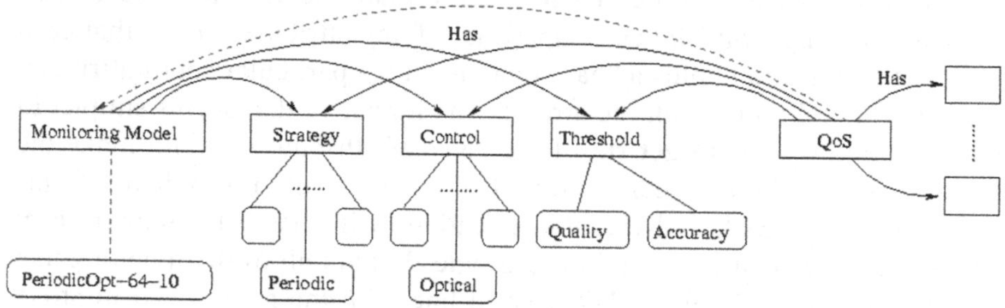

Figure 31-3. Levels of abstraction (2): Models and QoS. The dashed lines illustrate a possible alternative approach to the ontology design

The monitoring models, encapsulated in the mobile agents, dominate data collection during the runtime. No models can perfectly predict the future though. Being derived from the domain knowledge, history data, inference, and embedded statically into the agent a priori, a monitoring model may no longer fit the currently running application as time progresses.

In the face of this challenge, Mobile Surveyor dynamically analyzes the ongoing data and makes monitoring decisions on-the-fly. To achieve this, Mobile Surveyor allows controls over the monitoring strategy to meet the required quality by setting the quality of service specifications. Monitoring models are associated with other properties such as *Control* and *Threshold* in addition to *Strategy*. Having the control algorithm and threshold specification encapsulated along with the monitoring strategy, an agent is able to calibrate the monitoring accuracy (i.e., the boundary within which the observations can be left out safely) according to the quality required (i.e., the monitoring error allowed).

When talking about QoS, we generally mean the user's monitoring requirements that are represented as a set of QoS specifications. The requirements include the threshold specification (e.g., accuracy and quality) as well as other things the user wants to specify. For instance, what monitoring strategy and control algorithm they want to use, the importance level of the attributes being monitored, etc.

From the above analysis, we can see that *Monitoring Model* and *QoS* share some terms such as *Strategy*, *Control,* and *Threshold*. These terms can be designed as the properties of *Monitoring Model* and *QoS* separately, or can be regarded as independent entities that hold a "has" relation with *Monitoring Model* and *QoS*. Notice that the entity *Perceived Model* also shares at least *Strategy* with *Monitoring Model*. Thus *Strategy, Control,* and *Threshold* are created as independent and sharable concepts (Figure 31-3, solid lines).

Since *QoS* includes all the properties that a monitoring model has, it seems that *QoS* can have a "has" relation with *Monitoring Model*. An extreme alternative is that *QoS* only "has" *Monitoring Model* that only with the instances straightly (Figure 31-3, dashed lines). A problem of this approach is that when a user queries the ontology about what model is available and tries to specify the monitoring requirements, he does not have any flexible choices but to use the existing/defined instances.

3.1.4 Context and Credibility

Attributes of a system do not exist in isolation. The meaning of data would be weakened if the data were decoupled from the circumstances in which the event occurs. In this sense, recording only data values of an attribute during monitoring is insufficient. The entity *Context* is concerned with representing correlations and associations within data. There is context associated with each attribute, containing information about when, where, and how data was collected.

The context includes the identity of data sources of where data items are drawn upon, the observation, estimation, or transformation; the indication of what monitoring or perceived models are used to generate the particular data items; the record of parameters of the models, etc. The monitoring session is also an important property of the context since there would be different monitoring and perceived strategies in different sessions.

Due to the variety of data sources that provide information, it is necessary to rate the credibility of these data sources first of all to ensure that the knowledge inference will function well. The credibility shows how believable a data source is with respect to a particular view, and the rate of credibility provides a feasible way to cope with the uncertainty problem caused by the diversity of information sources. We identify a subclass of *Context*, the *Cred-Context*, to link the propositional attitude to the information and inferences of a domain. The credibility of a monitoring model used to obtain observations in a particular monitoring session indicates the degree of deviation of the model from the fact, while the credibility of a perceived model used to obtain estimations based on a particular monitoring session may reflect the confidence on the re-generated data items. When setting monitoring requirements, a user can choose an existing model according to its credibility, or he can propose a new model-based on the domain knowledge and there will be a credibility associated with this assertion.

There are subclasses *Param-Context* and *Thres-Context* of *Context* that are defined to represent the parameters (e.g., a and b for the linear model $f(x) = a * x + b$) and the threshold (i.e., the quality and accuracy specified) of a model, respectively.

3.1.5 Application-independent

In constructing the application-independent ontology for Mobile Surveyor, we have attempted to balance the modularity and straightforwardness of the structuralizing. Based on the above analysis and design, when applying Mobile Surveyor to any specific application, the only thing that distinguishes one application from another is the application name and the attribute set. To monitor the usage of system resources, the attributes may include CPU cycle, memory, and bandwidth. To monitor the running of a mobile agent, the primitive data states, suspend and resume of its execution, the message sending and receiving would be concerned. For other entities, relations, and instances, the addition of a new application is just an extension of the existing structure. The abstraction and modularity make Mobile Surveyor flexible to serve as a general monitoring tool and easy to be customized to any particular applications.

3.2 Rules and Reasonings

In addition to the analysis of what exists and their relations, we may need to make some statements about the information of a domain that can not be represented by a particular term or by the relationship between terms. Mobile Surveyor handles the representation of this kind of information by defining axioms that do not fit into the frame language but are supported by the extended Ontolingua Language and the Ontolingua Server.

An example that illustrates this design need is that for a user who wants to know about the credibility of a monitoring model for an attribute. There should be some rules defined to regulate this query since the credibility of a model used for an attribute is not always the same. It depends on the conditions such as what control algorithm the model has, what quality level is required, and what monitoring accuracy is specified. Even though the conditions are same, in which particular session the monitoring is performed also makes difference. To represent this kind of information, an axiom is defined to describe the implicit linking between *Attribute* and *Context* as the following:

```
;;; Credibility_Query
(Define-Axiom Credibility_Query "Not supplied yet."
:= (=> (And (Attribute ?attr) (Cred-Context ?cred-cont)
            (= (Run_Id ?attr) (Run_Id ?cred-cont))
            (= (Model_Id ?attr) (Model_Id ?cred-cont)))
      (And (Credibility ?cred) (Memory ?mem) (Stderr ?se))))
```

In addition to the use of mobile agents, Mobile Surveyor implements four classes of inference agents (IAs) that reside statically in the base station to accomplish the reasoning. The first two classes are estimation agents and transformation agents according to the classification of data sources. They aim to regenerate data points that are filtered out during monitoring and derive new variables from other data sources. The third class of IAs is identified as model building agents that are responsible for constructing data models. Each individual agent embodies a perspective on how to interpret a data set by implementing a particular algorithm and the corresponding rules. The last category of IAs falls into the ontology query class, about the structure as well as the rules. The querying agents seek to provide the high-level knowledge for the user to share the information of applications that Mobile Surveyor works on, make decisions for the future monitoring, extend and reuse Mobile Surveyor as an application-independent monitoring tool. In the next section we will demonstrate the use of an ontology query in the model-based monitoring of a mobile application.

4. CASE STUDY

4.1 Ontolingua Server and OKBC

We built Mobile Surveyor's ontology using the Ontolingua Server, a tool that is developed by Knowledge Systems Laboratory (KSL) at Stanford University to "enable wide access and provide users with the ability to publish, browse, create, and edit ontology stored on an ontology server"[5]. In addition to the support for the distributed, collaborative development of consensus ontology, Ontolingua Server provides facilities for ontology translation and run-time query by the programmatic agents via the network protocol, Open Knowledge Base Connectivity (OKBC)[15].

Even though designed based on the extended Knowledge Interchange Format (KIF), the Ontolingua language does not include commands for knowledge base queries or manipulation. Ontolingua Server uses OKBC as an API, which allows remote applications to talk to the server, to create a generic access and manipulation layer for knowledge sharing. The class of inference agents for ontology query in Mobile Surveyor is the OKBC client-side application that operates on the content of OKBC knowledge base for viewing and modifying. The Mobile Surveyor ontology can be found and accessed in the shared Ontolingua Ontology Library[22].

4.2 Ontology Mapping

The goal of creating ontology is not only to represent the world as stand-alone models but to glue the various sources of information together by ontology merging and reuse. This provides a global perspective of the world or permits a view of the domain in different points of view by ontology translation to realize the incorporation with other existing enterprise applications. Ontology translation has two major uses: translations between different ontology and translations between ontology and the information they describe in a system[23]. To distinguish the ontology language translation, we refer the latter use that connects ontology to the representation of information in an application system to the term *mapping*. The ontology mapping in Mobile Surveyor relates the ontology to its environment, that is, to transform the ontology into forms of the database schema to build a local database to store the actual contents of information from various data sources, as opposed to the remote knowledge base maintained in Ontolingua Server.

4.3 Testbed

Our test bed is a Palm Pilot Robot[24] (Figure 31-4). The robot is able to autonomously navigate and investigate its environment. Its primary sensors are three infrared detectors that serve as proximity sensors. The robot has three independent wheels that enable it to move in any direction on a two dimensional plane.

The robot is controlled by a Palm IIIxe, which uses a Motorola MC68EZ328 (Dragonball EZ) 16 MHz processor running PalmOS 3.5[25]. The Palm IIIxe provides eight megabytes of memory for applications and data, of which 256K of memory is referred to as the dynamic heap and is the

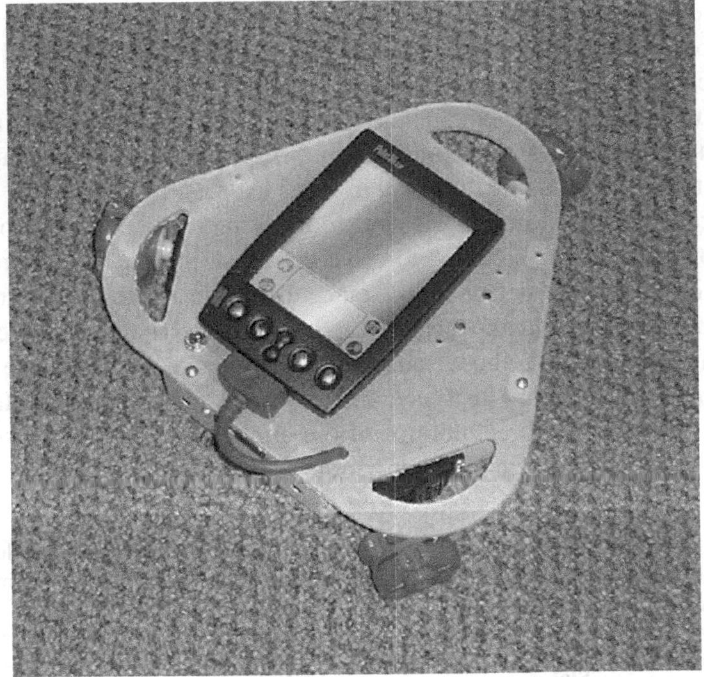

Figure 31-4. The Palm Pilot Robot that is being used as the current test bed

effective working space of programs. The remainder is designated as a persistent storage heap. All persistent information on the Palm OS, including applications and user data, is organized into related chunks kept in PDBs (Palm Databases). PalmOS is not a multi-tasking operating system as far as the developers are concerned. Hence Mobile Surveyor shares the mobile application's thread of control.

The disconnection aspect of mobile systems makes the communication of mobile entities to the base station difficult. Currently, communication between the robot and the base station is accomplished by physically moving the Palm Pilot to a docking cradle to transfer PDB files. Both mobile agents and observations are encoded as PDB files.

SuperWaba[26] is used for the implementation on the Palm Pilot (Palm IIIxe). SuperWaba is a Java-like environment that provides capabilities well suited to handheld devices. It was chosen in Mobile Surveyor due to the availability of drivers for the Palm Pilot Robot.

4.4 Model Building

The use of data models runs through the whole process of model-based monitoring. Building accurate and credible models is thus one of the primary goals in Mobile Surveyor. The construction and use of models is not limited to a single monitoring session. Instead, data modeling is an iterative process and can be refined and propagated between monitoring sessions, given that the application being monitored does not generally change between sessions since the underlying code remains the same. We give an example of building monitoring models for an attribute of a mobile application in this subsection to reflect the utility of using ontology in some aspects.

The running application we are monitoring is RobotController, an application that we implemented to drive the robot to map the environment. The proximity sensors detect the distance from the robot to obstacles and RobotController manipulates the robot to change directions whenever it gets close to an obstacle. We chose sensor data in this example because sensors are the most challenging test bed attributes to model. Other attributes, especially those under direct control of the application such as servo motor data, are more predictable and easier handle in the model building.

Table 31-1. A simplified fragment of the summary of the Mobile Surveyor knowledge base that is created by the inference (querying) agent KbOverview. The underlined terms are the frames that can be cross-referenced

Frame	**Type**	**Own Slots**		
		Slot	**Values**	**DValues**
Model	Class	Arity	1	
		Subclass-Of	Thing	
		Superclass-Of	Perceived-Model, Monitoring-Model	
		Instance-Of	Primitive, Class	
		Disjoint-Decomposition	Perceived-Model, Monitoring-Model	

4.4.1 Choose initial models

New users to Mobile Surveyor may want to get an overview of the system and its capabilities. One of the querying agents called *KbOverview*, being developed based on the OKBC example code, satisfies this need. Given an arbitrary OKBC Knowledge Base (KB), *KbOverview* generates a HTML page to show the contents of that KB by tabulating and cross-referencing the frames, including the slots, slot values, facets, facet values, and documentations on the frames in the KB. Table 31-1 shows a simplified fragment of the summary of Mobile Surveyor KB created by *KbOverview*.

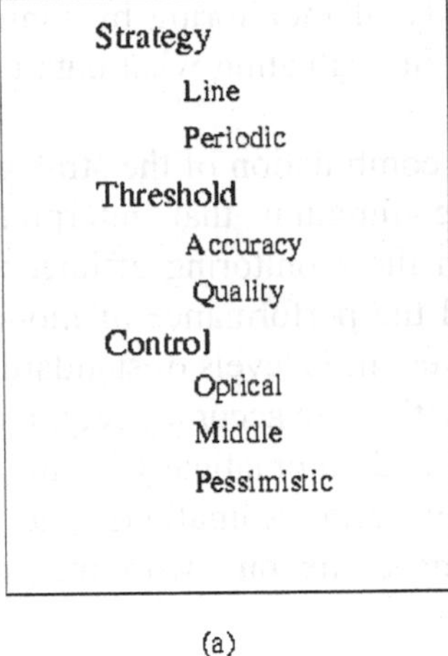

(a)

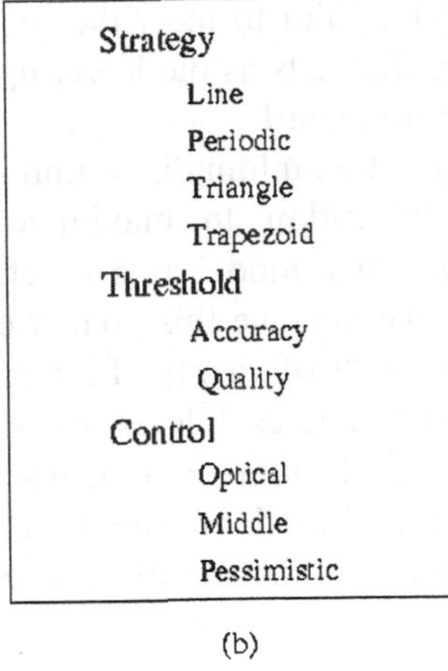

(b)

Figure 31-5. A snapshot of the result running ModelSummary agent before and after monitoring the mobile application RobotController

In the initial stage of monitoring a new application, the user knows little about the attributes to be monitored except for some domain knowledge so it is hard for the user to choose any specific models for the monitoring. Not to lose the generality, Mobile Surveyor provides two general strategies for the first monitoring session. One considers data as a sequence of line segments and another samples data periodically. After the first monitoring session, the monitoring and model building enter an iterative loop that is composed of data regeneration, agent construction and configuration. There is another querying agent called *ModelSummary* that simply provides information about the models in Mobile Surveyor. This agent just lists the strategies, control algorithms, and thresholds that are available to compose a model for the monitoring or data reconstruction. A snapshot of the result running *ModelSummary* agent before monitoring can be found in Figure 31-5(a). This information gives the user a reference of what models he can choose from the very beginning.

4.4.2 Model Building

Using general strategies for monitoring in the first several sessions, the user can heuristically add their own strategies based on the data collected. We tentatively distinguished two other attribute-specific strategies after several sessions. They modeled data as triangle and trapezoid waveforms considering the characteristic of sensor data in the way of the robot being driven. Based on the four strategies, the agent constructor generated a set of mobile agents in which each agent was the combination of a particular strategy and a control mechanism. The three control algorithms, as shown in

Figure 31-5, aim to meet the required quality of monitoring by tuning the accuracy that acts as the lower/upper bound in evaluating what data to drop and what to record.

The model building is to find an optimal combination of the strategy and control algorithm to maximize the score function that interprets the credibility of a model as a function of both the monitoring efficiency and quality[3]. To achieve this goal, we examined the performance of models on different levels of quality of service, which were nine levels of standard error from 2 to 10 and each level was associated with three accuracy requirements to start with. In total, 324 agents were generated automatically by the agent constructor. Based on the past observations and estimations, the agent configurator evaluated these agents and chose the one with the highest credibility to use in the next monitoring session. Theoretically, the search space of quality and accuracy levels in agent construction and model evaluation is a set of continuous real number, which means the set of agents could be infinite even though the space was bounded at [0,10]. Clearly, this is too large to search via brute force. The selection of nine-quality and three-accuracy levels was to narrow down the search space and provide a feasible and reasonable testing set.

The key of model building is to iteratively search the better models session by session. The criterion of this searching is the credibility of monitoring models. We built a local database based on the schema that is mapped from Mobile Surveyor ontology to store the actual contents of information from various sources, including observations, estimations, model parameters and credibility, etc. There is a table that records the credibility of each model in each monitoring session according to the axiom from ontology:

```
;;; Score_Function
(Define-Axiom Score_Function "Not supplied yet."
:= (=> (+ (* 0.5 (Memory ?mem)) (* 0.5 (Stderr ?se)))
        (Credibility ?cred)))
```

Usually, after a certain number of iterations, a particular model may demonstrate its superiority over others in monitoring an attribute. The statistics in this experiment showed that 50% of the time the model of triangle strategy with the optimistic control mechanism was chosen, also it indicated that the model worked best at a certain quality level. This result encouraged us to choose “TriOpt” model as the monitoring model for sensor data in the later sessions.

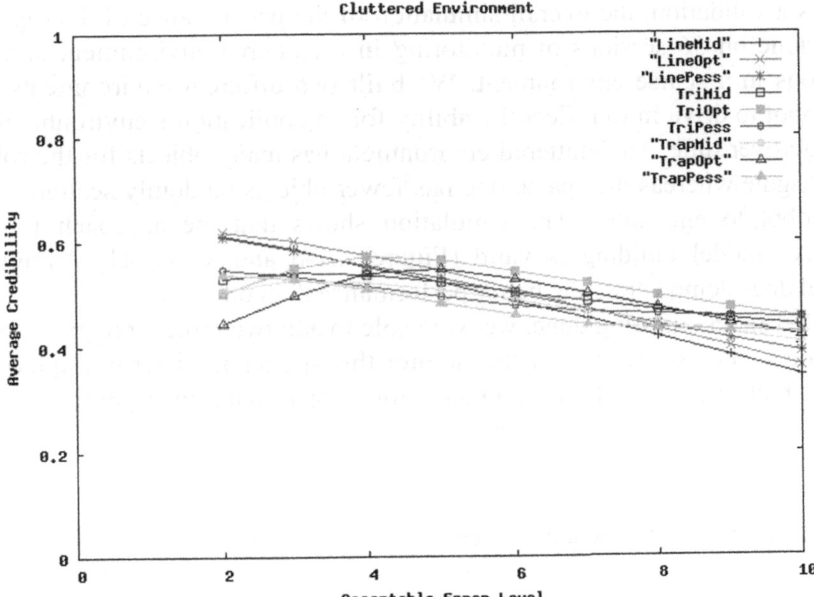

Figure 31-6. The performance of models in a cluttered environment: comparison of the average credibility versus the quality level. (The periodic models are ignored because of their inferior performance)

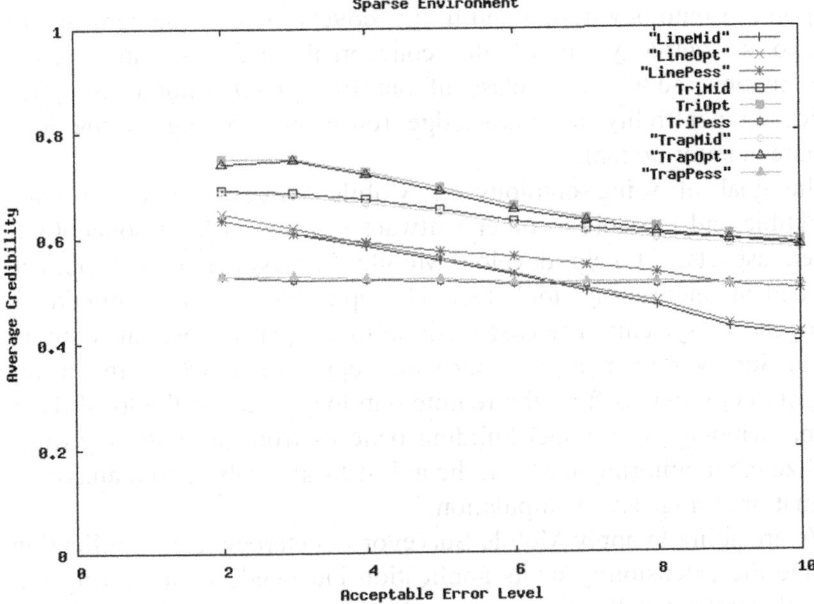

Figure 31-7. The performance of models in a sparse environment: comparison of the average credibility versus the quality level. (The periodic models are ignored because of their inferior performance)

As a validation, the overall simulation of the performance of 324 agents was done on 36 sessions of monitoring in a cluttered environment and 21 sessions in a sparse environment. We built two different environments for the robot to drive in to reflect the ability for an application's environment to change over time. The cluttered environment has many objects for the robot to navigate whereas the sparse one has fewer objects randomly scattered for the robot to encounter. The simulation shows that the approach to the iterative model building is valid (Figures 31-6 and 31-7). The "TriOpt" model does demonstrate the better performance than others do.

After the monitoring done, we were able to add two more strategies to the ontology. The user who needs to monitor this application later will query to know that there are four strategies for sensor data in Robotcontroller (Figure 31-5(b)) so that he can specify the QoS with more choices. The highest credibility of a model is also maintained in ontology as the axiom. It provides the user high-level information of which model is best without the need of accessing the local database.

5. CONCLUSIONS

This paper introduces the application of ontology in Mobile Surveyor, a model-based monitoring tool. It presents Mobile Surveyor from the viewpoint of ontology design and usage, covers the development of Mobile Surveyor's ontology in both conceptual analysis and language representation, adds a new class of ontology in Ontolingua Server, and provides a possibility for knowledge reuse and sharing in the area of software monitoring tool.

The goal of using ontology in Mobile Surveyor is to 1) make it compatible and reusable to other software systems in both conceptual and applied aspects; 2) help develop Mobile Surveyor into an application-independent monitoring tool that is applicable to all applications in heterogeneous systems. The case study in this paper demonstrates the use of Mobile Surveyor to monitor a particular application, where the utility of using ontology ranges from the remote ontology query to the local database schema mapping. The model building benefits from the ontology query to initialize the monitoring and with the aid of local database to manage all the information storage and manipulation.

We are going to apply Mobile Surveyor to heterogeneous applications to examine the extensibility of its application-independent monitoring feature and collaborate it with other systems to show its reusability in the future work.

REFERENCES

1. J. Han and M. Kamber, *Data Mining: Concept and Techniques* (Morgan Kaufmann Publishers, 2001).
2. X. Zheng and D. Hart, *Mobile agents for mobile monitoring,* in proc. of ISCA 16th Int. Conf. on Parallel and Distributed Computing Systems, pp. 405–410 (August 13-15, 2003).
3. X.Zheng, *Model-based Monitoring for Mobile Systems,* Ph.D. dissertation (University of Alabama in Huntsville, May, 2005).
4. B. Chandrasekaran, J. Josephson, and V. Benjamins, *Ontologies: What are they? Why do we need the?,* IEEE Intelligent Systems, **14**(1):20–26 (1999).
5. A. Farquhar, R. Fikes, and J. Rice, *The ontolingua server: A tool for collaborative ontology construction,* Technical Report No. Stanford KSL 96-26 (1996).
6. DAML+OIL (March 2001); http://www.daml.org/2001/03/daml+oil-index.html.
7. USC Information Sciences Institute/iSX Corporation (August, 1991); http://www.isi.edu/isd/LOOM/documentation/LOOM-DOCS.html.
8. A. Kabbaj, (September 2004); http://www.insea.ac.ma/CGTools/PROLOG+CG.htm.
9. G. Riley and et al, (September 2004); http://www.ghg.net/clips/CLIPS.html.
10. A. Valente, T. Russ, R. MacGregor, and W. Swartout, *Building and (re)using an ontology of air campaign planning,* IEEE Intelligent Systems, **14**(1):27–36 (1999).
11. H. S. Pinto, D. N. Peralta, and N. J. Mamede, *Using prot'eg'e-2000 in reuse processes,* in Proc. of the OntoWeb-SIG3 Workshop at the 13th Int. Conf. on Knowledge Engineering and Knowledge Management (EKAW 2002), pp. 15–26 (September, 2002).
12. W. Ceusters, B. Smith, and M. V. Mol, *Using ontology in query answering systems: Scenarios, requirements and challenges,* in Proc. of the 2nd CoLogNET-ElsNET Symposium, pp. 5–15 (2003).
13. J. Angele, E. Moench, H. Oppermann, S. Staab, and D. Wenke, *Ontology-based query and answering in chemistry: Ontonova @ project halo,* in Proc. of the 2nd Intl. Semantic Web Conf. (ISWC2003) (Springer, ed.), (Sanibel Island, FL, USA), (October, 2003).
14. M. Denny (November 2002); http://www.xml.com/pub/a/2002/11/06/ontologies.html.
15. V. K. Chaudhri, A. Farquhar, R. Fikes, P. D. Karp, and J. P. Rice., *Open knowledge base connectivity (okbc) specification document 2.0.3,* Technical Report, SRI Int. and Stanford University (KSL), (April, 1998).
16. M. R. Genesereth and R. E. Fikes, *Knowledge interchange format, version 3.0, reference manual,* Technical Report, Logic-92-1, Stanford University (1992).
17. X. Zheng, *Agent construction in mobile surveyor,* in proc. of the 42nd Annual ACM Southeast Conf., pp. 58–63, (ACM Press, New York, NY, USA), (April 2-3 2004).
18. H. Javitz and A. Valdes, *The SRI IDES statistical anomaly detector,* IEEE Symposium on Security and Privacy, pp. 316–326 (May, 1991).
19. G. Vigna and R. A. Kemmerer, *Netstat: A network-based intrusion detection approach,* in proc. of the 14th Annual Computer Security Conf., (Scottsdale, Arizona), pp. 25–, (December 1998).
20. L. Deri and S. Suin, *Improving network security using ntop,* in proc. of the RAID 2000 - Workshop on the Recent Advances in Intrusion Detection, (Toulouse, France), (October, 2000).
21. S. C. Chapra and R. P. Canale, *Numerical Methods for Engineers: With Software and Programming Applications* (McGraw-Hill Comp.: Elizabeth A. Jones 2001).
22. Stanford KSL Ontology Library (September, 2004); http://www-ksl-svc.stanford.edu:5915/.

23. H. Wache, T. Vogele, U. Visser, H. Stuckenschmidt, G. Schuster, H. Neumann, and S. Hubnet, *Ontology-based integration of information - a survey of existing approaches,* IJCAI Workshop on Ontologies and Information Sharing, pp. 108–117 (2001).
24. *Palm pilot robot kit* (September 2004); http://www.cs.cmu.edu/ pprk/.
25. C. Bey, E. Freeman, and J. Ostrem (September, 2004); http://www.palmos.com/dev/tech/docs/palmos/CompanionTOC.html.
26. A. Williams, *Java and the Waba toolkit* Dr. Dobb's Journal of Software Tools **26**(2):92, 94, 96, 98 (2001).

Chapter 32

THE NEWS ONTOLOGY FOR PROFESSIONAL JOURNALISM APPLICATIONS

Norberto Fernández-García, Luis Sánchez-Fernández, José M. Blázquez-del-Toro and Jesús Villamor-Lugo
Carlos III University of Madrid, Av. Universidad, 30, 28911 Leganés, Madrid, Spain

Abstract: In the Information Society, being well informed is a basic necessity. News agencies, journals, newspapers, and other communication media are required to provide fresh, relevant, high quality information to their clients. As partners of the NEWS (News Engine Web Services) EU IST project we believe that the usage of Semantic Web technologies may enable news providers to achieve these goals. So we are working on developing tools to bring Semantic Web technology into the world of professional journalism. As part of this process, we are currently developing an ontology for NEWS applications. It integrates current journalistic standards with existing top level ontologies and other metadata-related standards. In this chapter we describe the current state of that ontology, including aspects such as its intended usage, the development process and the architecture.

Key words: Semantic Web; ontologies; journalism; annotation; metadata

1. INTRODUCTION

It is probably true to say that the industry where the greatest amount of text and multimedia content is produced is the news industry. It is not by chance that this industry has long been aware of such things as metadata, formats for storing and exchanging content tagged with metadata, search and retrieval technologies, etc.

The news agencies are one of the main actors in the news business. The news agencies produce text and multimedia news items that will then be distributed to the mass media companies (journals, broadcast radios, television channels). Recently, they are also beginning to become interested in reaching the end user directly. The news agencies require a high quality production system for annotation, archiving, distribution, search and retrieval of content. Currently, the technologies used are:

- annotation: which is done by hand by journalists;
- distribution: which uses broadcast technologies (for instance, satellite transmission) or the Internet;
- archiving, search and retrieval: which are based on document databases and free-text search over selected fields of news items.

In practice the current situation is that news items have very reliable but limited annotations. For instance they can have annotations for category, date, author, rights owner, keywords and so on, but they do not place annotations on the entities referred to inside a news item (persons, companies, locations, etc.), because the cost of such annotations given the amount of content produced by the news agencies would be unaffordable. Even the cost of adding by hand the limited set of annotations currently used is large, so any tool support would be very valuable.

With respect to search and retrieval, the use of free-text search (over selected metadata fields or the news item content for text news items) and the lack of annotations make the results obtained open to improvement both in precision and recall. This is made more important by the huge amount of data archived.

The NEWS project aims to develop intelligent technology for the news domain in order to overcome these issues. This technology should improve the state of the art in news agencies' work processes by:

- developing a semantic annotation tool that will be able to categorize and annotate the content of a news item based on statistical and natural language processing technologies;
- developing a deductive database that will be able to perform semantic searches over the news items stored in such a database.

In accord with this vision, the goal of the NEWS project is to develop a standard vocabulary for the semantic annotation of news information objects, as well as a tool for its maintenance, which supports Semantic Web applications in the news domain.

Within the context of the project, the NEWS Ontology will serve as the knowledge representation and exchange language for all the content intelligence components in the NEWS system.

In this chapter we present a first version of the NEWS Ontology that is currently available for use. The rest of the chapter is structured as follows. Section 2 is devoted to providing a brief introduction to the NEWS Project. Section 3 gives an overview of existing ontologies. Section 4 analyzes

NEWS Ontology's intended application scenario and its effect on the design of the ontology. Following this, sections 5, 6, 7 and 8 describe each of the modules available in the current version of the NEWS Ontology. Concluding remarks are presented in section 9.

2. THE NEWS PROJECT

2.1 Description

The European FP6 001906 NEWS Project is an *Information Society and Technologies* (IST) program project, comprised by the *EFE* [1] and *ANSA* [2] News agencies, *Deutsches Forschungszentrum für Künstliche Intelligenz GmbH* (DFKI) [3] research institute, *Ontology Ltd* [4] company and *Universidad Carlos III de Madrid* [5].

As stated, the goal is to go beyond the current capabilities of news agencies in managing and delivering information. This includes reducing the gap that exists between the need for users to personalize content selection and presentation and what the news industry can offer. The use of Semantic Web technologies is the key element in obtaining better results than the filtering tools currently used can provide. These technologies are applied in this project along with elements that support them, keeping in mind always the importance of using standards.

In order to increase the impact of these technologies on users, news intelligence components with multilingual and multimedia capabilities are to be developed by this project, using automatic ontological annotation techniques.

This ontological annotation, together with news intelligence components will be integrated as Web Services into a standard interoperable platform, accessible by both users and applications.

2.2 Involved Technologies

Several emerging technologies in Web space, such as Semantic Web Technologies and (Semantic) Web Services, converge in the NEWS Project proposal.

1 http://www.efe.es.
2 http://www.ansa.it.
3 http://www.dfki.de.
4 http://www.ontology-ltd.com.
5 http://www.uc3m.es.

2.2.1 Semantic Web Technologies

The emergence of RDF-based semantic markup languages provides a way to use semantic-based querying (Maedche et al., 2003) (Broekstra et al., 2003) instead of the traditional keyword search. This is of great interest to news agencies, because of the huge amounts of information they manage. The use of Semantic technologies obtains better results in terms of precision/recall, which benefits both news agencies journalists and end users. This is achieved through the use of metadata to annotate documents, the creation of ontologies that describe the concepts and relationships present in the domain of interest, and the use of inference engines to extract implicit knowledge from the explicitly stated in databases.

As will be seen in following sections, the integration of RDF-based languages with international news standards, like NewsML, NITF, SRS and PRISM, into an ontology is mandatory in order to achieve these objectives.

2.2.2 (Semantic) Web Services

All these new developments might not be usable if they imposed considerable changes on the well-established workflows of news agencies. The use of a Service Oriented Architecture provides access to applications without modifying the agencies' workflow too much. This gives rise to a situation where remote software applications may work together. The elements of these applications may be heterogeneous and so a common platform is needed. (Semantic) Web Services provide such a platform through the use of XML documents, exchanged in an asynchronous fashion, usually (although it is not mandatory) over well-known protocols like HTTP and SMTP.

2.3 NEWS Workflow and Architecture

The integration of domain-specific knowledge models with existing upper-level ontologies and standards is crucial to furthering the success of the Semantic Web since it facilitates its leverage in new application areas.

Figure 32-1 shows the intended NEWS workflow. The journalist creates the news item and submits it in NITF format to the Annotation & Categorization system. This system analyzes the text and provides the most relevant entities inside the text as well as the SRS categories that better fit the content of the news item. The resulting document is returned to the journalist who checks its validity before sending it to a Heuristic and Deductive Database (HDDB). This element provides storage for the news

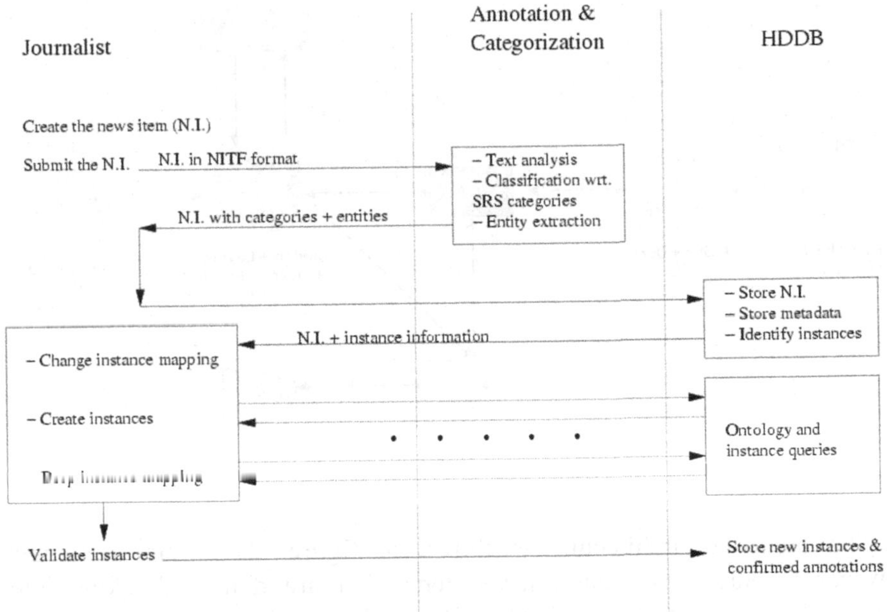

Figure 32-1. NEWS Intended Workflow

items and for the associated metadata. It also allows to map the extracted entities to instances of elements inside the ontology. For example, let us suppose that the Annotation & Categorization system has recognized, among others, the entity "Fernando Alonso". In addition, there exists an instance inside the ontology named `content:Fernando_Alonso`. In this case, the HDDB would map the entity to this instance. The set of all mappings is sent together with the news item back to the journalist who must verify them. The possibilities at this point are:

- commit: the mapping made by the HDDB is valid;
- select another instance: there exists another instance that matches the entity. This instance is obtained after querying the HDDB to retrieve all the available instances that could match the entity;
- create a new instance: none of the instances inside the ontology refer to the entity and this entity is important enough to create a new instance for it;
- drop the mapping: the entity is not relevant so there is no need to create a new instance for it.

After doing this for all the entities, the journalist sends the news item with the confirmed annotations to be stored into the HDDB.

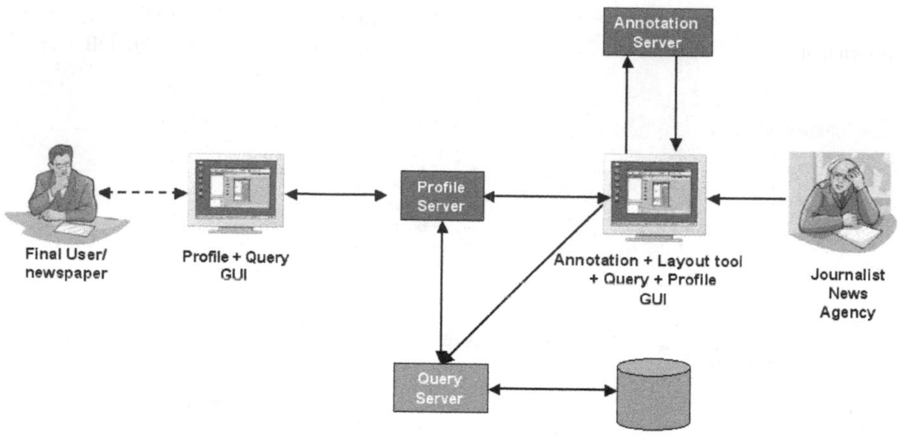

Figure 32-2. NEWS Architecture

The proposed architecture is shown in figure 32-2. End users and newspaper journalists request news items that are delivered taking into account the user profiles stored at the *Profile Server*.

Meanwhile, a journalist from the news agency can add new news items to this database. As can be seen in the figure, news items need to be annotated before their insertion in the database. The *Annotation Server* provides the necessary support for this task. But this is not the only feature offered to news agency's journalists because they can also query the database for related news items. In order to obtain better results they also have a profile in the *Profile Server*.

3. ONTOLOGIES: STATE OF THE ART

As we have seen in previous sections, applying Semantic Web technologies to the world of journalism requires the definition of ontologies which model the domain of interest. In our case such ontologies should be rich enough to provide us with:

- the elements (classes, properties) useful for news item descriptions, including aspects like priority, authorship and rights information, categorization, etc.;
- classes and properties to be used in news item content annotation. In practice this means including elements representing almost everything in the world;
- rules to make intelligent information retrieval possible.

We started by analyzing the state of the art in order to find the appropriate ontologies to be (re)used in the context of the NEWS project. We found several interesting resources, for instance:

SUMO SUMO (Suggested Upper Merged Ontology) (Niles and Pease, 2001) is a generic (top-level) ontology, developed by *Teknowledge Corporation* [6], which contains a set of general classes (such as, for example, `Agent`, `Process`, `Region`, `TimeInterval`, etc) and some properties (such as, for example, `meetsSpatially`, `meets Temporally`, `possesses`, `material`, etc.) suitable for use in a broad range of domains. It is one of the ontologies being worked on by the *IEEE Standard Upper Ontology Working Group*[7] in the process of development of its standard upper-level ontology. An OWL version of SUMO is freely available for download at (Teknowledge, 2003a).

MILO SUMO is a very generic ontology. To ease the task of developing specific domain ontologies taking SUMO as a basis, a mid-level ontology called MILO (MId-Level Ontology) (Niles and Terry, 2004) has also been developed by Teknowledge. A KIF version of MILO can be freely downloaded at (Teknowledge, 2003b) and used for non-commercial purposes. It contains concepts like `Newspaper`, `Publication`, `Sport`, `Government`, etc.

KIMO The KIM Ontology is a generic ontology developed by *Ontotext* [8] as part of its project KIM (Knowledge and Information Management) (Popov et al., 2004) where it is used, among others, as a basic vocabulary for the annotation of text resources. It contains about 250 classes (like `TimeUnit`, `Location`, `Agent`, `Event`, etc.) and 100 properties. An RDFS version of KIMO is freely available for download at (Ontotext, 2004).

PROTON PROTON (PROTo ONtology) (Terziev et al., 2005) is a basic upper-level lightweight ontology developed in the context of the project SEKT [9]. It is based on KIMO but is implemented in OWL Lite instead of RDFS. It contains about 250 classes and 100 properties, intended to provide basic elements for semantic annotation, indexing and retrieval. Some interesting concepts included in this ontology are for example: `Event`, `Person`, `Agent`, `Product`, `Number` or `Language`.

Upper Cyc Ontology The Upper Cyc Ontology is a generic ontology implemented in CycL and used as the upper level ontology in Cyc Knowledge Base (Lenat and Guha, 1990). It contains over 3,000 general terms (like `Country`, `Agent`, `SportsEvent`, etc.) and relations among them like `isa`, which relates instances with classes, or `genls`,

6 http://www.teknowledge.com.
7 http://suo.ieee.org.
8 http://www.ontotext.com.
9 http://www.sekt-project.com.

generalization, used for taxonomic relationships. A zipped MS Access MDB file containing Upper Cyc Ontology is freely available (for all purposes) at (Ontotext, 1997).

OpenCyc OpenCyc (OpenCyc, 2002b) is an open source version of Cyc. It consist of a general knowledge base and a reasoning engine. The knowledge base is written in CycL and can be accessed from Java programs using and open API. Version 1.0 of OpenCyc will contain more than 5,000 concepts (generic like for example `TimeInterval`, `Place`, `Agent`, `Event`, etc. and more specific like `BussinessEvent`, `Ambulance`, etc.) and 50,000 assertions. A free OWL version of OpenCyc Knowledge Base can be downloaded from (OpenCyc, 2002a). It is also one of the ontologies being worked on by the IEEE Standard Upper Ontology Working Group in the process of developing its standard upper-level ontology.

EuroWordNet Top Level EuroWordNet (Vossen, 1998; Vossen, 2001) is a multilingual database, developed in the context of European projects LE-2 4003 and LE-4 8328, containing information for several European languages (Dutch, Italian, Spanish, German, French, Czech and Estonian). The EuroWordNet Top Level ontology is a 64 class ontology, based on existing linguistic classifications, and developed to ease the task of encoding the different language resources in a uniform and interoperable way. It contains useful concepts such as `Building`, `Vehicle`, `Instrument`, `Place`, `Human`, etc.

SENSUS SENSUS (Knight and Whitney, 1994) is a taxonomy with 70,000 nodes containing terminological information. It is an extension and reorganization of WordNet (Fellbaum, 1998; Miller, 1995), written in the LOOM (MacGregor and Bates, 1987) language, and browsable via web using OntoSaurus (Swartout et al., 1996) at (Ontosaurus Loom Web Browser, 2003).

TAP Knowledge Base The TAP knowledge base (Guha and McCool, 2003) is developed by *Knowledge Systems Laboratory*[10] at *Stanford University* in collaboration with *Knowledge Management Group* at *IBM Almaden* [11] and *MIT/W3C* [12] members. It contains lexical and taxonomic information about popular objects, including for example: movies, authors, sports, places or companies. The full knowledge base coded in RDF(S) can be downloaded from (TAP, Building the Semantic Web, 2001).

UNSPSC The UNSPSC, United Nations Standard Products and Services Classification, developed by *ECCMA* (*Electronic Commerce Code Management Association*)[13] is a dictionary for service and product

10 http://ksl.stanford.edu.

11 http://www.almaden.ibm.com/software/km/index.shtml.

12 http://www.w3.org/2000/01/sw/.

13 http://www.eccma.org.

categorization. It contains over 20,000 items each of which is described by a code and a title. A code consists of four fields: segment, family, class and commodity, each two decimal digits. Basically, these four fields work as a four level taxonomy, the segments being the most general categories. For example, the identifier (10,10,17,01) represents `Live salmon`, which is a subclass of (10,10,17,00) `Live fish`, which is a subclass of (10,10,00,00) `Live animals`, which is a subclass of (10,00,00,00) `Live Plant and Animal Material and Accessories and Supplies`. Some currently available segments are for example: `Tools and General Machinery`, `Published Products`, `Editorial and Design and Graphic and Fine Art Services`, etc. DAML+OIL and RDFS versions of UNSPSC can be downloaded from (UNSPSC, 2003).

Analyzing in more detail the resources that we have introduced here, we have found them partialy useful for our purposes: most of them provide classes and relations for content annotation, and some of them (such as, for example, SUMO or OpenCyc) also provide rules for reasoning purposes. But in relation to news item descriptions and categorization, which require specific information from the journalism domain, we found these resources not to be very useful. Furthermore, no specific ontology for the journalism domain seems to be available in the state of the art. Nevertheless, some useful resources in this area are available, such as metadata standards for publication purposes (Dublin Core Metadata Initiative, 2005a; IDEAlliance, 2004) and journalism standards like NITF (IPTC, 2003a), NewsML (IPTC, 2004a) and IPTC [14] NewsCodes (IPTC, 2004b). The former are useful, but, since they are not specifically designed for the journalism domain, leave interesting aspects uncovered. The latter provide domain information covering all interesting aspects, but they are just XML schemata (NITF, NewsML) or controlled vocabularies providing values for some fields in the schema (NewsCodes), so they lack the degree of formalization of ontologies.

As a result of this analysis, we decided to develop the NEWS ontology. Our intention was to provide the basic elements required by professional semantic web based journalism applications. Of course, we will take as basis existing resources when possible, reusing and adapting them to our purposes. The next section will describe in more detail the design and implementation of this ontology.

[14] IPTC stands for International Press Telecommunications Council. It develops and maintains technical standards for improved news exchange that are used by virtually every major news organization in the world.

4. THE NEWS ONTOLOGY USAGE SCENARIO

As a first step in our process, we have analyzed the intended usage scenario of NEWS tools and how it might affect the design of the ontology. Some of the conditions introduced by the study of this scenario are:

Ontology Usage NEWS tools will provide:

- **Automatic news categorization** This consists of classifying news items using a taxonomy. The news item class can be used, for example, to decide which clients might be interested in a certain item and to send it to them (push model). Classification is currently done by hand using basic specific taxonomies [15]. In NEWS we propose to automate the process (with human supervision of the results) and define richer taxonomies, using mappings back to the old ones to achieve backwards compatibility.
- **Automatic news annotation** In the context of NEWS, this will include not only the whole item metadata currently added (mainly used for news item life cycle management), but also annotation of news contents (helpful for example in fine-grained news item selection by clients -pull model-). All these annotations will be added automatically (again with human supervision of the results).
- **Intelligent Information Retrieval** One of the main objectives of the NEWS project is to go beyond the classical text search facilities currently being used by news agencies and provide high quality information retrieval services. To do so, a reasoning-based query component will provide access to semantically annotated news items.

Conclusions for the NEWS Ontology design: Our ontology should provide the basic vocabulary for annotations and the taxonomy for news item classification. It should also provide the rules used by the reasoner for intelligent information retrieval.

News Representation Standards Compatibility Journalism standards like NewsML, or NITF are currently in use or are expected to be used in the future by news agencies to represent news items. Our metadata model should be compatible with these standards.

Conclusions for the NEWS Ontology design: We need to analyze journalism standards looking for information about what kind of metadata (global, inline) they support and where we can add metadata to news items represented using such standards.

Metadata Standards Compatibility Some standards like Dublin Core (DC), Publishing Requirements for Industry Standard Metadata (PRISM) or Subject Reference System (SRS) (IPTC, 2003b), could provide us with sets of standardized metadata. Compatibility with these standards is highly desirable because using such metadata, agencies can make their contents

[15] For example, taxonomy of ANSA consists of only 11 classes.

more accessible to other applications which are also compatible with them (for example, with editing applications from the field of communications media).

Conclusions for the NEWS Ontology design: These standards must be taken into account as a possible source of elements to be included in our ontology.

Fast Processing One of the requirements expressed by news agencies is *freshness*: news should be delivered to clients as fast as possible. With this requirement in mind it seems that the best solution is to avoid time-consuming inference processes, and develop a lightweight ontology. The problem with this solution is that it contradicts the requirement for the intelligent information retrieval function of NEWS tools: the lighter the ontology, the poorer the quality of intelligent information retrieval.

Conclusions for the NEWS Ontology design: A tradeoff should be reached. A first approach could be to develop a heavyweight ontology and try to obtain more efficiency at the reasoning level. We can later refine the results making the ontology lighter if required, until we reach the desired level of performance.

Range of Contents One of the biggest problems in building a content ontology which can be used to annotate the contents of a news item is that almost everything in the world can appear in a piece of news. It seems we need to model all things in the world, which is far from being an easy task. Some possibilities for dealing with this problem are:

- the use of already an existing general ontology, like OpenCyc, which provides concepts for a great number of application domains;
- the use of a top level ontology, such as, for example, SUMO, which provides general concepts independent of application domain;
- the definition of different ontologies for different domains, and the association of domain specific ontologies to news categories; that is, for instance, use a *sports ontology* to deal with news items in the *sports* category.

Conclusions for the NEWS Ontology design: Building an ontology to model a large set of entities is a hard task, so existing ontologies should be reused when possible. The content ontology should cover only the most important topics and domains for our application. Information about what these domains are may be inferred by looking at news categorization standards. So, a first approach could be a combination of two of the previous ones: to use a generic top level ontology and one domain specific ontology for each of the first level classes of IPTC SRS taxonomy (17 classes).

Multilingual Capabilities News agencies produce news items in several languages. For example, Spanish agency EFE produces items in Spanish, English, Brazilian, Arabic, and other languages. In such an environment, multilingual capabilities are crucial to allow, for example, cross-lingual query and retrieval: queries expressed in a certain language can (if the user requires it) be used to obtain relevant documents in other languages as a result. In the context of the NEWS project, we are mainly interested in dealing with news items in three languages: Spanish, English and Italian. In order to implement multilingual capabilities, we propose the usage of multilingual thesauri such as EuroWordNet, which relates words of different languages.

Conclusions for the NEWS Ontology design: Thesaurus words need to be mapped to ontology concepts, which is a time-consuming task, so we should find a way to minimize this time. A first step in this direction could be to use SUMO as a top-level ontology, because mappings from SUMO to WordNet already exist. Since WordNet and EuroWordNet are strongly related, the WordNet to SUMO mappings can be taken as a basis for the EuroWordNet to NEWS Ontology mapping task.

Ontology Standards Compatibility We are interested in compatibility with widely accepted ontology-related standards, such as W3C languages for ontology definition: RDFS (Brickley and Guha, 2004) and OWL (Dean and Schreiber, 2004). This requirement can be seen as being in contradiction with the need for rules for intelligent information retrieval, because neither RDFS nor OWL provides facilities for the definition of complex rules. Currently there is an initiative from the W3C to define a rule language for the Semantic Web, (Horrocks et al., 2004), but it is at an initial stage, so we need a different solution.

Conclusions for the NEWS Ontology design: We need an ontology language that is compatible with current W3C standards and which has complex rule definition capabilities. As we will see in section 5 our first choice has been TRIPLE (Sintek and Decker, 2002), a tool developed by members from DFKI, *Stanford University Database Group*[16] and *Digital Enterprise Research Institute*[17].

As conclusion to this analysis, we now outline the main characteristics of the NEWS Ontology:

1. It will provide:
   - basic vocabulary for semantic annotation of news items;
   - a taxonomy for news item classification;
   - rules for intelligent information retrieval.
2. In its design, standards such as NITF, NewsML, DC, SRS, etc, should be taken into account.
3. It will use SUMO as a basis for content annotation. Modules for each first level category of SRS taxonomy will also be provided.

[16] http://www-db.stanford.edu.

[17] http://sw.deri.ie.

4. It should be easy to map to a multilingual thesaurus like EuroWordNet.

As a consequence of this analysis for the NEWS Ontology, we have decided to structure the ontology into three main modules:

- a categorization module, containing the taxonomy for news item classification;
- an envelope metadata module, containing definitions for elements useful in the semantic annotation of news items with life cycle management metadata;
- a content annotation metadata module, containing definitions for elements useful in the semantic annotation of news item contents.

We also need an additional module because of the selection of TRIPLE as the ontology language: the Structural module. This is because TRIPLE has no fixed predefined semantics for object-oriented features such as classes and inheritance. Such semantics should be defined by users, and we do so in the Structural module.

This gives us the four modules which are now part of the current version of the NEWS Ontology. All these modules (with the exception of the Structural module which, as we have said, is a consequence of using TRIPLE) are related because some elements (classes and properties) in the Content Annotation module become parent elements of those in the other modules. The next sections will describe in more detail each of these modules.

5. TRIPLE AND THE STRUCTURAL MODULE

We have developed our ontology using TRIPLE as language. As we have seen in the previous section, TRIPLE does not have a predefined fixed semantics, so we need to define such a semantics in a special module of our ontology: the Structural module. This section provides a basic introduction to TRIPLE explaining its basic syntax, in order to make understandable the examples provided in the rest of this chapter. After this brief introduction, we describe the Structural module itself.

5.1 TRIPLE

Is a rule and query language based on Horn logic and built on top of the XSB inference engine (Sagonas et al., 1994).

An RDF statement can be expressed in TRIPLE as

```
subject[predicate->object].
```

For example:

```
instance:Medellin_City[content:is_city_of->instance:iso_country_CO].
```

The use of namespaces allows us to use different sources of data:

```
instance := "http://www.news-project.com/NEWSContentInstance#".
content := "http://www.news-project.com/ContentOntology#".
```

Reification is also supported through the use of "<" and ">". TRIPLE also provides means to simplify the writing of data:

```
content:Government_Colombia[content:is_government_of
   ->instance:iso_country_CO[content:capital_city-> content:Bogota_City]].
content:Michael_Douglas[content:has_function->content:Actor; content:husband->
   content:Catherine_Zeta_Jones].
```

The introduction of variables is through quantifiers: `FORALL` and `EXISTS`:

```
FORALL P1,P2 P1[news:has_less_prioriy->P2] <- P2[news:has_more_priority->P1].
```

Notice the syntax used in the implication. The consequent is expressed before the premises.

The last characteristic still to be mentioned is that TRIPLE is not only capable of being used to express rules or facts, but it can also be used as a query language. A query is a rule without head:

```
FORALL Q <- Q[content:occupiesPositionPredicatePosition->content:President].
```

In this example we look for all the elements in the database whose value for the property `content:occupiesPositionPredicate-Position` is `content:President`.

5.2 Structural module

One of the requirements of the NEWS Ontology scenario is to be compatible with languages like RDFS. Since we want to use TRIPLE as language, we need to define and axiomatize the semantics of RDFS in TRIPLE. In order to achieve this task, we need to define a set of rules such as, for example, the transitivity of `rdfs:subClassOf` and `rdfs:subPropertyOf`. The structural module of the NEWS Ontology covers these topics. In order to implement this module, we look at W3C documents defining RDF semantics such as (Hayes, 2004) and include the appropriate triples/rules in our ontology. Some of these are, for example:

```
// If S is subproperty of P all pairs of (O,V)
// related by S are also related by P (3)
FORALL O,V,P O[P->V] <-
  EXISTS S (S[rdfs:subPropertyOf->P] AND O[S->V]).

// All instances of a class are also instances of its superclasses
FORALL O,T O[rdf:type->T] <-
  EXISTS S (S[rdfs:subClassOf->T] AND O[rdf:type->S]).

// rdfs:subClassOf is transitive (3.4)
FORALL C1,C3 C1[rdfs:subClassOf->C3] <-
  EXISTS C2 (C1[rdfs:subClassOf->C2] AND C2[rdfs:subClassOf->C3]).

// rdfs:subPropertyOf is transitive (3.5)
FORALL C1,C3 C1[rdfs:subPropertyOf->C3] <-
  EXISTS C2 (C1[rdfs:subPropertyOf->C2] AND C2[rdfs:subPropertyOf->C3]).
```

6. IPTC SRS AND THE CATEGORIZATION TAXONOMY MODULE

One of the objectives of NEWS is to provide means for automatic news categorization. The Categorization Taxonomy module provides the basic vocabulary, the classes, used in such a process. It is based on the categorization system of the IPTC, the Subject Reference System, SRS. This section introduces the SRS system and describes in detail the implementation of the Categorization Taxonomy module.

6.1 SRS

NewsCodes, formerly known as Topic Sets, are controlled vocabularies defined by the IPTC which provide values for certain elements and attributes in NewsML or NITF documents. The most basic of these standardized NewsCodes (`Subject Code`, `Subject Qualifier`, `Media Type`, `NewsItem Type` and `Genre`) constitute the IPTC Subject Reference System (SRS). For categorization purposes two of these NewsCodes require special attention: the `Subject Code` and `Subject Qualifier` NewsCodes. Their values are used to represent `Subject References`.

A `Subject Reference` describes the content subject (or category) of a news object. It is identified by a fixed eight decimal digit string. The first two digits represent the `Subject`, which can take values in a range of 17 possibilities such as, for example, `Politics (11)`, `Labour (09)`, `Religion and Belief` (12), or `Science and Technology` (13). The following three digits represent the `Subject Matter` which is optional (000 means none). The last three digits can contain `000` (no value) or a number representing a `Subject Detail` (if `Subject Matter` exists) or a `Subject Qualifier` (in the case it does not). Basically the `Subject, Subject Matter` and `Subject Detail` act as a kind of three level taxonomy (from more general to more specific). Their values can be found in the `Subject Code` NewsCodes. The `Subject Qualifier` is used to make more precise a `Subject` and its values are defined in the `Subject Qualifier` NewsCodes. Apart from the numerical identifiers, subject references can have names in several languages. Finally, a single news object can provide information about different issues so it can have several subject references.

6.2 Categorization Module

As we have seen in subsection 6.1 SRS can be seen as a three level hierarchy consisting of `Subject, Subject Matter` and `Subject Detail`. Our NEWS Categorization module, takes these values and defines a tree of classes whose root is the `NewsItem` class defined in the content module (see section 8). The result is a taxonomy of over 1,200 classes.

The concrete news items generated by news agencies will be instances of one or more subclasses of `NewsItem`, so, for example, if we have a news item related with "economy" and "politics" topics, we can define for such a news item:

```
// IPTC Subject economy, business and finance
news_item_uri[rdf:type->iptc_subject:sr04000000].

// IPTC Subject politics
news_item_uri[rdf:type->iptc_subject:sr11000000].
```

In addition to the hierarchy, IPTC SRS defines a `Subject Qualifier`. It is used to make a `Subject` more precise. For instance, if a news item is talking about a sporting event (`Subject Sport` or `15000000`), we can add a `Subject Qualifier` saying if it is a male or female sporting event.

To link a `Subject` with a `Subject Qualifier` we have defined the classes `Subject` and `SubjectQualifier` in our ontology. The instances of `Subject` are the first level taxonomy classes. The instances of `SubjectQualifier` are taken from `Subject Qualifier` NewsCodes. Using a ternary relation we say that in a certain news item a concrete instance of `Subject` has a certain qualifier.

Note that instances of `Subject` are classes whose instances are concrete news items. The treatment of classes as instances is disallowed in OWL Lite and OWL DL, but not in RDFS, where, for example, the class `rdfs:Class` is an instance of itself.

In figure 32-3 we can see the taxonomy of NEWS Categorization module.

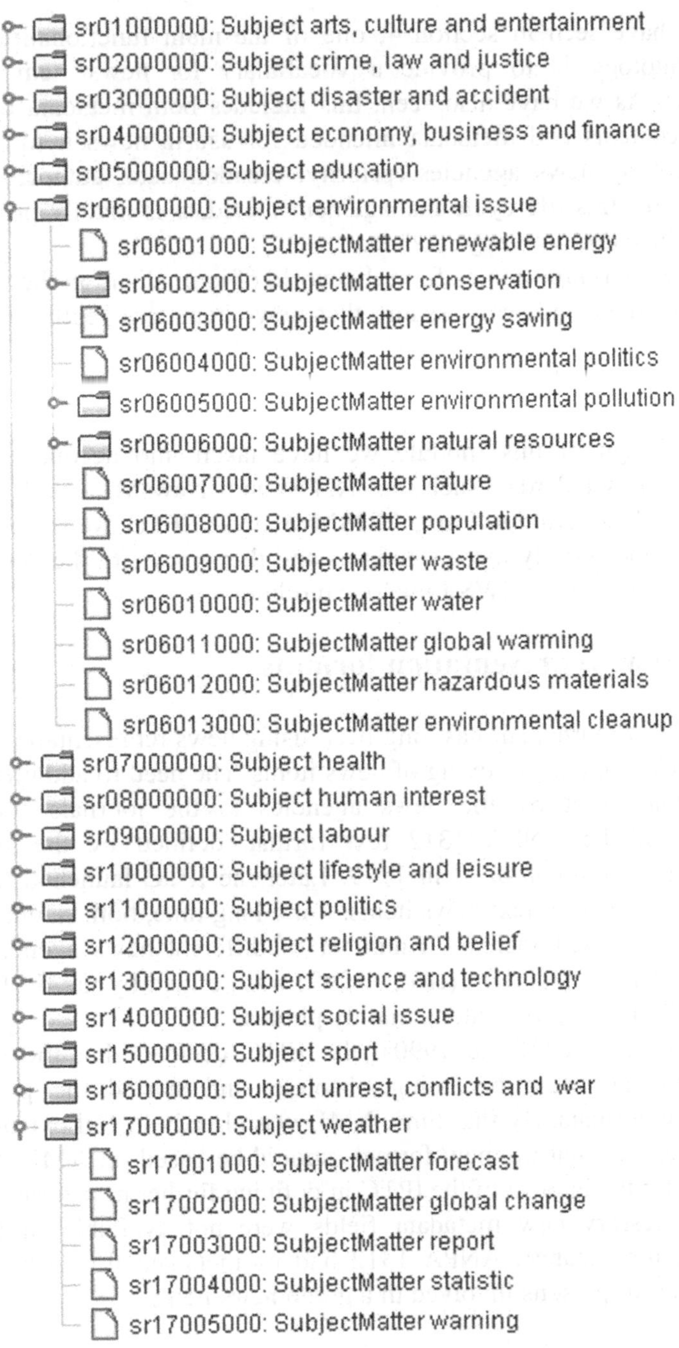

Figure 32-3. An excerpt of NEWS Categorization module taxonomy

7. ENVELOPE MODULE AND RELATED STANDARDS

As we have seen in section 4, one of the main functionalities of the NEWS Ontology is to provide a vocabulary for news item semantic annotations. As we have also seen, this includes both metadata describing the news contents and metadata intended for use in news item life cycle management by news agencies (priority, creation date, author, etc). The vocabulary for this life cycle management metadata is mainly provided by the News Envelope ontology module.

The name *envelope* comes from the world of journalism: in the context of the NEWS project, we can assume that news items are represented using XML-based IPTC standards like NITF or NewsML. Basically both standards can be seen as *envelopes* used to associate metadata to news contents, and this is the origin of the name.

In the design of this module we have taken into accout news item representation standards, such as NITF and NewsML, and metadata standards such as Dublin Core, PRISM and the IPTC NewsCodes. This section describes briefly these standards and then goes into the detail of the implementation of the NEWS Envelope module.

7.1 News representation formats

The field of journalism has long been using news representation formats both for exchange and archiving of news items. The need to add metadata to the text items sent by the news agencies to the journals forced the appearance of the ANPA 1312 text format, defined by the *American National Press Association* [18] in 1979. Later the IPTC launched the IPTC 7901 standard, also for text news items. For a long time, both standards have persisted, being used each by a number of different news agencies. Also another standard, named IIM (IPTC, 1999) was defined by the IPTC for the exchange of binary news content, mainly photos.

At the beginning of the 1990s, the IPTC decided that the currently available formats were becoming obsolete, and started the process of defining new formats. By that time, XML was already in full expansion, so the IPTC decided that the new formats should be based on XML. Some of the reasons for the interest of the IPTC in defining further new formats were:

- some necessary new metadata fields were not available in previous formats; for instance, ANPA 1312 had no metadata for describing the companies or persons involved in a given news item;

[18] http://www.naa.org.

- the support for multimedia was very limited or nonexistent; ANPA 1312 and IPTC 7901 are purely text formats; IIM can contain any binary document, but it is not able to structure the content (for instance, it is not possible to define in any standard way that a given text news item and a photo describe the same event);
- no support for the news life cycle was supported in previous formats: news item version, news item components, related news items, multilinguality, etc. were all unsupported.

The first of the new generation of news standards was named NITF (IPTC, 2003a) and was oriented towards text news items, although it allowed the embedding of multimedia content in the text. It was enriched with a broad set of metadata that can be defined for a news item as a whole (date, location, headline, etc.) and could also be used to tag entities that appear in the content of the news item (inline metadata) such as persons, companies, and so on.

A second new standard, named NewsML (IPTC, 2004a), was defined to support multimedia news items and their life cycle. NewsML is mainly an envelope for one or several news multimedia content items. Among others, NewsML provides the following features:

- support for news content in any media and format;
- rich metadata for description of a news item as a whole, including entities appearing in a news item;
- news items composition and structure;
- definition of news items relations;
- news item life cycle. News versions;
- rights information.

It has to be noted that NITF and NewsML should not be seen as competitors but as complementary standards. For instance, since NewsML is only an envelope for news content, it is not possible to tag entities inside a text news item content, as is the case in NITF. All the metadata present in a NewsML document refers to one content item as a whole (of the possible several content items described by the NewsML document). On the other hand, NITF has no support for structuring news content into subcomponents. In fact, IPTC recommends NITF as the preferred text format inside a NewsML document.

7.2 Metadata Standards

DC The Dublin Core Metadata Initiative is an open forum born in 1995 with the objective of developing a basic, easy to learn and use, multidomain vocabulary for resource description. The Dublin Core Metadata Element Set is standardized by ISO (ISO 15836:2003(E)) and has versions in 25 different languages. The basic element set consists of 15 elements such as, for example: `title`, `creator`, `subject`, `date`, `format`, `type`, `identifier`, `rights` and so on. This basic element set has been extended giving origin to DCMI Metadata Terms (Dublin Core Metadata Initiative, 2005b). The extension includes the addition of new elements (such as `abstract`, `references`, etc.), defining a vocabulary for values of `type` element (DCMI Type Vocabulary) and defining encoding schemes to be used as values for certain elements (for example `format` can take values from Internet Media Types).

PRISM Publishing Requirements for Industry Standard Metadata is developed by *IDEAlliance* (*International Digital Enterprise Alliance*) [19] and provides a vocabulary of metadata to be used in management and processing of any kind of content which can be published (books, journal content, etc.). PRISM provides both the elements used to describe content and the vocabularies supplying the possible values of those elements. The main purpose of PRISM metadata is to support the description of resources as a whole, the definition of management metadata (for example, rights), the specification of relations between resources, and the representation of inline metadata. The specification contains more than 70 elements, some of them obtained from the DC basic set. These elements are grouped into several categories:

- **General purpose** `dc:identifier`, `dc:title`, `dc:creator`, etc.
- **Provenance** `dc:publisher`, `prism:issn`, `dc:source`, etc.
- **Timestamps** `prism:creationDate`, `prism:modificationDate`, `prism:expirationDate`, etc.
- **Subject Description** `dc:coverage`, `dc:subject`, `prism:section`, etc.
- **Resource Relationships** `prism:isPartOf`, `prism:isBasedOn`, `prism:requires`, `prism:isReferencedBy`, etc.
- **Rights and Permissions** `dc:rights`, `prl:usage`, etc.
- **Controlled Vocabularies** `pcv:Descriptor`, `pcv:definition`, `pcv:label`, `pcv:vocabulary`, etc.
- **Inline markup** `pim:event`, `pim:industry`, `pim:location`, `pim:person`, etc.

IPTC NewsCodes

As we saw in subsection 6.1 NewsCodes (IPTC, 2004b) are controlled vocabularies that provide values for certain NewsML and NITF document fields. They can be defined by users, but for interoperability reasons, several

[19] http://www.idealliance.org.

essential NewsCodes are standardized by IPTC and their use is recommended. Other sets apart from those mentioned in subsection 6.1 are:

- **NewsItem Type** Contains values like `DTD`, `Alert`, `News` and so on.
- **Priority** Values from `1` (highest) to `9` (lowest), used to indicate the relative importance of a news item for distribution.
- **Format** `BMP`, `IIM`, `MP3`, `MPEG` or `NITF` among others.
- **Genre** `Current`, `History`, `Obituary`, etc.
- **Media Type** `Text`, `Graphic`, `Photo`, `Audio`, `Video` and `Animation`.

7.3 Envelope module

We started implementing this module by developing a first prototype (see (Fernández-García and Sánchez-Fernández, 2004)), inspired by NITF, PRISM and Dublin Core. The prototype was later refined by adding metadata components taken from NewsML (for example, specific information related with multimedia news items, which is not covered by the previous standards).

Basically, this module contains a set of definitions of properties which can be used to describe instances of the class `NewsItem`. Following the approach of NewsML, we can divide these properties according to their function into:

Management Metadata Properties These contain information relevant to the management process of a news item, as for example its urgency (`has_urgency`), its status (`has_status`, it is `usable`, `cancelled`, etc) or the UTC time it has been created (`has_creation_time_UTC`). An interesting special kind of property in this group consists of those which relate two news items, saying that one is an update of the other (`is_update_of`) or that one is derived from the other (`is_derived_from`), for example.

Administrative Metadata Properties These provide information about the provenance of a certain news item. Examples of these kind of properties are: `has_provider`, `has_creator` or `has_contributor` among others.

Rights-related Metadata Properties These contain information about the rights pertaining to a certain news item. For example: `has_rights_usage_type`, `has_right_geography`, `has_rights_start_date` or `has_rights_holder` among others.

Descriptive Metadata Properties These are used in relation to information describing the contents of a news item as a whole like, for example, the location where the news story has occurred `has_location`, the language used in elaborating the piece of news `has_language`, or the expected target audience of the item has_interest. A property which is specially important is the one which relates the news item with the entities that are explicitly mentioned in the contents of that news item has_entity_occurrence. The classes for these entities are provided by the NEWS Content Annotation module (see section 8).

Physical, content-related Metadata Properties These also provide information about the contents, but from the physical point of view: its binary size (has_binary_size), the codec used in coding it (for multimedia news items, has_audio_codec, has_video_codec), its MIME type (has_mime_type) or the number of words that it contains (for textual news items, has_word_count), among others.

Others These include keywords, the headline of the news item or its abstract are also included in the description as specific properties.

This module also includes the definition of some classes whose instances are used as a range of possible values for these properties. For instance, classes like Priority, Urgency, Genre or Format are defined here. Since IPTC NewsCodes that provide allowed values for these properties already exist, we have also populated this module with instances taken from such NewsCodes. The result is a module consisting of more than 50 classes, more than 90 properties and over 500 instances.

Another aspect which is covered by this module is the mapping between the priority system of IPTC (with 9 levels of priority) and the system currently used by EFE and ANSA news agencies, based on the one in ANPA (with only 5 levels of priority). Also, some rules and properties are defined to allow priority and urgency comparison, and the ordering of news items using such properties (thus allowing to obtain the news items with a bigger priority than a certain one, for instance).

In figure 32-4 we can see some relations between the NEWS Envelope module and the journalism and publishing standards which inspire its design. Note that in standards such as NITF or NewsML some metadata information can be added in different places. For instance, in NITF the language used to represent the contents can be specified in the lang attribute, as stated in the table, but it can also be added in the document header inside a meta element. So, the news agencies decide the place appropiate to the representation of certain information. Taking this into account, we must say that the information in NITF column has been taken from EFE NITF documents, whereas information from NewsML column has been taken from Reuters NewsML documents, with the exception of Characteristics. We have taken from NewsML 1.1 specification the suggested place for word count metadata. Other interesting points that we can abstract from the table are:

DC + DCMI Terms	PRISM	NITF	NewsML	NEWS Ontology
dc:date, created (DCMI Terms)	prism:creationDate	Element date.issue in docdata	Element FirstCreated child of NewsManagement	envelope:has_creation_time_UTC, envelope:has_creation_time_local
dc:language	dc:language	Attribute lang in element body	Element Language child of DescriptiveMetadata	envelope:has_language
extend (DCMI Terms)	prism:wordCount	Element meta inside body.head	Element Characteristics inside ContentItem	envelope:has_word_count
No content metadata available	prism:location, pim:location	Inline elements: city, country, region, sublocation	No inline metadata, element TopicOccurrence inside DescriptiveMetadata with appropiate topic.	envelope:has_entity_occurrence (with appropiate entity)
No available	No available	Element urgency inside docdata	Element Priority inside NewsEnvelope	envelope:has_priority

Figure 32-4. Translation of elements from standard languages to the NEWS Ontology

- specific concepts from journalism world (as for example the priority of a certain news item) are not directly covered by the standards such as DC and PRISM. These standards are designed to be used in a wide variety of domains and situations, so they do not include particular concepts for concrete domains such as journalism;
- NITF is not designed to be used in conjunction with multimedia content. This can be referenced from NITF documents, but cannot be embedded inside them. This was one of the reasons that motivated the development of NewsML. NewsML documents can have both textual or multimedia contents embedded inside them. So multimedia-related properties are included in NewsML but not directly in NITF;
- as NITF is specifically designed for text contents, its DTD includes elements for inline content annotation. As we can see, this is not the case of NewsML, where entities can only be referenced from the envelope (using for example a `TopicOccurrence` element). This is because NewsML contents can be binary multimedia items, so we may not assume that inline annotations are always possible;
- PRISM includes the basic DC elements, so for example the `dc:language` element is available in both specification. But as we can see in the table, some metadata for content annotation is included in PRISM, but not in DC nor in DC extensions (DCMI terms).

8. SUMO AND THE CONTENT ANNOTATION MODULE

The NEWS Content Annotation Module provides a basic vocabulary for news content annotation. It is also used to tie together the different NEWS Ontology modules. As we have seen in section 4, we propose a structure based on a top level ontology and several domain-specific ontologies. As we have said, we want to adapt already available ontologies when possible. In particular, we have decided to use a part of SUMO (Suggested Upper Merged Ontology) as our top level ontology. In the main, three particular points lend support to our choice:

- as we have seen in section 3, SUMO is an IEEE proposed standard;
- together with SUMO a set of domain ontologies have been developed (see (Pease, 2005)); they, in aggregation, are (claimed by the authors) to be "the largest public formal ontology in existence today". Since we have to develop a top level and also some domain-specific ontologies, we think that we could reuse not only SUMO, but also parts of the associate domain ontologies;
- as stated in section 4 we expect that the choice of SUMO will make easier the multilingual thesauri mapping process.

One of the problems with the choice of SUMO has its origin in a point of view oriented towards the ontology language: the SUMO ontology has been written using the SUO-KIF (IEEE, 2003) formalism, a variant of the KIF (Knowledge Interchange Format) language (Genesereth, 1998). We need to translate it to RDFS/TRIPLE, but the SUO-KIF format has many constructs that have no direct equivalent in RDFS/TRIPLE. In order to ease and automate the translation task, we have created a set of conversion rules. This section describes these translation rules and the resulting Content Annotation module.

8.1 From KIF to TRIPLE

A KIF model is a conceptualization of a given world in terms of objects and relations between objects. The concept of object is quite broad, so virtually anything can be considered as an object.

Relations A relation has in KIF its classical meaning, that is, an arbitrary set of tuples of objects. A first important difference with RDF/TRIPLE is that relations are not only binary, but also ternary, quaternary, etc.

Relations with more than two terms They will be substituted for a number of two argument relations (that is, triples susceptible to be converted to RDF). First we define the class `content:Predicate` as the class of all *n*-ary relations, Then we define a class in RDF whose elements map the tuples of the *n*-ary relation in KIF. Finally, for an *n*-ary KIF relation we define *n* predicates in TRIPLE to have all the information that was in the KIF relation.

Example: let us suppose that we have the statement `R(A,B,C)` over the ternary relation `R`. We define a key `K` that is an instance of a class defined for this translation. The elements inside the relation `R` are replaced by `R1(K,A)`, `R2(K,B)` and `R3(K,C)`. If we use now real elements taken from the SUMO ontology, we find:

```
(instance occupiesPosition TernaryPredicate)
(domain occupiesPosition 1 Human)
(domain occupiesPosition 2 Position)
(domain occupiesPosition 3 Organization)
(documentation occupiesPosition "(&%occupiesPosition ?PERSON ?POSITION ?ORG)
  means that ?PERSON holds the &%Position ?POSITION at
  &%Organization ?ORG.
  For example, (&%occupiesPosition &%TomSmith &%ResearchDirector
  &%AcmeLaboratory) means that &%TomSmith is a research director
  at Acme Labs.")
...
```

And the corresponding triples are:

```
// Decomposing occupiesPosition(Human, Position, Organization)
content:occupiesPositionPredicate[rdf:type->content:Predicate].
content:occupiesPositionPredicate[rdf:type->rdfs:Class].
content:occupiesPositionPredicateHuman[rdfs:domain->
  content:occupiesPositionPredicate].
content:occupiesPositionPredicateHuman[rdfs:range->content:Human].
content:occupiesPositionPredicatePosition[rdfs:domain->
  content:occupiesPositionPredicate].
content:occupiesPositionPredicatePosition[rdfs:range->content:Position].
content:occupiesPositionPredicateOrganization[rdfs:domain->
  content:occupiesPositionPredicate].
content:occupiesPositionPredicateOrganization[rdfs:range->content:Organization].
```

Relations with more than two terms are very generic so there are not any two-terms representations that belong to several relations at the same time.

Functions Functions are relations that hold that for a given set of arguments there is one only value as a result of the function. This property can be defined as an axiom. Therefore, we convert a function with *n* arguments and a given result in a relation with $(n + 1)$ arguments. The translation of a relation with more than 2 arguments has just been explained.

Example:

```
(instance GovernmentFn UnaryFunction)
(domain GovernmentFn 1 GeopoliticalArea)
(range GovernmentFn Government)
```

Translation to triples:

```
content:GovernmentFn[rdf:type->content:Predicate].
content:GovernmentFn[rdfs:domain-> content:GeopoliticalArea].
content:GovernmentFn[rdfs:range-> content:Government].
FORALL X,Y,Z Y[content:Equals->Z] <- X[content:GovernmentFn->Y]
AND X[content:GovernmentFn->Z].
```

Mapping of classes and properties: generalization When we find a subclass/instance/subproperty definition, for a number of reasons it may happen that we have decided not to have defined in the NEWS Ontology the superclass/class/superproperty. In that case we will generalize, that is, we will substitute the class or property we do not have for a class or property more general.

Example:

```
(subclass SelfConnectedObject Object)
(subclass CorpuscularObject SelfConnectedObject)
(subclass OrganicObject CorpuscularObject)
(subclass Organism OrganicObject)
(subclass Animal Organism)
(subclass Vertebrate Animal)
(subclass WarmBloodedVertebrate Vertebrate)
(subclass Mammal WarmBloodedVertebrate)
(subclass Primate Mammal)
(subclass Hominid Primate)
(subclass Human Hominid)
```

We do not have the classes `Vertebrate`, `WarmBloodedVertebrate`, `Mammal` and `Primate` in the NEWS Ontology, so we write:

```
content:Agent[rdfs:subClassOf->content:Object].
content:Organism[rdfs:subClassOf->content:Agent].
content:Animal[rdfs:subClassOf->content:Organism].
content:Hominid[rdfs:subClassOf->content:Animal].
content:Human[rdfs:subClassOf->content:Hominid].
```

Rules KIF provides the usual logical constructs to define rules: universal and existential quantifiers, logical operators *and*, *or*, *not*, implication and so on. In TRIPLE rules are defined by means of Horn clauses. Therefore a manual translation should be done, although usually this translation is straightforward.

8.1.1 Concepts treated specifically

Some concepts in SUMO are not translated following the rules stated before, but they are defined individually. They have RDF Schema counterparts or they are basic logical terms that are the basis for other definitions. Some of them are listed below.

instance Replaced by `rdf:type`.

BinaryPredicate Replaced by `rdf:Property`.

subclass Replaced by `rdfs:subClassOf`.

Relation Replaced by `content:Predicate`.

equality We define equality as `content:Equals` and add the following axioms (only defined what follows from equality):

```
content:Equals[rdf:type->rdf:Property]
content:Equals[rdfs:domain->content:Entity].
content:Equals[rdfs:range->content:Entity].

//Reflexive relation
// X = X
FORALL X X[content:Equals->X] <- X[rdf:type->content:Entity].

//Symmetric relation
// X = Y ⇔ Y = X
FORALL X,Y Y[content:Equals->X] <- X[content:Equals->Y].

//Equality axioms
// ∀ X, P, A, B  P(X,A) ∧ (A = B) ⇒ P(X, B)
FORALL X,P,A,B X[P -> B] <-X[P -> A] AND A[content:Equals -> B].

// ∀ X, P, A, B  P(A, X) ∧ (A = B) ⇒ P(B, X)
FORALL X,P,A,B B[P -> X] <-A[P -> X] AND A[content:Equals -> B].

// ∀ X, Y, P, Q  P(X, Y) ∧ (P = Q) ⇒ Q(X, Y)
FORALL X,Y,P,Q X[Q -> Y] <-X[P -> Y] AND P[content:Equals -> Q].
```

8.1.2 Limitations

The current implementation of the TRIPLE language is a layer on top of the XSB inference engine. The XSB inference engine uses a "closed world assumption", that is, all that cannot be proved is assumed to be false. This assumption is false in a context where we work with partial information, as is the case of the news domain. In practice, this means that we should not use the `NOT` operator in rules.

8.2 Content Annotation Module

This module has been built using SUMO as a basis, but some concepts from MILO have also been incorporated. The result is a generic top-level ontology with more than 200 classes, more than 100 properties and over 30 rules. It also contains more than 6,000 instances of different classes: countries, languages, currencies, cities, companies, persons, etc.

One of the main problems when building this ontology module was to select what concepts from SUMO/MILO should be included or discarded. SUMO/MILO are very wide ontologies with hundreds of concepts, but we feel that some of these concepts (like `Arthropod` or `ComplexNumber`) are of little utility in the news domain. So, a pruning strategy is needed to filter irrelevant concepts. The approach we have followed is to use a middle-out strategy, as suggested in ontology building methodologies such as (Uschold and Grüninger, 1996). The main idea is to look at the basic entities included in journalism standards (inline annotation elements from NITF, values of IPTC Topic Type NewsCodes, see table in figure 32-5) and map

NITF	IPTC Topic Type NewsCodes	NEWS Ontology
Chron	---	Date, Year, Instant, Interval
Event	Event	Process
Location	Location, Town, Country, Region	GeopoliticalArea, GeographicArea, Country, County, StateOrProvince, City, CityDistrict
Money	Currency	CurrencyMeasure, CurrencyMeasureUnit
Org	Organization, Company	Organization, Corporation, NonProfitOrganization, PoliticalOrganization, TerroristOrganization, ...
Person	Person	Human, Man, Woman
Function	Job	SocialRole, Position, Function
Num	---	Number
Postaddr	---	Address
Virtloc	---	URI, URN, URL
---	Language	Language, HumanLanguage
---	ProductOrService	Product, IntentionalProcess

Figure 32-5. Basic entities in NITF, IPTC Topic Type NewsCodes and the NEWS Ontology

these entities to classes in SUMO/MILO. These classes need to be included in our ontology in order for it to be compatible with standards. Once we have these seed classes we can start the process of pruning: for each seed we look at its ancestors up till the top concept of the ontology (`Entity`) and include them, obtaining as result a *seed tree*. For each class included in this tree we then look for non-included descendants, deciding to include them or not using criteria like:

- relation with at least one of the categories of SRS first level. For instance, the concept `Book` is related with IPTC subject `01000000`, which can be used as a type of news item talking about arts, culture and entertainment. We can think, for example, of a news item which talks about the presentation of a new book by a well-known writer;
- usefulness in other components of the NEWS Ontology. For example, the concept `HumanLanguage` is useful for the Envelope module, because instances of this concept are used as the range of one property of class `NewsItem` which relates the instance of news item with its language.

The resultant taxonomy is then reviewed in order to add/remove classes if needed.

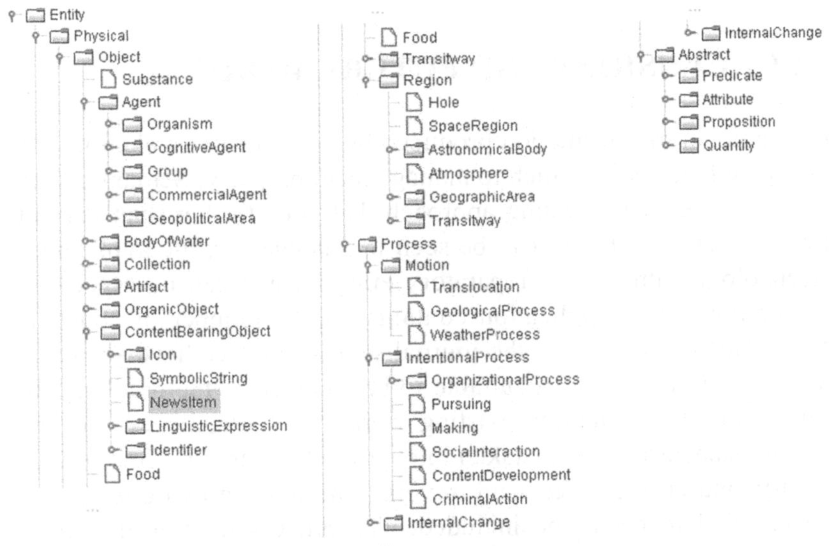

Figure 32-6. Taxonomy of NEWS Content Annotation Module

After deciding the concept taxonomy of the content module, we proceeded by analyzing SUMO/MILO relations which include at least one of the concepts of such a taxonomy. Again, using criteria of usefulness for news annotation, we decided which relations should be included. As a result, new concepts may also need to be included. When both concepts and relations from SUMO/MILO were defined, we proceeded by adding the rules and instances. The rules were taken both from SUMO/MILO or added by hand. There are three types of rules in this module:

- rules that tell if a property is transitive;
- rules that tell if a property is symmetric;
- Horn-like rules that allow to tell that *if propertyA and propertyB hold, then propertyC holds*.

The number of rules in this module is 30, which gives place to a lighter ontology than SUMO.

The instances used to populate the ontology were taken from different information sources like ISO languages standard (ISO 8601:2000), ISO country codes standard (ISO 3166:1997-1), CIA WorldFact Book (CIA, 2004), NASDAQ companies codes, SUMO/MILO instances, etc.

The current version of NEWS Content Annotation module does not include specific modules for each of the domains related with first level categories of SRS, but these modules are expected to be added in the near future. Figure 32-6 shows the tree with some of the elements included in this version.

9. CONCLUSIONS AND FUTURE WORK

The huge amount of information produced by news agencies clamour for innovative technologies with which to manage them properly. Semantic Web technologies provide an interesting approach that goes further than current keyword-based search tools. As can be seen in this chapter, the application of these technologies implies a preparatory effort, which can be especially difficult if the domain of application contains a large number of concepts and relations. This does occur in the journalism domain; we have seen that almost everything in the world is suitable to be included in the ontology. In order to ameliorate this situation, existing work must be analyzed. On the one hand, news standards must be taken into account due to their importance in the industry, and on the other hand, several ontologies provide us with a great number of elements to be included. The process of merging these sources of information must be handled carefully, so that the ontology does not become inconsistent. Furthermore, compromise must be obtained between simplification (news agencies need fast processing) and coverage.

The resultant modules of the ontology, explained in sections 5 to 8, have the following number of elements:

- **structural module**: It consists of 5 classes, 8 properties and 6 rules;
- **categorization module**: It includes over 1300 classes and 3 properties;

- **envelope module**: It consists of 52 classes, 96 properties, 21 rules and more than 500 instances;
- **content module**: It has 248 classes, 116 properties, 30 rules and thousands of instances.

In order to obtain all these elements two persons are needed, working full time for almost two months. The most time-consuming task is the choice of the classes that are relevant and the implications that this has in the selection of other classes.

Following all these steps an ontology to be used in the news industry has been developed. However there is more work to be done. At first, we want to extend our ontology by adding one module for each of the 17 first level categories of ITPC SRS. Another question to be solved is the maintenance: standards and information are evolving, so the development of a tool for ontology and knowledge maintenance is crucial. Finally, new features may be added if necessary, including:

- the addition of a user profiling module;
- future development of a new Time module; specially interesting is the addition of support for linking news events and time information.

ACKNOWLEDGEMENTS

This work has been partially funded by the European Comission under contract FP6-001906 in the framework of the Information Society Technologies (IST) programme and by the Spanish Ministry of Education and Science under contracts TSI2004-0042-E and TIC2003-07208. We wish to acknowledge the partners of the NEWS project for their cooperation in the work being done there. Helpful comments and suggestions made by Peter T. Breuer, Lars Zapf and Ansgar Bernardi are gratefully acknowledged.

REFERENCES

Allen, J., 1990, Maintaining knowledge about temporal intervals, in: *Expert systems: a software methodology for modern applications*, IEEE Computer Society Press, pp. 248-259.

Böhlen, M., 1994, *The Temporal Deductive Database System ChronoLog*, PhD thesis, Departement für Informatik, ETH Zurich.

Brickley, D. and Guha, R., 2004, RDF Vocabulary Description Language 1.0: RDF Schema, http://www.w3.org/TR/rdf-schema/.

Broekstra, J., Kampman, A. and van Harmelen, F., 2003, Sesame: An architecture for storing and querying RDF data and schema information, in: *Spinning the Semantic Web*, MIT Press, pp. 197-222.

CIA, 2004, World Factbook, http://www.cia.gov/cia/publications/factbook/.

Dean, M. and Schreiber, G., 2004, OWL Web Ontology Language Reference, http://www.w3.org/TR/owl-ref/.

Dublin Core Metadata Initiative, 2005a, http://dublincore.org.

Dublin Core Metadata Initiative, 2005b, DCMI Metadata Terms, http://dublincore.org/documents/dcmi-terms/.

Fellbaum, C., 1998, *WordNet: An Electronic Lexical Database*, The MIT Press.

Fernández-García, N. and Sánchez-Fernández, L., Building an ontology for NEWS applications. *ISWC'04*. Poster Session.

Genesereth, M., 1998, Knowledge Interchange Format, draft proposed American National Standard (dpANS) NCTIS.T2/98-004, http://logic.stanford.edu/kif/kif.html.

Guha, R. and McCool, R., 2003, TAP: A Semantic Web platform, *Computer Networks* **42**:557-577.

Hayes, P., 2004, RDF Semantics, http://www.w3.org/TR/rdf-mt/.

Hobbs, J., 2002, A DAML Ontology of Time, http://www.cs.rochester.edu/~ferguson/daml/.

Horrocks, I., Patel-Schneider, P., Boley, H., Tabet, S., Grosof, B. and Dean, M., 2004, SWRL: A Semantic Web Rule Language Combining OWL and RuleML, http://www.w3.org/Submission/2004/SUBM-SWRL-20040521/.

IDEAlliance, 2004, PRISM, Publishing Requirements for Industry Standard Metadata. Version 1.2, http://www.prismstandard.org.

IEEE, 2003, SUO-KIF, http://suo.ieee.org/SUO/KIF/.

IPTC, 1999, Information Interchange Model Version 4, http://www.iptc.org/download/download.php?fn=IIMV4.1.pdf.

IPTC, 2003a, NITF 3.2 DTD, with documentation embedded, http://www.nitf.org/IPTC/NITF/3.2/dtd/nitf-3-2.dtd.

IPTC, 2003b, Subject Reference System Guidelines, http://www.iptc.org/IPTC/NewsCodes/documentation/SRS-doc-Guidelines_3.pdf.

IPTC, 2004a, News ML 1.2 Guidelines V 1.0, http://www.newsml.org/IPTC/NewsML/1.2/documentation/NewsML_1.2-doc-Guidelines_1.00.pdf.

IPTC, 2004b, IPTC NewsCodes, http://www.iptc.org/NewsCodes/.

Knight, K. and Whitney, R., 1994, Building a large knowledge base for machine translation, *AAAI-94*, pp. 773-778.

Lenat, D. and Guha, R., 1990, *Building Large Knowledge-Based Systems: Representation and Inference in the Cyc Project*. Addison-Wesley Pub.

MacGregor, R. and Bates, R., 1987, The LOM knowledge representation language, *Technical report isi-rs-87-188*, USC Information Sciences Institute, Marina del Rey, CA.

Maedche, A., Steffen, S., Stojanovic, N., Studer, R. and Sure, Y., 2003, Semantic portal: The SEAL approach, in: *Spinning the Semantic Web*, MIT Press, pp. 317-359.

Miller, G. A., 1995, WordNet: A lexical database for English, *Commununications of the ACM* **38**(11), 39-41.

Niles, I. and Pease, A., 2001, Towards a standard upper ontology, *FOIS'01*, pp. 2-9.

Niles, I. and Terry, A., 2004, The MILO: A general-purpose, mid-level ontology, *IKE'04*, pp. 15-19.

Ontosaurus Loom Web Browser, 2003, http://www.isi.edu/isd/ontosaurus.html.

Ontotext, 1997, Upper Cyc download, http://www.ontotext.com/downloads/cyc_top_mdb.zip.

Ontotext, 2004, KIMO Ontology, http://www.ontotext.com/kim/kimo.rdfs.

OpenCyc.org, 2002a, OpenCyc download, http://sourceforge.net/project/showfiles.php?group_id=27274.

OpenCyc.org, 2002b, OpenCyc, Formalized Common Language, http://www.opencyc.org.

Pease, A., 2005, Ontology Portal, http://www.ontologyportal.org.

Popov, B., Kiryalov, A., Ognyanoff, D., Manov, D. and Kirilov, A., 2004, KIM - A semantic platform for information extraction and retrieval, *Nat. Lang. Eng.* **10**(3-4),375-392.

Sagonas, K., Swift, T. and Warren, D. S., 1994, XSB as an efficient deductive database engine, *SIGMOD '94*, ACM Press, pp. 442-453.

Sintek, M. and Decker, S.: 2002, A Query, Inference, and Transformation Language for the Semantic Web, *ISWC'02*, pp. 364-378.

Swartout, B., Patil, R., Knight, K. and Russ, T., 1996, Ontosaurus: a tool for browsing and editing ontologies, *KAW96*, pp. 69-1-69-12.

TAP, Building the Semantic Web, 2001, http://tap.stanford.edu/tap/download.html.

Teknowledge, 2003a, SUMO OWL, http://reliant.teknowledge.com/DAML/SUMO.owl.

Teknowledge, 2003b, MILO download http://einstein.teknowledge.com:8080/download/register.jsp?fileType=.zip&fileName=Milo.zip.

Terziev, I., Kiryakov, A. and Manov, D., 2005, D1.8.1 Base upper-level ontology (BULO) Guidance, http://proton.semanticweb.org/D1_8_1.pdf.

UNSPSC, 2003, http://www.unspsc.org/CodeDownload.asp?pageid=4.

Uschold, M. and Grüninger, M., 1996, Ontologies: Principles, Methods and Applications, *Knowledge Engineering Review*, **11**(2),93-155.

Vossen, P., 2001, EuroWordNet: Building a multilingual database with wordnets for several European languages, http://www.illc.uva.nl/EuroWordNet/.

Vossen, P. (ed.): 1998, *EuroWordNet: A Multilingual Database with Lexical Semantic Networks*, Kluwer Academic Publishers, Norwell, MA, USA

APPENDIX

```
<?xml version="1.0" encoding='iso-8859-1'?>
<!DOCTYPE nitf SYSTEM 'nitf-x020-strict.dtd'>
<nitf>
    <head>
        <title>P.VASCO-ATENTADOS MADRIDCámara Vasca condena "manipulación informativa"
                de Gobierno de PP</title>
        <meta name='wordcnt' content='531'/>
        <meta name='keyword' content='P.VASCO-ATENTADOS MADRID'/>
        <meta name='author-coded' content='099ZqLwKrw29ZqLwKp23nwJ'/>
        <meta name='author-decoded' content='efea0840/efea0828'/>
        <meta name='priority' content='R'/>
        <meta name='tabsposition' content=''/>
        <meta name='relevancy' content='C'/>
        <meta name='newtype' content='Avance'/>
        <meta name='category' content='POL'/>
        <meta name='category-full' content='POLITICA'/>
        <meta name='source' content='EFEDATA'/>
        <meta name='efe-extended-category' content='POL:POLITICA,PARLAMENTO,REGIONES-AUTONOMIAS
                TRI:JUSTICIA-INTERIOR-SUCESOS,TERRORISMO'/>
        <docdata>
            <doc-id id-string='VI9222'/>
            <date.issue  norm='20040507 112600'/>
        </docdata>
    </head>
    <body lang='es.es'>
        <body.head>
            <hedline>
                <hl1>P.VASCO-ATENTADOS MADRID</hl1>
                <hl2>Cámara Vasca condena "manipulación informativa" de Gobierno de PP</hl2>
            </hedline>
            <byline></byline>
            <dateline>
                <location>Vitoria</location>
            </dateline>
        </body.head>
        <body.content>
            <p> Vitoria, 7 may (EFE).- El Parlamento Vasco condenó hoy los "intentos de manipulación
                informativa" del Gobierno del PP, en torno a la autoría del atentado del 11 de marzo en
                Madrid, por considerar que "sólo tenía por objetivo la rentabilidad electoral partidista".
                La iniciativa, presentada por el PSE-EE, contó con el apoyo de PNV, EA y EB/IU. El PP
                respaldó sólo uno de sus puntos, a través del cual la institución se solidarizó con las
                víctimas del atentado; Sozialista Abertzaleak no participó en las votaciones.  En la
                proposición no de ley aprobada, también se manifiesta la solidaridad de la institución
                con la concejal socialista del Ayuntamiento de Vitoria, Natalia Rojo, el portavoz del
                PNV en las Juntas Generales de Alava, Alvaro Iturritxa, y con el parlamentario de EA
                Martín Aranburu.  Estos tres cargos están encausados por un presunto delito electoral,
                después de que el PP denunciase ante la Junta Electoral su participación en las
                concentraciones que se celebraron el 13 de marzo.  El parlamentario socialista Oscar
                Rodríguez consideró que las concentraciones del 13 de marzo fueron "espontáneas" y acusó
                al PP de "pretender empañar los resultados del 14 de marzo" y "perseguir penalmente la
                búsqueda de la verdad".EFE    ma/tr
            </p>
        </body.content>
    </body>
</nitf>
```

Figure 32-7. An example of an EFE NITF document

```
_20040507T112600_VI9222_POL_531[envelope:has_language->iso_language:es].
_20040507T112600_VI9222_POL_531_title_es[rdf:type->envelope:Label].
_20040507T112600_VI9222_POL_531_title_es[envelope:LBL_text->"P.VASCO-ATENTADOS MADRID
   Cámara Vasca condena 'manipulación informativa' de Gobierno de PP"].
_20040507T112600_VI9222_POL_531_title_es[envelope:LBL_language->iso_language:es].
_20040507T112600_VI9222_POL_531[envelope:has_headline->_20040507T112600_VI9222_POL_531_title_es].
_20040507T112600_VI9222_POL_531[envelope:has_keyword->"P.VASCO-ATENTADOS MADRID"].
_20040507T112600_VI9222_POL_531[envelope:has_creator->efea0840].
_20040507T112600_VI9222_POL_531[envelope:has_creator->efea0828].
_20040507T112600_VI9222_POL_531[envelope:has_priority->anpa_priority:routine].
_20040507T112600_VI9222_POL_531[envelope:has_creation_time_UTC->_20040507112600].
_20040507112600[rdf:type->time:Instant].
_20040507112600[time:has_year->2004].
_20040507112600[time:has_month->5].
_20040507112600[time:has_day->7].
_20040507112600[time:has_hour->11].
_20040507112600[time:has_minute->26].
_20040507112600[time:has_second->0].
_20040507T112600_VI9222_POL_531[rdf:type->iptc_subject:sr11009000].
_20040507T112600_VI9222_POL_531[rdf:type->iptc_subject:sr11012000].
_20040507T112600_VI9222_POL_531[rdf:type->iptc_subject:sr16001000].
_20040507T112600_VI9222_POL_531[envelope:has_location->content:Vitoria_City].
_20040507T112600_VI9222_POL_531[envelope:has_entity_ocurrence->content:Madrid_City].
_20040507T112600_VI9222_POL_531[envelope:has_entity_ocurrence->content:PP_Party]
_20040507T112600_VI9222_POL_531[envelope:has_entity_ocurrence->content:PSE-EE_Party].
_20040507T112600_VI9222_POL_531[envelope:has_entity_ocurrence->content:PNV_Party].
_20040507T112600_VI9222_POL_531[envelope:has_entity_ocurrence->content:EA_Party].
_20040507T112600_VI9222_POL_531[envelope:has_entity_ocurrence->content:Parlamento_Vasco].
_20040507T112600_VI9222_POL_531[envelope:has_entity_ocurrence->content:Ayuntamiento_de_Vitoria].
_20040507T112600_VI9222_POL_531[envelope:has_entity_ocurrence->content:Juntas_Generales_de_Alava].
_20040507T112600_VI9222_POL_531[envelope:has_entity_ocurrence->content:Alvaro_Iturritxa].
_20040507T112600_VI9222_POL_531[envelope:has_entity_ocurrence->content:Oscar_Rodriguez].
```

Figure 32-8. TRIPLE representation of the relevant information inside the previous NITF document.

INDEX

[illegible]
By Bookmasters

Printed in the United States
By Bookmasters